UNIVERSITY CASEBOOK SERIES®

FEDERAL HABEAS CORPUS

EXECUTIVE DETENTION AND POST-CONVICTION LITIGATION

by

BRANDON L. GARRETT
Roy L. and Rosamond Woodruff Morgan Professor of Law
University of Virginia School of Law

LEE KOVARSKY
Assistant Professor of Law
University of Maryland
Francis King Carey School of Law

FOUNDATION PRESS

University Casebook Series is a trademark registered in the U.S. Patent and Trademark Office.

© 2013 by LEG, Inc. d/b/a West Academic Publishing

610 Opperman Drive
St. Paul, MN 55123
1–800–313–9378
Printed in the United States of America

ISBN: 978–1–60930–188–0

Mat #41309375

To Kerry, Alex and Zack.

And to Cherie.

ACKNOWLEDGMENTS

For their invaluable comments on drafts of this manuscript, we thank Kerry Abrams, Michael Collins, Ashley Deeks, David Dow, Eric Freedman, Trevor Garmey, Aziz Huq, Frank Lancaster, Peter Low, David Martin, Daniel Medwed, and Sean Watts. We thank Aziz Huq and Constitutional Commentary for permission to reprint tables from Aziz Z. Huq, *What Good is Habeas?*, 26 Const. Commentary 385 (2010). We thank our research assistants for their help. Brandon Garrett wishes to thank University of Virginia law students Mark Johnson and Edward Ledford for their hard work on the manuscript, as well as students in his habeas corpus courses for their helpful feedback over the years. For their unflagging efforts to improve the form and content of the Book, Lee Kovarsky wishes to thank University of Maryland law students Leila Ameli-Grillon, Courtney Amelung, Nicole Barnard, Kari D'Ottavio, Sarah David, Laurie Holmes, Benjamin Levin, David Risk, and Blake Walsh.

SUMMARY OF CONTENTS

ACKNOWLEDGMENTS...V

TABLE OF CASES.. XIX

TABLE OF STATUTES.. XXV

TABLE OF SECONDARY AUTHORITIES XXIX

Chapter 1. Introduction and the Origins of Habeas Corpus..............1
1. The Birth of the Modern Writ in the United States 2
2. The English Common-law Writ 13
3. The Early Republic: Habeas Corpus, Article III, and Statutes 18
4. Post-Conviction Review 35

Chapter 2. Constitutional Structure of the Habeas Privilege 43
1. Introduction to Habeas and Constitutional Structure 43
2. The Drafting of the Suspension Clause and What The Habeas
    Privilege Meant to the Framers..44
3. How Does the Government "Suspend" the Privilege? 53
4. Does the Constitution Guarantee an Adequate Habeas Remedy? 64
5. Federal Supremacy and State Habeas 76
6. Original Habeas and the Exceptions Clause 87

**Chapter 3. The Scope of Federal Habeas Authority to Review
    State Convictions** 99
1. Origins of Federal Review of State Convictions 100
2. Scope of Modern Federal Review 133
3. Cognizability 141
4. Innocence..150

**Chapter 4. Procedural Limitations on Federal Post-Conviction
    Relief**..169
1. Exhaustion 173
2. Procedural Default..191
3. Successive Petitions...244
4. Statute of Limitations 266

Chapter 5. Federal Merits Review 299
1. "On the Merits" 301
2. Legal Defects in State Decisions..303
3. Factual Defects in State Decisions 358
4. Supplementing the State Record on Federal Review 378
5. Harmless Error 395

Chapter 6. Review of Federal Convictions 417
1. Introduction to 28 U.S.C. § 2255 417
2. AEDPA's Effects on § 2255..421
3. Procedural Default and Exhaustion of Appellate Remedies................426
4. The Constitution's Suspension Clause the § 2255 "Savings" Clause,
    and Post-Conviction Review Under § 2241. 432

5. The Innocence Protection Act 441

Chapter 7. Immigration Detention **443**
1. Introduction to Immigration Detention 444
2. Excludability and Deportability 446
3. Immigration Custody and the Suspension Clause 456
4. What Fact Review Does the Constitution Require? 474
5. The Real-ID Act 479
6. Length of Detention Pending Removal 489
7. Enemy Aliens 493

Chapter 8. Civil Detention **501**
1. Civil Detention Auxiliary to Military Necessity 502
2. Civil Detention Auxiliary to Criminal Process 512
3. Post-Conviction Civil Detention 517
4. Preventative and Public Health Detention 524
5. The Boundaries of Civil Detention: Child Custody 528

Chapter 9. Military Commissions **537**
1. Introductory Notes on the Law of War and Military Custody ... 537
2. The Suspension Clause and Law of War Commissions 543
3. Military Commission Procedures 555

Chapter 10. National Security Detention **571**
1. Introduction to Indefinite Detention 571
2. The *Boumediene* Decision 598
3. Post-*Boumediene* Developments 626

Chapter 11. Post-Conviction Procedure **653**
1. Conflicting Federal Rules of Procedure 653
2. The Boundaries With Section 1983 676

Chapter 12. The Future of Habeas Corpus **701**
1. Institutional Design 701
2. Revisiting the Constitutional Structure of Habeas Corpus 714

Statutory Appendix **721**

Appendix A **721**

Appendix B **723**

Appendix C **742**

Appendix D **746**

Appendix E **749**

INDEX 757

TABLE OF CONTENTS

ACKNOWLEDGMENTS..V

TABLE OF CASES...XIX

TABLE OF STATUTES...XXV

TABLE OF SECONDARY AUTHORITIES...XXIX

Chapter 1. Introduction and the Origins of Habeas Corpus.............1
    Introductory Note...1
1. The Birth of the Modern Writ in the United States.................................2
    Brown v. Allen...3
    Notes and Questions on Brown v. Allen...10
2. The English Common-law Writ...13
    Notes on Early English Origins...13
    Notes on The Case of the Five Knights..15
    Notes on the English Civil Wars and the Habeas Corpus Act of
        1679...16
3. The Early Republic: Habeas Corpus, Article III, and Statutes.................18
    Introductory Notes on the Suspension Clause.....................................18
    Notes on Section 14 of the Judiciary Act of 1789.................................20
    Introductory Note on Ex parte Bollman...21
    Ex parte Bollman...22
    Notes and Questions on Bollman..27
4. Post-Conviction Review...35
    Introductory Note on Post-Conviction Review.....................................35
    Ex parte Watkins...35
    Notes and Questions on Watkins..38
    Notes on Habeas Statutes...40

Chapter 2. Constitutional Structure of the Habeas Privilege..........43
1. Introduction to Habeas and Constitutional Structure.............................43
2. The Drafting of the Suspension Clause and What The Habeas
    Privilege Meant to the Framers...44
    Notes on the Drafting of the Suspension Clause.................................44
    Notes on the Scope of the Habeas Privilege......................................48
3. How Does the Government "Suspend" the Privilege?..............................53
    A. Executive Suspension..54
        Introductory Notes on Ex parte Merryman...............................54
        Ex Parte Merryman...56
        Notes and Questions on Merryman..60
    B. Authorization Versus Suspension...61
        Notes and Questions on the Relationship Between Suspension
            and the Underlying Legality of Custody.............................62
4. Does the Constitution Guarantee an Adequate Habeas Remedy?..........64
    A. Federal Detention and the "Adequate Substitute" Rule.................64
        Introductory Note on 28 U.S.C. § 2255 and United States v.
            Hayman..64
        United States v. Hayman..65

Notes and Questions on Hayman..67
Introductory Note on Detention by the District of Columbia
    and Swain v. Pressley 68
Swain v. Pressley 68
Notes and Questions on Pressley 71
B. Restrictions on Habeas Relief for State Prisoners 72
Introductory Notes on AEDPA and Habeas Relief for State
    Prisoners 72
Felker v. Turpin (Suspension Clause Holding) 73
Notes and Questions on Felker 75
5. Federal Supremacy and State Habeas 76
Introductory Notes on Antebellum State Habeas and Ableman v.
    Booth..76
Ableman v. Booth..78
Notes and Questions on Ableman..82
Notes on Ableman's Aftermath and Introduction to Tarble's Case 82
Tarble's Case 83
Notes and Questions on Tarble 85
6. Original Habeas and the Exceptions Clause 87
Note on the Reconstruction Act, Ex parte McCardle, and Ex parte
    Yerger 88
Ex parte McCardle..90
Notes and Questions on McCardle and Introductory Note to Ex
    parte Yerger..91
Ex parte Yerger...92
Notes and Questions on Yerger..94
Notes on AEDPA, Felker v. Turpin, and In re Davis 95

Chapter 3. The Scope of Federal Habeas Authority to Review
    State Convictions 99
Introductory Note on the Scope of the Post-Conviction Writ.................99
1. Origins of Federal Review of State Convictions 100
A. Classic Due Process Cases..100
Introductory Note on the Habeas Corpus Act of 1867 and the
    Classic Due Process Cases 100
Ex parte Siebold 101
Notes and Questions on Siebold..103
Introductory Note on Frank v. Mangum 105
Frank v. Mangum 106
Notes and Questions on Frank..111
Moore v. Dempsey 115
Notes and Questions on Moore..117
B. *Brown v. Allen* and the Modern Era of State Post-conviction
    Review..119
Introductory Note on Brown v. Allen...119
Brown v. Allen..119
Notes and Questions on Brown 128
2. Scope of Modern Federal Review 133
Introductory Note on the Modern Federal Habeas Statute 133
Note on the Custody Requirement..134

Notes on Habeas Filing Data 135
Notes on Common Constitutional Claims 137
3. Cognizability 141
Stone v. Powell 141
Notes and Questions on Powell 147
4. Innocence.. 150
Herrera v. Collins... 152
Notes and Questions on Herrera 158
Notes on State Innocence Statutes 162
Notes on "Sentencing" Innocence..................................... 165
Note on Innocence and Non-Capital Sentences 166

**Chapter 4. Procedural Limitations on Federal Post-Conviction
Relief**..169
Introductory Note on Procedural Doctrines 169
Note on the Three Phases of Review 170
1. Exhaustion 173
A. *Royall* and the Creation of the Exhaustion Rule 174
Introductory Note on Ex parte Royall........................... 174
Ex parte Royall 174
Notes and Questions on Royall and Supplementary Notes on
the Exhaustion Requirement.................................... 177
B. *Lundy* and "Mixed Petitions".. 181
Introductory Note on the Content of Federal Habeas
Petitions.. 181
Rose v. Lundy 182
Notes and Questions on Lundy and Mixed Petitions 187
2. Procedural Default.. 191
Introductory Note on Elements of Procedural Default...... 191
Note on Procedural Default Doctrine and Broader Trends in
Habeas Jurisprudence 191
A. Early Procedural Default Doctrine 192
Fay v. Noia... 192
Notes and Questions on Noia 199
B. The Modern Procedural Default Test 202
Wainwright v. Sykes 202
Notes and Questions on Sykes 211
Notes on the Mechanics of Procedural Default Inquiry 213
Introductory Note to Martinez v. Ryan 218
Martinez v. Ryan.. 220
Notes and Questions on Martinez.................................. 226
C. The Miscarriage of Justice Exception 229
Introductory Notes on the Origins of the Miscarriage-of-Justice
Exception 229
House v. Bell.. 231
Notes and Questions on House....................................... 241
3. Successive Petitions.. 244
Introductory Notes on Same-Claim and New-Claim Successive
Petitions.. 246
Introductory Note on McCleskey v. Zant....................... 248

McCleskey v. Zant...248
Notes and Questions on McCleskey v. Zant.......................257
Note on Previously-Asserted Claims Under 28 U.S.C. § 2244(b)(1)...264
Note on Authorization Procedure Under 28 U.S.C. § 2244(b)(3)........265
4. Statute of Limitations 266
   A. 28 U.S.C. § 2254(d)(1)—Statutory "Trigger Dates".........................268
      Notes on 28 U.S.C. § 2244(d)(1)(B)–(d)(1)(D): "Alternative"
      Triggers...268
      Note on 28 U.S.C. § 2244(d)(1)(A): The "Final Judgment"
      Trigger..270
   B. Subsection 2254(d)(2)—Statutory Tolling 271
      Notes on "Other Collateral Review"..............................271
      Notes on "Pending" 276
      Notes and Questions on "Properly Filed" 278
      Note on "Pertinent Judgment or Claim" 280
   C. Equitable Tolling..281
      Introductory Note on Equitable Tolling 281
      Holland v. Florida 282
      Notes and Questions on Holland and Equitable Tolling.............294
      Notes on Effect of Procedural Limitations 296

Chapter 5. Federal Merits Review 299
   Introduction to Federal Merits Review of State Convictions.............299
1. "On the Merits" 301
   Notes on Harrington v. Richter..301
2. Legal Defects in State Decisions..303
   A. Retroactivity 303
      Introductory Note on the Linkletter Standard 304
      Teague v. Lane 306
      Notes and Questions on Teague..................................312
   B. 28 U.S.C. § 2254(d)(1) 318
      Note on AEDPA Legislative History............................318
      Introductory Note on Terry Williams v. Taylor 321
      Terry Williams v. Taylor 322
      Notes and Questions on Terry Williams.......................332
      Notes on "Contrary To" 339
      Notes on "Unreasonable Application"...........................342
      Notes on "Cleary Established Federal Law" 344
      Notes on Order of Operations and Burden of Proof.......346
      Note on the Factual Record and Section 2254(d)(1) 347
      Cullen v. Pinholster 348
      Notes and Questions on Pinholster.............................354
3. Factual Defects in State Decisions 358
   Introductory Note on Miller-El v. Dretke.............................358
   Miller El v. Dretke 359
   Notes and Questions on Miller-El..374
4. Supplementing the State Record on Federal Review 378
   A. Evidentiary Hearings From *Townsend* to *Tamayo Reyes*...............379
      Notes and Questions on Townsend and Tamayo-Reyes 382

    B. AEDPA's Changes to Evidentiary Hearings.................................384
        Note on 28 U.S.C. § 2254(e)(1) 384
        Introductory Note on Federal Evidentiary Hearings 385
        Michael Williams v. Taylor...386
        Notes and Questions on Michael Williams............................391
5. Harmless Error 395
    Notes on Harmless Constitutional Error 396
    Notes on Structural Error 398
    Introductory Note on Brecht v. Abrahamson 400
    Brecht v. Abrahamson 401
    Notes and Questions on Brecht..407
    Notes on Harmless Error After AEDPA....................................414

Chapter 6. Review of Federal Convictions **417**
1. Introduction to 28 U.S.C. § 2255 417
    Notes on Cognizability..418
    Note on § 2255 Filing Data...420
    Note on the "Savings Clause" and Relationship to Habeas
        Practice 420
2. AEDPA's Effects on § 2255...421
    Note on Merits Review and Nonretroactivity 421
    Notes on Successive Petitions 422
    Notes on AEDPA Statute of Limitations.................................424
    Note on Evidentiary Hearings 425
3. Procedural Default and Exhaustion of Appellate Remedies..................426
    Note on Exhaustion of Appellate Remedies 426
    Introductory Note on Procedural Default..................................426
    United States v. Frady 426
    Notes and Questions on Frady..429
4. The Constitution's Suspension Clause the § 2255 "Savings" Clause,
    and Post-Conviction Review Under § 2241. 432
    Gilbert v. United States..433
    Notes and Questions on Gilbert 436
    Note on Coram Nobis..439
5. The Innocence Protection Act 441
    Notes and Comments on the Innocence Protection Act.............441

Chapter 7. Immigration Detention **443**
    Introductory Note on Immigration Law and Habeas Corpus 443
1. Introduction to Immigration Detention 444
    Notes on the Plenary Power Doctrine.......................................444
2. Excludability and Deportability 446
    Notes on Knauff 446
    Introductory Note on Shaughnessy v. Mezei 449
    Shaughnessy v. United States ex rel. Mezei 449
    Notes and Questions on Mezei 455
3. Immigration Custody and the Suspension Clause 456
    Note on Heikkila v. Barber...456
    Notes on Petitions for Review From 1961–1996 457
    Notes on AEDPA and IIRIRA 458

Introduction to Ins v. St. Cyr 461
INS v. St. Cyr 461
Notes and Questions on St. Cyr 472
4. What Fact Review Does the Constitution Require?...........474
Nishimura Ekiu v. U.S. 475
Notes and Questions on Ekiu 477
5. The Real-ID Act...479
Notes on Judicial Review Provisions 479
Notes on Questions of Law 481
Notes on Questions of Fact..483
Notes on the Current Uses of Immigration Habeas 485
Notes on Institutional Context of Removal Decisions 486
Note on Stays of Removal..488
Note on Extradition 488
6. Length of Detention Pending Removal 489
Notes on Length-of-Detention Challenges...........................489
7. Enemy Aliens 493
Ludecke v. Watkins 494
Notes and Questions on Ludecke...497
Notes on the USA Patriot Act 498

Chapter 8. Civil Detention 501
Introduction to Civil Detention...501
1. Civil Detention Auxiliary to Military Necessity 502
Note on Mitsuye Endo and American Detention of Japanese
    Americans During World War II....................................502
Ex parte Mitsuye Endo..503
Notes and Questions on Endo 510
2. Civil Detention Auxiliary to Criminal Process 512
Note on Pre-Trial Detention of Defendant Based on Flight Risk
    and Community Safety 512
Note on Material Witness Detention 514
Note on Civil Commitment Following Successful Insanity
    Defenses...517
3. Post-Conviction Civil Detention 517
Note on Post-Conviction Detention of Sexually Violent Predators 517
Seling v. Young 519
Notes and Questions on Young 522
Note on Incapacitation 523
4. Preventative and Public Health Detention........................524
Note on Preventative and Public Health Civil Detention ...524
Note on Civil Commitment for Mental Illness......................524
Note on Civil Commitment for Substance Abuse 526
Note on Civil Commitment for Public Health (Quarantine)...............526
5. The Boundaries of Civil Detention: Child Custody 528
Lehman v. Lycoming County Children's Services 528
Notes and Questions on Lehman 534

Chapter 9. Military Commissions..537
1. Introductory Notes on the Law of War and Military Custody..............537
    Notes on the Law of War..537
    Note on Courts Martial..541
    Note on Military Commissions...541
2. The Suspension Clause and Law of War Commissions 543
    Introductory Note on Ex parte Milligan...................................543
    Ex parte Milligan 544
    Notes and Questions on Milligan..549
    Notes on World War II Military Commissions...............................553
3. Military Commission Procedures...555
    Note on Military Detentions and Statutory Jurisdiction...................555
    Note on Determining Appropriate United States District Court 557
    Introductory Note on Detention in Foreign Jurisdictions..................557
    Johnson v. Eisentrager 557
    Notes and Questions on Eisentrager 562
    Notes on Hamdan v. Rumsfeld and Post-9/11 Military
        Commissions..566

Chapter 10. National Security Detention...............................571
    Introduction to National Security Detention 571
1. Introduction to Indefinite Detention 571
    Introductory Note on Hamdi v. Rumsfeld 572
    Hamdi v. Rumsfeld 573
    Notes and Questions on Hamdi and Indefinite Detention...................589
    Notes on the Post-9/11 Importance of Territorial Jurisdiction...........596
2. The *Boumediene* Decision..598
    Introductory Notes on Post-Hamdi Statutory Developments.............598
    Introductory Note on Boumediene v. Bush 600
    Boumediene v. Bush 601
    Notes and Questions on Boumediene 619
    Note on the Guantánamo Population 625
3. Post-*Boumediene* Developments 626
    A. Substantive Standards for Detention 626
        Introductory Notes on GTMO Detention After Boumediene 626
        Notes on the Scope of Detention Authority 629
        Note on the National Defense Authorization Act of 2012 630
        Notes on the Standard of Proof and Evidentiary Rules 631
        Notes on Discovery and Reliability 633
    B. The Return of Extraterritoriality 635
        Introductory Notes on New Extraterritorial Questions 635
        Introductory Note on Al-Maqaleh v. Gates and Bagram............637
        Al-Maqalah v. Gates 637
        Notes and Comments on Al-Maqaleh 643
    C. The Remedy of Release 645
        Introductory Note on Kiyemba v. Obama..........................645
        Kiyemba v. Obama (Kiyemba I) 645
        Notes and Questions on Kiyemba I..............................648
        Notes on the Future of National Security Detention.................650

Chapter 11. Post-Conviction Procedure 653
   Introduction 653
1. Conflicting Federal Rules of Procedure 653
   A. Pleading 654
      Granberry v. Greer 655
      Notes and Questions on Granberry 656
      Note on Trest v. Cain and Forfeiture of Procedural Default 659
      Notes on Day v. McDonough and Forfeiture of Limitations 659
   B. Post-Judgment Motions and Successive Petitions 661
      Gonzalez v. Crosby 662
      Notes and Questions on Gonzalez v. Crosby 666
   C. Certificates of Appealability 668
      Introductory Note on Slack v. McDaniel 668
      Slack v. McDaniel 669
      Notes and Questions on Slack and on § 2253 672
2. The Boundaries With Section 1983 676
   Introductory Note on Pre-Heck Cases 677
   Heck v. Humphrey 678
   Notes and Questions on Heck 681
   Notes on Parole Challenges 683
   Notes on DNA Exonerate Civil Suits 684
   Introductory Note on Access to Post-Conviction DNA Testing 686
   District Attorney's Office for Third Judicial Dist. v. Osborne 686
   Notes and Questions on Osborne and on Post-Conviction DNA
      Testing 693
   Hill v. McDonough 695
   Notes and Questions on Hill and on Method-of-Execution
      Challenges 697
   Notes on Bivens and National Security Detention 698

Chapter 12. The Future of Habeas Corpus 701
   Introduction 701
1. Institutional Design 701
   Notes on Federal Legislative Reform 701
   Notes on Habeas and the Role of Counsel 708
   Notes on National Security Courts 709
   Notes on State Habeas Reform 710
   Notes on Innocence Commissions 711
2. Revisiting the Constitutional Structure of Habeas Corpus 714
   Concluding Notes on the Suspension Clause 714
   Concluding Notes on Due Process 717
   Concluding Notes on Article III 718
   Concluding Note 718

Statutory Appendix 721

Appendix A 721

Appendix B 723

Appendix C 742

Appendix D **746**

Appendix E..**749**

INDEX 757

TABLE OF CASES

The principal cases are in bold type.

Cases

Ableman v. Booth -------- 49, **78**, 100
Addington v. Texas -------524, 578, 595
Afroyim v. Rusk ----------------------485
Ahrens v. Clark ---------------- 557, 596
Akins v. Texas -----------------------307
Al Alwi v. Obama --------------------634
Al Ginco v. Obama -------------------631
Al Odah v. United States-----------600
Al-Adahi v. Obama ------------ 628, 632
Al-Aulaqi v. Obama -----------------595
Al-Bihani v. Obama -----591, 627, 629,
   631, 634
Ali v. Mukasey----------------------484
Ali v. Rumsfeld ---------------------700
Allen v. McCurry -------------------682
Allen v. Siebert ---------------------660
Al-Maqaleh v. Gates --------------**637**
Amadeo v. Zant---------------- 216, 217
Amarjeet Singh v. Gonzales -------480
Amrine v. Bowersox-----------------394
Anam v. Obama ---------------------634
Anders v. California ----------------225
Ankenbrandt v. Richards -----------535
Ansari v. State----------------------514
Apprendi v. New Jersey ------------318
Arar v. Ashcroft --------------------699
Archuleta v. Hedrick ---------------523
Arizona v. Fulminante --------------398
Artuz v. Bennett -------------------278
Ashcroft v. al-Kidd -----------------515
Ashcroft v. Iqbal -------------------700
Ashford v. Gilmore -----------------322
Ashmus v. Woodford----------------704
Atkins v. Virginia- 140, 179, 263, 312,
   314, 342
Awad v. Obama ----------------511, 630
Ayanbadejo v. Chertoff-------------480
Babbitt v. Woodford----------------263
Bachman v. Bagley------------------281
Bagley v. U.S.-----------------------399
Bailey v. United States ------------438
Baldayaque v. United States------ 425
Barber v. Barber-------------------535
Barefoot v. Estelle ----------------668
Barrett v. Acevedo-----------------657
Bartlett v. Battaglia ---------------343
Batson v. Kentucky ----------- 359, 673
Baze v. Rees ------------------------698
Beard v. Kindler -------------------201
Beaty v. Brewer --------------------698
Beaulieu v. Minnesota -------------519
Began v. United States ------------433
Bell v. Cone------------------------343
Bensayah v. Obama-----------------629
Benslimane v. Gonzales -----------487
Berghuis v. Thompkins -------------346
Bismullah v. Gates -----------------627

Bivens v. Six Unknown Named
   Agents ------------------ 334, 516, 698
Bonhometre v. Gonzales ----------- 479
Booker v. United States-------419, 433
Boumediene v. Bush 16, 41, 48, 53,
   71, 556, 571, 600, **601**, 620, 623,
   627, 633, 638, 647, 714
Braden v. 30th Judicial Cir. Ct. - 557,
   596
Brady v. Maryland 138, 139, 153, 249,
   387
Brecht v. Abrahamson --------401, 410
Brewer v. Quarterman ------------- 345
Brock v. U.S. ----------------------- 418
Brown v. Allen ----------------3, **119**
Brown v. Board of Education of
   Topeka ------------------------------3
Brown v. United States ----------- 495
Burke v. United States ------------ 419
Burns v. Wilson -------------------- 557
Burris v. Parke----------------393, 423
Bushell's Case, Vaughan 135, 6 St.
   Tr. 231 (1670) ------------------- 39
Byers v. United States------------- 425
Byrnes v. Walker------------------- 96
Calcano-Martinez v. INS ---------- 474
Carey v. Musladin ----------------- 344
Carey v. Piphus-------------------- 717
Carey v. Saffold ------------------- 277
Casas-Castrillon v. DHS ----------- 493
Cassett v. Stewart ---------------- 189
Catwell v. Attorney General of U.S.
   ----------------------------------- 484
Chaapel v. Cochran---------------- 96
Chapman v. California -------395, 401
Chen v. Gonzales -------- 482, 483, 714
City of Canton v. Harris ----------- 685
Clay v. United States -------------- 424
Coleman v. Thompson - 211, 213, 214,
   215, 289, 302, 703
Cone v. Bell ----------------------- 302
Connecticut Dept. of Public Safety v.
   Doe----------------------------- 535
Connick v. Thompson -------------- 685
Crawford v. Washington ----------- 315
Critchley v. Thaler----------------- 268
Cullen v. Pinholster - 347, **348**, 415,
   693, 694, 710
Culombe v. Connecticut ----------- 199
Custis v. United States------------ 432
D'Ambrosio v. Bagley -------------- 658
Danforth v. Minnesota--------316, 422
Daniel v. Louisiana ---------------- 310
Dansby v. Hobbs------------------- 229
Darr v. Burford ----------------130, 178
Davis v. Blackburn ---------------- 148
Davis v. Terry --------------------- 97
Davis v. United States-- 147, 211, 420
Day v. McDonough------------------ 660
Delaware v. Van Arsdall----------- 397

Demore v. Kim ---------------------- 492
Desist v. United States ------------ 305
Dickerson v. United States -------- 150
DIOP v. ICE/Homeland Security - 493
**District Attorney's Office for
Third Judicial Dist. v. Osborne**
---------------------------------------**686**
Douglas v. California ---------- 171, 226
Dow v. Circuit Court of the First
Circuit--------------------------------528
Doyle v. Ohio -------------------------401
Dretke v. Haley---------- 166, 200, 431
Drinkard v. Johnson -----------------322
Duncan v. Kahahamoku------ 553, 584
Duncan v. Walker ------------- 266, 272
Earhart v. Johnson------------------658
Early v. Packer -----------------------340
Earp v. Ornoski ---------------------377
Edwards v. Arizona ------------------308
Edwards v. Balisok----------- 398, 683
Edwards v. Carpenter----------------216
Engle v. Isaac -----------------------213
Escobado v. Illinois-----------------316
Esmail v. Obama---------------------627
Esslinger v. Davis --------------------659
Evans v. Chavis -----------------------278
Evitts v. Lucey----------------- 150, 171
Ex parte Bollman -------------- 22, 75
Ex parte Dillon -----------------------527
Ex parte Grossman-------------- 88, 96
Ex parte Hawk ----------------------178
Ex parte Hayes ---------------------- 96
Ex parte Lange ----------------------103
Ex parte McCardle -------89, **90**, 100
Ex parte Merryman----------- 54, **56**
Ex parte Milligan - 61, 63, 510, 543,
544
Ex parte Milligan, ------------------542
Ex parte Mitsuye Endo---- **503**, 584
Ex parte Parks----------------------103
Ex parte Quirin --------------- 541, 584
Ex parte Royall -------- 129, 173, **174**
Ex parte Siebold----------------------101
Ex parte Watkins----- 35, 74, 105, 204
Ex parte Yerger--8, **92**, 95, 464, 469
Fassler v. U.S. -----------------------513
Fay v. Noia----- 49, 119, 130, 148, 192,
380
Felker v. Turpin------------------ 73, 95
**Felker v. Turpin (Suspension
Clause Holding)**73, 435, 464, 469,
609, 623
Fernandez v. Phillips----------------488
Fielder v. Varner---------------------281
Fleming v. Evans ---------------------395
Fleming v. Page ----------------------591
Fong Yue Ting v. United States---447
Ford v. Wainwright----- 140, 157, 264
Foucha v. Louisiana -----------------517
Francis S. v. Stone -------------------342
Francis v. Henderson--- 211, 429, 533
Frank v. Mangum 17, 101, 105, **106**
Frantz v. Hazey ----------------------343
Frazier v. Bouchard------------------357
Fry v. Pliler------------------------414

Furman v. Georgia ------------------ 140
Gherebi v. Obama------------------- 629
Gibbons v. Ogden-------------------- 501
Gibson v. Klinger------------------- 295
Gideon v. Wainwright--------315, 708
Gilbert v. United States -------- **433**
Gilberti v. United States ----------- 421
Gomez v. Dretke -------------------- 676
Gonzalez v. Crosby------------------ 662
Gonzalez v. Thaler---------654, 675
Gonzalez v. Wong ------------------- 357
Graham v. Florida ------------------ 166
Granberry v. Greer --- 179, 189, **655**
Graves v. Cockrell-------------------- 676
Graziano v. United States --------- 419
Great Northern Railway v. Sunburst
Oil & Refining Co.----------------- 303
Green v. French --------------------- 321
Greer v. Miller --------------------- 404
Gregg v. Georgia----------------140, 160
Griffith v. Kentucky ---------------- 307
Grullon v. Mukasey----------------- 461
Guidry v. Dretke-------------------- 375
Gul v. Obama----------------------- 650
Gulf Offshore Co. v. Mobil Oil Corp86
Habeas Corpus Res. Ctr. v. U.S.
Dep't of Justice--------------------- 705
Hall v. Luebbers -------------------- 704
Hamdan v. Rumsfeld--- 541, 566, 572,
598
Hamdan v. U.S.---------------------- 569
Hamdi v. Rumsfeld 60, 510, 537, 554,
571, **573**, 614, 633
Hampton v. Miller ------------------ 657
Hardiman v. Reynolds -------------- 659
Harlow v. Fitzgerald ---- 299, 334, 685
Harrington v. Richter -------------- 301
Harris v. Scully --------------------- 658
Harrison v. Ollison------------------ 439
Heck v. Humphrey ----677, **678**, 695
Heikkila v. Barber ------- 456, 464, 467
Herb v. Pitcairn--------------------- 195
Herbert v. Billy -------------------- 321
Hernandez v. Conway--------------- 189
Herrera v. Collins ---- 150, **152**, 625,
690, 691
Herring v. New York ---------------- 160
Herring v. United States----------- 299
Hill v. Lockhart -------------------340, 399
Hill v. McDonough ---------------- **695**
Hilton v. Guyot--------------------- 177
Hirota v. MacArthur ----------556, 635
Hohn v. United States -------------- 675
Holland v. Florida---- **282**, 356, 425,
702
Holland v. Tucker ------------------- 295
Holloway v. Horn-------------------- 394
Horn v. Banks --------------------- 335
House v. Bell--------- 161, 231, 244, 394
Howard v. U.S. --------------------- 269
Howard v. United States----------- 666
Hudson v. Michigan ---------------- 147
Hurles v. Ryan --------------------- 377
I.N.S. v. St. Cyr50, 443, 444, 615, 714
Ibarra v. Thaler-------------------- 228

In re An Investigation of The W. Va. State Police Crime Lab. --------- 708
In re Booth ------------------------------- 77
In re Clark ----------------------------- 163
In re Class Action Application of Habeas Corpus on Behalf of All Material Witnesses in the Western District of Texas ------------------ 515
In re D.W. ----------------------------- 515
In re Davenport --------------------- 439
In re Davis ------------------- 96, 97, 162
In re Dorsainvil ----------------------- 438
In re Guantanamo Bay Detainee Litig. -------------------------------- 628
In re Guantanamo Bay Detainee Litigation ------------------------- 628
In re Guantanamo Detainee Cases -------------------------------------- 598
In re Habeas Corpus Cases -------- 708
In re Hill ------------------------------ 265
In re Jones --------------------------- 439
In re Marriage of Osborne --------- 534
In re Nwanze ------------------------ 440
In re Ontiberos ---------------------- 519
In re Proportionality Review Project -------------------------------------- 708
In re Proportionality Review Project II ---------------------------------- 708
In re Provenzano -------------------- 263
In re Reyolds ------------------------ 86
In re Ross ---------------------------- 563
In re Tarble ------------------------- 86
In re Vial ---------------------------- 423
In re Walker ------------------------ 526
In re Webster ----------------------- 423
INS v. Elias-Zacarias --------------- 483
INS v. St. Cyr ---------------- 461, 714
Irons v. Carey ----------------------- 336
Jackson v. Denno ------------------- 203
Jackson v. Frank -------------------- 342
Jackson v. Indiana ------------------ 513
Jackson v. Kelly -------------------- 357
Jackson v. Norris ------------------- 393
Jackson v. Virginia ------- 161, 242, 398
Jacobson v. Massachusetts -------- 526
James v. Kentucky ------------------ 214
Jean-Pierre v. U.S. Atty. Gen. ----- 483
Jenkins v. Delaware ---------------- 305
Jenkins v. Director of Virginia Center for Behavioral Rehabilitation --------------------- 519
Jimenez v. Quarterman -------------- 270
John R. Sand & Gravel Co. v. United States ------------------------------ 660
Johnson v. Avery -------------------- 188
Johnson v. Eisentrager -- 557, 591, 606, 617, 700
Johnson v. New Jersey -------------- 307
Johnson v. Tara Sheneva Williams -------------------------------------- 303
Johnson v. United States---- 269, 270, 432
Jones v. Cunningham -------- 528, 532
Jones v. United States ------- 419, 517
Kamara v. Attorney Gen. of the United States --------------------- 483
Kansas v. Crane -------------- 518, 526

Kansas v. Hendricks --- 517, 518, 519, 521
Kaoru Yamataya v. Fisher -------- 497
Kaufman v. United States---- 142, 426
Keeney v. Tamayo-Reyes ----- 380, 389
Kelava v. Gonzales ------------------ 499
Kentucky v. Whorton --------------- 399
Khalid v. Bush ----------------------- 598
Kimmelman v. Morrison ------ 149, 150
Kinder v. Purdy ---------------------- 437
Kiyemba v. Obama (Kiyemba I) --------------------------------- 645, 649
Kiyemba v. Obama (Kiyemba II) - 649
Kiyemba v. Obama (Kiyemba III) 649
Korematsu v. United States ------- 511
Kotteakos v. United States --- 400, 401
Kuhlmann v. Wilson ---------- 230, 257
Kumarasamy v. Att'y Gen. --------- 480
Kyles v. Whitley --------------------- 139
LaFevers v. Gibson ----------------- 263
Lafler v. Cooper ----------- 340, 400, 709
Lambert v. Blackwell --------------- 377
Lambrix v. Singletary -------------- 217
Landon v. Plasencia ---------------- 455
Lawrence v. Florida ----- 181, 270, 277
Lawrence v. Texas ------------------ 314
Leavitt v. Arave--------------------- 228
Lee v. Kemna ----------------------- 214
Lee v. Lampert ---------------------- 296
Lehman v. Lycoming County Children's Services ------------- 528
Lindh v. Murphy -------------------- 300
Linkletter v. Walker ---------------- 304
Lockhart v. Fretwell---------------- 324
Lockyer v. Andrade ----------------- 335
Lolong v. Gonzales ------------------ 482
Lopes v. Gonzales ------------------- 480
Ludecke v. Watkins---------- 494, 499
Lundy v. Campbell------------------- 188
Machibroda v. United States ------ 425
Mackey v. United States ------ 305, 306
Madu v. U.S. Att'y Gen. ------------ 480
Magana-Pizano v. I.N.S. ----------- 458
Maples v. Thomas------------------- 218
Mapp v. Ohio ------------------ 143, 304
Marbury v. Madison------------ 22, 299
Mardesich v. Cate ------------------- 281
Martin v. Bartow -------------------- 523
Martinez v. Ryan ----- 213, 217, 218, 220, 356, 382, 430, 709
Martinez v. Stewart Villareal ----- 264
Massaro v. United States ---------- 430
Massiah v. United States---- 248, 257
Mathews v. Eldridge --- 578, 592, 610, 614, 717
Matteo v. Superintendent --------- 322
Matter of Silva-Trevino ----------- 484
Matter of Wilmer Rodrigo Castro Rodriguez ----------------------- 484
McCleskey v. Kemp------------ 160, 257
McCleskey v. Zant -------------- 75, 248
McCray v. New York ---------------- 306
McCurry v. Allen -------------------- 683
McFarland v. Scott ----------------- 383
McKaskle v. Wiggins---------------- 398
McNally v. Hill---------------------- 528
Medellín v. Dretke ------------------ 676

Medina v. California ---------------- 691
Medina v. People of the State of
    California-------------------------------- 513
Mercadel v. Cain -------------------- 189
Michael Williams v. Taylor ---- 385,
    386, 435
Michigan v. Long -------------- 201, 215
Miller El v. Dretke------------------**359**
Miller v. Alabama -------------------- 166
Miller v. N.J. State Dept. of Corr. 425
Miller–El v. Cockrell----------- 360, 673
Miller-El v. Dretke ------------------ 359
Mills v. Maryland-------------------- 335
Miranda v. Arizona 149, 202, 307, 316
Missouri v. Frye--------- 340, 400, 709
Mitchell v. Esparza------------------ 414
Mohammed v. Obama ----------------- 634
Moline v. City of Castle Rock ------ 526
Montero–Martinez v. Ashcroft----- 481
Mooney v. Holohan------------------- 119
Moore v. Dempsey ---- 101, 105, **115**
Moore v. Draper---------------------- 527
Morris v. Dretke --------------------- 180
Munaf v. Geren ---------------- 635, 714
Murphy v. Netherland --------------- 676
Murray v. Carrier--213, 216, 226, 230
Murray v. Giarratano --------- 172, 216
Myers v. Bethlehem Shipbuilding
    Corp. ------------------------------------ 173
Neal v. Puckett ---------------------- 343
Neelley v. Nagel --------------- 321, 322
Nelson v. Campbell------------------- 695
Nijhawan v. Holder ----------------- 484
Nishimura Ekiu v. U.S. -----------**475**
Nken v. Holder ---------------------- 488
Norfolk & Western R. Co. v. Train
    Dispatchers ----------------------------- 274
Noriega-Lopez v. Ashcroft----------- 461
O'Brien v. Dubois ------------------- 322
Oceanic Steam Navigation Co. v.
    Stranahan------------------------------- 446
Ochoa v. Sirmons -------------------- 265
O'Connor v. Donaldson-------------- 524
Oetjen v. Central Leather Co. ----- 648
O'Laughlin v. O'Brien --------------- 346
Omar v. McHugh --------------------- 636
O'Neal v. McAninch------------------ 410
Osborne v. District Attorney's Office
    ---------------------------------- 161, 165
O'Sullivan v. Boerckel -------------- 180
Outlaw v. Sternes-------------------- 265
Pace v. Diguglielmo ----- 279, 281, 290
Padilla v. Kentucky ----- 400, 459, 709
Padilla v. United States ------------ 437
Padilla v. Yoo ----------------------- 700
Palko v. Connecticut ---------------- 306
Panetti v. Quarterman-------- 141, 264
Pearson v. Callahan ---------- 335, 411
Pennsylvania v. Finley-172, 216, 690,
    691, 693
Penry v. Johnson-------------------- 345
Penry v. Lynaugh-------------------- 312
People v. Deskovic-------------------- 412
People v. Shilitano-------------------- 164

People's Mojahedin Organization of
    Iran v. U.S. Dept. of State ------- 499
Perillo v. Johnson ------------------- 704
Perkins v. McQuiggin --------------- 296
Pliler v. Ford------------------------- 190
Plunkett v. Johnson ----------------- 657
Porter v. McCollum ------------------ 344
Preiser v. Rodriguez----- 528, 678, 695
Price v. Johnston -------------------- 246
Prigg v. Pennsylvania---------------- 76
Prost v. Anderson ------------------- 437
Puri v Gonzales --------------------- 481
Purnell v. Missouri Dep't of
    Corrections ----------------------------- 394
Ramadan v. Gonzales --------------- 482
Ramdass v. Angelone ---------------- 341
Ramos-Martinez v. United States 425
Rasul v. Bush ------------------ 53, 597
Rasul v. Myers --------------------- 628
Reed v. Ross------------------------- 217
Reid v. Covert ---------------------- 563
Reyes–Requena v. United States- 439
Rhines .v. Weber-------------------- 357
Rhines v. Weber-----------------190, 272
Richardson v. Bowersox ------------ 322
Ring v. Arizona---------------------- 160
Rita v. United States---------------- 419
Roberts v. Ward---------------------- 321
Robinson v. California ------------- 526
Rochin v. California ---------------- 157
Rodriguez v. Sandstrom------------ 515
Rompilla v. Beard ------------------- 344
Roper v. Simmons ------------------- 314
Rose v. Clark------------------------ 398
Rose v. Lundy ---------------------- **182**
Ross v. Moffitt---------------------- 171
Rumsfeld v. Padilla-------------515, 596
Russello v. United States ---------- 424
Salahi v. Obama -------------------- 631
Salts v. Epps----------------------- 343
San Martin v. McNeil --------------- 295
Sanders v. United States ----119, 214,
    229, 247, 380
Sandvik v. United States ---------- 425
Sawyer v. Whitley--------------165, 230
Schall v. Martin---------------------- 513
Schlup v. Delo --------------------230, 260
Schmitt v. Maurer ------------------ 461
Schriro v. Landrigan ----------350, 379
Seling v. Young ---------------------- **519**
Sharrieff v. Cathel ----------------- 658
Shaughnessy v. Pedreiro----------- 457
Shaughnessy v. United States ex rel.
    Mezei-------------- 443, 449, 625, 647
Skinner v. Switzer ------------------ 165
Slack v. McDaniel ---------- 668, **669**
Smalls v. Batista -------------------- 322
Smith v. Baldi ---------------------- 128
Smith v. Dretke---------------------- 674
Smith v. Murray -------------------- 230
Smith v. Turner--------------------- 445
Solem v. Stumes -------------------- 308
Solomon v. United States ---------- 425
Souter v. Jones--------------------- 295
Spears v. Stewart ------------------- 704

Spencer v. Kemna ------------- 650, 683
Starns v. Andrews -------------------- 269
State v. Avery ------------------------- 412
State v. Peart ------------------------- 708
State, ex. rel. Dorsey, v. Haines --- 515
Stein v. New York -------------------- 515
Stewart v. Smith --------------------- 201
Stone v. Powell ---- 100, 141, 209, 304,
   409, 418, 703
Strait v. Laird ----------------------- 533
Strickler v. Greene ------------------ 216
Sullivan v. Louisiana ---------------- 413
Summerville v. Warden, State Prison
   --------------------------------------- 164
Swain v. Alabama ------------- 306, 358
Swain v. Pressley ----- 64, 68, 609, 615
Tafflin v. Levitt ----------------------- 86
Tarble's Case ------------------------- **83**
Tarble's Case ---------------- 49, 83, 100
Tart v. Massachusetts -------------- 148
Taylor v. Louisiana ------------------ 306
Taylor v. Maddox -------------------- 377
Teague v. Lane ----------- 300, 306, 708
Terry Williams v. Taylor ---- 299, 322,
   350
Thorne v. Warden, Brooklyn House of
   Detention of Men ----------------- 513
Timms v. Johns ---------------------- 519
Torzala v. U.S. ---------------------- 429
Townsend v. Sain - 119, 247, 377, 379,
   425
Trest v. Cain -------------------- 214, 659
Trevino v. Thaler -------------------- 229
Triestman v. United States -------- 423
Trinidad y Garcia v. Thomas 489, 637
Tucker v. Catoe --------------------- 704
U.S. ex rel. Toth v. Quarles -------- 557
U.S. v. Cook ------------------------- 418
U.S. v. Denedo ---------------------- 440
U.S. v. Dominguez Benitez -------- 411
U.S. v. Freeman --------------------- 420
U.S. v. Kwan ------------------------ 440
U.S. v. Maybeck --------------------- 431
U.S. v. Pettiford -------------------- 432
U.S. v. Pipito ----------------------- 513
U.S. v. Santos ----------------------- 419
United States ex rel. Bilokumsky v.
   Tod --------------------------------- 478
United States ex rel. Knauff v.
   Shaughnessy ----------- 447, 451, 625
United States ex rel. Siegel v.
   Shinnick --------------------------- 527
United States v. Addonizio --------- 418
United States v. Aguirre–Ganceda
   --------------------------------------- 425
United States v. Archer ------------- 433
United States v. Awadallah -------- 515
United States v. Ayala -------------- 422
United States v. Barrett ------------ 438
United States v. Beggerly ---------- 287
United States v. Boose ------- 441, 442
United States v. Brockamp --------- 287
United States v. Comstock --------- 519
United States v. Fasano ------------- 441
United States v. Frady ---- 217, **426**
United States v. Gabaldon --------- 425
United States v. Guillen ------------ 419

United States v. Hayman --- 64, **65**,
   417, 511, 609, 615
United States v. Hudson and
   Goodwin ---------------------------- 38
United States v. Jordan ------------ 441
United States v. Marcello ---------- 425
United States v. Martin ------------ 441
United States v. Martinez --------- 421
United States v. Mikalajunas ----- 431
United States v. More ------------- 104
United States v. Morgan ----------- 440
United States v. Olano ------------- 656
United States v. Peterman -------- 437
United States v. Petty ------------- 425
United States v. Richter ----------- 440
United States v. Salerno ----------- 513
United States v. Saro -------------- 425
United States v. Sisco -------------- 419
United States v. Sosa -------------- 425
United States v. White ------------ 420
United States v. Yazell ------------ 530
Valerio v. Crawford ---------------- 676
Vasquez v. Hillery ------------- 179, 398
Viracacha v. Mukasey -------------- 482
Wahem/Hunt v. Early -------------- 268
Wainwright v. Sykes --- 154, 192, 202,
   248, 428, 429
Walker v. Crosby --------------------- 281
Walker v. Martin -------------------- 201
Wallace v. Duckworth -------------- 148
Waller v. Georgia -------------------- 398
Wang v. Ashcroft -------------------- 489
Wang v. Attorney Gen. ------------- 487
Wang v. Department of Homeland
   Security ---------------------------- 487
Weinberger v. Salfi ------------------ 656
Welch v. U.S. ------------------------ 419
Whorton v. Bockting ----------- 315, 708
Wiggins v. Smith -------- 140, 344, 377
Wilkinson v. Dotson ----------------- 683
Williams v. Hobbs ------------------- 394
Williams v. Kaiser ------------------ 715
Winston v. Pearson ----------------- 357
Withrow v. Williams ----------- 150, 426
Wofford v. Scott --------------------- 439
Wong Doo v. United States --------- 246
Wong Yang Sung v. McGrath ----- 457
Wood v. Spencer --------------------- 269
Woodford v. Garceau ---------------- 266
Woodford v. Ngo --------------------- 214
Woodford v. Visciotti ---------------- 346
Woodson v. North Carolina -------- 160
Woolery v. Arave -------------------- 148
World-Wide Volkswagen Corp. v.
   Woodson ---------------------------- 621
Wright v. United States ------------ 528
Wright v. West ----------------- 315, 332
Yarborough v. Alvarado ------------ 342
Ylst v. Nunnemaker ---------------- 216
Yohey v. Collins --------------------- 513
Young v. Conway -------------------- 148
Younger v. Harris ------------- 299, 683
Zadvydas v. Davis 444, 490, 501, 578,
   595

TABLE OF STATUTES

Statutes

U.S. Const. Art. I, § 8 ---------------- 44
U.S. Const. Art. I, § 8, cl. 4 --------- 444
U.S. Const. Art. I, § 8, cl. 8 --------- 603
U.S. Const. Art. I, § 8, cl. 10 -------- 553
U.S. Const. Art. I, § 8, cl. 14 -------- 541
U.S. Const. Art. I, § 9 ---------------- 44
U.S. Const. Art. I, § 9, cl. 2 --2, 18, 43, 46, 54, 470
U.S. Const. Art. II, § 1, cl. 1 --------- 592
U.S. Const. Art. II, § 2, cl. 1 - 591, 592
U.S. Const. Art. II, § 3 --------------- 592
U.S. Const. Art. II, § 3, cl. 1 -------- 592
U.S. Const. Art. III, § 2 -------------- 88
U.S. Const. Art. III, § 3, cl. 1 ------- 582

5 U.S.C. § 706(2)(E) ----------- 479, 483

8 U.S.C. § 155(a) ---------------------- 456
8 U.S.C. § 1101(a)(13) --------------- 459
8 U.S.C. § 1101(a)(43) --------------- 463
8 U.S.C. § 1101(a)(43)(F) ------------ 463
8 U.S.C. § 1101(a)(43)(M)(i) -------- 463
8 U.S.C. § 1105 ----------------------- 457
8 U.S.C. § 1105a ---------------------- 458
8 U.S.C. § 1105a(a) ------------ 457, 469
8 U.S.C. § 1105a(a)(10) ------------- 469
8 U.S.C. § 1182(9)(A) ---------------- 650
8 U.S.C. § 1182(a) -------------------- 459
8 U.S.C. § 1182(a)(ii) ---------------- 480
8 U.S.C. § 1182(c) -------------------- 462
8 U.S.C. § 1189 ----------------------- 499
8 U.S.C. § 1225(a) -------------------- 489
8 U.S.C. § 1225(b)(1) ---------------- 624
8 U.S.C. § 1225(b)(1)(B)(iii)(IV) --- 489
8 U.S.C. § 1225(b)(1)(C) ------------ 485
8 U.S.C. § 1226(c)(1) ---------------- 489
8 U.S.C. § 1226a(a)(6) --------------- 499
8 U.S.C. § 1227(a) -------------------- 459
8 U.S.C. § 1227(a)(1)(A) ------------ 470
8 U.S.C. § 1227(a)(1)(C) ------------ 470
8 U.S.C. § 1227(a)(1)(G) ------------ 470
8 U.S.C. § 1227(a)(5) ---------------- 470
8 U.S.C. § 1227(B)(i) ---------------- 480
8 U.S.C. §§ 1228—1229a ----------- 459
8 U.S.C. § 1229a(c)(3)(A) ----------- 460
8 U.S.C. § 1229a(c)(4) --------------- 461
8 U.S.C. § 1229b(a)(3) --------------- 484
8 U.S.C. § 1231 ---------------- 488, 636
8 U.S.C. § 1231(a)(1) ---------------- 490
8 U.S.C. § 1231(a)(3) ---------------- 490
8 U.S.C. § 1252 ----------458, 467, 473
8 U.S.C. § 1252(a) -------------------- 480
8 U.S.C. § 1252(a)(1)---- 464, 466, 468, 470, 624
8 U.S.C. § 1252(a)(2)(B)(i) --------- 481
8 U.S.C. § 1252(a)(2)(B)(ii)-------- 481
8 U.S.C. § 1252(a)(2)(C) ----- 464, 466, 467, 469, 480

8 U.S.C. § 1252(a)(2)(D) ------- 479, 480
8 U.S.C. § 1252(a)(5) ----------------479
8 U.S.C. § 1252(a)(9) ----------------485
8 U.S.C. § 1252(b)(1) ----------- 470, 487
8 U.S.C. § 1252(b)(4)(A) -------------487
8 U.S.C. § 1252(b)(4)(B) -------------483
8 U.S.C. § 1252(b)(4)(D) -------------486
8 U.S.C. § 1252(b)(5)(B) ------- 485, 714
8 U.S.C. § 1252(b)(9) --------- 464, 466, 467, 468
8 U.S.C. § 1252(d)(1) ----------------461
8 U.S.C. § 1252(e) -------------------624
8 U.S.C. § 1252(e)(2) --- 469, 485, 624, 714
8 U.S.C. § 1252(e)(3) ----------------625
8 U.S.C. § 1252(e)(5) ----------------625
8 U.S.C. § 1252(f)(2)-----------------488
8 U.S.C. § 1534(a)--------------------499
8 U.S.C. § 1534(b)—(c) --------------499
8 U.S.C. § 1534(g)-------------------500

10 U.S.C. § 801 ----------------------599
10 U.S.C. § 821 ---------- 542, 567, 569
10 U.S.C. § 948c ---------------------627
10 U.S.C. § 948r(a) ------------------627
10 U.S.C. § 949a(b)(2)(C) -----------627
10 U.S.C. § 949a(b)(3)(D) -----------627
10 U.S.C. § 950t(25) -----------------568
10 U.S.C. § 950v(b)(25) --------------568

18 U.S.C. § 16 -----------------------463
18 U.S.C. § 924(a)-------------------431
18 U.S.C. § 924(c)-------------------438
18 U.S.C. § 1962(d) -----------------430
18 U.S.C. § 1983---------------------653
18 U.S.C. § 2339A—2339B---------499
18 U.S.C. § 3006A------- 173, 259, 383
18 U.S.C. § 3006A(a)(2)(B) ---------383
18 U.S.C. § 3144----------------------514
18 U.S.C. § 3145----------------------513
18 U.S.C. § 3599(a)(2) ---------------383
18 U.S.C. § 3600----------------------441
18 U.S.C. § 3600(a)-------------------442
18 U.S.C. § 3600(a)(1) -------- 441, 442
18 U.S.C. § 3600(a)(2)—(a)(5) ------442
18 U.S.C. § 3600(a)(3)----------------442
18 U.S.C. § 3600(a)(7) ---------------441
18 U.S.C. § 3600(g)-------------------442
18 U.S.C. § 3600(g)(2)----------------442
18 U.S.C. § 3600(h)-------------------442
18 U.S.C. § 4001(a) -----------575, 589
18 U.S.C. § 4243----------------------517
18 U.S.C. § 4243(c) ------------------517
18 U.S.C. § 4243(d) ------------------517
18 U.S.C. § 4248----------------------519

28 U.S.C. § 1005(e)(2)(C) -----------598
28 U.S.C. § 1005(h)(1) ---------------598
28 U.S.C. § 1257----------------------200
28 U.S.C. § 1257(a) ------------------200
28 U.S.C. § 1331----------------------131

28 U.S.C. § 1651(a)------------------ 440
28 U.S.C. § 1915A(a)—(b)----------- 684
28 U.S.C. § 1983 --------------------- 681
28 U.S.C. § 2111 -------------- 403, 404
28 U.S.C. § 2241 ----40, 134, 417, 433,
436, 438, 440, 457, 458, 460, 461,
464, 466, 468, 469, 480, 528, 529,
573, 577, 597, 598, 599, 601, 635
28 U.S.C. §§ 2241—2255 -------------50
28 U.S.C. § 2241(a)----------------40, 50
28 U.S.C. § 2241(b)------------------ 134
28 U.S.C. § 2241(c) ---------------------40
28 U.S.C. § 2241(d)------------------557
28 U.S.C. § 2241(d)(5) --------- 134, 528
28 U.S.C. § 2241(e)------------------601
28 U.S.C. § 2242 -----------------------41
28 U.S.C. § 2243 ----------------- 41, 196
28 U.S.C. § 2244 ----40, 134, 246, 250,
251, 253, 265, 275, 423
28 U.S.C. § 2244(b)-- 41, 73, 246, 251,
255, 256, 265, 422, 423, 663, 666
28 U.S.C. § 2244(b)(1) --245, 246, 264,
265, 422
28 U.S.C. § 2244(b)(1)—(b)(2)---- 245,
262
28 U.S.C. § 2244(b)(2) ----- 73, 74, 245,
246, 260, 262, 265, 393, 422
28 U.S.C. § 2244(b)(2)(A)----- 262, 269
28 U.S.C. § 2244(b)(2)(B)----- 269, 664
28 U.S.C. § 2244(b)(2)(B)(ii) ------- 243,
262, 263, 393, 422
28 U.S.C. § 2244(b)(3) ---- 95, 265, 665
28 U.S.C. § 2244(b)(3)(A)----------- 265
28 U.S.C. § 2244(b)(3)(B)----------- 265
28 U.S.C. § 2244(b)(3)(C)----------- 265
28 U.S.C. § 2244(b)(3)(D)----- 265, 423
28 U.S.C. § 2244(b)(3)(E) ------- 95, 265
28 U.S.C. § 2244(b)(4) --------- 246, 265
28 U.S.C. § 2244(d)------- 41, 265, 266,
287, 291, 292, 661, 665
28 U.S.C. § 2244(d)(1) --268, 281, 282,
659
28 U.S.C. § 2244(d)(1)(A)----- 268, 424
28 U.S.C. § 2244(d)(1)(B)----- 268, 292
28 U.S.C. § 2244(d)(1)(B)—(d)(1)(D)
-------------------------------------- 292
28 U.S.C. § 2244(d)(1)(C)----- 268, 269
28 U.S.C. § 2244(d)(1)(D)---- 268, 269,
295
28 U.S.C. § 2244(d)(2) --190, 271, 273,
274, 278, 282, 291, 292, 662
28 U.S.C. § 2246 ----------------------577
28 U.S.C. § 2253 ---------670, 671, 675
28 U.S.C. § 2253(c) ----------- 235, 668,
670, 675
28 U.S.C. § 2253(c)(1) ---------------674
28 U.S.C. § 2253(c)(2) --668, 674, 675,
676
28 U.S.C. § 2253(c)(3) --------- 668, 675
28 U.S.C. § 2254 -------------40, 41, 50,
134, 185, 245, 262, 346,
415, 431, 435, 531, 532, 668
28 U.S.C. § 2254(a)-------134, 203, 346
28 U.S.C. § 2254(a)(1) ---------------134
28 U.S.C. § 2254(b)------ 173, 178, 182,
183, 213, 274, 350
28 U.S.C. § 2254(b)(1) ---------------189

28 U.S.C. § 2254(b)(1)(B) ---------- 180
28 U.S.C. § 2254(b)(2)---------189, 245
28 U.S.C. § 2254(b)(3)--- 179, 190, 658
28 U.S.C. § 2254(c)------------183, 189
28 U.S.C. § 2254(c)(3) -------------- 668
28 U.S.C. § 2254(d) -------------41, 134,
227, 300, 301, 302, 318, 319, 320,
332, 335, 337, 338, 343, 346, 347,
349, 350, 354, 355, 375, 379, 384,
414, 415, 674, 685, 703
28 U.S.C. § 2254(d)(1)-- 300, 301, 303,
314, 318, 321, 322, 329, 330, 331,
332, 333, 334, 335, 336, 337, 338,
339, 340, 342, 343, 344, 347, 348,
349, 350, 351, 352, 353, 354, 355,
358, 376, 378, 379, 415
28 U.S.C. § 2254(d)(1)—(d)(2) ----- 302
28 U.S.C. § 2254(d)(2)-- 300, 301, 315,
347, 352, 353, 354, 355, 358, 360,
369, 374, 375, 376, 377, 378, 384,
385
28 U.S.C. § 2254(e) -------------41, 301,
347, 384
28 U.S.C. § 2254(e)(1)-- 360, 374, 377,
378, 384, 385, 395
28 U.S.C. § 2254(e)(2)-- 347, 350, 351,
352, 353, 355, 369, 384, 385, 388,
389, 390, 391, 393, 394, 395, 634
28 U.S.C. § 2254(e)(2)(A)(i)--------- 395
28 U.S.C. § 2254(e)(2)(A)(i)—
(e)(2)(A)(ii)-------------------------- 385
28 U.S.C. § 2254(e)(2)(A)(ii)--------369,
385, 391, 392, 393, 395
28 U.S.C. § 2254(e)(2)(B)----- 385, 388,
392, 395
28 U.S.C. § 2254(i) ------------------ 383
28 U.S.C. § 2255------------- 40, 41, 50,
64, 67, 68, 69, 134, 204, 247, 250,
251, 266, 269, 417, 418, 419, 424,
426, 427, 429, 430, 431, 432, 433,
434, 436, 438, 440, 441, 442, 531,
609, 668
28 U.S.C. § 2255(a) -------------418, 419
28 U.S.C. § 2255(b) ------------------ 425
28 U.S.C. § 2255(e) ---------65, 421, 433
28 U.S.C. § 2255(f) -------------269, 424
28 U.S.C. § 2255(f)(4) --------------- 269
28 U.S.C. § 2255(h) ------ 422, 423, 435
28 U.S.C. § 2255(h)(1) ----------422, 435
28 U.S.C. §§ 2261—2266------ 267, 704
28 U.S.C. § 2261(b) ------ 267, 704, 705
28 U.S.C. § 2263 ---------------------- 704
28 U.S.C. § 2263(a) -------------267, 704
28 U.S.C. § 2265(b) ------------------ 705
28 U.S.C. § 2266(b)(1)(A) -----267, 704
28 U.S.C. §§ 2341—2351----------- 457
28 U.S.C. § 2347 ---------------------- 487
28 U.S.C. § 2554(d) ------------------ 672

42 U.S.C. § 264---------------------- 527
42 U.S.C. § 1983 ---135, 164, 334, 522,
523, 653, 677, 678, 679, 680, 681,
682, 683, 684, 685, 686, 687, 688,
689, 692, 694, 695, 696, 697, 698,
707
42 U.S.C. § 2241 ---------------------- 594
42 U.S.C. § 2254 ---------------------- 681

50 U.S.C. § 21 ------------------------ 493

State Statutes
Alaska Stat. Ann. § 12.72.010 ----- 163
Alaska Stat. Ann. § 12.73.010 ----- 694
Ariz. Rev. Stat. Ann. § 13–4085--- 514
Iowa Code Ann. § 804.11 ------------ 514
N.C. Gen. Stat. § 15A-1460-------- 712
N.C. Gen. Stat. § 15A-211 --------- 712
N.C. Gen. Stat. §§ 15A-284.50—
15A-284.53---------------------------- 712
N.H. Rev. Stat. Ann. § 597:6 ------- 514
Wash. Admin. Code § 246–100–
    040(3)-------------------------------- 527
Wash. Admin. Code § 246–100–055
--------------------------------------- 527

Uniform Code of Military Justice
UCMJ § 802(a)(9)--------------------- 541
UCMJ § 818 -------------------------- 541
UCMJ §§ 877—934 ----------------- 541

TABLE OF SECONDARY AUTHORITIES

Abrams, Kerry, Immigration Law
and the Regulation of Marriage, 91
Minn. L. Rev. 1635 (2007) ------- 446

Abrams, Kerry, Polygamy,
Prostitution, and the
Federalization of Immigration
Law, 105 Colum. L. Rev. 641
(2005)---------------------------------- 445

Ackerman, Bruce, Terrorism and the
Constitutional Order, 75 Fordham
L. Rev. 475 (2006) ----------------- 571

Aleinikoff, Thomas Alexander, David
A. Martin, Hiroshi Motomura, &
Maryellen Fullerton, Immigration
and Citizenship: Process and Policy
1257, 1296–97 (7th ed. 2012) -- 482,
493

Aleinikoff, Thomas Alexander,
Detaining Plenary Power: The
Meaning And Impact Of Zadvydas
v. Davis, 16 Geo. Immigr. L.J. 365
(2002)--------------------------------- 491

Altman, Heidi, Prosecuting Post-
Padilla: State Interests and the
Pursuit of Justice for Noncitizen
Defendants, 101 Geo L. J. 1 (2012)
--------------------------------------- 400

Amar, Akhil Reed, Sovereignty and
Federalism, 86 Yale L.J. 1425
(1987)----------------------------------87

Amar, Akhil Reed, The Bill of Rights
and the Fourteenth Amendment,
101 Yale L.J. 1193 (1992) ---------47

Arkin, Marc M., The Ghost at the
Banquet: Slavery, Federalism, and
Habeas Corpus for State Prisoners,
70 Tul. L. Rev. 1 (1995) ------------86

Baldus, David C., Charles Pulaski,
and George Woodworth,
Comparative Review of Death
Sentences: An Empirical Study of
the Georgia Experience, Journal of
Criminal Law and Criminology
(Northwestern University) 74 (3):
661 (1983) --------------------------- 260

Baldus, David C., George
Woodworth, & Catherine M.
Grosso, Race and Proportionality
Since McCleskey v. Kemp (1987):
Different Actors with Mixed
Strategies of Denial and
Avoidance, 39 Colum. Hum. Rts. L.
Rev. 143 (2007) --------------------- 261

Bandes, Susan, Taking Justice to its
Logical Extreme: A Comment on
Teague v. Lane, 66 S. Cal. L. Rev.
2453 (1993) ------------------------- 317

Bator, Paul M., Finality in Criminal
Law and Federal Habeas Corpus
for State Prisoners, 76 Harv. L.

Rev. 441 (1963) 12, 39, 73, 101, 309,
319, 702

Baum, Lawrence, Judicial
Specialization and the
Adjudication of Immigration Cases,
59 Duke L.J. 1501 (2010) ------- 487

Berg, Nicholas, Turning a Blind Eye
to Innocence: The Legacy of
Herrera v. Collins, 42 Am. Crim. L.
Rev. 121 (2005)-------------------- 162

Bernhard, Adele, Justice Still Fails:
A Review of Recent Efforts to
Compensate Individuals Who Have
Been Unjustly Convicted and Later
Exonerated, 52 Drake L. Rev. 703
(2004) ------------------------------- 686

Bittker, Boris I., The World War II
German Saboteurs' Case and Writs
of Certiorari Before Judgment by
the Court of Appeals: A Tale of
Nunc Pro Tunc Jurisdiction, 14
Const. Comment. 431 (1997)---- 553

Blackstone, William, 1
Commentaries on the Laws of
England 137 (1756–1769) -----------1

Blume, John H., AEDPA: The 'Hype'
and the 'Bite,' 91 Cornell L. Rev.
259 (2006) ------------------------- 339

Blume, John H., and Stephen P.
Garvey, Harmless Error in Federal
Habeas Corpus after Brecht v.
Abrahamson, 35 Wm & Mary L.
Rev. 163 (1993)-------------------- 411

Blume, John H., Sheri Lynn Johnson,
& Keir M. Weyble, In Defense of
Noncapital Habeas: A Response to
Hoffmann and King, 96 Cornell L.
Rev. 435 (2011)--------------267, 706

Blume, John, & William Pratt,
Understanding Teague v. Lane, 18
N.Y.U. Rev. L. & Soc. Change 325
(1990–1991) ------------------------ 317

Bradley, Curtis A., & Jack L.
Goldsmith, Congressional
Authorization and the War on
Terrorism, 118 Harv. L. Rev. 2047
(2005) -------------------------568, 591

Bradley, Curtis A., Clear Statement
Rules And Executive War Powers,
33 Harv. J.L. & Pub. Pol'y 139
(2010) ------------------------------- 624

Bradley, Curtis A., The Story of Ex
parte Milligan: Military Trials,
Enemy Combatants, and
Congressional Authorization, in
Presidential Power Stories (2009)
--------------------------------------- 544

Brilmayer, R. Lea, State Forfeiture
Rules and Federal Review of State
Criminal Convictions, 49 U. Chi. L.
Rev. 741 (1982)-------------------- 212

Brown, George D., Counter-Counter-Terrorism Via Lawsuit—The Bivens Impasse, 82 S. Cal. L. Rev. 841 (2009) --------------------------- 699

Brown, Robbie, Judges Free Inmate on Recommendation of Special Panel, New York Times, February 17, 2010 ---------------------------- 713

Burns, Amy Knight, Insurmountable Obstacles: Structural Errors, Procedural Default, and Ineffective Assistance, 64 Stan. L. Rev. 727 (2012) -------------------------- 217, 399

Buxton, Michael J., No Habeas for You! Al Maqaleh v. Gates, The Bagram Detainees, and the Global Insurgency, 60 Am. U. L. Rev. 519 (2010) ---------------------------------- 644

Carbone, June, & Naomi Cahn, Judging Families, 77 UMKC L. Rev. 267 (2008) ---------------------- 534

Carpenter, A.H., Habeas Corpus in the Colonies, 8 Am. Hist. Rev. (1902) --------------------------------- 19

Carter, Linda E., The Sporting Approach to Harmless Error in Criminal Cases: The Supreme Court's "No Harm, No Foul" Debacle in Neder v. United States, 28 Am. J. Crim. L. 229 (2001)--- 413

Chafee, Zechariah Jr., The Most Important Human Right in the Constitution, 32 B.U. L. Rev. 143 (1952) --------------------------------- 20

Chapel, Charles S., The Irony of Harmless Error, 51 Okla. L. Rev 501 (1998) --------------------------- 413

Chemerinsky, Erwin, Closing the Courthouse Doors, 14 Green Bag 2d 375 (2011) ------------------------- 356

Chemerinsky, Erwin, No Harm, No Foul, 16 Cal. Law 27 (Jan 1996) 413

Chemerinsky, Erwin, Thinking About Habeas Corpus, 37 Case W. L. Rev. 748 (1987) ------------------ 100

Chen, Rebecca, Closing The Gaps in the U.S. and International Quarantine Systems: Legal Implications of the 2007 Tuberculosis Scare, 31 Hous. J. Int'l L. 83 (2008) -------------------- 527

Clarke, Alan W., Procedural Labyrinths And The Injustice Of Death: A Critique Of Death Penalty Habeas Corpus (Part One), 29 U. Rich. L. Rev. 1327 (1985) 657

Cody, Edward, Ex-Detainee Describes Struggle for Exoneration, Washington Post, May 26, 2009 ----------------------- 623

Cohen, Thomas H., & Brian A. Reaves, U.S. Dep't of Justice, Bureau of Justice Statistics, Felony Defendants in Large Urban Counties, 2002, at 27 tbl.28 (2006) --- 137

Cole, David, Enemy Aliens, 54 Stan. L. Rev. 953 (2002) ------------493, 511

Collings, Rex A., Habeas Corpus for Convicts-Constitutional Right or Legislative Grace?, 40 Cal. L. Rev. 335 (1952)------------------------49, 52

Collins, Michael G., Article III Cases, State Court Duties, and the Madisonian Compromise, 1995 Wis. L. Rev. 39 ----------------------- 87

Collins, Valerie L., Camouflaged Legitimacy: Civil Commitment, Property Rights, and Legal Isolation, 52 How. L. J. 407 (2009) -------------------------------- 524

Connolly, Jon, and Marc D. Falkoff, Habeas, Information Asymmetries, and the War on Terror, 41 Seton Hall L. Rev. 1361 (2011) --------- 649

Conrat, Maisie, & Richard Conrat, Executive Order 9066: The Internment of 110,000 Japanese Americans (1992)------------------ 502

Corrado, Michael Louis, Sex Offenders, Unlawful Combatants, and Preventive Detention, 84 N.C. L. Rev. 77 (2005)------------------ 511

Cortner, Richard C., A Mob Intent on Death: The NAACP and the Arkansas Riot Cases (1988)----- 118

Crawford, Sharon E., Felker Fingernail Scrapings Test Proves Inconclusive, Macon Telegraph, Dec. 12, 2000-------------------------- 76

Currie, David P., The Civil War Congress, 73 U. Chi. L. Rev. 1131 (2006) --------------------------------- 61

Currie, David P., Through the Looking Glass: The Confederate Constitution in Congress, 1861–1865, 90 Va. L. Rev. 1257 (2004) 61

Curry, Colleen, and Michael S. James, Troy Davis Executed After Stay Denied by Supreme Court, ABC News, Sept. 21, 2011 --------- 97

Cushman, Robert E., Ex parte Quirin et al.—The Nazi Saboteur Case, 28 Cornell L.Q. 54 (1942) ------------ 553

Davey, Monica, & Abbey Goodnough, Doubts Rise as States Hold Sex Offenders After Prison, N.Y. Times, Mar. 4, 2007-------------------------- 517

Deming, Adam, Sex Offender Civil Commitment Programs: Current Practices, Characteristics, and Resident Demographics, 36 J. Psychiatry & L. 439 (2009)------ 517

Dinnerstein, Leonard, The Leo Frank Case (1987)------------------------- 112

Dow, David R., Jared Tyler, Frances Burliot, and Jennifer Jeans, Is It Constitutional To Execute Someone Who Is Innocent (And If It Isn't, How Can It Be Stopped Following House v. Bell)?, 42 Tulsa L. Rev. 277 (2006) ----------------- 159

Drizin, Steven A., & Richard A. Leo,
The Problem of False Confessions
in the Post-DNA World, 82 N.C. L.
Rev. 891 (2004) -------------------- 199

Duker, William F., A Constitutional
History of Habeas Corpus (1980)
---------------------------13, 19, 47, 86

Dworkin, Ronald, Why It Was a
Great Victory, N.Y. Rev. Books,
Aug. 14, 2008 ----------------------- 619

Edwards, Abra, Note, Cornejo-
Barreto Revisited: The Availability
of a Writ of Habeas Corpus to
Provide Relief from Extradition
under the Torture Convention, 43
Va. J. Int'l L. 889 (2003)--------- 489

Edwards, Harry T., To Err Is
Human, But Not Always Harmless:
When Should Legal Error Be
Tolerated?, 70 N.Y.U. L. Rev. 1167
(1995)-------------------------- 397, 413

Emily, Jennifer, Death Penalty Case
that Highlighted Jury Bias Ends in
Plea Deal, Dallas Morning News,
March 20, 2008 --------------------- 378

Entzeroth, Lyn S., Struggling for
Federal Judicial Review of
Successive Claims of Innocence: A
Study of How Federal Courts
Wrestled with the AEDPA to
Provide Individuals Convicted of
Non-Existent Crimes with Habeas
Corpus Review, 60 U. Miami L.
Rev. 75 (2005)---------------------- 439

Fairman, Charles, Reconstruction
and Reunion, 1864–1888 (1971)--77

Falkoff, Marc D., Back to Basics:
Habeas Corpus Procedures and
Long-Term Executive Detention,
86 Den. U. L. Rev. 961 (2009)--- 633

Fallon, Richard H. Jr. and Daniel J.
Meltzer, New Law, Non-
Retroactivity, and Constitutional
Remedies, 104 Harv. L. Rev. 1731
(1991)-------------------------- 305, 317

Fallon, Richard H. Jr., and Daniel J.
Meltzer, Habeas Corpus
Jurisdiction, Substantive Rights,
and the War on Terror, 120 Harv.
L. Rev. 2029 (2007)---------------- 637

Fallon, Richard H. Jr., Essay, The
Supreme Court, Habeas Corpus,
and the War on Terror: An Essay
on Law and Political Science, 110
Colum. L. Rev. 352 (2010) -------555

Fallon, Richard H. Jr., et al., Hart
And Wechsler's The Federal Courts
And The Federal System 405 (6th
ed. 2009)-----------------------------87

Farber, Daniel A., Lincoln's
Constitution 87 (2003) ------------543

Farnsworth, Ward, Signatures of
Ideology: The Case of the Supreme
Court's Criminal Docket, 104 Mich.
L. Rev. 67 (2005) ------------------ 276

Farrelly, Jeremiah J., Denying
Formalism's Apologist's: Reforming

Immigration Law's CIMT Analysis,
82 U. Colo. L. Rev. 877 (2011)-- 484

Feldman, Noah, Scorpions: The
Battles and Triumphs of FDR's
Great Supreme Court Justices 235
(2010) ------------------------------- 503

Field, Martha A., Assessing the
Harmlessness of Federal
Constitutional Error—A Process in
Need of a Rationale, 125 U Pa. L.
Rev. 15 (1976) --------------------- 397

Findley, Keith A., Innocence
Protection in the Appellate
Process, 93 Marq. L. Rev. 591
(2009) ------------------------------- 711

Fisher, Stanley Z., Convictions of
Innocent Persons in
Massachusetts: An Overview, 12
B.U. Pub. Int. L.J. 1 (2002) ----- 713

Flango, Victor E., Nat'l Ctr. for State
Courts, Habeas Corpus in State
and Federal Courts 46 (1994) -- 138

Florendo, Bryan, Prost v. Anderson
and the Enigmatic Savings Clause
of § 2255: When is a Remedy by
Motion 'Inadequate or Ineffective'?,
89 Denv. U. L. Rev. 435 (2012)- 439

Forsyth, Clarke D., The Historical
Origins of Broad Federal Habeas
Review Reconsidered, 70 Notre
Dame L. Rev. 1079 (1995) ------- 104

Franklin, David, Enemy Combatants
and the Jurisdictional Fact
Doctrine, 29 Cardozo L. Rev. 1001
(2008) ------------------------------- 622

Freedman, Eric M., Habeas Corpus
in Three Dimensions: Dimension I:
Habeas as a Common Law Writ, 46
Harv C.R.-C.L. L. Rev. 591
(2011) ------------------------------- 715

Freedman, Eric M., Just Because
John Marshall Said It, Doesn't
Make It So: Ex parte Bollman and
the Illusory Prohibition on the
Federal Writ of Habeas Corpus for
State Prisoners in the Judiciary
Act of 1789, 51 Ala. L. Rev. 531
(2000) -------------------------- 34, 336

Freedman, Eric M., Leo Frank Lives:
Untangling the Historical Roots of
Meaningful Federal Habeas
Corpus Review of State
Convictions, 51 Ala. L. Rev. 1467
(2000) ------------------------------- 112

Freedman, Eric M., Milestones in
Habeas Corpus: Part II Leo Frank
Lives: Untangling the Historical
Roots of Meaningful Federal
Habeas Corpus Review of State
Convictions, 51 Ala. L. Rev. 1467
(2000) ------------------------------- 106

Freedman, Eric M., Milestones in
Habeas Corpus: Part III Brown v.
Allen: The Habeas Corpus
Revolution That Wasn't, 51 Ala. L.
Rev. 1541 (2000) --------- 3, 128, 318

Freedman, Eric M., The Revised ABA
    Guidelines and The Duties of
    Lawyers and Judges in Capital
    Post-conviction Proceedings, 5 J.
    App. Prac. & Proc. 325 (2003)--- 355
Freedman, Eric M., The Suspension
    Clause in the Ratification Debates,
    44 Buff. L. Rev. 451 (1996)------- 19
Frey, Robert Seitz, and Nancy
    Thompson-Frey, Charles and
    Louise Samuels, Night Fell on
    Georgia (1956) ----------------112
Frey, Robert Seitz, and Nancy
    Thompson-Frey, The Silent and the
    Damned (1988) ---------------112
Friedman, Barry, A Tale of Two
    Habeas, 73 Minn. L. Rev. 247
    (1988)-----------------------------149
Friendly, Henry J., Is Innocence
    Irrelevant? Collateral Attack on
    Criminal Judgments, 38 U. Chi. L.
    Rev. 142 (1970) ---71, 148, 150, 242,
    309, 702, 713
Garcia, Alfredo, The Right to Counsel
    Under Siege: Requiem for an
    Endangered Right?, 29 Am. Crim.
    L. Rev. 35 (1991) ------------------257
Garrett, Brandon L., & Tania Tetlow,
    Criminal Justice Collapse: The
    Constitution After Hurricane
    Katrina, 56 Duke L.J. 127
    (2006)---------------------------- 513, 514
Garrett, Brandon L., Aggregation in
    Criminal Law, 95 Calif. L. Rev. 383
    (2007)-------------------------------708
Garrett, Brandon L., Claiming
    Innocence, 92 Minn. L. Rev. 1629
    (2008)-------------------------------412
Garrett, Brandon L., Convicting the
    Innocent: Where Criminal
    Prosecutions Go Wrong 5, 235, 236
    (2011)-------------------- 150, 685, 686
Garrett, Brandon L., DNA and Due
    Process, 78 Ford. L. Rev. 2919
    (2010)-------------------------------693
Garrett, Brandon L., Habeas Corpus
    and Due Process, 98 Cornell L.
    Rev. 47 (2012)----594, 622, 701, 718
Garrett, Brandon L., Innocence,
    Harmless Error, and Federal
    Wrongful Conviction Law, 2005
    Wis. L. Rev. 35----------------------684
Garrett, Brandon L., Judging
    Innocence, 108 Colum. L. Rev. 55
    (2008)------------------- 150, 162, 243
Garrett, Brandon L., The Substance
    of False Confessions, 62 Stan. L.
    Rev. 1051 (2010) -------------------199
Ginsburg, Ruth Bader, In Memoriam:
    William H. Rehnquist, 119 Harv.
    L. Rev. 6 (2005)--------------------131
Glaberson, William, In Shift, Justices
    Agree to Review Detainees' Case,
    N.Y. Times, June 30, 2007 -------600
Glazier, David, Ignorance is Not
    Bliss: The Law of Belligerent
    Occupation and the U.S. Invasion

of Iraq, 58 Rutgers L. Rev. 121
    (2005) ------------------------------ 538
Glazier, David, Kangaroo Court or
    Competent Tribunal?: Judging the
    21st Century Military Commission,
    89 Va. L. Rev. 2005 (2003)------- 542
Goldblatt, Craig, Comment,
    Harmless Error as Constitutional
    Common Law: Congress' Power to
    Reverse Arizona v. Fulminante, 60
    U. Chi. L. Rev. 985 (1993) ------- 397
Golden, Harry, A Little Girl is Dead
    (1965) ------------------------------ 112
Goodman, Ryan, & Derek Jinks,
    International Law, U.S. War
    Powers, and the Global War on
    Terrorism, 118 Harv. L. Rev. 2653
    (2005) ------------------------------ 630
Green, Leslie C., The Contemporary
    Law of Armed Conflict (2d ed.
    2000) ------------------------------ 538
Grinberg, Emanuella, Exonerated
    death row inmate: 'Took 'em long
    enough,' CNN, May 13, 2009 --- 244
Hafetz, Jonathan, Habeas Corpus
    After 9/11 117 (2011)------------- 572
Hafetz, Jonathan, Habeas Corpus,
    Judicial Review, and Limits On
    Secrecy In Detentions At
    Guantánamo, 5 Cardozo Pub. L.
    Pol'y & Ethics J. 127 (2006)----- 594
Halliday, Paul D., & G. Edward
    White, The Suspension Clause:
    English Text, Imperial Contexts,
    and American Implications, 94 Va.
    L. Rev. 575 (2008) -- 28, 33, 47, 556,
    605, 620, 715
Halliday, Paul D., Habeas Corpus:
    From England to Empire 34, 108,
    109, 122–133 (2010) ----14, 534, 556
Hammel, Andrew, Diabolical
    Federalism: A Functional Critique
    and Proposed Reconstruction of
    Death Penalty Federal Habeas, 39
    Am. Crim. L. Rev. 1 (2002) ------ 706
Hanson, Roger A., & Henry W.K.
    Daley, U.S. Dep't of Justice,
    Bureau of Justice Statistics,
    Federal Habeas Corpus Review:
    Challenging State Court Criminal
    Convictions 17 (1995) ------------ 137
Harcourt, Bernard E., From the
    Asylum to the Prison: Rethinking
    the Incarceration Revolution, 84
    Tex. L. Rev. 1751 (2006)--------- 524
Hart, Henry M., Jr., Foreword: Time
    Chart of the Justices, 73 Harv. L.
    Rev. 84 (1959) --------------------- 118
Hart, Henry M., The Power of
    Congress to Limit the Jurisdiction
    of Federal Courts: An Exercise in
    Dialectic, 66 Harv. L. Rev. 1362
    (1953) ------------------------------ 448
Hartigan, Richard Shelly, Lieber's
    Code and the Law of War 20 (1983)
    ------------------------------------ 538

Hartnett, Edward A., The Constitutional Puzzle of Habeas Corpus, 46 B.C. L. Rev. 251 (2005)--------------------------------48

Hasday, Jill Elaine, Federalism and the Family Reconstructed, 45 UCLA L. Rev. 1297 (1998) ------- 535

Healy, Thomas, The Rise of Unnecessary Constitutional Rulings, 83 N.C. L. Rev. 847 (2005) -------------------------------------- 411

Henkin, Louis, The Constitution as Compact and as Conscience: Individual Rights Abroad and at Our Gates, 27 Wm. & Mary L. Rev. 11 (1985)---------------------------- 448

Hertz, Randy, & James S. Liebman, 1 Federal Habeas Corpus Practice and Procedure (2d ed. 1994)-------12

Hertz, Randy, & James S. Liebman, Federal Habeas Corpus Practice and Procedure §§ 11.4[b], 23.1, 23.4, 25.4, 32.2 (6th ed. 2011)-- 173, 180, 302, 313, 420, 426, 677, 684

Heytens, Toby J., Managing Transitional Moments in Criminal Cases, 115 Yale L.J. 922 (2006) 317

Hoffmann, Joseph L., Retroactivity and the Great Writ: How Congress Should Respond to Teague v. Lane, 1990 BYU L. Rev. 183------------ 317

Hoffmann, Joseph L., and Nancy J. King, Rethinking the Federal Role in State Criminal Justice, 84 N.Y.U. L. Rev. 89 (2009)--------- 706

Hoffstadt, Brian M., How Congress Might Redesign a Leaner, Cleaner Writ of Habeas Corpus, 49 Duke L.J. 947 (2000)--------------------- 703

Huq, Aziz Z., What Good is Habeas?, 26 Const. Commentary 385 (2010) -------------------------------------- 626

Hurd, R., Treatise on the Right of Personal Liberty, and On the Writ of Habeas Corpus and the Practice Connected with It: With a View of the Law of Extradition of Fugitives 166 (2d ed. 1876)-------------------86

Hutchinson, Dennis J., The Achilles Heel of the Constitution: Justice Jackson and the Japanese Exclusion Cases, in 2002 Sup. Ct. Rev. 455 ----------------------------511

Ides, Allan, Habeas Standards of Review Under 28 U.S.C. § 2254(d)(1): A Commentary on Statutory Text and Supreme Court Precedent, 60 Wash. & Lee L. Rev. 677 (2003) ----------------------------321

Isenberg, Nancy, Fallen Founder: The Life of Aaron Burr (2008) ----35

Jeffries, John C. Jr. & William J. Stuntz, Ineffective Assistance and Procedural Default in Federal Habeas Corpus, 57 U. Chi. L. Rev. 679 (1990) ----------------------------713

Jeffries, John C. Jr., Reversing the Order of Battle in Constitutional Torts, 2009 Sup. Ct. Rev. 115 -- 411

Kalhan, Anil, Rethinking Immigration Detention, 110 Colum. L. Rev. Sidebar 42 (2010) ------------------------------- 460

Kamin, Sam, Harmless Error and the Rights/Remedies Split, 88 Va. L. Rev. 1 (2002) ------------------397, 411

Kannenberg, Casey C., Wading Through The Morass Of Modern Federal Habeas Review Of State Capital Prisoners' Claims, 28 Quinnipiac L. Rev. 107 (2009)-- 705

Kassin, Saul M., & Holly Sukel, Coerced Confessions and the Jury: An Experimental Test of the Harmless Error Rule, 21 Law & Hum. Behav. 27 (1997) ----------- 399

Katyal, Neal K., & Laurence H. Tribe, Waging War, Deciding Guilt: Trying the Military Tribunals, 111 Yale L.J. 1259 (2002)------------- 568

Kaufman, Fred, Report of the Kaufman Commission on Proceedings Involving Guy Paul Morin (1998) ----------------------- 712

King, Nancy J., & Joseph L. Hoffman, Habeas for the Twenty-First Century: Uses, Abuses, and the Future of the Great Writ 70 ----------------------------------136, 706

King, Nancy J., Fred L. Cheesman II, & Brian J. Ostrom, Nat'l Ctr. for State Courts, Final Technical Report: Habeas Litigation in U.S. District Courts 19, 21, 27, 60 (2007) ------------- 137, 173, 181, 301

Klein, Adam, & Benjamin Wittes, Preventative Detention in American Theory and Practice, 2 Harv. Nat'l Sec. J. 85 (2011) ---- 524

Kovarsky, Lee B., A Constitutional Theory of Habeas Power, 97 Va. L. Rev. __ (2012)---------------------- 718

Kovarsky, Lee B., A Constitutional Theory of Habeas Power, 98 Va. L. Rev. __ (forthcoming 2013) - 48, 718

Kovarsky, Lee B., AEDPA's Wrecks: Comity, Finality, and Federalism, 82 Tul. L. Rev. 443 (2007) ------- 339

Kovarsky, Lee B., Death Ineligibility and Habeas Corpus, 925 Cornell L. Rev. 329 (2010)-------------------- 230

Kovarsky, Lee B., Habeas Verité, 47 Tulsa L. Rev. 13 (2011) ---------- 707

Kovarsky, Lee B., Lee Kovarsky, Custodial and Collateral Process: A Response to Professor Garrett, 98 Cornell L. Rev. Online 1 (2013) 701

Kovarsky, Lee B., Original Habeas Redux, 97 Va. L. Rev. 61 (2011) - 33

Landes, William M., and Richard A. Posner, Harmless Error, 30 J Legal Stud 161 (2001) ------------------- 397

Lane, Charles, Shanghaied, 7 Green Bag 2d 247 (2004)------------------565

Legomsky, Stephen H., The Detention of Aliens: Theories, Rules, and Discretion, 30 Univ. Miami Inter–Am. L. Rev. 531 (1999)--------------------------------447

Leiderman, Aaron G., Note, Preserving the Constitution's Most Important Human Right: Judicial Review of Mixed Questions Under the REAL ID Act, 106 Colum. L. Rev. 1367 (2006) --------------------482

Levenson, Laurie L., Detention, Material Witnesses & the War on Terrorism, 35 Loy. L.A. L. Rev. 1217 (2002) --------------------------515

Liebman, James S., & Randy Hertz, Brecht v. Abrahamson: Harmful Error in Habeas Corpus Law, 84 J. Crim. L. & Criminology 1109 (1994)--------------------------------411

Liebman, James S., & William F. Ryan, Some Effectual Power: The Quantity and Quality of Decisionmaking Required of Article III Courts, 98 Colum. L. Rev. 696 (1998)----------------------48, 336, 718

Liebman, James S., Apocalypse Next Time?: The Anachronistic Attack on Habeas Corpus/Direct Review Parity, 92 Colum. L. Rev. 1997 (1992)--------------------------------133

Liebman, James S., Jeffrey Fagan, & Valerie West, A Broken System: Error Rates in Capital Cases, 1973–1995 5 (2000) ---------------137

Liebman, James S., Opting for Real Death Penalty Reform, 63 Ohio St. L.J. 315 (2002)----------------------706

Liebman, James S., The Overproduction of Death, 100 Colum. L. Rev. 2030 (2000) ------706

Lin, Raymond Y., A Prisoner's Constitutional Right to Attorney Assistance, 83 Colum. L. Rev. 1279 (1983)--------------------------------188

Lincoln, Abraham, Message to Congress in Special Session (July 4, 1861)-------------------------------- 60

Lindsay, Matthew J., Immigration as Invasion: Sovereignty, Security, and the Origins of the Federal Immigration Power, 45 Harv. C.R.-C.L. L. Rev. 1 (2010) --------------446

Linzer, Dafna, and Glenn Kessler, Decision to Move Detainees Resolved Two-Year Debate Among Bush Advisers, Wash Post, Sept. 8, 2006--------------------------------568

Maiatico, Jerome M., All Eyes on Us: A Comparative Critique of the North Carolina Innocence Inquiry Commission, 56 Duke L.J. 1345 (2007)--------------------------------712

Marceau, Justin F., Challenging the Habeas Process Rather than the Result, 69 Wash. & Lee L. Rev. 85 (2012) ------------------------------- 356

Marceau, Justin F., Deference and Doubt: The Interaction of § AEDPA 2254(d)(2) and (e)(1), 82 Tulane L. Rev. 385 (2007)--------------------- 378

Marceau, Justin F., Don't Forget Due Process: The Path Not (Yet) Taken in § 2254 Habeas Corpus Adjudications, 62 Hastings L.J. 1 (2010) ------------------------------- 717

Martin, David A., Due Process and Membership in the National Community: Political Asylum and Beyond, 44 U. Pitt. L. Rev. 165 (1983) ------------------------------- 449

Martin, David A., Offshore Detainees and the Role of Courts After Rasul v. Bush: The Underappreciated Virtues of Deferential Review, 25 B.C. Third World L.J. 125 (2005) ------------------------------- 637

Martin, David A., The Graduated Application of Constitutional Protections for Aliens: The Real Meaning of Zadvydas v. Davis, 2001 Sup. Ct. Rev. 47 ------------ 491

Martin, Luther, The Genuine Information Delivered to the Legislature of the State of Maryland Relative to the Proceedings of the General Convention Lately Held at Philadelphia (1788)------------------ 47

Martinez, Jenny S., Process and Substance in the War on Terror, 108 Colum. L. Rev. 1013 (2008)594, 710

Mashaw, Jerry L., Federal Administration and Administrative Law in the Gilded Age, 119 Yale L.J. 1362 (2010)---------------------- 89

Mashaw, Jerry L., The Supreme Court's Due Process Calculus for Administrative Adjudication in Mathews v. Eldridge: Three Factors in Search of a Theory of Value, 44 U. Chi. L. Rev. 28 (1976) ------------------------------- 592

Matteson, Nicholas, Comment, Low Savings Rate: Applying the Section 2255 Savings Clause to Federal Sentencing Claims in Gilbert v. United States, 53 B.C. L. Rev. E. Supp. 61 (2012) ------------------ 437

Mazzetti, Mark, Eric Schmitt, and Robert F. Worth, Two-Year Manhunt Led to Killing of Awlaki in Yemen, N.Y. Times, Sept. 30, 2011 ------------------------------- 595

McConnell, David M., Judicial Review Under the Immigration and Nationality Act: Habeas Corpus And The Coming Of Real ID (1996–2005), 51 N.Y.L. Sch. L. Rev. 75 (2006–2007) -------------- 480

McCord, David, The Trial/Structural
Error Dichotomy: Erroneous, and
Not Harmless, 45 U. Kan. L. Rev.
1401 (1997) ------------------------ 399

Meador, Daniel John, Habeas Corpus
and Magna Carta: Dualism of
Power and Liberty 26 (1966) ------39

Meltzer, Daniel J., Habeas Corpus
Jurisdiction: The Limits of Models,
66 S. Cal. L. Rev. 2507 (1993) -- 317

Meltzer, Daniel J., Habeas Corpus,
Suspension, and Guantánamo: The
Boumediene Decision, 2008 Sup.
Ct. Rev. 1 --------------------------- 620

Meltzer, Daniel J., State Court
Forfeitures of Federal Rights, 99
Harv. L. Rev. 1128 (1986) ------- 212

Meyer, Linda, Nothing We Say
Matters: Teague and New Rules,
61 U. Chi. L. Rev. 423 (1994) --- 317

Mindes, Paula, Tuberculosis
Quarantine: A Review of Legal
Issues in Ohio and Other States,
10 J.L. & Health 403 (1995–96) 526

Mishkin, Paul J., Foreword: The
High Court, the Great Writ, and
the Due Process of Time and Law,
79 Harv. L. Rev. 56 (1965) ------- 305

Mitchell, Gregory, Against
Overwhelming Appellate Activism:
Constraining Harmless Error
Review, 82 Cal. L. Rev. 1335 (1994)
--- 397

Monahan, John, The Individual Risk
Assessment of Terrorism, 18
Psychol. Pub Polc'y & Law 167
(2012)-------------------------------- 650

Montgomery, Liam, The Unrealized
Promise of Section 1983 Method-of-
Execution Challenges, 94 Va. L.
Rev. 1987 (2008) -------------------- 698

Morrison, Trevor W., Hamdi's
Habeas Puzzle: Suspension as
Authorization?, 91 Cornell L. Rev.
411 (2006) ----------------------- 62, 594

Morrison, Trevor W., Suspension and
the Extrajudicial Constitution, 107
Colum. L. Rev. 1533 (2007) -------- 18

Morse, Stephen J., Blame and
Danger: An Essay on Preventive
Detention, 76 B.U. L. Rev. 113
(1996)-------------------------------- 524

Morse, Stephen J., Protecting Liberty
and Autonomy: Desert/Disease
Jurisprudence, 48 San Diego L.
Rev. 1077 (2011) ------------------- 518

Motomura, Hiroshi, Immigration
Law and Federal Court
Jurisdiction Through The Lens Of
Habeas Corpus, 91 Cornell L. Rev.
459 (2006) --------------------------- 486

Motomura, Hiroshi, The Curious
Evolution of Immigration Law:
Procedural Surrogates for
Substantive Constitutional Rights,
92 Colum. L. Rev. 1625 (1992)- 445,
449

Mulligan, Lumen N., Did the
Madisonian Compromise Survive
Detention at Guantánamo?, 85
N.Y.U. L. Rev. 535 (2010) ------- 621

Nesbitt, Nathaniel H., Note, Meeting
Boumediene's Challenge, 95 Minn.
L. Rev. 244 (2010)------------627, 633

Neuman, Gerald L., Discretionary
Deportation, 20 Geo. Immigr. L.J.
611 (2006) ------------------------- 446

Neuman, Gerald L., Federal Courts
Issues in Immigration Law, 78 Tex.
L. Rev. 1661 (2000) ---------------- 449

Neuman, Gerald L., Habeas Corpus,
Executive Detention, and the
Removal of Aliens, 98 Colum. L.
Rev. 961 (1998)---------------------- 14

Neuman, Gerald L., On the Adequacy
of Direct Review After the Real-ID
Act of 2005, 51 N.Y.L.S. Rev. 133
(2006–2007) ------------------------ 485

Neuman, Gerald L., Strangers to the
Constitution 35 (1996)------------ 445

Neuman, Gerald L., The
Constitutional Requirement of
'Some Evidence', 25 San Diego L.
Rev. 631 (1988)---------------475, 633

Neuman, Gerald L., The
Extraterritorial Constitution After
Boumediene v. Bush, 82 S. Cal. L.
Rev. 259 (2009)-------------------- 621

Neuman, Gerald L., The Habeas
Corpus Suspension Clause after
Boumediene v. Bush, 110 Colum.
L. Rev. 537 (2010)----- 624, 625, 715

Neuman, Gerald L., The Habeas
Corpus Suspension Clause After
INS v. St. Cyr, 33 Colum. Hum.
Rts. L. Rev. 555 (2002) -- 33, 34, 49,
473, 478

Niles, John D., Assessing the
Constitutionality of the Alien
Terrorist Removal Court, 57 Duke
L. J. 1833 (2008) ------------------ 500

Norland, Ray, As Bagram Detainees
are Transferred, U.S. Keeps its
Grip, N.Y. Times, May 30, 2012 644

Note, Multiparty Federal Habeas
Corpus, 81 Harv. L. Rev. 1482
(1968) --------------------------------- 707

Nott, C. C., The Mystery of the
Pinckney Draught (New York,
1908) ---------------------------------- 44

O'Neill, Timothy P., New Law, Old
Cases, Fair Outcomes: Why the
Illinois Supreme Court Must
Overrule People v. Flowers, 43 Loy.
U. Chi. L.J. 727 (2012)----------- 317

Oaks, Dallin H., Habeas Corpus in
the States—1776–1865, 32 U. Chi.
L. Rev. 243 (1965) ------------------ 19

Oaks, Dallin H., Legal History in the
High Court—Habeas Corpus, 64
Mich. L.Rev. 451 (1966) ----------- 70

Oaks, Dallin H., The 'Original' Writ
of Habeas Corpus in the Supreme

Court, 1962 Sup. Ct. Rev. 153
(1962)---------------------------------- 30

Obrien, David M., The Rehnquist
Court's Shrinking Plenary Docket,
81 Judicature 58 (1997)---------- 128

Ogletree, Charles J. Jr., The
Supreme Court, 1990 Term,
Comment: Arizona v. Fulminante:
The Harm Of Applying Harmless
Error To Coerced Confessions, 105
Harv. L. Rev. 152 (1991)--- 395, 399

Ogolla, Christopher, Non-Criminal
Habeas Corpus for Quarantine and
Isolation Detainees: Serving the
Private Right or Violating Public
Policy?, 14 DePaul J. Health Care
L. 135 (2011) ------------------------ 527

Oldham, James, and Michael J.
Wishnie, The Historical Scope of
Habeas Corpus and INS v. St. Cyr,
16 Geo. Immigr. L.J. 485 (2002)
------------------------------- 444, 474

Oney, Steve, And the Dead Shall Rise
324 (2003) ---------------------------- 112

Palmer, John R.B., Stephen W. Yale-
Loehr, & Elizabeth Cronin, Why
are so Many People Challenging
Board of Immigration Appeals
Decisions in Federal Court? An
Empirical Analysis of the Recent
Surge in Petitions for Review, 20
Geo. Immigr. L.J. 1 (2005) ------- 486

Parker, Dee Sanders, The
Antiterrorism and Effective Death
Penalty Act (AEDPA):
Understanding the Failures of
State Opt-In Mechanisms, 92 Iowa
L. Rev. 1969 (2007)---------------- 704

Paschal, Francis, The Constitution
and Habeas Corpus, 1970 Duke
L.J. 605 (1970) ------------- 19, 30, 32

Pearlstein, Deborah N., Detention
Debates, 110 Mich. L. Rev. 1045
(2012)---------------------------------- 651

Peller, Gary M., In Defense of
Federal Habeas Corpus
Relitigation, 16 Harv. C.R.-C.L. L.
Rev. 579 (1982) 12, 40, 73, 101, 132,
702

Pettys, Todd E., State Habeas Relief
for Federal Extrajudicial
Detainees, 92 Minn. L. Rev. 265
(2007)---------------------------- 82, 86

Pfander, James E., Jurisdiction
Stripping and the Supreme Court's
Power to Supervise Inferior
Tribunals, 78 Tex. L. Rev. 1433
(2000)---------------------------------- 104

Posner, Richard A., Report of the
Subcommittee on the Role of the
Federal Courts 468 (1990) ------- 379

Preston, Julia, Fewer Illegal
Immigrations Stopped for Traffic
Violations Will Face Deportation,
N.Y. Times, April 27, 2012------- 459

Preston, William Jr., Aliens and
Dissenters: Federal Suppression of
Radicals, 1903–1933 208 (1963) 493

Primus, Eve Brensike, A Structural
Vision of Habeas Corpus, 98 Cal. L.
Rev. 1 (2010) ------------------------ 707

Provost, Rene, Emergency Judicial
Relief for Human Rights Violations
in Canada and Argentina, 23 U.
Miami Inter-Am. L. Rev. 693
(1992) ------------------------------------1

Rago, John T., A Fine Line between
Chaos & Creation: Lessons on
Innocence Reform from the
Pennsylvania Eight, 12 Widener L.
Rev. 359 (2006)--------------------- 713

Ramji-Nogales, Jaya, Andrew I.
Schoenholtz, & Philip G. Schrag,
Refugee Roulette: Disparities in
Asylum Adjudication, 60 Stan. L.
Rev. 295 (2007)--------------------- 487

Raustiala, Kal, Al Maqaleh v. Gates,
605 F.3d 84. U.S. Court of Appeals
for the D.C. Circuit, May 21, 2010,
104 Am. J. Int'l L. 647 (2010)--- 644

Redish, Martin H., & Colleen
McNamara, Habeas Corpus, Due
Process and The Suspension
Clause: A Study in the
Foundations of American
Constitutionalism, 96 Va. L. Rev.
1361 (2010)--------------------- 19, 592

Rehnquist, William H., All The Laws
But One: Civil Liberties in
Wartime 18, 21–25 (1998) -- 55, 543

Reinert, Alexander A., Measuring the
Success of Bivens Litigation and its
Consequences for the Individual
Liability Model, 62 Stan. L. Rev.
809 (2010)--------------------------- 699

Resnik, Judith, Naturally Without
Gender: Women, Jurisdiction, and
the Federal Courts, 66 N.Y.U. L.
Rev. 1682 (1991) ------------------- 535

Roberts, Adam, & Richard Guelff,
Documents on the Laws of War (3d
ed. 2000)---------------------------- 538

Roberts, Caprice L., Rights,
Remedies, and Habeas Corpus—
The Uighurs, Legally Free while
Actually Imprisoned, 24 Geo. Imm.
L.J. 1 (2009)------------------------ 648

Roberts, Jenny, Proving Prejudice,
Post-Padilla, 54 How. L.J. 693
(2011) ------------------------------- 400

Robinson, Paul H., Punishing
Dangerousness: Cloaking
Preventive Detention as Criminal
Justice, 114 Harv. L. Rev. 1429
(2001) ------------------------------- 524

Rogers, O.A. Jr., The Elaine Race
Riots of 1919, 19 Ark. Hist. Q. 142
(1960) ------------------------------- 117

Roosevelt, Kermit III, A Little Theory
is a Dangerous Thing: The Myth of
Adjudicative Retroactivity, 31
Conn. L. Rev. 1075 (1999) ------- 317

Roosevelt, Kermit III, A Retroactivity Retrospective, with Thoughts for the Future: What the Supreme Court Learned from Paul Mishkin, and What It Might, 95 Calif. L. Rev. 1677, 1689–90 (2007) ------ 317

Roosevelt, Kermit III, Exhaustion under the Prison Litigation Reform Act: The Consequences of Procedural Error, 52 Emory L.J. 1771 (2003) ------------------------ 684

Rosenberg, Carol, Pentagon: 'No Vacancy' at Guantánamo Camps, Miami Herald, Oct. 18, 2011 ---- 626

Rubin, Edward L., Due Process and the Administrative State, 72 Cal. L. Rev. 1044 (1984)---------------- 592

Sanders Parker, Betsy Dee, The Antiterrorism and Effective Death Penalty Act (AEDPA): Understanding the Failures of State Opt-In Mechanisms, 92 Iowa L. Rev. 1969 (2007)---------------- 267

Saphire, Richard B., Procedural Justice, 78 S. Cal. L. Rev. 181 (2004)-------------------------------- 592

Saphire, Richard B., Specifying Due Process Values, 127 U. Pa. L. Rev. 111 (1978)-------------------------- 592

Scalia, John, U.S. Dep't of Justice, Bureau of Justice Statistics, Prisoner Petitions Filed in U.S. District Courts, 2000, with Trends, 1980–2000 1–2 (2002) ------------ 136

Schalock, R., et al., The Renaming of Mental Retardation: Understanding the Change to the Term Intellectual Disability, 45 Intellectual & Developmental Disabilities 116 (2007) ----------- 140

Scheck, Barry C., & Peter J. Neufeld, Toward the Formation of Innocence Commissions in America, 86 Judicature 98 (2002)-------------- 711

Schiff, Damien M., Purposivism and the 'Reasonable Legislator': A Review Essay of Justice Breyer's Active Liberty, 33 Wm. Mitchell L. Rev. 1081 (2007) -------------------- 276

Schlanger, Margo, Inmate Litigation, 116 Harv. L. Rev. 1557 (2003) -- 684

Schmitt, Eric, Closing Jail in Bagram is a Puzzle for Obama, N.Y. Times, Jan. 29, 2009 ----------------------- 644

Schriro, Dora, Amnesty International, Jailed without Justice: Immigration Detention in the USA (2009) -------------------- 460

Schriro, Dora, U.S. Dep't of Homeland Sec., Immigration Detention Overview and Recommendations 2 (Oct. 6, 2009) -------------------------------------- 460

Schuck, Peter H., The Transformation of Immigration Law, 84 Colum. L. Rev. 1 (1984)449

Scott, Ryan W., Inter-Judge Sentencing Disparity after Booker: A First Look, 63 Stanford L. Rev. 1 (2010) ------------------------------- 419

Seligman, Matthew, Note: Harrington's Wake: Unanswered Questions on AEDPA's Application to Summary Dispositions, 64 Stan. L. Rev. 469 (2012) ----------------- 302

Semeraro, Steven, A Reasoning-Process Review Model for Federal Habeas Corpus, 94 J. Crim. L. & Criminology 897 (2004)---------- 703

Shapiro, David L., Habeas Corpus, Suspension, and Detention: Another View, 82 Notre Dame L. Rev. 59 (2006) ------------------ 18, 63

Sholar, John A. Jr., Habeas Corpus and the War on Terror, 45 Duq. L. Rev. 661 (2007)---------------------- 19

Simon, Dan, A Third View of the Black Box: Cognitive Coherence in Legal Decision Making, 71 U. Chi. L. Rev. 511 (2004) ----------------- 413

Simon, James F., Lincoln and Chief Justice Taney: Slavery, Secession, and the President's War Powers 190 (2006) --------------------------- 55

Skeem, Jennifer L., & John Monahan, Current Directions in Violence Risk Assessment, 20 Current Directions Psychol. Sci. 38 (2011) ------------------------------- 518

Slobogin, Christopher, A Jurisprudence of Dangerousness, 98 Nw. U. L. Rev. 1 (2003) ------ 524

Slobogin, Christopher, Dangerousness and Expertise Redux, 56 Emory L. J. 275 (2006) ------------------------------- 518

Smith, Robert J., Recalibrating Constitutional Innocence Protection, 87 Wash. L. Rev. 139 (2012) ------------------------------- 244

Solomon, Jason M., Causing Constitutional Harm: How Tort Law Can Help Determine Harmless Error in Criminal Trials, 99 Nw. U. L. Rev. 1053 (2005) - 413

Stacy, Tom, & Kim Dayton, Rethinking Harmless Constitutional Error, 88 Colum. L. Rev. 79 (1988) --------------------- 397

Steiker, Carol S., & Jordan M. Steiker, A Tale of Two Nations: Implementation of the Death Penalty in 'Executing' Versus 'Symbolic' States in the United States, 84 Tex. L. Rev. 1869 (2006) ------------------------------------- 379

Steiker, Carol S., & Jordan M. Steiker, Part II: Report to the ALI Concerning Capital Punishment, 89 Tex. L. Rev. 367 (2010) ------ 707

Steiker, Jordan, Incorporating the Suspension Clause: Is There a Constitutional Right to Federal

Habeas Corpus for State Prisoners, 92 Mich. L. Rev. 862 (1994)------- 48

Steiker, Jordan, Innocence and Federal Habeas, 41 U.C.LA. L. Rev. 303 (1992) --------------------- 229

Steiker, Jordan, Restructuring Post-Conviction Review of Federal Constitutional Claims Raised by State Prisoners: Confronting the New Face of Excessive Proceduralism, 1998 U. Chi. Legal F. 315 -------------------------------- 705

Stevens, Jacqueline, U.S. Government Unlawfully Detaining and Deporting U.S. Citizens As Aliens, 18 Va. J. Soc. Pol'y & L. 606 (2011)------------------------------- 486

Stevenson, Bryan A., Confronting Mass Imprisonment and Restoring Fairness to Collateral Review of Criminal Cases, 41 Harv. C.R.-C.L. L. Rev. 339 (2006) ----------------- 212

Stevenson, Bryan A., The Politics of Fear and Death: Successive Problems in Capital Federal Habeas Cases, 77 N.Y.U. L. Rev. 699 (2002) --------------------------- 321

Stith, Kate, Arc of the Pendulum, 117 Yale L. J. 1420 (2008) ------------- 419

Stumpf, Juliet, The Crimmigration Crisis: Immigrants, Crime, and Sovereign Power, 56 Am. U. L. Rev. 367 (2006) --------------------- 458

Sulmasy, Glenn, The National Security Court System: A Natural Evolution of Justice in an Age of Terror 175 (2009) ------------------ 709

Sutton, Jane, Two Uighur Detainees Sent to El Salvador, N.Y. Times, April 20, 2012 ---------------------- 649

Swarns, Rachel L., Study Finds Disparities in Judges' Asylum Rulings, N.Y. Times, July 31, 2006, at A15 -------------------------------- 487

Tague, Peter W., Federal Habeas Corpus and Ineffective Assistance of Counsel: The Supreme Court Has Work to Do, 31 Stan. L. Rev. 1 (1978)---------------------------------212

Tilghman, Andrew, and S.K. Bardwell, City Looks to Ohio for Fix of Crime Lab Woes, Houston Chron., Aug. 19, 2004 ------------ 686

Tyler, Amanda L., Is Suspension a Political Question?, 59 Stan. L. Rev. 333 (2006) ----------- 18, 62, 594

Tyler, Amanda L., Suspension as an Emergency Power, 118 Yale L.J. 600 (2009) ---------------------- 20, 63

Tyler, Amanda L., The Forgotten Core Meaning of the Suspension Clause, 125 Harv. L. Rev. 901 (2012)----------------------45, 50, 555

Vladeck, Stephen I., AEDPA, Saucier, and the Stronger Case for Rights-First Constitutional Adjudication, 32 Seattle U. L. Rev. 595 (2009)----------------------339, 347

Vladeck, Stephen I., Deconstructing Hirota: Habeas Corpus, Citizenship, and Article III, 95 Geo. L. J. 1497 (2007) ------------- 556

Vladeck, Stephen I., The Case Against National Security Courts, 45 Willamette L. Rev. 505 (2009) -- 710

Vladeck, Stephen I., The D.C. Circuit After Boumediene, 41 Seton Hall L. Rev. 1451 (2011) --------------- 628

Vladeck, Stephen I., The Field Theory: Martial Law, The Suspension Power, And The Insurrection Act, 80 Temp. L. Rev. 391 (2007)---------------------------- 61

Vladeck, Stephen I., The New Habeas Revisionism, 124 Harv. L. Rev. 941 (2011)---------------- 33, 715

Vladeck, Stephen I., The New National Security Canon, 61 Am. U. L. Rev. 1295 (2012) ----------- 700

Vladeck, Stephen I., The Riddle of the One-Way Ratchet: Habeas Corpus and the District of Columbia, 12 Green Bag 2d 71 (2008) -------------------------------- 49

Vladeck, Stephen I., The Unreviewable Executive: Kiyemba, Maqaleh, and the Obama Administration, 26 Const. Comment. 603 (2010) -------644, 649

Walen, Alec, A Punitive Precondition for Preventive Detention: Lost Status as a Foundation for a Lost Immunity, 48 San Diego L. Rev. 1229 (2011)------------------------- 524

Waxman, Matthew C., Detention as Targeting: Standards Of Certainty And Detention Of Suspected Terrorists, 108 Colum. L. Rev. 1365 (2008) -------------------------- 630

Waxman, Matthew C., Guantanamo, Habeas, and Standards of Proof: Viewing the Law Through Multiple Lenses, 42 Case W. Res. J. Int'l L. 245 (2009)-------------------------- 633

Waxman, Seth P., & Trevor W. Morrison, What Kind of Immunity? Federal Officers, State Criminal Law, and the Supremacy Clause, 112 Yale L.J. 2195 (2003)--------- 87

Weisselberg, Charles D., The Exclusion and Detention of Aliens, Lessons from the Lives of Ellen Knauff and Ignatz Mezei, 143 U. Pa. L. Rev. 933 (1995)------------ 456

White, G. Edward, Felix Frankfurter's Soliloquy in Ex parte Quirin: Nazi Sabotage & Constitutional Conundrums, 5 Green Bag 2d 423 (2002)-------- 553

White, Josh, and William Branigin, Hamdan To Be Sent To Yemen: Bin Laden Driver Spent 7 Years at

Guantánamo, Washington Post, November 25, 2008 ---------------- 568

Wiecek, William, The Lost World of Classical Legal Thought: Law and Ideology in America 1886–1937 (1998) ------------------------------- 304

Wilkes, Donald E. Jr., From Oglethorpe to the Overthrow of the Confederacy: Habeas Corpus in Georgia, 1733–1865, 45 Ga. L. Rev. 1015 (2011) -------------------------- 19

Wilson, Scott, & Al Kamen, 'Global War on Terror' is Given a New Name, Wash. Post, March 25, 2009 --------------------------------- 571

Wiseman, Samuel R., Habeas After Pinholster, 53 B.C. L. Rev. 953 (2012) --------------------- 356, 716, 717

Witt, John Fabian, Lincoln's Code: The Laws of War in American History (2012) ---------------------- 538

Wittes, Benjamin et al., Brooking Inst., The Emerging Law of Detention: The Guantánamo Habeas Cases as Lawmaking (2010) ------------------------------- 627

Wittes, Benjamin, Law and the Long War: The Future of Justice in the Age of Terrorism 176 (2008) ----- 710

Woolhandler, Ann, and Michael G. Collins, The Story of Tarble's Case: State Habeas and Federal Detention, in Federal Courts Stories (Vicki C. Jackson & Judith Resnik eds., 2009) ------------------- 77

Woolhandler, Ann, Demodeling Habeas, 45 Stan. L. Rev. 575 (1993) ----------------- 38, 39, 133, 707

Worthington, Andy, Profiles: Odah and Boumediene, BBC News, Dec. 4, 2007 ------------------------------- 600

Yackle, Larry W., Federal Courts 135 (2d ed. 2003) --------------------------- 86

Yackle, Larry W., Federal Evidentiary Hearings Under the New Habeas Corpus Statute, 6 B.U. Pub. Int. L.J. 135 (1996) --- 377

Yackle, Larry W., State Convicts and Federal Courts: Reopening the Habeas Corpus Debate, 91 Cornell L. Rev. 541 (2006) ---------- 339, 705

Yackle, Larry W., The Exhaustion Doctrine in Federal Habeas Corpus: An Argument for a Return to First Principles, 44 Ohio St. L.J. 393 (1983) -------------------------- 179

Yackle, Larry W., The Figure in the Carpet, 78 Tex. L. Rev. 1731 (2000) --------------------------------------- 705

Yackle, Larry W., The Story of Fay v. Noia: Another Case About Another Federalism, in Federal Courts Stories 191 (Vicki Jackson & Judith Resnik eds., 2009) ------- 199

Yin, Tung, A Better Mousetrap: Procedural Default as a Retroactivity Alternative to Teague v. Lane and the Antiterrorism and Effective Death Penalty Act of 1996, 25 Am. J. Crim. L. 203 (1998) ------------------------------- 313

Yin, Tung, Procedural Due Process to Determine Enemy Combatant Status in the War on Terrorism, 73 Tenn. L. Rev. 351 (2006) -------- 593

FEDERAL HABEAS CORPUS

EXECUTIVE DETENTION AND POST-CONVICTION LITIGATION

CHAPTER 1

INTRODUCTION AND THE ORIGINS OF HABEAS CORPUS

INTRODUCTORY NOTE

The "Great Writ" of habeas corpus, Alexander Hamilton wrote, serves to protect "liberty and republicanism" against "arbitrary imprisonments" which had been "in all ages, the favorite and most formidable instruments of tyranny."[a] The trajectory of habeas law reflects the mundane needs of legal functionaries, the tragic wounds of war and rebellion, the ingenuity of King's Bench Justices in seventeenth-century England, and the unique federalism of American constitutional design. The United States Supreme Court has lauded the Great Writ as "indispensable," and one that "indisputably holds an honored position in our jurisprudence."[b]

The formal purpose of the writ has remained the same for centuries: to permit a prisoner to seek judicial review of any custody. If necessary, a judge may order the prisoner freed. The writ reaches even the most unpopular prisoners—enemies of the state, war criminals, and those convicted of heinous crimes. Because judges can terminate custody that they consider unlawful, habeas process implies an awesome power to define what "lawful custody" means. Habeas decisions therefore define the sovereign's authority to imprison its citizens and enemies.

Nor is the writ's influence limited to the domestic law of England and other common-law jurisdictions, as countries governed by civil law now have legal constructs with similar functions. For example, civil-law writs, such as the "amparo de libertad," are used throughout the Spanish-speaking world.[c] Customary international law also recognizes the importance of judicial remedies for wrongful custody and violations of liberty. Using language derived from habeas law, the 1966 International Covenant on Civil and Political Rights, to which the U.S. is a party, provides: "[n]o one shall be subjected to arbitrary arrest or detention" and any person "deprived of his liberty by arrest or detention shall be entitled to take proceedings before a court, in order that that court may decide without delay on the lawfulness of his detention and order his release if the detention is not lawful."[d] Hailing from humble common-law origins, the habeas writ has become the stuff of universal human rights.

Its pedigree notwithstanding, no Case Book has comprehensively examined how the habeas writ operates across the different types of custody. Habeas

---

[a] See The Federalist No. 84 (Alexander Hamilton). Hamilton also quoted Blackstone, who had called habeas the "stable bulwark" of English liberty. See William Blackstone, 1 Commentaries on the Laws of England 137 (1756–1769).

[b] Engle v. Isaac, 456 U.S. 107, 126 (1982).

[c] See, e.g., Rene Provost, *Emergency Judicial Relief for Human Rights Violations in Canada and Argentina*, 23 U. Miami Inter-Am. L. Rev. 693, 703–704 (1992) (exploring evolution of the amparo de libertad).

[d] See G.A. Res. 2200 A (xxi), U.N. GAOR, Supp. No. 16, arts. 9, 21, at 52, U.N. Doc. A/6316 (1966).

corpus is not just a loosely-related set of legal rules, each corresponding to a particular type of custody. In fact, habeas cases involving one category of custody liberally borrow principles from cases involving others. Only a unified treatment reveals what is perhaps the central insight into habeas law: that it generally evolves in ways that allow judges to define what it means for custody to be "lawful." Moreover, only by understanding that habeas was a means for defining lawful custody can students understand the writ's role in promoting modern concepts of individual liberty.

The chapters in this Book are roughly divided according to the two primary types of habeas review: (1) "post-conviction" review of a judgment in a criminal trial, and (2) review of noncriminal confinement, which includes civil detention, immigration decisions, and military custody. After two introductory chapters developing the origins and the constitutional structure of habeas corpus, the Book explores post-conviction review in Chapters 3 through 6. Chapters 7 through 10 are devoted to noncriminal confinement, including immigration detention (Chapter 7), civil detention (Chapter 8), and national-security detention exercised by the military (Chapters 9 and 10). Chapter 11 explores habeas rules for post-conviction proceedings and the boundary between habeas and other civil remedies. The Book concludes by examining reform proposals, and by reviewing common themes across categories of habeas review (Chapter 12).

This Chapter introduces the Book by exploring the genesis modern post-conviction review in Section 1, the English common-law origins of habeas corpus in Section 2, and the early development of U.S. habeas corpus review in Sections 3 and 4.

1. THE BIRTH OF THE MODERN WRIT IN THE UNITED STATES

Habeas corpus derives from the Latin phrase "you have the body," and a habeas corpus writ commands a jailor to bring "the body" to court for some purpose. English judges used several writs to issue such commands to jailers, and over time, judges developed the common-law habeas "privilege" into a powerful source of power for judges to examine whether a prisoner was lawfully detained. The Framers of the U.S. Constitution held the privilege in such high esteem that they included a Suspension Clause in Article I, stating that "[t]he Privilege of the Writ of Habeas Corpus shall not be suspended, unless when in Cases of Rebellion or Invasion the public Safety may require it." U.S. Const. art. I, § 9, cl. 2.

The scope of the privilege has grown over the course of American history. The First Judiciary Act, which Congress adopted in 1789 after the ratification of the Constitution, empowered federal judges to grant the writ to a narrow group of federal prisoners in pre-trial detention—but Congress did not statutorily extend habeas power to reach prisoners in custody of the states. The Civil War and Reconstruction dramatically altered the balance of state and federal power, and habeas law reflected that fundamental change in American governance. The Habeas Corpus Act of 1867 extended the general habeas jurisdiction of the federal courts to state prisoners for the first time.

As Chapter 3 will discuss, federal courts took decades to begin to exercise the broad, modern federal power over state custody: post-conviction authority to relieve constitutional violations sustained during state criminal process. For the most part, nineteenth-century federal courts observed the principle that custody could be lawful notwithstanding certain constitutional error in the underlying criminal process.

In the 1950s and 1960s, federal habeas review of state convictions became a more important feature of federal dockets and received increased attention as a political phenomenon. The big bang of modern post-conviction law is *Brown v. Allen,* 344 U.S. 443 (1953). Although we present the case with additional detail in Chapter 3, we present here the portions of *Brown v. Allen*[e] holding that federal habeas writs could remedy errors in the state criminal process—even errors that did not go to the jurisdiction of the convicting court. When the Warren Court developed new constitutional rights and incorporated them against States as part of the criminal procedure revolution of the 1950s and 1960s, *Brown v. Allen* ensured a primary enforcement role for habeas corpus.

In *Brown,* the Supreme Court heard the cases of four defendants— Clyde Brown, Raleigh Speller, Bennie Daniels, and Lloyd Ray Daniels. All were black men. Brown and Speller were separately convicted of different crimes, but both were convicted in North Carolina of raping white women, and both were sentenced to death. Bennie and Lloyd Ray Daniels' were cousins that were tried together in North Carolina, convicted of murdering a white taxicab driver, and sentenced to death.[f] After the Court denied them relief, all of the four defendants were executed in 1953. As you read the majority opinion, which describes a troubling confession and a pattern of persistent race discrimination in jury selection in the counties where the four men were tried, you can be forgiven for wondering why the Court's ruling was considered groundbreaking. As Chapter 3 will discuss further, however, many judges and scholars had argued that, before *Brown,* federal judges could issue relief only if the alleged error in the criminal process was something approximating a "jurisdictional" defect in the state conviction. The majority opinion in *Brown* reflected no such principle: the Court simply considered whether the prisoners had proven a constitutional violation. The possibility that federal courts could now closely regulate state criminal process deeply concerned Justice Jackson, who wrote a forceful concurring opinion. In the decades to come, Justice Jackson's concerns would become prominent in opinions by the Burger and Rehnquist Courts.

Brown v. Allen

United States Supreme Court
344 U.S. 443 (1953)

■ Mr. JUSTICE REED delivered the opinion of the Court.

Certiorari was granted to review judgments of the United States Court of Appeals for the Fourth Circuit. [There were three cases: *Brown v. Allen, Speller v. Allen,* and *Daniels v. Allen.* The Fourth Circuit had affirmed orders of the federal district court denying relief.] * * *

---

[e] We adopt the short form "*Brown v. Allen*" to avoid any potential confusion with *Brown v. Board of Education of Topeka, KS,* 347 U.S. 483 (1954).

[f] For a description of the factual background in each case and scholarly disputes over the significance of the ruling, see Eric M. Freedman, *Milestones In Habeas Corpus: Part III: Brown v. Allen: The Habeas Corpus Revolution that Wasn't,* 51 Ala. L. Rev. 1541, 1558–61 (2000).

First. We take up *Brown v. Allen,* a case that turns more generally than the others on the constitutional issues.

Petitioner, a Negro, was indicted on September 4, 1950, and tried in the North Carolina courts on a charge of rape, and, having been found guilty, he was sentenced to death on September 15, 1950. In the sentencing court petitioner made a timely motion to quash the bill of indictment, alleging discrimination against Negroes in the selection of grand jurors in contravention of the guarantees of the Fourteenth Amendment to the Federal Constitution. After the verdict, but before sentencing, petitioner, by a motion to set aside the verdict, sought to expand his constitutional attack on the selection of the grand jury to embrace the petit jury also. * * *

Petitioner's charge of discrimination against Negroes in the selection of grand and petit jurors in violation of his constitutional rights attacks the operation of a method used by North Carolina in selecting juries in Forsyth County. * * * It is petitioner's contention that no more than one or two Negroes at a time have ever served on a Forsyth County grand jury and that no more than five Negroes have ever previously served on a petit jury panel in the county. These contentions are the basis of the allegation that a system of discrimination is being employed against the Negro residents of the county. Petitioner offered no evidence to support his charge of limitation against the jury service of Negroes, except the fact that fewer Negroes than whites, having regard for their proportion of the population, appeared on the jury panels. * * * According to the unchallenged testimony of the * * * Supervisor in the office of the Tax Supervisor of Forsyth County, a list of names is compiled from a tabulation of all the county property and poll taxpayers who make returns and is thereafter tendered to the County Commissioners for use in jury selection. All males between 21 and 50 years of age are required to list themselves for poll tax as well as to list their property.

Discriminations against a race by barring or limiting citizens of that race from participation in jury service are odious to our thought and our Constitution. This has long been accepted as the law. * * * Our duty to protect the federal constitutional rights of all does not mean we must or should impose on states our conception of the proper source of jury lists, so long as the source reasonably reflects a cross-section of the population suitable in character and intelligence for that civic duty. Short of an annual census or required population registration, these tax lists offer the most comprehensive source of available names. * * *

Petitioner contends further that his conviction was procured in violation of the Fourteenth Amendment of the Federal Constitution because the trial judge permitted the jury to rely on a confession claimed by petitioner to be coerced in determining his guilt. * * * After hearing the testimony, the trial judge found that the petitioner's statements were freely and voluntarily given and declared them to be competent. Upon recall of the jury, the state introduced the statements in evidence, objections again being noted. * * *

A conviction by a trial court which has admitted coerced confessions deprives a defendant of liberty without due process of law. When the facts admitted by the state show coercion * * * a conviction will be set aside as violative of due process. * * * This is true even though the evidence apart from the confessions might have been sufficient to sustain the jury's verdict. * * *

The mere admission of the confessions by the trial judge constituted a use of them by the state, and if the confessions were improperly obtained, such a use constitutes a denial of due process of law as guaranteed by the Fourteenth Amendment. * * *

Petitioner's contention that he had a constitutional right to have his statements excluded from the record rests upon these admitted facts. He is an illiterate. He was held after arrest for five days before being charged with the crime for which he was convicted. He was not given a preliminary hearing until 18 days after his arrest. No counsel was provided for him in the period of his detention. The alleged confessions were taken prior to the preliminary hearing and appointment of counsel. There is no record of physical coercion or of that less painful duress generated by prolonged questioning. There is evidence that petitioner was told he could remain silent and that any statement he might make could be used against him. He chose to speak, and he made that choice without a promise of reward or immunity having been extended. He was never denied the right to counsel of his choice and was never without competent counsel from the inception of judicial proceedings. * * * Mere detention and police examination in private of one in official state custody do not render involuntary the statements or confessions made by the person so detained. Petitioner's constitutional rights were not infringed by the refusal of the trial court to exclude his confessions as evidence. * * *

Second. We examine the constitutional issues in * * * *Speller v. Allen.*

Petitioner, a Negro, was indicted and in August, 1949, tried in the Superior Court of Bertie County, North Carolina, upon a charge of rape. He has been convicted and sentenced to death on this charge three times, the first two convictions having been set aside on appeal by the Supreme Court of North Carolina on the ground of discriminatory selection of jurors. At this, his third trial, August Term 1949, petitioner made a timely motion to set aside the array of special veniremen called from Vance County, alleging discrimination against Negroes 'solely and wholly on account of their race and/or color' in the selection of the veniremen in contravention of the guarantees of the Fourteenth Amendment of the Federal Constitution. * * * Evidence was taken at length on this issue, although some evidence deemed material by petitioner was excluded. In particular, the trial judge, on the ground that it would be immaterial * * *, refused to permit petitioner to produce evidence as to all the scrolls in the jury box for the purpose of showing the existence of dots on the scrolls bearing the names of Negroes. The jury box was produced in court, opened, and counsel for defendant permitted to examine the scrolls. The trial judge made findings relating to the manner of selecting the veniremen, determining that no discrimination was practiced, and on these findings denied the motion to set aside the array. Petitioner was thereafter convicted for the third time, and sentenced to death.

On appeal petitioner asserted that his conviction violated the Equal Protection Clause of the Fourteenth Amendment, assigning the denial of his motion to set aside the array as error, and also assigning as error the trial court's ruling on his request for permission to examine into all the scrolls in the jury box. The Supreme Court of North Carolina had before it on that appeal as part of the record a mimeographed, narrative-style transcript of the entire proceedings below; petitioner makes no objection to the absence of any relevant evidence on that appeal, except that relating to all the scrolls which had been excluded by the trial court. Upholding the rulings of the trial court, the Supreme Court of North Carolina affirmed the conviction * * *.

Petitioner filed this petition for a writ of habeas corpus in the Federal District Court for the Eastern District of North Carolina after we denied certiorari on direct review of the state proceedings. The petition summarily recited the prior history of the litigation, and raised again the same federal question which had been passed upon by both North Carolina courts, and which had been offered to this Court on petition for certiorari, racial discrimination. The District Court heard all additional evidence the petitioner offered. This was in its discretion. * * * It better enabled that court to determine whether any violation of the Fourteenth Amendment occurred.

Petitioner's charge of discrimination against Negroes in the selection of petit jurors in violation of his constitutional rights attacks the operation of the system used by the North Carolina authorities to select juries in Vance County, from which county a special venire was obtained to try petitioner. The charge rests on petitioner's contentions (1) that no Negro within recent years had served on a jury in Vance County before this case, (2) that no Negro had been summoned to serve on a jury before this case, and (3) that the jury box in this case was so heavily loaded with names of white persons that the drawing could not fairly reflect a cross-section of those persons in the community qualified for jury service. Petitioner offered evidence to support each of these three contentions.

The evidence establishes the correctness of contentions [1] and (2). They are inapplicable to this case, however, under the circumstances of the filling of this particular jury box. * * * In Vance County, where the special venire for Speller's trial was drawn, the names of substantial numbers of Negroes appeared thereafter in the jury box. 145 Negroes out of a total of 2,126 names were in this jury box. As this venire was the first drawing of jurors from the box after its purge in July 1949, * * * the long history of alleged discrimination against its Negro citizens by Vance County jury commissioners is not decisive of discrimination in the present case. * * * Past practice is evidence of past attitude of mind. That attitude is shown to no longer control the action of officials by the present fact of colored citizens' names in the jury box.

It is suggested that the record shows that the names of colored persons in the jury box were marked with a dot or period on the scroll. This could be used for unlawful disposition of such scrolls when drawn. Such a scheme would be useless in the circumstances of this case. The record shows that the defendant and his counsel were present when the venire was drawn by a child, aged 5. All of the names drawn were given to the sheriff and summonses were issued. As a matter of fact the special venire contained the names of seven Negroes. Four appeared. None sat as jurors. Therefore the assertion as to the dots, even if true, means no more than that some unknown person desired to interfere with the fair drawing of juries in Vance County. * * *

This box was filled by names selected by the clerk of the jury commissioners and corrected by the commissioners. The names put in were substantially those selected by the clerk, who chose them from those on the tax lists who had 'the most property.' The clerk testified no racial discrimination entered into his selection. Since the effect of this possible objection to the selection of jurors on an economic basis was not raised or developed at the trial, on appeal to the State Supreme Court, on the former certiorari to this Court, or in the petition or brief on the present certiorari to this Court, it is not open to consideration here. Such an important national asset as state autonomy in local law enforcement must not be eroded through indefinite charges of unconstitutional actions. * * * The fact that causes further consideration in this case of the selection of prospective jurors is that the tax lists show 8,233 individual taxpayers in Vance County of whom 3,136 or 38% are Negroes. In the jury box involved, selected from that list, there were 2,126 names. Of that number 145 were Negroes, 7%. This disparity between the races would not be accepted by this Court solely on the evidence of the clerk of the commissioners that he selected names of citizens of 'good moral character and qualified to serve as jurors, and who had paid their taxes.' It would not be assumed that in Vance County there is not a much larger percentage of Negroes with qualifications of jurymen. The action of the commissioners' clerk, however, in selecting those with 'the most property,' an economic basis not attacked here, might well account for the few Negroes appearing in the box. Evidence of discrimination based solely on race on the selection actually made is lacking.

* * * It would require a conviction, by this Court, of violation of equal protection through racial discrimination to set aside this trial. Our delicate and serious responsibility of compelling state conformity to the Constitution by overturning state criminal convictions, should not be exercised without clear evidence of violation.

Disregarding, as we think we should, the clerk's unchallenged selections based on taxable property, there is no evidence of racial discrimination. Negroes names now appear in the jury box. If the requirement of comparative wealth is eliminated, and the statutory standards employed, the number would increase to the equality justified by their moral and educational qualification for jury service as compared with the white race. We do not think the small number, by comparison, of Negro names in this one jury box, is, in itself, enough to establish racial discrimination. * * *

We have spoken in this opinion of the change of practice in North Carolina in the selection of jurors. Our conclusions have been reached without regard to earlier incidents not connected with these juries or trials that suggest past discriminations. Since the states are the real guardians of peace and order within their boundaries, it is hoped that our consideration of these records will tend to clarify the requirements of the Federal Constitution in the selection of juries. Our Constitution requires that jurors be selected without inclusion or exclusion because of race. There must be neither limitation nor representation for color. By that practice, harmony has an opportunity to maintain essential discipline, without that objectionable domination which is so inconsistent with our constitutional democracy.

The judgments are affirmed.

■ Mr. JUSTICE FRANKFURTER [giving the Court's opinion as to the controlling effect to be given to prior state proceedings:]

I deem it appropriate to begin by making explicit some basic considerations underlying the federal habeas corpus jurisdiction. * * * [M]ost claims in these attempts to obtain review of State convictions are without merit. Presumably they are adequately dealt with in the State courts. * * * The meritorious claims are few, but our procedures must ensure that those few claims are not stifled by undiscriminating generalities. * * *

For surely it is an abuse to deal too casually and too lightly with rights guaranteed by the Federal Constitution, even though they involve limita-

tions upon State power and may be invoked by those morally unworthy.
* * *

Congress could have left the enforcement of federal constitutional rights governing the administration of criminal justice in the States exclusively to the State courts. These tribunals are under the same duty as the federal courts to respect rights under the United States Constitution. * * * It is for this Court to give fair effect to the habeas corpus jurisdiction as enacted by Congress. * * *

In exercising the power thus bestowed, the District Judge must take due account of the proceedings that are challenged by the application for a writ. All that has gone before is not to be ignored as irrelevant. But the prior State determination of a claim under the United States Constitution cannot foreclose consideration of such a claim, else the State court would have the final say which the Congress, by the Act of 1867, provided it should not have. * * * The prior State determination may guide his discretion in deciding upon the appropriate course to be followed in disposing of the application before him. * * *

I yield to no member of this Court in awareness of the enormity of the difficulties of dealing with crime that is the concomitant of our industrialized society. And I am deeply mindful of the fact that the responsibility for this task largely rests with the States. I would not for a moment hamper them in the effective discharge of this responsibility. Equally am I aware that misuse of legal procedures, whereby the administration of criminal justice is too often rendered leaden-footed, is one of the disturbing features about American criminal justice. On the other hand, it must not be lost sight of that there are also abuses by the law-enforcing agencies. * * *

The uniqueness of habeas corpus in the procedural armory of our law cannot be too often emphasized. It differs from all other remedies in that it is available to bring into question the legality of a person's restraint and to require justification for such detention. Of course this does not mean that prison doors may readily be opened. It does mean that explanation may be exacted why they should remain closed. It is not the boasting of empty rhetoric that has treated the writ of habeas corpus as the basic safeguard of freedom in the Anglo-American world. 'The great writ of habeas corpus has been for centuries esteemed the best and only sufficient defense of personal freedom.' Chief Justice Chase, writing for the Court, in Ex parte Yerger, 8 Wall. 85, 95. Its history and function in our legal system and the unavailability of the writ in totalitarian societies are naturally enough regarded as one of the decisively differentiating factors between our democracy and totalitarian governments. * * *

It is inadmissible to deny the use of the writ merely because a State court has passed on a Federal constitutional issue. The discretion of the lower courts must be canalized within banks of standards governing all Federal judges alike, so as to mean essentially the same thing to all and to leave only the margin of freedom of movement inevitably entailed by the nature of habeas corpus and the indefinable variety of circumstances which bring it into play.

■ Mr. JUSTICE JACKSON, concurring in the result.

Controversy as to the undiscriminating use of the writ of habeas corpus by federal judges to set aside state court convictions is traceable to three principal causes: (1) this Court's use of the generality of the Fourteenth Amendment to subject state courts to increasing federal control, especially in the criminal law field; (2) ad hoc determination of due process of law issues by personal notions of justice instead of by known rules of law; and (3) the breakdown of procedural safeguards against abuse of the writ.

1. In 1867, Congress authorized federal courts to issue writs of habeas corpus to prisoners 'in custody in violation of the Constitution or laws or treaties of the United States.' At that time, the writ was not available here nor in England to challenge any sentence imposed by a court of competent jurisdiction. The historic purpose of the writ has been to relieve detention by executive authorities without judicial trial. It might have been expected that if Congress intended a reversal of this traditional concept of habeas corpus it would have said so. However, this one sentence in the Act eventually was construed as authority for federal judges to entertain collateral attacks on state court criminal judgments. Whatever its justification, it created potentialities for conflict certain to lead to the antagonisms we have now, unless the power given to federal judges were responsibly used according to lawyerly procedures and with genuine respect for state court fact finding.

But, once established, this jurisdiction obviously would grow with each expansion of the substantive grounds for habeas corpus. The generalities of the Fourteenth Amendment are so indeterminate as to what state actions are forbidden that this Court has found it a ready instrument, in one field or another, to magnify federal, and incidentally its own, authority over the states. The expansion now has reached a point where any state court conviction, disapproved by a majority of this Court, thereby becomes unconstitutional and subject to nullification by habeas corpus.

This might not be so demoralizing if state judges could anticipate, and so comply with, this Court's due process requirements or ascertain any standards to which this Court will adhere in prescribing them. But they cannot. Of course, considerable uncertainty is inherent in decisional law which, in changing times, purports to interpret implications of constitutional provisions so cryptic and vagrant. How much obscurity is inevitable will be a matter of opinion. However, in considering a remedy for habeas corpus problems, it is prudent to assume that the scope and reach of the Fourteenth Amendment will continue to be unknown and unknowable, that what seems established by one decision is apt to be unsettled by another, and that its interpretation will be more or less swayed by contemporary intellectual fashions and political currents.

We may look upon this unstable prospect complacently, but state judges cannot. They are not only being gradually subordinated to the federal judiciary but federal courts have declared that state judicial and other officers are personally liable to federal prosecution and to civil suit by convicts if they fail to carry out this Court's constitutional doctrines. * * *

Conflict with state courts is the inevitable result of giving the convict a virtual new trial before a federal court sitting without a jury. Whenever decisions of one court are reviewed by another, a percentage of them are reversed. That reflects a difference in outlook normally found between personnel comprising different courts. However, reversal by a higher court is not proof that justice is thereby better done. There is no doubt that if there were a super-Supreme Court, a substantial proportion of our reversals of state courts would also be reversed. We are not final because we are infallible, but we are infallible only because we are final. * * *

Society has no interest in maintaining an unconstitutional conviction and every interest in preserving the writ of habeas corpus to nullify them when they occur. But the Constitution does not prevent the state courts from determining the facts in criminal cases. It does not make it unconstitutional for them to have a different opinion than a federal judge about the weight to be given to evidence. My votes in the cases under review and on other petitions and reviews will be guided as nearly as I can by the principles set forth herein.

I concur in the result announced by Mr. JUSTICE REED in these three cases.

■ Mr. JUSTICE BLACK, with whom Mr. JUSTICE DOUGLAS concurs, dissenting.

The four petitioners in these cases are under sentences of death imposed by North Carolina state courts. All are Negroes. Brown and Speller were convicted of raping white women; the two Daniels, aged 17 when arrested, were convicted of murdering a white man. The State Supreme Court affirmed and we denied certiorari in all the cases. These are habeas corpus proceedings which challenge the validity of the convictions.

I agree with the Court that the District Court had habeas corpus jurisdiction in all the cases including power to release either or all of the prisoners if held as a result of violation of constitutional rights. * * * I disagree with the Court's conclusion that petitioners failed to establish those contentions. The chief constitutional claims throughout have been and are: (a) extorted confessions were used to convict; (b) Negroes were deliberately excluded from service as jurors on account of their race. * * *

[Discussing Brown's jury selection claim:] Negroes are about one-third of Forsyth County's population. Consequently, the number of Negroes now called for jury duty is still glaringly disproportionate to their percentage of citizenship. * * * The jury that tried Speller was drawn from Vance County, North Carolina. Before this trial no Negro had served on a Vance County jury in recent years. No Negro had even been summoned. That this was the result of unconstitutional discrimination is made clear by the fact that Negroes constitute 45% of the county's population and 38% of its taxpayers. The Court holds, however, that this discrimination was completely cured by refilling the jury box with the names of 145 Negroes and 1,981 whites. Such a small number of Negro jurors is difficult to explain except on the basis of racial discrimination. * * * [Additional discussion of procedural rulings by the Court is omitted.]

[Dissenting opinions of Justice Frankfurter, joined by Justices Black and Douglas, are omitted, as is a concurring statement by Justices Burton and Clark]

NOTES AND QUESTIONS ON BROWN V. ALLEN

1) **The Modern Scope of the Writ.** In *Brown v. Allen,* the Supreme Court reviewed *de novo* the claims of the defendants, deciding whether their constitutional rights were violated. The portion excerpted here includes just some of their constitutional claims—Brown's jury selection and confession claims, and Speller's jury selection claim. Clyde Brown was an illiterate black teenager that had been arrested for raping and beating a white high school student in North

Carolina. As the Court noted, police held him without charges for five days, did not give him a hearing until his twenty-third day in custody, and withheld an appointed lawyer for three more days. He confessed during the five days he was detained without charges. An all-white jury convicted him and he was subject to a mandatory death sentence. Of course, the Court, having reached the merits, ultimately denied all relief to all claimants. Today, constitutional analysis of an involuntary-confession claim would be very different, and would focus on the voluntariness of the confession under the totality of the circumstances. The challenge to jury selection would also involve very different constitutional analysis, both as to who was included in the jury rolls and as to how jurors were selected at trial. We would not be so comfortable (and neither were Justices Black and Douglas) with such troubling statistics regarding the racial makeup of jury pool, with marking only the black residents' names with a dot, and with having a five-year old select the names of potential jurors to serve on a given jury.

Whether or not the Court correctly assessed the constitutional implications of the facts, *Brown v. Allen* stands as a historic development. The ruling validated a robust conception of federal habeas review of state convictions. The decision opened the door to new habeas challenges each time the Court announced a new right of criminal procedure. In the decades that followed, the Court developed what we consider the modern suite of criminal-procedure rights—and gradually incorporated each one against the states.

2)   The Custodian. Who was Allen? He was the warden of the Central Prison of the State of North Carolina. Habeas petitions are civil filings. In a post-conviction case like *Brown v. Allen*, federal habeas review is a federal post-conviction challenge that follows appellate review of the conviction and any state post-conviction proceedings. The nominal respondent in a federal habeas case is the state custodian—the state official with the power to release a prisoner. In practice, the nominal respondent has no courtroom presence. The State Attorney General's Office ordinarily handles the litigation as the nominal respondent's legal representative. The jailer no longer need appear personally in the courtroom to explain why the prisoner is confined.

3)   The Federal Filing. After losing their appeals and failing to obtain state post-conviction relief, the prisoners filed their habeas petitions in the federal District Court for the Eastern District of North Carolina. As the Supreme Court describes, such a petition will recite the prior litigation and specify the claims asserted, just like a complaint in a civil case. The district judge here "heard all additional evidence the petitioner offered." That is, the judge exercised "discretion" to hold a hearing and consider evidence supporting the claims—so that he would be "better enabled" to decide whether there was a constitutional violation. Such a rationale suggests a sweeping power to inquire into what happened in a state criminal case, hold hearings, develop facts, and then rule on constitutional claims.

4)   Federal Judges and State Judges. On the question of the preclusive effect to be given to prior state proceedings, Justice Frankfurter wrote for the Court. He acknowledged the problems that Justice Jackson identified, but considered those problems to be outweighed by the supremacy of the U.S. Constitution and the liberty interests of prisoners. Justice Jackson regarded the prospect of imposing Supreme Court-made constitutional criminal procedure on state criminal process with deep skepticism. He warned that "[c]onflict" would result—did he fear political backlash? He also feared that the result could harm habeas petitioners, because federal judges would struggle to find meritorious cases among piles of frivolous petitions. Judges, lawmakers, and scholars still debate whether habeas process should be tailored primarily to vindicate constitutional rights and to avert "miscarried" justice (Justice Frankfurter's themes), or whether that process should be limited to reflect the competence of state judges and the finality of criminal convictions (Justice Jackson's themes).

5)   Finality and History. Justice Jackson began his concurrence by emphasizing that the scope of federal habeas corpus review had traditionally been narrow. In particular, before the passage of the 1867 habeas statute, federal courts did not have general habeas jurisdiction to review state criminal convictions. Even after the passage of that statute, federal habeas review was quite constrained. The scholarly reaction to *Brown v. Allen*, by contrast, was swift and polarized. In a very influential article that this Book cites frequently, Professor Paul M. Bator developed the themes in Justice Jackson's concurrence. Professor Bator argued that *Brown* was a radical break from federal courts' prior practice of refusing the writ unless the trial error went to the state court's jurisdiction to enter a criminal judgment. See Paul M. Bator, *Finality in Criminal Law and Federal Habeas Corpus for State Prisoners*, 76 Harv. L. Rev. 441 (1963). As discussed in Chapter 3, some scholars have disputed Professor Bator's historical account. Professors Randy Hertz and James Liebman argued that *Brown v. Allen* "worked no revolution when it recognized the cognizability on habeas corpus of all federal constitutional claims presented by state prisoners." Randy Hertz & James S. Liebman, 1 *Federal Habeas Corpus Practice & Proc.* § 2.4[d][viii], at 73 (6th ed. 2011) (FHCPP). Professor Gary Peller argued that, before *Brown v. Allen*, federal courts granted habeas relief less frequently because habeas was a remedy for a thin due process right. Professor Peller reasoned that habeas relief was uncommon because fewer claims were cognizable under the federal Constitution, and because the habeas limits in the decisional law reflected only the Article III limits in on the Supreme Court's appellate jurisdiction. See Gary M. Peller, *In Defense of Federal Habeas Corpus Relitigation*, 16 Harv. C.R.-C.L. L. Rev. 579, 604–05 (1982). These responses notwithstanding, Professor Bator's account also has historical support. The same series of Supreme Court opinions forming the basis for Professor Bator's theory had prompted Justice Jackson to argue (in *Brown v. Allen*) that habeas corpus was only available to attack defects in the jurisdiction of the convicting court. Of course, the arguments of Professor Bator and Justice Jackson require us to address the meaning of the term "jurisdiction." *Ex parte Watkins*, presented at the end of this Chapter, will provide you with the opportunity to explore the origins that concept.

6)   Habeas Comes Full Circle. The debates between Justices Frankfurter and Jackson over the proper scope of the writ, between scholars over whether *Brown v. Allen* was a necessary revolution or an unwelcome intrusion, and between modern jurists over the role of federal courts in death row challenges, all share common features. The participants in the modern discourse have drawn different conclusions from the writ's common-law origins and from early Supreme Court decisions. To understand how habeas corpus assumed its modern form—and to assess the merits of each side in the aforementioned debates—you should first understand the writ's common-law history. The Sections that follow explore how the U.S. Constitution incorporated concepts from common-law habeas practice.

2. THE ENGLISH COMMON-LAW WRIT

The common-law features of the habeas writ are not of merely historical interest; they permeate the modern habeas regime. The Supreme Court often refers to the writ's historical development in deciding its habeas cases. For example, in the Warren Court's canonical (and highly controversial) habeas decision, *Fay v. Noia*, Justice William Brennan, writing for the Court, extolled "the historic office of the Great Writ" and emphasized the need to preserve its historical function. 372 U.S. 391, 423 (1963). Although other habeas opinions advance a history of the privilege sharply at odds with Justice Brennan's, judges have a tendency to view the Suspension Clause's reference to the "privilege of habeas corpus" as a reference to the privilege's common-law form. When judges try to ascertain the scope of the writ at common law, they plumb obscure common-law habeas procedure and practice, and they tend to view the Suspension Clause as incorporating the English writ into the U.S. constitutional system.

———

NOTES ON EARLY ENGLISH ORIGINS

The early English origins of the common-law writ are fairly modest. As William the Conqueror began to centralize the court system in England after the Norman Conquest in 1066, judges began to use standard forms that ordered people to appear before them for various reasons or to do various things. English parties could commence actions in local courts in any number of ways, but they needed to secure a "writ" before proceeding in a royal court exercising the power of the crown, something that English law treated as a "privilege." Judges exercising royal franchise could theoretically draft a writ to say anything, but in practice the various courts generally relied on standard form writs. Over the centuries, new types of writs quite literally created new types of relief, and resistance to new form writs grew over time. That resistance eventually precipitated rules confining each writ to a specific purpose. Thus, as Professor William F. Duker explained, "Habeas corpus originated as a device for compelling appearance before the King's judicial instrumentalities." William F. Duker, *A Constitutional History of Habeas Corpus* 62 (1980).

There were several types of habeas writs, and each type mandated the movement of prisoners through courts and jails for a different reason. Some resembled a modern-day subpoena, in which a judge orders a person to appear in court. One of those habeas writs was called "*habeas corpus ad subjiciendum et recipiendum*," meaning "you may have the body to undergo and receive." The purpose of this writ was to examine the circumstances of imprisonment. *Habeas corpus ad subjiciendum* was one of the "prerogative" writs that issued through the courts. *Habeas corpus ad subjiciendum* eventually evolved into what we call "the Great Writ," the instrument judges used to scrutinize the cause of commitment.

A habeas case began with the filing of a prayer for the writ. If granted, the writ permitted the judge to ask the custodian to produce the prisoner and also to explain the cause of the commitment. The judge sent a piece of parchment, the writ, to the custodian. The writ could be sent to jailors, other government officials detaining a person, and (occasionally) to courts; if they did not respond or comply, then they could face contempt and, in the most severe cases, jail. See Paul D. Halliday, *Habeas Corpus: From England to Empire* 109–111 (2010).

The "privilege" of the writ originally referred to the privilege of litigating in a royal court, which began with a petition filed by or on behalf of the prisoner. The court or judicial officer presiding over the habeas proceeding thereafter had several distinct powers: to issue the writ, requiring a return and production of the prisoner; to adjudicate the lawfulness of custody; and to order the prisoner discharged.

The custodian generally complied with the writ by producing the prisoner in court and by providing the judge with certain explanations: the cause for detention and, eventually, the cause for the initial arrest. The custodian would provide those explanations by sending a response called a "return."[g] In the return, the jailer could raise as a defense that the detention was authorized by common law, statute, or custom. If the custodian did not show that the detention was legally and factually authorized, then the judge could order the prisoner discharged from custody.

Anyone designated as a "judge" or a "justice" (and, actually, some officials with no formal judicial designation) could issue the writ, thereby demanding a return; but only those judicial officers who could *enforce* the command could do so with the expectation that the return would actually be provided. Barons of the Court of the Exchequer, Justices of Common Pleas, and Chancery could all send habeas writs, but only King's (or Queen's) Bench—the highest common-law court at Westminster—could be confident that the writ would be treated as a royal prerogative and that its command would be backed by the crown's effective monopoly on coercive sovereign power. The Bench began to use habeas writs not only to require jailers to produce prisoners, but also to require that an explanation be provided for the cause of imprisonment. Bench Justices conducted such inquiries even in cases in which another court ordered the detention, including other courts of record—even the powerful Privy Council and Star Chamber. Judges did not take the return on face value and "generated myriad ways to elicit evidence," including by demanding testimony in the courtroom and examining documents and sworn statements.[h] During the seventeenth century, the Bench seized the prerogative for itself, using habeas to scrutinize custody of any sort, including that ordered by the crown. Parliament eventually passed the famous 1679 Habeas Corpus Act, which specified certain practices for use of the writ and remains a model for many modern habeas statutes.

---

[g] Many courts and historians allude to a "rule against controverting the return," suggesting that the factual inquiry in a habeas proceeding was limited to the jailer's statement in support of detention. See, e.g., Frank v. Mangum, 237 U.S. 309, 330 (1915) ("The rule at the common law . . . seems to have been that a showing in the return to a writ of habeas corpus that the prisoner was held under final process based upon a judgment or decree of a court of competent jurisdiction, closed the inquiry."). Professor Halliday and others have described how the inflexibility of the rule can be overstated; judges employed a variety of procedures to conduct more intensive factual inquiries. The rule against controverting the return had origins in dicta by Lord Coke, which referenced an unrelated rule that an action for trespass or false imprisonment was necessary to seek damages. See Paul D. Halliday, *Habeas Corpus: From England to Empire* 108–111 (2010); see also Gerald Neuman, *Habeas Corpus, Executive Detention, and the Removal of Aliens*, 98 Colum. L. Rev. 961, 986 (1998) (arguing that the "general statement" that "the petitioner could not controvert the facts stated in the return" in fact "papered over exceptions").

[h] See Halliday, *supra* note g, at 109–111.

———

NOTES ON THE CASE OF THE FIVE KNIGHTS

Perhaps the most famous habeas case in all of English law marked the beginning of the writ's evolution during the seventeenth-century: the *Case of the Five Knights,* decided in 1627. Darnel's Case (The Case of the Five Knights) (1627), 3 How. St. Tr. 1 (K.B.). While earlier cases had established certain features of the common-law prerogative writ, *Five Knights* was "one of the most politically charged habeas corpus cases of any age," and it would alter the way the habeas writ was sought, litigated, issued, and honored.[i] King Charles I needed to finance unpopular wars in France and Spain, but he could not secure the approval of Parliament—because he had dissolved it. The King soon found another way to fund the wars: he forced wealthy subjects to loan him money. When Sir Thomas Darnel and four other noblemen refused to pay, the King decided to make an example of them. Darnel and the other knights were detained by the Privy Council (a high court of the King's advisors) at the Fleet Prison in London. In the habeas return, the warden of the Fleet Prison explained that the prisoners were "committed by the special command of his majesty." Royal commandment explained the cause of the detention, but it did not explain why they were arrested—for refusing to pay the forced loan to King Charles.

Prior to *Five Knights*, "writs of habeas corpus ad subjiciendum asked only for the cause of detention."[j] In order to prove that custody was lawful, "[a] jailer might [respond to a demand that cause for the commitment be shown] in rather vague language: 'because some legal officer with powers to order detention told me to detain this person.'"[k] The five knights argued that an order to show cause for detention required more—that it *implied* a demand that the Privy Council show cause for the underlying arrest. One of the knight's lawyers contended, for example, that "the return is too general" and that "there is no sufficient cause shewn."

The Attorney General responded, "But the King commits a subject, and expresseth no cause of the commitment. What then?" He added: "It may be divers men do suffer wrongfully in prison, but therefore shall all prisoners be delivered?" In short, *Five Knights* was about whether custody was lawful simply because the Crown ordered it. Was King Charles above the law?

In *Five Knights*, the Bench ultimately denied habeas relief, reasoning that it could not inquire into the cause for the arrest: "[I]f a man be committed by the commandment of the king, he is not to be delivered by a Habeas Corpus in this court, for we know not the cause of the commitment." Lord Chief Justice Hyde explained:

> The next thing is the main point in law, whether the substance or matter of the return be good or no: wherein the substance is this—[the Warden] doth certify that they are detained in prison by the special command of the King; and whether this be good in law or no, that is the question . . . The question now is, whether we may deliver these gentlemen or not . . . and

---

[i] *Id.* at 50.

[j] *Id.* at 49.

[k] *Id.*

this resolution of all the judges teacheth us; and what can we do but walk in the steps of our forefathers? . . . If in justice we ought to deliver you, we would do it; but upon these grounds and these records, and the precedents and resolutions, we cannot deliver you, but you must be remanded.

Although the decision depended more on prior judicial precedent on Privy Council custody and the language of the writs in question—which did not discuss the cause for the initial arrest—the outcome provoked strong public and institutional responses.

The legal response took both legislative and judicial forms. The legislative response came after many prominent lawyers took the problem of imprisonment orders issued without cause to the steps of Parliament. Parliament subsequently passed and Charles I assented to the Petition of Right in 1628, which decreed that no prisoner could be held "contrary to the laws and franchise of the land." Petition of Right, 1628, 3 Car., c. 1, §§ 1–11 (Eng); see also Boumediene v. Bush, 553 U.S. 723, 742 (2008) (explaining that the Petition of Right was a result of an "immediate outcry" over the *Five Knights* case). The judicial response was more subtle, but perhaps more important. After *Five Knights*, judges simply began to write the writ differently, adding a few words requiring that the custodian show not only cause for detention, but also cause for arrest.[1] Such writ language became standard, and the shift permitted the Bench to more carefully scrutinize new aspects of detention. It also allowed the Bench to check abusive detention undertaken at the behest of the King himself.

———

NOTES ON THE ENGLISH CIVIL WARS AND THE HABEAS CORPUS ACT OF 1679

The struggles among English governing institutions—the King, Parliament, and the Bench—were by no means finished. Shortly after the Petition of Right, the King again dissolved Parliament and, as the U.S. Supreme Court explained in *Boumediene v. Bush*:

When Parliament reconvened in 1640, it sought to secure access to the writ by statute. The Act of 164[1] . . . expressly authorized use of the writ to test the legality of commitment by command or warrant of the King or the Privy Council. Civil strife and the Interregnum soon followed, and not until 1679 did Parliament try once more to secure the writ, this time through the Habeas Corpus Act of 1679, [which] established procedures for issuing the writ; and it was the model upon which the habeas statutes of the 13 American Colonies were based . . .

553 U.S. 723 (2008).[m] The Supreme Court's language is perhaps too gentle: "civil strife" probably fails to capture the scope of the armed conflict, rebellion,

———

[1] *Id.* at 51.

[m] Some of the historical statements in this excerpt are wrong or debatable. First, *Boumediene* misdates the Star Chamber Act; it was passed in 1641, not 1650. See Halliday, *supra* note g, at 224–25, 421 n.10. Second, the Court states that the 1679 Habeas Corpus Act "established" procedures for issuing the writ, but the verb "confirmed" is probably more appropriate. Finally, not all (or even most) of the American colonies had habeas statutes, although the 1679 Habeas Corpus Act had been incorporated into the common law of most of those jurisdictions.

regicide, and revolution that characterized the reign of the Stuart Kings and the seventeenth-century English Civil Wars.

The English Habeas Corpus Act of 1679 has been treated—rightfully—as a landmark achievement in the advancement of human liberty. Students should nonetheless be cautious not to overestimate the Act's role in the development of Anglo-American habeas law. The Act supplemented and confirmed— but did not replace—the common-law writ. The historical account of how English common-law judges transformed a prerogative writ into a powerful tool for reviewing the legality of prisoners' detentions had been, until recently, incomplete. As Professor Paul Halliday has explained in his field-defining book, "Habeas Corpus: From England to Empire":

> Habeas corpus did not evolve. Judges made it, transforming a common device for moving people about in aid of judicial process into an instrument by which they supervised imprisonment orders made anywhere, by anyone, for any reason. The justices considered the writ's work to be so important that when jailers refused to answer commands made to them by habeas corpus, the court sometimes jailed the jailer himself.

See Halliday, *Habeas Corpus: From England to Empire*, at 9. Moreover, the judges wielded this power over jailers in the name of the monarch:

> The most important force driving the writ was the idea at its foundation: the prerogative, those aspects of legal authority possessed only by the monarch. As a prerogative writ, habeas corpus expressed the king's concern to know the circumstances whenever one of his subjects was imprisoned. By taking the idea and language of the prerogative into their own hands, the justices made a writ of majestic, even equitable sweep that made it possible to protect the king's subjects.

Id. No judge or historian before Professor Halliday had studied King's Bench records to determine when Justices actually issued the writ to jailers and what types of relief the prisoners obtained. Professor Halliday's data spans a five-hundred year period and allows us to understand how habeas practice changed over time, as judges defined the writ and as Parliament increasingly enacted statutes to both protect and suspend the privilege of habeas litigation.

Understanding that the habeas privilege had a complicated common-law evolution is important because the power that the modern writ gives a judge to inquire into the cause of a detention defies easy categorization. As Justice Oliver Wendell Holmes eloquently put it, "[H]abeas corpus cuts through all forms and goes to the very tissue of the structure. It comes in from the outside, not in subordination to the proceedings, and although every form may have been preserved, opens the inquiry whether they have been more than an empty shell." Frank v. Mangum, 237 U.S. 309, 346–347 (1915) (Holmes, J., dissenting). Professors Randy Hertz and James Liebman call habeas a kaleidoscope of "civil, appellate, collateral, equitable, common law and statutory procedure." 1 Hertz &. Liebman, *FHCPP* § 2.2. They could have added "criminal" and "constitutional" to that list. How can something be both appellate (direct review of the judgment by a superior court) and collateral (review after the judgment is final), or be both common law and statutory? The balance of this Chapter presents habeas corpus in its American institutional context.

3. THE EARLY REPUBLIC: HABEAS CORPUS, ARTICLE III, AND STATUTES

INTRODUCTORY NOTES ON THE SUSPENSION CLAUSE

The First Article of the U.S. Constitution contains the Suspension Clause, and the habeas privilege is the only remedy that the Constitution mentions explicitly. The Clause reads: "The Privilege of the Writ of Habeas Corpus shall not be suspended, unless when in Cases of Rebellion or Invasion the public Safety may require it." U.S. Const. art. I, § 9, cl. 2. The Clause appears to recognize a pre-existing privilege, but it neither indicates the constitutional source of that privilege nor explains what the privilege covers. The Suspension Clause then creates a limit on when the privilege may be suspended, but the Clause does not expressly create a suspension power. As a result, the meaning of the Suspension Clause remains indeterminate. Chapter 2 delves deeply into the various issues of constitutional interpretation, but here are some of the most important questions:

- What is the "privilege" and what does it entail?

- Does the privilege vest automatically, or does it require an enacting statute?

- Does the privilege afford a remedy for unlawful state custody, unlawful federal custody, or both?

- Which judges, state or federal, may grant the writ?

- Even though the "classic" habeas case is one in which the executive holds a prisoner without judicial process, can judges use habeas to review criminal convictions?

- Absent a suspension, does the privilege require the availability of certain judicial remedies?

- What officers or bodies can suspend the privilege? Although the Clause is an Article I limit on a suspension power, suggesting that Congress has it, does Congress share it with any other branch?

- What happens if the privilege is suspended?

- What entity decides whether the Clause's conditions, the existence of either rebellion or invasion, are satisfied? Is that conclusion subject to judicial review, or is it a nonjusticiable political question?

- Do prisoners have remedies for unlawful custody after the suspension is over?[n]

These questions represent a fraction of the potential constitutional issues, and the Supreme Court has answered only a subset of them. Congress has suspended the privilege four times, and the conditions for and implications of a

---

[n] Compare Trevor W. Morrison, *Suspension and the Extrajudicial Constitution*, 107 Colum. L. Rev. 1533, 1562 (2007) (arguing that suspension of the privilege removes merely a remedy for violation of underlying rights) with Amanda L. Tyler, *Is Suspension a Political Question?*, 59 Stan. L. Rev. 333, 383 (2006) (taking the position that a suspension would bar any remedy for unlawful custody during the suspension period); see also David L. Shapiro, *Habeas Corpus, Suspension, and Detention: Another View*, 82 Notre Dame L. Rev. 59, 87 (2006) (concurring generally with Professor Tyler).

suspension remain largely unlitigated. Starting in about 1996, however, Congress passed a series of statutes restricting the habeas privilege. As a result, the modern Court has considered, with increasing frequency, difficult questions involving the constitutionally-required scope of the privilege during periods of non-suspension.

In order to formulate modern constitutional rules of habeas law, courts consider what we know about the origins of the Suspension Clause at the Founding, but courts must also consider the limits of that knowledge. As developed in greater detail in Chapter 2, there was little discussion of the Suspension Clause during the Constitutional Convention. The Clause was not controversial, except to the extent that some delegates thought that the privilege should be inviolable.[o] In each of the thirteen colonies, prisoners enjoyed some form of a habeas privilege, usually the common-law writ, although one or more colonies also enacted statutes modeled on the Habeas Corpus Act of 1679.[p] (In Massachusetts, the Privy Council opposed an effort to do so.[q]) The precise form of the privilege varied by jurisdiction, as different colonial courts with different authority were established by different statutes and charters, but judges in all thirteen colonies employed the common-law habeas writ, based on English practices and the Habeas Corpus Act of 1679. Following independence, states then formally "received" common-law practices and statutes, including those concerning habeas corpus.

The Framers were familiar with aggressive suspension of the privilege. Lord North, King George's chief minister, pushed a suspension law in 1777 in order to detain, on the order of any magistrate and "without bail or mainprise," colonists who had "traitorously levied" rebellion in "certain of his majesty's colonies and plantations in America." 17 Geo. 3, c. 9 (1777). From 1777 to 1783, the English statute suspending the privilege in the American colonies was renewed five times.[r] This six-year suspension was the longest in English history. Critics deplored the suspensions as unjustified by any showing of necessity; England was not threatened by invasion or insurrection. Others, such as Edmund Burke, railed against the suspension statutes because they targeted spe-

---

[o] See William F. Duker, A Constitutional History of Habeas Corpus 129–31 (1980); Eric M. Freedman, *The Suspension Clause in the Ratification Debates*, 44 Buff. L. Rev. 451, 459 (1996); Martin H. Redish & Colleen McNamara, *Habeas Corpus, Due Process and The Suspension Clause: A Study in the Foundations of American Constitutionalism*, 96 Va. L. Rev. 1361, 1372–1375 (2010). Professor Francis Paschal has observed that the privilege-as-inviolable position is consistent with remarks of the pertinent drafters and committee members at the Constitutional Convention. See Francis Paschal, *The Constitution and Habeas Corpus*, 1970 Duke L.J. 605, 607 (1970).

[p] Although they "received" the common law, some colonies also formally adopted a habeas statute at the time of the founding, though the number that did so is in dispute. Professor Duker argues that, by the time of the Declaration of Independence, the principles of the Habeas Corpus Act were extended to Virginia, North Carolina, South Carolina, and Georgia— pursuant to instructions from the Crown. See Duker, supra note o, at 101-06. Several prominent academics, however, have stated that only South Carolina had a habeas statute. See A.H. Carpenter, *Habeas Corpus in the Colonies*, 8 Am. Hist. Rev. 18, 26 (1902); Dallin H. Oaks, *Habeas Corpus in the States—1776-1865*, 32 U. Chi. L. Rev. 243, 251 (1965).

[q] See John A. Sholar Jr., *Habeas Corpus and the War on Terror*, 45 Duq. L. Rev. 661, 671 (2007); Donald E. Wilkes Jr., *From Oglethorpe to the Overthrow of the Confederacy: Habeas Corpus in Georgia, 1733-1865*, 45 Ga. L. Rev. 1015 (2011); Redish and McNamara, *supra note* o, at 1369. For detailed historical accounts, see Duker, supra note o, at 98–116; A.H. Carpenter, *Habeas Corpus in the Colonies*, 8 Am. Hist. Rev. (1902).

[r] See 22 Geo. 3, c. 1 (1782) (renewal); 21 Geo. 3, c. 2 (1781) (renewal); 20 Geo. 3, c. 5 (1780) (renewal); 19 Geo. 3, c. 1 (1779) (renewal); 18 Geo. 3, c. 1 (1778) (renewal).

cific classes of people; the statutes were limited to certain subjects abroad. Professor Halliday has observed that, not only were hundreds of American sailors captured and denied use of the writ, but "[s]uffering the denial of habeas corpus became a marker of liberty and independence, a point of honor by which Americans would sustain rebellion." Halliday, *Habeas Corpus: From England to Empire*, at 253.

Having been on the receiving end of the English suspensions, the Framers included language in the Suspension Clause limiting suspension to "Cases of Rebellion or Invasion" when "the public Safety may require it." State constitutions had included similar suspension clauses (in addition to statutes providing for the privilege); indeed, five colonies had suspended the privilege during the American Revolution, and Massachusetts had suspended it after the Revolution, during Shay's Rebellion.[s] After ratification of the Constitution, Congress enacted federal statutes vesting in federal courts and judges the authority to issue habeas writs.

———

NOTES ON SECTION 14 OF THE JUDICIARY ACT OF 1789

At the Constitutional Convention, the delegates reached the "Madisonian Compromise"—giving Congress considerable power over the judicial branch—by agreeing that the Congress did not have to create any inferior Article III federal courts. Nevertheless, Congress promptly did just that when it enacted the Judiciary Act of 1789. The 1789 Judiciary Act also: (1) vested those courts with original jurisdiction, (2) created the United States Supreme Court, (3) specified the Supreme Court's appellate jurisdiction over the inferior tribunals, and (4) vested the Supreme Court with original jurisdiction. The 1789 Judiciary Act specified habeas jurisdiction as a power enjoyed by certain federal courts and judges. What particular types of habeas authority were vested in which courts and judges eventually became the subject of *Ex parte Bollman*, 4 Cranch (8 U.S.) 75 (1807), the early republic's defining habeas decision, discussed next. Much of the language of the 1789 Judiciary Act survives in Titles 16 and 28 of the modern United States Code. Specifically, Section 14 provided:

> That all the before-mentioned courts of the United States, shall have power to issue writs of *scire facias, habeas corpus,* and all other writs not specially provided for by statute, which may be necessary for the exercise of their respective jurisdictions, and agreeable to the principles and usages of law. And that either of the justices of the supreme court, as well as judges of the district courts, shall have power to grant writs of *habeas corpus* for the purpose of an inquiry into the cause of commitment.—*Provided,* That writs of *habeas corpus* shall in no case extend to prisoners in gaol, unless where they are in custody, under or by colour of the authority of the United States, or are committed for trial before some court of the same, or are necessary to be brought into court to testify.

———

[s] See Amanda L. Tyler, *Suspension as an Emergency Power,* 118 Yale L.J. 600, 622–28 (2009); see also Zechariah Chafee, Jr., *The Most Important Human Right in the Constitution,* 32 B.U. L. Rev. 143, 145–46 (1952) (noting North Carolina, Georgia, Massachusetts, New Hampshire, and Pennsylvania had such provisions).

1 Stat. 81–82. Section 14 thereby gave all federal judges the power to issue certain habeas writs.[t]

INTRODUCTORY NOTE ON EX PARTE BOLLMAN

Bollman, authored by Chief Justice John Marshall was one of the first Supreme Court decisions to discuss the statutory habeas remedy. *Bollman* is a complex opinion that resolved a politically charged case; its holdings continue to frame our modern habeas jurisprudence. The exchange between Chief Justice Marshall and Justice Johnson is a wonderful example of dueling statutory interpretation. *Bollman* raises difficult questions about the scope of the habeas privilege, including whether Congress must vest habeas jurisdiction in federal courts, the meaning of the Suspension Clause, whether habeas jurisdiction is a form of original or appellate power, and how the common-law habeas writ should function in a new constitutional environment. The opinion also embodies Chief Justice Marshall's cautious expansion of judicial power during an era when more ambitious assertions of jurisdiction could undermine judicial legitimacy. *Bollman* is not only one of the most important cases in the history of habeas law, but also one of the most important decisions about the scope of federal jurisdiction.

In *Bollman*, the Supreme Court ultimately ordered the release of two men facing a federal trial in a legally and politically sensational case. The men were associates of former Vice President Aaron Burr. They were accused of treason for assisting Burr with a plan to help southern states secede from the Union and to support Spain. In New Jersey, Burr had shot and mortally wounded Alexander Hamilton in a duel, and Burr was on the run. Burr made his way to New Orleans, where Burr raised money, met confederates, and gathered supporters. Historians have been unable to determine whether Burr was just trying to flee and make enough money to support himself, trying to raise a private army, or engaged in some sort of military mischief. Historians also cannot agree on Burr's geographic objective: Mexico, New Orleans, Florida, South America, or some other part of the United States (the Louisiana Territory had not yet been annexed). Perhaps Burr was trying to become "King of the West," or perhaps he was unsure where his plot was leading.

Louisiana Territory Gov. Gen. James Wilkinson, who met with and at least flirted with the idea of joining Burr, turned informant and forwarded some of Burr's incriminating letters to President Thomas Jefferson. President Jefferson declared the Burr activity a conspiracy. Gen. Wilkinson then declared martial law and arrested Burr, who was tried for treason. Gen. Wilkinson also arrested two of Burr's associates, Bollman and Swartwout. Neither Bollman nor Swartwout were not charged or tried. President Jefferson then asked Congress to suspend the privilege of habeas corpus so that he could detain the two men.[u] The Senate passed a suspension bill, but the House did not. Meanwhile,

---

[t] Section 14 limited federal habeas power only to cases involving federal custody, and did not extend such power to include state custody (except to those who are not challenging their detention, but are "necessary to be brought into court to testify").

[u] This request was ironic because Thomas Jefferson had urged, in his correspondence with James Madison, the inclusion in the Bill of Rights of a provision that habeas corpus could not be suspended. Letter from Thomas Jefferson to James Madison (Dec. 20, 1787), in 12 The Papers of Thomas Jefferson 438, 440 (Julian P. Boyd ed., 1955) (arguing that the Bill of Rights

the two men were detained without bail and charged with treason. The lower court denied habeas relief, so the men sought an "original" habeas writ from the U.S. Supreme Court, under Section 14.

There were two problems. First, the 1789 Judiciary Act § 14 did not, at least clearly, appear to vest the Supreme Court—as opposed to its individual Justices—with power to grant habeas relief. Second, even if § 14 did vest the Court with authority to issue an "original" habeas writ, *Marbury v. Madison*, 5 U.S. (1 Cranch) 137 (1803), held that Congress could not add to the Article III, § 2 jurisdiction of the Supreme Court that was denominated as original. The Supreme Court is limited under Article III, § 2, to "original jurisdiction" over "all cases affecting ambassadors, other public ministers and consuls, and those in which a state shall be party. However, that Section continues, "[i]n all the other cases before mentioned, the Supreme Court shall have appellate jurisdiction." For the Supreme Court to even hear *Bollman* and grant the writ, much less release the two prisoners, jurisdiction would have to be "appellate" in nature—as habeas corpus review of the custody of prisoners is not within the exclusive list of subjects falling within the Court's "original jurisdiction." Chief Justice Marshall had to conclude that § 14 of the Act authorized the Supreme Court to issue habeas writs and that Article III § 2 permitted the exercise of such jurisdiction; he also had to determine whether the Suspension Clause had anything to say about the jurisdiction of federal judges to grant habeas corpus relief.

Ex parte Bollman

United States Supreme Court
4 Cranch (8 U.S.) 75 (1807)

■ MARSHALL, CH. J. delivered the opinion of the court, as follows:

As preliminary to any investigation of the merits of this motion, this court deems it proper to declare that it disclaims all jurisdiction not given by the constitution, or by the laws of the United States.

Courts which originate in the common law possess a jurisdiction which must be regulated by their common law, until some statute shall change their established principles; but courts which are created by written law, and whose jurisdiction is defined by written law, cannot transcend that jurisdiction. * * * [F]or the meaning of the term *habeas corpus*, resort may unquestionably be had to the common law; but the power to award the writ by any of the courts of the United States, must be given by written law.

This opinion * * * extends only to the power of taking cognizance of any question between individuals, or between the government and individuals.

To enable the court to decide on such question, the power to determine it must be given by written law.

The inquiry therefore on this motion will be, whether by any statute, compatible with the constitution of the United States, the power to award a

---

should provide "clearly and without the aid of sophisms for . . . the eternal and unremitting force of the habeas corpus laws"). For a description of these events, including the suspension bill, see Duker, supra note o, at 135–37.

writ of *habeas corpus*, in such a case as that of Erick Bollman and Samuel Swartwout, has been given to this court.

The 14th section of the judicial act * * * has been considered as containing a substantive grant of this power.

It is in these words: 'That all the before mentioned courts of the United States shall have power to issue writs of *scire facias, habeas corpus*, and all other writs, not specially provided for by statute, which may be necessary for the exercise of their respective jurisdictions, and agreeable to the principles and usages of law. And that either of the justices of the supreme court, as well as judges of the district courts, shall have power to grant writs of *habeas corpus*, for the purpose of an inquiry into the cause of commitment.—*Provided*, that writs of *habeas corpus* shall in no case extend to prisoners in gaol, unless where they are in custody under or by colour of the authority of the United States, or are committed for trial before some court of the same, or are necessary to be brought into court to testify.'

The only doubt of which this section can be susceptible is, whether the restrictive words ["which may be necessary for the exercise of their respective jurisdictions"] limit the power to the award of such writs of *habeas corpus* as are necessary to enable the courts of the United States to exercise their respective jurisdictions in some cause which they are capable of finally deciding.

It has been urged, that in strict grammatical construction, these words refer to the last antecedent, which is, "all other writs not specially provided for by statute."

This criticism may be correct, and is not entirely without its influence; but the sound construction which the court thinks it safer to adopt, is, that the true sense of the words is to be determined by the nature of the provision, and by the context.

It may be worthy of remark, that this act was passed by the first congress of the United States, sitting under a constitution which had declared "that the privilege of the writ of *habeas corpus* should not be suspended, unless when, in cases of rebellion or invasion, the public safety might require it."

Acting under the immediate influence of this injunction, they must have felt, with peculiar force, the obligation of providing efficient means by which this great constitutional privilege should receive life and activity; for if the means be not in existence, the privilege itself would be lost, although no law for its suspension should be enacted. Under the impression of this obligation, they give, to all the courts, the power of awarding writs of *habeas corpus*.

It has been truly said, that this is a generic term, and includes every species of that writ. To this it may be added, that when used singly—when we say *the writ of habeas corpus*, without addition, we most generally mean that great writ which is now applied for; and in that sense it is used in the constitution.

The section proceeds to say, that "either of the justices of the supreme court, as well as judges of the district courts, shall have power to grant writs of *habeas corpus* for the purpose of an inquiry into the cause of commitment."

It has been argued that congress could never intend to give a power of this kind to one of the judges of this court, which is refused to all of them when assembled.

There is certainly much force in this argument, and it receives additional strength from the consideration, that if the power be denied to this court, it is denied to every other court of the United States; the right to grant this important writ is given, in this sentence, to every judge of the circuit, or district court, but can neither be exercised by the circuit nor district court. It would be strange if the judge, sitting on the bench, should be unable to hear a motion for this writ where it might be openly made, and openly discussed, and might yet retire to his chamber, and in private receive and decide upon the motion. This is not consistent with the genius of our legislation, nor with the course of our judicial proceedings. It would be much more consonant with both, that the power of the judge at his chambers should be suspended during his term, than that it should be exercised only in secret.

Whatever motives might induce the legislature to withhold from the *supreme* court the power to award the great writ of *habeas corpus*, there could be none which would induce them to withhold it from *every* court in the United States; and as it is granted to *all* in the *same sentence* and by the *same words*, the sound construction would seem to be, that the first sentence vests this power in all the courts of the United States; but as those courts are not always in session, the second sentence vests it in every justice or judge of the United States.

The doubt which has been raised on this subject may be further explained by examining the character of the various writs of *habeas corpus*, and selecting those to which this general grant of power must be restricted, if taken in the limited sense of being merely used to enable the court to exercise its jurisdiction in causes which it is enabled to decide finally.

The various writs of *habeas corpus*, as stated and accurately defined by judge Blackstone are, 1st. The writ of *habeas corpus ad respondendum*, "when a man hath a cause of action against one who is confined by the process of some inferior court; in order to remove the prisoner and charge him with this new action in the court above."

This case may occur when a party having a right to sue in this court, (as a state at the time of the passage of this act, or a foreign minister,) wishes to institute a suit against a person who is already confined by the process of an inferior court. This confinement may be either by the process of a court of the *United States*, or of a *state* court. If it be in a court of the United States, this writ would be inapplicable, because perfectly useless, and consequently could not be contemplated by the legislature. [The Court explained that *ad respondendum* writs would not be necessary to produce a federal prisoner in an original Supreme Court actions, and that they could not issue to state courts because they are not "inferior" courts. With respect to state courts, *Bollman* held that "[t]hey are not inferior courts because they emanate from a different authority, and are the creatures of a distinct government."]

2d. The writ of *habeas corpus ad satisfaciendum*, "when a prisoner hath had judgment against him in an action, and the plaintiff is desirous to bring him up to some superior court to charge him with process of execution."

This case can never occur in the courts of the United States. One court never awards execution on the judgment of another. Our whole juridical system forbids it.

3d. *Ad prosequendum, testificandum, deliberandum,* * * * "which issue when it is necessary to remove a prisoner, in order to prosecute, or bear testimony, in any court, or to be tried in the proper jurisdiction wherein the fact was committed."

This writ might unquestionably be employed to bring up a prisoner to bear testimony in a court, consistently with the most limited construction of the words in the act of congress; but the power to bring a person up that he may be tried in the proper jurisdiction is understood to be the very question now before the court.

4th, and last. The common writ *ad faciendum et recipiendum* ["*habeas corpus cum causa*"], which issues [from a superior to an inferior court with instructions for the latter] "to produce the body of the defendant, together with the day and cause of his caption and detainer, * * * to do and receive whatever the king's court shall consider in that behalf. This writ is grantable of common right, without any motion in court, and it instantly supersedes all proceedings in the court below."

Can a solemn grant of power to a court to award a writ be considered as applicable to a case in which that writ, if issuable at all, issues by law without the leave of the court?

It would not be difficult to demonstrate that the writ of *habeas corpus cum causa* cannot be the particular writ contemplated by the legislature in the section under consideration; but it will be sufficient to observe generally that the same act prescribes a different mode for bringing into the courts of the United States suits brought in a state court against a person having a right to claim the jurisdiction of the courts of the United States. He may [remove the cause] into the courts of the United States.

The only power then, which on this limited construction would be granted by the section under consideration, would be that of issuing writs of *habeas corpus ad testificandum*. The section itself proves that this was not the intention of the legislature. It concludes with the following proviso, "That writs of habeas corpus shall in no case extend to prisoners in jail, unless where they are in custody under or by colour of the authority of the United States, or are committed for trial before some court of the same, or are necessary to be brought into court to testify."

This proviso extends to the whole section. It limits the powers previously granted to the courts, because it specifies a case in which it is particularly applicable to the use of the power by courts:—where the person is necessary to be brought into court to testify. That construction cannot be a fair one which would make the legislature except from the operation of a proviso, limiting the express grant of a power, the whole power intended to be granted.

[The Court remarked that the restrictive reading is incompatible with the purposes for which Section 14 seems intended.]

[T]he 33d section throws much light upon this question. It contains these words: 'And upon all arrests in criminal cases, bail shall be admitted, except where the punishment may be death; in which cases it shall not be admitted but by the supreme or a circuit court, or by a justice of the supreme court, or a judge of a district court, who shall exercise their discretion therein, regarding the nature and circumstances of the offence, and of the evidence, and of the usages of law.'

The appropriate process of bringing up a prisoner, not committed by the court itself, to be bailed, is by the writ now applied for. Of consequence, a court possessing the power to bail prisoners not committed by itself, may award a writ of habeas corpus for the exercise of that power. The clause under consideration obviously proceeds on the supposition that this power was previously given, and is explanatory of the 14th section. * * *

If the act of congress gives this court the power to award a writ of *habeas corpus* in the present case, it remains to inquire whether that act be compatible with the constitution.

In [*Marbury* v. *Madison*], it was decided that this court would not exercise original jurisdiction except so far as that jurisdiction was given by the constitution. But so far as that case has distinguished between original and appellate jurisdiction, that which the court is now asked to exercise is clearly *appellate*. It is the revision of a decision of an inferior court, by which a citizen has been committed to jail.

It has been demonstrated at the bar, that the question brought forward on a *habeas corpus*, is always distinct from that which is involved in the cause itself. The question whether the individual shall be imprisoned is always distinct from the question whether he shall be convicted or acquitted of the charge on which he is to be tried, and therefore these questions are separated, and may be decided in different courts.

The decision that the individual shall be imprisoned must always precede the application for a writ of *habeas corpus*, and this writ must always be for the purpose of revising that decision, and therefore appellate in its nature.

If at any time the public safety should require the suspension of the powers vested by this act in the courts of the United States, it is for the legislature to say so.

That question depends on political considerations, on which the legislature is to decide. Until the legislative will be expressed, this court can only see its duty, and must obey the laws.

The motion, therefore, must be granted.

■ JOHNSON, J. [dissenting]:

* * * The original jurisdiction of this court is restricted to cases affecting ambassadors or other public ministers, and consuls, and those in which a state shall be a party. In all other cases within the judicial powers of the union, it can exercise only an appellate jurisdiction. The former it possesses independently of the will of any other constituent branch of the general government. Without a violation of the constitution, that division of our jurisdiction can neither be restricted or extended. In the latter its powers are subjected to the will of the legislature of the union, and it can exercise appellate jurisdiction in no case, unless expressly authorised to do so by the laws of congress. If I understand the case of *Marbury v. Madison*, it maintains this doctrine in its full extent. I cannot see how it could ever have been controverted.

It is incumbent, then, I presume, on the counsel, in order to maintain their motion, to prove that the issuing of this writ is an act within the power of this court in its original jurisdiction, or that, in its appellate capacity, the power is expressly given by the laws of congress. * * *

It is necessary to premise that the case of treason is one in which this court possesses neither original nor appellate jurisdiction. The 14th section of the judiciary act, so far as it has relation to this case, is in these words:— "All the beforementioned courts (of which this is one) of the United States shall have power to issue writs of scire facias, habeas corpus, and all other writs not specially provided for by statute, which may be necessary for the exercise of their respective jurisdictions, and agreeable to the principles and usages of law." I do not think it material to the opinion I entertain what construction is given to this sentence. If the power to issue the writs of scire facias and habeas corpus be not restricted to the cases within the original or appellate jurisdiction of this court, [*Marbury*] rejects the clause as unavailing; and if it relate only to cases within their jurisdiction, it does not extend to the case which is now moved for. But it is impossible to give a sensible construction to that clause without taking the whole together; it consists of but one sentence, intimately connected throughout, and has for its object the creation of those powers which probably would have vested in the respective courts without statutory provision, as incident to the exercise of their jurisdiction. To give to this clause the construction contended for by counsel, would be to suppose that the legislature would commit the absurd act of granting the power of issuing the writs of scire facias and habeas corpus, without an object or end to be answered by them. This idea is not a little supported by the next succeeding clause, in which a power is vested in the individual judges to issue the writ of habeas corpus, expressly for the purpose of inquiring into the cause of commitment. That part of the thirty-third section of the judiciary act which relates to this subject is in the following words:—"And upon all arrests in criminal cases, bail shall be admitted, except where the punishment is death, in which cases it shall not be admitted but by the supreme or a circuit court, or by a justice of the supreme court, or a judge of a district court, who shall exercise their discretion therein, regarding the nature and circumstances of the offence, and of the evidence, and usage of law."

On considering this act it cannot be denied that if it vests any power at all, it is an original power. "It is the essential criterion of appellate jurisdiction, that it revises and corrects the proceedings in a cause already instituted." * * *

* * * Let it be remembered that I am not disputing the power of the individual judges who compose this court to issue the writ of habeas corpus. This application is not made to us as at chambers, but to us as holding the supreme court of the United States—a creature of the constitution, and possessing no greater capacity to receive jurisdiction or power than the constitution gives it. We may in our individual capacities, or in our circuit courts, be susceptible of powers merely ministerial, and not inconsistent with our judicial characters, for on that point the constitution has left much to construction; and on such an application the only doubt that could be entertained would be, whether we can exercise any power beyond the limits of our respective circuits. On this question I will not now give an opinion. * * *

————

NOTES AND QUESTIONS ON BOLLMAN

1) Jurisdiction of the Supreme Court versus Habeas Jurisdiction of All Federal Courts. Why did the opinion begin the way it did? Before addressing the question of whether § 14 of the Act authorized the Supreme Court to entertain the original habeas petition, Chief Justice Marshall remarked, "[T]his court deems it proper to declare that it disclaims all jurisdiction not given by the constitution, or by the laws of the United States." Did Chief Justice Marshall mean that the Supreme Court's jurisdiction must be given by an enabling statute, or by some other "written law," or did he mean that the habeas jurisdiction common to all federal courts must be provided by an enabling statute? He then added, "[F]or the meaning of the term *habeas corpus*, resort may unquestionably be had to the common law; but the power to award the writ by any of the courts of the United States, must be given by written law." Perhaps he was merely "beginning on an ostensibly deferential note." Paul D. Halliday & G. Edward White, *The Suspension Clause: English Text, Imperial Contexts, and American Implications*, 94 Va. L. Rev. 575, 683 (2008). Chief Justice Marshall is known for his strategic introductory framing (most famously executed in *Marbury*). Although the Court would proceed to engage in a careful statutory analysis, notice how important common-law terms and practices were to its conclusions.

2) Overview of the Statutory Question: Did § 14 Authorize The Supreme Court to issue Writs of Habeas Corpus *Ad Subjiciendum*? Chief Justice Marshall and Justice Johnson disagree primarily on the answer to this question. If the 1789 Judiciary Act did not authorize the Supreme Court to issue the writ in question, then there was no need for *Bollman* to reach the constitutional question of whether such jurisdiction was permitted under Article III. The arguments about each part of § 14 are complex. In general, Chief Justice Marshall believed that each grant of power in § 14 was meant to ensure that federal courts can effectively exercise the most important type of habeas corpus review—that involving the prisoner's cause of commitment (or habeas corpus *ad subjuciendum*). Justice Johnson, in contrast, read § 14 in a more technical way. He views the text as clearly providing federal *courts* with jurisdiction to issue only auxiliary and mundane habeas writs, confining cause-of-commitment review to *judges*. Here is a table contrasting how Chief Justice Marshall and Justice Johnson interpreted each part of the statute.

Figure 1.1

Statutory Language	Chief Justice Marshall	Justice Johnson
That all the before-mentioned courts of the United States, shall have power to issue writs of *scire facias*, *habeas corpus*, and all other writs not specially provided for by statute, which may be necessary for the exercise of their respective jurisdictions, and agreeable to the principles and usages of law.	• "[W]hich may be necessary for the exercise of their respective jurisdictions" does not modify "habeas corpus" (last antecedent rule); so • All U.S. courts have jurisdiction to issue habeas writs to review cause of commitment.	• "[W]hich may be necessary for the exercise of their respective jurisdictions" modifies the entire sentence, including "habeas corpus;" so • The first sentence only grants to the Supreme Court the power to issue habeas writs auxiliary to some other source of jurisdiction.

And that either of the justices of the supreme court, as well as judges of the district courts, shall have power to grant writs of *habeas corpus* for the purpose of an inquiry into the cause of commitment.	• No negative implication for first sentence. This language reinforces the first sentence, by highlighting that individual judges may also grant habeas relief.	• The second sentence gives federal judicial officers authority to issue writs of habeas corpus *ad subjiciendum*; so • There is no need to strain the natural reading of the first sentence, which grants to federal courts only the power to issue auxiliary writs.
—*Provided*, That writs of *habeas corpus* shall in no case extend to prisoners in gaol, unless where they are in custody, under or by colour of the authority of the United States, or are committed for trial before some court of the same, or are necessary to be brought into court to testify.	• Proviso applies to first sentence; and • Congress would not have taken away exactly what the first sentence had given; and • The only auxiliary writ the first sentence could be referencing is the writ excluded under the proviso (to testify), so the first sentence must refer to cause-of-commitment writs.	• Proviso supplies a limit for habeas jurisdiction granted in first and second sentences, such that only individual judges may grant habeas corpus, but only to federal prisoners or for auxiliary reasons; and • Even if the first sentence describes auxiliary writs, it still grants habeas authority that is greater than what the proviso takes away.

3)   The Statutory Holding. First, Chief Justice Marshall broadly read § 14 of the Act as authorizing the Supreme Court, and not just individual Justices, to issue habeas writs for the purposes of scrutinizing custody. Marshall rejected what some argue is a more natural reading of § 14, a reading that would have assigned the power to issue habeas *ad subjiciendum* writs to individual Justices but would have withheld it from the entire Supreme Court. He read the first sentence of § 14—which empowered Article III courts "to issue writs of *scire facias, habeas corpus,* and all other writs not specially provided for by statute, which may be necessary for the exercise of their respective jurisdictions and agreeable to the principles and usages of law"—to refer to the Great Writ, rather than to other types of habeas writs.

Chief Justice Marshall argued that the term "habeas corpus" in the first sentence most naturally referred to the Great Writ because Congress did not specify the particular species of habeas writ to which that sentence might otherwise refer. Chief Justice Marshall then explained that the first sentence of § 14 must include a power to award writs of *habeas corpus ad subjiciendum* because such a power was necessarily contemplated by § 33, which prescribed how to decide bail in capital cases. Chief Justice Marshall reasoned that, because the process of admitting bail necessarily involved producing a prisoner in court and assessing whether there was continuing cause for detention, § 14 must have empowered the Court to grant the writ. Chief Justice Marshall also argued that "[i]t would be strange" to vest habeas power in judges and Justices, but not in Article III courts themselves.

4)   The First Sentence: Cause-of-commitment Versus Auxiliary Habeas Writs. One reason that key passages in *Bollman* are so impenetrable is that the Supreme Court's authority to issue the Great Writ turned partially on arcane distinctions between different types of common-law habeas process. Habeas corpus *ad subjiciendum*, used to examine the cause of a prisoner's commitment to custody, is the writ that is most important to us, and that was most important to the Court in *Bollman*. It was one of several common-law English habeas writs, and the others were more mundane and remained auxiliary to other sources of jurisdiction. In other words, auxiliary writs cannot be the source of a court's power over a particular dispute; they are simply available to help process a dispute over which a court enjoys jurisdiction arising under some other power, such as by allowing the court to bring in a witness to testify.

Chief Justice Marshall argued that the pertinent use of the term "habeas corpus" could not describe any of the auxiliary writs, except *ad testificandum*. He argued that the term encompassed more than the auxiliary writs—and that it included *ad subjiciendum*—because the proviso at the end of § 14 carves out jailed prisoners that "are necessary to be brought into court to testify." Congress could not have meant, Marshall reasoned, to use the § 14 proviso to take away the only jurisdiction granted in the first sentence. The first sentence must grant some jurisdiction other than just the power to demand that jailors produce witnesses to testify. It must give jurisdiction to examine the cause of a prisoner's commitment—which, after all, is the most substantial type of habeas review.

Justice Johnson's dissent was powerful, and some prominent scholars believe he got the better of Chief Justice Marshall—at least "with respect to technical construction." See Dallin Oaks, *The "Original" Writ of Habeas Corpus in the Supreme Court*, 1962 Sup. Ct. Rev. 153, 176 (1962); see also Francis Paschal, *The Constitution and Habeas Corpus*, 1970 Duke L.J. 605, 619 (1970) (reasoning that (1) the mention of *scire facias* proves that the first and second antecedents were qualified as writs "necessary for the exercise of their respective jurisdictions" and (2) § 14 plainly treated judges and courts differently). Pay particular attention to Justice Johnson's argument involving the first sentence of § 14:

> But it is impossible to give a sensible construction to [the first clause of the first sentence] without taking the whole [first sentence] together; [the first sentence is] intimately connected throughout, and has for its object the creation of those powers which probably would have vested in the respective courts without statutory provision, as incident to the exercise of their jurisdiction. To give to this clause the construction contended for by counsel, would be to suppose that the legislature would commit the absurd act of granting the power of issuing the writs of *scire facias* and *habeas corpus*, without an object or end to be answered by them. This idea is not a little supported by the next succeeding clause, in which a power is vested in the individual judges to issue the writ of *habeas corpus*, expressly for the purpose of inquiring into the cause of commitment.

Which side interpreted § 14 correctly?

5)   The Second Sentence: The Supreme Court versus Individual Justices. Chief Justice Marshall premised his statutory arguments concerning the second sentence of § 14 on what he described as a problematic alternative—the idea that individual Justices would have powers that the Supreme Court would not. In fact, individual English judges issued habeas writs all the time. One of the major purposes of the Habeas Corpus Act of 1679 was to provide statutory authority for judges to issue habeas writs while the courts over which they presided were in vacation.ᵛ Moreover, the 1789 Judiciary Act contemplated that each Supreme Court Justice would sit as a circuit judge (or "Circuit Justice") in one of the regional judicial districts housing a circuit court. The argument that Justices could issue habeas writs in their individual capacities, which Justice Johnson emphasized, sounds stranger now than it did to a contemporary practitioner, because we are unaccustomed to thinking of Justices as deciding cases—even habeas petitions—on their own.

6)   Overview of the Constitutional Question: Distinguishing Between the Supreme Court's "Appellate" and "Original" Jurisdiction. The narrow question that the Supreme Court faced was whether it could grant habeas relief to prisoners committed by order of a federal circuit court. At the time, federal circuit courts were the federal trial courts of general jurisdiction. After the Supreme Court determined that § 14 of the 1789 Judiciary Act vested it with original habeas jurisdiction, the Supreme Court had to confront the question of whether such a statutory grant was permitted under Article III, § 2 of the Constitution.

The idea that Congress could create *original* habeas authority was particularly problematic in light of *Marbury*, which had held, among other things, that the jurisdiction denominated as original in Article III, § 2 was an exhaustive list. In short, to permit Supreme Court jurisdiction, *Bollman* would have to hold that the Court's original habeas power was in fact an appellate authority.

Repeating the distinction made in *Marbury,* the Court distinguished its own original jurisdiction—which Congress may not expand beyond the scope specified in Article III ("In all Cases affecting Ambassadors, other public Ministers and Consuls, and those in which a State shall be Party")—from appellate jurisdiction (in "all the other Cases before mentioned" in Article III), which Congress can alter. U.S. Const. art. III, § 2, cl. 2. The Court observed that "[i]t is the essential criterion of appellate jurisdiction that it revises and corrects the proceedings in a cause already instituted, and does not create that cause." Provided that an original habeas petition seeks an order "revising" the lower court determination, Chief Justice Marshall reasoned, original jurisdiction is an appellate power.

Justice Marshall's resolution of the case, however, interpreted the appellate power of the Court fairly broadly. At this juncture in the *Bollman* litigation, there had been no trial. The lower-court "proceeding" that the Supreme Court was arguably revising was the (interlocutory) probable cause determination necessary to commit the two men pending further criminal process. One

---

ᵛ Indeed, Chief Justice Marshall acknowledged this practice in the Court's opinion, although he did not mention that enabling it was one of the major objectives of the 1679 Habeas Corpus Act. Moreover, Chief Justice Marshall argued that the practice supported his interpretation and that the only purpose of the *second* sentence in § 14 was to create this authority. The first sentence, he argued, simply vested the original habeas power while the Court was in term.

implication of *Bollman* is that no judge had decided that there was probable cause, then there would be no lower court determination to "revise," and therefore no appellate jurisdiction for the Supreme Court to exercise.

By contrast, an appeal from a final order occurs after a judgment of conviction. At the time, Congress had not vested the Supreme Court to hear ordinary appeals in federal criminal cases. In situations where a federal court conducts habeas review of a final state or federal conviction, then it is not hearing an appeal, but conducting a "collateral" proceeding. Collateral review that follows entry of a criminal judgment is called "post-conviction" review; post-conviction review is the subject five chapters of this Book. A recurring theme, particularly in early habeas cases, is the idea that habeas review can have the flavor of an appeal, at least when the Supreme Court uses it to review a proceeding in an inferior court. (The appellate "flavor" is not an accident or an artificial construct; King's Bench used habeas to review criminal sentences because it lacked appellate jurisdiction over appeals from other English Courts.)

7) **The Suspension Clause.** Chief Justice Marshall then (perhaps unnecessarily) addressed a larger constitutional question, alluding to the Suspension Clause. He wrote the Framers "must have felt, with peculiar force, the obligation of providing efficient means by which this great constitutional privilege should receive life and activity. . . [I]f the means be not in existence, the privilege itself would be lost, although no law for its suspension should be enacted." Chief Justice Marshall was suggesting that the Constitution does not create, of its own force, federal habeas jurisdiction, and that such jurisdiction requires an enabling statute. On the other hand, he also suggested that the Framers must have intended to provide "efficient means" to provide habeas review. Almost two hundred years later, Justices on the modern Court still dispute the relationship between the Suspension Clause and Article III jurisdiction. Scholars have disagreed just as intensely.[w] Would Congress be "suspending" the privilege by failing to vest federal courts and judges with power to issue it? Would suspension through legislative inaction be subject to constitutional challenge? Reading *Bollman* that way would render the proposition dicta—there was in fact a federal habeas statute—but dicta from Chief Justice Marshall would be "unusually authoritative."[x]

8) **Obligation Theory.** A different view of the relationship between the U.S. Constitution and the privilege is sometimes called the "Obligation Theory," evoking the language regarding the "peculiar force" with which the First Congress must have felt the "obligation" to enact a habeas statute. Obligation theory posits that, although there is no self-executing habeas jurisdiction, the Constitution required Congress to create some sort of meaningful habeas remedy.[y]

---

[w] Compare INS v. St. Cyr, 533 U.S. 289, 305 n.24 (2001) (reading the pertinent *Bollman* language to mean that a failure to enact a habeas statute would unconstitutionally restrict the privilege) with *id.* at 339 (Scalia, J., dissenting) (reading the pertinent *Bollman* language to mean that the Constitution does not require the existence of a federal habeas remedy). In *St. Cyr*, the Court's opinion on this question was dicta. In *Boumediene v. Bush*, however, the Court held that the Constitution barred Congress from stripping federal habeas jurisdiction over at least some kinds of custody. See 553 U.S. 723 (2008).

[x] *St. Cyr*, 533 U.S. at 339 (Scalia, J., dissenting). As discussed in Chapter 2, Justice Scalia is the only Justice to have suggested such a view of *Bollman*.

[y] For an even stronger view—that the Suspension Clause and/or Article III or other constitutional sources are self-executing, and that they directly provide federal judges with habeas jurisdiction, see Francis Paschal, *The Constitution and Habeas Corpus*, 1970 Duke L.J. 605, 607–08 (1970).

Is the Obligation Theory persuasive? What is the source of the obligation? The Suspension Clause? The Suspension Clause in combination with some other constitutional provision, such as the Supremacy Clause or the Fourteenth Amendment? In combination with Article III? What about the existence of the Supreme Court itself, required by the Constitution but in need of enacting legislation? Would a failure to enact "obligated legislation" be justiciable? Does this suggest that Congress must effectuate the writ to provide "efficient means" for courts to consider habeas petitions?

9) Written-Law Jurisdiction versus Common Law. Chief Justice Marshall wrote that common-law courts "possess a jurisdiction which must be regulated by their common law, until some statute shall change their established principles," but that U.S. courts "created by written law, and whose jurisdiction is defined by written law, cannot transcend that jurisdiction." Did the Court give the content of the Suspension Clause "short shrift" in a treatment that was "rather cursory"?[z] What is the power of judicial review if not, "strictly speaking, an exercise of judicial transcendence of written law"? Chief Justice Marshall promptly added that, although jurisdiction must be given by written law, a judge may "resort" to the common law to explain the content and meaning of the "term *habeas corpus*." If the power to grant the writ must arise out of written law, could a court still look to the common law? The *Bollman* Court certainly examined the term "habeas corpus" in light of common-law terminology and practice. If habeas jurisdiction arises under written law, but if the content of the privilege derives from the common law, then is the content of habeas frozen in time? Or can it change? These issues reflect broader debates over constitutional interpretation and statutory interpretation.

10) Practical Necessity. The Court did not mention practical reasons favoring *Bollman's* outcome. The Court did not have statutory certiorari jurisdiction when it decided *Bollman*. During the early nineteenth century, the Court generally exercised its appellate jurisdiction using a writ of error. The 1789 Judiciary Act authorized the Court to conduct writ-of-error review in civil cases, but not in criminal cases decided in lower federal courts. In fact, in 1807, there was no mandatory (as-of-right) appeal in criminal cases whatsoever. As a result, "a contrary ruling in *Bollman*—which would have eliminated original habeas authority—would have simply left the Court without any appellate jurisdiction over federal criminal confinement."[aa]

Aside from the need to have some vehicle for appellate review over federal criminal confinement, there was another practical reason for the outcome in *Bollman*. The District of Columbia had no state courts that could grant habeas relief for a prisoner detained in that jurisdiction. If the federal courts could not review the detentions, then there would be no remedy for illegal detention ordered by the lower court.[bb] The detentions were still more problematic; not only

[z] See Stephen I. Vladeck, *The New Habeas Revisionism*, 124 Harv. L. Rev. 941, 979–86 (2011) (describing the "consequences of the evisceration of common law habeas"). In an omitted passage, Chief Justice Marshall stated that it was "unnecessary to state the reasoning" supporting that claim and that it had "been repeatedly" made by the Court. However, "historians have not been able to find any instances of the 'reasoning' supporting" this view. See Paul D. Halliday & G. Edward White, *The Suspension Clause: English Text, Imperial Contexts, and American Implications*, 94 Va. L. Rev. 575, 695 (2008).

[aa] Lee Kovarsky, *Original Habeas Redux*, 97 Va. L. Rev. 61, 72 (2011).

[bb] Professor Gerald Neuman points out that "[a]llowing Congress to erect a habeas-free zone in the District of Columbia would have confirmed the direst warnings of the Antifederalists about the potential of the Seat of Government Clause to subvert liberty." Gerald L.

were the alleged acts committed far from the District, but "Bollman had been arrested by military authorities in New Orleans (then part of a territory), and brought to Washington in evasion of writs of habeas corpus issued by two other courts." Gerald L. Neuman, *The Habeas Corpus Suspension Clause After* INS v. St. Cyr, 33 Colum. Hum. Rts. L. Rev. 555, 597–98 (2002).

11) The Proviso: Federal Versus State Custody. Section 14 provides that federal judges could only grant habeas relief to federal prisoners:

> —*Provided,* That writs of *habeas corpus* shall in no case extend to prisoners in gaol, unless where they are in custody under or by colour of the authority of the United States, or are committed for trial before some court of the same, or are necessary to be brought into court to testify.

In *Bollman,* Chief Justice Marshall explained that writs of *habeas corpus ad respondendum* could not issue to state courts, which "are not inferior courts because they emanate from a different authority, and are the creatures of a distinct government." As a result, the 1789 Judiciary Act limits federal jurisdiction over prisoners in state custody; the Supreme Court could conduct writ-of-error review in cases decided by state supreme courts, but lower federal courts were not given explicit authority to review claims by state prisoners.[cc] State prisoners, therefore, could not seek review of factual determinations. Nor could they pursue collateral "cause-of-commitment" review in federal courts. Perhaps that reading was not inevitable—such as under a view that the third sentence of § 14 only limits the use of habeas corpus by individual judges. Regardless, it would not be until after the Civil War that Congress provided federal courts with broad power to review state prisoner claims.[dd]

12) The Suspension Power. The last two sentences of the Court's opinion contain sweeping dicta regarding the suspension power:

> If at any time the public safety should require the suspension of the powers vested by this act in the courts of the United States, it is for the legislature to say so.

> That question depends on political considerations, on which the legislature is to decide. Until the legislative will be expressed, this court can only see its duty, and must obey the laws.

Why do you think that *Bollman* returns full circle to the subject of Congressional power at the end of the opinion? Congress did not suspend the privilege, although President Jefferson tried to get Congress to do just that. Perhaps the Court ventured a theory of which branch can suspend the privilege, and under what conditions, out of a concern that the President could attempt to suspend it himself. *Bollman* treats suspension as a legislative power, but the text of the

---

Neuman, *The Habeas Corpus Suspension Clause After* INS v. St. Cyr, 33 Colum. Hum. Rts. L. Rev. 555, 597–98 (2002).

[cc] The proviso would appear to permit habeas writs to issue for prisoners that "are necessary to be brought into court to testify." Because the first two items in the proviso are expressly limited to prisoners in federal custody, the third, by negative implication, does not seem to be so limited.

[dd] See Eric Freedman, *Just Because John Marshall Said It Doesn't Make it So:* Ex Parte Bollman *and the Illusory Prohibition on the Federal Writ of Habeas Corpus for State Prisoners in the Judiciary Act of 1789,* 51 Ala. L. Rev. 531, 576–77, 596 (2000) (arguing that the provision in § 14 regarding ability to review detention of state prisoners limited only the jurisdiction of individual judges, but not courts).

Suspension Clause only places conditions on suspension (rebellion, invasion, and public safety). The Clause is located in Article I, but it does not expressly vest a suspension power in Congress. *Bollman* did not, apart from calling it a "political" matter for the legislature, detail how and when the habeas privilege may be suspended. In the next Chapter we will return to questions not answered here, such as whether Congress really has blank-check authority to suspend the privilege so long as public safety requires it.

13) The Aftermath. What happened to Bollman and Swartwout? The original habeas opinion was followed by lengthy hearings and a ruling eight days later. The Supreme Court ordered the prisoners released. The Court found insufficient evidence that Bollman and Swartwout had planned to levy war against the United States, although "both of the prisoners were engaged in a most culpable enterprize against the dominions of a power at peace with the United States." As to Swartwout; the only evidence involved a scheme "to carry an expedition to the Mexican territories." The Court noted that "[a]gainst Erick Bollman there is still less testimony." The Court concluded, "It is therefore the unanimous opinion of the court that they cannot be tried in this district." As for Aaron Burr, he was not convicted of treason, but of a misdemeanor for violating the U.S. treaty of neutrality with Mexico. He spent most of his remaining days in Europe.[ee]

4. POST-CONVICTION REVIEW

INTRODUCTORY NOTE ON POST-CONVICTION REVIEW

The focus of habeas scrutiny is the lawfulness of custody. Before the American Revolution, habeas review reached almost any form of custody exercised under color of English law—and some forms of custody that were claimed pursuant to no government authority whatsoever. The degree to which the habeas writ permitted King's Bench (or other courts and judicial officers) to scrutinize custody ordered pursuant to a criminal conviction remains disputed among lawyers and historians. Chapter 3 discusses that debate in more detail, but *Ex parte Watkins*, 28 U.S. 193 (1830), excerpted below, was the first major U.S. Supreme Court case to consider the relationship between habeas writs and criminal convictions. Bollman and Swartwout had been held in custody pending trial, but Tobias Watkins was being held after having been convicted of a crime in a lower federal court. After reading *Watkins*, you will be asked to consider how the form of detention affects the scope of habeas review.

Ex parte Watkins
United States Supreme Court
28 U.S. 193 (1830)

■ Mr. CHIEF JUSTICE MARSHALL delivered the opinion of the Court.

This is a petition for a writ of habeas corpus to bring the body of Tobias Watkins before this Court for the purpose of inquiring into the legality of his confinement in gaol. The petition states that he is detained in prison by virtue of a judgment of the Circuit Court of the United States for the County of Washington in the District of Columbia, rendered in a criminal prose-

---

[ee] For a recent biography of Burr, see Nancy Isenberg, *Fallen Founder: The Life of Aaron Burr* (2008).

cution carried on against him in that court. * * * [T]he motion [alleges] that the indictment charges no offense for which the prisoner was punishable in that court, or of which that court could take cognizance, and consequently that the proceedings are * * * totally void.

This application is made to a court which has no jurisdiction in criminal cases; which could not revise this judgment; could not reverse or affirm it, were the record brought up directly by writ of error. The power, however, to award writs of habeas corpus is conferred expressly on this Court by the fourteenth section of the Judicial Act, and has been repeatedly exercised. * * * [T]he question is whether this be a case in which it ought to be exercised. The cause of imprisonment is shown as fully by the petitioner as it could appear on the return of the writ; consequently the writ ought not to be awarded if the court is satisfied that the prisoner would be remanded to prison.

No law of the United States prescribes the cases in which this great writ shall be issued, nor the power of the court over the party brought up by it. The term is used in the Constitution as one which was well understood, and the Judicial Act authorizes this Court and all the courts of the United States and the judges thereof to issue the writ "for the purpose of inquiring into the cause of commitment." This general reference to a power which we are required to exercise, without any precise definition of that power, imposes on us the necessity of making some inquiries into its use, according to that law which is in a considerable degree incorporated into our own. The writ of habeas corpus is a high prerogative writ, known to the common law, the great object of which is the liberation of those who may be imprisoned without sufficient cause. It is in the nature of a writ of error to examine the legality of the commitment. The English judges, being originally under the influence of the Crown, neglected to issue this writ where the government entertained suspicions which could not be sustained by evidence, and the writ when issued was sometimes disregarded or evaded, and great individual oppression was suffered in consequence of delays in bringing prisoners to trial. To remedy this evil, the celebrated habeas corpus act of the 31st of Charles II was enacted, for the purpose of securing the benefits for which the writ was given. This statute may be referred to as describing the cases in which relief is, in England, afforded by this writ to a person detained in custody. It enforces the common law. This statute excepts from those who are entitled to its benefit, persons committed for felony or treason plainly expressed in the warrant, as well as persons convicted or in execution.

The exception of persons convicted applies particularly to the application now under consideration. The petitioner is detained in prison by virtue of the judgment of a court, which court possesses general and final jurisdiction in criminal cases. Can this judgment be reexamined upon a writ of habeas corpus?

This writ is, as has been said, in the nature of a writ of error which brings up the body of the prisoner with the cause of commitment. The court can undoubtedly inquire into the sufficiency of that cause, but if it be the judgment of a court of competent jurisdiction, especially a judgment withdrawn by law from the revision of this Court, is not that judgment in itself sufficient cause? Can the court, upon this writ, look beyond the judgment, and re-examine the charges on which it was rendered. A judgment, in its nature, concludes the subject on which it is rendered, and pronounces the law of the case. The judgment of a court of record whose jurisdiction is final is as conclusive on all the world as the judgment of this Court would be. It is as conclusive on this Court as it is on other courts. It puts an end to inquiry concerning the fact by deciding it.

The counsel for the prisoner admit the application of these principles to a case in which the indictment alleges a crime cognizable in the court by which the judgment was pronounced; but they deny their application to a case in which the indictment charges an offense not punishable criminally according to the law of the land. But with what propriety can this Court look into the indictment? We have no power to examine the proceedings on a writ of error, and it would be strange, if, under color of a writ to liberate an individual from unlawful imprisonment, we could substantially reverse a judgment which the law has placed beyond our control. An imprisonment under a judgment cannot be unlawful unless that judgment be an absolute nullity, and it is not a nullity if the court has general jurisdiction of the subject, although it should be erroneous. The Circuit Court for the District of Columbia is a court of record having general jurisdiction over criminal cases. An offense cognizable in any court is cognizable in that court. If the offense be punishable by law, that court is competent to inflict the punishment. The judgment of such a tribunal has all the obligation which the judgment of any tribunal can have. To determine whether the offense charged in the indictment be legally punishable or not is among the most unquestionable of its powers and duties. The decision of this question is the exercise of jurisdiction, whether the judgment be for or against the prisoner. The judgment is equally binding in the one case and in the other, and must remain in full force unless reversed regularly by a superior court capable of reversing it. * * *

Had any offense against the laws of the United States been in fact committed, the circuit court for the District of Columbia could take cognizance of it. The question whether any offense was, or was not committed, that is whether the indictment did or did not show that an offense had been committed, was a question which that court was competent to decide. If its judgment was erroneous, a point which this Court does not determine, still it is a judgment, and, until reversed, cannot be disregarded. * * *

The cases are numerous, which decide that the judgments of a court of record having general jurisdiction of the subject, although erroneous, are binding until reversed. It is universally understood that the judgments of the courts of the United States, although their jurisdiction be not shown in the pleadings, are yet binding on all the world, and that this apparent want of jurisdiction can avail the party only on a writ of error. This acknowledged principle seems to us to settle the question now before the Court. The judgment of the circuit court in a criminal case is of itself evidence of its own legality, and requires for its support no inspection of the indictments on which it is founded. The law trusts that court with the whole subject, and has not confided to this Court the power of revising its decisions. We cannot usurp that power by the instrumentality of the writ of habeas corpus. The judgment informs us that the commitment is legal, and with that information it is our duty to be satisfied. * * *

Without looking into the indictments under which the prosecution against the petitioner was conducted, we are unanimously of opinion that the judgment of a court of general criminal jurisdiction justifies his imprisonment, and that the writ of habeas corpus ought not to be awarded.

NOTES AND QUESTIONS ON WATKINS

1)   The Underlying Process in *Watkins*. Unlike in *Bollman*, in which the prisoners were not convicted of a crime and were held without bail, the prisoner in *Watkins* challenged a conviction that followed a criminal trial. Watkins was a federal official, an auditor working for the U.S. Treasury, charged with keeping certain accounts for the Navy Department. He was prosecuted for appropriating about three thousand dollars from the Treasury (a large sum in 1827) and for misappropriating money from another federal employee. He was sentenced to about nine months imprisonment and to pay fines approximating the money taken. Watkins, however, argued that defrauding the federal government was not a recognized state common-law offense or a federal crime. In 1827, there were very few federal criminal statutes and the Supreme Court had ruled that there were no federal common-law crimes.[ff]

2)   Looking at the Indictment Through the Conviction. Watkins sought to overturn his conviction by arguing that the indictment did not state a crime that was cognizable in a U.S. court. Habeas corpus relief for a conviction is an exception to ordinary principles of finality, in which a final judgment precludes subsequent litigation involving the same dispute. A judgment is final when direct review of the conviction concludes. Once direct review of a conviction ends, an interest in "finality" attaches, permitting "repose" so that the defendant, the victims, and the state can all behave as though the outcome of the criminal proceeding is conclusive. Final convictions are presumptively valid.

In *Watkins*, The Supreme Court held that any exception for habeas relief did not reach all questions subsumed in the conviction. Specifically, *Watkins* held that, because the lower court was a court of general jurisdiction (as opposed to a court having jurisdiction over only limited types of cases[gg]), its decision on whether the facts alleged in the indictment constituted a crime against the United States was not subject to a collateral challenge. In other words, the judgment of conviction in the lower federal court foreclosed challenges to the sufficiency of the indictment—a habeas writ did not permit a court to "look through" the conviction. Under *Watkins*, even a blatant charging error would not give rise to habeas relief. Moreover, at the time, federal criminal convictions were not appealable, so habeas review was the only way Watkins could challenge the conviction.

3)   The Common Law. The Supreme Court admitted that there were no obvious sources of U.S. law furnishing a rule to decide the question before it. Beginning with a description of a broad habeas power, the Court explained: "No law of the United States prescribes the cases in which this great writ shall be issued, nor the power of the court over the party brought up by it." Yet, because

---

[ff] See United States v. Hudson and Goodwin, 11 U.S. 32 (1812).

[gg] *Watkins* observes, "The petitioner is detained in prison by virtue of the judgment of a court, which court possesses general and final jurisdiction in criminal cases." In English law, "superior" courts "of general jurisdiction" were courts that had wide-ranging jurisdiction to decide most categories of cases and controversies cognizable under domestic law. They were contrasted with "inferior" courts, which exercised jurisdiction that was limited to a particular category of cases, usually by statute. In light of that distinction, can you make more sense of Chief Justice Marshall's statement, "Had any offense against the laws of the United States been in fact committed, the circuit court for the District of Columbia could take cognizance of it." How central is the attribute of general jurisdiction to *Watkins*? Appellate tribunals employed less deferential jurisdictional review when reviewing judgments of a court that was "inferior" in the sense just discussed. See Ann Woolhandler, *Demodeling Habeas*, 45 Stan. L. Rev. 575, 589 (1993).

the habeas privilege referenced in the Suspension Clause was "one which was well understood," the Court inquired into the practices and usages at common law. The Court ultimately denied relief on the ground that the lower court had jurisdiction to decide the question presented in the habeas petition—however, where did *Watkins'* rule against looking through the conviction come from? The Court did not cite to Article III or to a statutory command. It did, however, observe that "numerous" prior cases in the United States regarding this rule of finality. The Court alluded to the "celebrated" English Habeas Corpus Act of 1679, which differentiated between an inquiry into the cause of commitment, as in *Bollman,* versus an inquiry into the custody of a prisoner convicted after a criminal trial. A number of subsequent habeas decisions have used *Watkins* as authority for this proposition. Many scholars have criticized Chief Justice Marshall for improperly elevating the importance of the English statutory writ, when most of the work was done by the English common-law writ.[hh] Whether common-law practice or English statutes should be dispositive of an American legal question is, of course, a different issue.

4)   What is the Meaning of "Void"? Watkins argued that his conviction was "void" because the indictment did not state a crime. Post-conviction challenges are a form of collateral attack, and they are used to challenge a final judgment. One standard exception to the normal rule of finality—whether the issue is a civil or a criminal judgment—is that a judgment entered by a court without "jurisdiction" is void. *Watkins* held that the defect that the prisoner alleged would not have defeated the district court's "jurisdiction" or rendered the judgment void. Could there be an argument, however, that a federal court does not have jurisdiction in a criminal case if the indictment does not state a federal crime? As any student of civil procedure knows, the concept of "jurisdiction" is somewhat elastic. Professor Ann Woolhandler has argued that "jurisdiction" had assumed broader meaning when used to consider official action contrary to constitutional law. See Ann Woolhandler, *Demodeling Habeas,* 45 Stan. L. Rev. 575, 589–92 (1993).

5)   Two Limits. The Supreme Court's opinion reflects two limits on its habeas jurisdiction: (1) a limit on the use of its habeas jurisdiction as a substitute for ordinary appellate review, and (2) an intrinsic limit on the use of habeas to review criminal convictions ordered by jurisdictionally-competent courts. Subsequent Supreme Court decisions have read the second limit as a jurisdictional rule against habeas review of criminal convictions common to all federal courts. Professor Bator famously argued that, until late in the nineteenth century, federal courts followed the "black-letter principle of the common law that the writ was simply not available at all to one convicted of crime by a court of competent jurisdiction." Bator, *Finality in Criminal Law and Federal Habeas Corpus for State Prisoners,* 76 Harv. L. Rev. at 446. A number of important scholars have contested that characterization of the relevant nineteenth-century decisions, but Professor Bator's critique of *Watkins* and its progeny continues to influence

---

[hh] The Habeas Corpus Act made a category of prisoners eligible for a statutory writ, but it did not restrict the common-law privilege. See Daniel John Meador, *Habeas Corpus and Magna Carta: Dualism of Power and Liberty* 26 (1966). Professor Halliday writes that "judges performed their most innovative work using the common law writ, in part because the statute applied only to imprisonment for felony or treason." See Paul D. Halliday, *supra* note g , at 242. There were indeed at least some instances where the common-law writ issued to review criminal convictions. See Bushell's Case, Vaughan 135, 6 St. Tr. 231 (1670) (discharging through habeas a juror, sitting for the trial of William Penn and William Mead, criminally sentenced for contempt by a court of general jurisdiction).

habeas law today. Chapter 3 will explore Professor Bator's thesis, and the important responses to it, in great detail.

6)   "In the Nature of a Writ of Error." *Watkins* states that the habeas writ is "in the nature of a writ of error to examine the legality of the commitment." Generally speaking, a writ of error issues *from* an appellate court and *to* a lower court or judge of record, where the issuing court undertakes review of a judgment entered by the receiving court or judge. An appealing party is sometimes described as "suing for a writ of error" in the reviewing court. In what sense, then, is a habeas corpus writ "in the nature of a writ of error to examine the legality of confinement"? Can a habeas proceeding be like an appeal? Professor Gary Peller has argued that, because the "appellate" features of the writ were at issue in *Watkins*, the holding applies only to habeas process that substitutes for a formal appeal. Peller, *In Defense of Federal Habeas Corpus Relitigation*, 16 Harv. C.R.-C.L. L. Rev. at 611.

————————

NOTES ON HABEAS STATUTES

1)   Federal Habeas Statutes. *Bollman* discussed the first federal habeas statute, § 14 of the 1789 Judiciary Act. Habeas statutes have multiplied and expanded, but some features have not changed. Much of the first half of the Book discusses federal post-conviction petitions filed by prisoners convicted of crimes in state court. Filing and disposition of those habeas petitions is primarily regulated by 28 U.S.C. §§ 2244 & 2254. Chapters 3 through 5 explore post-conviction review of state convictions, including the substantive and procedural limits on relief. Federal prisoners who have been convicted of a crime (like Watkins) typically use a different statute, 28 U.S.C. § 2255, to attack their conviction collaterally. Section 2255 is discussed in Chapter 2 and is the sole subject of Chapter 6. Much of the second half of this Book explores habeas petitions by federal detainees, like Bollman and Swartwout, who have not been tried, and who bring habeas petitions to challenge their custody under the modern statutory source of habeas jurisdiction, 28 U.S.C. § 2241. Chapters 7 through 10 review challenges filed to noncriminal custody, frequently under § 2241. The full text of each statute is included in the Appendix.

2)   28 U.S.C. § 2241. The current federal statute governing executive detentions, 28 U.S.C. § 2241, retains much of the language from § 14 of the First Judiciary Act. Section 2241(a) should look familiar, and reads: "Writs of habeas corpus may be granted by the Supreme Court, any justice thereof, the district courts and any circuit judge within their respective jurisdictions." Indeed, § 2241 is considered the general grant of habeas authority. Section 2241 is sweeping in its scope. Section 2241(c) provides that a habeas petition may be filed by (1) any prisoner "in custody under or by color of the authority of the United States" or "committed for trial before some court thereof" or (2) a prisoner "in custody for an act done or omitted in pursuance of an Act of Congress, or an order, process, judgment or decree of a court or judge of the United States"; or (3) a prisoner "in custody in violation of the Constitution or laws or treaties of the United States." The statute covers prisoners who are citizens of foreign states and in custody based on foreign sanctions relating to the "law of nations" and, more mundanely, it covers prisoners who must be brought "into court to testify or for trial." This broad general grant of habeas jurisdiction is withheld in specific cases by other provisions in Title 28.

3) Companion Statutes to § 2241. Companion statutes describe the process for proceeding under § 2241. The prisoner first files a petition, which "shall allege the facts concerning the applicant's commitment or detention, the name of the person who has custody over him and by virtue of what claim or authority, if known." 28 U.S.C. § 2242. Under 28 U.S.C. § 2243, a judge may issue the writ, order a return, and then "determine the facts" to ascertain "the true cause of the detention." That process is little changed from common-law habeas practice.

4) Limits on § 2241. Other statutes carve out areas of habeas practice governed by different rules. Chapter 7 explains that habeas petitions lodging § 2241 attacks on immigration process—including challenges to "removal" orders—can include only certain types of issues. Instead, attacks on the process are funneled through an alternative procedure involving "petitions for review" filed in the U.S. Courts of Appeals. Chapters 9 and 10 describe how, after the attacks of September 11, 2001, Congress passed legislation concentrating most extra-territorial challenges to military custody in the U.S. Court of Appeals for the D.C. Circuit. Chapter 10 presents *Boumediene v. Bush*, 553 U.S. 723 (2008), the Supreme Court decision that ruled parts of the post-9/11 legislation to be in violation of the Suspension Clause.

5) 28 U.S.C. § 2254. After the Civil War, in 1867, Congress enacted legislation establishing federal habeas review of claims by state prisoners, making the writ available in "all cases where any person may be restrained of his or her liberty in violation of the constitution, or of any treaty or law of the United States." 14 Stat. 385 (1867). As you read in *Brown v. Allen*, the Supreme Court has interpreted the 1867 Habeas Corpus Act to vest federal courts with power to grant relief to state prisoners, notwithstanding the fact that the prisoners may have been convicted and sentenced by a competent state court of general jurisdiction.

28 U.S.C. § 2254 is a statutory descendant of the 1867 Act, reflecting the addition of new provisions and the modification of many original ones. Most dramatically, the Antiterrorism and Effective Death Penalty Act of 1996, Pub. L. No. 104–132, 110 Stat. 1214 (AEDPA), revised § 2254 and a raft of companion statutes. AEDPA also added new provisions, which Chapters 3 through 5 present in logical order. AEDPA, for example, fashioned new substantive limits on relief in § 2254(d), which are applicable to any state decision on the merits of a constitutional challenge. AEDPA also added or expanded a number of procedural restrictions on federal habeas relief for state prisoners, including: in § 2244(d), a new statute of limitations for filing federal habeas post-conviction petitions; in § 2254(e), more restrictive standards for obtaining federal evidentiary hearings; and in § 2244(b), jurisdictional limits on consideration of "successive" habeas petitions.

6) 28 U.S.C. § 2255. Chapter 6 explores the federal post-conviction remedy for federal prisoners. Although 28 U.S.C. § 2255, which contains the pertinent provisions, does not technically provide for habeas process, its provisions basically mirror post-conviction remedies available to state prisoners. Unlike habeas process, a proceeding under § 2255 takes place in the jurisdiction of conviction, rather than in the jurisdiction of confinement. Congress originally enacted this "habeas substitute" in 1948, and it periodically revises some of the provisions. AEDPA restricted § 2255 relief in language that paralleled limits on relief for state prisoners, but § 2255 remains—in subtle ways—a more robust remedy than its state-prisoner counterpart.

7)   State Habeas Statutes. States retain common law and statutory habeas power (although, as we will see in Chapter 2, they cannot grant habeas relief to federal prisoners). More states are enacting complicated post-conviction statutes. The application of federal habeas law can turn heavily on events in state post-conviction proceedings, and Chapters 3 through 5 will address the important features of state habeas law when they figure prominently in federal rules that the chapters cover.

8)   Written Law. These detailed statutes, along with many others referenced in this Book, comprise a vast expanse of habeas legislation. Although the "written law" to which *Bollman* alludes governs the modern habeas privilege, so does law made by judges. Judges have defined the written law, they have reconciled it with existing practice, and they have modified it to adapt the privilege to new sovereign challenges. *Bollman* reflects a tension between written law and judicial power that remains important and unresolved, and that is one of the central subjects of this Book.

CHAPTER 2

CONSTITUTIONAL STRUCTURE OF THE HABEAS PRIVILEGE

1. INTRODUCTION TO HABEAS AND CONSTITUTIONAL STRUCTURE

This Chapter explores the constitutional structure of the habeas privilege—which prisoners can invoke it, how courts can effectuate it, and when it may be suspended. As an introduction to the material, reconsider a passage from *Ex parte Watkins*, in which Chief Justice Marshall focused on a particularly important interpretive difficulty that the Suspension Clause creates:

> No law of the United States prescribes the cases in which this great writ shall be issued, nor the power of the court over the party brought up by it. The term is used in the Constitution as one which was well understood. . . . This general reference to a power which we are required to exercise, without any precise definition of that power, imposes on us the necessity of making some inquiries into its use, according to that law which is in a considerable degree incorporated into our own.

The relationship between the common-law writ and the Suspension Clause remains a source of uncertainty today. As you read this Chapter, think generally about which features of the common-law writ the Framers meant to incorporate into American governance.

Section 2 presents a brief history of the drafting of the Suspension Clause at the Constitutional Conviction. Habeas corpus is the only common-law writ and the only remedy that the Constitution mentions expressly. The Suspension Clause contains terms that were more familiar to eighteenth-century lawyers than to modern legal readers. The Suspension Clause reads: "The Privilege of the Writ of Habeas Corpus shall not be suspended, unless when in Cases of Rebellion or Invasion the public Safety may require it." U.S. Const. article I, § 9, cl. 2.

Section 3 explores the concept of suspension, including what the suspension power entails and the conditions for Congress to exercise it. There are not only differing views about Congressional power to regulate habeas jurisdiction during periods of non-suspension, but also differing views of the meaning of the Suspension Clause itself. The Suspension Clause states that, except under certain conditions, the government may not suspend a privilege—a privilege that the Clause does not expressly grant. In fact, many are surprised to learn that the Suspension Clause does not even expressly create a suspension power.

Section 4 considers which types of sovereign custody, state or federal, a federal judge may use habeas process to examine. The authority of a federal court to grant habeas relief to state prisoners remains a central and contested feature of modern federal power.

Section 5 explores the authority of *state* courts to use hear habeas petitions from *federal* prisoners, a practice that the Supreme Court ended in two cases bookending the Civil War. In the two cases, the Court articulated a view of exclusive federal authority that many scholars find to be a deeply troubling account of how the state and national governments share power.

Section 6 concludes the Chapter by inviting students to analyze the inaptly-named "original" habeas writ, referring to habeas relief sought in the first instance from the Supreme Court. The role of the original writ has changed over the course of American history, but it usually serves as a way to review custody over which Supreme Court review is otherwise foreclosed.

2. THE DRAFTING OF THE SUSPENSION CLAUSE AND WHAT THE HABEAS PRIVILEGE MEANT TO THE FRAMERS

NOTES ON THE DRAFTING OF THE SUSPENSION CLAUSE

The Framers drafted the Suspension Clause without lengthy or heated debate at the 1787 Constitutional Convention—probably because the Clause was uncontroversial. As discussed in Chapter 1, the Framers had been on the receiving end of Lord North's repeated suspensions. The Framers were also sensitive to interference with the habeas privilege because Massachusetts had suspended the privilege during Shay's Rebellion in 1786 and 1787.

The Suspension Clause was originally placed in the Article governing judicial power (what is now Article III), but the Clause was eventually moved to the Article governing legislative power (what is now Article I). As a limit on what would logically be a legislative power, the Suspension Clause appears to be properly situated in Article I. The exact language, however, leaves many questions unanswered. The Clause does not expressly create a suspension power, nor does it expressly create a privilege of habeas corpus for Congress to suspend. Like other clauses in Article I, § 9, the Suspension Clause limits a power that Congress might otherwise exercise enjoy under Article I, § 8.

During the debates at the Convention, the Framers did not focus on whether to expressly guarantee the privilege. They instead focused on whether the privilege of habeas corpus could ever be suspended and, if so, under what circumstances and for what duration.

Habeas corpus was discussed just four days into the Convention. On May 29, South Carolina delegate Charles Pinckney apparently submitted a "Draught of a Federal Government." No copy of Pinckney's Draught survives and we know of its content only from James Madison's notes, so the Draught's precise suspension language remains a matter of some speculation.[a] As Madison recorded it, the initial wording of the Suspension Clause stated:

> The United States shall not grant any title of Nobility—The Legislature of the United States shall pass no Law on the subject of Religion, nor touching or abridging the Liberty of the Press nor shall the Privilege of the Writ of Habeas Corpus ever be suspended except in case of Rebellion or Invasion.[b]

---

[a] See C. C. Nott, *The Mystery of the Pinckney Draught* (New York, 1908).

[b] See 1 The *Debates in the Several State Conventions, on the Adoption of the Federal Constitution 148* (Jonathan Elliot ed., 2d ed. 1881) (*Elliot's Debates*). Professor Amanda Tyler

That proposal was not very specific. Nonetheless, consider some of the subtle differences between the proposed language and the language that the Convention submitted to the States for ratification. At least initially, the suspension criteria did not include a "public safety" condition. In contrast to the bar on Nobility titles, which applied to the "United States," the suspension prohibition applied only to the "Legislature." Whatever its terminological nuances, Pinckney's Draught never made it to the Committee on Detail, which had been appointed to write a draft constitution reflecting the extant consensus of the delegates. The Committee on Detail instead worked off of the "Virginia Plan" submitted by Edmund Randolph. The Committee on Detail reported a draft to the Convention on August 6, but that document contained no suspension provision.

According to Madison's notes, on August 20, Charles Pinckney submitted a more familiar and more detailed draft of a Suspension Clause to the Convention, which provided that:

> The privileges and benefit of the Writ of Habeas corpus shall be enjoyed in this Government in the most expeditious and ample manner, and shall not be suspended by the legislature except upon the most urgent and pressing occasions, and for a limited time not exceeding __ months.[c]

The Pinckney draft contained language providing that: the writ be enjoyed "in" the federal government; the suspension conditions must be "urgent and pressing occasions" rather than "rebellion" and "invasion;" a suspension would be constitutionally capped for as specific duration; and the suspension prohibition applied to the legislature.[d]

The Convention began debate on Pinckney's proposal, slightly revised, on August 28. Pinckney raised the habeas issue as the Framers considered the article dealing with the judiciary, as an amendment to a section requiring jury trials. By August 28, the Convention had already concluded that the creation of lower federal courts would be subject to Congressional discretion (a decision now known as the "Madisonian Compromise"), as would much of the U.S. Supreme Court's appellate jurisdiction. The Madisonian Compromise meant that Congress would play an important role in regulating the scope of the federal judicial power. Perhaps Congress, vested with the "greater" power to create lower federal courts, could exercise the "lesser" power of restricting the habeas privilege in a way that falls short of a suspension.

Mr. Pinckney's version of the Clause included other important changes. The August 28 submission omitted any express requirement that the Govern-

---

notes that this proposal "may have derived from a number of sources, including possibly the Irish adoption of the 1679 Habeas Corpus Act ('An Act for Better Securing the Liberty of the Subject') in 1781, which imported the language of the 1679 Habeas Corpus Act verbatim, with one notable addition: a provision allowing the Irish Council to suspend the act 'during such time only as there shall be an actual invasion or rebellion in this kingdom or Great Britain.' " Amanda L. Tyler, *The Forgotten Core Meaning of the Suspension Clause*, 125 Harv. L. Rev. 901, 969 n.367 (2012) (citing An Act for Better Securing the Liberty of the Subject, 1781, 21 & 22 Geo. 3, c. 11, § XVI (Ir.)).

[c] 2 *The Records of the Federal Convention of 1787*, at 334 (Max Farrand ed. 1911) (*Farrand's Records*).

[d] On August 20, the delegates were also debating the Treason Clause, and Professor Tyler argues that, for this reason, the Framers "viewed the careful delineation of the crime of treason as connected to the provision for the privilege of the writ of habeas corpus along with its suspension." Tyler, supra note b, at 970.

ment provide for the writ. Such language was instead part of Mr. Pinckney's introductory remarks, and the reason that it was deleted from the Suspension Clause's formal text is not known. The debate over habeas, however, was not about whether the Constitution guaranteed the privilege. The disputes were over the breadth of the suspension power. John Rutledge, for example, "was for declaring the Habeas Corpus inviolable" because, according to Madison's notes, a nationwide suspension would never be necessary.[e] Similarly, Thomas Jefferson wrote to Madison that he opposed including a suspension clause, arguing that a suspension clause would be vulnerable to Congressional abuse.[f]

In response, Gouverneur Morris moved for a compromise, creating a more limited federal suspension power. Morris proposed that the language be: "The privilege of the writ of Habeas Corpus shall not be suspended, unless where in cases of Rebellion or invasion the public safety may require it." James Wilson continued to question whether there needed to be any suspension authority, noting that judges retained the ultimate discretion regarding conditions of release, and could deny bail in "important cases." This language was first placed in Article III, regarding judicial power, but the Committee on Style later moved it to Article I, reflecting its apparent status as a limitation on the power of Congress.[g]

Ten states voted on Mr. Morris' proposed wording. All ten agreed to the part of the Suspension Clause preceding the word "unless"—that "[t]he privilege of the writ of Habeas Corpus shall not be suspended." The remainder of Mr. Morris' proposed language, "unless where in cases of Rebellion or invasions the public safety may require it," was approved 7–3, with Geogia, North Carolina, and South Carolina voting no.[h] Sometime between that vote and the final draft of the Clause, the word "where" was changed to "when."

The Suspension Clause reads: "The Privilege of the Writ of Habeas Corpus shall not be suspended, unless when in Cases of Rebellion or Invasion the public Safety may require it." U.S. Const. article I, § 9, cl. 2. What inferences might you draw from the omission of Pinckney's original reference to "enjoyment"? Does that mean that the Constitution failed to guarantee the privilege? The strength of that conclusion might turn on how one views the votes of the states that resisted the proposed wording. For example, the three states that voted against the second part of Mr. Morris's formulation wanted there to be no suspension power whatsoever. There other evidence that Framers thought that the Clause would guarantee some form of habeas privilege. Mr. Wilson, for example, stated in a speech to the Pennsylvania Convention that "[he meant] to show the reason why the right of habeas corpus was secured by a particular provision in its favor."

Generally speaking, the historical record supports the idea that there existed some inviolable habeas privilege. In the Federalist Papers, Alexander Hamilton cited to the Suspension Clause as evidence that the Constitution pro-

---

[e] 2 *Farrand's Records*, supra note c, at 438.

[f] See Letter from Thomas Jefferson to James Madison (July 31, 1788), in 13 *The Papers of Thomas Jefferson* 440, 442 (Julian P. Boyd ed., 1956) ("for the few cases wherein the suspension of the hab. corp. has done real good, that operation is now become habitual, and the minds of the nation almost prepared to live under it's [sic] constant suspension.")

[g] *Id.* at 438, 576.

[h] The "yes" votes were New Hampshire, Massachusetts, Connecticut, Pennsylvania, Delaware, Maryland, and Virginia.

tected against abuses of the Crown. The lack of express language creating a habeas privilege notwithstanding, in Federalist 83, Hamilton stated that habeas corpus was "provided for . . . in the plan of the convention." Hamilton linked the Constitution's habeas and jury-trial guarantees to pre-Revolutionary English abuse of criminal process: "Arbitrary impeachments, arbitrary methods of prosecuting pretended offenses, and arbitrary punishments upon arbitrary convictions, have ever appeared to me to be the great engines of judicial despotism; and these have all relation to criminal proceedings." The Federalist No. 83 (Alexander Hamilton). In Federalist 84, he added: "The establishment of the writ of habeas corpus, the prohibition of ex post facto laws, and of titles of nobility, to which we have no corresponding provision in [the New York] Constitution, are perhaps greater securities to liberty and republicanism than any it contains." He called habeas corpus the "bulwark" of the U.S. Constitution. The Federalist No. 84 (Hamilton).[i] Federalist 84, in fact, was almost entirely dedicated to the idea that the failure to enumerate specific rights in the Constitution should not be interpreted as a failure to provide for or recognize them.[j]

The records of the Constitutional Convention are not, however, completely consistent with a strong federal habeas privilege. During ratification debates, opponents of the draft Constitution criticized the inclusion of a suspension power; Luther Martin prominently argued that the result gave the federal government power to "imprison . . . during its pleasure."[k] Thomas Jefferson wrote to Madison that the draft Constitution not only lacked a bill of rights, but also failed to provide for "the eternal and unremitting force of the habeas corpus laws"—objecting, like some at the Convention, to the language allowing Congress to suspend the privilege nationally.[l] Professor William Duker has argued that Jefferson's concern, as well as comments at state ratifying conventions, suggest that Framers viewed the Suspension Clause as pertaining to Congress' supposed authority to prevent state courts from granting habeas to federal prisoners. See William F. Duker, *A Constitutional History of Habeas Corpus* 133–35 (1980).

Put yourself in the Framers' shoes, and think about institutional design. Would you have included such a Suspension Clause at all? Why or why not? If you would have included it, how would you have drafted it? Would you have included a time limit for the term of a Suspension? Would you have included different conditions for the suspension of the privilege? Would you have includ-

---

[i] Hamilton paraphrased William Blackstone, who called the English Habeas Corpus Act of 1679 "that second *magna carta*, and stable bulwark of our liberties." 1 William Blackstone, *Commentaries on the Laws of England* 137. While one often encounters Blackstone's estimate of the Habeas Corpus Act of 1679 in cases and scholarship, some have argued that Blackstone improperly emphasizes Parliament's role in developing the writ. See, e.g., Paul Halliday & G. Edward White, *The Suspension Clause: English Text, Imperial Contexts, and American Implications*, 94 Va. L. Rev. 575, 611 (2008) (criticizing Blackstone's emphasis, at the expense of the judge-made common-law habeas writ, on the importance of the Habeas Corpus Act of 1679).

[j] In 1787, lawyers were parishioners of a common-law method in which legal authority "discovered" preexisting rights. As a corollary to law that was discovered rather than "created," many people would have read the Constitution's individual-rights provisions as declarative of a preexisting right, rather than as a freestanding source of the right itself. See Akhil Reed Amar, *The Bill of Rights and the Fourteenth Amendment*, 101 Yale L.J. 1193, 1205–12 (1992).

[k] Luther Martin, The Genuine Information Delivered to the Legislature of the State of Maryland Relative to the Proceedings of the General Convention Lately Held at Philadelphia (1788).

[l] See Letter from Thomas Jefferson to James Madison (Dec. 20, 1787), *in* 12 The Papers of Thomas Jefferson 438, 440 (Julian P. Boyd ed., 1955).

ed language regarding affirmative entitlement to and the scope of the writ itself?

———

NOTES ON THE SCOPE OF THE HABEAS PRIVILEGE

1)   The Debate over the Scope of the Habeas Privilege. The dearth of conclusive primary-source material frustrates scholarly unanimity about what the habeas privilege covers and suspension entails. Professor Edward Hartnett, for example, has called it a real "constitutional puzzle." Edward A. Hartnett, *The Constitutional Puzzle of Habeas Corpus*, 46 B.C. L. Rev. 251 (2005). These questions date back to the founding and made their way into Chief Justice Marshall's *Bollman* opinion: must habeas corpus be provided for by "written law"? What if Congress had not enacted the First Judiciary Act and had not given all federal judges the power to grant the writ? Was Congress under any "obligation" to give judges habeas power?

a)   The Suspension Clause as Source of Federal Habeas Jurisdiction. On one view, the Suspension Clause protects the privilege of habeas corpus in federal courts, and habeas jurisdiction requires no enacting legislation. Until recently, the Supreme Court had never squarely considered such a view of the Clause; in *Boumediene v. Bush*, 553 U.S. 723 (2008) the Court adopted a variation of the theory that the Constitution requires habeas process. *Boumediene* and the theory that habeas jurisdiction is self-executing are discussed extensively in Chapter 10. One of the authors has strongly criticized the proposition that the Suspension Clause could be the sole constitutional source of habeas jurisdiction. See Lee Kovarsky, *A Constitutional Theory of Habeas Power*, 98 Va. L. Rev. __ (forthcoming 2013).

b)   Other Constitutional Sources of Federal Habeas Jurisdiction. Other scholars argue that the habeas privilege to challenge sovereign custody is guaranteed by the Suspension Clause in combination with other constitutional provisions. See, e.g., Kovarsky, *A Constitutional Theory of Habeas Power* __ (arguing that the Suspension Clause and Article III combine to preclude any restriction on federal habeas jurisdiction over federal custody); James S. Liebman and William F. Ryan, *Some Effectual Power: The Quantity and Quality of Decisionmaking Required of Article III Courts*, 98 Colum. L. Rev. 696, 887 (1998) (reading the Suspension Clause in combination with the Supremacy Clause to guarantee federal review of state custody); Jordan Steiker, *Incorporating the Suspension Clause: Is There a Constitutional Right to Federal Habeas Corpus for State Prisoners*, 92 Mich. L. Rev. 862, 873 (1994) (answering the titular question in the affirmative on the ground that the Fourteenth Amendment incorporated the Suspension Clause against the states).

c)   Diffused Federal Habeas Jurisdiction. Another constitutional theory of the habeas privilege is that the document does not speak to the habeas authority of any court in particular, but instead requires only that a federal habeas remedy be available somewhere in the federal judicial system. We already know that Article III does not grant the Supreme Court original jurisdiction over habeas cases. Now suppose that Congress stripped the Supreme Court of appellate jurisdiction in such matters. If the lower courts retained habeas power, then would that allocation of jurisdiction violate some constitutional rule? Professor Gerald Neuman has argued that no particular federal court must be empowered with authority to issue habeas writs, but that some combination of federal courts must ensure that there exists an adequate and effective means of testing detention. See Gerald Neuman, *The Habeas Corpus Suspension Clause After INS v. St. Cyr*, 33 Colum. Hum. Rts. L. Rev. 555 (2002). If Professor Neuman and those who subscribe to this theory are correct, how far does that theory extend? For example, Professor Edward Hartnett has suggested that Congress could constitutionally strip the habeas jurisdiction of federal *courts* as long as habeas authority remained vested in Supreme Court Justices acting in their individual capacities. See Hartnett, *The Constitutional Puzzle of Habeas Corpus*, at 254. In a similar vein, Professor Stephen Vladeck has argued that Congress could constitutionally strip all habeas jurisdiction from federal courts other than the Superior Court of the District of Columbia—which, he argues, retains common-law habeas power. See Stephen I. Vladeck, *The Riddle of the One-Way Ratchet: Habeas Corpus and the District of Columbia*, 12 Green Bag 2d 71 (2008). Would an effort by Congress to remove habeas jurisdiction from lower federal courts, or to limit habeas jurisdiction to individual Supreme Court Justices, be faithful to constitutional design?

d) Federal Habeas Jurisdiction is not Self-Executing. Other scholars argue that the constitution simply provides no assurance that the habeas privilege be available in federal courts. See, e.g., Rex A. Collings, *Habeas Corpus for Convicts-Constitutional Right or Legislative Grace?*, 40 Cal. L. Rev. 335 (1952) (setting forth frequently-cited theory that the Suspension Clause does not guarantee any habeas review without an enacting statute). Under such theories, habeas jurisdiction (and the availability of the privilege) depends entirely on executing legislation—i.e., on the content of federal statutes. For proponents, the Constitution does no more than what the text of the Suspension Clause says: set the terms under which Congress may suspend the privilege. These scholars argue that, because Article III does not guarantee any jurisdiction of lower federal courts, federal judges must only exercise habeas power created by Congress. These theorists ultimately argue that Congress can eliminate habeas power without raising Suspension Clause problems.

e) The Suspension Clause as Guarantee of State Habeas Jurisdiction. Prominent historian William F. Duker argues that the Suspension Clause ensured that the *federal* government could not interfere with the authority of *state* courts to conduct habeas review of federal custody. See Duker, *A Constitutional History of Habeas Corpus*, at 126–80. Professor Duker's theory is particularly central to the discussion of *Ableman v. Booth*, 62 U.S. 506 (1859), and *Tarble's Case*, 80 U.S. 397 (1872), the two cases in which the Supreme Court decided that states could not conduct habeas review of federal custody. *Ableman* and *Tarble* receive extensive treatment later in this Chapter. Is Professor Duker's argument consistent with what you know about the drafting process: that the Suspension Clause was moved from the judicial to the legislative Article and that the debates involving the Clause centered on the issue of whether to provide that habeas be robustly enjoyed? Is Professor Duker's argument consistent with other ideas about the relationship among the suspension power, the privilege, and the sovereign custody for which the privilege serves as a remedy?

2) The Constitutionally Required Scope of a Common-law Habeas Privilege. Writing the majority opinion in *Fay v. Noia*, 372 U.S. 391 (1963), Justice William Brennan observed: "At the time that the Suspension Clause was written into our Federal Constitution and the first Judiciary Act was passed . . . there was respectable common-law authority for the proposition that habeas was available to remedy any kind of governmental restraint contrary to fundamental law."[m] (Justice Brennan's historical account remains a lightning rod.) On Justice Brennan's view, not only did the Suspension Clause incorporate the common-law privilege, but it also incorporated a particularly robust one. That view does have some support in the decisional law of the Supreme Court. Various decisions have relied on common-law practice in interpreting the meaning of the Suspension Clause, and some of those have suggested that the common-law practice sets constitutional boundaries of mandatory habeas jurisdiction. For example, Professor Amanda Tyler has argued that the common-law scope of the habeas privilege requires that the privilege be available for certain types of detainees and certain types of custody. See Amanda L. Tyler, *The Forgotten Core Meaning of the Suspension Clause*, 125 Harv. L. Rev. 901, 922–23 (2012) (arguing that the Framers viewed the writ as protecting citizens against detention without criminal charges absent a suspension of the writ).

3)   Statutory Sources of Modern Habeas Authority. In 1948, Congress created the modern statutes granting habeas jurisdiction to the federal courts, moving the provisions of the 1789 Judiciary Act into 28 U.S.C. §§ 2241–55. 28 U.S.C. Section 2241(a) now states that: "Writs of habeas corpus may be granted by the Supreme Court, any justice thereof, the district courts and any circuit judge within their respective jurisdictions." The 1948 Amendments also included special provisions for habeas challenges to state convictions (§ 2254), as well as a new post-conviction procedure for inmates convicted in a federal court (§ 2255). This Chapter will discuss these and other statutory changes as they become necessary to understanding the relevant subject matter.

4)   Constitutional Theory in Action: *INS v. St. Cyr,* **533 U.S. 289 (2001).** One of the central questions in modern habeas law is the scope of any constitutionally-required habeas privilege. This issue flared up in wake of the Antiterrorism and Effective Death Penalty Act of 1996 (AEDPA) and the Illegal Immigration Reform and Immigrant Responsibility Act of 1996 (IIRIRA). These statutes amended the Immigration and Nationality Act (INA) and stripped habeas jurisdiction over certain immigration proceedings. Prior to AEDPA and IIRIRA, the Attorney General (AG) had broad discretion to waive deportation or removal. Among other restrictions, IIRIRA narrowed the class of aliens eligible for a removal waiver, such that it was no longer available to anyone convicted of an aggravated felony. Other IIRIRA and AEDPA provisions also severely restricted judicial review over questions of waiver eligibility. Ten years after becoming a lawful resident, Enrico St. Cyr pled guilty to a Connecticut controlled-substance charge. St. Cyr's conviction made him removable, but he was eligible for a waiver when the criminal judgment issued. By the time his removal proceedings began, however, IIRIRA and AEDPA had restricted waiver eligibility for aggravated felons, and had imposed the new restrictions on judicial review of waiver determinations. St. Cyr filed a habeas petition challenging the application of the waiver restriction to aliens whose predicate conviction preceded the 1996 legislation. Lengthier excerpts of *St. Cyr* appear in Chapter 7, and what follows is only the content necessary to discuss the constitutional theory that is the subject of this Note.

---

[m] As Chapter 6 will explain, Justice Brennan's account of the writ's function at the Founding is contested. See, e.g., Wainwright v. Sykes, 433 U.S. 72, 81 (1977) (describing *Fay v. Noia*'s account of the writ as a "change in direction").

a)   **The Majority Opinion.** In *St. Cyr*, the Supreme Court held that there was a habeas forum for the petitioner to challenge IIRIRA, and that IIRIRA did not strip the federal courts of removal discretion over aliens who were convicted for predicate felonies prior to IIRIRA's enactment. On the question of whether there was a habeas forum for the challenge, the Court (in an opinion by Justice Stevens) held that: "[b]ecause of [the Suspension Clause], some judicial intervention in deportation cases is unquestionably required by the Constitution." In what has now become a standard hedge regarding the scope of that constitutional protection, the Court noted; "Regardless of whether the protection of the Suspension Clause encompasses all cases covered by the 1867 Amendment extending the protection of the writ to state prisoners, or by subsequent legal developments, at the absolute minimum, the Suspension Clause protects the writ as it existed in 1789." The Court explicitly stated its preference to interpret the statute so as to avoid the constitutional question and to allow the habeas challenge:

> In sum, even assuming that the Suspension Clause protects only the writ as it existed in 1789, there is substantial evidence to support the proposition that pure questions of law like the one raised by the respondent in this case could have been answered in 1789 by a common law judge with power to issue the writ of habeas corpus. It necessarily follows that a serious Suspension Clause issue would be presented if we were to accept the INS's submission that the 1996 statutes have withdrawn that power from federal judges and provided no adequate substitute for its exercise. The necessity of resolving such a serious and difficult constitutional issue—and the desirability of avoiding that necessity—simply reinforce the reasons for requiring a clear and unambiguous statement of constitutional intent.

Justice Stevens wrote the majority opinion and referenced a noteworthy passage in *Bollman*, which had stated that the First Congress passed a statute securing the habeas privilege under "immediate influence" of the Suspension Clause. (The *St. Cyr* excerpt is below.) Per *Bollman*—or at least the *St. Cyr* majority's gloss on it—the 1789 Judiciary Act secured an otherwise-unavailable habeas privilege and the First Congress thereby avoided a Suspension Clause violation. You may recognize this argument as the so-called "Obligation Theory." In dissent (explored in this Note's next subpart), Justice Scalia read the pertinent *Bollman* passage to express the idea that the Constitution *did not* require Congress to secure the habeas privilege at all. Justice Stevens responded:

> [Justice Scalia's] dissent reads into Chief Justice Marshall's opinion in *Bollman* support for a proposition that [Chief Justice Marshall] did not endorse, either explicitly or implicitly. He did note that "the first congress of the United States" acted under "the immediate influence" of the injunction provided by the Suspension Clause when it gave "life and activity" to "this great constitutional privilege" in the Judiciary Act of 1789, and that the writ could not be suspended until after the statute was enacted. That statement, however, surely does not imply that Marshall believed the Framers had drafted a Clause that would proscribe a temporary abrogation of the writ, while permitting its permanent suspension. Indeed, Marshall's comment expresses the far more sensible view that the Clause was intended to preclude any possibility that "the privilege itself would be lost" by either the inaction or the action of Congress.

Do you think that Justice Stevens properly characterizes *Bollman*?

b)   Justice Scalia's Dissent. Justice Scalia, joined in full by Chief Justice Rehnquist and Justice Thomas, and joined in part by Justice O'Connor, dissented. First, Justice Scalia argued that the statute plainly stripped habeas jurisdiction over the removal order in question, and he then reached the constitutional issue of whether the Suspension Clause permitted such legislation. Justice Scalia began by noting the absence of an express guarantee in the Suspension Clause: "Indeed, that was precisely the objection expressed by four of the state ratifying conventions—that the Constitution failed affirmatively to guarantee a right to habeas corpus."

Justice Scalia then distinguished between suspending the privilege and "permanently alter[ing] its content." He analogized the argument that the Suspension Clause required legislative grants of habeas authority to the argument that the Equal Protection Clause might require Congress to write laws to effectuate its purposes. Citing *Bollman*, Justice Scalia described Justice Marshall as having "specifically addresse[d] the Suspension Clause—not invoking it as a source of habeas jurisdiction, but to the contrary pointing out that without legislated habeas jurisdiction the Suspension Clause would have no effect." Justice Scalia then cited to several other passages in *Bollman* in support of the proposition that habeas authority be exercised pursuant to enabling legislation. For example, Chief Justice Marshall had stated that "[t]he power of taking cognizance of any question between individuals, or between the government and individuals . . . must be given by written law."

Then, assuming arguendo that the Suspension Clause did in fact protect some habeas authority, Justice Scalia considered two possible variations of such a theory. He first examined the idea that the Suspension Clause bars Congress from repealing habeas jurisdiction that Congress had previously provided to federal judges. He characterized that idea as an implausible "one-way ratchet." What are the problems with the "one-way ratchet" theory? In what ways might it be defensible? The second variation, which Justice Scalia took more seriously, was the argument that the Suspension Clause protected, at the very least, "the common law right of habeas corpus, as it was understood when the Constitution was ratified." Having assumed that the Constitution required some inherited common-law habeas process, Justice Scalia nonetheless rejected the proposition that the common-law habeas privilege included a right to have an Article III court adjudicate the exercise of removal discretion.

c)   A "Null-Set" Theory of the Habeas Privilege. Based on the Madisonian Compromise and on *Marbury*, Justice Scalia argued that the Constitution could not have required any federal habeas access because (1) Congress did not have to create the lower federal courts, and (2) Article III, § 2 does not specify habeas as a form of original jurisdiction. This first theory, already highlighted in Note 1.d, derives from Professor Rex Collings' influential law review article making the same argument. See Collings, *Habeas Corpus for Convicts-Constitutional Right or Legislative Grace?*, 40 Cal. L. Rev. 335. For Justice Scalia, that understanding of the Clause is consistent with its plain textual meaning, which "does not guarantee any content to (or even the existence of) the writ of habeas corpus, but merely provides that the writ shall not (except in case of rebellion or invasion) be suspended." Is Justice Scalia's assessment of the historical evidence correct on this score? Is there any significance to the fact that the Suspension Clause appears in Article I, as opposed to

Article III? What are other potential sources of the privilege, if not the text of the Suspension Clause? Can the text be reconciled with the notion that prisoners have some access to the privilege?

d)   Originalist Conceptions of the Privilege. Justice Scalia argued that, even if the Constitution does guarantee some quantum of habeas access, it does not guarantee habeas access to litigate the specific exercise of immigration authority at issue in *St. Cyr*. The scope of the habeas guarantee—in the context of executive detention—has taken center stage in much of the recent litigation over military confinement at various detention facilities around the globe. If the Constitution does protect some amount of habeas access, does Justice Scalia correctly argue that scope of the protected access must correspond to the habeas corpus remedies available in 1787? Is there any reason to distinguish between originalist arguments regarding habeas corpus and originalist arguments pertaining to other constitutional provisions? If one adopts the theory that the constitutional scope of the privilege was fixed at the Founding, then does that theory necessarily entail that all features of the privilege were also fixed—its territorial scope, the nationality of prisoners eligible for relief, and the sovereign status of the custodian that detains the prisoner?

5)   Coda to the *St. Cyr* Dissent. The originalist theory has emerged as a counterpoint to a more expansive reading of the habeas privilege's constitutional scope. One example is Justice Scalia's dissent in *Rasul v. Bush*, 542 U.S. 466 (2004), an important post-9/11 habeas case and the statutory precursor to *Boumediene v. Bush*, 553 U.S. 723 (2008). As did *St. Cyr*, *Rasul* reflects statutory interpretation designed to avoid a Suspension Clause question. In *Rasul*, the Court held that federal judges had jurisdiction over detainees held at the Guantánamo Bay Naval Base in Cuba ("GTMO"). Justice Scalia accused the majority of adopting a "strained construction" of the habeas statute in order to avoid having to decide whether there existed a "constitutional right to habeas."

After *Rasul*, Congress explicitly revoked habeas jurisdiction over certain categories of executive detainees. *Boumediene* held that such jurisdiction stripping was unconstitutional. Surprisingly, in *Boumediene*, not a single Justice expressed disagreement with the proposition that a "constitutional right to habeas" exists. Justice Scalia's *Boumediene* dissent, however, argued that a privilege with content fixed at the Founding should have been unavailable to the GTMO detainees. As Chapter 10 will discuss in detail, the *Boumediene* majority took the historical arguments quite seriously. The majority opinion offered a lengthy historical account of the common-law habeas writ. The majority, however, ultimately concluded that an incomplete historical record was incapable of providing definitive answers to questions about the scope of the habeas privilege.

3. HOW DOES THE GOVERNMENT "SUSPEND" THE PRIVILEGE?

Article I, § 9, cl. 2 sets forth conditions under which Congress may suspend the privilege of the writ of habeas corpus. Congress has invoked the suspension power four times: (1) in the middle of the Civil War, (2) during Reconstruction, (3) for the Philippines in 1905, and (4) in Hawaii during World War II. Where does the suspension power come from? Remember, the Suspension Clause just specifies limits on suspension power—it does not expressly create the power itself. In fact, the language of the Suspension Clause invites a host of other questions about the power to suspend, many of which Section 3 will explore: (1) which institutions have the power to suspend; (2) whether suspension can operate by means of congressional authorization followed by the exercise of an executive option; (3) whether the "public safety" requirement simply restates the "rebellion" and "invasion" limitations, or whether it is itself an additional limitation; (4) the justiciability of rebellion, invasion, and public safety determinations; and (5) whether a suspension of the habeas remedy actually affects the substantive legality of custody itself.

A. EXECUTIVE SUSPENSION

The limits on the suspension power—that it may be exercised only in response to rebellion or invasion, and that the public safety require it—appear in Article I, § 9, cl. 2, a constitutional provision that restricts the powers of Congress. If the limits on suspension arise under Article I, then one can probably assume that Congress may exercise the power to which those limits apply. What about the executive branch? Does it have the authority to suspend, arising from some other constitutional provision? Does the idea of a court "suspending" the privilege make any sense?

———

INTRODUCTORY NOTES ON EX PARTE MERRYMAN

The leading case on what branch may exercise the suspension power is *Ex parte Merryman*, 17 F.Cas. 144 (C.C.D. Md. 1861). Like many decisions, the text of the opinion fails to fully capture the personal, political, and institutional conflict that gave rise to the dispute. A thorough understanding of *Merryman* requires consideration of three factors: (1) the personal animus between President Abraham Lincoln and Supreme Court Chief Justice Roger Taney, (2) the political conflict between the remnants of Andrew Jackson's political coalition and the abolitionist Republican party, and (3) the Civil War-era struggle between the executive and judicial branches. As discussed in Section 5, *infra*, the 1840s and 1850s were an era of brutal struggle between abolitionist northern states and a Jacksonian coalition seeking to impose national compromises over slavery. Slave-holding Chief Justice Roger Taney, author of the infamous *Dred Scott* opinion, led the Jacksonian wing of the Court.

On April 13, 1861, Confederate forces attacked Fort Sumter. Congress was not in session, and there were few troops remaining in Washington, D.C. to defend the capital. The Confederate Army was camped in nearby Virginia. Meanwhile, Maryland was considering whether to secede; Confederate sympathizers burned Maryland railroad lines and incited violent riots in Baltimore. President Lincoln justifiably feared that the Confederacy would surround and quickly capture Washington, D.C. unless he took immediate action. Chief Justice Rehnquist, in his book on civil liberties during wartime, vividly describes the crisis:

> Baltimore was an absolutely critical rail junction for the purpose of bringing troops from the north or west into Washington, because the railroad coming down the coast from New York and Philadelphia, as well as the line from Harrisburg, ran through that city. . . . This strategic location, plus the substantial degree of secessionist sympathy in Baltimore, made the city the Achilles' heel of the early efforts to bring federal troops to de-

fend Washington. And the status of Maryland as a border state, whose adherence to the Union was problematic, exacerbated this difficulty. Maryland teetered both geographically and ideologically between North and South. If the secessionists were to gain the upper hand, the Union war effort could be seriously compromised.

William H. Rehnquist, *All the Laws But One: Civil Liberties in Wartime* 18 (1998). On April 19, a mob of 20,000 Confederate sympathizers attacked troops en route to Washington and burned railroad bridges near Baltimore. Federal troops would thereafter have to march off trains north of Baltimore, be ferried by ships to Annapolis, and then travel to Washington. Telegraph lines were also cut and mail service was uncertain: "the city of Washington seemed virtually cut off from the rest of the North."[n] Shortly thereafter, President Lincoln issued secret orders commanding military custodians not to respond to the writ of habeas corpus. On April 27, 1861, President Lincoln told Army Commander-in-Chief General Winfield Scott that, if the Army encountered resistance on the military line between Annapolis and Washington, then General Scott or a subordinate commander was authorized to "suspend" the writ. The order read:

> You are engaged in suppressing an insurrection against the laws of the United States. If at any point on or in the vicinity of any military line which is now or which shall be used between the city of Philadelphia and the city of Washington you find resistance which renders it necessary to suspend the writ of habeas corpus for the public safety, you personally or through the officer in command at the point at which resistance occurs, are authorized to suspend that writ.[o]

Several days later, a suspension order was given.[p]

John Merryman was a pro-Confederate member of the Maryland Militia, and he was arrested for treason after the Baltimore riots. Merryman's family attorney petitioned for a habeas writ from Chief Justice Taney, but in Taney's capacity as Circuit Justice. Chief Justice Taney—again, acting in his capacity as Circuit Justice—sent the writ to General John Cadawalder, the commanding officer at Fort McHenry, the military facility at which Merryman was detained. (Although Chief Justice Taney was acting in his capacity as Circuit Justice, he removed that designation from the writ.) Chief Justice Taney immediately traveled to Baltimore—a decision that many believe was designed to escalate the appearance of a direct confrontation with President Lincoln—where Taney ordered the production of Merryman. General Cadawalder provided a partial return, failing to produce Merryman. General Cadawalder did, however, send a subordinate to the Chief Justice to convey the message that the President had authorized a suspension. The subordinate also requested further time to allow General Cadawalder to secure Presidential guidance as to the appropriate manner of return. Incensed, Chief Justice Taney demanded that Merryman be produced in court and issued an attachment (a seizure order) against General Cadawalder.

---

[n] William H. Rehnquist, *All the Laws But One: Civil Liberties in Wartime* 22 (1998).

[o] See *id.* at 25.

[p] For more robust descriptions of these events, see Daniel Farber, *Lincoln's Constitution* 157–63, 188–92 (2003); Rehnquist, supra note n, at 20–25; James F. Simon, *Lincoln and Chief Justice Taney: Slavery, Secession, and the President's War Powers* 190 (2006).

The marshal was unable to serve Chief Justice Taney's orders at the facility the next day; sentries blocked access to Merryman. Chief Justice Taney's opinion issued on May 25.

————

Ex Parte Merryman

United States Circuit Court for the District of Maryland
17 F. Cas. 144 (1861)

■ CHIEF JUSTICE TANEY, sitting as Circuit Justice for the United States Circuit Court for the District of Maryland, delivered the opinion of the Court.

* * * [A] military officer, residing in Pennsylvania, issues an order to arrest a citizen of Maryland, upon vague and indefinite charges, without any proof, so far as appears; under this order, his house is entered in the night, he is seized as a prisoner, and conveyed to Fort McHenry, and there kept in close confinement; and when a habeas corpus is served on the commanding officer, requiring him to produce the prisoner before a justice of the supreme court, in order that he may examine into the legality of the imprisonment, the answer of the officer, is that he is authorized by the president to suspend the writ of habeas corpus at his discretion, and in the exercise of that discretion, suspends it in this case, and on that ground refuses obedience to the writ * * *.

* * * [The Suspension Clause] is devoted to the legislative department of the United States, and has not the slightest reference to the executive department. It begins by providing "that all legislative powers therein granted, shall be vested in a congress of the United States, which shall consist of a senate and house of representatives." And after prescribing the manner in which these two branches of the legislative department shall be chosen, it proceeds to enumerate specifically the legislative powers which it thereby grants [and legislative powers which it expressly prohibits]; and at the conclusion of this specification, a clause is inserted giving congress 'the power to make all laws which shall be necessary and proper for carrying into execution the foregoing powers, and all other powers vested by this constitution in the government of the United States, or in any department or officer thereof.'

The power of legislation granted by this latter clause is, by its words, carefully confined to the specific objects before enumerated. But as this limitation was unavoidably somewhat indefinite, it was deemed necessary to guard more effectually certain great cardinal principles, essential to the liberty of the citizen, and to the rights and equality of the states, by denying to congress, in express terms, any power of legislation over them. It was apprehended, it seems, that such legislation might be attempted, under the pretext that it was necessary and proper to carry into execution the powers granted; and it was determined, that there should be no room to doubt, where rights of such vital importance were concerned; and accordingly, this clause is immediately followed by an enumeration of certain subjects, to which the powers of legislation shall not extend. The great importance which the framers of the constitution attached to the privilege of the writ of habeas corpus, to protect the liberty of the citizen, is proved by the fact, that its suspension, except in cases of invasion or rebellion, is first in the list of prohibited powers; and even in these cases the power is denied, and its exercise prohibited, unless the public safety shall require it.

It is true, that in the cases mentioned, congress is, of necessity, the judge of whether the public safety does or does not require it; and their judgment is conclusive. But the introduction of these words is a standing admonition to the legislative body of the danger of suspending it, and of the extreme caution they should exercise, before they give the government of the United States such power over the liberty of a citizen.

It is the second article of the constitution that provides for the organization of the executive department, enumerates the powers conferred on it, and prescribes its duties. And if the high power over the liberty of the citizen now claimed, was intended to be conferred on the president, it would undoubtedly be found in plain words in this article; but there is not a word in it that can furnish the slightest ground to justify the exercise of the power.

[Chief Justice Taney specifies various forms of executive power and duty.]

Even if the privilege of the writ of habeas corpus were suspended by act of congress, and a party not subject to the rules and articles of war were afterwards arrested and imprisoned by regular judicial process, he could not be detained in prison, or brought to trial before a military tribunal, for the article in the amendments to the constitution immediately following the one above referred to (that is, the sixth article) provides, that 'in all criminal prosecutions, the accused shall enjoy the right to a speedy and public trial by an impartial jury of the state and district wherein the crime shall have been committed, which district shall have been previously ascertained by law; and to be informed of the nature and cause of the accusation; to be confronted with the witnesses against him; to have compulsory process for obtaining witnesses in his favor; and to have the assistance of counsel for his defence.'

The only power, therefore, which the president possesses, where the 'life, liberty or property' of a private citizen is concerned, is the power and duty prescribed in the third section of the second article, which requires 'that he shall take care that the laws shall be faithfully executed.' He is not authorized to execute them himself, or through agents or officers, civil or military, appointed by himself, but he is to take care that they be faithfully carried into execution, as they are expounded and adjudged by the coordinate branch of the government to which that duty is assigned by the constitution. It is thus made his duty to come in aid of the judicial authority, if it shall be resisted by a force too strong to be overcome without the assistance of the executive arm; but in exercising this power he acts in subordination to judicial authority, assisting it to execute its process and enforce its judgments. With such provisions in the constitution, expressed in language too clear to be misunderstood by any one, I can see no ground whatever for supposing that the president, in any emergency, or in any state of things, can authorize the suspension of the privileges of the writ of habeas corpus, or the arrest of a citizen, except in aid of the judicial power. He certainly does not faithfully execute the laws, if he takes upon himself legislative power, by suspending the writ of habeas corpus, and the judicial power also, by arresting and imprisoning a person without due process of law.

Nor can any argument be drawn from the nature of sovereignty, or the necessity of government, for self-defence in times of tumult and danger.

The government of the United States is one of delegated and limited powers; it derives it existence and authority altogether from the constitution, and neither of its branches, executive, legislative or judicial, can exercise any of the powers of government beyond those specified and granted; for the tenth article of the amendments to the constitution, in express terms, provides that 'the powers not delegated to the United States by the constitution, nor prohibited by it to the states, are reserved to the states, respectively, or to the people.'

Indeed, the security against imprisonment by executive authority, provided for in the fifth article of the amendments to the constitution, which I have before quoted, is nothing more than a copy of a like provision in the English constitution, which had been firmly established before the declaration of independence. Blackstone states it in the following words: 'To make imprisonment lawful, it must be either by process of law from the courts of judicature, or by warrant from some legal officer having authority to commit to prison.'

The people of the United Colonies, who had themselves lived under its protection, while they were British subjects, were well aware of the necessity of this safeguard for their personal liberty. And no one can believe that, in framing a government intended to guard still more efficiently the rights and liberties of the citizen, against executive encroachment and oppression, they would have conferred on the president a power which the history of England had proved to be dangerous and oppressive in the hands of the crown; and which the people of England had compelled it to surrender, after a long and obstinate struggle on the part of the English executive to usurp and retain it. * * *

[Chief Justice Taney further traces the history of the English common-law writ, which eventually defined the circumstances under which a prisoner's detention is lawful. He argues that Merryman's imprisonment, on vague charges, resembles the abuses to which the English writ was addressed.]

While the value set upon this writ in England has been so great, that the removal of the abuses which embarrassed its employment has been looked upon as almost a new grant of liberty to the subject, it is not to be wondered at, that the continuance of the writ thus made effective should have been the object of the most jealous care. Accordingly, no power in England short of that of parliament can suspend or authorize the suspension of the writ of habeas corpus. * * * If the president of the United States may suspend the writ, then the constitution of the United States has conferred upon him more regal and absolute power over the liberty of the citizen, than the people of England have thought it safe to entrust to the crown; a power which the queen of England cannot exercise at this day, and which could not have been lawfully exercised by the sovereign even in the reign of Charles the First.

* * * Mr. Justice Story, speaking, in his Commentaries, of the habeas corpus clause in the constitution, says:

> It is obvious that cases of a peculiar emergency may arise, which may justify, nay, even require, the temporary suspension of any right to the writ. But as it has frequently happened in foreign countries, and even in England, that the writ has, upon various pretexts and occasions, been suspended, whereby persons apprehended upon suspicion have suffered a long imprisonment, sometimes from design, and sometimes

because they were forgotten, the right to suspend it is expressly confined to cases of rebellion or invasion, where the public safety may require it. A very just and wholesome restraint, which cuts down at a blow a fruitful means of oppression, capable of being abused, in bad times, to the worst of purposes. Hitherto, no suspension of the writ has ever been authorized by congress, since the establishment of the constitution. It would seem, as the power is given to congress to suspend the writ of habeas corpus, in cases of rebellion or invasion, that the right to judge whether the exigency had arisen must exclusively belong to that body.

And Chief Justice Marshall, in delivering the opinion of the supreme court in the case of *Ex parte Bollman and Swartwout*, uses this decisive language:

> It may be worthy of remark, that this act (speaking of the one under which I am proceeding) was passed by the first congress of the United States, sitting under a constitution which had declared 'that the privilege of the writ of habeas corpus should not be suspended, unless when, in cases of rebellion or invasion, the public safety may require it.' Acting under the immediate influence of this injunction, they must have felt, with peculiar force, the obligation of providing efficient means, by which this great constitutional privilege should receive life and activity; for if the means be not in existence, the privilege itself would be lost, although no law for its suspension should be enacted. Under the impression of this obligation, they give to all the courts the power of awarding writs of habeas corpus. * * * If at any time, the public safety should require the suspension of the powers vested by this act in the courts of the United States, it is for the legislature to say so. That question depends on political considerations, on which the legislature is to decide; until the legislative will be expressed, this court can only see its duty, and must obey the laws.

I can add nothing to these clear and emphatic words of my great predecessor.

* * * [U]nder these circumstances, a military officer, stationed in Pennsylvania, without giving any information to the district attorney, and without any application to the judicial authorities, assumes to himself the judicial power in the district of Maryland; undertakes to decide what constitutes the crime of treason or rebellion; what evidence (if indeed he required any) is sufficient to support the accusation and justify the commitment; and commits the party, without a hearing, even before himself, to close custody, in a strongly garrisoned fort, to be there held, it would seem, during the pleasure of those who committed him.

* * * These great and fundamental laws [specified in the Constitution and the Bill], which congress itself could not suspend, have been disregarded and suspended, like the writ of habeas corpus, by a military order, supported by force of arms. Such is the case now before me, and I can only say that if the authority which the constitution has confided to the judiciary department and judicial officers, may thus, upon any pretext or under any circumstances, be usurped by the military power, at its discretion, the people of the United States are no longer living under a government of laws, but every citizen holds life, liberty and property at the will and pleasure of the army officer in whose military district he may happen to be found.

In such a case, my duty was too plain to be mistaken. I have exercised all the power which the constitution and laws confer upon me, but that power has been resisted by a force too strong for me to overcome. It is possible that the officer who has incurred this grave responsibility may have misunderstood his instructions, and exceeded the authority intended to be given him; I shall, therefore, order all the proceedings in this case, with my opinion, to be filed and recorded in the circuit court of the United States for the district of Maryland, and direct the clerk to transmit a copy, under seal, to the president of the United States. It will then remain for that high officer, in fulfillment of his constitutional obligation to 'take care that the laws be faithfully executed,' to determine what measures he will take to cause the civil process of the United States to be respected and enforced.

R.B. Taney,

Chief Justice of the Supreme Court of the United States.

————

NOTES AND QUESTIONS ON MERRYMAN

1) **Chief Justice Taney's Article I Argument.** Chief Justice Taney accords considerable weight to the fact that the Suspension Clause appears in Article I, § 9. Article I, § 8 enumerates congressional powers and gives to Congress all authority "necessary and proper" to the exercise of it. Section 9 generally restricts otherwise-available legislative power. As a result, most modern judges and scholars have agreed that, at least as far as constitutional structure is concerned, Chief Justice Taney correctly resolved the question. See, e.g., Hamdi v. Rumsfeld, 542 U.S. 507, 562 (2004) (Scalia, J., dissenting) ("Although [the Suspension Clause] does not state that suspension must be effected by, or authorized by, a legislative act, it has been so understood, consistent with English practice and the Clause's placement in Article I."). Look at Article I, § 8. To which enumerated power is a suspension a necessary and proper auxiliary?

2) **Lincoln's Argument for Article II Suspension Authority.** Arguing that other institutions should honor his suspension, President Lincoln beseeched Congress on the first day of a special session convened on July 4:

> Must [the law] be allowed to finally fail of execution, even had it been perfectly clear that by the use of the means necessary to their execution some single law, made in such extreme tenderness of the citizens' liberty that practically it relieves more of the guilty than of the innocent, should to a very limited extent be violated? To state the question more directly, Are all the laws *but one* to go unexecuted, and the Government itself go to pieces lest one law be violated? Even in such a case, would not the official oath be broken if the Government should be overthrown when it believed that disregarding the single law would tend to preserve it?[q]

In other words, Lincoln first argued that an executive suspension power derived from Article II, which obligates the President to faithfully execute the laws. That argument was largely rhetorical. President Lincoln's second and more serious legal argument was that the Constitution did not specify which branches had the power to suspend the habeas privilege, and that the Presi-

———

[q] Abraham Lincoln, Message to Congress in Special Session (July 4, 1861), in *Abraham Lincoln: Speeches and Writings* 1 859–1865, at 253 (Don E. Fehrenbacher ed., 1989).

dent's status as commander-in-chief implied such a power. Do you agree with President Lincoln's argument that, because the Suspension Clause does not specify which branch may exercise suspension power, the executive may do so? What do you make of President Lincoln's argument in light of the fact that Pinckney's draft suspension language drew a distinction between the privilege, which all people were to enjoy fully in the "Government," and the suspension criteria, which expressly restricted the legislature? If you agree with President Lincoln's argument, then do you think that the President should be able to delegate suspension authority to his military commanders?

3) Constitutional Integrity Versus Existential Imperative? One professor has summarized the dispute in *Merryman* as follows: "Taney had the Constitution's text and structure in his corner, along with dicta from [*Bollman*] suggesting that the power to suspend the writ rested entirely with the legislature. But Lincoln had rhetoric, exigency, and principle behind him." Stephen I. Vladeck, *The Field Theory: Martial Law, The Suspension Power, And The Insurrection Act*, 80 Temp. L. Rev. 391, 393 (2007). Is it fair to say that Chief Justice Taney was correct about the text and structure of the constitution, but that *Merryman* might have been the sort of "constitutional moment" that called for a more, shall we say, pragmatic interpretation of the Constitution?

4) Subsequent Congressional Authorization. *Merryman* looked like a prelude to a constitutional showdown that never materialized. The events in the days immediately after Fort Sumter were *sui generis*. Merryman himself was quietly released shortly after Taney's opinion, then indicted for treason, then released on bail, and never again tried (in part due to Chief Justice Taney's interference with treason cases in Maryland).[r] Through the Habeas Corpus Suspension Act of 1863, Congress formally authorized the President to suspend the privilege. Section 1 of the 1863 Act provided that "during the present rebellion, the President of the United States . . . is authorized to suspend the privilege of the writ of habeas corpus in any case throughout the United States." Act of Aug. 6, 1861, ch. 63, § 3, 12 Stat. 326, 326.[s] The Act expressed no legislative opinion on, and mooted the question of, whether Lincoln's prior suspension was constitutional. Although the subsequent legislation authorized the President to suspend the privilege, does it necessarily render lawful the President's failure to respond to the writ in *Merryman*? In light of the statutory authorization, would the President have to have suspended the privilege in a particular locale *before* deciding whether to respond to the return? You will encounter the provisions of the 1863 suspension statute again in Chapter 9, because they were ultimately litigated in *Ex parte Milligan*, 71 U.S. (4 Wall.) 2 (1866).

B. AUTHORIZATION VERSUS SUSPENSION

Does the power to suspend a remedy imply the substantive power to authorize detention for which that remedy would ordinarily be invoked?

---

[r] See Rehnquist, *All the Laws But One*, supra note n, at 39. Other federal judges also considered the constitutionality of Lincoln's suspension and generally agreed with Taney. See Stephen I. Vladeck, *The Field Theory: Martial Law, The Suspension Power, And The Insurrection Act*, 80 Temp. L. Rev. 391, 408–09 (2007). The Confederate Courts also considered questions regarding whether and when habeas corpus could be suspended during the Civil War. See David P. Currie, *Through the Looking Glass: The Confederate Constitution in Congress, 1861–1865*, 90 Va. L. Rev. 1257, 1326–44 (2004).

[s] For background concerning the passage of the Act, see David P. Currie, *The Civil War Congress*, 73 U. Chi. L. Rev. 1131, 1136–40 (2006).

The question has a surprisingly complex answer. Consider two separate questions. First, does the Suspension Clause permit Congress to pass a provision authorizing the custody to which the suspension applies? Second, is such a statute even necessary to render the custody "lawful" during the suspension period?

———

NOTES AND QUESTIONS ON THE RELATIONSHIP BETWEEN SUSPENSION AND THE UNDERLYING LEGALITY OF CUSTODY

1)   Note on Suspension and Predicate Detention Power at English Common Law. Does the power to suspend the habeas privilege also create the power to authorize the detention itself? In other words, if a prisoner is detained during a period of suspension under terms that would otherwise be illegal, can the prisoner challenge the detention using other remedies, or even sue for damages? Can the prisoners seek their release once the suspension period concludes? While an understanding of English common law is instructive, prominent commentators have disagreed sharply on whether English suspension power simultaneously authorized the predicate detention. Compare Trevor W. Morrison, *Hamdi's Habeas Puzzle: Suspension as Authorization?*, 91 Cornell L. Rev. 411, 426–42 (2006) (arguing that exercise of Suspension power is nothing more than the power to restrict the remedies of bail and discharge), with Amanda L. Tyler, *Is Suspension a Political Question?*, 59 Stan. L. Rev. 333, 386 (2006) (arguing that Suspension power does include power to authorize emergency detention). Chapter 11 explores the modern Supreme Court cases regarding circumstances in which prisoners may sue using civil rights statutes, rather than pursue habeas corpus remedies.

2)   The Structure of English Suspensions. Describing pre-Revolutionary War pieces of English legislation as "habeas suspension statutes" is a bit misleading. None used the term "suspend" or "habeas corpus." Instead, they created royal authority to arrest and to detain. More precisely, the statutes empowered the Crown to lawfully arrest and imprison without "bail or mainprise." For example, the English suspension of habeas corpus during the American Revolution authorized the detention "without bail or mainprize" of persons who "have been, or shall hereafter be seised or taken in the act of high treason . . . or who are or shall be charged with or suspected of the crime of high treason . . . and who have been, or shall be committed . . . for such crimes . . . or for suspicion of such crimes." 17 Geo. 3, c. 9 (1777). Nothing in these suspension statutes actually interrupted the habeas "power" to hear a habeas motion. As a result, English judges could continue to entertain petitions and even consider the question of lawfulness. English judges were simply unable to order a prisoner discharged during the suspension period. English judges frequently ordered prisoners discharged on the first day after a suspension period ended.

The American colonial suspension statutes exhibited virtually the same structures as their English counterparts. For example, the Virginia legislature enacted the following suspension statute during the Revolutionary War:

> The Governor, with advice of the Council, is . . . hereby empowered to apprehend . . . and commit[] to close confinement, any person or persons whatsoever, whom they may have just cause to suspect disaffection to the

independence of the United States or of attachment to their enemies, and such person or persons shall not be set at liberty by bail, mainprise or habeas corpus.

Act of May 1781, ch. 7, *reprinted in* 10 *The Statutes at Large, Being a Collection of All the Laws of Virginia, from the First Session of the Legislature in the Year 1619*, at 413–16 (1822). Is there any reason to believe that the Constitution changed the way suspension was to operate in America?[t] Could one argue that the Suspension Clause empowers Congress to enhance detention power during a suspension period, but that Congress has to pass a separate statutory provision to that effect?

3)   Note on *Ex Parte Milligan* and The Relationship Between Power To Suspend And Power To Authorize Detention. Suspension is one of the most dramatic acts that the federal government can take, and the powers that the federal government enjoys pursuant to a suspension are, after September 11, 2001, a source of intense academic dispute. There is no controlling legal authority on the question of whether a suspension can enlarge the substantive scope of legal custody—which, of course, would have the effect of precluding other remedies for that detention. What little discussion the U.S. Reporter does contain appears in *Ex Parte Milligan*, 71. U.S. (4 Wall.) 2 (1866), a case featured in Chapter 9. Writing for the Court, Justice Davis observed in passing that the "suspension of the writ does not authorize the arrest of anyone, but simply denies to one arrested the privilege of this writ in order to obtain his liberty." Chief Justice Chase, joined by Justices Wayne, Swayne, and Miller, disagreed on two points: (1) "that, in our judgment, when the writ is suspended, the Executive is authorized to arrest, as well as to detain," and (2) that there are "cases in which, the privilege of the writ being suspended, trial and punishment by military commission, in states where civil courts are open, may be authorized by Congress, as well as arrest and detention." In short, the two *Milligan* opinions disagreed over whether the power to suspend also included (1) the power to enlarge arresting authority and (2) the power to constitute military commissions notwithstanding the availability of criminal process in an Article III court.

Roughly speaking, the *Milligan* majority provides a "minimalist" account of the suspension power, and the dissent provides a "maximalist" account of that authority. A maximalist would argue that because the English "suspension" acts generally restricted discharge *and* augmented arrest authority, the constitution permits a properly-executed suspension statute to include enhanced arrest and detention provisions.[u] A minimalist, by contrast, would argue that English suspension acts generally had no effect on the availability of other remedies for unlawful detention, and that one cannot infer that such de-

---

[t] For a more far-ranging discussion of colonial suspension statutes, see Amanda Tyler, *Suspension as an Emergency Power*, 118 Yale L.J. 600, 622 (2009).

[u] One would presumably be more comfortable with a maximalist account of suspension authority if the conditions under which the power could be exercised were more restrictive. See Tyler, supra note t, 118 Yale L.J. at 606 ("it is precisely because of the dramatic effects of a suspension on individual liberty that a decision by the political branches to invoke the authority should not be understood as categorically immune from judicial review"). Whether legislation that simply says that the privilege is "suspended" operates to enhance arresting and detention authority is probably a separate question of statutory interpretation. But see David L. Shapiro, *Habeas Corpus, Suspension, and Detention: Another View*, 82 Notre Dame L. Rev. 59, 89–90 (2006) (suggesting that statutory suspension language is in and of itself sufficient to authorize detention).

tention became, in any formal sense, "legal" during the suspension period. As one might imagine, how the Court resolves such a question will be extremely important to how the government adjudicates the modern detention of alleged terrorists. If Congress were to suspend the privilege, the answer to this question would dictate the government's substantive authority to detain prisoners.[v]

4. DOES THE CONSTITUTION GUARANTEE AN ADEQUATE HABEAS REMEDY?

This Section explores *what kind* of habeas privilege the Constitution might protect. The Supreme Court has settled on the rule that, during periods of non-suspension, there has to be habeas or some alternate remedy that allows a prisoner to make certain types of challenges to the lawfulness of custody. The Supreme Court has emphasized this rule in a series of decisions describing the requirement with some variation: that the remedy be "adequate and effective" to test detention, that it be an "adequate and effective substitute" for habeas, or that it merely be an "adequate" (not "effective") substitute. Whether the Court intended the terminological variation to be meaningful is not clear.

A. FEDERAL DETENTION AND THE "ADEQUATE SUBSTITUTE" RULE

Until *Boumediene*, there were two leading cases on this subject. The first is *United States v. Hayman*, 342 U.S. 205 (1952), which dealt with the constitutionality of a habeas-like remedy for inmates convicted in a federal court. The second is *Swain v. Pressley*, 430 U.S. 372 (1977), which involved a similar remedy for inmates convicted in a District of Columbia court of local jurisdiction. As you read these two cases, pay careful attention to (1) the genesis of the "adequate and effective substitute" rule and (2) what each decision rejects as a procedure or circumstance that would render the substitute invalid.

INTRODUCTORY NOTE ON 28 U.S.C. § 2255 AND UNITED STATES V. HAYMAN

Because federal prisons were concentrated in a few states, and because habeas process formally requires prisoners to seek relief from courts physically located in the territorial jurisdiction where the prisoners are confined, the federal courts in the states with federal prisoners had almost unmanageable habeas dockets. Moreover, requiring that habeas proceedings take place in the jurisdiction of confinement meant that witnesses—including attorneys and law enforcement officials—often had to travel great distances to participate.

The 1948 revision of the Judicial Code created a habeas-like remedy designed to limit post-conviction litigation to the jurisdiction where the federal prisoner was convicted. See 28 U.S.C. § 2255. Section 2255, which is the subject of Chapter 6, provides that prisoners in custody under sentence of a federal court may move the sentencing court to vacate, set aside, or correct a sentence

---

[v] Even in the absence of a suspension, the federal government has authorized detentions that have triggered damages actions for imprisonment, torture, and other rights violations.

otherwise subject to a habeas challenge. The remedy was not denominated as "habeas relief," but it contained virtually identical features—except for the requirement that the proceeding take place in the jurisdiction of confinement.

Section 2255(e) also includes a Savings Clause providing that a writ of habeas corpus "shall not be entertained" when a sentencing court denies relief, "unless it also appears that the remedy by motion is inadequate or ineffective to test the legality of [a prisoner's] detention."

United States v. Hayman

United States Supreme Court
342 U.S. 205 (1952)

■ Mr. CHIEF JUSTICE VINSON delivered the opinion of the Court.

[Hayman had been convicted and sentenced to twenty years' imprisonment in federal district court. He subsequently alleged that he was denied effective assistance of counsel under the Sixth Amendment. The district court denied Hayman's motion to vacate and for a new trial. The Ninth Circuit held that the § 2255 procedure was not adequate and effective to test Hayman's detention, and, in the alternative, that any statutory language precluding access to federal habeas procedure was an unconstitutional suspension of the writ.]

* * * *First*. The need for Section 2255 is best revealed by a review of the practical problems that had arisen in the administration of the federal courts' habeas corpus jurisdiction.

Power to issue the writ of habeas corpus, "the most celebrated writ in the English law," was granted to the federal courts in the Judiciary Act of 1789. Since Congress had not defined the term "habeas corpus," resort to the common law was necessary. Although the objective of the Great Writ long has been the liberation of those unlawfully imprisoned, at common law a judgment of conviction rendered by a court of general criminal jurisdiction was conclusive proof that confinement was legal. Such a judgment prevented issuance of the writ without more.

In 1867, Congress changed the common law rule by extending the writ of habeas corpus to "all cases where any person may be restrained of his or her liberty in violation of the constitution, or of any treaty or law of the United States," and providing for inquiry into the facts of detention. * * * [T]his Court has [made clear that, under the 1867 Habeas Corpus Act, a prisoner in custody pursuant to the final judgment of a jurisdictionally-competent court may have judicial inquiry into the cause of his detention.] * * * Under the 1867 Act, United States District Courts have jurisdiction to determine whether a prisoner has been deprived of liberty in violation of constitutional rights, although the proceedings resulting in incarceration may be unassailable on the face of the record. Under that Act, a variety of allegations have been held to permit challenge of convictions on facts dehors the record.

One aftermath of these developments in the law has been a great increase in the number of applications for habeas corpus filed in the federal courts by state and federal prisoners. The annual volume of applications had nearly tripled in the years preceding enactment of Section 2255. In addition to the problems raised by a large volume of applications for habeas corpus that are repetitious and patently frivolous, serious administrative problems developed in the consideration of applications which appear meritorious on their face. Often, such applications are found to be wholly lacking in merit when compared with the records of the sentencing court. But, since a habeas corpus action must be brought in the district of confinement, those records are not readily available to the habeas corpus court.

* * * These practical problems have been greatly aggravated by the fact that the few District Courts in whose territorial jurisdiction major federal penal institutions are located were required to handle an inordinate number of habeas corpus actions far from the scene of the facts, the homes of the witnesses and the records of the sentencing court solely because of the fortuitous concentration of federal prisoners within the district.

Second. * * * [A Statement of the Judicial Conference recommending the creation of the § 2255 remedy], stressing the practical difficulties encountered in [habeas] hearings held in the district of confinement, rather than the district of sentence, described the [§ 2255 remedy] as follows:

> This section applies only to Federal sentences. It creates a statutory remedy consisting of a motion before the court where the movant has been convicted. The remedy is in the nature of, but much broader than, coram nobis. The motion remedy broadly covers all situations where the sentence is 'open to collateral attack.' As a remedy, it is intended to be as broad as habeas corpus.

* * * According to the Reviser's Note on Section 2255:

> This section restates, clarifies and simplifies the procedure in the nature of the ancient writ of error coram nobis. It provides an expeditious remedy for correcting erroneous sentences without resort to habeas corpus. It has the approval of the Judicial Conference of the United States. Its principal provisions are incorporated in H.R. 4233, Seventy-ninth Congress [the so-called jurisdictional bill].

> * * *

This review of the history of Section 2255 shows that it was passed at the instance of the Judicial Conference to meet practical difficulties that had arisen in administering the habeas corpus jurisdiction of the federal courts. Nowhere in the history of Section 2255 do we find any purpose to impinge upon prisoners' rights of collateral attack upon their convictions. On the contrary, the sole purpose was to minimize the difficulties encountered in habeas corpus hearings by affording the same rights in another and more convenient forum.

Third. [The Court determined that, for § 2255 to be adequate and effective in this case, it had to provide for notice to Hayman and allow for Hayman's presence at a hearing. It also determined that the district court was in violation of § 2255 when it failed to meet these requirements.]

Fourth. Nothing has been shown to warrant our holding at this stage of the proceeding that the Section 2255 procedure will be "inadequate or ineffective" if respondent is present for a hearing in the District Court on remand of this case. In a case where the Section 2255 procedure is shown to be "inadequate or ineffective," the Section provides that the habeas corpus remedy shall remain open to afford the necessary hearing. Under such circumstances, we do not reach constitutional questions. This Court will not pass upon the constitutionality of an act of Congress where the question is properly presented unless such adjudication is unavoidable, much less anticipate constitutional questions.

* * *

Vacated and remanded.

Mr. JUSTICE BLACK and Mr. JUSTICE DOUGLAS concur in the result.

Mr. JUSTICE MINTON took no part in the consideration or decision of this case.

NOTES AND QUESTIONS ON HAYMAN

1)   Habeas by any Other Name. Does § 2255 raise a Suspension Clause problem just because it provides an alternative remedy that is not called "a writ of habeas corpus?" The Supreme Court emphasizes that the statute was designed to simplify housekeeping problems in the federal courts—to solve problems involving the appropriate territorial forum in which to bring a habeas petition. Should the Court have approved a statute that limited the ability of a federal judge to engage in habeas corpus review? Or is the same type of review, by another name, constitutional as long as the review is just as "effective" as a habeas proceeding? Could the Court affirm a statute designed to alleviate administrative problems facing the federal courts, even if it did alter federal judicial power to grant the writ?

2)   The Savings Clause in *Hayman*. One might describe *Hayman* as a case with constitutional overtones, but it was really a statutory-interpretation opinion. *Hayman* did not state a constitutional rule requiring that a habeas substitute be adequate and effective to test detention. *Hayman* involved the statutory interpretation of the § 2255 *savings clause*, which stated that, if § 2255 were inadequate and ineffective to test detention, then a habeas writ would be available. The Court held that the district court violated the statute when it failed to provide Hayman with notice and an opportunity to be heard, so nothing in § 2255 rendered the substitute remedy inadequate or ineffective to test detention.

3)   Adequacy and Effectiveness. Later cases have held that a substitute remedy must be an adequate and effective stand-in for a habeas proceeding. *Hayman* was more directly focused on ensuring that the specific prisoner receives adequate review. *Hayman* held that the substitute has to be adequate and effective to test detention, or to "afford the necessary hearing."

4)   Ineffective Assistance of Counsel. *Hayman* is your first encounter with a claim that a convicted prisoner received "ineffective assistance of counsel" under the Sixth Amendment (an "IAC" claim). (The constitutional source of the right can be a little more complicated, but understanding it as a Sixth Amendment claim suffices for now.) IAC claims are among the most frequently litigated post-conviction challenges, and you will read a great deal about them in this Book. Such challenges are more common today than they were when *Hayman* was decided.

5)   Criminal Conviction as Proof of Lawfulness. *Hayman* stated that "a judgment of conviction rendered by a court of general criminal jurisdiction was conclusive proof that confinement was legal." Does this assertion (regardless of its accuracy) mean that, absent the 1867 statutory enactment expressly expanding the habeas jurisdiction of federal courts, federal courts lacked power to grant relief in cases where the return attached a criminal judgment? If a criminal judgment was "conclusive proof" of lawfulness at common law, is there a reason why its conclusiveness may have diminished?

———————

INTRODUCTORY NOTE ON DETENTION BY THE DISTRICT OF COLUMBIA AND SWAIN V. PRESSLEY

In the District of Columbia Court Reform and Criminal Procedure Act of 1970, Congress created a new local court system for the District of Columbia. Among other things, it vested in a Superior Court all of the local jurisdiction previously exercised by the United States District Court for the District of Columbia. The Act established a process for post-conviction review similar to that enacted in 28 U.S.C. § 2255. The Supreme Court adjudicated the constitutionality of that remedy in *Swain v. Pressley*, 430 U.S. 372 (1977).

Swain v. Pressley
United States Supreme Court
430 U.S. 372 (1977)

■ Mr. JUSTICE STEVENS delivered the opinion of the Court, in which BRENNAN, WHITE, MARSHALL, and POWELL, JJ., joined, and in Part I of which BURGER, C.J., and BLACKMUN and REHNQUIST, JJ., joined.

[Pressley] is in custody pursuant to a sentence imposed by the Superior Court of the District of Columbia. He has filed an application for a writ of habeas corpus in the United States District Court for the District of Columbia asking that court to review the constitutionality of the proceedings that led to his conviction and sentence. The question presented to us is whether § 23–110(g) of the District of Columbia Code prevents the District Court from entertaining the application.

* * * Section 23–110(g) provides:

> An application for a writ of habeas corpus in behalf of a prisoner who is authorized to apply for relief by motion pursuant to this section shall not be entertained by the Superior Court or by any Federal or State court if it appears that the applicant has failed to make a motion for relief under this section or that the Superior Court has denied him relief, unless it also appears that the remedy by motion is inadequate or ineffective to test the legality of his detention.

On the authority of this provision, the District Court dismissed [Pressley's] application. The Court of Appeals reversed. Largely because of its doubts concerning the constitutionality of a statutory curtailment of the District Court's jurisdiction to issue writs of habeas corpus, the Court of Appeals construed the statute as merely requiring exhaustion of local remedies before a habeas corpus petition could be filed in the District Court[, and remanded the case for merits consideration.]

I

[The Court held that § 23–110(g) does not just require exhaustion of local remedies as a precondition for seeking habeas relief.]

II

[Pressley] argues that § 23–110(g), if read literally, violates Art. I, § 9, cl. 2, of the United States Constitution, which provides: "The Privilege of the Writ of Habeas Corpus shall not be suspended, unless when in Cases of Rebellion or Invasion the public Safety may require it."

His argument is made in two steps: (1) that the substitution of a remedy that is not "exactly commensurate" with habeas corpus relief available in a district court is a suspension of the writ within the meaning of the Clause; and (2) that, because the judges of the Superior Court of the District of Columbia do not enjoy the life tenure and salary protection which are guaranteed to district judges by Art. III, § 1, of the Constitution, the collateral review procedure authorized by § 23–110(g) of the District of Columbia Code is not exactly commensurate with habeas corpus relief in the district courts.

The Government disputes both propositions. First, it contends that the constitutional provision merely prohibits suspension of the writ as it was being used when the Constitution was adopted; at that time, the writ was not employed in collateral attacks on judgments entered by courts of competent jurisdiction. Second, it contends that the procedure authorized by § 23–110(g) is "exactly commensurate" with the preexisting habeas corpus remedy.

We are satisfied that the statute is valid, but we do not rest our decision on either of the broad propositions advanced by the Government. We are persuaded that the final Clause in § 23–110(g) avoids any serious question about the constitutionality of the statute. That clause allows the District Court to entertain a habeas corpus application if it "appears that the remedy by motion is inadequate or ineffective to test the legality of [Pressley's] detention." Thus, the only constitutional question presented is whether the substitution of a new collateral remedy which is both adequate and effective should be regarded as a suspension of the Great Writ within the meaning of the Constitution. The obvious answer to this question is provided by the Court's opinion in *United States v. Hayman*:

> In a case where the Section 2255 procedure is shown to be "inadequate or ineffective," the Section provides that the habeas corpus remedy shall remain open to afford the necessary hearing. Under such circumstances, we do not reach constitutional questions.

The Court implicitly held in *Hayman*, as we hold in this case, that the substitution of a collateral remedy which is neither inadequate nor ineffective to test the legality of a person's detention does not constitute a suspension of the writ of habeas corpus.

The question which remains is whether the remedy in the Superior Court of the District of Columbia created by § 23–110 is "inadequate or ineffective." We have already construed the remedy created by 28 U.S.C. § 2255 as the exact equivalent of the pre-existing habeas corpus remedy. Since the scope of the remedy provided by § 23–210 is the same as that provided by § 2255, it is also commensurate with habeas corpus in all respects save one—the judges who administer it do not have the tenure and salary protection afforded by Art. III of the Constitution.

We are fully cognizant of the critical importance of life tenure, particularly when judges are required to vindicate the constitutional rights of persons who have been found guilty of criminal offenses[, but] the Constitution does not require that all persons charged with federal crimes be tried in Art. III courts. That holding necessarily determines that the judges of the Superior Court of the District of Columbia must be presumed competent to decide all issues, including constitutional issues, that routinely arise in the trial of criminal cases. We must, therefore, presume that the collateral relief available in the Superior Court is neither ineffective nor inadequate simply because the judges of that court do not have life tenure.

This conclusion is consistent with the settled view that elected judges of our state courts are fully competent to decide federal constitutional issues, and that their decisions must be respected by federal district judges in processing habeas corpus applications pursuant to 28 U.S.C. § 2254. Normally a state judge's resolution of a factual issue will be presumed to be correct unless the factfinding procedure employed by the state court was not adequate. It is equally permissible to presume that the judges of the Superior Court of the District of Columbia will correctly resolve constitutional issues unless it has been demonstrated, in accordance with the final clause of § 23–110(g), that the remedy afforded by that court is "inadequate or ineffective."

Finding no reason to doubt the adequacy of the remedy provided by § 23–110, and having noted that its scope is commensurate with habeas corpus relief, we hold that § 23–110(g) has not suspended the writ of habeas corpus within the meaning of Art.I, § 9, cl. 2.

The judgment of the Court of Appeals is reversed.

It is so ordered.

[The opinion of Mr. JUSTICE POWELL, concurring, is omitted.]

■ Mr. CHIEF JUSTICE BURGER, with whom Mr. JUSTICE BLACKMUN and Mr. JUSTICE REHNQUIST Join, concurring in part and concurring in the judgment.

I join Part I of the Court's opinion and concur in the Court's judgment. However, I find it unnecessary to examine the adequacy of the remedy provided by § 23–110(g), for I do not consider that the statute in any way implicates the respondent's rights under the Suspension Clause * * *.

The sweep of the Suspension Clause must be measured by reference to the intention of the Framers and their understanding of what the writ of habeas corpus meant at the time the Constitution was drafted. The scope of the writ during the 17th and 18th centuries has been described as follows:

> [O]nce a person had been convicted by a superior court of general jurisdiction, a court disposing of a habeas corpus petition could not go behind the conviction for any purpose other than to verify the formal jurisdiction of the committing court.

[Dallin] Oaks, *Legal History in the High Court—Habeas Corpus*, 64 MICH. L.REV. 451, 468 (1966). Thus, at common law, the writ was available (1) to compel adherence to prescribed procedures in advance of trial; (2) to inquire into the cause of commitment not pursuant to judicial process; and (3) to inquire whether a committing court had proper jurisdiction. The writ in 1789 was not considered "a means by which one court of general jurisdiction exercises post-conviction review over the judgment of another court of like authority." * * * [I]n defining the scope of federal collateral remedies, the Court has invariably engaged in statutory interpretation, construing what Congress has actually provided, rather than what it constitutionally must provide. Judge Friendly has expressed this view clearly: "It can scarcely be doubted that the writ protected by the suspension clause is the writ as known to the framers, not as Congress may have chosen to expand it or, more pertinently, as the Supreme Court has interpreted what Congress did." Friendly, *Is Innocence Irrelevant? Collateral Attack on Criminal Judgments*, 38 U. Chi. L. Rev. 142, 170 (1970).

Since I do not believe that the Suspension Clause requires Congress to provide a federal remedy for collateral review of a conviction entered by a court of competent jurisdiction, I see no issue of constitutional dimension raised by the statute in question. * * * However, I agree with Part I of the Court's opinion, namely that § 23–110(g) was designed to preclude access to the District Court, not merely to assure exhaustion of local remedies, and I would end the inquiry there. Congress has not provided access to the District Court, and is under no compulsion to do so. I would therefore reverse the judgment on this basis.

———

NOTES AND QUESTIONS ON PRESSLEY

1) **Necessary Versus Sufficient.** In *Pressley*, the Court held that (1) in order for a substitute remedy to be constitutionally adequate and effective to test the lawfulness of detention, it does not need to be "exactly commensurate" with habeas relief; and (2) the absence of Article III restrictions on salary and life tenure did not render a remedy inadequate or ineffective. Even if a substitute remedy is constitutional because it is adequate and effective to test detention, does that mean the substitute remedy is *unconstitutional* when it is *not adequate or effective* to test detention? Do you think there are situations where Congress may constitutionally restrict remedies for detention in ways that render them less efficacious than habeas remedies?

2) **Originalism and the Suspension Clause.** In Chief Justice Burger's dissent, you again see the twin propositions that (1) the Suspension Clause protects the habeas remedy as understood in 1789, and (2) the scope of the remedy at that time did not include post-conviction review. Subsequent Chapters will explore both the interpretive and historical cases to be made for each proposition.

3) **Adequacy and Article III appointments.** Do you think that losing the opportunity to present a claim to a federal, life-tenured Article III judge is a constitutional concern? Does the absence of Article III protection for judges render a substitute remedy inadequate or ineffective? Inadequate and ineffective in what sense—to adjudicate criminal liability under a federal statute or to perform functions analogous to a habeas corpus proceeding? The Supreme Court is certainly correct in observing that non-Article III courts routinely decide cases under federal law. What implications does that observation have for the adequacy-and-effectiveness inquiry?

4) **Post-9/11 Detention.** Detentions following the September 11, 2001 attacks produced a series of decisions involving the substantive constitutional rights of detainees, as well as the degree to which they should have access to habeas as a vehicle for asserting those rights. The decisions culminated in *Boumediene v. Bush*, 553 U.S. 723 (2008), probably the most important Suspension Clause case in American constitutional law. *Boumediene* is extensively excerpted and analyzed in Chapter 10. You should briefly understand the connection to *Hayman* and *Swain* here. In 2006, the Military Commissions Act ("MCA") stripped the federal district courts of habeas jurisdiction over GTMO detention. In *Boumediene*, all nine Justices appeared to agree that a habeas

restriction, other than a suspension, was unconstitutional if it was an inadequate substitute for habeas corpus. The Justices then split 5–4 on the issue of whether the process provided to GTMO prisoners, pursuant to Department of Defense procedures and Congressional legislation, was adequate and effective. The majority relied on *Hayman* and *Swain* not just to support the holding that the Suspension Clause prohibited Congress from replacing habeas with an inadequate and ineffective substitute, but also to contrast the process provided to GTMO prisoners with the process under the pertinent post-conviction statutes—process that was not intended to narrow the scope of judicial review.

B. RESTRICTIONS ON HABEAS RELIEF FOR STATE PRISONERS

Courts and habeas scholars disagree about the Constitution's habeas requirements on many fronts, but a point of near-unanimous consensus is that the Constitution did not require federal habeas relief for state prisoners, at least during the first part of the nineteenth century. The scope of the modern federal habeas remedy for state imprisonment is nonetheless a source of considerable dispute, for at least two reasons. First, over the course of American history, Congress has gradually used statutes to make the federal writ available to state prisoners. That process creates myriad questions of statutory interpretation that play a significant role in cases featured in subsequent Chapters. Second, when modern laws restrict habeas access for state prisoners, they raise the question whether the Constitution now protects federal review of state confinement.

———

INTRODUCTORY NOTES ON AEDPA AND HABEAS RELIEF FOR STATE PRISONERS

1) The Historical Availability of Habeas Relief for State Prisoners. Under the terms of the 1789 Judiciary Act, habeas relief was not available for prisoners convicted by a state court of general jurisdiction. In two pieces of pre-Civil War legislation, Congress created limited statutory entitlements to federal habeas review of state detention. First, in response to South Carolina's threats to "nullify" federal tax law, Congress passed the 1833 Force Act, which allowed federal officers (e.g., tax collectors) to obtain federal habeas relief were they to be detained by a State. 4 Stat. 632 (1833).[w] Second, in response to a diplomatic debacle, Congress passed the Habeas Act of 1842. 5 Stat 539 (1842).[x]

The Habeas Corpus Act of 1867, however, forever altered the balance of power between the federal government and the states. First and foremost, the 1867 Act extended the habeas jurisdiction of the federal courts to include re-

---

[w] Because South Carolina never nullified the federal law, the 1833 Force Act was never used for its intended purpose. Instead, the Force Act was used primarily by federal officials arrested in Northern states for enforcing the Fugitive Slave Act.

[x] Alexander McLeod was a British citizen indicted by a New York Court for his role in the British assault on the *Caroline*, a ship bringing supplies to Canadian insurgents fighting the British in Ontario. McLeod had been acting on direct orders of the Crown, and most historians believe that, had he not been acquitted by the New York Court, American and England would have gone to war. After McLeod's acquittal, New York arrested another participant in the *Caroline* raid. Congress then enacted legislation that allowed a state prisoner to obtain federal habeas review where the prisoner claimed to have been acting under color of a foreign state's authority.

view of state criminal confinement. 14 Stat. 385 (1867). There remains an ongoing dispute as to the degree of review the federal courts were intended to conduct under that statute—whether they were to grant relief only for jurisdictional error, for failure to conduct full and fair process, or for any constitutional
infirmity. Compare Paul M. Bator, *Finality in Criminal Law and Federal Habeas Corpus for State Prisoners*, 76 Harv. L. Rev. 441 (1963) (arguing that habeas review was confined only to jurisdictional error and instances where state
courts failed to provide full and fair review), with Gary Peller, *In Defense of
Federal Habeas Corpus Relitigation*, 16 Harv. Civ. R. and Civ. L. L. Rev 579
(1982) (arguing that observed absence of habeas relief for procedural error was
in fact attributable to a narrower conception of due process, rather than to any
limit on the habeas remedy). The strength of each account will consume much
of Chapter 3, but for now you should understand (1) that the 1867 Habeas Corpus Act statutorily entitled convicted state prisoners to federal habeas review,
and (2) that the scope of the review to which they were entitled under the 1867
statute remains hotly disputed.

2)   AEDPA and the Abuse-of-the Writ Doctrine. After the Oklahoma City
bombing, Congress passed AEDPA by overwhelming majorities. AEDPA is the
starting point for most federal post-conviction inquiry. One of the things
AEDPA did was reconstitute the judicially-created "abuse-of-the-writ" defense
as a jurisdictional bar. "Abuse-of-the-writ" was a state defense asserted when a
habeas petitioner made a claim for the first time in a "successive" petition. The
term "abuse-of-the-writ" can be misleading, because there might be perfectly
legitimate reasons for failing to include a claim in a prior petition. For example,
the factual or legal basis for the claim might have been unavailable when the
first petition was filed. For that reason, the judicially-created rule allowed
claims asserted for the first time to proceed in certain circumstances. AEDPA
modified 28 U.S.C. § 2244(b)(2), which gives statutory form to the abuse-of-the
writ rule, and to some of the exceptions to it. The following excerpt from *Felker
v. Turpin*, 518 U.S. 1051 (1996), considers whether the AEDPA's statutory restrictions on federal habeas relief for state prisoners are unconstitutional under
the Suspension Clause.

Felker v. Turpin (Suspension Clause Holding)
United States Supreme Court
518 U.S. 651 (1996)

■ CHIEF JUSTICE REHNQUIST delivered the opinion of the Court.

[A jury convicted Wayne Felker of murder, rape, aggravated sodomy,
and false imprisonment; it sentenced him to death. The Georgia Supreme
Court affirmed his conviction and sentence, and the U.S. Supreme Court
denied certiorari. A state trial court denied collateral relief, and no other
court exercised discretionary appellate review. The Petitioner was unable
to obtain relief in his initial federal habeas proceeding.]

* * * [AEDPA] Subsections 106(b)(1) and (b)(2) specify the conditions
under which claims in second or successive applications must be dismissed,
amending 28 U.S.C. § 2244(b) to read:

(1) A claim presented in a second or successive habeas corpus application under section 2254 that was presented in a prior application shall
be dismissed.

(2) A claim presented in a second or successive habeas corpus application under section 2254 that was not presented in a prior application shall be dismissed unless

    (A) the applicant shows that the claim relies on a new rule of constitutional law, made retroactive to cases on collateral review by the Supreme Court, that was previously unavailable; or

    (B) (i) the factual predicate for the claim could not have been discovered previously through the exercise of due diligence; and

        (ii) the facts underlying the claim, if proven and viewed in light of the evidence as a whole, would be sufficient to establish by clear and convincing evidence that, but for constitutional error, no reasonable factfinder would have found the applicant guilty of the underlying offense.

* * * On May 2, 1996, petitioner filed in the United States Court of Appeals for the Eleventh Circuit a motion for stay of execution and a motion for leave to file a second or successive federal habeas corpus petition under § 2254. Petitioner sought to raise two claims in his second petition, the first being that the state trial court violated due process by equating guilt "beyond a reasonable doubt" with "moral certainty" of guilt in *voir dire* and jury instructions. He also alleged [that post-conviction expert reports established a colorable claim of actual innocence].

The Court of Appeals denied both motions the day they were filed, concluding that petitioner's claims had not been presented in his first habeas petition, that they did not meet the standards of [§ 2244(b)(2)], and that they would not have satisfied pre-Act standards for obtaining review on the merits of second or successive claims. Petitioner filed in this Court a pleading styled a "Petition for Writ of Habeas Corpus, for Appellate or Certiorari Review of the Decision of the United States Circuit Court for the Eleventh Circuit, and for Stay of Execution." On May 3, we granted petitioner's stay application and petition for certiorari.

* * * [W]e consider whether [AEDPA] suspends the writ of habeas corpus in violation of Article I, § 9, clause 2, of the Constitution. This clause provides that "[t]he Privilege of the Writ of Habeas Corpus shall not be suspended, unless when in Cases of Rebellion or Invasion the public Safety may require it."

The writ of habeas corpus known to the Framers was quite different from that which exists today. As we explained previously, the first Congress made the writ of habeas corpus available only to prisoners confined under the authority of the United States, not under state authority. The class of judicial actions reviewable by the writ was more restricted as well. In *Ex parte Watkins*, 3 Pet. 193 (1830), we denied a petition for a writ of habeas corpus from a prisoner "detained in prison by virtue of the judgment of a court, which court possesses general and final jurisdiction in criminal cases." Reviewing the English common law which informed American courts' understanding of the scope of the writ, we held that "[t]he judgment of the circuit court in a criminal case is of itself evidence of its own legality," and that we could not "usurp that power by the instrumentality of the writ of habeas corpus."

It was not until 1867 that Congress made the writ generally available in "all cases where any person may be restrained of his or her liberty in violation of the constitution, or of any treaty or law of the United States." And it was not until well into this century that this Court interpreted that provision to allow a final judgment of conviction in a state court to be collaterally attacked on habeas. But we assume, for purposes of decision here, that the Suspension Clause of the Constitution refers to the writ as it exists today, rather than as it existed in 1789.

The Act requires a habeas petitioner to obtain leave from the court of appeals before filing a second habeas petition in the district court. But this requirement simply transfers from the district court to the court of appeals a screening function which would previously have been performed by the district court as required by 28 U.S.C. § 2254 Rule 9(b). The Act also codifies some of the pre-existing limits on successive petitions, and further restricts the availability of relief to habeas petitioners. But we have long recognized that "the power to award the writ by any of the courts of the United States, must be given by written law," *Ex parte Bollman*, 4 Cranch 75, 94 (1807), and we have likewise recognized that judgments about the proper scope of the "writ are normally for Congress to make."

The new restrictions on successive petitions constitute a modified *res judicata* rule, a restraint on what is called in habeas corpus practice "abuse of the writ." In *McCleskey v. Zant*, 499 U.S. 467 (1991), we said that "the doctrine of abuse of the writ refers to a complex and evolving body of equitable principles informed and controlled by historical usage, statutory developments, and judicial decisions." The added restrictions which the Act places on second habeas petitions are well within the compass of this evolutionary process, and we hold that they do not amount to a "suspension" of the writ contrary to Article I, § 9.

[The Court denies the original habeas writ on the merits.]

It is so ordered.

———

NOTES AND QUESTIONS ON FELKER

1)   **The Writ as it Exists Today.** The Supreme Court did not assume that the constitutionally-required scope of the writ is confined to what it was in 1789. Instead, the Court assumed *arguendo* that the constitutionally-required scope of the writ has "evolved." The Court then described that "evolutionary process" in some detail. Why does the Court assume *arguendo* that the scope of the writ's constitutional protection was fixed in 1789 for some cases, and assume *arguendo* that it evolves for others? When the Court decided *Boumediene*, it took a similar tack by assuming *arguendo* that the privilege protected by the Constitution *did not* grow over time, and that even an originalist interpretation of the Clause would have required a habeas remedy for the detainees in question. What do you think of the Court's failure to commit to an interpretive rule? Is the uncertainty good for litigants or other courts? Is there some other reason why it might be desirable?

2)   **Post-Felker claims that AEDPA Suspended the Privilege.** On multiple occasions, the Supreme Court has been presented with the opportunity to hold that the Constitution does not compel state post-conviction review. It has thus far declined to do so. If you believe that the Constitution does not oblige Congress to provide a federal habeas remedy for state prisoners, then is there any Article III problem with limiting such a remedy? In other words, should the power to withhold the greater include the power to withhold the lesser?

3)   Ellis Wayne Felker. Felker was executed in 1996. In 2000, a Georgia judge ruled that DNA testing would be performed posthumously. Such a procedure marked the first time that forensic experts attempted post-execution DNA testing in the United States. The results were inconclusive—they neither inculpated nor exculpated Felker.[y] No court needed to reach the question, then, of whether to posthumously vacate a conviction.

5. FEDERAL SUPREMACY AND STATE HABEAS

The degree to which state courts have historically exercised habeas authority—particularly over federal custody—figures prominently in the development of constitutional habeas law. First, a number of influential scholars have argued that the Suspension Clause protected the power of state courts to conduct habeas review of federal custody. Second, decisions about state habeas review had featured roles in developing federal Supremacy doctrine before, during, and after the Civil War. Section 5 explores this material.

INTRODUCTORY NOTES ON ANTEBELLUM STATE HABEAS AND ABLEMAN V. BOOTH

This Book has thus far focused on the habeas power of federal judges, but state judges can also issue habeas writs. Modern state judges can generally issue writs for prisoners detained under color of state law, but can no longer do so for federal detention. Federal prisoners, however, were not always beyond the reach of state habeas process. Two United States Supreme Court cases out of Wisconsin, bookending the Civil War, foreclosed state judges from using habeas writs to review federal custody.

The Suspension Clause directly precedes a clause specifying rules for "migration and importation" of slaves, and the relationship of antebellum state habeas to federal detention in many ways reflects the struggle over slavery. The Fugitive Slave Act of 1793 provided for extraterritorial capture and rendition of slaves. Northern States passed laws that criminalized fugitive slave capture, but the Supreme Court held such laws unconstitutional in *Prigg v. Pennsylvania*, 41 U.S. 539 (1842). Following *Prigg* and through "personal liberty laws," many Northern States passed statutes that—although not criminalizing slave recapture—prohibited the use of state law enforcement resources to enforce it. The insistence by Northern States that the Fugitive Slave Act be enforced only with federal resources precipitated the Compromise of 1850, which actually consisted of four statutes. One of those statutes was, colloquially, an 1850 Fugitive Slave Act, which neutered the post-*Prigg* personal liberty laws and enraged constituencies in Northern States.[z]

Two types of habeas power figured prominently in the post-1850 fight over slavery: (1) federal habeas power over state custody, and (2) state habeas power over federal custody. First, federal judges used habeas writs to free from state confinement U.S. Marshals who were responsible for enforcing the various

---

[y] See Sharon E. Crawford, *Felker Fingernail Scrapings Test Proves Inconclusive*, Macon Telegraph, Dec. 12, 2000.

[z] See Fugitive Slave Act, ch. 60, §§ 1–10 9 Stat. 462 (1850) (repealed 1864).

statutory and constitutional fugitive slave provisions. Specifically, Northern States more systematically arrested federal officers who effectuated violent slave recapture. Eventually, because the federal officers were enforcing federal law, they successfully invoked the habeas provisions of the 1833 "Force Act"— originally passed to allow federal tax collectors to remove South Carolina cases to federal court during the nullification controversy—to secure their release.

In 1854, United States Marshal Stephen Ableman arrested abolitionist Sherman Booth for aiding a fugitive slave's escape to Canada. Ableman had given fiery speeches that incited an angry crowd to break into the jail and free the slave.[aa] Booth was held under a federal judicial warrant issued under the 1850 Fugitive Slave Act. The federal commissioner committed Booth to the custody of Ableman, a U.S. Marshal. The day after Booth's commitment, he applied to a Wisconsin Supreme Court Justice for a habeas writ, arguing that the 1850 Fugitive Slave Act was unconstitutional. The Wisconsin Justice issued the writ, and Ableman made his return and produced Booth. The Wisconsin judge took umbrage at the "degrading insinuation" that state judges could not decide federal subject matter, and asserted a solemn responsibility "to interpose a resistance . . . to every assumption of power on the part of the general government, which is not expressly granted or necessarily implied in the federal constitution." In re Booth, 3 Wis. 1, 23, 35 (1854) (Smith, J.). Then, the Wisconsin Supreme Court, finding the Fugitive Slave Act unconstitutional, issued state habeas relief to free Booth. The U.S. Supreme Court issued a writ of error to review the case, and Wisconsin complied.

Before the Supreme Court completed appellate review in that case, however, a Wisconsin federal district court convicted and sentenced Booth. Booth again sought habeas relief in the Wisconsin Supreme Court, arguing that (1) the fugitive slave laws were unconstitutional, (2) the district court had no jurisdiction to try or punish him, and (3) the trial and sentence were nullities. The Wisconsin Supreme Court issued the writ, decided that Booth's detention was illegal, and ordered him discharged.

No counsel appeared for Wisconsin before the U.S. Supreme Court, but the Court deemed the certified records sufficient to adjudicate the disputes. In the first case, the Wisconsin courts claimed habeas authority to discharge a prisoner committed by a federal commissioner pending trial. In the second case, the Wisconsin courts claimed habeas authority to void the conviction of a jurisdictionally-competent federal court. In the second case, the Wisconsin Supreme Court instructed the state clerk to ignore the writ of error from the Supreme Court, issued to conduct appellate review. The U.S. Supreme Court, reviewing the case on writ of error, finally resolved *Ableman v. Booth* against Wisconsin four years later, in an opinion by Chief Justice Roger Taney. As you read the opinion, pay attention to the grounds upon which the court invalidates the Wisconsin writ.

[aa] For a vivid description of the underlying events leading to both *Booth* and *Tarble*, see Ann Woolhandler and Michael G. Collins, *The Story of* Tarble's Case: *State Habeas and Federal Detention*, in Federal Courts Stories (Vicki C. Jackson & Judith Resnik eds., 2009). For a broader history of the litigation challenging the legality of Reconstruction, see Charles Fairman, *Reconstruction and Reunion, 1864–1888* (1971).

Ableman v. Booth

United States Supreme Court
62 U.S. 506 (1859)

■ CHIEF JUSTICE TANEY delivered the opinion of the court.

* * * [T]he supremacy of the State courts over the courts of the United States, in cases arising under the Constitution and laws of the United States, is now for the first time asserted and acted upon in the Supreme Court of a State.

* * * [T]heir commentaries upon the provisions of [the fugitive slave] law, and upon the privileges and power of the writ of habeas corpus, were out of place, and their judicial action upon them without authority of law, unless they had the power to revise and control the proceedings in the criminal case of which they were speaking, and their judgments releasing the prisoner and disregarding the writ of error from this court can rest upon no other foundation.

If the judicial power exercised in this instance has been reserved to the States, no offence against the laws of the United States can be punished by their own courts without the permission and according to the judgment of the courts of the State in which the party happens to be imprisoned, for if the Supreme Court of Wisconsin possessed the power it has exercised in relation to offences against the act of Congress in question, it necessarily follows that they must have the same judicial authority in relation to any other law of the United States, and, consequently, their supervising and controlling power would embrace the whole criminal code of the United States, and extend to offences against our revenue laws, or any other law intended to guard the different departments of the General Government from fraud or violence. And it would embrace all crimes, from the highest to the lowest; including felonies, which are punished with death, as well as misdemeanors, which are punished by imprisonment. And, moreover, if the power is possessed by the Supreme Court of the State of Wisconsin, it must belong equally to every other State in the Union when the prisoner is within its territorial limits, and it is very certain that the State courts would not always agree in opinion, and it would often happen that an act which was admitted to be an offence, and justly punished, in one State would be regarded as innocent, and indeed as praiseworthy, in another.

[A statement of that result] is, of itself, a sufficient and conclusive answer, for no one will suppose that a Government which has now lasted nearly seventy years, enforcing its laws by its own tribunals and preserving the union of the States, could have lasted a single year, or fulfilled the high trusts committed to it, if offences against its laws could not have been punished without the consent of the State in which the culprit was found.

* * * There can be no such thing as judicial authority unless it is conferred by a Government or sovereignty, and if the judges and courts of Wisconsin possess the jurisdiction they claim, they must derive it either from the United States or the State. It certainly has not been conferred on them by the United States, and * * * no State can authorize one of its judges or courts to exercise judicial power, by habeas corpus or otherwise, within the jurisdiction of another and independent Government. [Wisconsin's] sovereignty is limited and restricted by the Constitution of the United States. And the powers of the General Government, and of the State, although both exist and are exercised within the same territorial limits, are yet separate and distinct sovereignties, acting separately and independently of each other within their respective spheres. * * *

But * * * questions of this kind must always depend upon the Constitution and laws of the United States, and not of a State. * * * [It] was felt by the [framers and adopters of the U.S. Constitution] that it was necessary that many of the rights of sovereignty which the States then possessed should be ceded to the General Government, and that, in the sphere of action assigned to it, it should be supreme, and strong enough to execute its own laws by its own tribunals, without interruption from a State or from State authorities. And it was evident that anything short of this would be inadequate to the main objects for which the Government was established, and that local interests, local passions or prejudices, incited and fostered by individuals for sinister purposes, would lead to acts of aggression and injustice by one State upon the rights of another, which would ultimately terminate in violence and force unless there was a common arbiter between them, armed with power enough to protect and guard the rights of all by appropriate laws to be carried into execution peacefully by its judicial tribunals.

The language of the Constitution by which this power is granted is too plain to admit of doubt or to need comment. It declares that[:]

> [T]his Constitution, and the laws of the United States which shall be passed in pursuance thereof, and all treaties made, or which shall be made, under the authority of the United States, shall be the supreme law of the land, and the judges in every State shall be bound thereby, anything in the Constitution or laws of any State to the contrary notwithstanding.

But the supremacy thus conferred on this Government could not peacefully be maintained unless it was clothed with judicial power equally paramount in authority to carry it into execution, for if left to the courts of justice of the several States, conflicting decisions would unavoidably take place, and the local tribunals could hardly be expected to be always free from the local influences of which we have spoken. And the Constitution and laws and treaties of the United States, and the powers granted to the Federal Government, would soon receive different interpretations in different States, and the Government of the United States would soon become one thing in one State and another thing in another. It was essential, therefore, * * * that a tribunal should be established in which all cases which might arise under the Constitution and laws and treaties of the United States, whether in a State court or a court of the United States, should be finally and conclusively decided. Without such a tribunal, * * * there would be no uniformity of judicial decision, and that the supremacy, (which is but another name for independence) so carefully provided in the clause of the Constitution above referred to could not possibly be maintained peacefully unless it was associated with this paramount judicial authority.

Accordingly, [the U.S. Constitution declares] that its judicial power shall (among other subjects enumerated) extend to all cases in law and equity arising under the Constitution and laws of the United States, and that, in such cases, as well as the others there enumerated, this court shall have appellate jurisdiction both as to law and fact, with such exceptions and under such regulations as Congress shall make. The appellate power, it will be observed, is conferred on this court in all cases or suits in which such a question shall arise. It is not confined to suits in the inferior courts of the United States, but extends to all cases where such a question arises, whether it be in a judicial tribunal of a State or of the United States. And it is manifest that this ultimate appellate power in a tribunal created by the Constitution itself was deemed essential to secure the independence and supremacy of the General Government in the sphere of action assigned to it, to make the Constitution and laws of the United States uniform, and the same in every State, and to guard against evils which would inevitably arise from conflicting opinions between the courts of a State and of the United States, if there was no common arbiter authorized to decide between them.

The importance which the framers of the Constitution attached to such a tribunal [is demonstrated by the Clause sensibly requiring that State parties submit to the jurisdiction of the Supreme Court.]

The same purposes are clearly indicated by the different language employed when conferring supremacy upon the laws of the United States, and jurisdiction upon its courts. In the first case, it provides that this Constitution, and the laws of the United States which shall be made in pursuance thereof, shall be the supreme law of the land, and obligatory upon the judges in every State.

* * * And as the courts of a State, and the courts of the United States, might, and indeed certainly would, often differ as to the extent of the powers conferred by the General Government, it was manifest that serious controversies would arise between the authorities of the United States and of the States, which must be settled by force of arms unless some tribunal was created to decide between them finally and with out appeal.

The Constitution has accordingly provided, as far as human foresight could provide, against this danger. And, in conferring judicial power upon the Federal Government, it declares that the jurisdiction of its courts shall extend to all cases arising under "this Constitution" and the laws of the United States * * *. The judicial power covers every legislative act of Congress, whether it be made within the limits of its delegated powers or be an assumption of power beyond the grants in the Constitution.

This judicial power was justly regarded as indispensable not merely to maintain the supremacy of the laws of the United States, but also to guard the States from any encroachment upon their reserved rights by the General Government. And as the Constitution is the fundamental and supreme law, if it appears that an act of Congress is not pursuant to and within the limits of the power assigned to the Federal Government, it is the duty of the courts of the United States to declare it unconstitutional and void * * *.

In organizing [the Supreme Court to be the highest appellate tribunal], * * * it was not left to Congress to create it by law, for the States could hardly be expected to confide in the impartiality of a tribunal created exclusively by the General Government without any participation on their part. * * * So long, therefore, as this Constitution shall endure, this tribunal must exist with it . * * *

* * * [A]rticle 1, section 8, paragraph 18, in the following words: "To make all laws which shall be necessary and proper to carry into execution the foregoing powers, and all other powers vested by this Constitution in the Government of the United States, or in any department or officer thereof." * * * [B]y the 25th section of the act of 1789, Congress authorized writs of error to be issued from this court to a State court whenever a right had been claimed under the Constitution or laws of the United States and the decision of the State court was against it. And to make this appellate

power effectual and altogether independent of the action of State tribunals, this act further provides that, upon writs of error to a State court, instead of remanding the cause for a final decision in the State court, this court may, at their discretion, if the cause shall have been once remanded before, proceed to a final decision of the same and award execution. * * *

In the case before the Supreme Court of Wisconsin, a right was claimed under the Constitution and laws of the United States, and the decision was against the right claimed, and it refuses obedience to the writ of error, and regards its own judgment as final. It has not only reversed and annulled the judgment of the District Court of the United States, but it has reversed and annulled the provisions of the Constitution itself, and the act of Congress of 1789, and made the superior and appellate tribunal the inferior and subordinate one.

We do not question the authority of State court or judge who is authorized by the laws of the State to issue the writ of habeas corpus to issue it in any case where the party is imprisoned within its territorial limits, provided it does not appear, when the application is made, that the person imprisoned is in custody under the authority of the United States. * * * But, after the return is made and the State judge or court judicially apprized that the party is in custody under the authority of the United States, they can proceed no further. They then know that the prisoner is within the dominion and jurisdiction of another Government, and that neither the writ of habeas corpus nor any other process issued under State authority can pass over the line of division between the two sovereignties. * * * If he has committed an offence against their laws, their tribunals alone can punish him. If he is wrongfully imprisoned, their judicial tribunals can release him and afford him redress. And although, as we have said, it is the duty of the marshal or other person holding him to make known, by a proper return, the authority under which he detains him, it is at the same time imperatively his duty to obey the process of the United States, to hold the prisoner in custody under it, and to refuse obedience to the mandate or process of any other Government. * * * [I]f the authority of a State, in the form of judicial process or otherwise, should attempt to control the marshal or other authorized officer or agent of the United States in any respect, in the custody of his prisoner, it would be his duty to resist it, and to call to his aid any force that might be necessary to maintain the authority of law against illegal interference. No judicial process, whatever form it may assume, can have any lawful authority outside of the limits of the jurisdiction of the court or judge by whom it is issued, and an attempt to enforce it beyond these boundaries is nothing less than lawless violence. * * *

* * * [I]f there was any defect of power in the commissioner, or in his mode of proceeding, it was for the tribunals of the United States to revise and correct it, and not for a State court. And as regards the decision of the District Court, it had exclusive and final jurisdiction by the laws of the United States, and neither the regularity of its proceedings nor the validity of its sentence could be called in question in any other court, either of a State or the United States, by habeas corpus or any other process.

[The Court then held the Fugitive Slave Law to be constitutional.]

The judgment of the Supreme Court of Wisconsin must therefore be reversed * * * .

NOTES AND QUESTIONS ON ABLEMAN

1)   The Supreme Court Supreme. The United States Supreme Court was perfectly able, and did, reverse the Wisconsin Supreme Court on appeal. The U.S. Supreme Court used writ-of-error procedure to address both the state court's habeas grant as well as the merits of the state-court ruling on the constitutionality of the Fugitive Slave Act. Why, then, was it necessary to create a blanket rule that state courts may not grant habeas relief to federal convicts? State courts ordinarily hear federal claims. Was there anything inadequate about the Article III process by which the Supreme Court may normally review state supreme court decisions on appeal?

2)   *Ableman's* View of Federalism. The Court wrote, "the powers of the General Government, and of the State, although both exist and are exercised within the same territorial limits, are yet separate and distinct sovereignties, acting separately and independently of each other within their respective spheres." The notion of separate spheres may describe some aspects of our federal system, but does it describe how the separate court systems interact? After all, state courts hear Article III subject matter routinely. Indeed, all "federal question" claims under the U.S. Constitution were brought, following the First Judiciary Act, in state courts. Such claims could implicate the sovereign authority of the federal government. Again, why are claims raised in habeas petitions any different?

3)   The Role of a Federal Conviction. To what extent is *Booth* a rule about the availability of state habeas relief for federal prisoners *subject to a criminal conviction*, and to what extent is *Booth* a rule about the availability of habeas relief to *any* federal prisoners? In other words, after *Booth*, would a prisoner in the federal custody of an executive officer and not subject to a criminal judgment be able to avail himself of state habeas relief? Could a federal court have issued a habeas writ to review the criminal judgment of the federal court sitting in Wisconsin?

4)   Refusing to Appear. Chief Justice Taney was clearly infuriated by Wisconsin's failure to respond to the writ of error. To what extent does that circumstance limit some of *Booth's* applicability? If the concern with treating fifty different state courts as "supreme" is attributable to the idea that they do not participate in proceedings before the United States Supreme Court, then is such logic equally applicable where a State *does* respond to a writ of error?

5)   Booth. Booth was later pardoned by President Buchanan, after remaining in custody when he completed his sentence for refusing to pay the $1,000 fine under the Fugitive Slave Act.[bb]

NOTES ON ABLEMAN'S *AFTERMATH AND INTRODUCTION TO* TARBLE'S CASE

Did *Booth* spell the end of state review of federal custody? In the years immediately following *Booth*, many courts read it narrowly as barring only the exercise of state habeas jurisdiction over inmates subject to federal criminal convictions. See Todd E. Pettys, *State Habeas Relief for Federal Extrajudicial*

[bb] See Woolhandler and Collins, *The Story of Tarble's Case*, supra note aa, at 148.

Detainees, 92 Minn. L. Rev. 265, 284–87 (2007). At first glance, this reading seems implausible, as the opinion devotes considerable space to the *Booth* case involving no federal conviction. Is it possible to read the "first" case, *Ableman v. Booth*, as dicta in light of the opinion in the "second" case, *United States v. Booth*? The motivation for reading *Booth* narrowly might have come from something else—the sense that, when the framers barred a privilege against suspension, they meant to preserve the well-established role of state habeas practice at the founding. The Supreme Court finally decided the question of *Booth's* breadth and the surviving state habeas authority in *Tarble's Case*, 80 U.S. 397 (1871), which is excerpted below.

Tarble's Case
United States Supreme Court
80 U.S. (13 Wall.) 397 (1871)

■ Mr. JUSTICE FIELD delivered the opinion of the Court.

[A military recruiting officer held Edward Tarble, who was awaiting military trial for desertion and for swearing a false oath that he was twenty-one when he enlisted. Tarble's father sought state habeas relief from a Wisconsin state commissioner, alleging that Tarble was held unlawfully because he had enlisted under a false name without his father's knowledge and consent. The petition also alleged that Tarble's confinement was in violation of a federal statute requiring his father's consent for enlistment. The Wisconsin state judge ordered Tarble's release. The Wisconsin Supreme Court affirmed the ruling, and the United States Supreme Court issued a writ of error to review the case.]

* * * The question presented may be more generally stated thus: whether any judicial officer of a state has jurisdiction to issue a writ of habeas corpus or to continue proceedings under the writ when issued for the discharge of a person held under the authority, or claim and color of the authority, of the United States by an officer of that government. * * * It may even reach to parties imprisoned under sentence of the national courts, after regular indictment, trial, and conviction, for offenses against the laws of the United States. * * * [The Supreme Court of Wisconsin] asserts * * * the right to determine upon habeas corpus in all cases whether that court ever had such jurisdiction. In the case of *Booth*, which subsequently came before this Court, it not only sustained the action of one of its justices in discharging a prisoner held in custody by a marshal of the United States under a warrant of commitment for an offense against the laws of the United States issued by a commissioner of the United States, but it discharged the same prisoner when subsequently confined under sentence of the district court of the United States for the same offense, after indictment, trial, and conviction, on the ground that in its judgment the act of Congress creating the offense was unconstitutional, and in order that its decision in that respect should be final and conclusive, directed its clerk to refuse obedience to the writ of error issued by this Court, under the act of Congress, to b[r]ing up the decision for review.

It is evident [from the decision in *Booth* that], if the power asserted by that state court existed, no offense against the laws of the United States could be punished by their own tribunals without the permission and according to the judgment of the courts of the state in which the parties happen to be imprisoned[.] * * *

* * * There are within the territorial limits of each state two governments, restricted in their spheres of action but independent of each other and supreme within their respective spheres. Each has its separate departments, each has its distinct laws, and each has its own tribunals for their enforcement. Neither government can intrude within the jurisdiction, or authorize any interference therein by its judicial officers with the action of the other. The two governments in each state stand in their respective spheres of action in the same independent relation to each other, except in one particular, that they would if their authority embraced distinct territories. That particular consists in the supremacy of the authority of the United States when any conflict arises between the two governments. * * *

Whenever, therefore, any conflict arises between the enactments of the two sovereignties or in the enforcement of their asserted authorities, those of the national government must have supremacy until the validity of the different enactments and authorities can be finally determined by the tribunals of the United States. This temporary supremacy until judicial decision by the national tribunals, and the ultimate determination of the conflict by such decision, are essential to the preservation of order and peace, and the avoidance of forcible collision between the two governments. * * *

Such being the distinct and independent character of the two governments within their respective spheres of action, it follows that neither can intrude with its judicial process into the domain of the other except so far as such intrusion may be necessary on the part of the national government to preserve its rightful supremacy in cases of conflict of authority. * * *

[The Supreme Court held that the power to punish enlistment violations is necessary and proper to both the power "to raise and support armies" and the power "to provide for the government and regulation of the land and naval forces." Fearing post-Civil War hostility towards national government, it also held that appellate proceedings would be insufficient to remedy erroneous state action.]

State judges and state courts, authorized by laws of their states to issue writs of habeas corpus, have undoubtedly a right to issue the writ in any case where a party is alleged to be illegally confined within their limits, unless it appear upon his application that he is confined under the authority or claim and color of the authority of the United States by an officer of that government. If such fact appear upon the application, the writ should be refused. If it do not appear, the judge or court issuing the writ has a right to inquire into the cause of imprisonment and ascertain by what authority the person is held within the limits of the state, and it is the duty of the marshal or other officer having the custody of the prisoner to give, by a proper return, information in this respect. His return should be sufficient in its detail of facts to show distinctly that the imprisonment is under the authority or claim and color of the authority of the United States and to exclude the suspicion of imposition or oppression on his part. And the process or orders under which the prisoner is held should be produced with the return and submitted to inspection in order that the court or judge issuing the writ may see that the prisoner is held by the officer in good faith under the authority or claim and color of the authority of the United States, and not under the mere pretense of having such authority.

[The Court quotes *Ableman* extensively for the proposition that habeas cannot allow one sovereignty to adjudicate questions arising under the other's laws.]

Some attempt has been made in adjudications, to which our attention has been called, to limit the decision of this Court in *Ableman v. Booth* and *United States v. Booth* to cases where a prisoner is held in custody under undisputed lawful authority of the United States, as distinguished from his imprisonment under claim and color of such authority. But it is evident that the decision does not admit of any such limitation. It would have been unnecessary to enforce by any extended reasoning such as the Chief Justice uses, the position that when it appeared to the judge or officer issuing the writ that the prisoner was held under undisputed lawful authority, he should proceed no further. No federal judge even could, in such case, release the party from imprisonment except upon bail when that was allowable. The detention being by admitted lawful authority, no judge could set the prisoner at liberty except in that way at any stage of the proceeding. All that is meant by the language used is that the state judge or state court should proceed no further when it appears from the application of the party or the return made that the prisoner is held by an officer of the United States under what in truth purports to be the authority of the United States—that is, an authority, the validity of which is to be determined by the Constitution and laws of the United States. If a party thus held be illegally imprisoned it is for the courts or judicial officers of the United States, and those courts or officers alone, to grant him release.

* * * The United States are as much interested in protecting the citizen from illegal restraint under their authority, as the several states are to protect him from the like restraint under their authority, and are no more likely to tolerate any oppression. Their courts and judicial officers are clothed with the power to issue the writ of habeas corpus in all cases where a party is illegally restrained of his liberty by an officer of the United States, whether such illegality consist in the character of the process, the authority of the officer, or the invalidity of the law under which he is held. * * *

[The Court held that the state court lacked jurisdiction to issue the writ because it appeared from the face of the application that Tarble was detained under color of federal authority, and therefore declined to reach evidentiary issues involving Tarble's age.]

Judgment reversed.

■ Chief JUSTICE CHASE, dissenting.

[Chief Justice Chase first stated that state courts had the right to scrutinize federal jurisdiction in light of the fact that the Supreme Court had writ-of-error review over the case. Second, he stated that the absence of judicial process was a significant determinant of state jurisdiction.]

――――――

NOTES AND QUESTIONS ON TARBLE

1)   **Historical Criticism of** *Ableman* **and** *Tarble***.** *Tarble* has proven remarkably durable in the face of criticism by federal courts scholars. There are at least two elements of *Tarble* that have emerged as particularly problematic. First, *Tarble* is inconsistent with the generally-accepted premise that, barring legislation, state courts were considered competent to consider the same federal questions as an Article III federal tribunal. (See Note 2, below.) Second, *Tarble*

fails to grapple with the fact that early nineteenth-century state courts *did* issue habeas writs to federal custodians.[cc]

2)   Overinvesting the Supremacy Clause? If *Tarble* is understood to say that the Supremacy Clause, by its own force and without statutory enactment, forecloses state habeas jurisdiction over all forms of federal confinement, then what are the textual, structural, and practical justifications for such a holding? State courts adjudicate Article III subject matter routinely, and such adjudication is pursuant to constitutional design. See Gulf Offshore Co. v. Mobil Oil Corp, 453 U.S. 473, 478 (1981) (citing The Federalist No. 82 (A. Hamilton)). On an influential theory of constitutional structure, the Madisonian Compromise meant that the Constitution did not, for Article III subject matter within the Supreme Court's appellate jurisdiction, foreclose the original-but-concurrent jurisdiction of state courts. See, e.g., Tafflin v. Levitt, 493 U.S. 455, 459 (1990) (referring to the "deeply rooted presumption in favor of concurrent state court jurisdiction"). Moreover, if Congress wanted certain subject matter to be cognizable in some lower court, Congress could do so by creating inferior Article III tribunals. Do you think the Court should treat habeas the same way it treats other Article III subject matter, or is there something unique about habeas corpus that distinguishes it from other forms of jurisdiction specified in Article III, § 2? See generally Larry W. Yackle, Federal Courts 135–36 (2d ed. 2003) (arguing that *Tarble* ignored "the conventional understanding that Congress might never have created the lower federal courts and might have relied, instead, on state courts to police the system").

3)   Writ of Error Review. Note that the Wisconsin Supreme Court took direct aim at the United States Justices, describing them as a group that "was denying to one of an oppressed race born on our soil the poor privilege of even suing for his rights in a federal court." *In re Tarble*, 25 Wis. 390, 394–95 (1870).[dd] *Booth* and *Tarble* held that Supreme Court writ-of-error review was an insufficient vehicle for enforcing federal supremacy in cases coming from state courts. If the federal system has a vehicle to ensure Supreme Court review of state habeas decisions, then did the Court appropriately determine that such an appellate remedy was not "expedient enough" to survive a Supremacy Clause challenge?

4)   Reading *Ableman* Narrowly. Recall from the Notes and Comments appearing after this Chapter's *Booth* excerpt that, in that decision's immediate aftermath, courts generally read the decision as a narrower rule applicable only to federal convictions and not to all forms of federal custody. What role does the dispute over *Booth's* "narrowness" play in *Tarble?*

[cc] See William F. Duker, *A Constitutional History of Habeas Corpus* 178 n.92 (1980) (collecting cases); In re Reyolds, 20 Fed. Cas. 592 (N.Y. 1867) (same). See also R. Hurd, *Treatise on the Right of Personal Liberty, and On the Writ of Habeas Corpus and the Practice Connected with It: With a View of the Law of Extradition of Fugitives* 166 (2d ed. 1876) ("It may be considered that state courts may grant the writ in all cases of illegal confinement under the authority of the United States."); Marc M. Arkin, *The Ghost at the Banquet: Slavery, Federalism, and Habeas Corpus for State Prisoners*, 70 Tul. L. Rev. 1, 7 (1995) ("At the very beginning of the nineteenth century, most state courts continued to draw their authority to issue the writ from their common-law powers which preceded independence.")

[dd] Professor Todd Pettys gives a detailed account of the Wisconsin Supreme Court opinion, which seethed at the Supreme Court for the Court's tolerance of slavery. See Todd E. Pettys, *State Habeas Relief for Federal Extrajudicial Detainees*, 92 Minn. L. Rev. 265, 288–90 (2007).

5)   The Riddle. *Tarble* is difficult to reconcile with the following combination of propositions: that Congress did not have to establish inferior federal courts (the Madisonian Compromise); that the Supreme Court lacks original jurisdiction to grant habeas writs (*Marbury*); and that the Constitution guarantees some quantum of habeas access. If one of those three propositions or *Tarble* has to be wrong, then many distinguished scholars have pointed the finger directly at *Tarble*. In fact, Chief Justice Chase, the lone *Tarble* dissenter and an abolitionist lawyer, believed that the Suspension Clause reflected original intent to guarantee access to state habeas for federal prisoners. Recall Professor Duker's theory, mentioned in Subsection 2.B of this Chapter, which presents a historical argument for such an interpretation. Contrary to what *Booth* and *Tarble* imply, use of state habeas writs to free federal prisoners was fairly robust during the first sixty years of the country's existence. Might there be a way to distinguish that historical practice from the holding in *Booth*, but not the holding in *Tarble*? Cf. Michael G. Collins, *Article III Cases, State Court Duties, and the Madisonian Compromise*, 1995 Wis. L. Rev. 39, 101–02 (observing that, if Congress did not have to create lower federal courts and that, if *Tarble* correctly held that the Constitution forbade state habeas jurisdiction in federal-custody cases, then there would be no forum for redressing the federal grievance).

6)   Reconciling *Tarble*. In an effort to reconcile *Tarble* with the Madisonian Compromise and the Suspension Clause, some scholars have argued that *Tarble* can be justified as a "sub-constitutional" ruling that functions as a statutory preemption case.[ee] The Judiciary Act of 1789 granted lower federal courts the habeas authority to scrutinize military detention, so *Tarble* might be justified on the ground that the 1789 Act's grant of such jurisdiction was *exclusive*, and therefore preempted state habeas jurisdiction over that form of confinement. There is no express exclusivity in the 1789 Judiciary Act. Should *Tarble*, in light of its extensive reliance on *Booth*, be understood as an implied exclusivity case? Does the language towards the end of the opinion, discussing the sufficiency of federal habeas review, support this reading of the case? Implied exclusivity is an especially heavy lift under modern preemption theory, but could *Tarble* continue be read as an implied exclusivity case if, under preemption doctrine prevailing when the case was decided, that rationale would have been more persuasive? In light of *Tarble's* potentially far-reaching implications, would courts be justified in adopting a narrow reading of the opinion?

6. ORIGINAL HABEAS AND THE EXCEPTIONS CLAUSE

Recall the brief discussion of the Judiciary Act of 1789, *Marbury v. Madison*, and *Ex Parte Bollman* at the beginning of Chapter 1. The Judiciary Act of 1789 gave the Supreme Court the authority to issue "original" habeas writs. After *Marbury* held that Congress could not add to the origi-

---

[ee] See, e.g., Richard H. Fallon Jr., et al., *Hart and Wechsler's The Federal Courts and The Federal System* 405 (6th ed. 2009) (suggesting that Tarble might "be justified on the ground that federal statutes (and not the Constitution of its own force) impliedly establish habeas corpus for persons in federal custody as a domain of exclusive federal jurisdiction."); Akhil Reed Amar, *Sovereignty and Federalism*, 86 Yale L.J. 1425, 1510 (1987) ("[Booth and Tarble] can be justified only if they are understood simply as attributing to Congress a desire for exclusive federal court jurisdiction in habeas proceedings against federal officers."); Seth P. Waxman & Trevor W. Morrison, *What Kind of Immunity? Federal Officers, State Criminal Law, and the Supremacy Clause*, 112 YALE L.J. 2195, 2225–26 (2003) (arguing that Tarble is predicated on the idea that the habeas statutes "reflected an implicit congressional determination that state jurisdiction was not appropriate").

nal jurisdiction assigned to the Court under Article III, § 2, and because § 2 did not mention original habeas jurisdiction, most assumed that *Bollman* would invalidate the Court's practice of issuing original writs. Writing for the Court in *Bollman*, Chief Justice Marshall preserved the constitutionality of original habeas process by characterizing it as an appellate remedy. To be a constitutional exercise of appellate power, however, the original writ had to revise inferior judicial proceedings.

The story of original habeas process, therefore, is not as much about the grant of original jurisdiction in Article III, § 2 as it is about the constitutionality of restrictions on the Supreme Court's appellate jurisdiction, also specified in that Section. The "Exceptions Clause" provides: "In all the other cases before mentioned, the Supreme Court shall have appellate jurisdiction, both as to law and fact, *with such exceptions, and under such regulations as the Congress shall make.*" (Emphasis added.) More precisely, original habeas authority has been invoked repeatedly as the residual appellate jurisdiction that avoids problems under the Exceptions Clause—problems that the Court would have to resolve if a statute were interpreted to strip all of its appellate authority over a particular piece of subject matter, including its original habeas power.

Because the Supreme Court lacked other forms of appellate jurisdiction over final criminal judgments in lower federal courts, original habeas process actually emerged as an important source of Court authority over criminal proceedings. As Congress has created new forms of appellate jurisdiction by which the Supreme Court could review lower-court decisions—including rights of appeal and statutory certiorari jurisdiction—the importance of original habeas process as an appellate power declined.

The last time the original writ was granted was in 1925. See *Ex parte Grossman*, 267 U.S. 87 (1925). The Supreme Court and the Justices can exercise their original habeas powers to transfer a petition for an original writ to a district court, and the only such transfer ordered in the last fifty years was an August 2009 ruling in *In re Davis*, which is discussed shortly. Instead, the original habeas power is invoked in disputes about other forms of appellate jurisdiction, in which the Court will cite its original habeas authority to support the idea that legislation stripping other forms of appellate jurisdiction does not entirely foreclose Supreme Court review.

This pattern plays out in each of two historical episodes excerpted below. Although these episodes are separated by over a century, they reflect a similar pattern. In each episode, Congress severely restricted the appellate jurisdiction in the Supreme Court—in language that could be interpreted to strip original habeas jurisdiction along with all other forms of appellate power over certain subject matter. And each time, the Supreme Court responded to Congress by declaring that it retained original habeas jurisdiction, thereby avoiding the question of whether the "Exceptions Clause" of Article III, § 2 permits Congress to strip *all* of the Court's appellate jurisdiction over a particular type of question.

NOTE ON THE RECONSTRUCTION ACT, EX PARTE MCCARDLE, AND EX PARTE YERGER

After the end of the Civil War, Congressional Republicans implemented a plan for Reconstruction. Congress passed the Military Reconstruction Act over

President Andrew Johnson's veto, dividing the South into military districts. See Act of Mar. 2, 1867, ch. 153, 14 Stat. 428. Congress then passed the Tenure of Office Act, to prevent the President from dismissing executive officers, which President Johnson refused to execute; Congress tried and failed to impeach Johnson. See Tenure of Office Act, ch. 154, 14 Stat. 430 (1867) (repealed 1887).[ff] Congress passed a host of other bills providing for Congressionally-controlled Reconstruction, and the noncompliant states faced the prospect of military rule.

In large part to effectuate Reconstruction, the Habeas Corpus Act of 1867 authorized federal judges to grant habeas writs to any person detained in violation of federal (constitutional) law. Habeas jurisdiction—particularly over state detention—was crucial to enforcing constitutional laws in favor of newly-freed African Americans and their supporters. In addition to vesting habeas jurisdiction in federal judges, the 1867 Habeas Act also created an as-of-right appeal from the federal circuit courts to the United States Supreme Court.

In Vicksburg, Mississippi, the military arrested William McCardle for publishing agitprop opposing Reconstruction. While McCardle, a former Confederate solider, was awaiting trial before a commission constituted under the Military Reconstruction Act, he filed a habeas petition in the federal circuit court for the Southern District of Mississippi. The circuit court denied relief, and McCardle appealed.

The Supreme Court denied the Government's motion to dismiss, holding that it had jurisdiction to entertain the appeal. The Court emphasized the breadth of the 1867 Act, which extended to "all cases where any person may be restrained of his or her liberty in violation of the Constitution." The Court noted: "This legislation is of the most comprehensive character. It brings within the habeas corpus jurisdiction of every court and of every judge every possible case of privation of liberty contrary to the National Constitution, treaties, or laws. It is impossible to widen this jurisdiction." Ex parte McCardle, 73 U.S. (6 Wall.) 318, 325–26 (1868).

Congressional Republicans believed that the Military Reconstruction Act could be ruled unconstitutional were the Justices to decide the merits—given the outcome in the *Ex parte Milligan*. While the *McCardle* appeal was pending, congressional Republicans slipped a rider into a bill committed for the purposes of creating Supreme Court jurisdiction over civil cases involving Internal Revenue Service officers. That rider was designed to strip Supreme Court jurisdiction over appeals from circuit courts in habeas cases. It provided that "[S]o much of the [1867 Habeas Act amendments to the 1789 Judiciary Act] as authorize[] an appeal from the judgment of the circuit court to the Supreme Court of the United States, or the exercise of any such jurisdiction by said Supreme Court on appeals which have been or may hereafter be taken, be, and the same is, hereby repealed." Congress ultimately passed the repeal over President Johnson's veto. While the legislation was being considered and then enacted, the Court carried the case over to the next term.

[ff] For a description of these events, see Jerry L. Mashaw, *Federal Administration and Administrative Law in the Gilded Age*, 119 Yale L.J. 1362, 1383–84, 1462–63 (2010).

Ex parte McCardle

United States Supreme Court
74 U.S. (7 Wall.) 506 (1869)

■ The CHIEF JUSTICE delivered the opinion of the court.

The first question necessarily is that of jurisdiction, for if the act of March, 1868, takes away the jurisdiction defined by the act of February, 1867, it is useless, if not improper, to enter into any discussion of other questions.

* * * [T]he appellate jurisdiction of this court is not derived from acts of Congress. It is, strictly speaking, conferred by the Constitution. But it is conferred "with such exceptions and under such regulations as Congress shall make."

It is unnecessary to consider whether, if Congress had made no exceptions and no regulations, this court might not have exercised general appellate jurisdiction under rules prescribed by itself. For among the earliest acts of the first Congress, at its first session, was the act of September 24th, 1789, to establish the judicial courts of the United States. That act provided for the organization of this court, and prescribed regulations for the exercise of its jurisdiction.

The source of that jurisdiction, and the limitations of it by the Constitution and by statute, have been on several occasions subjects of consideration here. In the case of *Durousseau v. The United States* particularly, the whole matter was carefully examined, and the court held that, while "the appellate powers of this court are not given by the judicial act, but are given by the Constitution," they are, nevertheless, "limited and regulated by that act, and by such other acts as have been passed on the subject." The court said further that the judicial act was an exercise of the power given by the Constitution to Congress "of making exceptions to the appellate jurisdiction of the Supreme Court." "They have described affirmatively," said the court, its jurisdiction, and this affirmative description has been understood to imply a negation of the exercise of such appellate power as is not comprehended within it.

The principle that the affirmation of appellate jurisdiction implies the negation of all such jurisdiction not affirmed having been thus established, it was an almost necessary consequence that acts of Congress, providing for the exercise of jurisdiction, should come to be spoken of as acts granting jurisdiction, and not as acts making exceptions to the constitutional grant of it.

The exception to appellate jurisdiction in the case before us, however, is not an inference from the affirmation of other appellate jurisdiction. It is made in terms. The provision of the act of 1867 affirming the appellate jurisdiction of this court in cases of habeas corpus is expressly repealed. It is hardly possible to imagine a plainer instance of positive exception.

We are not at liberty to inquire into the motives of the legislature. We can only examine into its power under the Constitution, and the power to make exceptions to the appellate jurisdiction of this court is given by express words.

What, then, is the effect of the repealing act upon the case before us? We cannot doubt as to this. Without jurisdiction, the court cannot proceed at all in any cause. Jurisdiction is power to declare the law, and, when it ceases to exist, the only function remaining to the court is that of announcing the fact and dismissing the cause. And this is not less clear upon authority than upon principle. * * *

It is quite clear, therefore, that this court cannot proceed to pronounce judgment in this case, for it has no longer jurisdiction of the appeal, and judicial duty is not less fitly performed by declining ungranted jurisdiction than in exercising firmly that which the Constitution and the laws confer.

Counsel seem to have supposed, if effect be given to the repealing act in question, that the whole appellate power of the court, in cases of habeas corpus, is denied. But this is an error. The act of 1868 does not except from that jurisdiction any cases but appeals from Circuit Courts under the act of 1867. It does not affect the jurisdiction which was previously exercised.

The appeal of the petitioner in this case must be dismissed for want of jurisdiction. * * *

NOTES AND QUESTIONS ON MCCARDLE AND INTRODUCTORY NOTE TO EX PARTE YERGER

1) **Deliberate Delay.** Why did Supreme the Court postpone merits consideration in *McCardle*? The Court waited until Congress enacted the pending 1868 legislation. The Court knew that legislation was specifically designed to strip the Court of jurisdiction over McCardle's appeal, which had the potential to undermine Reconstruction authority.

2) **Alternative Appellate Vehicles.** The 1868 Act was quite narrow, as it was drafted to target *McCardle* during the pendency of the case. The Act only affected "an appeal from the judgment of the circuit court to the Supreme Court of the United States." In *McCardle*, the Court was careful to note that "[i]t does not affect the jurisdiction which was previously exercised." For example, appeals from habeas petitions filed in the district courts could still reach the Supreme Court through other channels—i.e., the Supreme Court could still exercise its original habeas power. What would the Court have done had Congress sought to restrict the Court's "whole appellate power?"

3) **Separation of Powers.** Recognition of a Congressional power to repeal Supreme Court jurisdiction in a particular case seems to present serious separation-of-powers concerns. Insofar as we are talking about separation of powers, is there any reason to distinguish between jurisdiction stripping in an appellate and in an original context? Is this risk something that the Exceptions Clause seems to contemplate? If some type of appellate review remains open, then does *McCardle* mean that Congress can freely burden or eliminate other types of appellate review?

4) **Introduction to *Yerger*.** *McCardle* is the central case in the scholarly debate over whether the Exceptions Clause permits Congress to strip *all* Supreme Court appellate jurisdiction over Article III subject matter. Prominent scholars have argued credibly on both sides of this issue, but the Court has been extremely careful to avoid having to rule on it. One of the ways the Court has avoided the question has been by imposing a "super-clear-statement rule" for any legislation that purports to strip its jurisdiction to review inferior judicial process. Pursuant to that rule, the Court will not infer the elimination of a specific appellate power; the statute must strip that specific appellate power

expressly. Consider this principle as it applies to the Supreme Court's original habeas jurisdiction in *Ex Parte Yerger*.

Ex parte Yerger
United States Supreme Court
75 U.S. (8 Wall.) 85 (1868)

■ The CHIEF JUSTICE delivered the opinion of the Court.

* * * The general question of jurisdiction in this case resolves itself necessarily into two other questions:

1. Has the court jurisdiction, in a case like the present, to inquire into the cause of detention, alleged to be unlawful, and to give relief if the detention be found to be in fact unlawful, by the writ of habeas corpus under the Judiciary Act of 1789.

2. If, under that act, the court possessed this jurisdiction, has it been taken away by the second section of the act of March, 27, 1868, repealing so much of the Act of February 5, 1867, as authorizes appeals from circuit courts to the Supreme Court?

[T]he terms of [the Suspension Clause] necessarily imply judicial action. In England, all the higher courts where open to applicants for the writ, and it is hardly supposable that, under the new government founded on more liberal ideas and principles, any court would be intentionally closed to them.

[The 1789 Judiciary Act granted the Supreme Court authority to issue habeas writs.]. It would have been, indeed, a remarkable anomaly if this Court * * * had been denied, under a constitution which absolutely prohibits the suspension of the writ except under extraordinary exigencies, that power in cases of alleged unlawful restraint which the Habeas Corpus Act of Charles II expressly declares those courts to possess.

But the power vested in this Court is * * * appellate, whereas that of the English courts, though declared and defined by statutes, is derived from the common law and is original. * * *

The doctrine of the Constitution and of the cases thus far may be summed up in these propositions:

(1) The original jurisdiction of this Court cannot be extended by Congress to any other cases than those expressly defined by the Constitution.

(2) The appellate jurisdiction of this Court, conferred by the Constitution, extends to all other cases within the judicial power of the United States.

(3) This appellate jurisdiction is subject to such exceptions and must be exercised under such regulations as Congress, in the exercise of its discretion, has made or may see fit to make.

(4) Congress not only has not excepted writs of habeas corpus and mandamus from this appellate jurisdiction, but has expressly provided for the exercise of this jurisdiction by means of these writs.

We come, then, to consider the first great question made in the case now before us.

* * * [T]his Court, under the act of 1789, and under all the subsequent acts, giving jurisdiction in cases of habeas corpus may, in the exercise of its

appellate power, revise the decisions of inferior courts of the United States and relieve from unlawful imprisonment authorized by them except in cases within some limitations of the jurisdiction by Congress.

* * * [C]an this Court inquire into the lawfulness of detention, and relieve from it if found unlawful, when the detention complained of is not by civil authority under a commitment made by an inferior court, but by military officers, for trial before a military tribunal, after an examination into the cause of detention by the inferior court, resulting in an order remanding the prisoner to custody?

[The idea that the Supreme Court lacks habeas jurisdiction in any case where judgment is imposed by a tribunal over which it lacks appellate jurisdiction] seems to assert not only that the decision to be revised upon habeas corpus must have been made by a court of the United States, subject to the ordinary appellate jurisdiction of this Court, but that having been so made, it must have resulted in an order of commitment to civil authority subject to the control of the court making it.

* * * The action which we are asked to revise was that of a tribunal whose decisions are subject to revision by this Court in ordinary modes. We need consider, therefore, [whether] the action of the inferior court must have resulted in a commitment for trial in a civil court, and the inference drawn from it that no relief can be had here by habeas corpus from imprisonment under military authority to which the petitioner may have been remanded by such a court.

This proposition certainly is not supported by authority. * * *

As limited by the act of 1789, [authority to issue habeas writs] did not extend to cases of imprisonment after conviction under sentences of competent tribunals, nor to prisoners in jail unless in custody under or by color of the authority of the United States or committed for trial before some court of the United States or required to be brought into court to testify. But this limitation has been gradually narrowed, and the benefits of the writ have been extended * * *.

We are obliged to hold, therefore, that in all cases where a circuit court of the United States has, in the exercise of its original jurisdiction, caused a prisoner to be brought before it and has, after inquiring into the cause of detention, remanded him to the custody from which he was taken, this Court, in the exercise of its appellate jurisdiction, may, by the writ of habeas corpus, aided by the writ of certiorari, revise the decision of the circuit court, and if it be found unwarranted by law, relieve the prisoner from the unlawful restraint to which he has been remanded.

This conclusion brings us to the inquiry whether the 2d section of the Act of March 27, 1868, takes away or affects the appellate jurisdiction of this Court under the Constitution and the acts of Congress prior to 1867. * * *

[The 1867 Habeas Corpus Act extended the original habeas jurisdiction] of the district and circuit courts and of the several judges of these courts to all cases of restraint of liberty in violation of the Constitution, treaties, or laws of the United States. This act authorized appeals to this Court from judgments of the circuit court, but did not repeal any previous act conferring jurisdiction by habeas corpus, unless by implication. * * *

The effect of the [1868 repealer] act was to oust the Court of its jurisdiction of the particular case then before it on appeal, and it is not to be doubted that such was the effect intended. Nor will it be questioned that legislation of this character is unusual and hardly to be justified except upon some imperious public exigency.

* * * [I]t is not to be presumed that an act, passed under such circumstances, was intended to have any further effect than that plainly apparent from its terms. It is quite clear that the words of the act reach not only all appeals pending, but all future appeals to this Court under the act of 1867, but they appear to be limited to appeals taken under that act.

The words of the repealing section are,

> That so much of the Act approved February 5, 1867, as authorizes an appeal from the judgment of the circuit court to the Supreme Court of the United States, or the exercise of any such jurisdiction by said Supreme Court on appeals which have been or may be hereafter taken be, and the same is hereby, repealed.

These words * * * repeal only so much of the act of 1867 as authorized appeals or the exercise of appellate jurisdiction by this Court. They affected only appeals and appellate jurisdiction authorized by that act. They do not purport to touch the appellate jurisdiction conferred by the Constitution or to except from it any cases not excepted by the act of 1789. They reach no act except the act of 1867.

It has been suggested, however, that the act of 1789, so far as it provided for the issuing of writs of habeas corpus by this Court, was already repealed by the act of 1867. We have already observed that there are no repealing words in the act of 1867. If it repealed the act of 1789, it did so by implication, and any implication which would give to it this effect upon the act of 1789 would give it the same effect upon the acts of 1833 and 1842. If one was repealed, all were repealed.

Repeals by implication are not favored. They are seldom admitted except on the ground of repugnancy, and never, we think, when the former act can stand together with the new act. * * *

Our conclusion is that none of the acts prior to 1867 authorizing this Court to exercise appellate jurisdiction by means of the writ of habeas corpus was repealed by the act of that year, and that the repealing section of the act of 1868 is limited in terms, and must be limited in effect to the appellate jurisdiction authorized by the act of 1867.

We could come to no other conclusion without holding that the whole appellate jurisdiction of this Court, in cases of habeas corpus, conferred by the Constitution, recognized by law, and exercised from the foundation of the government hitherto, has been taken away, without the expression of such intent and by mere implication, through the operation of the acts of 1867 and 1868.

* * * [T]he jurisdiction of the court to issue the writ prayed for is Affirmed.

———

NOTES AND QUESTIONS ON YERGER

1) **Applying the "Presumption Against Repeals By Implication" Broadly.** In both *Yerger* and *McCardle*, the Supreme Court refused to infer Congressional intent to repeal the Court's original habeas jurisdiction, but the

presumption against implied repeals has been applied much more broadly. First, *Yerger* and *McCardle* rejected the argument that a repeal could be implied by a new grant of jurisdiction. Second, in *Yerger* and *McCardle* the Court refused to infer a repeal of its *appellate* jurisdiction; subsequent decisions have applied that presumption to the original jurisdiction of district courts in habeas cases.

2) Epilogue. In 1885, Congress passed a statute that restored Supreme Court jurisdiction taken away in the 1869 Act. When Congress did that, it did not repeal the 1867 Act expanding scope of federal habeas review to include review of state convictions. Why did Congress again intervene, this time to *expand* the appellate power of the Supreme Court? By 1885, lower courts were granting habeas corpus relief to state prisoners, especially in the South. Congressional attitudes towards Reconstruction had changed, and Congress may have perceived that the Supreme Court would restrain habeas grants by lower courts.

NOTES ON AEDPA, FELKER V. TURPIN, *AND* IN RE DAVIS

1) Abuse of the Writ and 28 U.S.C. § 2244(b). Recall from discussion of *Felker v. Turpin*, 518 U.S. 1051 (1996)—which introduced the post-conviction Suspension Clause question—that AEDPA modified § 2244(b). Section 2244(b) operated as a statutory abuse-of-the-writ rule, but one that differed in several respects from the prior judge-made law. One of those differences was that, under § 2244(b)(3), a federal appeals court must authorize any successive petition before the claims therein proceed in district court. And, under § 2244(b)(3)(E), an order denying authorization "shall not be appealable and shall not be the subject of a petition for rehearing or for a writ of certiorari." That restriction on appellate jurisdiction was the subject of a separate Exceptions Clause challenge in *Felker.*

Although there were supplemental concurrences, Chief Justice Rehnquist wrote for a unanimous Court. *Felker* starts with a discussion of *Yerger*:

> More than a century ago, we considered whether a statute barring review by appeal of the judgment of a circuit court in a habeas case also deprived this Court of power to entertain an original habeas petition. Ex parte Yerger, 8 Wall. 85 (1869). We consider the same question here.... In *Yerger*, we considered whether the Act of 1868 deprived us not only of power to hear an appeal from a inferior court's decision on a habeas petition, but also of power to entertain a habeas petition to this Court under § 14 of the Act of 1789. We concluded that the 1868 Act did not affect our power to entertain such habeas petitions. We explained that the 1868 Act's text addressed only jurisdiction over appeals conferred under the Act of 1867, not habeas jurisdiction conferred under the Acts of 1789 and 1867. We rejected the suggestion that the Act of 1867 had repealed our habeas power by implication. Repeals by implication are not favored, we said, and the continued exercise of original habeas jurisdiction was not "repugnant" to a prohibition on review by appeal of circuit court habeas judgments.

Next, the Court concluded that, because of the absence of a clear statement rule, AEDPA did not repeal its "authority to entertain original habeas petitions," for reasons similar to those stated in *Yerger*:

> No provision . . . mentions our authority to entertain original habeas petitions. . . Although §106(b)(3)(E) precludes us from reviewing, by appeal or petition for certiorari, a judgment on an application for leave to file a second habeas petition in district court, it makes no mention of our authority to hear habeas petitions filed as original matters in this Court."

Felker then cited the *Yerger* presumption against implied jurisdiction stripping. *Felker* observed that the existence of original habeas jurisdiction eliminates any issue under the Exceptions Clause: "[The presence of original habeas jurisdiction] obviates one of the constitutional challenges raised [because] it does not repeal our authority to entertain a petition for habeas corpus. [T]here can be no plausible argument that the Act has deprived this Court of appellate jurisdiction in violation of Article III, § 2."

2)   *In re Davis* and Exercising Original Jurisdiction. In *McCardle*, the Supreme Court held that Congress could constitutionally strip certain appellate jurisdiction because the Court retained its authority to exercise its original habeas power. The Court signaled its willingness to use that power in *Yerger*. Over a hundred years later and in a similar spirit of constitutional avoidance, the Court sustained AEDPA's appellate-jurisdiction stripping as constitutional on the ground that the Court could exercise an original habeas power that it had not actually exercised since 1973.[gg] Perhaps *Felker's* recognition of the original habeas power was in name only—a way to avoid the question of whether Congress could entirely foreclose the Court's appellate jurisdiction in habeas cases.

The legal community was quite surprised when, in the summer of 2009, the Supreme Court ordered an original habeas petition transferred to a district court. The case, *In re Davis*, 330 S.Ct. 1 (2009), was the first time the Court had exercised any post-AEDPA original habeas authority. Davis had sought authorization from the Eleventh Circuit to file a successive petition after seven of the nine witnesses that had testified in his capital murder trial recanted. The Eleventh Circuit denied Davis authorization to proceed, and the Supreme Court lacked certiorari jurisdiction over that order. The Court nonetheless allowed the case to go forward by exercising its original habeas power to transfer the case to a district court with authority to decide the merits of Mr. Davis' innocence claim. Justice Stevens explained, in a three-Justice concurrence to the order:

> [S]even of the State's key witnesses have recanted their trial testimony; several individuals have implicated the State's principal witness as the shooter; and "no court," state or federal, "has ever conducted a hearing to assess the reliability of the score of [post-conviction] affidavits that, if reliable, would satisfy the threshold showing for a truly persuasive demon-

---

[gg] Actually, the Court itself had not exercised the authority to transfer a petition pursuant to its original habeas power since 1962. *See* Byrnes v. Walker, 371 U.S. 937, 937 (1962); Chaapel v. Cochran, 369 U.S. 869, 869 (1962). Justice Douglas transferred a case in his capacity as an individual Justice in 1973. *See* Ex parte Hayes, 414 U.S. 1327, 1329 (1973). The Court had not ordered a prisoner released pursuant to its original habeas power since 1925. *See* Ex parte Grossman, 267 U.S. 87 (1925).

stration of actual innocence[.]" The substantial risk of putting an innocent man to death clearly provides an adequate justification for holding an evidentiary hearing.

Justice Scalia, joined by Justice Thomas dissented:

> Today this Court takes the extraordinary step—one not taken in nearly 50 years—of instructing a district court to adjudicate a state prisoner's petition for an original writ of habeas corpus. The Court proceeds down this path even though every judicial and executive body that has examined petitioner's stale claim of innocence has been unpersuaded, and (to make matters worse) even though it would be impossible for the District Court to grant any relief.

After the remand to the district court, the district court denied relief on the ground that Mr. Davis was not innocent. See In re Davis, No. CV409–130, 2010 WL 3385081 (S.D. Ga. Aug. 24, 2010). On September 21, 2011, the Georgia Board of Pardons and Paroles, which had exclusive jurisdiction over clemency decisions, denied Mr. Davis's clemency petition—despite a high profile national and international campaign on his behalf. One million people apparently signed a petition in support of relief and a number of high profile leaders spoke out in the case. Georgia executed him the next day, after the Supreme Court declined to grant eleventh-hour relief.[hh]

Setting aside the complex issues surrounding adjudication of the inmate's guilt, *Davis* constitutes a powerful reminder that the modern Court remains extremely skeptical of any Congressional attempt to completely eliminate its appellate jurisdiction over Article III subject matter adjudicated in inferior federal courts. In the *Davis* opinions, the Justices fought over whether Davis could ultimately obtain relief, but not a single Justice suggested that the Court lacked the authority to grant the original habeas transfer.

In *Davis*, what do you think drove the Supreme Court to send the case to the district court to hear Davis's new evidence? Could it have been the fact that *Davis* was a capital case with strong evidence of actual innocence? Do you think *Davis* is the start of a trend, or that it is an aberration in an otherwise constant state of original habeas inactivity? What are some of the problems with the idea that the Court would use its original habeas power to superintend habeas outcomes in lower federal courts? Does it matter that the Court did not grant original habeas relief, but merely ordered a transfer? Finally, for an inmate whose case is transferred to a district court under the original habeas provisions, what is the appropriate court in which to lodge an appeal from the judgment in the transferee court—the Supreme Court or the court of appeals?[ii]

[hh] See Colleen Curry and Michael S. James, *Troy Davis Executed After Stay Denied by Supreme Court*, ABC News, Sept. 21, 2011.

[ii] The district court noted, "The jurisdictional effects of this transfer, especially with respect to appeal, are unclear." In re Davis, No. CV409–130, 2010 WL 3385081 *1 (S.D. Ga. Aug. 24, 2010). The judge added, "Functionally[,] . . . this Court is operating as a magistrate for the Supreme Court, which suggests appeal of this order would be directly to the Supreme Court. However, this Court has been unable to locate any legal precedent or legislative history on point." The Eleventh Circuit agreed that any appeal would lie with the Supreme Court. See Davis v. Terry, 625 F.3d 716 (11th Cir. 2010). The Supreme Court then denied cert.

CHAPTER 3

THE SCOPE OF FEDERAL HABEAS AUTHORITY TO REVIEW STATE CONVICTIONS

INTRODUCTORY NOTE ON THE SCOPE OF THE POST-CONVICTION WRIT

Today, petitions brought by state prisoners dominate the federal habeas docket. For almost eighty years after the First Judiciary Act, however, federal courts did not and could not exercise general habeas jurisdiction over state convictions. The absence of a federal habeas remedy notwithstanding, state prisoners were not entirely without recourse to the federal judiciary. The Supreme Court could exercise direct appellate review of state criminal convictions through writs of error issued to the highest state courts.

The Civil War permanently altered the relationship between the national and state governments. The Thirteenth, Fourteenth, and Fifteenth Amendments to the Constitution, as well as the accompanying Reconstruction legislation, reflected robust conceptions of federal and judicial power—paradigms that differed substantially from their antebellum predecessors. As part of these changes, Congress enacted the Habeas Corpus Act of 1867, which extended federal habeas corpus review to state prisoners. This new habeas jurisdiction did not immediately result in a broad pattern of judges granting habeas relief. In 1867, and for decades afterwards, there were few rules of constitutional criminal procedure. As a result, few habeas claims were available to state prisoners. According to many habeas scholars, habeas review was also narrower because, during this era, the writ issued only to address "jurisdictional" errors.

The landmark Supreme Court decision in *Brown v. Allen,* 344 U.S. 443 (1953), announced—or affirmed, depending on who you talk to—the broad view that constitutional errors in state criminal process were cognizable on federal habeas review. Under the stewardship of the Warren Court, habeas corpus played an important role in the mid-century revolution in criminal procedure. Legal revolutions can have foils, and the Warren Court's revolution in criminal procedure—and in habeas process—was followed by a counter-revolution on the Burger and Rehnquist courts. Broadly speaking, the Burger and Rehnquist Courts believed that Warren-era habeas jurisprudence invited too much post-conviction activity. The Burger and Rehnquist Courts pared back the scope of habeas review, narrowed the set of cognizable claims, and erected procedural barriers to relief.

While the Justices tried to ground competing visions of habeas in history, the debates were also influenced by the politics of crime. The Warren Court revolutionized criminal procedure at the same time that crime rates were growing, and the twin dynamics produced a new national politics surrounding criminal procedure and law enforcement. Dean Erwin Chemerinsky writes, "Conservatives view habeas corpus as the vehicle that guilty people use to escape convictions and sentences." See Erwin Chemerinsky, *Thinking About Habeas Corpus*, 37 Case W. L. Rev. 748, 750 (1987). As a result, many conservative judges and commentators emphasize social interests in comity, finality, and federalism, and they express skepticism about federal involvement in local policing, prosecution, and adjudication. Dean Chemerinsky explains that, in contrast, "Liberals see habeas corpus as an essential protection against individuals being held in violation of the Constitution." Speaking generally, liberal jurists and commentators believe that the interest in liberty dominates others, and they distrust the ability of states and localities to enforce constitutional rules of criminal procedure.

This Chapter proceeds in four parts. Section 1 traces the scope of state-prisoner review from the Habeas Corpus Act of 1867 through *Brown v. Allen*. Section 2 explores the modern scope of the writ, in part by explaining the most commonly-litigated claims. Section 3 explores limits on the cognizability, or the ability to assert, certain federal habeas claims. Most prominently, the Supreme Court ruled, in *Stone v. Powell*, 428 U.S. 465 (1976), that habeas relief may not issue for violations of the Fourth Amendment. Section 4 presents another cognizability issue: whether federal habeas relief may issue for a "freestanding" claim of "actual innocence"—a claim in which the absence of guilt is asserted as the sole basis for constitutional challenge. Freestanding innocence questions are an entrée into broader questions about the appropriate role of role innocence in habeas litigation.

1. ORIGINS OF FEDERAL REVIEW OF STATE CONVICTIONS

A. CLASSIC DUE PROCESS CASES

INTRODUCTORY NOTE ON THE HABEAS CORPUS ACT OF 1867 AND THE CLASSIC DUE PROCESS CASES

Passed alongside the Civil War Amendments, the Habeas Corpus Act of 1867 permitted all state prisoners to file habeas petitions in federal court. (There were narrower grants of federal habeas authority to review certain types of state custody in 1833 and 1842.) The 1867 Act "grant[s] the courts the power to issue writs of habeas corpus in all cases where any person may be restrained of his or her liberty in violation of the constitution, or any treaty or law of the United States." Act of Feb. 5, 1867, ch. 28, §1, 14 Stat. 385, 386. Many argue that Congress intended and understood the 1867 Act to permit federal courts to exercise habeas jurisdiction over every type of state custody. In the first of the *McCardle* cases, the Supreme Court observed that "[t]his legislation is of the most comprehensive character. It brings within the *habeas corpus* jurisdiction of every court and of every judge every possible case of privation of liberty contrary to the National Constitution, treaties, or laws. It is impossible to widen this jurisdiction." Ex Parte McCardle, 73 U.S. 318, 325–26 (1867).

Such language from *McCardle* notwithstanding, the degree of habeas power that the 1867 Act actually conferred upon federal courts is subject to considerable dispute. The statute effectively gives all federal judges the power to overturn state criminal convictions, and the justification required for judges to do so is not clear. If one reads *Ableman v. Booth*, 62 U.S. 506 (1859), and *In re Tarble*, 80 U.S. 397 (1871), presented in Chapter 2, to repudiate the idea that state courts can issue habeas writs to federal custodians, the 1867 Act expressly sanctions the opposite of that process—federal judges could send writs to state jailors. Federal habeas decisions sometimes held that if the state court was a court of competent jurisdiction, then the federal judge could not review the conviction. Of course, these earlier cases did not reflect opinions about the collateral cognizability of most modern criminal procedure rights because the Supreme Court had yet either to announce the rights themselves or to incorporate them against the states. Until the middle of the twentieth century, there were few constitutional rights for petitioners to assert, and federal judges were not very receptive when those rights were asserted in post-conviction proceedings.

Modern federal habeas review of criminal convictions looks much different than it did in the late nineteenth-century. Federal courts may now grant relief for almost all species of constitutional errors in state proceedings, regardless of whether those errors go to the jurisdiction of the convicting court. For quite some time, however, there was a dispute over whether habeas relief could issue for state inmates held pursuant to constitutional error that did not qualify as jurisdictional. This dispute culminated in *Brown v. Allen*, which is presented in this Chapter, after presenting the Court's earlier decisions.

In an enormously influential article, Professor Paul M. Bator argued that *Brown v. Allen* was a break from a rule that habeas writs would not issue unless there was some jurisdiction-like flaw in the state criminal judgment. See Paul M. Bator, *Finality in Criminal Law and Federal Habeas Corpus for State Prisoners*, 76 Harv. L. Rev. 441, 463–499 (1963) (hereinafter *Finality in Criminal Law*). Scholars have responded to Professor Bator's historical account and the normative principles that sprung from it. An influential response was written by Professor Gary Peller, who argued that what Professor Bator was describing as a limited habeas remedy actually reflected a thin due process right and the limited scope of Supreme Court appellate jurisdiction. See Gary M. Peller, *In Defense of Federal Habeas Corpus Relitigation*, 16 Harv. C.R.-C.L. L. Rev. 579, 604–05 (1982). Although there are a number of late-nineteenth and early-twentieth century cases that are pertinent to this dispute and that pave the way to *Brown v. Allen*, three stand out as most important: *Ex parte Siebold*, 100 U.S. 371 (1879); *Frank v. Mangum*, 237 U.S. 309 (1915); and *Moore v. Dempsey*, 261 U.S. 86 (1923).

When you read these cases, consider the question that was paramount for the Supreme Court in *Brown v. Allen* and for Professor Bator: whether habeas relief may issue for constitutional violations that do not go to the jurisdiction of the convicting court. Do the limits on habeas relief reflect a narrow due process right, or do they reflect a narrow habeas remedy?

Ex parte Siebold

United States Supreme Court
100 U.S. 371 (1879)

■ Mr. JUSTICE BRADLEY delivered the opinion of the court.

The petitioners in this case, Albert Siebold, Walter Tucker, Martin C. Burns, Lewis Coleman, and Henry Bowers, were judges of election at different voting precincts in the city of Baltimore at the election held in that city [for representatives to the 46th Congress].

* * * [T]hey were severally tried, convicted, and sentenced * * * to fine and imprisonment. They now apply to this court for a writ of habeas corpus to be relieved from imprisonment.

* * * [The] indictments were framed partly under sect. 5515 and partly under sect. 5522 of the Revised Statutes of the United States; and the principal questions raised by the application are whether those sections, and certain sections of the title of the Revised Statutes relating to the elective franchise which they are intended to enforce, are within the constitutional power of Congress to enact. If they are not, then it is contended that the Circuit Court has no jurisdiction of the cases, and that the convictions and sentences of imprisonment of the several petitioners were illegal and void.

The jurisdiction of this court to hear the case is the first point to be examined. * * * [One such limitation arises] from the nature and objects of the writ itself, as defined by the common law, from which its name and incidents are derived. It cannot be used as a mere writ of error. * * * [T]he general rule is [] that a conviction and sentence by a court of competent jurisdiction is lawful cause of imprisonment, and no relief can be given by habeas corpus.

The only ground on which this court, or any court, without some special statute authorizing it, will give relief on *habeas corpus* to a prisoner under conviction and sentence of another court is the want of jurisdiction in such court over the person or the cause, or some other matter rendering its proceedings void.

This distinction between an erroneous judgment and one that is illegal or void is well illustrated by the two cases of *Ex parte Lange* and *Ex parte Parks*. In the former case, we held that the judgment was void, and released the petitioner accordingly; in the latter, we held that the judgment, whether erroneous or not, was not void, because the court had jurisdiction of the cause, and we refused to interfere.

[King's Bench] Chief Justice Abbot * * * said: "'It is a general rule that, where a person has been committed under the judgment of another court of competent criminal jurisdiction, [King's Bench] cannot review the sentence upon a return to a habeas corpus. In such cases, this court is not a court of appeal.'"

It is stated, however, in Bacon's Abridgment, * * * that, "if the commitment be against law, as being made by one who had no jurisdiction of the cause, or for a matter for which by law no man ought to be punished, the court are to discharge." The latter part of this rule, when applied to imprisonment under conviction and sentence, is confined to cases of clear and manifest want of criminality in the matter charged such as in effect to render the proceedings void. * * *

* * * [W]e are clearly of opinion that the question raised in the cases before us is proper for consideration on *habeas corpus*. The validity of the judgments is assailed on the ground that the acts of Congress under which the indictments were found are unconstitutional. If this position is well taken, it affects the foundation of the whole proceedings. An unconstitutional law is void, and is as no law. An offence created by it is not a crime. A conviction under it is not merely erroneous, but is illegal and void, and cannot be a legal cause of imprisonment. * * * [P]ersonal liberty is of so great moment in the eye of the law that the judgment of an inferior court affecting it is not deemed so conclusive but that, as we have seen, the question of the court's authority to try and imprison the party may be reviewed

on habeas corpus by a superior court or judge having authority to award the writ. * * *

We proceed, therefore, to examine the cases on their merits. * * * We think that the cause of commitment in these cases was lawful, and that the application for the writ of habeas corpus must be denied.

Application denied.

[The dissenting opinions of JUSTICE CLIFFORD and JUSTICE FIELD have been omitted.]

NOTES AND QUESTIONS ON SIEBOLD

1)   *Lange* **and** *Parks*. *Ex parte Lange*, 85 U.S. 163 (1873) and *Ex parte Parks*, 93 U.S. 18 (1876), share common language, but point in different directions. *Lange* was a major Supreme Court foray into the Fifth Amendment's Double Jeopardy Clause. Lange was convicted of a federal misdemeanor— appropriating a mail-bag worth less than twenty-five dollars—and the federal court sentenced him to one-year imprisonment *and* a fine of two-hundred dollars. The pertinent statute, however, was worded in the disjunctive; the punishment was supposed to be the jail term *or* the fine. After Lange paid the fine and had served five days in jail, the judge vacated the sentence and imposed a new sentence consisting only of the jail time. Lange filed a habeas petition challenging the new sentence under the Double Jeopardy clause, and the Supreme Court upheld the challenge. The Court reasoned:

> [The lower] court . . . could render no second judgment against the prisoner. Its authority was ended. All further exercise of it in that direction was forbidden by the common law, by the Constitution, and by the dearest principles of personal rights, which both of them are supposed to maintain.

> There is no more sacred duty of a court than, in a case properly before it, to maintain unimpaired those securities for the personal rights of the individual which have received for ages the sanction of the jurist and the statesman; and in such cases no narrow or illiberal construction should be given to the words of the fundamental law in which they are embodied. . . [T]he sentence of the Circuit Court under which the petitioner is held a prisoner was pronounced without authority, and he should therefore be discharged.

In *Parks*, the petitioner was convicted of forgery in federal district court, and argued on habeas that the crime for which he was convicted was not a crime against the United States. The Court explained that:

> Whether an act charged in an indictment is or is not a crime by the law which the court administers (in this case the statute law of the United States), is a question which has to be met at almost every stage of criminal proceedings; on motions to quash the indictment, on demurrers, on motions to arrest judgment . . .

The Supreme Court ultimately explained that it could not use habeas process to review the district court's decision that the act charged was a federal crime:

If [we find] that the court below has transcended its powers, [we] will grant the writ and discharge the prisoner, even after judgment. But if the court had jurisdiction and power to convict and sentence, the writ cannot issue to correct a mere error. We have shown that the court below had power to determine the question before it[.] . . .

In *Ex parte Lange* we proceeded on the ground, that, when the court rendered its second judgment, the case was entirely out of its hands. It was *functus officio* in regard to it. The judgment first rendered had been executed and satisfied. The subsequent proceedings were, therefore, according to our view, void.

But, in the case before us, the District Court had plenary jurisdiction, both of the person, the place, the cause, and every thing about it. To review the decision of that court by means of the writ of habeas corpus would be to convert that writ into a mere writ of error, and to assume an appellate power which has never been conferred upon this court.

On what basis can *Lange* and *Parks* be distinguished? The Supreme Court says that the sentencing court was not "jurisdictionally competent" in *Lange*, but that the sentencing court was "jurisdictionally competent" in *Parks*. What does that distinction mean? What type of challenge does *Lange* involve that *Parks* does not?

2)   Limits on Appellate Jurisdiction versus Limits on Habeas Jurisdiction. Think about *Seibold's* procedural posture—use of the Supreme Court's "original" habeas jurisdiction to review a criminal judgment of a lower court. In fact, the Court decided a number of cases in such a posture, frequently making it difficult to isolate the source of any jurisdictional limit. *Siebold* does a particularly good job of specifying which limits flow from which concepts. The Court observed that one such limitation arises "from the nature and objects of the writ itself as defined by the common law, from which its name and incidents are derived." Where else might the limitation come from, if not from the writ?

Until a series of late-nineteenth and early-twentieth century modifications to the Court's appellate jurisdiction, habeas corpus was the vehicle by which the Court conducted direct review of federal criminal convictions.[a] By contrast, Section 25 of the 1789 Judiciary Act did create a general appellate power over state convictions.[b]

Several scholars have argued that during the early eighteenth century, the Supreme Court's habeas review was largely a substitute for formal writ-of-error jurisdiction over federal conviction. See Clarke D. Forsyth, *The Historical Origins of Broad Federal Habeas Review Reconsidered*, 70 Notre Dame L. Rev. 1079, 1147–48 (1995). That habeas jurisdiction was the means by which the Supreme Court exercised appellate power over early and mid-eighteenth-century federal criminal convictions seems clear; but the degree to which the scope of such review approximates the authority the Court would have under a more-general appellate power is a far more difficult question.

Use of habeas jurisdiction as a stand-alone appellate power over criminal proceedings is also not without precedent in English law. In one high profile

[a] Cf. United States v. More, 7 U.S. (3 Cranch) 159, 173–74 (1805) (holding that the 1789 Judiciary Act did not create general appellate jurisdiction over federal criminal convictions).

[b] See James E. Pfander, *Jurisdiction Stripping and the Supreme Court's Power to Supervise Inferior Tribunals*, 78 Tex. L. Rev. 1433, 1467 n.147 (2000).

case, the Court of Common Pleas issued a habeas writ to a lower court that had jailed jurors who had voted to acquit in a high-profile case against William Penn. That exercise of habeas power was particularly noteworthy because King's Bench—not Common Pleas—had general appellate jurisdiction over the conviction. See *Bushell's Case*, 124 Eng. Rep. 1006 (C.P. 1670).

3) Looking "Inside" the Conviction. If a criminal conviction does not suffice to satisfy a habeas inquiry, then must a court be able to look "inside" a conviction to determine the result on collateral review? In *Siebold*, the Court assessed the constitutionality of the sentence, but in *Parks* the Court says it lacks power to "correct a mere error." How much more than "mere error" triggers habeas jurisdiction? The Supreme Court defines one category of justiciable habeas claims as those involving matters for which "by law no man ought to be punished . . ." How broad is that category? Does the category of matters that "ought" not to be punished include those involving factual errors, or just legal errors? How broad should the cognizable set of legal errors be? Should it be limited to convictions under unconstitutional statutes, or did it include due process violations?

4) A "Superior Court." Note that *Siebold* uses the term "superior court." Obviously, that term does not refer to a "supreme court." It actually refers to a court that has broad subject matter jurisdiction ("general jurisdiction") subject to parliamentary exception or deference owed to another sovereign. In England, King's Bench, Common Pleas, Chancery, the Barons of Exchequer, and some other courts claimed general jurisdiction. Recall from the discussion of *Ex parte Watkins*, 28 U.S. 193 (1833), in Chapter 1—specifically, the Note pertaining to courts of general jurisdiction—that a reviewing court owed more deference to "jurisdictional" determinations of superior courts.

5) Federal versus State Custody. In *Lange, Parks,* and *Siebold*, the petitioner was the subject of a federal conviction and sentence. Would a rule for post-conviction review function differently if the prisoner were in state custody? Are the limits expressed in *Siebold* and its antecedents applicable to state custody cases? If so, are there reasons for even greater limits in such cases? What sorts of interests does habeas review promote and compromise?

6) Stay Tuned. According to an influential theory of habeas history, *Lange, Parks,* and *Siebold* mark the beginning of a period in which the court began to use a more elastic concept of "jurisdiction" as a touchstone for federal habeas power. Whether or not those cases were indeed deviations from earlier authority, the early twentieth-century Supreme Court certainly became more aggressive in its use of "due process violations" to justify habeas interventions. The seminal entries in that story are *Frank v. Mangum* and *Moore v. Dempsey*, each excerpted below.

INTRODUCTORY NOTE ON FRANK V. MANGUM

  Many habeas scholars consider *Siebold's* ruling that federal habeas relief could issue to relieve a conviction under an unconstitutional statute to be a significant development. *Siebold*, however, was not addressed to questions of error at trial. In two early twentieth-century cases, *Frank v. Mangum,* 237 U.S. 309 (1915), and *Moore v. Dempsey,* 261 U.S. 86 (1923), the Supreme Court was confronted with claims of mob-dominated trials, but there was no question as to the constitutionality of the underlying statute of conviction. In both cases, the trial court denied motions for a new trial. In both cases, the Court had to address whether such proceedings violated Due Process and whether a habeas corpus remedy could correct the violation.

Leo M. Frank was a part owner and the superintendent of the National Pencil Factory in Atlanta, Georgia. He was "a rising member of the Jewish community who had been elected president of the local B'nai B'rith the previous year." Eric M. Freedman, *Milestones in Habeas Corpus: Part II Leo Frank Lives: Untangling the Historical Roots of Meaningful Federal Habeas Corpus Review of State Convictions*, 51 Ala. L. Rev. 1467, 1475 (2000) (hereinafter "Leo Frank Lives"). In 1913, a night watchman found the body of a 13-year-old white girl who worked at the factory. In Atlanta, the newspaper coverage was sensational, and people throughout the South followed the four-week trial closely. Justice Holmes, in his dissent, described the trial atmosphere as follows:

> The trial began on July 28, 1913, at Atlanta, and was carried on in a court packed with spectators and surrounded by a crowd outside, all strongly hostile to the petitioner. On Saturday, August 23, this hostility was sufficient to lead the judge to confer in the presence of the jury with the chief of police of Atlanta and the colonel of the Fifth Georgia Regiment, stationed in that city, both of whom were known to the jury. On the same day, the evidence seemingly having been closed, the public press, apprehending danger, united in a request to the court that the proceedings should not continue on that evening. Thereupon the court adjourned until Monday morning. On that morning, when the solicitor general entered the court, he was greeted with applause, stamping of feet and clapping of hands, and the judge, before beginning his charge, had a private conversation with the petitioner's counsel in which he expressed the opinion that there would be "probable danger of violence" if there should be an acquittal or a disagreement, and that it would be safer for not only the petitioner but his counsel to be absent from court when the verdict was brought in. At the judge's request they agreed that the petitioner and they should be absent, and they kept their word. When the verdict was rendered, and before more than one of the jurymen had been polled, there was such a roar of applause that the polling could not go on until order was restored. The noise outside was such that it was difficult for the judge to hear the answers of the jurors, although he was only 10 feet from them. With these specifications of fact, the petitioner alleges that the trial was dominated by a hostile mob and was nothing but an empty form.

When you read the Court's decision in *Frank*, consider whether this sort of due process violation goes to the "jurisdiction" of the convicting court.

Frank v. Mangum
United States Supreme Court
237 U.S. 309 (1915)

■ Mr. JUSTICE PITNEY * * * delivered the opinion of the Court:

The points raised by the appellant may be reduced to the following:

(1) * * * [the trial proceedings] amounted to mob domination, that [the judge and jury both "succumbed" to it], and that * * * the proceedings were *coram non judice*.

(2) That [defendant-petitioner] Frank's right to be present [through] the verdict was an essential part of the [unwaivable] right of * * * trial by jury * * *.

(3) That his presence was so essential to a proper hearing that the reception of the verdict [in his absence and that of his counsel] was a departure from the due process * * * sufficient to bring about a loss of jurisdiction of the trial court, and to render the verdict and judgment absolute nullities.

(4) That the failure of Frank and his counsel, upon the first motion for a new trial, to allege as a ground of that motion * * * Frank's absence at the reception of the verdict, or to raise any jurisdictional question based upon it, did not deprive him of the right to afterwards attack the judgment as a nullity * * * .

* * * [I]n order to entitle [Frank] to [habeas relief, his custody must violate] the Constitution of the United States. Moreover, if he is held in custody by reason of his conviction upon a criminal charge before a court having plenary jurisdiction over the subject matter or offense, the place where it was committed, and the person of the prisoner, it results from the nature of the writ itself that he cannot have relief on habeas corpus. Mere errors in point of law, however serious, committed by a criminal court in the exercise of its jurisdiction over a case properly subject to its cognizance cannot be reviewed by habeas corpus. That writ cannot be employed as a substitute for the writ of error.

As to the "due process of law" that is required by the 14th Amendment, * * * a criminal prosecution in the courts of a state, based upon a law not in itself repugnant to the Federal Constitution, and conducted according to the settled course of judicial proceedings as established by the law of the state, so long as it includes notice and a hearing, or an opportunity to be heard, before a court of competent jurisdiction, according to established modes of procedure, is "due process" in the constitutional sense.

* * * [T]he writ of habeas corpus will lie only in case the judgment under which the prisoner is detained is shown to be absolutely void for want of jurisdiction in the court that pronounced it, either because such jurisdiction was absent at the beginning, or because it was lost in the course of the proceedings. And since no question is made respecting the original jurisdiction of the trial court, the contention is and must be that by the conditions that surrounded the trial, and the absence of defendant when the verdict was rendered, the court was deprived of jurisdiction to receive the verdict and pronounce the sentence.

But it would be clearly erroneous to confine the inquiry to the proceedings and judgment of the trial court. The laws of the state of Georgia * * * provide for an appeal in criminal cases to the Supreme Court of that state upon divers grounds, including such as those upon which it is here asserted that the trial court was lacking in jurisdiction. * * * [W]here such an appeal is provided for, and the prisoner has had the benefit of it, the proceedings in the appellate tribunal are to be regarded as a part of the process of law under which he is held in custody by the state, and to be considered in determining any [Fourteenth Amendment] question * * *.

* * * The [due process restriction] is addressed to the state; if it be violated, it makes no difference in a court of the United States by what agency of the state this is done; so, if a violation be threatened by one agency of the state, but prevented by another agency of higher authority, there is no violation by the state. * * * [T]he question whether a state is depriving a pris-

oner of his liberty without due process of [a constitutional] law * * * cannot ordinarily be determined * * * until the conclusion of the course of justice in its [state] courts.

* * * [W]here it is made to appear to a court of the United States that an applicant for habeas corpus is in the custody of a state officer in the ordinary course of a criminal prosecution, under a law of the state not in itself repugnant to the Federal Constitution, the writ, in the absence of very special circumstances, ought not to be issued until the state prosecution has reached its conclusion, and not even then until the Federal questions arising upon the record have been brought before this Court upon writ of error. * * *

* * * [W]here, as here, a criminal prosecution has proceeded through all the courts of the state, * * * the result of the appellate review cannot be ignored when, afterwards, the prisoner applies for his release on the ground of a deprivation of Federal rights sufficient to oust the state of its jurisdiction to proceed to judgment and execution against him. This is not a mere matter of comity, as seems to be supposed. The rule stands upon a much higher plane, for it arises out of the very nature and ground of the inquiry into the proceedings of the state tribunals, and touches closely upon the relations between the state and the Federal governments. * * *

It is objected by [Georgia] that the alleged loss of jurisdiction cannot be shown by evidence outside of the record * * *. The rule at the common law, and under [Parliamentary acts], seems to have been that a showing in the return to a writ of habeas corpus that the prisoner was held under final process based upon a judgment or decree of a court of competent jurisdiction closed the inquiry. So it was held under [the 1789 Judiciary Act in *Watkins*]. And the rule seems to have been the same under the [habeas provisions enacted in 1833 and 1842]. But when Congress, in the [1867 Judiciary Act], extended the writ of habeas corpus to all cases of persons restrained of their liberty in violation of the Constitution or a law or treaty of the United States, procedural regulations were included * * *. These require that the application for the writ shall be made by complaint in writing, signed by the applicant and verified by his oath, setting forth the facts concerning his detention, in whose custody he is detained, and by virtue of what claim or authority, if known; require that the return shall certify the true cause of the detention; and provide that the prisoner may, under oath, deny any of the facts set forth in the return, or allege other material facts, and that the court shall proceed in a summary way to determine the facts by hearing testimony and arguments, and thereupon dispose of the party as law and justice require. The effect is to substitute for the bare legal review * * * a more searching investigation * * *.

* * * [I]t results that under the sections cited a prisoner in custody pursuant to the final judgment of a state court of criminal jurisdiction may have a judicial inquiry in a court of the United States into the very truth and substance of the causes of his detention, although it may become necessary to look behind and beyond the record of his conviction to a sufficient extent to test the jurisdiction of the state court to proceed to judgment against him.

In the light, then, of these established rules and principles: that the due process of law guaranteed by the 14th Amendment has regard to substance of right, and not to matters of form or procedure; that it is open to the courts of the United States, upon an application for a writ of habeas corpus, to look beyond forms and inquire into the very substance of the matter, to the extent of deciding whether the prisoner has been deprived of his liberty without due process of law, and for this purpose to inquire into jurisdictional facts, whether they appear upon the record or not; that an investigation into the case of a prisoner held in custody by a state on conviction of a criminal offense must take into consideration the entire course of proceedings in the courts of the state, and not merely a single step in those proceedings; * * * — we proceed to consider the questions presented.

1. And first, the question of the disorder and hostile sentiment that are said to have influenced the trial court and jury to an extent amounting to mob domination.

* * * There is no doubt of the jurisdiction to issue the writ of habeas corpus. The question is as to the propriety of issuing it in the present case. * * *

Now the obligation resting upon us, as upon the district court, to look through the form and into the very heart and substance of the matter applies as well to the averments of the petition as to the proceedings which the petitioner attacks. * * * [T]he petition contains a narrative of disorder, hostile manifestations, and uproar which, if it stood alone, and were to be taken as true, may be conceded to show an environment inconsistent with a fair trial and an impartial verdict. * * *

[T]he allegations were considered by [the state appellate] courts, successively, at times and places and under circumstances wholly apart from the atmosphere of the trial, and free from any suggestion of mob domination or the like * * *. [T]he allegations of disorder were found by both of the state courts to be groundless except in a few particulars [found to be harmless error] * * *.

Whatever question is raised about the jurisdiction of the trial court, no doubt is suggested but that the [state] Supreme Court had full jurisdiction to determine the matters of fact and the questions of law arising out of this alleged disorder; nor is there any reason to suppose that it did not fairly and justly perform its duty. * * * It is a fundamental principle of jurisprudence, arising from the very nature of courts of justice and the objects for which they are established, that a question of fact or of law distinctly put in issue and directly determined by a court of competent jurisdiction cannot afterwards be disputed between the same parties. * * *

However, it is not necessary, for the purposes of the present case, to invoke the doctrine of *res judicata*; and, in view of the impropriety of limiting in the least degree the authority of the courts of the United States in investigating an alleged violation by a state of the due process of law guaranteed by the Fourteenth Amendment, we put out of view for the present the suggestion that even the questions of fact bearing upon the jurisdiction of the trial court could be conclusively determined against the prisoner by the decision of the state court of last resort.

But this does not mean that that decision may be ignored or disregarded. To do this, as we have already pointed out, would be not merely to disregard comity, but to ignore the essential question before us, which is not the guilt or innocence of the prisoner, or the truth of any particular fact asserted by him, but whether the state, taking into view the entire course of its procedure, has deprived him of due process of law. This familiar phrase does not mean that the operations of the state government shall be conducted without error or fault in any particular case, nor that the Federal courts may substitute their judgment for that of the state courts, or exercise any general review over their proceedings, but only that the fundamental rights of the prisoner shall not be taken from him arbitrarily or without the right to be heard according to the usual course of law in such cases.

We, of course, agree that if a trial is in fact dominated by a mob, so that the jury is intimidated and the trial judge yields, and so that there is an actual interference with the course of justice, there is, in that court, a departure from due process of law in the proper sense of that term. And if the state, supplying no corrective process, carries into execution a judgment of death or imprisonment based upon a verdict thus produced by mob domination, the state deprives the accused of his life or liberty without due process of law.

But the state may supply such corrective process as to it seems proper. Georgia has adopted the familiar procedure of a motion for a new trial, followed by an appeal to its Supreme Court, not confined to the mere record of conviction, but going at large, and upon evidence adduced outside of that record, into the question whether the processes of justice have been interfered with in the trial court. Repeated instances are reported of verdicts and judgments set aside and new trials granted for disorder or mob violence interfering with the prisoner's right to a fair trial.

Such an appeal was accorded to the prisoner in the present case, in a manner and under circumstances already stated, and the Supreme Court, upon a full review, decided appellant's allegations of fact, so far as matters now material are concerned, to be unfounded. * * * [S]uch a determination of the facts as was thus made by the court of last resort of Georgia respecting the alleged interference with the trial through disorder and manifestations of hostile sentiment cannot, in this collateral inquiry, be treated as a nullity, but must be taken as setting forth the truth of the matter; certainly, until some reasonable ground is shown for an inference that the court which rendered it either was wanting in jurisdiction or at least erred in the exercise of its jurisdiction, and that the mere assertion by the prisoner that the facts of the matter are other than the state court, upon full investigation, determined them to be, will not be deemed sufficient to raise an issue respecting the correctness of that determination; especially not, where the very evidence upon which the determination was rested is withheld by him who attacks the finding.

It is argued that if, in fact, there was disorder such as to cause a loss of jurisdiction in the trial court, jurisdiction could not be restored by any decision of the Supreme Court. This, we think, embodies more than one error of reasoning. It regards a part only of the judicial proceedings, instead of considering the entire process of law. It also begs the question of the existence of such disorder as to cause a loss of jurisdiction in the trial court, which should not be assumed, in the face of the decision of the reviewing court, without showing some adequate ground for disregarding that decision. * * * The rule of law that in ordinary cases requires a prisoner to exhaust his remedies within the state before coming to the courts of the United States for redress would lose the greater part of its salutary force if the prisoner's mere allegations were to stand the same in law after as before the state courts had passed judgment upon them. * * *

The Georgia courts, in the present case, proceeded upon the theory that Frank would have been entitled to this relief had his charges been true, and they refused a new trial only because they found his charges untrue save in a few minor particulars not amounting to more than irregularities, and not prejudicial to the accused. There was here no denial of due process of law. * * *

4. To conclude: taking appellant's petition as a whole, and not regarding any particular portion of it to the exclusion of the rest,—dealing with its true and substantial meaning, and not merely with its superficial import,—it shows that Frank, having been formally accused of a grave crime, was placed on trial before a court of competent jurisdiction, with a jury lawfully constituted; he had a public trial, deliberately conducted, with the benefit of counsel for his defense; he was found guilty and sentenced pursuant to the laws of the state; twice he has moved the trial court to grant a new trial, and once to set aside the verdict as a nullity; three times he has been heard upon appeal before the court of last resort of that state, and in every instance the adverse action of the trial court has been affirmed; his allegations of hostile public sentiment and disorder in and about the courtroom, improperly influencing the trial court and the jury against him, have been rejected because found untrue in point of fact upon evidence presumably justifying that finding, and which he has not produced in the present proceeding; his contention that his lawful rights were infringed because he was not permitted to be present when the jury rendered its verdict has been set aside because it was waived by his failure to raise the objection in due season when fully cognizant of the facts. In all of these proceedings, the state, through its courts, has retained jurisdiction over him, has accorded to him the fullest right and opportunity to be heard according to the established modes of procedure, and now holds him in custody to pay the penalty of the crime of which he has been adjudged guilty. In our opinion, he is not shown to have been deprived of any right guaranteed to him by the 14th Amendment or any other provision of the Constitution or laws of the United States; on the contrary, he has been convicted, and is now held in custody, under "due process of law" within the meaning of the Constitution.

The final order of the District Court, refusing the application for a writ of habeas corpus, is affirmed.

[The dissenting opinion of JUSTICE HOLMES, joined by JUSTICE HUGHES, is omitted.]

————

NOTES AND QUESTIONS ON FRANK

1) The Frank Murder Trial. Leo Frank's trial was a state and national sensation from the beginning; it was a hurricane of political, cultural, and racial resentment. The court convicted and sentenced Frank for murder. The pencil plant's night watchman found the girl's body on his way to the "colored" bathroom. The police eventually suspected Frank because he had not answered his phone when called about the attack, he was nervous when questioned, and he had been inappropriately suggestive to several young women around the plant. The police were believed to have applied coercive tactics to secure the cooperation of several witnesses.

Frank was Jewish, and his trial in Marietta, Georgia, stoked cultural resentment blotting the Deep South. Frank was cast as a Yankee Jew who took the life of a young Christian girl. Frank's legal team, in turn, argued that at least one prosecution witness was not credible because he was a black man. The defense's closing described the witness as a "dirty, filthy, black, drunken, lying, nigger."[c] Most historians now believe that the witness was in fact the murderer, but many white people did not believe that a black man was capable of executing such a "sophisticated" crime. At trial, Frank took the stand in his own defense, telling the jury, "I know nothing whatever of the death of little Mary Phagan." The atmosphere was so circus-like, with a crowd of five thousand people outside the courthouse, that the judge had to make sure that Frank and his attorneys were not present when the court read the jury's verdict. The judge reasoned that the crowd might harm Frank and his defense team if Frank were found innocent.

Frank was found guilty and lost his Supreme Court appeal. Lame-duck Governor John Slaton reviewed a mountain of evidence—including much that had not been presented at trial—and commuted Frank's sentence the day before Frank was to hang. Governor Slaton gave the statement:

> Two thousand years ago another Governor washed his hands of a case and turned a Jew over to a mob. For two thousand years that Governor's name has been accursed. If today another Jew were lying in his grave because I had failed to do my duty I would all through life find his blood on my hands and would consider myself an assassin through cowardice.

Under the influence of the Governor-elect, however, a group of prominent local officials organized a band of "Knights of Mary Phagan" to lynch Frank. Knight membership included various police officers, the mayor of Marietta, a former governor, a sheriff, an ex-sheriff, a clergyman, and two former judges. On August 16, 1915, about twenty-five of the Knights kidnapped Frank from the prison farm (which only had two guards) and hung him. Crowds gathered to watch and snap photos; families came to examine the corpse. Merchants sold pictures of the hanging as postcards. 3,000 Jewish people left Georgia after the hanging. Frank was pardoned posthumously in 1986, after his then-elderly office boy came forward with a credible affidavit that one of the witnesses had committed the murder. Many books have been written about the case (including the David Mamet book "The Old Religion"), and it has inspired movies, a mini-series, and a musical.[d]

2)   Understanding the Arguments. To understand exactly why *Frank* was so legally significant, you should understand precisely the relief that Frank sought. He wanted a declaration that: (1) mob domination affected the judge's rulings and the jury's verdict; (2) because he was absent for most of the proceedings, the judgment abrogated his fair-trial rights; (3) his absence amounted to a due process violation that, in turn, robbed the trial court of its jurisdictional competency; (4) Frank's failure to include some of the arguments in his new trial motion before the state court did not bar federal habeas relief. *Frank* therefore addressed both the jurisdiction of the federal court and the propriety of granting relief when prior state process could have addressed the question.

---

[c] Steve Oney, *And the Dead Shall Rise* 324 (2003). The paragraphs that follow draw from Oney's account and that of Leonard Dinnerstein. See Leonard Dinnerstein, *The Leo Frank Case* (1987). For an excellent detailed discussion of *Frank*, focusing on its importance for federal habeas corpus, see Eric M. Freedman, *Leo Frank Lives: Untangling the Historical Roots of Meaningful Federal Habeas Corpus Review of State Convictions*, 51 Ala. L. Rev. 1467 (2000).

[d] See, e.g., Harry Golden, *A Little Girl is Dead* (1965), and Robert Seitz Frey and Nancy Thompson-Frey, Charles and Louise Samuels, *Night Fell on Georgia* (1956), *The Silent and the Damned* (1988). Dramatic works include: *They Won't Forget* (1937) (film of fictionalized retelling); *The Murder of Mary Phagan* (1988) (dramatized miniseries), *Parade (1998)* (musical), *The People v. Leo Frank* (2009) (docudrama).

In light of the facts presented in Note 1, do you think that, in the new trial motion, Frank should have been required to present his claim of mob domination to the trial court?

3)   Features of "Jurisdictional Competence." *Frank* says that habeas relief is available only where the trial court lacked (or lost) jurisdiction over the subject matter or the person. How consistent is that proposition with *Siebold*, *Parks*, and *Lange*? For example, in *Lange*, the Supreme Court ordered habeas relief for a prisoner who had been sentenced in violation of the Double Jeopardy Clause. In what sense does a Double Jeopardy violation deprive the trial court of personal or subject-matter jurisdiction?

4)   Features of "Due Process." The Supreme Court held that due process required that the conviction and sentence not be under law repugnant to the Federal Constitution, be imposed "according to the settled course of judicial proceedings as established by the law of the state," and reflect a "notice and a hearing, or an opportunity to be heard, before a court of competent jurisdiction, according to established modes of procedure . . ." Although the Court in *Frank* held that a habeas writ could not serve as a remedy for run-of-the-mill error, the Court also held that habeas could, to some extent, serve as a remedy for due process violations. Is the concept of due process in *Frank* broad or narrow, from the perspective of then-controlling precedent? Does it include deviations from ordinary state process? Under *Frank's* reasoning, is any constitutional violation a due process violation?

To put these questions a slightly different way, was the Court saying that habeas could remedy certain due process violations, but only if those due process violations related to the "jurisdiction" of the convicting court? Or was the Court positioning habeas as a remedy for a larger set of due process violations, where the important variable for determining whether relief should issue involved the availability of state corrective process? You might recognize some of the examples of the due process right identified by the court—subject matter jurisdiction,[e] notice of a hearing, and opportunity to be heard—as "jurisdictional" phenomena you encountered in your first-year civil procedure course. In civil cases, of course, there are many due process violations that do not go the jurisdiction of the court that has entered judgment against a defendant, and the due process violations that do not go to the jurisdiction of the judgment-entering court are generally not subject to collateral attack. Should the concept of a court's jurisdiction be the same in civil and criminal contexts?

5)   The Role of State Appellate Remedies. *Frank* emphasizes the role of state appellate review both in assessing the existence of a due process violation and in determining the propriety of a federal habeas remedy. How does the availability of a state remedy function in each context? Do you agree that the state may "cure" any trial due process violations by supplying corrective process on appeal? Ideally, the availability of state corrective process means that a state court will produce a decision on the constitutional question presented. Does additional process reach the point of diminishing returns, or is there something important and different that a federal judge can contribute?

---

[e] The question of subject matter jurisdiction is usually considered a function of Article III, § 2 of the Constitution, and not of either the Fifth or Fourteenth Amendment Due Process clauses.

6) ***Res Judicata.*** *Frank* noted briefly that *res judicata*, which bars
relitigation between the same parties of the same claim after there has been a
final judgment, posed no obstacle to reviewing the decision by the state court.
Federal post-conviction review is usually treated as a *res judicata* exception,
and subsequent decisions by the Court would more explicitly state as much.
Treating post-conviction review as a *res judicata* exception means that a prior
judgment between two parties does not preclude a habeas challenge to the merits of something that prior judgment may have encompassed. Because habeas is
treated as a *res judicata* exception, courts have the power to examine issues
fairly encompassed by the criminal judgment of a jurisdictionally-competent
court.

7)   Fact Review. *Frank* did not hold that the federal *Constitution* requires
that there be habeas authority to revisit fact questions decided by a state court,
but the Supreme Court identified a *statutory* right to fact disposition in the
1867 Habeas Corpus Act. In *Frank*, however, the Court also held that the state
disposition of the mob-domination claim could not be disregarded, even though
the federal courts technically had jurisdiction to re-determine fact questions.
How should federal judges proceed if they are trying to honor *Frank's* holding
that federal judges have jurisdiction to review—but should not vacate—factual
determinations made by state courts?

8)   Comity. Comity is a concept rooted in international law and means,
roughly, that one sovereign should recognize and enforce judgments of another.
In what sense does federal post-conviction review implicate comity concerns?
How much should comity justify results in state convictions that differ from
legal outcomes that would have been reached in federal court? Does comity apply equally to specific determinations of fact and to disposition of particular
claims—or does it apply more broadly to anything fairly encompassed within a
judgment? Moreover, the Supreme Court stated that comity requires some deference to appellate fact review. The Court reasoned that comity requires more
than just sequencing—more than the ability of a state to decide constitutional
questions and related issues first.

(9)   The Holmes Dissent. Justice Holmes, in dissent, argued forcefully that
the judgment should be reversed:

> Whatever disagreement there may be as to the scope of the phrase "due
> process of law," there can be no doubt that it embraces the fundamental
> conception of a fair trial, with opportunity to be heard. Mob law does not
> become due process of law by securing the assent of a terrorized jury. We
> are not speaking of mere disorder, or mere irregularities in procedure, but
> of a case where the processes of justice are actually subverted. In such a
> case, the Federal court has jurisdiction to issue the writ.

In a passage describing the function of habeas corpus, Justice Holmes wrote
that the Justices could "lay on one side" any procedural defects, such as whether the petitioner did or did not waive an argument about jury polling:

> [H]abeas corpus cuts through all forms and goes to the very tissue of the
> structure. It comes in from the outside, not in subordination to the pro-
> ceedings, and although every form may have been preserved, opens the in-
> quiry whether they have been more than an empty shell.

Justice Holmes dissented in *Frank*, but secured a majority for a similar position eight years later, in *Moore v. Dempsey*, 261 U.S. 86 (1923).

Moore v. Dempsey

United States Supreme Court
261 U.S. 86 (1923)

■ Mr. JUSTICE HOLMES delivered the opinion of the Court.

* * * The ground of the petition for the writ is that the proceedings in the State Court, although a trial in form, were only a form, and that the appellants were hurried to conviction under the pressure of a mob without any regard for their rights and without according to them due process of law.

* * * On the night of September 30, 1919, a number of colored people assembled in their church were attacked and fired upon by a body of white men, and in the disturbance that followed, a white man was killed. The report of the killing caused great excitement, and was followed by the hunting down and shooting of many negroes and also by the killing on October 1 of one Clinton Lee, a white man, for whose murder the petitioners were indicted. They seem to have been arrested with many others on the same day. The petitioners say that Lee must have been killed by other whites, but that we leave on one side, as what we have to deal with is not the petitioners' innocence or guilt, but solely the question whether their constitutional rights have been preserved. They say that their meeting was to employ counsel for protection against extortions practiced upon them by the landowners, and that the landowners tried to prevent their effort, but that again we pass by as not directly bearing upon the trial. * * *

A Committee of Seven was appointed by the Governor in regard to what the committee called the "insurrection" in the county. The newspapers daily published inflammatory articles. On the 7th, a statement by one of the committee was made public to the effect that the present trouble was "a deliberately planned insurrection of the negroes against the whites, directed by an organization known as the 'Progressive Farmers' and Household Union of America' established for the purpose of banding negroes together for the killing of white people." According to the statement, the organization was started by a swindler to get money from the blacks.

Shortly after the arrest of the petitioners, a mob marched to the jail for the purpose of lynching them, but were prevented by the presence of United States troops and the promise of some of the Committee of Seven and other leading officials that, if the mob would refrain, as the petition puts it, they would execute those found guilty in the form of law. The Committee's own statement was that the reason that the people refrained from mob violence was "that this Committee gave our citizens their solemn promise that the law would be carried out." According to affidavits * * *, the Committee made good their promise by calling colored witnesses and having them whipped and tortured until they would say what was wanted, among them being the two relied on to prove the petitioners' guilt. However this may be, a grand jury of white men was organized on October 27 with one of the Committee of Seven and, it is alleged, with many of a posse organized to fight the blacks upon it, and, on the morning of the 29th, the indictment was returned. On November 3, the petitioners were brought into Court, informed that a certain lawyer was appointed their counsel, and were placed on trial before a white jury—blacks being systematically excluded from both grand and petit juries. The Court and neighborhood were thronged with an adverse crowd that threatened the most dangerous consequences to anyone interfering with the desired result. The counsel did not venture to demand delay or a change of venue, to challenge a juryman or to ask for separate trials. He had had no preliminary consultation with the accused, called no witnesses for the defence, although they could have been produced, and did not put the defendants on the stand. The trial lasted about three-quarters of an hour, and in less than five minutes, the jury brought in a verdict of guilty of murder in the first degree. According to the allegations and affidavits, there never was a chance for the petitioners to be acquitted; no juryman could have voted for an acquittal and continued to live in Phillips County, and if any prisoner by any chance had been acquitted by a jury, he could not have escaped the mob.

The averments as to the prejudice by which the trial was environed have some corroboration in appeals to the Governor, about a year later, earnestly urging him not to interfere with the execution of the petitioners. One came from five members of the Committee of Seven, and stated, in addition to what has been quoted heretofore, that "all our citizens are of the opinion that the law should take its course." Another, from a part of the American Legion, protests against a contemplated commutation of the sentence of four of the petitioners and repeats that a "solemn promise was given by the leading citizens of the community that, if the guilty parties were not lynched, and let the law take its course, that justice would be done and the majesty of the law upheld." A meeting of the Helena Rotary Club, attended by members representing, as it said, seventy-five of the leading industrial and commercial enterprises of Helena, passed a resolution approving and supporting the action of the American Legion post. The Lions Club of Helena, at a meeting attended by members said to represent sixty of the leading industrial and commercial enterprises of the city, passed a resolution to the same effect. In May of the same year, a trial of six other negroes was coming on, and it was represented to the Governor by the white citizens and officials of Phillips County that, in all probability, those negroes would be lynched. It is alleged that, in order to appease the mob spirit and in a measure secure the safety of the six, the Governor fixed the date for the execution of the petitioners at June 10, 1921, but that the execution was stayed by proceedings in Court; we presume the proceedings before the Chancellor to which we shall advert.

In *Frank v. Mangum*, it was recognized, of course, that if, in fact, a trial is dominated by a mob so that there is an actual interference with the course of justice, there is a departure from due process of law, and that, "if the State, supplying no corrective process, carries into execution a judgment of death or imprisonment based upon a verdict thus produced by mob domination, the State deprives the accused of his life or liberty without due process of law." We assume in accordance with that case that the corrective process supplied by the State may be so adequate that interference by habeas corpus ought not to be allowed. It certainly is true that mere mistakes of law in the course of a trial are not to be corrected in that way. But if the case is that the whole proceeding is a mask — that counsel, jury and judge were swept to the fatal end by an irresistible wave of public passion, and that the State Courts failed to correct the wrong; neither perfection in the machinery for correction nor the possibility that the trial court and counsel saw no other way of avoiding an immediate outbreak of the mob can prevent this Court from securing to the petitioners their constitutional rights.

In this case, a motion for a new trial on the ground alleged in this petition was overruled, and, upon exceptions and appeal to the Supreme Court, the judgment was affirmed. The Supreme Court said that the complaint of discrimination against petitioners by the exclusion of colored men from the jury came too late, and, by way of answer to the objection that no fair trial could be had in the circumstances, stated that it could not say "that this must necessarily have been the case"; that eminent counsel was appointed to defend the petitioners, that the trial was had according to law, the jury correctly charged, and the testimony legally sufficient. On June 8, 1921, two days before the date fixed for their execution; a petition for habeas corpus was presented to the Chancellor, and he issued the writ and an injunction against the execution of the petitioners; but the Supreme Court of the State held that the Chancellor had no jurisdiction under the state law, whatever might be the law of the United States. * * * [The federal habeas petition] was presented to the District Court on September 21. We shall not say more concerning the corrective process afforded to the petitioners than that it does not seem to us sufficient to allow a Judge of the United States to escape the duty of examining the facts for himself when, if true as alleged, they make the trial absolutely void. We have confined the statement to facts admitted by the demurrer. We will not say that they cannot be met, but it appears to us unavoidable that the District Judge should find whether the facts alleged are true and whether they can be explained so far as to leave the state proceedings undisturbed.

Order reversed. The case to stand for hearing before the District Court.

[The dissenting opinion of JUSTICE MCREYNOLDS is omitted.]

NOTES AND QUESTIONS ON MOORE

1) **The Elaine Race Riots.** As the Supreme Court opinion explains, the black tenant farmers union was meeting inside a Phillips, Arkansas church. Some members of the union or its sympathizers exchanged fire with the group of white men outside the church. A white railroad security employee was killed, and the "Elaine Race Riots" ensued. The governor led federal troops into the countryside and arrested hundreds of black people. The State restricted the movement of many others. Almost 250 black people and at least 4 white people were killed in the violence. See Freedman, *Leo Frank Lives*, 51 Ala. L. Rev. at 1503. For a more detailed historical account of the riots, see O.A. Rogers, Jr., *The Elaine Race Riots of 1919*, 19 Ark. Hist. Q. 142 (1960).

After the riots, an all-white grand jury did not charge the potential black defendants who chose to testify against other alleged rioters. The rest were indicted. Law enforcement officers elicited much of the relevant testimony through illegal beatings and torture. Frank Moore was among the black defendants charged with and sentenced to die for murder. The defense lawyer, whom the defendants did not meet until the trial, called no witnesses and presented no evidence. The trial took less than an hour, and the jury deliberations took less than ten minutes. A white mob surrounded the courthouse and plainly intimidated the jurors.

When the proceedings concluded, the trial court sentenced twelve black defendants to death. Thirty-six black defendants pleaded guilty to second-degree murder, and sixty-seven others were convicted and imprisoned. The Supreme Court's decision in *Moore* remanded the case to the trial court to assess the truth of the pleadings. The trial court released Moore, and the rest of those sentenced in the wake of the Elaine race riot. For an account of the legal battle, see Richard C. Cortner, *A Mob Intent on Death: The NAACP and the Arkansas Riot Cases* (1988).

2)   A "Sham" Proceeding. *Moore* is a big step, notwithstanding the argument about whether the "step" is a growth in due process rights or the scope of the habeas remedy. In *Moore*, the Court clearly did not want to require federal habeas relief for all trial injustices, so the Court characterizes its due process ruling as affecting those cases where the "whole proceeding is a mask." What were the attributes of the sham proceeding? Is the failure of counsel sufficient to qualify a proceeding as a sham?

3)   The Sufficiency of State Corrective Process. In *Frank*, the Court ruled that the adequacy of state appellate process cured the due process violation. In *Moore*, the Court held that "[w]e shall not say more concerning the corrective process afforded to the petitioners than that it does not seem to us sufficient to allow a Judge of the United States to escape the duty of examining the facts for himself when, if true as alleged, they make the trial absolutely void." What distinguishes the corrective process in *Frank* from that in *Moore*? Both were presumably conducted in the same shadow of violence. Why might the Court strain for a very narrow ruling in *Moore*?

4)   Does *Moore* Overrule *Frank*? There exists academic disagreement about whether *Moore* overruled *Frank*, and the focus on state corrective process is key to understanding the dispute. Professor Henry Hart, Jr., stated that "*Frank v. Mangum* was substantially discredited eight years later in *Moore v. Dempsey*." Henry M. Hart, Jr., *Foreword: Time Chart of the Justices*, 73 Harv. L. Rev. 84, 105 (1959). In his *Moore* dissent, Justice McReynolds accused the majority of overruling *Frank*. Professor Bator, however, argued that *Moore* and *Frank* can be reconciled:

> What is striking is that in *Moore*, unlike in *Frank*, the state supreme court did not conduct any proceeding or make any inquiry into the truth of the allegations of mob domination, and made no findings with respect to them; its opinion refers to the charge that fair trial was impossible in the trial court solely by commenting, laconically, that it could not say "that this must necessarily have been the case."

Bator, *Finality in Criminal Law*, 76 Harv. L. Rev. at 488. In fact, Justices McKenna and Van Devanter joined the majorities in both *Moore* and *Frank*. Do you think *Moore* overrules *Frank*, or do you think they are distinguishable? If they are, then is the availability of state corrective process the key to distinguishing them?

5)   Innocence. Justice Holmes argued that whether the defendants are innocent or not is beside the point. For the *Frank* majority, the question was simply whether the defendants were denied due process. How exactly is due process bound up with innocence? Is it not possible that a court could sentence an innocent man while being faithful to the procedural guarantees in the Federal Constitution? How about the converse situation—should federal habeas relief concern itself with constitutional violations that do not go to the ultimate issue of innocence?

B. *BROWN V. ALLEN* AND THE MODERN ERA OF STATE POST-CONVICTION REVIEW

The scope of the writ expanded gradually after *Moore*, as the Supreme Court developed more procedures for evaluating state sentences imposed absent statutory authority, some other jurisdictional requirement, and, gradually, due or corrective process. For example, in *Mooney v. Holohan*, 294 U.S. 87 (1935), the Court held that a conviction lacked due process if it was obtained pursuant to knowingly perjured testimony—the Court sent the case back for "corrective process" in the state courts.

INTRODUCTORY NOTE ON BROWN V. ALLEN

The next case, *Brown v. Allen*, 344 U.S. 443 (1953), is generally considered the big bang of modern post-conviction jurisprudence. After *Brown v. Allen*, from the 1950s through the early 1970s, a series of Supreme Court cases affirmed the use of the writ to enforce new rules of criminal procedure against the states. For example, in a trilogy of 1963 rulings, *Fay v. Noia*, 372 U.S. 391 (1963), *Townsend v. Sain*, 372 U.S. 293 (1963), and *Sanders v. United States*, 373 U.S. 1 (1963), the Court recognized relatively permissive "gateways" for prisoners to bypass procedural defects in federal habeas petitions.

Chapter 1 contained an excerpt from *Brown v. Allen*, which involved the merits of the claims that the four defendants raised in their consolidated cases. Excerpted below is the Court's more general ruling concerning the scope of habeas corpus relief available to state inmates. As you read the majority opinion in *Brown*—part of it by Justice Reed, and part by Justice Frankfurter—focus on: (1) whether a prior disposition in a state proceeding or on a certiorari petition should limit the scope of federal habeas review; (2) whether the habeas statute requires that state remedies be exhausted before pursuing federal habeas review; (3) whether a federal judge may conduct a hearing to explore the facts in the case; and (4) whether any constitutional claim may be asserted in a federal habeas petition challenging a state conviction (as opposed to simply questions of the trial court's "jurisdiction"). When reflecting on those issues, also consider Justice Jackson's concurring opinion, which objects to the expansion of federal review of state convictions. Try to identify the elements of his critique that relate to (1) the intrusion of federal habeas review on state judicial power, (2) the burden that federal habeas review places on federal judges, and (3) the counterproductive consequences for the prisoner-litigants themselves.

Brown v. Allen[f]
United States Supreme Court
344 U.S. 443 (1953)

■ Mr. JUSTICE REED delivered the opinion of the Court.

Certiorari was granted to review judgments of the United States Court of Appeals for the Fourth Circuit. [There were three cases: *Brown v. Allen*,

[f] As the introductory Note indicated, the Supreme Court decided four consolidated cases: *Brown v. Allen, (Bennie and Lloyd Ray) Daniels v. Allen*, and *Allen v. Smith*.

Speller v. Allen, and *Daniels et al. v. Allen*. The Fourth Circuit had affirmed orders of the federal district court denying relief.] * * * *

It is to be noted that an applicant is barred unless he has "exhausted the remedies available in the courts of the State . . . by any available procedure." * * * When, in April 1948, Judge Maris presented the Judicial Conference draft of § 2254 to the Senate Judiciary Subcommittee, the language of the revision of 28 U.S.C., on which the hearings were being held, set out three bases for exercise of federal jurisdiction over applications for habeas corpus from state prisoners[:] (1) that the applicant had exhausted the remedies available in the courts of the state, or (2) where there was no adequate remedy available in such courts, or (3) where such courts had denied the applicant a fair adjudication of the legality of his detention under the Constitution and laws of the United States. In accepting the recommendation of the Judicial Conference, the Congress eliminated the third basis of jurisdiction * * *:

> "The second purpose is to eliminate, as a ground of Federal jurisdiction to review by habeas corpus judgments of State courts, the proposition that the State court has denied a prisoner a 'fair adjudication of the legality of his detention under the Constitution and laws of the United States.' The Judicial Conference believes that this would be an undesirable ground for Federal jurisdiction in addition to exhaustion of State remedies or lack of adequate remedy in the State courts because it would permit proceedings in the Federal court on this ground before the petitioner had exhausted his State remedies. This ground would, of course, always be open to a petitioner to assert in the Federal court after he had exhausted his State remedies or if he had no adequate State remedy.["] * * * *

If the substitution for "adequate remedy available" of the present definition was intended by the Congress to eliminate the right of a state prisoner to apply for relief by habeas corpus to the lower federal courts, we do not think that the report would have suggested that a remedy for denial of a "fair adjudication" was in the federal court. The suggested elimination of district and circuit courts does not square with the other statutory habeas corpus provisions. We are unwilling to conclude without a definite congressional direction that so radical a change was intended. * * * *

II. Effect of Former Proceedings

* * * * A. *Effect of Denial of Certiorari.*—[Justice Reed, who did not write for the Court on this point, would accord prior denials of certiorari potentially significant but not *res judicata* on subsequent federal habeas applications. On this point, the opinion of Mr. Justice Frankfurter, excerpted below, was the majority position of the Court.]

B. *Effect of State Court Adjudications.*—* * * So far as weight to be given the proceedings in the courts of the state is concerned, a United States district court, with its familiarity with state practice is in a favorable position to recognize adequate state grounds in denials of relief by state courts without opinion. *A fortiori*, where the state action was based on an adequate state ground, no further, examination is required, unless no state remedy for the deprivation of federal constitutional rights ever existed. Furthermore, where there is material conflict of fact in the transcripts of evidence as to deprivation of constitutional rights, the District Court may properly depend upon the state's resolution of the issue. In other circumstances the state adjudication carries the weight that federal practice gives to the conclusion of a court of last resort of another jurisdiction on federal constitutional issues. It is not res judicata. * * * *

The District Court and the Court of Appeals recognized the power of the District Court to reexamine federal constitutional issues even after trial and review by a state and refusal of certiorari in this Court. * * *

III. Right to Plenary Hearing.

* * * [T]he writ of habeas corpus was refused on the entire record of the respective state and federal courts. It is petitioner's contention, however, that the District Court committed error when it took no evidence and heard no argument on the federal constitutional issues. * * * He argues that the Federal District Court * * * must exercise its judicial power to hear again the controversy notwithstanding prior determinations of substantially identical federal issues by the highest state court * * *.

Jurisdiction over applications for federal habeas corpus is controlled by statute. The Code directs a court entertaining an application to award the writ. But an application is not "entertained" by a mere filing. Liberal as the courts are and should be as to practice in setting out claimed violations of constitutional rights, the applicant must meet the statutory test of alleging facts that entitle him to relief.

The word "entertain" presents difficulties. * * * [But] we think it means a federal district court's conclusion, after examination of the application with such accompanying papers as the court deems necessary, that a hearing on the merits legal or factual is proper. Even after deciding to entertain the application, the District Court may determine later from the return or otherwise that the hearing is unnecessary.

It is clear by statutory enactment that a federal district court is not required to entertain an application for habeas corpus if it appears that "the legality of such detention has been determined by a judge or court of the United States on a prior application for a writ of habeas corpus." The Reviser's Notes to this [provision] say that no material change in existing practice is intended. Nothing else indicates that the purpose of Congress was to restrict by the adoption of the Code of 1948 the discretion of the District Court, if it had such discretion before, to entertain petitions from state prisoners which raised the same issues raised in the state courts.

Furthermore, in enacting 28 U.S.C. 2254, dealing with persons in custody under state judgments, Congress made no reference to the power of a federal district court over federal habeas corpus for claimed wrongs previously passed upon by state courts. A federal judge on a habeas corpus application is required to "summarily hear and determine the facts, and dispose of the matter as law and justice require[.]" This has long been the law. * * *

Applications to district courts on grounds determined adversely to the applicant by state courts should follow the same principle—a refusal of the writ without more, if the court is satisfied, by the record, that the state process has given fair consideration to the issues and the offered evidence, and has resulted in a satisfactory conclusion. Where the record of the application affords an adequate opportunity to weigh the sufficiency of the allegations and the evidence, and no unusual circumstances calling for a hearing are presented, a repetition of the trial is not required. However, a trial may be had in the discretion of the federal court or judge hearing the new application. A way is left open to redress violations of the Constitution. [See, *inter alia*, Moore v. Dempsey, 261 U.S. 86.] Although they have the power, it is not necessary for federal courts to hold hearings on the merits, facts or law a second time when satisfied that federal constitutional rights have been protected. It is necessary to exercise jurisdiction to the extent of determining by examination of the record whether or not a hearing would serve the ends of justice. As the state and federal courts have the same responsibilities to protect persons from violation of their constitutional rights, we conclude that a federal district court may decline, without a rehearing of the facts, to award a writ of habeas corpus to a state prisoner where the legality of such detention has been determined, on the facts presented, by the highest state court with jurisdiction * * *.

As will presently appear, this case involves no extraordinary situation. Since the complete record was before the District Court, there was no need for rehearing or taking of further evidence. Treating the state's response to the application as a motion to dismiss, the court properly granted that motion. Discharge from conviction through habeas corpus is not an act of judicial clemency but a protection against illegal custody.

The need for argument is a matter of judicial discretion. All issues were adequately presented. There was no abuse.

IV. Disposition of Constitutional Issues.

Next we direct our attention to the records which were before the District Court in order to review that court's conclusions that North Carolina accorded petitioners a fair adjudication of their federal questions. Questions of discrimination and admission of coerced confessions lie in the compass of the Due Process and Equal Protection Clauses of the Fourteenth Amendment. Have petitioners received hearings consonant with standards accepted by this Nation as adequate to justify their convictions? * * *

We take up *Brown v. Allen*, * * * a case that turns more generally than the others on the constitutional issues.

Petitioner, a Negro, was indicted on September 4, 1950, and tried in the North Carolina courts on a charge of rape, and, having been found guilty, he was sentenced to death on September 15, 1950. [The petitioner made timely challenges on the basis that his grand and petit juries were constituted in violation of the Fourteenth Amendment, and that the sentencing court admitted a coerced confession.]

A. [The Court determined, on the merits, that the petitioner sustained no Fourteenth Amendment violation because of the way his grand and petit juries were constituted.]

B. Petitioner contends further that his conviction was procured in violation of the Fourteenth Amendment of the Federal Constitution because the trial judge permitted the jury to rely on a confession claimed by petitioner to be coerced in determining his guilt. * * *

A conviction by a trial court which has admitted coerced confessions deprives a defendant of liberty without due process of law. When the facts admitted by the state show coercion, a conviction will be set aside as violative of due process. This is true even though the evidence apart from the confessions might have been sufficient to sustain the jury's verdict.

Therefore, it does not matter in this case whether or not the jury was acquainted with all the facts laid before the judge upon which petitioner now relies or whether the jury heard or did not hear the petitioner testify. Neither does it matter that there possibly is evidence in the record independent of the confessions which could sustain the verdict. The mere admission of the confessions by the trial judge constituted a use of them by the state, and if the confessions were improperly obtained, such a use constitutes a denial of due process of law as guaranteed by the Fourteenth Amendment. In determining whether a confession has been used by the state in violation of the constitutional rights of a petitioner, a United States court appraises the alleged abuses by the facts as shown at the hearing or admitted on the record.

[The Court concluded that the Petitioner's "constitutional rights were not infringed by the refusal of the trial court to exclude his confessions as evidence."]

* * *

The judgments are affirmed.

■ Mr. JUSTICE FRANKFURTER. [Dissenting in *Brown*, but writing for the Court on the issue of the controlling effect of prior state proceedings and certiorari review:[g]]

* * *

I.

[The Court held that a denial of certiorari on review of the conviction should not be given any preclusive effect in a subsequent collateral proceeding.]

II.

The issue of the significance of the denial of certiorari raises a sharp division in the Court. This is not so as to the bearing of the proceedings in the State courts upon the disposition of the application for a writ of habeas corpus in the Federal District Courts. This opinion is designed to make explicit and detailed matters that are also the concern of Mr. Justice Reed's opinion. The uncommon circumstances in which a district court should entertain an application ought to be defined with greater particularity, as should be the criteria for determining when a hearing is proper. The views of the Court on these questions may thus be drawn from the two opinions jointly.

I deem it appropriate to begin by making explicit some basic considerations underlying the federal habeas corpus jurisdiction. * * * [M]ost claims in these attempts to obtain review of State convictions are without merit. Presumably they are adequately dealt with in the State courts. * * * [That the] wholesale opening of State prison doors by federal courts is * * * not at all the real issue before us is best indicated by a survey recently prepared in the Administrative Office of the United States Courts for the Conference of Chief Justices: of all federal question applications for habeas corpus, some not even relating to State convictions, only 67 out of 3,702 applications were granted in the last seven years. And "only a small number" of these 67 applications resulted in release from prison: "a more detailed

---

[g] Justice Frankfurter's opinion, presented here, is available in *Daniels v. Allen*, 344 U.S. 443 (1953). As the Notes below explain, the denomination of opinions in the consolidated cases is somewhat complex. The syllabus in *Brown v. Allen* states that Justice Frankfurter wrote for the Court on the preclusive effective of a prior certiorari denial, but Justice Frankfurter's entire opinion is "for the Court" in *Daniels*. As a result, most consider Justice Frankfurter's statement as to the effect of prior state proceedings, although not technically designated by the *Brown* syllabus as controlling on that question, to be the opinion of "the Court" in the consolidated cases.

study over the last four years shows that out of 29 petitions granted, there were only 5 petitioners who were released from state penitentiaries." The meritorious claims are few, but our procedures must ensure that those few claims are not stifled by undiscriminating generalities. * * *

For surely it is an abuse to deal too casually and too lightly with rights guaranteed by the Federal Constitution, even though they involve limitations upon State power and may be invoked by those morally unworthy. Under the guise of fashioning a procedural rule, we are not justified in wiping out the practical efficacy of a jurisdiction conferred by Congress on the District Courts. Rules which in effect treat all these cases indiscriminately as frivolous do not fall far short of abolishing this head of jurisdiction.

Congress could have left the enforcement of federal constitutional rights governing the administration of criminal justice in the States exclusively to the State courts. These tribunals are under the same duty as the federal courts to respect rights under the United States Constitution. Indeed, the jurisdiction given to the federal courts to issue writs of habeas corpus by the First Judiciary Act extended only to prisoners in custody under authority of the United States. It was not until the Act of 1867 that the power to issue the writ was extended to an applicant under sentence of a State court. It is not for us to determine whether this power should have been vested in the federal courts. * * * By giving the federal courts that jurisdiction, Congress has imbedded into federal legislation the historic function of habeas corpus adapted to reaching an enlarged area of claims.

In exercising the power thus bestowed, the District Judge must take due account of the proceedings that are challenged by the application for a writ. All that has gone before is not to be ignored as irrelevant. But the prior State determination of a claim under the United States Constitution cannot foreclose consideration of such a claim, else the State court would have the final say which the Congress, by the Act of 1867, provided it should not have. A State determination may help to define the claim urged in the application for the writ and may bear on the seriousness of the claim. That most claims are frivolous has an important bearing upon the procedure to be followed by a district judge. The prior State determination may guide his discretion in deciding upon the appropriate course to be followed in disposing of the application before him. The State record may serve to indicate the necessity of further pleadings or of a quick hearing to clear up an ambiguity, or the State record may show the claim to be frivolous or not within the competence of a federal court because solely dependent on State law. * * * *

Of course, experience cautions that the very nature and function of the writ of habeas corpus precludes the formulation of fool-proof standards * * * . * * * [I]t is important, in order to preclude individualized enforcement of the Constitution in different parts of the Nation, to lay down as specifically as the nature of the problem permits the standards or directions that should govern the District Judges in the disposition of applications for habeas corpus by prisoners under sentence of State courts.

[JUSTICE FRANKFURTER then explained the need to adopt clear rules.]

First. Just as in all other litigation, a prima facie case must be made out by the petitioner. The application should be dismissed when it fails to state a federal question, or fails to set forth facts which, if accepted at face value, would entitle the applicant to relief. * * *

Second. Failure to exhaust an available State remedy is an obvious ground for denying the application. * * * *

Third. If the record of the State proceedings is not filed, the judge is required to decide, with due regard to efficiency in judicial administration, whether it is more desirable to call for the record or to hold a hearing. * * * *

Fourth. When the record of the State court proceedings is before the court, it may appear that the issue turns on basic facts and that the facts (in the sense of a recital of external events and the credibility of their narrators) have been tried and adjudicated against the applicant. Unless a vital flaw be found in the process of ascertaining such facts in the State court, the District Judge may accept their determination in the State proceeding and deny the application. On the other hand, State adjudication of questions of law cannot, under the habeas corpus statute, be accepted as binding. It is precisely these questions that the federal judge is commanded to decide. * * * *

Fifth. Where the ascertainment of the historical facts does not dispose of the claim but calls for interpretation of the legal significance of such facts, the District Judge must exercise his own judgment on this blend of facts and their legal values. Thus, so-called mixed questions or the application of constitutional principles to the facts as found leave the duty of adjudication with the federal judge. * * * *

Sixth. A federal district judge may under § 2244 take into consideration a prior denial of relief by a federal court, and in that sense § 2244 is of course applicable to State prisoners. * * * *

These standards, addressed as they are to the practical situation facing the District Judge, recognize the discretion of judges to give weight to whatever may be relevant in the State proceedings, and yet preserve the full implication of the requirement of Congress that the District Judge decide constitutional questions presented by a State prisoner even after his claims have been carefully considered by the State courts. Congress has the power to distribute among the courts of the States and of the United States jurisdiction to determine federal claims. It has seen fit to give this Court power to review errors of federal law in State determinations, and in addition to give to the lower federal courts power to inquire into federal claims, by way of habeas corpus. * * *

* * * Insofar as this jurisdiction enables federal district courts to entertain claims that State Supreme Courts have denied rights guaranteed by the United States Constitution, it is not a case of a lower court sitting in judgment on a higher court. It is merely one aspect of respecting the Supremacy Clause of the Constitution whereby federal law is higher than State law. It is for the Congress to designate the member in the hierarchy of the federal judiciary to express the higher law. The fact that Congress has authorized district courts to be the organ of the higher law rather than a Court of Appeals, or exclusively this Court, does not mean that it allows a lower court to overrule a higher court. It merely expresses the choice of Congress how the superior authority of federal law should be asserted. * * * *

It is inadmissible to deny the use of the writ merely because a State court has passed on a federal constitutional issue. The discretion of the lower courts must be canalized within banks of standards governing all federal judges alike, so as to mean essentially the same thing to all and to leave only the margin of freedom of movement inevitably entailed by the nature of habeas corpus and the indefinable variety of circumstances which bring it into play. * * * *

■ Mr. JUSTICE JACKSON, concurring in the result.[h]

Controversy as to the undiscriminating use of the writ of habeas corpus by federal judges to set aside state court convictions is traceable to three principal causes: (1) this Court's use of the generality of the Fourteenth Amendment to subject state courts to increasing federal control, especially in the criminal law field; (2) ad hoc determination of due process of law issues by personal notions of justice, instead of by known rules of law; and (3) the breakdown of procedural safeguards against abuse of the writ.

1. In 1867, Congress authorized federal courts to issue writs of habeas corpus to prisoners "in custody in violation of the Constitution or laws or treaties of the United States." At that time, the writ was not available here nor in England to challenge any sentence imposed by a court of competent jurisdiction. The historic purpose of the writ has been to relieve detention by executive authorities without judicial trial. It might have been expected that, if Congress intended a reversal of this traditional concept of habeas corpus, it would have said so. However, this one sentence in the Act eventually was construed as authority for federal judges to entertain collateral attacks on state court criminal judgments. * * *

But, once established, this jurisdiction obviously would grow with each expansion of the substantive grounds for habeas corpus. The generalities of the Fourteenth Amendment are so indeterminate as to what state actions are forbidden that this Court has found it a ready instrument, in one field or another, to magnify federal, and incidentally its own, authority over the states. The expansion now has reached a point where any state court conviction, disapproved by a majority of this Court, thereby becomes unconstitutional and subject to nullification by habeas corpus.

This might not be so demoralizing if state judges could anticipate, and so comply with, this Court's due process requirements or ascertain any standards to which this Court will adhere in prescribing them. But they cannot. * * *

They are not only being gradually subordinated to the federal judiciary but federal courts have declared that state judicial and other officers are personally liable to federal prosecution and to civil suit by convicts if they fail to carry out this Court's constitutional doctrines.

2. * * * A manifestation of [the increasingly ad hoc character of federal habeas review] is seen in the diminishing respect shown for state court adjudications of fact. Of course, this Court never has considered itself foreclosed by a state court's decision as to the facts when that determination results in alleged denial of a federal right. But captious use of this power was restrained by observance of a rule, elementary in all appellate procedure, that the findings of fact on a trial are to be accepted by an appellate court in absence of clear showing of error. The trial court, seeing the demeanor of witnesses, hearing the parties, giving to each case far more time than an appellate court can give, is in a better position to unravel disputes of fact than is an appellate court on a printed transcript. Recent decisions avow no candid alteration of these rules, but revision of state fact finding has grown by emphasis, and respect for it has withered by disregard.

---

[h] The text returns now to *Brown v. Allen*, 344 U.S. 443 (1953).

3. * * * It must prejudice the occasional meritorious application to be buried in a flood of worthless ones. He who must search a haystack for a needle is likely to end up with the attitude that the needle is not worth the search. Nor is it any answer to say that few of these petitions in any court really result in the discharge of the petitioner. That is the condemnation of the procedure which has encouraged frivolous cases. In this multiplicity of worthless cases, states are compelled to default or to defend the integrity of their judges and their official records, sometimes concerning trials or pleas that were closed many years ago. State Attorneys General recently have come habitually to ignore these proceedings, responding only when specially requested and sometimes not then. Some state courts have wearied of our repeated demands upon them, and have declined to further elucidate grounds for their decisions. * * *

* * * Once upon a time, the writ could not be substituted for appeal or other reviewing process, but challenged only the legal competence or jurisdiction of the committing court. We have so departed from this principle that the profession now believes that the issues we actually consider on a federal prisoner's habeas corpus are substantially the same as would be considered on appeal.

Conflict with state courts is the inevitable result of giving the convict a virtual new trial before a federal court sitting without a jury. Whenever decisions of one court are reviewed by another, a percentage of them are reversed. That reflects a difference in outlook normally found between personnel comprising different courts. However, reversal by a higher court is not proof that justice is thereby better done. There is no doubt that, if there were a super-Supreme Court, a substantial proportion of our reversals of state courts would also be reversed. We are not final because we are infallible, but we are infallible only because we are final.

* * * Since the Constitution and laws made pursuant to it are the supreme law, and since the supremacy and uniformity of federal law are attainable only by a centralized source of authority, denial by a state of a claimed federal right must give some access to the federal judicial system. But federal interference with state administration of its criminal law should not be premature, and should not occur where it is not needed. Therefore, we have ruled that a state convict must exhaust all remedies which the state affords for his alleged grievance before he can take it to any federal court by habeas corpus.

* * * No very close personal consideration can be given by each Justice to such a multiplicity of these petitions as we have had and, as a class, they are so frivolous * * * that this worthlessness of the class discredits each individual application. * * * The fact is that superficial consideration of these cases is the inevitable result of depreciation of the writ. The writ has no enemies so deadly as those who sanction the abuse of it, whatever their intent.

* * * My conclusion is that whether or not this Court has denied certiorari from a state court's judgment in a habeas corpus proceeding, no lower federal court should entertain a petition except on the following conditions: (1) that the petition raises a jurisdictional question involving federal law on which the state law allowed no access to its courts, either by habeas corpus or appeal from the conviction and that he therefore has no state remedy; or (2) that the petition shows that, although the law allows a remedy, he was actually improperly obstructed from making a record upon which the question could be presented, so that his remedy by way of ultimate application

to this Court for certiorari has been frustrated. There may be circumstances so extraordinary that I do not now think of them which would justify a departure from this rule, but the run-of-the-mill case certainly does not.
* * *

I concur in the result announced by Mr. JUSTICE REED in these three cases.

[The dissenting opinion of Mr. JUSTICE BLACK, with whom Mr. JUSTICE DOUGLAS joins, is omitted.]

———

NOTES AND QUESTIONS ON BROWN

1)   **Clyde Brown.** All of the defendants—Clyde Brown, Raleigh Speller, Bennie Daniels and Lloyd Ray Daniels—were executed in North Carolina in 1953. Clyde Brown was an illiterate black teenager who was arrested for raping and beating a white high school student in North Carolina. Law enforcement held him without charges for five days, did not give him a hearing until his twenty-third day in custody, and did not permit him to communicate with a court-appointed lawyer until twenty-six days after the arrest. Brown confessed during the five-day period for which he was detained without charges. An all-white jury convicted him, and he was subject to a mandatory death sentence.

Brown argued that his confession was coerced, and he challenged the constitutionality of the grand and petit jury composition. He appealed to the North Carolina Supreme Court, where he lost, and he unsuccessfully sought a petition for certiorari from the U.S. Supreme Court. Brown then went to federal district court, which denied habeas relief on the ground that there was nothing "unusual" about the conviction. The Fourth Circuit affirmed and the Supreme Court granted certiorari in Brown's case, alongside others that involved similar issues of North Carolina grand and petit jury selection.

2)   **The Prior Effect of Certiorari Denials.** Before reaching the preclusive effect to be given prior state adjudication, *Brown* and *Daniels* decided that a Supreme Court order denying certiorari to review a state judgment did not affect the merits of a federal court's habeas review of that claim. Many scholars believe that the issue of the preclusive effect to be given a prior denial of certiorari in a collateral proceeding was the issue the Court had originally wanted to resolve in *Brown v. Allen*. See Eric M. Freedman, *Milestones in Habeas Corpus: Part III Brown v. Allen: The Habeas Corpus Revolution That Wasn't*, 51 Ala. L. Rev. 1541, 1551 (2000) (citing Smith v. Baldi, 344 U.S. 561 (1953)). The Court can grant a writ of certiorari on the votes of four Justices, although many Justices used to offer a "join-3" when three other Justices voted for review. See David M. Obrien, *The Rehnquist Court's Shrinking Plenary Docket*, 81 Judicature 58 (1997). The four-vote certiorari requirement is sometimes described as a "rule of four." The Supreme Court rules set forth several criteria for certiorari grants, and error correction is not among them. Generally speaking, the Supreme Court uses certiorari to decide nationally-important questions or to smooth inter-jurisdictional legal conflict. Among those who vote to deny certiorari review of a state judgment, there will almost certainly be Justices who believe the state adjudication was not in error. Is there any way to give effect to certiorari denials in situations where they do express a merits determination? Would it make sense to have some sort of requirement that the Court provide

an explanation for certiorari denials in such cases? What are the practical reasons for not doing that?

3)   **Counting Votes.** *Brown v. Allen* and the companion decisions require careful attention to how the Justices voted in each of the consolidated cases. Reading *Brown v. Allen* in a vacuum will not provide a clear picture of the alignment of the Justice across the decisions, but Justice Reed—along with Justices Vinson, Minton, Burton, Clark, and Jackson, would have denied all relief to Brown. Justices Frankfurter, Douglas, and Black would have granted relief to Brown. Justices Burton and Clark, while voting to deny relief to Brown, joined Justice Frankfurter's opinion in *Daniels*—along with Justices Douglas and Black—to form a five-Justice majority setting forth the principles about how state adjudication of constitutional claims would affect subsequent federal habeas proceedings. Justice Frankfurter's opinion is the "opinion of the Court" in *Daniels*, but the formal syllabus to *Brown v. Allen* only implies that Justice Frankfurter announces the Court's Opinion on the effect of the Court's prior denial of certiorari. Justice Frankfurter's opinion is nonetheless considered the most important opinion in the consolidated cases, and is generally the one against which Justice Jackson's *Brown v. Allen* concurrence is measured.

(4)   **Nascent Procedural Doctrine.** One under-appreciated feature of the *Brown v. Allen* litigation is the degree to which the holding foreshadows many of the modern procedural restrictions on relief. First, the Supreme Court emphasized that the petitioners must present, or "exhaust," their claims in the state courts. (To be clear, the exhaustion rule dates back to *Ex parte Royall*, 117 U.S. 241 (1881).)

Second, the Supreme Court held that certain claims no longer capable of state merits disposition were procedurally defaulted. The Court held that the claims were defaulted even though the default was apparently due to mistakes by the claimants' lawyer, who filed a statement of the case for appeal 61 days after trial. (State rules required filing within 60 days.) The Court concluded that "[a] period of limitation accords with our conception of proper procedure." Is this a different version of adequate "corrective process"? Justice Frankfurter dissented on this point, noting that the state rule was not fixed—that North Carolina courts had discretion to hear the appeal even if the statement was filed late. He viewed the state decision not to hear the appeal as "an act so arbitrary and so cruel in its operation, considering that life is at stake, that in the circumstances of this case it constitutes a denial of due process in its rudimentary procedural aspect."

Third, *Brown v. Allen* agreed that the district court properly decided not to conduct an evidentiary hearing to review the facts supporting the petitioners' claims. The Supreme Court emphasized that the statute gives federal judges discretion to decide whether to conduct a hearing or not. The subject of federal fact development has emerged as a contentious topic in modern habeas cases, and Chapter 5 will explore that issue.

5)   **Statistics.** Justice Frankfurter correctly observes that the overwhelming majority of federal habeas cases lack merit, but what is the appropriate way to quantify the volume of meritorious claims? Justice Frankfurter noted that only 67 out of 3,702 federal habeas applications were granted, but does that fraction necessarily speak to the "merits" of the federal claims that the federal proceedings decided—especially if many courts were deciding them under unnecessarily stringent standards?

6)   Justice Frankfurter's Theory of Article III Jurisdiction. Justice Frankfurter states that the 1867 habeas provisions were the first time Congress vested in Article III courts a power to grant habeas relief to state prisoners. In what sense is Justice Frankfurter correct in this history, and in what sense is he wrong? Does this idea run counter to the proposition that habeas jurisdiction identified in the Constitution is self-executing? If some habeas jurisdiction identified in the Constitution is self-executing, does that jurisdiction include power over writs filed by state prisoners?

Justice Frankfurter's opinion for the Court also states that the Federal Constitution contemplates a central role for state judges in adjudication of Article III subject matter. On what basis does Justice Frankfurter draw that conclusion? Under what "head" of jurisdiction does habeas authority over state custody fall? Why does Justice Frankfurter believe that giving too much preclusive effect to state judgments would eliminate the jurisdiction Congress gave to federal judges in 1867? Does this argument strike you as a strong or as a weak one?

7)   Exhaustion. Justice Frankfurter's opinion affirms that a failure to exhaust state remedies—that is, the failure to have previously presented a given claim to the state courts—is a reason for a judge to *deny* a habeas application. Exhaustion is the subject of Section 1 in Chapter 4. The modern exhaustion rule is statutory, and unexhausted claims are *dismissed without prejudice*. What is the difference between a denial and a dismissal, and do you think Justice Frankfurter meant to approve of the idea of a prejudiced denial? In what sense is a non-prejudiced denial just a rule of sequencing? On a slightly different note, should exhaustion require that a state prisoner seek certiorari review of all state judgments before filing a federal habeas petition? In *Darr v. Burford*, 339 U.S. 200 (1950), the Supreme Court held that exhaustion should ordinarily require such prisoner to seek Supreme Court review before seeking federal habeas relief in district court. *Darr* grounded that requirement in "comity," but in what sense does including certiorari proceedings within an exhaustion rule promote comity? *Darr* was later overruled by *Fay v. Noia*, 372 U.S. 391 (1963).

8)   Binding Effect of Prior Fact Adjudication. Justice Frankfurter's opinion for the Court stated that, "unless a vital flaw be found in the process of ascertaining such facts in the State court," a federal district court exercising habeas jurisdiction *may* accept state-court factfinding as valid. Why do you think Justice Frankfurter makes the rule permissive, and what are the implications of that decision? Why is sufficient process the touchstone of acceptable factfinding—can you imagine facts found pursuant to impeccable process that are nonetheless wrong? Is the deference to procedurally sound fact-finding more a function of comity, or is it more a critique of redundant process? Finally, what does it mean for state factfinding to be without a "vital flaw"—does this concept refer to any situation other than those suffused with "mob domination" (as in *Frank* and *Moore*), or does it include others?

9)   Independent Review of Mixed and Legal Questions. By orders of magnitude, the most important ruling in *Brown v. Allen* was that the 1867 Habeas Act required federal judges to exercise independent judgment about whether legal and mixed challenges to state judgments were meritorious. In other words, *Brown v. Allen* permitted federal habeas claimants to "relitigate" such challenges in federal court, notwithstanding a state criminal judgment that may not have directly addressed the issue. Are federal judges likely to resolve constitutional claims differently than state judges and, if so, why? Even if state judges do resolve claims differently than federal judges do, why should a state disposition be subject to review in an inferior federal court? State judges determine federal questions all of the time. The Constitution permits (and sometimes requires) that state courts take part in adjudication of federal questions. Recall the Madisonian Compromise, which made inferior federal courts voluntary. The Framers seemed to contemplate a legal regime in which state courts shouldered the primary responsibility for deciding state questions. In 1801, Congress briefly vested inferior federal courts with original jurisdiction over federal questions. That jurisdiction was quickly revoked, however, and Congress did not restore it until 1875, enacting what is now codified at 28 U.S.C. § 1331. Does *Brown v. Allen* make state judges "second class jurists" in a system where, for over a century, state judges had exercised original (and at least concurrent) jurisdiction over many federal questions?

10) The Dissenters' View. The *Brown v. Allen* dissenters wanted to grant relief. Justice Black, who wrote the dissent, described the pertinent counties' disturbing history of racial discrimination in jury selection. For example, in the county where Daniels was convicted, "Negroes constituted about 47% of the population of the county and about one-third of the taxpayers. But the jury box of 10,000 names included at most 185 Negroes." Justice Black argued that the mere fact that the state courts had denied relief should not absolve the federal district court from carefully examining whether the constitutional claims related to confessions and jury selection had merit. Echoing Justice Holmes (dissenting in *Frank* and writing for the Court in *Moore*), he concluded:

> I read Moore v. Dempsey as standing for the principle that it is never too late for courts in habeas corpus proceedings to look straight through procedural screens in order to prevent forfeiture of life or liberty in flagrant defiance of the Constitution. Perhaps there is no more exalted judicial function. I am willing to agree that it should not be exercised in cases like these except under special circumstances or in extraordinary situations. But I cannot join in any opinion that attempts to confine the Great Writ within rigid formalistic boundaries.

11) Justice Jackson's Law Clerk. Justice Jackson was apparently urged to write his famous *Brown* concurrence by his law clerk, William Rehnquist.[i] Justice Jackson's influence on Chief Justice Rehnquist was also undeniable and is captured perfectly with the mentor's observation in *Brown v. Allen*: "We are not final because we are infallible, but we are infallible only because we are final." Justice Ruth Bader Ginsburg, *In Memoriam: William H. Rehnquist*, 119 Harv. L. Rev. 6, 7 (2005). Justice Jackson's broadside against robust habeas adjudication continues to resonate in cases today—not surprisingly, in light of the prominent role his clerk would assume in the Nixon administration and on the United States Supreme Court. As you read many of the cases that follow, ask yourself whether, paraphrasing Justice Jackson slightly, the needle in the haystack is worth the search. What do you make of the argument that habeas filings were surging as the Court was beginning to recognize new constitutional

---

[i] See Habeas Corpus, Then and Now, Or, 'If I Can Just Find the Right Judge, Over These Prison Walls I Shall Fly,' Memorandum from Law Clerk Rehnquist to Justice Jackson in McGee (1951 Term, No. 517), in *Robert H. Jackson Papers*, Library of Congress, Container 120 (Opinion Notes: Habeas Corpus) (Legal File 1952 Term, Brown v. Allen, Nos. 32, 22, 20, 31).

rights? Is that now the job of a federal judge—to search for the rare meritorious habeas petition? Does doing so "trivializ[e]" the writ—as compared with the prior practice in cases like *Frank*?

12) Scholarly Debate. *Brown v. Allen* remains the central case in a longstanding disagreement over the proper relationship between federal habeas review and state criminal adjudication. Notwithstanding that neither wrote the "primary" opinion, the opinions of Justice Frankfurter and Justice Jackson have been the most intellectually durable. In Professor Bator's classic treatment (much cited by the Supreme Court), he argued that the *Brown v. Allen* opinions do not "deal adequately with the grave problems of federalism created by the doctrine of that case," and he noted the "unanimity of the resentment among state law-enforcement officials and judges" in response to the decision, particularly where the opinion did not provide "principled institutional justification" for the power of "a federal judge to reverse the action of the highest court of the state." Bator, *Finality in Criminal Law*, 76 Harv. L. Rev. at 504-05. In Professor Bator's view, habeas corpus was traditionally confined to cases where the state court lacked jurisdiction, and should not be expanded to include other constitutional claims. Professor Bator added:

> The problem of federalism created by *Brown v. Allen* should not be seen in terms of the possible irritation of state judges at being reversed by federal district judges. The crucial issue is the possible damage done to the inner sense of responsibility, to the pride and conscientiousness, of a state judge in doing what is, after all, under the constitutional scheme a part of *his* business: the decision of federal questions properly raised in state litigation. And the problem must be further analyzed in terms of its effect on the integrity and effectiveness of the substantive criminal law of the states.

Professor Bator then turned to the federal judiciary:

> [T]he doctrine of *Brown v. Allen* must be assessed in light of the strains put on the federal judicial system itself by the ever increasing flood of habeas petitions from state prisoners. It is, of course, notorious that most of these petitions are frivolous. . . I have suggested before that this matter should be seen not only in terms of time and money but in terms of husbanding the intellectual and moral energies and intensities of our judges.

Professor Gary Peller offered a contrary view, that *Brown v. Allen* had the history right. See Gary Peller, *In Defense of Federal Habeas Corpus Relitigation*, 16 Harv. C.R.-C.L. L. Rev. 579, 621–22 (1982). According to Professor Peller, the nineteenth-century Supreme Court cases denying habeas relief should not be conceptualized as limiting habeas jurisdiction, but as reflecting thin due process right. Professor Peller argued:

> [A]lthough [Professor Bator] primarily relies on habeas cases in which petitioners claimed that trial errors violated their due process rights, Bator does not consider the extant scope of the due process clause. . . [A]t that point in history, criminal due process encompassed only the right not to be detained unless the detention was pursuant to the judgment of a court of competent jurisdiction, acting in substantial conformity with its usual processes. The Court, therefore, disposed of due process claims on direct and habeas review by determining whether the state court had jurisdiction. Thus, when the Court held that a habeas petition must be denied because

the alleged trial error did not impugn the state court's jurisdiction, it decided on *the merits* that a due process claim had not been stated, not that habeas jurisdiction was unavailable.

Professor Anne Woolhandler has argued that the truth is somewhere in between what she calls Professor Bator's "institutional competence" model and Professor Peller's "full review" model. The space between the two accounts, she contends, reflects the difficulty in translating the concept of "unlawful" custody from English common law to the American constitutional environment:

> The revised history suggests that the institutional competence model, which sees habeas as historically limited to issues of jurisdiction, oversimplifies a complex, evolving pattern of constitutional law and federal jurisdiction. As a consequence, the Supreme Court's reliance on this narrow version of habeas history to justify further restrictions is misplaced. The competing claim that habeas historically demanded full review is also flawed. It fails to acknowledge that, for a time, the Court restricted federal trial court jurisdiction so as not to police the full range of potential constitutional violations, particularly those involving random illegal acts by government officials. Nevertheless, I will argue that the process of transforming common law violations into constitutional violations supports a full review model for habeas, even if claiming for it an evolutionary rather than a static pedigree.

Ann Woolhandler, *Demodeling Habeas*, 45 Stan. L. Rev. 575, 580–81 (1993). Professor James Liebman argued that *Brown v. Allen* was not all that revolutionary, and that it did little more than summarize holdings that had accumulated over quite some time:

> *Brown* is anticlimax. True, between two majority opinions, the case did nicely catalogue the governing habeas corpus principles. But those principles already were long established, to anyone with the patience to search them out from among the literally hundreds of individually unimportant cases in which they lay dispersed.

See James S. Liebman, *Apocalypse Next Time?: The Anachronistic Attack on Habeas Corpus/Direct Review Parity*, 92 Colum. L. Rev. 1997, 2083 (1992) (hereinafter *Apocalypse Next Time*). Based on your knowledge of *Brown v. Allen*, the "canonical" due process cases, and common law writ history, whose account do you find most persuasive?

2. SCOPE OF MODERN FEDERAL REVIEW

INTRODUCTORY NOTE ON THE MODERN FEDERAL HABEAS STATUTE

Since the Supreme Court decided *Brown v. Allen*, Congress has revised the federal habeas statute on several occasions. Professor Liebman concluded that the 1966 legislative revisions to the habeas statutes effectively codified *Brown v. Allen*:

> Congress knew that federal habeas corpus courts were reviewing pure and mixed legal questions *de novo* and aimed to preserve that standard of review. Hence, when the drafters of the 1966 amendments left intact the 1948 (and 1867) provisions requiring that "a district court shall entertain

an application for a writ of habeas corpus in behalf of a person . . . in custody in violation of the Constitution," they meant what they said: that it was the "district court," and not the state court, that had the duty to determine the constitutional question.

Liebman, *Apocalypse Next Time*, 92 Colum. L. Rev. at 2091. Modern federal habeas law is mostly an evolving creature of statute. The most recent major revision was the Antiterrorism and Effective Death Penalty Act of 1996 (AEDPA). Pub. L. No. 104–132, 110 Stat. 1214 (codified as amended in scattered sections of 28 U.S.C.). 28 U.S.C. § 2241(b) creates the generally-applicable federal habeas power.

The main federal habeas provisions governing state-prisoner petitions are §§ 2244 & 2254. Section 2244 sets forth a number of procedural restrictions on federal habeas relief, including limits pertaining to successive petitions and the statute of limitations. Section 2254 contains a number of limits on relief for prisoners held pursuant to a state conviction, and § 2255 sets forth requirements for prisoners convicted in federal court. Section 2254(a) supplements the global grant of habeas power in 28 U.S.C. § 2241, and it states:

> The Supreme Court, a Justice thereof, a circuit judge, or a district court shall entertain an application for a writ of habeas corpus in behalf of a person in custody pursuant to the judgment of a State court only on the ground that he is in custody in violation of the Constitution or laws or treaties of the United States.

This Chapter focuses on the "cognizability" of various claims lodged in federal post-conviction challenges, Chapter 4 will explore the many judge-made procedural rules that Congress has codified (and some that had no common law antecedent), and Chapter 5 will focus on "substantive limits on relief" in § 2254(d).

––––––––––

NOTE ON THE CUSTODY REQUIREMENT

In general, 28 U.S.C. § 2241 extends the federal habeas power only to cases involving prisoners who are "in custody."[j] The additional grant of power in 28 U.S.C. § 2254(a)(1) also empowers federal judicial officers to review "custody." What does it mean for a person to be in custody? Certainly, someone subject to state criminal detention qualifies, as do many prisoners detained under noncriminal process.

A related question involves *when* a prisoner must be in custody for the purposes of a habeas claim. Custody is assessed at the time the habeas petition is filed. Incarceration satisfies the requirement, but "custody" has a broader meaning. Custody is also satisfied if the prisoner was released but remains on probation or parole, or if the prisoner is in civil or criminal detention of any kind, including in a mental institution.[k] Persons are not "in custody" simply

––––––––––

[j] The only exception is in 28 U.S.C. § 2241(d)(5), which allows a federal court to issue a writ to allow "prisoners" to testify. Of course, one might legitimately ask when someone might be a "prisoner" but not be "in custody," but suffice it to say that Subsection (d)(5) is nonetheless the only part of § 2241 to which the "in custody" requirement does not formally apply.

[k] See, e.g., Jones v. Cunningham, 371 U.S. 236, 243 (1963) (parole); Dow v. Circuit Court of the First Circuit, 995 F.2d 922, 923 (9th Cir. 1993) (rehabilitation program); Wright v. United States, 732 F.2d 1048, 1050 (2d Cir. 1983) (probation).

because they must pay fines, have had driver's licenses revoked, are subject to professional discipline, suffer dignitary harm, or lose the right to vote.

The "custody" requirement empowers federal courts to hear several different types of challenges: challenges to a conviction (this Book has already presented a number of those); challenges to a sentence (e.g., a claim that a person is ineligible for execution due to mental retardation); challenges to conditions of confinement; and challenges to parole board determinations. As Chapter 11 discusses, prisoners can bring some of those challenges under other civil rights statutes, such as 42 U.S.C. § 1983, and the Supreme Court has repeatedly ruled on what can or must be brought in a federal habeas petition.

NOTES ON HABEAS FILING DATA

What does the federal habeas docket look like? Recall how, in *Brown v. Allen*, Justice Jackson bemoaned the surge in federal habeas filings. The yearly filings in 1953 numbered in the hundreds—now they number in the tens of thousands. Changes in habeas law—both decisional and statutory—have altered the mix of claims that prisoners bring and the rate at which they obtain relief. Notwithstanding this caveat, however, Justice Jackson's quip about searching for a needle in a haystack remains prescient: very few habeas petitioners receive relief. Table 6.1 shows the growth of state-prisoner habeas filings in federal court.[1]

Table 6.1

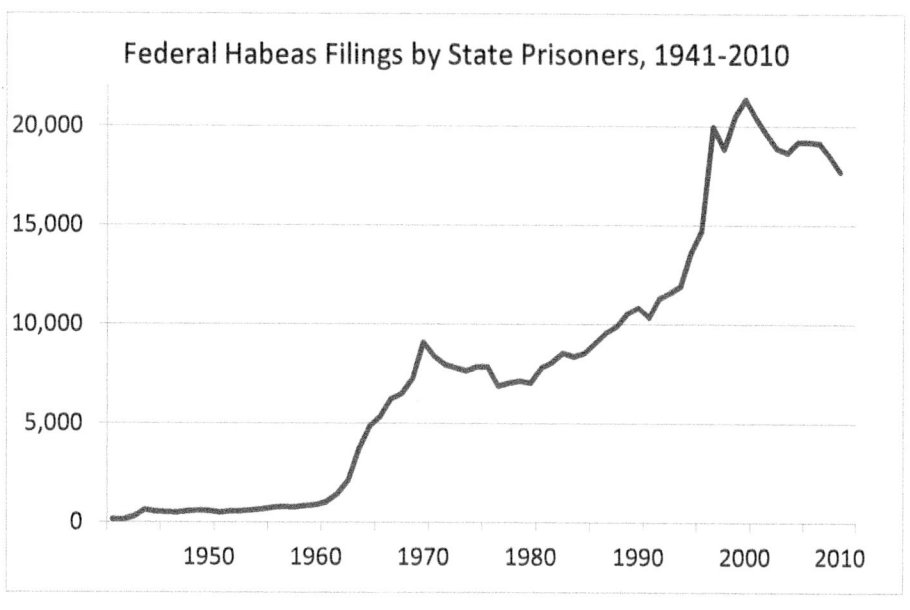

Was there cause to fear a flood of habeas petitions in the 1950s and 1960s? Do people have more cause to worry now? Is the steady rise in habeas filings

---

[1] These data are compiled from Annual Reports of the Administrative Office of the U.S. Courts.

during the 1980s and 1990s more puzzling? As we will see in the next Chapter, that was an era in which the Supreme Court announced a series of rulings that created or heightened a number of procedural obstacles to relief.

Since *Brown v. Allen*, prison populations have exploded, from less than 150,000 prisoners in the 1940s to about 1,400,000 prisoners today. In isolation, the increase in habeas filings might seem large; the increased volume of habeas activity, however, largely mirrors increased prisoner populations and increased civil filings. As a result, the habeas filings per prisoner has remained roughly constant. Table 6.2 shows the number of federal habeas filings as a percentage of the state prison population (with data on prison populations compiled from Bureau of Justice Statistics).

Table 6.2

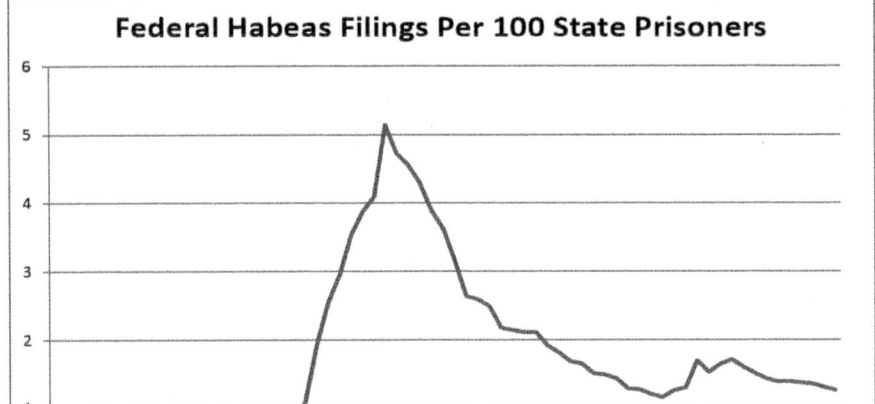

As Professors Nancy King and Joseph Hoffman write, "The modern explosion in state prisoner populations overwhelmed, and masked, a long and gradual decline in the rate of habeas filings per prisoner." Nancy King & Joseph Hoffman, *Habeas For the Twenty-First Century* 70 (2011). Table 6.1 shows that, as a fraction of the overall prison population, few prisoners actually file federal habeas petitions. In 2000, as habeas filings were rising rapidly, less than 2% of state prisoners filed federal habeas petitions—a rate approaching levels observed during the mid-1960s. Who are the prisoners who file habeas petitions? Predictably, they are the prisoners convicted of the most serious crimes and those facing the longest sentences.[m]

According to a study by Professor Nancy J. King, Fred L. Cheesman II, and Brian J. Ostrom, *Final Technical Report: Habeas Litigation in U.S. District Courts: An Empirical Study of Habeas Corpus Cases Filed by State Prisoners Under the Antiterrorism and Effective Death Penalty Act of 1996* ("2007 Habeas Study"), 28.2% of federal habeas petitioners were convicted of a homicide and

---

[m] See John Scalia, U.S. Dep't of Justice, Bureau of Justice Statistics, *Prisoner Petitions Filed in U.S. District Courts, 2000, with Trends, 1980–2000* 1-2 (2002) (stating that in year 2000, for every 1,000 inmates in state prisons, 17 inmates filed habeas petitions).

15.4% were convicted of sexual assault.[n] The *2007 Habeas Study* found that, of habeas petitioners for whom sentencing information was available, 27.7% were serving life sentences and the rest were sentenced to an average of twenty years.[o] Convictions for serious crimes, such as murder and rape, are not common. According to the Bureau of Justice Statistics (BJS), only 0.7% of felony defendants are convicted of murder and only 0.8% are convicted of rape.[p]

There is a logical explanation for the disproportionate number of prisoners found guilty of serious criminal offenses among habeas filers. Considerable time must pass before a prisoner can even file for federal habeas relief; the shortest sentences will almost certainly lapse before a federal habeas claim ripens. In order to "exhaust" a constitutional challenge, a state prisoner must seek both appellate review of the conviction and state collateral relief. Doing so may take years.

The success rate of one group of habeas petitioners stands out: prisoners sentenced to death. For example, in the mid-1990s, capital claimants filed less than one percent of state-prisoner petitions, but accounted for almost forty percent of all grants.[q] Professor James Liebman and several colleagues reviewed all post-conviction filings by death row inmates from 1973 through 1995, and they found that 68% of those inmates had their death sentences reversed.[r] This success rate differs markedly from that of noncapital inmates. During the same period over which the researchers measured the 68% grant rate for capital prisoners, the researchers found that roughly 1% of non-capital petitions were granted. Sixty-three percent were dismissed summarily, and many of those were tossed for procedural reasons; only 35% were denied on the merits. AEDPA, discussed extensively in the next chapters, appears to have further depressed the grant rate to around 12%. See King et al., *2007 Habeas Study*, at 2. Suffice it to say (1) that very few state-prisoner petitions result in federal relief, but (2) that federal judges seem to review the merits more carefully and grant relief more often in cases involving severe sentences.

NOTES ON COMMON CONSTITUTIONAL CLAIMS

What types of claims do the many thousands of state prisoners bring in their habeas petitions? The typical habeas petition is filed *pro se*—without a lawyer—and it may include many different federal claims. The most frequently litigated constitutional claim is that a prisoner's trial or appellate lawyer was ineffective under the Sixth Amendment (IAC or "ineffective-assistance-of-counsel" claims). Another frequently litigated habeas claim is that the prosecu-

---

[n] See Nancy J. King, Fred L. Cheesman II & Brian J. Ostrom, Nat'l Ctr. for State Courts, *Final Technical Report: Habeas Litigation in U.S. District Courts* 19–20 (2007) ("2007 Habeas Study").

[o] See *id.* at 20.

[p] See Thomas H. Cohen & Brian A. Reaves, U.S. Dep't of Justice, Bureau of Justice Statistics, *Felony Defendants in Large Urban Counties, 2002*, at 27 tbl.28 (2006).

[q] See Roger A. Hanson & Henry W.K. Daley, U.S. Dep't of Justice, Bureau of Justice Statistics, *Federal Habeas Corpus Review: Challenging State Court Criminal Convictions* 17 (1995).

[r] See James S. Liebman, Jeffrey Fagan & Valerie West, *A Broken System: Error Rates in Capital Cases, 1973–1995* 5 (2000).

tion unconstitutionally withheld exculpatory evidence, in violation of *Brady v. Maryland*, 373 U.S. 83 (1963) ("*Brady*" claims).

1)   Ineffective Assistance of Counsel (IAC) Claims. *Gideon v. Wainwright* held that indigent defendants are entitled to state-provided counsel at their criminal trials. See 372 U.S. 335, 344 (1963). The Supreme Court eventually held that a right to appointed counsel implied a right to a constitutionally-effective representative—"effective assistance of counsel." Under *Strickland v. Washington*, an IAC claimant must show (1) that the trial attorney's representation was so deficient as to not be reasonably effective, and (2) that the attorney's ineffectiveness materially prejudiced the outcome at trial, so that "there is a reasonable probability that, but for counsel's unprofessional errors, the result of the proceeding would have been different." 466 U.S. 668, 693–94 (1984).[s] The *2007 Habeas Study* found that 50.4% of noncapital claimants and 81% of capital claimants raised IAC claims relating to the performance of trial or appellate counsel.[t]

In elaborating on the first prong of *Strickland*, the Supreme Court explained that "the proper standard for attorney performance is that of reasonably effective assistance." The Court noted that trial counsel "also has a duty to bring to bear such skill and knowledge as will render the trial a reliable adversarial testing process." The Court added:

> Prevailing norms of practice as reflected in American Bar Association standards and the like . . . are guides to determining what is reasonable, but they are only guides. No particular set of detailed rules for counsel's conduct can satisfactorily take account of the variety of circumstances faced by defense counsel or the range of legitimate decisions regarding how best to represent a criminal defendant. Any such set of rules would interfere with the constitutionally protected independence of counsel and restrict the wide latitude counsel must have in making tactical decisions.

The Court also underscored that "[j]udicial scrutiny of counsel's performance must be highly deferential." The Court wrote:

> A fair assessment of attorney performance requires that every effort be made to eliminate the distorting effects of hindsight, to reconstruct the circumstances of counsel's challenged conduct, and to evaluate the conduct from counsel's perspective at the time. Because of the difficulties inherent in making the evaluation, a court must indulge a strong presumption that counsel's conduct falls within the wide range of reasonable professional assistance; that is, the defendant must overcome the presumption that, under the circumstances, the challenged action "might be considered sound trial strategy."

Finally, the Court stated that "[t]he reasonableness of counsel's actions may be determined or substantially influenced by the defendant's own statements or actions. Counsel's actions are usually based, quite properly, on informed stra-

---

[s] We refer to the effective assistance of *trial* counsel, but prisoners also have a federal constitutional right to effective assistance to *appellate* counsel, and the same *Strickland v. Washington* standard is used for such claims. See Evitts v. Lucey, 469 U.S. 387 (1985).

[t] See King et al., 2007 Habeas Study, supra note o, at 28; see also Victor E. Flango, Nat'l Ctr. for State Courts, *Habeas Corpus in State and Federal Courts* 46–47 (1994) (finding slightly lower incidence of such claims in sample data).

tegic choices made by the defendant and on information supplied by the defendant."

As to *Strickland's* "prejudice" prong, the Supreme Court rejected the two extreme positions. First, it held that "[i]t is not enough for the defendant to show that the errors had some conceivable effect on the outcome of the proceeding. Virtually every act or omission of counsel would meet that test." But it also rejected the most exacting standard: "we believe that a defendant need not show that counsel's deficient conduct more likely than not altered the outcome in the case." Instead, to show prejudice, a claimant must prove that "there is a reasonable probability that, but for counsel's unprofessional errors, the result of the proceeding would have been different. A reasonable probability is a probability sufficient to undermine confidence in the outcome." The Court added:

> In making this determination, a court hearing an ineffectiveness claim must consider the totality of the evidence before the judge or jury. Some of the factual findings will have been unaffected by the errors, and factual findings that were affected will have been affected in different ways. Some errors will have had a pervasive effect on the inferences to be drawn from the evidence, altering the entire evidentiary picture, and some will have had an isolated, trivial effect. Moreover, a verdict or conclusion only weakly supported by the record is more likely to have been affected by errors than one with overwhelming record support. Taking the unaffected findings as a given, and taking due account of the effect of the errors on the remaining findings, a court making the prejudice inquiry must ask if the defendant has met the burden of showing that the decision reached would reasonably likely have been different absent the errors.

Strickland claims are difficult (but not impossible) to win. Most trial decisions can be fairly viewed as strategic. Moreover, even egregious failings can be affirmed as nonprejudicial if sufficient evidence of guilt supports the conviction (or if evidence of aggravation supports a capital sentence—more on that below).

Although a small fraction of *Strickland* claims are successful, the sheer volume of such claims means that more prisoners prevail on IAC theories than on any others. One reason that IAC claims are so common is that many states provided inadequate funding for defending indigent defendants, resulting in persistently poor assistance of trial counsel. Another reason is that claims regarding trial strategy and prejudice can present a way for prisoners to indirectly relitigate questions of guilt and culpability.

2) Brady Claims. *Brady v. Maryland*, 373 U.S. 83, 87 (1963), established the due process right to have the State disclose of all material evidence of innocence. The Court held that "the suppression by the prosecution of evidence favorable to an accused upon request violates due process where the evidence is material either to guilt or to punishment, irrespective of the good faith or bad faith of the prosecution." Brady claims have roughly the same structure as Strickland claims—the prosecution has to withhold material, exculpatory evidence, and the omitted evidence has to prejudice the verdict. Specifically, *Brady* prejudice requires a prisoner to show a reasonable probability that suppressing the evidence of innocence (or impeachment of other favorable evidence) prejudiced the outcome at trial.

One of the most significant *Brady* cases was *Kyles v. Whitley*, 514 U.S. 419 (1995), which addressed the situation in which *police* withhold exculpatory evidence from *prosecutors*. The Supreme Court held that the State must disclose exculpatory evidence in the possession of the police. *Kyles* applied *Brady* to a very complicated (and fascinating) set of facts, concluding that the materiality and prejudice analysis must be cumulative—a court must assess how various pieces of suppressed evidence may have together affected the trial. The Court explained that the definition of materiality should be "considered collectively, not item by item." Although, to be sure, "the Constitution is not violated every time the government fails or chooses not to disclose evidence that might prove helpful to the defense," the reviewing court must ask whether "disclosure of the suppressed evidence to competent counsel would have made a different result reasonably probable." The full story of the case makes for dramatic reading; for a book-length treatment, see Jed Horne, *Desire Street: A True Story of Death and Deliverance in New Orleans* (2005).

3)   Special Claims in Capital Cases. A capital sentence is a product of unique trial procedure, in that a jury must deliver separate guilt-phase and punishment-phase verdicts. The Supreme Court invalidated the death penalty in *Furman v. Georgia*, 408 U.S. 238 (1972), but affirmed the constitutionality of "bifurcated" capital sentencing four years later. See Gregg v. Georgia, 428 U.S. 153 (1976). Substantive capital sentencing law is terrifically complicated, but there are at least three frequently-litigated habeas claims that are specific to death penalty litigation.

The first major capital-specific challenge is called a *"Wiggins"* claim, named after *Wiggins v. Smith*, 539 U.S. 510 (2003). Capital sentencing schemes vary from state to state, but every jurisdiction must have a vehicle for the punishment-phase jury to consider "mitigating" evidence—evidence that tends to diminish the defendant's culpability for the murder. Capital defense attorneys have certain obligations to put on a mitigation case. A *Wiggins* claim is a species of IAC claim where the petitioner asserts that trial counsel failed to adequately investigate mitigating evidence. For punishment-phase IAC claims, "prejudice" is the effect that the deficient performance had on the capital-sentencing verdict. Do you see why the same attorney error could create different amounts of prejudice in different jurisdictions?

The second major capital-specific challenge is an *"Atkins"* claim, named after *Atkins v. Virginia*, 536 U.S. 304 (2002). An *Atkins* claim alleges that a prisoner is categorically ineligible for the death penalty due to mental retardation (MR).[u] Although the Supreme Court did not formally impose an exact definition of MR on the states, an offender can usually show *Atkins* ineligibility by proving: (1) substantially below-average intellectual functioning (low IQ); (2) significant deficits in adaptive functioning; and (3) onset before age 18. There is considerable federal litigation over the legal standards states are using to adjudicate MR, including over the role of "clinical" versus "lay" observation.

The third major capital-specific challenge is a claim that an offender is ineligible to be executed due to mental incompetence. These are sometimes called *"Ford"* claims, after *Ford v. Wainwright*, 477 U.S. 399 (1986). Mental incompetence and MR are distinct conditions, with mental incompetence more closely

---

[u] Many standard-setting bodies and clinicians have abandoned the term "mental retardation" and now denominate the condition as "intellectual disability." See R. Schalock, et al., *The Renaming of Mental Retardation: Understanding the Change to the Term Intellectual Disability*, 45 Intellectual & Developmental Disabilities 116 (2007). This Book uses the term "mental retardation" (MR) because the relevant case law continues to rely on that term.

resembling the traditional concept of insanity. A *Ford* claim involves an inquiry into a capital prisoner's mental state at the time an execution is to be carried out. For that reason, *Ford* claims remain unripe until a state issues a death warrant and (usually) sets an execution date. *Ford* claims are likely to become an increasingly fertile ground of capital post-conviction litigation after *Panetti v. Quarterman*, 551 U.S. 930 (2007). In *Panetti,* the Supreme Court stopped short of announcing a substantive standard for competency, but it did say that it required more than a prisoner's rational awareness of the execution. *Panetti* also imposed several procedural requirements on courts adjudicating the competency issue. Because *Ford* claims are usually premature until well after direct review of the conviction concludes, there is quite a bit of federal habeas litigation on the question of competency.

There are other capital-specific claims, but there is not space to cover all of them here. Is there a reason why society expends so many resources on capital litigation? If society expends so many resources on these questions in trial proceedings, then what is the justification for spending even more resources on collateral scrutiny? In what ways is a death sentence less severe than life in prison? How do you feel about the punishment-related proposition that "death is different?" The unique place of capital punishment in our criminal justice system will resurface throughout the habeas cases in this Chapter and in those to come.

3. COGNIZABILITY

This Chapter has presented the major cases involved in the debate over whether of the scope of the writ has expanded following the 1867 Habeas Corpus Act. Depending on which side of the debate one takes, *Brown v. Allen* either affirmed the existing habeas powers of federal courts or created new ones. Either way, *Brown v. Allen* was an important moment; after 1953, the federal habeas statute undoubtedly permitted state prisoners to "relitigate" their legal and factual challenges to convictions in collateral federal proceedings. Federal post-conviction review reached a zenith or a nadir—again, depending on the view you take—in a series of 1963 Warren Court decisions excerpted in Chapter 4. Under the influence of Professor Bator and of Justice Jackson's famous *Brown v. Allen* concurrence, a more restrained paradigm of habeas review eventually gained traction on the Supreme Court. In 1976, the Burger Court decided *Stone v. Powell*, 428 U.S. 465, excerpted below and which held that Fourth Amendment claims of state prisoners were not cognizable in federal habeas proceedings. Some observers believed that *Stone* was the beginning of *Brown v. Allen's* demise, but such predictions never materialized.

Stone v. Powell

United States Supreme Court
428 U.S. 465 (1976)

■ Mr. JUSTICE POWELL delivered the opinion of the Court.

* * * The question presented is whether a federal court should consider, in ruling on a petition for habeas corpus relief filed by a state prisoner, a claim that evidence obtained by an unconstitutional search or seizure was introduced at his trial, when he has previously been afforded an opportunity for full and fair litigation of his claim in the state courts. * * *

I

* * *

A

Respondent Lloyd Powell was convicted of murder * * * after trial in a California state court. * * * *

In August, 1971, Powell filed an amended petition for a writ of federal habeas corpus under 28 U.S.C. § 2254 in the United States District Court for the Northern District of California, contending that the testimony * * * should have been excluded as the fruit of an illegal search. * * * The District Court concluded that * * * the deterrent purpose of the exclusionary rule does not require that it be applied to bar admission of the fruits of a search incident to an otherwise valid arrest. * * *

In December, 1974, the Court of Appeals for the Ninth Circuit reversed. * * * *

II

The authority of federal courts to issue the writ of habeas corpus *ad subjiciendum* was included in the first grant of federal court jurisdiction, made by the Judiciary Act of 1789, with the limitation that the writ extend only to prisoners held in custody by the United States. The original statutory authorization did not define the substantive reach of the writ. * * * The courts defined the scope of the writ in accordance with the common law, and limited it to an inquiry as to the jurisdiction of the sentencing tribunal.

In 1867, the writ was extended to state prisoners. Under the 1867 Act, federal courts were authorized to give relief in "all cases where any person may be restrained of his or her liberty in violation of the constitution, or of any treaty or law of the United States . . ." But the limitation of federal habeas corpus jurisdiction to consideration of the jurisdiction of the sentencing court persisted. And, although the concept of "jurisdiction" was subjected to considerable strain as the substantive scope of the writ was expanded, this expansion was limited to only a few classes of cases until *Frank v. Mangum.* * * * The Court recognized * * * that if a habeas corpus court found that the State had failed to provide adequate "corrective process" for the full and fair litigation of federal claims, whether or not "jurisdictional," the court could inquire into the merits to determine whether a detention was lawful.

In the landmark decision in *Brown v. Allen*, the scope of the writ was expanded still further. * * * Despite the apparent adequacy of the state corrective process, the Court reviewed the denial of the writ of habeas corpus and held that Brown was entitled to a full reconsideration of these constitutional claims, including, if appropriate, a hearing in the Federal District Court. * * * *

During the period in which the substantive scope of the writ was expanded, the Court did not consider whether exceptions to full review might exist with respect to particular categories of constitutional claims. * * *

Kaufman [*v. United States*, 394 U. S. 217 (1969)] * * * held that search and seizure claims are cognizable in § 2255 proceedings. The Court noted that "the federal habeas remedy extends to state prisoners alleging that unconstitutionally obtained evidence was admitted against them at trial" and concluded, as a matter of statutory construction, that there was no basis for restricting "access by federal prisoners with illegal search and sei-

zure claims to federal collateral remedies, while placing no similar restriction on access by state prisoners." * * *

* * * Upon examination, we conclude, in light of the nature and purpose of the Fourth Amendment exclusionary rule, that this view is unjustified. * * *

III

The Fourth Amendment assures the "right of the people to be secure in
their persons, houses, papers, and effects, against unreasonable searches
and seizures." * * *

The exclusionary rule was a judicially created means of effectuating
the rights secured by the Fourth Amendment. * * * [T]he exclusionary rule
was [eventually] held applicable to the States in *Mapp v. Ohio*, 367 U. S.
643 (1961).

* * * The *Mapp* majority justified the application of the rule to the
States on several grounds, but relied principally upon the belief that exclusion would deter future unlawful police conduct.

Although our decisions often have alluded to the "imperative of judicial
integrity," they demonstrate the limited role of this justification in the determination whether to apply the rule in a particular context. Logically extended, this justification would require that courts exclude unconstitutionally seized evidence despite lack of objection by the defendant, or even over
his assent. * * * While courts, of course, must ever be concerned with preserving the integrity of the judicial process, this concern has limited force
as a justification for the exclusion of highly probative evidence. The force of
this justification becomes minimal where federal habeas corpus relief is
sought by a prisoner who previously has been afforded the opportunity for
full and fair consideration of his search and seizure claim at trial and on
direct review.

The primary justification for the exclusionary rule then is the deterrence of police conduct that violates Fourth Amendment rights. Post-*Mapp*
decisions have established that the rule is not a personal constitutional
right. It is not calculated to redress the injury to the privacy of the victim of
the search or seizure * * * . Instead,

> "the rule is a judicially created remedy designed to safeguard Fourth
> Amendment rights generally through its deterrent effect . . ."

* * * *

IV

* * * The question is whether state prisoners—who have been afforded
the opportunity for full and fair consideration of their reliance upon the
exclusionary rule with respect to seized evidence by the state courts at trial
and on direct review—may invoke their claim again on federal habeas corpus review. * * *

The costs of applying the exclusionary rule even at trial and on direct
review are well known: the focus of the trial, and the attention of the participants therein, are diverted from the ultimate question of guilt or innocence that should be the central concern in a criminal proceeding. Moreover, the physical evidence sought to be excluded is typically reliable and
often the most probative information bearing on the guilt or innocence of
the defendant. * * * Application of the rule thus deflects the truthfinding
process, and often frees the guilty. * * * [A]lthough the rule is thought to

deter unlawful police activity in part through the nurturing of respect for Fourth Amendment values, if applied indiscriminately, it may well have the opposite effect of generating disrespect for the law and administration of justice. These long-recognized costs of the rule persist when a criminal conviction is sought to be overturned on collateral review on the ground that a search and seizure claim was erroneously rejected by two or more tiers of state courts.

Evidence obtained by police officers in violation of the Fourth Amendment is excluded at trial in the hope that the frequency of future violations will decrease. Despite the absence of supportive empirical evidence, we have assumed that the immediate effect of exclusion will be to discourage law enforcement officials from violating the Fourth Amendment by removing the incentive to disregard it. More importantly, over the long-term, this demonstration that our society attaches serious consequences to violation of constitutional rights is thought to encourage those who formulate law enforcement policies, and the officers who implement them, to incorporate Fourth Amendment ideals into their value system.

We adhere to the view that these considerations support the implementation of the exclusionary rule at trial and its enforcement on direct appeal of state court convictions. But the additional contribution, if any, of the consideration of search and seizure claims of state prisoners on collateral review is small in relation to the costs. * * * The view that the deterrence of Fourth Amendment violations would be furthered rests on the dubious assumption that law enforcement authorities would fear that federal habeas review might reveal flaws in a search or seizure that went undetected at trial and on appeal. Even if one rationally could assume that some additional incremental deterrent effect would be present in isolated cases, the resulting advance of the legitimate goal of furthering Fourth Amendment rights would be outweighed by the acknowledged costs to other values vital to a rational system of criminal justice.

In sum, we conclude that, where the State has provided an opportunity for full and fair litigation of a Fourth Amendment claim, a state prisoner may not be granted federal habeas corpus relief on the ground that evidence obtained in an unconstitutional search or seizure was introduced at his trial. In this context, the contribution of the exclusionary rule, if any, to the effectuation of the Fourth Amendment is minimal, and the substantial societal costs of application of the rule persist with special force.

Accordingly, the judgments of the Courts of Appeals are

Reversed.

[The concurring opinion of CHIEF JUSTICE BURGER is omitted.]

■ Mr. JUSTICE BRENNAN, with whom Mr. JUSTICE MARSHALL concurs, dissenting.

* * * Today's holding portends substantial evisceration of federal habeas corpus jurisdiction, and I dissent.* * *

I

Much of the Court's analysis implies that respondents are not entitled to habeas relief because they are not being unconstitutionally detained. Although purportedly adhering to the principle that the Fourth and Fourteenth Amendments "require exclusion" of evidence seized in violation of their commands, the Court informs us that there has merely been a "view" in our cases that "the effectuation of the Fourth Amendment . . . requires the granting of habeas corpus relief when a prisoner has been convicted in state court on the basis of evidence obtained in an illegal search or seizure . . ."

Understandably, the Court must purport to cast its holding in constitutional terms, because that avoids a direct confrontation with the incontrovertible facts that the habeas statutes have heretofore always been construed to grant jurisdiction to entertain Fourth Amendment claims of both state and federal prisoners, that Fourth Amendment principles have been applied in decisions on the merits in numerous cases on collateral review of final convictions, and that Congress has legislatively accepted our interpretation of congressional intent as to the necessary scope and function of habeas relief. * * *

* * * When a state court admits [unconstitutionally seized] evidence, it has committed a constitutional error, and, unless that error is harmless under federal standards * * * it follows ineluctably that the defendant has been placed "in custody in violation of the Constitution" within the comprehension of 28 U.S.C. § 2254. In short, it escapes me as to what logic can support the assertion that the defendant's unconstitutional confinement obtains during the process of direct review, no matter how long that process takes, but that the unconstitutionality then suddenly dissipates at the moment the claim is asserted in a collateral attack on the conviction.

The only conceivable rationale upon which the Court's "constitutional" thesis might rest is the statement that "the [exclusionary] rule is not a personal constitutional right . . . Instead, 'the rule is a judicially created remedy designed to safeguard Fourth Amendment rights generally through its deterrent effect.'" * * * However, * * * the prevailing constitutional *rule* is that unconstitutionally seized evidence *cannot be admitted* in the criminal trial of a person whose federal constitutional rights were violated by the search or seizure. The erroneous admission of such evidence is a violation of the Federal Constitution—*Mapp* inexorably means at least this much, or there would be no basis for applying the exclusionary rule in state criminal proceedings—and an accused against whom such evidence is admitted has been convicted in derogation of rights mandated by, and is "in custody in violation of," the Constitution of the United States. Indeed, since state courts violate the strictures of the Federal Constitution by admitting such evidence, then, even if federal habeas review did not directly effectuate Fourth Amendment values, a proposition I deny, that review would nevertheless serve to effectuate what is concededly a constitutional principle concerning admissibility of evidence at trial. * * * *

II

Therefore, the real ground of today's decision—a ground that is particularly troubling in light of its portent for habeas jurisdiction generally—is the Court's novel reinterpretation of the habeas statutes; this would read the statutes as requiring the district courts routinely to deny habeas relief to prisoners "in custody in violation of the Constitution or laws . . . of the United States" as a matter of judicial "discretion"—a "discretion" judicially manufactured today contrary to the express statutory language—because such claims are "different in kind" from other constitutional violations in that they "do not impugn the integrity of the factfinding process," and because application of such constitutional strictures "often frees the guilty." Much in the Court's opinion suggests that a construction of the habeas statutes to deny relief for non-"guilt-related" constitutional violations, based on this Court's vague notions of comity and federalism, is the actual premise for today's decision, and * * * those premises mark this case as a harbinger of future eviscerations of the habeas statutes that plainly does violence to congressional power to frame the statutory contours of habeas jurisdiction. * * * I am therefore justified in apprehending that the groundwork is being laid today for a drastic withdrawal of federal habeas jurisdiction, if not for all grounds of alleged unconstitutional detention, then at least for claims—for example, of double jeopardy, entrapment, self-incrimination, Miranda violations, and use of invalid identification procedures—that this Court later decides are not "guilt-related."

* * * There is no foundation in the language or history of the habeas statutes for discriminating between types of constitutional transgressions, and efforts to relegate certain categories of claims to the status of "second-class rights" by excluding them from that jurisdiction have been repulsed. Today's opinion, however, marks the triumph of those who have sought to establish a hierarchy of constitutional rights, and to deny for all practical purposes a federal forum for review of those rights that this Court deems less worthy or important. * * *

The procedural safeguards mandated in the Framers' Constitution are not admonitions to be tolerated only to the extent they serve functional purposes that ensure that the "guilty" are punished and the "innocent" freed; rather, every guarantee enshrined in the Constitution * * * is by it endowed with an independent vitality and value, and this Court is not free to curtail those constitutional guarantees even to punish the most obviously guilty. * * * Enforcement of federal constitutional rights that redress constitutional violations directed against the "guilty" is a particular function of federal habeas review, lest judges trying the "morally unworthy" be tempted not to execute the supreme law of the land. State judges popularly elected may have difficulty resisting popular pressures not experienced by federal judges given lifetime tenure designed to immunize them from such influences * * *.

* * * To the extent state trial and appellate judges faithfully, accurately, and assiduously apply federal law and the constitutional principles enunciated by the federal courts, such determinations will be vindicated on the merits when collaterally attacked. But to the extent federal law is erroneously applied by the state courts, there is no authority in this Court to deny defendants the right to have those errors rectified by way of federal habeas; indeed, the Court's reluctance to accept Congress' desires along these lines can only be a manifestation of this Court's mistrust for federal judges. Furthermore, some might be expected to dispute the academic's dictum seemingly accepted by the Court that a federal judge is not necessarily more skilled than a state judge in applying federal law. For the Supremacy Clause of the Constitution proceeds on a different premise, and Congress, as it was constitutionally empowered to do, made federal judges (and initially federal district court judges) "the primary and powerful reliances for vindicating every right given by the Constitution, the laws, and treaties of the United States."

If proof of the necessity of the federal habeas jurisdiction were required, the disposition by the state courts of the underlying Fourth Amendment issues presented by these cases supplies it. [Justice Brennan would have invalidated the statutes at issue as, among other things, void for vagueness.] * * * *

IV

* * * Until this decision, our cases have never departed from the construction of the habeas statutes as embodying a congressional intent that, however substantive constitutional rights are delineated or expanded, those rights may be asserted as a procedural matter under federal habeas jurisdiction. * * * [A]s a practical matter, the only result of today's holding will be that denials by the state courts of claims by state prisoners of violations of their Fourth Amendment rights will go unreviewed by a federal tribunal. I fear that the same treatment ultimately will be accorded state prisoners' claims of violations of other constitutional rights; thus, the potential ramifications of this case for federal habeas jurisdiction generally are ominous. The Court, no longer content just to restrict forthrightly the constitutional rights of the citizenry, has embarked on a campaign to water down even such constitutional rights as it purports to acknowledge by the device of foreclosing resort to the federal habeas remedy for their redress.

I would affirm the judgments of the Court[ ] of Appeals.

[The dissenting opinion of JUSTICE WHITE is omitted.]

NOTES AND QUESTIONS ON POWELL

1)   **Competing Versions of the Fourth Amendment Exclusionary Rule.**
Per the *Powell* majority, the Exclusionary Rule is a judicially-created remedy designed to deter Fourth Amendment violations by law enforcement. Per the *Powell* dissent, admission of unlawfully-seized evidence is itself a Fourth Amendment violation. In a series of cases over the course of the last few years, the Supreme Court has moved decisively towards the *Powell* Majority position.[v] What role does the substantive account of the Fourth Amendment right play in the Court's remedial holding? Is it possible that the remedial ruling could be justified even under a broader conception of the Fourth Amendment?

2)   **Balancing.** *Powell* reflects, at least in part, the Supreme Court's determination that the benefits of relitigating Fourth-Amendment claims are outweighed by the costs of such a practice. Should habeas jurisdiction turn on the efficacy of a suppression remedy? Consider the question of whether, under such a balancing approach, the Court might restrict habeas relief for other kinds of constitutional violations having a suppression remedy.

3)   **"Full and Fair" Corrective Process.** *Powell* used "magic words" of sorts. In a nod to Professor Bator, the Supreme Court held that the opportunity for "full and fair" state consideration precluded relitigation of a claim in federal habeas proceedings. Professor Bator's critique of federal habeas review involved the epistemic limits of human knowledge and the fallibility of institutions we use to discover "the truth." His critique argued that, without some reason to believe state consideration of a claim was legally or factually defective—that it was not "full and fair"—then there was no reason to permit federal courts to revisit the same question. Relitigation of such claims yields no incremental

----

[v] See, e.g., Davis v. United States, 131 S.Ct. 2419 (2011) (holding that the exclusionary rule does not apply to a police search made in objectively reasonable reliance on binding appellate precedent); Herring v. United States; 555 U.S. 135 (2009) (holding that the exclusionary rule did not apply to good-faith mistakes made by police in the course of investigating crime); Hudson v. Michigan, 547 U.S. 586 (2006) (holding that violations of the so-called knock-and-announce rule do not require suppression).

truth discovery. Federal judges are not, according to Professor Bator, more institutionally competent to decide constitutional challenges in federal habeas proceedings. How does the availability of "state corrective process" figure into the *Powell* outcome? Would an absence of state corrective process render the trial not "full and fair?"

In his *Powell* dissent, Justice Brennan largely repeats the thrust of his controversial opinion for the Supreme Court in *Fay v. Noia*, 372 U.S. 391 (1963), arguing that "all constitutional claims have . . . been cognizable on federal habeas corpus." By the time the Court decided *Powell*, Professor Bator's critique of *Brown v. Allen* was already entrenched as the primary counterpoint to the narrative Justice Brennan had announced for the Court in *Noia*. Is Justice Brennan's view, expressed in his *Powell* dissent, consistent with *Lange*, *Parks*, *Siebold*, and *Moore*? Is it consistent with *Brown v. Allen*? Justice Brennan believed that *Powell* was just the beginning of a process by which the Burger Court would chisel away at its predecessor's view of expansive habeas authority. In his words, the decision "portends substantial evisceration of federal habeas corpus jurisdiction."

4)   A Waivable Defense? In response to Justice Brennan's arguments concerning the erosion of habeas jurisdiction, the Supreme Court explained, in omitted footnote 37, that "we hold only that a federal court need not apply the exclusionary rule on habeas review of a Fourth Amendment claim absent a showing that the state prisoner was denied an opportunity for a full and fair litigation of that claim at trial and on direct review. Our decision does not mean that the federal court lacks jurisdiction over such a claim . . ." Several appeals courts have applied footnote 37 and concluded that the *Powell* rule is non-jurisdictional. These courts reason that, if the State waives a *Powell* objection to a Fourth Amendment exclusionary rule claim, then the federal judge has discretion to consider it.[w]

5)   Innocence and the Scope of the Writ. The Supreme Court underscores the idea that suppression of evidence only allows guilty prisoners to go free. Do you agree that a Fourth Amendment violation "has no bearing on the basic justice of [the defendant's] incarceration"? Should habeas corpus be limited only to claims that have a bearing on the ultimate question of guilt? In other words, should innocence restrict the scope of habeas relief? What if you take into account an expanding definition of due process? For an argument that innocence should guide federal courts in deciding the substantive scope of relief, see Henry J. Friendly, *Is Innocence Irrelevant? Collateral Attack on Criminal Judgments*, 38 U. Chi. L. Rev. 142, 160 (1970). (The following Section considers the topic of innocence and discusses Judge Friendly's famous article in a little more detail.) While Congress and the Supreme Court have built the concept of inno-

---

[w] See Young v. Conway, 698 F.3d 69, 85 (2d Cir. 2012) ("We hold that, because the *Stone* rule is non-jurisdictional, it is waivable by the State, and we decline in the exercise of our discretion to consider it on appeal."); Tart v. Massachusetts, 949 F.2d 490, 497 n.6 (1st Cir. 1991) (ruling on the merits of Fourth Amendment claim, where *Powell* argument waived); Davis v. Blackburn, 803 F.2d 1371, 1372–73 (5th Cir. 1986) (per curiam) (divided panel) ("a federal court is not foreclosed from sua sponte applying the principles of *Stone*" but *Stone* is a "prudential" not a "jurisdictional" rule); Wallace v. Duckworth, 778 F.2d 1215, 1220 n.1 (7th Cir. 1985) (holding that where the State "never raised any *Stone*[ ] argument, and since the rule of Stone[ ] is not a jurisdictional rule, we need not raise the issue sua sponte." (citation omitted)). But see Woolery v. Arave, 8 F.3d 1325, 1328 (9th Cir. 1993) (stating that *Powell* is "a categorical limitation on the applicability of fourth amendment exclusionary rules in habeas corpus proceedings").

cence into various procedural inquiries, they have not incorporated that aspect of *Powell* into rules about the cognizability of other types of claims.

6)   Lower Federal Courts. As a result of *Powell*, federal district courts generally cannot reverse Fourth Amendment exclusionary-rule holdings of state courts. Is there something unseemly about the idea of a lower federal court overruling a state court? Is there something especially unseemly about such a decision in the exclusionary rule context? Keep in mind that the Supreme Court continues to be able to take Fourth Amendment cases on certiorari review of the conviction and of any state collateral proceeding. For the view that habeas review in federal district court should function as a substitute for direct review in the Supreme Court, see Barry Friedman, *A Tale of Two Habeas*, 73 Minn. L. Rev. 247, 335–38 (1988).

7)   *Powell* and Other Constitutional Claims—The Sixth Amendment. Ten years after *Powell*, the Court considered whether that decision controlled Sixth Amendment IAC claims involving a defense lawyer's failure to make a timely Fourth Amendment suppression motion. In *Kimmelman v. Morrison*, 477 U.S. 365 (1986), the Court held that such Sixth-Amendment IAC claims remained cognizable on federal habeas review. A New Jersey court convicted Neil Morrison of raping a 15-year old girl. At trial, the prosecution introduced a bed sheet that police seized in violation of the Fourth Amendment. Defense counsel lodged an untimely Fourth Amendment objection to the evidence. Morrison argued that his counsel's failure to move in a timely fashion for suppression under the Fourth Amendment constituted a violation of his Sixth Amendment right to counsel. The federal district court found Morrison's Sixth Amendment IAC claim meritorious, but held that *Powell* barred consideration of the underlying Fourth Amendment challenge. The federal appeals court affirmed. At the outset, the Supreme Court held that:

> We do not share petitioners' perception of the identity between [Morrison's] Fourth and Sixth Amendment claims. While defense counsel's failure to make a timely suppression motion is the primary manifestation of incompetence and source of prejudice advanced by respondent, the two claims are nonetheless distinct, both in nature and in the requisite elements of proof.

The Court (with Justice Brennan writing) then explained that, whereas *Powell* reflected the sub-constitutional status of the exclusionary rule, an IAC claim is separate and asserts a Sixth Amendment right. In addition, part of the reasoning in *Powell* was that the exclusionary rule claim can be presented to the state courts; if counsel is ineffective and fails to do so, then there has been no such full and fair opportunity for review in the state courts. On remand, Morrison received a new trial. How prominently should a distinction between right and remedy figure in whether a habeas claim is cognizable? Under *Powell's ratio decidendi*, should it have mattered that the harm from the asserted Fourth Amendment violation only arose by way of a Sixth Amendment claim about the conduct of the defense lawyer?

8)   *Powell* and Other Constitutional Claims—*Miranda*. Under *Miranda v. Arizona*, 384 U.S. 436 (1966), law enforcement officers were required, in any custodial interrogation, to administer a now-familiar script of constitutional warnings. Unlike the Sixth Amendment question at issue in *Morrison*, there remained some question as to whether *Miranda* was perhaps some type of prudential, "sub-constitutional" rule. (The Court did not conclusively establish the "full" constitutional status of *Miranda* until *Dickerson v. United States*, 530 U.S. 428 (**2000**), which struck down a federal statute purporting to overturn *Miranda*.) In *Withrow v. Williams*, 507 U.S. 680 (1993), while the constitutional status of *Miranda* remained uncertain, the Supreme Court nevertheless declined to extend *Powell* to *Miranda* claims. *Withrow* reasoned that *Miranda* was a personal right, both to protect against unlawful self-incrimination and coercion during interrogations, and to ensure a fair trial free from unreliable confession statements. Justice O'Connor, joined by Chief Justice Rehnquist partially concurred, arguing: "Unlike involuntary or compelled statements—which are of dubious reliability and are therefore inadmissible for any purpose—confessions obtained in violation of Miranda are not necessarily untrustworthy." Given *Powell's* stated rationale, did Justice O'Connor properly consider the truth-seeking function of the constitutional right at issue? What does *Withrow* say about the Court's willingness to apply *Powell* to any new contexts? In what sense does *Withrow* signal the end of the Court's flirtation with Professor Bator's "full and fair" model of federal habeas review?

4. INNOCENCE

Historically, habeas review enabled judges to consider whether custody was lawful by reference to the authority of the jailing entity—not by reference to the guilt or innocence of the inmate. Is innocence still irrelevant? In his influential 1970 article, Judge Henry Friendly asked whether innocence should determine substantive and procedural features of habeas review. He provocatively argued that innocence should be both sufficient and necessary for habeas relief—that it should be a ground for relief unto itself, and that prisoners unable to show innocence should have their claims dismissed. See Henry J. Friendly, *Is Innocence Irrelevant?: Collateral Attack on Criminal Judgments*, 38 U. Chi. L. Rev. 142, 158–60 & n.87 (1970). While many constitutional criminal procedure rights "promote the ultimate objective that the guilty be convicted and the innocent go free," they "are granted to the innocent and the guilty alike." Kimmelman v. Morrison, 477 U.S. 365, 379-80 (1986) (quoting Evitts v. Lucey, 469 U.S. 387, 394 (1985)). Beginning with *Herrera v. Collins*, 506 U.S. 390 (1993) (excerpted below), the Court has avoided any holding that a "freestanding" claim of actual innocence would be sufficient to entitle a claimant to relief. (Innocence is *necessary* to overcome a host of procedural obstacles to habeas relief, many of which Chapter 4 discusses.)

In the last twenty years, courts have had a new reason to focus on innocence claims—a revolution in forensic DNA testing, which allows inmates to prove innocence, even decades after their convictions. There have been more than 300 post-conviction "DNA exonerations," convictions vacated based on new DNA evidence supporting claims of innocence. Most exonerated prisoners had been convicted of very serious crimes—for example, aggravated rape and murder—and spent an average of 13 years in prison before they were exonerated. Until DNA evidence freed them, courts had rejected all of their innocence claims. The DNA evidence frequently exonerated people for whom any trial error had been found harmless or for whom appellate and post-conviction judges had concluded that there was "overwhelming" evidence of guilt. See Brandon L. Garrett, *Convicting the Innocent: Where Criminal Prosecutions Go Wrong* 5 (2011); Brandon L. Garrett, *Judging Innocence*, 108 Colum. L. Rev. 55, 108 (2008). A nationwide network of innocence projects and law school innocence clinics now seek potentially meritorious innocence claims and provide pro bono legal assistance for potentially innocent prisoners.

In addition to changes in technology and the rise of innocence clinics, several other developments drive the new focus on innocence. First, in *Herrera*, the Supreme Court gestured cautiously at the idea that a freestanding innocence claim might be cognizable. What would a "freestanding" innocence claim look like? It would have to be denominated as a *constitutional* claim, perhaps arising under the Due Process Clause or the Eighth Amendment. It would likely require an extremely strong showing of innocence. Notwithstanding the failure of the Supreme Court to recognize freestanding innocence claims formally, prisoners are filing increasing numbers of them in federal courts. Westlaw and Lexis searches for titles of the Supreme Court cases that signal such arguments suggest a growing body of case law. The *2007 Habeas Study* found that 3.9% of noncapital petitioners raised newly-discovered-evidence-of-innocence claims, as did 10.8% of capital petitioners; 18.9% of non-capital petitioners and 25.5% of capital petitioners raised sufficiency of the evidence claims. See King et al., *2007 Habeas Study*, at 29–30. Interestingly, the *2007 Habeas Study* revealed that habeas petitioners who raise innocence claims obtain relief at a much higher rate—"a claim raising new evidence of innocence or guilt was related to a higher likelihood of a grant [of reversal], raising it by about 11 percentage points"—even though a freestanding innocence claim was itself *never* granted. What might explain that effect of innocence claims—claims that the habeas judges did not actually grant?

Second, the value placed on finality has diminished. In response to the DNA revolution, state legislatures have enacted DNA-access statutes to allow DNA testing and to promote consideration of other evidence of innocence. These statutes provide for state-financed DNA testing. They enable judicial scrutiny, even long after a conviction becomes final and after otherwise-applicable limitations periods expire. Newly-discovered evidence need not be biological; there have been hundreds of inmates exonerated by non-DNA evidence. Professor Samuel Gross and the Center of Wrongful Convictions maintain a "National Registry of Exonerations" detailing such cases.[x]

Even though the Court has not formally recognized innocence as an independent ground for habeas relief—it has elevated innocence as a consideration for several procedural inquiries. Statutory and decisional law now contain a number of procedural bars to relief—where claims are untimely, abusively withheld from a prior habeas petition, or not litigated in state court. In most instances, the Court has created innocence "gateways" that allow merits consideration of the underlying claim notwithstanding a procedural defect in the petition. For example, a sufficient showing of actual innocence excuses a claim that is procedurally defaulted—i.e., that is forfeited because a state rejected it on "adequate and independent" state grounds. AEDPA has also incorporated innocence-based exceptions into several key provisions of the habeas statute, and those provisions are described in Chapter 4. The focus of this Chapter's material is on whether a claim of innocence is *sufficient* to entitle a prisoner to habeas relief. The entry point for this complex question is the Court's decision in *Herrera v.*

---

[x] See National Registry of Exonerations, *http://www.law.umich.edu/special/exoneration/Pages/about.aspx* (last visited on December 5, 2012) (recording over 1,000 exonerations).

Collins, which rejected—but assumed the hypothetical existence of—a free-standing actual innocence claim.

Herrera v. Collins
United States Supreme Court
506 U.S. 390 (1993)

■ CHIEF JUSTICE REHNQUIST delivered the opinion of the Court.

Petitioner Leonel Torres Herrera was convicted of capital murder and sentenced to death in January 1982. He unsuccessfully challenged the conviction on direct appeal and state collateral proceedings in the Texas state courts, and in a federal habeas petition. In February 1992—10 years after his conviction—he urged in a second federal habeas petition that he was "actually innocent" of the murder for which he was sentenced to death, and that the Eighth Amendment's prohibition against cruel and unusual punishment and the Fourteenth Amendment's guarantee of due process of law therefore forbid his execution. He supported this claim with affidavits tending to show that his now-dead brother, rather than he, had been the perpetrator of the crime. [Herrera] urges us to hold that this showing of innocence entitles him to relief in this federal habeas proceeding. We hold that it does not.

[In September 1981, Texas Department of Public Safety Officer David Rucker was found lying next to his patrol car, shot in the head.] At about the same time, Los Fresnos Police Officer Enrique Carrisalez observed a speeding vehicle traveling west towards Los Fresnos, away from the place where Rucker's body had been found, along the same road. Carrisalez, who was accompanied in his patrol car by Enrique Hernandez, turned on his flashing red lights and pursued the speeding vehicle. [The car eventually pulled over, and the police car pulled behind it.] Carrisalez took a flashlight and walked toward the car of the speeder. The driver opened his door and exchanged a few words with Carrisalez before firing at least one shot at Carrisalez' chest. The officer died nine days later.

Petitioner Herrera was arrested a few days after the shootings and charged with the capital murder of both Carrisalez and Rucker. He was tried and found guilty of the capital murder of Carrisalez in January 1982, and sentenced to death. In July 1982, [Herrera] pleaded guilty to the murder of Rucker.

At [Herrera]'s trial for the murder of Carrisalez, Hernandez, who had witnessed Carrisalez' slaying from the officer's patrol car, identified [Herrera] as the person who had wielded the gun. A declaration by Officer Carrisalez to the same effect, made while he was in the hospital, was also admitted. Through a license plate check, it was shown that the speeding car involved in Carrisalez' murder was registered to [Herrera]'s "live-in" girlfriend. [Herrera] was known to drive this car, and he had a set of keys to the car in his pants pocket when he was arrested. Hernandez identified the car as the vehicle from which the murderer had emerged to fire the fatal shot. He also testified that there had been only one person in the car that night.

The evidence showed that Herrera's Social Security card had been found alongside Rucker's patrol car on the night he was killed. Splatters of blood on the car identified as the vehicle involved in the shootings, and on [Herrera]'s blue jeans and wallet were identified as type A blood—the same type which Rucker had. (Herrera has type O blood.) Similar evidence with respect to strands of hair found in the car indicated that the hair was Rucker's and not Herrera's. A handwritten letter was also found on the person of [Herrera] when he was arrested, which strongly implied that he had killed Rucker.

[Herrera] appealed his conviction and sentence, arguing, among other things, that Hernandez' and Carrisalez' identifications were unreliable and improperly admitted. The Texas Court of Criminal Appeals affirmed, and we denied certiorari. [Herrera]'s application for state habeas relief was denied. [Herrera] then filed a federal habeas petition, again challenging the identifications offered against him at trial. This petition was denied and we again denied certiorari.

[Herrera] next returned to state court and filed a second habeas petition, raising, among other things, a claim of "actual innocence" based on newly discovered evidence. In support of this claim [Herrera] presented the affidavits of Hector Villarreal, an attorney who had represented [Herrera]'s brother, Raul Herrera, Sr., and of Juan Franco Palacious, one of Raul, Senior's former cellmates. Both individuals claimed that Raul, Senior, who died in 1984, had told them that he—and not [Herrera]—had killed Officers Rucker and Carrisalez. The State District Court denied this application, finding that "no evidence at trial remotely suggest[ed] that anyone other than [Herrera] committed the offense." The Texas Court of Criminal Appeals affirmed, and we denied certiorari.

In February 1992, [Herrera] lodged the instant habeas petition—his second—in federal court, alleging, among other things, that he is innocent of the murders of Rucker and Carrisalez, and that his execution would thus violate the Eighth and Fourteenth Amendments. In addition to proffering the above affidavits, [Herrera] presented the affidavits of Raul Herrera, Jr., Raul Senior's son, and Jose Ybarra, Jr., a schoolmate of the Herrera brothers. Raul, Junior, averred that he had witnessed his father shoot Officers Rucker and Carrisalez and [Herrera] was not present. Raul, Junior, was nine years old at the time of the killings. Ybarra alleged that Raul, Senior, told him one summer night in 1983 that he had shot the two police officers. [Herrera] alleged that law enforcement officials were aware of this evidence, and had withheld it in violation of *Brady v. Maryland*, 373 U.S. 83 (1963).

[The District Court granted a stay of execution for [Herrera] to present a claim of actual innocence in state court. The Court of Appeals vacated the stay of execution.] We granted certiorari and the Texas Court of Criminal Appeals stayed [Herrera's] execution. We now affirm.

[Herrera] asserts that the Eighth and Fourteenth Amendments to the United States Constitution prohibit the execution of a person who is innocent of the crime for which he was convicted. This proposition has an elemental appeal, as would the similar proposition that the Constitution prohibits the imprisonment of one who is innocent of the crime for which he was convicted. After all, the central purpose of any system of criminal justice is to convict the guilty and free the innocent. But the evidence upon which [Herrera's] claim of innocence rests was not produced at his trial, but rather eight years later. In any system of criminal justice, "innocence" or "guilt" must be determined in some sort of a judicial proceeding. [Herrera's] showing of innocence, and indeed his constitutional claim for relief based upon that showing, must be evaluated in the light of the previous proceedings in this case, which have stretched over a span of 10 years.

A person when first charged with a crime is entitled to a presumption of innocence, and may insist that his guilt be established beyond a reasonable doubt. Other constitutional provisions also have the effect of ensuring against the risk of convicting an innocent person. * * * In capital cases, we have required additional protections because of the nature of the penalty at stake. * * * All of these constitutional safeguards, of course, make it more difficult for the State to rebut and finally overturn the presumption of innocence which attaches to every criminal defendant. But we have also observed that "[d]ue process does not require that every conceivable step be taken, at whatever cost, to eliminate the possibility of convicting an innocent person." To conclude otherwise would all but paralyze our system for enforcement of the criminal law.

Once a defendant has been afforded a fair trial and convicted of the offense for which he was charged, the presumption of innocence disappears. * * * Here, it is not disputed that the State met its burden of proving at trial that [Herrera] was guilty of the capital murder of Officer Carrisalez beyond a reasonable doubt. Thus, in the eyes of the law, [Herrera] does not come before the Court as one who is "innocent," but, on the contrary, as one who has been convicted by due process of law of two brutal murders.

Based on affidavits here filed, [Herrera] claims that evidence never presented to the trial court proves him innocent notwithstanding the verdict reached at his trial. Such a claim is not cognizable in the state courts of Texas. For to obtain a new trial based on newly discovered evidence, a defendant must file a motion within 30 days after imposition or suspension of sentence. The Texas courts have construed this 30-day time limit as jurisdictional.

Claims of actual innocence based on newly discovered evidence have never been held to state a ground for federal habeas relief absent an independent constitutional violation occurring in the underlying state criminal proceeding. * * * This rule is grounded in the principle that federal habeas courts sit to ensure that individuals are not imprisoned in violation of the Constitution—not to correct errors of fact. * * * The guilt or innocence determination in state criminal trials is "a decisive and portentous event." *Wainwright v. Sykes, 433 U.S. 72, 90 (1977).* "Society's resources have been concentrated at that time and place in order to decide, within the limits of human fallibility, the question of guilt or innocence of one of its citizens." *Ibid.* Few rulings would be more disruptive of our federal system than to provide for federal habeas review of freestanding claims of actual innocence. * * *

[Herrera] asserts that this case is different because he has been sentenced to death. But we have "refused to hold that the fact that a death sentence has been imposed requires a different standard of review on federal habeas corpus." * * *

Alternatively, [Herrera] invokes the Fourteenth Amendment's guarantee of due process of law in support of his claim that his showing of actual innocence entitles him to a new trial, or at least to a vacation of his death sentence. "[B]ecause the States have considerable expertise in matters of criminal procedure and the criminal process is grounded in centuries of common-law tradition," we have "exercis[ed] substantial deference to legislative judgments in this area." * * *

The Constitution itself, of course, makes no mention of new trials. New trials in criminal cases were not granted in England until the end of the

17th century. * * * The practice in the States today, while of limited relevance to our historical inquiry, is divergent. Texas is one of 17 States that requires a new trial motion based on newly discovered evidence to be made within 60 days of judgment. One State adheres to the common-law rule and requires that such a motion be filed during the term in which judgment was rendered. Eighteen jurisdictions have time limits ranging between one and three years, with 10 States and the District of Columbia following the 2-year federal time limit. Only 15 States allow a new trial motion based on newly discovered evidence to be filed more than three years after conviction. Of these States, four have waivable time limits of less than 120 days, two have waivable time limits of more than 120 days, and nine States have no time limits. * * *

[W]e cannot say that Texas' refusal to entertain [Herrera]'s newly discovered evidence eight years after his conviction transgresses a principle of fundamental fairness "rooted in the traditions and conscience of our people." This is not to say, however, that [Herrera] is left without a forum to raise his actual innocence claim. For under Texas law, [Herrera] may file a request for executive clemency. Clemency is deeply rooted in our Anglo-American tradition of law, and is the historic remedy for preventing miscarriages of justice where judicial process has been exhausted.

Executive clemency has provided the "fail safe" in our criminal justice system. * * * It is an unalterable fact that our judicial system, like the human beings who administer it, is fallible. But history is replete with examples of wrongfully convicted persons who have been pardoned in the wake of after-discovered evidence establishing their innocence. In his classic work, Professor Edwin Borchard compiled 65 cases in which it was later determined that individuals had been wrongfully convicted of crimes. Clemency provided the relief mechanism in 47 of these cases; the remaining cases ended in judgments of acquittals after new trials. Recent authority confirms that over the past century clemency has been exercised frequently in capital cases in which demonstrations of "actual innocence" have been made. * * *

As the foregoing discussion illustrates, in state criminal proceedings the trial is the paramount event for determining the guilt or innocence of the defendant. Federal habeas review of state convictions has traditionally been limited to claims of constitutional violations occurring in the course of the underlying state criminal proceedings. Our federal habeas cases have treated claims of "actual innocence," not as an independent constitutional claim, but as a basis upon which a habeas [Herrera] may have an independent constitutional claim considered on the merits, even though his habeas petition would otherwise be regarded as successive or abusive. * * *

We may assume, for the sake of argument in deciding this case, that in a capital case a truly persuasive demonstration of "actual innocence" made after trial would render the execution of a defendant unconstitutional, and warrant federal habeas relief if there were no state avenue open to process such a claim. But because of the very disruptive effect that entertaining claims of actual innocence would have on the need for finality in capital cases, and the enormous burden that having to retry cases based on often stale evidence would place on the States, the threshold showing for such an assumed right would necessarily be extraordinarily high. The showing made by [Herrera] in this case falls far short of any such threshold.

[Herrera's] newly discovered evidence consists of affidavits. In the new trial context, motions based solely upon affidavits are disfavored because the affiants' statements are obtained without the benefit of cross-examination and an opportunity to make credibility determinations. * * * [Herrera]'s affidavits are particularly suspect in this regard because, with the exception of Raul Herrera, Jr.'s affidavit, they consist of hearsay. * * *

The affidavits filed in this habeas proceeding were given over eight years after [Herrera's] trial. No satisfactory explanation has been given as to why the affiants waited until the 11th hour—and, indeed, until after the alleged perpetrator of the murders himself was dead—to make their statements. * * * Equally troubling, no explanation has been offered as to why [Herrera], by hypothesis an innocent man, pleaded guilty to the murder of Rucker.

Moreover, the affidavits themselves contain inconsistencies, and therefore fail to provide a convincing account of what took place on the night Officers Rucker and Carrisalez were killed. For instance, the affidavit of Raul, Junior, who was nine years old at the time, indicates that there were three people in the speeding car from which the murderer emerged, whereas Hector Villarreal attested that Raul, Senior, told him that there were two people in the car that night. Of course, Hernandez testified at [Herrera]'s trial that the murderer was the only occupant of the car. The affidavits also conflict as to the direction in which the vehicle was heading when the murders took place and [Herrera]'s whereabouts on the night of the killings.

Finally, the affidavits must be considered in light of the proof of [Herrera]'s guilt at trial—proof which included two eyewitness identifications, numerous pieces of circumstantial evidence, and a handwritten letter in which [Herrera] apologized for killing the officers and offered to turn himself in under certain conditions. That proof, even when considered alongside [Herrera]'s belated affidavits, points strongly to [Herrera]'s guilt.

This is not to say that [Herrera]'s affidavits are without probative value. Had this sort of testimony been offered at trial, it could have been weighed by the jury, along with the evidence offered by the State and [Herrera], in deliberating upon its verdict. Since the statements in the affidavits contradict the evidence received at trial, the jury would have had to decide important issues of credibility. But coming 10 years after [Herrera]'s trial, this showing of innocence falls far short of that which would have to be made in order to trigger the sort of constitutional claim which we have assumed, *arguendo*, to exist.

The judgment of the Court of Appeals is

Affirmed.

■ JUSTICE O'CONNOR, with whom JUSTICE KENNEDY joins, concurring.

I cannot disagree with the fundamental legal principle that executing the innocent is inconsistent with the Constitution. * * * Dispositive to this case, however, is an equally fundamental fact: [Herrera] is not innocent, in any sense of the word. * * * *

Our society has a high degree of confidence in its criminal trials, in no small part because the Constitution offers unparalleled protections against convicting the innocent. The question similarly would be answered in the negative today, except for the disturbing nature of the claim before us. * * *

Unless federal proceedings and relief—if they are to be had at all—are reserved for "extraordinarily high" and "truly persuasive demonstration[s] of 'actual innocence'" that cannot be presented to state authorities, the federal courts will be deluged with frivolous claims of actual innocence. * * *

Ultimately, two things about this case are clear. First is what the Court does not hold. Nowhere does the Court state that the Constitution permits the execution of an actually innocent person. Instead, the Court assumes for the sake of argument that a truly persuasive demonstration of actual innocence would render any such execution unconstitutional and that federal habeas relief would be warranted if no state avenue were open to process the claim. Second is what [Herrera] has not demonstrated. [Herrera] has failed to make a persuasive showing of actual innocence. * * * Accordingly, the Court has no reason to pass on, and appropriately reserves, the question whether federal courts may entertain convincing claims of actual innocence. That difficult question remains open. If the Constitution's guarantees of fair procedure and the safeguards of clemency and pardon fulfill their historical mission, it may never require resolution at all.

■ JUSTICE SCALIA, with whom JUSTICE THOMAS joins, concurring.

We granted certiorari on the question whether it violates due process or constitutes cruel and unusual punishment for a State to execute a person who, having been convicted of murder after a full and fair trial, later alleges that newly discovered evidence shows him to be "actually innocent." I would have preferred to decide that question, particularly since, as the Court's discussion shows, it is perfectly clear what the answer is: There is no basis in text, tradition, or even in contemporary practice (if that were enough) for finding in the Constitution a right to demand judicial consideration of newly discovered evidence of innocence brought forward after conviction. * * *

With any luck, we shall avoid ever having to face this embarrassing question again, since it is improbable that evidence of innocence as convincing as today's opinion requires would fail to produce an executive pardon.

My concern is that in making life easier for ourselves we not appear to make it harder for the lower federal courts * * *. A number of Courts of Appeals have hitherto held * * * that newly discovered evidence relevant only to a state prisoner's guilt or innocence is not a basis for federal habeas corpus relief. I do not understand it to be the import of today's decision that those holdings are to be replaced with a strange regime that assumes permanently, though only "*arguendo*," that a constitutional right exists, and expends substantial judicial resources on that assumption. * * *

[The concurring opinion of JUSTICE WHITE is omitted.]

■ JUSTICE BLACKMUN, with whom JUSTICE STEVENS and JUSTICE SOUTER join with respect to Parts I-IV, dissenting.

Nothing could be more contrary to contemporary standards of decency, *see Ford v. Wainwright*, 477 U.S. 399, 406 (1986), or more shocking to the conscience, *see Rochin v. California*, 342 U.S. 165, 172 (1952), than to execute a person who is actually innocent.

I therefore must disagree with the long and general discussion that precedes the Court's disposition of this case. * * * Because I believe that in the first instance the District Court should decide whether [Herrera] is entitled to a hearing and whether he is entitled to relief on the merits of his claim, I would reverse the order of the Court of Appeals and remand this case for further proceedings in the District Court. * * *

The Eighth Amendment prohibits "cruel and unusual punishments." This proscription is not static but rather reflects evolving standards of decency. I think it is crystal clear that the execution of an innocent person is "at odds with contemporary standards of fairness and decency." * * *

Execution of the innocent is equally offensive to the Due Process Clause of the Fourteenth Amendment. The majority's discussion misinterprets [Herrera]'s Fourteenth Amendment claim as raising a procedural, rather than a substantive, due process challenge. * * *

Whatever procedures a State might adopt to hear actual-innocence claims, one thing is certain: The possibility of executive clemency is *not* sufficient to satisfy the requirements of the Eighth and Fourteenth Amendments. The majority correctly points out: "A pardon is an act of grace." The vindication of rights guaranteed by the Constitution has never been made to turn on the unreviewable discretion of an executive official or administrative tribunal. * * *

* * * I would hold that, to obtain relief on a claim of actual innocence, [Herrera] must show that he probably is innocent. This standard is supported by several considerations. First, new evidence of innocence may be discovered long after the defendant's conviction. Given the passage of time, it may be difficult for the State to retry a defendant who obtains relief from his conviction or sentence on an actual-innocence claim. The actual-innocence proceeding thus may constitute the final word on whether the defendant may be punished. In light of this fact, an otherwise constitutionally valid conviction or sentence should not be set aside lightly. Second, conviction after a constitutionally adequate trial strips the defendant of the presumption of innocence. * * *

Just as an execution without adequate safeguards is unacceptable, so too is an execution when the condemned prisoner can prove that he is innocent. The execution of a person who can show that he is innocent comes perilously close to simple murder.

NOTES AND QUESTIONS ON HERRERA

1) What was the Holding? Chief Justice Rehnquist wrote the Supreme Court's opinion, formally joined by Justices O'Connor, Scalia, Kennedy, and Thomas. That opinion did not recognize a freestanding innocence claim, but assumed *arguendo* that one might exist in order to hold that Herrera's petition would not meet the standard. Justice O'Connor wrote for herself and for Justice Kennedy, stating that the execution of an actually innocent person would be unconstitutional. Like Chief Justice Rehnquist, Justices O'Connor and Kennedy explicitly reserved on the question of what standards would govern a freestanding innocence claim in a case where a claimant could make a sufficiently persuasive factual showing. Justice White concurred in the judgment, in a brief opinion omitted here, stating that he would recognize a freestanding innocence claim only in situations where no rational trier of fact, in light of the new evidence, could have found the offender guilty beyond a reasonable doubt. Only Justices Scalia and Thomas would have rejected outright the recognition of freestanding innocence claims as "constitutional." Justice Blackmun, joined by Justices Stevens and Souter, would have held that a freestanding innocence claim was cognizable under the Constitution. In light of this alignment, and the designation of Chief Justice Rehnquist's opinion as that of the Court, how would you answer the question, "what is *Herrera's* holding?"

To add another layer of complexity to the question, consider the varying rationales advanced for the freestanding innocence claim: the Eighth Amendment, as well as substantive and procedural theories under the Fourteenth Amendment Due Process Clause. Again, count the votes. Justices Scalia and Thomas would not recognize any such constitutional right. The Chief Justice would only recognize one *arguendo*, and did not specify the constitutional provision from which the hypothetical right would arise. Justices White, O'Connor, and Kennedy—although willing to recognize a constitutional right—also failed to specify an originating constitutional provision. They provided the Chief Justice with a majority and would not reach such issues in this case. Only the three dissenters—Justices Blackmun, Stevens, and Souter—would have expressly premised a constitutional right to present an actual innocence claim on an Eighth Amendment or, alternatively, a substantive due process rationale. Even if there were six votes to recognize, in theory, an actual innocence claim, the Court declined to do so in this case.

2)   What Showing? Chief Justice Rehnquist assumed *arguendo* that the standard to prevail on a hypothetical actual innocence claim would be "a truly persuasive demonstration of 'actual innocence.'" He added that it would be an "extraordinarily high burden." How much evidence would suffice to make that kind of showing? Enough so that a reasonable juror could not convict—given the "beyond a reasonable doubt" standard at trial? Enough so that, more likely than not, no reasonable juror could convict? Substantial or "clear and convincing" evidence of innocence? The dissenters advanced a different standard. Justice Blackmun, joined by two other Justices suggested a "probably innocent" standard for showing innocence. What kind of evidence would that standard require?

What is your assessment of Herrera's innocence evidence? Should the Court have ordered a hearing, as the dissenters suggested, for a district court to evaluate whether that evidence met certain evidentiary thresholds?

3)   Corrective Process. The Court underscores the availability of state motions for new trial, and also the availability of state clemency. Clemency usually takes the form of an executive order that a sentence not be carried out. When the clemency order discharges the prisoner, it is called a pardon. When it transforms a death sentence into a term of life, the order "commutes" the sentence. Clemency power is usually vested in an executive or in a board, and sometimes it is vested in both simultaneously. For a state-by-state breakdown of state clemency procedures involving actual innocence claims, see David R. Dow, Jared Tyler, Frances Burliot, and Jennifer Jeans, *Is It Constitutional To Execute Someone Who Is Innocent (And If It Isn't, How Can It Be Stopped Following House v. Bell)?*, 42 Tulsa L. Rev. 277, Appendix B (2006).

Do you agree with the suggestion that clemency provides the appropriate "fail safe" to prevent wrongful convictions or executions? Consider the distortions that elections create. Are there reasons to think that clemency is less "blind" than other forms of criminal justice? How comfortable are you with the frank acknowledgment "that our judicial system, like the human beings who administer it, is fallible"? Is the Court's reference to clemency fulfilling the same role as the appellate process fulfilled in *Frank*?

4)   Finality. Assume for the sake of argument that, contrary to the views expressed by a number of the Justices, Herrera presented a nontrivial claim of actual innocence. One rationale of the Court's opinion was that "finality" would be undermined by permitting inmates like Herrera to litigate freestanding actual innocence claims. Finality is one interest that tips a post-conviction scale towards a decision to deny relief. Is finality an interest of litigants, of courts, of the public, or some combination thereof? In what sense would other potential outcomes in *Herrera*—either an order for a new trial or an order to discharge the prisoner—undermine finality? Is the interest in finality diminished in these situations, or is that perhaps the wrong way to answer the question? Is there a better way to ask whether other interests dominate the interest in finality when a prisoner alleges actual innocence? Is there a way to define or measure the finality interest that could be compared across cases? Would it be unseemly for a federal court to entertain new evidence of innocence where the state, like Texas, has a statute prohibiting motions based on new evidence of innocence brought after a short limitations period has expired?

5)   Accuracy. Did the Court place enough value on accuracy in criminal cases—the value in ensuring that "the guilty be convicted and the innocent go free"? Herring v. New York, 422 U.S. 853, 863 (1975). How would you precisely articulate in the interest in "accuracy"? Does the question involve anything more than the increment of accuracy added by an additional proceeding? As with the interest in finality, is there any way to state the interest in accuracy rigorously enough such that it seems to drive, rather than reflect, the outcome in the case? Compare the interest in accuracy at issue in *Herrera* with the interest at issue in *Powell*. In which case does an accuracy inquiry seem most appropriate?

6)   Is Death Different? One of the more controversial propositions in all of criminal punishment is the idea that "death is different"—that capital proceedings deserve extra procedural protection, appellate scrutiny, and collateral review.[y] One approach suggests that, because a capital sentence is the most extreme punishment, death should be imposed with more certainty than any other criminal sentence. Under another approach, all criminal sentences—at least the severe ones—deserve the same amount of process and scrutiny. For the purposes of due process, does death require a greater confidence in the verdict? Should the habeas remedy be more robust in the capital context? Certainly, the Eighth Amendment, concerned with cruel and unusual punishment, might have far more to say about an execution of an innocent person; an actual innocence claim grounded in the Due Process Clause, in contrast, might extend more broadly to other types of non-capital cases.

7)   Innocence Gateways and *House v. Bell*. Recall that *Herrera* involved a question as to the cognizability of a freestanding innocence claim—whether an innocence showing is *sufficient* to obtain habeas relief. The other salient question is whether, for cases in certain procedural postures, an innocence allega-

---

[y] Although the Justices do not all agree about what role a "death-is-different" proposition should play in American law, it is frequently mentioned in some of the most important criminal procedure cases. See, e.g., Ring v. Arizona, 536 U.S. 584, 605-06 (2002) ("[T]here is no doubt that '[d]eath is different.'") (alteration in original); Atkins v. Virginia, 536 U.S. 304, 337 (2002) (Scalia, J., dissenting) (describing that the *Atkins* rule that states cannot execute offenders with mental retardation as the "pinnacle of . . . death-is-different jurisprudence"); McCleskey v. Kemp, 481 U.S. 279, 340 (1987) (Brennan, J., dissenting) ("It hardly needs reiteration that this Court has consistently acknowledged the uniqueness of the punishment of death."); Woodson v. North Carolina, 428 U.S. 280, 305 (1976) (opinion of Stewart, Powell, & Stevens, JJ.) ("[T]he penalty of death is qualitatively different from a sentence of imprisonment, however long."); Gregg v. Georgia, 428 U.S. 153, 188 (1976) (opinion of Stewart, Powell, & Stevens, JJ.) ("[T]he penalty of death is different in kind from any other punishment . . . .").

tion is *necessary* to obtaining merits review. In *House v. Bell*, 547 U.S. 518 (2006), the Supreme Court affirmed the existence of an innocence gateway that allowed state inmates to excuse procedurally defaulted claims. Chapter 4 contains a lengthy *House* excerpt and a robust discussion thereof. There are similar innocence gateways for several other procedural obstacles. *House*, like many cases in which the Court considered both an innocence gateway and a *Herrera* claim, decided the former and expressly reserved the latter. The Court explained:

> We conclude here, much as in *Herrera*, that whatever burden a hypothetical freestanding innocence claim would require, this petitioner has not satisfied it. To be sure, House has cast considerable doubt on his guilt—doubt sufficient to satisfy [the] gateway standard for obtaining federal review despite a state procedural default. In *Herrera*, however, the Court described the threshold for any hypothetical freestanding innocence claim as "extraordinarily high." . . . House's showing falls short of the threshold implied in *Herrera*.

How should the different functions of innocence—as a freestanding basis for relief and as a means for excusing procedural defects—influence rules that develop in each context?

8) Sufficiency of the Evidence Claims *Herrera* distinguished a freestanding innocence claim from a sufficiency of the evidence claim, relying on the decision in *Jackson v. Virginia*, 443 U.S. 307 (1979). *Jackson* held that a Due Process Clause violation occurs when a claimant is convicted on evidence insufficient to justify a jury finding of guilt beyond a reasonable doubt. The *Jackson* inquiry is highly deferential: "the relevant question is whether, after viewing the evidence in the light most favorable to the prosecution, any rational trier of fact could have found the essential elements of the crime beyond a reasonable doubt." That standard, however, "does not permit a court to make its own subjective determination of guilt or innocence . . ." Nor does that standard permit the court to consider newly discovered evidence of innocence that was not part of the trial record.

9) *Osborne.* The discussion in *Herrera* was limited to whether a capitally-sentenced prisoner could litigate a freestanding innocence claim. In *Osborne v. District Attorney's Office*, 129 S.Ct. 2308 (2009), a decision presented in Chapter 11 that chiefly considered a procedural due process right to post-conviction DNA testing, the Supreme Court again "assume[d] without deciding" that a freestanding innocence claim exists. *Osborne* was a non-capital case, however, perhaps indicating that *Herrera* claims may be viable in such contexts. Freestanding innocence claims may require factual consideration by federal judges. *Osborne* also noted that a federal district court has authority to order discovery, including post-conviction DNA testing, relevant to such a hypothetical *Herrera* claim.

10) A Strange Regime. Concurring in *Herrera*, Justice Scalia predicted "a strange regime that assumes permanently, though only '*arguendo*,' that a constitutional right exists, and expends substantial judicial resources on that assumption." He was right. Lower federal courts now entertain *Herrera* claims of actual innocence. Although those courts assume the claim exists, they have denied relief on all *Herrera* claims, perhaps because of the extraordinarily high evidentiary burden that such claims must meet. See Nicholas Berg, *Turning a Blind Eye to Innocence: The Legacy of Herrera v. Collins*, 42 Am. Crim. L. Rev.

121, 130–26 (2005). Among those who have tried and failed to assert a *Herrera* claim were several who were later exonerated by DNA testing. See Garrett, *Judging Innocence,* 108 Colum. L. Rev. at 111–12.

11) Having it Both Ways? Although harmless error and other doctrines permit a court to deny habeas relief based on the strength of trial evidence of guilt, innocence is not a basis for relief—at least as habeas "claims" have historically been conceptualized. Justice Blackmun added, in his *Herrera* dissent, "[H]aving held that a prisoner who is incarcerated in violation of the Constitution must show he is actually innocent to obtain relief, the majority would now hold that a prisoner who is actually innocent must show a constitutional violation to obtain relief." He concluded, "The only principle that would appear to reconcile these two positions is the principle that habeas relief should be denied whenever possible." Is Justice Blackmun right? Or does the principle of finality explain the two positions?

12) Herrera's Execution. Herrera maintained his innocence until the end. His final words were, "I am innocent, innocent, innocent. Something terribly wrong is happening here tonight." See Amnesty International, *United States of America: Killing Without Mercy: Clemency Procedures in Texas* (1999). The Amnesty Report noted that the Texas Board of Pardons and Paroles has rarely recommended clemency in death penalty cases and, for Herrera, did not recommend a hearing to evaluate the claim. Given that virtually every single prisoner subject to the death penalty seeks clemency, is there anything unusual about the failure of the clemency board to hold hearings? In 1992, Texas governor Anne Richards granted a 30-day reprieve to a mentally-troubled inmate named Johnny Frank Garrett, after being urged to do so by Pope John Paul II. The reprieve was followed by a hearing, and then a 17–0 Texas Board vote to carry out the execution.

13) The Troy Davis Case. A *Herrera* claim was also important to the *Troy Davis* case, discussed in Chapter 2. See In re Davis, 130 S.Ct. 1 (2009). Recall that Davis came forward with a freestanding innocence claim in a successive petition. The Eleventh Circuit did not authorize the petition, and the Supreme Court exercised its original habeas jurisdiction to transfer the case to a district court for a merits determination. Justice Scalia dissented from the transfer order, joined by Justice Thomas, calling the district court proceeding a "fool's errand." Justice Scalia argued that there was no point in transferring *Davis* for adjudication of the innocence claim, because an innocence challenge was not a "constitutional" claim and the district court did not have habeas jurisdiction to grant relief. The district court ultimately mooted the cognizability issue, finding that Davis was guilty of the offense for which he was convicted, and he was later executed.

———

NOTES ON STATE INNOCENCE STATUTES

1) Finality Reconsidered. Early federal practice would permit consideration of new-trial motions only during the same term in which judgment was entered; in 1946, the federal rules committee adopted a two-year limitations period for filing new-trial motions. As the Supreme Court emphasized in *Herrera*, state courts traditionally adopted limitation periods for collateral challenges to criminal convictions. Inmates and defendants could argue that they were innocent—and even use evidence not presented at trial to do it—but they were usually subject to some state period of limitation when doing so.

Recall that, in *Herrera*, the Supreme Court observed that freestanding innocence litigation would be "disruptive" of finality. The Court explained that, under Texas law, Herrera could obtain an evidentiary hearing on new evidence of innocence within 30 days of the imposition of the sentence. The Court also observed that, at common law, courts granted new trial motions infrequently. *Herrera* noted "divergent" practices in the states, with Texas being one of 17 states (in the early 1990s) that required a new trial motion based on newly dis- covered evidence to be made within 60 days of judgment. Eighteen states had time limits ranging between one and three years, fifteen states allowed a new trial motion based on newly discovered evidence to be filed more than three years after conviction, and nine states had no time limits.[z]

Accuracy was one reason why the finality interest predominated—because a new proceeding might be far less accurate than the trial held years before, much closer to when the crime took place. *Herrera*, for example, emphasized how "the passage of time only diminishes the reliability of criminal adjudica- tions" due to the "erosion of memory and dispersion of witnesses." As several recent Roberts Court decisions have acknowledged, DNA testing may change the calculus, making new, more accurate evidence available long after trial. DNA-testing technology can sometimes resolve innocence claims with great certainty—particularly in rape cases—and tests can yield perfectly accurate results even decades after a conviction. For a long time, however, older rules vindicating the state interest in finality made DNA testing difficult to obtain in situations where prosecutors were unwilling to agree to conduct the tests. Earl Washington, Jr., was a well-known case exhibiting this problem. In 1993, de- spite obtaining DNA tests that cleared him, Washington could not obtain any relief based on that new evidence of innocence in the courts. Virginia had a rule that new evidence of innocence could only be asserted within twenty-one days of the criminal trial. The rule read as follows: "All final judgments, orders, and decrees, irrespective of terms of court, shall remain under the control of the trial court and subject to be modified, vacated, or suspended for twenty-one days after the date of entry, and no longer." As in other states, Virginia courts interpreted the rule to permit, after the 21-day period, a judge to correct only inadvertent clerical errors. Washington's trial was in 1984, long before DNA testing was available, so his 1993 DNA request came nine years too late. He was able to obtain partial clemency from the Governor, but was not exonerated until 2000. See Garrett, *Convicting the Innocent*, at 219–227.

2) State Innocence Claims. Most states now permit freestanding claims of innocence, including those based on newly-discovered evidence. Pertinent state statutes typically require that the petitioner have exercised due diligence and have sought relief in good faith as soon as the new evidence of innocence be- came available.[aa] Claims of innocence not involving DNA evidence, however,

---

[z] State post-conviction remedies were less common, but where they existed they tended to be very restrictive. The trend towards statutes of limitation is a more recent phenomenon. As of 1970, three states "had a principal postconviction remedy with a statute of limitations," but by 2006 that number was thirty-seven. *See* Donald Wilkes, *State Postconviction Remedies and Relief* § 1:7 (2007 Edition).

[aa] See, e.g. Alaska Stat. § 12.72.010, 12.72.01020 (excusing otherwise applicable time bars and permitting relief based on "evidence of material facts, not previously presented and heard by the court, that requires vacation of the conviction or sentence in the interest of justice"); In re Clark, 5 Cal. 4th 750, 790 (Cal. 1993) ("[T]he scope of review on habeas corpus in this state

may face higher hurdles. The new evidence may resemble material introduced at trial, and courts may discount the motives of witnesses who come forward years later. For example, courts have historically been highly suspicious of witness recantations; one court commented, "There is no form of proof so unreliable as recanting testimony." People v. Shilitano, 218 N.Y. 161 (1916). On the other hand, evidence of innocence that the State suppressed at trial by may be the subject of a *Brady* claim, and need not be the basis for a freestanding innocence challenge.

3) DNA Access Statutes. In response to the advent of DNA-testing technology, jurisdictions relaxed the traditional rules of finality by enacting new DNA-testing provisions and providing for "writs of innocence." In 1999, ten years after the first post-conviction DNA exoneration, only New York and Illinois had passed this type of statute.[bb] Now, forty-nine states, the District of Columbia, and the federal government have all enacted statutes regarding post-conviction DNA testing and relief. Some of those statutes permit motions based on new non-DNA and non-biological evidence of innocence. The federal Innocence Project Act, discussed in Chapter 6, provides for access to DNA testing and vests courts with the power to vacate a conviction based on such evidence.

4) Restrictions. Prosecutors now typically agree to conduct post-conviction DNA tests, without the need for the inmate to file a formal motion. However, when the formal motion using a DNA testing statute must be filed, gaining access to DNA testing is not a given. Despite statutory access to and procedures for litigating newly-discovered evidence of innocence, the post-conviction DNA provisions routinely impose procedural limitations on access to DNA testing and relief. Nearly all statutes require a showing of some likelihood, typically a "reasonable probability," that the petitioner would not have been convicted had DNA tests been performed at trial. Two states have "more probable than not" standards, and two states require "clear and convincing" or substantial evidence that DNA would alter the result. Many states bar access to petitioners who pleaded guilty or whose attorney failed to request DNA testing at trial, or they bar testing that was available at the time of the trial. Statutes also impose other substantive and procedural hurdles, and courts have adopted restrictive interpretations of some of those provisions.[cc]

5) Due Process Remedies. What remedy does a convict have if a prosecutor refuses to voluntarily agree to conduct post-conviction DNA testing, and then a state court denies access to DNA testing or to relief? The answer appears to be, "probably none." *Osborne*, however, did state that, if a state order denying relief under a post-conviction DNA access statute is arbitrary, then a prisoner might seek relief using a § 1983 lawsuit in federal court, using a procedural due pro-

---

is not limited to error of constitutional dimension. Newly discovered evidence may also be the basis for relief."); Summerville v. Warden, State Prison, 229 Conn. 397, 422 (Conn. 1994) ("We now hold . . . that a substantial claim of actual innocence is cognizable by way of a petition for a writ of habeas corpus, even in the absence of proof by the petitioner of an antecedent constitutional violation that affected the result of his criminal trial.").

[bb] See Act of May 9, 1997, Pub. Act No. 90–0141, 1997 Ill. Laws 2461 (codified at 725 Ill. Comp. Stat. 5/116–3(a) (2007)); Act of Oct. 18, 1999, ch. 560, 1999 N.Y. Laws 3247 (codified at N.Y. Crim. Proc. Law § 440.30(1-a) (McKinney 2005)).

[cc] For a survey of the first forty-five such statutes and discussion of judicial approaches towards their provisions, see Brandon L. Garrett, *Claiming Innocence*, 92 Minn. L. Rev. 1629 (2008). That data has been updated here to include the statutes now present in 49 states and the District of Columbia.

cess theory. See Skinner v. Switzer, 131 S.Ct. 1289 (2011); District Attorney's Office v. Osborne, 557 U.S. 52 (2009). Chapter 11 explores those decisions in greater detail, as they implicate the boundaries between habeas corpus litigation and other types of civil proceedings.

———

NOTES ON "SENTENCING" INNOCENCE

1) **Defining Innocence.** The term "innocence" is potentially broad, and the definition could be limited merely to claims that another person committed the crime. The definition of innocence might, however, extend to cases where no crime occurred, where a jury could not have determined that an element of the crime was satisfied "beyond a reasonable doubt," or where a defendant is categorically exempt from a sentence. "Innocent" is not a legally-defined status in American law. A person may be found guilty or not guilty, but courts do not make determinations of "innocence" except under a state post-conviction statute that requires such a finding. Sentencing errors, however, are of increasing importance—longer sentences produce greater incentives to mount sentencing challenges. As explained below, the Supreme Court has only recognized "sentencing innocence" claims primarily (but not exclusively) in capital cases, and usually (but not always) as gateways to excuse procedural defects in underlying claims. If the sentencing innocence claim is "freestanding" or is in a noncapital case, then the law is murky. Moreover, changes in AEDPA have created questions about the degree to which the Court's pre-AEDPA decisions recognizing sentencing-innocence claims survive that legislation. The Notes below touch on some of those questions, and some of them are addressed in Chapter 4.

2) **The *Sawyer* Standard.** In *Sawyer v. Whitley,* 505 U.S. 333 (1992), the Court concluded that, although the petitioner would ordinarily be prohibited from bringing a claim because he did not bring it in an earlier federal habeas petition, the bar could be excused based on a showing "by clear and convincing evidence that, but for a constitutional error, no reasonable juror would have found the petitioner eligible for the death penalty under the applicable state law." The Court explained that "actual innocence" has a different meaning "in the setting of capital punishment." After all, "[a] prototypical example of 'actual innocence' in a colloquial sense is the case where the State has convicted the wrong person of the crime." However, "[t]he phrase 'innocent of death' is not a natural usage of those words. . ."

As mentioned earlier in this Chapter, death sentences are imposed based on factors that limit the class of offenders eligible for the death penalty. Broadly speaking, state statutes define a capital crime as a subset of first-degree murder. If a person is found guilty, a sentencing-phase jury will usually consider whether the presence of "aggravating" factors justifies the death penalty or whether "mitigating" factors cut the other way. The precise balance of aggravating and mitigating factors sufficient to trigger a death penalty varies by state, subject to Eighth Amendment rules beyond the scope of this discussion.

Sawyer is a case involving an "actual innocence of the death penalty" gateway—the Court did not recognize a freestanding sentencing innocence claim. In Sawyer's case, the jury sentenced him to death based on three statutory aggravating factors: "(1) that [Sawyer] was engaged in the commission of aggravated arson, (2) that the offense was committed in an especially cruel, atrocious and heinous manner, and (3) that [Sawyer] had previously been convicted of an unrelated murder." The Louisiana Supreme Court held that the last aggravating circumstance was not supported by the evidence. Sawyer argued that a procedural bar should be excused in a capital case where "there is a 'fair probability' that the admission of false evidence, or the preclusion of true mitigating evidence, [caused by a constitutional error] resulted in a sentence of death." The Supreme Court held that the "actual innocence" requirement must focus solely on the aggravating elements that render a defendant eligible for the death penalty, and "not on additional mitigating evidence that was prevented from being introduced as a result of a claimed constitutional error." In addition, the petitioner must present substantial evidence, or "clear and convincing evidence that but for constitutional error, no reasonable juror would find him eligible for the death penalty" under state law.

Given the subjectivity of some aggravating factors, such as whether the offense was committed in an "especially cruel, atrocious and heinous manner," and that the jury need only find one aggravating factor present, how easy is it to satisfy the *Sawyer* gateway? Remember, the *Sawyer* standard is not a standard for a freestanding sentencing innocence claim, and the contents of a freestanding standard remain a matter of speculation.

NOTE ON INNOCENCE AND NON-CAPITAL SENTENCES

Why not extend the same logic to sentencing errors in non-death penalty cases?[dd] If the factual predicates necessary to impose a sentence are not satisfied, then should the federal constitution offer relief? In Dretke v. Haley, 541 U.S. 386 (2004) the Court declined to address non-capital sentencing innocence claims. In 1997, Michael Wayne Haley was arrested after stealing a calculator from a local Wal-Mart and attempting to exchange it for other merchandise. He was charged and found guilty of stealing property valued at less than $1,500. Because he had two prior theft convictions, however, Haley was charged as a "habitual offender" and faced a far more serious sentence. The indictment alleged he had two prior felony convictions. The timing was important because, under the Texas statute, a defendant could be sentenced as a habitual offender only if the second prior conviction was for an offense occurring after the first conviction became final.

During the sentencing phase of his trial, the State introduced records showing that Haley was convicted of delivery of amphetamine on October 18, 1991, and attempted robbery on September 9, 1992. However, the attempted robbery had actually occurred on October 15, 1991, three days *before* his first conviction became final. No one at trial—not the prosecutor, defense lawyer or judge—noticed this problem. The jury returned a verdict of guilty on the habitual offender charge and recommended a sentence of 16 1/2 years, which the

---

[dd] In a series of recent cases, the Supreme Court has basically barred the imposition of life-without-parole (LWOP) on juveniles. In *Graham v. Florida*, 130 S.Ct. 2011 (2010), the Court prohibited the imposition of LWOP on juveniles that committed non-homicide offenses. Then, in *Miller v. Alabama*, 132 S.Ct. 2455 (2012), the Court all but foreclosed the possibility of LWOP sentences for any juvenile offender. (*Miller* left open the possibility that, after individualized sentencing, a court might be able to impose LWOP, but also telegraphed that such a sentence would also run a very high risk of being struck down as unconstitutional.) This Chapter omits extensive discussion of the juvenile LWOP cases.

judge followed. Haley did not raise the objection on appeal—the sentencing error was raised for the first time in a state habeas petition. The state habeas court rejected the claim, stating that it should have been raised at trial or on direct appeal. When Haley filed a *pro se* habeas petition in federal court, the State conceded that he was erroneously sentenced as a habitual offender, but that the argument was procedurally defaulted. The Magistrate Judge, however, recommended excusing the procedural default and granting the claim because respondent was "actually innocent of a sentence for a second-degree felony." The District Court agreed and the Court of Appeals for the Fifth Circuit affirmed, holding that the actual innocence exception "applies to noncapital sentencing procedures involving a career or habitual felony offender."

The Supreme Court noted a split in the federal circuits on the issue, but declined to address the issue in *Haley*. The Court noted that "such claims are likely to present equally difficult questions regarding the scope of the actual innocence exception itself. Whether and to what extent the exception extends to noncapital sentencing error is just one example." Is the problem of assuring correct sentencing calculations more complex? What of challenges to interpretations of non-binding sentencing guidelines provisions? Justice Stevens dissented:

> Because, as all parties agree, there is no factual basis for respondent's conviction as a habitual offender, it follows inexorably that respondent has been denied due process of law. And because that constitutional error clearly and concededly resulted in the imposition of an unauthorized sentence, it also follows that respondent is a "victim of a miscarriage of justice," [he is] entitled to immediate and unconditional release.

Justice Stevens concluded that "the Court unquestionably has the authority to recognize a narrow exception for the unusual case that is as clear as this one." Do you agree with Justice Stevens, or do you agree with the majority that noncapital sentencing error is too complex a subject to be recognized as a cognizable claim in federal habeas proceedings?

CHAPTER 4

PROCEDURAL LIMITATIONS ON FEDERAL POST-CONVICTION RELIEF

INTRODUCTORY NOTE ON PROCEDURAL DOCTRINES

Before a federal court can reach the "merits" of a constitutional claim asserted in a habeas proceeding, a prisoner must overcome a number of procedural obstacles. Courts and Congress have crafted these obstacles in various forms: affirmative defenses that the State can forfeit or waive, jurisdictional limits, and prohibitions that federal courts may impose *sua sponte*. Lawyers, claimants, and judges often find these procedural rules maddening—frequently because the rules seem unnecessarily complex. Federal courts, the complaint goes, could more easily reject most claims on the merits, and avoid these thorny procedural questions. In *Coleman v. Thomson*, Justice Blackmun wrote: "I believe that the Court is creating a Byzantine morass of arbitrary, unnecessary, and unjustifiable impediments to the vindication of federal rights." 501 U.S. 722, 759 (1991) (Blackmun, J., dissenting). Notwithstanding powerful critiques like Justice Blackmun's, courts and Congress developed rules to protect the important government interests in the finality of criminal judgments and in the promotion of comity between state and federal sovereigns.

Each procedural doctrine generates its own idiosyncratic questions, but the doctrines share common issues and implicate common themes. As a result, decisions formally involving one procedural doctrine often cross-reference decisions formally addressing others. The cases presented in this Chapter are, therefore, incapable of perfect sequencing. Generally speaking, the presentation of the procedural doctrines corresponds with the order in which courts developed them. We do not organize the Chapter to reflect the ideal sequence in which a federal court might actually consider the rules—an "order of battle," so to speak—because the actual sequence of consideration depends too much on the forum and the litigation choices of the parties. The pleading requirements for each doctrine are developed in more detail in Chapter 11.

This Chapter begins with a Section on the exhaustion rule, which requires that federal prisoners exhaust all available state remedies before seeking federal habeas relief. The second Section explores "procedural default," the exhaustion corollary generally barring federal habeas review of claims that state courts rejected on adequate and independent (for example, "procedural") grounds. The third Section considers the unique issues created by "successive petitions," which can include both new and previously-presented claims. The fourth Section concludes the Chapter with a discussion of AEDPA's statute of limitations—which, alone among the procedural doctrines, lacks a common law antecedent.[a]

---

[a] Absent from this Chapter is a Section on "nonretroactivity." Including a nonretroactivity Section would have been appropriate before 1996, but AEDPA largely incorporated the Su-

---

NOTE ON THE THREE PHASES OF REVIEW

Before discussing the procedural limits on federal habeas relief, we first describe the process that precedes those questions. Specifically, we review the structure of criminal process in state courts, which occurs before a case reaches federal habeas review. Each step in that state process, along with the procedural history that the state litigation generates, dictates whether and how procedural doctrines apply on federal habeas review. Three types of review ordinarily follow a state criminal conviction: (1) the direct review of the conviction (what we ordinarily think of as the appeal); (2) state post-conviction review, or state habeas (including appellate review of any lower-state habeas disposition); and (3) federal post-conviction or federal habeas corpus review, which is our focus. The diagram below illustrates these three types of review.

Figure 4.1. Three Levels of Criminal Review

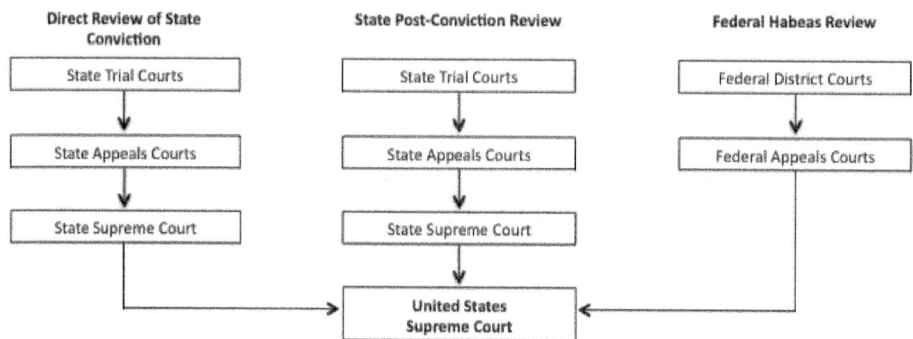

1)   Criminal Convictions. Before any appeal or collateral proceeding commences, a prisoner has to be convicted. A conviction follows a report of a crime, a criminal investigation, an arrest, and then—for most criminal defendants who are indigent—the appointment of a lawyer. While trial courts may conduct preliminary hearings to review the status of the case, the vast majority of criminal cases are resolved without a trial—over 95% of criminal defendants plead guilty.[b] Defendants that "plead out" are convicted after a brief court proceeding in which the judge reviews the admission of guilt along with the terms of the plea agreement. The defendants are then sentenced, and a clerk of the court ultimately enters a criminal judgment of conviction. As a condition of their pleas, defendants typically waive most procedural rights, including the right to pursue any appeal and many post-conviction remedies. Criminal trials are actually very rare, and happen in less than five percent of criminal cases. In those rare instances, most criminal defendants are convicted. A conviction is a find-

---

preme Court's prior nonretroactivity jurisprudence into 28 U.S.C. § 2254(d)(1), which is a substantive limit on relief. Discussion of the nonretroactivity cases therefore appears in Chapter 5.

[b] See Bureau of Justice Statistics, U.S. Dep't of Justice, *Felony Defendants in Large Urban Counties, 2006* 10 (May 2010).

ing of guilt by the jury (or by a judge, if the proceeding is a bench trial). As with guilty pleas, a guilty verdict is ultimately entered as a judgment of conviction by the court clerk. The sentence assessed in conjunction with judgment—the punishment bearing the imprimatur of the court—may be entered on the docket by a separate order. Defendants who have not waived procedural remedies may appeal the conviction, the sentence, or both.

2)   First Phase: Direct Appeals. All fifty states allow criminal convicts to appeal (as long as the right was not waived in a plea agreement). The state appellate process will usually involve an as-of-right appeal to an intermediate state appellate court, and some form of appeal to or discretionary review by a state supreme court.

   a)   Constitutional Rights in As-of-Right Appeals. The Supreme Court has held that there is no constitutional right of appeal to a superior state court, but that, if a state provides for an as-of-right appeal, indigent state defendants also have a constitutional right to a lawyer during the appellate proceeding, grounded in the Equal Protection Clause of the Fourteenth Amendment. See Douglas v. California, 372 U.S. 353, 356–57 (1963).[c] In addition, the Court has held that a criminal defendant has a right to effective appellate assistance, extending to appeals the same ineffective assistance of counsel (IAC) analysis that measures the effectiveness of a trial lawyer. See Evitts v. Lucey, 469 U.S. 387, 396 (1985). A prisoner may assert ineffective assistance of *appellate* counsel when, for example, an appellate lawyer failed to file an appeal, omitted claims, or otherwise blundered sufficiently to be both constitutionally ineffective and to have prejudiced the appellate outcome.

   b)   Claims on Appeal. Most state courts limit appellate review to claims based on the trial record. In such situations, a prisoner cannot introduce evidence or raise issues outside the record that the trial court created. After the highest available state court denies relief on direct review, an inmate has 90 days to seek certiorari review from the Supreme Court. The Court can only review cases in which there is no "adequate and independent" state ground for affirming the conviction. Once direct review is complete,[d] the conviction becomes "final."

3)   Second Phase: State-Post-conviction Review. The second phase of the criminal process is state post-conviction review. Very few criminal appeals succeed, but an inmate can still challenge a conviction or sentence "collaterally." There are both state and federal post-conviction proceedings. The formal name for the state post-conviction process varies by jurisdiction; some call it "state habeas," some call it "state post-conviction" review, and some states use other names. Most state collateral-review procedures are specified statutorily, but some more exotic, obscure post-conviction remedies—such as *coram nobis*—are available at common law. The civil-versus-criminal denomination of state collateral proceedings also varies by jurisdiction. (The federal proceeding is considered civil, even though the underlying conviction derives from a criminal proceeding.) This second round of review—following an appeal of the convic-

---

[c] The Supreme Court, however, has held that an indigent appellant does not have a right to have counsel appointed by the state for a purely discretionary appeal. See Ross v. Moffitt, 417 U.S. 600, 616 (1974).

[d] If an inmate does not obtain Supreme Court review, a conviction becomes final when the certiorari petition is denied or, if the inmate does not certiorari review, upon the lapse of the 90-day window for doing so.

tion—is usually subject to some statute of limitations triggered by the conclusion of direct review. For example, a state rule may provide that the state post-conviction petition must be brought within 60 days of the decision by the highest court regarding the appeal. Some states, however, permit collateral proceedings to begin while direct review of the conviction remains ongoing.

a) Claims Raised in Post-conviction Proceedings. Why permit a second round of challenges to the criminal conviction? Recall that, on appeal, the inmate may be limited to raising claims based on the trial record. During state post-conviction review, inmates may pursue some claims that involve issues outside the trial record, including the most commonly raised claims: *Strickland v. Washington* claims of ineffective assistance of trial counsel (IAC claims) and *Brady* claims concerning evidence that the prosecution may have unconstitutionally suppressed. (Chapter 3 described each of these challenges in considerable detail.) Keep in mind that the trial lawyer may also be the appellate counsel; that lawyer may not be the best person do decide whether to raise appellate challenges to the effectiveness of trial representation. In part because of such potential conflicts of interest, states typically allow inmates to pursue many claims on state post-conviction review. States, however, constrain state post-conviction litigation in other ways: states often forbid collateral review of claims that could have been raised at trial or on appeal, as well as re-litigation of claims already rejected on the merits. As a remedy, an inmate may receive, among other things: a discharge from custody; a vacatur setting aside a conviction or a sentence or both; a dismissal of charges; an order setting aside probation or a parole revocation; or an order setting aside some administrative outcome.

b) No Constitutional Right to State Post-Conviction Counsel. Most state post-conviction claimants appear so *pro se*, meaning without the assistance of counsel. There is no federal constitutional right to a lawyer during state post-conviction review, even if the inmate is indigent and state post-conviction review is the first phase at which the inmate may raise a particular type of claim. The Supreme Court has not held that fundamental fairness or access to courts require that an inmate have a lawyer during state post-conviction review. See Pennsylvania v. Finley, 481 U.S. 551, 555–57, 559 (1987). Notwithstanding *Finley*, concurring and dissenting Justices in Murray v. *Giarratano*, 492 U.S. 1, 12–13 (1989), raised sufficient concerns about unrepresented state post-conviction litigation to cause most states to require that counsel be appointed in capital cases.

While the byzantine procedural requirements for filing state post-conviction petitions can flummox even experienced lawyers, many prisoners must navigate this process without the assistance of legal counsel. Unsurprisingly, the grant rate in state post-conviction proceedings is very low, and relief is frequently denied in brief and unreasoned summary orders. An inmate may appeal any state trial-court order denying post-conviction relief and may seek certiorari review from the U.S. Supreme Court. If a prisoner is denied or does not seek certiorari review of an order denying state post-conviction relief, state post-conviction review is complete. State post-conviction review may take many years and is therefore almost always useless to inmates serving short sentences.

4) Third Phase: Federal Habeas Review. Inmates that fail to obtain appellate or state post-conviction relief may file a habeas corpus petition in a federal district court. Similarly, inmates who file federal habeas petitions tend to be serving long sentences; the inmates must complete state appeals and state post-conviction review before filing their federal habeas petition. The 2007 Habeas Study, discussed in Chapter 3, showed an average interval of over 7 years between state judgments and federal habeas filings; one in ten cases took more than 13.8 years to reach federal court. See Nancy J. King, Fred L. Cheesman II & Brian J. Ostrom, Nat'l Ctr. for State Courts, *Final Technical Report: Habeas Litigation in U.S. District Courts* 21 (2007) (*2007 Habeas Study*).

As the last Chapter explained, the federal habeas petition may attack the lawfulness of a state conviction by raising federal claims that arise under the Constitution, a treaty, or a statute. A prisoner's conviction becomes final when direct review concludes; so federal habeas review is a civil, collateral attack on a criminal judgment or sentence. There is also no constitutional right to a lawyer in federal habeas proceedings, but federal courts are statutorily required to appoint lawyers in capital cases and may appoint them in non-capital cases, where the "interests of justice" require legal representation. See 18 U.S.C. § 3006A. This Chapter turns now to the procedural doctrines that limit federal habeas corpus review of state-prisoner petitions. As mentioned in this Chapter's Introductory Note, the precise application of a federal habeas doctrine will often turn on a prisoner's state litigation history.

1. EXHAUSTION

Many legal claims have exhaustion requirements. For example, in administrative law, courts may require a claimant to exhaust administrative remedies before seeking judicial remedies. See Myers v. Bethlehem Shipbuilding Corp., 303 U.S. 41 (1938). Such requirements allow administrative officials, rather than judges, the first chance to correct mistakes—both in deference to administrative expertise and authority, and to conserve judicial resources. In federal habeas proceedings involving state prisoners, the exhaustion requirement serves similar goals. The federal habeas exhaustion requirement reflects the principle that state judges, who are required to enforce the federal constitution, should be given the first opportunity to correct state judicial errors and to remedy unlawful state custody. The habeas exhaustion requirement works together with "procedural default" rules to require a prisoner to present a claim to a state court before seeking federal habeas relief. The Supreme Court first imposed the exhaustion requirement in *Ex parte Royall*, 117 U.S. 241 (1886), excerpted below. Conforming to a pattern that you will soon appreciate, Congress then codified the judicially-created rule in 1948, shortly after the Supreme Court updated and refurbished the judicially-created version exhaustion rule.[e] AEDPA altered it slightly in 1996. See 28 U.S.C. § 2254(b) (setting forth the current statutory exhaustion rules).

The exhaustion requirement might seem straightforward, but it remains a source of considerable federal litigation. A single prisoner can have many claims, and they must all be presented to a state court for adjudication. Following the appeal, prisoners will typically litigate those claims *pro se*. As you read the cases that follow, consider the following questions: what

---

[e] See Ex parte Hawk, 321 U.S. 114, 117 (1944) (explaining state of judge-made exhaustion law prior to statutory codification). For discussion of the theory and original application of the exhaustion doctrine, see Randy Hertz & James S. Liebman, *Federal Habeas Corpus Practice and Procedure* § 23.1 & n.7 (6th ed. 2011) (*FHCPP*).

does exhaustion require the prisoner to do in state court? If exhaustion facilitates federalism, is it something more than a rule of sequencing? Is it an ironclad rule with no exceptions? Under what circumstances should federal courts excuse a failure to exhaust?

A. *ROYALL* AND THE CREATION OF THE EXHAUSTION RULE

INTRODUCTORY NOTE ON EX PARTE ROYALL

W.L. Royall was indicted for selling past-due bond coupons without a license and for failure to pay the necessary tax. After his arrest, Royall petitioned for federal habeas relief in the Eastern district of Virginia. Royall claimed that the Virginia statute penalizing the coupon sale violated Article 1, § 10 of the federal Constitution. Royall argued that Virginia could not levy a tax on the bonds at the same time that it did not readily accept the bonds as payment due the Commonwealth. Under Virginia law, the coupons could only be acceptable for such payment after Royall paid a series of taxes necessary to enforce a judgment on coupon terms. He also alleged that several of these taxes violated Article 1, § 10. The case ultimately involved two petitions collectively presenting the various issues that the court decided.

Ex parte Royall

Supreme Court of the United States
117 U.S. 241 (1886)

■ Mr. JUSTICE HARLAN delivered the opinion of the Court * * *:

The first question to be considered is whether the circuit courts have jurisdiction on *habeas corpus* to discharge from custody one who is restrained of his liberty in violation of the national constitution, but who, at the time, is held under state process for trial on an indictment charging him with an offense against the laws of the State. * * *

The grant to the circuit courts in section 751 of jurisdiction to issue writs of habeas corpus is in language as broad as could well be employed. While it is attended by the general [but implied] condition * * * that the authority conferred must be exercised agreeably to the principles and usages of law, the only express limitation imposed is that the * * * courts and the judicial officers named shall not have power to award the writ to [] any prisoner in jail, except in specified cases, one of them being where he is alleged to be held in custody in violation of the constitution. The latter class of cases was first distinctly provided for by the [1867 Habeas Act]." * * * [T]he circuit court has, by the express words of the statute, jurisdiction on *habeas corpus* to inquire into the cause for which he is restrained of his liberty, and to dispose of him "as law and justice require."

It may be suggested that the state court is competent to decide whether [Royall] is * * * illegally restrained of his liberty; that the appropriate time for [that] determination * * * is at the trial of the indictment; and that his detention for the purpose simply of securing his attendance at the trial ought not to be deemed an improper exercise by that court of its power to hear and decide the case. The first of these propositions is undoubtedly sound, for * * * "a state court of original jurisdiction, having the parties before it, may, consistently with existing federal legislation, determine cases at law or in equity, arising under the constitution and laws of the United

States, or involving rights dependent upon such constitution or laws;" and that, "upon the state courts, equally with the courts of the Union, rests the obligation to guard, enforce, and protect every right granted or secured by the constitution of the United States, and the laws made in pursuance thereof, whenever those rights are involved in any suit or proceeding before them."

But with respect to the other propositions, it is clear that if the local statute under which Royall was indicted be repugnant to the constitution, the * * * entire proceeding against him is a nullity. * * * [I]f the statute prescribing the offense [for which prisoners were convicted] was void, the court which tried them was without jurisdiction, and they were entitled to be discharged. * * * The statute evidently contemplated that cases might arise when the power thus conferred should be exercised during the progress of proceedings instituted against the petitioner in a state court or by or under authority of a State, on account of the very matter presented for determination by the writ of habeas corpus; for care is taken to provide that any such proceedings, pending the hearing of the case upon the writ, and until final judgment, and after the prisoner is discharged, shall be null and void. * * * That the petitioner is held under the authority of a State cannot affect the question of the power or jurisdiction of the circuit court to inquire into the cause of his commitment, and to discharge him, if he be restrained of his liberty in violation of the constitution. * * * We are therefore of opinion that the circuit court has jurisdiction, upon writ of habeas corpus, to inquire into the cause of appellant's commitment, and to discharge him if he be held in custody in violation of the constitution.

It remains, however, to be considered whether the refusal of that court to issue the writ * * * can be sustained upon any other ground than the one upon which it proceeded. * * * If, however, it is apparent upon the petition that the writ, if issued, ought not * * * to result in the immediate discharge of the accused from custody, the court is not bound to award it as soon as the application is made. What law and justice may require in a particular case is often an embarrassing question to the court or to the judicial officer before whom the petitioner is brought. * * * [I]t is not alleged, and it does not appear, in either case that he is unable to give security for his appearance in the state court, or that reasonable bail is denied him, or that his trial will be unnecessarily delayed. The question as to the constitutionality of the law under which he is indicted must necessarily arise at his trial under the indictment, and it is one upon which, as we have seen, it is competent for the state court to pass. Under such circumstances, does the statute imperatively require the circuit court, by writ of *habeas corpus*, to wrest the petitioner from the custody of the state officers in advance of his trial in the state court? We are of opinion that * * * it is not bound in every case to exercise such a power immediately upon application being made for the writ. * * * The injunction to hear the case summarily, and thereupon "to dispose of the party as law and justice require," does not deprive the court of discretion as to the time and mode in which it will exert the powers conferred upon it. That discretion should be exercised in the light of the relations existing, under our system of government, between the judicial tribunals of the Union and of the States, and in recognition of the fact that the public good requires that those relations be not disturbed by unnecessary conflict between courts equally bound to guard and protect rights secured by the constitution. When the petitioner is in custody by state authority for an act done or omitted to be done in pursuance of a law of the United States, or of an order, process, or decree of a court of judge thereof; or where, being a subject or citizen of a foreign state, the validity and effect [of foreign state activity] depend upon the law of nations—in such and like cases of urgency, involving the authority and operations of the general government, the obligations of this country to or its relations with foreign nations, the courts of the United States have frequently interposed by writs of *habeas corpus*, and discharged prisoners who were held in custody under state authority. * * * Nor do their circumstances, as detailed in the petitions, suggest any reason why the state court of original jurisdiction may not, without interference upon the part of the courts of the United States, pass upon the question which is raised as to the constitutionality of the statutes under which the appellant is indicted. The circuit court was not at liberty, under the circumstances disclosed, to presume that the decision of the state court would be otherwise than is required by the fundamental law of the land, or that it would disregard the settled principles of constitutional law announced by this Court, upon which is clearly conferred the power to decide ultimately and finally all cases arising under the constitution and laws of the United States. * * *

[Courts should] "give preference to such principles and methods of procedure as shall seem to conciliate the distinct and independent tribunals of the states and of the Union, so that they may co-operate as harmonious members of a judicial system co-extensive with the United States, and submitting to the paramount authority of the same constitution, laws, and federal obligations." * * * ["T]he forbearance which courts of co-ordinate jurisdiction, administered under a single system, exercise towards each other, whereby conflicts are avoided, by avoiding interference with the process of the other, is a principle of comity, with perhaps no higher sanction than the utility which comes from concord; but between state courts and those of the United States it is something more. It is a principle of right and of law, and therefore of necessity."

* * * [T]his Court holds that, where a person is in custody, under process from a state court of original jurisdiction, for an alleged offense against the laws of such State, and it is claimed that he is restrained of his liberty in violation of the Constitution of the United States, the Circuit Court has a discretion whether it will discharge him upon habeas corpus, in advance of his trial in the court in which he is indicted; that discretion, however, to be subordinated to any special circumstances requiring immediate action. When the state court shall have finally acted upon the case, the Circuit Court has still a discretion whether, under all the circumstances then existing, the accused, if convicted, shall be put to his writ of error from the highest court of the State, or whether it will proceed, by writ of *habeas corpus*, summarily to determine whether the petitioner is restrained of his liberty in violation of the constitution of the United States. * * *

* * * [W]e are of opinion that the judgment in each case must be affirmed, but without prejudice to the right of the petitioner to renew his application to that court at some future time should the circumstances render it proper to do so. Affirmed.

———

NOTES AND QUESTIONS ON ROYALL AND SUPPLEMENTARY NOTES ON THE EXHAUSTION REQUIREMENT

1)   **The Scope of Pre-Conviction Federal Power Over State Proceedings.** Consider *Royall's* language in light of the "cognizability" questions posed in Chapter 3. A prisoner in custody before a trial has not yet been subject to a judgment by the trial court. Do you think the Supreme Court was correct in holding that a district court has the power to grant habeas relief before the conclusion of state trial proceedings? Note *Royall's* reliance on *Siebold* for the proposition that a conviction under an unconstitutional statute is "void" and, therefore falls under the federal habeas statute. How should an exhaustion requirement work with respect to a claim of unlawful pre-trial detention? Should exhaustion require anything more than the trial itself, or should the state courts also be given a chance to decide any appeals?

2)   **The Scope of Post-Conviction Federal Power Over State Proceedings.** Notice how the Supreme Court urges federal judges to deny habeas relief to people in state custody in advance of a trial, subject to exception only in "special circumstances." Further, note how the Court suggests that waiting until the conclusion of an appeal is more appropriate, and that the Court can itself review the case on "writ of error from the highest court of the State." The Court is saying, in effect, that the need for federal habeas review diminishes when the Court itself can review cases on direct appeal. To the extent *Royall* reflects such a norm of habeas non-intervention, that norm was undermined when the Court switched to *certiorari* review of state judgments. Certiorari procedure made Supreme Court review almost entirely discretionary. Now, consider what sorts of questions a federal court should be deciding on federal habeas review. What authority does a federal court have to review questions that the state court *actually decided* in the state proceeding? Is there language in *Royall* supporting the idea that federal habeas review is a vehicle for relitigation of certain questions?

3)   **Comity and the Law of Nations.** *Royall* seems to root the exhaustion requirement in comity, rather than in federalism. Comity is a concept that originated in the Law of Nations and generally expresses the idea that the courts of a forum sovereign should exercise restraint and forbearance when a foreign sovereign has an interest in the judicial proceeding. The canonical statement of the Law of Nations comity interest appears in Justice Gray's opinion for the Court in *Hilton v. Guyot*, 159 U.S. 113 (1895):

> "Comity," in the legal sense, is neither a matter of absolute obligation, on the one hand, nor of mere courtesy and good will, upon the other. But it is the recognition which one nation allows within its territory to the legislative, executive or judicial acts of another nation, having due regard both to international duty and convenience, and to the rights of its own citizens, or of other persons who are under the protection of its laws.

In what ways is the concurrent jurisdiction of federal and state courts like the international law doctrine that Justice Gray describes? In what ways does it differ? Are you surprised that the Supreme Court borrowed international law to decide a question of domestic habeas practice?

The Supreme Court held that the habeas authority of district courts is subject to the implied condition that it be exercised consistent with the "principles and usages" of law. *Royall* then positioned the exhaustion rule as a principle of law—but not as a principle unique to habeas law:

> That discretion should be exercised in the light of the relations existing, under our system of government, between the judicial tribunals of the Union and of the States, and in recognition of the fact that the public good requires that those relations be not disturbed by unnecessary conflict between courts equally bound to guard and protect rights secured by the constitution.

The federal Constitution permits—and in some cases mandates—state adjudication of questions to which Article III judicial power extends. (Again, recall an American legal environment contemplated by the Madisonian compromise.) In what ways does the structure of federal adjudication respect the power of state courts to decide Article III subject matter? Consider both the appellate jurisdiction of the United States Supreme Court and the original jurisdiction of inferior courts.

Is there a comity interest that goes beyond respecting the role of states in adjudicating federal disputes? How would a pre-conviction intervention by a federal court affect the ability of states to enforce state criminal law? If *Royall* is a decision about pre-conviction intervention, how suitable is the case as precedent for post-conviction cases?

How much work should comity do? Does it require that state adjudication be given *res judicata* effect, or does it simply require the federal court to wait and give the state court the first opportunity to review a claim? Consider the following passage from *Darr v. Burford*, 339 U.S. 200 (1950):

> As it would be unseemly in our dual system of government for a federal district court to upset a state court conviction without an opportunity to the state courts to correct a constitutional violation, the federal courts sought a means to avoid such collisions. Solution was found in the doctrine of comity between courts, a doctrine which teaches that one court should defer action on causes properly within its jurisdiction until the courts of another sovereignty with concurrent powers, and already cognizant of the litigation, have had an opportunity to pass upon the matter.

> Since habeas corpus is a discretionary writ, federal courts had authority to refuse relief as a matter of comity until state remedies were exhausted. Through this comity, the doctrine of exhaustion of state remedies has developed steadily from cases refusing federal habeas corpus before state trial to a statutory direction that federal courts shall not grant the writ to a state prisoner until state remedies have been exhausted.

Is the "unseemliness" of federal habeas review limited to situations where the state has not had an opportunity to address the prisoner's claim? In what circumstances should a failure to exhaust be excused?

4) The Modern Habeas Statute. In *Ex parte Hawk*, 321 U.S. 114 (1944), the Supreme Court explained that "[o]rdinarily an application for habeas corpus by one detained under a state court judgment of conviction for crime will be entertained by a federal court only after all state remedies available, including all appellate remedies in the state courts and in this Court by appeal or writ of certiorari, have been exhausted." In 1948, Congress statutorily incorporated the *Hawk* description of the exhaustion rule. 28 U.SC. § 2254(b) now states:

(1) An application for a writ of habeas corpus on behalf of a person in custody pursuant to the judgment of a State court shall not be granted unless it appears that—(A) the applicant has exhausted the remedies available in the courts of the State; or (B) (i) there is an absence of available State corrective process; or (ii) circumstances exist that render such process ineffective to protect the rights of the applicant.

Subsection (c) further provides that an applicant does not meet the exhaustion requirement if the applicant "has the right under the law of the State to raise, by any available procedure, the question presented."

5)   State Waiver. In contrast to the rule described by *Royall*, the modern statutory exhaustion requirement is more or less mandatory. When Congress first codified the exhaustion requirement in 1948, it did not address the possibility of State waiver. In *Granberry v. Greer*, 481 U.S. 129 (1987), the Supreme Court held that, when the State fails to raise a nonexhaustion defense in the district court, the appellate court should use discretion to determine, on a case-by-case basis, whether the interests of comity, federalism, and justice would be better served by addressing the merits of the case or by requiring that the claim be exhausted. (*Granberry* is one of the major cases presented in Chapter 11.)

Under AEDPA, enacted in 1996, Congress statutorily allowed the State to waive the exhaustion requirement—but only if it does so expressly. 28 U.S.C. § 2254(b)(3) states that "[a] State shall not be deemed to have waived the exhaustion requirement or be estopped from reliance upon the requirement unless the State, through counsel, expressly waives the requirement." Is a mandatory exhaustion rule consistent with *Royall*, or with the law-of-nations comity described in Note 4? For an argument that subsequent courts have erroneously treated exhaustion as a quasi-jurisdictional rule, see Larry W. Yackle, *The Exhaustion Doctrine in Federal Habeas Corpus: An Argument for a Return to First Principles*, 44 Ohio St. L.J. 393, 394–95 (1983).

6)   What is a "Claim"? One way to exhaust a claim is to "present" it to a state court. The exhaustion inquiry is focused the substance of the prisoner's arguments to the state court, not on the decision that the state court actually made. When is a prisoner litigating the same "claim" raised and presented in state court? Surely the identity between the state and federal claim must be more than just a common denomination or shared constitutional origin. In other words, a claim is not exhausted unless the common facts and legal theory supporting relief were presented (or could no longer be presented) to the state court. The particular combination of facts and legal theory must be in "substance" the same as were presented to a state court. How should a federal court treat a legal theory that a prisoner presents to it if the prisoner supported that theory with different evidence before the state court? Can the claim always be treated as exhausted? Cf. Vasquez v. Hillery, 474 U.S. 254, 257–58 (1986) ("We have never held that presentation of additional facts to the district court, pursuant to that court's directions, evades the exhaustion requirement when the prisoner has presented the substance of his claim to the state courts.").

Should the exhaustion determination turn on whether the newly-presented evidence was "materially different" from that presented to the state court? Consider a situation in which a prisoner alleges that his mental retardation renders him ineligible for execution under *Atkins v. Virginia*, 536 U.S. 304 (2002). The prisoner argues that he has mental retardation in state court, and presents evidence of low IQ. He does not, however, present the state court with a subsequently-obtained low IQ score. He then presents the latter IQ score to the federal court, alleging that he did not present the evidence to the state because he lacked state funding for expert assistance. Is the claim exhausted? See Morris v. Dretke, 413 F.3d 484 (5th Cir. 2005) (holding that the new evidence merely supplemented and did not fundamentally alter the claim).

7)   Notes on the Mechanics of Exhaustion. Under the exhaustion requirement, a state prisoner must present the claim to state courts. In light of complicated state appellate and post-conviction procedure—as well as certiorari review of state judgments—exactly what such "presentation" entails can be confusing. What follows are Notes clarifying some of the exhaustion requirement's finer procedural points.

a)   A Prisoner Need Only Present a Claim to a State Court Once to Exhaust It. Exhaustion does not require that a claim be pursued in both state appellate and state post-conviction proceedings—just that the claim was pursued all the way up to the state Supreme Court in either the appeal directly reviewing the conviction or the post-conviction proceeding. See O'Sullivan v. Boerckel, 526 U.S. 838, 844 (1999). In *Boerckel*, the Court added: "Section 2254(c) requires only that state prisoners give state courts a fair opportunity to act on their claims." Thus, "state prisoners must give the state courts one full opportunity to resolve any constitutional issues by invoking one complete round of the State's established appellate review process." The Court did rule, however, that Boerckel was required not just to complete the direct appeal through the Illinois intermediate court, but also to pursue the purely discretionary review by the Illinois Supreme Court, because that procedure did remain "available." Does that ruling unnecessarily burden state supreme courts?

(b)   Claims Exhausted by the Absence of Available Remedies. Remember, a claim is exhausted not only if it *was* presented to a state court, but also if it *can no longer be* presented to a state court. Put another way, a claim is only *unexhausted* if an inmate can still obtain a merits ruling on it in state court. In some cases, the inmate may not be at fault for the fact that the claim is not exhausted. Notice how Section 2254(b)(1)(B) provides that, if there is an "absence of state corrective process" or other "circumstances exist that render such process ineffective," then the federal court can still entertain the application. That exception, however, is not implicated as long as the state really does have a procedure through which the claim could have been raised. Only in very rare cases—when state litigation would be "futile," when there is inordinate delay, where the State interferes with litigation in state courts, or when further delay would risk a miscarriage of justice—do federal courts excuse nonexhaustion. See Randy Hertz & James S. Liebman, *Federal Habeas Corpus Practice and Procedure* § 23.4 (6th ed. 2011) (*FHCPP*).

How would you approach claims that can no longer be raised in state court because doing so would violate a state procedural rule—for example, because a claim would be untimely under state law? Why would a federal court impose an exhaustion bar on claims a prisoner can still assert in state court but not on claims that a prisoner has forfeited in the state forum? The forfeited claims are considered exhausted because there is no available state remedy, but the inmate is punished more severely for the forfeiture under a different doctrine— the doctrine of procedural default, to which we turn in the next Section.

c)   Certiorari Not Required for Exhaustion. In light of the language in *Royall* and *Hawk*, as well as the language in *Boerckel* requiring a state prisoner to seek discretionary state supreme court review, do you think that a prisoner fails to exhaust a claim if the prisoner does not seek certiorari review of the conviction from the U.S. Supreme Court? Consider this question in light of the twin purposes of exhaustion that flow from *Royall*: (1) preserving the power of state courts to adjudicate federal subject matter, and (2) allowing states to complete criminal proceedings without federal interference. Should the exhaustion requirement work differently depending on whether the pertinent certiorari proceeding involves direct review of the conviction or direct review of a state post-conviction proceeding? The Supreme Court has held that "state prisoners need not petition for certiorari to exhaust state remedies." Lawrence v. Florida, 549 U.S. 327, 332–333 (2007).

8)   Exhaustion Incentives. What incentives does the exhaustion rule create? What should you advise a lawyer to do when filing a state habeas petition? File every conceivable claim? But would that also prejudice the client? How does the exhaustion rule affect state courts—does it always inure to their benefit? Note that the exhaustion requirement affects finality in conflicting ways. On the one hand, it ensures that state prisoners must fairly present their claims to the state courts before a federal court will conduct a review that could unsettle the state conviction. On the other hand, when the federal court requires the state prisoner to return to state court to exhaust a claim, the appeals take more time to resolve, further burdening state courts. Consider the tension between comity and finality as you read the next case, which adopted a "total exhaustion" rule for federal habeas petitions.

B. *LUNDY* AND "MIXED PETITIONS"

INTRODUCTORY NOTE ON THE CONTENT OF FEDERAL HABEAS PETITIONS

Federal habeas petitions can (and usually do) contain more than one claim.[f] The exhaustion requirement is an inquiry that applies on a claim-by-claim basis. The federal judge must sort out what the claims in a the federal petition are—which can be a substantial task in *pro se* cases—and must then review the entire procedural history of the case to assess which claims were fairly presented to the state judiciary. The Supreme Court eventually had to confront the still-more-complicated question of what federal courts should do in situations where only a subset of the claims in a federal petition are exhausted. What are the options for processing the federal petition? What are the interests promoted by each option?

---

[f] One study found that the average number of claims was five or fewer in 77% of the cases where they had information on this, and the average number was far higher, 28 claims, in capital cases. See Nancy J. King, Fred L. Cheesman II & Brian J. Ostrom, Nat'l Ctr. for State Courts, *Final Technical Report: Habeas Litigation in U.S. District Courts* 27 (2007) (*2007 Habeas Study*).

Rose v. Lundy

United States Supreme Court
455 U.S. 509 (1982)

■ JUSTICE O'CONNOR delivered the opinion of the Court, except as to Part III-C.

In this case, we consider whether the exhaustion rule in 28 U.S.C. §§ 2254(b), (c) requires a federal district court to dismiss a petition for a writ of habeas corpus containing any claims that have not been exhausted in the state courts. Because a rule requiring exhaustion of all claims furthers the purposes underlying the habeas statute, we hold that a district court must dismiss such "mixed petitions," leaving the prisoner with the choice of returning to state court to exhaust his claims or of amending or resubmitting the habeas petition to present only exhausted claims to the district court.

I

[Following an unsuccessful appeal of his Tennessee conviction for rape and crimes against nature, Lundy] subsequently filed a petition in Federal District Court for a writ of habeas corpus under 28 U.S.C. § 2254, alleging four grounds for relief: (1) that he had been denied the right to confrontation because the trial court limited the defense counsel's questioning of the victim; (2) that he had been denied the right to a fair trial because the prosecuting attorney stated that [Lundy] had a violent character; (3) that he had been denied the right to a fair trial because the prosecutor improperly remarked in his closing argument that the State's evidence was uncontradicted; and (4) that the trial judge improperly instructed the jury that every witness is presumed to swear the truth. After reviewing the state court records, however, the District Court concluded that it could not consider claims three and four "in the constitutional framework" because [Lundy] had not exhausted his state remedies for those grounds. The court nevertheless stated that "in assessing the atmosphere of the cause taken as a whole these items may be referred to collaterally."

Apparently in an effort to assess the "atmosphere" of the trial, the District Court reviewed the state trial transcript and identified 10 instances of prosecutorial misconduct, only five of which [Lundy] had raised before the state courts. * * * In short, the District Court considered several instances of prosecutorial misconduct never challenged in the state trial or appellate courts, or even raised in [Lundy]'s habeas petition.

The Sixth Circuit affirmed[.] * * *

II

[Tennessee] urges this Court to apply a "total exhaustion" rule requiring district courts to dismiss every habeas corpus petition that contains both exhausted and unexhausted claims. [Tennessee] argues at length that such a rule furthers the policy of comity underlying the exhaustion doctrine because it gives the state courts the first opportunity to correct federal constitutional errors and minimizes federal interference and disruption of state judicial proceedings. [Tennessee] also believes that uniform adherence to a total exhaustion rule reduces the amount of piecemeal habeas litigation.

Under [Tennessee's] approach, [the prisoner would have a] choice of returning to state court to litigate his unexhausted claims, or of proceeding with only his exhausted claims in federal court. [Tennessee] believes that a prisoner would be reluctant to choose the latter route, since a district court could * * * dismiss subsequent federal habeas petitions as an abuse of the writ. In other words, if the prisoner amended the petition to delete the unexhausted claims or immediately refiled in federal court a petition alleging only his exhausted claims, he could lose the opportunity to litigate his presently unexhausted claims in federal court. * * *

III

A

[The extant version of 28 U.S.C. § 2254] does not directly address the problem of mixed petitions. To be sure, the provision states that a remedy is not exhausted if there exists a state procedure to raise "the question presented," but we believe this phrase to be too ambiguous to sustain the conclusion that Congress intended to either permit or prohibit review of mixed petitions. * * * Congress never thought of the problem. Consequently, we must analyze the policies underlying the statutory provision to determine its proper scope.

B

The exhaustion doctrine is principally designed to protect the state courts' role in the enforcement of federal law and prevent disruption of state judicial proceedings. * * * [F]ederal and state "courts [are] equally bound to guard and protect rights secured by the Constitution." Because "it would be unseemly in our dual system of government for a federal district court to upset a state court conviction without an opportunity to the state courts to correct a constitutional violation," federal courts apply the doctrine of comity * * *.

A rigorously enforced total exhaustion rule will encourage state prisoners to seek full relief first from the state courts, thus giving those courts the first opportunity to review all claims of constitutional error. As the number of prisoners who exhaust all of their federal claims increases, state courts may become increasingly familiar with, and hospitable toward, federal constitutional issues. Equally as important, federal claims that have been fully exhausted in state courts will more often be accompanied by a complete factual record to aid the federal courts in their review. * * *

* * *[O]ur interpretation of §§ 2254(b), (c) provides a simple and clear instruction to potential litigants: before you bring any claims to federal court, be sure that you first have taken each one to state court. Just as *pro se* petitioners have managed to use the federal habeas machinery, so too should they be able to master this straightforward exhaustion requirement. * * *

* * * [S]trict enforcement of the exhaustion requirement will encourage habeas petitioners to exhaust all of their claims in state court and to present the federal court with a single habeas petition. To the extent that the exhaustion requirement reduces piecemeal litigation, both the courts and the prisoners should benefit * * *.

C

[JUSTICE O'CONNOR, joined by CHIEF JUSTICE BURGER, JUSTICE POWELL, and JUSTICE REHNQUIST, concluded in Part III-C that the total exhaustion rule does not impair the state prisoner's interest in obtaining speedy federal relief on his claim; rather than returning to state court to exhaust all of his claims, a prisoner can always amend the petition to delete the unexhausted claims, although, by doing so, the prisoner would risk dismissal of subsequent federal petitions.]

IV

* * * Accordingly, the judgment of the Court of Appeals is reversed, and the case is remanded for proceedings consistent with this opinion.

It is so ordered.

■ JUSTICE BLACKMUN, concurring in the judgment.

* * * What troubles me is that the "total exhaustion" rule, now adopted by this Court, can be read into the statute, as the Court concedes, * * * only by sheer force; that it operates as a trap for the uneducated and indigent *pro se* prisoner-applicant; that it delays the resolution of claims that are not frivolous; and that it tends to increase, rather than to alleviate, the caseload burdens on both state and federal courts. * * *

Although purporting to rely on the policies upon which the exhaustion requirement is based, the Court uses that doctrine as "a blunderbuss to shatter the attempt at litigation of constitutional claims without regard to the purposes that underlie the doctrine and that called it into existence." Those purposes do not require the result the Court reaches * * *. * * *

I

A

* * * Although this Court's precedents do not address specifically the appropriate treatment of mixed habeas petitions, they plainly suggest that state courts need not inevitably be given every opportunity to safeguard a prisoner's constitutional rights and to provide him relief before a federal court may entertain his habeas petition.

B

* * * I cannot agree that [the policies underlying the exhaustion rule] will be sacrificed by permitting district courts to consider *exhausted* habeas claims.

The first interest relied on by the Court involves an offshoot of the doctrine of federal-state comity. The Court hopes to preserve the state courts' role in protecting constitutional rights, as well as to afford those courts an opportunity to correct constitutional errors and—somewhat patronizingly—to "become increasingly familiar with and hospitable toward federal constitutional issues." * * *

In some respects, the Court's ruling appears more destructive than solicitous of federal-state comity. Remitting a habeas petitioner to state court to exhaust a patently frivolous claim before the federal court may consider a serious, exhausted ground for relief hardly demonstrates respect for the state courts. The state judiciary's time and resources are then spent rejecting the obviously meritless unexhausted claim, which doubtless will receive little or no attention in the subsequent federal proceeding that focuses on the substantial exhausted claim. * * *

The second set of interests relied upon by the Court involves those of federal judicial administration—ensuring that a § 2254 petition is accompanied by a complete factual record to facilitate review and relieving the district courts of the responsibility for determining when exhausted and unexhausted claims are interrelated. If a prisoner has presented a particular challenge in the state courts, however, the habeas court will have before it the complete factual record relating to that claim. And the Court's Draconian approach is hardly necessary to relieve district courts of the obligation to consider exhausted grounds for relief when the prisoner also has advanced interrelated claims not yet reviewed by the state courts. When the district court believes, on the facts of the case before it, that the record is inadequate or that full consideration of the exhausted claims is impossible, it has always been free to dismiss the entire habeas petition pending resolution of unexhausted claims in the state courts. Certainly, it makes sense to commit these decisions to the discretion of the lower federal courts, which will be familiar with the specific factual context of each case.

* * * In order to comply with the Court's ruling, a federal court now will have to review the record in a § 2254 proceeding, at least summarily, in order to determine whether all claims have been exhausted. In many cases, a decision on the merits will involve only negligible additional effort. And in other cases, the court may not realize that one of a number of claims is unexhausted until after substantial work has been done. If the district court must nevertheless dismiss the entire petition until all grounds for relief have been exhausted, the prisoner will likely return to federal court eventually, thereby necessitating duplicative examination of the record and consideration of the exhausted claim — perhaps by another district judge. Moreover, when the § 2254 petition does find its way back to federal court, the record on the exhausted grounds for relief may well be stale, and resolution of the merits more difficult.

The interest of the prisoner and of society in [preserving the writ of habeas corpus as a swift and imperative remedy in all cases of illegal restraint or confinement] is the final policy consideration to be weighed in the balance. Compelling the habeas petitioner to repeat his journey through the entire state and federal legal process before receiving a ruling on his exhausted claims obviously entails substantial delay. * * *

II

The Court's misguided approach appears to be premised on the specter of "the sophisticated litigious prisoner intent upon a strategy of piecemeal litigation . . . ," whose aim is to have more than one day in court. * * * [The Court's] ruling today will not frustrate the Perry Masons of the prison populations[, who] will simply include only exhausted claims in each of many successive habeas petitions. * * *

Instead of deterring the sophisticated habeas petitioner who understands, and wishes to circumvent, the rules of exhaustion, the Court's ruling will serve to trap the unwary *pro se* prisoner who is not knowledgeable about the intricacies of the exhaustion doctrine, and whose only aim is to secure a new trial or release from prison. He will consolidate all conceivable grounds for relief in an attempt to accelerate review and minimize costs. But, under the Court's approach, if he unwittingly includes in a § 2254 motion a claim not yet presented to the state courts, he risks dismissal of the entire petition and substantial delay before a ruling on the merits of his exhausted claims. * * *

III

* * * [I would direct] that the courts below dismiss [Lundy]'s unexhausted claims and examine those that have been properly presented to the state courts in order to determine whether they are interrelated with the unexhausted grounds and, if not, whether they warrant collateral relief.

[The dissenting opinion of JUSTICE BRENNAN, with whom JUSTICE MARSHALL joins, is omitted.]

■ JUSTICE WHITE, concurring in part and dissenting in part.

* * * I would not require a "mixed" petition to be dismissed in its entirety, with leave to resubmit the exhausted claims. The trial judge cannot rule on the unexhausted issues, and should dismiss them. But he should rule on the exhausted claims unless they are intertwined with those he must dismiss or unless the habeas petitioner prefers to have his entire petition dismissed. In any event, if the judge rules on those issues that are ripe and dismisses those that are not, I would not tax the petitioner with abuse of the writ if he returns with the latter claims after seeking state relief.

■ JUSTICE STEVENS, dissenting.

* * * [T]he District Judge properly exercised his statutory duty to consider the merits of the claims advanced by [Lundy] that previously had been rejected by the Tennessee courts. The District Judge exceeded, however, what I regard as proper restraints on the scope of collateral review of state court judgments. * * *

I

[Lundy] was convicted in state court of rape and a crime against nature. * * * [T]rial error occurred. * * *

Because these [two of the four claims on federal habeas review] had not been presented to the Tennessee Court of Criminal Appeals, the Federal District Judge concluded that he could "not consider them in the constitutional framework." He added, however, that, "in assessing the atmosphere of the cause, taken as a whole, these items may be referred to collaterally." * * *

The Court holds, however, that the District Court committed two procedural errors. "Unquestionably," according to the Court, it was wrong for the District Court to consider the portions of the trial record described in the unexhausted claims in evaluating those claims that had been exhausted. More fundamentally, according to the Court, it was wrong for the District Court even to consider the merits of the exhausted claims, because the prisoner had included unexhausted claims in his pleadings. Both of the Court's holdings are unsatisfactory for the same basic reason: the Court assumes that the character of all claims alleged in habeas corpus petitions is the same. Under the Court's analysis, *any* unexhausted claim asserted in a habeas corpus petition—no matter how frivolous—is sufficient to command the district judge to postpone relief on a meritorious exhausted claim, no matter how obvious and outrageous the constitutional violation may be. * * *

In this case, I think it is clear that neither the exhausted claims nor the unexhausted claims describe any error demonstrating that [Lundy]'s trial was fundamentally unfair. Since his lawyer found insufficient merit in the two unexhausted claims to object to the error at trial or to raise the claims on direct appeal, I would expect that the Tennessee courts will consider them to have been waived as a matter of state law; thereafter, under the teaching [of procedural default law discussed in Section 2, *infra*, those claims] will not support federal relief. This case is thus destined to return to the Federal District Court and the Court of Appeals where, it is safe to predict, those courts will once again come to the conclusion that the writ should issue. The additional procedure that the Court requires before considering the merits will be totally unproductive.

If my appraisal of [Lundy]'s exhausted claims is incorrect—if the trial actually was fundamentally unfair to [Lundy]—postponing relief until another round of review in the state and federal judicial systems has been completed is truly outrageous. The unnecessary delay will make it more difficult for the prosecutor to obtain a conviction on retrial if [Lundy] is, in fact, guilty; if he is innocent, requiring him to languish in jail because he made a pleading error is callous indeed.

There are some situations in which a district judge should refuse to entertain a mixed petition until all of the prisoner's claims have been exhausted. If the unexhausted claim appears to involve error of the most serious kind, and if it is reasonably clear that the exhausted claims do not, addressing the merits of the exhausted claims will merely delay the ultimate disposition of the case. Or if an evidentiary hearing is necessary to decide the merits of both the exhausted and unexhausted claims, a procedure that enables all fact questions to be resolved in the same hearing should be followed. I therefore would allow district judges to exercise discretion to determine whether the presence of an unexhausted claim in a habeas corpus application makes it inappropriate to consider the merits of a properly pleaded exhausted claim. The inflexible, mechanical rule the Court adopts today arbitrarily denies district judges the kind of authority they need to administer their calendars effectively. * * *

I respectfully dissent.

———

NOTES AND QUESTIONS ON LUNDY AND MIXED PETITIONS

1)   Subsequent Treatment of Unexhausted Claims. A petition containing both exhausted and unexhausted claims is called a "mixed petition." Prior to *Lundy*, two circuits prohibited review of exhausted claims in a mixed petition and eight circuits permitted it. *Lundy* held that, on federal habeas review, a court must dismiss all claims in a mixed petition. The dismissal is almost always without prejudice. Only Justices Blackmun and Stevens dissented from the "total exhaustion" rule.

Justice O'Connor did not garner a majority of the Justices regarding the treatment of the unexhausted claims, expressed in Part III.C of her opinion. In Part III.C, Justice O'Connor argued that, if a prisoner files a mixed petition and then amends it to delete unexhausted claims, the deleted claims may be not be raised in a subsequent habeas petition because of "abuse-of-the-writ" rules. An abuse-of-the-writ finding bars consideration of certain claims, raised in a subsequent habeas petition, on the ground that they were omitted from a prior habeas petition without sufficient cause. (This Chapter explores abuse-of-the-writ law in Section 3.) Justices White, Blackmun, Brennan, and Marshall rejected Justice O'Connor's conclusion that "abuse of the writ" would bar the previously-deleted claims in such a situation and Justice Stevens did not reach the question.

2)   Alternate Strategies. After *Lundy*, state prisoners who raise both exhausted and unexhausted claims face a choice. They may either proceed with federal litigation of the exhausted claims, or they may wait until they have fully exhausted all of the claims in state court and *then* proceed with federal litigation on all of the challenges. In what ways do each of these strategies promote comity and finality?

3) Perry Masons. Justices O'Connor and Blackmun appear to have very different types of prisoners in mind. Justice O'Connor seems to be concerned about the ability of more sophisticated prisoners to game the system by raising some claims in state courts and then strategically raising other claims for the first time in federal court. Justice Blackmun, by contrast, is concerned about the total exhaustion rule becoming a "trap for the unwary." In state proceedings, recall that indigent prisoners receive appointed counsel during an appeal, but not in post-conviction proceedings. Does that bolster Justice Blackmun's concern? Does your assessment of the archetypes change if you are told that many prisoners have access to either jailhouse lawyers or "writ writers" who assist in preparing post-conviction claims?[g] How sensitive should the rule be to the increasing number of claims that can only be asserted on collateral review?

4) State Judges. Justice O'Connor argues that one benefit of the total exhaustion rule is that more prisoners will exhaust federal claims and, as a result, that state judges "may become increasingly familiar with, and hospitable toward, federal constitutional issues." Do you agree that the total exhaustion rule helps to accomplish that educational goal? Does the practice of requiring a prisoner to exhaust futile, unmeritorious claims—that a federal judge could readily dismiss on the merits—benefit state judges? Does it promote comity?

5) Coda on Lundy. On remand, the Sixth Circuit commented that "[t]he case has been in litigation and in the appellate process, in both state and federal courts, including the United States Supreme Court, continuously for sixteen years." *Lundy v. Campbell*, 888 F.2d 467, 468 (6th Cir. 1989). The Sixth Circuit went on to describe that, following the Supreme Court's ruling:

> Lundy therefore returned to the state courts of Tennessee, filing a petition for post-conviction relief with the Criminal Court of Knox County on July 6, 1982. The court denied the petition, and the Tennessee Court of Criminal Appeals affirmed. However, on June 4, 1984, the Tennessee Supreme Court reversed, and remanded for further proceedings. Following a hearing conducted in February 1986, the Criminal Court of Knox County again dismissed Lundy's petition for post-conviction relief, and, in December 1987, the Tennessee Court of Criminal Appeals again affirmed. On March 14, 1988, the Tennessee Supreme Court denied permission to appeal. His state remedies finally exhausted, Lundy returned once again to the district court, filing the instant petition for habeas corpus on May 21, 1988. The district court again granted Lundy's petition on September 21, 1988, and this appeal followed.

The Sixth Circuit concluded that, "if reprosecution is feasible at all, it will be undertaken seventeen years after the alleged offense was committed . . . Neither Lundy, the state of Tennessee, the criminal justice system, nor the federal constitutional principles in support of which we undertake today's duty have been well served no matter what the outcome in this sixteen-year-old litigation." The Sixth Circuit reversed the district court and dismissed the petition. Another state appeal was later dismissed. What does the aftermath of the

---

[g] In Johnson v. Avery, 393 U.S. 483 (1969) the Supreme Court held that inmates may not be foreclosed from access to writ writers, absent some state-provided alternative to help inmates in their preparation of petitions for post-conviction relief. Allowing access to writ writers has been criticized on the ground that the writ writers are ineffective and that the practices creates threats to prison security. See Raymond Y. Lin, *A Prisoner's Constitutional Right to Attorney Assistance*, 83 Colum. L. Rev. 1279, 1314 n. 227 (1983).

Court's decision in *Rose v. Lundy* tell you, one way or the other, about the practical impact of the total exhaustion rule? What would the outcome have been under the rule that Justice Stevens preferred, in which the judge could consider unexhausted claims if the trial was "fundamentally unfair"?

6) Note on AEDPA and Exhaustion. AEDPA made several changes to the statutory exhaustion rules. It altered both the structure and the substance of the portion of § 2254 codifying the exhaustion rule. AEDPA divided the statutory provisions into three subsections. Before considering each, take note of the definition of "exhaustion" in § 2254(c): "An applicant shall not be deemed to have exhausted the remedies available in the courts of the State, within the meaning of this section, if he has the right under the law of the State to raise, by any available procedure, the question presented."

a) Section 2254(b)(1). Subsection (1) sets forth the basic rule of exhaustion for three situations, and reads as follows:

(1) An application for a writ of habeas corpus on behalf of a person in custody pursuant to the judgment of a State court shall not be granted unless it appears that—(A) the applicant has exhausted the remedies available in the courts of the State; or (B)(i) there is an absence of available State corrective process; or (ii) circumstances exist that render such process ineffective to protect the rights of the applicant.

b) Section 2254(b)(2). Second, consider the situation where the judge knows that the claim lacks merit, but the claim is unexhausted. Congress responded to Justice Blackmun's concern that the "state judiciary's time and resources are then spent rejecting the obviously meritless unexhausted claim" by enacting § 2254(b)(2), which deviates from the complete exhaustion rule: "An application for a writ of habeas corpus may be denied on the merits, notwithstanding the failure of the applicant to exhaust the remedies available in the courts of the State." Is the exception for adverse merits adjudication an improvement over the prior rule—or should a court invoke this subsection only if it is sure the claim substantially lacks merit? The Circuits are divided on whether a federal judge enjoys considerable discretion to deny the petition on the merits or whether the judge should only deny an unexhausted claim on the merits if the prisoner "obviously" cannot prevail on it. Some Circuit Courts, relying on language in *Granberry v. Greer*, 481 U.S. 129 (1987), have indicated that a federal court may deny an unexhausted claim only if it is "perfectly clear" that the claim lacks merit, or if the claim "obviously lacks merit," or if the claim is "patently frivolous."[h] What is the problem with the converse rule: why would it be problematic to allow federal courts to grant relief on plainly meritorious claims? Would such a rule not have similar benefits in terms of efficiency?

c) Section 2254(b)(3). Third, consider a situation in which the State fails to assert an exhaustion bar. In *Granberry*, the Supreme Court ruled that a federal court could impose an exhaustion bar even if the State forfeited exhaustion as a defense. The Court explained: "When the State answers a habeas corpus petition, it has a duty to advise the district court whether the prisoner has, in fact, exhausted all available state remedies." The Court, however, noted that

---

[h] See, e.g., Cassett v. Stewart, 406 F.3d 614, 623 (9th Cir. 2005) (using "perfectly clear" language); Mercadel v. Cain, 179 F.2d 271, 276 (5th Cir. 1999) ("obviously" lacks merit and "frivolous"); Hernandez v. Conway, 485 F.Supp.2d 266, 273 (W.D.N.Y.2007) ("patently frivolous"); see also Hertz & Liebman, *FHCPP, supra* note e, at § 23.1 n.5 (collecting more cases).

"there are exceptional cases in which the State fails, whether inadvertently or otherwise, to raise an arguably meritorious nonexhaustion defense." The Court held:

> The State's omission in such a case makes it appropriate for the court of appeals to take a fresh look at the issue. The court should determine whether the interests of comity and federalism will be better served by addressing the merits forthwith or by requiring a series of additional state and district court proceedings before reviewing the merits of the petitioner's claim.

AEDPA codified a more deferential rule in the new Section 2254(b)(3): "A State shall not be deemed to have waived the exhaustion requirement or be estopped from reliance upon the requirement unless the State, through counsel, expressly waives the requirement." When would the State ever explicitly waive its own defense? What purposes does this new rule serve? What does it change about *Granberry*? Why does federal law treat forfeitures by the claimant and forfeitures by the state differently?

7) Total Exhaustion and the Federal Limitations Rule. *Lundy* was decided before AEDPA created a statute of limitations applicable to federal habeas petitions. According to the 2007 Habeas Study, fairly few habeas cases had claims dismissed as unexhausted (5.7% of all non-capital cases and just 2.4% of capital cases), but one reason might be that more cases are both resolved on the merits; in addition, more cases are dismissed based on the new AEDPA statute of limitations. See King et al., *2007 Habeas Study*, at 47 (setting forth statistics). If the one-year limitations period is tolled only by the pendency of a *state* post-conviction proceeding—as § 2244(d)(2) states—then what happens to the limitations period applicable to exhausted claims dismissed under *Lundy*? Those claims were pending in *federal* court. What happens if the mixed petition was pending in federal court for over a year? The limitations period would seem to bar the prisoner from reasserting even the exhausted claims. As the Court put it in *Pliler v. Ford*, 542 U.S. 225 (2004):

> The combined effect of [*Lundy*] and AEDPA's limitations period is that if a petitioner comes to federal court with a mixed petition toward the end of the limitations period, a dismissal of his mixed petition could result in the loss of all of his claims—including those already exhausted—because the limitations period could expire during the time a petitioner returns to state court to exhaust his unexhausted claims.

The imposition of a limitations period under such circumstances is an undeniably harsh result, and courts may issue "stay and abeyance" orders that suspend litigation over the exhausted claims without dismissing them. A prisoner may then exhaust the other claims in state court. See Rhines v. Weber, 544 U.S. 269, 274 (2005). Specifically, a court using stay-and-abeyance procedure should (1) dismiss the unexhausted claims without prejudice; (2) stay and hold in abeyance the proceedings involving the exhausted claims; and (3) after the previously-unexhausted claims are sufficiently presented to state courts, allow the prisoner to add them to the pending federal petition via amendment. Do you think a federal court *must* tell a state prisoner about the availability of stay-and-abeyance procedure? The Supreme Court stated in *Pliler*: "Without addressing the propriety of this stay-and-abeyance procedure, we hold that federal district judges are not required to give *pro se* litigants these two warnings." Justice Breyer dissented on this point, emphasizing the "importance of maintaining a prisoner's access to a federal habeas court and the comparatively minor interference that the Ninth Circuit's procedure creates with comity or other AEDPA concerns," and reasoning that the judge "should have informed [petitioner] of this important rights-preserving option."

Rhines held that a district court does not always need to issue a stay-and-abeyance order. Instead, a district court should grant a stay where: (1) the prisoner has good cause for failure to exhaust; (2) the unexhausted claims have merit; (3) there is no sign of intentional delay. What type of *pro-se* prisoner does a *Rhines* stay reflect: an unwarily-trapped one or a Perry Mason?[i]

2. PROCEDURAL DEFAULT

INTRODUCTORY NOTE ON ELEMENTS OF PROCEDURAL DEFAULT

The concept of "procedural default" goes hand-in-glove with the exhaustion requirement. Whereas the exhaustion rule requires a prisoner to pursue all available state remedies before seeking federal habeas relief, the procedural default rule penalizes a prisoner who failed to exhaust a claim, and may no longer raise that claim because of the state court's procedural rules. Specifically, a claim is procedurally defaulted if there is an "adequate and independent" ground on which the state courts rejected or could have rejected the claim. AEDPA, however, says nothing about procedural default rules. In fact, the habeas statutes have never referred to the concept of a procedural default.

The absence of statutory content notwithstanding, readers familiar with Supreme Court jurisdiction will recognize the "adequate and independent state ground" requirement. An adequate and independent state ground is a jurisdictional bar to Supreme Court review of cases appealed directly from state courts. Unlike the rule of Supreme Court jurisdiction over state judgments, however, a procedural default is not a jurisdictional bar to federal habeas review. Even if there is an adequate and independent ground for the denial of state post-conviction relief, there are several categories of "excuses" that permit a federal court to consider an otherwise-defaulted claim. The scope of these excuses has changed radically over the past few decades and they have been a source of intense debate among the Supreme Court Justices. Procedural default is one the most common reasons for the dismissal of claims filed by prisoners.[j]

NOTE ON PROCEDURAL DEFAULT DOCTRINE AND BROADER TRENDS IN HABEAS JURISPRUDENCE

There is a great deal of consensus about the arc of late-twentieth century federal post-conviction review. The Warren Court (1) located in the first ten

---

[i] The *2007 Habeas Study* also found that quite a few capital cases (17%) had at least one period of time when the petition was stayed pending exhaustion, but that in non-capital cases, only 2.6% were stayed for exhaustion. See King et al., *2007 Habeas Study*, supra note f, at 31-33. Why do you think that judges are more willing to grant stays in capital cases? Or could the explanation simply be that capital habeas petitioners have lawyers who may cautiously file a petition even though some claims may be unexhausted?

[j] The *2007 Habeas Study*, for example, found that over 13.3% of non-capital cases and 42% of capital cases included a ruling that at least one claim was barred by a procedural default. See King et al., *2007 Habeas Study*, supra note f, at 48.

Amendments a number of procedural rights applicable to criminal trials; (2) used the Due Process Clause of the Fourteenth Amendment to "incorporate" those rights against the states; and (3) used habeas corpus as the primary remedy to implement these changes. The Burger and Rehnquist Courts very forcefully pushed back against the use of habeas to effectuate any revolution in criminal procedure.

Perhaps the cases that best illustrate the changes in the Supreme Court's approach towards federal habeas corpus are *Fay v. Noia*, 372 U.S. 391 (1963), and *Wainwright v. Sykes*, 433 U.S. 72 (1977)—both excerpted below. *Noia*, decided by the Warren Court, is generally considered the "high water mark" of federal habeas relief. *Sykes*, in turn, is considered a seminal entry in a set of Burger and Rehnquist Court decisions that pared back the availability of habeas relief to state prisoners. On a doctrinal level, *Fay* and *Sykes* set out standards for deciding when a procedural default is excused. These two decisions, however, are a microcosm of the larger shift in habeas paradigms on the Court.

A. EARLY PROCEDURAL DEFAULT DOCTRINE

During the fifteen years preceding *Fay v. Noia*, 372 U.S. 391 (1963), many legislative proposals seeking to restrict the writ met a terminal fate in various phases of congressional consideration. The Warren Court habeas paradigms were still ascendant, and *Noia* became a vehicle for two ideas. First, the decision formulated a legal rule for excusing forfeitures that occurred in state proceedings. Second, it established an atmosphere of habeas process that favored the liberty interest of robust constitutional review over competing state interests in comity and federalism.

Fay v. Noia
Supreme Court of the United States
372 U.S. 391 (1963)

■ Mr. JUSTICE BRENNAN delivered the opinion of the Court.

This case presents important questions touching the federal habeas corpus jurisdiction * * * in its relation to state criminal justice. The narrow question is whether the respondent Noia may be granted federal habeas corpus relief from imprisonment under a New York conviction now admitted by the State to rest upon a confession obtained from him in violation of the Fourteenth Amendment, after he was denied state post-conviction relief because the coerced confession claim had been decided against him at the trial and Noia had allowed the time for a direct appeal to lapse without seeking review by a state appellate court.

Noia was convicted [in New York for felony murder] in 1942 with Santo Caminito and Frank Bonino * * *. The sole evidence against each defendant was his signed confession. Caminito and Bonino, but not Noia, appealed their convictions to the Appellate Division of the New York Supreme Court. These appeals were unsuccessful, but subsequent legal proceedings resulted in the releases of Caminito and Bonino on findings that their confessions had been coerced and their convictions therefore procured in violation of the Fourteenth Amendment. * * * [T]he coercive nature of Noia's confession was also established, [but] the United States District Court for the Southern District of New York held in Noia's federal habeas corpus proceeding that, because of his failure to appeal, he must be denied [habeas relief.] * * * The Court of Appeals for the Second Circuit reversed * * * and ordered that Noia's conviction be set aside and that he be discharged from custody unless given a new trial forthwith. * * *

We granted certiorari. We affirm the judgment of the Court of Appeals but reach that court's result by a different course of reasoning. We hold: (1) Federal courts have *power* under the federal habeas statute to grant relief despite the applicant's failure to have pursued a state remedy not available to him at the time he applies; the doctrine under which state procedural defaults are held to constitute an adequate and independent state law ground barring direct Supreme Court review is not to be extended to limit the power granted the federal courts under the federal habeas statute. * * * (3) Noia's failure to appeal cannot, under the circumstances, be deemed an intelligent and understanding waiver of his right to appeal such as to justify the withholding of federal habeas corpus relief.

I

* * * We do well to bear in mind the extraordinary prestige of the Great Writ * * * in Anglo-American jurisprudence * * *. It is "a writ antecedent to statute, and throwing its root deep into the genius of our common law * * *. It is perhaps the most important writ known to the constitutional law of England, affording as it does a swift and imperative remedy in all cases of illegal restraint or confinement. * * *" Received into our own law in the colonial period, given explicit recognition in the [Suspension Clause], incorporated in the first grant of federal court jurisdiction [under the 1789 Judiciary Act], habeas corpus was early confirmed by Chief Justice John Marshall to be a "great constitutional privilege." * * *

These are not extravagant expressions. Behind them may be discerned the unceasing contest between personal liberty and government oppression. It is no accident that habeas corpus has time and again played a central role in national crises, wherein the claims of order and of liberty clash most acutely, not only in England in the seventeenth century, but also in America from our very beginnings, and today. Although in form the Great Writ is simply a mode of procedure, its history is inextricably intertwined with the growth of fundamental rights of personal liberty. For its function has been to provide a prompt and efficacious remedy for whatever society deems to be intolerable restraints. Its root principle is that in a civilized society, government must always be accountable to the judiciary for a man's imprisonment: if the imprisonment cannot be shown to conform with the fundamental requirements of law, the individual is entitled to his immediate release. Thus there is nothing novel in the fact that today habeas corpus in the federal courts provides a mode for the redress of denials of due process of law. Vindication of due process is precisely its historic office. * * *

Of course standards of due process have evolved over the centuries. But the nature and purpose of habeas corpus have remained remarkably constant. History refutes the notion that until recently the writ was available only in a very narrow class of lawless imprisonments. For example, it is not true that at common law habeas corpus was exclusively designed as a remedy for executive detentions; it was early used by the great common-law courts to effect the release of persons detained by order of inferior courts.

Thus, at the time that the Suspension Clause was written into our Federal Constitution and the first Judiciary Act was passed conferring habeas corpus jurisdiction upon the federal judiciary, there was respectable common-law authority for the proposition that habeas was available to remedy any kind of governmental restraint contrary to fundamental law. In this connection it is significant that neither the Constitution nor the Judiciary Act anywhere defines the writ, although the Act does intimate that its issuance is to be "agreeable to the principles and usages of law";—the common law, presumably. * * *

This marked a return to the common-law principle that restraints contrary to fundamental law, by whatever authority imposed, could be redressed by writ of habeas corpus. * * *

The same principles have consistently been applied in cases of state prisoners seeking habeas corpus in the federal courts, although the development of the law in this area was at first delayed for several reasons. The first Judiciary Act did not extend federal habeas to prisoners in state custody; and shortly after Congress removed this limitation in 1867, it withdrew from this Court jurisdiction of appeals from habeas decisions by the lower federal courts and did not restore it for almost 20 years. Moreover, it was not until this century that the Fourteenth Amendment was deemed to apply some of the safeguards of criminal procedure contained in the Bill of Rights to the States. Yet during the period of the withdrawal of the Supreme Court's jurisdiction of habeas appeals, the lower federal courts did not hesitate to discharge state prisoners whose convictions rested on unconstitutional statutes or had otherwise been obtained in derogation of constitutional rights. * * *

We do not suggest that this Court has always followed an unwavering line in its conclusions as to the availability of the Great Writ. Our development of the law of federal habeas corpus has been attended, seemingly, with some backing and filling. * * *

II

* * * Despite the Court's refusal to give binding weight to state court determinations of the merits in habeas, it has not infrequently suggested that, where the state court declines to reach the merits because of a procedural default, the federal courts may be foreclosed from granting the relief sought on habeas corpus. * * *

* * * [R]arely, if ever, has the Court predicated its deference to state procedural rules on a want of power to entertain a habeas application where a procedural default was committed by the defendant in the state courts. Typically, the Court, like the District Court in the instant case, has approached the problem as an aspect of the rule requiring exhaustion of state remedies, which is not a rule distributing power as between the state and federal courts. * * * The same considerations of comity that led the Court to refuse relief to one who had not yet availed himself of his state remedies likewise prompted the refusal of relief to one who had inexcusably failed to tender the federal questions to the state courts. Either situation poses a threat to the orderly administration of criminal justice that ought, if possible, to be averted. * * * [T]he Court, by relying upon a rule of discretion, avowedly flexible, yielding always to "exceptional circumstances," has refused to concede jurisdictional significance to the abortive state court proceeding.

III

* * * It is a familiar principle that this Court will decline to review state court judgments which rest on independent and adequate state grounds, notwithstanding the co-presence of federal grounds. * * * Thus, a

default such as Noia's, if deemed adequate and independent (a question on which we intimate no view), would cut off review by this Court of the state *coram nobis* proceeding in which the New York Court of Appeals refused him relief. It is contended that it follows from this that the remedy of federal habeas corpus is likewise cut off.

The fatal weakness of this contention is its failure to recognize that the adequate state ground rule is a function of the limitations of *appellate* review. * * * [T]he adequate state ground rule is a consequence of the Court's obligation to refrain from rendering advisory opinions or passing upon moot questions.[40]

But while our appellate function is concerned only with the judgments or decrees of state courts, the habeas corpus jurisdiction of the lower federal courts is not so confined. The jurisdictional prerequisite is not the judgment of a state court, but detention *simpliciter*. * * *

* * * And the only concrete impact the assumption of federal habeas jurisdiction in the face of a procedural default has on the state interest we have described, is that it prevents the State from closing off the convicted defendant's last opportunity to vindicate his constitutional rights, thereby punishing him for his default and deterring others who might commit similar defaults in the future.

* * * While [this Court] has deferred to state substantive grounds so long as they are not patently evasive of or discriminatory against federal rights, it has sometimes refused to defer to state procedural grounds only because they made burdensome the vindication of federal rights. That the Court nevertheless ordinarily gives effect to state procedural grounds may be attributed to considerations which are peculiar to the Court's role and function, and have no relevance to habeas corpus proceedings in the Federal District Courts: the unfamiliarity of members of this Court with the minutiae of 50 States' procedures; the inappropriateness of crowding our docket with questions turning wholly on particular state procedures; the web of rules and statutes that circumscribes our appellate jurisdiction, and the inherent and historical limitations of such a jurisdiction.

A practical appraisal of the state interest here involved plainly does not justify the federal courts' enforcing on habeas corpus a doctrine of forfeitures under the guise of applying the adequate state ground rule. We fully grant * * * that the exigencies of federalism warrant a limitation whereby the federal judge has the discretion to deny relief to one who has deliberately sought to subvert or evade the orderly adjudication of his federal defenses in the state courts. Surely no stricter rule is a realistic necessity. A man under conviction for crime has an obvious inducement to do his very best to keep his state remedies open, and not stake his all on the outcome of a federal habeas proceeding which, in many respects, may be less advantageous to him than a state court proceeding. And if, because of inadvertence or neglect, he runs afoul of a state procedural requirement, and thereby forfeits his state remedies, appellate and collateral, as well as di-

---

[40] "The reason (for the adequate state ground rule) is so obvious that it has rarely been thought to warrant statement. It is found in the partitioning of power between the state and federal judicial systems and in the limitations of our own jurisdiction. Our only power over state judgments is to correct them to the extent that they incorrectly adjudge federal rights. And our power is to correct wrong judgments, not to revise opinions. We are not permitted to render an advisory opinion, and if the same judgment would be rendered by the state court after we corrected its views of federal laws, our review could amount to nothing more than an advisory opinion." Herb v. Pitcairn, 324 U.S. 117, 125–126 (1945). * * *

rect review thereof in this Court, those consequences should be sufficient to vindicate the State's valid interest in orderly procedure. Whatever residuum of state interest there may be under such circumstances is manifestly insufficient in the face of the federal policy, drawn from the ancient principles of the writ of habeas corpus, embodied both in the Federal Constitution and in the habeas corpus provisions of the Judicial Code, and consistently upheld by this Court, of affording an effective remedy for restraints contrary to the Constitution. For these several reasons, we reject as unsound in principle, as well as not supported by authority, the suggestion that the federal courts are without power to grant habeas relief to an applicant whose federal claims would not be heard on direct review in this Court because of a procedural default furnishing an adequate and independent ground of state decision.

What we have said substantially disposes of the further contention that 28 U.S.C. § 2254 embodies a doctrine of forfeitures and cuts off relief when there has been a failure to exhaust state remedies no longer available at the time habeas is sought. This contention is refuted by the language of the statute and by its history. * * * Very little support can be found in the long course of previous decisions by this Court elaborating the rule of exhaustion for the proposition that it was regarded at the time of the revision of the Judicial Code as jurisdictional, rather than merely as a rule ordering the state and federal proceedings so as to eliminate unnecessary federal-state friction. There is thus no warrant for attributing to Congress, in the teeth of the language of 2254, intent to work a radical innovation in the law of habeas corpus. We hold that § 2254 is limited in its application to failure to exhaust state remedies still open to the habeas applicant at the time he files his application in federal court. * * *

V

Although we hold that the jurisdiction of the federal courts on habeas corpus is not affected by procedural defaults incurred by the applicant during the state court proceedings, we recognize a limited discretion in the federal judge to deny relief to an applicant under certain circumstances. Discretion is implicit in the statutory command that the judge, after granting the writ and holding a hearing of appropriate scope, "dispose of the matter as law and justice require," 28 U.S.C. § 2243; and discretion was the flexible concept employed by the federal courts in developing the exhaustion rule. Furthermore, habeas corpus has traditionally been regarded as governed by equitable principles. Among them is the principle that a suitor's conduct in relation to the matter at hand may disentitle him to the relief he seeks. Narrowly circumscribed, in conformity to the historical role of the writ of habeas corpus as an effective and imperative remedy for detentions contrary to fundamental law, the principle is unexceptionable. We therefore hold that the federal habeas judge may, in his discretion, deny relief to an applicant who has deliberately bypassed the orderly procedure of the state courts and in so doing has forfeited his state court remedies.

But we wish to make very clear that this grant of discretion is not to be interpreted as a permission to introduce legal fictions into federal habeas corpus. The classic definition of waiver * * *—"an intentional relinquishment or abandonment of a known right or privilege"—furnishes the controlling standard. If a habeas applicant, after consultation with competent counsel or otherwise, understandingly and knowingly forewent the privilege of seeking to vindicate his federal claims in the state courts, whether for strategic, tactical, or any other reasons that can fairly be described as the deliberate bypassing of state procedures, then it is open to the federal court on habeas to deny him all relief if the state courts refused to entertain his federal claims on the merits — though, of course, only after the federal court has satisfied itself, by holding a hearing or by some other means, of the facts bearing upon the applicant's default. At all events, we wish it clearly understood that the standard here put forth depends on the considered choice of the petitioner. A choice made by counsel not participated in by the petitioner does not automatically bar relief. Nor does a state court's finding of waiver bar independent determination of the question by the federal courts on habeas, for waiver affecting federal rights is a federal question.

[The Court determined that Noia had not deliberately bypassed his appellate remedy.] * * *

VI

* * * Our decision today swings open no prison gates. Today as always few indeed is the number of state prisoners who eventually win their freedom by means of federal habeas corpus. Those few who are ultimately successful are persons whom society has grievously wronged and for whom belated liberation is little enough compensation. Surely no fair-minded person will contend that those who have been deprived of their liberty without due process of law ought nevertheless to languish in prison. * * *

Affirmed.

[The Dissenting Opinion of Mr. JUSTICE CLARK is omitted.]

■ Mr. JUSTICE HARLAN, whom Mr. JUSTICE CLARK and Mr. JUSTICE STEWART join, dissenting.

* * * [T]he federal courts have no power, statutory or constitutional, to release the respondent Noia from state detention. This is because his custody by New York does not violate any federal right, since it is pursuant to a conviction whose validity rests upon an adequate and independent state ground which the federal courts are required to respect.

[Brown v. Allen] substantially expanded the scope of inquiry on an application for federal habeas corpus. Frank v. Mangum and Moore v. Dempsey had denied that the federal courts in habeas corpus sat to determine whether errors of law, even constitutional law, had been made in the original trial and appellate proceedings. Under * * * Brown, if a petitioner could show that the validity of a state decision to detain rested on a determination of a constitutional claim, and if he alleged that determination to be erroneous, the federal court had the right and the duty to satisfy itself of the correctness of the state decision.

But what if the validity of the state decision to detain rested not on the determination of a federal claim, but rather on an adequate nonfederal ground which would have barred direct review by this Court? * * *

II

CONSTITUTIONAL BARRIER

The true significance of today's decision can perhaps best be laid bare in terms of a hypothetical case presenting questions of the powers of this Court on direct review, and of a Federal District Court on habeas corpus.

1. On direct review.—Assume that a man is indicted, and held for trial in a state court, by a grand jury from which members of his race have been systematically excluded. Assume further that the State requires any objec-

tion to the composition of the grand jury to be raised prior to the verdict, that no such objection is made, and that the defendant seeks to raise the point for the first time on appeal from his conviction. If the state appellate court refuses to consider the claim because it was raised too late, and if certiorari is sought and granted, the initial question before this Court will be whether there was an adequate state ground for the judgment below. If the petitioner was represented by counsel not shown to be incompetent, and if the necessary information to make the objection is not shown to have been unavailable at the time of trial, it is certain that the judgment of conviction will stand, despite the fact the indictment was obtained in violation of the petitioner's constitutional rights.

What is the reason for the rule that an adequate and independent state ground of decision bars Supreme Court review of that decision — a rule which, of course, is as applicable to procedural as to substantive grounds? * * * [U[nder the governing statute (i) the Court did not have jurisdiction, on review of a state decision, to examine and decide "questions not of a Federal character," and (ii) an erroneous decision of a federal question by a state court could not warrant reversal if there were:

"any other matter or issue adjudged by the State court which is sufficiently broad to maintain the judgment of that court notwithstanding the error in deciding the issue raised by the Federal question."

* * * [T]he adequate state ground rule has roots far deeper than the statutes governing our jurisdiction, and rests on fundamentals that touch this Court's habeas corpus jurisdiction equally with its direct reviewing power. * * *

* * * For this Court to go beyond the adequacy of the state ground and to review and determine the correctness of that ground on its merits would, in our hypothetical case, be to assume full control over a State's procedures for the administration of its own criminal justice. This is and must be beyond our power if the federal system is to exist in substance, as well as form. The right of the State to regulate its own procedures governing the conduct of litigants in its courts, and its interest in supervision of those procedures, stand on the same constitutional plane as its right and interest in framing "substantive" laws governing other aspects of the conduct of those within its borders. * * *

2. *On habeas corpus.* — The adequate state ground doctrine thus finds its source in basic constitutional principles, and the question before us is whether this is as true in a collateral attack in habeas corpus as on direct review. Assume, then, that, after dismissal of the writ of certiorari in our hypothetical case, the prisoner seeks habeas corpus in a Federal District Court, again complaining of the composition of the grand jury that indicted him. Is that federal court constitutionally more free than the Supreme Court on direct review to "ignore" the adequate state ground, proceed to the federal question, and order the prisoner's release?

The answer must be that it is not. * * * The fact that a District Court on habeas has fewer choices than the Supreme Court, since it can only act on the body of the prisoner, does not alter the significance of the exercise of its power. In habeas, as on direct review, ordering the prisoner's release invalidates the judgment of conviction and renders ineffective the state rule relied upon to sustain that judgment. Try as the majority does to turn habeas corpus into a roving commission of inquiry into every possible invasion of the applicant's civil rights that may ever have occurred, it cannot divorce the writ from a judgment of conviction if that judgment is the basis of the detention.

[Justice Harlan would not have found that the absence of a deliberate bypass entitled the federal court to conduct habeas review.]

IV

ADEQUACY OF THE STATE GROUND HERE INVOLVED

[Justice Harlan would have held that the state ground was adequate.] Since Noia is detained pursuant to a state judgment whose validity rests on an adequate and independent state ground, the judgment below should be reversed.

———————

NOTES AND QUESTIONS ON NOIA

1) Coerced Confessions. Noia claimed a constitutional violation occurred during the investigation: that his confession was coerced.[k] Such a claim does not go to the jurisdiction of the trial court. The reasons why a coerced confession might concern a habeas judge, however, are obvious. Concerns with the unreliability of coerced confessions date back to Roman and medieval law (which approved the use of torture under strict rules in certain capital cases). We now know more about the role of false confessions in wrongful convictions, particularly based on high-profile DNA exonerations in cases that involved seemingly powerful confessions. In the 1950s and early 1960s, police had not fully adopted modern psychological interrogation techniques, and some police still used outright torture. During that time, the Court increasingly highlighted concerns about brutal "third degree" techniques and the unreliability of statements produced using torture, particularly when vulnerable individuals were interrogated.[l] Confession evidence is extremely powerful—and in Noia's case it was the sole evidence of his guilt. Should the application of habeas procedure turn, at least to some extent, on the type of constitutional challenge at issue? Should a federal judge be able to bend the rules because a coerced confession might be false and the inmate might be "actually innocent"?

———————

[k] For a description of the history of Charles Noia's case, see Larry Yackle, *The Story of Fay v. Noia: Another Case About Another Federalism, in* Federal Courts Stories 191 (Vicki Jackson & Judith Resnik eds., 2009). Professor Yackle suggests that the search for the participants in this mugging, where a victim was shot near Coney Island in Brooklyn, NY, may have been particularly aggressive because a police officer was killed during a similar robbery later the same night. Professor Yackle explained that the defendants alleged that a number of police officers involved in the interrogation had "slapped, punched, kicked, threatened, yanked [them] by the hair, and deprived [them] of food," as well as threatened to arrest their family members if they did not confess. The defendants said that the detectives had told them exactly what to say in their confession statements. The detectives denied such abuses, but admitted that teams of detectives interrogated the men for more than 27 hours; that the interogees were not allowed to see an attorney or family member; and that the interrogators used several deceptive tactics—including a female police officer impersonating a fictitious eyewitness, who claimed to identify the defendants as the culprits.

[l] See, e.g. Culombe v. Connecticut, 367 U.S. 568, 572–74 (1961) (explaining the role of "physical brutality" in modern interrogation); Steven A. Drizin & Richard A. Leo, *The Problem of False Confessions in the Post-DNA World*, 82 N.C. L. Rev. 891, 894–900 (2004) (describing causes and examples of false confessions); Brandon L. Garrett, *The Substance of False Confessions*, 62 Stan. L. Rev. 1051, 1110 (2010) (explaining that, during the 1950s and 1960s, the Supreme Court was particularly concerned with the physical abuse that interrogation techniques favored).

2)   Historiography and the Writ. Historiography is the study of how a group constructs the history of a particular phenomenon or event. How accurate is Justice Brennan's account of habeas history? What are the authoritative sources for writ history, and how have they shaped what we now treat as an "objective" account of the role that habeas has played in Anglo-American government? Many judicial decisions contain their own version of habeas history, almost always for the purpose of situating a particular decision in what appears to be a natural extension of the existing state of habeas process. One of the most important considerations—particularly when you read accounts of the writ from the Warren, Burger, Rehnquist and Roberts Courts—is the state of conflict over the historical record. *Noia* is considered a high water mark in one version of habeas history. Judges and academics have subjected Justice Brennan's historical account to withering attacks, and—in our opinion—with good reason. Is "vindication of due process" really the "historic office" of the writ, or was habeas chiefly a remedy only for custody ordered without proper jurisdiction? Does the writ really "stem[] ultimately from Magna Charta," or does it have more mundane roots in moving prisoners from one form of custody to another? How does common-law history translate to habeas corpus under the U.S. Constitution? In what sense is the writ "embodied in the written Constitution"?

3)   Relationship to Direct Review. The concepts of "adequacy" and "independence" originate from a different context—the rules regulating the Supreme Court's certiorari jurisdiction over the decisions of a state's highest court, as set forth in 28 U.S.C. § 1257(a):

> Final judgments or decrees rendered by the highest court of a State in which a decision could be had, may be reviewed by the Supreme Court by writ of certiorari where the validity of a treaty or statute of the United States is drawn in question or where the validity of a statute of any State is drawn in question on the ground of its being repugnant to the Constitution, treaties, or laws of the United States, or where any title, right, privilege, or immunity is specially set up or claimed under the Constitution or the treaties or statutes of, or any commission held or authority exercised under, the United States.

On direct review, the Supreme Court cannot reach even federal questions in state judgments that rest on "adequate and independent" procedural grounds. The rule for procedural default on federal habeas review grew out of that doctrine.

The concepts of "adequacy and independence," however, operate differently in the direct review and in the habeas contexts. Whereas an adequate and independent state ground disables the Supreme Court's appellate *jurisdiction* under 28 U.S.C. § 1257, an adequate and independent state ground is merely a *prudential* bar to federal habeas review. See Dretke v. Haley, 541 U.S. 386, 392 (2004). Do you find this distinction persuasive? In dissent, Justice Harlan argued that the adequate state ground rule nevertheless "rests on fundamentals" that relate to questions of jurisdiction and "basic constitutional principles." Who gets the better of the argument, Justice Brennan or Justice Harlan?

4)   Adequacy. Before a court even reaches the deliberate bypass questions, a claim cannot be defaulted unless the state procedural rule was both "adequate" to support the judgment and "independent" of a federal question. A state ground is adequate if it is firmly established and regularly followed. A discretionary state rule can qualify provided it meets those criteria. See Beard v. Kindler, 558 U.S. 53 (2009).

Consider the following situation. State X does not allow appeals of lower-state-court orders denying state habeas relief, and instead requires a state prisoner to file an original habeas petition in the State X Supreme Court—confined to habeas issues raised in the lower court. State X has no fixed limitations period for filing in the state Supreme Court, although the prisoner is subject to a "reasonableness" standard for timely filing. The State X Supreme Court sometimes dismisses the original petitions as untimely, citing a particular and recurrent line of state cases. The State X Supreme Court will sometimes decide late-filed petitions on the merits, and it will not cite the line of cases that controls the timeliness inquiry. Is a discretionary "reasonableness" rule for timely filing a "firmly established" criterion? How does the citation of state precedent affect the determination of whether the state law is "regularly" followed? The Supreme Court worked its way through this issue in *Walker v. Martin*, 131 S.Ct. 1120 (2011).

5)   Independence. What does it mean for a state procedural rule to be "independent" of state law? Here, the Supreme Court has also drawn from the concept of "independence" native to its direct-review case law. In *Michigan v. Long*, 463 U.S. 1062 (1983), the Supreme Court held that:

> [W]hen, as in this case, a state court decision fairly appears to rest primarily on federal law, or to be interwoven with the federal law, and when the adequacy and independence of any possible state law ground is not clear from the face of the opinion, we will accept as the most reasonable explanation that the state court decided the case the way it did because it believed that federal law required it to do so. If a state court chooses merely to rely on federal precedents as it would on the precedents of all other jurisdictions, then it need only make clear by a plain statement in its judgment or opinion that the federal cases are being used only for the purpose of guidance, and do not themselves compel the result that the court has reached. . . If the state court decision indicates clearly and expressly that it is alternatively based on bona fide separate, adequate, and independent grounds, we, of course, will not undertake to review the decision.

One recurrent issue in both direct and collateral contexts involves the "independence" of waiver rules and plain-error bars that contain exceptions for constitutional error or fundamental rights. In *Ake v. Oklahoma*, the Court held that a state waiver provision was not "independent" because, by its own terms, the state waiver statute did not apply to "fundamental" trial error. Although the Supreme Court has never formally and expressly held that the holding of *Ake* applies in federal habeas proceedings, the Court has made that assumption. See Stewart v. Smith, 536 U.S. 856 (2002).[m]

6)   What is a Deliberate Bypass? The Supreme Court's decision in *Noia* marked a departure from the rule of *Daniels v. Allen*, 344 U.S. 443 (1953), where the Court held that a failure to comply with a state procedural rule would result in forfeiture and the dismissal of a federal habeas claim. In *Noia*, the Court held that a federal judge should excuse the procedural default unless

---

[m] Coleman v. Thompson, 501 U.S. 722, 741, describes *Ake* as a direct review case, but in dicta, *Coleman* states: "We have never applied its rule regarding independent state grounds in federal habeas. But even if *Ake* applies here, it does Coleman no good because the Virginia Supreme Court relied on an independent state procedural rule."

a prisoner "deliberately bypassed" state remedies. What would a state respondent have to show to prove that a prisoner deliberately bypassed a claim? Presumably, a garden-variety failure of diligence would not be enough. The Court emphasized that "inadvertence or neglect" by the prisoner (or the prisoner's lawyer) should not trigger an inexcusable procedural default. The Court explained that, for the state ground to be "adequate and independent" in a sense that would bar federal review of the criminal judgment, an inmate must have knowingly decided not to pursue state remedies "after consultation with competent counsel or otherwise[.]" Only the knowing forfeiture of state court remedies, "whether for strategic, tactical, or any other reasons [could be] fairly be described as the deliberate bypassing of state procedures." Why would a prisoner ever decide not to pursue state remedies? Under *Noia's* formulation, very few state forfeitures would represent decisions to "deliberately bypass" state remedies.

7)   Noia's Decision not to Appeal. The Court discussed how Noia, having originally received a life sentence, might have appealed and obtained a retrial at which he could have been resentenced to death. The Court stated that "[h]e declined to play Russian roulette in this fashion." The Court added, however: "This was a choice by Noia not to appeal, but under the circumstances it cannot realistically be deemed a merely tactical or strategic litigation step, or in any way a deliberate circumvention of state procedures." Do you agree that Noia did not deliberately bypass the state appellate remedy? The Court added that the facts of each case are different, and not all situations in which a person might face a more severe penalty provide an acceptable reason to forgo state court remedies. Does that suggest any clear limit to what counts as a deliberate bypass?

B. THE MODERN PROCEDURAL DEFAULT TEST

The Supreme Court crafted the modern approach to procedural default questions in the case that follows, *Wainwright v. Sykes*, 433 U.S. 72 (1977). Notice how *Sykes* rejects the deliberate bypass standard from *Noia*, in favor of a cause-and-prejudice test—but the Court does not precisely define those terms. As in *Noia*, *Sykes* left the contours of its test somewhat open. By the time the Court decided *Sykes*, the *Noia* approach to procedural defaults— i.e., the deliberate-bypass standard—had become the operative excuse rule for other procedural doctrines. As a result, federal judges had wide discretion to excuse procedural defects that did not reflect deliberate, strategic decisions of a lawyer or client. Repeating the pattern of cross-pollination among procedural doctrines, the Court would eventually apply the cause-and-prejudice test for excusing a procedural default from *Sykes* to other types of procedural defects. When you read *Sykes*, consider the type of prisoner that the Court seems to have in mind, and compare it to the type of prisoner that the Court had in mind when deciding *Noia*.

Wainwright v. Sykes

United States Supreme Court
433 U.S. 72 (1977)

■ Mr. JUSTICE REHNQUIST delivered the opinion of the Court.

We granted certiorari to consider the availability of federal habeas corpus to review a state convict's claim that testimony was admitted at his trial in violation of his rights under *Miranda v. Arizona*, 384 U. S. 436

(1966), a claim which the Florida courts have previously refused to consider on the merits because of noncompliance with a state contemporaneous objection rule. * * *

Respondent Sykes was convicted of third-degree murder after a jury trial in the Circuit Court of DeSoto County. He testified at trial that, on the evening of January 8, 1972, he told his wife to summon the police because he had just shot Willie Gilbert. Other evidence indicated that, when the police arrived at [Sykes]'s trailer home, they found Gilbert dead of a shotgun wound, lying a few feet from the front porch. Shortly after their arrival, [Sykes] came from across the road and volunteered that he had shot Gilbert, and a few minutes later [Sykes]'s wife approached the police and told them the same thing. Sykes was immediately arrested and taken to the police station.

Once there, it is conceded that he was read his *Miranda* rights, and that he declined to seek the aid of counsel and indicated a desire to talk. He then made a statement, which was admitted into evidence at trial through the testimony of the two officers who heard it, to the effect that he had shot Gilbert from the front porch of his trailer home; there were several references during the trial to [Sykes]'s consumption of alcohol during the preceding day and to his apparent state of intoxication, facts which were acknowledged by the officers who arrived at the scene. At no time during the trial, however, was the admissibility of any of [Sykes]'s statements challenged by his counsel on the ground that [Sykes] had not understood the *Miranda* warnings. Nor did the trial judge question their admissibility on his own motion or hold a factfinding hearing bearing on that issue.

[Sykes] appealed his conviction, but apparently did not challenge the admissibility of the inculpatory statements. He later filed in the trial court a motion to vacate the conviction and, in the State District Court of Appeals and Supreme Court, petitions for habeas corpus. These filings, apparently for the first time, challenged the statements made to police on grounds of involuntariness. In all of these efforts, [Sykes] was unsuccessful.

Having failed in the Florida courts, [Sykes] initiated the present action under 28 U.S.C. § 2254, asserting the inadmissibility of his statements by reason of his lack of understanding of the *Miranda* warnings. The United States District Court for the Middle District of Florida ruled that *Jackson v. Denno*, 378 U. S. 368 (1964), requires a hearing in a state criminal trial prior to the admission of an inculpatory out-of-court statement by the defendant. It held further that [Sykes] had not lost his right to assert such a claim by failing to object at trial or on direct appeal, since only "exceptional circumstances" of "strategic decisions at trial" can create such a bar to raising federal constitutional claims in a federal habeas action. The court stayed issuance of the writ to allow the state court to hold a hearing on the "voluntariness" of the statements.

[The Warden appealed the decision to the Fifth Circuit, which affirmed.]

The simple legal question before the Court calls for a construction of the language of 28 U.S.C. § 2254(a), which provides that the federal courts shall entertain an application for a writ of habeas corpus "in behalf of a person in custody pursuant to the judgment of a state court only on the ground that he is in custody in violation of the Constitution or laws or treaties of the United States." But, to put it mildly, we do not write on a clean slate in construing this statutory provision. Its earliest counterpart, applicable only to prisoners detained by federal authority, is found in the Judiciary Act of 1789. Construing that statute for the Court in *Ex parte Watkins*, 3 Pet. 193, 28 U. S. 202 (1830), Mr. Chief Justice Marshall said:

"An imprisonment under a judgment cannot be unlawful unless that judgment be an absolute nullity; and it is not a nullity if the Court has general jurisdiction of the subject, although it should be erroneous."

In 1867, Congress expanded the statutory language so as to make the writ available to one held in state, as well as federal, custody. For more than a century since the 1867 amendment, this Court has grappled with the relationship between the classical common law writ of habeas corpus and the remedy provided in 28 U.S.C. § 2254. * * *

The area of controversy which has developed has concerned the reviewability of federal claims which the state court has declined to pass on because [the claims were] not presented in the manner prescribed by its procedural rules. The adequacy of such an independent state procedural ground to prevent federal habeas review of the underlying federal issue has been treated very differently than where the state law ground is substantive.

In *Brown [v. Allen]*, [the] lawyer [in a consolidated case] had failed to mail the appeal papers to the State Supreme Court on the last day provided by law for filing, and hand delivered them one day after that date. Citing the state rule requiring timely filing, the Supreme Court of North Carolina refused to hear the appeal. This Court * * * held that federal habeas was not available to review a constitutional claim which could not have been reviewed on direct appeal here because it rested on an independent and adequate state procedural ground.

In *Fay v. Noia* respondent Noia sought federal habeas to review a claim that his state-court conviction had resulted from the introduction of a coerced confession in violation of the Fifth Amendment to the United States Constitution. While the convictions of his two codefendants were reversed on that ground in collateral proceedings following their appeals, Noia did not appeal, and the New York courts ruled that his subsequent coram nobis action was barred on account of that failure. This Court held that petitioner was nonetheless entitled to raise the claim in federal habeas, and thereby overruled its decision 10 years earlier in *Brown v. Allen* * * *.

As a matter of comity, but not of federal power, the Court acknowledged "a limited discretion in the federal judge to deny relief . . . to an applicant who had deliberately by-passed the orderly procedure of the state courts, and, in so doing, has forfeited his state court remedies." In so stating, the Court made clear that the waiver must be knowing and actual— "an intentional relinquishment or abandonment of a known right or privilege." * * *

A decade later, we decided *Davis v. United States*, in which a federal prisoner's application under 28 U.S.C. § 2255 sought for the first time to challenge the makeup of the grand jury which indicted him. * * * We noted that the * * * *Fay v. Noia* concept of waiver should [control federal habeas review of federal convictions]. * * *[W]e concluded that review of the claim should be barred on habeas, as on direct appeal, absent a showing of cause for the noncompliance and some showing of actual prejudice resulting from the alleged constitutional violation.

Last Term, in *Francis v. Henderson* the rule of *Davis* was applied to the parallel case of a state procedural requirement that challenges to grand jury composition be raised before trial. The Court noted that there was power in the federal courts to entertain an application in such a case, but rested its holding on "considerations of comity and concerns for the orderly administration of criminal justice * * *." While there was no counterpart provision of the state rule which allowed an exception upon some showing of cause, the Court concluded that the standard derived from the Federal Rule should nonetheless be applied in that context, since "'[t]here is no reason to * * * give greater preclusive effect to procedural defaults by federal defendants than to similar defaults by state defendants.'" As applied to the federal petitions of state convicts, the Davis "cause- and-prejudice" standard was thus incorporated directly into the body of law governing the availability of federal habeas corpus review.

To the extent that the dicta of *Fay v. Noia* may be thought to have laid down an all-inclusive rule rendering state contemporaneous objection rules ineffective to bar review of underlying federal claims in federal habeas proceedings—absent a "knowing waiver" or a "deliberate bypass" of the right to so object—its effect was limited by *Francis*, which applied a different rule and barred a habeas challenge to the makeup of a grand jury. Petitioner Wainwright in this case urges that we further confine its effect by applying the principle enunciated in *Francis* to a claimed error in the admission of a defendant's confession.

* * * We thus come to the crux of this case. Shall the rule of *Francis v. Henderson*, barring federal habeas review absent a showing of "cause" and "prejudice" attendant to a state procedural waiver, be applied to a waived objection to the admission of a confession at trial? We answer that question in the affirmative.

* * * We leave open for resolution in future decisions the precise definition of the "cause" and "prejudice" standard, and note here only that it is narrower than the standard set forth in dicta in *Fay v. Noia*, which would make federal habeas review generally available to state convicts absent a knowing and deliberate waiver of the federal constitutional contention. It is the sweeping language of *Fay v. Noia*, going far beyond the facts of the case eliciting it, which we today reject.

The reasons for our rejection of it are several. The contemporaneous objection rule itself is by no means peculiar to Florida, and deserves greater respect than *[Noia]* gives it, both for the fact that it is employed by a coordinate jurisdiction within the federal system and for the many interests which it serves in its own right. A contemporaneous objection enables the record to be made with respect to the constitutional claim when the recollections of witnesses are freshest, not years later in a federal habeas proceeding. It enables the judge who observed the demeanor of those witnesses to make the factual determinations necessary for properly deciding the federal constitutional question. * * *

A contemporaneous-objection rule may lead to the exclusion of the evidence objected to, thereby making a major contribution to finality in criminal litigation. Without the evidence claimed to be vulnerable on federal constitutional grounds, the jury may acquit the defendant, and that will be the end of the case; or it may nonetheless convict the defendant, and he will have one less federal constitutional claim to assert in his federal habeas petition. If the state trial judge admits the evidence in question after a full hearing, the federal habeas court pursuant to the 1966 amendment to § 2254 will gain significant guidance from the state ruling in this regard. Subtler considerations as well militate in favor of honoring a state contemporaneous objection rule. An objection on the spot may force the prosecution to take a hard look at its hole card, and, even if the prosecutor thinks that the state trial judge will admit the evidence, he must contemplate the possibility of reversal by the state appellate courts or the ultimate issuance of a federal writ of habeas corpus based on the impropriety of the state court's rejection of the federal constitutional claim.

We think that the rule of *Fay v. Noia*, broadly stated, may encourage "sandbagging" on the part of defense lawyers, who may take their chances on a verdict of not guilty in a state trial court with the intent to raise their constitutional claims in a federal habeas court if their initial gamble does not pay off. The refusal of federal habeas courts to honor contemporaneous objection rules may also make state courts themselves less stringent in their enforcement. Under the rule of *Fay v. Noia*, state appellate courts know that a federal constitutional issue raised for the first time in the proceeding before them may well be decided in any event by a federal habeas tribunal. Thus, their choice is between addressing the issue notwithstanding the petitioner's failure to timely object, or else face the prospect that the federal habeas court will decide the question without the benefit of their views.

The failure of the federal habeas courts generally to require compliance with a contemporaneous objection rule tends to detract from the perception of the trial of a criminal case in state court as a decisive and portentous event. * * * Any procedural rule which encourages the result that those proceedings be as free of error as possible is thoroughly desirable, and the contemporaneous objection rule surely falls within this classification.

We believe the adoption of the *Francis* rule in this situation will have the salutary effect of making the state trial on the merits the "main event," so to speak, rather than a "tryout on the road" for what will later be the determinative federal habeas hearing. There is nothing in the Constitution or in the language of § 2254 which requires that the state trial on the issue of guilt or innocence be devoted largely to the testimony of fact witnesses directed to the elements of the state crime, while only later will there occur in a federal habeas hearing a full airing of the federal constitutional claims which were not raised in the state proceedings. If a criminal defendant thinks that an action of the state trial court is about to deprive him of a federal constitutional right, there is every reason for his following state procedure in making known his objection.

The "cause"-and-"prejudice" exception of the *Francis* rule will afford an adequate guarantee, we think, that the rule will not prevent a federal habeas court from adjudicating for the first time the federal constitutional claim of a defendant who, in the absence of such an adjudication, will be the victim of a miscarriage of justice. Whatever precise content may be given those terms by later cases, we feel confident in holding without further elaboration that they do not exist here. [Sykes] has advanced no explanation whatever for his failure to object at trial, and, as the proceeding unfolded, the trial judge is certainly not to be faulted for failing to question the admission of the confession himself. The other evidence of guilt presented at trial, moreover, was substantial to a degree that would negate any possibility of actual prejudice resulting to [Sykes] from the admission of his inculpatory statement.

We accordingly conclude that the judgment of the Court of Appeals for the Fifth Circuit must be reversed, and the cause remanded to the United

States District Court for the Middle District of Florida with instructions to dismiss [Sykes]'s petition for a writ of habeas corpus.

It is so ordered.

[The concurring opinions of Mr. Chief Justice Burger, Justice Stevens, and Mr. Justice White are omitted.]

■ Mr. JUSTICE BRENNAN, with whom Mr. JUSTICE MARSHALL joins, dissenting.

Over the course of the last decade, the deliberate bypass standard announced in *Fay v. Noia* has played a central role in efforts by the federal judiciary to accommodate the constitutional rights of the individual with the States' interests in the integrity of their judicial procedural regimes. The Court today decides that this standard should no longer apply with respect to procedural defaults occurring during the trial of a criminal defendant. In its place, the Court adopts the two-part "cause"-and-"prejudice" test * * *.

* * * Today's decision makes no effort to provide concrete guidance as to the content of those terms. More particularly, left unanswered is the thorny question that must be recognized to be central to a realistic rationalization of this area of law: how should the federal habeas court treat a procedural default in a state court that is attributable purely and simply to the error or negligence of a defendant's trial counsel? * * *

I

I begin with the threshold question: what is the meaning and import of a procedural default? If it could be assumed that a procedural default, more often than not, is the product of a defendant's conscious refusal to abide by the duly constituted, legitimate processes of the state courts, then I might agree that a regime of collateral review weighted in favor of a State's procedural rules would be warranted. *[Noia]*, however, recognized that such rarely is the case, and therein lies [its] basic unwillingness to embrace a view of habeas jurisdiction that results in "an airtight system of [procedural] forfeitures."

This, of course, is not to deny that there are times when the failure to heed a state procedural requirement stems from an intentional decision to avoid the presentation of constitutional claims to the state forum. *[Noia]* was not insensitive to this possibility. Indeed, the very purpose of its bypass test is to detect and enforce such intentional procedural forfeitures of outstanding constitutionally based claims. *[Noia]* does so through application of the longstanding rule used to test whether action or inaction on the part of a criminal defendant should be construed as a decision to surrender the assertion of rights secured by the Constitution: to be an effective waiver, there must be "an intentional relinqishment or abandonment of a known right or privilege." * * * For this reason, the Court's assertion that it "think[s]" that the *[Noia]* rule encourages intentional "sandbagging" on the part of the defense lawyers is without basis; certainly the Court points to no cases or commentary arising during the past 15 years of actual use of the *[Noia]* test to support this criticism. * * *

But having created the bypass exception to the availability of collateral review, *[Noia]* recognized that intentional, tactical forfeitures are not the norm upon which to build a rational system of federal habeas jurisdiction. In the ordinary case, litigants simply have no incentive to slight the state tribunal, since constitutional adjudication on the state and federal levels are not mutually exclusive. Under the regime of collateral review recognized since the days of *Brown v. Allen* and enforced by the *[Noia]* bypass test, no rational lawyer would risk the "sandbagging" feared by the Court. * * *

In brief then, any realistic system of federal habeas corpus jurisdiction must be premised on the reality that the ordinary procedural default is born of the inadvertence, negligence, inexperience, or incompetence of trial counsel. The case under consideration today is typical. The Court makes no effort to identify a tactical motive for the failure of Sykes' attorney to challenge the admissibility or reliability of a highly inculpatory statement. * * * Indeed, there is no basis for inferring that Sykes or his state trial lawyer was even aware of the existence of his claim under the Fifth Amendment; for this is not a case where the trial judge expressly drew the attention of the defense to a possible constitutional contention or procedural requirement, or where the defense signals its knowledge of a constitutional claim by abandoning a challenge previously raised. Rather, any realistic reading of the record demonstrates that we are faced here with a lawyer's simple error. * * *

II

What are the interests that Sykes can assert in preserving the availability of federal collateral relief in the face of his inadvertent state procedural default? Two are paramount.

As is true with any federal habeas applicant, Sykes seeks access to the federal court for the determination of the validity of his federal constitutional claim. Since at least *Brown v. Allen*, it has been recognized that the "fair effect [of] the habeas corpus jurisdiction as enacted by Congress" entitles a state prisoner to such federal review. While some of my Brethren may feel uncomfortable with this congressional choice of policy, the Legislative Branch nonetheless remains entirely free to determine that the constitutional rights of an individual subject to state custody * * * are best preserved by "interpos[ing] the federal courts between the States and the people, as guardians of the people's federal rights * * *."

With respect to federal habeas corpus jurisdiction, Congress explicitly chose to effectuate the federal court's primary responsibility for preserving federal rights and privileges by authorizing the litigation of constitutional claims and defenses in a district court after the State vindicates its own interest through trial of the substantive criminal offense in the state courts. This, of course, was not the only course that Congress might have followed: as an alternative, it might well have decided entirely to circumvent all state procedure through the expansion of existing federal removal statutes * * *, thereby authorizing the pretrial transfer of all state criminal cases to the federal courts whenever federal defenses or claims are in issue. But liberal post-trial federal review is the redress that Congress ultimately chose to allow and the consequences of a state procedural default should be evaluated in conformance with this policy choice. Certainly we can all agree that, once a state court has assumed jurisdiction of a criminal case, the integrity of its own process is a matter of legitimate concern. The *[Noia]* bypass test, by seeking to discover intentional abuses of the rules of the state forum, is, I believe, compatible with this state institutional interest. But whether *[Noia]* was correct in penalizing a litigant solely for his intentional forfeitures properly must be read in light of Congress' desired norm of widened post-trial access to the federal courts. If the standard adopted today is later construed to require that the simple mistakes of attorneys are to be treated as binding forfeitures, it would serve to subordinate the fundamental rights contained in our constitutional charter to inadvertent defaults of rules promulgated by state agencies, and would essentially leave it to the States, through the enactment of procedure and the certification of the competence of local attorneys, to determine whether a habeas applicant will be permitted the access to the federal forum that is guaranteed him by Congress.

* * * But federal review is not the full measure of Sykes' interest, for there is another of even greater immediacy: assuring that his constitutional claims can be addressed to some court. For the obvious consequence of barring Sykes from the federal courthouse is to insulate Florida's alleged constitutional violation from any and all judicial review because of a lawyer's mistake. * * *

* * * That the State legitimately desires to preserve an orderly and efficient judicial process is undeniable. But similar interests of efficiency and the like also can be identified with respect to other state institutions, such as its law enforcement agencies. Yet, as was only recently reconfirmed, we would not permit and have not permitted the state police to enhance the orderliness and efficiency of their law enforcement activities by embarking on a campaign of acquiring inadvertent waivers of important constitutional rights.

A procedural default should be treated accordingly. Indeed, a recent development in the law of habeas corpus suggests that adherence to the deliberate-bypass test may be more easily justified today than it was when [Noia] was decided. It also suggests that the "prejudice" prong of the Court's new test may prove to be a redundancy. Last Term, the Court ruled that alleged violations of the Fourth Amendment in most circumstances no longer will be cognizable in habeas corpus. Stone v. Powell, 428 U. S. 465 (1976). While, for me, the principle that generated this conclusion was not readily apparent, I expressed my concern that the Stone decision contains the seeds for the exclusion from collateral review of a variety of constitutional rights that my Brethren somehow deem to be unimportant—perhaps those that they are able to conclude are not "guilt-related." If this trail is to be followed, it would be quite unthinkable that an unintentional procedural default should be allowed to stand in the way of vindication of constitutional rights bearing upon the guilt or innocence of a defendant. Indeed, if, as has been argued, a key to decision in this area turns upon a comparison of the importance of the constitutional right at stake with the state procedural rule, then the Court's threshold effort to identify those rights of sufficient importance to be litigated collaterally should largely predetermine the outcome of this balance. * * *

III

A regime of federal habeas corpus jurisdiction that permits the reopening of state procedural defaults does not invalidate any state procedural rule as such; Florida's courts remain entirely free to enforce their own rules as they choose, and to deny any and all state rights and remedies to a defendant who fails to comply with applicable state procedure. The relevant inquiry is whether * * * the fulfillment of important interests of the State necessitates that federal courts be called upon to impose additional sanctions for inadvertent noncompliance with state procedural requirements such as the contemporaneous objection rule involved here.

* * * The strict enforcement of procedural defaults * * * may be seen as a means of deterring any tendency on the part of the defense to slight the state forum, to deny state judges their due opportunity for playing a meaningful role in the evolving task of constitutional adjudication, or to mock the needed finality of criminal trials. * * *

The question remains, however, whether any of these policies or interests are efficiently and fairly served by enforcing both intentional and inadvertent defaults pursuant to the identical stringent standard. * * * [N]o standard stricter than *[Noia's]* deliberate-bypass test is realistically defensible.

Punishing a lawyer's unintentional errors by closing the federal courthouse door to his client is both a senseless and misdirected method of deterring the slighting of state rules. It is senseless because unplanned and unintentional action of any kind generally is not subject to deterrence; and, to the extent that it is hoped that a threatened sanction addressed to the defense will induce greater care and caution on the part of trial lawyers, thereby forestalling negligent conduct or error, the potential loss of all valuable state remedies would be sufficient to this end. And it is a misdirected sanction because, even if the penalization of incompetence or carelessness will encourage more thorough legal training and trial preparation, the habeas applicant, as opposed to his lawyer, hardly is the proper recipient of such a penalty. Especially with fundamental constitutional rights at stake, no fictional relationship of principal-agent or the like can justify holding the criminal defendant accountable for the naked errors of his attorney. This is especially true when so many indigent defendants are without any realistic choice in selecting who ultimately represents them at trial. Indeed, if responsibility for error must be apportioned between the parties, it is the State, through its attorney's admissions and certification policies, that is more fairly held to blame for the fact that practicing lawyers too often are ill-prepared or ill-equipped to act carefully and knowledgeably when faced with decisions governed by state procedural requirements.

* * * I can understand the Court's wistfully wishing for the day when the trial was the sole, binding and final "event" of the adversarial process * * *. But it should be plain that, in the real world, the interest in finality is repeatedly compromised in numerous ways that arise with far greater frequency than do procedural defaults. The federal criminal system, to take one example, expressly disapproves of interlocutory review in the generality of cases even though such a policy would foster finality by permitting the authoritative resolution of all legal and constitutional issues prior to the convening of the "main event." Instead, it relies on the belated correction of error, through appeal and collateral review, to ensure the fairness and legitimacy of the criminal sanction. Indeed, the very existence of the well established right collaterally to reopen issues previously litigated before the state courts represents a congressional policy choice that is inconsistent with notions of strict finality * * *. Ultimately, all of these limitations on the finality of criminal convictions emerge from the tension between justice and efficiency in a judicial system that hopes to remain true to its principles and ideals. Reasonable people may disagree on how best to resolve these tensions. But the solution that today's decision risks embracing seems to me the most unfair of all: the denial of any judicial consideration of the constitutional claims of a criminal defendant because of errors made by his attorney which lie outside the power of the habeas petitioner to prevent or

deter and for which, under no view of morality or ethics, can he be held responsible. * * *

IV

* * * [T]he only thing clear about the Court's "cause"-and-"prejudice" standard is that it exhibits the notable tendency of keeping prisoners in jail without addressing their constitutional complaints. Hence, as of today, all we know of the "cause" standard is its requirement that habeas applicants bear an undefined burden of explanation for the failure to obey the state rule. Left unresolved is whether a habeas petitioner like Sykes can adequately discharge this burden by offering the commonplace and truthful explanation for his default: attorney ignorance or error beyond the client's control. The "prejudice" inquiry, meanwhile, appears to bear a strong resemblance to harmless error doctrine. I disagree with the Court's appraisal of the harmlessness of the admission of [Sykes]'s confession, but if this is what is meant by prejudice, [Sykes]'s constitutional contentions could be as quickly and easily disposed of in this regard by permitting federal courts to reach the merits of his complaint. * * *

NOTES AND QUESTIONS ON SYKES

1)   Overruling *Noia*. *Sykes* and *Noia* both involved the standard for "excusing" a procedural default. *Noia* crafted a "deliberate bypass" standard, and *Sykes* required a showing of "cause and prejudice." *Sykes* did not formally overrule *Noia*; by its own terms, *Sykes* just cabined Justice Brennan's famous 1963 opinion to the specific instances of attorney conduct that *Noia* involved. But did *Sykes* really just limit *Noia* to its facts? Or was it part of an effort to eradicate "deliberate bypass" entirely? Why do you think the Court did not overturn *Noia* in 1977? Finally, in 1991, came the denouement:

> We now make it explicit: In all cases in which a state prisoner has defaulted his federal claims in state court pursuant to an independent and adequate state procedural rule, federal habeas review of the claims is barred unless the prisoner can demonstrate cause for the default and actual prejudice as a result of the alleged violation of federal law, or demonstrate that failure to consider the claims will result in a fundamental miscarriage of justice. [*Noia*] was based on a conception of federal/state relations that undervalued the importance of state procedural rules. The several cases after [*Noia*] that applied the cause and prejudice standard to a variety of state procedural defaults represent a different view. We now recognize the important interest in finality served by state procedural rules, and the significant harm to the States that results from the failure of federal courts to respect them.

Coleman v. Thompson, 501 U.S. 722, 750 (1991).

2)   Tracing the Precedent. *Sykes* grounds the cause-and-prejudice standard in two prior decisions: *Davis v. United States,* 411 U.S. 233 (1973) and *Francis v. Henderson,* 425 U.S. 536 (1976). *Davis* applied a cause-and-prejudice standard to a failure to lodge a pre-trial objection to federal jury composition. *Francis* then applied the same standard to an objection to a state jury composition. *Francis*, in part, was premised on the idea that there should not be a different standard for forfeiture based on whether the case was tried before a state or a federal jury. How can such a difference be reconciled with the purposes behind the procedural default doctrine? What inevitably happens if the Supreme Court articulates a less deferential rule for federal trials, then ultimately seeks uniform treatment of state and federal forfeiture? For an argument that the cause-and-prejudice rule restricts relief more dramatically than does any Court-announced limit on cognizability, see Peter W. Tague, *Federal Habeas Corpus and Ineffective Assistance of Counsel: The Supreme Court Has Work to Do*, 31 Stan. L. Rev. 1, 4 (1978).

3)   Sandbagging. *Sykes* expresses concern about the prospect of "sandbagging." A prisoner sandbags a claim by not raising the challenge in the hopes of litigating the claim in some future proceeding, presumably before a more favorable forum. If Sykes's lawyer was trying to sandbag, then the lawyer must have made a trial decision not to challenge Sykes' ability to understand the *Miranda* warnings. The lawyer must have hoped, the logic goes, that the jury would find Sykes not guilty at trial. If Sykes lost, he would have a "trump" card to raise on appeal—the claim that those inculpatory statements were unconstitutionally introduced at trial. Do you think that Sykes' lawyer was thinking that strategically? Or was the lawyer just ineffective? According to the Court, why is the "deliberate-bypass" standard insufficient to deal with the problem? Justice Brennan seems particularly troubled by the Court's argument: "the Court points to no cases or commentary arising during the past 15 years of actual use of the *Fay* test to support this criticism." Why does Justice Brennan think that the deliberate-bypass standard works well enough?

The sandbagging concern recurs throughout the jurisprudence of the Burger, Rehnquist, and Roberts Courts.[n] Several prominent academics have argued that the risk of sandbagging is actually quite small. See, e.g., Daniel J. Meltzer, *State Court Forfeitures of Federal Rights*, 99 Harv. L. Rev. 1128, 1197 (1986) (observing that "strong countervailing pressures against intentionally withholding a claim for later consideration in a federal habeas corpus proceeding"); Bryan A. Stevenson, *Confronting Mass Imprisonment and Restoring Fairness to Collateral Review of Criminal Cases*, 41 Harv. C.R.-C.L. L. REV. 339, 351 (2006) (characterizing the sandbagging claim as being subject to "serious doubt"). Are there greater incentives to sandbag the court with particular types of claims? Based on what you know, have the incentives to sandbag changed since *Sykes*?

4)   Attorney Error. Justice Brennan argues that the standard for excusing procedural defaults must, above all else, grapple with the incidence and consequences of attorney error. What reasons exist for penalizing a prisoner for an attorney's mistake? What are the judicial challenges to a system that seeks to distinguish between attorney mistakes in which the client was complicit and those in which the client was not? Consider how the standard might vary depending on whether the attorney error occurred on direct review of the conviction or on collateral review. Moreover, should there be a different system for prisoners who proceed *pro se*, as they often do in state collateral proceedings?

---

[n] Professor R. Lea Brilmayer captures the gist of the difference in the views of the Warren and Burger Courts: "[I]t may be important whether the procedural irregularity was an innocent and somewhat technical mistake or a deliberate flouting of proper procedures. The Warren Court was relatively willing to characterize defense mistakes as innocent; the Burger Court sees them as likely sandbagging[.]" R. Lea Brilmayer, *State Forfeiture Rules and Federal Review of State Criminal Convictions*, 49 U. Chi. L. Rev. 741, 773 (1982).

5)   Contemporaneous Objection. The particular state rule here, a contemporaneous-objection rule, involves a decision that is particularly subject to attorney's control. During trial, will the defendant be able to tap counsel on the shoulder and insist that he object at the moment that evidence is to be introduced? The contemporaneous-objection rule nonetheless serves the important interest of incentivizing trial adjudication of objections—when any error can be corrected at the "main event," as the Court puts it. However, the Court applies the procedural default doctrine to other state rules, including those that do not apply during a trial—but rather those during post-trial, appeals, or post-conviction proceedings. See Engle v. Isaac, 456 U.S. 107, 129 (1982) ("The costs outlined above do not depend upon the type of claim raised by the prisoner."); Murray v. Carrier, 477 U.S. 478, 493–496 (1986) (rejecting the proposition that the cause-and-prejudice inquiry should be part of an overall assessment of justice). Should the application of the procedural default rule reflect a particularized state interest in state forfeiture criteria, or a particularized assessment of the constitutional violation involved?

6)   Coleman v. Thompson. In *Coleman v. Thompson,* 501 U.S. 722 (1991), the Court extended the cause-and-prejudice analysis to all types of procedural defaults. Coleman's lawyers filed a state habeas petition, which the state trial court dismissed. The lawyers then filed a defective notice of appeal in state court, which was arguably filed one day late. The Court held that the untimely state appellate filing procedurally defaulted every claim in the state habeas petition, including an IAC claim. Coleman could only excuse the procedural default by showing cause and prejudice under the *Sykes* test. Theoretically, the inmate in *Sykes* could have sought to excuse his defaulted claim by arguing that his lawyer was ineffective for failing to make the contemporaneous objection. The Court held that Coleman could not invoke the inadequacy of his post-conviction his lawyer as cause for default of the IAC claim, because there is no right to effective assistance of counsel during post-conviction proceedings. The result of *Coleman,* then, was that bad lawyering would never excuse a state forfeiture unless the forfeiture occurred in a forum where an inmate had a constitutional right to effective assistance. Is that result problematic? There are certain claims that are difficult to raise during direct review—the only phase of criminal process where there is a constitutional right to counsel—including claims challenging the effectiveness of the trial lawyer's representation. The Court revisited that problem in *Martinez v. Ryan,* 132 S.Ct. 1309 (2012), the case discussed after the Notes that follow.

NOTES ON THE MECHANICS OF PROCEDURAL DEFAULT INQUIRY

Determining whether a claim was procedurally defaulted involves a careful analysis of the procedural history of the litigation, of the pertinent state court rulings, and of state law and procedure in general. Just like the exhaustion analysis, the procedural default analysis applies on a "claim-by-claim" basis, rather than on a "petition-by-petition" basis. In other words, a procedural bar is applied against a *claim* made *in* a habeas petition, not against a *habeas petition* as a whole. Note, however, an important difference between this procedural default analysis and the exhaustion analysis. The exhaustion analysis is set out in detail in 28 U.S.C. § 2254(b), and Congress revised the procedures in

AEDPA. In contrast, the habeas statute has never referred to the doctrine of procedural default. The procedural default inquiry is exclusively judge-made.

After the state pleads procedural default—or the court raises the issue *sua sponte*—the inquiry proceeds in two parts. First, a federal court must decide whether the claim is procedurally defaulted—whether there is an adequate and independent state ground that forms the basis for a state order denying a claim. Second, a federal court must decide whether the default is nonetheless "excused," either because the claimant can show "cause and prejudice" or a "miscarriage of justice."

1) An Adequate and Independent State Rule.

a) Pleading Procedural Default. The State should assert procedural default as an affirmative defense, but a federal court may assert the procedural default rule *sua sponte*. Cf. Trest v. Cain, 522 U.S. 87 (observing the prevailing lower-court rule that procedural default should function as an affirmative defense that a court can nonetheless consider *sua sponte*). Even though a federal court can raise procedural default on its own initiative, a court is not required to do so, and the State may be deemed to have waived the defense. See Lee v. Kemna, 534 U.S. 36, 376 n.8 (2002).

b) Adequacy. The main issue, of course, is *what* the State has to plead: adequate and independent state grounds. Adequacy ensures that a procedural rule is regularly applied in a way that does not discriminate against federal rights—that it is a "firmly established and regularly followed" state practice. James v. Kentucky, 466 U.S. 341 (1984) (defining "adequacy" in direct-review case).

c) Independence. Independence ensures that the state court denied relief on a ground that does not involve a subsidiary and substantial ruling of federal law. See Coleman v. Thompson, 501 U.S. 722, 725 (1991).

d) Forfeited Claims. Often a claim is unexhausted because the prisoner simply failed to include bring that claim in state court proceedings. State statutes of limitations will typically bar the prisoner from trying to assert that claim in a second state court proceeding. Where a claim is unexhausted but the prisoner will surely violate a procedural rule were the litigation to return to state court, must an inmate go back to state court to take a futile stab at state relief? Federal law does not require state prisoners to return to state court in such circumstances; a federal court may simply treat the claim as defaulted and then determine whether the default is excused. Cf. Woodford v. Ngo, 548 U.S. 81, 92–93 (2006) ("In habeas, state-court remedies are described as having been 'exhausted' when they are no longer available, regardless of the reason for their unavailability[; but the claims are procedurally defaulted]"); *Coleman*, 501 U.S. at 732 ("A habeas petitioner who has defaulted his federal claims in state court meets the technical requirements for exhaustion; there are no state remedies any longer 'available' to him.")

e) State Grounds for Denying Relief. A procedural default, unless the claim is never presented to state courts, requires that a state court have *actually* relied upon the adequate and independent state ground asserted as the basis for its ruling. If the state court discussed the merits of a federal claim or referred to a federal law standard, without citing to any state law reason for denying relief, then there is no question that the state court relied on federal grounds when it denied relief. State post-conviction rulings, however, are often summary orders that do not clearly provide the reasoning of the court that issues them. How should a federal judge interpret such decisions by state courts?

f)   Ambiguous State Court Rulings. The short answer is that ambiguous state court rulings are typically presumed to rely on adequate and independent state grounds. Some explanation is in order. One approach could have been to follow the Supreme Court's rule for direct-review cases, in which there exists a presumption that, in ambiguous cases, a state decision does not rely on an adequate and independent basis. See Michigan v. Long, 463 U.S. 1032 (1983). In *Coleman v. Thompson*, 501 U.S. 722 (1991), however, the Court rejected that approach for federal habeas corpus review. The Court reasoned that the direct-review presumption was premised on an empirical generalization that ambiguous state judgments usually rested on federal grounds. *Coleman* held that, as an empirical matter, such generalizations did not describe run-of-the-mill orders denying state post-conviction relief. *Coleman* also grounded the rule on the "dignitary interest" of the States:

> State courts presumably have a dignitary interest in seeing that their state law decisions are not ignored by a federal habeas court, but most of the price paid for federal review of state prisoner claims is paid by the State. When a federal habeas court considers the federal claims of a prisoner in state custody for independent and adequate state law reasons, it is the State that must respond. It is the State that pays the price in terms of the uncertainty and delay added to the enforcement of its criminal laws. It is the State that must retry the petitioner if the federal courts reverse his conviction. If a state court, in the course of disposing of cases on its overcrowded docket, neglects to provide a clear and express statement of procedural default, or is insufficiently motivated to do so, there is little the State can do about it. Yet it is primarily respect for the State's interests that underlies the application of the independent and adequate state ground doctrine in federal habeas.

> A broad presumption would also put too great a burden on the state courts. It remains the duty of the federal courts, whether this Court on direct review, or lower federal courts in habeas, to determine the scope of the relevant state court judgment. We can establish a *per se* rule that eases the burden of inquiry on the federal courts in those cases where there are few costs to doing so, but we have no power to tell state courts how they must write their opinions. We encourage state courts to express plainly, in every decision potentially subject to federal review, the grounds upon which its judgment rests, but we will not impose on state courts the responsibility for using particular language in every case in which a state prisoner presents a federal claim—every state appeal, every denial of state collateral review—in order that federal courts might not be bothered with reviewing state law and the record in the case.

What happens if the state court did not clearly articulate a reason for dismissing the prisoner's claims? *Coleman* held that, even if the state court opinion was ambiguous, so long as the state court did not expressly rely on federal law or discuss the merits of the federal claim, the federal judge should assume that the state court relied on the procedural default—the adequate and independent state law ground.

g)   Looking Back to Lower State Court Rulings. State post-conviction rulings are commonly summary orders, but the existence of a summary order from a state supreme court does not necessarily end the inquiry. *Coleman* only sets up a presumption. The federal judge may look at prior rulings in the case to try to infer the basis for state disposition. In the *Coleman* companion case, *Ylst v. Nunnemaker*, 501 U.S. 797 (1991), the Supreme Court held that a federal court may use the "last reasoned opinion on the claim" to identify the state court's ground for denying relief: "where there has been one reasoned state judgment rejecting a federal claim, later unexplained orders upholding that judgment or rejecting the same claim rest upon the same ground . . ."

2)   Cause and Prejudice. After a state respondent proves that a state court denied relief based on an adequate-and-independent state ground, a claimant may seek to "excuse" the procedural default, either by showing "cause and prejudice" or by demonstrating that a default would result in a "miscarriage of justice." *Sykes* introduced "cause and prejudice" into the procedural default jurisprudence, but *Sykes* did not precisely define what cause, prejudice, or miscarriage of justice meant. It left the content of those inquiries for future decisions.

a)   Cause. A state prisoner shows that there is "cause" for a procedural default by proving that something *external*—"some objective factor external to the defense," such as government interference—resulted in the failure to comply with state procedures. See Murray v. Carrier, 477 U.S. 478, 488 (1986). The Court has resisted attempts to have it declare an exhaustive catalogue of what can provide cause. See, e.g., Edwards v. Carpenter, 529 U.S. 466, 451 (2000) ("[W]e have not identified with precision exactly what constitutes 'cause' to excuse a procedural default.")

The Court has nonetheless clarified that certain events qualify and certain events do not. For example, if the government concealed a written policy of discrimination regarding jury selection, then there is cause for default. See Amadeo v. Zant, 486 U.S. 214 (1988); see also Strickler v. Greene, 527 U.S. 263 (1998) (finding that state suppression of documents constituted cause for default of *Brady* claim). Why does the Court focus so intensely on the requirement that the cause be "external" to the defense? Should new law or newly discovered facts count as "cause" for a default?

The most common form of cause asserted is ineffective legal representation: that the convict's lawyer failed to comply with a state procedural rule. In *Murray v. Carrier*, 477 U.S. 478 (1986), the Court held that as "long as a defendant is represented by counsel whose performance is not constitutionally ineffective under [*Strickland*], we discern no inequity in requiring him to bear the risk of attorney error that results in a procedural default." As a result, ineffective assistance of counsel can constitute "cause" for a procedural default, but only if a prisoner can show that the lawyer's ineffectiveness rose to a level that satisfied *Strickland*. In contrast, substandard legal representation usually cannot excuse a default where no right to effective assistance of counsel attaches. The Supreme Court has repeatedly held that there is no constitutional right to counsel in post-conviction proceedings. See, e.g., Murray v. Giarratano, 492 U.S. 1, 6 (1989) (Opinion of Rehnquist, J.) ("[We have] ruled that neither the Due Process Clause of the Fourteenth Amendment nor the equal protection guarantee of 'meaningful access' required the State to appoint counsel for indigent prisoners seeking state postconviction relief."); Pennsylvania v. Finley, 481 U.S. 551 (1987) ("We have never held that prisoners have a constitutional right to counsel when mounting collateral attacks upon their convictions . . .

and we decline to so hold today."). *Coleman* emphasized that deficient performance of state post-conviction counsel cannot ordinarily excuse default because there is no constitutional right to effective assistance during state post-conviction proceedings. The exception to that general rule is the subject of *Martinez v. Ryan*, 132 S.Ct. 1309 (2012), excerpted below.

b)   Prejudice. Before a prisoner can satisfy the cause-and-prejudice gateway, there has to be prejudice. Just as the Supreme Court has not provided a detailed definition of "cause," the Court has also failed to provide a single formal definition of prejudice. The Court has said that a prisoner must show more than a "possibility of prejudice." United States v. Frady, 456 U.S. 152 (1982). The Court's formulations of the prejudice requirement, however, have varied considerably. The issue of prejudice in the cause-and-prejudice inquiry is often discussed by reference the requirement that an IAC claimant show prejudice—that there be a "reasonable probability" that the constitutionally deficient legal representation was outcome affective. No matter how the standard is articulated, the Supreme Court has made clear that a prisoner must show "actual prejudice"—not just the possibility thereof—but what that showing requires is far from clear.[o] If you were constructing a prejudice standard, what would it look like? Would the amount of prejudice necessary to satisfy the default rule vary with respect to the constitutional claim at issue?

3)   The Miscarriage of Justice Exception. The second excuse mentioned in *Sykes,* but not defined in that decision, permits a court to revive a procedurally defaulted claim when a failure to do so would result in a "fundamental miscarriage of justice." Recall from the last chapter that, although *Herrera v. Collins* did not recognize a freestanding innocence claim, the Supreme Court was careful to note "that is not to say that our habeas jurisprudence casts a blind eye toward innocence." The Court observed that, in a series of cases, it had recognized an innocence-based "fundamental miscarriage of justice exception" as "a gateway through which a habeas petitioner must pass to have his otherwise barred constitutional claim considered on the merits." The Subsection after next develops, in greater detail, the standards for applying that innocence "gateway."

4)   Order of Operation. The Supreme Court has indicated that a federal judge should typically address questions regarding exhaustion and procedural default before addressing the merits: "the procedural-bar issue should ordinarily be considered first." Lambrix v. Singletary, 520 U.S. 518, 524 (1997). The

---

[o] Professors Randy Hertz and James Liebman analyzed the decisional law and listed the various prejudice standards in increasing order of stringency: (1) a "harmless beyond a reasonable doubt" standard from *Chapman v. California*, 386 U.S. 18 (1967), used in direct review of constitutional errors in criminal convictions; (2) a "substantial and injurious effect on the verdict" standard from *Kotteakos v. United States*, 328 U.S. 750 (1946), used in direct review of nonconstitutional errors in criminal convictions; (3) a "but for which a prisoner might not have been convicted of murder" standard from *Reed v. Ross*, 468 U.S. 1 (1984); (4) a "reasonable or significant likelihood that error affected the judgment" standard borrowed from *Brady* cases; and (5) a "reasonable probability that the judgment would have been different" standard borrowed from the prejudice prong of IAC analysis. See Hertz & Liebman, *FHCPP, supra* note e, at § 26.3[c], p. 1509–11 (collecting cases). To compound the confusion, some errors are sufficiently egregious that a court presumes prejudice under the procedural default inquiry. See, e.g., Amadeo v. Zant, 486 U.S. 214, 228 n.6 (1988) (holding that intentional racial discrimination in constructing jury lists was a structural error for which a federal court should presume prejudice). For a piece exploring the Circuit splits and uncertainties in the meaning of the "prejudice" requirement, see Amy Knight Burns, *Insurmountable Obstacles: Structural Errors, Procedural Default, and Ineffective Assistance*, 64 Stan. L. Rev. 727 (2012).

Court added that one reason for this order of operation is that "Constitutional issues are generally to be avoided." The Court, however, also noted that "[j]udicial economy might counsel" addressing a merits question first (there an issue of nonretroactivity), "if it were easily resolvable against the habeas petitioner, whereas the procedural-bar issue involved complicated issues of state law."

5) Review. Consider the following hypothetical scenarios and answer whether each claim would be considered procedurally defaulted and, if prompted, whether that default would be excused:

a) The federal habeas petitioner had filed a timely state post-conviction petition, but the state court denied leave to amend the petition to add an IAC claim. State court rules give district courts discretion over whether to give leave to amend habeas petitions. Is the IAC claim defaulted?

b) Same as above, but state courts may only grant leave to amend a state habeas petition within 30 days of filing the original. The petitioner asked to add the IAC claim 45 days after filing the original petition. Is the IAC claim defaulted?

c) Same as (b), but the state judge also stated *both* that amendment was untimely and that "petitioner's *Strickland v. Washington* claim lacks merit."

d) Same as (c), but the state supreme court affirmed the district court's denial of relief, stating only "denial of the lower court is affirmed."

e) Same as (c), but the state supreme court affirmed the district court's denial of relief, stating that "we agree that the amended petition was filed late."

f) What if a *Brady* claim that was not included in the first state post-conviction petition. A concealed forensic laboratory report provided strong evidence of innocence, but it was not uncovered until a lab official disclosed its existence for the first time shortly before the federal habeas petition was filed. It is now one year too late, under state rules, to file a state post-conviction petition; when the second state post-conviction petition was filed with the *Brady* claim, it was dismissed as untimely. Can the petitioner show "cause and prejudice" to excuse the default in the federal proceeding?

g) Suppose that the forensic report in (f) would have powerfully affected the jury. Assume that it was a test on bandana worn by the assailant, and that the test results conclusively excluded the prisoner and pointed to another unknown individual. Would that make the case for showing "cause and prejudice" stronger? Without knowing yet the details of the standards for making such a showing, do you think that such a case should instead be analyzed separately as a possible "miscarriage of justice"?

INTRODUCTORY NOTE TO MARTINEZ V. RYAN

The Supreme Court significantly amended the cause-and-prejudice rule in two cases argued on the same day: *Maples v. Thomas*, 132 S.Ct. 912 (2012) and *Martinez v. Ryan*, 132 S.Ct. 1309 (2012). Recall *Coleman's* holdings that: there is no constitutional right to counsel in state post-conviction proceedings, there can be no IAC claim arising out of a proceeding where there is no right to counsel, and attorney error cannot constitute excuse a procedural default unless the error rises to the level of a formal IAC claim. The Court explained that "[a]ttorney ignorance or inadvertence is not 'cause' because the attorney is the petitioner's agent when acting, or failing to act, in furtherance of the litigation, and the petitioner must bear the risk of attorney error." *Coleman* also contained an important caveat to its otherwise-categorical holding that an attorney's state post-conviction performance cannot constitute excuse an otherwise-defaulted claim:

> We reiterate that counsel's ineffectiveness will constitute cause only if it is an independent constitutional violation. [Prior cases establish the general rule that] there is no right to counsel in state collateral proceedings. For Coleman to prevail, therefore, there must be an exception to the [general rule] where state collateral review is the first place a prisoner can present a challenge to his conviction. We need not answer this question broadly, however, [because Coleman's state post-conviction counsel was effective before the trial court, and his argument is limited to attorney performance of the state post-conviction appeal].

Coleman therefore left two questions open. The first was an abandonment issue—what happens when a state post-conviction attorney is "acting, or failing to act, in furtherance of the litigation[.]" The second involved situations where "state collateral review is the first place a prisoner can present a challenge to his conviction."

With respect to abandonment, in 2012, the Supreme Court decided *Maples v. Thomas*. Alabama capitally sentenced Cory Maples in 1997, for killing two people. Maples' trial lawyers were underfunded and had almost no experience in capital cases. Maples eventually filed a state post-conviction application, alleging ineffective assistance of trial counsel. In state post-conviction proceedings, he was represented *pro bono* by two attorneys from a prominent New York law firm. Maples also had local counsel, with the understanding that local counsel's responsibilities were limited to facilitating the appearance of the out-of-state attorneys and that local counsel would undertake no substantive representation. While the state post-conviction petition remained pending, the out-of-state-attorneys changed jobs and stopped representing Maples. They did not notify the court or facilitate substitution of counsel. Because Maples had no attorney that was actually representing him, his time to appeal the state post-conviction order lapsed; at that point, his claim was procedurally defaulted under federal law.

The Supreme Court held that the ineffective assistance of state post-conviction counsel could provide "cause" for the procedural default of Maples' underlying *Strickland* claim, citing equitable concerns and the fact that the state post-conviction proceedings were the first available opportunity to present the IAC claim. The Court held that Maples had shown "cause" sufficient to excuse the procedural default, reasoning that attorney abandonment is an "extraordinary circumstance"—an external event beyond his control—that caused his default. In an opinion by Justice Ginsburg, the Court observed: "Abandoned by counsel, Maples was left unrepresented at a critical time for his state postconviction petition, and he lacked a clue of any need to protect himself *pro se*. In these circumstances, no just system would lay the default at Maples' death-cell door." The Court remanded the case for the lower federal courts to decide prejudice. After *Maples*, attorney abandonment excuses the procedural default of a claim at the state post-conviction phase—even though there is no constitutional right to counsel in that proceeding.

The Court heard *Martinez v. Ryan*, excerpted below, the same day it heard *Maples*. In *Martinez*, the prisoner was not abandoned. Instead, the issue was the major one that the Court left open in *Coleman*—whether, under certain circumstances, ineffective assistance of *post-conviction* counsel could constitute cause to excuse the procedural default of a claim otherwise forfeited in the state post-conviction proceedings. The Court addressed whether a pro se litigant that inadvertently failed to assert a *Strickland* claim in the first available state proceedings would similarly have that default excused by a federal habeas court. As you read *Martinez*, consider the logical limits of the holding. Moreover, think about the implications of state institutional design on the treatment of claims during federal habeas review.

Martinez v. Ryan

United States Supreme Court
132 S.Ct. 1309 (2012)

■ JUSTICE KENNEDY delivered the opinion of the Court.

The State of Arizona does not permit a convicted person alleging ineffective assistance of trial counsel to raise that claim on direct review. Instead, the prisoner must bring the claim in state collateral proceedings. In the instant case, however, [Martinez]'s postconviction counsel did not raise the ineffective-assistance claim in the first collateral proceeding, and, indeed, filed a statement that, after reviewing the case, she found no meritorious claims helpful to [Martinez]. On federal habeas review, and with new counsel, [Martinez] sought to argue he had received ineffective assistance of counsel at trial and in the first phase of his state collateral proceeding. Because the state collateral proceeding was the first place to challenge his conviction on grounds of ineffective assistance, [Martinez] maintained he had a constitutional right to an effective attorney in the collateral proceeding. While [Martinez] frames the question in this case as a constitutional one, a more narrow, but still dispositive, formulation is whether a federal habeas court may excuse a procedural default of an ineffective-assistance claim when the claim was not properly presented in state court due to an attorney's errors in an initial-review collateral proceeding.

I

A jury convicted petitioner, Luis Mariano Martinez, of two counts of sexual conduct with a minor under the age of 15. The prosecution introduced a videotaped forensic interview with the victim, Martinez's 11–year–old stepdaughter. It also put in evidence the victim's nightgown, with traces of Martinez's DNA. As part of his defense, Martinez introduced evidence of the victim's recantations, including testimony from the victim's grandmother and mother and a second videotaped interview in which the victim denied any abuse. The victim also denied any abuse when she testified at trial. To explain the inconsistencies, a prosecution expert testified that recantations of child-abuse accusations are caused often by reluctance on the part of the victim's mother to lend support to the child's claims. After considering the conflicting evidence, the jury convicted Martinez. He was sentenced to two consecutive terms of life imprisonment with no possibility of parole for 35 years.

The State appointed a new attorney to represent Martinez in his direct appeal. She made numerous arguments on Martinez's behalf, including a claim that the evidence was insufficient and that newly discovered evidence warranted a new trial. Arizona law, however, did not permit her to argue on direct appeal that trial counsel was ineffective. Arizona instead requires claims of ineffective assistance at trial to be reserved for state collateral proceedings.

While Martinez's direct appeal was pending, the attorney began a state collateral proceeding by filing a "Notice of Post–Conviction Relief." * * * Despite initiating this proceeding, counsel made no claim trial counsel was ineffective and later filed a statement asserting she could find no colorable claims at all. The state trial court hearing the collateral proceeding gave Martinez 45 days to file a *pro se* petition in support of postconviction relief and to raise any claims he believed his counsel overlooked. Martinez did not respond. He later alleged that he was unaware of the ongoing collateral proceedings and that counsel failed to advise him of the need to file a *pro se* petition to preserve his rights. The state trial court dismissed the action for postconviction relief, in effect affirming counsel's determination that Martinez had no meritorious claims. The Arizona Court of Appeals affirmed Martinez's conviction, and the Arizona Supreme Court denied review.

About a year and a half later, Martinez, now represented by new counsel, filed a second notice of postconviction relief in the Arizona trial court. Martinez claimed his trial counsel had been ineffective for failing to challenge the prosecution's evidence. He argued, for example, that his trial counsel should have objected to the expert testimony explaining the victim's recantations or should have called an expert witness in rebuttal. Martinez also faulted trial counsel for not pursuing an exculpatory explanation for the DNA on the nightgown. Martinez's petition was dismissed, in part in reliance on an Arizona Rule barring relief on a claim that could have been raised in a previous collateral proceeding. Martinez, the theory went, should have asserted the claims of ineffective assistance of trial counsel in his first notice for postconviction relief. The Arizona Court of Appeals agreed. It denied Martinez relief because he failed to raise his claims in the first collateral proceeding. The Arizona Supreme Court declined to review Martinez's appeal.

Martinez then sought relief in United States District Court for the District of Arizona, where he filed a petition for a writ of habeas corpus, again raising the ineffective-assistance-of-trial-counsel claims. * * *

* * * [T]he District Court denied the petition, ruling that Arizona's preclusion rule was an adequate and independent state-law ground to bar federal review. * * * [The Ninth Circuit affirmed.]

II

Coleman v. Thompson left open, and the Court of Appeals in this case addressed, a question of constitutional law: whether a prisoner has a right to effective counsel in collateral proceedings which provide the first occasion to raise a claim of ineffective assistance at trial. These proceedings can be called, for purposes of this opinion, "initial-review collateral proceedings." *Coleman* had suggested, though without holding, that the Constitution may require States to provide counsel in initial-review collateral proceedings because "in [these] cases . . . state collateral review is the first place a prisoner can present a challenge to his conviction." As *Coleman* noted, this makes the initial-review collateral proceeding a prisoner's "one and only appeal" as to an ineffective-assistance claim, and this may justify an exception to the constitutional rule that there is no right to counsel in collateral proceedings.

This is not the case, however, to resolve whether that exception exists as a constitutional matter. The precise question here is whether ineffective assistance in an initial-review collateral proceeding on a claim of ineffective assistance at trial may provide cause for a procedural default in a federal habeas proceeding. To protect prisoners with a potentially legitimate claim of ineffective assistance of trial counsel, it is necessary to modify the unqualified statement in *Coleman* that an attorney's ignorance or inadvertence in a postconviction proceeding does not qualify as cause to excuse a procedural default. This opinion qualifies *Coleman* by recognizing a narrow exception: Inadequate assistance of counsel at initial-review collateral proceedings may establish cause for a prisoner's procedural default of a claim of ineffective assistance at trial.

A

* * * The doctrine barring procedurally defaulted claims from being heard is not without exceptions. A prisoner may obtain federal review of a defaulted claim by showing cause for the default and prejudice from a violation of federal law. There is no dispute that Arizona's procedural bar on successive petitions is an independent and adequate state ground. Thus, a federal court can hear Martinez's ineffective-assistance claim only if he can establish cause to excuse the procedural default.

Coleman held that "[n]egligence on the part of a prisoner's postconviction attorney does not qualify as 'cause.'" *Coleman* reasoned that "because the attorney is the prisoner's agent . . . under 'well-settled principles of agency law,' the principal bears the risk of negligent conduct on the part of his agent."

Coleman, however, did not present the occasion to apply this principle to determine whether attorney errors in initial-review collateral proceedings may qualify as cause for a procedural default. The alleged failure of counsel in *Coleman* was on appeal from an initial-review collateral proceeding, and in that proceeding the prisoner's claims had been addressed by the state habeas trial court.

As *Coleman* recognized, this marks a key difference between initial-review collateral proceedings and other kinds of collateral proceedings. When an attorney errs in initial-review collateral proceedings, it is likely that no state court at any level will hear the prisoner's claim. This Court on direct review of the state proceeding could not consider or adjudicate the claim. And if counsel's errors in an initial-review collateral proceeding do not establish cause to excuse the procedural default in a federal habeas proceeding, no court will review the prisoner's claims. * * *

Where, as here, the initial-review collateral proceeding is the first designated proceeding for a prisoner to raise a claim of ineffective assistance at trial, the collateral proceeding is in many ways the equivalent of a prisoner's direct appeal as to the ineffective-assistance claim. This is because the state habeas court "looks to the merits of the clai[m]" of ineffective assistance, no other court has addressed the claim, and "defendants pursuing first-tier review * * * are generally ill equipped to represent themselves" because they do not have a brief from counsel or an opinion of the court addressing their claim of error. * * *

* * * Claims of ineffective assistance at trial often require investigative work and an understanding of trial strategy. When the issue cannot be raised on direct review, moreover, a prisoner asserting an ineffective-assistance-of-trial-counsel claim in an initial-review collateral proceeding cannot rely on a court opinion or the prior work of an attorney addressing that claim. To present a claim of ineffective assistance at trial in accordance with the State's procedures, then, a prisoner likely needs an effective attorney.

The same would be true if the State did not appoint an attorney to assist the prisoner in the initial-review collateral proceeding. The prisoner, unlearned in the law, may not comply with the State's procedural rules or may misapprehend the substantive details of federal constitutional law. While confined to prison, the prisoner is in no position to develop the evidentiary basis for a claim of ineffective assistance, which often turns on evidence outside the trial record.

A prisoner's inability to present a claim of trial error is of particular concern when the claim is one of ineffective assistance of counsel. The right to the effective assistance of counsel at trial is a bedrock principle in our justice system. * * * Indeed, the right to counsel is the foundation for our adversary system. Defense counsel tests the prosecution's case to ensure that the proceedings serve the function of adjudicating guilt or innocence, while protecting the rights of the person charged. * * *

This is not to imply the State acted with any impropriety by reserving the claim of ineffective assistance for a collateral proceeding. Ineffective-assistance claims often depend on evidence outside the trial record. Direct appeals, without evidentiary hearings, may not be as effective as other proceedings for developing the factual basis for the claim. Abbreviated deadlines to expand the record on direct appeal may not allow adequate time for an attorney to investigate the ineffective-assistance claim. Thus, there are sound reasons for deferring consideration of ineffective-assistance-of-trial-counsel claims until the collateral-review stage, but this decision is not without consequences for the State's ability to assert a procedural default in later proceedings. By deliberately choosing to move trial-ineffectiveness claims outside of the direct-appeal process, where counsel is constitutionally guaranteed, the State significantly diminishes prisoners' ability to file such claims. It is within the context of this state procedural framework that counsel's ineffectiveness in an initial-review collateral proceeding qualifies as cause for a procedural default.

The rules for when a prisoner may establish cause to excuse a procedural default are elaborated in the exercise of the Court's discretion. These rules reflect an equitable judgment that only where a prisoner is impeded or obstructed in complying with the State's established procedures will a federal habeas court excuse the prisoner from the usual sanction of default. Allowing a federal habeas court to hear a claim of ineffective assistance of trial counsel when an attorney's errors (or the absence of an attorney) caused a procedural default in an initial-review collateral proceeding acknowledges, as an equitable matter, that the initial-review collateral proceeding, if undertaken without counsel or with ineffective counsel, may not have been sufficient to ensure that proper consideration was given to a substantial claim. From this it follows that, when a State requires a prisoner to raise an ineffective-assistance-of-trial-counsel claim in a collateral proceeding, a prisoner may establish cause for a default of an ineffective-assistance claim in two circumstances. The first is where the state courts did not appoint counsel in the initial-review collateral proceeding for a claim of ineffective assistance at trial. The second is where appointed counsel in the initial-review collateral proceeding, where the claim should have been raised, was ineffective under the standards of *Strickland v. Washington,* 466 U.S. 668 (1984). To overcome the default, a prisoner must also demonstrate that the underlying ineffective-assistance-of-trial-counsel claim is a substantial one, which is to say that the prisoner must demonstrate that the claim has some merit.

Most jurisdictions have in place procedures to ensure counsel is appointed for substantial ineffective-assistance claims. Some States, including Arizona, appoint counsel in every first collateral proceeding. Some States appoint counsel if the claims require an evidentiary hearing, as claims of ineffective assistance often do. * * * Other States appoint counsel if the claims have some merit to them or the state habeas trial court deems the record worthy of further development. It is likely that most of the attorneys appointed by the courts are qualified to perform, and do perform, according to prevailing professional norms; and, where that is so, the States may enforce a procedural default in federal habeas proceedings.

B

This limited qualification to *Coleman* * * * * ought not to put a significant strain on state resources. When faced with the question whether there is cause for an apparent default, a State may answer that the ineffective-assistance-of-trial-counsel claim is insubstantial, *i.e.,* it does not have any merit or that it is wholly without factual support, or that the attorney in the initial-review collateral proceeding did not perform below constitutional standards.

This is but one of the differences between a constitutional ruling and the equitable ruling of this case. A constitutional ruling would provide defendants a freestanding constitutional claim to raise; it would require the appointment of counsel in initial-review collateral proceedings; it would impose the same system of appointing counsel in every State; and it would require a reversal in all state collateral cases on direct review from state courts if the States' system of appointing counsel did not conform to the constitutional rule. An equitable ruling, by contrast, permits States a variety of systems for appointing counsel in initial-review collateral proceedings. And it permits a State to elect between appointing counsel in initial-review collateral proceedings or not asserting a procedural default and raising a defense on the merits in federal habeas proceedings. In addition, state collateral cases on direct review from state courts are unaffected by the ruling in this case.

The rule of *Coleman* governs in all but the limited circumstances recognized here. The holding in this case does not concern attorney errors in other kinds of proceedings, including appeals from initial-review collateral proceedings, second or successive collateral proceedings, and petitions for discretionary review in a State's appellate courts. * * *

In addition, the limited nature of the qualification to *Coleman* adopted here reflects the importance of the right to the effective assistance of trial counsel and Arizona's decision to bar defendants from raising ineffective-assistance claims on direct appeal. * * *

III

Where, under state law, claims of ineffective assistance of trial counsel must be raised in an initial-review collateral proceeding, a procedural default will not bar a federal habeas court from hearing a substantial claim of ineffective assistance at trial if, in the initial-review collateral proceeding, there was no counsel or counsel in that proceeding was ineffective.

In this case Martinez's attorney in the initial-review collateral proceeding filed a notice akin to an *Anders* brief, in effect conceding that Martinez lacked any meritorious claim, including his claim of ineffective assistance at trial. See *Anders v. California,* 386 U.S. 738 (1967). Martinez argued before the federal habeas court that filing the *Anders* brief constituted ineffective assistance. The Court of Appeals did not decide whether that was so. Rather, it held that because Martinez did not have a right to an attorney in the initial-review collateral proceeding, the attorney's errors in the initial-review collateral proceeding could not establish cause for the failure to comply with the State's rules. Thus, the Court of Appeals did not determine whether Martinez's attorney in his first collateral proceeding was ineffective or whether his claim of ineffective assistance of trial counsel is substantial. And the court did not address the question of prejudice. These issues remain open for a decision on remand. * * *

The judgment of the Court of Appeals is reversed, and the case is remanded for further proceedings consistent with this opinion.

It is so ordered.

■ JUSTICE SCALIA, with whom JUSTICE THOMAS joins, dissenting.

* * * Let me get this straight: Out of concern for the values of federalism; to preserve the ability of our States to provide prompt justice; and in light of our longstanding jurisprudence holding that there is no constitutional right to counsel in state collateral review; the Court, in what it portrays as an admirable exercise of judicial restraint, abstains from holding that there is a constitutional right to counsel in initial-review state habeas. After all, that would have meant, in a case such as the one before us, that failing to provide assistance of counsel, or providing assistance of counsel that falls below the *Strickland* standard, would constitute cause for excusing procedural default. Instead of taking that radical step, the Court holds that, *for equitable reasons,* in a case such as the one before us, failing to provide assistance of counsel, or providing assistance of counsel that falls below the *Strickland* standard, constitutes cause for excusing procedural default. The result, of course, is precisely the same.

Ah, but perhaps the explanation of why the Court's action today amounts to praiseworthy self-restraint is this: It pronounces this excuse from the usual rule of procedural default only in initial-review state habeas raising an ineffective-assistance-of-trial-counsel claim. But it could have limited its invention of a new constitutional right to collateral-review counsel in precisely the same fashion—and with precisely the same consequences. Moreover, no one really believes that the newly announced "equitable" rule will remain limited to ineffective-assistance-of-trial-counsel cases. There is not a dime's worth of difference in principle between those cases and many other cases in which initial state habeas will be the first opportunity for a particular claim to be raised: claims of "newly discovered" prosecutorial misconduct, * * * claims based on "newly discovered" exculpatory evidence or "newly discovered" impeachment of prosecutorial witnesses, and claims asserting ineffective assistance of appellate counsel. The Court's soothing assertion that its holding "addresses only the constitutional claims presented in this case," insults the reader's intelligence. * * *

Of course even the *appointment* of state-collateral-review counsel will not guarantee that the State's criminal proceeding can be concluded without years-long federal retrial. Appointment of counsel may, as I have said, avoid federal review of the adequacy of representation that occurred years ago, at the original trial. But since, under today's opinion, the condition for exclusion of federal habeas is the very same condition that would apply if appointment of state-collateral-review counsel were constitutionally required, it will remain to be determined in federal habeas review *whether the state-appointed counsel was effective.* * * *

Rejection of the argument in *Coleman* was compelled by our jurisprudence pertaining to cause for excusing procedural default, and in particular *Murray v. Carrier,* 477 U.S. 478 (1986). *Carrier* involved the failure of a defendant's attorney to raise a claim on direct appeal. This failure did not constitute cause, we explained, because it was not an "objective factor *external* to the defense." This external-factor requirement reflects the judgment that States should not be forced to undergo federal habeas review of a defaulted claim unless a factor not attributable to the prisoner obstructed his compliance with state procedures.

Although this externality requirement has been the North Star of our excuse-for-cause jurisprudence, today's opinion does not whisper its name— no doubt because it is impossible to say that Martinez's procedural default was caused by a factor external to his defense. * * *

Far from avoiding the consequences a constitutional holding would have imposed on the States, today's holding as a practical matter requires States to appoint counsel in initial-review collateral proceedings—and, to boot, eliminates the pre-existing assurance of escaping federal-habeas review for claims that appointed counsel fails to present. Despite the Court's protestations to the contrary, the decision is a radical alteration of our habeas jurisprudence that will impose considerable economic costs on the States and further impair their ability to provide justice in a timely fashion. The balance it strikes between the finality of criminal judgments and the need to provide for review of defaulted claims of ineffective assistance of trial counsel grossly underestimates both the frequency of such claims in federal habeas, and the incentives to argue (since it is a free pass to federal habeas) that appointed counsel was ineffective in failing to raise such claims. The balance might have been close (though it would disregard our established jurisprudence) if the Court merely held that uncounseled failure to raise ineffective assistance of trial counsel would not constitute default. But in *adding* to that the rule that *counseled* failure to raise it may also provide an excuse, the Court creates a monstrosity. For these reasons, I respectfully dissent.

———

NOTES AND QUESTIONS ON MARTINEZ

1) Direct Appeals and IAC Claims. The Supreme Court has held that there is a constitutional right to appellate counsel under the Fourteenth Amendment's Equal Protection Clause, rather than under the Sixth Amendment. See Douglas v. California, 372 U.S. 353, 357 (1963). Consider the practical issues with raising IAC claims during direct-review proceedings. Arizona was not unique; most states do not permit prisoners, during appellate review of the conviction, to raise claims involving matters outside the trial record. As a result, most IAC claims—and other claims that necessarily raise issues outside the trial record—are litigated for the first time during state post-conviction proceedings. Even in states where an appellate court may entertain IAC claims on direct review of the conviction, there are additional questions about whether direct review provides an adequate opportunity to litigate IAC claims. Would a new trial motion be sufficient to get the pertinent information into the appellate record? If the trial lawyer is also handling the appeal, then there are obvious reasons why that lawyer might be reluctant to assert such a claim. As a question of institutional design, do you think that these practical factors properly overcome the traditional paradigm whereby all constitutional issues should be raised as quickly as possible?

2) **A Remedy without a Right.** Professor Steven Vladeck described *Martinez* as having announced a "remedy without a right."[p] Before reading further, consider the basis for that description and whether you agree with it. *Coleman v. Thompson* had earlier affirmed the proposition that there is no constitutional obligation for the state to provide counsel after the direct appeal is over. In *Martinez*, the Supreme Court was clear that it did not reach the question of whether there should be a constitutional rule obliging representation—much less effective representation—during state post-conviction proceedings. As a matter of state law, *Martinez* observes that only "some" jurisdictions provide attorneys to inmates pursuing state post-conviction appeals, except in capital cases and in cases involving "substantial" claims. Does the *Martinez* rule encourage states to pay to provide post-conviction counsel to more state inmates? Is Justice Scalia right that the result will impose "considerable economic costs" on states?

3) **Distinguishing Coleman.** How effectively did *Martinez* distinguish *Coleman*? In *Coleman*, the state post-conviction attorney failed to file a timely notice to appeal a trial-court judgment dismissing the state post-conviction petition. Martinez's IAC claim, by contrast, was omitted entirely from the first state post-conviction filing. Indeed, Martinez's lawyer actually filed a notice stating that she would file no post-conviction claims, because the lawyer believed that none of the claims had merit. *Martinez* distinguished *Coleman* because, in *Coleman*, the inmate at least had a trial forum in which he received adequate assistance for litigating the IAC claim. Are you persuaded that the distinction should yield different outcomes? What is special about that initial opportunity to present a constitutional claim? Given the direction the Court's procedural default jurisprudence took in *Sykes* and then in *Coleman*, were you surprised to see seven Justices in *Martinez* agree to recognize an excuse permitting a federal court to review otherwise procedurally defaulted claims?

4) **Equity and State Post-Conviction Counsel.** The Court was careful to explain that its rule was not constitutional, but grounded in equity and the discretion of the federal judge. *Martinez* was the Court's attempt to reconcile Rehnquist-era procedural default jurisprudence with the role that AEDPA and the Court contemplate for state post-conviction review. The Court emphasized that IAC litigation requires the construction of a substantial record regarding, among other things, the actions and omissions of the trial lawyer. As we will see in the next Chapter, the federal judge's inquiry under 28 U.S.C. § 2254(d) is typically confined to the factual record developed in state court. For that rea-

---

[p] Steve Vladeck, *Opinion Analysis: A new remedy, but no right*, SCOTUSblog, March 21, 2012.

son, and because of the practical limitations involved with litigating IAC claims on appeal of the conviction itself, the state post-conviction proceeding is often the "main event." As a theoretical matter, is that forum the most institutionally appropriate place for the main event? Moreover, think about the source of power asserted to craft the practical rule: equity. The idea that the Court enjoys considerable equitable authority to calibrate the habeas remedy appears in a number of the cases in this Chapter, and reflects a principle that the Court sometimes invokes when it makes law in different custodial categories.

5)   Substantiality. Why did the Court limit the new exception to "substantial" claims of ineffective assistance of counsel? Do you think Martinez's particular claim, regarding his trial lawyer's failure to challenge expert evidence and provide an explanation for the DNA test results, was likely a "substantial" claim of ineffective assistance? Some post-*Martinez* dispositions have denied relief because the prisoners did not show that their claims were sufficiently "substantial." See, e.g., Leavitt v. Arave, 2012 WL 1995091 *1 (D. Idaho June 1, 2012). What would happen if there were no such limitation? Considerable confusion exists over what, precisely, a "substantial" IAC claim is. Do you think the substantiality requirement is a good way to circumscribe the new exception, or do you think it invites more trouble than it is worth?

6)   The Prejudice Inquiry. Ultimately, *Martinez* recognized that ineffective assistance of state post-conviction counsel could excuse forfeiture of a trial-phase IAC claim. But "cause" is only half of the excuse showing that a state inmate must make in order to obtain merits review of the underlying IAC claim. What about the prejudice inquiry? In fact, in a *Martinez* situation, there are really two prejudice inquires—maybe even three. Can you distinguish them conceptually? Even though they are conceptually distinct, do you think an inmate needs to show different things to meet each one, or is a showing of prejudice native to the trial-phase IAC claim sufficient to satisfy the various prejudice requirements?

7)   Extending Martinez to other Types of Claims. *Martinez* applies, as a formal matter, only for IAC claims. Was Justice Scalia correct to observe that the reasoning of the Court could be extended to other post-conviction claims that are "substantial" or that could only be raised for the first time in a state post-conviction proceedings? What should a federal habeas judge do when confronted with deficient post-conviction lawyering of a *Brady* claim? Is there language in *Martinez* that might distinguish IAC claims from *Brady* claims? Would extending the reasoning of *Martinez* in effect eliminate the procedural default doctrine, or is there a natural stopping point that prevents the exception from swallowing the rule? If Justice Scalia correctly predicts that *Martinez* will lead to analogous exceptions for claims that are similarly beyond face of the trial record, then is that outcome a good or a bad thing?

8)   Limiting Martinez based on the Formal Availability of Appellate Review. The Fifth Circuit has held that *Martinez* "does not apply" to Texas claimants, because, at least as a theoretical matter, those claimants can raise an IAC claim on direct review of the conviction. See Ibarra v. Thaler, 687 F.3d 222 (5th Cir. 2012). Specifically, the Fifth Circuit reasoned, IAC claimants could use new-trial motions and appellate remedies to redress their constitutional grievances. What language in *Martinez* supports the rule in *Ibarra*? Is *Ibarra* correct, or did the Court intend a more functional rule focused on whether raising an IAC on direct review of the claim is practical? The degree to which *Ibarra* will gain traction in other jurisdictions is unclear at this time, although at least one other circuit has adopted a similar rule. See Dansby v. Hobbs, 691 F.3d 934 (8th Cir. 2012). The U.S. Supreme Court has just accepted certiorari to review the *Ibarra* question.[q]

C. THE MISCARRIAGE OF JUSTICE EXCEPTION

INTRODUCTORY NOTES ON THE ORIGINS OF THE MISCARRIAGE-OF-JUSTICE EXCEPTION

1)   Miscarriage of Justice as an Excuse for Procedural Default. Recall the steps of the procedural default inquiry. First, the state decision must have been based on an adequate and effective state ground; at that point, the claim is procedurally defaulted and the only question is whether the default is excused. The last Subsection dealt with the first excuse doctrine, "cause and prejudice." The second excuse doctrine involves the "miscarriage of justice" exception, and refers generally to claims of innocence or claims that an offender is categorically ineligible for a punishment. As you proceed through the Notes and the cases excerpted in Subsection C, think about the degree to which the miscarriage-of-justice exception reflects the equitable flavor of habeas jurisprudence, and about how that calculus might change if Congress were to enact more restrictive standards.

2)   Early Concern with Miscarriages of Justice. The Supreme Court had long emphasized that an interest in avoiding a great injustice might excuse a procedural defect that might otherwise preclude relief on the merits. For example, in *Sanders v. United States*, 373 U.S. 1 (1963), the Court held that a habeas court must hear an otherwise-barred claim when required to do so by the "ends of justice," quoting the language from the then-operative Title 28 successive-petition provision. The Court mentioned a miscarriage-of-justice exception again in *Sykes*. The miscarriage-of-justice exception developed in an era before DNA testing showed that wrongful convictions occur far more frequently than many had previously anticipated. Do you think that the miscarriage-of-justice exception should reach all evidence of innocence? Do you think it should reach *only* evidence of innocence? For the argument that the federal habeas standard should reflect Federal Rule of Criminal Procedure 52(b), which includes a "miscarriage-of-justice" standard that reaches non-innocence claims, see Jordan Steiker, *Innocence and Federal Habeas*, 41 U.C.LA. L. Rev. 303, 340 (1992).

3)   Miscarriage-of-Justice Law as a Distinct Excuse for Default. Think about the relationship between the cause-and-prejudice excuse and the miscarriage-of-justice rule. In *Engle v. Isaac,* the Court noted that, in "appropriate cases" the principles underlying the cause-and-prejudice test "must yield to the imperative of correcting a fundamentally unjust incarceration ..." 456 U.S. 107, 135 (1982). There, however, the Court suggested that it was "confident" that any "victims of a fundamental miscarriage of justice will meet the cause-and-prejudice standard." The idea that any miscarriage of justice would satisfy the cause-and-prejudice inquiry is almost certainly wrong; can you explain why? The Court subsequently decided that a miscarriage-of-justice showing would be treated as a stand-alone excuse for procedural defaults—that is, independent of the cause-and-prejudice inquiry. In three decisions handed down in

---

[q] See Trevino v. Thaler, 133 S.Ct. 544 (Oct. 29, 2012).

1986, the Court emphasized that the traditional miscarriage-of-justice exception remained alive and well across multiple categories of procedural doctrines, despite revisions in the federal habeas statute. See Smith v. Murray (applying miscarriage-of-justice gateway to procedurally defaulted claim regarding sentencing error); Murray v. Carrier (affirming the procedural-default gateway "where a constitutional violation has probably resulted in the conviction of one who is actually innocent, a federal habeas court may grant the writ even in the absence of a showing of cause for the procedural default."); Kuhlmann v. Wilson, 477 U.S. 436, 452 (1986) (plurality opinion) (recognizing a successive-petition excuse where habeas petitioner "supplements his constitutional claim with a colorable showing of factual innocence"). For an extensive discussion of how the miscarriage-of-justice gateways developed across the procedural doctrines, see Lee B. Kovarsky, *Death Ineligibility and Habeas Corpus*, 925 Cornell L. Rev. 329, 333–42 (2010).

4) *Schlup v. Delo.* In *Schlup v. Delo*, 513 U.S. 298 (1995), the Court further refined the standard that a prisoner must meet in order to satisfy the miscarriage-of-justice gateway. *Schlup* was technically a successive-petition decision, but federal courts (including the Supreme Court) have referred generally to the "*Schlup* standard" across the various procedural doctrines. Schlup brought IAC and *Brady* claims in a successive petition. Schlup had omitted those claims from his first federal petition and could not show cause for that omission. In particular, Schlup presented sworn statements by several eyewitnesses that he was not involved in the prison murder for which he was convicted. The new evidence also showed that he could not have made it from the scene of the murder to the prison dining room—where a video showed him in line waiting for food. That evidence supported his trial contention that the timing of the crime was such that it would have been impossible for him to have committed it and then be seen on video just moments later.

The lower court borrowed the miscarriage-of-justice standard from *Sawyer v. Whitley*, 505 U.S. 333 (1992) which applied to capital sentencing challenges. That miscarriage-of-justice standard (mentioned in Chapter 3) provided that, in order to satisfy the miscarriage of justice gateway, a prisoner had to show "by clear and convincing evidence that but for a constitutional error, no reasonable juror would have found the petitioner eligible for the death penalty." In *Schlup*, the Supreme Court rejected the more stringent standard from *Sawyer*, instead adopting what amounts to a preponderance of the evidence standard: that a prisoner show that "a constitutional violation has probably resulted in the conviction of one who is actually innocent." The *Schlup* Court explained:

> We note finally that the *Carrier* standard requires a petitioner to show that it is more likely than not that "no reasonable juror" would have convicted him. The word "reasonable" in that formulation is not without meaning. It must be presumed that a reasonable juror would consider fairly all of the evidence presented. It must also be presumed that such a juror would conscientiously obey the instructions of the trial court requiring proof beyond a reasonable doubt.

Why is innocence so important to whether there was a miscarriage of justice? "To ensure that the fundamental miscarriage of justice exception would remain 'rare' and would only be applied in the 'extraordinary case,' while at the same time ensuring that the exception would extend relief to those who were truly deserving, the Court has explicitly tied the miscarriage of justice exception to the petitioner's innocence."

5) Passing Through the Gateway. What happens if a prisoner satisfies the miscarriage-of-justice standard? In other words, what happens if the prisoner "passes through" the gateway? As the term suggests, a gateway showing is not sufficient to entitle a prisoner to relief, because a court must still decide the merits of the constitutional claim. In the course of clarifying the standard, the Court was careful to distinguish a "procedural" *Schlup* argument from a "substantive" *Herrera* claim of freestanding innocence. (The latter might entitle a prisoner to relief solely based on a showing of innocence.) Why is the Court more willing to consider innocence as an excuse permitting consideration of procedurally defaulted claims, but unwilling to recognize—except hypothetically—a constitutional claim of freestanding innocence? Does it have to do with the Court's attitude towards claims of innocence? Or do you think the Court can more freely elaborate equitable exceptions to court-made habeas doctrines than it can recognize new constitutional rights?

6) Applying *Schlup*. How should courts, in practice, conduct the *Schlup* inquiry; how does a judge decide whether new evidence would more likely than not lead to a different result at a trial? The case that follows, *House v. Bell*, 547 U.S. 518 (2006), provided the Court with an opportunity to revisit how judges should apply the *Schlup* standard, and also an opportunity to revisit whether to recognize a freestanding innocence claim. When you read the case, ask yourself which evidence most strongly influenced the majority, and why the dissent was not convinced.

House v. Bell
United States Supreme Court
547 U.S. 518 (2006)

■ JUSTICE KENNEDY delivered the opinion of the Court.

Some 20 years ago in rural Tennessee, Carolyn Muncey was murdered. A jury convicted petitioner Paul Gregory House of the crime and sentenced him to death, but new revelations cast doubt on the jury's verdict. House, protesting his innocence, seeks access to federal court to pursue habeas corpus relief based on constitutional claims that are procedurally barred under state law. * * * In certain exceptional cases involving a compelling claim of actual innocence * * * the state procedural default rule is not a bar to a federal habeas corpus petition. * * * [W]e conclude that House has made the stringent showing required by this exception [and] that his federal habeas action may proceed.

I

* * * Around 3 p.m. on Sunday, July 14, 1985, two local residents found [Mrs. Muncey's] body concealed amid brush and tree branches on an embankment roughly 100 yards up the road from her driveway. Mrs. Muncey had been seen last on the evening before, when, around 8 p.m., she and her two children—Lora Muncey, age 10, and Matthew Muncey, age 8—visited their neighbor, Pam Luttrell. According to Luttrell, Mrs. Muncey mentioned her husband, William Hubert Muncey, Jr., known in the community as "Little Hube" and to his family as "Bubbie." As Luttrell recounted Mrs. Muncey's comment, Mr. Muncey "had gone to dig a grave, and he hadn't come back, but that was all right, because [Mrs. Muncey] was going

to make him take her fishing the next day[.]" Mrs. Muncey returned home, and some time later, before 11:00 p.m. at the latest, Luttrell "heard a car rev its motor as it went down the road," something Mr. Muncey customarily did when he drove by on his way home. * * *

The next afternoon Billy Ray Hensley, the victim's first cousin, heard of Mrs. Muncey's disappearance and went to look for Mr. Muncey. As he approached the Munceys' street, Hensley allegedy "saw Mr. House come out from under a bank, wiping his hands on a black rag." Just when and where Hensley saw House, and how well he could have observed him, were disputed at House's trial.

* * * As he traveled up the road, Hensley saw House traveling in the opposite direction in the white Plymouth. House "flagged [Hensley] down" through his windshield, and the two cars met about 300 feet up the road from the Munceys' driveway. According to Hensley, House said he had heard Mrs. Muncey was missing and was looking for her husband. Though House had only recently moved to the area, he was acquainted with the Munceys, had attended a dance with them, and had visited their home. He later told law enforcement officials he considered both of the Munceys his friends. According to Hensley, House said he had heard that Mrs. Muncey's husband, who was an alcoholic, was elsewhere "getting drunk."

As Hensley drove off, he "got to thinking to [him]self—he's hunting Little Hube, and Little Hube drunk—what would he be doing off that bank * * * ." His suspicion aroused, Hensley later returned to the Munceys' street with a friend named Jack Adkins. The two checked different spots on the embankment, and though Hensley saw nothing where he looked, Adkins found Mrs. Muncey. Her body lay across from the sawmill near the corner where House's car had been parked, dumped in the woods a short way down the bank leading toward a creek.

Around midnight, Dr. Alex Carabia, a practicing pathologist and county medical examiner, performed an autopsy. Dr. Carabia put the time of death between 9 and 11 p.m. * * * The cause of death, in Dr. Carabia's view, was a severe blow to the left forehead * * *.

The county sheriff, informed about Hensley's earlier encounter with House, questioned House shortly after the body was found. That evening, House answered further questions during a voluntary interview at the local jail. Special Agent Ray Presnell of the Tennessee Bureau of Investigation (TBI) prepared a statement of House's answers, which House signed. Asked to describe his whereabouts on the previous evening, House claimed— falsely, as it turned out—that he spent the entire evening with his girl-friend, Donna Turner, at her trailer. Asked whether he was wearing the same pants he had worn the night before, House replied—again, falsely— that he was. House was on probation at the time, having recently been re-leased on parole following a sentence of five years to life for aggravated sexual assault in Utah. House had scratches on his arms and hands, and a knuckle on his right ring finger was bruised. He attributed the scratches to Turner's cats and the finger injury to recent construction work tearing down a shed. The next day House gave a similar statement to a different TBI agent, Charles Scott.

In fact House had not been at Turner's home. After initially supporting House's alibi, Turner informed authorities that House left her trailer around 10:30 or 10:45 p.m. to go for a walk. According to Turner's trial tes-timony, House returned later—she was not sure when—hot and panting, missing his shirt and his shoes. House, Turner testified, told her that while he was walking on the road near her home, a vehicle pulled up beside him, and somebody inside "called him some names and then they told him he didn't belong here anymore." House said he tried to ignore the taunts and keep walking, but the vehicle pulled in behind him, and "one of them got out and grabbed him by the shoulder * * * and [House] swung around with his right hand" and "hit something." According to Turner, House said "he took off down the bank and started running and he said that he—he said it seemed forever where he was running. And he said they fired two shots at him while he took off down the bank . . ." House claimed the assailants "grabbed ahold of his shirt," which Turner remembered as "a blue tank top, trimmed in yellow," and "they tore it to where it wouldn't stay on him and he said—I just throwed it off when I was running." Turner, noticing House's bruised knuckle, asked how he hurt it, and House told her "that's where he hit." Turner testified that she "thought maybe my ex-husband had something to do with it."

Although the white Plymouth House drove the next day belonged to Turner, Turner insisted House had not used the car that night. No forensic evidence connected the car to the crime; law enforcement officials inspected a white towel covering the driver seat and concluded it was clean. Turner's trailer was located just under two miles by road, through hilly terrain, from the Muncey residence.

Law enforcement officers also questioned the victim's husband. Though Mrs. Muncey's comments to Luttrell gave no indication she knew this, Mr. Muncey had spent the evening at a weekly dance at a recreation center roughly a mile and a half from his home. In his statement to law enforcement—a statement House's trial counsel claims he never saw—Mr. Muncey admitted leaving the dance early, but said it was only for a brief trip to the package store to buy beer. He also stated that he and his wife had had sexual relations Saturday morning.

Late in the evening on Monday, July 15—two days after the murder—law enforcement officers visited Turner's trailer. With Turner's consent, Agent Scott seized the pants House was wearing the night Mrs. Muncey disappeared. The heavily soiled pants were sitting in a laundry hamper; years later, Agent Scott recalled noticing "reddish brown stains" he "suspected" were blood. Around 4 p.m. the next day, two local law enforcement officers set out for the Federal Bureau of Investigation in Washington, D.C., with House's pants, blood samples from the autopsy, and other evidence packed together in a box. They arrived at 2:00 a.m. the next morning. On July 17, after initial FBI testing revealed human blood on the pants, House was arrested.

II

The State of Tennessee charged House with capital murder. At House's trial, the State presented testimony by Luttrell, Hensley, Adkins, Lora Muncey, Dr. Carabia, the sheriff, and other law enforcement officials. * * * Central to the State's case, however, was what the FBI testing showed—that semen consistent (or so it seemed) with House's was present on Mrs. Muncey's nightgown and panties, and that small bloodstains consistent with Mrs. Muncey's blood but not House's appeared on the jeans belonging to House.

Regarding the semen, FBI Special Agent Paul Bigbee, a serologist, testified that the source was a "secretor," meaning someone who "secrete[s] the ABO blood group substances in other body fluids, such as semen and saliva"—a characteristic shared by 80 percent of the population, including House. Agent Bigbee further testified that the source of semen on the gown was blood-type A, House's own blood type. As to the semen on the panties, Agent Bigbee found only the H blood-group substance * * *.

In the defense case House called Hankins, Clinton, and Turner, as well as House's mother, who testified that House had talked to her by telephone around 9:30 p.m. on the night of the murder and that he had not used her car that evening. House also called the victim's brother, Ricky Green, as a witness. Green testified that on July 2, roughly two weeks before the murder, Mrs. Muncey called him and "said her and Little Hube had been into it and she said she was wanting to leave Little Hube, she said she was wanting to get out—out of it, and she was scared." Green recalled that at Christmastime in 1982 he had seen Mr. Muncey strike Mrs. Muncey after returning home drunk. * * *

In the State's rebuttal, after defense counsel questioned House's motive "to go over and kill a woman that he barely knew[,][w]ho was still dressed, still clad in her clothes," the prosecutor referred obliquely to the semen stains. While explaining that legally "it does not make any difference under God's heaven, what the motive was," the prosecutor told the jury, "you may have an idea why he did it[]":

> "The evidence at the scene which seemed to suggest that he was subjecting this lady to some kind of indignity, why would you get a lady out of her house, late at night, in her night clothes, under the trick that her husband has had a wreck down by the creek? . . . Well, it is because either you don't want her to tell what indignities you have subjected her to, or she is unwilling and fights against you, against being subjected to those indignities. In other words, it is either to keep her from telling what you have done to her, or it is that you are trying to get her to do something that she nor any mother on that road would want to do with Mr. House, under those conditions, and you kill her because of her resistance. That is what the evidence at the scene suggests about motive."

* * * And the prosecution reiterated the importance of the blood. "[D]efense counsel," he said, "does not start out discussing the fact that his client had blood on his jeans on the night that Carolyn Muncey was killed . . . He doesn't start with the fact that nothing that the defense has introduced in this case explains what blood is doing on his jeans, all over his jeans, that is scientifically, completely different from his blood." The jury found House guilty of murder in the first degree.

The trial advanced to the sentencing phase. As aggravating factors to support a capital sentence, the State sought to prove: (1) that House had previously been convicted of a felony involving the use or threat of violence; (2) that the homicide was especially heinous, atrocious, or cruel in that it involved torture or depravity of mind; and (3) that the murder was committed while House was committing, attempting to commit, or fleeing from the commission of, rape or kidnapping. After presenting evidence of House's parole status and aggravated sexual assault conviction, the State rested. As mitigation, the defense offered testimony from House's father and mother, as well as evidence, presented through House's mother, that House attempted suicide after the guilt-phase verdict. Before the attempt House wrote his mother a letter professing his innocence.

In closing the State urged the jury to find all three aggravating factors and impose death. As to the kidnaping or rape factor, the prosecution suggested Mrs. Muncey was "decoy[ed] or entic[ed] . . . away from her family, and confin[ed] her against her will because you know that as she was being beaten to death." "We also think," the prosecutor added, "the proof shows strong evidence of attempted sexual molestation of the victim to accompany the taking away and murdering her." Later the prosecutor argued, "I think the proof shows in the record that it is more likely than not that having been through the process before and having been convicted of a crime involving the threat of violence, or violence to another person, aggravated sexual assault, that the defendant cannot benefit from the type of rehabilitation that correction departments can provide." The jury unanimously found all three aggravating factors and concluded "there are no mitigating circumstances sufficiently substantial to outweigh the statutory aggravating circumstance or circumstances." The jury recommended a death sentence, which the trial judge imposed.

III

The Tennessee Supreme Court affirmed House's conviction and sentence, describing the evidence against House as "circumstantial" but "quite strong." Two months later, in a state trial court, House filed a *pro se* petition for postconviction relief, arguing he received ineffective assistance of counsel at trial. * * * The trial court dismissed the petition * * *. On appeal House's attorney renewed only the jury-instructions argument. In an unpublished opinion the Tennessee Court of Criminal Appeals affirmed, and both the Tennessee Supreme Court and this Court denied review.

House filed a second postconviction petition in state court reasserting his ineffective-assistance claim and seeking investigative and/or expert assistance. After extensive litigation regarding whether House's claims were procedurally defaulted the Tennessee Supreme Court held that House's claims were barred under a state statute providing that claims not raised in prior postconviction proceedings are presumptively waived * * *. This Court denied certiorari.

House next sought federal habeas relief, asserting numerous claims of ineffective assistance of counsel and prosecutorial misconduct. * * * Presenting evidence we describe in greater detail below, House attacked the semen and blood evidence used at his trial and presented other evidence, including a putative confession, suggesting that Mr. Muncey, not House, committed the murder. The District Court nevertheless denied relief, holding that House had neither demonstrated actual innocence of the murder under *Schlup* nor established that he was ineligible for the death penalty under Sawyer.

The Court of Appeals for the Sixth Circuit granted a certificate of appealability under 28 U.S.C. § 2253(c) as to all claims in the habeas petition. On the merits a divided panel affirmed, but its opinion was withdrawn and the case taken en banc. A divided en banc court certified state-law questions to the Tennessee Supreme Court. Concluding that House had made a compelling showing of actual innocence, and recognizing that in *Herrera v. Collins*, this Court assumed without deciding that "in a capital case a truly persuasive demonstration of 'actual innocence' made after trial would render the execution of a defendant unconstitutional, and warrant federal habeas relief if there were no state avenue open to process such a claim," the six-judge majority certified questions to the State Supreme Court. The questions sought "to ascertain whether there remains a 'state avenue open to process such a claim' in this case." Four dissenting judges argued the court should have reached the merits, rather than certifying questions to the state court; these judges asserted that House could not obtain relief under *Schlup*, let alone *Sawyer* and *Herrera*. A fifth dissenter explained that while he agreed with the majority that House "presents a strong claim for habeas relief, at least at the sentencing phase of the case," he objected to the certification of questions to the Tennessee high court. This Court denied certiorari.

The State urged the Tennessee Supreme Court not to answer the Court of Appeals' certified questions, and the state court did not do so. The case returned to the United States Court of Appeals for the Sixth Circuit. * ** [A]n eight-judge majority [of the Sixth Circuit *en banc* panel] affirmed the District Court's denial of habeas relief. Six dissenters argued that House not only had met the actual innocence standard for overcoming procedural default but also was entitled to immediate release under *Herrera*. * * * A seventh dissenter (the same judge who wrote separately in the previous en banc decision) described the case as "a real-life murder mystery, an authentic 'who-done-it' where the wrong man may be executed." * * *

We granted certiorari, and now reverse.

IV

As a general rule, claims forfeited under state law may support federal habeas relief only if the prisoner demonstrates cause for the default and prejudice from the asserted error. * * * The bar is not, however, unqualified. * * * "[I]n appropriate cases," the Court has said, "the principles of comity and finality that inform the concepts of cause and prejudice 'must yield to the imperative of correcting a fundamentally unjust incarceration.'"

In *Schlup*, the Court * * * held that prisoners asserting innocence as a gateway to defaulted claims must establish that, in light of new evidence, "it is more likely than not that no reasonable juror would have found petitioner guilty beyond a reasonable doubt." * * *

For purposes of this case several features of the *Schlup* standard bear emphasis. First, although "[t]o be credible" a gateway claim requires "new reliable evidence * * * that was not presented at trial," the habeas court's analysis is not limited to such evidence. There is no dispute in this case that House has presented some new reliable evidence * * *. * * * Based on this total record, the court must make "a probabilistic determination about what reasonable, properly instructed jurors would do." The court's function is not to make an independent factual determination about what likely occurred, but rather to assess the likely impact of the evidence on reasonable jurors.

Second, it bears repeating that the *Schlup* standard is demanding and permits review only in the "extraordinary" case. * * * At the same time, though, the *Schlup* standard does not require absolute certainty about the petitioner's guilt or innocence. A petitioner's burden at the gateway stage is to demonstrate that more likely than not, in light of the new evidence, [a] reasonable juror would have reasonable doubt. * * * The State also argues that the District Court's findings in this case tie our hands, precluding a ruling in House's favor absent a showing of clear error as to the District Court's specific determinations.

This view overstates the effect of the District Court's ruling. Deference is given to a trial court's assessment of evidence presented to it in the first instance. Yet the *Schlup* inquiry, we repeat, requires a holistic judgment about "'all the evidence'" * * * and its likely effect on reasonable jurors applying the reasonable-doubt standard. As a general rule, the inquiry does not turn on discrete findings regarding disputed points of fact, and "[i]t is not the district court's independent judgment as to whether reasonable doubt exists that the standard addresses." Here, although the District Court attentively managed complex proceedings, carefully reviewed the extensive record, and drew certain conclusions about the evidence, the court did not clearly apply *Schlup's* predictive standard regarding whether reasonable jurors would have reasonable doubt. * * * With this background in mind we turn to the evidence developed in House's federal habeas proceedings.

DNA Evidence

First, in direct contradiction of evidence presented at trial, DNA testing has established that the semen on Mrs. Muncey's nightgown and panties came from her husband, Mr. Muncey, not from House. The State, though conceding this point, insists this new evidence is immaterial. At the guilt phase at least, neither sexual contact nor motive were elements of the offense, so in the State's view the evidence, or lack of evidence, of sexual assault or sexual advance is of no consequence. We disagree. In fact we consider the new disclosure of central importance.

From beginning to end the case is about who committed the crime. When identity is in question, motive is key. The point, indeed, was not lost on the prosecution, for it introduced the evidence and relied on it in the final guilt-phase closing argument. Referring to "evidence at the scene," the prosecutor suggested that House committed, or attempted to commit, "some indignity" on Mrs. Muncey that neither she "nor any mother on that road would want to do with Mr. House." Particularly in a case like this where the proof was, as the State Supreme Court observed, circumstantial, we think a jury would have given this evidence great weight. Quite apart from providing proof of motive, it was the only forensic evidence at the scene that would link House to the murder.

Law and society, as they ought to do, demand accountability when a sexual offense has been committed, so not only did this evidence link House to the crime; it likely was a factor in persuading the jury not to let him go free. At sentencing, moreover, the jury came to the unanimous conclusion, beyond a reasonable doubt, that the murder was committed in the course of a rape or kidnaping. The alleged sexual motivation relates to both those determinations. This is particularly so given that, at the sentencing phase, the jury was advised that House had a previous conviction for sexual assault.

A jury informed that fluids on Mrs. Muncey's garments could have come from House might have found that House trekked the nearly two miles to the victim's home and lured her away in order to commit a sexual offense. By contrast a jury acting without the assumption that the semen could have come from House would have found it necessary to establish some different motive, or, if the same motive, an intent far more speculative. When the only direct evidence of sexual assault drops out of the case, so, too, does a central theme in the State's narrative linking House to the crime. In that light, furthermore, House's odd evening walk and his false statements to authorities, while still potentially incriminating, might appear less suspicious.

Bloodstains

The other relevant forensic evidence is the blood on House's pants, which appears in small, even minute, stains in scattered places. As the prosecutor told the jury, they were stains that, due to their small size, "you or I might not detect[,] [m]ight not see, but which the FBI lab was able to find on [House's] jeans." The stains appear inside the right pocket, outside that pocket, near the inside button, on the left thigh and outside leg, on the seat of the pants, and on the right bottom cuff, including inside the pants. Due to testing by the FBI, cuttings now appear on the pants in several places where stains evidently were found. (The cuttings were destroyed in the testing process, and defense experts were unable to replicate the tests.) At trial, the government argued "nothing that the defense has introduced in this case explains what blood is doing on his jeans, all over [House's] jeans, that is scientifically, completely different from his blood." House, though not disputing at this point that the blood is Mrs. Muncey's, now presents an alternative explanation that, if credited, would undermine the probative value of the blood evidence.

During House's habeas proceedings, Dr. Cleland Blake, an Assistant Chief Medical Examiner for the State of Tennessee and a consultant in forensic pathology to the TBI for 22 years, testified that the blood on House's pants was chemically too degraded, and too similar to blood collected during the autopsy, to have come from Mrs. Muncey's body on the night of the crime. The blood samples collected during the autopsy were placed in test tubes without preservative. * * * Dr. Blake thus concluded the blood on the jeans came from the autopsy samples, not from Mrs. Muncey's live (or recently killed) body.

Other evidence confirms that blood did in fact spill from the vials. It appears the vials passed from Dr. Carabia, who performed the autopsy, into the hands of two local law enforcement officers, who transported it to the FBI, where Agent Bigbee performed the enzyme tests. The blood was contained in four vials, evidently with neither preservative nor a proper seal. The vials, in turn, were stored in a styrofoam box, but nothing indicates the box was kept cool. Rather, in what an evidence protocol expert at the habeas hearing described as a violation of proper procedure, the styrofoam box was packed in the same cardboard box as other evidence including House's pants (apparently in a paper bag) and other clothing (in separate bags). The cardboard box was then carried in the officers' car while they made the 10-hour journey from Tennessee to the FBI lab. Dr. Blake stated that blood vials in hot conditions (such as a car trunk in the summer) could blow open; and in fact, by the time the blood reached the FBI it had hemolyzed, or spoiled, due to heat exposure. By the time the blood passed from the FBI to a defense expert, roughly a vial and a half were empty, though Agent Bigbee testified he used at most a quarter of one vial. Blood, moreover, had seeped onto one corner of the styrofoam box and onto packing gauze inside the box below the vials.* * *

Thus, whereas the bloodstains, emphasized by the prosecution, seemed strong evidence of House's guilt at trial, the record now raises substantial questions about the blood's origin.

A Different Suspect

Were House's challenge to the State's case limited to the questions he has raised about the blood and semen, the other evidence favoring the prosecution might well suffice to bar relief. There is, however, more; for in the post-trial proceedings House presented troubling evidence that Mr. Muncey, the victim's husband, himself could have been the murderer.

At trial, as has been noted, the jury heard that roughly two weeks before the murder Mrs. Muncey's brother received a frightened phone call from his sister indicating that she and Mr. Muncey had been fighting, that she was scared, and that she wanted to leave him. The jury also learned that the brother once saw Mr. Muncey "smac[k]" the victim. House now has produced evidence from multiple sources suggesting that Mr. Muncey regularly abused his wife. * * *

Of most importance is the testimony of Kathy Parker and her sister Penny Letner. They testified at the habeas hearing that, around the time of House's trial, Mr. Muncey had confessed to the crime. Parker recalled that she and "some family members and some friends [were] sitting around drinking" at Parker's trailer when Mr. Muncey "just walked in and sit down." Muncey, who had evidently been drinking heavily, began "rambling off . . . [t]alking about what happened to his wife and how it happened and he didn't mean to do it." According to Parker, Mr. Muncey "said they had been into [an] argument and he slapped her and she fell and hit her head and it killed her and he didn't mean for it to happen." Parker said she "freaked out and run him off."

Letner similarly recalled that at some point either "during [House's] trial or just before," Mr. Muncey intruded on a gathering at Parker's home. Appearing "pretty well blistered," Muncey "went to crying and was talking about his wife and her death and he was saying that he didn't mean to do it." * * *

It bears emphasis, finally, that Parker's and Letner's testimony is not comparable to the sort of eleventh-hour affidavit vouching for a defendant and incriminating a conveniently absent suspect that Justice O'Connor described in her concurring opinion in Herrera as "unfortunate" and "not uncommon" in capital cases; nor was the confession Parker and Letner described induced under pressure of interrogation. The confession evidence here involves an alleged spontaneous statement recounted by two eyewitnesses with no evident motive to lie. For this reason it has more probative value than, for example, incriminating testimony from inmates, suspects, or friends or relations of the accused.

The evidence pointing to Mr. Muncey is by no means conclusive. If considered in isolation, a reasonable jury might well disregard it. In combination, however, with the challenges to the blood evidence and the lack of motive with respect to House, the evidence pointing to Mr. Muncey likely would reinforce other doubts as to House's guilt.

Other Evidence

Certain other details were presented at the habeas hearing. * * *

The victim's daughter, Lora Muncey (now Lora Tharp), also testified at the habeas hearing. She repeated her recollection of hearing a man with a deep voice like her grandfather's and a statement that her father had had a wreck down by the creek. She also denied seeing any signs of struggle or hearing a fight between her parents, though she also said she could not recall her parents ever fighting physically. * * *

Finally, House himself testified at the habeas proceedings. He essentially repeated the story he allegedly told Turner about getting attacked on the road. The District Court found, however, based on House's demeanor, that he "was not a credible witness."

Conclusion

This is not a case of conclusive exoneration. Some aspects of the State's evidence—Lora Muncey's memory of a deep voice, House's bizarre evening walk, his lie to law enforcement, his appearance near the body, and the blood on his pants—still support an inference of guilt. Yet the central forensic proof connecting House to the crime—the blood and the semen—has been called into question, and House has put forward substantial evidence pointing to a different suspect. Accordingly, and although the issue is close, we conclude that this is the rare case where—had the jury heard all the conflicting testimony—it is more likely than not that no reasonable juror viewing the record as a whole would lack reasonable doubt.

V

In addition to his gateway claim under *Schlup*, House argues that he has shown freestanding innocence and that as a result his imprisonment and planned execution are unconstitutional. * * * House urges the Court to answer the question left open in *Herrera* and hold not only that freestanding innocence claims are possible but also that he has established one.

We decline to resolve this issue. We conclude here, much as in *Herrera*, that whatever burden a hypothetical freestanding innocence claim would require, this petitioner has not satisfied it. * * *

House has satisfied the gateway standard set forth in *Schlup* and may proceed on remand with procedurally defaulted constitutional claims. The judgment of the Court of Appeals is reversed, and the case is remanded for further proceedings consistent with this opinion.

It is so ordered.

■ Chief Justice Roberts, with whom Justice Scalia and Justice Thomas join, concurring in the judgment in part and dissenting in part.

* * * The question is not whether House was prejudiced at his trial because the jurors were not aware of the new evidence, but whether all the evidence, considered together, proves that House was actually innocent, so that no reasonable juror would vote to convict him. Considering all the evidence, and giving due regard to the District Court's findings on whether House's new evidence was reliable, I do not find it probable that no reasonable juror would vote to convict him, and accordingly I dissent. * * *

The majority's assessment of House's new evidence is precisely the summary judgment-type inquiry *Schlup* said was inappropriate. By casting aside the District Court's factual determinations made after a comprehensive evidentiary hearing, the majority has done little more than reiterate the factual disputes presented below. * * *

The majority states that if House had presented just one of his three key pieces of evidence—or even two of the three—he would not pass through the *Schlup* gateway. * * * Because the case against House remains substantially unaltered from the case presented to the jury, I disagree.

* * * The jury rejected House's attempt to implicate Mr. Muncey, and the District Court was not persuaded by House's attempt to supplement this evidence at the evidentiary hearing, finding that his new witnesses were not credible. * * *

House's single victory at the evidentiary hearing was new DNA evidence proving that the semen was deposited by Mr. Muncey. The majority identifies the semen evidence as "[c]entral to the State's case" against House, but House's jury would probably be quite surprised by this characterization. At trial, Agent Bigbee testified that from the semen stains on Mrs. Muncey's clothing, he could determine that the man who deposited the semen had type A blood, and was a secretor. Agent Bigbee also testified that House and Mr. Muncey both have type A blood, that House is a secretor, and that "[t]here is an *eighty (80%) percent* chance that [Mr. Muncey] is a secretor." Moreover, Agent Bigbee informed the jury that because 40 percent of people have type A blood, and 80 percent of those people are secretors, the semen on Mrs. Muncey's clothing could have been deposited by roughly one out of every three males. * * *

The majority describes House's sexual motive as "a central theme in the State's narrative linking House to the crime," and states that without the semen evidence, "a jury . . . would have found it necessary to establish some different motive, or, if the same motive, an intent far more speculative." The State, however, consistently directed the jury's attention away from motive, and sexual motive was far from a "central theme" of the State's case--presumably because of the highly ambiguous nature of the semen evidence recounted above. * * * After the State's equivocal presentation of the semen evidence through Agent Bigbee's testimony at trial, the State again made no reference to the semen evidence or to a motive in its closing argument, prompting the defense to again highlight this omission. * * *

The majority aphoristically states that "[w]hen identity is in question, motive is key." Not at all. Sometimes, when identity is in question, alibi is key. Here, House came up with one—and it fell apart, later admitted to be fabricated when his girlfriend would not lie to protect him. Scratches from a cat, indeed. Surely a reasonable juror would give the fact that an alibi had been made up and discredited significant weight. People facing a murder charge, who are innocent, do not make up a story out of concern that the truth might somehow disturb their parole officer. And people do not lie to the police about which jeans they were wearing the night of a murder, if they have no reason to believe the jeans would be stained with the blood shed by the victim in her last desperate struggle to live. * * *

Given the District Court's reliability findings about the first two pieces of evidence, the evidence before us now is not substantially different from that considered by House's jury. I therefore find it more likely than not that in light of this new evidence, at least one juror, acting reasonably, would vote to convict House. The evidence as a whole certainly does not establish that House is actually innocent of the crime of murdering Carolyn Muncey, and accordingly I dissent.

Notes and Questions on House

1) DNA and Other Forensic Evidence. The Supreme Court did not address problems with the trial forensics. At House's trial, the FBI analyst testified that the defendant was an "A secretor," but that the victim's stained underwear yielded only "H" antigens. Rather than tell the jury that no "A" antigens were detected in that stain, thus *excluding* House as the source, the analyst speculated that the A material could have "degraded," yielding a different antigen type. This "vanishing A" testimony was "sheer nonsense," according to *amici* in the case. *House* did acknowledge, however, the central role that DNA technology can play when the Court held that the inmate showed, using post-conviction DNA testing, a reasonable probability that he was innocent. Specifically, the post-conviction DNA testing showed that semen obtained from the victim's clothes did not match Paul House. How should the innocence gateways accommodate DNA evidence? Why and in what ways might post-conviction rules *over*-compensate for DNA evidence?

2)   A Holistic Gateway Inquiry. The Court emphasized the "holistic" nature of the inquiry. While lower courts had considered evidence piece by piece, the Court emphasized that is to consider whether "all the evidence" taken together would cause a reasonably jury, more likely than not, to reach a different outcome. In his influential law review article, Judge Henry Friendly defined a "colorable showing of innocence" as follows:

> The petitioner for collateral attack must show a fair probability that, in light of all the evidence, including that alleged to have been illegally admitted (but with due regard to any unreliability of it) and evidence tenably claimed to have been wrongly excluded or to have become available only after the trial, the trier of fact would have entertained a reasonable doubt of his guilt.

Henry J. Friendly, *Is Innocence Irrelevant? Collateral Attacks on Criminal Judgments*, 38 U. Chi. L. Rev. 142 (1970). *House* endorses the idea that the innocence inquiry involves an assessment of what the record should have looked like in front of the jury, but that a federal court should not weigh the evidence taken in isolation. What are the other alternative standards? Consider the "clear and convincing evidence" standard, adopted in *Sawyer*, for claims regarding evidence of death ineligibility. Or consider the deferential standard in *Jackson v. Virginia*, 443 U.S. 307 (1979): whether, in light of trial evidence viewed in the light most favorable to the prosecution, any rational juror could have found sufficient evidence to convict. Consider the "truly persuasive demonstration of actual innocence" that the *Herrera* posited as a potential freestanding innocence rule. Which standard is best suited to the underlying purposes of the miscarriage-of-justice exception?

3)   Passing through the Gateway. What evidence do you think was most important to the Supreme Court when finding that House satisfied the *Schlup* standard? The Court held that the record did not disclose a "conclusive" exoneration, and it again refused to decide whether a *Herrera* claim is cognizable under the constitution. On other words, more than a decade after *Herrera* and in a case that involved DNA tests, the Court remained unwilling to clarify the constitutional status of freestanding innocence claims. Consider the following hypotheticals:

> (1) Suppose that the evidence was otherwise as described in *House*, except that the post-conviction testing of DNA on the victim's clothes was not a match for House or Mr. Muncey, but rather belonged to an unknown third party.

> (2) Suppose that the evidence was otherwise as described in *House*, but that new FBI documentation was obtained, post-conviction, showing that the blood on House's pants was from spilled vials of the victim's blood.

(3) Suppose that the evidence was otherwise as described in *House*, but that Mr. Muncey made a post-conviction confession to House's lawyers, and also signed an affidavit stating that he in fact did murder his wife.

Under each of these three scenarios, explain whether House would be able to make a stronger or a weaker showing that a reasonable jury would not convict? Do you think that, under any of these scenarios, the Court would have reached the question whether to recognize an freestanding innocence claim?

4)   The Subsequent Merits Adjudication. The Supreme Court was not willing to go "all the way" and order that House be released, but it held that his constitutional claim should be considered on the merits because the procedural default was excused. Having passed through the "gateway" and shown a miscarriage of justice, House would then have to litigate his underlying ineffective assistance of counsel claim. What are the possible results for House on remand? More and more habeas petitions involve innocence evidence, and the presence of such evidence meaningfully increases the likelihood of a grant. The *2007 Habeas Study*, discussed throughout this Book, showed that "a claim raising new evidence of innocence of guilt was related to a higher likelihood of a grant [of reversal], raising it by about 11 percentage points"—even though the innocence claim itself was never credited as the basis of relief. See King et al., *2007 Habeas Study*, at 64. The Study Report concluded, "it appeared that the presence of an innocence claim operated somehow to make a grant of relief on a different claim more likely." See King et al., *2007 Habeas Study*, at 89.[r] Why would that be the case? Will the findings the Court made regarding evidence of House's possible innocence impact the rulings on the underlying constitutional claims having to do with effectiveness of the trial lawyer's assistance?

5)   A *Martinez* Hypothetical. Had *Martinez* been decided before *House*, might the district court have considered House's IAC claim on a different theory? House, proceeding *pro se*, had waived the ineffective assistance of counsel claims regarding failure to call a series of witnesses at trial. House later had an appointed lawyer litigate the state post-conviction petition. Proceeding on appeal *pro se*, however, he omitted those IAC claims. On the one hand, and as in *Coleman,* these claims were waived after the initial opportunity to litigate them in at least one state post-conviction forum. On the other hand, House argued that the ineffective state post-conviction assistance occurred when his lawyer inadequately litigated his IAC claims at the forum where House had representation. In arguing the IAC claim, House's lawyer presented nothing except the trial record; House's lawyer introduced no witness testimony or other proof. Would that type of performance satisfy *Martinez*?

6)   AEDPA versus *Schlup*. As discussed in the next Section, the innocence gateway for successive petitions is now statutory. In 28 U.S.C. § 2244(b)(2)(B)(ii), AEDPA codified a rule far more stringent than the *Schlup* standard, and which requires in part that new facts would establish innocence "by clear and convincing evidence." There is no comparable AEDPA standard for treatment of procedurally defaulted claims. In an omitted portion of the opinion, the Supreme Court made clear that nothing in AEDPA affects the availability of the innocence gateway for procedural default. The rules remain

---

[r] Similarly, a study by one of the authors of post-conviction DNA exoneree litigation found that all exonerees who raised innocence claims ultimately failed, but most who won interim reversals had judges assess trial evidence and even comment on possible innocence. See Brandon L. Garrett, *Judging Innocence*, 108 Colum. L. Rev. 55, 113 (2008).

subject to all pre-AEDPA decisional law. Is there a logical rationale for having different standards for procedural default and for successive petitions? In other words, should innocence more readily excuse a procedural default than a failure to include a claim in a prior federal petition?

7)   Innocence Protection. Professor Robert J. Smith has argued that trial's role as the primary forum for "innocence protection" is in decline. See Robert J. Smith, Recalibrating Constitutional Innocence Protection, 87 Wash. L. Rev. 139 (2012). Reciting the specific types of evidence that have proven particularly problematic—eyewitness identifications and false confessions, among others—and observing that penal institutions can now incapacitate defendants for lengthier periods during which a guilt determination is pending, he argues that the "center of gravity" for innocence protection ought to shift backwards in the criminal process, to include more post-conviction proceedings. Set aside the dispute about whether Professor Smith's proposal is a good or a bad idea, and consider several other questions. First, in what ways does such a proposal conflict with the Supreme Court's emphasis on the criminal trial as the "main event"? Second, what institutions would be most appropriate to conduct the sort of post-conviction innocence protection that Professor Smith is promoting?

(8)   Coda on Paul House. In 2008, after the Supreme Court remanded the case, the federal district judge granted House's habeas petition and ordered House freed on bond and released unless the District Attorney retried him. See House v. Bell, 2007 WL 4568444 *9 (E.D.Tenn. 2007). The district judge emphasized that the new evidence of innocence powerfully supported House's claim that his trial lawyer should have called witnesses that, for example, could have corroborated testimony tending to inculpate the victim's husband. Experts conducted several new DNA tests. Perhaps coming as a surprise to those that had focused on the theory that the culprit might have been the victim's husband, House's DNA did not match DNA found under the victim's fingernails and on her clothes—nor was that DNA profile of the victim's husband. The district attorney declined to try House again, noting "the new evidence (including the forensic examinations) raises a reasonable doubt that he acted alone and the possibility that others were involved in the crime."[s] Assume that House had been retried. If the DNA evidence excludes House, but it also excluded the alternate theory upon which he based his defense—that Mr. Muncey was the perpetrator—then how should the DNA be treated?

3. SUCCESSIVE PETITIONS

How many habeas petitions can a prisoner file? A "successive" habeas petition is, as the term implies, a petition that is not a "first" petition. Although judges and lawmakers have developed procedures to address subsequent habeas filings, some prisoners might have understandable reasons for failing to include claims in a first habeas petition. What reasons are sound? What if new facts come to light after the first habeas petition was filed and dismissed? What if a new constitutional right is recognized by the Supreme Court? What if the prisoner was *pro se* and inadvertently left out a potentially meritorious claim? *Res judicata* does not formally apply to habeas judgments. Because a successive petition involves claims attacking the same custody and involving the same parties as a first petition, however,

---

[s] See Emanuella Grinberg, *Exonerated death row inmate: 'Took 'em long enough,'* CNN, May 13, 2009.

successive-petition rules are strongly influenced by *res judicata* principles. Courts have long wrestled with how to best reconcile the interest in avoiding unlawful custody—which the very existence of the writ implies—with the interest in finality that *res judicata* embodies. Congress has now enacted legislation addressing this problem, although AEDPA does not appear to have increased the proportion of habeas filings dismissed on successive petition grounds; perhaps it simply discouraged such filings.[t]

Successive-petition laws have developed along two distinct threads, depending on the nature of the claim asserted in the successive petition. The first thread involves claims that were already asserted in a prior petition. Such claims are "successive claims." Successive petitions containing only successive claims are sometimes called "same-claim" successive petitions. The second thread involves claims asserted in a successive petition that *were not* asserted in a prior or first petition. These claims are called "new claims," and successive petitions containing only new claims are sometimes called "new-claim" successive petitions. A new claim that is impermissibly asserted in a successive petition is called an "abuse of the writ."

The post-AEDPA structure of the federal habeas statute reflects the distinction between successive claims and new claims. Compare 28 U.S.C. § 2244(b)(1) (successive claims) and § 2254(b)(2) (new or abusive claims). The rule for successive claims is quite clear: "A claim presented in a second or successive habeas corpus application under section 2254 that was presented in a prior application shall be dismissed." 28 U.S.C. § 2244(b)(1). The rules for new claims in successive petitions contain more latent ambiguities, and appear in Subsection (b)(2):

> (2) A claim presented in a second or successive habeas corpus application under section 2254 that was not presented in a prior application shall be dismissed unless—
>
> (A) the applicant shows that the claim relies on a new rule of constitutional law, made retroactive to cases on collateral review by the Supreme Court, that was previously unavailable; or
>
> (B)(i) the factual predicate for the claim could not have been discovered previously through the exercise of due diligence; and (ii) the facts underlying the claim, if proven and viewed in light of the evidence as a whole, would be sufficient to establish by clear and convincing evidence that, but for constitutional error, no reasonable factfinder would have found the applicant guilty of the underlying offense.

28 U.S.C. § 2244(b)(2). The first subsection, roughly speaking, permits inmates to assert new claims based on new rules of constitutional law announced after the inmate's conviction became final. The second subsection, also speaking roughly, permits inmates to assert a new claim if that claim (1) alleges constitutional error *and* (2) is predicated on actual innocence of the offense charged.

Successive-claim and "abuse of the writ" arguments had historically been affirmative defenses that the state had to plead and prove, just like the defenses of exhaustion and procedural default. AEDPA, however, reconstituted these affirmative defenses as *jurisdictional* conditions for habeas relief. 28 U.S.C. § 2244(b)(1)-(2) contain the content of the successive petition standards, but § 2244(b) has other rules pertaining to the how var-

---

[t] The *2007 Habeas Study* found that 6.9% of non-capital cases and just 3.8% of capital cases involved successive petitions. See King et al., *2007 Habeas Study*, supra note f, at 47.

ious federal courts apply the standards. The § 2244(b)(1) and (b)(2) conditions must be considered at two different phases of the federal habeas process. First, any successive petition (whatever combination of new or successive claims it contains) must be "authorized" by a three-judge panel of federal appellate judges, and the successive petition may be filed in the district court only if the inmate makes a prima facie case for relief under Subsection (b). Next, if the successive petition is authorized, a district court must then reconsider the jurisdictional question in view of a more robust record. See 28 U.S.C. § 2244(b)(4). Working through the intricacies of § 2244(b) is challenging. The task is complicated by the fact that § 2244(b) is a Subsection that the Supreme Court interprets in light of the writ's common law history and the Court's own prior rulings.

INTRODUCTORY NOTES ON SAME-CLAIM AND NEW-CLAIM SUCCESSIVE PETITIONS

1) *Wong Doo*, *Price*, **and the 1948 Legislation.** *Res judicata* means a "matter already judged," and it corresponds to what we think of as claim preclusion. Normally, a claim that was or could have been decided in a previous action between two litigants cannot be asserted in subsequent litigation. In *Wong Doo v. United States*, 265 U.S. 239 (1924), the Supreme Court explained:

> [T]he courts below erred in applying the inflexible doctrine of res judicata. But it does not follow that the judgment should be reversed; for it plainly appears that the situation was one where, according to a sound judicial discretion, controlling weight must have been given to the prior refusal. . . The petitioner had full opportunity to offer proof of it at the hearing on the first petition, and, if he was intending to rely on that ground, good faith required that he produce the proof then. To reserve the proof for use in attempting to support a later petition, if the first failed, was to make an abusive use of the writ of habeas corpus.

Price v. Johnston, 334 U.S. 266 (1948) followed almost a quarter-century later and dealt with a prisoner's fourth habeas petition. *Price* contained some dicta that compromised the relative clarity of *Wong Doo*, stating that the three previously-dismissed petitions had "no bearing or weight on the disposition to be made of the new matter raised in the fourth petition." Shortly after *Price*, Congress enacted the first version of what is now 28 U.S.C. § 2244:

> No circuit or district judge shall be required to entertain an application for a writ of habeas corpus to inquire into the detention of a person pursuant to a judgment of a court of the United States, or of any State, if it appears that the legality of such detention has been determined by a judge or court of the United States on a prior application for a writ of habeas corpus and the petition presents no new ground not theretofore presented and determined, and the judge or court is satisfied that the ends of justice will not be served by such inquiry.

As you read the cases that follow (and the discussion of *Sanders*), pay attention to what Congress did when it passed the 1948 legislation. Did it pass a rule regarding successive petitions? What does the "ends of justice" mean? Does it remind you of any concepts you have encountered thus far in this Chapter?

(2) *Sanders* and Deliberate Bypass. The habeas procedural doctrines did not develop independently. In 1963, the Warren Court announced deliberate bypass standards for three important habeas doctrines—abusive petitions, procedurally defaulted claims, and introduction of new evidence in federal hearings—within the span of a month. The decision to craft identical standards for the procedural penalty in each context could not have been an accident. We read *Fay v. Noia,* the procedural default decision. The second decision, *Townsend v. Sain,* 372 U.S. 293 (1963), set forth the standard for providing an evidentiary hearing to develop the facts surrounding a claim in a federal habeas petition. The third decision, *Sanders v. United States,* 373 U.S. 1 (1963) was an abusive-claim case. *Sanders,* however, involved a § 2255 petition of a *federal* prisoner, a feature that distinguished it from its two historical-companion cases. Sanders had been arrested for robbing a federally insured bank. He declined counsel, waived his indictment and pleaded guilty. Sanders then filed a § 2255 petition alleging IAC, the invalidity of his indictment, and that his plea was coerced and uncounseled. In a subsequent federal petition, Sanders alleged that he had been incompetent to stand trial.

a) *Res Judicata* in *Sanders*. Recall that decisional law frequently identified habeas as an exception to *res judicata* because, at common law, habeas judgments were not appealable. Writing for the Court in *Sanders,* however, Justice Brennan attempts to ground the exception in a more philosophical feature of the writ: "Conventional notions of finality of litigation have no place where life or liberty is at stake and infringement of constitutional rights is alleged. . . The inapplicability of *res judicata* to habeas, then, is inherent in the very role and function of the writ." Do you agree that a claim should be excepted from *res judicata* rules every time it implicates life or liberty? Would such a regime be administrable? Conversely, should courts give *res judicata* effect to a prior habeas petition simply because some appellate relief was available from the originating decision?

b) New Claims and the "Deliberate Withholding" Standard. *Sanders* immediately distinguished between claims in subsequent petitions that had been the subject of a prior merits determination and those that had not. With respect to claims that had been subject to an adverse prior merits determination, *Sanders* held that the prior result should be given dispositive weight unless renewed consideration would promote "the ends of justice." For claims that were not denied on the merits in a previous application, *Sanders* held that a federal court could withhold merits consideration only if the habeas remedy had been "abused," a defense that the United States must plead specifically. Quoting language from *Wong Doo* that premised denial in part on the fact that the prisoner should have presented the claim in the first petition "in good faith," *Sanders* equated "abuse of the writ" with instances in which the prisoner "deliberately withheld" a claim from a prior petition.

c) Addressing the 1948 Statute. Whereas *Wong Doo* and *Price* had been decided before there was federal statutory language on point, recall the statutory provision that Congress passed in 1948. The express language of that provision applied only to claims presented and decided on the merits in a prior petition, and required that they be considered only if "the ends of justice" necessitated such treatment. *Sanders* rejected the argument that the 1948 revision was meant to apply to claims *not* presented in a prior petition. Moreover, the Court observed that the 1948 revision was not intended to effect any change in substantive law: "[I]t was plainly not intended to change the law as judicially evolved. Not only does the Reviser's note disclaim any such intention, but language in the original bill which would have injected *res judicata* into habeas corpus was deliberately eliminated . . ." When Congress passed the statute in 1948, then, what was the state of the law with respect to previously-omitted claims?

d)   The Harlan Dissent. Justice Harlan, joined by Justice Clark, dissented. Justice Harlan described *Sanders* and the other two cases as constituting the "trilogy of guideline decisions in which the Court has undertaken to restate the responsibilities of federal courts in federal post-conviction proceedings." He criticized the trilogy on the ground that it "relegate[d] to a back seat, as it affects state and federal criminal cases finding their way into federal post-conviction proceedings, the principle that there must be some end to litigation." Why did Justice Harlan focus on finality, rather than on the "comity" interest present in so many of the other cases? In what ways would Justice Brennan say that the deliberate bypass rule accommodates the public interest in finality? If the deliberate bypass standard is over-inclusive—i.e., if it protects more than those claimants who acted in good faith when they filed their initial petitions—then is the interest in "just" consideration of previously-omitted claims greater than the interest in finality?

INTRODUCTORY NOTE ON MCCLESKEY V. ZANT

Recall that, in *Wainwright v. Sykes*, 432 U.S. 72 (1977), the Supreme Court changed the standard for excusing a procedural default from the deliberate-bypass rule to the cause-and-prejudice standard. Previously-omitted claims were also, under *Sanders*, subject to a deliberate-bypass rule. In *McCleskey v. Zant*, 499 U.S. 467 (1991), excerpted below, the Court heightened the excuse standard in the abuse-of-the-writ context as well. Do procedural default, successive petition, and abuse-of-the-writ doctrines share enough standards and reflect enough common policy to justify common excuses? Consider that question as you read *McCleskey*.

McCleskey v. Zant
Supreme Court of the Untied States
499 U.S. 467 (1991)

■ JUSTICE KENNEDY delivered the opinion of the Court.

The doctrine of abuse of the writ defines the circumstances in which federal courts decline to entertain a claim presented for the first time in a second or subsequent petition for a writ of habeas corpus. Petitioner Warren McCleskey in a second federal habeas petition presented a claim under *Massiah v. United States*, 377 U.S. 201 (1964), that he failed to include in his first federal petition. [We hold] that the petitioner here abused the writ * * *.

I

McCleskey and three other men, all armed, robbed a Georgia furniture store in 1978. One of the robbers shot and killed an off duty policeman who entered the store in the midst of the crime. McCleskey confessed to the police that he participated in the robbery. When on trial for both the robbery and the murder, however, McCleskey renounced his confession after taking the stand with an alibi denying all involvement. To rebut McCleskey's testimony, the prosecution called Offie Evans, who had occupied a jail cell next to McCleskey's. Evans testified that McCleskey admitted shooting the officer during the robbery and boasted that he would have shot his way out of the store even in the face of a dozen policemen.

* * * The portion of the appeal relevant for our purposes involves McCleskey's attack on Evans' rebuttal testimony. McCleskey contended [that the prosecution had impermissibly withheld the statement to Evans,] in violation of *Brady v. Maryland*, 373 U.S. 83 (1963). [McCleskey failed to obtain any relief on the *Brady* claim.]

McCleskey then initiated [state] postconviction proceedings, * * * [raising] 23 challenges to his murder conviction and death sentence. * * * [Among them], McCleskey alleged that admission of Evans' testimony violated the Sixth Amendment right to counsel as construed in *[Massiah]*. On this theory, "[t]he introduction into evidence of [his] statements to [Evans], elicited in a situation created to induce [McCleskey] to make incriminating statements without the assistance of counsel, violated [McCleskey's] right to counsel under the Sixth Amendment to the Constitution of the United States." * * *

* * * [McCleskey's first federal] petition failed to allege the *Massiah* claim, but it did reassert *Giglio* and *Brady* claims * * * [that had been alleged in the state proceedings. McCleskey did not obtain relief on those claims.] * * *

In July 1987, McCleskey filed a second federal habeas action, the one we now review. In the District Court, McCleskey asserted seven claims, including a *Massiah* challenge to the introduction of Evans' testimony. McCleskey had presented a *Massiah* claim, it will be recalled, in his first state habeas action when he alleged that the conversation recounted by Evans at trial had been "elicited in a situation created to induce" him to make an incriminating statement without the assistance of counsel. The first federal petition did not present a *Massiah* claim. The proffered basis for the *Massiah* claim in the second federal petition was a 21-page signed statement that Evans made to the Atlanta Police Department on August 1, 1978, two weeks before the trial began. The department furnished the document to McCleskey one month before he filed his second federal petition.

The statement related pretrial jailhouse conversations that Evans had with McCleskey and that Evans overheard between McCleskey and Bernard Dupree. By the statement's own terms, McCleskey participated in all the reported jail cell conversations. Consistent with Evans' testimony at trial, the statement reports McCleskey admitting and boasting about the murder. It also recounts that Evans posed as [an accomplice]'s uncle and told McCleskey he had talked with Wright about the robbery and the murder.

In his second federal habeas petition, McCleskey asserted that the statement proved Evans "was acting in direct concert with State officials" during the incriminating conversations with McCleskey, and that the authorities "deliberately elicited" inculpatory admissions in violation of McCleskey's Sixth Amendment right to counsel [as held in *Massiah*]. * * *

[The federal court had a hearing surrounding the circumstances of McCleskey's cell placement. The hearing focused considerably on the Ulysses Worthy, a Fulton county jail officer who stated that someone asked that

Evans be moved near McCleskey's cell. The opinion indicates that Worthy's testimony was confusing and unreliable.]

[In] 1987, the District Court granted McCleskey relief based upon a violation of *Massiah*. * * *

In granting habeas relief, the District Court rejected the State's argument that McCleskey's * * * *Massiah* claim [was] * * * an abuse of the writ. The court ruled that McCleskey did not deliberately abandon the claim after raising it in his first state habeas petition. * * * The District Court also determined that when McCleskey filed his first federal petition, he did not know about either the 21-page Evans document or the identity of Worthy, and that the failure to discover the evidence for the first federal petition "was not due to [McCleskey's] inexcusable neglect."

The Eleventh Circuit reversed, holding that the District Court abused its discretion by failing to dismiss McCleskey's *Massiah* claim as an abuse of the writ. * * *.

II

The * * * government has the burden of pleading abuse of the writ, and * * * the petitioner must [then] show that he has not abused the writ in seeking habeas relief. Much confusion exists though, on the standard for determining when a petitioner abuses the writ. * * *

B

At common law, res judicata did not attach to a court's denial of habeas relief. * * * The rule made sense because at common law an order denying habeas relief could not be reviewed. Successive petitions served as a substitute for appeal.

As appellate review became available from a decision in habeas refusing to discharge the prisoner, courts began to question the continuing validity of the common-law rule allowing endless successive petitions. * * *

[Our decisions have] reaffirmed that res judicata does not apply [to orders denying habeas relief.] They recognized, however, that the availability of appellate review required a modification of the common-law rule allowing endless applications. * * *

[The Court explained the relationship between *Wong Doo*, *Price*, and the 1948 revisions to 28 U.S.C. § 2244. That relationship is the subject of Introductory Note 1, *supra*.] * * *

* * * [T]he Reviser's Note to the 1948 statute made clear that as a general matter Congress did not intend the new section to disrupt the judicial evolution of habeas principles, and we confirmed in *Sanders v. United States* that Congress' silence on the standard for abuse of the writ involving a new claim was "not intended to foreclose judicial application of the abuse-of-writ principle as developed in *Wong Doo* and *Price*."

Sanders also recognized our special responsibility in the development of habeas corpus with respect to * * * 28 U.S.C. § 2255. The statute created a new postconviction remedy for federal prisoners with a provision for repetitive petitions different from the one found in § 2244. While § 2244 permitted dismissal of subsequent habeas petitions that "present[ed] no new ground not theretofore presented and determined," § 2255 allowed a federal district court to refuse to entertain a subsequent petition seeking "similar relief." On its face, § 2255 appeared to announce a much stricter abuse of the writ standard than its counterpart in § 2244. We concluded in *Sanders*, however, that the language in § 2255 [should be] construed * * * to be the "material equivalent" of the abuse standard in § 2244. * * *.

Three years after Sanders, Congress once more amended the habeas corpus statute. The amendment was an attempt to alleviate the increasing burden on federal courts caused by successive and abusive petitions by "introducing a greater degree of finality of judgments in habeas corpus proceedings." * * *

* * * Subparagraph (b) establishes a "qualified application of the doctrine of res judicata." It states that a federal court "need not entertain" a second or subsequent habeas petition "unless" the petitioner satisfies two conditions. First, the subsequent petition must allege a new ground, factual or otherwise. Second, the applicant must satisfy the judge that he did not deliberately withhold the ground earlier or "otherwise abus[e] the writ." * * *

Section 2244(b) * * * does not state the limits on the district court's discretion to entertain abusive petitions. Nor does the statute define the term "abuse of the writ." * * *

* * * Congress did not intend § 2244(b) to foreclose application of the court announced principles defining and limiting a district court's discretion to entertain abusive petitions.

Rule 9(b) of the Rules Governing Habeas Corpus Proceedings, promulgated in 1976, also speaks to the problem of new grounds for relief raised in subsequent petitions. It provides:

> "A second or successive petition may be dismissed if the judge finds that it fails to allege new or different grounds for relief and the prior determination was on the merits or, if new and different grounds are alleged, the judge finds that the failure of the petitioner to assert those grounds in a prior petition constituted an abuse of the writ."

Like 28 U.S.C. § 2244(b), Rule 9(b) "incorporates the judge made principle governing the abuse of the writ set forth in Sanders." The Advisory Committee Notes make clear that a new claim in a subsequent petition should not be entertained if the judge finds the failure to raise it earlier "inexcusable." The Notes also state that a retroactive change in the law and newly discovered evidence represent acceptable excuses for failing to raise the claim earlier. * * *

III

* * * Although our decisions on the subject do not all admit of ready synthesis, one point emerges with clarity: Abuse of the writ is not confined to instances of deliberate abandonment. * * *

* * * [A]petitioner may abuse the writ by failing to raise a claim through inexcusable neglect. * * *

* * * [A] review of our habeas corpus precedents leads us to decide that the same standard used to determine whether to excuse state procedural defaults should govern the determination of inexcusable neglect in the abuse of the writ context.

The prohibition against adjudication in federal habeas corpus of claims defaulted in state court is similar in purpose and design to the abuse of the writ doctrine, which in general prohibits subsequent habeas consideration of claims not raised, and thus defaulted, in the first federal habeas proceeding. The terms "abuse of the writ" and "inexcusable neglect," on the one hand, and "procedural default," on the other, imply a background norm of procedural regularity binding on the petitioner. This explains the presumption against habeas adjudication both of claims defaulted in state court and of claims defaulted in the first round of federal habeas. * * *

The doctrines of procedural default and abuse of the writ implicate nearly identical concerns flowing from the significant costs of federal habeas corpus review. To begin with, the writ strikes at finality. One of the law's very objects is the finality of its judgments. Neither innocence nor just punishment can be vindicated until the final judgment is known. * * * And when a habeas petitioner succeeds in obtaining a new trial, the "'erosion of memory' and 'dispersion of witnesses' that occur with the passage of time" prejudice the government and diminish the chances of a reliable criminal adjudication. Though *Fay v. Noia* may have cast doubt upon these propositions, since [*Noia]* we have taken care in our habeas corpus decisions to reconfirm the importance of finality.

Finality has special importance in the context of a federal attack on a state conviction. * * * Our federal system recognizes the independent power of a State to articulate societal norms through criminal law; but the power of a State to pass laws means little if the State cannot enforce them.

Habeas review extracts further costs. Federal collateral litigation places a heavy burden on scarce federal judicial resources, and threatens the capacity of the system to resolve primary disputes. Finally, habeas corpus review may give litigants incentives to withhold claims for manipulative purposes and may establish disincentives to present claims when evidence is fresh. * * *

If reexamination of a conviction in the first round of federal habeas stretches resources, examination of new claims raised in a second or subsequent petition spreads them thinner still. These later petitions deplete the resources needed for federal litigants in the first instance, including litigants commencing their first federal habeas action. * * * And if reexamination of convictions in the first round of habeas offends federalism and comity, the offense increases when a State must defend its conviction in a second or subsequent habeas proceeding on grounds not even raised in the first petition.

The federal writ of habeas corpus overrides all these considerations, essential as they are to the rule of law, when a petitioner raises a meritorious constitutional claim in a proper manner in a habeas petition. Our procedural default jurisprudence and abuse of the writ jurisprudence help define this dimension of procedural regularity. Both doctrines impose on petitioners a burden of reasonable compliance with procedures designed to discourage baseless claims and to keep the system open for valid ones; both recognize the law's interest in finality; and both invoke equitable principles to define the court's discretion to excuse pleading and procedural requirements for petitioners who could not comply with them in the exercise of reasonable care and diligence. It is true that a habeas court's concern to honor state procedural default rules rests in part on respect for the integrity of procedures "employed by a coordinate jurisdiction within the federal system," and that such respect is not implicated when a petitioner defaults a claim by failing to raise it in the first round of federal habeas review. Nonetheless, the doctrines of procedural default and abuse of the writ are both designed to lessen the injury to a State that results through reexamination of a state conviction on a ground that the State did not have the opportunity to address at a prior, appropriate time; and both doctrines seek to vindicate the State's interest in the finality of its criminal judgments.

We conclude from the unity of structure and purpose in the jurisprudence of state procedural defaults and abuse of the writ that the standard for excusing a failure to raise a claim at the appropriate time should be the same in both contexts. We have held that a procedural default will be excused upon a showing of cause and prejudice. We now hold that the same standard applies to determine if there has been an abuse of the writ through inexcusable neglect.

In procedural default cases, the cause standard requires the petitioner to show that "some objective factor external to the defense impeded counsel's efforts" to raise the claim in state court. Objective factors that constitute cause include "'interference by officials'" that makes compliance with the State's procedural rule impracticable, and "a showing that the factual or legal basis for a claim was not reasonably available to counsel." In addition, constitutionally "ineffective assistance of counsel . . . is cause." Attorney error short of ineffective assistance of counsel, however, does not constitute cause and will not excuse a procedural default. Once the petitioner has established cause, he must show "'actual prejudice' resulting from the errors of which he complains."

Federal courts retain the authority to issue the writ of habeas corpus in a further, narrow class of cases despite a petitioner's failure to show cause for a procedural default. These are extraordinary instances when a constitutional violation probably has caused the conviction of one innocent of the crime. We have described this class of cases as implicating a fundamental miscarriage of justice.

The cause and prejudice analysis we have adopted for cases of procedural default applies to an abuse of the writ inquiry in the following manner. When a prisoner files a second or subsequent application, the government bears the burden of pleading abuse of the writ. * * * To excuse his failure to raise the claim earlier, [the petitioner] must show cause for failing to raise it and prejudice therefrom as those concepts have been defined in our procedural default decisions. * * * If petitioner cannot show cause, the failure to raise the claim in an earlier petition may nonetheless be excused if he or she can show that a fundamental miscarriage of justice would result from a failure to entertain the claim. * * *

* * * In addition, the exception to cause for fundamental miscarriages of justice gives meaningful content to the otherwise unexplained "ends of justice" inquiry mandated by *Sanders*. *Sanders* drew the phrase "ends of justice" from the 1948 version of § 2244. Although the 1966 revision to the habeas statute eliminated any reference to an "ends of justice" inquiry, a plurality of the Court [has] held that this inquiry remained appropriate, and required federal courts to entertain successive petitions when a petitioner supplements a constitutional claim with a "colorable showing of factual innocence." The miscarriage of justice exception to cause serves as "an additional safeguard against compelling an innocent man to suffer an unconstitutional loss of liberty" guaranteeing that the ends of justice will be served in full.

* * * The [inexcusable neglect] standard is an objective one, and can be applied in a manner that comports with the threshold nature of the abuse-of-the-writ inquiry. * * *

The cause and prejudice standard should curtail the abusive petitions that in recent years have threatened to undermine the integrity of the habeas corpus process. * * *

IV

[The Court first determined that McCleskey could not show cause for failure to raise the *Massiah* claim in the initial federal habeas petition.]

For cause to exist, the external impediment, whether it be government interference or the reasonable unavailability of the factual basis for the claim, must have prevented petitioner from raising the claim * * *. The requirement of cause in the abuse- of-the-writ context is based on the principle that petitioner must conduct a reasonable and diligent investigation aimed at including all relevant claims and grounds for relief in the first federal habeas petition. If what petitioner knows or could discover upon reasonable investigation supports a claim for relief in a federal habeas petition, what he does not know is irrelevant. Omission of the claim will not be excused merely because evidence discovered later might also have supported or strengthened the claim.

[The Court also determined that it would not "exercise its equitable discretion to correct a miscarriage of justice."]

* * * The judgment of the Court of Appeals is

Affirmed.

■ JUSTICE MARSHALL, with whom JUSTICE BLACKMUN and JUSTICE STEVENS join, dissenting.

* * * Without even the most casual admission that it is discarding longstanding legal principles, the Court radically redefines the content of the "abuse of the writ" doctrine, substituting the strict-liability "cause and prejudice" standard of *Wainwright v. Sykes* for the good-faith "deliberate abandonment" standard of *Sanders v. United States*. * * *

I

* * * What emerges from *Sanders* and its predecessors is essentially a good-faith standard. * * * [T]he principal form of bad faith that the "abuse of the writ" doctrine is intended to deter is the deliberate abandonment of a claim the factual and legal basis of which are known to the petitioner (or his counsel) when he files his first petition. The Court in Sanders stressed this point by equating its analysis with that of *Fay v. Noia*, which established the then-prevailing "deliberate bypass" test for the cognizability of claims on which a petitioner procedurally defaulted in state proceedings. A petitioner also abuses the writ under *Sanders* when he uses the writ to achieve some end other than expeditious relief from unlawful confinement — such as "to vex, harass, or delay." * * *

"Cause and prejudice"—the standard currently applicable to procedural defaults in state proceedings—imposes a much stricter test. As this Court's precedents make clear, a petitioner has cause for failing effectively to present his federal claim in state proceedings only when "some objective factor external to the defense impeded counsel's efforts to comply with the State's procedural rule . . ." * * * In this sense, the cause component of the *Wainwright v. Sykes* test establishes a strict-liability standard.

Equally foreign to our abuse-of-the-writ jurisprudence is the requirement that a petitioner show "prejudice." Under *Sanders*, a petitioner who articulates a justifiable reason for failing to present a claim in a previous habeas application is not required in addition to demonstrate any particular degree of prejudice before the habeas court must consider his claim. * * *

II

* * *

A

Incorporation of the cause-and-prejudice test into the abuse-of-the-writ doctrine cannot be justified as an exercise of this Court's common-lawmaking discretion, because this Court has no discretion to exercise in this area. Congress has affirmatively ratified the *Sanders* good-faith standard in the governing statute and procedural rules, thereby insulating that standard from judicial repeal.

The abuse-of-the-writ doctrine is embodied in 28 U.S.C. § 2244(b) and in Habeas Corpus Rule 9(b). Enacted three years after Sanders, § 2244(b) recodified the statutory authority of a district court to dismiss a second or successive petition, amending the statutory language to incorporate the *Sanders* criteria * * * . Consistent with *Sanders*, the purpose of the recodification was to spare a district court the obligation to entertain a petition "containing allegations identical to those asserted in a previous application that has been denied, or predicated upon grounds *obviously well known to [the petitioner] when [he] filed the preceding application*." Rule 9(b) likewise adopts Sanders' terminology * * *.

* * * There can be no question that § 2244(b) and Rule 9(b) codify Sanders. The legislative history of, and Advisory Committee's Notes to, Rule 9(b) expressly so indicate, and such has been the universal understanding of this Court * * *.

The majority * * * concludes nonetheless that Congress did "not answer" all of the "questions" concerning the abuse-of-the-writ doctrine. The majority emphasizes that § 2244(b) refers to second or successive petitions from petitioners who have "deliberately withheld the newly asserted ground . . . *or otherwise abused the writ*" without exhaustively cataloging the ways in which the writ may "otherwise" be "abused." From this "silenc[e]," the majority infers a congressional delegation of lawmaking power broad enough to encompass the engrafting of the cause-and-prejudice test onto the abuse-of-the-writ doctrine.

It is difficult to take this reasoning seriously. Because "cause" under *Sykes* makes the mental state of the petitioner (or his counsel) irrelevant, "cause" completely subsumes "deliberate abandonment." Thus, if merely failing to raise a claim without "cause"—that is, without some external impediment to raising it—necessarily constitutes an abuse of the writ, the statutory reference to *deliberate* withholding of a claim would be rendered superfluous. Insofar as *Sanders* was primarily concerned with limiting dismissal of a second or subsequent petition to instances in which the petitioner had deliberately abandoned the new claim, the suggestion that Congress invested courts with the discretion to read this language out of the statute is completely irreconcilable with the proposition that § 2244(b) and Rule 9(b) codify Sanders.

To give content to "otherwise abus[e] the writ" as used in § 2244(b), we must look to *Sanders*. As I have explained, the Court in *Sanders* identified two broad classes of bad-faith conduct that bar adjudication of a claim not raised in a previous habeas application: the deliberate abandonment or withholding of that claim from the first petition; and the filing of a petition aimed at some purpose other than expeditious relief from unlawful confinement, such as "to vex, harass, or delay." By referring to second or successive applications from habeas petitioners who have "deliberately withheld the newly asserted ground or otherwise abused the writ," § 2244(b) tracks this division. Congress may well have selected the phrase "otherwise abused the writ" with the expectation that courts would continue to elaborate upon the types of dilatory tactics that, in addition to deliberate abandonment of a known claim, constitute an abuse of the writ. But consistent with Congress' intent to codify Sanders' good-faith test, such elaborations must be confined to circumstances in which a petitioner's omission of an unknown claim is conjoined with his intentional filing of a petition for an improper purpose, such as "to vex, harass or delay." * * *

B

* * * [T]he majority's abrupt change in law subverts the policies underlying 2244(b) and unfairly prejudices the petitioner in this case.

The majority premises adoption of the cause-and-prejudice test almost entirely on the importance of "finality." At best, this is an insufficiently developed justification for cause-and-prejudice or any other possible conception of the abuse-of-the-writ doctrine. For the very essence of the Great Writ is our criminal justice system's commitment to suspending "[c]onventional notions of finality of litigation . . . where life or liberty is at stake and infringement of constitutional rights is alleged." * * *

* * * This Court's precedents on the procedural-default doctrine identify two purposes served by the cause-and-prejudice test. The first purpose is to promote respect for a State's legitimate procedural rules. * * * The second purpose of the cause-and-prejudice test is to preserve the connection between federal collateral review and the general "deterrent" function served by the Great Writ." * * * With regard to both of these purposes, the strictness of the cause-and-prejudice test has been justified on the ground that the defendant's procedural default is akin to an independent and adequate state-law ground for the judgment of conviction.

Neither of these concerns is even remotely implicated in the abuse-of-the-writ setting. The abuse-of-the-writ doctrine clearly contemplates a situation in which a petitioner (as in this case) has complied with applicable state-procedural rules and effectively raised his constitutional claim in state proceedings; were it otherwise, the abuse-of-the-writ doctrine would not perform a screening function independent from that performed by the procedural-default doctrine and by the requirement that a habeas petitioner exhaust his state remedies. Because the abuse-of-the-writ doctrine presupposes that the petitioner has effectively raised his claim in state proceedings, a decision by the habeas court to entertain the claim notwithstanding its omission from an earlier habeas petition will neither breed disrespect for state-procedural rules nor unfairly subject state courts to federal collateral review in the absence of a state-court disposition of a federal claim.

* * * A habeas petitioner's own interest in liberty furnishes a powerful incentive to assert in his first petition all claims that the petitioner (or his counsel) believes have a reasonable prospect for success. Sanders' bar on the later assertion of claims omitted in bad faith adequately fortifies this natural incentive. At the same time, however, the petitioner faces an effective disincentive to asserting any claim that he believes does not have a

reasonable prospect for success: the adverse adjudication of such a claim will bar its reassertion under the successive-petition doctrine, whereas omission of the claim will not prevent the petitioner from asserting the claim for the first time in a later petition should the discovery of new evidence or the advent of intervening changes in law invest the claim with merit.

The cause-and-prejudice test destroys this balance. By design, the cause-and-prejudice standard creates a near-irrebuttable presumption that omitted claims are permanently barred. This outcome not only conflicts with Congress' intent that a petitioner be free to avail himself of newly discovered evidence or intervening changes in law, but also subverts the statutory disincentive to the assertion of frivolous claims. Rather than face the cause-and-prejudice bar, a petitioner will assert all conceivable claims, whether or not these claims reasonably appear to have merit. * * *

III

[Justice Marshall would have held that the case should have been remanded for consideration of the facts in light of the new standard.] * * *

I dissent.

NOTES AND QUESTIONS ON MCCLESKEY V. ZANT

1) *Massiah* **Claims.** McCleskey alleged a "*Massiah*" claim—a claim that law enforcement deliberately elicited incriminating statements by placing an informant in an adjacent cell. See Massiah v. United States, 377 U.S. 201 (1964). Generally speaking, *Massiah* held that, once adversary proceedings have commenced, an accused has a Sixth Amendment right to the presence of an attorney anytime law enforcement deliberately elicits responses to questioning. In *McCleskey v. Zant*,[u] the Supreme Court determined that, even though the state wrongfully concealed a document disclosing how police placed an informant in the adjacent jail cell, McCleskey could not show cause for failing to include the claim in his original petition. When McCleskey filed his first habeas proceeding, the Court reasoned, he knew he had spoken to the jailhouse informant, and that the informant had some connection to the police.[v]

2) **The Statutory Argument.** In 1966, three years after *Sanders*, Congress added Subsection (b) to Section 2244. The pertinent language of 28 U.S.C. § 2244(b) provided:

> When after an evidentiary hearing on the merits of a material factual issue, or after a hearing on the merits of an issue of law, a person in custody pursuant to the judgment of a State court has been denied by a court of the United States or a justice or judge of the United States release from custody or other remedy on an application for a writ of habeas corpus, a subsequent application for a writ of habeas corpus on behalf of such person need not be entertained by a court of the United States or a justice or judge of the United States unless the application alleges and is predicated

---

[u] We use the short form "*McCleskey v. Zant*" to avoid any confusion with *McCleskey v. Kemp*, 481 U.S. 279 (1987), which is discussed in Note 9, *infra*.

[v] For an extended discussion of the role *Massiah* plays in balancing the right-to-counsel against the police interest in informants, see Alfredo Garcia, *The Right to Counsel Under Siege: Requiem for an Endangered Right?*, 29 Am. Crim. L. Rev. 35, 62–78 (1991). In fact, *Kuhlmann v. Wilson*, 477 U.S. 436 (1986), which affirmed an "ends of justice" gateway for successive-petition claims, was also a *Massiah* case.

on a factual or other ground not adjudicated on the hearing of the earlier application for the writ, and unless the court, justice, or judge is satisfied that the applicant has not on the earlier application deliberately withheld the newly asserted ground or otherwise abused the writ."

Under that statute, a federal court "need not entertain" a subsequent habeas petition "unless" the petitioner satisfies "the judge that he did not deliberately withhold the ground from the initial petition or "otherwise abuse[] the writ." *McCleskey v. Zant* read this provision as requiring that deliberate omission trigger a finding of writ abuse, and as delegating authority to identify other instances where forfeiture of a previously-omitted claim is appropriate. Justice Marshall, by contrast, believed that "otherwise abused the writ" referred to forms of writ abuse described in *Sanders*—to "vex, harass, or delay." Setting aside any assessment of the policy, which Justice had the better argument as to statutory construction? Justice Kennedy, in an omitted passage, referred to Congressional "silences" in both the earlier 1948 version of the statute and the 1966 version. Was the statute silent on the question before the Court? Or did Congress intend to codify *Sanders*? Does Justice Kennedy ignore *Sanders'* influence of the 1966 Amendments, or does Justice Marshall make too much of it?

(3) Deliberate Abandonment Versus Excusable Neglect. *McCleskey v. Zant* is part of a broader shift in habeas jurisprudence, and it parallels the Court's earlier 1977 ruling in *Sykes,* which introduced cause-and-prejudice analysis for procedural defaults. The core of *McCleskey v. Zant* is the rule elevating the level of diligence a prisoner must show to obtain merits consideration of claims based on new facts. One way to think about the excusable neglect rule is as a rule about "forfeiture"—when a prisoner forfeits a claim that involves facts "in existence" at the time the petitioner filed the initial petition without the omitted claim. When the Warren Court decided the 1963 habeas trilogy, *Sanders* restricted forfeiture to instances in which the prisoner deliberately withheld the claim from an initial petition. *McCleskey v. Zant* rejected the "deliberate bypass" standard to permit consideration of the omitted claim in a subsequent petition, and instead adopts the *Sykes* standard of "cause and prejudice," requiring a prisoner to show that some "external circumstance" prevented the claim from appearing in the first petition. In an opinion excerpt omitted here, *McCleskey* held that there was no cause for failing to include the *Massiah* claim.

Rather than focusing on whether the prisoner knew about the 21-page memo and about Officer Worthy, the decision focused on the availability of the "predicate" information that the memo and the officer referenced. Specifically, the Supreme Court reasoned that McCleskey forfeited his *Massiah* claim because: (1) McCleskey was party to the conversations with Evans and knew their underlying contents and (2) McCleskey knew about Evans and his relationship with the police when he filed his first federal petition. Why did the Court focus on the predicate facts rather than the documents or testimony that contained them? Did the Court need to announce the cause-and-prejudice rule, or would it have been possible to deny relief based on the deliberate abandonment standard from *Sanders*?

4) A Reasonable Investigation Rule. Interpret the following language from *McCleskey v. Zant*: "If what petitioner knows or could discover upon reasonable investigation supports a claim for relief in a federal habeas petition, what he does not know is irrelevant." How would you describe that diligence standard? Would it be fair to call the diligence standard a "reasonable investigation" rule? Non-capital prisoners, however, are not statutorily (or constitutionally) entitled to lawyers in federal habeas proceedings—although some do have counsel appointed under the Criminal Justice Act, 18 U.S.C. § 3006A. Should the "standard of care" depend on whether a prisoner is represented? Why would such a rule be conceptually or practically problematic? In other cases, the "reasonable investigation" rule frequently operates not as a rule about what the prisoner (a principal) should have done, but rather as a rule about what the lawyer representing the prisoner (an agent) should have done. Given that the rule pertains more to the investigation performed by a prisoner's lawyer than to the prisoner's own decisions, what sorts of additional information might you need to know in order to evaluate the efficacy of the rule? Should a prisoner be charged with forfeiture because an attorney failed to conduct a reasonable investigation?

5) **Incentives.** What other sorts of incentives does the *McCleskey* rule generate? Obviously, a prisoner has an increased incentive to conduct an investigation. What sorts of incentives does the rule create for the timing of a federal filing? Will the rule increase the number of claims asserted before the prisoner is fully prepared to litigate them? Is "premature" filing a real problem, or does it depend largely on how much a prisoner is allowed to develop the claim in the federal habeas proceeding?

6) **Equating Abuse of the Writ with Procedural Default.** *McCleskey* is one of a long line of cases in which procedural default and abuse-of-the-writ doctrines cross-pollinate. Specifically, the decision states: "We conclude from the unity of structure and purpose in the jurisprudence of state procedural defaults and abuse of the writ that the standard for excusing a failure to raise a claim at the appropriate time should be the same in both contexts." Evaluate the question posed in the paragraph introducing the case: do you agree that the two doctrines share enough "unity of structure and purpose?"

McCleskey v. Zant explains that, because the procedural default and successive petition and abuse of the writ doctrines serve largely the same interests, the standards for excuse should be identical. Should any differences between the two doctrines—and the interests they promote—cause the excuse standards to diverge? Does a more permissive abusive-writ standard compromise state procedural rules or preclude states from having the first crack at deciding a constitutional claim? Although there are "federalism" interests at work in abusive-writ law, those interests generally reflect a state's role as a litigant, not as an adjudicator. Should that be enough to support the analogy? Do the two rules reflect a similar interest in finality?

7) **"External Factor" As Cause.** According to *Sykes* and *McCleskey v. Zant*, "cause" must be something "external" to the petitioner. What sorts of "external" obstacles might there be? Would a rule prohibiting a prisoner's use of library be an "external obstacle?" Suppose that a court, when faced with a mixed petition, erroneously refuses to stay and abate the exhausted claim. Instead, it proceeds on the exhausted claim and forces the prisoner to come back and re-petition for relief on the previously-unexhausted claim after the prisoner litigates it in state court. Would that error be an external cause? What about the performance of an attorney? The court makes clear that constitutionally ineffective performance by an attorney can constitute cause, but the most common attor-

ney errors offered as cause will occur in post-conviction proceedings, in which there is no constitutional right to counsel.

8)   A *Martinez* Exception? In *Martinez v. Ryan*, presented earlier in the Chapter, the Supreme Court held that, for claims that can be asserted for the first time only on collateral review, deficient state post-conviction counsel constitutes "cause" for procedural default of a trial-phase IAC claim. Should the Court extend *Martinez* to abuse-of-the-writ-excuses? Does the answer depend on a comparison of the general quality of representation in state versus federal post-conviction proceedings? Might *Martinez* be an inappropriate rule for abuse-of-the-writ inquiries, even if federal post-conviction representation in the initial habeas proceeding is abysmal?

9)   Miscarriage of Justice and *Schlup v. Delo*. The Court concluded that McCleskey could not satisfy the miscarriage of justice exception, given the strength of the inculpatory evidence. Recall the discussion of *Schlup v. Delo*, 513 U.S. 298 (1995), from the procedural default section—where the Supreme Court considered the standard for the "miscarriage of justice" exception to which the Court alluded in *McCleskey v. Zant*. Schlup, a Missouri prisoner, had been convicted of killing another inmate while incarcerated. Schlup alleged, in a second habeas petition, that trial error kept the jury from hearing evidence that would have established his innocence. The lower federal courts held that the new evidence would have to have proven innocence under a "clear and convincing" standard, but the Court held that Schlup only had to show that he was "probably" innocent—that innocence was "more likely than not." That "more likely than not" requirement, however, was merely a "gateway" to a merits review of the underlying constitutional claim—satisfying the requirement did not entitle Schlup to relief. The *Schlup* gateway is important for at least two reasons. First, you will have to reconcile the "probably innocent" standard with the new text of § 2244(b)(2), which displaced the *Schlup* standard for abusive claims entirely. Second, recall that, whatever the reading of § 2244(b)(2), *House v. Bell* reiterated that the *Schlup* standard remains the "innocence gateway" rule for procedural doctrines that are not embodied in a statute—i.e., for procedural default.

10)   Warren McCleskey. *McCleskey v. Zant* is only the second most famous decision involving Warren McCleskey, who the State of Georgia executed in the fall of 1991. The Supreme Court decided *McCleskey v. Kemp*, 481 U.S. 279 in 1987, and that case presented the question of whether a state's capital punishment scheme could be constitutional despite the statistically significant presence of race as a sentence determinant. Specifically, McCleskey challenged his capital sentence under the Eighth Amendment and the Fourteenth Amendment's Equal Protection clause.

Professor David Baldus, a recently-deceased law professor at the University of Iowa, led a group that coded data for over 2,000 murder cases in Georgia. See David C. Baldus, Charles Pulaski, and George Woodworth, *Comparative Review of Death Sentences: An Empirical Study of the Georgia Experience*, Journal of Criminal Law and Criminology (Northwestern University) 74 (3): 661–753 (1983) (Baldus Study). The Baldus Study showed that black defendants were 1.7 times more likely to receive the death penalty than white defendants. The Baldus Study also found that defendants accused of killing white victims were 4.3 times more likely than defendants accused of killing black victims to receive the death penalty.

The Court first addressed the Equal Protection argument. With Justice Powell writing, the majority held that the Baldus study was insufficient to support an inference that any of the decision makers in McCleskey's case acted with a discriminatory purpose. Similarly, the majority held that the Baldus study could not support an inference that the Georgia legislature enacted the capital sentencing scheme for racially discriminatory reasons. The Court also rejected McCleskey's Eighth Amendment challenge:

> At most, the Baldus study indicates a discrepancy that appears to correlate with race. Apparent disparities in sentencing are an inevitable part of our criminal justice system. The discrepancy indicated by the Baldus study is "a far cry from the major systemic defects identified in *Furman.*" As this Court has recognized, any mode for determining guilt or punishment "has its weaknesses and the potential for misuse." Specifically, "there can be no perfect procedure for deciding in which cases governmental authority should be used to impose death." Despite these imperfections, our consistent rule has been that constitutional guarantees are met when "the mode [for determining guilt or punishment] itself has been surrounded with safeguards to make it as fair as possible." Where the discretion that is fundamental to our criminal process is involved, we decline to assume that what is unexplained is invidious. In light of the safeguards designed to minimize racial bias in the process, the fundamental value of jury trial in our criminal justice system, and the benefits that discretion provides to criminal defendants, we hold that the Baldus study does not demonstrate a constitutionally significant risk of racial bias affecting the Georgia capital sentencing process.

Justices Brennan, Marshall, Blackmun, and Stevens all dissented.

Professor Baldus later wrote that *McCleskey* "nearly eliminated the incentive of federal and state courts and legislatures to address meaningfully the issue of racial discrimination in the administration of the death penalty and has provided them with a political and legal framework for denying and avoiding the issue." David C. Baldus, George Woodworth & Catherine M. Grosso, *Race and Proportionality Since McCleskey v. Kemp (1987): Different Actors with Mixed Strategies of Denial and Avoidance*, 39 Colum. Hum. Rts. L. Rev. 143, 144 (2007).

11)   AEDPA and the Abuse-of-the-Writ Rule. AEDPA altered the abuse-of-the writ rule. There is no detailed legislative history regarding these changes. Congress generally noted: "This title incorporates reforms to curb the abuse of the statutory writ of habeas corpus, and to address the acute problems of unnecessary delay and abuse in capital cases." H.R. Rep. No. 104–518, at 111 (1996) (Conf. Rep.). Recall that, when the Supreme Court decided it, McCleskey's case had been pending for over a decade. AEDPA was in part a response to the Oklahoma City bombing, and the prospect of executing Timothy McVeigh loomed in the background. Many elected officials paired the interest in passing the legislation with the interest in avoiding delays in capital litigation. For example, AEDPA supporter Rep. Henry Hyde said that, "in death penalty cases, it normally takes 8 years to exhaust the appeals. It is ridiculous, 8 years is ridiculous; 15 and 17 years is even more so." 142 Cong. Rec. H3606 (daily ed. Apr. 18, 1996) (statement of Rep. Hyde). Of course, the changes to the successive-petition and abuse-of-the-writ rules applied in both capital and noncapital cases.

The interests in speedy resolution of capital cases and in "curbing" writ abuse were embodied in statutory provisions that largely incorporate the outcome in *McCleskey v. Zant*. To the extent that there is deviation between the outcome in the case and the text of the statute, the legislation is more restrictive. For example, under the decisional law, the government pleaded writ abuse by showing that a subsequent federal petition contained a new claim that an earlier petition omits. Then the burden shifted to the petitioner to show either (1) cause and prejudice from a failure to include the claim in the prior petition; or (2) a miscarriage of justice.

AEDPA reconstituted the abuse-of-the-writ defense (and its partner, the successive petition bar) as jurisdictional preconditions to relief. See 28 U.S.C. § 2244(b)(1)-(b)(2). Specifically, § 2244(b)(2) states that: "A claim presented in a second or successive habeas corpus application under section 2254 that was not presented in a prior application shall be dismissed." Then, § 2244(b)(2) creates two exceptions. One exception is for new law, and one is for newly-discovered facts:

> (A) the applicant shows that the claim relies on a new rule of constitutional law, made retroactive to cases on collateral review by the Supreme Court, that was previously unavailable; or

> (B)(i) the factual predicate for the claim could not have been discovered previously through the exercise of due diligence; and (ii) the facts underlying the claim, if proven and viewed in light of the evidence as a whole, would be sufficient to establish by clear and convincing evidence that, but for constitutional error, no reasonable factfinder would have found the applicant guilty of the underlying offense.

28 U.S.C. § 2244(b)(2).

a) **New Law.** One reason a claim might not have been included in an initial habeas petition is that, at the time the initial petition was filed, the claim was not cognizable in federal court. Prisoners can, in limited circumstances, invoke "new rules" of constitutional law as a basis for federal habeas relief. Usually, prisoners will have to litigate a habeas claim involving the new rule in a successive petition. You might think of 28 U.S.C. § 2244(b)(2)(A) as the "new law" exception to the statutory abuse-of-the-writ rule. The provision states that a petitioner may proceed with a claim not included in a prior federal petition if the claim relies on a rule "made retroactive to cases on collateral review by the Supreme Court." What does it mean for a case to be "made retroactive"? You will learn more about retroactivity in Chapter 5, but for now you should simply understand that the Supreme Court makes a new rule retroactive when the rule may be invoked not just by prisoners against whom criminal proceedings are pending, but also by prisoners whose convictions are final upon the conclusion of direct review.

b) **New Facts**. Turn to the second exception, which requires an inmate to show particular types of cause and prejudice. Cause requires a showing that new facts were not previously discoverable using due diligence. A prisoner satisfies the prejudice requirement if those facts "would be sufficient to establish by clear and convincing evidence that, but for constitutional error, no reasonable factfinder would have found the applicant guilty of the underlying offense." In what way is § 2244(b)(2)(B)(ii) a combination of the cause-and-prejudice and miscarriage-of-justice inquiries from earlier decisional law?

c)   A Statutory Mash-up. Note that the § 2244(b)(2)(B)(ii) inquiries no longer reflect distinct exceptions for consideration of a new claim. Before AEDPA, a prisoner could secure merits review of a new claim by satisfying *either* the cause-and-prejudice inquiry or by showing a miscarriage of justice. Section 2244(b)(2)(B)(ii) merges the inquiries in two ways.

First, § 2244(b)(2)(B)(ii) includes "but for" language that requires a nexus between the new claim and the evidence of innocence. Under *McCleskey*, the new claim did not have to be related to the guilt or innocence of the prisoner, and unrelated evidence of innocence could permit the claim to pass through the miscarriage of justice exception. Second, § 2244(b)(2)(B)(ii) requires that there be a particular type of cause, where the claim must involve underlying facts not previously available "through the exercise of due diligence," in order to assert any new evidence of innocence. *Schlup* imposed no such requirement. Do you think that AEDPA sensibly combined the two gateways—was there any need for them to be separate?

d)   Other Differences Between § 2244(b) and the Antecedent Decisional Law? There are other differences between AEDPA and prior decisional law. Under AEDPA, the prisoner must show "by *clear and convincing evidence* that, but for constitutional error, no reasonable factfinder would have found the applicant guilty of the underlying offense." (Emphasis added.) Under *Schlup*, the evidence to satisfy the miscarriage-of-justice gateway needed only to show that "a constitutional violation has *probably resulted* in the conviction of one who is actually innocent." (Emphasis added.) *Schlup* specifically rejected a "clear and convincing evidence" standard. In light of concerns about increased habeas filings, did Congress sensibly raise the burden of proof associated with innocence claims? Should the excuse standard for successive petitions be different than the one for procedurally defaulted claims?

What about new evidence that a sentence is unconstitutional—can new facts showing the defendant should not have received a capital sentence satisfy the provisions regarding whether a reasonable factfinder "would have found the applicant guilty of the underlying offense"? Congress cribbed some language from *Sawyer* when it crafted § 2244(b)(2)(B)(ii)—could Congress have nonetheless intended to bar *Sawyer* claims themselves? Take one example of a rule that was frequently the subject of successive habeas litigation: the rule announced in *Atkins v. Virginia*, 536 U.S. 304 (2002). *Atkins* held that inmates with mental retardation could not be executed. What would happen if an inmate had new evidence of mental retardation that would preclude an execution under *Atkins*? Under a literal interpretation of the statute, would a sentencing challenge satisfy an AEDPA successive-petition gateway? If you are unwilling to adopt a literalist interpretation, then do you think the fact that the statutory language seems to exclude *Sawyer* claims was simply an oversight by Congress? Even if the omission were inadvertent, do federal courts really have any special license to correct it? The question remains open.[w]

---

[w] See, e.g., LaFevers v. Gibson, 238 F.3d 1263, 1267 (10th Cir. 2001) (interpreting 2244(b)(2)(B) as permitting second or successive challenges to death sentences); Babbitt v. Woodford, 177 F.3d 744, 746 (9th Cir. 1999) (same). In contrast, some Circuits have held that "innocence" means only innocence of the crime, and not the sentence. See, e.g. In re Provenzano, 215 F.3d 1233, 1237 (11th Cir. 2000) (holding that the "2244(b)(2)(B) exception does not fit sentence stage claims" (internal quotation marks and citations omitted)).

NOTE ON PREVIOUSLY-ASSERTED CLAIMS UNDER 28 U.S.C. § 2244(b)(1)

Successive petitions may include claims that were raised in prior petitions, and also new claims that were not. Only the latter category is governed by § 2244(b)(2) and the abuse-of-the-writ rules. The former category—claims asserted in some prior federal petition—are categorically excluded, subject to no exceptions. 28 U.S.C. § 2244(b)(1) provides: "A claim presented in a second or successive habeas corpus application under section 2254 that was presented in a prior application shall be dismissed." Despite that AEDPA language, the Supreme Court has adopted somewhat more flexible (and perhaps strained) interpretations of Subsection (b)(1) in order to avoid the harshest outcomes of the statute's categorical language.

In *Panetti v. Quarterman*, 127 S.Ct. 2842 (2007), the Court dealt with the Eighth Amendment rule that states cannot execute incompetent offenders. Cf. Ford v. Wainwright, 477 U. S. 399, 409–410 (1986) ("[T]he Eighth Amendment prohibits a State from carrying out a sentence of death upon a prisoner who is insane.") "*Ford* challenges" are tricky, because the claim is not ripe until an execution is imminent—probably until a state has issued a death warrant that identifies an execution date. Under a literal reading of § 2244(b)(1), a prisoner would face a stark choice: either assert unripe *Ford* claims in an initial habeas petition (those proceedings would begin long before a state issued a death warrant), or wait and assert the *Ford* claim in a subsequent habeas petition that is filed after the *Ford* claim ripens.

In *Panetti*, the Court held that a *Ford* claim would not be disqualified under Subsection (b)(1) simply because a prisoner had failed to assert a premature version in an initial habeas petition. The Court stated, "[W]e have confirmed that claims of incompetency to be executed remain unripe at early stages of the proceedings." It then explained:

> In the usual case, a petition filed second in time and not otherwise permitted by the terms of § 2244 will not survive AEDPA's "second or successive" bar. There are, however, exceptions. We are hesitant to construe a statute, implemented to further the principles of comity, finality, and federalism, in a manner that would require unripe (and, often, factually unsupported) claims to be raised as a mere formality, to the benefit of no party.

> The statutory bar on "second or successive" applications does not apply to a *Ford* claim brought in an application filed when the claim is first ripe.

Do you think that the Court faithfully interpreted the statute, that it was permissibly correcting a drafting oversight, or that it was improperly defeating the will of the legislature? *Panetti* was not, in fact, the first time the Court strained to adopt a more-workable interpretation of § 2244(b)(1). See, e.g., Martinez v. Stewart Villareal, 523 U.S. 637 (1998) (deciding a similar issue with respect to a *Ford* claim).

———

NOTE ON AUTHORIZATION PROCEDURE UNDER 28 U.S.C. § 2244(b)(3)

Not only did AEDPA reconstitute the successive and abusive claim rules as jurisdictional limits, AEDPA also created an "authorization" procedure—an appeals-panel preclearance necessary to proceed on a successive petition in district court. See 28 U.S.C. § 2244(b)(3). Subsection (b)(3)(A) requires a federal petitioner, prior to proceeding on a successive habeas application in the district court, to make a motion asking an appeals court for authorization. Subsection (b)(3)(B) requires that a three-judge panel of that court decide the authorization motion.

Subsection (b)(3)(C) states that the appeals panel "may authorize the filing of a second or successive application only if it determines that the application makes a prima facie showing that the application satisfies the requirements of this subsection." Subsection (b)(3)(D) states that the appeals panel shall decide the motion within 30 days, although the time limit is purely aspirational and is infrequently observed.

Finally, Subsection (b)(3)(E) states that the order granting or denying the authorization motion cannot "be the subject of a petition for rehearing or for a writ of certiorari." Recall the excerpts and discussions of *Felker v. Turpin*, 518 U.S. 1051 (1996), from Chapter 2. In *Felker*, the Court considered the constitutionality of the certiorari restriction—namely, whether it ran afoul of the Article, III § 2 "Exceptions Clause" by stripping the Supreme Court's appellate jurisdiction over federal judicial subject matter. The Court concluded that § 2244(b)(3)(E) was constitutional, after interpreting it only to strip certiorari jurisdiction. In the various *Felker* opinions, the Justices underscored that the Court retained other forms of appellate jurisdiction over authorization orders.

After a *petition* is authorized under Subsection (b)(3)—because it contains a claim that satisfies either Subsection (b)(1) or (b)(2)—then the district court has to re-apply Subsections (b)(1) and (b)(2), in full, to every claim in the petition. While the authorization inquiry only looked to determine whether the petition states a "prima facie" case for relief under § 2244(b), the statute also directs that, after a petition is authorized, a district court "shall dismiss any claim presented in a second or successive application that the court of appeals has authorized to be filed unless the applicant shows that the claim satisfies the requirements of this *section*." (Emphasis added.)

There are at least three important differences between the § 2244(b)(3) authorization inquiry and the § 2244(b)(4) district court inquiry. First, the authorization inquiry is a determination about whether the petition contains a claim meeting either Subsection (b)(1) or (b)(2). In contrast, the district court applies that test on a claim-by-claim basis and examines each claim in the entire petition. Second, the statutory division of labor directs the court of appeals to authorize a petition that satisfies the standards in § 2244(b). In contrast, the district court must then apply the rest of § 2244 (including the statute of limitations in § 2244(d)).[x] Third, an authorization proceeding requires that an ap-

---

[x] The courts of appeals, however, are divided on the issue of whether an authorization panel can consider other affirmative defenses, including the § 2244(d) limitations period. Compare, e.g., Ochoa v. Sirmons, 485 F.3d 538, (10th Cir. 2007) (per curiam) (holding that the authorization panel may consider only whether the claimant has stated a prima facie entitlement to relief under § 2244(b)), with In re Hill, 437 F.3d 1080, 1083 (11th Cir. 2006) (asserting gatekeeping authority to time-bar a successive petition) and Outlaw v. Sternes, 233 F.3d 453,

peals court determine that a prisoner make a "prima facie" case, whereas the district court must apply the standards in full.

What are the advantages of an authorization proceeding? Are there some questions that you think are appropriate for resolution in such a proceeding, and others that you think are more appropriate for a district court?

4. STATUTE OF LIMITATIONS

AEDPA created, for the first time, a statute of limitations applicable to federal habeas claims of state prisoners. See 28 U.S.C. § 2244(d).[y] Of the many changes that AEDPA made to post-conviction law, the statute of limitations was, along with § 2254(d), perhaps the biggest break from prior practice. The statute of limitations, unlike the other procedural limits discussed in this Chapter, had no common-law antecedent.[z] The limitations rule has become one of the most frequently-litigated habeas issues in the federal courts. According to the *2007 Habeas Study*, the statute of limitations is now the most common reason why habeas claims are dismissed.[aa]

The limitations period was designed to put in place a one-year time period for filing certain federal habeas litigation. See H.R. Conf. Rep. No. 104–518, at 111 (AEDPA Committee Report describing § 2244(d) as setting "a one-year limitation on an application for a habeas writ[]"). The Supreme Court has explained that the statute of limitations "quite plainly serves the well-recognized interest in the finality of state court judgments." Duncan v. Walker, 533 U.S. 167, 179 (2001). After all, a central goal in enacting AEDPA was to "reduce delays in the execution of state and federal criminal sentences, particularly in capital cases." Woodford v. Garceau, 538 U.S. 202, 206 (2003).

Section 2244(d) raised, both on its face and in combination with other procedural rules, some difficult issues that Congress almost certainly failed to anticipate. (If Congress did anticipate them, then the statute's legislative history failed to memorialize that awareness.) As a result, the Supreme Court has been called on to interpret the provision many, many times in the last fifteen years. Section 2244(d) provides:

(1) A 1-year period of limitation shall apply to an application for a writ of habeas corpus by a person in custody pursuant to the judgment of a State court. The limitation period shall run from the latest of—

---

455 (7th Cir. 2000) (holding in the alternative that authorization be denied because the petition would be time-barred).

[y] There is an analogous period of limitation applicable to federal-prisoner claims under 28 U.S.C. § 2255 ¶(f).

[z] Federal judges, however, did follow timeliness rules under Habeas Rule 9(a), and would exercise discretion to dismiss dilatory habeas filings under a "prejudicial delay" standard. That rule was deleted in 2004 as unnecessary, given the AEDPA limitations statute. See Advisory Committee Notes to Rule 9 of the Rules Governing Section 2254 Cases in the United States District Courts (2004 Amendments).

[aa] The *2007 Habeas Study* revealed that 18.1% of non-capital cases were barred by the statute of limitations. See King et al., *2007 Habeas Study*, supra note f, at 47. Contrast that figure with the one in capital cases, where the limitations defense "was employed infrequently;" only 3% of capital cases (just 11 cases in the sample) involved a ruling that a claim was time-barred. Given that Congressional intent was plainly to focus on expediting capital litigation, do you find the disparity between capital and noncapital timeliness figures problematic? What do you think explains it?

(A) the date on which the judgment became final by the conclusion of direct review or the expiration of the time for seeking such review;

(B) the date on which the impediment to filing an application created by State action in violation of the Constitution or laws of the United States is removed, if the applicant was prevented from filing by such State action;

(C) the date on which the constitutional right asserted was initially recognized by the Supreme Court, if the right has been newly recognized by the Supreme Court and made retroactively applicable to cases on collateral review; or

(D) the date on which the factual predicate of the claim or claims presented could have been discovered through the exercise of due diligence.

(2) The time during which a properly filed application for State post-conviction or other collateral review with respect to the pertinent judgment or claim is pending shall not be counted toward any period of limitation under this subsection.

The statute of limitations commences on one of the four "trigger dates" specified in Subsection (d)(1). Subsection (d)(2) provides a statutory tolling mechanism. Chapter 11 explores the pleading requirements applicable to the limitations period, which is formally an "affirmative defense" that is subject to some unusual forfeiture rules.

A more restrictive statute of limitations—along with other, more stringent procedures—might apply in capital cases. Congress enacted, as part of AEDPA, a set of procedural defenses that death-penalty states could invoke if they "opted-in" by providing competent counsel to death row inmates during state post-conviction proceedings. Specifically, the opt-in provisions would shorten the applicable limitations period to 180 days, and they would require a federal judge to rule on a habeas petition within 180 days of when the inmate files it. See 28 U.S.C. §§ 2263(a) & 2266(b)(1)(A).

These capital opt-in provisions, 28 U.S.C. §§ 2261–2266, remain dormant. No death-penalty state has successfully opted in by providing sufficiently competent counsel to death row inmates. 28 U.S.C. § 2261(b). As Chapter 12 describes in more detail, federal courts have rejected every attempt that states have made to obtain certification for complying with opt-in conditions. Congress made it possible for the AG to certify state compliance, but efforts to draft guidelines for the AG certification process have stalled. So far, then, Congress's attempt at a quid pro quo—with states providing better state post-conviction lawyers in exchange for more favorable federal habeas defenses—has failed. See generally John H. Blume, Sheri Lynn Johnson & Keir M. Weyble, *In Defense of Noncapital Habeas: A Response to Hoffmann and King*, 96 Cornell L. Rev. 435, 469–70 (2011) (using opt-in regime as example of state resistance to providing adequate capital post-conviction representation); Betsy Dee Sanders Parker, *The Antiterrorism and Effective Death Penalty Act ("AEDPA"): Understanding the Failures of State Opt-In Mechanisms*, 92 Iowa L. Rev. 1969 (2007) (discussing shortcomings of the opt-in regime). The limitations cases are good illustrations both of why the opt-in project has been such a colossal failure and of how the Supreme Court has crafted other strategies to improve state post-conviction representation. When you read the statute of limitations cases, ask yourself whether AEDPA legislation or judge-made decisional law provides better incentives for states to invest in effective post-conviction representation.

A. 28 U.S.C. § 2244(d)(1)—STATUTORY "TRIGGER DATES"

Section 2244(d)(1) specifies four "trigger dates"—the dates on which the statute of limitations "clock" begins to run. Although there are trigger dates for claims that could not be asserted because of state interference (Subsection (d)(1)(B)), claims that arise from new and retroactive Supreme Court decisions (Subsection (d)(1)(C)), and claims that relate to newly-discovered evidence (Subsection (d)(1)(D)), the most frequently-implicated trigger date appears in Subsection (d)(1)(A), which is the date on which "the judgment became final by the conclusion of direct review or the expiration of the time for seeking such review[.]"

NOTES ON 28 U.S.C. § 2244(d)(1)(B)–(d)(1)(D): "ALTERNATIVE" TRIGGERS

Much, but not all, of the discussion in this Section involves issues that Subsection (d)(1)(A) raises. The other trigger dates nonetheless merit a brief discussion. Subsection (d)(1)(B) provides, as an alternative trigger date, "the date on which the impediment to filing an application created by State action in violation of the Constitution or laws of the United States is removed, if the applicant was prevented from filing by such State action." For the Subsection (d)(1)(B) trigger, the state-created impediment must have been a violation of federal law that prevented the filing of a habeas petition.[bb] Suppose that the deficient representation of a state-appointed lawyer delayed the filing of a federal claim. How is the standard for the § 2244(d)(1)(B) trigger more severe than the standard for excusing procedural default of the same claim? Do you think Congress intended to make excuses for untimely filings harder to come by than excuses for forfeiting claims in state court? Is there another feature of the limitations statute that might accommodate the problems created by the inept-lawyer scenario? (Hint: think about what the Court might do with the tolling mechanism.)

Subsection (d)(1)(C) commences a limitations period on "the date on which the constitutional right asserted was initially recognized by the Supreme Court," and when that new right was "newly recognized by the Supreme Court and made retroactively applicable to cases on collateral review." This new-law trigger roughly corresponds to the new-law exception in the successive-petition context. We will tackle retroactivity in the next Chapter, but for now consider how the limitations statute and the successive-petition rules work together in order to clear procedural obstacles that might otherwise frustrate the vindication of a newly-announced constitutional right. Also, given the fact that § 2244(d)(1)(C) actually has two conditions that need not occur simultaneous-

---

[bb] For a collection of cases on the § 2244(d)(1)(B) questions, see Hertz & Liebman, *FHCPP*, *supra* note e, at § 5.2[b][i] & n.54. See also, e.g., Critchley v. Thaler, 586 F.3d 318, 321 (5th Cir. 2009) (finding that claims were subject to § 2244(d)(1)(B) limitations period because state court officials twice failed to file prisoner's properly submitted state habeas petition); Wahem/Hunt v. Early, 233 F.3d 1146, 1148 (9th Cir. 2000) (en banc) (suggesting that the unavailability of materials in prison library might support the use of a § 2244(d)(1)(B) limitations period.).

ly—the announcement of a new rule an finding that it applies retroactively—think about whether the limitations period starts from the announcement of the new rule or only after the retroactivity of that rule is decided.[cc]

The third alternative trigger, appearing in Subsection (d)(1)(D), commences a limitations period on "the date on which the factual predicate of the claim or claims presented could have been discovered through the exercise of due diligence." Unlike the other trigger dates, the new-facts trigger is perhaps more lenient than its counterparts in other procedural doctrine. The new-facts trigger does not require that the new factual evidence go to innocence or set forth a particular standard of proof. Cf. 28 U.S.C. § 2244(b)(2)(B) (successive-petition rule requiring that claims based on new facts demonstrate innocence by clear and convincing evidence). The new-facts trigger, however, is not entirely toothless. For the pertinent limitations period to apply, the new evidence must be part of the claim's "factual predicate"—i.e., it must be essential evidence—and there must have been diligence and "cause" for failing to discover it at an earlier time.[dd]

The Supreme Court has ruled at least once on an alternative trigger, albeit in a 28 U.S.C. § 2255 federal-inmate case.[ee] In *Johnson v. United States*, 544 U.S. 295 (2005), the Court decided when the new-fact trigger in § 2255(f)(4) triggered a particular period of limitation. Section 2255(f)(4) provides that a limitations period commences on "the date on which the facts supporting the claim or claims presented could have been discovered through the exercise of due diligence." Johnson's federal sentence had been enhanced by the presence of a prior state conviction. Twenty-one months after he was convicted in federal court, he mounted a successful state collateral attack on his prior state conviction. He thereafter sought, via a § 2255 petition, to have his federal sentence reduced, as there was no longer a state conviction upon which to predicate the enhancement. The Supreme Court ruled that the order vacating his state conviction was a "new fact" that could commence a § 2244(d)(1)(C) statute of limitations. The Court nonetheless refused to recognize a new limitations period for Johnson because he had not exhibited prevacatur diligence; he had waited 21 months to seek state post-conviction relief. The Court observed:

[cc] For a collection of cases on the § 2244(d)(1)(C) questions, Hertz & Liebman, *FHCPP*, *supra* note e, at § 5.2[b][i] & n.55. For an example of a parallel § 2255 case discussing the requirement and noting a lack of guidance on the "made retroactive" language, see Howard v. U.S., 374 F.3d 1068 (11th Cir. 2004). Although there has been no formal holding under § 2244(d)(1)(C) that the Supreme Court has to be the entity declaring the rule retroactive, *Tyler v. Cain* held that, under the complementary successive-petition rule § 2244(b)(2)(A), the retroactivity of the new rule requires a high court finding. See 533 U.S. 656, 668 (2001).

[dd] For a collection of cases on the § 2244(d)(1)(D) questions, Hertz & Liebman, FHCPP, *supra* note e, at § 5.2[b][i] & n.56. See also, e.g., Starns v. Andrews, 524 F.3d 612 (5th Cir. 2008) (finding Subsection (d)(1)(C) triggered upon post-conviction receipt of statement by victim's former employer); The First Circuit has defined the due diligence test as "objective, not subjective . . . . [W]e are concerned less with what [the defendant's] counsel believed and more with what knowledge fairly may be imputed to him." Wood v. Spencer, 487 F.3d 1, 5 (1st Cir. 2007).

[ee] Chapter 9 discusses 28 U.S.C. § 2255, which provides for and limits habeas-like relief for federal inmates. (The representative new-fact-trigger case, Johnson v. United States, involved a federal-inmate petition.) Section 2255(f) includes a one-year statute of limitations. Federal inmates, however, require no statutory tolling for state collateral review. Section 2255(f) warrants discussion on its own merits (and receives it in Chapter 9), and the Court frequently interprets the state-inmate limitations period in light of parallel language in or its prior rulings on the federal-inmate limitations period.

Johnson has offered no explanation for this delay, beyond observing that he was acting *pro se* and lacked the sophistication to understand the procedures. But the Court has never accepted *pro se* representation alone or procedural ignorance as an excuse for prolonged inattention when a statute's clear policy calls for promptness. On this record, Johnson fell far short of reasonable diligence in challenging the state conviction.

Do you think that the Court's reasoning is consistent with the underlying concerns expressed in more recent procedural-defect cases, such as *Martinez v. Ryan*? What if a prisoner sought a post-conviction DNA test? The majority reasoned that the results might be exculpatory, but that "the due diligence requirement would say that the test result only triggers a new 1-year period if the petitioner began the testing process with reasonable promptness once the DNA sample and testing technology were available." The majority reasoned that the prisoner could wait "untold years"—maybe even until a key prosecution witness died—before requesting that DNA test. The dissent responded that the majority should not have discussed a DNA issue not presented in the case and that, furthermore, the DNA scenario implicated no analogous questions about whether a prisoner diligently sought to invalidate a conviction. In the dissent's view, the diligence requirement only applied to behavior following the order vacating the state conviction. The dissent argued that no federal rule was necessary because states have their own timeliness requirements for state collateral challenges. Which position do you find more persuasive?

NOTE ON 28 U.S.C. § 2244(d)(1)(A): THE "FINAL JUDGMENT" TRIGGER

The most important limitations period commences under Subsection (d)(1)(A), when the defendant receives a "final judgment" in state court and direct review of that judgment concludes. Consistent with what appears to be the plain language of the statute, the Supreme Court has ruled that the Subsection (d)(1)(A) trigger does not take effect until "the judgment became final" when either the Supreme Court denies certiorari review of the conviction or, if the petitioner seeks no certiorari review, when the 90-day window for seeking such review expires. See Jimenez v. Quarterman, 555 U.S. 113, 118 (2009). By contrast, the "pendency" of a state post-conviction claim, for the purposes of computing statutory tolling, does not include the window of time for seeking certiorari review. See Lawrence v. Florida, 549 U.S. 327, 337 (2007).

President Clinton signed AEDPA into law on April 24, 1996. All the circuits that addressed the issue decided that prisoners whose convictions became final prior to that date would have a one-year "grace period" during which to file their habeas claims.[ff] Of course, these prisoners still had to contend with all the other procedural limits on relief; but courts treated AEDPA limitations periods as though they commenced on the statute's effective date, rather than on any prior dates on which inmates' convictions became final. What arguments might you make for, or against, a constructive trigger date of April 24, 1996?

[ff] For a collection of cases on the constructive trigger date, see Hertz & Liebman, *FHCPP, supra* note e, at § 5.2[a] & n.22. See also Johnson v. United States, 544 U.S. 295, 300 (2005) ("Courts of Appeals" had "uniformly" provided a "1-year grace period running from the new statute's effective date" to prisoners whose convictions became final before AEDPA's enactment).

B. SUBSECTION 2244(d)(2)—STATUTORY TOLLING

AEDPA's statutory tolling provision states: "The time during which a properly filed application for State post-conviction or other collateral review with respect to the pertinent judgment or claim is pending shall not be counted toward any period of limitation under this subsection." 28 U.S.C. § 2244(d)(2). Because Congress pegged the tolling mechanism to other features of the complex and jurisdictionally-varied state post-conviction process, a straightforward application of the federal tolling provision is frequently impossible. A few questions emerge from the tolling provision's text. What does it mean for the referenced application to be "properly filed?" When is the application "pending," and does the pendency include any certiorari period? Does "other collateral review" refer only to other *state* collateral review, or does it also encompass *federal* habeas review? Does the state post-conviction pendency of one claim always toll the limitations period for all of the other claims in a habeas petition?

The tolling decisions are of extraordinary practical significance, as the limitations defense is raised in and results in the dismissal of so many habeas cases. The decisions are also pedagogically and conceptually significant because courts so frequently interpret the statute of limitations by recourse to the "purposes" of habeas or the statutes that prescribe its role. As you read the various cases in this Subsection, consider how the Supreme Court balances "comity, finality, and federalism" against the interest in providing federal remedy for constitutional violations.

NOTES ON "OTHER COLLATERAL REVIEW"

1)   Introduction to the Question. AEDPA's statutory tolling provision states that "[t]he time during which a properly filed application for *State post-conviction or other collateral review* with respect to the pertinent judgment or claim *is pending* shall not be counted toward any period of limitation under this subsection." (Emphasis added.) Some of the most important statutory tolling questions have involved interpretation of the italicized language. One of the first questions that the Supreme Court had to decide was whether, under § 2244(d)(2), the word "State" modified both "post-conviction" and "other collateral." Technically, the question was whether the phrase could be interpreted to mean "*state* post-conviction or other *state* collateral review." If so, then the pendency of a federal petition would not toll the applicable limitations period. This question is particularly important because habeas petitioners, frequently proceeding *pro se*, often file federal petitions prematurely—before all the claims in the petition are exhausted.

2)   Problems for Similarly-Situated Prisoners. Consider the scenario in which Inmates A and B have identical, unexhausted *Brady* claims, and each files a federal habeas petition containing the unexhausted claim with six months left in the limitations period. The federal judge takes five months to adjudicate Inmate A's petition, and another federal judge takes seven months to adjudicate Inmate B's petition. If the pendency of the federal proceeding does not toll the statutory limitations period, Inmate B will lose the opportunity to litigate the claim in federal court. Inmate A would have a month left on the limitations period and could litigate the claim.

More problematically, consider this issue in light of *Lundy's* bar on "mixed petitions." If an inmate has an exhausted claim that appears in a federal petition also containing an unexhausted one, then *Lundy* requires the federal judge to dismiss the entire petition. Assume Inmate C has an unexhausted *Brady* claim with six months remaining in the limitations period. If the pendency of the federal habeas petition does not toll the limitations period for the *Brady* claim, and if the federal court must dismiss the mixed petition, then the *Brady* claim would be time-barred if the federal court takes more than six months to dismiss the mixed petition. Even if the federal court takes less than six months to dismiss the entire petition, Inmate C might have very little time to exhaust that *Brady* claim in state court. (The pendency of the state proceeding would not count against Inmate C, because pending state post-conviction proceedings unquestionably toll the limitations period.)

3)   Stay and Abeyance. The Supreme Court addressed this problem in *Rhines v. Weber*, 544 U.S. 269 (2005). The Court acknowledged the problem discussed above, that "if a district court dismisses a mixed petition close to the end of the 1-year period, the petitioner's chances of exhausting his claims in state court and refiling his petition in federal court before the limitations period runs are slim." Justice O'Connor, the author of *Rose v. Lundy,* wrote the majority opinion, and noted how AEDPA "reinforces the importance of *Lundy's* simple and clear instruction to potential litigants: before you bring any claims to federal court, be sure that you first have taken each one to state court."

The Supreme Court endorsed a "stay-and-abeyance" procedure to maintain the pendency of the exhausted claims in federal court while the prisoner exhausted the other claims in state post-conviction proceedings. The Court acknowledged the complicating effects that *Rhines* stays have on a limitations provision designed to promote finality: "Staying a federal habeas petition frustrates AEDPA's objective of encouraging finality by allowing a petitioner to delay the resolution of the federal proceedings." The Court's endorsement of stay-and-abeyance procedure was restrained:

> [S]tay and abeyance is only appropriate when the district court determines there was good cause for the petitioner's failure to exhaust his claims first in state court. Moreover, even if a petitioner had good cause for that failure, the district court would abuse its discretion if it were to grant him a stay when his unexhausted claims are plainly meritless.

The Court added that, even when stay and abeyance is appropriate, its use is limited by the "timeliness concerns reflected in AEDPA." Where capital petitioners might "deliberately engage in dilatory tactics," district courts should impose "reasonable limits on a petitioner's trip to state court and back." The Court indicated that, if the inmate is not deliberately delaying punishment, a district court abuses its discretion by refusing a *Rhines* stay. Do the conditions on stay-and-abeyance orders reflect the "deliberate bypass" paradigm of the Warren Court and the cause-and-prejudice paradigms of its successors? Is stay-and-abeyance procedure consistent with AEDPA's statutory goals?

4)   *Duncan v. Walker.* The Supreme Court wrestles with many of these issues in *Duncan v. Walker*, 533 U.S. 167 (2001). In reading through the *Duncan* excerpts in the Notes, consider how the Court reconciles these problematic outcomes with the interests of comity, finality, and federalism.

a)   The Majority Opinion. In her opinion for the Court, Justice O'Connor framed the question:

> Our task is to construe what Congress has enacted. We begin, as always, with the language of the statute. [Walker, the prisoner] reads § 2244(d)(2) to apply the word "State" only to the term "post-conviction" and not to the phrase "other collateral." Under this view, a properly filed federal habeas petition tolls the limitation period. [New York] contends that the word "State" applies to the entire phrase "post-conviction or other collateral review." Under this view, a properly filed federal habeas petition does not toll the limitation period.

In expressing agreement with the State, Justice O'Connor applied a series of interpretive canons to the text of the provision:

> The essence of respondent's position is that Congress used the phrase "other collateral review" to incorporate federal habeas petitions into the class of applications for review that toll the limitation period. But a comparison of the text of § 2244(d)(2) with the language of other AEDPA provisions supplies strong evidence that, had Congress intended to include federal habeas petitions within the scope of § 2244(d)(2), Congress would have mentioned "Federal" review expressly. . .

> Section 2244(d)(2), by contrast, employs the word "State," but not the word "Federal," as a modifier for "review." It is well settled that "'[w]here Congress includes particular language in one section of a statute but omits it in another section of the same Act, it is generally presumed that Congress acts intentionally and purposely in the disparate inclusion or exclusion.'"
> . . .

> Further, were we to adopt [Walker's] construction of the statute, we would render the word "State" insignificant, if not wholly superfluous. . . We are especially unwilling to do so when the term occupies so pivotal a place in the statutory scheme as does the word "State" in the federal habeas statute. But under [Walker's] rendition of § 2244(d)(2), Congress' inclusion of the word "State" has no operative effect on the scope of the provision. If the phrase "State post-conviction or other collateral review" is construed to encompass both state and federal collateral review, then the word "State" places no constraint on the class of applications for review that toll the limitation period. The clause instead would have precisely the same content were it to read "post-conviction or other collateral review." . . .

> Congress also may have employed the construction "post-conviction or other collateral" in recognition of the diverse terminology that different States employ to represent the different forms of collateral review that are available after a conviction. In some jurisdictions, the term "post-conviction" may denote a particular procedure for review of a conviction that is distinct from other forms of what conventionally is considered to be postconviction review.

The Court concluded with an evaluation of how AEDPA's omnipresent purposes affected the Court's interpretation of the statute:

> [New York's] interpretation of the statute is consistent with "AEDPA's purpose to further the principles of comity, finality, and federalism." Specifically, under [Walker's] construction, § 2244(d)(2) promotes the exhaus-

tion of state remedies while respecting the interest in the finality of state court judgments. . .

The tolling provision of § 2244(d)(2) balances the interests served by the exhaustion requirement and the limitation period. Section 2244(d)(2) promotes the exhaustion of state remedies by protecting a state prisoner's ability later to apply for federal habeas relief while state remedies are being pursued. At the same time, the provision limits the harm to the interest in finality by according tolling effect only to "properly filed application[s] for State post-conviction or other collateral review."

By tolling the limitation period for the pursuit of state remedies and not during the pendency of applications for federal review, § 2244(d)(2) provides a powerful incentive for litigants to exhaust all available state remedies before proceeding in the lower federal courts. But if the statute were construed so as to give applications for federal review the same tolling effect as applications for state collateral review, then § 2244(d)(2) would furnish little incentive for individuals to seek relief from the state courts before filing federal habeas petitions. The tolling provision instead would be indifferent between state and federal filings. While other statutory provisions, such as § 2254(b) itself, of course, would still provide individuals with good reason to exhaust, § 2244(d)(2) would be out of step with this design. At the same time, [Walker's] interpretation would further undermine the interest in finality by creating more potential for delay in the adjudication of federal law claims.

A diminution of statutory incentives to proceed first in state court would also increase the risk of the very piecemeal litigation that the exhaustion requirement is designed to reduce. . . Tolling the limitation period for a federal habeas petition that is dismissed without prejudice would thus create more opportunities for delay and piecemeal litigation without advancing the goals of comity and federalism that the exhaustion requirement serves. We do not believe that Congress designed the statute in this manner.

Judges may rely on canons to interpret the text of statutes. *Ejusdem generis* is the interpretive rule that "when a general term follows a specific one, the general term should be understood as a reference to subjects akin to the one with specific enumeration." Norfolk & Western R. Co. v. Train Dispatchers, 499 U.S. 117, 129 (1991). How does that particular canon apply to the statutory tolling provision? Do you think that the specification of "state" post-conviction review means that the "other collateral" review referenced in the statute is also limited to state proceedings? *Ejusdem generis* is not the only canon at work in the Court's opinion. The Court also invoked an interpretive principle you might recognize as "the rule against surplusage"—the idea that a statute should be interpreted, if possible, so that every word has some operative effect. Could the term "state" add any meaning if "other collateral review" included federal habeas proceedings? If not, is the rule against surplusage a useful guide for statutory meaning? Why or why not?

b)   The Breyer Dissent. Justice Breyer wrote a dissent disputing the textual exegesis of the tolling provision, and also taking issue with what he perceived to be sloppy deployment of legislative purpose in favor of restrictive statutory interpretations. First, he argued that the statutory language was indeterminate:

The statute's language, read by itself, does not tell us whether the words "State post-conviction or other collateral review" include federal habeas proceedings... Indeed, most naturally read, the statute refers to two distinct kinds of applications: (1) applications for "State post-conviction" review and (2) applications for "other collateral review," a broad category that, on its face, would include applications for federal habeas review. The majority's reading requires either an unusual intonation—"*State* post-conviction-or-other-collateral *review*"—or a slight rewrite of the language, by inserting the word "State" where it does not appear, between "other" and "collateral." ... The statute's words, by themselves, have no singular "plain meaning."

Neither do I believe that the various interpretive canons to which the majority appeals can solve the problem...

[O]ther statutory neighbors show that, when Congress wished unambiguously to limit tolling to state proceedings, "it knew how to do so." ... Does Congress's failure to include a similar qualification in § 2244's tolling provision show that it means that provision to cover both federal and state proceedings? In fact, the "argument from neighbors" shows only that Congress might have spoken more clearly than it did. It cannot prove the statutory point.

The majority also believes that only its interpretation gives effect to every word in the statute—in particular the word "State." ...

But this argument proves too much, for one can ask with equal force: If Congress intended to exclude federal habeas proceedings, why does the word "post-conviction" appear in the statute? State post-conviction proceedings are a form of collateral review. So, had Congress meant to exclude federal collateral proceedings, it could have just said "State collateral review," thereby clearly indicating that the phrase applies only to state proceedings.

In fact, this kind of argument, viewed realistically, gets us nowhere. Congress probably picked out "State post-conviction" proceedings from the universe of collateral proceedings and mentioned it separately because State post-conviction proceedings are a salient example of collateral proceedings. But to understand this is not to understand whether the universe from which Congress picked "State post-conviction" proceedings as an example is the universe of *all* collateral proceedings, or the universe of *state* collateral proceedings. The statute simply does not say...

Aside from state post-conviction remedies, what else might constitute "other collateral review," if not federal habeas remedies? Do you think that the statutory text is indeterminate? If so, do you think the best way to interpret the rule is by reference to legislative purpose—the methodology that, although they reach different conclusions, both opinions use? Justice Breyer concludes:

Congress would not have intended to shorten that time dramatically, at random, and perhaps erase it altogether ... simply because the technical nature of the habeas rules led a prisoner initially to file a petition in the wrong court.

The majority's argument assumes a congressional desire to strengthen the prisoners' incentive to file in state court first. But that is not likely to be the result of today's holding. After all, virtually every state prisoner already knows that he must first exhaust state-court remedies; and I imagine that virtually all of them now try to do so. The problem arises because the vast majority of federal habeas petitions are brought without legal representation. . .

Nor is it likely that prisoners will deliberately seek to delay by repeatedly filing unexhausted petitions in federal court, as the Court suggests. First, prisoners not under a sentence of death (the vast majority of habeas petitioners) have no incentive to delay adjudication of their claims. . . Second, the prisoner who chooses to go into federal court with unexhausted claims runs the risk that the district court will simply deny those claims on the merits . . . before the prisoner has had the opportunity to develop a record in state court. . .

Finally, the majority's construction of the statute will not necessarily promote comity. Federal courts, understanding that dismissal for nonexhaustion may mean the loss of any opportunity for federal habeas review, may tend to read ambiguous earlier state-court proceedings as having adequately exhausted a federal petition's current claims. For similar reasons, wherever possible, they may reach the merits of a federal petition's claims without sending the petitioner back to state court for exhaustion. To that extent, the majority's interpretation will result in a lesser, not a greater, respect for the state interests to which the majority refers. In addition, by creating pressure to expedite consideration of habeas petitions and to reach the merits of arguably exhausted claims, it will impose a heavier burden on the district courts.

In fact, Justice Breyer's *Duncan* dissent is considered by some to be a seminal entry in his canon of purposivist interpretation. See Damien M. Schiff, *Purposivism and the "Reasonable Legislator": A Review Essay of Justice Breyer's Active Liberty*, 33 Wm. Mitchell L. Rev. 1081, 1099–1104 (2007).

Who gets the better of the argument about statutory purpose, Justice O'Connor or Justice Breyer? What does Justice Breyer mean when he says that noncapital prisoners do not share an incentive to delay with capitally-sentenced inmates? For an argument that statutory interpretation on the *Duncan* issue reflects the broader problem that AEDPA does not lend itself to useful "legal metrics" for comparing different statutory interpretations, see Ward Farnsworth, *Signatures of Ideology: The Case of the Supreme Court's Criminal Docket*, 104 Mich. L. Rev. 67, 84–88 (2005).

————

NOTES ON "PENDING"

1)   State Post-conviction Applications. The prior Notes dealt with questions about what types of proceedings toll the limitations period. This Note and the next one deal more specifically with the how state post-conviction proceedings can effect the limitations period through tolling. Under 28 U.S.C. § 2244(d)(2), the limitations period is only tolled while a "properly filed" state post-conviction application is "pending." When is an application for post-conviction review "pending?" An application would certainly be pending while under active consideration by a court, but what about periods between a trial-court disposition and when the appeal commences? What if the appeal is discretionary?

2)   Not Pending During Certiorari Review. The application is not "pending" during a certiorari proceeding in the United States Supreme Court, or—if the prisoner does not seek certiorari review—before the lapse of the period during which the prisoner remained eligible to do so. See Lawrence v. Florida, 549 U.S. 327, 337 (2007). In *Lawrence,* the Court explained that, "allowing the statute of limitations to be tolled by certiorari petitions would provide incentives for state prisoners to file certiorari petitions as a delay tactic." The Court added that such a tolling rule "would provide an incentive for prisoners to file certiorari petitions—regardless of the merit of the claims asserted—so that they receive additional time to file their habeas applications." Justice Ginsburg, joined by three other Justices, dissented, arguing that, "Until we have disposed of the petition for certiorari, the application remains live as one for state postconviction relief; it is not transformed into a federal application simply because the state-court applicant petitions for this Court's review."

3)   State Discretionary Review. The state post-conviction landscape varies considerably across jurisdictions, and different states have different processes for reviewing post-conviction adjudication in lower state courts. In *Carey v. Saffold,* 536 U.S. 214 (2002), the Supreme Court considered whether a state post-conviction application was pending during the period between the conclusion of a post-conviction proceeding in a state trial court and the initiation of discretionary review in a state appeals court. Justice Breyer wrote for the Court, beginning the opinion with textualist logic:

> The dictionary defines "pending" (when used as an adjective) as "in continuance" or "not yet decided." Webster's Third New International Dictionary 1669 (1993). It similarly defines the term (when used as a preposition) as "through the period of continuance . . . of," "until the . . . completion of." That definition, applied in the present context, means that an application is pending as long as the ordinary state collateral review process is "in continuance"—i.e., "until the completion of" that process. In other words, until the application has achieved final resolution through the State's post-conviction procedures, by definition it remains "pending."

Consistent with a sequence that should now be becoming familiar, the Court then proceeded to justify the favored interpretation of the statute by reference to the purposes of the habeas provisions in Title 28:

> California's reading would also produce a serious statutory anomaly. A federal habeas petitioner must exhaust state remedies before he can obtain federal habeas relief. The statute makes clear that a federal petitioner has not exhausted those remedies as long as he maintains "the right under the law of the State to raise" in that State, "by any available procedure, the question presented." We have interpreted this latter provision to require the federal habeas petitioner to "invok[e] one complete round of the State's established appellate review process." The exhaustion requirement serves AEDPA's goal of promoting "comity, finality, and federalism[ ]" . . . by giving state courts "the first opportunity to review [the] claim," and to "correct" any "constitutional violation in the first instance." And AEDPA's limitations period—with its accompanying tolling provision—ensures the achievement of this goal because it "promotes the exhaustion of state remedies while respecting the interest in the finality of

state court judgments." California's interpretation violates these principles by encouraging state prisoners to file federal habeas petitions *before* the State completes a full round of collateral review.

Justice Kennedy wrote the dissent for four of the Justices. Justice Kennedy emphasized some complicated features of California's system of appellate review of a collateral judgment. Specifically, the California Supreme Court reviewed the lower-court habeas judgment using an "original" habeas writ. (The petitioner missed his 10-day window to file a standard appeal following the lower court's judgment.) Because the original habeas writ was not the preferred vehicle for appellate review of lower-court state habeas decisions, Justice Kennedy argued that the period between the conclusion of the lower court proceeding and the filing of the original writ application should not be treated as a period of "pendency" under § 2244(d)(2).[gg]

NOTES AND QUESTIONS ON *"PROPERLY FILED"*

1)   "Conditions for Filing" Versus "Conditions for Relief." Congress has concluded that a state prisoner should not be able to statutorily toll the limitations period by frivolously filing collateral attacks on a conviction. Under 28 U.S.C. § 2244(d)(2), the federal limitations period is not statutorily tolled unless a pending application for state post-conviction review is "properly filed." Of course, whether an application should be treated as "properly filed" is not always a simple determination. States have all sorts of rules that can preclude relief on a claim, apart from an adverse determination on the merit of the constitutional challenge: a technical defect in the form of a filing, a lapsed state limitations period, or a determination that a state challenge is an abuse of the writ (under state law). What kinds of defects render an application "not properly filed" within the meaning of the federal limitations statute?

The Supreme Court addressed this question for the first time in *Artuz v. Bennett*, 531 U.S. 4 (2000), in the context of a New York state court order denying relief for failure to raise the claim through the proper procedural channels. Bennett, the prisoner, argued that an application was properly filed as long as it complied with "with all mandatory state-law procedural requirements that would bar review of the merits of the application." The Court, in a unanimous opinion by Justice Scalia, disagreed. Justice Scalia wrote for the Court in *Bennett*, holding that "[a]n application is 'filed,' as that term is commonly understood, when it is delivered to, and accepted by, the appropriate court officer for

---

[gg] In *Evans v. Chavis*, 546 U.S. 189 (2006), the Supreme Court returned to the unusual system of appellate review in California, and clarified when state post-conviction applications are not "pending" on review in the state supreme Court. California requires that the functional equivalent of a notice of appeal must be filed within a "reasonable time." The Supreme Court held that an unexplained six-month delay between a state post-conviction judgment and the notice of appeal, and then a three year delay in filing the petition for review in the California Supreme Court, was "unreasonable." Even though the California Supreme Court order disclosed no basis for its decision—i.e., that the state supreme court disposition could theoretically have been on the merits—the limitations period was not statutorily tolled. The Supreme Court concluded that, because the California Supreme Court was silent about whether it denied his petition for timeliness reasons or for merits reasons, a federal court must "simply to ask and . . . decide whether the state prisoner made the relevant filing within a reasonable time." The Court concluded that an unexplained six-month delay in filing the notice of appeal was not reasonable, and that the post-conviction application was not "pending" within the meaning of the statutory tolling mechanism during that delay.

placement into the official record." Justice Scalia then explained that an application is "'properly filed' when its delivery and acceptance are in compliance with the applicable laws and rules governing filings." The Court listed some rules that it considered to be conditions for filing: the form of the document, time limits on delivery, and a filing fee. The Court was careful to distinguish between post-conviction claims, which may or may not have been properly raised, and applications, which are more appropriately described as having been either filed or not filed. The rule that most take away from *Bennett* is that, when a pending state post-conviction application failed to meet a "condition for relief," the limitations period is tolled. When such an application does not satisfy a "condition for filing," however, the limitations period continues to run.

The Supreme Court reserved an important question in footnote 2 of the opinion: "We express no view on the question whether the existence of certain exceptions to a timely filing requirement can prevent a late application from being considered improperly filed." The Court was alluding to state laws that impose a limitations period on state post-conviction applications, but contain exceptions requiring a court to evaluate the merits of a claim presented in an otherwise untimely application. Would such a rule be a "condition for filing" for which the limitations period would not be tolled, or a "condition for relief?"

2)   *Pace v. Diguglielmo.* In *Pace v. Diguglielmo*, 544 U.S. 408 (2005), the Supreme Court took up the question left open in *Bennett*: whether a state post-conviction application that failed to meet an exception to a state timeliness requirement was "properly filed." In February 1986, Pace pleaded guilty to second-degree murder in Pennsylvania state court; he was sentenced to life without the possibility of parole. He filed no motion to withdraw his guilty plea and did not file a direct appeal. In August 1986, Pace filed a state post-conviction application under the then-applicable state statute; those proceedings concluded in September 1992. The default trigger date for AEDPA claims relating to convictions that were final prior to its passage was the enactment date of April 24, 1996.

On November 27, 1996, Pace filed another state application under a new state post-conviction statute. The new Pennsylvania statute included a statute of limitations that had three exceptions. The state courts concluded that the claim was untimely, reasoning Bennett had neither "alleged nor proven" that he fell within a statutory exception. The Pennsylvania Supreme Court denied review of that issue on July 29, 1999. On December 24, 1999, Pace filed a federal habeas petition. The U.S. Supreme Court had to decide whether the second state application was "properly filed" because the exceptions to the state post-conviction statute were "conditions for relief," or whether the federal limitations period was not statutorily tolled because the exceptions were "conditions for filing."

a)   The Majority Opinion. Chief Justice Rehnquist wrote for the Court, holding that "a petition filed after a time limit, and which does not fit within any exceptions to that limit, is no more 'properly filed' than a petition filed after a time limit that permits no exception." A contrary ruling, the Court reasoned, would turn the statutory tolling provision "into a *de facto* extension mechanism, quite contrary to the purpose of AEDPA, and open the door to abusive delay." Does the Court's opinion turn at all on the nature of the exceptions? What if one of the exceptions is something that involves a quasi-merits assessment of a claim, such as a determination of whether a claimant makes a "prima facie" showing? Note the analogy to procedural default jurisprudence, and the similarity to the question of whether an independent and adequate state ground exists.

b)   Finality and Capital Versus Noncapital Prisoners. Is there a reason to believe that capital and noncapital prisoners behave differently? Justice Stevens argued in dissent that "[m]ost prisoners have precisely the opposite incentive because delaying the initiation of federal postconviction relief will almost assuredly maximize their periods of incarceration." Many judicial opinions seem to treat a capital prisoner, with a clear incentive to delay imposition of a capital sentence, as the archetypal post-conviction claimant. As some of the statistics presented in this Book have indicated, the typical habeas claimant is a noncapital prisoner, who arguably lacks the same incentive for filings that frustrate final adjudication of a sentence.

c)   Piecemeal Litigation. Justice Stevens also argued that the Court's rule would result in piecemeal litigation, as claimants made protective federal filings and then sought to stay the federal proceeding to exhaust the challenge in state court:

> Unfortunately, the most likely consequence of the Court's new rule will be to increase, not reduce, delays in the federal system. The inevitable result of today's decision will be a flood of protective filings in the federal district courts. As the history of this case demonstrates, litigants, especially those proceeding *pro se*, cannot predict accurately whether a state court will find their application timely filed. Because a state court's timeliness ruling cannot be predicted with certainty, prisoners who would otherwise run the risk of having the federal statute of limitations expire while they are exhausting their state remedies will have no choice but to file premature federal petitions accompanied by a request to stay federal proceedings pending the exhaustion of their state remedies.

First, do you recognize the mechanism by which the prisoners would be seeking to stay the federal proceeding? Second, is Justice Stevens trying to have his cake and eat it too? On the one hand, he argues that *pro se* litigants are unsophisticated and unable to predict state timeliness determinations. On the other hand, he argues that their litigation will be piecemeal because they will invoke a fairly complicated procedure to hold their federal litigation in abeyance to exhaust the pertinent claim.

3)   Authorization Procedures. Consider other types of state habeas procedures, and whether they are "conditions to filing" or "conditions for relief." Many states have an "authorization procedure" for successive state petitions, much like the federal rules for authorizing successive federal petitions. If a state supreme court does not authorize a successive state petition, is the unauthorized petition "properly filed?" Is there any principled way of distinguishing conditions for filing from conditions for relief based on *Bennett* and *Pace*?

———

NOTE ON "PERTINENT JUDGMENT OR CLAIM"

Note that the limitations period is statutorily tolled only for the pendency of properly-filed collateral attacks "with respect to the pertinent judgment or claim." Would the pendency of a state post-conviction application involving one claim toll the limitations period for other claims? The language of the statute might suggest that any attack on the "pertinent judgment" tolls the federal limitations period for other attacks on the same judgment. Does such a reading of the statute render the language "or claim" surplusage? A contrary interpretation, whereby the limitations period is tolled only on a claim-by-claim basis, is equally susceptible to the criticism that it moots other language in the provision—then what work does "judgment" do?

The "judgment" versus "claim-by-claim" question may lead to different results depending on whether the question involves the trigger or the tolling mechanism. The Eleventh Circuit has held that, because the trigger provisions apply to an "application," the latest potentially-applicable trigger date sets the period of limitation for all claims collaterally attacking the same judgment. See Walker v. Crosby, 341 F.3d 1240, 1243 (11th Cir.2003). The Third, Sixth, and Ninth circuits, by contrast, have held that each claim is subject to a different limitations period. See Mardesich v. Cate, 668 F.3d 1164, 1170 (9th Cir. 2012); Bachman v. Bagley, 487 F.3d 979, 984 (6th Cir. 2007); Fielder v. Varner, 379 F.3d 113, 117–18 (3d Cir. 2004). The weight of circuit authority probably reflects that, in *Pace*, the Supreme Court suggested that "claim-by-claim consideration" was appropriate when applying the limitations triggers. See *Pace*, 544 U.S. at 416 n. 6.

The more pertinent question here is whether the *tolling* provision should apply on a claim-by-claim basis, or to the petition as a whole. Consider a specific case in which a prisoner has an *Atkins* claim. The Supreme Court decided *Atkins* in March 2002, and assume the state inmate's conviction became final sometime in late 2001. Would the pendency of a properly-filed state *Atkins* application toll the limitations period for other claims that accrued when the conviction became final? If any state collateral attack on the judgment tolls the limitations period for all other claims, then the pendency of the state *Atkins* litigation will stop the limitations clock in for all claims in federal court. But if the limitations period is tolled only for the "pertinent claim," then only the limitations period applicable to the *Atkins* claim is tolled.

Is there any way to read § 2244(d)(2) so as to give effect to both parts of the phrase "pertinent judgment or claim?" Recall that § 2244(d)(1) has some statutory triggers for claims that accrue upon the conviction becoming final, and other statutory triggers for other claims that do not accrue until some later date—e.g., upon a Supreme Court decision announcing a new and retroactive constitutional rule. What do you think about the possibility that Congress meant for "tolling to follow the trigger"—that tolling applies on a "judgment" basis for all claims that accrue for a trigger that is pegged to the date the judgment becomes final, and that tolling applies on a claim-by-claim basis for all claims that accrue for a trigger that is pegged to the accrual of a specific claim? How should the answer to that question reflect the approaches to statutory interpretation that the Court uses to answer limitations questions?

C. EQUITABLE TOLLING

INTRODUCTORY NOTE ON EQUITABLE TOLLING

28 U.S.C. § 2244(d)(2) expressly provides a prerequisite for tolling the limitations period in § 2244(d)(1): the pendency of a properly-filed state collateral attack on the pertinent judgment or claim. Are there other circumstances that

would toll the limitations period? After AEDPA, every U.S. court of appeals held that the limitations period could be *equitably* tolled. The Supreme Court, however, had only assumed the existence of equitable tolling arguendo; the existence of statutory conditions for tolling arguably suggests, by negative implication, that tolling is unavailable in other circumstances.

Some argued that the need for equitable tolling was particularly extreme in situations where an inmate was either not represented or was represented by a lawyer whose performance was defective. As you read the following case, keep two questions in mind. First, should there be an equitable tolling rule for such situations? Second, if there should be a rule, what should the standard for tolling be?

Holland v. Florida

United States Supreme Court
130 S.Ct. 2549 (2010)

■ Justice Breyer delivered the opinion of the Court.

We here decide that the timeliness provision in the federal habeas corpus statute is subject to equitable tolling. * * * In the Court of Appeals' view, when a petitioner seeks to excuse a late filing on the basis of his attorney's unprofessional conduct, that conduct, even if it is "negligent" or "grossly negligent," cannot "rise to the level of egregious attorney misconduct" that would warrant equitable tolling unless the petitioner offers "proof of bad faith, dishonesty, divided loyalty, mental impairment or so forth." In our view, this standard is too rigid. We therefore reverse the judgment of the Court of Appeals and remand for further proceedings.

I

AEDPA states that "[a] 1-year period of limitation shall apply to an application for a writ of habeas corpus by a person in custody pursuant to the judgment of a State court." § 2244(d)(1). It also says that "[t]he time during which a properly filed application for State post-conviction . . . review" is "pending shall not be counted" against the 1-year period. § 2244(d)(2).

On January 19, 2006, Albert Holland filed a *pro se* habeas corpus petition in the Federal District Court for the Southern District of Florida. Both Holland (the petitioner) and the State of Florida (the respondent) agree that, unless equitably tolled, the statutory limitations period applicable to Holland's petition expired approximately five weeks before the petition was filed. * * *

A

In 1997, Holland was convicted of first-degree murder and sentenced to death. The Florida Supreme Court affirmed that judgment. On *October 1, 2001*, this Court denied Holland's petition for certiorari. And on that date—the date that our denial of the petition ended further direct review of Holland's conviction—the 1-year AEDPA limitations clock began to run.

Thirty-seven days later, on *November 7, 2001*, Florida appointed attorney Bradley Collins to represent Holland in all state and federal postconviction proceedings. By *September 19, 2002*—316 days after his appointment and 12 days before the 1-year AEDPA limitations period expired—Collins, acting on Holland's behalf, filed a motion for postconviction relief in the state trial court. That filing automatically stopped the running of the AEDPA limitations period [with] 12 days left on the clock.

For the next three years, Holland's petition remained pending in the state courts. During that time, Holland wrote Collins letters asking him to make certain that all of his claims would be preserved for any subsequent federal habeas corpus review. Collins wrote back, stating, "I would like to reassure you that we are aware of state-time limitations and federal exhaustion requirements." He also said that he would "presen[t] . . . to the . . . federal courts" any of Holland's claims that the state courts denied. In a second letter Collins added, "should your Motion for Post-Conviction Relief be denied" by the state courts, "your state habeas corpus claims will then be ripe for presentation in a petition for writ of habeas corpus in federal court."

In mid-May 2003 the state trial court denied Holland relief, and Collins appealed that denial to the Florida Supreme Court. Almost two years later, in February 2005, the Florida Supreme Court heard oral argument in the case. But during that 2-year period, relations between Collins and Holland began to break down. Indeed, between April 2003 and January 2006, Collins communicated with Holland only three times—each time by letter.

Holland, unhappy with this lack of communication, twice wrote to the Florida Supreme Court, asking it to remove Collins from his case. In the second letter, filed on June 17, 2004, he said that he and Collins had experienced "a complete breakdown in communication." Holland informed the court that Collins had "not kept [him] updated on the status of [his] capital case" and that Holland had "not seen or spoken to" Collins "since April 2003." He wrote, "Mr. Collins has abandoned [me]" and said, "[I have] no idea what is going on with [my] capital case on appeal." He added that "Collins has never made any reasonable effort to establish any relationship of trust or confidence with [me]," and stated that he "does not trust" or have "any confidence in Mr. Collin's ability to represent [him.]" Holland concluded by asking that Collins be "dismissed (removed) off his capital case" or that he be given a hearing in order to demonstrate Collins' deficiencies. The State responded that Holland could not file any *pro se* papers with the court while he was represented by counsel, including papers seeking new counsel. The Florida Supreme Court agreed and denied Holland's requests.

During this same period Holland wrote various letters to the Clerk of the Florida Supreme Court. In the last of these he wrote, "[I]f I had a competent, conflict-free, postconviction, appellate attorney representing me, I would not have to write you this letter. I'm not trying to get on your nerves. I just would like to know exactly what is happening with my case on appeal to the Supreme Court of Florida." During that same time period, Holland also filed a complaint against Collins with the Florida Bar Association, but the complaint was denied.

Collins argued Holland's appeal before the Florida Supreme Court on February 10, 2005. Shortly thereafter, Holland wrote to Collins emphasizing the importance of filing a timely petition for habeas corpus in federal court once the Florida Supreme Court issued its ruling. Specifically, on March 3, 2005, Holland wrote:

"Dear Mr. Collins, P. A.:

"How are you? Fine I hope.

"I write this letter to ask that you please write me back, as soon as possible to let me know what the status of my case is on appeal to the Supreme Court of Florida.

"If the Florida Supreme Court denies my [postconviction] and State Habeas Corpus appeals, please *file my 28 U. S. C. 2254 writ of Habeas Corpus petition, before my deadline to file it runs out (expires)*. ([E]mphasis added [by the Court]).

"Thank you very much.

"Please have a nice day." ([E]mphasis added [by the Court]).

Collins did not answer this letter.

On June 15, 2005, Holland wrote again:

"Dear Mr. Collins:

"How are you? Fine I hope.

"On March 3, 2005 I wrote you a letter, asking that you let me know the status of my case on appeal to the Supreme Court of Florida.

"*Also, have you begun preparing my 28 U. S. C. § 2254 writ of Habeas Corpus petition? Please let me know, as soon as possible.*

"*Thank you.*" ([E]mphasis added [by the Court]).

But again, Collins did not reply.

Five months later, in November 2005, the Florida Supreme Court affirmed the lower court decision denying Holland relief. Three weeks after that, on *December 1, 2005*, the court issued its mandate, making its decision final. At that point, the AEDPA federal habeas clock again began to tick—with 12 days left on the 1-year meter. Twelve days later, on *December 13, 2005*, Holland's AEDPA time limit expired.

B

Four weeks after the AEDPA time limit expired, on January 9, 2006, Holland, still unaware of the Florida Supreme Court ruling issued in his case two months earlier, wrote Collins a third letter:

"Dear Mr. Bradley M. Collins:

"How are you? Fine I hope.

"I write this letter to ask that you please let me know the status of my appeals before the Supreme Court of Florida. Have my appeals been decided yet?

"Please send me the [necessary information] * * * so that I can determine when the deadline will be to file my 28 U. S. C. Rule 2254 Federal Habeas Corpus Petition, in accordance with all United States Supreme Court and Eleventh Circuit case law and applicable "Antiterrorism and Effective Death Penalty Act," if my appeals before the Supreme Court of Florida are denied.

"Please be advised that I want to preserve my privilege to federal review of all of my state convictions and sentences.

"Mr. Collins, would you please also inform me as to which United States District Court my 28 U. S. C. Rule 2254 Federal Habeas Corpus Petition will have to be timely filed in and that court's address?

"Thank you very much."

Collins did not answer.

Nine days later, on January 18, 2006, Holland, working in the prison library, learned for the first time that the Florida Supreme Court had issued a final determination in his case and that its mandate had issued— five weeks prior. He immediately wrote out his own *pro se* federal habeas petition and mailed it to the Federal District Court for the Southern District of Florida the next day. The petition begins by stating,

"Comes now Albert R. Holland, Jr., a Florida death row inmate and states that court appointed counsel has failed to undertake timely action to seek Federal Review in my case by filing a 28 U. S. C. Rule 2254 Petition for Writ of Habeas Corpus on my behalf."

It then describes the various constitutional claims that Holland hoped to assert in federal court.

The same day that he mailed that petition, Holland received a letter from Collins telling him that Collins intended to file a petition for certiorari in this Court from the State Supreme Court's most recent ruling. Holland answered immediately:

"Dear Mr. Bradley M. Collins:

* * * * * *

"Since recently, the Supreme Court of Florida has denied my [postconviction] and state writ of Habeas Corpus Petition. I am left to understand that you are planning to seek certiorari on these matters.

"It's my understanding that the AEDPA time limitations is not tolled during discretionary appellate reviews, such as certiorari applications resulting from denial of state post conviction proceedings.

"Therefore, I advise you *not* to file certiorari if doing so affects or jeopardizes my one year *grace* period as prescribed by the AEDPA.

"Thank you very much." ([S]ome emphasis deleted [by the Court]).

Holland was right about the law.

On January 26, 2006, Holland tried to call Collins from prison. But he called collect and Collins' office would not accept the call. Five days later, Collins wrote to Holland and told him for the very first time that, as Collins understood AEDPA law, the limitations period applicable to Holland's federal habeas application had in fact expired in 2000—*before* Collins had begun to represent Holland. Specifically, Collins wrote:

"Dear Mr. Holland:

"I am in receipt of your letter dated January 20, 2006 concerning operation of AEDPA time limitations. One hurdle in our upcoming efforts at obtaining federal habeas corpus relief will be that the one-year statutory time frame for filing such a petition began to run after the case was affirmed on October 5, 2000 [when your] Judgment and Sentence * * * were affirmed by the Florida Supreme Court. However, it was not until November 7, 2001, that I received the Order appointing me to the case. As you can see, *I was appointed about a year after your case became final* . . .

"[T]he AEDPA time period [thus] had run before my appointment and therefore before your [postconviction] motion was filed." ([E]mphasis added [by the Court]).

Collins was wrong about the law. As we have said, Holland's 1-year limitations period did not begin to run until *this* Court denied Holland's petition for certiorari from the state courts' denial of relief on direct review, which occurred on October 1, 2001. And when Collins was appointed (on November 7, 2001) the AEDPA clock therefore had 328 days left to go.

Holland immediately wrote back to Collins, pointing this out.

"Dear Mr. Collins:

"I received your letter dated January 31, 2006. You are incorrect in stating that 'the one-year statutory time frame for filing my 2254 petition began to run after my case was affirmed on October 5, 2000, by the Florida Supreme Court.' As stated on page three of [the recently filed] Petition for a writ of certiorari, October 1, 2001 is when the United States Supreme Court denied my initial petition for writ of certiorari and that is when my case became final. That meant that the time would be tolled once I filed my [postconviction] motion in the trial court.

"Also, Mr. Collins you never told me that my time ran out (expired). I told you to timely file my 28 U. S. C. 2254 Habeas Corpus Petition before the deadline, so that I would not be time-barred.

"You never informed me of oral arguments or of the Supreme Court of Florida's November 10, 2005 decision denying my postconviction appeals. You never kept me informed about the status of my case, although you told me that you would immediately inform me of the court's decision as soon as you heard anything.

"Mr. Collins, I filed a motion on January 19, 2006 [in federal court] to preserve my rights, because I did not want to be time-barred. Have you heard anything about the aforesaid motion? Do you know what the status of aforesaid motion is?

"Mr. Collins, please file my 2254 Habeas Petition immediately. Please do not wait any longer, even though it will be untimely filed at least it will be filed without wasting anymore time. (valuable time).

"Again, please file my 2254 Petition at once.

"Your letter is the first time that you have ever mentioned anything to me about my time had run out, before you were appointed to represent me, and that my one-year started to run on October 5, 2000.

"Please find out the status of my motion that I filed on January 19, 2006 and let me know.

"Thank you very much."

Collins did not answer this letter. Nor did he file a federal habeas petition as Holland requested.

On March 1, 2006, Holland filed another complaint against Collins with the Florida Bar Association. This time the bar asked Collins to respond, which he did, through his own attorney, on March 21. And the very next day, over three months after Holland's AEDPA statute of limitations had expired, Collins mailed a proposed federal habeas petition to Holland, asking him to review it.

But by that point Holland had already filed a *pro se* motion in the District Court asking that Collins be dismissed as his attorney. The State responded to that request by arguing once again that Holland could not file a *pro se* motion seeking to have Collins removed while he was represented by counsel, *i.e.*, represented by Collins. But this time the court considered Holland's motion, permitted Collins to withdraw from the case, and appointed a new lawyer for Holland. * * *

C

After considering the briefs, the Federal District Court held that the facts did not warrant equitable tolling and that consequently Holland's petition was untimely. * * * [It held] that Collins' professional conduct in the case was at worst merely "negligent." But the court rested its holding on an alternative rationale: It wrote that, even if Collins' "behavior could be characterized as an 'extraordinary circumstance,'" Holland "did not seek any help from the court system to find out the date [the] mandate issued denying his state habeas petition, nor did he seek aid from 'outside supporters.'" [(Alteration in original.)] Hence, the court held, Holland did not "demonstrate" the "due diligence" necessary to invoke "equitable tolling."

On appeal, the Eleventh Circuit agreed with the District Court that Holland's habeas petition was untimely. The Court of Appeals first agreed with Holland that "'[e]quitable tolling can be applied to . . . AEDPA's statutory deadline.'" But it also held that equitable tolling could not be applied in a case, like Holland's, that involves no more than "[p]ure professional negligence" on the part of a petitioner's attorney because such behavior can never constitute an "extraordinary circumstance." * * * Holland made "no allegation" that Collins had made a "knowing or reckless factual misrepresentation," or that he exhibited "dishonesty," "divided loyalty," or "mental impairment." Hence, the court held, equitable tolling was *per se* inapplicable to Holland's habeas petition. The court did not address the District Court's ruling with respect to Holland's diligence.

* * * [W]e granted the petition [for certiorari].

II

* * * [L]ike all 11 Courts of Appeals that have considered the question, we hold that § 2244(d) is subject to equitable tolling in appropriate cases.

We base our conclusion on the following considerations. First, the AEDPA "statute of limitations defense . . . is not 'jurisdictional.'" * * *

We have previously made clear that a nonjurisdictional federal statute of limitations is normally subject to a "rebuttable presumption" in *favor* "of equitable tolling."

In the case of AEDPA, the presumption's strength is reinforced by the fact that "'equitable principles'" have traditionally "'governed'" the substantive law of habeas corpus, for we will "not construe a statute to displace courts' traditional equitable authority absent the 'clearest command.'" The presumption's strength is yet further reinforced by the fact that Congress enacted AEDPA after this Court decided *Irwin* and therefore was likely aware that courts, when interpreting AEDPA's timing provisions, would apply the presumption.

Second, the statute here differs significantly from the statutes at issue in United *States v. Brockamp*, 519 U. S. 347 (1997), and *United States v. Beggerly*, 524 U. S. 38 (1998), two cases in which we held that *Irwin's* presumption had been overcome. In *Brockamp*, we interpreted a statute of limitations that was silent on the question of equitable tolling as foreclosing application of that doctrine. But in doing so we emphasized that the statute at issue (1) "se[t] forth its time limitations in unusually emphatic form"; (2) used "highly detailed" and "technical" language "that, linguistically speaking, cannot easily be read as containing implicit exceptions"; (3) "reiterate[d] its limitations several times in several different ways"; (4) related to an "underlying subject matter," nationwide tax collection, with respect to which the practical consequences of permitting tolling would have been substantial; and (5) would, if tolled, "require tolling, not only procedural limitations, but also substantive limitations on the amount of recovery—a kind of tolling for which we . . . found no direct precedent." And in *Beggerly* we held that *Irwin's* presumption was overcome where (1) the 12-year statute of limitations at issue was "unusually generous" and (2) the underlying claim "deal[t] with ownership of land" and thereby implicated landowners' need to "know with certainty what their rights are, and the period during which those rights may be subject to challenge."

By way of contrast, AEDPA's statute of limitations, unlike the statute at issue in *Brockamp*, does not contain language that is "unusually emphatic," nor does it "re-iterat[e]" its time limitation. Neither would application of equitable tolling here affect the "substance" of a petitioner's claim. Moreover, in contrast to the 12-year limitations period at issue in *Beggerly*, AEDPA's limitations period is not particularly long. And unlike the subject matters at issue in both *Brockamp* and *Beggerly*—tax collection and land claims—AEDPA's subject matter, habeas corpus, pertains to an area of the law where equity finds a comfortable home. In short, AEDPA's 1-year limit reads like an ordinary, run-of-the-mill statute of limitations.

Respondent, citing *Brockamp*, argues that AEDPA should be interpreted to foreclose equitable tolling because the statute [sets forth tolling conditions statutorily and does not authorize equitable tolling.] * * * But the fact that Congress *expressly* referred to tolling during state collateral review proceedings is easily explained without rebutting the presumption in favor of equitable tolling. A petitioner cannot bring a federal habeas claim without first exhausting state remedies—a process that frequently takes longer than one year. Hence, Congress had to explain how the limitations statute accounts for the time during which such state proceedings are pending. This special need for an express provision undermines any temptation to invoke the interpretive maxim *inclusio unius est exclusio alterius* (to include one item * * * is to exclude other similar items * * *).

Third, and finally, we disagree with respondent that equitable tolling undermines AEDPA's basic purposes. We recognize that AEDPA seeks to eliminate delays in the federal habeas review process. But AEDPA seeks to do so without undermining basic habeas corpus principles and while seeking to harmonize the new statute with prior law, under which a petition's timeliness was always determined under equitable principles. When Congress codified new rules governing this previously judicially managed area of law, it did so without losing sight of the fact that the "writ of habeas corpus plays a vital role in protecting constitutional rights." It did not seek to end every possible delay at all costs. * * *

III

[In cases assuming *arguendo* the existence of equitable tolling, we] have previously made clear that [the AEDPA limitations statute is tolled only if a petitioner] shows "(1) that he has been pursuing his rights diligently, and (2) that some extraordinary circumstance stood in his way" and prevented timely filing. In this case, the "extraordinary circumstances" at issue involve an attorney's failure to satisfy professional standards of care. The Court of Appeals held that, where that is so, even attorney conduct that is "grossly negligent" can never warrant tolling absent "bad faith, dishonesty, divided loyalty, mental impairment or so forth on the lawyer's part." But in our view, the Court of Appeals' standard is too rigid.

We have said that courts of equity "must be governed by rules and precedents no less than the courts of law." But we have also made clear that often the "exercise of a court's equity powers . . . must be made on a case-by-case basis." * * * [Equity] courts exercise judgment in light of prior precedent, but with awareness of the fact that specific circumstances, often hard to predict in advance, could warrant special treatment in an appropriate case.

We recognize that, in the context of procedural default, we have previously stated, without qualification, that a petitioner "must 'bear the risk of attorney error.'" *Coleman v. Thompson*, 501 U. S. 722, 752–753 (1991). But *Coleman* was "a case about federalism," in that it asked whether *federal* courts may excuse a petitioner's failure to comply with a *state court's* procedural rules, notwithstanding the state court's determination that its own rules had been violated. Equitable tolling, by contrast, asks whether federal courts may excuse a petitioner's failure to comply with *federal* timing rules, an inquiry that does not implicate a state court's interpretation of state law. * * *

We have previously held that "a garden variety claim of excusable neglect[,]" * * *, such as a simple "miscalculation" that leads a lawyer to miss a filing deadline[,] * * *, does not warrant equitable tolling. But the case before us does not involve * * * a "garden variety claim" of attorney negligence. Rather, the facts of this case present far more serious instances of attorney misconduct. And, as we have said, although the circumstances of a case must be "extraordinary" before equitable tolling can be applied, we hold that such circumstances are not limited to those that satisfy the test that the Court of Appeals used in this case.

IV

The record facts that we have set forth in Part I of this opinion suggest that this case may well be an "extraordinary" instance in which petitioner's attorney's conduct constituted far more than "garden variety" or "excusable neglect." * * * Here, Collins failed to file Holland's federal petition on time despite Holland's many letters that repeatedly emphasized the importance of his doing so. Collins apparently did not do the research necessary to find out the proper filing date, despite Holland's letters that went so far as to identify the applicable legal rules. Collins failed to inform Holland in a timely manner about the crucial fact that the Florida Supreme Court had decided his case, again despite Holland's many pleas for that information. And Collins failed to communicate with his client over a period of years, despite various pleas from Holland that Collins respond to his letters.

A group of teachers of legal ethics tells us that these various failures violated fundamental canons of professional responsibility, which require attorneys to perform reasonably competent legal work, to communicate with their clients, to implement clients' reasonable requests, to keep their clients informed of key developments in their cases, and never to abandon a client. And in this case, the failures seriously prejudiced a client who thereby lost what was likely his single opportunity for federal habeas review of the lawfulness of his imprisonment and of his death sentence.

We do not state our conclusion in absolute form, however, because more proceedings may be necessary. The District Court rested its ruling not on a lack of extraordinary circumstances, but rather on a lack of diligence—

a ruling that respondent does not defend. We think that the District Court's conclusion was incorrect. The diligence required for equitable tolling purposes is ["reasonable diligence"], not ["maximum feasible diligence."] Here, Holland not only wrote his attorney numerous letters seeking crucial information and providing direction; he also repeatedly contacted the state courts, their clerks, and the Florida State Bar Association in an effort to have Collins—the central impediment to the pursuit of his legal remedy—removed from his case. And, the very day that Holland discovered that his AEDPA clock had expired due to Collins' failings, Holland prepared his own habeas petition *pro se* and promptly filed it with the District Court.

Because the District Court erroneously relied on a lack of diligence, and because the Court of Appeals erroneously relied on an overly rigid per se approach, no lower court has yet considered in detail the facts of this case to determine whether they indeed constitute extraordinary circumstances sufficient to warrant equitable relief. * * * Thus, because we conclude that the District Court's determination must be set aside, we leave it to the Court of Appeals to determine whether the facts in this record entitle Holland to equitable tolling, or whether further proceedings, including an evidentiary hearing, might indicate that respondent should prevail.

The judgment below is reversed, and the case is remanded for further proceedings consistent with this opinion.

It is so ordered.

■ JUSTICE ALITO, concurring in part and concurring in the judgment.

* * * I agree with the Court's conclusion that equitable tolling is available under AEDPA. I also agree with much of the Court's discussion concerning whether equitable tolling is available on the facts of this particular case. * * *

* * * I think that the majority does not do enough to explain the right standard [for assessing extraordinary circumstances]. * * * I therefore write separately to set forth my understanding of the principles governing the availability of equitable tolling in cases involving attorney misconduct.

I

"Generally, a litigant seeking equitable tolling bears the burden of establishing two elements: (1) that he has been pursuing his rights diligently, and (2) that some extraordinary circumstance stood in his way." *Pace v. DiGuglielmo*, 544 U. S. 408, 418 (2005). The dispute in this case concerns whether and when attorney misconduct amounts to an "extraordinary circumstance" that stands in a petitioner's way and prevents the petitioner from filing a timely petition. * * * [I]t is useful to note that several broad principles may be distilled from this Court's precedents.

First, our prior cases make it abundantly clear that attorney negligence is not an extraordinary circumstance warranting equitable tolling. * * *

Second, the mere fact that a missed deadline involves "gross negligence" on the part of counsel does not by itself establish an extraordinary circumstance. * * * [T]he principal rationale for disallowing equitable tolling based on ordinary attorney miscalculation is that the error of an attorney is constructively attributable to the client and thus is not a circumstance beyond the litigant's control. * * *

II

Although attorney negligence, however styled, does not provide a basis for equitable tolling, the AEDPA statute of limitations may be tolled if the missed deadline results from attorney misconduct that is not constructively attributable to the petitioner. In this case, petitioner alleges facts that amount to such misconduct. In particular, he alleges that his attorney essentially "abandoned" him, as evidenced by counsel's near-total failure to communicate with petitioner or to respond to petitioner's many inquiries and requests over a period of several years. Petitioner also appears to allege that he made reasonable efforts to terminate counsel due to his inadequate representation and to proceed *pro se*, and that such efforts were successfully opposed by the State on the perverse ground that petitioner failed to act through appointed counsel.

If true, petitioner's allegations would suffice to establish extraordinary circumstances beyond his control. Common sense dictates that a litigant cannot be held constructively responsible for the conduct of an attorney who is not operating as his agent in any meaningful sense of that word. That is particularly so if the litigant's reasonable efforts to terminate the attorney's representation have been thwarted by forces wholly beyond the petitioner's control. The Court of Appeals apparently did not consider petitioner's abandonment argument or assess whether the State improperly prevented petitioner from either obtaining new representation or assuming the responsibility of representing himself. Accordingly, I agree with the majority that the appropriate disposition is to reverse and remand so that the lower courts may apply the correct standard to the facts alleged here.

■ JUSTICE SCALIA, with whom JUSTICE THOMAS joins as to all but Part I, dissenting.

* * * In my view § 2244(d) leaves no room for equitable exceptions, and Holland could not qualify even if it did.

I

The Court is correct that we ordinarily presume federal limitations periods are subject to equitable tolling unless tolling would be inconsistent with the statute. That is especially true of limitations provisions applicable to actions that are traditionally governed by equitable principles—a category that includes habeas proceedings. If § 2244(d) merely created a limitations period for federal habeas applicants, I agree that applying equitable tolling would be appropriate.

But § 2244(d) does much more than that, establishing a detailed scheme regarding the filing deadline that addresses an array of contingencies. * * * It also expressly tolls the limitations period during the pendency of a properly filed application for state collateral relief. § 2244(d)(2). Congress, in short, has considered and accounted for specific circumstances that in its view excuse an applicant's delay.

The question, therefore, is not whether § 2244(d)'s time bar is subject to tolling, but whether it is consistent with § 2244(d) for federal courts to toll the time bar for *additional* reasons beyond those Congress included.

In my view it is not. It is fair enough to infer, when a statute of limitations says nothing about equitable tolling, that Congress did not displace the default rule. But when Congress has codified that default rule and specified the instances where it applies, we have no warrant to extend it to other cases. * * * We should assume * * * that by specifying situations in which an equitable principle applies to a specific requirement, Congress has displaced courts' discretion to develop ad hoc exceptions.

The Court's responses are unpersuasive. It brushes aside § 2244(d)(1)(B)–(D), apparently because those subdivisions merely delay the *start* of the limitations period but do not suspend a limitations period already underway. But the Court does not explain why that distinction makes any difference * * * .

The Court does address § 2244(d)(2), which undeniably provides for poststart tolling, but dismisses it on the basis that Congress had to resolve a contradiction between § 2244(d)'s 1-year time bar and [the exhaustion rule]. But there is no contradiction to resolve unless, in the absence of a statutory tolling provision, equitable tolling would not apply to a state prisoner barred from filing a federal habeas application while he exhausts his state remedies. * * *

II

A

Even if § 2244(d) left room for equitable tolling in some situations, tolling surely should not excuse the delay here. Where equitable tolling is available, we have held that a litigant is entitled to it only if he has diligently pursued his rights and—the requirement relevant here—if "'some extraordinary circumstances stood in his way.'" Because the attorney is the litigant's agent, the attorney's acts (or failures to act) within the scope of the representation are treated as those of his client, * * * and thus such acts (or failures to act) are necessarily not extraordinary circumstances.

To be sure, the rule that an attorney's acts and oversights are attributable to the client is relaxed where the client has a constitutional right to effective assistance of counsel. Where a State is constitutionally obliged to provide an attorney but fails to provide an effective one, the attorney's failures * * * are chargeable to the State, not to the prisoner. But where the client has no right to counsel—which in habeas proceedings he does not— the rule holding him responsible for his attorney's acts applies with full force.[4] Thus, when a state habeas petitioner's appeal is filed too late because of attorney error, the petitioner is out of luck—no less than if he had proceeded *pro se* and neglected to file the appeal himself.

Congress could, of course, have included errors by state-appointed habeas counsel as a basis for delaying the limitations period, but it did not. Nor was that an oversight: Section 2244(d)(1)(B) expressly allows tolling for state-created impediments that prevent a prisoner from filing his application, but only if the impediment violates the Constitution or federal law.

* * * Why Collins did not notify Holland or file a timely federal application for him is unclear, but none of the plausible explanations would support equitable tolling. By far the most likely explanation is that Collins * * * assumed incorrectly that the pendency of a petition for certiorari in this Court seeking review of the denial of Holland's state habeas petition would toll AEDPA's time bar under § 2244(d)(2). That mistake would also be insufficient, as [we held in *Lawrence v. Florida*], to warrant tolling. * * *

The Court insists that Collins's misconduct goes beyond garden-variety neglect and mine-run miscalculation. But the only differences it identifies

---

[4] The Court dismisses *Coleman* as "a case about federalism" and therefore inapposite here. I fail to see how federalism concerns are not implicated by ad hoc exceptions to the statute of limitations for attempts to overturn state-court convictions. * * *

had no effect on Holland's ability to file his federal application on time. The Court highlights Collins's nonresponsiveness while Holland's state postconviction motions were still pending. But even taken at face value, Collins's silence *prior* to November 10, 2005, did not prevent Holland from filing a timely federal application once the Florida courts were finished with his case. The Court also appears to think significant Collins's correspondence with Holland in January 2006, *after* the limitations period had elapsed. But unless Holland can establish that the time-bar should be tolled due to events before December 15, 2005, any misconduct by Collins after the limitations period elapsed is irrelevant. Even if Collins's conduct *before* November 10 and after December 15 was "extraordinary," Holland has not shown that it "stood in his way and prevented timely filing." * * *

B

[The Court] concludes only that the Eleventh Circuit applied the wrong rule and remands the case for a re-do. * * *

* * * [E]ven if the Eleventh Circuit had adopted an entirely inflexible rule, it is simply untrue that, as the Court appears to believe, all general rules are *ipso facto* incompatible with equity. * * *

* * * [T]he Court offers almost no clue about what test that court should have applied. The Court * * * [provides] no explanation besides the assertion that [the Eleventh Circuit's] test left out cases where tolling might be warranted, and no precise indication of what those cases might be. The Court says that "courts can easily find precedents that can guide their judgments," citing several Court of Appeals opinions that (in various contexts) permit tolling for attorney error—but notably omitting opinions that disallow it * * * [even in situations where the conduct can be described as grossly or willfully negligent].

The only thing the Court offers that approaches substantive instruction is its implicit approval of "fundamental canons of professional responsibility," articulated by an ad hoc group of legal-ethicist *amici* consisting mainly of professors of that least analytically rigorous and hence most subjective of law-school subjects, legal ethics. The Court does not even try to justify importing into equity the "prevailing professional norms" we have held implicit in the right to counsel. In his habeas action Holland has no right to counsel. I object to this transparent attempt to smuggle [a constitutional right to counsel] into a realm the Sixth Amendment does not reach.

C

* * * [I]t is not even clear that Holland acted with the requisite diligence. Although Holland repeatedly contacted Collins and the state courts, there were other reasonable measures Holland could have pursued. For example, * * * Holland might have filed a [protective] federal habeas application and asked the District Court to stay the federal action until his state proceedings had concluded. He also presumably could have checked the court records in the prison's writ room—from which he eventually learned of the state court's decision—on a more regular basis. And he could have sought permission from the state courts to proceed pro se and thus remove Collins from the equation. This is not to say the District Court was correct to conclude Holland was not diligent; but the answer is not as obvious as the Court would make it seem.

* * *

* * * I respectfully dissent.

_____

NOTES AND QUESTIONS ON HOLLAND AND EQUITABLE TOLLING

1)   The Text. The statute discusses a one-year limitations period and a series of triggering events, together with other events that statutorily toll the limitations period—but nowhere does it mention equitable tolling. Yet the Court highlights that the limitations rule is not "inflexible." Why did so many lower courts, and then the Supreme Court, recognize the existence of equitable tolling? If applying similar equitable concepts in other contexts is "customary," is doing so particularly warranted in the federal habeas context, which involves a remedy frequently described as "equitable" in its nature? Or does equitable tolling contravene Congress' intent in enacting detailed statutory limitations provisions? In short, do you agree with the majority position as to the existence of equitable tolling, or with Justice Scalia's?

2)   The Two-Pronged Test for Equitable Tolling. _Holland_ held that in order to receive equitable tolling, an inmate must show that some "extraordinary circumstance" prevented timely filing and that there was no lapse in diligence. Compare the equitable tolling rule to the judge-made excuses for other procedural habeas defects. Is the rule closer to the deliberate-bypass paradigms or to the cause-and-prejudice paradigms? Do you think the Court was consciously trying to develop a parallel habeas excuse doctrine, or was it simply borrowing the broadly-used equitable tolling standard from other contexts?

3)   Extraordinary Circumstances. The Supreme Court held that the misconduct of Holland's attorney was an "extraordinary circumstance." _Holland_, however, seemed to foreclose the possibility that ordinary attorney negligence might constitute cause: the Court indicated that equitable tolling was inappropriate when the conduct of an attorney was not "far more than 'garden variety' or 'excusable neglect.'" Is it possible to anchor the requisite level of attorney error to the concept of "external factors" that create cause for excusing other kinds of procedural defects? If the attorney error has to be classifiable as an "external factor," then how serious does it have to be? Does it have to rise to the level of abandonment—and what does the presence of Justice Alito's concurrence affect the answer? What other types of situations might justify equitable tolling? Some of the situations in the following hypotheticals have been recognized as presenting extraordinary circumstances that justify equitable tolling.

a)   Judicial omissions or error. What if a judge failed to provide notice of a discretionary filing deadline or instructed an inmate that the inmate had more time to file than the inmate actually had?

b)   Government interference. What if a government entity failed to provide the required transcript of the trial record, or failed to provide an inmate other access to information that the inmate might need to lodge a federal claim?

c)   Defective representation? What if counsel were negligent by failing to understand certain questions of federal habeas law?

d)   Mental competence? Should an inmate have to show a nexus between mental incompetence and the missed deadline and, if so, how exacting should the competency inquiry be?

4) Diligence. The equitable tolling standard has two parts: extraordinary circumstances and reasonable diligence. In the context of habeas law, what is the difference between "reasonable diligence" and maximum feasible diligence? *Holland* did not reach a conclusion as to diligence, but instead remanded the case for the lower federal court to decide that question. Does the diligence standard depend on whether or not the prisoner was represented by a lawyer? Justice Scalia argued that Holland was not sufficiently diligent because he did not file a protective federal petition, frequently check records, or more proactively seek to remove his lawyer. If Justice Scalia believed that such failures preclude a diligence finding, then was his disagreement with the factual proposition that Holland's diligence was reasonable or with the legal proposition that no more than "reasonable diligence" is required?

5) Attorney-Client Agency. Identify the factors that prevented Holland from filing his federal habeas petition. Justice Alito would have held that these obstacles added up to "extraordinary circumstances," but he disagreed with the majority's definition of that requirement. Specifically, he did not believe that even gross attorney negligence necessarily triggers tolling. In what way does his argument about attorney abandonment reflect a concept of agency? If Justice Alito's argument was that equitable tolling should be limited to situations where the lawyer no longer serves (constructively) as the client's agent, then what are the limitations of such a theory? Agent-principle law developed generally as a way of mediating commercial relationships; is its utility in a criminal context limited and, if so, why? Think about how Justice Alito's theory of agency might have applied to the excuse doctrine for other procedural defects. How would the agency theory have worked in *Martinez*?

6) On Remand. On remand, the federal district court reached the merits and granted the habeas petition in part. See Holland v. Tucker, 854 F.Supp.2d 1229 (S.D.Fla. 2012). The court's order granting relief began by noting that the facts were "unusual and highly unlikely to be repeated in the future." Holland obtained relief on his claim that the trial judge's refusal to allow Holland to represent himself violated the Sixth Amendment. (At the time of this publication, Holland's retrial is delayed pending further litigation regarding his ability to represent himself at trial.)

(7) Innocence. Should evidence of innocence justify equitable tolling? What if there is evidence of innocence, but the petitioner did not pursue it diligently? In other words, what happens if the circumstances under which that evidence arises would prevent an inmate from satisfying § 2244(d)(1)(D) language that initiates a limitations period on "the date on which the factual predicate of the claim or claims presented could have been discovered through the exercise of due diligence[?]" Federal courts have equitably tolled the AEDPA statute of limitations on the grounds of actual innocence.[hh] Some courts have accom-

---

[hh] See, e.g., San Martin v. McNeil, 633 F.3d 1257, 1267–68 (11th Cir.2011) ("A court also may consider an untimely § 2254 petition if, by refusing to consider the petition for untimeliness, the court thereby would endorse a fundamental miscarriage of justice because it would require that an individual who is actually innocent remain imprisoned."); Souter v. Jones, 395 F.3d 577, 602 (6th Cir. 2005) ("[W]here an otherwise time-barred habeas petitioner can demonstrate that it is more likely than not that no reasonable juror would have found him guilty beyond a reasonable doubt, the petitioner should be allowed to pass through the gateway and argue the merits of his underlying constitutional claims."); Gibson v. Klinger, 232 F.3d 799, 808 (10th Cir. 2000) ("Equitable tolling would be appropriate, for example, when a prisoner is actually innocent . . . .").

plished the same result as an equitable tolling approach by reading a "miscarriage of justice" exception into the statute of limitations.[ii]

Adopting the equitable tolling approach, the Ninth Circuit, for example, explained: "As with equitable tolling based on diligence and extraordinary circumstances, [citing *Holland*] we conclude that Congress intended for the actual innocence exception to apply to AEDPA's statute of limitations." Lee v. Lampert, 653 F.3d 929, 934 (9th Cir. 2011) (en banc). The Ninth Circuit referenced the *Schlup* standard, noting that: "[a]t the time of AEDPA's passage, federal courts had equitable discretion to hear the merits of procedurally-defaulted habeas claims where the failure to do so would result in a 'fundamental miscarriage of justice,' such as the conviction of an actually innocent person." The U.S. Supreme Court has granted certiorari on whether the statute of limitations has a miscarriage of justice exception as a feature of equitable tolling. See Perkins v. McQuiggin, 133 S.Ct. 527 (2012). What are the consequences of using a miscarriage-of-justice paradigm to address the issue of innocence in tolling cases? Is the innocence showing in miscarriage-of-justice cases *higher* than the showing necessary to satisfy an ordinary new-fact inquiry?

NOTES ON EFFECT OF PROCEDURAL LIMITATIONS

1)   Responding to a Habeas Petition. Consider which procedural defenses you might assert in response to a habeas petition if you represented the State. Some defenses might be more burdensome to investigate than others. Now assume the role of the federal judge. Consider what information you would need to assess whether a particular defense is meritorious or not. Recall that we did not organize the Chapter to reflect the sequence in which a federal court might actually consider the rules—because the parties may decide which defenses to assert and contest—and because the judge may decide where to begin, depending on which defenses are the most straightforward. If the procedural history of a case in state court is particularly hard to untangle, then the judge may focus on a potentially more straightforward AEDPA statute of limitations defense. Or, if claims are obviously unexhausted or are being raised again in a second federal habeas petition, then the judge may address those defenses first. Taken together, how do you think these procedural defenses impact the role of a federal judge, when reviewing habeas petitions by state prisoners? How do you think that they impact the way that a prisoner litigates in state court? How do these rules impact the way that prisoners litigate in federal court? Could these rules even impact the way that criminal investigations and trials are conducted, or are habeas procedures too far downstream?

2)   Unintended Consequences and Federal Habeas Policy. Each procedural doctrine discussed in this Chapter was designed to expedite and impose order on prisoner litigation. Have the statutory and judge-made doctrines served their goals? Take AEDPA's statute of limitations as an example. AEDPA has not reduced delays between the state judgment and federal habeas disposition. The *2007 Habeas Study* found that, rather than accomplish this goal, "the average period has increased from about five years before AEDPA to over six years for the cases in this study filed in 2003 and 2004." See King et al., *2007 Habeas Study*, at 55. One reason why the statute of limitations may not have reduced delays involves its interaction with other AEDPA changes to the federal habeas statutes. The *2007 Habeas Study* also noted that the complexity of

---

[ii] See Hertz & Liebman, *FHCPP*, *supra* note e, at § 5.2[b] & n.85 (collecting cases).

habeas filings has increased: "The proportion of non-capital cases with four or more claims has greatly increased." The Study continues, "AEDPA's limits on successive petitions may be prompting more petitioners to bring all of their allegations of error at once in a single petition." Do some of these procedural rules work at cross-purposes? Should Congress or the Supreme Court reconsider some of the doctrines described in this Chapter? Which ones? Consider that question again when you turn from procedural limitations on habeas relief to substantive questions regarding review of the merits of claims, the subject of the next Chapter.

CHAPTER 5

FEDERAL MERITS REVIEW

INTRODUCTION TO FEDERAL MERITS REVIEW
OF STATE CONVICTIONS

Under Article III, federal courts have "the judicial Power"—and an obligation, recognized in *Marbury*, to say what the Constitution means and what federal law requires in a particular case. As Chief Justice Marshall wrote in *Marbury's* most famous sentence: "It is emphatically the province and duty of the judicial department to say what the law is." *Marbury v. Madison.* In *Brown v. Allen,* the Supreme Court described habeas corpus as giving "the final say" to federal courts on questions of constitutional law, thereby "respecting the Supremacy Clause of the Constitution[.]" 344 U.S. 443 (1953) (Opinion of Frankfurter, J.). In *Terry Williams v. Taylor,* 529 U.S. 362 (2000), an important case presented in this Chapter, the Court again emphasized that "federal courts, even on habeas, have an independent obligation to say what the law is." (Citations and quotations marks omitted.) Why did the Court find it necessary to affirm the independent obligation, *"even on habeas,"* and what does the independent obligation entail?

The availability of a habeas remedy cannot follow, *ipso facto*, from the existence of a constitutional grievance. That a constitutional violation does not give rise to every remedy is a staple of modern legal thought. For example, in civil rights litigation, qualified immunity doctrine partially protects government officials from having to pay damages, even when they have violated a person's constitutional rights. See Harlow v. Fitzgerald, 457 U.S. 800 (1982).[a] In the policing context, the Supreme Court has created a "good faith" exception to the Fourth Amendment exclusionary rule. See Herring v. United States, 555 U.S. 135, 144–46 (2009). For all types of constitutional questions, federal courts abstain from considering civil lawsuits that might interfere with pending state litigation. See, e.g., Younger v. Harris, 401 U.S. 37 (1971). This Chapter will explore important "substantive" limits on the federal post-conviction remedy.

Federal merits review of state criminal decisions is now more complicated than it once was. Before AEDPA, a federal judge would begin by considering any of the procedural obstacles discussed in the previous Chapter. If a claim survived those restrictions, then the judge could ask a simple question: whether a constitutional claim had merit. If so, then a federal court could grant relief, unless the constitutional violation was harmless. The federal habeas "review" of the state decision itself was *de novo*. Or, put another way, there was no review of the state decision at all; the federal judge decided whether a prisoner was entitled to relief under federal law.

After AEDPA, a federal court may no longer grant habeas relief merely because it believes that a constitutional violation contributed to the prisoner's conviction. Instead, the federal judge must conclude that the state court had denied relief in a decision that was legally or factually unreason-

---

[a] The analogy between qualified immunity and post-conviction review is developed in Section 2.

able. Congress enacted revisions to 28 U.S.C. § 2254(d), which fundamentally altered the role of federal courts by barring them (in most instances) from reviewing the *claim*. Instead, federal judges must review a state *decision*, and only for its "reasonableness." What "reasonableness" review entails, however, is not always clear. Justice David Souter famously remarked that, "in a world of silk purses and pigs' ears, [AEDPA] is not a silk purse of the art of statutory drafting." Lindh v. Murphy, 521 U.S. 320, 338 (1997). Section 2254(d) presents interpretive challenges that are, to say the least, daunting. It provides:

> **(d)** An application for a writ of habeas corpus on behalf of a person in custody pursuant to the judgment of a State court shall not be granted with respect to any claim that was adjudicated on the merits in State court proceedings unless the adjudication of the claim—
>
> > **(1)** resulted in a decision that was contrary to, or involved an unreasonable application of, clearly established Federal law, as determined by the Supreme Court of the United States; or
> >
> > **(2)** resulted in a decision that was based on an unreasonable determination of the facts in light of the evidence presented in the State court proceeding.

Section 2254(d) begins with preambular text that applies its two subsections only to state merits adjudications; if a state decision is not on the merits, then a prisoner may receive a straightforward federal merits adjudication of the claim. If, however, the state decision is a merits adjudication, then Subsection (d) requires a prisoner to satisfy one of two independent clauses. The satisfaction of either provides a way for a prisoner obtain merits review on a claim. Roughly speaking, Subsection (d)(1) permits a prisoner to obtain a merits adjudication if the state decision involves an unreasonable legal determination, and Subsection (d)(2) permits a prisoner to obtain a merits adjudication if there the state decision is based on an unreasonable factual determination. With that order of operation in mind, this Chapter presents the federal "merits inquiry" as follows:

(1) **On the Merits.** First, the judge must decide, under the preambular text of § 2254(d), whether a state decision was adjudicated on the merits. If it was not (and if no procedural bar applies), then the federal court simply decides the claim under the appropriate federal rule of decision.

(2) **Non-retroactivity.** Second, the judge must decide whether, under the Supreme Court's decision in *Teague v. Lane*, 489 U.S. 288 (1989), the inmate has based a claim on a "new rule" of constitutional law, and whether doing so is permissible.

(3) **The Substantive Limits on Relief.** Third, if the claim was adjudicated on the merits in state court, then the inmate must show that the state merits decision was either legally unreasonable under § 2254(d)(1) or factually unreasonable under (d)(2). Only if an inmate can meet one of those conditions may a federal court grant relief on the merits.

(4) **The State Record.** Fourth, if an inmate is seeking to demonstrate that a claim satisfies the limits on relief in § 2254(d), the inmate may only rely on the evidence presented to the state court. Only after an inmate makes the pertinent § 2254(d) showing is the inmate potentially entitled to relief on that claim.

(5) **Evidentiary Hearing.** Fifth, the inmate may or may not need a federal evidentiary hearing to show entitlement to relief on a claim, and § 2254(e) provides the standard for deciding whether inmates may obtain an evidentiary hearing. Such evidentiary hearings are quite rare.[b]

(6) **Harmless Error.** Finally, in situations in which a federal court must determine whether the claim has merit, the inmate may have to show that the error was not harmless.

1. "ON THE MERITS"

28 U.S.C. § 2254(d) does not apply to every federal habeas challenge by a state prisoner; the preambular language states that § 2254(d) only applies when a federal claim is "adjudicated on the merits in State court proceedings." What does it mean for the state court to have adjudicated a claim "on the merits"? Does the provision mean that the state court must have discussed the merits of the claim? Does the claim have to be identified as "federal"? State courts can issue decisions that are not accompanied by a written opinion, or that are single-sentence-boilerplate denials. These state decisions are often called "summary" or "postcard" denials. Because there are so many applications, state post-conviction dispositions frequently come in the form of unreasoned summary orders. If the state adjudication was "on the merits," then a prisoner cannot obtain relief without satisfying either § 2254(d)(1) or (d)(2). If the state adjudication was not "on the merits," however, then a prisoner can obtain federal relief by simply showing that the claim is meritorious.

NOTES ON HARRINGTON V. RICHTER

1) Summary Denials are "On the Merits." In *Harrington v. Richter*, 131 S.Ct. 770 (2011), the Supreme Court held that summary denials should ordinarily be treated as decisions on the merits:

> [D]etermining whether a state court's decision resulted from an unreasonable legal or factual conclusion does not require that there be an opinion from the state court explaining the state court's reasoning. . . . Where a state court's decision is unaccompanied by an explanation, the habeas petitioner's burden still must be met by showing there was no reasonable basis for the state court to deny relief. This is so whether or not the state court reveals which of the elements in a multipart claim it found insufficient, for § 2254(d) applies when a "claim," not a component of one, has been adjudicated.

In *Richter*, the Court was unsympathetic to the argument that § 2254(d) would encourage state courts to withhold explanations for their decisions: "Opinion-writing practices in state courts are influenced by considerations other than avoiding scrutiny by collateral attack in federal court." Formally speaking,

---

[b] See Nancy J. King, Fred L. Cheesman II & Brian J. Ostrom, Nat'l Ctr. for State Courts, *Final Technical Report: Habeas Litigation in U.S. District Courts* 60 (2007) (2007 Habeas Study) (finding hearings granted in non-capital cases at a rate of 0.4%, noting a prior pre-AEDPA study reported a higher rate of 1.1%; only 9.5% of the capital cases in the sample included an evidentiary hearing, compared to 19% prior to AEDPA).

Richter establishes a presumption that an unreasoned order denying state post-conviction relief is "on the merits" and that the presumption can be overcome when there is some other basis for the decision.

2) The Pricing of Deference. One might argue that, for the purposes of § 2254(d), a decision be treated as "on the merits" only when the state court denies the claim in a reasoned opinion. As you will see, the remainder of § 2254(d) focuses on the reasoning that a state judge used to adjudicate the federal claim. On the one hand, perhaps a federal judge ought to defer to the reasoning of a state judge only when the state judge memorialized a rationale for the decision. On the other hand, the vast majority of state dispositions are in the form of summary orders; state adjudication would be far more costly if only reasoned orders receive "deference" on federal habeas review. Do you think the Supreme Court was right not to require state courts to write a reasoned opinion for their decisions to receive "deference" under § 2254(d)(1)-(2)?[c] In other words, from a policy perspective, do you think that the presumption that summary denials are merits determination is desirable? Should state courts be forced to signal whether the state adjudication reflected a merits disposition?

3) Consistency with Procedural Default Jurisprudence. Notice that the presumption in *Richter* is the opposite of the presumption regarding silence of state judges in the procedural default context. In *Coleman v. Thompson*, 501 U.S. 722 (1991), the Supreme Court held that state summary orders are presumed to have been based on an independent and adequate state ground—i.e., they are presumed *not* to have been based on the merits of the federal claim. What explains the different presumption adopted for § 2254(d)?

4) *De Novo* Review of Non-Adjudicated Claims. The procedural default standard interacts with the Court's interpretation of § 2254(d) in a more significant way. If a state decision is not on the merits, then a claim must be reviewed *de novo*.[d] Such a scenario, however, would probably be a hollow victory for a state inmate. Although any merits inquiry would be *de novo*, an order denying relief that is not on the merits will probably be based on an adequate and independent state ground, and will trigger the procedural default rules. Is there any scenario in which a non-merits decision would not necessitate a default inquiry?

5) Overcoming the Presumption. What sorts of rulings might overcome the presumption that a state court denied a claim on the merits? What happens if a state order denying relief is reasoned with respect to one claim, and not reasoned with respect to another? Should the disposition of the claim without corresponding reasoning be treated as an order "on the merits?" What about where the same type of trial error is cognizable as a violation of both state and federal constitutions, where the state constitutional standard is less exacting,

---

[c] For an analysis of whether a summary disposition by a state court should be treated differently when the claim is based on new evidence that was not part of the trial record and when a summary disposition meant that the state court never examined that new evidence, see Matthew Seligman, *Note: Harrington's Wake: Unanswered Questions on AEDPA's Application to Summary Dispositions*, 64 Stan. L. Rev. 469 (2012); see also Randy Hertz & James S. Liebman, Federal Habeas Corpus Practice and Procedure § 32.2 (6th ed. 2011) (FHCPP) (arguing that Section 2254(d) requires that the federal court evaluate the state court's reasoning and that this analysis "cannot be performed if the state court failed to articulate its reasoning sufficiently").

[d] See, e.g., Cone v. Bell, 129 S.Ct. 1769, 1784 (2009) (Applying Section 2254(d), and noting that, where the state court "did not reach the merits[,] . . . the claim is reviewed *de novo*.").

and where the state decision only invokes state law? In *Johnson v. Tara Sheneva Williams*, 133 S.Ct. 1088 (U.S. 2013), the Supreme Court addressed a variation on this scenario. In dismissing a state post-conviction challenge involving a jury-trial right, the California Supreme Court did not explicitly decide the inmate's claim under the Sixth Amendment of the federal constitution. The state court had dismissed all of the prisoner's claims, but had discussed its reasoning primarily by reference to state precedent, and those state court decisions had discussed the federal right. In *Tara Sheneva Williams*, the Supreme Court concluded that following the "*Richter* presumption," federal courts should presume that state courts adjudicated the federal claim on the merits. The Supreme Court explained that the presumption could be rebutted only in "limited circumstances," such as in a case where the state court "inadvertently overlooked" the federal claim.

2. LEGAL DEFECTS IN STATE DECISIONS

We now consider the relationship between legal error by state judges and habeas relief. Although the inquiry is now governed primarily by 28 U.S.C. § 2254(d)(1), our consideration must begin with the concept of "retroactivity," the judge-made precursor to the statutory provision. Retroactivity law specifies who can enjoy the benefits of new Supreme Court decisions. The Supreme Court's retroactivity doctrine permits inmates to obtain habeas relief based on a "new rule" of constitutional law only if their convictions were pending on direct review—subject to two exceptions that we will discuss momentarily. In other words, inmates whose convictions are final upon the conclusion of direct review cannot enjoy the benefits of any new rule. That retroactivity doctrine, while largely supplanted by AEDPA, informs the central requirement of § 2254(d)(1), which provides that state inmates seeking federal habeas relief can only invoke legal rules that the Supreme Court had "clearly established" when the state court decided the merits of the federal claim.

A. RETROACTIVITY

28 U.S.C. § 2254(d)(1) now provides that a state prisoner may obtain relief if, among other things, a state merits adjudication "resulted in a decision that was contrary to, or involved an unreasonable application of, clearly established Federal law, as determined by the Supreme Court of the United States[.]" In order to understand the rationale for the "clearly established" requirement, you should first understand the habeas law of "retroactivity."

When the Supreme Court announces a decision interpreting the constitution, litigants will dispute whether the decision announced a "new" rule or simply clarified an "old" one. Moreover, even when the Court does announce a fairly novel constitutional rule, it will often decline to position its ruling as a complete break from the past, but instead will try to ground its decision as a logical progression from prior precedent. This issue relates to age-old questions about whether the Court discovers law or makes it.[e]

---

[e] In the 1930s and 1940s, the Supreme Court undermined a number of propositions at the heart of what might be described as "legal formalism" or "classicism," in which judges were thought to be engaged in an enterprise of legal discovery. See, e.g., Great Northern Railway v. Sunburst Oil & Refining Co., 287 U.S. 358 (1932) (questioning the premise that judges declared preexisting law). See generally, William Wiecek, *The Lost World of Classical Legal*

The formalist paradigm of legal discovery animated the concern expressed by Justice Jackson's dissent in *Brown v. Allen*, 344 U.S. 443 (1953), when he argued that state judges would find it increasingly "demoralizing" if they could not "anticipate, and so comply with, this Court's due process requirements or ascertain any standards to which this Court will adhere in prescribing them." Should defendants who had been convicted under the "old" rule be able to obtain relief when a "new" rule is adopted by a federal court? Or, put another way, which categories of prisoners should get the benefit of a "new" constitutional decision?

INTRODUCTORY NOTE ON THE LINKLETTER *STANDARD*

These questions arose more frequently during and immediately after the criminal procedure revolution initiated by the Warren Court. For example, in *Mapp v. Ohio*, 367 U.S. 643 (1961), the Warren Court issued a landmark decision requiring state courts to exclude evidence seized in violation of the Fourth Amendment. *Mapp* was a major legal event—it incorporated the exclusionary rule against the states. In *Linkletter v. Walker*, 381 U.S. 618 (1965), the Court discussed whether prisoners whose convictions were final when *Mapp* was decided should be able to obtain habeas relief when a state court improperly applied the exclusionary rule.[f]

Linkletter conceded that judges traditionally extended Supreme Court rulings retroactively:

> At common law there was no authority for the proposition that judicial decisions made law only for the future. Blackstone stated the rule that the duty of the court was not to "pronounce a new law, but to maintain and expound the old one." This Court followed that rule [in older cases]. The judge rather than being the creator of the law was but its discoverer.

The question in *Linkletter* reflected the previously-mentioned debate about whether a legal decision "makes" law or "discovers" it. In *Linkletter*, the Court ultimately decided that *Mapp* should not be available to prisoners whose convictions were final when *Mapp* was decided. *Mapp*, however, was not "purely prospective." *Mapp* (the case) reversed the conviction of Mapp (the prisoner), and was applied to cases "still pending on direct review at the time [*Mapp*] was rendered." The Court cast the retroactivity rule as prudential: "the Constitution neither prohibits nor requires retrospective effect." Under *Linkletter*, the retroactive application of a rule was determined by examining the "prior history of the rule in question, its purpose and effect, and whether retrospective operation will further or retard its operation." With respect to the exclusionary rule at issue in *Linkletter*, the Court observed that, although the rule's purpose is to deter law enforcement from conducting illegal searches and seizures, a new-trial remedy does not directly accomplish that goal. Moreover, *Linkletter* reasoned, when a Fourth Amendment violation occurs, law enforcement may have

---

Thought: Law and Ideology in America 1886–1937 (1998) (tracing the American historical arc of classical legal thought).

[f] *Stone v. Powell*, 428 U.S. 465 (1976), which you encountered in Chapter 3 and which held that Fourth Amendment claims were not cognizable on federal habeas review, had not yet been decided.

improperly obtained evidence, but the "fairness of the trial is not under attack. All that petitioner attacks is the admissibility of evidence, the reliability and relevancy of which is not questioned, and which may well have had no effect on the outcome."

Students who have taken criminal procedure will recognize *Linkletter's* observation about the relationship between the constitutional violation and the reliability of the unlawfully-obtained evidence as representative of modern Fourth Amendment decisions scaling back the scope of the exclusionary rule. In a spirited *Linkletter* dissent, Justice Black argued:

> If the exclusionary rule has the high place in our constitutional plan of "ordered liberty," which this Court in *Mapp* and other cases has so frequently said that it does have, what possible valid reason can justify keeping people in jail under convictions obtained by wanton disregard of a constitutional protection which the Court itself in *Mapp* treated as being one of the "constitutional rights of the accused."

Consider each view of the exclusionary rule: (1) that the exclusionary rule is a judicially-created remedy for a Fourth Amendment violation and (2) that the federal constitution requires exclusion because the admission of impermissibly-obtained evidence is itself a constitutional violation. How should the retroactive application of the exclusionary rule depend on what view of the rule you take?

An extensive retroactivity debate followed *Linkletter*. See generally Richard H. Fallon, Jr. and Daniel J. Meltzer, *New Law, Non-Retroactivity, and Constitutional Remedies,* 104 Harv. L. Rev. 1731, 1738–49 (1991) (presenting the historical arc of the discussion among judges and scholars). Professor Paul Mishkin, for example, influentially argued that new decisions should always be retroactive to decisions pending on direct appeal. See Paul J. Mishkin, *Foreword: The High Court, the Great Writ, and the Due Process of Time and Law,* 79 Harv. L. Rev. 56, 77–86 (1965).

Some Justices preferred that constitutional decisions not be retroactive because such a paradigm made otherwise-disruptive constitutional rulings more palatable. In a famous concurrence, Justice Harlan called non-retroactivity "a technique that provided an impetus . . . for the implementation of long overdue reforms, which otherwise could not practicably be effected." *Mackey v. United States,* 401 U.S. 667, 676 (1971) (Harlan, J., concurring in part and dissenting in part) (quoting *Jenkins v. Delaware,* 395 U.S. 213, 218 (1969)) (internal quotation marks omitted). Justice Harlan objected both to *ad hoc* retroactivity rules for prisoners whose convictions were not final and to such rules for prisoners for whom direct review was over.

How would the *Miranda* revolution have proceeded if the decision were given retroactive effect? *Mackey* was one in a series of opinions by Justice Harlan arguing that the Court needed to "rethink" its retroactivity jurisprudence. See also *Desist v. United States,* 394 U.S. 244, 258 (1969) (Harlan, J., dissenting) ("I can no longer, however, remain content with the doctrinal confusion that has characterized our efforts to apply the basic *Linkletter* principle. 'Retroactivity' must be rethought."). He believed that only rules falling into two categories were important enough to be given full retroactive effect. First, Justice Harlan argued that federal courts should give retroactive effect to decisions that constitutionally prohibited the punishment of previously-punishable conduct. Second, he argued that federal courts should give retroactive effect to newly-announced procedural rules that are "implicit in the concept of ordered liberty." *Mackey*, 401 U.S. at 692–93 (Harlan, J., concurring in part and dissenting in part) (quoting *Palko v. Connecticut*, 302 U.S. 319, 325 (1937)). What kinds of rulings would fall into each category? Would *Mapp* qualify for either exception?

Justice Harlan's position never secured a majority on the Warren Court, but its influence persisted. Keep Justice Harlan's views in mind when you read *Teague v. Lane*, 489 U.S. 288 (1989), the leading case on retroactivity. Teague was a black man convicted of a number of crimes by an all-white Illinois jury. During jury selection, the prosecution used all ten of its peremptory challenges to exclude black members of the venire. The prosecution argued that it was trying to achieve a balance of men and women on the jury. On appeal and on habeas review, Teague argued that he was entitled to a jury comprised of a fair community "cross section." On federal habeas review, Teague argued that the Supreme Court, through various opinions concurring in or dissenting from a denial of certiorari in *McCray v. New York*, 461 U.S. 961 (1983), had invited reexamination of *Swain v. Alabama*, 380 U.S. 202 (1965). *Swain* "prohibited States from purposefully and systematically denying blacks the opportunity to serve on juries." The federal appeals court ruled against Teague on the ground that the "fair cross-section" requirement applied only to the jury venire, and not to the petit jury.

Teague v. Lane
United States Supreme Court
489 U.S. 288 (1989)

■ JUSTICE O'CONNOR announced the judgment of the Court and delivered the opinion of the Court with respect to Parts I, II, and III, and an opinion with respect to Parts IV and V, in which [ ] CHIEF JUSTICE [REHNQUIST], JUSTICE SCALIA, and JUSTICE KENNEDY join.

In *Taylor v. Louisiana*, 419 U.S. 522 (1975), this Court held that the Sixth Amendment required that the jury venire be drawn from a fair cross section of the community. The Court stated, however, that "in holding that petit juries must be drawn from a source fairly representative of the community we impose no requirement that petit juries actually chosen must mirror the community and reflect the various distinctive groups in the population. Defendants are not entitled to a jury of any particular composition." The principal question presented in this case is whether the Sixth Amendment's fair cross section requirement should now be extended to the petit jury. Because we adopt Justice Harlan's approach to retroactivity for cases on collateral review, we leave the resolution of that question for another day. * * *

IV

[Teague's] third and final contention is that the Sixth Amendment's fair cross section requirement applies to the petit jury. As we noted at the outset, *Taylor* expressly stated that the fair cross section requirement does not apply to the petit jury. [Teague] nevertheless contends that the *ratio decidendi* of *Taylor* cannot be limited to the jury venire, and he urges adoption of a new rule. Because we hold that the rule urged by [Teague] should not be applied retroactively to cases on collateral review, we decline to address [Teague]'s contention.

A

* * * [W]e think it is time to clarify how the question of retroactivity should be resolved for cases on collateral review. * * *

In our view, the question "whether a decision [announcing a new rule should] be given prospective or retroactive effect should be faced at the time of [that] decision." Retroactivity is properly treated as a threshold question, for, once a new rule is applied to the defendant in the case announcing the rule, evenhanded justice requires that it be applied retroactively to all who are similarly situated. Thus, before deciding whether the fair cross section requirement should be extended to the petit jury, we should ask whether such a rule would be applied retroactively to the case at issue. This retroactivity determination would normally entail application of the *Linkletter* standard, but we believe that our approach to retroactivity for cases on collateral review requires modification.

It is admittedly often difficult to determine when a case announces a new rule, and we do not attempt to define the spectrum of what may or may not constitute a new rule for retroactivity purposes. In general, however, a case announces a new rule when it breaks new ground or imposes a new obligation on the States or the Federal Government. To put it differently, a case announces a new rule if the result was not *dictated* by precedent existing at the time the defendant's conviction became final. Given the strong language in *Taylor* and our statement in *Akins v. Texas*, 325 U.S. 398, 403 (1945), that "[f]airness in [jury] selection has never been held to require proportional representation of races upon a jury," application of the fair cross section requirement to the petit jury would be a new rule.

Not all new rules have been uniformly treated for retroactivity purposes. Nearly a quarter of a century ago, in *Linkletter,* the Court attempted to set some standards by which to determine the retroactivity of new rules. * * *

The *Linkletter* retroactivity standard has not led to consistent results. Instead, it has been used to limit application of certain new rules to cases on direct review, other new rules only to the defendants in the cases announcing such rules, and still other new rules to cases in which trials have not yet commenced. * * *

Application of the *Linkletter* standard led to the disparate treatment of similarly situated defendants on direct review. For example, in *Miranda v. Arizona*, 384 U.S. 436, 467–73 (1966), the Court held that, absent other effective measures to protect the Fifth Amendment privilege against self-incrimination, a person in custody must be warned prior to interrogation that he has certain rights, including the right to remain silent. The Court applied that new rule to the defendants in *Miranda* and its companion cases, and held that their convictions could not stand because they had been interrogated without the proper warnings. In *Johnson v. New Jersey*, 384 U.S. 719, 733–35 (1966), the Court held, under the *Linkletter* standard, that *Miranda* would only be applied to trials commencing after that decision had been announced. Because the defendant in *Johnson,* like the defendants in *Miranda,* was on direct review of his conviction, the Court's refusal to give *Miranda* retroactive effect resulted in unequal treatment of those who were similarly situated. * * *

In *Griffith v. Kentucky*, 479 U.S. 314 (1987), we rejected as unprincipled and inequitable the *Linkletter* standard for cases pending on direct review at the time a new rule is announced, and adopted the first part of the retroactivity approach advocated by Justice Harlan. We agreed with Justice Harlan that "failure to apply a newly declared constitutional rule to criminal cases pending on direct review violates basic norms of constitutional adjudication." We gave two reasons for our decision. First, because we can only promulgate new rules in specific cases and cannot possibly decide all cases in which review is sought, "the integrity of judicial review" requires the application of the new rule to "all similar cases pending on direct review." * * *

Second, because "selective application of new rules violates the principle of treating similarly situated defendants the same," we refused to continue to tolerate the inequity that resulted from not applying new rules retroactively to defendants whose cases had not yet become final. Although new rules that constituted clear breaks with the past generally were not given retroactive effect under the *Linkletter* standard, we held that "a new rule for the conduct of criminal prosecutions is to be applied retroactively to all cases, state or federal, pending on direct review or not yet final, with no exception for cases in which the new rule constitutes a clear break with the past."

The *Linkletter* standard also led to unfortunate disparity in the treatment of similarly situated defendants on collateral review. An example will best illustrate the point. In *Edwards v. Arizona*, 451 U.S. 477, 484–87 (1981), the Court held that once a person invokes his right to have counsel present during custodial interrogation, a valid waiver of that right cannot be inferred from the fact that the person responded to police-initiated questioning. It was not until *Solem v. Stumes*, 465 U.S. 638 (1984), that the Court held, under the *Linkletter* standard, that *Edwards* was not to be applied retroactively to cases on collateral review. In the interim, several lower federal courts had come to the opposite conclusion and had applied *Edwards* to cases that had become final before that decision was announced. Thus, some defendants on collateral review whose *Edwards* claims were adjudicated prior to *Stumes* received the benefit of *Edwards,* while those whose *Edwards* claims had not been addressed prior to *Stumes* did not. * * *

B

Justice Harlan believed that new rules generally should not be applied retroactively to cases on collateral review. He argued that retroactivity for cases on collateral review could "be responsibly [determined] only by focusing, in the first instance, on the nature, function, and scope of the adjudicatory process in which such cases arise. The relevant frame of reference, in other words, is not the purpose of the new rule whose benefit the [defendant] seeks, but instead the purposes for which the writ of habeas corpus is made available." * * *

Justice Harlan identified only two exceptions to his general rule of nonretroactivity for cases on collateral review. First, a new rule should be applied retroactively if it places "certain kinds of primary, private individual conduct beyond the power of the criminal law-making authority to proscribe." Second, a new rule should be applied retroactively if it requires the observance of "those procedures that . . . are 'implicit in the concept of ordered liberty.'"

* * *[W]e have recognized that interests of comity and finality must also be considered in determining the proper scope of habeas review. Thus, if a defendant fails to comply with state procedural rules and is barred from

litigating a particular constitutional claim in state court, the claim can be considered on federal habeas only if the defendant shows cause for the default and actual prejudice resulting therefrom. We have declined to make the application of the procedural default rule dependent on the magnitude of the constitutional claim at issue, or on the State's interest in the enforcement of its procedural rule.

This Court has not "always followed an unwavering line in its conclusions as to the availability of the Great Writ. Our development of the law of federal habeas corpus has been attended, seemingly, with some backing and filling." Nevertheless, it has long been established that a final civil judgment entered under a given rule of law may withstand subsequent judicial change in that rule. * * *

These underlying considerations of finality find significant and compelling parallels in the criminal context. Application of constitutional rules not in existence at the time a conviction became final seriously undermines the principle of finality which is essential to the operation of our criminal justice system. * * * The fact that life and liberty are at stake in criminal prosecutions "shows only that 'conventional notions of finality' should not have *as much* place in criminal as in civil litigation, not that they should have *none*." Friendly, *Is Innocence Irrelevant? Collateral Attacks on Criminal Judgments*, 38 U. Chi. L. Rev. 142, 150 (1970). "[I]f a criminal judgment is ever to be final, the notion of legality must at some point include the assignment of final competence to determine legality." Bator, *Finality in Criminal Law and Federal Habeas Corpus for State Prisoners*, 76 Harv. L. Rev. 441, 450–451 (1963). * * *

We find these criticisms to be persuasive, and we now adopt Justice Harlan's view of retroactivity for cases on collateral review. Unless they fall within an exception to the general rule, new constitutional rules of criminal procedure will not be applicable to those cases which have become final before the new rules are announced.

V

[Teague's] conviction became final in 1983. As a result, the rule [Teague] urges would not be applicable to this case, which is on collateral review, unless it would fall within an exception.

The first exception suggested by Justice Harlan—that a new rule should be applied retroactively if it places "certain kinds of primary, private individual conduct beyond the power of the criminal law-making authority to proscribe"—is not relevant here. Application of the fair cross section requirement to the petit jury would not accord constitutional protection to any primary activity whatsoever.

The second exception suggested by Justice Harlan—that a new rule should be applied retroactively if it requires the observance of "those procedures that . . . are implicit in the concept of ordered liberty[,]"—we apply with a modification. The language used by Justice Harlan in *Mackey* leaves no doubt that he meant the second exception to be reserved for watershed rules of criminal procedure:

> "Typically, it should be the case that any conviction free from federal constitutional error at the time it became final, will be found, upon reflection, to have been fundamentally fair and conducted under those procedures essential to the substance of a full hearing. However, in some situations it might be that time and growth in social capacity, as well as judicial perceptions of what we can rightly demand of the adju-

dicatory process, will properly alter our understanding of the *bedrock procedural elements* that must be found to vitiate the fairness of a particular conviction. For example, such, in my view, is the case with the right to counsel at trial now held a necessary condition precedent to any conviction for a serious crime."

* * * Because we operate from the premise that such procedures would be so central to an accurate determination of innocence or guilt, we believe it unlikely that many such components of basic due process have yet to emerge. We are also of the view that such rules are "best illustrated by recalling the classic grounds for the issuance of a writ of habeas corpus—that the proceeding was dominated by mob violence; that the prosecutor knowingly made use of perjured testimony; or that the conviction was based on a confession extorted from the defendant by brutal methods."

An examination of our decision in *Taylor* applying the fair cross section requirement to the jury venire leads inexorably to the conclusion that adoption of the rule [Teague] urges would be a far cry from the kind of absolute prerequisite to fundamental fairness that is "implicit in the concept of ordered liberty." The requirement that the jury venire be composed of a fair cross section of the community is based on the role of the jury in our system. Because the purpose of the jury is to guard against arbitrary abuses of power by interposing the commonsense judgment of the community between the State and the defendant, the jury venire cannot be composed only of special segments of the population. * * * But as we stated in *Daniel v. Louisiana*, 420 U.S. 31, 32 (1975), which held that *Taylor* was not to be given retroactive effect, the fair cross section requirement "[does] not rest on the premise that every criminal trial, or any particular trial, [is] necessarily unfair because it [is] not conducted in accordance with what we determined to be the requirements of the Sixth Amendment." Because the absence of a fair cross section on the jury venire does not undermine the fundamental fairness that must underlie a conviction or seriously diminish the likelihood of obtaining an accurate conviction, we conclude that a rule requiring that petit juries be composed of a fair cross section of the community would not be a "bedrock procedural element" that would be retroactively applied under the second exception we have articulated. * * *

We therefore hold that, implicit in the retroactivity approach we adopt today, is the principle that habeas corpus cannot be used as a vehicle to create new constitutional rules of criminal procedure unless those rules would be applied retroactively to *all* defendants on collateral review through one of the two exceptions we have articulated. Because a decision extending the fair cross section requirement to the petit jury would not be applied retroactively to cases on collateral review under the approach we adopt today, we do not address [Teague]'s claim.

For the reasons set forth above, the judgment of the Court of Appeals is affirmed.

It is so ordered.

[JUSTICE WHITE concurred only in Parts I, II, and III, and concurred in the judgment.]

[JUSTICE BLACKMUN, concurred in the judgment on the *Swain* claim and joined Part I of the opinion of JUSTICE STEVENS, which concurred in part and concurred in the judgment.]

■ JUSTICE STEVENS, with whom JUSTICE BLACKMUN joins as to Part I, concurring in part and concurring in the judgment.

I

* * * I do not agree * * * with the plurality's dicta proposing a "modification" of Justice Harlan's fundamental fairness exception. * * * Justice Harlan expressly rejected a previous statement linking the fundamental fairness exception to factual innocence.

* * * I cannot agree that it is "unnecessarily anachronistic" to issue a writ of habeas corpus to a petitioner convicted in a manner that violates fundamental principles of liberty. Furthermore, a touchstone of factual innocence would provide little guidance in certain important types of cases, such as those challenging the constitutionality of capital sentencing hearings. Even when assessing errors at the guilt phase of a trial, factual innocence is too capricious a factor by which to determine if a procedural change is sufficiently "*bedrock*" or "watershed" to justify application of the fundamental fairness exception. In contrast, given our century-old proclamation that the Constitution does not allow exclusion of jurors because of race, a rule promoting selection of juries free from racial bias clearly implicates concerns of fundamental fairness.

As a matter of first impression, therefore, I would conclude that a guilty verdict delivered by a jury whose impartiality might have been eroded by racial prejudice is fundamentally unfair. * * *

■ JUSTICE BRENNAN, with whom JUSTICE MARSHALL joins, dissenting.

* * * [T]he plurality would for the first time preclude the federal courts from considering on collateral review a vast range of important constitutional challenges; where those challenges have merit, it would bar the vindication of personal constitutional rights and deny society a check against further violations until the same claim is presented on direct review. * * *

These are massive changes, unsupported by precedent. They also lack a reasonable foundation. By exaggerating the importance of treating like cases alike and granting relief to all identically positioned habeas petitioners or none, "the Court acts as if it has no choice but to follow a mechanical notion of fairness without pausing to consider sound principles of decisionmaking." Certainly it is desirable, in the interest of fairness, to accord the same treatment to all habeas petitioners with the same claims. Given a choice between deciding an issue on direct or collateral review that might result in a new rule of law that would not warrant retroactive application to persons on collateral review other than the petitioner who brought the claim, we should ordinarily grant certiorari and decide the question on direct review. * * * [A] new rule would apply equally to all persons whose convictions had not become final before the rule was announced, whereas habeas petitioners other than the one whose case we decided might not benefit from such a rule if we adopted it on collateral review. Taking cases on direct review ahead of those on habeas is especially attractive because the retrial of habeas petitioners usually places a heavier burden on the States than the retrial of persons on direct review. Other things being equal, our concern for fairness and finality ought to therefore lead us to render our decision in a case that comes to us on direct review.

Other things are not always equal, however. Sometimes a claim which, if successful, would create a new rule not appropriate for retroactive application on collateral review is better presented by a habeas case than by one on direct review. In fact, sometimes the claim is *only* presented on collateral review. In that case, while we could forgo deciding the issue in the hope that it would eventually be presented squarely on direct review, that hope might be misplaced, and even if it were in time fulfilled, the opportunity to check constitutional violations and to further the evolution of our thinking in some area of the law would in the meanwhile have been lost. In addition, by preserving our right and that of the lower federal courts to hear such claims on collateral review, we would not discourage their litigation on federal habeas corpus and thus not deprive ourselves and society of the benefit of decisions by the lower federal courts when we must resolve these issues ourselves.

The plurality appears oblivious to these advantages of our settled approach to collateral review. Instead, it would deny itself these benefits because adherence to precedent would occasionally result in one habeas petitioner's obtaining redress while another petitioner with an identical claim could not qualify for relief. In my view, the uniform treatment of habeas petitioners is not worth the price the plurality is willing to pay. Permitting the federal courts to decide novel habeas claims not substantially related to guilt or innocence has profited our society immensely. Congress has not seen fit to withdraw those benefits by amending the statute that provides for them. And although a favorable decision for a petitioner might not extend to another prisoner whose identical claim has become final, it is at least arguably better that the wrong done to one person be righted than that none of the injuries inflicted on those whose convictions have become final be redressed, despite the resulting inequality in treatment. * * *

Perfectly evenhanded treatment of habeas petitioners can by no means justify the plurality's *sua sponte* renunciation of the ample benefits of adjudicating novel constitutional claims on habeas corpus that do not bear substantially on guilt or innocence.

NOTES AND QUESTIONS ON TEAGUE

1) Adoption of the Teague Plurality Approach. The *Teague* opinion itself was only for a Supreme Court plurality (Justice Blackmun did not join Part IV), but a majority of the Justices soon adopted the approach. See Penry v. Lynaugh, 492 U.S. 302 (1989) (abrogated on other grounds by *Atkins v. Virginia*, 536 U.S. 304 (2002)). Under the prevailing approach, a rule must first be classified as new or old. Old rules apply to all prisoners and defendants. New rules do not apply retroactively, except to those defendants with direct-review proceedings that are pending, and to other inmates when the decision satisfies one of the two *Teague* exceptions.

2) Timing. The *Teague* plurality explained that "new" rules should be retroactively applied to cases that are pending on direct review when the new rule is announced. Which cases fit this description? Recall that convictions are not final until the direct appeal is complete. That occurs when the highest state court denies relief on the appeal and the U.S. Supreme Court denies certiorari.[g] All proceedings initiated after that last denial of the direct appeal are collateral, including state and federal habeas corpus challenges. Thus, prisoners with pending state or federal habeas challenges may not take advantage of a "new" rule that does not meet a *Teague* exception. To perform the *Teague* analysis, one must examine the following dates: (1) the date when direct review ended,

[g] In cases where a defendant does not seek certiorari review of the conviction, the conviction becomes final when the 90-day period for seeking a petition for a writ of certiorari lapses.

and (2) the date of the Supreme Court or Circuit Court decision announcing the purportedly "new" rule. (Perhaps one might also have to examine (3), the date that the court subsequently declares the "newness" of a rule announced in a prior decision.)

3) What is a "New" Rule? Most claimants must argue that new precedent did not amount to a new rule under *Teague*—that the precedent was an extension of old law. But what makes a rule new? The *Teague* plurality noted that a case may announce a new rule "when it breaks new ground or imposes a new obligation on the States or the Federal Government." Do rulings often "break new ground"? The plurality explained, "[t]o put it differently, a case announces a new rule if the result was not *dictated* by precedent existing at the time the defendant's conviction became final." Indeed, those are very different formulations. Many rulings are not strictly "dictated" by prior precedent. Might a rule fall somewhere between those that break new ground and those that are not completely dictated by prior precedent? In your view, what should count as precedent—decisional law from the Supreme Court, or from lower federal courts as well?

Professor Tung Yin points out that, despite the lengthy opinion explaining its new retroactivity analysis, "the Court spent a grand total of one third of one paragraph analyzing why the rule urged by Teague would be a new rule." Tung Yin, *A Better Mousetrap: Procedural Default as a Retroactivity Alternative to Teague v. Lane and the Antiterrorism and Effective Death Penalty Act of 1996*, 25 Am. J. Crim. L. 203, 257 (1998). Was the "newness" of the rule established by "strong language" in *Taylor*—that racially proportionate representation was not required on petit juries, even if it was required in the jury venire from which the petit jury would be drawn?

4) The End of Habeas Review as an Appellate Substitute. Recall that, during the Warren era, the Supreme Court functionally deputized lower federal courts to conduct what amounted to appellate review of state criminal process. How does *Teague* change that equation? If only cases pending on direct review can benefit from a "new rule," then consider what happens when an inmate presents a novel constitutional theory to a federal district judge. Can the judge interpret the constitution and decide whether a new constitutional approach is justified? If lower-court judges are foreclosed from granting relief in such situations, then can the law develop outside of the Supreme Court? Professors Randy Hertz and James Liebman comment that the *Teague* plurality approach "forbids judges to interpret the United States Constitution in habeas corpus cases and relegates those judges to the virtually ministerial task of putting into operation decisions that the Supreme Court renders on direct review." Randy Hertz & James S. Liebman, *Federal Habeas Corpus Practice and Procedure* § 25.4 (6th ed. 2011) (*FHCPP*).[h]

Teague, to a certain extent, recognized this effect on federal habeas: "habeas corpus cannot be used as a vehicle to create new constitutional rules of criminal procedure unless those rules would be applied retroactively to all defendants on collateral review." The Supreme Court seemed comfortable with that state of affairs. Will the result provoke defendants to file more certiorari

---

[h] See also Tung Yin, A Better Mousetrap: Procedural Default as a Retroactivity Alternative to Teague v. Lane and the Antiterrorism and Effective Death Penalty Act of 1996, 25 Am. J. Crim. L. 203, 283 (1998) (as a result of Teague, "the lower federal courts are essentially removed from the development of constitutional law.").

petitions with the Supreme Court, alleging novel constitutional theories? Will the result deprive federal judges of the ability to develop constitutional criminal procedure? Or do Professors Hertz and Liebman provide an account of retroactivity jurisprudence that is too dire? What are the other channels through which constitutional rules of criminal procedure might develop? What are the reasons to prefer one channel to another?

5)   Conflict with the Statute. When the Supreme Court decided *Teague*, the federal habeas statute instructed—as it had since 1867—that federal courts "shall" entertain an application for a writ of habeas corpus filed by a person in custody asserting constitutional violations. 28 U.S.C. § 2254(a). Does *Teague* contradict the admonition in the habeas statute that federal judges shall entertain constitutional challenges? If not, why not?

6)   Relationship to Procedural Defenses. *Teague* involved a nonretroactivity defense that a state could assert in federal habeas litigation. Because nonretroactivity was a defense, the state could also waive it. Retroactivity, however, is conceptually different than the other procedural doctrines presented in Chapter 4. Although retroactivity is pleaded the same way as other procedural doctrines and is subject to the same waiver rules, it also requires a unique assessment of any new decision in light of existing law. While some believe the "*Teague* bar" was inconsistent with the federal habeas statute at the time, AEDPA mooted that dispute by changing the statute. *Teague* is now a judge-made precursor to § 2254(d)(1), discussed in the next Section, which was enacted as part of AEDPA, and which created a new substantive restriction on relief. Because *Teague* introduces questions most relevant and important for understanding § 2254(d)(1), we present it here, rather than in Chapter 4.

7)   Treatment of Similarly-Situated Prisoners. The Court repeatedly alludes to the unfairness of the *Linkletter* regime, emphasizing the differential treatment of similarly-situated prisoners. In what sense are the prisoners under discussion similarly situated? How much weight should the interest in identical treatment of similarly-situated prisoners carry? The law, of course, treats prisoners that commit the same crime differently all the time. Those differences might be based on when the crime was committed, when a prisoner is charged, how quickly a court delivers a verdict, or how quickly an appeal proceeds. What implications do these variables have for the interest in treating similarly-situated prisoners—in the sense *Teague* invokes—the same way? Is Justice Brennan making a similar point in dissent, or is he talking about something else? Does Justice Brennan himself exaggerate the plurality's exaggeration?

8)   The First *Teague* Exception. The first *Teague* exception involves "new" decisions that place certain types of conduct beyond the authority of state punishment. One example is *Lawrence v. Texas*, 539 U.S. 558 (2003), which struck down state anti-sodomy laws as violating the Due Process Clause. Two other prominent examples are: *Atkins v. Virginia*, 536 U.S. 304 (2002), which the Court held that offenders with mental retardation cannot be sentenced to death, and *Roper v. Simmons*, 543 U.S. 551 (2005), which also barred the capital sentencing of juvenile offenders. Both are cases dealing with who is eligible for the death penalty; are those cases an easy fit for the first *Teague* exception?

9)   The Second *Teague* Exception. The second *Teague* exception refers to certain "watershed" rules of criminal procedure. What is a "watershed" procedural rule? The Court describes such a rule as one that exists to prevent an "impermissibly large risk" of a wrongful conviction. The Court also describes such a rule as related to the "bedrock procedural elements" of a fair trial. What sorts of procedural rules might be "bedrock" rules, but ones that do not go to a question of a defendant's guilt?

The Court has subsequently indicated that one case would have satisfied the second *Teague* exception, had it been decided under that retroactivity framework—*Gideon v. Wainwright*, 372 U.S. 335 (1963). *Gideon* required that state courts provide any indigent felony defendant with a lawyer. How does *Gideon* prevent wrongful convictions? Compare *Gideon* to the "Confrontation Clause" rule announced in *Crawford v. Washington*, 541 U.S. 36 (2004), a case that changed the way the Sixth Amendment restricted the admissibility of hearsay evidence at trial. The Ninth Circuit held that *Crawford* "rework[ed] our understanding of bedrock criminal procedure." Other Courts of Appeals disagreed, and the Supreme Court subsequently held, in *Whorton v. Bockting*, 549 U.S. 406 (2007), that although *Crawford* was a "new rule" of criminal procedure, it was not of the "watershed" variety. *Bockting* underscored the Court's hesitation to place any constitutional rules within the second *Teague* exception: "in the years since *Teague*, we have rejected every claim that a new rule satisfied the requirements for watershed status." Is there any hypothetical rule of criminal procedure as groundbreaking as *Gideon*'s requirement that criminal defendants be provided with a lawyer? Why does the Court maintain the "watershed" rule exception, if no rule can satisfy it?

10) An Upgrade from *Linkletter*? *Teague* pointed to a number of flaws in the *Linkletter* retroactivity paradigm. Among other things, the Court focused on the uncertainty created by not knowing whether a new rule would be retroactive or not. Does the new approach create greater certainty about the retroactive effect of Supreme Court decisions? Now all "new" rules will be retroactive—but only to cases pending on direct appeal.

11) *Teague* and Distinguishing Questions of Law and Mixed Questions. The Court announced *Teague* in 1989. By the mid-1990's, the Justices began to disagree quite conspicuously over how *Teague* applied to issues beyond the pure legal question of what constitutional rule could be applied in a prisoner's case. If *Teague* applied to mixed questions—involving the application of an "old" rule to the facts of a prisoner's case—then *Teague* would more sharply limit much of what courts historically did when considering the merits of a claim raised in a habeas petition. Take, for example, an IAC claim requiring an inquiry into whether a deficient trial representation constituted objectively unreasonable performance and whether it prejudiced the trial outcome. The IAC rule has two longstanding criteria, but applying them in a particular case may be quite fact-dependent. If one could argue that state judges deserve deference when making errors in applying an old rule to an inmate's case, then *Teague* would bar relief in the vast majority of habeas filings. Justice Thomas most prominently argued that state decisions deserved deference unless they were "patently unreasonable" in their application of law to the facts. See Wright v. West, 505 U.S. 207 (1992) (Opinion of Thomas, J.). The Court ultimately failed to adopt Justice Thomas' view, perhaps because—as discussed in the next Section—AEDPA adopted a statutory rule requiring deference to state decisions that did not "unreasonably" apply law to facts. See 28 U.S.C. § 2254(d)(2).

12) Announcing New Rules. After *Teague*, should the Court be clear that a decision announces a "new" constitutional right applicable to cases pending on direct review? Perhaps that would eliminate uncertainty and place states on notice that a new rule of constitutional law must be applied retroactively. The Justices, however, seem to avoid using opinions to specify the retroactivity status of the decisions that they explain.

Consider an example involving *Padilla v. Kentucky*, 559 U.S. 356 (2010), in which the Supreme Court announced that a prisoner may state a federal IAC claim if a trial attorney failed to advise the prisoner about the risk of deportation associated with a guilty plea in a criminal proceeding. *Padilla* was an application of *Strickland's* two-pronged approach to IAC claims, but the opinion itself did not disclose whether the rule of decision it announced was retroactive. Was *Padilla* new and therefore nonretroactive, or was it "old" law under *Strickland*? In *Chaidez v. United States*, 133 S.Ct. 1103 (U.S. 2013) the Court held that *Padilla* was a new rule and was not retroactively applicable to cases that were pending on direct review when *Padilla* was announced. *Chaidez* clarified that "*Padilla* would not have created a new rule had it only applied *Strickland's* general standard to yet another factual situation." The Court did observe that, "despite the many different settings in which it has been applied, we have never found that an application of *Strickland* resulted in a new rule." The Court, however, ultimately distinguished *Padilla*. It reasoned that what made *Padilla* "new" was that it resolved an unsettled preliminary question—whether deportation is collateral to a conviction and whether that status bars relief on an IAC claim alleging that a trial attorney did not advise a criminal defendant about deportation consequences. Justice Sonia Sotomayor dissented, pointing out that *Padilla* itself disregarded any distinction between direct and collateral consequences as being "irrelevant to the issue it ultimately decided." Justice Sotomayor concluded, "In *Padilla*, we did nothing more than apply *Strickland*." Do you agree with the *Teague* analysis in *Chaidez*?

13) *Teague* and State Adjudication. *Teague* set forth a retroactivity rule, but a rule for which courts? In *Danforth v. Minnesota*, 552 U.S. 264 (2008), the Court held that states need not follow the *Teague* approach in their own postconviction proceedings. Justice Stevens, writing for the majority, explained: "Neither *Linkletter* nor *Teague* explicitly or implicitly constrained the authority of the States to provide remedies for a broader range of constitutional violations than are redressable on federal habeas." He observed that the applicability of a retroactivity rule to the states was not a new issue. Although the Supreme Court had not given retroactive effect to the rule announced in *Escobado v. Illinois*, 378 U.S. 478 (1964), and *Miranda v. Arizona*, 384 U.S. 436 (1966), the Oregon Supreme Court decided that those decisions could be given retroactive effect in state proceedings. Justice Stevens reasoned that "*Teague's* general rule of nonretroactivity was an exercise of this Court's power to interpret the federal habeas statute,"—particularly 28 U.S.C. § 2243, which provides that judges may resolve habeas petitions "as law and justice require." Justice Stevens emphasized that "[f]ederalism and comity considerations are unique to *federal* habeas review of state convictions. If anything, considerations of comity militate in favor of allowing state courts to grant habeas relief to a broader class of individuals than is required by *Teague*."

Is non-retroactivity a limitation on the substantive right at issue, or on the ability of the prisoner to obtain a habeas remedy? With that in mind, consider Chief Justice Roberts' dissent:

> This Court has held that the question whether a particular ruling is retro-active is itself a question of federal law. It is basic that when it comes to any such question of federal law, it is "the province and duty" of this Court "to say what the law is." *Marbury v. Madison.* State courts are the final arbiters of their own state law; this Court is the final arbiter of federal law. State courts are therefore bound by our rulings on whether our cases construing federal law are retroactive.

He emphasized the interest in treating similarly-situated offenders the same way, an interest that *Teague* itself expressed. Chief Justice Roberts wrote: "The end result is startling: Of two criminal defendants, each of whom committed the same crime, at the same time, whose convictions became final on the same day, and each of whom raised an identical claim at the same time under the Federal Constitution, one may be executed while the other is set free." Finally, Chief Justice Roberts emphasized the view that *Teague* "is not about remedy; it is about choice of law new or old." Therefore, "[t]here is no reason to believe, either legally or intuitively, that States should have any authority over this question when it comes to which *federal* constitutional rules of criminal proce-dure to apply." Why is Chief Justice Roberts so concerned with rebutting the proposition that non-retroactivity is a feature of the remedy? Alternatively, is it wrong for a state court to follow *Teague,* given the reasoning that state judges should be situated to remedy federal constitutional errors in the first instance? See Timothy P. O'Neill, *New Law, Old Cases, Fair Outcomes: Why the Illinois Supreme Court Must Overrule* People v. Flowers, 43 Loy. U. Chi. L.J. 727 (2012).

14) Scholarly Debate. We mentioned Paul Mishkin's influential work in the wake of *Linkletter.* Scholarly debate surrounding how the Supreme Court should approach non-retroactivity analysis did not abate after *Teague.* For the view that decisions should not necessarily be retroactive even to cases pending on direct appeal, see Toby J. Heytens, *Managing Transitional Moments in Criminal Cases,* 115 Yale L.J. 922, 979 (2006). For the view that the *Teague* analysis should be abandoned, see Kermit Roosevelt III, *A Little Theory is a Dangerous Thing: The Myth of Adjudicative Retroactivity,* 31 Conn. L. Rev. 1075 (1999). For additional scholarship, selecting from a voluminous literature, see Susan Bandes, *Taking Justice to its Logical Extreme: A Comment on Teague v. Lane,* 66 S. Cal. L. Rev. 2453, 2453 (1993) (exploring the relationship among *Teague,* federal jurisdiction, and substantive constitutional law); John Blume & William Pratt, *Understanding Teague v. Lane,* 18 N.Y.U. Rev. L. & Soc. Change 325, 326 (1990–1991) (arguing that *Teague* failed to make retroactivity out-comes more predictable); Richard H. Fallon, Jr. & Daniel J. Meltzer, *New Law, Non-Retroactivity, and Constitutional Remedies,* 104 Harv. L. Rev. 1731, 1758 (1991) (theorizing that "new law" doctrines are best analyzed through remedial paradigms); Joseph L. Hoffman, *Retroactivity and the Great Writ: How Con-gress Should Respond to Teague v. Lane,* 1990 BYU L. Rev. 183, 210 (favoring a statutory approach to non-retroactivity doctrine); Daniel J. Meltzer, *Habeas Corpus Jurisdiction: The Limits of Models,* 66 S. Cal. L. Rev. 2507, 2516 (1993) (emphasizing the role that *Teague* plays in balancing powers); Linda Meyer, *"Nothing We Say Matters": Teague and New Rules,* 61 U. Chi. L. Rev. 423, 424–25 (1994) (criticizing *Teague* on various grounds, including the conceptual diffi-culties of connecting "newness" and "holdings"); Kermit Roosevelt III, *A Retro-activity Retrospective, with Thoughts for the Future: What the Supreme Court Learned from Paul Mishkin, and What It Might,* 95 Calif. L. Rev. 1677, 1689–

90 (2007) (considering the application of the retroactivity framework to line of cases under *Apprendi v. New Jersey*, 530 U.S. 466 (2000)).

B. 28 U.S.C. § 2254(d)(1)

In *Teague*, Justice White noted that, if the Supreme Court was taking the wrong approach to retroactivity, then Congress could correct it. In 1996, Congress incorporated *Teague* into a substantive limit on relief, 28 U.S.C. § 2254(d)(1). Section 2254(d) only applies where a claim has been adjudicated on the merits in state courts. Section 2254(d) then supplies, in each of two subsections, criteria for granting relief on such a claim. A claim subject to state merits disposition need not satisfy both subsections, but must satisfy at least one for the state prisoner to obtain federal relief.

The first of those subsections, § 2254(d)(1), provides that a federal court may grant habeas relief if a state merits adjudication "resulted in a decision that was contrary to, or involved an unreasonable application of, clearly established Federal law, as determined by the Supreme Court of the United States[.]" Section 2254(d)(1), among other things, reconstituted the *Teague* bar as a substantive limit on relief. The language regarding "clearly established" law reflects the obvious concern with "new rules" and the retroactivity jurisprudence that developed to address them. Although *Teague* itself still applies in limited circumstances, understanding the reach of § 2254(d)(1) is far more important. What else did Congress intend to accomplish by enacting § 2254(d)(1)?

––––––

NOTE ON AEDPA LEGISLATIVE HISTORY

AEDPA represents the culmination of longstanding efforts to limit federal habeas review of state prisoner claims. Resistance to broad federal habeas review is nothing new. The opening salvo in that fight was *Brown v. Allen*, 344 U.S. 443 (1953), which held that the federal habeas statute permitted state prisoners to relitigate the merits of constitutional questions that state courts had decided against them.[i] (*Brown v. Allen* is excerpted in Chapters 1 and 4.) If you review *Noia* in Chapter 4, you get a strong sense that Justice Brennan was staking out a position in a fight about the proper scope of federal postconviction review.

Although AEDPA's legislative history has been important to judges trying to interpret the statute, insights about the process are often reduced to the fairly simplistic proposition that prisoners should lose close interpretive questions. AEDPA's genesis can be traced to two different threads of habeas restrictions: the first involves substantive limits on a federal authority to hear state-prisoner cases; the second involves procedural limits and is responsive to delays in the imposition of capital sentences.

First, in the 1940s, a conference of Senior Circuit Judges chaired by Judge John J. Parker ("Parker Committee") drafted a model habeas jurisdiction-stripping proposal. Congress rejected the jurisdiction-stripping proposal in 1948, opting instead for more moderate procedural reform—including the mod-

––––––

[i] For the view that many overstate the role of *Brown v. Allen* in modern disputes over the writ's scope, see Eric M. Freedman, *Milestones in Habeas Corpus: Part III*, Brown v. Allen: *The Habeas Corpus Revolution That Wasn't*, 51 Ala. L. Rev. 1541 (2000).

ern exhaustion requirement. Most legislative proposals focused on increasing the preclusive effect afforded to state judgments. The most prominent legislative opponent of these restrictive proposals was the Democratic Senate Majority Leader, Lyndon B. Johnson. The case for habeas restrictions got a shot in the arm in 1963, when Professor Paul Bator wrote a famous Harvard Law Review article arguing that federal habeas law should give preclusive effect to the criminal judgments of jurisdictionally competent state courts, as long as the process used to adjudicate a constitutional claim was "full and fair." See Paul M. Bator, *Finality in Criminal Law and Federal Habeas Corpus for State Prisoners*, 76 Harv. L. Rev. 441 (1963). Professor Bator's article—almost surely the most influential post-conviction article ever written—came out just as the Court was deciding *Noia*. His "full-and-fair" principle ultimately became the centerpiece of habeas proposals advanced to limit the scope of federal review. The Parker Committee backed a full-and-fair proposal in 1964, and variants appeared alongside bills that ultimately comprised the 1968 Omnibus Crime Control and Safe Streets Act. Those full-and-fair provisions provoked much opposition, and Congressional Republicans withdrew them.

In 1973, a young Department of Justice (DOJ) official named William Rehnquist began to vocally promote a full-and-fair proposal, and Senator Roman Hruska eventually introduced the DOJ's preferred language in a Senate bill that never reached the floor. The Reagan DOJ pushed for a moderated full-and-fair rule, accompanied by proposed statutory commentary reserving for federal courts the authority to reconsider even soundly-adjudicated state decisions. In 1991, another effort to introduce a full-and-fair rule failed. The 1991 amendment would have provided for a full-and-fair rule and clarified that a state decision was not full and fair if it "was contrary to or involved an arbitrary or unreasonable interpretation or application of clearly established Federal law" or if it "involved an arbitrary or unreasonable determination of the facts in light of the evidence presented." 137 Cong. Rec. H7996 (daily ed. Oct. 17, 1991). That language appears to be the most direct ancestor of what is now Section 2254(d).

At the same time that the full-and-fair concept was getting tryouts in various legal institutions, there was a second movement to impose a variety of procedural restrictions on relief—particularly in capital cases. In 1989, Chief Justice Rehnquist chartered a committee, chaired by then-retired Associate Justice Louis Powell, to consider the prudence of legislation "directed toward avoiding delay and the lack of finality in capital cases in which the prisoner had or had been offered counsel."[j] The "Powell Committee" reported out a series of recommendations, the unifying theme of which was the idea of a quid pro quo whereby the states provided inmates with adequate post-conviction representation in exchange for more favorable defenses on federal habeas review. The Powell Committee and the legislators who embraced its proposal were primarily concerned with the delay that federal habeas proceedings caused in capital cases. Senator Arlen Specter eventually emerged as the leader of the Senate contingent most aggressively seeking to implement the Powell Committee recommendations.

---

[j] Judicial Conference of the U.S., Ad Hoc Comm. on Fed. Habeas Corpus in Capital Cases, Comm. Rep. and Proposal 3 (Aug. 23, 1989), *reprinted in* Habeas Corpus Legislation: Hearings on H.R. 4737 H.R. 1090, H.R. 1953, and H.R. 32584 Before the H. Subcomm. on Courts, Intellectual Property, and the Administration of Justice of the H. Comm. on the Judiciary, 101st Cong. 46 (1990) (internal quotation marks omitted).

The movements for substantive and procedural reform converged toward the end of President Clinton's first term. In 1994, Newt Gingrich and House Republicans won a majority for the first time in forty ears. Then, on April 19, 1995, United States Army Veteran and militia sympathizer Timothy McVeigh detonated a truck bomb at the Murrah Federal Building in Oklahoma City. The Oklahoma City Bombing killed 168 people and remains the deadliest act of domestic terrorism in American history. Congress eventually added habeas reform to the pending antiterrorist legislation—accounting for AEDPA's name. AEDPA ultimately incorporated changes to the substantive "standard of review" in § 2254(d) and to procedural restrictions in *all* cases—not just those involving capital sentences.

In the 104th Congress, Representative Christopher Cox introduced an amendment to a Republican bill, tracking the 1991 full-and-fair effort to limit federal habeas review. Supporters of the full-and-fair bill still needed the votes of Senator Specter and the thirty-four Senators who were most interested in procedural limits that derived from the Powell Committee recommendations. The Hatch and Specter contingents forged a compromise bill, which did not contain a full-and-fair proposal. The compromise bill instead provided that a state prisoner could not obtain federal habeas relief unless, under what is now Section 2254(d), a state merits adjudication was legally or factually unreasonable. That bill ultimately passed both chambers and became AEDPA.

There are no House or Senate committee reports describing the meaning and intent behind AEDPA revisions there is only a Conference Committee report. It explains:

> The title incorporates reforms to curb the abuse of the statutory writ of habeas corpus, and to address the acute problems of unnecessary delay and abuse in capital cases. It sets a one year limitation on an application for a habeas writ and revises the procedures for consideration of a writ in federal court. It provides for the exhaustion of state remedies and requires deference to the determinations of state courts that are neither "contrary to," nor an "unreasonable application of," clearly established federal law.[k]

That statement did not explain what the new standards of review meant or what their effect might be. President William J. Clinton issued a statement upon signing the legislation on April 24, 1996: "I have signed this bill because I am confident that the Federal courts will interpret these provisions to preserve independent review of Federal legal claims and the bedrock constitutional principle of an independent judiciary."[l] Far less sanguine was Senator Patrick Moynihan, one of the main critics of the statute, who objected: "We are about to enact a statute which would hold that constitutional protections do not exist unless they have been unreasonably violated, an idea that would have confounded the framers." He added, "Thus we introduce a virus that will surely spread throughout our system of laws."[m] Then-Senator Joe Biden also described his concern with a standard of review that would limit relief to situations in which the state court was "not merely wrong but unreasonable."[n]

---

[k] H.R. Conf. Rep. 104–518, 94th Cong., 2d Sess. 111 (1996).

[l] *Statement of the President on Signing the Antiterrorism and Effective Death Penalty Act of 1996*, 32 Weekly Comp. Pres. Doc. 719 (April 26, 1996).

[m] See 142 Cong. Rec. S3427–04, S3438 (1996).

[n] 141 Cong. Rec. S7842 (daily ed. June 7, 1995) (statement of Sen. Biden).

AEDPA co-sponsor Senator Arlen Specter countered that, although he was not "entirely comfortable" with the standard, he believed "that the standard in the bill will allow Federal courts sufficient discretion to ensure that convictions in State court have been obtained in conformity with the Constitution."[o] Perhaps more ambiguously, Senator Orrin Hatch argued that the standard of review still "enables the Federal court to overturn State court positions that clearly contravene Federal law. It further allows the Federal courts to review State court decisions that improperly apply clearly established Federal law."[p]

Both defenders and objectors found themselves wanting for clarity in explaining the statute's operative language and its intended effects on judicial review; some argue that, as a result, the legislative history of AEDPA is not particularly informative. For example, Professor Bryan Stevenson has written that "AEDPA was drafted, enacted, and signed in an atmosphere of fear. The legislation, which includes substantial cutbacks in the federal habeas corpus remedy, was Congress's response to the tragedy of the Oklahoma City bombing." Bryan A. Stevenson, *The Politics of Fear and Death: Successive Problems in Capital Federal Habeas Cases*, 77 N.Y.U. L. Rev. 699, 701 (2002); see also Allan Ides, *Habeas Standards of Review Under 28 U.S.C. § 2254(d)(1): A Commentary on Statutory Text and Supreme Court Precedent*, 60 Wash. & Lee L. Rev. 677, 696 (2003) ("to the extent that the legislative history is informative, it reveals some concern that the 'unreasonable application' standard of review might be read to preclude federal court review of a state court decision that could be described as wrong-but-reasonable."). Consider the interpretive significance of the statutory history as we turn to § 2254(d)(1) and how federal courts apply it.

INTRODUCTORY NOTE ON TERRY WILLIAMS V. TAYLOR

The relationship between the statute and *Teague* notwithstanding, 28 U.S.C. § 2254(d)(1) represents an important break from the pre-AEDPA standard for federal merits review. Federal courts no longer decide whether a claim simply has merit. Instead, they scrutinize state decisions for reasonableness. *Teague* had been a state procedural defense, formally having to do with a pure question of law—whether a "new" rule could be applied in a given case. If the rule the Court announced in a particular decision was not "new," then the prisoner could invoke the decision.

By contrast, § 2254(d)(1) is a substantive limit on relief. AEDPA provided that a state prisoner can satisfy § 2254(d)(1) only if the state court's decision denying relief on a claim was either "contrary to" or an "unreasonable application of" clearly established U.S. Supreme Court law. Following the enactment of AEDPA, the circuits quickly split on the interpretation of the new federal rule. The most deferential approaches were adopted by the Fourth, Fifth, Sixth, Tenth, and Eleventh circuits, in which a state legal determination was honored unless it was decided "in a manner that reasonable jurists would *all agree* is unreasonable." Green v. French, 143 F.3d 865, 873–74 (4th Cir. 1998).[q] The

---

[o] 142 Cong. Rec. S3472 (daily ed. April 17, 1996) (statement of Sen. Specter).

[p] 141 Cong. Rec. S7846 (daily ed. June 7, 1995) (statement of Sen. Hatch).

[q] See also Roberts v. Ward, 176 F.3d 489 (10th Cir. 1999) (applying the "all reasonable jurists" standard); Herbert v. Billy, 160 F.3d 1131, 1135 (6th Cir. 1998) (same); Neelley v. Nagel,

First, Third, and Eighth Circuits rejected the "all reasonable jurists" standard.[r] The circuits also split over other concepts. The Fifth, Seventh, and Eleventh Circuits applied the "contrary to" language to questions of law and the "unreasonable application" language to mixed questions of law and fact.[s] The Second, Ninth, and Tenth Circuits had not adopted any clear means of distinguishing decisions that were contrary to federal law from decisions that unreasonably applied it, and panels applied "apparently inconsistent standards."[t] In *Terry Williams v. Taylor*, 529 U.S. 362 (2000), the Supreme Court set forth how the federal judiciary was to apply § 2254(d)(1). Focus on how Justice O'Connor, writing for the Court on this question, gave independent meaning to the key phrases in § 2254(d)(1)—particularly to the terms "contrary to" and "unreasonable application."

Terry Williams v. Taylor

United States Supreme Court, 2000
529 U.S. 362 (2000)

■ JUSTICE STEVENS announced the judgment of the Court and delivered the opinion of the Court with respect to Parts I, III, and IV, and an opinion with respect to Parts II and V.

The questions presented are whether Terry Williams' constitutional right to the effective assistance of counsel as defined in *Strickland v. Washington*, 466 U.S. 668 (1984), was violated, and whether the judgment of the Virginia Supreme Court refusing to set aside his death sentence "was contrary to, or involved an unreasonable application of, clearly established Federal law, as determined by the Supreme Court of the United States," within the meaning of 28 U.S.C. § 2254(d)(1). We answer both questions affirmatively.

I

On November 3, 1985, Harris Stone was found dead in his residence on Henry Street in Danville, Virginia. Finding no indication of a struggle, local officials determined that the cause of death was blood alcohol poisoning, and the case was considered closed. Six months after Stone's death, Terry Williams, who was then incarcerated in the "I" unit of the city jail for an unrelated offense, wrote a letter to the police stating that he had killed "'that man down on Henry Street'" and also stating that he "'did it'" to that "'lady down on West Green Street'" and was "'very sorry.'" The letter was unsigned, but it closed with a reference to "I cell." The police readily identified Williams as its author, and, on April 25, 1986, they obtained several statements from him. In one Williams admitted that, after Stone refused to lend him "'a couple of dollars,'" he had killed Stone with a mattock and tak-

---

138 F.3d 917, 924 (11th Cir. 1998) (same); Drinkard v. Johnson, 97 F.3d 751, 767–68 (5th Cir. 1996) (same).

[r] See O'Brien v. Dubois, 145 F.3d 16, 24 (1st Cir. 1998); Matteo v. Superintendent, 171 F.3d 877 (3d Cir. 1999) (en banc); Richardson v. Bowersox, 188 F.3d 973, 977–78 (8th Cir. 1999); see also Hertz & Liebman, *FHCPP*, supra note c, at § 32.3 & n.21 (collecting cases).

[s] See Ashford v. Gilmore, 167 F.3d 1130, 1134 (7th Cir. 1999); *Neelley*, 138 F.3d at 924; *Drinkard*, 97 F.3d at 767–68.

[t] See Hertz & Liebman, *FHCPP*, supra note c, at §32.3 & n.24; see, e.g. Smalls v. Batista, 191 F.3d 272, 278 (2d Cir. 1999) ("We need not join either side of the existing circuit split on this issue").

en the money from his wallet.[1] In September 1986, Williams was convicted of robbery and capital murder.

At Williams' sentencing hearing, the prosecution proved that Williams had been convicted of armed robbery in 1976 and burglary and grand larceny in 1982. The prosecution also introduced the written confessions that Williams had made in April. The prosecution described two auto thefts and two separate violent assaults on elderly victims perpetrated after the Stone murder. * * * Williams had also been convicted of arson for setting a fire in the jail while awaiting trial in this case. Two expert witnesses employed by the State testified that there was a "high probability" that Williams would pose a serious continuing threat to society.

The evidence offered by Williams' trial counsel at the sentencing hearing consisted of the testimony of Williams' mother, two neighbors, and a taped excerpt from a statement by a psychiatrist. One of the neighbors had not been previously interviewed by defense counsel, but was noticed by counsel in the audience during the proceedings and asked to testify on the spot. The three witnesses briefly described Williams as a "nice boy" and not a violent person. The recorded psychiatrist's testimony did little more than relate Williams' statement during an examination that in the course of one of his earlier robberies, he had removed the bullets from a gun so as not to injure anyone.

* * * In closing argument, Williams' counsel characterized Williams' confessional statements as "dumb," but asked the jury to give weight to the fact that he had "turned himself in, not on one crime but on four . . . that the [police otherwise] would not have solved." The weight of defense counsel's closing, however, was devoted to explaining that it was difficult to find a reason why the jury should spare Williams' life.[2]

The jury found a probability of future dangerousness and unanimously fixed Williams' punishment at death. The trial judge concluded that such punishment was "proper" and "just" and imposed the death sentence. The Virginia Supreme Court affirmed the conviction and sentence. * * *

State Habeas Proceedings

In 1988 Williams filed for state collateral relief in the Danville Circuit Court. The petition was subsequently amended, and the Circuit Court (the

---

[1] "'I had gone to Dee Dee Stone's house on Henry Street, Dee Dee's father was there. No one else was there except him. He had been drinking a lot. He was on the bed. He asked me if I wanted a drink. I told him, 'No.' I asked him if I could borrow a couple of dollars and he told me, 'No.' We started arguing and things started going around in my head. I just wanted to get back at him. I don't know what. He just laid back like he had passed out. He was laying there talking and moaning to himself. I went into the kitchen. I saw the butcher knife. I didn't want to use it. I was looking for something to use. I went into the bathroom and I saw the mattock. I picked up the mattock and I came back into the room where he was at. He was laying on the bed. He was laying on his back. I took the mattock and I hit him on the chest with it. He raised up and was gasping for his breath. He fell over to his side and I hit him in the back with the mattock. He fell back on the bed. I went and put the mattock back in the bathroom. I came back into the room. I took his wallet from his pocket. He had three dollars in it. I got the three dollars from it. I left him there. He was still grasping for breath.'"

[2] In defense counsel's words: "I will admit too that it is very difficult to ask you to show mercy to a man who maybe has not shown much mercy himself. I doubt very seriously that he thought much about mercy when he was in Mr. Stone's bedroom that night with him. I doubt very seriously that he had mercy very highly on his mind when he was walking along West Green and the incident with Alberta Stroud. I doubt very seriously that he had mercy on his mind when he took two cars that didn't belong to him. Admittedly it is very difficult to get us and ask that you give this man mercy when he has shown so little of it himself. But I would ask that you would."

same judge who had presided over Williams' trial and sentencing) held an evidentiary hearing on Williams' claim that trial counsel had been ineffective. Based on the evidence adduced after two days of hearings, Judge Ingram found that Williams' conviction was valid, but that his trial attorneys had been ineffective during sentencing. Among the evidence reviewed that had not been presented at trial were documents prepared in connection with Williams' commitment when he was 11 years old that dramatically described mistreatment, abuse, and neglect during his early childhood, as well as testimony that he was "borderline mentally retarded," had suffered repeated head injuries, and might have mental impairments organic in origin. The habeas hearing also revealed that the same experts who had testified on the State's behalf at trial believed that Williams, if kept in a "structured environment," would not pose a future danger to society.

Counsel's failure to discover and present this and other significant mitigating evidence was "below the range expected of reasonable, professional competent assistance of counsel." Counsel's performance thus "did not measure up to the standard required under the holding of *Strickland v. Washington*, 466 U.S. 668 (1984), and [if it had,] there is a reasonable probability that the result of the sentencing phase would have been different." Judge Ingram therefore recommended that Williams be granted a rehearing on the sentencing phase of his trial.

The Virginia Supreme Court did not accept that recommendation. Although it assumed, without deciding, that trial counsel had been ineffective, * * * it disagreed with the trial judge's conclusion that Williams had suffered sufficient prejudice to warrant relief. Treating the prejudice inquiry as a mixed question of law and fact, the Virginia Supreme Court accepted the factual determination that available evidence in mitigation had not been presented at the trial, but held that the trial judge had misapplied the law in two respects. First, relying on our decision in *Lockhart v. Fretwell*, 506 U.S. 364 (1993), the court held that it was wrong for the trial judge to rely "'on mere outcome determination'" when assessing prejudice. Second, it construed the trial judge's opinion as having "adopted a *per se* approach" that would establish prejudice whenever any mitigating evidence was omitted.

The court then reviewed the prosecution evidence supporting the "future dangerousness" aggravating circumstance, reciting Williams' criminal history, including the several most recent offenses to which he had confessed. In comparison, it found that the excluded mitigating evidence— which it characterized as merely indicating "that numerous people, mostly relatives, thought that defendant was nonviolent and could cope very well in a structured environment,"— "barely would have altered the profile of this defendant that was presented to the jury." On this basis, the court concluded that there was no reasonable possibility that the omitted evidence would have affected the jury's sentencing recommendation, and that Williams had failed to demonstrate that his sentencing proceeding was fundamentally unfair.

[Williams sought federal habeas relief. The federal district court granted habeas relief, and the Fourth Circuit reversed. The Supreme Court granted certiorari.]

II

[JUSTICE STEVENS was joined in Part II only by JUSTICE SOUTER, GINSBURG, and BREYER. JUSTICE O'CONNOR wrote an opinion for the Court on the issue discussed in Part II.]

* * * It is * * * well settled that the fact that constitutional error occurred in the proceedings that led to a state-court conviction may not alone be sufficient reason for concluding that a prisoner is entitled to the remedy of habeas. On the other hand, errors that undermine confidence in the fundamental fairness of the state adjudication certainly justify the issuance of the federal writ. The deprivation of the right to the effective assistance of counsel recognized in *Strickland* is such an error.

* * * The relevant portion of [28 U.S.C. § 2254] provides:

"(d) An application for a writ of habeas corpus on behalf of a person in custody pursuant to the judgment of a State court shall not be granted with respect to any claim that was adjudicated on the merits in State court proceedings unless the adjudication of the claim—

"(1) resulted in a decision that was contrary to, or involved an unreasonable application of, clearly established Federal law, as determined by the Supreme Court of the United States . . ." * * *

As the Fourth Circuit would have it, a state-court judgment is "unreasonable" in the face of federal law only if all reasonable jurists would agree that the state court was unreasonable. * * * But the statute says nothing about "reasonable judges," presumably because all, or virtually all, such judges occasionally commit error; they make decisions that in retrospect may be characterized as "unreasonable." Indeed, it is most unlikely that Congress would deliberately impose such a requirement of unanimity on federal judges. * * *

* * * A construction of AEDPA that would require the federal courts to cede this authority to the courts of the States would be inconsistent with the practice that federal judges have traditionally followed in discharging their duties under Article III of the Constitution. If Congress had intended to require such an important change in the exercise of our jurisdiction, we believe it would have spoken with much greater clarity than is found in the text of AEDPA. * * *

The "clearly established law" requirement

* * * The antiretroactivity rule recognized in *Teague*, which prohibits reliance on "new rules," is the functional equivalent of a statutory provision commanding exclusive reliance on "clearly established law." * * * It is perfectly clear that AEDPA codifies *Teague* to the extent that *Teague* requires federal habeas courts to deny relief that is contingent upon a rule of law not clearly established at the time the state conviction became final.

Teague's core principles are therefore relevant to our construction of this requirement. * * * *Teague* * * * [explained] that a federal habeas court operates within the bounds of comity and finality if it applies a rule "dictated by precedent existing at the time the defendant's conviction became final." * * *

To this, AEDPA has added, immediately following the "clearly established law" requirement, a clause limiting the area of relevant law to that "determined by the Supreme Court of the United States." If this Court has not broken sufficient legal ground to establish an asked-for constitutional principle, the lower federal courts cannot themselves establish such a principle with clarity sufficient to satisfy the AEDPA bar. * * *

* * * [R]ules of law may be sufficiently clear for habeas purposes even when they are expressed in terms of a generalized standard rather than as a bright-line rule. * * * Moreover, the determination whether or not a rule is clearly established at the time a state court renders its final judgment of conviction is a question [that the federal courts must decide].

* * * The *Teague* cases reflect this Court's view that habeas corpus is not to be used as a second criminal trial, and federal courts are not to run roughshod over the considered findings and judgments of the state courts that conducted the original trial and heard the initial appeals. * * * We are convinced that in the phrase, "clearly established law," Congress did not intend to modify [the] independent obligation [to say what the law is].

The "contrary to, or an unreasonable application of," requirement

The message that Congress intended to convey by using the phrases, "contrary to" and "unreasonable application of" is not entirely clear. We are not persuaded that the phrases define two mutually exclusive categories of questions. * * *

* * * The statutory text likewise does not obviously prescribe a specific, recognizable standard of review for dealing with either phrase. Significantly, it does not use any term, such as "*de novo*" or "plain error," that would easily identify a familiar standard of review. Rather, the text is fairly read simply as a command that a federal court not issue the habeas writ unless the state court was wrong as a matter of law or unreasonable in its application of law in a given case. * * * Whether or not a federal court can issue the writ "under [the] 'unreasonable application' clause," the statute is clear that habeas may issue under § 2254(d)(1) if a state-court "decision" is "contrary to . . . clearly established Federal law." We thus anticipate that there will be a variety of cases, like this one, in which both phrases may be implicated.

Even though we cannot conclude that the phrases establish "a body of rigid rules," they do express a "mood" that the federal judiciary must respect. In this respect, it seems clear that Congress intended federal judges to attend with the utmost care to state-court decisions, including all of the reasons supporting their decisions, before concluding that those proceedings were infected by constitutional error sufficiently serious to warrant the issuance of the writ. * * * AEDPA plainly sought to ensure a level of "deference to the determinations of state courts," provided those determinations did not conflict with federal law or apply federal law in an unreasonable way. * * *

On the other hand, it is significant that the word "deference" does not appear in the text of the statute itself. Neither the legislative history, nor the statutory text, suggests any difference in the so-called "deference" depending on which of the two phrases is implicated. Whatever "deference" Congress had in mind with respect to both phrases, it surely is not a requirement that federal courts actually defer to a state-court application of the federal law that is, in the independent judgment of the federal court, in error. * * *

The simplest and first definition of "contrary to" as a phrase is "in conflict with." Webster's Ninth New Collegiate Dictionary 285 (1983). In this sense, we think the phrase surely capacious enough to include a finding that the state-court "decision" is simply "erroneous" or wrong. * * * Moreover, state-court decisions that do not "conflict" with federal law will rarely be "unreasonable" under either the Court's reading of the statute or ours. We all agree that state-court judgments must be upheld unless, after the closest examination of the state-court judgment, a federal court is firmly convinced that a federal constitutional right has been violated. Our difference is as to the cases in which, at first blush, a state-court judgment seems entirely reasonable, but thorough analysis by a federal court produces a firm conviction that that judgment is infected by constitutional error. In our view, such an erroneous judgment is "unreasonable" within the meaning of the Act even though that conclusion was not immediately apparent.

In sum, the statute directs federal courts to attend to every state-court judgment with utmost care, but it does not require them to defer to the opinion of every reasonable state-court judge on the content of federal law. If, after carefully weighing all the reasons for accepting a state court's judgment, a federal court is convinced that a prisoner's custody—or, as in this case, his sentence of death—violates the Constitution, that independent judgment should prevail. Otherwise the federal "law as determined by the Supreme Court of the United States" might be applied by the federal courts one way in Virginia and another way in California. In light of the well-recognized interest in ensuring that federal courts interpret federal law in a uniform way, we are convinced that Congress did not intend the statute to produce such a result.

III

[The Court set out the IAC standard and concluded that the Virginia decision was contrary to and involved an unreasonable application of *Strickland*.]

IV

[The Court rejected the argument that subsequent precedent had modified the *Strickland* inquiry as the Virginia Supreme Court had maintained in its decision.]

The trial judge analyzed the ineffective-assistance claim under the correct standard; the Virginia Supreme Court did not.

We are likewise persuaded that the Virginia trial judge correctly applied both components of that standard to Williams' ineffectiveness claim. Although he concluded that counsel competently handled the guilt phase of the trial, he found that their representation during the sentencing phase fell short of professional standards—a judgment barely disputed by the State in its brief to this Court. The record establishes that counsel did not begin to prepare for that phase of the proceeding until a week before the trial. They failed to conduct an investigation that would have uncovered extensive records graphically describing Williams' nightmarish childhood, not because of any strategic calculation but because they incorrectly thought that state law barred access to such records. Had they done so, the jury would have learned that Williams' parents had been imprisoned for the criminal neglect of Williams and his siblings, that Williams had been severely and repeatedly beaten by his father, that he had been committed to the custody of the social services bureau for two years during his parents' incarceration (including one stint in an abusive foster home), and then, after his parents were released from prison, had been returned to his parents' custody.

Counsel failed to introduce available evidence that Williams was "borderline mentally retarded" and did not advance beyond sixth grade in school. They failed to seek prison records recording Williams' commendations for helping to crack a prison drug ring and for returning a guard's missing wallet, or the testimony of prison officials who described Williams as among the inmates "least likely to act in a violent, dangerous or provocative way." Counsel failed even to return the phone call of a certified public accountant who had offered to testify that he had visited Williams frequently when Williams was incarcerated as part of a prison ministry program, that Williams "seemed to thrive in a more regimented and structured environment," and that Williams was proud of the carpentry degree he earned while in prison.

Of course, not all of the additional evidence was favorable to Williams. The juvenile records revealed that he had been thrice committed to the juvenile system—for aiding and abetting larceny when he was 11 years old, for pulling a false fire alarm when he was 12, and for breaking and entering when he was 15. But as the Federal District Court correctly observed, the failure to introduce the comparatively voluminous amount of evidence that did speak in Williams' favor was not justified by a tactical decision to focus on Williams' voluntary confession. Whether or not those omissions were sufficiently prejudicial to have affected the outcome of sentencing, they clearly demonstrate that trial counsel did not fulfill their obligation to conduct a thorough investigation of the defendant's background.

We are also persuaded, unlike the Virginia Supreme Court, that counsel's unprofessional service prejudiced Williams within the meaning of *Strickland*. After hearing the additional evidence developed in the postconviction proceedings, the very judge who presided at Williams' trial, and who once determined that the death penalty was "just" and "appropriate," concluded that there existed "a reasonable probability that the result of the sentencing phase would have been different" if the jury had heard that evidence. * * *

The Virginia Supreme Court's own analysis of prejudice reaching the contrary conclusion was thus unreasonable in at least two respects. First, as we have already explained, the State Supreme Court mischaracterized at best the appropriate rule, made clear by this Court in *Strickland*, for determining whether counsel's assistance was effective within the meaning of the Constitution. While it may also have conducted an "outcome determinative" analysis of its own, * * * it is evident to us that the court's decision turned on its erroneous view that a "mere" difference in outcome is not sufficient to establish constitutionally ineffective assistance of counsel. Its analysis in this respect was thus not only "contrary to," but also, inasmuch as the Virginia Supreme Court relied on the inapplicable exception recognized in *Lockhart*, an "unreasonable application of" the clear law as established by this Court.

Second, the State Supreme Court's prejudice determination was unreasonable insofar as it failed to evaluate the totality of the available mitigation evidence—both that adduced at trial, and the evidence adduced in the habeas proceeding in reweighing it against the evidence in aggravation. * * *

* * * [T]he graphic description of Williams' childhood, filled with abuse and privation, or the reality that he was "borderline mentally retarded," might well have influenced the jury's appraisal of his moral culpability. The circumstances recited in his several confessions are consistent with the view that in each case his violent behavior was a compulsive reaction rather than the product of cold-blooded premeditation. Mitigating evidence

unrelated to dangerousness may alter the jury's selection of penalty, even if it does not undermine or rebut the prosecution's death-eligibility case. The Virginia Supreme Court did not entertain that possibility. It thus failed to accord appropriate weight to the body of mitigation evidence available to trial counsel.

V

* * * Accordingly, the judgment of the Court of Appeals is reversed, and the case is remanded for further proceedings consistent with this opinion.

It is so ordered.

■ JUSTICE O'CONNOR delivered the opinion of the Court with respect to Part II (except as to the footnote), concurred in part, and concurred in the judgment. [JUSTICE KENNEDY joins the opinion in its entirety; CHIEF JUSTICE REHNQUIST and JUSTICE THOMAS join Part II; and JUSTICE SCALIA joins Part II, with the exception of footnote 1.[u]]

II

A

* * * [F]or Williams to obtain federal habeas relief, he must first demonstrate that his case satisfies the condition set by §2254(d)(1). That provision modifies the role of federal habeas courts in reviewing petitions filed by state prisoners. Justice STEVENS' opinion in Part II essentially contends that §2254(d)(1) does not alter the previously settled rule of independent review. Indeed, the opinion concludes its statutory inquiry with the somewhat empty finding that §2254(d)(1) does no more than express a " 'mood' that the federal judiciary must respect." For Justice STEVENS, the congressionally enacted "mood" has two important qualities. First, "federal courts [must] attend to every state-court judgment with utmost care" by "carefully weighing all the reasons for accepting a state court's judgment." Second, if a federal court undertakes that careful review and yet remains convinced that a prisoner's custody violates the Constitution, "that independent judgment should prevail."

* * * Justice STEVENS' interpretation of §2254(d)(1) gives the 1996 amendment no effect whatsoever. The command that federal courts should now use the "utmost care" by "carefully weighing" the reasons supporting a state court's judgment echoes our pre-AEDPA statement * * * that federal habeas courts "should, of course, give great weight to the considered conclusions of a coequal state judiciary." Similarly, the requirement that the independent judgment of a federal court must in the end prevail essentially repeats the conclusion we reached [in a pre-AEDPA case.] * * *

That Justice STEVENS would find the new § 2254(d)(1) to have no effect on the prior law of habeas corpus is remarkable given his apparent acknowledgment that Congress wished to bring change to the field. That acknowledgment is correct and significant to this case. It cannot be disputed that Congress viewed § 2254(d)(1) as an important means by which its goals for habeas reform would be achieved.

Justice STEVENS arrives at his erroneous interpretation by means of one critical misstep. He fails to give independent meaning to both the "contrary to" and "unreasonable application" clauses of the statute. By reading

---

[u] Footnote 1 of the Opinion contained supportive references to legislative history, and is not reproduced here.

§ 2254(d)(1) as one general restriction on the power of the federal habeas court, Justice STEVENS manages to avoid confronting the specific meaning of the statute's "unreasonable application" clause and its ramifications for the independent-review rule. It is, however, a cardinal principle of statutory construction that we must "'give effect, if possible, to every clause and word of a statute.'" * * * Under the statute, a federal court may grant a writ of habeas corpus if the relevant state-court decision was either (1) "*contrary to* . . . clearly established Federal law, as determined by the Supreme Court of the United States," or (2) "*involved an unreasonable application of* . . . clearly established Federal law, as determined by the Supreme Court of the United States." (Emphasis added [by the Court].)

* * * A state-court decision will certainly be contrary to our clearly established precedent if the state court applies a rule that contradicts the governing law set forth in our cases. Take, for example, our decision in *Strickland*. * * * If a state court were to reject a prisoner's claim of ineffective assistance of counsel on the grounds that the prisoner had not established by a preponderance of the evidence that the result of his criminal proceeding would have been different, that decision would be "diametrically different," "opposite in character or nature," and "mutually opposed" to our clearly established precedent because we held in *Strickland* that the prisoner need only demonstrate a "reasonable probability that . . . the result of the proceeding would have been different." A state-court decision will also be contrary to this Court's clearly established precedent if the state court confronts a set of facts that are materially indistinguishable from a decision of this Court and nevertheless arrives at a result different from our precedent. * * *

On the other hand, a run-of-the-mill state-court decision applying the correct legal rule from our cases to the facts of a prisoner's case would not fit comfortably within § 2254(d)(1)'s "contrary to" clause. Assume, for example, that a state-court decision on a prisoner's ineffective-assistance claim correctly identifies *Strickland* as the controlling legal authority and, applying that framework, rejects the prisoner's claim. Quite clearly, the state-court decision would be in accord with our decision in *Strickland* as to the legal prerequisites for establishing an ineffective-assistance claim, even assuming the federal court considering the prisoner's habeas application might reach a different result applying the *Strickland* framework itself. It is difficult, however, to describe such a run-of-the-mill state-court decision as "diametrically different" from, "opposite in character or nature" from, or "mutually opposed" to *Strickland*, our clearly established precedent. Although the state-court decision may be contrary to the federal court's conception of how *Strickland* ought to be applied in that particular case, the decision is not "mutually opposed" to *Strickland* itself.

Justice STEVENS would instead construe § 2254(d)(1)'s "contrary to" clause to encompass such a routine state-court decision. That construction, however, saps the "unreasonable application" clause of any meaning. If a federal habeas court can, under the "contrary to" clause, issue the writ whenever it concludes that the state court's *application* of clearly established federal law was incorrect, the "unreasonable application" clause becomes a nullity. * * * Reading § 2254(d)(1)'s "contrary to" clause to permit a federal court to grant relief in cases where a state court's error is limited to the manner in which it *applies* Supreme Court precedent is suspect given the logical and natural fit of the neighboring "unreasonable application" clause to such cases.

* * * First, a state-court decision involves an unreasonable application of this Court's precedent if the state court identifies the correct governing legal rule from this Court's cases but unreasonably applies it to the facts of the particular state prisoner's case. Second, a state-court decision also involves an unreasonable application of this Court's precedent if the state court either unreasonably extends a legal principle from our precedent to a new context where it should not apply or unreasonably refuses to extend that principle to a new context where it should apply.

A state-court decision that correctly identifies the governing legal rule but applies it unreasonably to the facts of a particular prisoner's case certainly would qualify as a decision "involv[ing] an unreasonable application of . . . clearly established Federal law." * * *

B

There remains the task of defining what exactly qualifies as an "unreasonable application" of law under § 2254(d)(1). * * * Defining an "unreasonable application" by reference to a "reasonable jurist[]" * * * is of little assistance to the courts that must apply § 2254(d)(1) and, in fact, may be misleading. Stated simply, a federal habeas court making the "unreasonable application" inquiry should ask whether the state court's application of clearly established federal law was objectively unreasonable. The federal habeas court should not transform the inquiry into a subjective one by resting its determination instead on the simple fact that at least one of the Nation's jurists has applied the relevant federal law in the same manner the state court did in the habeas petitioner's case. The "all reasonable jurists" standard would tend to mislead federal habeas courts by focusing their attention on a subjective inquiry rather than on an objective one. * * *

The term "unreasonable" is no doubt difficult to define. That said, it is a common term in the legal world and, accordingly, federal judges are familiar with its meaning. For purposes of today's opinion, the most important point is that an *unreasonable* application of federal law is different from an *incorrect* application of federal law. * * * Under § 2254(d)(1)'s "unreasonable application" clause, then, a federal habeas court may not issue the writ simply because that court concludes in its independent judgment that the relevant state-court decision applied clearly established federal law erroneously or incorrectly. Rather, that application must also be unreasonable. * * *

Throughout this discussion the meaning of the phrase "clearly established Federal law, as determined by the Supreme Court of the United States" has been put to the side. That statutory phrase refers to the holdings, as opposed to the dicta, of this Court's decisions as of the time of the relevant state-court decision. In this respect, the "clearly established Federal law" phrase bears only a slight connection to our *Teague* jurisprudence. With one caveat, whatever would qualify as an old rule under our *Teague* jurisprudence will constitute "clearly established Federal law, as determined by the Supreme Court of the United States" under § 2254(d)(1). The one caveat, as the statutory language makes clear, is that § 2254(d)(1) restricts the source of clearly established law to this Court's jurisprudence.

In sum, § 2254(d)(1) places a new constraint on the power of a federal habeas court to grant a state prisoner's application for a writ of habeas corpus with respect to claims adjudicated on the merits in state court. Under § 2254(d)(1), the writ may issue only if one of the following two conditions is satisfied–the state-court adjudication resulted in a decision that (1) "was contrary to . . . clearly established Federal law, as determined by the Supreme Court of the United States," or (2) "involved an unreasonable application of . . . clearly established Federal law, as determined by the Supreme Court of the United States." Under the "contrary to" clause, a federal habeas court may grant the writ if the state court arrives at a conclusion opposite to that reached by this Court on a question of law or if the state court decides a case differently than this Court has on a set of materially indistinguishable facts. Under the "unreasonable application" clause, a federal habeas court may grant the writ if the state court identifies the correct governing legal principle from this Court's decisions but unreasonably applies that principle to the facts of the prisoner's case.

III

Although I disagree with Justice STEVENS concerning the standard we must apply under §2254(d)(1) in evaluating Terry Williams' claims on habeas, I agree with the Court that the Virginia Supreme Court's adjudication of Williams' claim of ineffective assistance of counsel resulted in a decision that was both contrary to and involved an unreasonable application of this Court's clearly established precedent. * * *

Accordingly, although I disagree with the interpretation of §2254(d)(1) set forth in Part II of Justice STEVENS' opinion, I join Parts I, III, and IV of the Court's opinion and concur in the judgment of reversal.

[CHIEF JUSTICE REHNQUIST, joined by JUSTICES SCALIA AND THOMAS, agreed with the Court's interpretation of § 2254(d), but would not have granted relief in this case. That dissenting opinion is omitted.]

NOTES AND QUESTIONS ON TERRY WILLIAMS

1)   **The "Opinion of the Court."** The two subsections of § 2254(d) apply only to claims adjudicated on the merits by the state court. If the state court decides the case on the merits, then the next step in the analysis requires a federal court to scrutinize the decision involving that claim. Therefore, § 2254(d) analysis must be conducted for each claim that the petitioner raises. Assuming a state merits adjudication, § 2254(d)(1) permits habeas relief where state decisions are either "contrary to" or an "unreasonable application of" clearly established federal law. Justice Stevens formally "wrote for the Court," but, on the key question regarding the interpretation of Section 2254(d)(1), it was Part II of Justice O'Connor's opinion that garnered a majority of the Justices' votes. What were the key differences between Justice O'Connor's interpretation of Section 2254(d)(1) and Justice Stevens' interpretation? Over which of the two § 2254(d)(1) clauses do Justices O'Connor and Stevens disagree?

2)   **Independent Review and "Interpretive Mood."** The Supreme Court held that, when applying § 2254(d)(1), a federal court no longer scrutinizes the *claim*, and instead assesses whether the state *decision* is "reasonable." The terminology in the statute, as well as language in excerpted parts of Justice O'Connor's opinion for the Court, reflects a concept most prominently appearing in a pre-AEDPA opinion by Justice Thomas. In *Wright v. West*, 505 U.S. 277 (1992), no opinion garnered a Court majority, but Justice Thomas advanced the argument that *Teague* should extend to mixed questions of law and fact, so that claims would be *Teague*-barred unless the "state court's decision rejecting the claim . . . is patently unreasonable." The Court never adopted such a view of

Teague, but Congress arguably enacted something along those lines in § 2254(d)(1).

In the portion of his *Terry Williams* opinion that did not garner a majority, Justice Stevens argued that § 2254(d)(1) permits a federal court to evaluate the claim *simpliciter.* Justice Stevens also believed that the language reflects more of a "mood" than a set of marching orders. What kind of "mood" might § 2254(d)(1) reflect, and what does it require of federal judges? Does the fact that the mood is restrictive support statutory interpretations that promote "deference"? How does that interpretive mood reflect AEDPA's legislative history? Does Justice O'Connor respond correctly when she says that notwithstanding whatever mood the language expresses, that mood cannot be invoked to frustrate the principle that each clause or phrase in a statute be given independent meaning?

Think of "contrary to" and "unreasonable application of" as two members of a single provision. If you agree that the canon of giving independent effect to each member of the provision should control, then what exactly do those members mean? Will the Court ever state what is "contrary to" or what results in "an unreasonable application of" federal law with a more meaningful level of specificity? And, if it cannot, then did Congress prudently vest discretion over what constitutes a "reasonable" state decision in lower federal judges?

3) The "Contrary To" Clause. Writing for the Court on the issue, Justice O'Connor gives the "contrary to" and "unreasonable application of" phrases distinct meanings. Justice Stevens would have interpreted the "contrary to or resulted in an unreasonable application of" language as expressing single directive to perform federal habeas review deferentially. Under the controlling interpretation of § 2254(d)(1), however, a case is "contrary to" clearly established law when "a state court arrives at a conclusion opposite to that reached by this Court on a question of law or if the state court decides a case differently than this Court has on a set of materially indistinguishable facts." Justice Stevens, however, would have read "contrary to" to mean "in conflict with," therefore giving it broader effect. How would his reading have rendered the "unreasonable application" language superfluous?

The first category of "contrary to" decisions—those in which a state court "arrives at a conclusion opposite to that reached by" the Supreme Court on a question of law—seems straightforward and represents a helpful clarification. The example that the Court provides in *Terry Williams* involves the prejudice prong of an IAC claim. The law requires that a prisoner show a "reasonable probability" that a sentencing outcome would be different, and a state decision that specifies something other than a "reasonable probability" standard would be "contrary to" federal law. What are some other examples? How easy will it be to show that a state incorrectly applied governing Supreme Court law? Will it still be possible to show that a state court got governing Supreme Court law wrong if the state court issued a summary opinion that did not provide reasons? How wrong must the state court be about Supreme Court law? Completely wrong? "Diametrically different"?

More problematic is the second category of "contrary to" decisions—those in which a state court "decides a case differently than this Court has on a set of materially indistinguishable facts." Obviously, no cases have facts that are indistinguishable. Presumably Justice O'Connor includes the word "material" to address this observation, but what sort of work can "material" do? If the facts are "materially different," does the state decision become the subject of the "unreasonable application" clause?

In *Terry Williams,* the Justices agreed that the Virginia decision was "contrary to" clearly established IAC law. The Virginia Supreme Court sidestepped the prejudice requirement. Despite evidence of grossly ineffective assistance, the Virginia Supreme Court stated that evidence of prejudice could be disregarded, based on "proper attention to whether the result of the criminal proceeding was fundamentally unfair or unreliable." Thus, the Virginia Supreme Court really did apply the wrong standard, failing to ask whether the ineffective assistance prejudiced, with a reasonable probability, the outcome at sentencing.

4)   The "Unreasonable Application" Clause. A state decision applies clearly established federal law unreasonably "if the state court identifies the correct governing legal principle from this Court's decisions but unreasonably applies that principle to the facts of the prisoner's case." The application of federal law must be "objectively unreasonable." What cases satisfy the "unreasonable application" language of § 2254(d)(1)? As noted, before the Court decided *Terry Williams,* there were massive Circuit splits on what this wording meant. Recall how the Fourth Circuit, for example, had used an "all reasonable jurists" standard. Under such a reading of § 2254(d)(1), a federal judge would have to believe that none of the judges on the Virginia Supreme Court were reasonable people. The U.S. Supreme Court rejected that type of subjective inquiry. How "incorrectly" must a court apply law in order to render the decision "unreasonable"? Does it depend on how flexible or inflexible the underlying legal rule is?

5)   Clearly Established Law. Notice that § 2254(d)(1) permits a state prisoner to obtain relief only if the state decision runs afoul of law that the Supreme Court "clearly established." Does § 2254(d)(1) therefore mean that state courts need not follow interpretations of the federal constitution set out by federal district courts and courts of appeals? Moreover, consider the Court's statement regarding the concept of "clearly established" law in *Terry Williams*: that "[clearly established law] refers to the holdings, as opposed to the dicta, of this Court's decisions as of the time of the relevant state-court decision." Ironically, because *Terry Williams* was a case about the meaning of the "contrary to" and "unreasonable application of" language, the Court's statement about dicta was itself dictum.

6)   The Qualified Immunity Analogy. The term "clearly established" has a history of usage in the qualified immunity context. State officers can be sued for damages under 42 U.S.C. § 1983, and federal officers can be sued under *Bivens v. Six Unknown Named Agents,* 403 U.S. 388 (1971). Qualified immunity is designed to protect government officials from damages liability "insofar as their conduct does not violate clearly established statutory or constitutional rights of which a reasonable person would have known." Harlow v. Fitzgerald, 457 U.S. 800, 818 (1981). The qualified immunity rules are designed to give officials "fair notice" of what the constitution requires. Perhaps Congress had qualified immunity in mind when requiring state courts to be insulated from reversal based on what law was "clearly established" at the time of the state court decision. Under qualified immunity doctrine, the official may have gotten it wrong, but deserves some extra layer of deference when facing a civil rights lawsuit seeking monetary damages; the goal is to protect public servants acting in good faith from burdensome litigation. The archetypical case was that of a police officer acting "reasonably" when conducting a search or a seizure under the Fourth Amendment and having to make a quick judgment call on the scene. See Pearson v. Callahan, 555 U.S. 223, 231 (2009). Is the Fourth-Amendment scenario a sound analogy for state judges ruling on constitutional claims brought by prisoners?

7) Codifying _Teague_? After _Terry Williams_, what is the relationship between _Teague_ and § 2254(d)(1)? _Teague_ generally barred the application of "new" decisions on collateral review, and defined "new" decisions as those not "dictated by precedent." Section 2254(d)(1) also bars relief based on new decisions—habeas writs may issue only for claims based on law that the Supreme Court had "clearly established." In _Horn v. Banks_, 536 U.S. 266 (2002), however, the Court held that § 2254(d)(1) did not displace _Teague_. After Banks' direct appeal ended, he filed a state post-conviction petition. The Pennsylvania Supreme Court denied relief despite _Mills v. Maryland_, 486 U.S. 367 (1988), an intervening U.S. Supreme Court decision barring states from imposing unanimity requirements on mitigating circumstances at issue in the punishment phase of a bifurcated death penalty trial. Banks had been sentenced using such a unanimity requirement. The federal district court denied relief under § 2254(d)(1), but the court of appeals reversed, granting Banks relief. The Third Circuit did not conduct a _Teague_ inquiry because it reasoned that § 2254(d)(1) replaced _Teague_ with the rule that an inmate may invoke only law that was clearly established at the time the state court adjudicated the claim. The Supreme Court reversed. It held that "none of our post-AEDPA cases have suggested that a writ of habeas corpus should automatically issue if a prisoner satisfies the AEDPA standard, or that AEDPA relieves courts from the responsibility of addressing properly raised _Teague_ arguments."

Having established that AEDPA does not formally displace _Teague_, however, students should understand that, in the vast majority of state prisoner cases, any decision that can satisfy § 2254(d)(1) will also clear the _Teague_ bar. Section 2254(d)(1) and _Teague_ overlap in many respects—and perhaps for that reason, post-AEDPA dismissals of habeas petitions on _Teague_ grounds have become fairly uncommon. But one should apply both _Teague_ and § 2254(d)(1), in case the state decision is part of the small group that _Teague_ would disqualify but that § 2254(d) would not. For example, only _Teague_ applies when a federal claim was not adjudicated "on the merits" by a state court.

Section 2254(d)(1) differs from _Teague_ in several other respects. First, _Teague_ has narrower coverage; it addresses only the pure legal question of whether a rule can support a claim at all. Section 2254(d)(1) has the "contrary to" clause, which relates to such pure legal questions, but it also has real bite in the "mixed-question" situation dealing with application of law to facts. Second, even as to pure legal questions, the timing of the restrictions is different. Section 2254(d)(1) focuses on "the time the state court renders its decision." Lockyer v. Andrade, 538 U.S. 63, 71–72 (2003). The question is whether the ruling by the state court was "contrary to" or an "unreasonable application of" Supreme Court precedent _at the time that the claim was adjudicated by the state court._ Under _Teague_, by contrast, an inmate may get the benefit of a new rule if it is announced while the prisoner's case is at any phase of direct review. Finally, _Teague_ and § 2254(d)(1) refer to different bodies of precedent. For _Teague_, the new rule could have been announced by a Court of Appeals. For § 2254(d)(1), it must consist of U.S. Supreme Court decisions.

8)   Stacking Different Reasonableness Inquiries. Note that, when adjudicating an IAC claim, a state post-conviction court must determine whether trial counsel was reasonably effective. A federal court reviewing the state judge's ruling must then ask whether the state judge reasonably concluded that counsel was reasonably effective. The word "reasonable" means different things in each context, of course. For the underlying IAC analysis, the question is what an objectively competent attorney would do in the circumstances, based on standards of trial representation and the types of tactical decisions appropriate to the case. For the AEDPA analysis, the question is directed to state judges, not trial lawyers, and identifies reasonable judicial interpretations of the governing precedent at the time a collaterally-attacked judgment issued. Thus, § 2254(d)(1) focuses on the reasonableness of the state judges' decision, which is not always explicit from the face of the opinion.

9)   Is Section 2254 Constitutional? There are objections to the constitutionality of § 2254(d)(1), and they come in different forms. See, e.g., James S. Liebman & William F. Ryan, *"Some Effectual Power": The Quantity and Quality of Decisionmaking Required of Article III Courts*, 98 Colum. L. Rev. 696 (1998) (contending that the most restrictive readings of § 2254(d)(1) violate the Supremacy Clause). The most common objection is that the provision violates the Suspension Clause by imposing an impermissibly severe burden on state prisoners. See, e.g., Eric Freedman, *Just Because John Marshall Said It, Doesn't Make It So:* Ex parte Bollman *and the Illusory Prohibition on the Federal Writ of Habeas Corpus for State Prisoners in the Judiciary Act of 1789*, 51 Ala. L. Rev. 531 (2000) (arguing that the prevailing assumption that the Suspension Clause protected only federal prisoners is a mistake). How would you evaluate this argument, in light of the fact that federal habeas relief was not generally available to state prisoners until 1867—and, even then, only by statute?

Consider a slightly different argument, raised by Judge John T. Noonan in a Ninth Circuit case, *Irons v. Carey*, 505 F.3d 846 (9th Cir. 2007):

Proper resolution of this case . . . involves the clash of two constitutional principles of importance to every inhabitant of our country:

Congress has the power to determine the jurisdiction of all federal courts.

Congress does not have the power to determine how a federal court shall decide a case.

An easy solution of the clash is to say that the greater power includes the lesser. [Judge Noonan calls this Euclidean logic.] If Congress can determine jurisdiction and so take away any judicial supervision of the subject, a fortiori Congress can specify what materials the courts may use in deciding the case. . .

This line of argument [is] . . . mistaken. Euclidean logic does not dominate a judge's careful consideration of all the aspects of matters that are far from linear. A simple example: The power to kill is greater than the power to torture. The state may kill individuals. It may not torture them. . .

The great writ exists, by negative implication, in Article I . . . It was initially understood to extend only to prisoners in the custody of the United States. It was extended by statute in 1867 to embrace prisoners of a state in custody in violation of the Constitution of the United States. . . It is not, however, necessary to maintain that habeas corpus today is a requirement of due process. What is most relevant is that if Congress does provide for habeas in the federal courts, Congress cannot then instruct the federal courts, whether acting in a federal or in a state case, how to think, how to ascertain the law, how to judge.

Fundamentally, the Euclidean line of argumentation advanced above is based on a profound misunderstanding of the judicial power and the role that judges, uncontrolled in their reasoning by the legislature, perform to make it work. Legislatures exist to make laws. Courts exist to decide cases. The separation of these functions is part of our democratic system of government. To allow the legislature to decide a case is to deny the separation. To allow the legislature to tell a court how a case should be decided is worse. It allows the legislature to mask itself under judicial robes. It puts forward as the judgment of a court what in actuality is the judgment of the legislature. . .

Do you think the separation between "making law" and "deciding cases" is artificial, or is it a meaningful way of conceptualizing the responsibilities of judicial and legislative institutions that share power in a national government? In accusing AEDPA of usurping the role of judges, Judge Noonan compared § 2254(d)(1) to rules as to the form and manner of judicial proceedings:

It may be said that Congress has the power to approve or disapprove the Federal Rules of Procedure, and these rules play a part in the decision of a case. It may be further argued that Congress can determine the number of judges, where they shall sit, how many assistants they may have, and what appeals may be taken, and that all these determinations have an impact on how a particular case will be decided.

. . . The number, venue, and assistance given the judges point to no particular outcome in the decision of a case, nor does the path provided for appeal. The Federal Rules, formulated by judges, operate impartially in all cases. They preordain a decision in none. Even more importantly, they do not determine the law the judges must apply.

In what ways does § 2254(d)(1) differ from the form-and-manner rules described by Judge Noonan? Judge Noonan then took square aim at the role of "dicta" and § 2254(d)(1):

AEDPA specifies that an application for a writ of habeas corpus "shall not be granted with respect to any claim that was adjudicated on the merits in State court proceedings unless the adjudication of the claim (1) resulted in a decision that was contrary to, or involved an unreasonable application of, clearly established Federal law, as determined by the Supreme Court of the United States . . ." 28 U.S.C. § 2254(d).

Concurring in [Terry] *Williams v. Taylor*, Justice O'Connor glossed "clearly established" to mean a holding by the Supreme Court, not a dictum. Justice O'Connor's concurrence was adopted by a majority of the Court. Her gloss on "clearly established" was itself dictum because it was not necessary to the decision of the case. It is a dictum that has banished dicta from the grounds for granting habeas corpus. It is a dictum necessarily narrowing the normal way in which decisions of the highest court are read and applied.

AEDPA does operate over the whole class of cases of habeas corpus. It does not require a result in any particular case. What it does do is to strike at the center of the judge's process of reasoning. It shuts the judge off from the judge's normal sources of law and curbs that use of analogy which is the way the mind of a judge works. In our system of law where precedent prevails and is developed, AEDPA denies the judge the use of circuit precedent, denies development of Supreme Court and circuit precedent, denies the deference due the penumbra and emanations of precedent, and even denies the courts the power to follow the law as now determined by the Supreme Court—the precedent to be applied must have been in existence at the earlier moment when a state decision occurred. A more blinkered concept of law cannot be imagined—law, particularly constitutional law—is treated as what once was the law. The development of doctrine is despised. That despisal is a direct legislative interference in the independence of the judiciary.

It could be said that the ban on using Supreme Court decisions issued later than the relevant state court determination is a ban on the retroactivity of such decisions; and the Supreme Court has more than once announced constitutional decisions that are good for the future but cannot be read back into the past. True as that is, for the Supreme Court to choose not to make its decisions retroactive is not the same as Congress choosing to do it. The latter action is an interference with a prerogative that goes with wise judging. Whether to judge only for the future is for the judge to decide.

It might equally be asserted that the exclusion of a circuit court's precedents from consideration by the circuit is simply a limitation on the jurisdiction of circuit courts. So it might be said, but far from accurately. AEDPA does not address jurisdiction: it addresses the materials for judging. It deprives a whole class of cases of their normal value as governing authority for the circuit which has decided them.

Does § 2254(d)(1) arrest the process of judging as severely as Judge Noonan describes? Are there other ways that precedent might develop in the federal courts? Of course, Judge Noonan has a point—Congress cannot use its authority over jurisdiction to tell courts how to decide cases. Why can it do the same thing by circumscribing the authority from which a federal court extracts a rule? Do you agree that such a restriction is less troublesome if the Supreme Court imposes it in the form of a retroactivity rule than if Congress imposes it as a substantive limit on relief? Would the Congressionally-imposed rule be on stronger ground if it were conceptualized as a restriction on the right or on the remedy?

10) More Legislative History. One reason why the Justices did not dwell on the legislative history of § 2254(d) in *Terry Williams* may be that it is fairly impenetrable. Two lead sponsors and drafters of Bill were Orrin Hatch and Arlen Specter. Senator Hatch said of § 2254(d): "[T]his standard essentially gives the Federal court the authority to review, de novo, whether the State court decided the claim in contravention of Federal law." This observation suggests that federal courts are to conduct independent de novo review, a task very different from what the Supreme Court identified in *Terry Williams*. In the same statement, Senator Hatch interpreted his own remarks:

What does this mean? It means that if the State court reasonably applied Federal law, its decision must be upheld. Why is this a problematic standard? After all, Federal habeas review exists to correct fundamental defects in the law. After the State court has reasonably applied Federal law it is hard to say that a fundamental defect exists.[v]

Senator Specter was no more instructive, noting that "there still is latitude for the Federal judge to disagree with the determination made by the State court judge." He added, "It is my sense, having litigated these cases . . . that where there is a miscarriage of justice, the Federal court can come to a different decision than was made in the State court proceedings."[w] Finally, recall that when signing the legislation, President Clinton noted, "I have signed this bill because I am confident that the federal courts will interpret these provisions to preserve independent review of federal legal claims." Was this confidence misplaced, or did *Terry Williams* preserve independent review? Does this legislative history support the view that the statute preserves a deferential "mood" but not a precise set of marching orders? Or does it suggest that federal courts will play an important role in interpreting the language?

11) Bibliography. There has been substantial academic criticism of the approach the Court has taken when interpreting § 2254(d). For examples, see Lee Kovarsky, *AEDPA's Wrecks: Comity, Finality, and Federalism*, 82 Tul. L. Rev. 443, 470 (2007) (observing that AEDPA is the hurried product of a transitory political coalition that combined sometimes-inconsistent habeas proposals that had been languishing in Congressional committees for decades); Stephen I. Vladeck, *AEDPA, Saucier, and the Stronger Case for Rights-First Constitutional Adjudication*, 32 Seattle U. L. Rev. 595 (2009) (arguing that AEDPA should be applied by first determining whether a constitutional violation occurred, then by determining whether it was an unreasonable application of clearly established federal law); Larry W. Yackle, *State Convicts and Federal Courts: Reopening the Habeas Corpus Debate*, 91 Cornell L. Rev. 541, 542, 553 (2006) (arguing, on the basis that "[t]he circumstances in which [AEDPA] was adopted defy any serious expectation that it may yet work if given the chance[,]"the habeas statute conform to a "hybrid model" that increases access to deferential habeas review in federal courts). For the view that the "bite" of the AEDPA has not been as large as commonly supposed, see John H. Blume, *AEDPA: The "Hype" and the "Bite,"* 91 Cornell L. Rev. 259 (2006).

12) Terry Williams. Following the Supreme Court's ruling, Terry Williams accepted an offer of a life sentence without the possibility of parole.[x]

NOTES ON "CONTRARY TO"

1) When is a State Decision Contrary to Clearly Established Federal Law? 28 U.S.C. § 2254(d)(1) permits a prisoner to obtain federal merits relief if the state decision "resulted in a decision that was *contrary to* . . . clearly established Federal law, as determined by the Supreme Court of the United States[.]" (Emphasis added.) Of all of the definitions offered in *Terry Williams*

---

[v] 142 Cong. Rec. S3446–02 (daily ed. Apr. 17, 1996) (statement by Sen. Hatch).

[w] 141 Cong. Rec. S7803–01 (daily ed. June 7, 1995) (statement by Sen. Specter).

[x] See Brooke A. Master, *Deal Gets Inmate Off Death Row*, Wash. Post, Nov. 15, 2000, at B1.

concerning the language in § 2254(d)(1), the definition of "contrary to" appears the most straightforward and limited. The Court held that a state decision is "contrary to . . . clearly established federal law" when "a state court arrives at a conclusion opposite to that reached by this Court on a question of law or if the state court decides a case differently than this Court has on a set of materially indistinguishable facts." The second scenario—deciding a case on a "materially" indistinguishable" set of facts—is more common than the first. Interpreting the "contrary to" clause as it applies to the second scenario comes very close to the operation of the "unreasonable application" clause. Can you see why?

2) Is a State Decision "Contrary to" Clearly Established Federal Law if it does not Cite Supreme Court Law? Is a state decision contrary to federal law if it does not expressly apply federal precedent to resolve a case? In *Early v. Packer*, 537 U.S. 3 (2002), the Supreme Court held that a state decision is not "contrary to" clearly established federal law even if it does not cite to the applicable Supreme Court decisions. The Court explained: "Avoiding these pitfalls does not require citation of our cases-indeed, it does not even require *awareness* of our cases, so long as neither the reasoning nor the result of the state-court decision contradicts them."

3) A Plea Bargaining Example. In *Lafler v. Cooper*, 132 S.Ct. 362 (2012), and *Missouri v. Frye*, 132 S.Ct. 1399 (2012), the Supreme Court considered IAC claims pertaining to the plea bargaining phase of a criminal proceeding. In *Hill v. Lockhart*, 474 U.S. 52 (1985), the Supreme Court held that a prisoner could state a Sixth Amendment IAC claim based on an inadequately-counseled guilty plea. In *Lafler* and *Frye*, the Court considered an IAC claim based on a decision *not* to accept a plea offer. *Lafler* was a federal habeas case, and *Frye* was on certiorari review of the state post-conviction disposition. Both cases also involved a question about what the proper scope of the remedy for plea-phase IAC should be.

In *Lafler*, the prisoner's lawyer was ineffective for advising him not to accept a favorable plea deal yielding a term of incarceration that was far below the mandatory minimum sentence he subsequently received at trial. (In *Frye*, the prisoner later accepted plea bargain inferior to the one ineffective assistance caused him to reject.) One of the questions the *Lafler* Court had to resolve was whether the Michigan decision was contrary to clearly established Supreme Court law. Justice Kennedy, writing for the Court, emphasized that "the Michigan Court of Appeals identified respondent's ineffective-assistance-of-counsel claim but failed to apply *Strickland* to assess it. Rather than applying *Strickland*, the state court simply found that respondent's rejection of the plea was knowing and voluntary." The Court added:

> After stating the incorrect standard, moreover, the state court then made an irrelevant observation about counsel's performance at trial and mischaracterized respondent's claim as a complaint that his attorney did not obtain a more favorable plea bargain. By failing to apply Strickland to assess the ineffective-assistance-of-counsel claim respondent raised, the state court's adjudication was contrary to clearly established federal law. And in that circumstance the federal courts in this habeas action can determine the principles necessary to grant relief.

The Supreme Court also assumed that this view of *Strickland v. Washington* was "clearly established" in 2005, when the state court had ruled. The Michigan Court of Appeals decision in question read as follows:

To establish ineffective assistance, the defendant must demonstrate that his counsel's performance fell below an objective standard of reasonableness and that counsel's representation so prejudiced the defendant that he was deprived of a fair trial. With respect to the prejudice aspect of the test, the defendant must demonstrate a reasonable probability that, but for counsel's errors, the result of the proceedings would have been different, and that the attendant proceedings were fundamentally unfair and unreliable.

Defendant challenges the trial court's finding after a [] hearing that defense counsel provided effective assistance to defendant during the plea bargaining process. He contends that defense counsel failed to convey the benefits of the plea offer to him and ignored his desire to plead guilty, and that these failures led him to reject a plea offer that he now wishes to accept. However, the record shows that defendant knowingly and intelligently rejected two plea offers and chose to go to trial. The record fails to support defendant's contentions that defense counsel's representation was ineffective because he rejected a defense based on [a] claim of self-defense and because he did not obtain a more favorable plea bargain for defendant.

Justice Scalia, joined by Chief Justice Roberts and Justice Thomas, dissented, arguing that, in *Lafler* and *Frye,* "the Court . . . opens a whole new field of constitutionalized criminal procedure: plea-bargaining law." They argued that these decisions departed substantially from *Strickland*, which had focused on the underlying right to a fair trial: "It is also apparent from *Strickland* that bad plea bargaining has nothing to do with ineffective assistance of counsel in the constitutional sense." The dissenters argued that the state court did in fact apply *Strickland* analysis and denied relief, and that the state court had ruled that there was not "anything 'fundamentally unfair' about Cooper's conviction and sentence, so that no *Strickland* prejudice had been shown." Justice Scalia added that "The state court's analysis was admittedly not a model of clarity, but federal habeas corpus is a guard against extreme malfunctions in the state criminal justice systems, not a license to penalize a state court for its opinion-writing technique." Which side do you think has the better interpretation of the state court opinion and whether it was "contrary to" Supreme Court law?

4)   Indistinguishable Facts. Regarding the second way in which a state decision may be "contrary to" clearly established federal law—where the state court confronts "materially indistinguishable" facts—the Court has explained that a prisoner satisfies § 2254(d)(1) if the state court "reaches a different result from one of our cases despite confronting indistinguishable facts." Ramdass v. Angelone, 530 U.S. 156, 165–66 (2000). In *Ramdass*, the Court found the factual circumstances to be sufficiently distinguishable from the prior ruling that the state decision was not contrary to clearly established federal law. Justice O'Connor concurred, and noted that, even if the facts are somewhat different, as long as the relevant "circumstances" make the particular legal result "foreordained," then the decision would have been "contrary to" Supreme Court law. Even with that additional gloss, is the "indistinguishable facts" category of "contrary to" cases still miniscule?

———————

NOTES ON "UNREASONABLE APPLICATION"

1)   What is Unreasonable? 28 U.S.C. § 2254(d)(1) also permits a prisoner to obtain federal merits relief if the state process "resulted in a decision that . . . involved an *unreasonable application* [of] clearly established Federal law, as determined by the Supreme Court of the United States[.]" (Emphasis added.) To repeat a question that we have raised before: to what degree must a state decision deviate from the way a federal court would resolve an issue before the state decision becomes legally "unreasonable" under 28 U.S.C. § 2254(d)(1). Since deciding *Terry Williams,* courts have struggled with this question. Whether a state involves an unreasonable application of federal law may depend not only on how one defines "unreasonable," but also on, among other things: (1) is the clarity of the underlying law, (2) the precision (granularity) of that law, (3) the difficulty of applying the underlying law to the facts, and (4) the actual reasoning of the state court, if that reasoning is apparent from the decision. Some discussions of the unreasonable application clause frame the provision as though erroneous decisions may not trigger federal habeas relief. Is there a more benign way of framing the question—maybe in terms of the deviation between the state decision and the way the federal court would have resolved the issue had the federal court confronted it first? Does the "unreasonable application" clause really bar relief for certain erroneous state decisions, or does it bar relief in situations where there is reasonable disagreement over whether error exists?

2)   Unreasonability and the Generality of the Law. The Court has noted, "The more general the rule, the more leeway courts have in reaching outcomes in case-by-case determinations." Yarborough v. Alvarado, 541 U.S. 652, 654 (2004). In *Panetti v. Quarterman,* the Court again underscored that general rules can still applied unreasonably: "That the standard is stated in general terms does not mean the application was reasonable." 551 U.S. 930 (2007). Can you anticipate problems when the Supreme Court announces a rule at an extremely high degree of generality? Consider *Atkins v. Virginia,* 536 U.S. 304 (2002). The Supreme Court offenders with mental retardation (MR) were ineligible for the death penalty, but left the enforcement specifics to the state. Could this delegation be so broad as to include the power to define MR itself? How far outside consensus definitions of MR can states go without running afoul of the "unreasonable application" clause? Does the fact that the Supreme Court actually relied on certain definitions—without requiring that states follow them—change your assessment of what applications are reasonable?

3)   What Increment of Incorrectness is Unreasonable? The lower courts have struggled with the how-much-error-is-unreasonable question. (Or, in the alternative phrasing of the question, how much deviation from the district court's preferred result is "unreasonable.") For example, the Second Circuit has held that that "some increment of incorrectness beyond error is required. We caution, however that the increment need not be great; otherwise, habeas relief would be limited to state court decisions so far off the mark as to suggest judicial incompetence." Francis S. v. Stone, 221 F.3d 100, 111 (2nd Cir. 2000) (internal quotation marks omitted). Contrast the holding in *Francis* with this statement from the Seventh Circuit: "habeas relief should not be granted if the state court decision can be said to be one of several equally-plausible outcomes." Jackson v. Frank, 348 F.3d 658, 662 (7th Cir.2003) (internal citation omitted). Or with another statement from the Seventh Circuit—that an "unreasonable application" is "something like lying well outside the boundaries of permissible differences of opinion." Bartlett v. Battaglia, 453 F.3d 796, 800 (7th Cir. 2006) (internal citations omitted). The upshot is that there exists very little consensus about what constitutes an unreasonable application of law.

4) The State Court's Actual Reasons. The Supreme Court has also indicated that a federal court must also attend to the actual reasons given by the state court. For example, in *Panetti*, the Court observed that part of the inquiry involves whether the reasoning of the state-court decision contradicts prior Supreme Court rulings. In contrast, in *Bell v. Cone*, 542 U.S. 447 (2004) (per curiam) the Court noted that the failure of the state court to cite its earlier decisions did not deserve reversal "on the basis of nothing more than a lack of citation," where the state court had applied the proper "construction in respondent's case."

Exploring this proposition in greater detail, the Ninth Circuit has explained that "if we were to defer to some *hypothetical* alternative rationale when the state court's *actual* reasoning evidences a 2254(d)(1) error, we would distort the purpose of AEDPA." Frantz v. Hazey, 513 F.3d 1002, 1011–1012 (9th Cir. 2008) (en banc). The Fifth Circuit, however, seems to observe a contrary rule: "it is not immediately clear to us whether a federal habeas court looks exclusively to the objective reasonableness of the state court's ultimate conclusion or must also consider the method by which the state court arrives at its conclusions." Neal v. Puckett, 286 F.3d 230, 244 (5th Cir. 2002) (en banc). The Fifth Circuit more recently clarified that, although it will ask whether a state court could have reasonably applied the correct rules, a judge may not "assume a state court applied legal rules it did not, and then ask whether such rules could still reasonably support the result." Salts v. Epps, 676 F.3d 468, 480 (5th Cir. 2012). Of course, the state court may have issued a summary order without providing any reasoning—but if the state decision is memorialized in a reasoned opinion, then habeas review must scrutinize the reasons that the state court actually used.

5) Antecedent Due Process Violations. What happens when a state decision is the result of defective process? What happens under the "unreasonable application" clause of § 2254(d)(1), and how does that affect the rest of the federal inquiry? To put the question in concrete terms, consider the situation in which a state proceeding fails to provide a constitutionally sufficient forum for a prisoner to be heard on an *Atkins* (mental retardation) or *Ford* (incompetence) claim. Does the "antecedent" deprivation of due process mean that the prisoner satisfies § 2254(d)(1) and that a federal court may decide the claim on the merits? *Panetti* strongly suggests that a due process violation eliminates the restrictions on relief in § 2254(d):

> When a state court's adjudication of a claim is dependent on an antecedent unreasonable application of federal law, the requirement set forth in § 2254(d)(1) is satisfied. A federal court must then resolve the claim without the deference AEDPA otherwise requires. Here, due to the state court's unreasonable application of *Ford*, the factfinding procedures upon which the court relied were "not adequate for reaching reasonably correct results" or, at a minimum, resulted in a process that appeared to be "seriously inadequate for the ascertainment of the truth." We therefore consider petitioner's claim on the merits and without deferring to the state court's finding of competency.

How does this passage in *Panetti* bear on the issue of whether a federal court is to scrutinize the reasonableness of a state outcome versus a state court's reasoning?

6)   Partial Analysis. What if the state court analyzes one portion or prong of the federal claim, but not the other portions of the required analysis? This partial analysis often occurs with respect to IAC claims in which the state court either addresses whether counsel was effective, or whether there was prejudice, but not both. The Supreme Court has stated that a federal court should review *de novo* the portion of the IAC analysis that the state decision did not address. See Porter v. McCollum, 130 S.Ct. 447, 452 (2009) (per curiam) ("Because the state court did not decide whether [petitioner's] counsel was deficient, we review this element of [petitioner's] *Strickland* claim *de novo.*"); Rompilla v. Beard, 545 U.S. 374, 390 (2005) (holding that, because the state court did not address prejudice prong, it should be reviewed *de novo*); Wiggins v. Smith, 539 U.S. 510, 534 (2003) (conducting *de novo* review of prejudice, where state court analyzed only inadequate performance); see also Hertz & Liebman, *FHCPP*, at § 32.2 n.7 (collecting cases on this issue).

———

NOTES ON "CLEARY ESTABLISHED FEDERAL LAW"

1)   What is "Clearly Established" Supreme Court law? 28 U.S.C. § 2254(d)(1) permits a prisoner to obtain federal merits relief if the state decision "resulted in a decision that was contrary to, or involved an unreasonable application of, *clearly established Federal law, as determined by the Supreme Court of the United States*[.]" (Emphasis added.) *Terry Williams* did not carefully define what constitutes "clearly established" Federal law, as determined by the Supreme Court. As discussed earlier, however, the Court did say that only the Court's holdings, and not its dicta, would count as "clearly established" law. What are the virtues and vices of such a rule?

2)   The Dicta Question in Action: *Carey v. Musladin.* In *Carey v. Musladin*, 549 U.S. 70 (2006), the Supreme Court further addressed the "clearly established law" requirement. The case involved the allegedly-prejudicial conduct of courtroom spectators, relatives of the victim who wore buttons bearing the victim's image. The Court stated that "the effect on a defendant's fair-trial rights of the spectator conduct to which Musladin objects is an open question in our jurisprudence." The Court believed that, although there was clearly established law as to prejudicial *state* conduct, there was not clearly established law as to prejudicial *spectator* conduct: "[r]eflecting the lack of guidance from this Court, lower courts have diverged widely in their treatment of defendants' spectator-conduct claims." In a concurring opinion, Justice Stevens made the following observation:

> [Justice O'Connor's *Terry Williams* dictum about the inapplicability of dicta in § 2254(d)(1) determinations of what constitutes "clearly established law"] represents an incorrect interpretation of the statute's text, and . . . its repetition today is wholly unnecessary . . . Virtually every one of the Court's opinions announcing a new application of a constitutional principle contains some explanatory language that is intended to provide guidance to lawyers and judges in future cases. . . The text of AEDPA itself provides

sufficient obstacles to obtaining habeas relief without placing a judicial thumb on the warden's side of the scales.

Do you think the reference to "clearly established law" should include dicta? How should the law accommodate frequent disagreement over what parts of opinions are "holdings" and what parts are "dicta?"

3)   Clearly Established Capital Sentencing Law: The *Penry* Cases. Consider an additional example from the capital sentencing context. In *Brewer v. Quarterman*, 550 U.S. 286 (2007), the Supreme Court held that the Texas capital sentencing rules did not adequately permit consideration of mitigating evidence during the punishment phase of a capital case. At the punishment phase of the capital trial, the state court had excluded evidence of the prisoner's mental illness and substance abuse. The Supreme Court held that doing so contravened the Court's earlier decision in *Penry v. Johnson*, 532 U.S. 782 (2001), which held that the sentencing instructions violated the Eighth and Fourteenth Amendments because the instructions did not allow the jury to consider giving "full effect" to such mitigation evidence. Thus, the court held that "the Texas state court's decision to deny relief to Brewer under [*Penry*] was both contrary to and involved an unreasonable application of, clearly established Federal law, as determined by the Supreme Court of the United States." (Internal quotation marks omitted.) The prior precedent regarding the effect that a jury had to give mitigating evidence, however, was set forth in a combination of cases decided on direct and collateral review. Chief Justice Roberts, dissenting along with three Associate Justices, countered:

> When this Court considers similar challenges to the same jury instructions five separate times, it usually is not because the applicable legal rules are "clearly established." The Court today nonetheless picks from the five precedents the one that ruled in favor of the defendant ... and anoints that case as the one embodying "clearly established Federal law." In doing so the Court fails to give any meaningful weight to the two pertinent precedents subsequent to [that case,] even though those [subsequent] cases adopted a more "limited view" of [the original rule] than the Court embraces today. . .
>
> When the state courts considered these cases, our precedents did not provide them with "clearly established" law, but instead a dog's breakfast of divided, conflicting, and ever-changing analyses. That is how the Justices on this Court viewed the matter, as they shifted from being in the majority, plurality, concurrence, or dissent from case to case, repeatedly lamenting the failure of their colleagues to follow a consistent path. Whatever the law may be today, the Court's ruling that 'twas always so—and that state courts were "objectively unreasonable" not to know it—is utterly revisionist.

In areas particularly regulated by complex decisional law—where the law might be a "dog's breakfast" of prior decisions, in Chief Justice Roberts' colorful terminology—can you ever have "clearly established" precedent? When can a line of cases clearly establish a rule?

4)   Lower Courts. As with the other AEDPA requirements, uncertainty about the appropriate interpretation of "clearly established Federal law" has divided lower federal courts. They have disagreed about the extent to which the general principle of Supreme Court law must have been clearly established, or whether that rule must also have been extended to the factual scenario in a given case. Even though AEDPA limits "clearly established Federal law" to Supreme Court decisions, lower federal courts may have to look at Court of Appeals precedent to determine whether a given jurisdiction treats a Supreme Court ruling as clearly established.[y] There are additional complications. Lower courts are divided over whether, in situations in which an IAC claim involves a failure to lodge a constitutional objection at trial, the underlying violation must be "clearly established."[z] Are these issues unavoidable any time a legislature cabins the set of precedent from which a court may draw in making decisions?

NOTES ON ORDER OF OPERATIONS AND BURDEN OF PROOF

1) The Petitioner's Burden of Proof. Because 28 U.S.C. § 2254(d) is a substantive limit on relief, and not a defense, prisoners must prove that they satisfy the limit to prevail in the district court. Thus, the Supreme Court has since explained that not only does § 2254(d)(1) provide for a "highly deferential standard for evaluating state-court rulings," but that the petitioner carries the burden of proof that the one of the Subsections of 2254(d) are satisfied. Woodford v. Visciotti, 537 U. S. 19, 24–25 (2002) (per curiam).

2) Separating § 2254(d) and "The Merits" Inquiry. Remember that a federal court will usually rule on procedural defenses before reaching the merits—at least for colorable claims. Ordinarily, a federal court is supposed to decide whether the limit on relief in § 2254(d) applies and, if not, only then does it decide the merits of the claim itself. Does a federal court always have to apply § 2254(d) before it considers the merits? In a recent case, *Berghuis v. Thompkins*, 130 S.Ct. 2250 (2010), the Court considered that question in the context of an IAC claim:

> It is unclear what prejudice standard the state court applied. The Court of Appeals ruled that the state court used the incorrect standard for assessing prejudice under *Strickland*. Even if the state court used an incorrect legal standard, we need not determine whether AEDPA's deferential standard of review, 28 U.S.C. § 2254(d), applies in this situation. That is because, even if AEDPA deference does not apply, Thompkins cannot show prejudice under de novo review, the more favorable standard of review for Thompkins. Courts cannot grant writs of habeas corpus under § 2254 by engaging only in de novo review when it is unclear whether AEDPA deference applies, § 2254(d). In those situations, courts must resolve whether AEDPA deference applies, because if it does, a habeas petitioner may not be entitled to a writ of habeas corpus under § 2254(d). Courts can, however, deny writs of habeas corpus under § 2254 by engaging in de novo review when it is unclear whether AEDPA deference applies, because a habeas petitioner will not be entitled to a writ of habeas corpus if his or her claim is rejected on de novo review, see § 2254(a).

---

[y] See, e.g., O'Laughlin v. O'Brien, 568 F.3d 287, 304–5 (1st Cir. 2009) ("we are not precluded from looking at other federal court decisions that may help guide us in applying [the constitutional standard]"); see also Hertz & Liebman, FHCPP, supra note c, at §32.3 n.9 (collecting cases).

[z] See Hertz & Liebman, FHCPP, supra note c, at § 32.3 n.7 (collecting cases).

Is there anything wrong with the idea that lower courts can rely on the easiest available vehicle for denying the claim? In such a situation, what happens when an appellate court reverses the district court and finds the claim meritorious? Cf. Stephen I. Vladeck, *AEDPA, Saucier, and the Stronger Case for Rights-First Constitutional Adjudication*, 32 Seattle U. L. Rev. 595 (2009) (arguing that federal courts should determine whether a constitutional violation occurred before applying § 2254(d)).

NOTE ON THE FACTUAL RECORD AND SECTION 2254(d)(1)

28 U.S.C. § 2254(d)(1) permits a state habeas petitioner to obtain relief if a state merits adjudication "resulted in a decision that was contrary to, or involved an unreasonable application of, clearly established Federal law, as determined by the Supreme Court of the United States[.]" Section 2254(d)(2) permits a state habeas petitioner to obtain relief if a state merits adjudication "resulted in a decision that was based on an unreasonable determination of the facts *in light of the evidence presented in the State court proceeding.*" (Emphasis added.) Subsection 2 requires an assessment of whether state factual determinations were unreasonable in light of the record, but Subsection 1 lacks analogous language—does § 2254(d)(1) nonetheless limit the inquiry to the evidence in the state record?

To answer that question, we need to look at the AEDPA standards for obtaining federal evidentiary hearings. 28 U.S.C. § 2254(e)(2) provides:

(2) If the applicant has failed to develop the factual basis of a claim in State court proceedings, the court shall not hold an evidentiary hearing on the claim unless the applicant shows that—

(A) the claim relies on—

(i) a new rule of constitutional law, made retroactive to cases on collateral review by the Supreme Court, that was previously unavailable; or

(ii) a factual predicate that could not have been previously discovered through the exercise of due diligence; and

(B) the facts underlying the claim would be sufficient to establish by clear and convincing evidence that but for constitutional error, no reasonable factfinder would have found the applicant guilty of the underlying offense.

In *Cullen v. Pinholster*, 131 S.Ct. 1388 (2011), excerpted below, the Supreme Court concluded that a federal court cannot answer § 2254(d)(1) by reference to anything other than the state record. As you read *Pinholster*, consider not only the technical strength of the argument, but also the role that federal evidentiary hearings now play in a set of laws in which § 2254(d) does not permit consideration of evidence outside of the state record. In other words, how does the Court's interpretation of § 2254(d)(1) affect the role of § 2254(e)?

Cullen v. Pinholster

United States Supreme Court
131 S.Ct. 1388 (2011)

■ JUSTICE THOMAS delivered the opinion of the Court [JUSTICES GINSBURG and KAGAN joined only Part II of the opinion].

* * * A jury convicted [Scott Lynn] Pinholster of first-degree murder, and he was sentenced to death.

After the California Supreme Court twice unanimously denied Pinholster habeas relief, a Federal District Court held an evidentiary hearing and granted Pinholster habeas relief under 28 U.S.C. § 2254. The District Court concluded that Pinholster's trial counsel had been constitutionally ineffective at the penalty phase of trial. Sitting en banc, the Court of Appeals for the Ninth Circuit affirmed. Considering the new evidence adduced in the District Court hearing, the Court of Appeals held that the California Supreme Court's decision "was contrary to, or involved an unreasonable application of, clearly established Federal law." § 2254(d)(1).

We granted certiorari and now reverse.

I

* * *

C

In August 1993, Pinholster filed his first state habeas petition. Represented by new counsel, Pinholster alleged, *inter alia,* ineffective assistance of counsel at the penalty phase of his trial. * * * The California Supreme Court unanimously and summarily denied Pinholster's penalty-phase ineffective-assistance claim "on the substantive ground that it is without merit."

Pinholster filed a federal habeas petition in April 1997. He reiterated his previous allegations about penalty-phase ineffective assistance and also added new allegations that his trial counsel had failed to furnish [the psychiatric expert] Dr. Stalberg with adequate background materials. In support of the new allegations, Dr. Stalberg provided a declaration stating that in 1984, Pinholster's trial counsel had provided Dr. Stalberg with only some police reports and a 1978 probation report. Dr. Stalberg explained that, had he known about the material that had since been gathered by Pinholster's habeas counsel, he would have conducted "further inquiry" before concluding that Pinholster suffered only from a personality disorder. He noted that Pinholster's school records showed evidence of "some degree of brain damage." Dr. Stalberg did not, however, retract his earlier diagnosis. * * * [T]he federal petition was held in abeyance to allow Pinholster to go back to state court.

In August 1997, Pinholster filed his second state habeas petition, this time including [the expert's] declaration and requesting judicial notice of the documents previously submitted in support of his first state habeas petition. His allegations of penalty-phase ineffective assistance of counsel mirrored those in his federal habeas petition. The California Supreme Court again unanimously and summarily denied the petition "on the substantive ground that it is without merit."

Having presented Dr. Stalberg's declaration to the state court, Pinholster returned to the District Court. In November 1997, he filed an amended petition for a writ of habeas corpus. His allegations of penalty-phase ineffective assistance of counsel were identical to those in his second state habeas petition. * * *

The District Court concluded that [AEDPA] did not apply and granted an evidentiary hearing. * * * [Pinholster] presented two new medical experts: Dr. Sophia Vinogradov, a psychiatrist who diagnosed Pinholster with organic personality syndrome and ruled out antisocial personality disorder, and Dr. Donald Olson, a pediatric neurologist who suggested that Pinholster suffers from partial epilepsy and brain injury. The State called Dr. F. David Rudnick, a psychiatrist who, like Dr. Stalberg, diagnosed Pinholster with antisocial personality disorder and rejected any diagnosis of bipolar disorder.

D

* * * On rehearing en banc, the Court of Appeals * * * determined that new evidence from the hearing could be considered in assessing whether the California Supreme Court's decision "was contrary to, or involved an unreasonable application of, clearly established Federal law" under § 2254(d)(1). Taking the District Court evidence into account, the en banc court determined that the California Supreme Court unreasonably applied *Strickland* * * * in denying Pinholster's claim of penalty-phase ineffective assistance of counsel. * * *

We granted certiorari to resolve two questions. First, whether review under § 2254(d)(1) permits consideration of evidence introduced in an evidentiary hearing before the federal habeas court. Second, whether the Court of Appeals properly granted Pinholster habeas relief on his claim of penalty-phase ineffective assistance of counsel.

II

We first consider the scope of the record for a § 2254(d)(1) inquiry. The State argues that review is limited to the record that was before the state court that adjudicated the claim on the merits. Pinholster contends that evidence presented to the federal habeas court may also be considered. We agree with the State.

A

* * * If an application includes a claim that has been "adjudicated on the merits in State court proceedings," § 2254(d), an additional restriction applies. Under § 2254(d), that application "shall not be granted with respect to [such a] claim . . . unless the adjudication of the claim":

> "(1) resulted in a decision that was contrary to, or involved an unreasonable application of, clearly established Federal law, as determined by the Supreme Court of the United States; or

> "(2) resulted in a decision that was based on an unreasonable determination of the facts in light of the evidence presented in the State court proceeding." * * *

* * * We now hold that review under § 2254(d)(1) is limited to the record that was before the state court that adjudicated the claim on the merits. Section 2254(d)(1) refers, in the past tense, to a state-court adjudication that "resulted in" a decision that was contrary to, or "involved" an unreasonable application of, established law. This backward-looking language requires an examination of the state-court decision at the time it was made. It follows that the record under review is limited to the * * * record before the state court.

This understanding of the text is compelled by "the broader context of the statute as a whole," which demonstrates Congress' intent to channel prisoners' claims first to the state courts. * * * Section 2254(b) requires that prisoners must ordinarily exhaust state remedies before filing for federal habeas relief. It would be contrary to that purpose to allow a petitioner to overcome an adverse state-court decision with new evidence introduced in a federal habeas court and reviewed by that court in the first instance effectively *de novo*.

Limiting § 2254(d)(1) review to the state-court record is consistent with our precedents interpreting that statutory provision. Our cases emphasize that review under § 2254(d)(1) focuses on what a state court knew and did. State-court decisions are measured against this Court's precedents as of "the time the state court renders its decision." To determine whether a particular decision is "contrary to" then-established law, a federal court must consider whether the decision "applies a rule that contradicts [such] law" and how the decision "confronts [the] set of facts" that were before the state court. If the state-court decision "identifies the correct governing legal principle" in existence at the time, a federal court must assess whether the decision "unreasonably applies that principle to the facts of the prisoner's case." It would be strange to ask federal courts to analyze whether a state court's adjudication resulted in a decision that unreasonably applied federal law to facts not before the state court.[3]

Our recent decision in *Schriro v. Landrigan*, 550 U.S. 465, 836 (2007), is consistent as well with our holding here. We explained that "[b]ecause the deferential standards prescribed by § 2254 control whether to grant habeas relief, a federal court must take into account those standards in deciding whether an evidentiary hearing is appropriate." In practical effect, we went on to note, this means that when the state-court record "precludes habeas relief" under the limitations of § 2254(d), a district court is "not required to hold an evidentiary hearing." * * *[5]

B

Pinholster's contention that our holding renders § 2254(e)(2) superfluous is incorrect. Section 2254(e)(2) imposes a limitation on the discretion of federal habeas courts to take new evidence in an evidentiary hearing. * * * Section 2254(e)(2) continues to have force where § 2254(d)(1) does not bar federal habeas relief. For example, not all federal habeas claims by state prisoners fall within the scope of § 2254(d), which applies only to claims "adjudicated on the merits in State court proceedings." * * *

---

[3] Justice SOTOMAYOR argues that there is nothing strange about allowing consideration of new evidence under § 2254(d)(1) because, in her view, it would not be "so different" from some other tasks that courts undertake. * * * What makes the consideration of new evidence strange is not how "different" the task would be, but rather the notion that a state court can be deemed to have unreasonably applied federal law to evidence it did not even know existed. We cannot comprehend how exactly a state court would have any control over its application of law to matters beyond its knowledge. Adopting Justice SOTOMAYOR's approach would not take seriously AEDPA's requirement that federal courts defer to state-court decisions and would effectively treat the statute as no more than a " 'mood' that the Federal Judiciary must respect," Terry Williams, 529 U.S., at 386 (opinion of Stevens, J.).

[5] Justice SOTOMAYOR's suggestion that Michael Williams "rejected" the conclusion here, see post, at 1420–1421, is thus quite puzzling. In the passage that she quotes, see ibid., the Court merely explains that § 2254(e)(2) should be interpreted in a way that does not preclude a state prisoner, who was diligent in state habeas court and who can satisfy § 2254(d), from receiving an evidentiary hearing.

Although state prisoners may sometimes submit new evidence in federal court, AEDPA's statutory scheme is designed to strongly discourage them from doing so. Provisions like §§ 2254(d)(1) and (e)(2) ensure that "[f]ederal courts sitting in habeas are not an alternative forum for trying facts and issues which a prisoner made insufficient effort to pursue in state proceedings." * * *

III

[The Court rejected the IAC claim on the basis of the record before the state court, finding that the state court was not unreasonable in finding that there was not deficient attorney performance and that there was not prejudice.] * * *

The judgment of the United States Court of Appeals for the Ninth Circuit is reversed.

It is so ordered.

[The Opinion of JUSTICE ALITO, concurring in part and concurring in the judgment, is omitted.]

■ JUSTICE BREYER, concurring in part and dissenting in part.

* * * Like the Court, I believe that its understanding of 28 U.S.C. § 2254(d)(1) does not leave AEDPA's hearing section, § 2254(e), without work to do. An offender who believes he is entitled to habeas relief must first present a claim (including his evidence) to the state courts. If the state courts reject the claim, then a federal habeas court may review that rejection on the basis of the materials considered by the state court. If the federal habeas court finds that the state-court decision fails (d)'s test (or if (d) does not apply), then an (e) hearing may be needed.

For example, if the state-court rejection assumed the habeas petitioner's facts (deciding that, *even if* those facts were true, federal law was not violated), then (after finding the state court wrong on a (d) ground) an (e) hearing might be needed to determine whether the facts alleged were indeed true. Or if the state-court rejection rested on a state ground, which a federal habeas court found inadequate, then an (e) hearing might be needed to consider the petitioner's (now unblocked) substantive federal claim. Or if the state-court rejection rested on only one of several related federal grounds (*e.g.,* that counsel's assistance was not "inadequate"), then, if the federal court found that the state court's decision in respect to the ground it decided violated (d), an (e) hearing might be needed to consider other related parts of the whole constitutional claim (*e.g.,* whether the counsel's "inadequate" assistance was also prejudicial). There may be other situations in which an (e) hearing is needed as well.

In this case, however, we cannot say whether an (e) hearing is needed until we know whether the state court, in rejecting Pinholster's claim on the basis presented to that state court, violated (d). * * *

■ JUSTICE SOTOMAYOR, with whom JUSTICE GINSBURG and JUSTICE KAGAN join as to Part II, dissenting.

Some habeas petitioners are unable to develop the factual basis of their claims in state court through no fault of their own. Congress recognized as much when it enacted [AEDPA], and permitted therein the introduction of new evidence in federal habeas proceedings in certain limited circumstances. Under the Court's novel interpretation of § 2254(d)(1), however, federal courts must turn a blind eye to new evidence in deciding whether a petitioner has satisfied § 2254(d)(1)'s threshold obstacle to federal habeas relief—even when it is clear that the petitioner would be entitled to relief in light of that evidence. * * *

I also disagree with the Court that, even if the § 2254(d)(1) analysis is limited to the state-court record, respondent Scott Pinholster failed to demonstrate that the California Supreme Court's decision denying his [IAC] claim was an unreasonable application of *Strickland* * * *.

I

The Court first holds that, in determining whether a state-court decision is an unreasonable application of Supreme Court precedent under § 2254(d)(1), "review . . . is limited to the record that was before the state court that adjudicated the claim on the merits." New evidence adduced at a federal evidentiary hearing is now irrelevant to determining whether a petitioner has satisfied § 2254(d)(1). This holding is unnecessary to promote AEDPA's purposes, and it is inconsistent with the provision's text, the structure of the statute, and our precedents.

A

* * * AEDPA's entire structure—which gives state courts the opportunity to decide factual and legal questions in the first instance—ensures that evidentiary hearings in federal habeas proceedings are very rare. Even absent the new restriction created by today's holding, AEDPA erects multiple hurdles to a state prisoner's ability to introduce new evidence in a federal habeas proceeding. * * *

To the limited extent that federal evidentiary hearings are available under AEDPA, they ensure that petitioners who diligently developed the factual basis of their claims in state court, discovered new evidence after the state-court proceeding, and cannot return to state court retain the ability to access the Great Writ. * * * Allowing a petitioner to introduce new evidence at a hearing in the limited circumstance permitted by § 2254(e)(2) does not upset the balance that Congress struck in AEDPA between the state and federal courts. By construing § 2254(d)(1) to do the work of other provisions in AEDPA, the majority has subverted Congress' careful balance of responsibilities. * * *

B

The majority's interpretation of § 2254(d)(1) finds no support in the provision's text or the statute's structure as a whole.

1

Section 2254(d)(1) requires district courts to ask whether a state-court adjudication on the merits "resulted in a decision that was contrary to, or involved an unreasonable application of, clearly established Federal law, as determined by the Supreme Court of the United States." Because this provision uses "backward-looking language"—*i.e.*, past-tense verbs—the majority believes that it limits review to the state-court record. But both §§ 2254(d)(1) and 2254(d)(2) use "backward-looking language," and § 2254(d)(2)—unlike § 2254(d)(1)—expressly directs district courts to base their review on "the evidence presented in the State court proceeding." If use of the past tense were sufficient to indicate Congress' intent to restrict analysis to the state-court record, the phrase "in light of the evidence presented in the State court proceeding" in § 2254(d)(2) would be superfluous. The majority's construction of § 2254(d)(1) fails to give meaning to Congress' decision to include language referring to the evidence presented to the state court in § 2254(d)(2).

Ignoring our usual "reluctan[ce] to treat statutory terms as surplusage in any setting," the majority characterizes the phrase appearing in § 2254(d)(2) as mere "clarifying language." * * * The argument that this phrase is merely "clarifying" might have more force, however, had Congress included this phrase in § 2254(d)(1) but not in § 2254(d)(2). As between the two provisions, § 2254(d)(2)—which requires review of the state court's "determination of the facts"—more logically depends on the facts presented to the state court. Because this provision needs less clarification on this point than § 2254(d)(1), it is all the more telling that Congress included this phrase in § 2254(d)(2) but elected to exclude it from § 2254(d)(1).

Unlike my colleagues in the majority, I refuse to assume that Congress simply engaged in sloppy drafting. * * *

2

[AEDPA's broader context] reinforces this conclusion. In particular, Congress' decision to include * * * § 2254(e)(2), [a provision] that permits federal evidentiary hearings in certain circumstances[,] provides further evidence that Congress did not intend to limit the § 2254(d)(1) inquiry to the state-court record in every case.

We have long recognized that some diligent habeas petitioners are unable to develop all of the facts supporting their claims in state court. As discussed above, in enacting AEDPA, Congress generally barred evidentiary hearings for petitioners who did not "exercise diligence in pursuing their claims" in state court. * * *

The majority charts a * * * novel course that, so far as I am aware, no court of appeals has adopted: § 2254(d)(1) continues to apply when a petitioner has additional evidence that he was unable to present to the state court, but the district court cannot consider that evidence in deciding whether the petitioner has satisfied § 2254(d)(1). The problem with this approach is its potential to bar federal habeas relief for diligent habeas petitioners who cannot present new evidence to a state court. * * *

The majority's interpretation of § 2254(d)(1) thus suggests the anomalous result that petitioners with new claims based on newly obtained evidence can obtain federal habeas relief if they can show cause and prejudice for their default but petitioners with newly obtained evidence supporting a claim adjudicated on the merits in state court cannot obtain federal habeas relief if they cannot first satisfy § 2254(d)(1) without the new evidence. * * *

The majority responds to this anomaly by suggesting that my hypothetical petitioner "may well [have] a new claim." This suggestion is puzzling. New evidence does not usually give rise to a new claim; it merely provides additional proof of a claim already adjudicated on the merits. The majority presumably means to suggest that the petitioner might be able to obtain federal-court review of his new evidence if he can show cause and prejudice for his failure to present the "new" claim to a state court. In that scenario, however, the federal court would review the purportedly "new" claim *de novo*. The majority's approach thus threatens to replace deferential review of new evidence under § 2254(d)(1) with *de novo* review of new evidence in the form of "new" claims. Because it is unlikely that Congress intended *de novo* review—the result suggested by the majority's opinion—it must have intended for district courts to consider newly discovered evidence in conducting the § 2254(d)(1) analysis.

* * * By reading § 2254(d)(1) to do the work of § 2254(e)(2), the majority gives § 2254(e)(2) an unnaturally cramped reading. As a result, the ma-

jority either has foreclosed habeas relief for diligent petitioners who, through no fault of their own, were unable to present exculpatory evidence to the state court that adjudicated their claims or has created a new set of procedural complexities for the lower courts to navigate to ensure the availability of the Great Writ for diligent petitioners. * * *

II

[JUSTICE SOTOMAYOR would have held that Pinholster satisfied § 2254(d)(1) on the basis of the state court record. JUSTICE GINSBURG and JUSTICE KAGAN joined only Part II.] * * *

NOTES AND QUESTIONS ON PINHOLSTER

1)   **Understanding the Holding.** Pinholster was advancing the same IAC claim on federal habeas review that he pressed on state post-conviction review. Why were the facts Pinholster sought to present on habeas review new? The federal district court had already held the case in abeyance for Pinholster to return to state court to present the affidavit of Dr. Stalberg. In other words, the Stalberg affidavit was not part of Pinholster's second habeas petition. Why did the Supreme Court hold that, under § 2254(d)(1), the district court could properly consider Dr. Stalberg's affidavit, but not the opinions of the two new medical experts, Dr. Vinogradov and Dr. Olson?

2)   **The Argument from Text.** Section 2254(d)(2) permits a state prisoner to obtain federal habeas relief if the state decision is based on an unreasonable factual determination "in light of the evidence presented in the State court proceeding." Section 2254(d)(1), by contrast, does not expressly limit evidence to what was presented to the state court. Only Justice Sotomayor, however, would have held that, by negative implication of the express reference to the state record in § 2254(d)(2), under § 2254(d)(1) a federal judge may consider new evidence adduced outside of the state record. What does Justice Sotomayor mean when she rejects the Supreme Court's treatment of that distinction as "sloppy drafting?" You have already encountered the view that AEDPA is not a model of legislative precision; does that justify the Court's decision not to treat the record limitation differently under the two § 2254(d) subsections?

   Justice Thomas, writing for the Court, reasoned that § 2254(d)(1) contains "backward looking language" and that the assessment of the state decision's legal reasonableness should therefore reflect only the evidence before the state court. To what "backwards looking language" does he refer? Section 2254(d)(1) requires that any rule upon which a state prisoner relies be "clearly established;" that a state merits adjudication must have "resulted in" a certain type of decision; and that the state decision might have "involved" an unreasonable application of federal law. Do these past-tense verbs require that the § 2254(d)(1) inquiry be limited to the state record?

3)   **The Argument from Purpose.** The Supreme Court held that allowing new evidence to satisfy § 2254(d)(1) would "allow a petitioner to overcome an adverse state-court decision with new evidence introduced in a federal habeas court and reviewed by that court in the first instance effectively *de novo*." Is Justice Thomas rightly concerned that, if the purpose of AEDPA was to give states the first crack at disposition of the legal and factual grounds for relief, then allowing new federal evidence to satisfy § 2254(d)(1) undermines that ob-

jective? On the other hand, AEDPA has provisions that express that purpose, but other provisions that limit it. For example, federal courts can consider claims *de novo* if the state made no merits decision. Or—more central to the argument in *Pinholster*—§ 2254(e)(2) provides a statutory mechanism for introducing new evidence in a federal evidentiary hearing. This issue obviously implicates a much bigger interpretive question. If one section of a statute embodies a purpose and another section of the statute embodies a limit on that purpose, how do you interpret ambiguous text—to be consistent with the purpose, or with the limit on it? Do you agree with the premise and the conclusion expressed by the Court, that § 2254(d)(1) "focuses on what the state court knew and did" and that no decision could be "contrary to" or "involve an unreasonable application of clearly established federal law" based on new evidence not presented to state courts?

4)   28 U.S.C. § 2254(e)(2). One of the objections that Justice Sotomayor lodged against the Supreme Court's interpretation of § 2254(d)(2) was that it mooted the restrictions on federal evidentiary hearings in § 2254(e)(2). Section 2254(e)(2) restricts the availability of evidentiary hearings to situations in which prisoners can make certain showings, including the presence of "a factual predicate that could not have been previously discovered through the exercise of due diligence[.]" For that reason, Justice Sotomayor accused the majority of "reading § 2254(d)(1) to do the work of § 2254(e)(2)," and of giving "§ 2254(e)(2) an unnaturally cramped reading." Does the presence of § 2254(e)(2) suggest that federal evidentiary hearings should be available in a broader category of cases than those amenable to such hearings after *Pinholster*?

Setting aside the merits of Justice Sotomayor's critique, what work is left for § 2254(e)(2)? We include Justice Breyer's concurrence to illustrate some of the situations in which § 2254(e)(2) remains salient. Justice Breyer's explanation provides insight not only into how to interpret § 2254(e)(2), but also into how to think about § 2254(d) in relation to the "merits" of the claim. If § 2254(e)(2) mediates the introduction of new evidence, and if a § 2254(d) inquiry can involve no new federal evidence, then—by definition—§ 2254(e)(2) can only apply in situations in which § 2254(d) does not limit relief. Section 2254(d) would not limit relief in at least two situations: (1) where, under the preambular language, the state decision is not "on the merits;" or (2) where a state prisoner satisfies one of the subsections and is therefore entitled to a straightforward merits determination. In what other situations might a federal evidentiary hearing be necessary? (Hint: think about factual issues that might be necessary to resolve procedural defenses.)

5)   Money for Investigation. How do you think *Pinholster* should affect the approval of attorneys' fees and investigative costs? Should a court approve the resources necessary for federal factfinding even if it thinks the new facts cannot be considered under § 2254(d)? What other purposes might newly-found facts serve under the statute, even if § 2254(d)(1) inquiry excludes them? Specifically, in order to obtain a certificate of appealability, a prisoner must make "a substantial showing of the denial of a constitutional right." In other words, the showing for a COA does not relate to the limit on relief in § 2254(d), but to the merits of the claim. See Eric M. Freedman, *The Revised ABA Guidelines and The Duties of Lawyers and Judges in Capital Post-conviction Proceedings*, 5 J. App. Prac. & Proc. 325, 341–43 (2003) (explaining that duties of federally-appointed counsel include overcoming defective state trial representation). If a court aggressively invokes *Pinholster* to foreclose money for investigating the claim itself (not just a hearing on it), does it unfairly prejudice the ability of a prisoner to appeal an adverse habeas disposition from the federal district court?

6)   The Current State of State Post-Conviction Review. State post-conviction proceedings rarely involve evidentiary hearings. How can diligent inmates avoid losing their chance to create a factual record? Presumably they must do it through paper submissions, if the court will not conduct a hearing. Similarly, inmates must try to uncover facts on their own if the state court will not grant discovery or an opportunity to question witnesses in court. In his concurrence, Justice Breyer noted that Pinholster "can always return to state court presenting new evidence not previously presented." How could Pinholster do that? On the "enormous premium" *Pinholster* places on state habeas fact development, see Samuel Wiseman, *Habeas After Pinholster,* 53 Boston College L. Rev. 953 (2012).[aa] Is Justice Breyer's scenario a tactical reality for prisoners that proceed *pro se*? Whether the hearing is live or on paper, indigent state prisoners proceeding without a lawyer will frequently have difficulty constructing a useful record and carefully observing the complex state post-conviction procedures necessary to preserve it for state review.

7)   A Renewed Emphasis on State-Post Conviction Review. *Pinholster* might be viewed as the flip side of cases like *Holland v. Florida,* 130 S.Ct. 2549 (2010) (recognizing equitable tolling for gross negligence of state post-conviction lawyer) and *Martinez v. Ryan,* 132 S.Ct. 1309 (2012) (recognizing an excuse for procedurally defaulted IAC claim where state post-conviction lawyer was ineffective). Although the Supreme Court has stopped short of creating rights to effective representation in state post-conviction proceedings, it has recognized the problems that poor state post-conviction representation has created for the preservation of viable federal claims. While *Pinholster* requires that state inmates litigate from the platform of a state post-conviction record, cases like *Holland* and *Martinez* provide some relief for situations in which that record is inadequate. Is the Supreme Court making state post-conviction review "the main event"—from two different angles? If so, do the incentives for adequate state post-conviction representation offset the penalty for failing to present evidence in support of a claim to the state court?

8)   The Diligent State Prisoner. Consider a hypothetical posed by Justice Sotomayor in an omitted portion of the dissent:

> A petitioner who diligently attempted in state court to develop the factual basis of a claim that prosecutors withheld exculpatory witness statements in violation of *Brady v. Maryland.* The state court denied relief on the ground that the withheld evidence then known did not rise to the level of materiality required under Brady. Before the time for filing a federal habeas petition has expired, however, a state court orders the State to disclose additional documents the petitioner had timely requested under the State's public records Act. The disclosed documents reveal that the State withheld other exculpatory witness statements, but state law would not permit the petitioner to present the new evidence in a successive petition.

[aa] For additional literature discussing the impact of *Pinholster,* see Erwin Chemerinsky, *Closing the Courthouse Doors,* 14 Green Bag 2d 375, 382–83 (2011); Justin F. Marceau, *Challenging the Habeas Process Rather than the Result,* 69 Wash. & Lee L. Rev. 85 (2012).

How does a federal district court treat the claim? Do you see why this hypothetical is probably not an issue of procedural default? Moreover, there is no issue with diligence, as the state withheld the witness statements that made the *Brady* claim much stronger. This hypothetical underscores Justice Sotomayor's central concern—that the rule is unduly harsh on prisoners that, acting diligently, discover new evidence supporting a claim after the state decision issues. Justice Thomas, in footnote that we omitted from the Court's opinion, responded that "Justice Sotomayor's hypothetical involving new evidence of withheld exculpatory witness statements . . . may well present a new claim." That new claim would not have been adjudicated on the merits in state court, however, and the prisoner would be required to show cause and prejudice it if was now defaulted. Moreover, that footnote added "we do not decide where to draw the line between new claims and claims adjudicated on the merits." Is that a convincing answer to the problem identified by Justice Sotomayor? How might Justice Breyer suggest that this problem be resolved; is there a way to present the new evidence to the state court?

9)   Capital Cases. *Pinholster* has had perhaps the greatest impact on capital cases, which had been far more likely than noncapital cases to receive an evidentiary hearing in federal court. Consider the following scenario. A prisoner was convicted of rape and murder and sentenced to death. A state habeas petition was dismissed without an evidentiary hearing. The strongest nondefaulted claim was one of failure of trial counsel to offer mitigating evidence during the penalty phase. The trial attorney did not interview petitioner's brother and sister, who could have testified to "devastating physical and psychological abuse he suffered at the hands of his biological father and stepfather." Jackson v. Kelly, 699 F. Supp. 2d 838, 843 (E.D. Va. 2010). Based on a two-day evidentiary hearing developing this mitigation evidence, the judge granted habeas relief and ordered that a new penalty hearing be conducted, or that the defendant be resentenced to life in prison. The appeals court reversed based on *Pinholster,* stating that this new evidence could not be considered. See Jackson v. Kelly, 650 F.3d 477 (4th Cir. 2011). For a similar ruling, see Frazier v. Bouchard, 661 F.3d 519 (11th Cir. 2011). For a post-*Pinholster* ruling that, where an IAC claim was presented to state courts that refused to allow the inmate to develop the record or conduct an evidentiary hearing, then the claim was not "adjudicated on the merits," and would therefore be reviewed de novo, see *Winston v. Pearson,* 683 F.3d 489, 501 (4th Cir. 2012).

10)   Stay and Abeyance. As long as the state prisoner has not filed the claim in a federal habeas petition, presenting new evidence to a state court after an initial disposition of a state post-conviction claim is straightforward enough. But what happens when a state prisoner has already filed a federal habeas petition? Some courts have tried staying a federal petition and holding it in abeyance so that the petitioner can present the new evidence to the state court. You studied this stay-and-abeyance procedure when you read the Notes on *Rhines .v. Weber,* in Chapter 4. A stay-and-abeyance order allows the prisoner to "present" the new evidence to the state court, thereby bringing the evidence within the purview of what the federal court could consider under the § 2254(d)(1) inquiry. Cf. Gonzalez v. Wong, 667 F.3d 965, 979–80 (9th Cir. 2011) ("This course provides the state court with the first opportunity to resolve this claim. It also protects Gonzales's interest in obtaining federal review of his claim."). What are some of the problems with the idea that new evidence introduced under such circumstances is then "presented" such that it could be considered under

§ 2254(d)(1)? If the evidence is presented in a posture that makes state courts unlikely to consider it, then what good does the stay-and-abeyance procedure do?

3. FACTUAL DEFECTS IN STATE DECISIONS

The prior Section dealt with 28 U.S.C. § 2254(d)(1), which is one of the two provisions a state prisoner may satisfy in order to obtain federal merits relief. Section 2254(d)(2) is the other, and Subsection (d)(2) permits the federal judge to grant relief when state merits adjudication "resulted in a decision that was based an unreasonable determination of the facts in light of the evidence presented in the State court proceeding." As with § 2254(d)(1), a showing that satisfies § 2254(d)(2) is not *sufficient* to entitle a prisoner to merits relief; it is simply a precondition to straightforward merits adjudication. Most elementally, what is an unreasonable determination of fact? Perhaps unreasonable factfinding *procedures* qualify, but what are some other examples? Moreover, in what situations is a decision "based on" an unreasonable factual determination?

INTRODUCTORY NOTE ON MILLER-EL V. DRETKE

American trial practice usually allows the defense and the prosecution to exercise a certain number of "peremptory strikes" on members of the venire (the jury pool) that appear to be unfavorably disposed to one side or the other. Peremptory challenges are, for the most part, honored without review by the trial judge. Peremptory challenges are separate from challenges "for cause," which require the striking party to provide a reason for the strike and that are reviewable by the judge presiding over voir dire.

The Supreme Court considered racially-disparate peremptory strike practice in *Swain v. Alabama*, 380 U.S. 202 (1965). For many years, black members of a venire were disproportionately subject to peremptory strikes because they tended to distrust law enforcement were less likely to vote for a death sentence in capital cases. (Black venire members were not the only people who the prosecution struck for such predispositions.) In tracing the historic roots of preemptory strike practice, the Court explained Alabama's argument:

> In providing for jury trial in criminal cases, Alabama adheres to the common-law system of trial by an impartial jury of 12 men who must unanimously agree on a verdict, the system followed in the federal courts by virtue of the Sixth Amendment. As part of this system it provides for challenges for cause and substitutes a system of strikes for the common-law method of peremptory challenge. Alabama contends that its system of peremptory strikes—challenges without cause, without explanation and without judicial scrutiny—affords a suitable and necessary method of securing juries which in fact and in the opinion of the parties are fair and impartial. This system, it is said, in and of itself, provides justification for striking any group of otherwise qualified jurors in any given case, whether they be Negroes, Catholics, accountants or those with blue eyes. Based on the history of this system and its actual use and operation in this country, we think there is merit in this position.

The Court ultimately rejected Alabama's position, at least with respect to race. It held that a peremptory strike practice motivated by intentional discrimination was unconstitutional, but it set a fairly high bar for making the showing necessary to prevail on such a claim.

The Supreme Court eventually found this rule for racially-motivated jury strikes unworkable, and crafted a new Equal Protection rule in *Batson v. Kentucky*, 476 U.S. 79 (1986). Under *Batson*, federal courts apply a three-step inquiry to claims of racially-motivated jury strikes. First, a defendant or post-conviction claimant must make out a prima facie case of discrimination by showing that the prosecution struck a potential juror because of race. Second, after a prima facie case is established, the State must articulate a race-neutral reason for striking the juror(s) in question. Finally, the court must determine whether a defendant has carried a burden of showing purposeful discrimination. *Batson* also relaxed the standard on the third step, in the sense that it disavowed the evidentiary requirements for showing discrimination that might have been inherited from *Swain*.

Miller-El v. Dretke, 545 U.S. 231 (2005) ("*Miller-El II*"), excerpted below, involves a *Batson* challenge to preemptory strikes at a Dallas County capital trial. The Supreme Court had already decided another issue that the case presented in *Miller-El v. Cockrell* ("*Miller-El I*"). In *Miller-El I*, the Court determined that the lower federal courts had erroneously denied Miller-El a certificate of appealability (COA) on the *Batson* issue. In other words, the Supreme Court held that Miller-El had made "a substantial showing of the denial of a constitutional right." For that reason, *Miller-El II* contains many references to reasoning present in the various opinions from *Miller-El I*.

Miller El v. Dretke

United States Supreme Court
545 U.S. 231 (2005)

■ JUSTICE SOUTER delivered the opinion of the Court.

Two years ago, we ordered * * * review of the District Court's rejection of the claim that prosecutors in [Miller-El's] capital murder trial made peremptory strikes of potential jurors based on race. Today we find Miller-El entitled to prevail on that claim and order relief under §2254.

I

* * * During jury selection in Miller-El's trial for capital murder, prosecutors used peremptory strikes against 10 qualified black venire members. Miller-El objected that the strikes were based on race and could not be presumed legitimate, given a history of excluding black members from criminal juries by the Dallas County District Attorney's Office. * * *

While an appeal was pending, this Court decided *Batson v. Kentucky*, 476 U.S. 79 (1986), which [formulated a new] threshold requirement to prove systemic discrimination under a Fourteenth Amendment jury claim, with the rule that discrimination by the prosecutor in selecting the defendant's jury sufficed to establish the constitutional violation. * * *

[The Texas and lower federal courts all denied relief on the *Batson* claim.] We grant[ ] certiorari[ ] and * * * reverse.

II

A

* * * Defendants are harmed * * * when racial discrimination in jury selection compromises the right of trial by impartial jury, but racial minorities are harmed more generally, for prosecutors drawing racial lines in picking juries establish "state-sponsored group stereotypes rooted in, and reflective of, historical prejudice."

Nor is the harm confined to minorities. When the government's choice of jurors is tainted with racial bias, that "overt wrong . . . casts doubt over the obligation of the parties, the jury, and indeed the court to adhere to the law throughout the trial . . ." * * * So, "[f]or more than a century, this Court consistently and repeatedly has reaffirmed that racial discrimination by the State in jury selection offends the Equal Protection Clause." * * *

[*Swain v. Alabama's*] demand to make out a continuity of discrimination over time, however, turned out to be difficult to the point of unworkable, and in *Batson v. Kentucky*, we recognized that this requirement to show an extended pattern imposed a "crippling burden of proof" that left prosecutors' use of peremptories "largely immune from constitutional scrutiny." By *Batson's* day, the law implementing equal protection elsewhere had evolved into less discouraging standards for assessing a claim of purposeful discrimination, and we accordingly held that a defendant could make out a prima facie case of discriminatory jury selection by "the totality of the relevant facts" about a prosecutor's conduct during the defendant's own trial. "Once the defendant makes a prima facie showing, the burden shifts to the State to come forward with a neutral explanation for challenging . . . jurors" within an arguably targeted class. * * * "The trial court then will have the duty to determine if the defendant has established purposeful discrimination." * * *

B

Under [AEDPA], Miller-El may obtain relief only by showing the Texas conclusion to be "an unreasonable determination of the facts in light of the evidence presented in the State court proceeding." 28 U.S.C. § 2254(d)(2). Thus we presume the Texas court's factual findings to be sound unless Miller-El rebuts the "presumption of correctness by clear and convincing evidence." §2254(e)(1). The standard is demanding but not insatiable; as we said the last time this case was here, "[d]eference does not by definition preclude relief." *Miller–El v. Cockrell*, 537 U.S., at 340.

III

A

The numbers describing the prosecution's use of peremptories are remarkable. Out of 20 black members of the 108-person venire panel for Miller-El's trial, only 1 served. Although 9 were excused for cause or by agreement, 10 were peremptorily struck by the prosecution. * * *

More powerful than these bare statistics, however, are side-by-side comparisons of some black venire panelists who were struck and white panelists allowed to serve. If a prosecutor's proffered reason for striking a black panelist applies just as well to an otherwise-similar nonblack who is permitted to serve, that is evidence tending to prove purposeful discrimination to be considered at *Batson's* third step. * * * [T]he prosecution's reasons for exercising peremptory strikes against some black panel members appeared equally on point as to some white jurors who served. The details of two panel member comparisons bear this out.[2]

The prosecution used its second peremptory strike to exclude Billy Jean Fields, a black man who expressed unwavering support for the death penalty. On the questionnaire filled out by all panel members before individual examination on the stand, Fields said that he believed in capital punishment, and during questioning he disclosed his belief that the State acts on God's behalf when it imposes the death penalty. * * * He testified that he had no religious or philosophical reservations about the death penalty and that the death penalty deterred crime. He twice averred, without apparent hesitation, that he could sit on Miller-El's jury and make a decision to impose this penalty.

Although at one point in the questioning, Fields indicated that the possibility of rehabilitation might be relevant to the likelihood that a defendant would commit future acts of violence, he responded to ensuing questions by saying that although he believed anyone could be rehabilitated, this belief would not stand in the way of a decision to impose the death penalty[.] * * *

Fields also noted on his questionnaire that his brother had a criminal history. During questioning, the prosecution went into this, too:

"Q Could you tell me a little bit about that?"

"A He was arrested and convicted on [a] number of occasions for possession of a controlled substance."

"Q Was that here in Dallas?"

"A Yes. "

"Q Was he involved in any trials or anything like that?"

"A I suppose of sorts. I don't really know too much about it."

"Q Was he ever convicted?"

"A Yeah, he served time."

"Q Do you feel that that would in any way interfere with your service on this jury at all?"

"A No."

Fields was struck peremptorily by the prosecution, with prosecutor James Nelson offering a race-neutral reason:

"[W]e . . . have concern with reference to some of his statements as to the death penalty in that he said that he could only give death if he thought a person could not be rehabilitated and he later made the comment that any person could be rehabilitated if they find God or are

---

[2] The dissent contends that comparisons of black and nonblack venire panelists, along with Miller-El's arguments about the prosecution's disparate questioning of black and nonblack panelists and its use of jury shuffles, are not properly before this Court, not having been "put before the Texas courts." But the dissent conflates the difference between evidence that must be presented to the state courts to be considered by federal courts in habeas proceedings and theories about that evidence. There can be no question that the transcript of voir dire, recording the evidence on which Miller-El bases his arguments and on which we base our result, was before the state courts, nor does the dissent contend that Miller-El did not "fairly presen[t]" his Batson claim to the state courts. Only as to the juror questionnaires and information cards is there question about what was before the state courts. Unlike the dissent, we reach no decision about whether the limitation on evidence in § 2254(d)(2) is waiveable.

introduced to God and the fact that we have a concern that his religious feelings may affect his jury service in this case."

Thus, Nelson simply mischaracterized Fields's testimony. He represented that Fields said he would not vote for death if rehabilitation was possible, whereas Fields unequivocally stated that he could impose the death penalty regardless of the possibility of rehabilitation. * * *

If, indeed, Fields's thoughts on rehabilitation did make the prosecutor uneasy, he should have worried about a number of white panel members he accepted with no evident reservations. Sandra Hearn said that she believed in the death penalty "if a criminal cannot be rehabilitated and continues to commit the same type of crime." Hearn went so far as to express doubt that at the penalty phase of a capital case she could conclude that a convicted murderer "would probably commit some criminal acts of violence in the future." "People change," she said, making it hard to assess the risk of someone's future dangerousness. "[T]he evidence would have to be awful strong." But the prosecution did not respond to Hearn the way it did to Fields, and without delving into her views about rehabilitation with any further question, it raised no objection to her serving on the jury. White panelist Mary Witt said she would take the possibility of rehabilitation into account in deciding at the penalty phase of the trial about a defendant's probability of future dangerousness, but the prosecutors asked her no further question about her views on reformation, and they accepted her as a juror. Latino venireman Fernando Gutierrez, who served on the jury, said that he would consider the death penalty for someone who could not be rehabilitated, but the prosecutors did not question him further about this view. In sum, nonblack jurors whose remarks on rehabilitation could well have signaled a limit on their willingness to impose a death sentence were not questioned further and drew no objection, but the prosecution expressed apprehension about a black juror's belief in the possibility of reformation even though he repeatedly stated his approval of the death penalty and testified that he could impose it according to state legal standards even when the alternative sentence of life imprisonment would give a defendant (like everyone else in the world) the opportunity to reform.

The unlikelihood that his position on rehabilitation had anything to do with the peremptory strike of Fields is underscored by the prosecution's response after Miller-El's lawyer pointed out that the prosecutor had misrepresented Fields's responses on the subject. A moment earlier the prosecutor had finished his misdescription of Fields's views on potential rehabilitation with the words, "Those are our reasons for exercising our . . . strike at this time." When defense counsel called him on his misstatement, he neither defended what he said nor withdrew the strike. Instead, he suddenly came up with Fields's brother's prior conviction as another reason for the strike.

It would be difficult to credit the State's new explanation, which reeks of afterthought. While the Court of Appeals tried to bolster it with the observation that no seated juror was in Fields's position with respect to his brother, the court's readiness to accept the State's substitute reason ignores not only its pretextual timing but the other reasons rendering it implausible. Fields's testimony indicated he was not close to his brother, * * * and the prosecution asked nothing further about the influence his brother's history might have had on Fields * * *. There is no good reason to doubt that the State's afterthought about Fields's brother was anything but makeweight. * * *

In sum, when we look for nonblack jurors similarly situated to Fields, we find strong similarities as well as some differences. But the differences seem far from significant, particularly when we read Fields's *voir dire* testimony in its entirety. Upon that reading, Fields should have been an ideal juror in the eyes of a prosecutor seeking a death sentence, and the prosecutors' explanations for the strike cannot reasonably be accepted.

The prosecution's proffered reasons for striking Joe Warren, another black venireman, are comparably unlikely. Warren gave this answer when he was asked what the death penalty accomplished:

"I don't know. It's really hard to say because I know sometimes you feel that it might help to deter crime and then you feel that the person is not really suffering. You're taking the suffering away from him. So it's like I said, sometimes you have mixed feelings about whether or not this is punishment or, you know, you're relieving personal punishment."

The prosecution said nothing about these remarks when it struck Warren from the panel, but prosecutor Paul Macaluso referred to this answer as the first of his reasons when he testified at the later *Batson* hearing:

"I thought [Warren's statements on voir dire] were inconsistent responses. At one point he says, you know, on a case-by-case basis and at another point he said, well, I think—I got the impression, at least, that he suggested that the death penalty was an easy way out, that they should be made to suffer more."

On the face of it, the explanation is reasonable from the State's point of view, but its plausibility is severely undercut by the prosecution's failure to object to other panel members who expressed views much like Warren's. Kevin Duke, who served on the jury, said, "sometimes death would be better to me than—being in prison would be like dying every day and, if you were in prison for life with no hope of parole, I['d] just as soon have it over with than be in prison for the rest of your life." Troy Woods, the one black panelist to serve as juror, said that capital punishment "is too easy. I think that's a quick relief . . . I feel like [hard labor is] more of a punishment than putting them to sleep." Sandra Jenkins, whom the State accepted (but who was then struck by the defense) testified that she thought "a harsher treatment is life imprisonment with no parole." Leta Girard, accepted by the State (but also struck by the defense) gave her opinion that "living sometimes is a worse—is worse to me than dying would be." The fact that Macaluso's reason also applied to these other panel members, most of them white, none of them struck, is evidence of pretext.

The suggestion of pretext is not, moreover, mitigated much by Macaluso's explanation that Warren was struck when the State had 10 peremptory challenges left and could afford to be liberal in using them. If that were the explanation for striking Warren and later accepting panel members who thought death would be too easy, the prosecutors should have struck Sandra Jenkins, whom they examined and accepted before Warren. Indeed, the disparate treatment is the more remarkable for the fact that the prosecutors repeatedly questioned Warren on his capacity and willingness to impose a sentence of death and elicited statements of his ability to do so if the evidence supported that result and the answer to each special question was yes, whereas the record before us discloses no attempt to determine whether Jenkins would be able to vote for death in spite of her view that it was easy on the convict. Yet the prosecutors accepted the white panel member Jenkins and struck the black venireman Warren. * * *

The Court of Appeals pretermitted these difficulties by stating that the prosecution's reason for striking Warren was a more general ambivalence about the penalty and his ability to impose it. But this rationalization was erroneous as a matter of fact and as a matter of law.

As to fact, Macaluso said nothing about any general ambivalence. He simply alluded to the possibility that Warren might think the death penalty too easy on some defendants, saying nothing about Warren's ability to impose the penalty when it appeared to be warranted. * * *

As for law, the rule in *Batson* provides an opportunity to the prosecutor to give the reason for striking the juror, and it requires the judge to assess the plausibility of that reason in light of all evidence with a bearing on it. [A]nd it can sometimes be hard to say what the reason is. But when illegitimate grounds like race are in issue, a prosecutor simply has got to state his reasons as best he can and stand or fall on the plausibility of the reasons he gives. A *Batson* challenge does not call for a mere exercise in thinking up any rational basis. If the stated reason does not hold up, its pretextual significance does not fade because a trial judge, or an appeals court, can imagine a reason that might not have been shown up as false. The Court of Appeals's and the dissent's substitution of a reason for eliminating Warren does nothing to satisfy the prosecutors' burden of stating a racially neutral explanation for their own actions. * * *

B

The case for discrimination goes beyond these comparisons to include broader patterns of practice during the jury selection. The prosecution's shuffling of the venire panel, its enquiry into views on the death penalty, its questioning about minimum acceptable sentences: all indicate decisions probably based on race. Finally, the appearance of discrimination is confirmed by widely known evidence of the general policy of the Dallas County District Attorney's Office to exclude black venire members from juries at the time Miller-El's jury was selected.

The first clue to the prosecutors' intentions, distinct from the peremptory challenges themselves, is their resort during voir dire to a procedure known in Texas as the jury shuffle. In the State's criminal practice, either side may literally reshuffle the cards bearing panel members' names, thus rearranging the order in which members of a venire panel are seated and reached for questioning. Once the order is established, the panel members seated at the back are likely to escape *voir dire* altogether, for those not questioned by the end of the week are dismissed. As we previously explained,

> "the prosecution's decision to seek a jury shuffle when a predominant number of African-Americans were seated in the front of the panel, along with its decision to delay a formal objection to the defense's shuffle until after the new racial composition was revealed, raise a suspicion that the State sought to exclude African-Americans from the jury. Our concerns are amplified by the fact that the state court also had before it, and apparently ignored, testimony demonstrating that the Dallas County District Attorney's Office had, by its own admission, used this process to manipulate the racial composition of the jury in the past."

In this case, the prosecution and then the defense shuffled the cards at the beginning of the first week of *voir dire*; the record does not reflect the changes in order. At the beginning of the second week, when a number of black members were seated at the front of the panel, the prosecution shuffled. At the beginning of the third week, the first four panel members were black. The prosecution shuffled, and these black panel members ended up at the back. Then the defense shuffled, and the black panel members again appeared at the front. The prosecution requested another shuffle, but the trial court refused. Finally, the defense shuffled at the beginning of the fourth and fifth weeks of *voir dire*; the record does not reflect the panel's racial composition before or after those shuffles.

* * * [N]o racially neutral reason [for the shuffle] has ever been offered in this case, and nothing stops the suspicion of discriminatory intent from rising to an inference.

The next body of evidence that the State was trying to avoid black jurors is the contrasting *voir dire* questions posed respectively to black and nonblack panel members, on two different subjects. First, there were the prosecutors' statements preceding questions about a potential juror's thoughts on capital punishment. Some of these prefatory statements were cast in general terms, but some followed the so-called graphic script, describing the method of execution in rhetorical and clinical detail. It is intended, Miller-El contends, to prompt some expression of hesitation to consider the death penalty and thus to elicit plausibly neutral grounds for a peremptory strike of a potential juror subjected to it, if not a strike for cause. If the graphic script is given to a higher proportion of blacks than whites, this is evidence that prosecutors more often wanted blacks off the jury, absent some neutral and extenuating explanation.

* * * [F]or 94% of white venire panel members, prosecutors gave a bland description of the death penalty before asking about the individual's feelings on the subject. The abstract account went something like this:

> "I feel like it [is] only fair that we tell you our position in this case. The State of Texas . . . is actively seeking the death penalty in this case for Thomas Joe Miller-El. We anticipate that we will be able to present to a jury the quantity and type of evidence necessary to convict him of capital murder and the quantity and type of evidence sufficient to allow a jury to answer these three questions over here in the affirmative. A yes answer to each of those questions results in an automatic death penalty from Judge McDowell."

Only 6% of white venire panelists, but 53% of those who were black, heard a different description of the death penalty before being asked their feelings about it. This is an example of the graphic script:

> "I feel like you have a right to know right up front what our position is. Mr. Kinne, Mr. Macaluso and myself, representing the people of Dallas County and the state of Texas, are actively seeking the death penalty for Thomas Joe Miller-El . . ."

> "We do that with the anticipation that, when the death penalty is assessed, at some point Mr. Thomas Joe Miller-El—the man sitting right down there—will be taken to Huntsville and will be put on death row and at some point taken to the death house and placed on a gurney and injected with a lethal substance until he is dead as a result of the proceedings that we have in this court on this case. So that's basically our position going into this thing."

The State concedes that this disparate questioning did occur but argues that use of the graphic script turned not on a panelist's race but on expressed ambivalence about the death penalty in the preliminary questionnaire. Prosecutors were trying, the argument goes, to weed out noncommittal or uncertain jurors, not black jurors. And while some white venire members expressed opposition to the death penalty on their questionnaires, they were not read the graphic script because their feelings were already clear. The State says that giving the graphic script to these panel members would only have antagonized them.

This argument, however, first advanced in dissent when the case was last here, and later adopted by the State and the Court of Appeals, simply does not fit the facts. Looking at the answers on the questionnaires, and at *voir dire* testimony expressly discussing answers on the questionnaires, we find that black venire members were more likely than nonblacks to receive the graphic script regardless of their expressions of certainty or ambivalence about the death penalty, and the State's chosen explanation for the graphic script fails in the cases of four out of the eight black panel members who received it. * * *

The State's purported rationale fails again if we look only to the treatment of ambivalent panel members, ambivalent black individuals having been more likely to receive the graphic description than ambivalent nonblacks. * * *

The State's attempt at a race-neutral rationalization thus simply fails to explain what the prosecutors did. But if we posit instead that the prosecutors' first object was to use the graphic script to make a case for excluding black panel members opposed to or ambivalent about the death penalty, there is a much tighter fit of fact and explanation. Of the 10 nonblacks whose questionnaires expressed ambivalence or opposition, only 30% received the graphic treatment. But of the seven blacks who expressed ambivalence or opposition, 86% heard the graphic script. As between the State's ambivalence explanation and Miller-El's racial one, race is much the better, and the reasonable inference is that race was the major consideration when the prosecution chose to follow the graphic script.

The same is true for another kind of disparate questioning, which might fairly be called trickery. The prosecutors asked members of the panel how low a sentence they would consider imposing for murder. Most potential jurors were first told that Texas law provided for a minimum term of five years, but some members of the panel were not, and if a panel member then insisted on a minimum above five years, the prosecutor would suppress his normal preference for tough jurors and claim cause to strike. Two Terms ago, we described how this disparate questioning was correlated with race:

> "Ninety-four percent of whites were informed of the statutory minimum sentence, compared [with] only twelve and a half percent of African-Americans. No explanation is proffered for the statistical disparity. . . . Indeed, while [Miller-El]'s appeal was pending before the Texas Court of Criminal Appeals, that court found a *Batson* violation where this precise line of disparate questioning on mandatory minimums was employed by one of the same prosecutors who tried the instant case."

The State concedes that the manipulative minimum punishment questioning was used to create cause to strike, but now it offers the extenuation that prosecutors omitted the 5-year information not on the basis of race, but on stated opposition to the death penalty, or ambivalence about it, on the questionnaires and in the *voir dire* testimony. On the State's identification of black panel members opposed or ambivalent, all were asked the trick question. But the State's rationale flatly fails to explain why most white panel members who expressed similar opposition or ambivalence were not subjected to it. * * * [O]nly 27% of nonblacks questioned on the subject who expressed these views were subjected to the trick question, as against 100% of black members. Once again, the implication of race in the prosecutors' choice of questioning cannot be explained away.

There is a final body of evidence that confirms this conclusion. We know that for decades leading up to the time this case was tried prosecutors in the Dallas County office had followed a specific policy of systematically excluding blacks from juries, as we explained the last time the case was here.

> "Although most of the witnesses [presented at the *Swain* hearing in 1986] denied the existence of a systematic policy to exclude African-Americans, others disagreed. A Dallas County district judge testified that, when he had served in the District Attorney's Office from the late-1950's to early-1960's, his superior warned him that he would be fired if he permitted any African-Americans to serve on a jury. Similarly, another Dallas County district judge and former assistant district attorney from 1976 to 1978 testified that he believed the office had a systematic policy of excluding African-Americans from juries."

> "Of more importance, the defense presented evidence that the District Attorney's Office had adopted a formal policy to exclude minorities from jury service ... A manual entitled 'Jury Selection in a Criminal Case' [sometimes known as the Sparling Manual] was distributed to prosecutors. It contained an article authored by a former prosecutor (and later a judge) under the direction of his superiors in the District Attorney's Office, outlining the reasoning for excluding minorities from jury service. Although the manual was written in 1968, it remained in circulation until 1976, if not later, and was available at least to one of the prosecutors in Miller-El's trial." * * *

Prosecutors here "marked the race of each prospective juror on their juror cards."

The Court of Appeals concluded that Miller-El failed to show by clear and convincing evidence that the state court's finding of no discrimination was wrong, whether his evidence was viewed collectively or separately. We find this conclusion as unsupportable as the "dismissive and strained interpretation" of his evidence that we disapproved when we decided Miller-El was entitled to a certificate of appealability. It is true, of course, that at some points the significance of Miller-El's evidence is open to judgment calls, but when this evidence on the issues raised is viewed cumulatively its direction is too powerful to conclude anything but discrimination.

In the course of drawing a jury to try a black defendant, 10 of the 11 qualified black venire panel members were peremptorily struck. At least two of them, Fields and Warren, were ostensibly acceptable to prosecutors seeking a death verdict, and Fields was ideal. The prosecutors' chosen race-neutral reasons for the strikes do not hold up and are so far at odds with the evidence that pretext is the fair conclusion, indicating the very discrimination the explanations were meant to deny.

The strikes that drew these incredible explanations occurred in a selection process replete with evidence that the prosecutors were selecting and rejecting potential jurors because of race. At least two of the jury shuffles conducted by the State make no sense except as efforts to delay consideration of black jury panelists to the end of the week, when they might not even be reached. The State has in fact never offered any other explanation. Nor has the State denied that disparate lines of questioning were pursued: 53% of black panelists but only 3% of nonblacks were questioned with a graphic script meant to induce qualms about applying the death penalty (and thus explain a strike), and 100% of blacks but only 27% of nonblacks were subjected to a trick question about the minimum acceptable penalty for murder, meant to induce a disqualifying answer. The State's attempts to explain the prosecutors' questioning of particular witnesses on nonracial grounds fit the evidence less well than the racially discriminatory hypothesis.

If anything more is needed for an undeniable explanation of what was going on, history supplies it. The prosecutors took their cues from a 20-year-old manual of tips on jury selection, as shown by their notes of the race of each potential juror. By the time a jury was chosen, the State had peremptorily challenged 12% of qualified nonblack panel members, but eliminated 91% of the black ones.

It blinks reality to deny that the State struck Fields and Warren, included in that 91%, because they were black. The strikes correlate with no fact as well as they correlate with race, and they occurred during a selection infected by shuffling and disparate questioning that race explains better than any race-neutral reason advanced by the State. The State's pretextual positions confirm Miller-El's claim, and the prosecutors' own notes proclaim that the * * * emphasis on race was on their minds when they considered every potential juror.

The state court's conclusion that the prosecutors' strikes of Fields and Warren were not racially determined is shown up as wrong to a clear and convincing degree; the state court's conclusion was unreasonable as well as erroneous. The judgment of the Court of Appeals is reversed, and the case is remanded for entry of judgment for [Miller-El] together with orders of appropriate relief.

It is so ordered.

[A concurring opinion by JUSTICE BREYER is omitted]

■ JUSTICE THOMAS, with whom THE CHIEF JUSTICE and JUSTICE SCALIA join, dissenting.

* * *

II

Not even the majority is willing to argue that the evidence before the state court shows that the State discriminated against black veniremen. Instead, it bases its decision on juror questionnaires and juror cards that Miller-El's new attorneys unearthed during his federal habeas proceedings and that he never presented to the state courts. Worse still, the majority marshals those documents in support of theories that Miller-El never argued to the state courts. AEDPA does not permit habeas petitioners to engage in this sort of sandbagging of state courts.

A

The majority discusses four types of evidence: (1) the alleged similarity between black veniremen who were struck by the prosecution and white veniremen who were not; (2) the apparent disparate questioning of black and white veniremen with respect to their views on the death penalty and their ability to impose the minimum punishment; (3) the use of the "jury shuffle" by the prosecution; and (4) evidence of historical discrimination by the D.A.'s Office in the selection of juries. Only the last was ever put before the Texas courts—and it does not prove that any constitutional violation occurred at Miller-El's trial. The majority's discussion of the other types of evidence relies on documents like juror questionnaires and juror cards that were added to the record before the District Court.

The majority's willingness to reach outside the state-court record and embrace evidence never presented to the Texas state courts is hard to fathom. AEDPA mandates that the reasonableness of a state court's factual findings be assessed "in light of the evidence presented in the State court proceeding," 28 U.S.C. § 2254(d)(2), and also circumscribes the ability of federal habeas litigants to present evidence that they "failed to develop" before the state courts. §2254(e)(2). Miller-El did not argue disparate treatment or disparate questioning at the *Batson* hearing, so he had no reason to submit the juror questionnaires or cards to the trial court. However, Miller-El could have developed and presented all of that evidence at the *Batson* hearing. Consequently, he must satisfy §2254(e)(2)'s requirements to adduce the evidence in federal court—something he cannot do. For instance, there is no doubt that Miller-El's supplemental material could have been "previously discovered through the exercise of due diligence." §2254(e)(2)(A)(ii).

* * * By crediting evidence that Miller-El never placed before the state courts, the majority flouts AEDPA's plain terms and encourages habeas applicants to attack state judgments collaterally with evidence never tested by the original triers of fact. * * *

III

Even taken on its own terms, Miller-El's cumulative evidence does not come remotely close to clearly and convincingly establishing that the state court's factual finding was unreasonable. * * *

A

The majority devotes the bulk of its opinion to a side-by-side comparison of white panelists who were allowed to serve and two black panelists who were struck, Billy Jean Fields and Joe Warren. The majority argues that the prosecution's reasons for striking Fields and Warren apply equally to whites who were permitted to serve, and thus those reasons must have been pretextual. The *voir dire* transcript reveals that the majority is mistaken.

* * * Warren was obviously equivocal about the death penalty. In the end, the majority's case reduces to a single venireman, Fields, and its reading of a 20-year-old *voir dire* transcript that is ambiguous at best. This is the antithesis of clear and convincing evidence.

1

From the outset of questioning, Warren did not specify when he would vote to impose the death penalty. When asked by prosecutor Paul Macaluso about his ability to impose the death penalty, Warren stated, "[T]here are some cases where I would agree, you know, and there are others that I don't." Macaluso then explained at length the types of crimes that qualified as capital murder under Texas law, and asked whether Warren would be able to impose the death penalty for those types of heinous crimes. Warren continued to hedge: "I would say it depends on the case and the circumstances involved at the time." He offered no sense of the circumstances that would lead him to conclude that the death penalty was an appropriate punishment.

Macaluso then changed tack and asked whether Warren believed that the death penalty accomplished any social purpose. Once again, Warren proved impossible to pin down: "Yes and no. Sometimes I think it does and sometimes I think it don't. Sometimes you have mixed feelings about things like that." Macaluso then focused on what the death penalty accomplished in those cases where Warren believed it useful. Even then, Warren expressed no firm view:

> "I don't know. It's really hard to say because I know sometimes you feel that it might help to deter crime and then you feel that the person is not really suffering. You're taking the suffering away from him. So it's like I said, sometimes you have mixed feelings about whether or not this is punishment or, you know, you're relieving personal punishment."

While Warren's ambivalence was driven by his uncertainty that the death penalty was severe enough, that is beside the point. Throughout the examination, Warren gave no indication whether or when he would prefer the death penalty to other forms of punishment, specifically life imprisonment. To prosecutors seeking the death penalty, the reason for Warren's ambivalence was irrelevant.

At *voir dire*, there was no dispute that the prosecution struck Warren not for his race, but for his ambivalence on the death penalty. Miller-El's attorneys did not object to the State's strikes of Warren or Paul Bailey, though they objected to the removal of every other black venireman. Both Bailey and Warren shared the same characteristic: It was not clear, based on their questionnaires and *voir dire* testimony, that they could impose the death penalty. * * *

There also was no question at the *Batson* hearing why the prosecution struck Warren. Macaluso testified:

> "I thought [Warren's statements on *voir dire*] were inconsistent responses. At one point he says, you know, on a case-by-case basis and at another point he said, well, I think–I got the impression, at least, that he suggested that the death penalty was an easy way out, that they should be made to suffer more."

In addition, Macaluso noted that Warren's brother recently had been convicted for a crime involving food stamps. This suggested that Warren might be more sympathetic to defendants than other jurors. * * *

The majority points to four other panel members * * * who supposedly expressed views much like Warren's, but who were not struck by the State. According to the majority, this is evidence of pretext. But the majority's premise is faulty. None of these veniremen was as difficult to pin down on the death penalty as Warren. * * *

Nevertheless, even assuming that any of these veniremen expressed views similar to Warren's, [several of the compared jurors] were questioned much later in the jury selection process, when the State had fewer peremptories to spare. * * *

The majority thinks it can prove pretext by pointing to white veniremen who match only one of the State's proffered reasons for striking Warren. This defies logic. "'Similarly situated' does not mean matching any one of several reasons the prosecution gave for striking a potential juror—it means matching *all* of them." Given limited peremptories, prosecutors often must focus on the potential jurors most likely to disfavor their case. By ignoring the totality of reasons that a prosecutor strikes any particular venireman, it is the majority that treats potential jurors as "products of a set of cookie cutters[ ]"—as if potential jurors who share only some among many traits must be treated the same to avoid a *Batson* violation. Of course jurors must not be "identical in all respects" to gauge pretext, but to isolate race as a variable, the jurors must be comparable in all respects that the prosecutor proffers as important. This does not mean "that a defendant cannot win a *Batson* claim unless there is an exactly identical white juror." It means that a defendant cannot support a *Batson* claim by comparing veniremen of different races unless the veniremen are truly similar.

2

The second black venireman on whom the majority relies is Billy Jean Fields. Fields expressed support for the death penalty, but Fields also expressed views that called into question his ability to impose the death penalty. Fields was a deeply religious man, and prosecutors feared that his religious convictions might make him reluctant to impose the death penalty. Those fears were confirmed by Fields' view that all people could be rehabilitated if introduced to God, a fear that had special force considering the special-issue questions necessary to impose the death penalty in Texas. One of those questions asked whether there was a probability that the defendant would engage in future violence that threatened society. * * *

* * * Fields indicated that the possibility of rehabilitation was ever-present and relevant to whether a defendant might commit future acts of violence. In light of that view, it is understandable that prosecutors doubted whether he could vote to impose the death penalty.

Fields did testify that he could impose the death penalty, even on a defendant who could be rehabilitated. For the majority, this shows that the State's reason was pretextual. But of course Fields said that he could fairly consider the death penalty—if he had answered otherwise, he would have been challengeable for cause. The point is that Fields' earlier answers cast significant doubt on whether he could impose the death penalty. The very purpose of peremptory strikes is to allow parties to remove potential jurors whom they suspect, but cannot prove, may exhibit a particular bias. * * *

The majority dismisses as "makeweight" the State's justification as to Fields' brother, ante, but it is the majority's arguments that are contrived. The State questioned Fields during *voir dire* about his brother's drug offenses, where the offenses occurred, whether his brother had been tried, whether his brother had been convicted, and whether his brother's criminal history would affect Fields' ability to serve on the jury. The State did not fail to engage in a "'meaningful *voir dire* examination,'" as the majority contends. * * *

B

Miller-El's claims of disparate questioning also do not fit the facts. Miller-El argues, and the majority accepts, that the prosecution asked different questions at *voir dire* of black and nonblack veniremen on two subjects: (1) the manner of execution and (2) the minimum punishment allowed by state law. * * *

* * * The State questioned panelists differently when their questionnaire responses indicated ambivalence about the death penalty. Any racial disparity in questioning resulted from the reality that more nonblack veniremen favored the death penalty and were willing to impose it.

1

While most veniremen were given a generic description of the death penalty at the outset of their *voir dire* examinations, some were questioned with a "graphic script" that detailed Texas' method of execution. According to Miller-El and the majority, prosecutors used the graphic script to create cause for removing black veniremen who were ambivalent about or opposed to the death penalty. This is incorrect.

The jury questionnaires asked two questions directly relevant to the death penalty. Question 56 asked, "Do you believe in the death penalty?" * * * Question 58 asked, "Do you have any moral, religious, or personal beliefs that would prevent you from returning a verdict which would ultimately result in the execution of another human being?" and offered panelists only the chance to circle "yes" or "no."

According to the State, those veniremen who took a consistent stand on the death penalty—either for or against it—did not receive the graphic script. These prospective jurors either answered "no" to question 56 and "yes" to question 58 (meaning they did not believe in the death penalty and had qualms about imposing it), or answered "yes" to question 56 and "no" to question 58 (meaning they did believe in the death penalty and had no qualms about imposing it). Only those potential jurors who answered inconsistently, thereby indicating ambivalence about the death penalty, received the graphic script.

The questionnaires bear out this distinction. Fifteen blacks were questioned during *voir dire*. Only eight of them—or 53%—received the graphic script. All eight had given ambivalent questionnaire answers regarding their ability to impose the death penalty. * * *

Of the seven blacks who did not receive the graphic script, six took a stand on the death penalty—either for or against it—in their questionnaires. There was no need to use the graphic script to clarify their positions. * * *

Thus far, the State's explanation for its use of the graphic script fares far better than Miller-El's or the majority's. Questionnaire answers explain prosecutors' use of the graphic script with 14 out of the 15 blacks, or 93%. By contrast, race explains use of the script with only 8 out of 15 veniremen, or 53%. * * *

The State's explanation also accounts for its treatment of the 12 nonblack veniremen (10 whites, 1 Hispanic, and 1 Filipino) on whom the majority relies. * * *

First, of the five nonblacks who received the graphic script[,] * * * four were ambivalent. * * *

Of the seven nonblacks who allegedly did not receive the graphic script, four were strongly opposed to the death penalty. * * * Administering the graphic script to these potential jurors would have been useless. "No trial lawyer would willingly antagonize a potential juror ardently opposed to the death penalty with an extreme portrait of its implementation." * * *

In any event, again the State's explanation fares well. The State's explanation accounts for prosecutors' choice between the abstract and graphic scripts for 9 of 12 nonblack veniremen, or 75%. * * * However, the majority's theory accounts for the State's treatment of only 6 of 12 nonblacks, or 50%. * * *

Finally, the majority cannot take refuge in any supposed disparity between use of the graphic script with ambivalent black and nonblack veniremen. The State gave the graphic script to 8 of 9 ambivalent blacks, or 88%, and 5 of 7 ambivalent nonblacks, or 71%. This is hardly much of a difference. * * *

In sum, the State can explain its treatment of 23 of 27 potential jurors, or 85%, while the majority can only account for the State's treatment of 18 of 27 potential jurors, or 67%. This is a far cry from clear and convincing evidence of racial bias.

2

Miller-El also alleges that the State employed two different scripts on the basis of race when asking questions about imposition of the minimum sentence. * * * The evidence confirms that, as the State argues, prosecutors used different questioning on minimum sentences to create cause to strike veniremen who were ambivalent about or opposed to the death penalty.

Of the 15 blacks, 7 were given the minimum punishment script (MPS). All had expressed ambivalence about the death penalty, either in their questionnaires * * * or during *voir dire* * * *. * * * However, even assuming that the State should have used the MPS on these 3 veniremen, the State's explanation still accounts for 7 of the 10 ambivalent blacks, or 70%.

The majority does not seriously contest any of this. Instead, it contends that the State used the MPS less often with nonblacks, which demonstrates that the MPS was a ruse to remove blacks. This is not true: The State used the MPS more often with ambivalent nonblacks who were not otherwise removable for cause or by agreement. * * *

C

Miller-El's argument that prosecutors shuffled the jury to remove blacks is pure speculation. At the *Batson* hearing, Miller-El did not raise, nor was there any discussion of, the topic of jury shuffling as a racial tactic. The record shows only that the State shuffled the jury during the first three weeks of jury selection, while Miller-El shuffled the jury during each of the five weeks. This evidence no more proves that prosecutors sought to eliminate blacks from the jury, than it proves that Miller-El sought to eliminate whites even more often.

Miller-El notes that the State twice shuffled the jury (in the second and third weeks) when a number of blacks were seated at the front of the panel. According to the majority, this gives rise to an "inference" that prosecutors were discriminating. But Miller-El should not be asking this Court to draw "inference[s]"; he should be asking it to examine clear and convincing proof. And the inference is not even a strong one. We do not know if the nonblacks near the front shared characteristics with the blacks near the front, providing race-neutral reasons for the shuffles. We also do not know the racial composition of the panel during the first week when the State shuffled, or during the fourth and fifth weeks when it did not.

More importantly, any number of characteristics other than race could have been apparent to prosecutors from a visual inspection of the jury panel. Granted, we do not know whether prosecutors relied on racially neutral reasons, but that is because Miller-El never asked at the *Batson* hearing. It is Miller-El's burden to prove racial discrimination, and the jury-shuffle evidence itself does not provide such proof.

D

The majority's speculation would not be complete, however, without its discussion * * * of the history of discrimination in the D.A.'s Office. This is nothing more than guilt by association that is unsupported by the record. Some of the witnesses at the *Swain* hearing did testify that individual prosecutors had discriminated. However, no one testified that the prosecutors in Miller-El's trial * * * had ever been among those to engage in racially discriminatory jury selection.

The majority then tars prosecutors with a manual entitled Jury Selection in a Criminal Case * * * authored by John Sparling, a former Dallas County prosecutor. There is no evidence, however, that [the prosecutors in Miller-El's case] had ever read the Manual—which was written in 1968, almost two decades before Miller-El's trial. * * * The majority simply assumes that all Dallas County prosecutors were racist and remained that way through the mid-1980's. * * *

Finally, the majority notes that prosecutors "marked the race of each prospective juror on their juror cards." This suffers from the same problems as Miller-El's other evidence. Prosecutors did mark the juror cards with the jurors' race, sex, and juror number. We have no idea—and even the majority cannot bring itself to speculate—whether this was done merely for identification purposes or for some more nefarious reason. * * *

Thomas Joe Miller-El's charges of racism have swayed the Court, and AEDPA's restrictions will not stand in its way. But Miller-El has not established, much less established by clear and convincing evidence, that prosecutors racially discriminated in the selection of his jury—and he certainly has not done so on the basis of the evidence presented to the Texas courts. On the basis of facts and law, rather than sentiments, Miller-El does not merit the writ. I respectfully dissent.

NOTES AND QUESTIONS ON MILLER-EL

1) AEDPA and Factual Findings. The Supreme Court quoted the § 2254(d)(2) standard, and, citing to § 2254(e)(1), noted that it would "presume the Texas court's factual findings to be sound unless Miller–El rebuts" the presumption by clear and convincing evidence. Without explaining how the § 2254(d)(2) standard worked with the § 2254(e)(1) presumption, the Court simply noted that "[t]he standard is demanding but not insatiable; as we said the last time this case was here, '[d]eference does not by definition preclude relief.'" Does the Court mean that "deference" is the product of the paired operation of the two provisions? Notice how, in the concluding paragraph, the Court found the state court's factual findings to be both "wrong to a clear and convincing degree" and unreasonable. Would it have been possible in different circumstances for a state court to be wrong to that degree but not unreasonable, or the converse?

2)   Aggregating Differences in Factual Assessment. Justice Thomas attacks each of the four evidentiary arguments in favor of the *Batson* violation: (1) that the prosecution struck black venire members with profiles that were otherwise materially indistinguishable from white venire members; (2) that race accounted for the use of different voir dire "scripts," with certain scripts designed to elicit disqualifying responses from black venire members; (3) jury shuffles consistent with the purpose of moving black members to the end of venire queue, thereby decreasing the odds that they served on the petit jury; and (4) a history of Dallas County prosecutors striking black jurors based on race. The Supreme Court concluded that the evidence on these issues established that the state decision was unreasonable. What role does aggregation of questionable factual determinations play in determining "unreasonability" under § 2254(d)(2)? If no individual finding rises to the level of being unreasonable, can several questionable-but-not-unreasonable findings be aggregated to determine that a state decision was factually unreasonable? Do you think the Court appropriately assessed the totality of the evidence in *Miller-El*?

3)   New Evidence on § 2254(d)(2) Inquiry. Consider Justice Thomas' critique of what he perceives to be the liberal use of material not forming the basis of the state decision:

> The majority's willingness to reach outside the state-court record and embrace evidence never presented to the Texas state courts is hard to fathom. AEDPA mandates that the reasonableness of a state court's factual findings be assessed "in light of the evidence presented in the State court proceeding," 28 U.S.C. § 2254(d)(2), and also circumscribes the ability of federal habeas litigants to present evidence that they "failed to develop" before the state courts. [citing § 2254(e)(2).]

Separate Justice Thomas's criticism into two parts: one involving the source of record material available for § 2254(d)(2) analysis, and one involving what a federal court is allowed to do with the material that is before the state court.

a)   Whether § 2254(d)(2) Inquiry Is Limited to the State Record. First, the text of § 2254(d)(2) does seem to foreclose use of material outside the state record for the purposes of that inquiry; the statute contains the phrase, "in light of the evidence presented in the State court proceeding." We will use the term "intrinsic review" to describe § 2254(d) review that involves only the state record. ("Intrinsic" simply signals that the reasonableness of the premises and factual analysis is assessed without reference to other cases, facts *dehors* the record, etc.) In footnote 2, the Majority states that it does not resolve whether the rule of intrinsic review is waivable, a proposition that Justice Thomas finds deeply problematic. In light of what you know about how § 2254(d) evolved from a nonretroactivity defense, do you think that intrinsic review is waivable? Is § 2254(d) an affirmative defense?[bb] If intrinsic review is not waivable, then which of the evidence considered by *Miller-El II* would be improper?

b)   Whether a State Factual Determination may be Unreasonable under § 2254(d)(2) if it Involves an Updated Theory on the Evidence. Justice Thomas also argued that Miller-El should be foreclosed from arguing evidentiary theories that, even though they were based on evidence before the

---

[bb] For an example of a case stating that the intrinsic review condition is waivable, see Guidry v. Dretke, 429 F.3d 154, 160 (5th Cir 2005).

state court, were presented to the state court differently. The majority has a rejoinder on this point: "But the dissent conflates the difference between evidence that must be presented to the state courts to be considered by federal courts in habeas proceedings and theories about that evidence." Is the fact that the voir dire transcripts were before the state court, and that Miller-El properly presented a *Batson* claim based on voir dire, enough to satisfy an intrinsic review condition? How close is close enough? Can Miller-El's federal arguments be considered part of intrinsic review if he made any arguments about disparate juror treatment to the state courts? Or should the Supreme Court have required that he identify the similarly-situated jurors with particularity?

4)   Is *Miller-El* a Special Case? The Supreme Court has not given much guidance about exactly what counts as a factually unreasonable determination. In *Miller-El II*, the Court points to four categories of evidence that support its conclusion. Do you think there is a reason that the *Miller-El II* Court may have been particularly primed to rule on the unreasonability of the state findings? Does the degree of factual analysis—there was much more excised from the opinion presented here—surprise you?

Remember that the Court had decided *Miller-El I* and, in that decision, the Court granted to Miller-El the certificate of appealability (COA) necessary to obtain appellate review of his claims. *Miller-El I*, while limited to the narrow question of whether a COA should issue, contained very strong language—in an opinion by Justice Kennedy, frequently a swing Justice—indicating that the Court believed that the *Batson* claim was meritorious. Justice Thomas dissented in *Miller-El I*, outlining an argument with respect to the similarly situated jurors that, on remand, the Fifth Circuit panel adopted—in places verbatim. One might read the particularly detailed account of the evidentiary analysis present in *Miller-El II* as an expression of irritation with the Fifth Circuit panel's decision to adopt large chunks of Justice Thomas's dissent in *Miller-El I*.

5)   Factual Unreasonableness as a Limit on Relief. The Majority opinion concludes by stating, "[T]he state court's conclusion was unreasonable as well as erroneous." Why does the Court say that the conclusion was unreasonable *and* erroneous? One might argue that any *conclusion* that is unreasonable is, by definition, erroneous. Consider, however, the relationship between an unreasonable factual determination (or an unreasonable decision) and whether a prisoner should prevail on a claim. A factual determination might have been unreasonable, but a claim might fail on the merits for some other reason. For example, despite the state court having made one unreasonable factual determination, other more important factual determinations might have been reasonable and supported the court's denial of relief on the claim. For that reason, think of § 2254(d)(2) much like § 2254(d)(1), as a "limit on relief." If a prisoner shows that the state decision was based on an unreasonable determination of fact, then the federal court must assess the claim *de novo* to determine whether the prisoners show a constitutional violation.

6)   "Procedural" Versus "Substantive" Unreasonableness. In *Wood v. Allen*, the Supreme Court observed that, for the purposes of § 2254(d)(2) inquiry, "the term unreasonable is difficult to define." 130 S. Ct. 841, 849 (2010) (internal punctuation, alterations, and quotation marks omitted). The Court has repeatedly observed that a decision is not unreasonable simply because if a federal court were assessing the record independently, it would reach a different conclusion. When dealing with a concept that is as elastic as "factual unreasonability," perhaps it helps to subdivide decisions that are based on factually unreasonable determinations into two categories. You might think of the first category as decisions that are based on unreasonable factual determinations because the *procedures* used to find facts were defective. Some courts hold that the failure of the state court to hold a "full and fair hearing" should affect whether the state court's factual findings are reasonable. See, e.g., Hurles v. Ryan, 650 F.3d 1301, 1311 (9th Cir. 2011) (finding state factfinding "fundamentally flawed" when the state court did not offer an "opportunity . . . to develop" the claim.)[cc] You might think of the second category as decisions that are factually unreasonable because they partially rely on the factual determinations that are *substantively* unreasonable. Into which category would you place *Miller-El II*?

7) *Wiggins.* In *Wiggins v. Smith*, 539 U.S. 510 (2003), the Supreme Court held that the prisoner satisfied § 2254(d)(2) because the state court relied on a description of the record's factual content that was demonstrably false. *Wiggins* was a landmark IAC case regarding the obligation of capital defense attorneys to conduct reasonable mitigation investigations. The Court faulted the factfinding by the state court, noting that the Maryland Court of Appeals had "based its conclusion, in part, on a clear factual error—that the 'social service records . . . recorded incidences of . . . sexual abuse.'" The Supreme Court emphasized that, because those "records contain no mention of sexual abuse, much less of the repeated molestations and rapes of petitioner[,]" Wiggins' trial lawyers were constitutionally ineffective for failing to locate the mitigating evidence concerning the abuse their client had suffered as a child. *Wiggins* rejected the Maryland court's "assumption that the records documented instances of this abuse has been shown to be incorrect by 'clear and convincing evidence,' 28 U.S.C. § 2254(e)(1)," and moreover, it emphasized that the "partial reliance on an erroneous factual finding further highlights the unreasonableness of the state court's decision." Thus, as did *Miller-El II, Wiggins* invoked § 2254(d)(2) and § 2254(e)(1) in combination. We turn to that problematic pairing now.

8) Relationship Between 28 U.S.C. § 2254(d)(2) & (e)(1). One of the most persistent sources of interpretive confusion involves the relationship between 28 U.S.C. § 2254(d)(2), the substantive limit on relief for reasonable state factfinding, and § 2254(e)(1), a provision that requires state factual determinations to be presumed correct unless refuted by clear and convincing evidence. In both *Miller-El* cases, the Supreme Court assumed that the § 2254(e)(1) "clear and convincing" standard is incorporated as the standard for unreasonableness in § 2254(d)(2). Reading the two statutes together (*in pari materia*), what is your initial reaction to that treatment? Does § 2254(e)(1) provide the standard for intrinsic review? Or might it supply the standard for something that you

---

[cc] See, e.g., Lambert v. Blackwell, 387 F.3d 210, 239 (3d Cir. 2004) (holding that "[t]he extent to which a state court afforded a defendant adequate procedural means to develop a factual record—whether the defendant was afforded a 'full and fair hearing,' to put it in the parlance of the pre-AEDPA statute—may well affect whether a state court's factual determination was 'reasonable' in 'light of the evidence presented in the State court proceeding' or whether the petitioner has adequately rebutted a presumption that the state court's determination is correct."); Taylor v. Maddox, 366 F.3d 992 (9th Cir. 2004) (holding that the prisoner satisfied § 2254(d)(2) because the state court failed to afford him a hearing to present evidence). In order to assess the reasonableness of the state factfinding, some courts have even imported factors from *Townsend v. Sain*, 372 U.S. 293 (1963) (excerpted later in this Chapter). See, e.g., Earp v. Ornoski 431 F.3d 1158, 1167 (9th Cir. 2005) (citing *Townsend*, 372 U.S. at 313). Some scholars have also advocated such an approach. See Larry W. Yackle, *Federal Evidentiary Hearings Under the New Habeas Corpus Statute*, 6 B.U. Pub. Int. L.J. 135, 140 (1996).

might conceptualize as "extrinsic review"—a federal decision based on evidence outside the state record?

Notwithstanding the Supreme Court's assumption in the *Miller-El* cases, in subsequent opinions it has made clear that the precise interplay between 28 U.S.C. § 2254(e)(1) and (d)(2) remains unresolved. In *Wood v. Allen*, 130 S.Ct. 841, 851 (2010), the Court noted that "[b]ecause the resolution of this case does not turn on them, we leave for another day the questions of how and when § 2254(e)(1) applies in challenges to a state court's factual determinations under § 2254(d)(2)." The Court did note that the word "unreasonable" means something other than "wrong": "It suffices to say, however, that a state-court factual determination is not unreasonable merely because the federal habeas court would have reached a different conclusion in the first instance." For a careful explanation of the argument that the "presumption of correctness" in (e)(1) should be read as independent of the (d)(2) "unreasonableness" requirement, and that state fact-finding should not be presumed correct if it was conducted in a way that was procedurally unfair, see Justin F. Marceau, *Deference and Doubt: The Interaction of § AEDPA 2254(d)(2) and (e)(1)*, 82 Tulane L. Rev. 385 (2007).

In what way are facts to be evaluated differently under § 2254(e)(1) and under § 2254(d)(2)? Perhaps the presumption of correctness in § 2254(e)(1) is the *result* of a determination that the state decision was reasonable under § 2254(d)(2), rather than part of the *process* by which the reasonableness determination is made. What would you say to an interpretation of the statute by which the presumption of correctness and clear and convincing evidence standard from § 2254(e)(1) applied to subsidiary determinations of fact, and where "more global" factual decisions are assessed for reasonableness? Of the various possible interpretations advanced in this Note, which do you find most persuasive and why?

9)   Thomas Jo Miller-El. The legal community watched the *Miller-El* litigation with extraordinary anticipation. At one level, the Supreme Court was confronting complex questions of statutory interpretation and constitutional law. At another level, the Court was wading into the notorious mid-century legacy of the Dallas County prosecutor's office, which had—as the opinion mentions—a well-documented history of adverting to race in its prosecutorial practice. Miller-El was convicted of killing a hotel clerk in the course of a robbery. Twenty years after the litigation started, Thomas Jo Miller-El took a plea deal in which he basically waived his right to an appeal in exchange for a life sentence.[dd]

4. SUPPLEMENTING THE STATE RECORD ON FEDERAL REVIEW

Until *Pinholster*, federal courts frequently conducted evidentiary hearings to determine whether the state decision was unreasonable, particularly under § 2254(d)(1). Recall that § 2254(d)(2) has language requiring that the factual unreasonableness determination be made "in light of" the state record, and that *Pinholster* held that the § 2254(d)(1) inquiry was similarly limited to an assessment of evidence before the state court. After *Pinholster*, however, there are still two major situations in which federal

---

[dd] See Jennifer Emily, Death Penalty Case that Highlighted Jury Bias Ends in Plea Deal, Dallas Morning News, March 20, 2008.

factfinding may be necessary: (1) to conduct merits review when the limit on relief in § 2254(d) does not apply; and (2) to resolve non-merits questions that nonetheless require certain factual determinations. This Section explores when and how federal courts conduct such factfinding.

In pre-*Pinholster* situations in which a federal court looked at new evidence to resolve the reasonableness of a state decision, as well as in situations where federal courts continue to resolve habeas challenges *simpliciter*, the fact intensiveness of the state and federal inquiries varies by claim. Some claims may embody a straightforward challenge to a state court's application of a legal rule. Other claims may require detailed investigation and factfinding. Such fact-intensive claims include the most common constitutional challenge to criminal convictions: IAC claims. IAC claims require analysis of what a defense lawyer did and should have done, along with how effective representation would have affected the outcome of the criminal proceeding. With respect to IAC claims, and to many other types of constitutional challenges, federal adjudication might require: background investigations, mental and physical evaluations, outside interviews, and forensic inquiry. As you read this Section, consider the following over-arching question: Why does habeas law usually foreclose the consideration of new evidence on federal review and, in situations where new evidence is permitted, how must a court balance the new evidence against the evidence adduced in the state proceeding?

A. EVIDENTIARY HEARINGS FROM *TOWNSEND* TO *TAMAYO REYES*

Evidentiary hearings are rare. The Rules Governing Section 2254 Cases (the "2254 Rules" are presented in Appendix E) now provide for the appointment of counsel to conduct discovery (2254 Rule 6(a)), and Section 2254 Rule 8 now provides for the appointment of counsel in a state-inmate case if an evidentiary hearing is ordered. Evidentiary hearings are more common in capital cases, where a prisoner has had appointed counsel from the start. The *2007 Habeas Study* found that less than ten percent of capital cases and less than .03 percent of noncapital cases had evidentiary hearings. *Pinholster* held that a decision's legal reasonableness under 28 U.S.C. § 2254(d)(1) must be measured against the state record, and § 2254(d)(2) expressly requires that the factual reasonableness of the state decision be assessed in light of that state record—so both subsections of § 2254(d) involve "intrinsic review" and no new federal evidence.

Pre-AEDPA, pre-*Pinholster* law worked very differently. A pre-AEDPA study concluded that federal courts held hearings in approximately one percent of habeas cases.[ee] The likelihood of a hearing depended largely on the preference of the presiding judge.[ff] In *Townsend v. Sain*, 372 U.S. 293 (1963), the Supreme Court held that, when the facts in a habeas petition were in dispute, a federal court had to hold an evidentiary hearing unless the inmate had received a "full and fair" hearing in state court or if the in-

---

[ee] See Richard A. Posner, *Report of the Subcommittee on the Role of the Federal Courts* 468–515 (1990); see also Schriro v. Landrigan, 550 U.S. 465 (2007) (Stevens, J., dissenting) ("habeas cases requiring evidentiary hearings have been 'few in number'").

[ff] See Carol S. Steiker & Jordan M. Steiker, *A Tale of Two Nations: Implementation of the Death Penalty in "Executing" Versus "Symbolic" States in the United States*, 84 Tex. L. Rev. 1869, 1902 (2006).

mate deliberately bypassed the opportunity to present the pertinent evidence. The Court explained:

> [S]tate factual determinations not fairly supported by the record cannot be conclusive of federal rights. . . [Moreover, even] if all the relevant facts were presented in the state-court hearing, it may be that the fact-finding procedure there employed was not adequate for reaching reasonably correct results. If the state trial judge has made serious procedural errors[,] . . . a federal hearing is required. Even where the procedure employed does not violate the Constitution, if it appears to be seriously inadequate for the ascertainment of the truth, it is the federal judge's duty to disregard the state findings and take evidence anew. . . Where newly discovered evidence is alleged in a habeas application, evidence which could not reasonably have been presented to the state trier of facts, the federal court must grant an evidentiary hearing.

To determine what evidence was "reasonably" omitted before the state court, The Court adopted a "deliberate bypass" rule:

> If, for any reason not attributable to the inexcusable neglect of petitioner, evidence crucial to the adequate consideration of the constitutional claim was not developed at the state hearing, a federal hearing is compelled. The standard of inexcusable default set down in *Fay v. Noia* adequately protects the legitimate state interest in orderly criminal procedure, for it does not sanction needless piecemeal presentation of constitutional claims in the form of deliberate by-passing of state procedures.

The deliberate-bypass standard should be familiar; recall from the last Chapter that deliberate bypass had been the Warren Court's standard for excusing claims that were either procedurally defaulted or abusive. See Sanders v. United States 373 U.S. 1 (1963) (abuse of the writ); Fay v. Noia, 372 U.S. 391 (1963) (procedural default). Like the deliberate-bypass standards articulated in *Noia* and *Sanders*, the *Townsend* rule is no longer good law.

In *Keeney v. Tamayo-Reyes,* 504 U.S. 1 (1992), the Supreme Court overruled *Townsend's* deliberate-bypass standard in favor of the cause-and-prejudice inquiry that was ascendant in both procedural default and abusive claim doctrine. The Court held, in an opinion by Justice White:

> As in cases of state procedural default, application of the cause-and-prejudice standard to excuse a state prisoner's failure to develop material facts in state court will appropriately accommodate concerns of finality, comity, judicial economy, and channeling the resolution of claims into the most appropriate forum. Applying the cause-and-prejudice standard in cases like this will obviously contribute to the finality of convictions, for requiring a federal evidentiary hearing solely on the basis of a habeas petitioner's negligent failure to develop facts in state-court proceedings dramatically increases the opportunities to relitigate a conviction.

In devising the new rule for when prisoners could obtain federal evidentiary hearings, *Tamayo-Reyes* also analogized to claim exhaustion:

> Furthermore, ensuring that full factual development of a claim takes place in state court channels the resolution of the claim to the most appropriate forum. The state court is the appropriate forum for resolution of factual issues in the first instance, and creating incentives for

the deferral of factfinding to later federal court proceedings can only degrade the accuracy and efficiency of judicial proceedings. This is fully consistent with, and gives meaning to, the requirement of exhaustion. . . Comity concerns dictate that the requirement of exhaustion is not satisfied by the mere statement of a federal claim in state court. Just as the State must afford the petitioner a full and fair hearing on his federal claim, so must the petitioner afford the State a full and fair opportunity to address and resolve the claim on the merits.

The Court emphasized that "applying the cause-and-prejudice standard in this case also advances uniformity in habeas law. There is no good reason to maintain in one area of habeas law a standard that has been rejected in the area in which it was principally enunciated." Finally, the Court adopted a "narrow exception to the cause-and-prejudice requirement" where the petitioner can show that a "fundamental miscarriage of justice would result from failure to hold a federal evidentiary hearing."

Justice O'Connor and three other Justices dissented, arguing that the claim warranted factual development: "Jose Tamayo-Reyes' habeas petition stated that, because he does not speak English, he pleaded nolo contendere to manslaughter without any understanding of what 'manslaughter' means. If this assertion is true, his conviction was unconstitutionally obtained, and Tamayo-Reyes would be entitled to a writ of habeas corpus." The dissent also described how, at the state post-conviction hearing, the state court heard very little evidence about the language barrier: "Tamayo-Reyes was the only witness to testify, but his attorney did not ask him whether his interpreter had translated 'manslaughter' for him." His lawyer introduced only "the deposition testimony of the interpreter, who admitted that he had translated 'manslaughter' only as 'less than murder.'" The dissent emphasized that *Townsend* had not affected the principle that state factfinding be entitled to real weight. The dissent also argued that *Townsend* merely adopted a careful standard to ensure that an evidentiary hearing would be held only if the state court "fairly considered the relevant evidence" and only if the petitioner did not "deliberately [withhold] evidence from the state [court.]"

The dissenters also argued that the federalism concerns underlying procedural default doctrine are different than the federalism concerns present in the evidentiary hearing context. They concluded, "Federalism, comity, and finality are all advanced by declining to permit relitigation of claims in federal court in certain circumstances; these interests are less significantly advanced, once relitigation properly occurs, by permitting district courts to resolve claims based on an incomplete record."

Finally, the dissenters raised a statutory argument: "The Court's decision today cannot be reconciled with subsection (d) of 28 U.S.C. 2254, which Congress enacted only three years after we decided *Townsend*." The dissenters noted that Subsection (d) of the then-controlling statute (as noted, Section 2254(e) now includes some of this language) provided that state court factfinding "shall be presumed to be correct, unless the applicant shall establish" one of eight listed circumstances—circumstances which were chiefly "taken word for word from *Townsend*," including where "the material facts were not adequately developed at the State court hearing."

Not only did the dissenting Justices argue that "overruling *Townsend* would frustrate the evident intent of Congress," but they also identified the bind now facing state inmates. They reasoned that a typical case "will very likely be like this one, where the material facts were not developed because of attorney error." They noted that "effect is more than a little ironic," because a failure to develop material facts at trial would violate *Strickland* and require a new trial. However, "[w]here, as in this case, the state factfinding occurs at a postconviction proceeding, the petitioner has no constitutional right to the effective assistance of counsel, so counsel's poor performance can never constitute 'cause' under the cause and prejudice standard." That is, the decision creates a bind analogous to the one discussed in *Coleman v. Thompson*—a bind that the Court started to address in *Martinez v. Ryan*, 132 S.Ct. 1309 (2012), presented in Chapter 4.

Do you think the cause and prejudice standard for procedural default context works in what we might call an "evidentiary default" context? A consideration common to both contexts is the incentive that federal habeas law creates for state courts to develop a factual record. Over time, federal law has increasingly required greater deference to state findings that are products of reliable procedure. What incentives does a cause-and-prejudice standard create to generate a reliable factual record, with respect to both prisoners and to state courts? How effectively can *pro se* litigants develop such facts during state habeas proceedings—given, as the dissent notes, that they have no entitlement to constitutionally effective counsel? What role should *Townsend* have played in the interpretation of the then-controlling version of § 2254? Four years after *Tamayo-Reyes*, Congress enacted AEDPA, which revised § 2254 in ways that created new interpretive questions for courts confronted with requests for evidentiary hearings.

———

NOTES AND QUESTIONS ON TOWNSEND AND TAMAYO-REYES

1) **The Fundamental Question in *Townsend* and *Tamayo-Reyes*.** The basic question in *Townsend* and *Tamayo-Reyes* involves the circumstances under which a federal court may conduct new factfinding. A federal court might want to conduct factfinding because the state record is incomplete. As you proceed through this Section, think about the different types of interests the federal hearing rules should accommodate, and about how effective the rules are in promoting those interests. Moreover, consider how those interests should affect the interpretation of statutory federal-hearing rules. *Townsend* and *Tamayo-Reyes* are no longer "the law," mostly in the sense that AEDPA replaced them with a set of statutory rules—although the prestatutory decisional law obviously influences how courts interpret habeas provisions.

2) **The Composition of the State Record provided to Federal Courts.** The State does not have to answer a federal habeas petition unless a federal court issues an order requiring it to do so. Once ordered to respond to the petition, however, the State has to specify which documents memorialize the state proceedings. Specifically, Section 2254 Rule 5(c) states: "The answer must also indicate what transcripts (of pretrial, trial, sentencing, or post-conviction proceedings) are available, when they can be furnished, and what proceedings have been recorded but not transcribed." After specifying which material is available, the State then usually has to supply the relevant transcripts, briefs, and court orders. The record may be supplemented on motion by the prisoner or by *sua sponte* order of the federal court. See Section 2254 Rule 7(a).

3) **Access to Counsel.** Federal habeas representation requires: sophisticated legal assessment of the trial record; robust investigation of the circumstances that influenced the proceeding; careful construction of an evidentiary record to support the post-conviction claim; and, of course, competent litigation of the claim itself. There is, however, no constitutional right to have appointed counsel in a federal habeas proceeding.

Few non-capital habeas petitioners are represented by counsel. In non-capital cases, judges may appoint counsel if the "interests of justice" require doing so, see 18 U.S.C. § 3006A(a)(2)(B), and the judges typically make appointments if evidentiary hearings are necessary. In non-capital cases, judges also typically appoint counsel in potentially meritorious and complex cases, cases involving disabled or mentally ill petitioners, or if discovery or expert development of claims is required. See Section 2254 Rule 6(a). Even if the petitioner is represented, however, there is no remedy if the federal habeas lawyer provides ineffective assistance. See 28 U.S.C. § 2254(i).

As of 1988, all capital prisoners are statutorily entitled to appointed federal counsel. See 18 U.S.C. § 3599(a)(2). In *McFarland v. Scott*, 512 U.S. 849 (1994), the Supreme Court held that the district court may appoint counsel even before a habeas petition is filed, so that a lawyer may help draft the petition itself. What sorts of limits would you place on *McFarland*? Should capital prisoners really have access to a lawyer to help write even frivolous habeas petitions? For example, how would you apply *McFarland* to a request for attorney assistance in preparing what seems to be a nonmeritorious *Atkins* claim?

4) Discovery Rule 6. As in any civil case, federal district courts have discretion to order appropriate discovery. Section 2254 Rule 6(a) provides for discovery in habeas proceedings if the petitioner shows "good cause." The Rule reads:

> (a) Leave of Court Required. A judge may, for good cause, authorize a party to conduct discovery under the Federal Rules of Civil Procedure and may limit the extent of discovery. If necessary for effective discovery, the judge must appoint an attorney for a petitioner who qualifies to have counsel appointed under 18 U.S.C. § 3006A.

> (b) Requesting Discovery. A party requesting discovery must provide reasons for the request. The request must also include any proposed interrogatories and requests for admission, and must specify any requested documents.

The Habeas Rules provide for more limited discovery than that permissible under the more generally-applicable Federal Rules of Civil Procedure (FRCP). Under the FRCP, parties are first compelled to make initial automatic disclosures; those are followed by document discovery, written interrogatories, and lengthy witness depositions. They often conclude with expert reports and depositions. See FRCP 26. The process proceeds liberally, and the FRCP permit discovery of "any matter," if non-privileged and not unduly burdensome, that is "relevant to any party's claim or defense." FRCP 26(b). Then again, the Section 2254 Rules allow more liberal discovery than what is available under Rule 16 of the Federal Rules of Criminal Procedure—which is limited to discrete items and does not even include the prosecution's witness list. Do you think that habeas discovery should be closer to the discovery practice in civil or in criminal proceedings?

B. AEDPA'S CHANGES TO EVIDENTIARY HEARINGS

NOTE ON 28 U.S.C. § 2254(e)(1)

You have already encountered 28 U.S.C. § 2254(e)(1) in Section 3, which explores factual defects in state decisions. The sequencing of § 2254(e)(1) requires some explanation. Section 2254(e)(1) provides: "In a proceeding instituted by an application for a writ of habeas corpus by a person in custody pursuant to the judgment of a State court, a determination of a factual issue made by a State court shall be presumed to be correct. The applicant shall have the burden of rebutting the presumption of correctness by clear and convincing evidence." Section 2254(e)(1) is, as the Notes following *Miller-El II* indicate, neither fish nor fowl, in the following sense—it is used both as a feature of what we have called "intrinsic" review under § 2254(d) and as a standard for "extrinsic" review under § 2254(e)(2). The role of § 2254(e)(1) during intrinsic review remains disputed. Understanding § 2254(e)(1) requires an examination of the prior version of § 2254(d) that controlled from 1966 to 1996, which provided:

> In any proceeding instituted in a Federal court by an application for a writ of habeas corpus by a person in custody pursuant to the judgment of a State court, a determination after a hearing on the merits of a factual issue, made by a State court of competent jurisdiction in a proceeding to which the applicant for the writ and the State or an officer or agent thereof were parties, evidenced by a written finding, written opinion, or other reliable and adequate written indicia, shall be presumed to be correct, unless the applicant shall establish or it shall otherwise appear, or the respondent shall admit—

> [the statute then listed various potential defects in the State factfinding procedure, plus a scenario in which "the Federal court on a consideration of such part of the record as a whole concludes that such factual determination is not fairly supported by the record."]

> And in an evidentiary hearing in the proceeding in the Federal court, when due proof of such factual determination has been made, unless [one or more of the defective condition specified exists], the burden shall rest upon the applicant to establish by convincing evidence that the factual determination by the State Court was erroneous.

Note the structure of the then-controlling statute: there was intrinsic review, and if the State prevailed on the intrinsic review, then any factual determination by the state court had to be overcome by clear and convincing evidence; if the prisoner prevailed, then the federal court simply made its own finding based on whatever evidence it wanted (extrinsic review). In other words, the pre-AEDPA version of § 2254(d) included both intrinsic and extrinsic review instructions.

AEDPA has confused courts because, as explained in the notes following *Miller-El II*, some have read the new § 2254(e)(1) as providing a standard for the intrinsic review process. Under that interpretation, the rules for intrinsic review are spread across § 2254(d) and § 2254(e). In *Wood v. Allen*, also discussed in the notes following *Miller-El II*, the Supreme Court acknowledged this confusion and observed that the issue remained open. The interpretation under which § 2254(e)(1) furnishes rules for intrinsic review is explored in the Section on § 2254(d)(2). This Note, by contrast, explores a different interpretation: that § 2254(e)(1) specifies rules for extrinsic review—a presumption of correctness that attaches to determinations involving new evidence and a "clear and convincing" standard for overcoming that presumption.

Consider the breadth of the presumption. It certainly applies to explicit findings of fact made by the state court, but what about findings that are not express? How does the presumption work with respect to "implicit" findings? Should the presumption attach to findings that are supportive of the state outcome or, more rigorously, just those findings that are logically *necessary* to it? In any event, the presumption can be overcome with a showing of clear and convincing evidence.

INTRODUCTORY NOTE ON FEDERAL EVIDENTIARY HEARINGS

28 U.S.C. § 2254(d)(2) permits a state prisoner to obtain habeas relief if the state decision was based on an unreasonable factual determination, but there are other habeas provisions that deal with factual determinations during habeas review. 28 U.S.C. § 2254(e)(1) requires that "a determination of a factual issue made by a State court shall be presumed to be correct[,]" and adds that a state inmate "shall have the burden of rebutting the presumption of correctness by clear and convincing evidence." We will now focus on § 2254(e)(2), which essentially replaces *Tamayo-Reyes*. Section 2254(e)(2) provides that, if the habeas petitioner "failed to develop the factual basis of a claim in State court proceedings, the court shall not hold an evidentiary hearing on the claim" unless very restrictive conditions in subsections (A) and (B) are met. Under these restrictions, the petitioner must show that the particular claim relies on "a new rule of constitutional law, made retroactive to cases on collateral review by the Supreme Court, that was previously unavailable[,]" or on "a factual predicate that could not have been previously discovered through the exercise of due diligence." 28 U.S.C. § 2254(e)(2)(A)(i)-(A)(ii). The petitioner must also show that "the facts underlying the claim would be sufficient to establish by clear and convincing evidence that, but for constitutional error, no reasonable factfinder would have found the applicant guilty of the underlying offense." 28 U.S.C. § 2254(e)(2)(B).

So, to be clear: a prisoner must show *either* that there is a new claim under § 2254(e)(2)(A)(i) or a new factual predicate under § 2254(e)(2)(A)(ii) (one that is newly discovered not for lack of diligence), and then must show that the new claim or factual predicate would qualify the habeas challenge under § 2254(e)(2)(B). *Michael Williams v. Taylor*, 529 U.S. 420 (2000) (excerpted below), was decided the same day as *Terry Williams v. Taylor*, and interpreted § 2254(e)(2). Michael Williams was capitally sentenced for murder. In pursuing federal habeas relief, he conceded that he would not meet the stringent standards for a new federal hearing if he "failed to develop the factual basis of a claim in State court proceedings," per the globally-applicable language in § 2254(e)(2). The Court's decision in *Michael Williams* was unanimous.

Michael Williams v. Taylor

United States Supreme Court
529 U.S. 420 (2000)

■ JUSTICE KENNEDY delivered the opinion of the Court. * * *

I

On the evening of February 27, 1993, Verena Lozano James dropped off [Williams] and his friend Jeffrey Alan Cruse near a local store in a rural area of Cumberland County, Virginia. The pair planned to rob the store's employees and customers using a .357 revolver [Williams] had stolen in the course of a quadruple murder and robbery he had committed two months earlier. Finding the store closed, [Williams] and Cruse walked to the [Morris and Mary Elizabeth] Kellers' home. [Williams] was familiar with the couple, having grown up down the road from where they lived. He told Cruse they would have "a couple thousand dollars." Cruse, who had been holding the .357, handed the gun to [Williams] and knocked on the door. When Mr. Keller opened the door, [Williams] pointed the gun at him as the two intruders forced their way inside. [Williams] and Cruse forced Mr. Keller to the kitchen, where they discovered Mrs. Keller. [Williams] ordered the captives to remove their clothing. While [Williams] kept guard on the Kellers, Cruse searched the house for money and other valuables. He found a .38-caliber handgun and bullets. Upon Cruse's return to the kitchen, [Williams] had Cruse tie their captives with telephone cords. The Kellers were confined to separate closets while the intruders continued ransacking the house.

When they gathered all they wanted, [Williams] and Cruse decided to rape Mrs. Keller. With Mrs. Keller pleading with them not to hurt her or her husband, [Williams] raped her. Cruse did the same. [Williams] then ordered the Kellers to shower and dress and "take a walk" with him and Cruse. As they were leaving, [Williams] told Mrs. Keller he and Cruse were going to burn down the house. Mrs. Keller begged to be allowed to retrieve her marriage license, which she did, guarded by [Williams].

As the prosecution later presented the case, details of the murders were as follows. [Williams], now carrying the .38, and Cruse, carrying the .357, took the Kellers to a thicket down a dirt road from the house. With [Williams] standing behind Mr. Keller and Cruse behind Mrs. Keller, [Williams] told Cruse, "We'll shoot at the count of three." At the third count, [Williams] shot Mr. Keller in the head, and Mr. Keller collapsed to the ground. Cruse did not shoot Mrs. Keller at the same moment. Saying "he didn't want to leave no witnesses," [Williams] urged Cruse to shoot Mrs. Keller. Cruse fired one shot into her head. Despite his wound, Mr. Keller stood up, but [Williams] shot him a second time. To ensure the Kellers were dead, [Williams] shot each of them two or three more times.

After returning to the house and loading the stolen property into the Kellers' jeep, [Williams] and Cruse set fire to the house and drove the jeep to Fredericksburg, Virginia, where they sold some of the property. They threw the remaining property and the .357 revolver into the Rappahannock River and set fire to the jeep.

Pursuing a lead from Verena James, the police interviewed Cruse about the fire at the Kellers' home. [Williams] had fled to Florida. Cruse provided no useful information until the police discovered the bodies of the victims, at which point Cruse consulted counsel. In a plea bargain Cruse agreed to disclose the details of the crimes in exchange for the Commonwealth's promise not to seek the death penalty against him. Cruse described the murders but made no mention of his own act of rape. When the Commonwealth discovered the omission, it revoked the plea agreement and charged Cruse with capital murder.

[Williams] was arrested and charged with robbery, abduction, rape, and the capital murders of the Kellers. At trial in January 1994, Cruse was the Commonwealth's main witness. He recounted the murders as we have just described. Cruse testified [that Williams] raped Mrs. Keller, shot Mr. Keller at least twice, and shot Mrs. Keller several times after she had been felled by Cruse's bullet. He also described [Williams] as the mastermind of the murders. The circumstances of the first plea agreement between the Commonwealth and Cruse and its revocation were disclosed to the jury. Testifying on his own behalf, [Williams] admitted he was the first to shoot Mr. Keller and it was his idea to rob the store and set fire to the house. He denied, however, raping or shooting Mrs. Keller, and claimed to have shot Mr. Keller only once. [Williams] blamed Cruse for the remaining shots and disputed some other parts of Cruse's testimony.

The jury convicted [Williams] on all counts [and sentenced him to death]. * * * [All courts denied relief on direct appeal of the conviction.] * * * Cruse pleaded guilty to the capital murder of Mrs. Keller and the first-degree murder of Mr. Keller. After the prosecution asked the sentencing court to spare his life because of his testimony against [Williams], Cruse was sentenced to life imprisonment.

[Williams] filed a habeas petition in state court alleging, in relevant part, that the Commonwealth failed to disclose a second [informal] agreement it had reached with Cruse after the first one was revoked. * * * Finding no merit to [Williams'] claims, the Virginia Supreme Court dismissed the habeas petition, and we again denied certiorari.

[Williams] filed a habeas petition in the United States District Court for the Eastern District of Virginia on November 20, 1996. In addition to his claim regarding the alleged undisclosed agreement between the Commonwealth and Cruse, the petition raised three claims relevant to questions now before us. First, [Williams] claimed the prosecution had violated *Brady v. Maryland*, 373 U.S. 83 (1963), in failing to disclose a report of a confidential pre-trial psychiatric examination of Cruse. Second, [Williams] alleged his trial was rendered unfair by the seating of a juror who at *voir dire* had not revealed possible sources of bias. Finally, [Williams] alleged one of the prosecutors committed misconduct in failing to reveal his knowledge of the juror's possible bias.

* * * [T]he District Court [ultimately denied] an evidentiary hearing and dismissed the petition, having determined [Williams] could not satisfy § 2254(e)(2)'s requirements.

The Court of Appeals affirmed. * * *

II

A

* * * The Commonwealth argues AEDPA bars [Williams] from receiving an evidentiary hearing on any claim whose factual basis was not developed in state court, absent narrow circumstances not applicable here. [Williams] did not develop, or raise, his claims of juror bias, prosecutorial misconduct, or the prosecution's alleged *Brady* violation regarding Cruse's psy-

chiatric report until he filed his federal habeas petition. [Williams] explains he could not have developed the claims earlier because he was unaware, through no fault of his own, of the underlying facts. As a consequence, [Williams] contends, AEDPA erects no barrier to an evidentiary hearing in federal court.

Section 2254(e)(2), the provision which controls whether [Williams] may receive an evidentiary hearing in federal district court on the claims that were not developed in the Virginia courts, becomes the central point of our analysis. It provides as follows:

"If the applicant has failed to develop the factual basis of a claim in State court proceedings, the court shall not hold an evidentiary hearing on the claim unless the applicant shows that—

"(A) the claim relies on—

"(i) a new rule of constitutional law, made retroactive to cases on collateral review by the Supreme Court, that was previously unavailable; or

"(ii) a factual predicate that could not have been previously discovered through the exercise of due diligence; and

"(B) the facts underlying the claim would be sufficient to establish by clear and convincing evidence that but for constitutional error, no reasonable factfinder would have found the applicant guilty of the underlying offense."

By the terms of its opening clause the statute applies only to prisoners who have "failed to develop the factual basis of a claim in State court proceedings." * * * Here, [Williams] concedes his case does not comply with § 2254(e)(2)(B), so he may receive an evidentiary hearing only if his claims fall outside the opening clause.

* * * [Williams] * * * says the phrase "failed to develop" means lack of diligence in developing the claims, a defalcation he contends did not occur since he made adequate efforts during state-court proceedings to discover and present the underlying facts. * * * We agree with [Williams] * * * that "failed to develop" implies some lack of diligence; but, unlike the Court of Appeals, we find no lack of diligence on [Williams]'s part with regard to two of his three claims.

B

We start, as always, with the language of the statute. Section 2254(e)(2) begins with a conditional clause, "[i]f the applicant has failed to develop the factual basis of a claim in State court proceedings," which directs attention to the prisoner's efforts in state court. We ask first whether the factual basis was indeed developed in state court * * *. Here the answer is no.

The Commonwealth would have the analysis begin and end there. Under its no-fault reading of the statute, if there is no factual development in the state court, the federal habeas court may not inquire into the reasons for the default when determining whether the opening clause of § 2254(e)(2) applies. We do not agree with the Commonwealth's interpretation of the word "failed."

* * * In its customary and preferred sense, "fail" connotes some omission, fault, or negligence on the part of the person who has failed to do something. * * * Had Congress intended a no-fault standard, it would have

had no difficulty in making its intent plain. It would have had to do no more than use, in lieu of the phrase "has failed to," the phrase "did not."

Under the opening clause of § 2254(e)(2), a failure to develop the factual basis of a claim is not established unless there is lack of diligence, or some greater fault, attributable to the prisoner or the prisoner's counsel. * * *

Our interpretation of § 2254(e)(2)'s opening clause has support in *Keeney* v. *Tamayo-Reyes,* 504 U.S. 1 (1992), a case decided four years before AEDPA's enactment. * * * [Tamayo-Reyes] had not developed the facts of his claim in state collateral proceedings, an omission caused by the negligence of his state postconviction counsel. The Court characterized this as the "prisoner's failure to develop material facts in state court." We required the prisoner to demonstrate cause and prejudice excusing the default before he could receive a hearing on his claim * * * .

Section 2254(e)(2)'s initial inquiry into whether "the applicant has failed to develop the factual basis of a claim in State court proceedings" echoes *Keeney*'s language regarding "the state prisoner's failure to develop material facts in state court." In *Keeney*, the Court borrowed the cause and prejudice standard applied to procedurally defaulted claims, deciding there was no reason "to distinguish between failing to properly assert a federal claim in state court and failing in state court to properly develop such a claim." As is evident from the similarity between the Court's phrasing in *Keeney* and the opening clause of § 2254(e)(2), Congress intended to preserve at least one aspect of *Keeney*'s holding: prisoners who are at fault for the deficiency in the state-court record must satisfy a heightened standard to obtain an evidentiary hearing. To be sure, in requiring that prisoners who have not been diligent satisfy § 2254(e)(2)'s provisions rather than show cause and prejudice, and in eliminating a freestanding "miscarriage of justice" exception, Congress raised the bar *Keeney* imposed on prisoners who were not diligent in state-court proceedings. * * *

We are not persuaded by the Commonwealth's further argument that anything less than a no-fault understanding of the opening clause is contrary to AEDPA's purpose to further the principles of comity, finality, and federalism. * * *

It is consistent with these principles to give effect to Congress' intent to avoid unneeded evidentiary hearings in federal habeas corpus, while recognizing the statute does not equate prisoners who exercise diligence in pursuing their claims with those who do not. * * * Yet comity is not served by saying a prisoner "has failed to develop the factual basis of a claim" where he was unable to develop his claim in state court despite diligent effort. In that circumstance, an evidentiary hearing is not barred by § 2254(e)(2).

III

Now we apply the statutory test. If there has been no lack of diligence at the relevant stages in the state proceedings, the prisoner has not "failed to develop" the facts under § 2254(e)(2)'s opening clause, and he will be excused from showing compliance with the balance of the subsection's requirements. We find lack of diligence as to one of the three claims but not as to the other two.

A

[Williams] did not exercise the diligence required to preserve the claim that nondisclosure of Cruse's psychiatric report was in contravention of *Brady*. * * * There are repeated references to a "psychiatric" or "mental health" report in a transcript of Cruse's sentencing proceeding, a copy of which [Williams'] own state habeas counsel attached to the state habeas petition he filed with the Virginia Supreme Court. The transcript reveals that Cruse's attorney described the report with details that should have alerted counsel to a possible *Brady* claim. * * *

* * * [W]e must determine if the requirements in the balance of § 2254(e)(2) are satisfied so that [Williams]'s failure is excused. Subparagraph (B) of § 2254(e)(2) conditions a hearing upon a showing, by clear and convincing evidence, that no reasonable factfinder would have found [Williams] guilty of capital murder but for the alleged constitutional error. [Williams] concedes he cannot make this showing * * *. * * * [W]e affirm the Court of Appeals' judgment barring an evidentiary hearing on this claim.

B

We conclude [Williams] has met the burden of showing he was diligent in efforts to develop the facts supporting his juror bias and prosecutorial misconduct claims in collateral proceedings before the Virginia Supreme Court.

[Williams]'s claims are based on two of the questions posed to the jurors by the trial judge at *voir dire*. First, the judge asked prospective jurors, "Are any of you related to the following people who may be called as witnesses?" Then he read the jurors a list of names, one of which was "Deputy Sheriff Claude Meinhard." Bonnie Stinnett, who would later become the jury foreperson, had divorced Meinhard in 1979, after a 17-year marriage with four children. Stinnett remained silent, indicating the answer was "no." Meinhard, as the officer who investigated the crime scene and interrogated Cruse, would later become the prosecution's lead-off witness at trial.

After reading the names of the attorneys involved in the case, including one of the prosecutors, Robert Woodson, Jr., the judge asked, "Have you or any member of your immediate family ever been represented by any of the aforementioned attorneys?" Stinnett again said nothing, despite the fact Woodson had represented her during her divorce from Meinhard. * * *

The trial record contains no evidence which would have put a reasonable attorney on notice that Stinnett's non-response was a deliberate omission of material information. * * * Counsel had no reason to believe Stinnett had been married to Meinhard or been represented by Woodson. The underdevelopment of these matters was attributable to Stinnett and Woodson, if anyone. * * * [I]f the prisoner has made a reasonable effort to discover the claims to commence or continue state proceedings, § 2254(e)(2) will not bar him from developing them in federal court. * * * Because of Stinnett and Woodson's silence, there was no basis for an investigation into Stinnett's marriage history. Section 2254(e)(2) does not apply to [Williams]'s related claims of juror bias and prosecutorial misconduct.

Our analysis should suffice to establish cause for any procedural default [Williams] may have committed in not presenting these claims to the Virginia courts in the first instance. Questions regarding the standard for determining the prejudice that [Williams] must establish to obtain relief on these claims can be addressed by the Court of Appeals or the District Court in the course of further proceedings. * * *

The judgment of the Court of Appeals is affirmed in part and reversed in part, and the case is remanded for further proceedings consistent with this opinion.

It is so ordered.

NOTES AND QUESTIONS ON MICHAEL WILLIAMS

1) **"Failed to develop."** Pay attention to the part of the statute that *Michael Williams* interprets. In full, 28 U.S.C. § 2254(e)(2) provides:

> **(2)** If the applicant has failed to develop the factual basis of a claim in State court proceedings, the court shall not hold an evidentiary hearing on the claim unless the applicant shows that—
>
> > **(A)** the claim relies on—
> >
> > > (i) a new rule of constitutional law, made retroactive to cases on collateral review by the Supreme Court, that was previously unavailable; or
> > >
> > > (ii) a factual predicate that could not have been previously discovered through the exercise of due diligence; and
> >
> > **(B)** the facts underlying the claim would be sufficient to establish by clear and convincing evidence that but for constitutional error, no reasonable factfinder would have found the applicant guilty of the underlying offense.

Michael Williams is a decision about the preambular text of 28 U.S.C. § 2254(e)(2), which requires a court to apply subsections (A) and (B) only when "the applicant has failed to develop the factual basis of a claim in State court proceedings." Virginia wanted a reading of the statute that would not turn on diligence. Why would Virginia's preferred reading be described as a "no fault" standard?

The Supreme Court rejected Virginia's preferred reading. *Michael Williams* held that a prisoner does not "fail to develop" a claim in state court unless there was a lack of diligence. But does § 2254(e)(2) already have a diligence rule in Subsection (A)(ii)? What is the effect of reading a diligence standard into the globally-applicable language? In other words, what does a state prisoner avoid by making a showing of diligence that stops the § 2254(e)(2) inquiry before it reaches Subsections (A) and (B)?

Or, consider the possibility—ultimately endorsed by the Supreme Court—that the diligence required by the globally-applicable "failed to develop" language and the "diligence" required by § 2254(e)(2)(A)(ii) require a prisoner to be diligent about different things. In a passage omitted from the main excerpt, the Court elaborated:

> Diligence for purposes of the opening clause depends upon whether the prisoner made a reasonable attempt, in light of the information available at the time, to investigate and pursue claims in state court ... Though lack of diligence will not bar an evidentiary hearing if efforts to discover

the facts would have been in vain, see § 2254(e)(2)(A)(ii), and there is a convincing claim of innocence, see § 2254(e)(2)(B), only a prisoner who has neglected his rights in state court need satisfy these conditions. The statute's later reference to diligence pertains to cases in which the facts could not have been discovered, whether there was diligence or not. In this important respect §2254(e)(2)(A)(ii) bears a close resemblance to (e)(2)(A)(i), which applies to a new rule that was not available at the time of the earlier proceedings

Are you convinced by the Court's distinction between the two types of "diligence"?

2) Applying the "Diligence" Rule. The Supreme Court held that Williams was not diligent in his presentation of the *Brady* claim, but that there was no failure of diligence in his presentation of the claims based on juror bias and prosecutorial misconduct. The Court held that that Williams was not diligent (and therefore failed to develop the *Brady* claim) because the psychiatric report—the *Brady* material at issue—was discussed in some of the hearings. The Court, however, held that there was no lapse of diligence—as to the juror bias and prosecutorial misconduct claims—when Williams' attorneys failed to check county marital records. Did the Court draw the right line in applying the diligence standard it announced?

3) Treatment of *Keeney* v. *Tamayo-Reyes*. In *Michael Williams*, the Court remarked: "Congress intended to preserve at least one aspect of *Keeney*'s holding: prisoners who are at fault for the deficiency in the state-court record must satisfy a heightened standard to obtain an evidentiary hearing."[gg] Recall that *Tamayo-Reyes* incorporated the cause and prejudice standard from procedural default law and applied it to what we have been calling "evidentiary default" for the purposes of obtaining a federal hearing. Consider two objections to the Court's appropriation of *Tamayo-Reyes*. First, is the standard of diligence articulated by *Michael Williams* closer to the cause-and-prejudice rule or to some earlier variant of the deliberate bypass standard that it displaced? In other words, is the degree of fault for the failure to develop the claim really calibrated at a level consistent with *Tamayo-Reyes*? Second, to the extent that § 2254(e)(2) was supposed to incorporate *Tamayo-Reyes*, do you think that work is done by the globally-applicable "failed to develop" language, or by the cause-and-prejudice rules in § 2254(e)(2)(A)(ii) and (2)(B), respectively? If the latter, then would the result in *Michael Williams* be different?

4) The Role of Attorney Error. *Michael Williams* reflects the prevailing understanding of a lawyer's relationship to a client as that between an agent and a principal. For that reason, a lack of diligence on the part of a prisoner's attorney-agent is charged to the prisoner-principal. When the Court says that Williams "failed to develop" the *Brady* claim, it simply means that Williams' attorney was on notice that there was potentially-supportive evidence. Should we punish federal habeas claimants for the failures of their counsel? And, if the answer is yes, then should there be a difference when the defective representation occurs during trial or direct review, as opposed to during post-conviction proceedings?

[gg] In *Michael Williams*, the Court refers to *Keeney v. Tamayo-Reyes* using the short form "*Keeney*", but we use the short form *Tamayo-Reyes*. This Book observes the general rule that the short-form citation of a habeas case should use the name of the prisoner, not the institutional officer. (*Strickland* is the major exception.) Tamayo-Reyes was the prisoner in the case.

To take the last question from the previous paragraph a step further, what happens if the lawyer representing the petitioner was ineffective and did not develop crucial facts at the state post-conviction hearing? Is "diligence" the same level of performance as is "constitutionally effective" under *Strickland*— the law for IAC purposes? Do you think that the decision in *Martinez*, which recognizes that deficient state post-conviction representation can constitute cause for excusing procedural default of an IAC claim, will affect the Court's interpretation of "failed to develop" in § 2254(e)(2)? Or do you think that *Michael Williams* already decided that issue?

5) Actual Innocence and Death Ineligibility. *Michael Williams* discusses AEDPA's statutory changes to the treatment of "innocence" for the purposes of obtaining a federal evidentiary hearing. Do you understand the difference? What is the effect of eliminating the "miscarriage of justice" exception for federal hearings—which included innocence claims—and instead making innocence the touchstone of the prejudice inquiry? What would happen if a prisoner had powerful evidence of innocence that the prisoner failed to develop in federal court? If Williams had failed to develop the innocence claim in state court, and if he had not been diligent within the meaning of § 2254(e)(2)(A)(ii), then what would the result have been under the rest of the § 2254(e)(2) inquiry? Would a non-diligent prisoner with even the strongest innocence claim be entitled to a federal evidentiary hearing? And if the prisoner is not entitled to such a hearing, then how else might the prisoner obtain some sort of federal relief on the claim?

Consider how the change in wording affects claims of death ineligibility. How would an *Atkins* claimant—with cause—fare under § 2254(e)(2)? The prejudice requirement provides that a prisoner must show that "no reasonable factfinder would have found the applicant guilty of the underlying offense." This seems to leave no room for evidentiary hearings involving death ineligibility claims for which the prisoner can show cause and prejudice, despite the way that the provision, just as the provision in 2244(b)(2)(B)(ii) regarding successive petitions, appeared to borrow its "clear and convincing" evidence standard from the *Sawyer v. Whitley* standard for death-ineligibility challenges. Do you think the text reflects a drafting error? If so, how should courts treat it? As Chapter 4 notes in the discussion of the similar successive petition provision, lower courts are divided on this issue.[hh]

6) Comparison to the Successive Petition Provisions. There is an important difference in the structure of § 2254(e)(2) and § 2244(b)(2). The evidentiary hearing provision has different conjunctions, and requires the heightened showing of innocence for both excuses related to new rules of constitutional law and new facts. The successive petition provisions in § 2244(b)(2), in contrast, permits an excuse based on new rules of constitutional law and a second excuse based on new facts with a heightened showing of innocence. Is the discrepancy a drafting error, or did Congress mean to require, in the evidentiary hearing section, that a prisoner satisfy the heightened showing of innocence for both the new-law and new-fact excuses? The Supreme Court has noted that, although AEDPA changes to the successive petition and evidentiary hearing rule adopt a

---

[hh] Compare, e.g., Burris v. Parke, 116 F.3d 256, 258 (7th Cir. 1997) ("We have held that identical language in § 2244(b)(2)(B)(ii) refers unambiguously to the offense of conviction and does not permit proceedings concerning the sentence.") and, e.g., Jackson v. Norris, 615 F.3d 959, 962 (8th Cir. 2010) ("An Atkins hearing is not barred by 28 U.S.C. § 2254(e)(2).").

standard "similar" to *Sawyer,* there is no analogous AEDPA provision governing procedural defaults. Therefore, the Court has reasoned, the statutory provisions are "inapplicable" and the *Schlup* standard still applies in the procedural default context. See House v. Bell, 547 U.S. 518, 539 (2006). Would Congress have intended to leave a less restrictive miscarriage-of-justice or innocence-related excuse in the procedural default context than it requires in the successive petition and evidentiary hearing contexts?

7) Section 2254(e)(2) Restrictions on State Parties. In 2010, the Supreme Court denied a certiorari petition in a case in which the Eighth Circuit reversed a district court habeas grant. The appeals court held that the district court order was based on a federal evidentiary hearing that should not have happened. The State, however, had not asserted its § 2254(e)(2) objection to the hearing until *after* the hearing had concluded. Justice Sotomayor, joined by Justice Ginsburg, dissented from the order denying certiorari and stated:

> Today the Court refuses to review the Eighth Circuit's conclusion that a State may withhold an objection to a federal habeas evidentiary hearing until after the hearing is complete, the constitutional violation established, and habeas relief granted. Because I believe such a rule enables, and even invites, States to manipulate federal habeas proceedings to their own strategic advantage at an unacceptable cost to justice, I respectfully dissent.

Williams v. Hobbs, 131 S.Ct 558 (2010) (Sotomayor, J., dissenting).

In that case, Justice Sotomayor pointed out that, "rather than reveal an objection to the hearing, the record indicates that the State affirmatively consented to the hearing and sought to use the hearing to its own strategic advantage." Indeed, the State had "relied on new evidence *developed at the hearing* to contest the court's prior conclusion, *on the state-court record,* that defense counsel's performance had been deficient." Justice Sotomayor concluded: "I simply cannot see how this record suggests anything other than a deliberate strategy by the State to use the hearing to fortify the record in support of the state-court decision and to object to the hearing only if and when that strategy failed."

Justice Sotomayor highlights an important difference in the way that 28 U.S.C. § 2254(e)(2) applies to prisoner and government parties. Section 2254(e)(2) restricts the ability of prisoners to introduce new evidence in federal habeas proceedings, but does not formally apply to state respondents. Under federal habeas law, states are permitted to introduce evidence that they "failed to raise" in state proceedings. What policies might support a distinction between a state and a petitioner? Should there be party parity on this question?

8) Hearings on Non-merits Questions. *Michael Williams* and most of the supplementing Notes involve hearings on the merits of a claim, but federal evidentiary hearings may be necessary for many things *other than* constitutional merit. A judge might require an evidentiary hearing to decide a procedural defense discussed in Chapter 4, for example.[ii] An evidentiary hearing might be

---

[ii] See, e.g., Holloway v. Horn, 355 F.3d 707, 716 (3rd Cir. 2004) (hearing on procedural default questions of cause and prejudice); Amrine v. Bowersox, 128 F.3d 1222, 1228–29 (8th Cir. 1997) (hearing on whether a prisoner satisfied the *Schlup* exception for a "miscarriage of justice"); Purnell v. Missouri Dep't of Corrections, 753 F.2 703, 708 (8th Cir. 1985) (hearing on whether a prisoner failed to exhaust).

necessary to determine, among other things, whether there is cause for procedural default, whether a claim was "available" within the meaning of certain statutory language, or whether a prisoner showed some quantum of diligence. What are some other examples where a state prisoner might require a federal evidentiary hearing that does not involve a final merits assessment?

After you have become comfortable with the concept of a non-merits hearing in federal court, try to think about how the existence of such hearings influences your interpretation of the statute. For example, can § 2254(e)(2) even apply to an issue—such as whether the statute of limitations should be equitably tolled—that is never developed in state court because it is not ever a question a state decides? Cf. Fleming v. Evans, 481 F.3d 1249, 1256–57 (10th Cir. 2007) (remanding case for evidentiary hearing on equitable tolling). Could § 2254(e)(1) still apply in situations in which the federal procedural question involves some evidentiary fact that was adjudicated in the process of deciding a related question in federal court?

9)　The Balance of 28 U.S.C. § 2254(e)(2). Remember that *Michael Williams* only deals with the globally-applicable "failed to develop" language in § 2254(e)(2). There are, however, other parts of § 2254(e)(2) that courts must interpret and apply. Section 2254(e)(2)(A)(i) sets forth a "new rule" exception for federal evidentiary hearings, and § 2254(e)(2)(A)(ii) sets forth an exception for newly discovered facts (with a diligence requirement). Section 2254(e)(2)(B) is effectively a prejudice showing, which a prisoner must make irrespective of whether the hearing is sought under Subsection (e)(2)(A)(i) or (e)(2)(A)(ii). Why is there a cause (diligence) requirement for a new factual predicate, but not for new law? In order to meet the prejudice requirement, a prisoner must show that "the facts underlying the claim would be sufficient to establish by clear and convincing evidence that but for constitutional error, no reasonable factfinder would have found the applicant guilty of the underlying offense." Is that standard of prejudice too high when the question is just whether a federal evidentiary hearing should happen?

5. HARMLESS ERROR

As Professor Charles Ogletree explains, "Traditionally at common law, even the most technical error at trial resulted in automatic reversal." Charles J. Ogletree, Jr., *The Supreme Court, 1990 Term, Comment: Arizona v. Fulminante: The Harm Of Applying Harmless Error To Coerced Confessions*, 105 Harv. L. Rev. 152, 156 (1991). Over time, the practice came under fire because even picayune and technical errors required reversal. Modern procedure, with its incredible complexity, could not accommodate the *per se* rule. The federal courts began using a harmless error rule in 1919, which is now reflected in Fed. R. Crim. P. 52(a). By 1967, when the U.S. Supreme Court issued its first major harmless error opinion, all fifty states had some harmless error rule in criminal cases. See Chapman v. California, 386 U.S. 18, 22 (1967). On appeal and in post-conviction proceedings, judges must now decide which mistakes are serious enough to require a new trial.

Chief Justice Roger Traynor spent three decades as a California Justice, served seven years as the Chief Justice, and is considered one of this country's greatest state jurists. In a oft-cited book passage, he poetically captures the many dimensions of the harmless-error concept:

> Errors are the insects in the world of law, traveling through it in swarms, often unnoticed in their endless procession. Many are plainly harmless; some appear ominously harmful. Some, for all the benign appearance of their spindly traces, mark the way for a plague of followers that deplete trials of fairness.
>
> The well-being of the law encompasses a tolerance for harmless errors adrift in an imperfect world. Its well-being must also encompass the capacity to ward off the destroyers. So an inquiry into what makes an error harmless, though one of philosophical tenor, is also an intensely practical inquiry into the health and sanitation of the law.
>
> From the traffic pattern of errors we have much to learn about judicial discretion in the countless leeways where judges and can raise or lower the standards of judicial responsibility.

Roger J. Traynor, *The Riddle of Harmless Error* ix (1970). As Chief Justice Traynor describes, trial mistakes are legion: judges improperly admit or exclude evidence; juries may receive improper instructions; courts violate enacted rules of procedure; lawyers are constitutionally ineffective; prosecutors withhold evidence; attorneys with conflicting interests represent clients; trials are not speedy; verdicts reflect the wrong standard of proof—and so on and so forth.

NOTES ON HARMLESS CONSTITUTIONAL ERROR

1)   Emergence of Harmless Error Rules. Prior to 1967, constitutional rights were not subject to harmless error analysis; the only errors that could be harmless were non-constitutional. In the meantime, however, the Federal Rules of Civil and Criminal Procedure adopted harmless error rules, as did many state courts. In *Chapman*, however, the Supreme Court concluded that constitutional error could be harmless. Writing for the Court, Justice Black emphasized the important role that the harmless error concept plays in American law: "All of these rules, state or federal, serve a very useful purpose insofar as they block setting aside convictions for small errors or defects that have little, if any, likelihood of having changed the result of the trial."

2)   A Generous Rule. Although *Chapman* held that there was such a thing as harmless constitutional error, it set a standard for harmlessness that—at least from a more modern perspective—seems favorable to defendants. This slant was no accident; the Supreme Court intervened in *Chapman* because the California state rule set too high a bar for harmfulness. The Court ruled that the standard should be whether "there is a reasonable possibility that the evidence complained of might have contributed to the conviction." Putting it differently, the state would have to show that error was "harmless beyond a reasonable doubt." The harmless-error test would therefore avoid retrial for insignificant errors—what we might think of as technicalities—but not those for which there is some reasonable possibility that they affected the trial outcome. The Supreme Court was careful to note that some constitutional errors— "structural errors"—are not amenable to harmless error analysis. Justice Black wrote that some "constitutional rights [are] so basic to a fair trial that their infraction can never be treated as harmless." (We will have more to say about what these types of errors are shortly.)

3) Ubiquity of Harmless Error Defenses. Empirically speaking, the government frequently argues harmless error as a defense on appeal from criminal convictions. See William M. Landes and Richard A. Posner, *Harmless Error*, 30 J Legal Stud 161, 161 (2001). The development of the harmless-error doctrine reflects the principle that "the Constitution entitles a criminal defendant to a fair trial, not a perfect one." Delaware v. Van Arsdall, 475 U.S. 673, 681 (1985). *Van Arsdall* explained that harmless error is designed to reinforce the trial as the main event for fact-finding: "[t]he harmless-error doctrine recognizes the principle that the central purpose of a criminal trial is to decide the factual question of the defendant's guilt or innocence." At this point, you can probably guess both that harmless error doctrine migrated from appellate to post-conviction review and that the rules diverge somewhat in the two contexts.

4) The Judicial Approach. How does a court decide whether the trial was fair enough? The reviewing judge must analyze whether an error affected the outcome, which can be difficult when the analysis involves only a written trial record. After all, the jury is a something of a black box, and no outside observer can know for certain which information drove the verdict. Nevertheless, to make the best assessment of prejudice possible, the harmless error analysis requires holistic scrutiny of the trial. Whether a particular act or omission is harmful depends substantially on the circumstances under which it occurred. What factors do you think should be important in assessing harm? For example, how can you tell what role that an improperly-admitted confession or piece of eyewitness testimony played at trial? Conversely, what factors might determine the effect of improperly excluding evidence that *should* have been admitted at trial—if, for example, the court should have allowed the defense to conduct a DNA test?

5) Bibliography. For scholarship on harmless error, see Harry T. Edwards, *To Err Is Human, But Not Always Harmless: When Should Legal Error Be Tolerated?*, 70 N.Y.U. L. Rev. 1167, 1205–09 (1995) (favoring an "effect-on-the-verdict" approach to harmless error over a "guilt-based" approach); Martha A. Field, *Assessing the Harmlessness of Federal Constitutional Error—A Process in Need of a Rationale*, 125 U Pa. L. Rev 15, 60–61 (1976) (favoring a test that considers primarily whether the error influenced the verdict, with allowances made for situations where erroneously-admitted evidence is cumulative); Sam Kamin, *Harmless Error and the Rights/Remedies Split*, 88 Va. L. Rev. 1, 72, 78–86 (2002) (arguing that harmless-error rules are uniquely responsible for stagnating the development of constitutional law); Gregory Mitchell, *Against "Overwhelming" Appellate Activism: Constraining Harmless Error Review*, 82 Cal. L. Rev. 1335, 1341 (1994) (providing empirical analysis of wide variation in judicial application of harmless error doctrines); Tom Stacy & Kim Dayton, *Rethinking Harmless Constitutional Error*, 88 Colum. L. Rev. 79, 82–83 (1988) (urging a harmless error doctrine unrelated to truth-determination). Is the concept of harmless error a creature of "constitutional common law" that Congress could reverse? See Craig Goldblatt, *Comment, Harmless Error as Constitutional Common Law: Congress' Power to Reverse Arizona v. Fulminante*, 60 U. Chi. L. Rev. 985, 1004 (1993).

NOTES ON STRUCTURAL ERROR

1)   The Concept of Structural Error. Although some constitutional errors can be harmless, others are presumptively harmful—in other words, claims of certain kind of constitutional error require no showing of actual prejudice to the trial result. In *Arizona v. Fulminante*, 499 U.S. 279 (1991), the Court addressed whether the erroneous admission of a coerced confession can ever be harmless. Affirming the principle that some types of constitutional error require new trials without inquiry into how the error affects the result, *Fulminante* observed that "structural" errors "defy analysis by 'harmless-error' standards." Structural errors are those "affecting the framework within which the trial proceeds, rather than simply an error in the trial process itself." Other errors that the Court has designated as structural—or has otherwise exempt from harmless error analysis—include: the Equal Protection right to be free from exclusion of members of defendant's race from a grand jury, *Vasquez v. Hillery*, 474 U.S. 254 (1986); the Sixth Amendment right to self-representation at trial, *McKaskle v. Wiggins*, 465 U.S. 168, 177–178, n. 8 (1984); the Sixth Amendment right to a public trial, *Waller v. Georgia*, 467 U.S. 39, 49, n. 9 (1984); the right to an impartial judge, *Edwards v. Balisok*, 520 U.S. 641, 647 (1997); and the right to trial by jury, *Rose v. Clark*, 478 U.S. 570, 577–78 (1986). For a comprehensive list of additional types of errors that the Court has found to be "structural," see Hertz & Liebman, *FHCPP*, at § 31.3.

2)   Can Serious Error be Harmless? Returning to the precise question in *Fulminante*, can an erroneous admission of a coerced confession be harmless error? Justice White, in a dissenting portion of his *Fulminante* opinion (he otherwise wrote for the Court), argued that "*Chapman* specifically noted three constitutional errors that could not be categorized as harmless error: using a coerced confession against a defendant in a criminal trial, depriving a defendant of counsel, and trying a defendant before a biased judge." He reasoned that "[a] defendant's confession is probably the most probative and damaging evidence that can be admitted against him, so damaging that a jury should not be expected to ignore it even if told to do so, and because in any event it is impossible to know what credit and weight the jury gave to the confession." (Internal citations and quotation marks omitted.)

Chief Justice Rehnquist, who authored the majority opinion on this point, countered that "[t]his Court has applied harmless-error analysis to the violation of other constitutional rights similar in magnitude and importance and involving the same level of police misconduct." Injecting a note of legal realism, he added that:

> Of course an involuntary confession may have a more dramatic effect on the course of a trial than do other trial errors—in particular cases it may be devastating to a defendant—but this simply means that a reviewing court will conclude in such a case that its admission was not harmless error; it is not a reason for eschewing the harmless-error test entirely.

In what kind of case could you imagine that introducing an involuntary confession at trial would be a harmless error?

3)   The Current Boundaries. The distinctions between errors that can be harmless and those that are structural are not always clear. Failure to instruct a jury on the reasonable doubt standard is not analyzed using a harmless error test. See Jackson v. Virginia, 443 U.S. 307, 320, n. 14 (1979). Contrast *Jackson*, however, with Kentucky v. Whorton, 441 U.S. 786 (1979), which held that failure to instruct the jury on the presumption of innocence was *not* structural error. Can you articulate a meaningful principle for distinguishing between structural and harmless instructional error?

4) Native Prejudice Inquiries. Other errors require no harm inquiry because they already contain a harm standard that is "native" to the constitutional claim itself. For example, an IAC claim requires a showing of ineffectiveness, but also a showing of a "reasonable probability" that the ineffectiveness prejudiced the outcome. The harmless-error inquiry is effectively built into the IAC prejudice prong, so courts do not require a showing of harm beyond that necessary to establish the IAC claim itself. Similarly, because there is a showing of harmfulness native to *Brady* claims—"a reasonable probability that, had the evidence been disclosed to the defense, the result of the proceeding would have been different"—no harmless-error analysis is necessary. The Court adopted that approach in *Bagley v. U.S.* 473 U.S. 667, 682 (1985). In a sense, the prejudice requirement of harmless error has been incorporated or built into the constitutional claim itself.

Both constitutional claims—IAC and *Brady* claims—were developed by the Supreme Court on habeas review, and their structure reflected the Court's growing concern with limiting habeas reversals to outcome-affective errors. As we will discuss in the next set of Notes, however, the Supreme Court—having incorporated the "prejudice" requirement piecemeal into perhaps the two most significant constitutional rights litigated in federal habeas cases—would ultimately use *Brecht v. Abrahamson* to extend that prejudice requirement to all other constitutional claims. At the time the opinions announcing them came down, IAC and *Brady* claims may have seemed like exceptions to the generally-applicable harmless error standard (*Chapman*); but, after *Brecht*, those early decisions look more like the precursors to the *Brecht* harmless error rule, discussed below.

5) Bibliography. For scholarship exploring and critiquing the concept of structural error, see Amy Knight Burns, *Insurmountable Obstacles: Structural Errors, Procedural Default, and Ineffective Assistance of Counsel*, 64 Stan. L. Rev. 727 (2012) (arguing in favor of increased use of "presumed" error in procedural default analysis); David McCord, *The "Trial"/"Structural" Error Dichotomy: Erroneous, and Not Harmless*, 45 U. Kan. L. Rev. 1401 (1997) (arguing that the analytic distinction between trial and structural error is logically flawed); Charles J. Ogletree, Jr., *Arizona v. Fulminante: The Harm of Applying Harmless Error to Coerced Confessions*, 105 Harv. L. Rev. 152, 161–65 (1991) (criticizing the use of harmless error doctrine for coerced confessions). For experimental work examining impact of evidence on mock-jurors, see Saul M. Kassin & Holly Sukel, *Coerced Confessions and the Jury: An Experimental Test of the "Harmless Error" Rule*, 21 Law & Hum. Behav. 27, 28 (1997).

6) Plea Bargaining and Prejudice. Recall from the previous Section that the Supreme Court has extended IAC framework to the plea bargaining phase of the criminal process. In doing so, the Court has raised difficult questions about what the requirement of "prejudice" means where there is no trial outcome against which to evaluate harm. In *Hill v. Lockhart*, 474 U.S. 52, 59 (1985), the Court first extended the *Strickland v. Washington* test to plea bargaining and gave the following test for prejudice: whether "but for counsel's errors, [the defendant] would not have pleaded guilty and would have insisted on going to trial." What does that formulation mean: does the court conduct an objective inquiry into what a defendant would have done during a plea negotiation? Is the inquiry limited to whether the defendant would have fared worse by taking the case to a trial? Or does the inquiry permit a realistic assessment of what alternative plea offers might have been forthcoming? In *Padilla v. Kentucky*, 130 S. Ct. 1473, 1485 (2010), the Court explained that, to show prejudice, "a petitioner must convince the court that a decision to reject the plea bargain would have been rational under the circumstances." In *Lafler v. Cooper*, 132 S.Ct. 362 (2012), and *Missouri v. Frye*, 132 S.Ct. 1399 (2012), the Supreme Court held that a prisoner can establish prejudice if counsel failed to convey a plea offer or gave incorrect advice about the risks of going to trial.

The Supreme Court has moved towards a contextual understanding of what prejudice means during plea bargaining, but a host of unanswered questions remain. For a detailed explanation of the problem of prejudice during plea bargaining, see Jenny Roberts, *Proving Prejudice, Post*-Padilla, 54 How. L.J. 693, 733 (2011). Professor Roberts argues that prejudice in the plea bargaining context should also encompass the situations in which there is a "(1) reasonable probability of a second plea that is more favorable to the defendant; or (2) reasonable probability of a sentence that is more favorable with effective assistance than it was with ineffective assistance." Do you think that a post-conviction judge should consider prejudice in the context of what plea deals the prosecution might have otherwise offered? How should post-conviction judges weigh the impact that potential deportation would have on non-citizens facing conviction for an offense that makes them eligible for removal, and where the defense lawyer incorrectly or failed to advise the client concerning those immigration consequences? For an analysis of unresolved questions regarding the immigration consequences of a guilty plea and prejudice, see Heidi Altman, *Prosecuting Post*-Padilla*: State Interests and the Pursuit of Justice for Noncitizen Defendants*, 101 Geo L. J. 1, 38–40 (2012).

INTRODUCTORY NOTE ON BRECHT V. ABRAHAMSON

Thus far, the harmless-error discussion has involved mostly assessments of harm made on direct appellate review of a conviction. Under *Chapman*, a constitutional error evaluated in such a posture would be treated as harmful, thereby requiring reversal and retrial, if it was not harmless beyond a reasonable doubt. Federal courts, however, operated with a different standard for direct review of *nonconstitutional* trial error in federal criminal cases. In *Kotteakos v. United States*, 328 U.S. 750 (1946), the Supreme Court announced the standard for determining whether such nonconstitutional error was harmless: whether the error had "substantial and injurious effect or influence" in determining the jury verdict. That standard was based on the 1919 federal harmless-error statute, which stated: "in any case, civil or criminal, the court shall give judgment after an examination of the entire record before the court, without regard to technical errors, defects, or exceptions which do not affect the substantial rights of the parties."

Chapman and *Kotteakos* each announced a harmless error standard for *direct* review of a conviction, but the question remained—what should be the harmless-error standard for collateral review? The *Chapman* standard was an obvious candidate and, by the early 1990s, some courts also viewed the

Kotteakos standard as an option. In *Brecht v. Abrahamson*, 507 U.S. 619 (1993), excerpted below, the Supreme Court addressed this question.

Brecht v. Abrahamson

Supreme Court of the United States
507 U.S. 619 (1993)

■ CHIEF JUSTICE REHNQUIST delivered the opinion of the Court.

In *Chapman v. California*, 386 U.S. 18, 24 (1967), we held that the standard for determining whether a conviction must be set aside because of federal constitutional error is whether the error "was harmless beyond a reasonable doubt." In this case we must decide whether the *Chapman* harmless-error standard applies in determining whether the prosecution's use for impeachment purposes of petitioner's post-*Miranda* silence, in violation of due process under *Doyle v. Ohio*, 426 U.S. 610 (1976), entitles petitioner to habeas corpus relief. We hold that it does not. Instead, the standard for determining whether habeas relief must be granted is whether the *Doyle* error "had substantial and injurious effect or influence in determining the jury's verdict." *Kotteakos v. United States*, 328 U.S. 750, 776 (1946). The *Kotteakos* harmless-error standard is better tailored to the nature and purpose of collateral review than the *Chapman* standard, and application of a less onerous harmless-error standard on habeas promotes the considerations underlying our habeas jurisprudence. Applying this standard, we conclude that petitioner is not entitled to habeas relief.

[Brecht murdered a man in Wisconsin. After he fled, he drove a car into a ditch in a nearby town. When a police officer stopped to help, Brecht told him that he had called Ms. Hartman and that a tow truck was on the way. Brecht then hitched a ride to Winona, Minnesota, where he was stopped and arrested. When he was told that he was being arrested for the shooting, he told officers that "it was a big mistake" and asked to speak with "somebody that would understand" him." Brecht was returned to Wisconsin and *Mirandized* at his arraignment. At his subsequent first-degree murder trial, Brecht took the stand and claimed that the shooting was an accident. Brecht claimed that, after the shooting, Hartman disappeared. Brecht said that he went looking for Hartman, but panicked and fled after he saw Hartman at his neighbor's door. The state argued that Brecht's account was inconsistent with his decisions to flee the scene, to lie to the police officer about having called Ms. Hartman, and to omit reference to the shooting when interacting with several people after the incident.]

* * * Over the objections of defense counsel, the State also asked [Brecht] during cross-examination whether he had told anyone at any time before trial that the shooting was an accident, to which [Brecht] replied "no," and made several references to [Brecht's] pretrial silence during closing argument.[2] Finally, the State offered extrinsic evidence tending to con-

---

[2] The State's cross-examination of petitioner included the following exchange:

"Q. In fact the first time you have ever told this story is when you testified here today was it not? . . . . .

"A. You mean the story of actually what happened?

"Q. Yes.

tradict [Brecht's] story, including the path the bullet traveled through Mr. Hartman's body (horizontal to slightly downward) and the location where the rifle was found after the shooting (outside), as well as evidence of motive (petitioner's hostility toward Mr. Hartman because of his disapproval of [Brecht] sexual orientation).

The jury returned a guilty verdict, and [Brecht] was sentenced to life imprisonment. The Wisconsin Court of Appeals set the conviction aside on the ground that the State's references to [Brecht's] post-*Miranda* silence violated due process under [*Doyle*] and that this error was sufficiently "prejudicial" to require reversal. The Wisconsin Supreme Court reinstated the conviction. * * *

[Brecht sought federal habeas relief, reasserting the *Doyle* claim. The district court found both a *Doyle* violation and that the error was not harmless beyond a reasonable doubt, and set aside the conviction.] * * * The Court of Appeals for the Seventh Circuit reversed[, applying the *Kotteakos* standard on harmless error.] * * *

We granted certiorari to resolve a conflict between Courts of Appeals on the question whether the *Chapman* harmless error standard applies on collateral review of *Doyle* violations, and now affirm. * * *

In [*Doyle*], we held that "the use for impeachment purposes of [a defendant's] silence, at the time of arrest and after receiving *Miranda* warnings, violate[s] the Due Process Clause of the Fourteenth Amendment." * * * [T]he Constitution does not prohibit the use for impeachment purposes of a defendant's silence prior to arrest, or after arrest if no *Miranda* warnings are given. Such silence is probative and does not rest on any implied assurance by law enforcement authorities that it will carry no penalty.

This case illustrates the point well. The first time [Brecht] claimed that the shooting was an accident was when he took the stand at trial. It was entirely proper—and probative—for the State to impeach his testimony by pointing out that petitioner had failed to tell anyone before the time he received his *Miranda* warnings at his arraignment about the shooting being an accident. Indeed, if the shooting was an accident, petitioner had every reason—including to clear his name and preserve evidence supporting his version of the events—to offer his account immediately following the shooting. On the other hand, the State's references to petitioner's silence after that point in time, or more generally to petitioner's failure to come forward with his version of events at any time before trial crossed the *Doyle* line. For it is conceivable that, once [Brecht] had been given

"A. I knew what happened, I'm just telling it the way it happened, yes, I didn't have a chance to talk to anyone, I didn't want to call somebody from a phone and give up my rights, so I didn't want to talk about it, no sir." App. 22–23.

Then on re-cross-examination, the State further inquired:

"Q. Did you tell anyone about what had happened in Alma?"

"A. No I did not." *Id.*, at 23.

During closing argument, the State urged the jury to "remember that Mr. Brecht never volunteered until in this courtroom what happened in the Hartman residence...." *Id.*, at 30. It also made the following statement with regard to petitioner's pretrial silence: "He sits back here and sees all of our evidence go in and then he comes out with this crazy story...." *Id.*, at 31. Finally, during its closing rebuttal, the State said: "I know what I'd say [had I been in petitioner's shoes], I'd say, 'hold on, this was a mistake, this was an accident, let me tell you what happened,' but he didn't say that did he. No, he waited until he hears our story." *Id.*, at 36.

his *Miranda* warnings, he decided to stand on his right to remain silent because he believed his silence would not be used against him at trial.

* * * [W]e think *Doyle* error fits squarely into the category of constitutional violations which we have characterized as "trial error." Trial error * * * is amenable to harmless error analysis because it "may ... be quantitatively assessed in the context of other evidence presented in order to determine [the effect it had on the trial]." At the other end of the spectrum of constitutional errors lie "structural defects in the constitution of the trial mechanism, which defy analysis by 'harmless-error" standards." * * * Since our landmark decision in [*Chapman*], we have applied the harmless-beyond-a-reasonable-doubt standard in reviewing claims of constitutional error of the trial type. * * *

Chapman reached this Court on direct review, as have most of the cases in which we have applied its harmless-error standard. * * * [W]e have yet squarely to address [*Chapman's*] applicability on collateral review. * * *

* * * The [federal habeas corpus] statute says nothing about the standard for harmless-error review in habeas cases. [The State] urges us to fill this gap with the *Kotteakos* standard, under which an error requires reversal only if it "had substantial and injurious effect or influence in determining the jury's verdict." This standard is grounded in the federal harmless-error statute. 28 U. S. C. § 2111. On its face § 2111 might seem to address the situation at hand, but to date we have limited its application to claims of nonconstitutional error in federal criminal cases.

[Brecht] asserts that Congress' failure to enact various proposals since *Chapman* was decided that would have limited the availability of habeas relief amounts to legislative disapproval of application of a less stringent harmless-error standard on collateral review of constitutional error. * * *

As a general matter, we are [hesitant to infer things from Congressional inaction.] * * * We have filled the gaps of the habeas corpus statute with respect to other matters, and find it necessary to do so here. * * *

The principle that collateral review is different from direct review resounds throughout our habeas jurisprudence. Direct review is the principal avenue for challenging a conviction. * * *

Recognizing the distinction between direct and collateral review, we have applied different standards on habeas than would be applied on direct review with respect to matters other than harmless-error analysis. Our recent retroactivity jurisprudence is a prime example. Although new rules always have retroactive application to criminal cases on direct review, we have held that they seldom have retroactive application to criminal cases on federal habeas. * * *

The reason most frequently advanced in our cases for distinguishing between direct and collateral review is the State's interest in the finality of convictions that have survived direct review within the state court system. We have also spoken of comity and federalism. * * * Finally, we have recognized that "[l]iberal use of the writ ... degrades the prominence of the trial itself" and at the same time encourages habeas petitioners to relitigate their claims on collateral review.

In light of these considerations, we must decide whether the same harmless-error standard that the state courts applied on direct review of petitioner's *Doyle* claim also applies in this habeas proceeding. * * * State courts are fully qualified to identify constitutional error and evaluate its prejudicial effect on the trial process under *Chapman,* and state courts often occupy a superior vantage point from which to evaluate the effect of trial error. For these reasons, it scarcely seems logical to require federal habeas courts to engage in the identical approach to harmless-error review that *Chapman* requires state courts to engage in on direct review.

[Brecht] argues that application of the *Chapman* harmless-error standard on collateral review is necessary to deter state courts from relaxing their own guard in reviewing constitutional error and to discourage prosecutors from committing error in the first place. Absent affirmative evidence that state-court judges are ignoring their oath, we discount [Brecht's] argument that courts will respond to our ruling by violating their Article VI duty to uphold the Constitution. * * *

Overturning final and presumptively correct convictions on collateral review because the State cannot prove that an error is harmless under *Chapman* undermines the States' interest in finality and infringes upon their sovereignty over criminal matters. Moreover, granting habeas relief merely because there is a "reasonable possibility" that trial error contributed to the verdict is at odds with the historic meaning of habeas corpus—to afford relief to those whom society has "grievously wronged." Retrying defendants whose convictions are set aside also imposes significant "social costs," including the expenditure of additional time and resources for all the parties involved, the "erosion of memory" and "dispersion of witnesses" that accompany the passage of time and make obtaining convictions on retrial more difficult, and the frustration of "society's interest in the prompt administration of justice." And since there is no statute of limitations governing federal habeas, and the only laches recognized is that which affects the State's ability to defend against the claims raised on habeas, retrials following the grant of habeas relief ordinarily take place much later than do retrials following reversal on direct review.

The imbalance of the costs and benefits of applying the *Chapman* harmless-error standard on collateral review counsels in favor of applying a less onerous standard on habeas review of constitutional error. The *Kotteakos* standard, we believe, fills the bill. The test under *Kotteakos* is whether the error "had substantial and injurious effect or influence in determining the jury's verdict." Under this standard, habeas petitioners may obtain plenary review of their constitutional claims, but they are not entitled to habeas relief based on trial error unless they can establish that it resulted in "actual prejudice." The *Kotteakos* standard is thus better tailored to the nature and purpose of collateral review and more likely to promote the considerations underlying our recent habeas cases. Moreover, because the *Kotteakos* standard is grounded in the federal harmless-error rule, 28 U. S. C. § 2111, federal courts may turn to an existing body of case law in applying it. * * *

* * *[9] All that remains to be decided is whether petitioner is entitled to relief under this standard based on the State's *Doyle* error. * * *

---

[9] Our holding does not foreclose the possibility that in an unusual case, a deliberate and especially egregious error of the trial type, or one that is combined with a pattern of prosecutorial misconduct, might so infect the integrity of the proceeding as to warrant the grant of habeas relief, even if it did not substantially influence the jury's verdict. Cf. *Greer v. Miller,* 483 U.S. 756, 769 (1987) (STEVENS, J., concurring in judgment). We, of course, are not presented with such a situation here.

The State's references to petitioner's post-*Miranda* silence were infrequent, comprising less than two pages of the 900-page trial transcript in this case. And in view of the State's extensive and permissible references to petitioner's pre-*Miranda* silence—*i.e.*, his failure to mention anything about the shooting being an accident to the officer who found him in the ditch, the man who gave him a ride to Winona, or the officers who eventually arrested him—its references to petitioner's post-*Miranda* silence were, in effect, cumulative. Moreover, the State's evidence of guilt was, if not overwhelming, certainly weighty. The path of the bullet through Mr. Hartman's body was inconsistent with petitioner's testimony that the rifle had discharged as he was falling. The police officers who searched the Hartmans' home found nothing in the downstairs hallway that could have caused petitioner to trip. The rifle was found outside the house (where Hartman was shot), not inside where petitioner claimed it had accidently fired, and there was a live round rammed in the gun's chamber, suggesting that petitioner had tried to fire a second shot. Finally, other circumstantial evidence, including the motive proffered by the State, also pointed to petitioner's guilt.

In light of the foregoing, we conclude that the *Doyle* error that occurred at [Brecht's] trial did not "substantial[ly] . . . influence" the jury's verdict. Petitioner is therefore not entitled to habeas relief, and the judgment of the Court of Appeals is

Affirmed.

[The concurring opinion of JUSTICE STEVENS is omitted.]

■ JUSTICE WHITE, with whom JUSTICE BLACKMUN joins, and with whom JUSTICE SOUTER joins in part, dissenting.

* * * As a result of today's decision, in short, the fate of one in state custody turns on whether the state courts properly applied the Federal Constitution as then interpreted by decisions of this Court, and on whether we choose to review his claim on certiorari. Because neither the federal habeas corpus statute nor our own precedents can support such illogically disparate treatment, I dissent. * * *

Chapman v. California established the federal nature of the harmless-error standard to be applied when constitutional rights are at stake. * * * Ultimately, the central question is whether States may detain someone whose conviction was tarnished by a constitutional violation that is not harmless beyond a reasonable doubt. *Chapman* dictates that they may not; the majority suggests that, so long as direct review has not corrected this error in time, they may. If state courts remain obliged to apply *Chapman,* and in light of the infrequency with which we grant certiorari, I fail to see how this decision can be reconciled with Congress' intent. * * *

Our habeas jurisprudence is taking on the appearance of a confused patchwork in which different constitutional rights are treated according to their status, and in which the same constitutional right is treated differently depending on whether its vindication is sought on direct or collateral review. I believe this picture bears scant resemblance either to Congress' design or to our own precedents. The Court of Appeals having yet to apply *Chapman* to the facts of this case, I would remand to that court for determination of whether the *Doyle* violation was harmless beyond a reasonable doubt. I dissent.

[The dissenting opinion of JUSTICE BLACKMUN is omitted.]

■ JUSTICE O'CONNOR, dissenting.

I have no dispute with the Court's observation that "collateral review is different from direct review." Just as the federal courts may decline to adjudicate certain issues of federal law on habeas because of prudential concerns, so too may they resolve specific claims on habeas using different and more lenient standards than those applicable on direct review. But decisions concerning the Great Writ "warrant restraint," for we ought not take lightly alteration of that "'fundamental safeguard against unlawful custody.'"

In my view, restraint should control our decision today. The issue before us is not whether we should remove from the cognizance of the federal courts on habeas a discrete prophylactic rule unrelated to the truth finding function of trial * * * . Rather, we are asked to alter a standard that not only finds application in virtually every case of error but that also may be critical to our faith in the reliability of the criminal process. Because I am not convinced that the principles governing the exercise of our habeas powers—federalism, finality, and fairness—counsel against applying *Chapman's* harmless-error standard on collateral review, I would adhere to our former practice of applying it to cases on habeas and direct review alike. I therefore respectfully dissent.

* * * When a prisoner asserts the violation of a core constitutional privilege critical to the reliability of the criminal process, he has a strong claim that fairness favors review; but if the infringement concerns only a prophylactic rule, divorced from the criminal trial's truthfinding function, the prisoner's claim to the equities rests on far shakier ground. * * *

Petitioner in this case alleged a violation of *[Doyle]*, an error the Court accurately characterizes as constitutional trial error. But the Court's holding today, it turns out, has nothing to do with *Doyle* error at all. Instead, the Court announces that the harmless-error standard of *Chapman* * * *, which requires the prosecution to prove constitutional error harmless beyond a reasonable doubt, no longer applies to *any* trial error asserted on habeas, whether it is a *Doyle* error or not. In *Chapman's* place, the Court substitutes the less rigorous standard of *Kotteakos v. United States.*

A repudiation of the application of *Chapman* to *all* trial errors asserted on habeas should be justified, if at all, based on the nature of the *Chapman* rule itself. Yet, as Justice White observes, one searches the majority opinion in vain for a discussion of the basis for *Chapman's* harmless-error standard. We are left to speculate whether *Chapman* is the product of constitutional command or a judicial construct that may overprotect constitutional rights. More important, the majority entirely fails to discuss the *effect* of the *Chapman* rule. If there is a unifying theme to this Court's habeas jurisprudence, it is that the ultimate equity on the prisoner's side—the possibility that an error may have caused the conviction of an actually innocent person—is sufficient by itself to permit plenary review of the prisoner's federal claim. Whatever the source of the *Chapman* standard, the equities may favor its application on habeas if it substantially promotes the central goal of the criminal justice system—accurate determinations of guilt and innocence.

In my view, the harmless-error standard often will be inextricably intertwined with the interest of reliability. By now it goes without saying that harmless-error review is of almost universal application; there are few errors that may not be forgiven as harmless. * * * Proof of harmlessness beyond a reasonable doubt, however, sufficiently restores confidence in the verdict's reliability that the conviction may stand despite the potentially accuracy impairing error. Such proof demonstrates that, even though the error had the *potential* to induce the jury to err, in fact there is no reasonable possibility that it did. Rather, we are confident beyond a reasonable doubt that the error had no influence on the jury's judgment at all.

At least where errors bearing on accuracy are at issue, I am not persuaded that the *Kotteakos* standard offers an adequate assurance of reliability. * * * By tolerating a greater probability that an error with the potential to undermine verdict accuracy was harmful, the Court increases the likelihood that a conviction will be preserved despite an error that actually affected the reliability of the trial. * * *

To be sure, the harmless-error inquiry will not always bear on reliability. If the trial error being reviewed for harmlessness is not itself related to the interest of accuracy, neither is the harmless-error standard. Accordingly, in theory it would be neither illogical nor grudging to reserve *Chapman* for errors related to the accuracy of the verdict, applying *Kotteakos'* more lenient rule whenever the error is of a type that does not impair confidence in the trial's result. But the Court draws no such distinction. On the contrary, it holds *Kotteakos* applicable to *all* trial errors, whether related to reliability or not. * * *

Nor does the majority demonstrate that the *Kotteakos* standard will ease the burden of conducting harmless-error review in those cases to which it does apply. * * * *Kotteakos* is unlikely to lighten the load of the federal judiciary at all. The courts still must review the entire record in search of conceivable ways the error may have influenced the jury; they still must conduct their review *de novo;* and they still must decide whether they have sufficient confidence that the verdict would have remained unchanged even if the error had not occurred. The only thing the Court alters today is the degree of confidence that suffices. * * *

Finally, the majority considers the costs of habeas review generally. Once again, I agree that those costs—the effect on finality, the infringement on state sovereignty, and the social cost of requiring retrial, sometimes years after trial and at a time when a new trial has become difficult or impossible—are appropriate considerations. But the Court does not explain how those costs set the harmless-error inquiry apart from any other question presented on habeas; such costs are inevitable *whenever* relief is awarded. Unless we are to accept the proposition that denying relief whenever possible is an unalloyed good, the costs the Court identifies cannot by themselves justify the lowering of standards announced today. * * * Because I would remand the case to the Court of Appeals for application of *Chapman*'s more demanding harmless-error standard, I respectfully dissent.

[The dissenting opinion of JUSTICE SOUTER is omitted.]

___

NOTES AND QUESTIONS ON BRECHT

1) *Doyle* **Error and Holistic Assessment of Harm.** Under *Doyle*, there is constitutional error when post-*Miranda* silence is used to impeach a witness-defendant; the admission of that information violates due process. What is the *Doyle* error in *Brecht,* and how damaging was that error at the trial? There are several instances in which Brecht remained silent, but introducing the fact of such silence was not always *Doyle* error. In what situations was silence used as impeachment, but did not create *Doyle* error? Moreover, what other evidence of guilt or impeachment was in the record, and how persuasive was it? Assessing the probative weight of the wrongfully-admitted evidence is a key analytic step in performing any harmless error inquiry.

2)   Substantial and Injurious Effect. *Brecht* requires that a federal judge apply a standard of harmlessness that requires a "substantial and injurious effect," or a standard requiring a showing of "actual prejudice." In contrast, the *Chapman* test required the State to make a far stronger showing that error was "harmless beyond a reasonable doubt." If *Brecht* truly incorporates the standard that had been adopted in *Kotteakos*, based on the federal harmless-error statute used in § 2255 federal-prisoner cases, then a harmless error would be one that "did not influence the jury" or "had very slight effect." In Brecht's case, do you think the *Doyle* error was harmless under *Kotteakos*? Was the error harmless under *Chapman* and, if it was harmless under the prior standard, then should the Court have reached the question whether to adopt a new harmless error rule for federal habeas corpus in *Brecht*?

In an omitted concurring opinion, Justice Stevens, who provided the fifth vote, explained that, to apply the *Kotteakos* standard, the judge must "make a *de novo* examination of the trial record" in order to "consider all the ways that error can infect the course of a trial." Justice Stevens noted that a full application of the *Kotteakos* standard "places the burden on prosecutors to explain why those errors were harmless." Justice Stevens added that, because the inquiry is holistic, "[a]lthough our adoption of *Kotteakos* does impose a new standard in this context, it is a standard that will always require the discrimination . . . of judgment transcending confinement by formula or precise rule." (Internal citation omitted.)

3)   (Non-)Parity on Direct and Collateral Review. Even if the standard requires a holistic judgment, which cannot be reduced to a precise rule, *Brecht* certainly made the federal habeas harmless-error standard more restrictive. Why do federal courts, on collateral review, use a more deferential standard than *Chapman* requires state judges to use in direct-review cases? The answer, once again, had to do with the interests of comity, finality, and federalism. As the Court says: "Overturning final and presumptively correct convictions on collateral review because the State cannot prove that an error is harmless under *Chapman* undermines the States' interest in finality and infringes upon their sovereignty over criminal matters." Does the premise do enough work to justify the result? When the Supreme Court reviews federal questions in state criminal cases, does it not interfere with precisely these same interests to precisely the same degree? Might the justification be more effectively stated in terms of *which* federal court most permissibly interfere with these interests?

Brecht also justifies the incorporation of the *Kotteakos* standard on the ground that the *Chapman* standard would impose significant social costs. Those costs actually subdivide into two categories—those associated with the actual practice of habeas review and those associated with having to conduct a new trial. With respect to the first category, Justice O'Connor argues that the Court's recourse to comity, finality, and federalism cannot do all of the analytic work "[u]nless we are to accept the proposition that denying relief whenever possible is an unalloyed good[.] [T]he costs the Court identifies cannot by themselves justify the lowering of standards announced today." Those tripartite interests animate the Court's move to more restrictive rules in many areas of habeas law, a point that Justice O'Connor makes when she observes that "the Court does not explain how those costs set the harmless-error inquiry apart from any other question presented on habeas; such costs are inevitable *whenever* relief is awarded." In what other situations has the Court invoked comity, finality, and federalism to justify a more restrictive rule, and, in *those* situations, has the Court explained why it ultimately decided to draw the line where it did? Even if those costs are always created when a court grants habeas relief, are they not created less frequently when the harmless error standard is higher?

With respect to the second category of costs—those associated with habeas review itself—the Supreme Court held (in an unexcerpted passage) that a *Chapman* standard required federal courts to expend too many resources scrutinizing trial records. Justice O'Connor responded that federal courts incur the cost of reviewing the record no matter what the standard for harmless error is. Is the Court not correct, however, in observing that the *Kotteakos* standard relieves the court from having to conduct other types of inquiry? Are those savings worth the costs?

Ultimately, consider Justice White's objection to the absence of parity between direct and collateral review. Should there be parity, or does the majority opinion persuade you that the standard—whatever it is—should be different on collateral review?

4) Reliability. Fourth Amendment violations are not cognizable under *Stone v. Powell*; what other violations do not undermine the reliability of a guilt determination? What does Justice O'Connor mean by reliability? Is she referring only to trial errors, to wrongful convictions, to structural errors, to sentencing errors, or to some combination thereof? She ultimately suggests applying *Chapman* to constitutional errors that go to reliability, and that *Kotteakos* be used for constitutional errors that do not. In light of what you know about habeas generally, should the standard for harmless error turn on whether the constitutional violation goes to the reliability of the conviction and sentence? Is Justice O'Connor adopting Judge Henry Friendly's premise from his article *Is Innocence Irrelevant*?

5) Policing the States. The Supreme Court bristled at the idea that the *Chapman* standard might be appropriate because it deterred states from constitutional violations: "Absent affirmative evidence that state-court judges are ignoring their oath, we discount [Brecht's] argument that courts will respond to our ruling by violating their Article VI duty to uphold the Constitution." You have encountered the debate over whether habeas should play a deterrent role in policing state criminal process before. Might there be a need for deterrence even if state court judges were not "ignoring their oath?" What structural conditions place pressure on state judges that are not present for federal judges? Are these structural differences enough to justify the state-deterrence rationale? Moreover, does review of harmlessness go to the question of whether judges are faithfully applying the Constitution, or does the answer to that question turn solely on review of the constitutional error itself?

6) The Exception for Deliberate and Egregious Error. The general rule from *Brecht* is that error must "substantially influence" the verdict to warrant federal habeas relief. The Court reserved an exception to this general rule in footnote 6, leaving open the possibility that, for "a deliberate and especially egregious error of the trial type," or for one that is "combined with a pattern of prosecutorial misconduct," habeas relief might be appropriate without a specific finding of harm.[jj] Perhaps the exception might be explained the following way: if state actors are deliberately or systematically violating constitutional rights of criminal defendants, then there is a greater need for habeas serve a deterrent function.

7)   Pleading Harmlessness. Harmless error is an affirmative defense that the state must plead either plead or waive. See Hertz & Liebman, *FHCPP*, at § 31.2[a]. Because harmless error is generally pleaded by the State and treated like an affirmative defense, the State must show that the error lacked a "substantial and injurious effect." In contrast, under the *Chapman* standard, the State has the more onerous burden to show that the error was harmless beyond a reasonable doubt. In *O'Neal v. McAninch*, 513 U.S. 432, 435 (1995), the Supreme Court addressed the pleading issue, which the Justices did not squarely address in *Brecht*. The Court rejected the notion that the inmate should bear the burden of showing whether the error was prejudicial. Adopting the view of Justice Stevens' *Brecht* concurrence, that the Court adopted the entire *Kotteakos* standard, which placed the burden on the State to show that the error was harmless. The Court held that: "When a federal judge in a habeas proceeding is in grave doubt about whether a trial error of federal law had 'substantial and injurious effect or influence in determining the jury's verdict,' that error is not harmless. And, the petitioner must win."

In the harmless-error context, the term "burden of proof" is perhaps inappropriate, because a harmless-error defense necessarily involves an assessment of the entire trial record. The Court explained that, conceptually, the harmless-error standard was not subject to what we ordinarily think of as a burden of proof:

> [W]e note that we deliberately phrase the issue in this case in terms of a judge's grave doubt, instead of in terms of "burden of proof." The case before us does not involve a judge who shifts a "burden" to help control the presentation of evidence at a trial, but rather involves a judge who applies a legal standard (harmlessness) to a record that the presentation of evidence is no longer likely to affect. In such a case, we think it conceptually clearer for the judge to ask directly, "Do I, the judge, think that the error substantially influenced the jury's decision?" than for the judge to try to put the same question in terms of proof burdens (*e.g.*, "Do I believe the party has borne its burden of showing . . . ?").

The Court held that, where the question of harmlessness under the *Kotteakos* standard is close to 50/50—when "the matter is so evenly balanced that [the court feels itself] in virtual equipoise as to the harmlessness of the error"—the prisoner should receive the benefit of the doubt. Did the Court in effect adopt the view of Justice Stevens' *Brecht* concurrence: that the standard is not intended to be precise, but rather reflects a judicial mindset that the error was not trivial? If the state has the burden to show that the error did not have a substantial and injurious effect, then a showing that the error did prejudice the outcome permits relief, as does a showing that leaves the judge in doubt as to how prejudicial the error was.

[jj] See also *Fry v. Pliler*, 551 U.S. 112, 117 (2007) (noting that *Brecht* left open "an exception" for "deliberate and especially egregious error") (quoting *Brecht*, 507 U.S. at 638 n.9).

8) Order of Operations. Does harmless error doctrine encourage federal judges to avoid the merits and to simply rule that, even if there was an error, it was harmless? Should we discourage judges from making unnecessary constitutional rulings for minor violations? Cf. Thomas Healy, *The Rise of Unnecessary Constitutional Rulings,* 83 N.C. L. Rev. 847, 894 (2005) (criticizing approaches that encourage gratuitous rulings on constitutional questions). Or does a judge ruling on the merits of a constitutional claim, while finding the error harmless and denying relief, further encourage the development of constitutional law? Scholars have also debated the broader questions regarding "order of battle" in deciding constitutional questions, particularly given the Supreme Court's decision in *Pearson v. Callahan,* 555 U.S. 223 (2009). After *Pearson,* federal courts considering qualified immunity defenses no longer need resolve constitutional questions before deciding whether the constitutional rule was clearly established. Cf. John C. Jeffries, Jr., *Reversing the Order of Battle in Constitutional Torts,* 2009 Sup. Ct. Rev. 115 (using *Pearson* as a platform for discussing how remedies should vary across different rights).

9) How Much Does the Harmless Error Standard Matter? Justice Scalia commented, in *U.S. v. Dominguez Benitez,* 542 U.S. 74 (2004), that quantifying the impact of incremental changes to the harmless error standard is impossible:

> Such ineffable gradations of probability seem to me quite beyond the ability of the judicial mind (or any mind) to grasp, and thus harmful rather than helpful to the consistency and rationality of judicial decisionmaking. That is especially so when they are applied to the hypothesizing of events that never in fact occurred. Such an enterprise is not factfinding, but closer to divination.

> For purposes of estimating what would have happened, it seems to me that the only serviceable standards are the traditional "beyond a reasonable doubt" and "more likely than not." We should not pretend to a higher degree of precision.

What is the implication of that view; does it suggest that an imprecise standard will lead to unduly imprecise rulings, or does it suggest that district judges should simply be given a fair amount of discretion?

10) Empirical Data. For reactions to *Brecht,* predicting or describing adverse consequences for the quality of habeas review, see, e.g., John H. Blume and Stephen P. Garvey, *Harmless Error in Federal Habeas Corpus after Brecht v. Abrahamson,* 35 Wm & Mary L. Rev. 163 (1993) (arguing that the differences between the different harmless error standards are not ultimately that great); Sam Kamin, *Harmless Error and the Rights/Remedies Split,* 88 Va. L. Rev. 1, 7 (2002) ("[In] a database of nearly 300 California Supreme Court decisions in death penalty cases, . . . during a ten year period, over ninety percent of death sentences imposed by trial courts were upheld on appeal even though nearly every case was found to have been tainted by constitutional error."). See also James S. Liebman & Randy Hertz, Brecht v. Abrahamson: *Harmful Error in Habeas Corpus Law,* 84 J. Crim. L. & Criminology 1109, 1110–11 (1994) (considering how federal courts should apply the different harmless error rules after *Brecht*).

11) Innocence and Harmless Error. In examining claims raised by 250 people later freed by DNA tests, one of the authors found that appellate and

post-conviction judges producing written opinions invoked harmless error (or
lack of prejudice) as a reason to deny relief in 38% of the cases. See Brandon L.
Garrett, *Convicting the Innocent* 201 (2011). Even more exonerees had judges
simply label them as people who were likely guilty of the crime; courts referred
to the likely guilt of the convicts in 47% of the cases, typically by underscoring
the reliability of the prosecution evidence. In 10% of the cases, courts went farther and called the evidence overwhelming. Take the case of Jeffrey Deskovic,
for whom the appellate court cited "overwhelming evidence of the defendant's
guilt in the form of the defendant's own multiple inculpatory statements, as
corroborated by such physical evidence as the victim's autopsy findings."[kk] Or
the case of Leonard McSherry, in which the court referred to "the unusual circumstances in this case, overwhelmingly identifying appellant as the perpetrator."[ll] In retrospect, now that DNA has proved the innocence of those convicts,
many of those cases no longer look so strong. Judges also apply harmless-error-
like standards when deciding whether to grant access to DNA tests or to grant
relief based on new evidence of innocence. For example, after DNA test results
excluded Stephen Avery, a man convicted of a rape and attempted murder of a
woman in Wisconsin, the state intermediate court nevertheless denied his appeal.[mm] The court concluded that even DNA evidence did not meet the fairly
lenient reasonable-probability standard under a state new-trial statute, concluding that "the presence of DNA from an unidentified third party did not create a reasonable probability of a different result on retrial." The court relied on
the certainty of the victim who identified Avery; the victim said, "It's as if I
have a photograph in my mind." A court did not vacate Avery's conviction until
six years later, in 2002, when more powerful DNA testing confirmed the exclusion and also resulted in a cold hit matching a prisoner who was incarcerated
for crimes similar to the ones for which Avery was convicted. See Brandon L.
Garrett, *Claiming Innocence,* 92 Minn. L. Rev. 1629, 1713–14 (2008).

12) Guilt-Based Analysis. If a constitutional error occurred during a criminal trial, there are multiple ways to examine the degree to which error contributed to a conviction. One way to ask that question is what weight was accorded
to the evidence that was tainted by error. Some judges have suggested that,
instead, courts ought to imagine a trial in which there had been no error, and
simply ask whether there would still be enough evidence for the jury to have
convicted the defendant. Can you see why that second, "guilt-based" approach
is far more tolerant of error? The Supreme Court has rejected that guilt-based
analysis and has held that the question a judge asks when conducting harmless
error analysis is *not* whether there was, apart from the tainted evidence,
enough evidence of guilt to convict. Specifically, the Court has explained that:

> The inquiry . . . is . . . whether the guilty verdict actually rendered in this
> trial was surely unattributable to the error. The must be so, because to
> hypothesize a guilty verdict that was never in fact rendered—no matter
> how inescapable the findings to support that verdict might be—would vio-
> late the jury-trial guarantee.

[kk] People v. Deskovic, 607 N.Y.S.2d 957, 958 (N.Y. App. Div. 1994).
[ll] People v. McSherry, 14 Cal. Rptr. 2d 630, 636 (Cal. Ct. App. 1992) (depublished).
[mm] See State v. Avery, 570 N.W.2d 573, 580 (Wis. Ct. App. 1997).

Sullivan v. Louisiana, 508 U.S. 275, 279 (1993).[nn] Thus, the question is whether the error reasonably contributed to the outcome. Can federal judges reading a written trial record ever be expected to put out of their minds the "inescapable" other evidence of guilt?

Judge Harry Edwards explained how, if a case is reversed, "the government and the trial court will be forced to undergo the time and expense of retrying a case in which there appears to be little doubt of the defendant's guilt. (And in many criminal cases, the expense and time involved are enormous.)" Harry T. Edwards, *To Err Is Human, But Not Always Harmless: When Should Legal Error Be Tolerated?*, 70 N.Y.U. L. Rev. 1167 (1995). Judge Edwards explained that, as a result, judges may be tempted to conduct a guilt-based analysis asking no more than whether the properly-admitted evidence would be enough to convict. He gave the example of "Joe Didit," a defendant who was seen robbing a convenience store by four customers, and then shooting the owner in the head. Joe Didit also confessed—but the confession was coerced; he was also beaten and he was not properly *Mirandized*. Was admission of the coerced confession harmless because a jury could have convicted based on the four eyewitnesses alone? There is no question, however, that the confession had a substantial impact on the jury. Judge Edwards explained:

> I believe that, more often than not, we review the record to determine how we might have decided the case; the judgment as to whether an error is harmless is therefore dependent on our judgment about the factual guilt of the defendant. I call this application of harmless error the "guilt-based approach."

He calls that approach "dangerously seductive." He noted that, in his hypothetical example, if the court affirms the conviction crediting the eyewitness testimony, then "this result will likely undermine the integrity of the criminal justice system by sending dubious messages to the police officer who brutalized the defendant and thereby gained the coerced confession, to the prosecutor who introduced the evidence at trial, and to the trial judge who erroneously admitted it." A series of scholars have criticized use of the guilt-based approach, and the Supreme Court has not condoned it.[oo]

Psychologically speaking, can a judge really be expected to be able to assess the outcome of the counterfactual trial without giving subconscious weight to the fact that the defendant was convicted—or to the nature of evidence that was unconstitutionally admitted at trial? For example, judges may be susceptible to "confirmation bias" and may tend to credit the evidence supporting the guilty verdict, and they may tend to discredit contrary evidence. See Dan Simon, *A Third View of the Black Box: Cognitive Coherence in Legal Decision Making*, 71 U. Chi. L. Rev. 511, 576 (2004). On the other hand, do these biases

---

[nn] Justice Stevens, concurring in *Brecht*, reasoned, "The habeas court cannot ask only whether it thinks the petitioner would have been convicted even if the constitutional error had not taken place." 507 U.S. at 632 (Stevens, J., concurring).

[oo] For the argument that a guilt-based approach to harmless error runs afoul of the right to trial by jury, see Linda E. Carter, *The Sporting Approach to Harmless Error in Criminal Cases: The Supreme Court's "No Harm, No Foul" Debacle in Neder v. United States*, 28 Am. J. Crim. L. 229, 239–45 (2001). For other scholars criticizing a guilt-based approach, see Charles S. Chapel, *The Irony of Harmless Error*, 51 Okla. L. Rev 501, 506 (1998); Erwin Chemerinsky, *No Harm, No Foul*, 16 Cal Law 27 (Jan 1996); Brandon L. Garrett, *Innocence, Innocence, Harmless Error and Federal Wrongful Conviction Law*, 2005 Wisc. L. Rev. 35; Jason M. Solomon, *Causing Constitutional Harm: How Tort Law Can Help Determine Harmless Error in Criminal Trials*, 99 Nw. U. L. Rev. 1053, 1059–64 (2005).

inhere in any form of direct or collateral review? Does the existence of harmless error doctrine reflect the fact that society will tolerate such biases?

NOTES ON HARMLESS ERROR AFTER AEDPA

1) *Fry v. Pliler* **and Whether AEDPA Modified** *Brecht.* Congress passed AEDPA in 1996, and the Supreme Court eventually had to confront the ways in which AEDPA potentially interacted with *Brecht*. In *Fry v. Pliler*, 551 U.S. 112 (2007), the Court addressed whether, under AEDPA, a federal court applied the *Brecht* "substantial and injurious effect" test or the *Chapman* "harmless beyond a reasonable doubt" test when the state court did not itself apply *Chapman*. In Fry's case, the Court assumed that § 2254(d) did not apply because the state court did not conduct a harmless error analysis. Fry argued that, when deciding the claim *simpliciter*, absent the § 2254(d) restriction on relief, the federal judge should use the *Chapman* harmless error test. Fry also argued that AEDPA displaced the *Brecht* test entirely, such that if § 2254(d) did apply, and the state court had conducted a harmless error analysis, then the federal judge would ask whether the state court reached an "unreasonable" harmless error determination using the *Chapman* test.

Justice Scalia, writing for the Court and rejecting that argument, began with an assessment of whether the Court had intended *Brecht* to apply only to situations in which the state did its own harmless error analysis:

> The primary reasons *Brecht* gave for adopting a less onerous standard on collateral review of state-court criminal judgments did not turn on whether the state court itself conducted Chapman review. The opinion explained that application of *Chapman* would [undermine the States interest in finality, would infringe upon the States' sovereignty over criminal matters, would undercut the historic limitation of habeas relief to those "grievously wronged," and would impose significant societal costs], Since each of these concerns applies with equal force whether or not the state court reaches the *Chapman* question, it would be illogical to make the standard of review turn upon that contingency.

> The opinion in Brecht clearly assumed that the *Kotteakos* standard would apply in virtually all § 2254 cases. It suggested an exception only for the "unusual case" in which "a deliberate and especially egregious error of the trial type, or one that is combined with a pattern of prosecutorial misconduct . . . infect[s] the integrity of the proceeding."

Justice Scalia then turned to the argument that AEDPA displaced the principle that *Brecht* applied without respect to the state court's application of *Chapman*:

> Petitioner contends that, even if *Brecht* adopted a categorical rule, post-*Brecht* developments require a different standard of review. Three years after we decided Brecht, Congress passed, and the President signed, [AEDPA], under which a habeas petition may not be granted unless the state court's adjudication "resulted in a decision that was contrary to, or involved an unreasonable application of, clearly established Federal law, as determined by the Supreme Court of the United States . . ." In *Mitchell v. Esparza*, 540 U.S. 12 (2003) (per curiam), we held that, when a state court determines that a constitutional violation is harmless, a federal

court may not award habeas relief under § 2254 unless the harmlessness determination itself was unreasonable. Petitioner contends that § 2254(d)(1), as interpreted in *Esparza*, eliminates the requirement that a petitioner also satisfy Brecht's standard. We think not. That conclusion is not suggested by *Esparza*, which had no reason to decide the point. Nor is it suggested by the text of AEDPA, which sets forth a precondition to the grant of habeas relief . . . , not an entitlement to it. Given our frequent recognition that AEDPA limited rather than expanded the availability of habeas relief, it is implausible that, without saying so, AEDPA replaced the *Brecht* standard . . . with the more liberal AEDPA/*Chapman* standard . . . That said, it certainly makes no sense to require formal application of both tests (AEDPA/Chapman and Brecht) when the latter obviously subsumes the former.

2) Applying Harmless Error After AEDPA. After AEDPA, the Court held that *Brecht* still applies whether or not § 2254(d) limits relief. Section 2254(d) will not limit relief if a state court failed to make a required harmless error finding. If, however, § 2254(d) does not limit relief, then a federal court must still decide whether habeas relief should issue for the constitutional violation. Such a determination may require the judge to apply the *Brecht* harmless error test. However, if the state court did make a harmless error finding, the federal judge still applies *Brecht*:

> [I]n § 2254 proceedings a court must assess the prejudicial impact of constitutional error in a state-court criminal trial under the "substantial and injurious effect" standard set forth in *Brecht,* whether or not the state appellate court recognized the error and reviewed it for harmlessness under the "harmless beyond a reasonable doubt" standard set forth in *Chapman.*

Do you think the Court was right to hold that *Brecht* still applies regardless whether AEDPA's deferential merits limitations apply? Did the Court adopt a simpler test, rather than trying to accommodate AEDPA's requirements? Or do you think Fry had the better argument, that state courts should not get deference when they do not conduct harmless error analysis?

3) Prejudice and *Pinholster*. Recall *Cullen v. Pinholster,* 131 S.Ct. 1388 (2011), where that the California Supreme Court had found an IAC claim to lack merit—but did so without having considered the evidence developed at a subsequent hearing in front of the federal judge. The California Supreme Court had ruled on both prongs of the IAC analysis, finding no prejudice caused by any omissions of counsel. The U.S. Supreme Court repeated the prejudice standard as one requiring the inmate to show a "reasonable probability," which means a "probability sufficient to undermine confidence in the outcome," or a "substantial" and not just a "conceivable" chance that that the outcome would be different. That standard is not meaningfully different than the *Brecht* standard, although the burden is placed on the inmate. There is, however, a difference so far as AEDPA is concerned. The Court distinguished the treatment of the "prejudice" inquiry native to an IAC claim, stating that it must receive "doubly deferential" treatment, both due to the prejudice requirement, and the deference required by 2254(d). The Court noted that in prior cases, such as *Terry Williams,* the state court had not applied, or misapplied, the prejudice test, giving the Court no occasion to define AEDPA treatment of the prejudice standard. The Court concluded that Pinholster had to show that "the California Supreme Court must have unreasonably concluded that Pinholster was not prejudiced." Why do you think that the ineffective assistance of counsel prejudice requirement receives this "double deferential" treatment? Does this result follow from the way that the prejudice test is incorporated into the ineffective assistance of counsel claim?

4)   A *Brecht* Hypothetical. Assume counterfactually that *Brecht* is an AEDPA case, brought in the present day, and that the federal judge is considering granting relief on Brecht's claim. What questions would a federal judge have to ask? Does Brecht's claim satisfy those standards?

CHAPTER 6

REVIEW OF FEDERAL CONVICTIONS

1. INTRODUCTION TO 28 U.S.C. § 2255

Post-conviction review for federal inmates operates in a universe large-ly parallel to the system of federal collateral review for state prisoners. The First Judiciary Act permitted federal prisoners to seek habeas corpus re-view, but not state prisoners. As described, this changed after the Civil War, and now state prisoners use habeas corpus to challenge their criminal judgments. Federal prisoners now chiefly use a habeas-like post-conviction remedy to challenge their convictions and sentences. In 1948, Congress en-acted 28 U.S.C. § 2255, a statute requiring proceedings that mimicked ha-beas review in all important respects save one—the statute changed the forum of appropriate filing in order to streamline post-conviction review.

Congress was responding to a geographic problem when it enacted § 2255. A habeas petition, filed under 28 U.S.C. § 2241, had to be filed against the custodian in the district where the prisoner was in custody. Most federal inmates were held in just a few districts housing the largest federal prison facilities. The forum-of-custody filing rule disproportionately burdened districts in which the prisoners were located. Moreover, because prisoners had to file their habeas petitions in districts other than the ones where they were originally convicted, the habeas proceedings would take place in courts that lacked ready access to the records. A different U.S. At-torney's Office, unfamiliar with the case, might be asked to defend the con-viction. The House Report explained that § 2255 "provides an expeditious remedy for correcting erroneous sentences without resort to habeas cor-pus." 80th Congress House Report No. 308. Congress' purpose in enacting § 2255 was not to change the substance of post-conviction remedies for fed-eral prisoners, but to streamline *where* those applications were handled. As the Supreme Court put it in *United States v. Hayman*, 342 U.S. 205 (1952) (presented in Chapter 2), "the sole purpose was to minimize the difficulties . . . by affording the same rights in another and more convenient forum."

A § 2255 motion differs in form from a habeas petition. In contrast to habeas review, which occurs in a court having personal jurisdiction over the custodian, § 2255 requires federal post-conviction review to occur in the sentencing court. The § 2255 proceeding is considered "a further step in the criminal case in which petitioner is sentenced," and it vests the trial judge with powers to make post-judgment modifications on the conviction and sentence. S. Rep. 1526, 80th Cong., 2d Sess., 2 (1948). Virtually all of the post-conviction practice for federal prisoners involves § 2255 motions, and not habeas corpus motions under § 2241. We will discuss the exceptions later.

NOTES ON COGNIZABILITY

1)   Cognizability of Sentencing Claims. Section 2255 permits a range of additional claims that are not within the scope of § 2254. Section 2255(a) reads as follows:

> (a) A prisoner in custody under sentence of a court established by Act of Congress claiming the right to be released upon the ground that the sentence was imposed in violation of the Constitution or laws of the United States, or that the court was without jurisdiction to impose such sentence, or that the sentence was in excess of the maximum authorized by law, or is otherwise subject to collateral attack, may move the court which imposed the sentence to vacate, set aside or correct the sentence.

A prisoner in federal custody may assert violations of federal law (including constitutional violations), a lack of jurisdiction, or a sentencing challenge. The prisoner "may move the court which imposed the sentence to vacate, set aside or correct the sentence." 28 U.S.C. § 2255(a). Thus, aside from the geographic change, § 2255 differs from § 2254 in that it also expressly permits federal relief for a sentencing error. Of course, state inmates may still get relief from certain sentencing errors, but the habeas statute does not expressly provide for the availability of such relief.

Despite broad statutory language, the Court has held that § 2255 does not encompass "all claimed errors in conviction and sentencing." United States v. Addonizio, 442 U.S. 178, 185 (1979). The Court held that an error of law, as distinguished from a constitutional error, is cognizable under § 2255 only if it "constituted a fundamental defect which inherently results in a complete miscarriage of justice." In that case, the prisoner complained that the judge erred in calculating the sentence, because parole policies had changed in a way that should have been taken into account. The Court explained:

> The claimed error here—that the judge was incorrect in his assumptions about the future course of parole proceedings—does not meet any of the established standards of collateral attack. There is no claim of a constitutional violation; the sentence imposed was within the statutory limits; and the proceeding was not infected with any error of fact or law of the "fundamental" character that renders the entire proceeding irregular and invalid.

In short, the Court re-aligned the § 2255 practice with the practice under the habeas statute applicable to state inmates. Other questions about the cognizability of certain § 2255 claims remain unanswered by the Court. For example, some courts have extended the rule of *Stone v. Powell*, barring collateral litigation of Fourth Amendment exclusionary claims, to § 2255 motions.[a] Do you think those courts are right to do so? What policy interests did *Stone v. Powell* vindicate, and do those interests play out differently in the federal-inmate context?

---

[a] See, e.g., Brock v. United States, 573 F.3d 497, 500 (7th Cir. 2009) ("This Court has determined that the principles of Stone apply equally to § 2255 motions.") ; United States v. Cook, 997 F.2d 1312, 1317 (10th Cir. 1993) ("Today, we . . . hold that Fourth Amendment violations are not reviewable in a § 2255 motion when the federal prisoner has had a full and fair opportunity to litigate the Fourth Amendment claim at trial and present issues on direct appeal.").

2) Post-*Booker* Sentencing Challenges. The *Addonizio* case is somewhat outdated, because sentencing and parole outcomes now turn heavily on guidelines issued by the United States Sentencing Commission ("Sentencing Guidelines" or "Guidelines"). The Guidelines were, for some time, more or less mandatory. A federal judge would compute the Guidelines range based on a number of variables, and sentence the convicted prisoner within that range. The variables would generally relate either to offense conduct (43 offense levels) or to criminal history (six categories). The Guidelines are extremely complex, and, following *Booker v. United States*, 543 U.S. 220 (2005), they are only advisory. *Booker* held that, because Guidelines findings were judicial determinations not made by a jury beyond a reasonable doubt, they could not be mandatory sentencing rules. The Supreme Court has nonetheless permitted federal courts of appeals to apply a "presumption of reasonableness" to Guidelines sentences. See *Rita v. United States*, 551 U.S. 339 (2007). As Professor Kate Stith has put it, while the Guidelines remain the "starting point for all sentences," they also remain "the frame, in both law and practice, in which sentences are viewed."[b] The combination of judicial discretion and Guidelines complexity nonetheless creates divergent interpretation of sentencing provisions,[c] which in turn leads to appeals and § 2255 proceedings involving federal sentences.[d]

"Departures" are sentences that fall out of the recommended Guideline range, sometimes called the "heartland." Some Circuits have held that federal inmates may not use § 2255 to challenge Guidelines departures, thereby limiting § 2255 sentencing challenges to other types of sentencing errors.[e] For example, the Seventh Circuit states: "we have held that deviations from the Sentencing Guidelines generally are not cognizable on a § 2255 motion," but explained that in the different situation "where a change in law reduces the defendant's statutory maximum sentence below the imposed sentence, have long been cognizable on collateral review." Welch v. U.S., 604 F.3d 408, 412 (7th Cir. 2010). What is the difference between an ordinary Guidelines departure from the heartland and the situation described in *Welch*? In part, that court relied on the fact that § 2255(a) includes in its statutory scope challenges to a sentence "in excess of the maximum authorized by law." Other courts of appeals have similarly held that § 2255 may be used to challenge sentences in excess of the statutory maximum.[f]

---

[b] Kate Stith, *Arc of the Pendulum*, 117 Yale L. J. 1420, 1496 (2008).

[c] For a general discussion and empirical analysis of the divergence in Guidelines application, see Ryan W. Scott, *Inter-Judge Sentencing Disparity after* Booker: *A First Look*, 63 Stanford L. Rev. 1 (2010).

[d] For just one fascinating example of a § 2255 sentencing challenge, see U.S. v. Santos, 553 U.S. 507 (2008), raising the question how a sentencing judge should consider the proceeds of an illegal gambling operation for sentencing under the federal money laundering statute.

[e] See, e.g., United States v. Mikalajunas, 186 F.3d 490, 495–96 (4th Cir.1999) (collecting cases); Jones v. United States, 178 F.3d 790, 796 (6th Cir.1999) ("Moreover, an error in the application of the Sentencing Guidelines does not warrant collateral relief under § 2255 absent a complete miscarriage of justice."); Burke v. United States, 152 F.3d 1329, 1332 (11th Cir.1998) ("a claim that the sentence imposed is contrary to a post-sentencing clarifying amendment is a non-constitutional issue that does not provide a basis for collateral relief in the absence of a complete miscarriage of justice."); Graziano v. United States, 83 F.3d 587, 590 (2d Cir.1996) (collecting cases).

[f] See, e.g. United States v. Sisco ("We have repeatedly held that, in the face of a valid appeal waiver, any sentence within the statutory range is not subject to appeal."); United States v. Guillen ("Guillen was entitled to appeal her sentence if it was above the statutory maximum or departed upward from the Guideline range.").

3) Cognizability of Challenges to Guilty pleas. Just as in state courts, the vast majority of federal defendants plead guilty. Plea agreements usually require that the defendant not only waive the right to appeal, but also the right to "collaterally attack the conviction and sentence" under § 2255. See United States v. Freeman, 131 S.Ct. 2685, 2699 (2011). The guilty plea, however, may not bar challenges to the formation of the plea itself, including IAC claims and challenges to the voluntariness of the plea. Moreover, a plea agreement cannot waive § 2255 claims challenging the imposition of the sentence after the plea was entered.[g] For example, related to the prior Note, courts have held that an appeal waiver in a plea agreement may result in a "miscarriage of justice" if the "sentence exceeds the statutory maximum." United States v. White, 584 F.3d 935, 948 (10th Cir. 2009).

———

NOTE ON § 2255 FILING DATA

Despite procedural restrictions adopted by AEDPA, the number of § 2255 filings grew somewhat steadily over time, as the table below displays.[h]

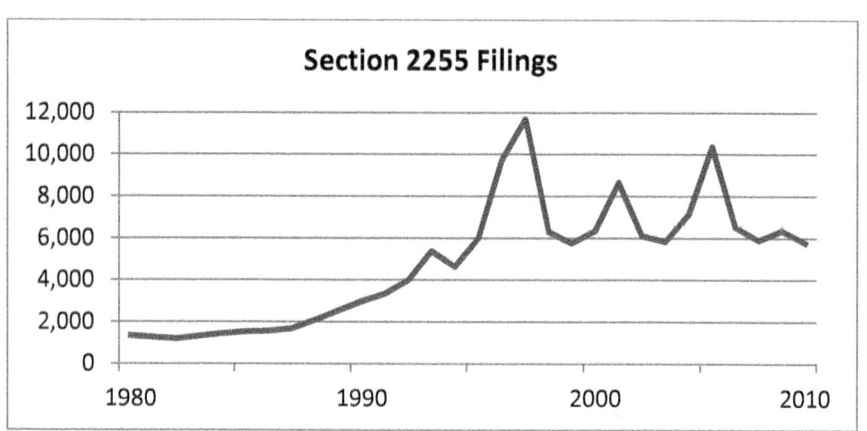

Section 2255 petitions are an important part of the federal docket. Recall that state prisoners file about 20,000 federal habeas petitions a year—§ 2255 petitions compose one third to one-half of the number of federal habeas petitions filed by state prisoners.

———

NOTE ON THE "SAVINGS CLAUSE" AND RELATIONSHIP TO HABEAS PRACTICE

By enacting § 2255, Congress meant to "afford federal prisoners a remedy identical in scope to federal habeas corpus." Davis v. United States, 417 U.S. 333, 343 (1974). Section 2255, however, does not have an identical scope and

---

[g] See Randy Hertz & James S. Liebman, *Federal Habeas Corpus Practice and Procedure* at § 41.7[b] (6th ed. 2011) (FHCPP) (collecting cases).

[h] These data are compiled from the Sourcebook of Criminal Justice Statistics, at http://www.albany.edu/sourcebook/pdf/t5652009.pdf (last visited on Feb. 12, 2013).

nor does it *completely* replace habeas corpus for federal prisoners. By adding a savings clause in the statute, Congress provided that a habeas petition under § 2241 may still be filed if remedies under § 2255 are "inadequate or ineffective." Specifically, § 2255(e) provides:

> An application for a writ of habeas corpus in behalf of a prisoner who is authorized to apply for relief by motion pursuant to this section, shall not be entertained if it appears that the applicant has failed to apply for relief, by motion, to the court which sentenced him, or that such court has denied him relief, *unless it also appears that the remedy by motion is inadequate or ineffective to test the legality of his detention.*

(Emphasis added.) How does the Savings Clause map on to the constitutional requirement that any substitute habeas remedy be "adequate and effective?"

Cases developing the meaning of the Savings Clause will be explored further below. Consider, though, whether adequate and effective review of detention necessarily means that a judge should use the same procedures when examining the convictions of state and federal prisoners. On the one hand, judges may adopt stricter restrictions on habeas relief for state inmates because of interests in federalism and comity. After all, the Court developed doctrines in the § 2254 state prisoner context that are animated by federalism and comity interests. Although federal judges might be expected to defer to state judges and state sovereignty in § 2254 cases, federalism is simply not relevant in § 2255 cases, in which federal judges review federal convictions. On the other hand, a divergence in a federal judge's treatment of state and federal post-conviction review seems troubling. Why should two prisoners subject to identical procedural errors be treated differently by a federal judge? The next Section explores how the Court has interpreted § 2255 to include procedural doctrines borrowed from § 2254 decisional law.

2. AEDPA's EFFECTS ON § 2255

NOTE ON MERITS REVIEW AND NONRETROACTIVITY

A federal judge conducts more deferential merits review for state inmates than for federal inmates. This is because of § 2254(d): the substantive limit on relief applicable to state inmates, which defers to a state judge's reasoning where a state court adjudicated a claim on the merits. There is no analogous provision in § 2255. Under § 2255, a judge reviews a claim *de novo* and may grant relief if a claim has merit. Why do you think Congress declined to include a provision like § 2254(d) in the statutes governing federal-inmate proceedings? Are there features of § 2254(d) that should be applied in the § 2255 context?

Although AEDPA did not alter the standard for § 2255 merits review, federal courts hold that *Teague* applies in § 2255 proceedings. Moreover, the lower federal courts apply *Teague* even though the federalism concerns that animate the *Teague* rule are not present in the § 2255 context. The lower federal courts that apply *Teague* instead usually cite a finality interest.[i] The Supreme Court,

---

[i] See, e.g., United States v. Martinez, 139 F.3d 412, 416 (4th Cir. 1998) ("Because each of those cases presented the retroactivity issue in the context of convictions under federal criminal law, it can safely be assumed that the Court would apply Teague 's nonretroactivity principle to suits under § 2255. Indeed, the purpose of collateral relief under § 2255 is identical to that of the habeas writ generally."); Gilberti v. United States, 917 F.2d 92, 94 (2d Cir. 1990) ("The general principle of nonretroactivity on collateral review is not limited to state convic-

however, has reserved the question of whether *Teague* applies in § 2255 proceedings. See Danforth v. Minnesota, 552 U.S. 264, 269 n. 4 (2008).

NOTES ON SUCCESSIVE PETITIONS

1) AEDPA's § 2255 Successive Petition Rule. AEDPA added an express successive-petition provision, which now appears 28 U.S.C. § 2255(h). That provision reads as follows:

> (h) A second or successive motion must be certified as provided in section 2244 by a panel of the appropriate court of appeals to contain—

> (1) newly discovered evidence that, if proven and viewed in light of the evidence as a whole, would be sufficient to establish by clear and convincing evidence that no reasonable factfinder would have found the movant guilty of the offense; or

> (2) a new rule of constitutional law, made retroactive to cases on collateral review by the Supreme Court, that was previously unavailable.

The provision mostly resembles its analogue in § 2244(b), with several noteworthy differences.

2) No Express Successive-Claim Requirement. Unlike its sister provision applicable to state prisoners in 28 U.S.C. § 2244(b)(1), § 2255 does not contain any provision applicable to claims that have been raised in a prior petition. Section 2244(b)(2) states categorically that "[a] claim presented in a second or successive habeas corpus application under section 2254 that was presented in a prior application shall be dismissed." How should a federal court interpret the absence of a provision expressly foreclosing relief for successive claims that have been raised in prior petitions?

3) The Diligence Requirement for Abusive Claims. Second, the language of § 2255(h)(1) imposes no diligence requirement for newly-discovered facts. Section 2244(b)(2)(B)(ii), which is the analogous provision applicable to state-inmate petitions, does not permit relief upon discovery of new facts unless "the factual predicate for the claim could not have been discovered previously through the exercise of due diligence[.]" How should courts interpret that difference in the statutory text?

4) Freestanding Innocence Claims. Unlike 28 U.S.C. § 2244(b)(2)(B)(ii), § 2255 seems to permit "freestanding innocence" claims to pass through the successive-petition bar. Section 2244(b)(2)(B)(ii) permits merits consideration with respect to claims for which a state inmate can show cause, when "the facts underlying the claim, if proven and viewed in light of the evidence as a whole, would be sufficient to establish by clear and convincing evidence that, *but for constitutional error,* no reasonable factfinder would have found the applicant guilty of the underlying offense." (Emphasis added.) Section 2255(h) requires no nexus between the new evidence and constitutional error. Should this differ-

---

tions. Although Teague did involve the habeas corpus petition of a state prisoner, there is no indication that the Court intended its analysis to be limited to state convictions."); United States v. Ayala, 894 F.2d 425, 429 n.8 (D.C. Cir. 1990) (citing *Teague*-barred claim as an example of a challenge that a federal prisoner could not make in § 2255 proceeding).

ence be interpreted to mean that federal prisoners can bring successive claims of freestanding innocence, but state prisoners cannot?

5) Innocence of Sentence. Does § 2255(h) permit a federal judge to consider second or successive claims asserting "innocence" of the sentence? Some courts have ruled that, as with § 2244(b), the language regarding finding the movant "guilty of the offense" bars second or successive claims asserting "innocence" of the sentence. For example, the Fifth Circuit concluded that "there is no reason to believe that Congress intended the language 'guilty of the offense' to mean 'eligible for a death sentence.'" In re Webster, 605 F.3d 256, 257–58 (5th Cir. 2010). Judge Jacques L. Weiner, Jr. concurred with the panel's ruing, stating, "I write separately to emphasize the absurdity of its Kafkaesque result: Because Webster seeks to demonstrate only that he is constitutionally ineligible for the death penalty—and not that he is factually innocent of the crime—we must sanction his execution."[j]

6) Authorization Requirements. 28 U.S.C. § 2255(h) has preambular language requiring that a "second or successive motion must be certified as provided in section 2244 by a panel of the appropriate court of appeals[.]" Federal courts have interpreted that provision to mean that federal inmates must seek and obtain precisely the same authorization orders as do their state counterparts. The authorization requirements for state and federal inmates, however, have some important differences. First, there is no express provision that bars certiorari review of an order denying authorization under § 2255, whereas § 2244(b)(3)(E) states that "[t]he grant or denial of an authorization by a court of appeals to file a second or successive application shall not be appealable and shall not be the subject of a petition for rehearing or for a writ of certiorari." Federal courts have nonetheless read this requirement into the federal authorization procedure, relying on the language in § 2255 stating that a successive motion must be certified "as provided in section 2244."[k]

7) Second, § 2255(h) does not expressly require the *district court* to apply the restrictions on *each claim* after the appeals court has determined that *the petition* contains at least one claim that meets those restrictions. Section 2255(h) does not have any instructions for the district court upon consideration of a successive petition, whereas § 2244(b)(4) requires a district court to "dismiss any claim presented in a second or successive application that the court of appeals has authorized to be filed unless the applicant shows that the claim satisfies the requirements of [§ 2244]."

---

[j] See also Burris v. Parke, 116 F.3d 256, 258–59 (7th Cir. 1997) ("We have held that identical language in § 2244(b)(2)(B)(ii) refers unambiguously to the offense of conviction and does not permit proceedings concerning the sentence"); In re Vial, 115 F.3d 1192, 1198 & n.12 (4th Cir. 1997) (en banc) (declining to address whether § 2255(h) permits a second or successive petition alleging innocence of the death penalty, but holding that inmate "cannot pursue this claim under the 'newly discovered evidence' exception to the bar on second and successive § 2255 proceedings because that exception applies only to challenges to the underlying conviction; it is not available to assert sentencing error").

[k] See, e.g., Triestman v. United States ("In the absence of such a specification, it is logical to assume that Congress intended to refer to all of the subsections of § 2244 dealing with the authorization of second and successive motions, including § 2244(b)(3)(D).").

NOTES ON AEDPA STATUTE OF LIMITATIONS

1) AEDPA Statute of Limitations. AEDPA enacted a one-year statute of limitations for actions under 28 U.S.C. § 2255. Specifically, § 2255(f) provides:

> (f) A 1-year period of limitation shall apply to a motion under this section. The limitation period shall run from the latest of—

> (1) the date on which the judgment of conviction becomes final;

> (2) the date on which the impediment to making a motion created by governmental action in violation of the Constitution or laws of the United States is removed, if the movant was prevented from making a motion by such governmental action;

> (3) the date on which the right asserted was initially recognized by the Supreme Court, if that right has been newly recognized by the Supreme Court and made retroactively applicable to cases on collateral review; or

> (4) the date on which the facts supporting the claim or claims presented could have been discovered through the exercise of due diligence.

The state-inmate analogue for § 2255(f) is § 2244(d)(1), presented in Chapter 4, which sets forth four statutory trigger dates for the inception of the limitations period.

2) Federal Inmate Trigger Dates. The major difference between state and federal trigger dates involves the language of the first trigger, the finality date of the conviction. Compare § 2255(f)(1) with the language from § 2244(d)(1)(A): "the date on which the judgment became final *by the conclusion of direct review or the expiration of the time for seeking such review*" (Emphasis added.) What, if any, is the significance of the italicized language? Does a state conviction "become final" at a different point than does a federal conviction? After all, "When Congress includes particular language in one section of a statute but omits it in another section of the same Act, we have recognized, it is generally presumed that Congress acts intentionally and purposely in the disparate inclusion or exclusion." Russello v. United States, 464 U.S. 16, 23 (1983) (citations and internal quotation marks omitted.) In *Clay v. United States*, 537 U.S. 522 (2003), however, the Supreme Court resolved a split among the Circuits, and held that the state-inmate and federal-inmate trigger dates were the same. The Court noted that "Finality is variously defined; like many legal terms, its precise meaning depends on context." The Court explained that in the post-conviction context, "[f]inality attaches when this Court affirms a conviction on the merits on direct review or denies a petition for a writ of certiorari, or when the time for filing a certiorari petition expires." What rationale might exist for more carefully specifying the finality rule in the state inmate-context?

As for the rest of the triggers, § 2255 has much the same exceptions as in the parallel provision in § 2244(d)(1) applicable to state convicts, permitting filing within a year: after a government impediment to the motion was removed, a new right was recognized and "made retroactively applicable to cases on collateral review" by the Supreme Court, or the date on which new facts "could have been discovered through the exercise of due diligence."

3) Equitable Tolling. Of course, § 2255 reflects the fact that federal-inmate proceedings lack the complications created by state post-conviction adjudication. As a result, there is no statutory tolling mechanism pegged to the pendency of state post-conviction applications. Can you see why there nonetheless exists a need for an equitable tolling rule? Recall that *Holland v. Florida*, 130 S.Ct. 2549 (2010) announced that equitable tolling was available to state inmates that could show (1) extraordinary circumstances and (2) diligence. Although the Supreme Court has yet to expressly decide the issue, every federal court of appeals to have considered the issue has held that there is also an equitable tolling rule for federal inmates seeking relief under § 2255.[1]

NOTE ON EVIDENTIARY HEARINGS

AEDPA also enacted a provision for evidentiary hearings involving federal inmates, which uses a standard that is more forgiving than the standard for state inmates. Specifically, 28 U.S.C. § 2255(b) provides in pertinent part:

> Unless the motion and the files and records of the case conclusively show that the prisoner is entitled to no relief, the court shall cause notice thereof to be served upon the United States attorney, grant a prompt hearing thereon, determine the issues and make findings of fact and conclusions of law with respect thereto.

Compare the § 2255 conditions for evidentiary hearings with those in § 2254(e), which are applicable in state-inmate challenges. In contrast to the extraordinarily restrictive standard in § 2254(e)(2), under § 2255 a district court should conduct a hearing "unless the facts alleged are contradicted by the record or are inherently incredible and to the extent that they are merely conclusions rather than statements of fact." Machibroda v. United States, 368 U.S. 487, 494–95 (1962). Thus, in the § 2255 context, the pre-AEDPA standard for evidentiary hearings, originally derived from *Townsend v. Sain*, is still in place. Why would Congress enact a less permissive rule for federal evidentiary hearings involving federal inmates? Does the rule reflect that there is no need for deference to state factfinding? Does it reflect that there may be no factfinding at all, at least for certain types of claims? What types?

---

[1] See Ramos-Martinez v. United States, 638 F.3d 315 (1st Cir. 2011); United States v. Aguirre–Ganceda, 592 F.3d 1043, 1045 (9th Cir.2010); Byers v. United States, 561 F.3d 832, 836 (8th Cir.2009); United States v. Petty, 530 F.3d 361, 364 (5th Cir.2008) (per curiam); United States v. Gabaldon, 522 F.3d 1121, 1124 (10th Cir.2008); Solomon v. United States, 467 F.3d 928, 935 (6th Cir.2006); United States v. Sosa, 364 F.3d 507, 512 (4th Cir.2004); Baldayaque v. United States, 338 F.3d 145, 150 (2d Cir.2003); United States v. Marcello, 212 F.3d 1005, 1010 (7th Cir.2000); Sandvik v. United States, 177 F.3d 1269, 1271 (11th Cir.1999) (per curiam); Miller v. N.J. State Dept. of Corr., 145 F.3d 616, 619 n. 1 (3d Cir.1998). The Court of Appeals for the District of Columbia has assumed arguendo that the § 2255 limitations period can be equitably tolled. See, e.g. United States v. Saro, 252 F.3d 449, 453–54 (D.C. Cir. 2001).

3. PROCEDURAL DEFAULT AND EXHAUSTION OF APPELLATE REMEDIES

NOTE ON EXHAUSTION OF APPELLATE REMEDIES

One major difference between § 2254 and § 2255 involves the requirements for exhaustion and procedural default. For obvious reasons, there is no requirement that a federal inmate seeking relief under § 2255 exhaust state post-conviction proceedings. A federal inmate, however, must exhaust federal appellate remedies: federal courts typically will not permit § 2255 motions to be brought while an appeal is pending. See Randy Hertz & James S. Liebman, *Federal Habeas Corpus Practice and Procedure* at § 41.4[a] (6th ed. 2011) (FHCPP). However, claims that have already been rejected on direct review will ordinarily not be entertained under § 2255. The Supreme Court has emphasized district court "discretion" to decline to reach the merits of a federal claim previously raised and dismissed during the appeal. See Kaufman v. U.S., 394 U.S. 217, 227, n. 8 (1969).[m] The pertinent language in *Kaufman* is dicta, but many federal courts rely on it. The decisional law, however, does recognize exceptions where the claim relies on new law or new evidence—or where IAC explains why the claim was not presented during the direct appeal.[n] Whereas the state-inmate exhaustion provision would require the federal court to send the claim back to state court, the § 2255 exhaustion doctrine does not require a claimant to return to a federal court of appeals to exhaust appellate remedies. Why are the rules different in the two contexts?

INTRODUCTORY NOTE ON PROCEDURAL DEFAULT

There is no "adequate and independent state ground" doctrine for claims that are defaulted by federal inmates; § 2255 proceedings involve only federal questions. The comity and federalism concerns that animate procedural default doctrine for state inmates are absent in § 2255 proceedings. If there are no comity and federalism interests at stake, what might nonetheless prompt the Supreme Court to craft a procedural default rule? Would you expect that rule to be more or less forgiving than its state-inmate counterpart? Why?

United States v. Frady
Supreme Court of the United States
456 U.S. 152 (1982)

■ JUSTICE O'CONNOR delivered the opinion of the Court.

Rule 52(b) of the Federal Rules of Criminal Procedure permits a criminal conviction to be overturned on direct appeal for "plain error" in the jury instructions, even if the defendant failed to object to the erroneous instructions before the jury retired, as required by Rule 30. In this case we are

---

[m] See also Withrow v. U.S., 507 U.S. 680, 720–721 (1993) (Scalia, J., concurring in part and dissenting in part) (collecting cases and noting that "a prior opportunity for full and fair litigation is normally dispositive of a federal prisoner's habeas claim.").

[n] See Hertz & Liebman, *FHCPP, supra* note g at § 41.7.

asked to decide whether the same standard of review applies on a collateral challenge to a criminal conviction brought under 28 U.S.C. § 2255. * * *

Joseph Frady, the respondent, does not dispute that 19 years ago he and Richard Gordon killed Thomas Bennett in the front room of the victim's house in Washington, D. C. * * *

Although Frady now admits that the evidence that he and Gordon caused Bennett's death was "overwhelming," at his trial in the United States District Court for the District of Columbia Frady defended solely by denying all responsibility for the killing, suggesting through his attorney that another man, the real murderer, had been seen leaving the victim's house while the police were preoccupied apprehending Frady and Gordon. Consistent with this theory, Frady did not raise any justification, excuse, or mitigating circumstance. A jury convicted Frady of first-degree murder and robbery, and sentenced him to death by electrocution.

Sitting en banc, the Court of Appeals for the District of Columbia Circuit upheld Frady's first-degree murder conviction by a vote of 8–1. [However, the appellate court set aside Frady's death sentence and he was resentenced to life in prison. He then filed a series of collateral attacks: Frady filed four motions to vacate or reduce his sentence in 1965, and one each in 1974, 1975, 1976, and 1978. The 1978 motion resulted in a Court of Appeals decision ruling that Frady's sentences for robbery and murder run concurrently rather than consecutively.] * * *

Frady initiated the present action by filing a motion under 28 U.S.C. § 2255 seeking the vacation of his sentence because the jury instructions used at his trial in 1963 were defective. Specifically, Frady argued that the Court of Appeals, in cases decided after his trial and appeal, had disapproved instructions identical to those used in his case. As determined by these later rulings, the judge at Frady's trial had improperly equated intent with malice by stating that "a wrongful act ... intentionally done ... is therefore done with malice aforethought." * * * Also, the trial judge had incorrectly instructed the jury that "the law infers or presumes from the use of such weapon in the absence of explanatory or mitigating circumstances the existence of the malice essential to culpable homicide." * * * In his § 2255 motion Frady contended that these instructions compelled the jury to presume malice and thereby wrongfully eliminated any possibility of a manslaughter verdict, since manslaughter was defined as culpable homicide without malice.

Nineteen years after his crime, Frady now complains he was convicted by a jury erroneously instructed on the meaning of malice. At trial, however, Frady did not object to the instructions, nor did he raise the issue on direct appeal. Rule 30 of the Federal Rules of Criminal Procedure declares in pertinent part:

"No party may assign as error any portion of the charge or omission therefrom unless he objects thereto before the jury retires to consider its verdict, stating distinctly the matter to which he objects and the grounds of his objection."

Rule 52(b), however, somewhat tempers the severity of Rule 30. It grants the courts of appeals the latitude to correct particularly egregious errors on appeal regardless of a defendant's trial default:

"Plain errors or defects affecting substantial rights may be noticed although they were not brought to the attention of the court."

* * * Because it was intended for use on direct appeal, however, the "plain error" standard is out of place when a prisoner launches a collateral attack against a criminal conviction after society's legitimate interest in the finality of the judgment has been perfected by the expiration of the time allowed for direct review or by the affirmance of the conviction on appeal. Nevertheless, in 1980 the Court of Appeals applied the "plain error" standard to Frady's long-delayed § 2255 motion, as though the clock had been turned back to 1965 when Frady's case was first before the court on direct appeal. In effect, the court allowed Frady to take a second appeal 15 years after the first was decided. * * * We reaffirm the well-settled principle that to obtain collateral relief a prisoner must clear a significantly higher hurdle than would exist on direct appeal. * * *

We believe the proper standard for review of Frady's motion is the "cause and actual prejudice" standard enunciated in *Davis v. United States*, 411 U.S. 233 (1973), and later confirmed and extended in * * * *Wainwright v. Sykes*, 433 U.S. 72 (1977). Under this standard, to obtain collateral relief based on trial errors to which no contemporaneous objection was made, a convicted defendant must show both (1) "cause" excusing his double procedural default, and (2) "actual prejudice" resulting from the errors of which he complains. In applying this dual standard to the case before us, we find it unnecessary to determine whether Frady has shown cause, because we are confident he suffered no actual prejudice of a degree sufficient to justify collateral relief 19 years after his crime. * * *

So stated, Frady's claim of actual prejudice has validity only if an error in the instructions concerning an element of the crime charged amounts to prejudice *per se*, regardless of the particular circumstances of the individual case. Our precedents, however, hold otherwise. Contrary to Frady's suggestion, he must shoulder the burden of showing, not merely that the errors at his trial created a possibility of prejudice, but that they worked to his actual and substantial disadvantage, infecting his entire trial with error of constitutional dimensions.

This Frady has failed to do. At the outset, we emphasize that this would be a different case had Frady brought before the District Court affirmative evidence indicating that he had been convicted wrongly of a crime of which he was innocent. But Frady, it must be remembered, did not assert at trial that he and Richard Gordon beat Thomas Bennett to death without malice. Instead, Frady claimed he had nothing whatever to do with the crime. The evidence, however, was overwhelming, and Frady promptly abandoned that theory on appeal. Since that time, Frady has never presented colorable evidence, even from his own testimony, indicating such justification, mitigation, or excuse that would reduce his crime from murder to manslaughter. * * *

In sum, Frady has fallen far short of meeting his burden of showing that he has suffered the degree of actual prejudice necessary to overcome society's justified interests in the finality of criminal judgments. Therefore, the judgment of the Court of Appeals is reversed, and the case is remanded for further proceedings consistent with this opinion.

So ordered.

[The CHIEF JUSTICE and JUSTICE MARSHALL took no part in the decision. JUSTICE STEVENS and JUSTICE BLACKMUN each wrote concurring opinions that are omitted. JUSTICE BRENNAN'S dissenting opinion is omitted.]

———

NOTES AND QUESTIONS ON FRADY

1) **"Procedural Default" and Excuse Thereof in § 2255 Cases.** What are the interests justifying the Court's application of the procedural default rule developed for state-inmate challenges? The Court had previously explained, "Plainly the interest in finality is the same with regard to both federal and state prisoners. . . There is no reason to . . . give greater preclusive effect to procedural defaults by federal defendants than to similar defaults by state defendants." Francis v. Henderson, 425 U.S. 536, 542 (1976) (citations omitted and alterations in original). Do you agree that the finality interest is the same? Does the state inmate rule reflect anything other than that finality interest? *Frady* also reasoned that a "federal prisoner . . . unlike his state counterparts, has already had an opportunity to present his federal claims in federal trial and appellate forums." Has a prisoner necessarily had the opportunity to receive a merits adjudication? Does this comment in *Frady* apply for all types of claims?

2) **Frady's Claim.** Is the argument for applying a procedural default rule in § 2255 (and failing to excuse it) stronger in a case like Frady's, where there was no objection to the jury instructions at trial, than in a case where a claim was, say, omitted by counsel during the direct appeal or his prior § 2255 motion? What if it was a claim that could not be brought during the direct appeal? What if Frady had argued that his lawyer was ineffective for failing to object to the jury instructions at trial? What is the difference between these two types of situations, and why does the distinction matter? Note also that, to the extent that finality was a concern in Frady's case, AEDPA's bar on successive petitions (had previously filed a § 2255 motion) and AEDPA's statute of limitations would be reasons to dispose of his claim were he to bring it today.

3) **The Dissent.** Justice Brennan, in a dissenting opinion that was not excerpted, argued that there is no similar tension between sovereigns when a federal court reviews a federal conviction: "Under § 2255, the prisoner is directed back to the same court that first convicted him." Justice Brennan added "that this is not the first instance in which the Court has obscured the distinction between § 2254 and § 2255." He pointed out that in prior decisions, such as *Wainwright v. Sykes*, the Court had relied on the Federal Rules of Criminal Procedure to import stricter rules into civil federal habeas proceedings. The origins of the cause-and-prejudice standard were a brief reference in Fed. R. Crim. Pro. 12(b)(2), which had provided that failure of a defendant to assert a defense could be excused "for cause shown." See Davis v. United States, 411 U.S. 233, 243–245 (1973). In *Frady*, Justice Brennan noted, the Court did the opposite, and rejected the plain error rule for federal criminal appeals in favor of a more restrictive procedural default rule.

4) **Waiver.** Recall that in the § 2254 context federal courts usually treat a forfeited procedural default defense as waived. A federal court, however, is permitted to impose the bar *sua sponte*. Similarly, federal courts will usually give effect to a waived procedural default defense in § 2255 proceedings.[o]

---

[o] See, e.g., Torzala v. U.S., 545 F.3d 517, 522 (7th Cir. 2008) ("Because the government did not assert procedural default as a defense in this action but instead chose to respond on the merits, however, the government has waived the procedural default.").

5)   *Massaro v. United States.* The Supreme Court elaborated on the § 2255
procedural default rules in *Massaro v. United States,* 538 U.S. 500 (2003). The
Court explained the facts as follows:

> [Massaro] was indicted on federal racketeering charges, including murder
> in aid of racketeering, 18 U.S.C. § 1962(d), in connection with the shooting
> death of Joseph Fiorito. He was tried in the United States District Court
> for the Southern District of New York. The day before Massaro's trial was
> to begin, prosecutors learned of what appeared to be a critical piece of evi-
> dence: a bullet allegedly recovered from the car in which the victim's body
> was found. They waited for several days, however, to inform defense coun-
> sel of this development. Not until the trial was underway and the defense
> had made its opening statement did they make this disclosure. After the
> trial court and the defense had been informed of the development but still
> during the course of trial, defense counsel more than once declined the tri-
> al court's offer of a continuance so the bullet could be examined. Massaro
> was convicted and sentenced to life imprisonment.

The federal district court dismissed Massaro's § 2255 petition, holding that the
ineffective assistance claim that it contained was procedurally defaulted. The
Second Circuit affirmed. The Supreme Court ultimately reversed the Second
Circuit, and explained: "The procedural-default rule is neither a statutory nor a
constitutional requirement, but it is a doctrine adhered to by the courts to conserve judicial resources and to respect the law's important interest in the finality of judgments." The Court held that "requiring a criminal defendant to bring
ineffective-assistance-of-counsel claims on direct appeal does not promote these
objectives." The Court criticized the practical implications of requiring § 2255
claimants to "preserve" their IAC claims by asserting them on appeal:

> As Judge Easterbrook has noted, "[r]ules of procedure should be designed
> to induce litigants to present their contentions to the right tribunal at the
> right time." [citation omitted]. Applying the usual procedural-default rule
> to ineffective-assistance claims would have the opposite effect, creating the
> risk that defendants would feel compelled to raise the issue before there
> has been an opportunity fully to develop the factual predicate for the
> claim. Furthermore, the issue would be raised for the first time in a forum
> not best suited to assess those facts. This is so even if the record contains
> some indication of deficiencies in counsel's performance. The better-
> reasoned approach is to permit ineffective-assistance claims to be brought
> in the first instance in a timely motion in the district court under § 2255.
> We hold that an ineffective-assistance-of-counsel claim may be brought in
> a collateral proceeding under § 2255, whether or not the petitioner could
> have raised the claim on direct appeal.

Does this exception to the procedural default rule make sense? The Court also
reasoned that, otherwise, appellate lawyers would be in an awkward relationship, relying on trial counsel to make sense of a "lengthy record on a short
deadline," but also potentially impugning the effectiveness of trial counsel.
Having already been through the procedural default rules for § 2254 cases,
perhaps *Massaro* foreshadows the Court's subsequent decision in *Martinez v.
Ryan*, discussed in Chapter 4—at least insofar as it is an exception for IAC
claims to the general procedural default rule.

6)   Actual Innocence. Notice that the Court did state that an innocence exception (miscarriage of justice) might apply to a § 2255 procedural default rule.

In *Bousley v. United States*, the Court ordered a remand for the judge to assess whether that prisoner satisfied the miscarriage of justice exception, citing to the *Schlup* standard asking whether "more likely than not" no reasonable juror would have voted to convict the inmate. 524 U.S. 614, 623–25 (1998). Is there any reason why the miscarriage of justice gateway may be different in § 2255 litigation than in state-inmate cases?

7) Actual Innocence (Sentence). Because § 2255 claims often involve sentencing errors, courts frequently encounter the argument that "sentencing innocence" constitutes an excuse for deciding the merits of an otherwise-defaulted claim. For example, the Fourth Circuit excused a procedural default where, based on his report that he was convicted of "armed burglary" in 1973, a prisoner had pleaded guilty and received a "career offender" sentencing enhancement. In fact, the inmate was convicted of "attempted third degree burglary of a drug store" which did not qualify for the enhancement. See U.S. v. Maybeck, 23 F.3d 888, 890–91 (4th Cir. 1994). The *Maybeck* court concluded that "[t]here is no question . . . that on the record we review, Maybeck is actually innocent of being a career offender as defined in § 4B1.1 of the Guidelines." Recall that cases where the innocence-gateway applies to sentencing claims usually involve capital inmates. *Maybeck*, however, held that noncapital sentencing claims could still satisfy the innocence gateway in § 2255 cases:

> The government urges that the actual innocence defense is inapplicable here because it applies only to death penalty habeas challenges otherwise procedurally barred. We disagree. Except for the obvious difference in the severity of the sentences, we see little difference between holding that a defendant can be innocent of the acts required to enhance a sentence in a death case and applying a parallel rationale in non-capital cases.

Was that approach to correcting a sentencing error satisfactory? The Fourth Circuit later limited the rule to the career-offender or other habitual-offender guideline provisions—and held it inapplicable other types of sentencing errors. See United States v. Mikalajunas, 186 F.3d 490, 494–95 (4th Cir.1999). That court explained that any other reading would be "absurdly broad," because, if the actual innocence gateway "is available anytime a guideline is misapplied [then] . . . the actual innocence exception would swallow the rule that issues not raised on appeal cannot be considered in a § 2255 motion absent a showing of cause and prejudice to excuse the default." The court also detailed how other circuits typically had held that "errors of guideline interpretation or application ordinarily fall short of a miscarriage of justice."

Recall *Dretke v. Haley*, 541 U.S. 386 (2004), from Chapter 3. In *Haley*, the Supreme Court expressed concern over "a growing divergence of opinion in the Courts of Appeals regarding the availability and scope of the actual innocence exception in the noncapital sentencing context." The Court, however, declined to address the broad question of whether noncapital-sentencing-innocence showings could satisfy the miscarriage-of-justice gateway. Instead, *Haley* remanded and held that a federal court should first address non-defaulted claims and other possible grounds for cause to excuse the default.

8) Vacated State Convictions. Some § 2255 motions are premised on prior state proceedings, making them, in that way, more like § 2254 cases. That is because a federal prisoner may argue that his sentence is erroneous if an enhancement to the sentence—say, under the Sentencing Guidelines or the Armed Career Criminal Act of 1984, 18 U.S.C. § 924(a)—was premised on prior state convictions that have since been vacated. The Supreme Court has suggested that a federal prisoner might, if the state predicate convictions were vacated, "then apply for reopening of any federal sentence enhanced by the state sentences." Custis v. United States, 511 U.S. 485, 497 (1994). Lower courts have permitted such § 2255 motions.[p]

4. THE CONSTITUTION'S SUSPENSION CLAUSE THE § 2255 "SAVINGS" CLAUSE, AND POST-CONVICTION REVIEW UNDER § 2241.

As described in this Chapter's introductory material, § 2255 includes a "Savings Clause" that permitted a federal inmate to file a habeas corpus petition if the § 2255 remedy was inadequate or ineffective. Specifically, § 2255(e) provides:

> An application for a writ of habeas corpus in behalf of a prisoner who is authorized to apply for relief by motion pursuant to this section, shall not be entertained if it appears that the applicant has failed to apply for relief, by motion, to the court which sentenced him, or that such court has denied him relief, unless it also appears that the remedy by motion is inadequate or ineffective to test the legality of his detention.

28 U.S.C. § 2255(e). Before we spend a little more time with the Savings Clause, it is worth noting that, although § 2255(e) provides statutorily for some situations where federal habeas review should be used as the vehicle for post-conviction challenges, there are others. A federal inmate may file a habeas proceeding under § 2244—rather than a challenge under § 2255—for claims relating to: parole; computation of good time credits or other prison-administered rules regarding length of sentences; and other administrative decisions by prisons, such as discipline or transfer. Such challenges are discussed further in Chapter 11.

When can the § 2255(e) Savings Clause be used by a federal prisoner to file a habeas petition? Federal courts have also found that it may permit claims of innocence to be raised if there is no "adequate" or "effective" way to raise such a claim using § 2255. Moreover, AEDPA's changes to § 2255 have created more incentives for prisoners to denominate their post-conviction challenges as § 2241 habeas petitions, because such styling allows them to avoid the statute of limitations and successive-petition restrictions that § 2255 now contains.

That incentive notwithstanding, many jurisdictions have read § 2255(e) fairly broadly, in keeping with the idea that the Suspension Clause requires there to be some vehicle to adequately and effectively challenge confinement. For example, in *Triestman v. United States,* 124 F.3d 361 (2d Cir.1997), the court of appeals said:

> We have already stated that "inadequate or ineffective" is not limited merely to the practical considerations suggested by the government, but refers to something that is still less than the full set of cases in

---

[p] See, e.g., U.S. v. Pettiford ("In accordance with this line of cases, this court, when reviewing sentences imposed under the career offender guideline, has concluded that sentence enhancements based on previous convictions should be reconsidered if those convictions are later vacated.") The Supreme Court has added, however, that the federal convict must act diligently to obtain the state court vacatur. Johnson v. United States.

which § 2255 is either unavailable or unsuccessful. We now hold that
that "something" is, at the least, the set of cases in which the petitioner cannot, for whatever reason, utilize § 2255, and in which the failure
to allow for collateral review would raise serious constitutional questions.

When would inability to use § 2255 raise serious constitutional questions?
In an *en banc* decision, the Eleventh Circuit addressed this problem and
reviewed the state of the caselaw on the meaning of the Savings Clause.

Gilbert v. United States

Eleventh Circuit Court of Appeals
640 F.3d 1293 (11th Cir. 2011)

■ CARNES, Circuit Judge:

[Federal prisoner Ezell Gilbert was sentenced for possession with intent to distribute crack cocaine in 1997, eight years before the decision in
United States v. Booker, 543 U.S. 220 (2005), made the Guidelines discretionary. In addition, he received enhancements as a career offender based
on two prior convictions—one of which involved carrying a concealed weapon, which he argued was not a crime of violence within the meaning of the
Guideline provision, U.S.S.G. § 4B1.1. The enhancement elevated his sentence substantially, from a Guidelines range of 151 to 188 months, to a
range of 292 to 365 months. The judge sentenced him to 292 months, the
bottom of the range, after making it "abundantly clear that he would have
preferred to give Gilbert a shorter term of imprisonment." Gilbert's direct
appeal and pro se 28 U.S.C. § 2255 motions were denied. However, following the Circuit's interpretation of the Supreme Court's decision in *Began v.
United States*, 553 U.S. 137 (2008), the Eleventh Circuit ruled in 2008 in
United States v. Archer, 531 F.3d 1347, 1352 (11th Cir. 2008) that it no
longer considered carrying a concealed weapon as a "violent felony" subject
to the career-offender-enhancement provision. Gilbert filed a habeas petition seeking to take advantage of that new Eleventh Circuit ruling. He conceded that the § 2255(h) bar on second and successive petitions prevented
raising his sentencing claims in a § 2255 motion. The district court granted
his habeas petition. The district court was reversed by an appeals court
panel and rehearing en banc was granted.]

   * * * The text of the savings clause itself does not indicate that it authorizes the filing of a § 2241 petition to remedy a miscalculation of the
sentencing guidelines that already has been, or may no longer be, raised in
a § 2255 motion. The language of the savings clause provides that it applies, and a § 2241 petition may be filed, only when "the remedy by [§ 2255]
motion is inadequate or ineffective to test the legality of [the petitioner's]
detention." 28 U.S.C. § 2255(e). The history behind the savings clause does
not provide much help with its meaning. * * * What does the provision
mean? This is one of those times when it is easier to determine something
that a provision does not mean, and that determination is enough to dispose of this case.

3. *The Relationship of § 2255(e) and 2255(h)*

   Assuming that a sentencing guidelines error that resulted in a longer
sentence may be remedied in a collateral proceeding, the reason Gilbert
cannot obtain relief through a § 2255 motion now is that he unsuccessfully
filed one earlier (six years before he filed this motion), and § 2255(h) ex-

pressly bars him from filing another one. The existence of the statutory bar on second and successive motions cannot mean that § 2255 is "inadequate or ineffective" to test the legality of Gilbert's detention within the meaning of the savings clause. If it did, the savings clause would eviscerate the second or successive motions bar, and prisoners could file an endless stream of § 2255 motions, none of which could be dismissed without a determination of the merits of the claims they raise.

That simply cannot be, as every circuit to address the matter has pointed out. * * * We join all of those other circuits in refusing to interpret the savings clause in a way that would drop the § 2255(h) bar on second and successive motions, defeat its purpose, and render it pointless.

Fundamental canons of statutory construction support the conclusion that the generally worded and ambiguous savings clause, which was first enacted in 1947, cannot override the specifically worded and clear statutory bar on second or successive motions that was enacted as part of AEDPA in 1996. An ambiguous or general statutory provision enacted at an earlier time must yield to a specific and clear provision enacted at a later time. * * *

4. Finality Interests

The critically important nature of the finality interests safeguarded by § 2255(h) also weighs heavily against an interpretation of the savings clause that would lower the second or successive motions bar and permit guidelines-based attacks years after the denial of an initial § 2255 motion. Sentencing guidelines provisions are many and complex, the English language and those who use it are imperfect, and the case law about what various and sundry guidelines mean and whether they apply in different factual situations is in a constant state of flux. * * *

The single guidelines term that gave rise to this litigation illustrates the phenomenon. Many are the decisional oars that have churned the law about the meaning of "crime of violence," as it appears in § 4B1.1. * * *And there will undoubtedly be more churning to come as additional decisions are issued refining the term "crime of violence" as it applies to hundreds of crimes variously defined in the codes of the fifty states and in the federal criminal code that might be classified as violent. From 1991 to 2004 the § 4B1.1 career offender guideline was applied in 2,906 cases in this circuit alone. It was applied in 16,049 cases nationwide during that same period. Id.

* * * The rule Gilbert asks us to create for his benefit would apply to every type and kind of enhancement, of which there are scores in the sentencing guidelines Many of those enhancements turn on terms whose precise meaning is not manifestly clear even where the terms are defined in the guidelines. Definitions employ their own terms, the meaning of which can also be debatable, as the whole saga with the § 4B1.1 term "crime of violence" and its § 4B1.2(a) definition of that term proves. Consider just a few examples of enhancement terms which lend themselves to litigation about their extent and scope, and thereby open up the possibility of clarifying case law years after sentences are imposed: "physical contact," "bodily injury," "substantial bodily injury," "permanent or life-threatening bodily injury," "reckless conduct," "custody, care or supervisory control of the defendant," "uncontrollable circumstances," "substantial disruption of public, governmental, or business functions or services," "a pattern of activity," "a substantial part of a fraudulent scheme," "personal information," and

"abuse of a position of trust." Those terms, and many others like them, form a seed bed from which decisions can sprout, undermining sentencing calculations that were made years before.

And the rule Gilbert is seeking could not be confined to sentence miscalculations based on enhancement errors. If the savings clause operates to allow attacks on old sentences that were lengthened by enhancements that later decisions have called into doubt, there is no reason it would not also operate to do the same with any other guidelines calculation error. * * *

As we have pointed out more than once, "one of the principal functions of AEDPA was to ensure a greater degree of finality for convictions." The Supreme Court has reached the same conclusion we have about what Congress did and why, observing that "AEDPA's purpose [is] to further the principles of comity, finality, and federalism." *Williams v. Taylor*, 529 U.S. 420, 436 (2000). * * * The statutory bar against second or successive motions is one of the most important AEDPA safeguards for finality of judgment. * * * If second and successive motions are not "greatly restrict[ed]," there will be no end to collateral attacks on convictions and sentences, and there will be no finality of judgment. * * * We believe that for claims of sentence error, at least where the statutory maximum was not exceeded, the point where finality holds its own against error correction is reached not later than the end of the first round of collateral review. * * *

6. *The Suspension Clause*

None of the other circuits that have refused to apply the savings clause of § 2255(e) to sentencing claims have felt that by declining to do so they were violating the Suspension Clause of the Constitution, Art. I, § 9. Nor do we. * * *

The Supreme Court did have something to say in *Felker v. Turpin*, 518 U.S. 651, (1996), about the Suspension Clause as it involves the AEDPA's clamp down on second or successive petitions in 28 U.S.C. § 2254 cases. What the Court decided in Felker is that the increased restrictions that the statute placed on second or successive habeas petitions do not violate the Suspension Clause. * * * Describing the law restricting second and successive filings as "a complex and evolving body of equitable principles informed and controlled by historical usage, statutory developments, and judicial decisions," the Court concluded that "[t]he added restrictions which the Act places on second or successive petitions are well within the compass of this evolutionary process, and we hold that they do not amount to a 'suspension' of the writ contrary to Article I, § 9." * * * Although *Felker* was a § 2254 case, the Suspension Clause issue is essentially the same in § 2255 cases. * * * There is no savings clause in § 2254. Yet the Supreme Court held in *Felker* that § 2254's restrictions on second or successive petitions, which are materially identical to those in § 2255, do not violate the Suspension Clause. * * * We conclude, in keeping with the Supreme Court's decision in *Felker*, that the restrictions § 2255(h) places on second or successive motions do not violate the Suspension Clause. * * *

7. *The Actual Innocence Exceptions*

Section 2255(h) itself contains an actual innocence exception to its bar against second or successive motions, but it is a narrow one. The exception applies only when the claim is based on "newly discovered evidence that, if proven and viewed in light of the evidence as a whole, would be sufficient to establish by clear and convincing evidence that no reasonable factfinder would have found the movant guilty of the offense." 28 U.S.C. § 2255(h)(1).

As Gilbert concedes, this exception is of no help to him because his claim is not based on newly discovered evidence, and he does not pretend to be innocent of the offense for which he was convicted, possessing crack cocaine with intent to distribute.

A number of courts have held that the savings clause permits a claim of actual innocence of the crime of conviction to be brought in a § 2241 petition when it cannot be brought in a second or successive motion because of § 2255(h). This decisional law exception is broader than the statutory one contained in § 2255(h)(1), because it encompasses innocence based on changes in the law where the evidence remains the same. * * * Unable to colorably contend that he was convicted of a nonexistent crime, Gilbert asserts instead that he "is actually innocent of being a career offender, factually and legally." Put in its best light, Gilbert's argument assumes that he was convicted of the nonexistent offense of being a career offender with only one qualifying predicate offense. But he wasn't. As the indictment and the judgment in this case show, Gilbert was not charged with, nor was he convicted of, being a career offender. A defendant who is convicted and then has the § 4B1.1 career offender enhancement, or any other guidelines enhancement, applied in the calculation of his sentence has not been convicted of being guilty of the enhancement. * * *

To put our reasoning and the result in the broader terms with which we began this opinion, a federal prisoner's right to have errors in the calculation of his sentence corrected is not without limits. After a case has passed the stage of a first § 2255 proceeding, the right to error correction is narrowly limited by principles of policy that reside in the finality of judgment neighborhood of the law—principles which further critically important interests. The restrictions that those finality of judgment principles place on error correction have been reinforced and strengthened by AEDPA provisions such as § 2255(e) & (h), and they have been embodied in decisions of the Supreme Court and this Court. The result in this case is that Gilbert must serve the sentence that was imposed on him fourteen years ago.[22]

AFFIRMED.

[Concurring opinions by Judges DUBINA; TJOFLAT, joined by Judge EDMONSON; and PRYOR are omitted. Dissenting opinions by Judge BARKETT, joined by Judge HILL; Judge MARTIN, joined by Judges BARKETT and HILL; and Judge HILL, joined by Judge BARKETT are omitted.]

NOTES AND QUESTIONS ON GILBERT

1)   **The Savings Clause.** What purpose does § 2255(e) serve, according to the Eleventh Circuit? Does it provide access to the type of review that might otherwise be available using habeas corpus, or does it provide only access to unusual remedies where there would otherwise be a Suspension Clause concern? Which view of the Savings Clause is, from your perspective, more desirable? For a detailed discussion of the procedural history of the *Gilbert* case, and critical analysis of the panel's holding, see Nicholas Matteson, Comment, *Low Sav-*

---

[22] After the panel issued its decision, it ordered Gilbert released from prison immediately. That order, which was issued on July 1, 2010, is rescinded immediately on the date this opinion is issued.

ings Rate: Applying the Section 2255 "Savings Clause" to Federal Sentencing Claims in Gilbert v. United States, 53 B.C. L. Rev. E. Supp. 61 (2012). In one of the three separate concurring opinions, Judge William H. Pryor, Jr. strongly agreed with the panel's analysis, adding: "The dissents trivialize the Great Writ when they argue that it must issue to reverse the sentence of a confessed and recidivist drug dealer, who has already challenged his conviction and sentence both on direct and collateral review. . .."

2) *Felker* **or** *Boumediene?* The *Gilbert* en banc decision also produced three separate dissenting opinions. Judge Rosemary Barkett dissented, stating:

> In a recent landmark decision comprehensively interpreting the Suspension Clause, the Supreme Court squarely held that the Suspension Clause is violated when a prisoner is denied "a meaningful opportunity to demonstrate that he is being held pursuant to the erroneous application or interpretation of relevant law." *Boumediene v. Bush.* Thus, where the application of the statutory bar in § 2255(h) would deny a federal prisoner such a meaningful opportunity, the savings clause must apply in order to avoid an unconstitutional suspension of the writ of habeas corpus.

The majority opinion instead relied on *Felker v. Turpin.* In countering the dissent, the majority noted, that "[t]he *Boumediene* case did not involve prisoners who had been convicted and sentenced by a federal district court, whose convictions and sentences had been reviewed by a federal appeals court, and whose previous collateral challenges to those convictions and sentences had been decided by a federal district court and court of appeals. Instead, *Boumediene* was an executive detention case." Therefore, the "question was not whether the detainees in *Boumediene* were entitled to multiple rounds of habeas review of their detention but whether they were entitled to any habeas review at all." The majority concluded: "The Suspension Clause decision about restrictions on second or successive petitions and motions attacking judgments of conviction and sentences is *Felker*. This case is governed by the *Felker* decision." Which Supreme Court precedent do you think is most on point?

3) **Innocence Claims.** Other Circuits had permitted federal inmates to invoke § 2255(e) to assert innocence-of-conviction claims, but not to assert sentencing errors. The rationale used by the other appeals courts was similar, in that they expressed reluctance to undercut the purposes of AEDPA's successive-petition requirements.[q] Other courts emphasized the concern, expressed in *Gilbert*, with allowing the Savings Clause to permit litigants to avoid AEDPA restrictions. See, e.g. Prost v. Anderson, 636 F.3d 578, 586 (10th Cir. 2011) ("If the rule were otherwise—if the § 2255 remedial mechanism could be deemed 'inadequate or ineffective' any time a petitioner is barred from raising a meritorious second or successive challenge to his conviction—subsection (h) would

---

[q] See, e.g., Kinder v. Purdy, 222 F.3d 209 (5th Cir.2000) ("Kinder's argument that he is actually innocent of being a career offender in light of [a later decision], however, is not the type of argument that courts have recognized may warrant review under § 2241"); see also Padilla v. United States, 416 F.3d 424, 427 (5th Cir. 2005) ("Thus, because Padilla does not attack his conviction and his claims challenge only the validity of his sentence, Padilla's § 2241 petition does not fall within the savings clause of § 2255."); United States v. Peterman, 249 F.3d 458 (6th Cir. 2001) ("The circumstances in which § 2255 is inadequate and ineffective are narrow, for to construe § 2241 relief much more liberally than § 2255 relief would defeat the purpose of the restrictions Congress placed on the filing of successive petitions for collateral relief").

become a nullity, 'a meaningless gesture.'" (citations omitted)).ʳ The Tenth Circuit opinion in *Prost* also reasoned that given the purpose of Congress in enacting § 2255, the concerns may have been limited to those arising from changing the venue:

> Simply put, Congress included the savings clause to ensure that those who couldn't comply with § 2255's new venue mandate were *still* provided with at least one opportunity to challenge their detentions. This isn't to say that the language Congress employed in the savings clause is necessarily limited only to remedying venue problems. But it is to say that the history of the clause illustrates that Congress's purpose in enacting it surely wasn't to ensure that a prisoner will win relief on a meritorious successive motion, or receive multiple bites at the apple.

Do you agree with that reasoning? On the other hand, the text of the Savings Clause describes the situation in which § 2255 is "inadequate or ineffective *to test the legality of* [the prisoner's] *detention* " (emphasis added). As the Second Circuit put it, that language "seems to get at legal inadequacies, not practical ones." *Triestman*, 124 F.3d at 376.

4) *Bailey* Claims. The Eleventh Circuit did acknowledge that the Savings Clause has had the "primary function to date" "to permit claims based on Bailey v. United States, 516 U.S. 137 (1995)." *Bailey* held that passive possession of a firearm during a drug crime was not "use" within the meaning of 18 U.S.C. § 924(c). Federal prisoners sought release, arguing they had been convicted of passive possession of a firearm, which was in fact not a crime after *Bailey*. A series of courts had held that the prisoners, despite the otherwise-applicable bar on second or successive petitions, could use the Savings Clause to bring *Bailey* claims in a § 2241 habeas petition.ˢ *Bailey* claims can be distinguished from the claim raised by Gilbert; they involve the definition of the crime itself and not the interpretation of sentencing guideline provisions.

5) Voided Crimes and the Savings Clause. The Fifth Circuit has expressed the principle at work in the *Bailey* context in more abstract terms:

> The savings clause applies only to claims that were foreclosed by circuit law at the time when the claim should have been raised in the petitioner's trial, appeal, or first § 2255 motion, if the claims are based on a retroactively applicable Supreme Court decision which establishes that petitioner may have been convicted of a nonexistent offense.

ʳ See also United States v. Barrett, 178 F.3d 34, 50 (1st Cir.1999) ("A petition under § 2255 cannot become 'inadequate or ineffective,' thus permitting the use of § 2241, merely because a petitioner cannot meet the AEDPA 'second or successive' requirements. Such a result would make Congress's AEDPA amendment of § 2255 a meaningless gesture."); In re Davenport, 147 F.3d 605, 608 (7th Cir.1998) (rejecting the argument that "when the new limitations [on second or successive motions] prevent the prisoner from obtaining relief under 2255, his remedy under that section is inadequate and he may turn to 2241," with this explanation: "That can't be right; it would nullify the limitations."); *Triestman*, 124 F.3d at 376 ("If it were the case that any prisoner who is prevented from bringing a § 2255 petition could, without more, establish that § 2255 is 'inadequate or ineffective' . . . then Congress would have accomplished nothing at all in its attempts—through statutes like the AEDPA—to place limits on federal collateral review.").

ˢ See, e.g., Reyes–Requena v. United States, 243 F.3d 893, 904–06 (5th Cir.2001); In re Jones, 226 F.3d 328, 333–34 (4th Cir. 2000); In re Davenport, 147 F.3d 605, 607–11 (7th Cir. 1998); *Triestman*, 124 F.3d at 376–80; In re Dorsainvil, 119 F.3d 245, 248 (3d Cir. 1997).

Reyes–Requena v. United States, 243 F.3d 893, 904 (5th Cir. 2001). Professor Lyn Entzeroth has surveyed the caselaw concerning *Bailey* claims and AEDPA restrictions, and proposes that AEDPA include a more general innocence exception to the successive petition restriction. Lyn S. Entzeroth, *Struggling for Federal Judicial Review of Successive Claims of Innocence: A Study of How Federal Courts Wrestled with the AEDPA to Provide Individuals Convicted of Non-Existent Crimes with Habeas Corpus Review*, 60 U. Miami L. Rev. 75, 82–83 (2005). Do you find it odd that, for the Fifth Circuit, a non-retroactivity rule, rather than an innocence argument, is used to justify availability of the habeas corpus alternative to § 2255? Do you think the Suspension Clause requires such a statutory interpretation? If it does, what other types of claims should the Savings Clause reach?

6) Other Approaches to the Savings Clause. The Fourth and Eleventh Circuits adopt the same innocence and retroactivity approach as does the Fifth Circuit. See Wofford v. Scott, 177 F.3d 1236, 1242–44 (11th Cir. 1999), In re Jones, 226 F.3d 328, 333–34 (4th Cir. 2000). Other Circuits, however, focus on whether the claim could have been raised in a first § 2255 motion. The Seventh Circuit, for example, asks whether the inmate had a prior "unobstructed procedural shot" at raising the claim. In re Davenport, 147 F.3d 605, 609 (7th Cir. 1998). The Ninth Circuit also asks whether a petitioner had an "unobstructed procedural shot," but qualifies that question. It assesses whether there was a "material" change in the law after the first § 2255 motion, and whether the change justifies a Savings Clause exception to permit an otherwise barred post-conviction application. Harrison v. Ollison, 519 F.3d 952, 959–60 (9th Cir. 2008). The Second Circuit interprets the Clause more generally to include: "the set of cases in which the petitioner cannot, for whatever reason, utilize § 2255, and in which the failure to allow for collateral review would raise serious constitutional questions." *Triestman*, 124 F.3d at 377. For an analysis of the circuit split and a call for the Supreme Court to intervene and provide more guidance for how to interpret the Savings Clause, and how it interacts with AEDPA successive petition restrictions, see Bryan Florendo, *Prost v. Anderson and the Enigmatic Savings Clause of § 2255: When is a Remedy by Motion "Inadequate or Ineffective"?*, 89 Denv. U. L. Rev. 435 (2012).

7) Floodgates. Do you agree that recognizing a sentencing-error claim of the sort contemplated in *Gilbert* would fling open "floodgates"? Do you agree that such a state of affairs would do unacceptable violence to the principle of finality? Judge Hill, also dissenting in *Gilbert*, countered, "A judicial system that values finality over justice is morally bankrupt. That is why Congress provided in § 2255 an avenue to relief in circumstances just such as these." Suppose that an inmate was convicted of several offenses, one of which was later determined to be incorrectly defined and is now a "nonexistent" offense. Is there something more unjust about being convicted of a nonexistent crime than of an incorrect sentence above a statutory maximum?

―――――――

NOTE ON CORAM NOBIS

Not only does the Savings Clause permit narrow resort to habeas corpus, but there is an unrelated residual remedy available to federal inmates—the common-law writ of *coram nobis*. That writ is available under "extraordinary" circumstances to correct "a legal or factual error" and "to achieve justice." U.S. v. Denedo, 129 S.Ct. 2213, 2221 (2009). As the Court explained:

> The writ of coram nobis is an ancient common-law remedy designed to correct errors of fact. United States v. Morgan, 346 U.S. 502, 507 (1954). In American jurisprudence the precise contours of coram nobis have not been well defined, but the writ traces its origins to the King's Bench and the Court of Common Pleas. In English practice the office of the writ was to foster respect for judicial rulings by enabling the same court where the action was commenced and where the judgment was rendered to avoid the rigid strictures of judgment finality by correcting technical errors such as happened through the fault of the clerk in the record of the proceedings prior to the judgment.
>
> Any rationale confining the writ to technical errors, however, has been superseded; for in its modern iteration coram nobis is broader than its common-law predecessor. This is confirmed by our opinion in *Morgan*. In that case we found that a writ of coram nobis can issue to redress a fundamental error, there a deprivation of counsel in violation of the Sixth Amendment, as opposed to mere technical errors. The potential universe of cases that range from technical errors to fundamental ones perhaps illustrates, in the case of coram nobis, the "tendency of a principle to expand itself to the limit of its logic." B. Cardozo, The Nature of the Judicial Process 51 (1921). To confine the use of coram nobis so that finality is not at risk in a great number of cases, we were careful in *Morgan* to limit the availability of the writ to "extraordinary" cases presenting circumstances compelling its use "to achieve justice." Another limit, of course, is that an extraordinary remedy may not issue when alternative remedies, such as habeas corpus, are available.

Coram nobis is not a separate collateral civil proceeding, like habeas, but is a type of "belated extension" of the original criminal case. State courts may entertain such common-law writs; in federal courts, the authority to grant such a common-law writ comes from the All Writs Act, which allows federal courts to issue "all writs necessary or appropriate in aid of their respective jurisdictions." 28 U.S.C. § 1651(a).

Sometimes *coram nobis* has been used when a prisoner is no longer in custody, and cannot file a habeas petition. See U.S. v. Kwan, 407 F.3d 1005 (9th Cir. 2005). Courts may grant such a remedy when other remedies are unavailable or inadequate, and where there were valid reasons for not having earlier pursued those other remedies.[t] (*Coram nobis* was the remedy granted to Fred Korematsu many years after he was released from his World War II internment.) Some federal courts have suggested that a new legal claim may be asserted using an even-more-obscure common-law writ, *audita querela*, where no relief would be permitted under §§ 2255 or 2241.[u]

---

[t] For a case suggesting *coram nobis* could be used to challenge a sentence under *Bailey*, see *In re Nwanze*, 242 F.3d 521, 526 (3d Cir. 2001).

[u] See United States v. Richter, 510 F.3d 103, 104 (2d Cir. 2007); Hertz & Liebman, FHCPP, supra note g at § 41.2[b].

5. THE INNOCENCE PROTECTION ACT

NOTES AND COMMENTS ON THE INNOCENCE PROTECTION ACT

1) Innocence Claims and Federal Prisoners. Congress enacted the Innocence Protection Act of 2004 to provide a set of statutory remedies for federal prisoners seeking to make claims of innocence based on post-conviction DNA testing. Rather than argue that a miscarriage of justice might excuse a late filing, and rather than make Savings Clause arguments, those inmates may instead take advantage of remedies under the Act.

2) Enactment. The Innocence Protection Act of 2004 was passed as part of the Justice for All Act of 2004, and includes provisions for access to post-conviction DNA testing and relief. See 118 Stat. 2260, codified at 18 U.S.C. § 3600. The statute creates an exception to the rules that would otherwise bar a § 2255 application. That exception allows a federal prisoner to seek post-conviction DNA testing that might shed light on a claim of innocence. See United States v. Boose, 498 F. Supp.2d 887, 888 (N.D. Miss. 2007) ("the entire purpose of the statute is to permit collateral review of convictions through DNA testing—no matter how much time has transpired—or what other deadlines have passed. What the statute seeks—with its narrow tailoring—is justice itself.").

3) Reasonable Probability of Innocence. The inmate must assert "under penalty of perjury, that the applicant is actually innocent." 18 U.S.C. § 3600(a)(1). Among other requirements, the applicant must show that the requested testing would support a theory of the defense, and "raise a reasonable probability that the applicant did not commit the offense." 18 U.S.C. § 3600(a)(7). What is a "reasonable probability" of innocence? Some courts have denied DNA testing requests, emphasizing "overwhelming" evidence of the defendant's guilt.[v] Other courts emphasize that the prosecution theory would not be undercut by the presence of someone else's DNA on a weapon or other exculpatory crime-scene evidence.[w] If there were an untested hair on a victim's body, under what other circumstances would testing be proper, and under what other circumstances would it be improper? The question whether there is a "reasonable probability" that the DNA tests could show innocence has been held to be a question of law and entitled to *de novo* review.[x] Why do you think that courts have adopted a *de novo* standard of review for that question?

4) Additional Prerequisites for Testing. A showing that the result could provide some reasonable probability of exculpatory evidence is only one of the conditions for obtaining the DNA test. Other prerequisites to obtaining DNA testing include: that the evidence to be tested must have been secured as part of the investigation or prosecution; that it have been in the possession of the

---

[v] See, e.g., United States v. Martin, 377 Fed. Appx. 395 (5th Cir. 2010) (unpublished) (affirming dismissal of DNA testing application under Act where applicant failed to provide "nonfrivolous" arguments that statutory provisions were satisfied and citing "overwhelming" evidence of guilt).

[w] See, e.g., United States v. Jordan, 594 F.3d 1265 (10th Cir. 2010) (affirming dismissal of application for testing under the Act, noting that the strength and reliability of the government's case would not be altered by the presence of another suspect's DNA on crime scene objects).

[x] See United States v. Fasano, 577 F.3d 572, 575 (5th Cir.2009) ("We see the readings by the district court of Sections (a)(4) and (a)(8) as questions of law and we review them de novo.").

Government with adequate chain of custody; and that it either must not have previously been tested or a new testing technology must be available.[y] See 18 U.S.C. §3600(a)(2)–(5). A judge may deny testing if, at some prior proceeding, the applicant knowingly waived the right to DNA testing. See 18 U.S.C. §3600(a)(3).

5)   Relief Based on DNA. If the DNA test results exclude the applicant as a perpetrator, then the court may entertain a motion for a new trial or resentencing. 18 U.S.C. §3600(g). The standard for granting relief is whether the test results, "when considered with all other evidence in the case (regardless of whether such evidence was introduced at trial), establish by compelling evidence that a new trial would result in an acquittal" or a reduced sentence. 18 U.S.C. §3600(g)(2). The statute adds that the new-trial or resentencing motion is not considered a § 2255 or a habeas corpus proceeding, and that the motion does not affect any other remedies. 18 U.S.C. §3600(h). What do you think Congress sought to achieve by preventing courts from denominating DNA motions as § 2255 proceedings?

6)   Sanctions. On the other hand, if the DNA results inculpate the applicant, the judge may determine whether the applicant committed perjury under 18 U.S.C. § 3600(a)(1) and may hold the applicant in contempt. The judge must also charge the applicant for the cost of the DNA testing, and may forward the finding of perjury to the Director of the Bureau of Prisons and to the United States Parole Commission (which may use the finding of perjury in their assessment of the applicant's behavior).

REVIEW EXERCISE

What if, four years after a federal court denied a federal inmate's § 2255 motion, a DNA test result from material on the mask left at the crime scene by a gunman-perpetrator strongly suggests that the inmate was not the one who robbed the convenience store. Suppose that a federal judge denies the inmate's motion for relief under the Innocence Protection Act, stating in a summary order that the DNA evidence was not sufficiently "compelling." As counsel for the inmate, you believe that this DNA test provides clear and convincing evidence of innocence. What options do you now have? Could you file another § 2255 motion? Could you file a habeas petition, arguing that the petition triggers the Savings Clause? Could you file a writ of coram nobis? If you have multiple options, which would be wisest to pursue first?

---

[y] For example, courts have denied requests for DNA tests where the new technology was not much more probative than the DNA tests already conducted. See, e.g., United States v. Boose, 498 F. Supp.2d 887, 890 (N.D. Miss. 2007) ("The defendant's DNA was previously tested by the FBI and, although new testing methods have been developed, the new methods are less probative than the previous test because they are designed for circumstances not present in this case.").

CHAPTER 7

IMMIGRATION DETENTION

INTRODUCTORY NOTE ON IMMIGRATION LAW AND HABEAS CORPUS

The United States is a nation of immigrants. In *Arizona v. United States*, the Supreme Court explained: "The history of the United States is in part made of the stories, talents, and lasting contributions of those who crossed oceans and deserts to come here." 132 S.Ct. 2492, 2510 (2012). The Court added that the "[n]ational Government has significant power to regulate immigration." That power includes the ability to define who may lawfully enter the country, and who may be detained at and removed from our borders. As a check on that broad power, the Court has long permitted habeas scrutiny of immigration custody. As the federal government began to regulate immigration by excluding, detaining, and deporting immigrants, habeas corpus became a crucial instrument to protect aliens from unlawful removal and detention. As the Court put it in the most important of its recent immigration habeas rulings: "At its historical core, the writ of habeas corpus has served as a means of reviewing the legality of Executive detention, and it is in that context that its protections have been strongest." INS v. St. Cyr, 533 U.S. 289, 302 (2001).

Habeas corpus is a tool used by noncitizens to challenge immigration decisions, but the availability of habeas corpus has also shaped the structure of judicial review of immigration decisions. Beginning with the earliest restrictive federal immigration laws, the Supreme Court has emphasized that Congress cannot eliminate noncitizens' access to habeas review. For example, in its 1888 ruling regarding the Chinese Exclusion Acts—laws that excluded Chinese laborers from entering the country—the Court emphasized, "We see nothing in these acts which in any manner affects the jurisdiction of the courts of the United States to issue a writ of habeas corpus." *Jung Ah Lung*, 124 U.S. 621, 626–32 (1888). Congress has largely supplanted habeas process with statutes that provide for judicial review in the federal courts of appeals. This does not mean that habeas corpus plays no role; some residual uses of habeas remain. Perhaps more importantly, Congress drafted immigration judicial-review statutes with Supreme Court Suspension Clause rulings in mind. Congress sought to preserve adequate and effective means to obtain review of immigration custody, and judges have interpreted the statutes in keeping with Supreme Court habeas jurisprudence. That is not to say that our current statutes regulating judicial review of immigration decisions are well drafted, or that judges should find all of the provisions constitutional. One thing is clear, though—habeas review has played a central role in defining the structure of judicial review of immigration decisions.

The first Section of this Chapter describes the origins of the federal immigration power recognized by the Supreme Court. This Section emphasizes the crucial constitutional and statutory distinction between noncitizens who were *excludable* and those who were *deportable*. The second Section further explores the limitations of the Due Process Clause in immigration cases, focusing on the Supreme Court's decision in *Shaughnessy v. United States ex rel. Mezei*, 345 U.S. 206 (1953), which held that a noncitizen detained outside the territory of the United States lacks due process rights but may nevertheless obtain habeas corpus review on the question of whether immigration custody was authorized by written law.

The third Section turns to the Suspension Clause and the minimal process it requires for noncitizens facing removal from the United States. The Section provides an overview of how administrative immigration judges conduct removal hearings, as well as when and how government officials place noncitizens in detention pending removal from the United States. The section focuses on the central Supreme Court decision in immigration habeas, *INS v. St. Cyr*, 533 U.S. 289 (2001), in which the Court narrowly construed statutes that limited judicial review of removal orders, in order to avoid a Suspension Clause issue. *St. Cyr* has played an important role in subsequent habeas jurisprudence, particularly in challenges to national security detention following the September 11, 2001 attacks. An important aspect of *St. Cyr* was its emphasis on the Suspension Clause's requirement of a judicial forum in which to raise questions of law. In contrast, the fourth Section discusses questions of fact, examining whether a noncitizen is entitled under the Constitution to challenge factual determinations that provide the basis for custody. The fifth Section turns to Congress' statutory response to the *St. Cyr* ruling. In enacting the REAL-ID Act of 2005, Congress structured the statute to avoid potential Suspension Clause concerns suggested by the Court.

The sixth Section explores a different area in which habeas litigation has played an important role: challenges to the length of immigration detention, focusing on the Supreme Court's decision in *Zadvydas v. Davis*, 533 U.S. 678 (2001). Finally, the seventh Section discusses the Court's rulings concerning "enemy aliens," or citizens of nations with which the United States is at war. The recent material-support-of-terrorism statutes and Alien Terrorist Removal Court provisions offer an opportunity to discuss the ways that immigration removal can be used to accomplish national security goals and the role that habeas corpus plays in that context. The connections between immigration and national-security habeas jurisprudence are an important theme of the Chapters that follow.

1. INTRODUCTION TO IMMIGRATION DETENTION

NOTES ON THE PLENARY POWER DOCTRINE

1) **Immigration Law at the Founding.** The original Articles of the Constitution do not include an express federal immigration power.[a] Article I, § 8, clause 4 gives Congress the power to "establish an uniform Rule of Naturalization"—rules for granting citizenship to those not born on U.S. soil. The Fourteenth Amendment guarantees citizenship to those who were. Apart from the conditions for naturalization, however, those constitutional provisions do not mention the separate issue of regulating noncitizens. Nor do they discuss entry to and removal from the United States. The federal immigration power, which includes the power to detain noncitizens for certain immigration purposes,

---

[a] Few records of colonial opinions regarding immigration detentions exist. We do know, however, that colonial habeas writ practice reached the executive custody of non-citizens, and that judges used the writ to scrutinize the lawfulness of custody that was based on the immigration status of the person being detained. See James Oldham and Michael J. Wishnie, *The Historical Scope of Habeas Corpus and INS v. St. Cyr*, 16 Geo. Immigr. L.J. 485, 496 (2002).

flows from the power to conduct foreign relations and from other aspects of constitutional structure, such as federal supremacy over issues concerning national security. The Supreme Court began to define the immigration power in the late-nineteenth century.

2) Early Federal Immigration Regulation and the Rise of Plenary Power. The earliest federal immigration measures, enacted in 1798, did not regulate immigration generally, but instead targeted noncitizens perceived to be national security threats. The Alien Enemies Act of 1798 empowered government officials to arrest and deport citizens of nations against which the United States had formally declared war. See Alien Enemies Act, ch. 58, 1 Stat. 570 (1798). The Alien Friends Act, a broader and far more controversial companion statute (it expired two years later), permitted the President to approve summary arrest and deportation of aliens found to be "dangerous to the peace and safety of the United States," or involved in "secret machinations against" the United States. See Alien Friends Act, ch. 58, 1 Stat. 577 (1798).

3) Regulation of the Slave Trade. Until the 1870s, Congress passed no other federal statutes regulating immigration. The states regulated their own borders. The slave trade was the main objective of slave states' immigration regulation. The slave trade also drove immigration policy in many free states, some of which barred the importation of slaves from abroad or from other states. Some states barred entry of all black people, even those who were legally free. In all slave and some free states there was detailed antebellum legislation regulating the movement of free black people.[b] Many early nineteenth-century states were under-populated and generally welcomed settlement, so— apart from slavery-driven immigration policy—they had little reason to adopt restrictive immigration laws. However, many states did regulate the entry of persons deemed undesirable, such as convicts, paupers, and persons posing a public health threat.[c]

4) Federal Regulation. By the mid-nineteenth century, as immigration intensified, some states tried to stem the tide by either excluding or taxing arriving immigrants, especially people from Ireland and Germany. The Supreme Court decided the so-called *Passenger Cases* in 1849, which struck down such efforts and determined that immigration was of federal concern. See Smith v. Turner, 48 U.S. (7 How.) 283 (1849). Yet for decades, Congress did not adopt federal immigration statutes. The Civil War, however, ended the conflict over state regulation of slave-related migration. By the late nineteenth century, Congress was under increasing political pressure—in response to anti-Chinese sentiment in Western states and other concerns—to broadly regulate immigration federally. The Page Law of 1875 and the Chinese Exclusion Act of 1882 sharply restricted Chinese immigration.[d]

5) Plenary Power Doctrine. In *Chae Chan Ping v. United States* (the "Chinese Exclusion Case"), decided in 1889, the Supreme Court upheld the

---

[b] Although it would have been an important subject for federal regulation, the Migration or Importation Clause of the Constitution stated that the federal government could not interfere with the slave trade until 1808; Congress did so after 1808, but interstate slave trade was not federally regulated. See Gerald Neuman, *Strangers to the Constitution* 35–40 (1996).

[c] See Neuman, supra note b, at 21-25, 33–34.

[d] See Kerry Abrams, *Polygamy, Prostitution, and the Federalization of Immigration Law*, 105 Colum. L. Rev. 641 (2005); Hiroshi Motomura, *The Curious Evolution of Immigration Law: Procedural Surrogates for Substantive Constitutional Rights*, 92 Colum. L. Rev. 1625, 1626, 1632–33 (1992).

Chinese Exclusion Act. See 130 U.S. 581 (1889). The *Chinese Exclusion Case* identified, for the first time, an inherent federal immigration power, which it grounded in the power of a sovereign nation to protect itself against foreign nations sending "vast hordes of its people crowding in upon us."[e] Thus, the federal power to regulate immigration derives in part from a national defense power.[f] Congress's "plenary power" to regulate immigration is crucial to understanding immigration habeas. In the *Chinese Exclusion Case*, the Court found immigration legislation "conclusive upon the judiciary." The Court elaborated: "Whatever license . . . Chinese laborers may have obtained . . . to return to the United States after their departure, is held at the will of the government, revocable at any time, at its pleasure." Thus, Congress has faced little substantive limit in its decisions about who to admit into or exclude from the country. The Supreme Court has noted: "over no conceivable subject is the legislative power of Congress more complete than it is over [the power to exclude aliens]." *Oceanic Steam Navigation Co. v. Stranahan*, 214 U.S. 320, 339 (1909). Further, the Government appeared to have very broad discretion to apply those criteria. As a result, "the substantive criteria for entry to or removal from the United States became immunized from judicial review." Gerald L. Neuman, *Discretionary Deportation*, 20 Geo. Immigr. L.J. 611, 618 (2006). Broad authority grounded in plenary power creates a backdrop for highly deferential judicial review.

6)   Habeas Review. At the same time, however, the Court rejected arguments that immigration legislation foreclosed habeas relief. In *United States v. Jung Ah Lung*, decided the year before the *Chinese Exclusion Case* established the plenary power doctrine, the Court recognized a federal immigration power implicitly, but concluded, "We see nothing in these acts which in any manner affects the jurisdiction of the courts of the United States to issue a writ of habeas corpus." 124 U.S. 621, 626–32 (1888). Since the inception of federal immigration law, immigration outcomes and procedure have been subject to judicial challenge on many grounds, including due process. Habeas is a standard vehicle for such challenges. While broad legal challenges to official admissions criteria might be futile in light of plenary power, the Government must often litigate whether the criteria are correctly applied to a particular person.

2. EXCLUDABILITY AND DEPORTABILITY

NOTES ON KNAUFF

1)   Traditional Immigration Nomenclature: Exclusion and Deportation. In criminal cases, a prisoner generally seeks habeas relief only after a trial and an appeal. In immigration cases, a noncitizen seeks review where the prior process was largely administrative. Judicial review of immigration decisions can hinge on the status of the noncitizen. The distinction between noncitizens who were *excludable* and those who were *deportable* was crucial to the development of immigration law before statutory changes made in 1996—and it still remains important today. "Exclusion" referred to a decision to refuse a noncitizen entry into the United States. "Deportation" referred to a decision to

---

[e] See also Kerry Abrams, *Immigration Law and the Regulation of Marriage*, 91 Minn. L. Rev. 1635, 1641 (2007) (tracing history of plenary power doctrine).

[f] See Matthew J. Lindsay, *Immigration as Invasion: Sovereignty, Security, and the Origins of the Federal Immigration Power*, 45 Harv. C.R.-C.L. L. Rev. 1 (2010).

physically expel a noncitizen who had already entered the country. Violation of certain laws, including immigration law itself, provided the grounds for deportation. The Supreme Court has long said that both exclusion and deportation are "but parts of one and the same power"—the plenary immigration power. Fong Yue Ting v. United States, 149 U.S. 698, 713 (1893). They remain important and distinct forms of enforcement, however, and different statutes and different constitutional rules apply to each form. This conceptual distinction shapes rules of judicial review in profound ways.[g] Although Congress abandoned the terms "exclusion" and "deportation" in 1996, many practitioners still use them and the distinction remains embedded in the case law. Most conspicuously, the Supreme Court has held that a noncitizen seeking entry to the country may be excluded without constitutional due process protections. The *Knauff* and *Mezei* decisions, explored below, famously cemented this principle.

2)   *Knauff v. Shaughnessy*. In *United States ex rel. Knauff v. Shaughnessy*, 338 U.S. 537 (1950), the federal Government had excluded, without a hearing, Ellen Knauff, the noncitizen wife of a citizen who sought admission to be naturalized under the War Brides Act of 1945, a law which allowed spouses and children of U.S. military to be admitted to the country. When she sought to enter the country after she married Knauff, she was detained at Ellis Island in New York Harbor, considered not to be within the territory of the United States. Reviewing the matter, an Assistant Commissioner of Immigration and Naturalization recommended that "she be permanently excluded without a hearing on the ground that her admission would be prejudicial to the interests of the United States." That same day, "the Attorney General adopted this recommendation and entered a final order of exclusion." The decision was made on the basis of confidential information. The Attorney General "denied her a hearing on the matter because, in his judgment, the disclosure of the information on which he based that opinion would itself endanger the public security."

Knauff filed a habeas petition, which was dismissed by the district court, and the Court of Appeals affirmed. The Supreme Court also affirmed, citing to a 1941 statute providing authority that the Attorney General interpreted to permit him (1) to exclude aliens without a hearing, and (2) to issue an executive order, a proclamation calling for additional restrictions on admission of aliens. Emergency regulations issued by the Secretary of State and the Attorney General "specified the classes of aliens whose entry into the United States was deemed prejudicial to the public interest" and the regulations "provided that the Attorney General might deny an alien a hearing before a board of inquiry in special cases where he determined that the alien was excludable under the regulations on the basis of information of a confidential nature, the disclosure of which would be prejudicial to the public interest."

The Court emphasized that "an alien who seeks admission to this country may not do so under any claim of right. Admission of aliens to the United States is a privilege granted by the sovereign United States Government." Similarly, rejecting the claim that the legislation and regulations were unconstitutionally broad delegations, the Court found "there is no question of inappropriate delegation of legislative power involved here. The exclusion of aliens is a fundamental act of sovereignty." Finally, rejecting the claim that the hearing procedures violated due process, the Court explained:

---

[g] See Stephen H. Legomsky, The Detention of Aliens: Theories, Rules, and Discretion, 30 Univ. Miami Inter–Am. L. Rev. 531 (1999).

The action of the executive officer under such authority is final and conclusive. Whatever the rule may be concerning deportation of persons who
have gained entry into the United States, it is not within the province of
any court, unless expressly authorized by law, to review the determination
of the political branch of the Government to exclude a given alien. . . Normally Congress supplies the conditions of the privilege of entry into the
United States. But because the power of exclusion of aliens is also inherent in the executive department of the sovereign, Congress may in broad
terms authorize the executive to exercise the power, e.g., as was done here,
for the best interests of the country during a time of national emergency. . .

Whatever the procedure authorized by Congress is, it is due process as far
as an alien denied entry is concerned.

The Court denied relief, concluding, "we have no authority to retry the determination of the Attorney General."

2)   The *Knauff* Dissent. Dissenting, Justice Jackson wrote, "I do not find
that Congress has authorized an abrupt and brutal exclusion of the wife of an
American citizen without a hearing." He added,

Security is like liberty in that many are the crimes committed in its name.
The menace to the security of this country, be it great as it may, from this
girl's admission is as nothing compared to the menace to free institutions
inherent in procedures of this pattern. In the name of security the police
state justifies its arbitrary oppressions on evidence that is secret, because
security might be prejudiced if it were brought to light in hearings.

He concluded that Congress "will have to be much more explicit before I can
agree that it authorized a finding of serious misconduct against the wife of an
American citizen without notice of charges, evidence of guilt and a chance to
meet it."

3)   The Residual Role of Habeas Corpus. As important as what the Supreme Court did say is what it did not say. Nowhere did the Court suggest that
it lacked ability to review Knauff's habeas petition. To be sure, after reviewing
the Attorney General's statutory and regulatory authority, the Court found the
detention justified. So, although no due process right required that it "retry"
the Attorney General's determination or that the Attorney General provide
more procedures before reaching a decision, the Court still conducted a habeas
corpus inquiry into whether the detention was authorized. Habeas corpus review, albeit a limited review, was conducted and it resulted in no relief.

4)   Scholarly Appraisals. In his classic dialogue, Professor Henry Hart criticized *Knauff*, arguing that it ignored the "great and generating principle of
this whole body of law—that the Constitution always applies when a court is
sitting with jurisdiction in habeas corpus." Henry M. Hart, *The Power of Congress to Limit the Jurisdiction of Federal Courts: An Exercise in Dialectic*, 66
Harv. L. Rev. 1362, 1393 (1953). Is it the notion that the Constitution requires
a remedy and no right problematic? Are there parallel examples for this phenomenon in other forms of habeas review?

Knauff has been subject to substantial criticism arguing that the distinction between admitted and physically-present noncitizens is artificial, and that,
in other contexts, noncitizens receive constitutional protection. See, e.g., Louis

Henkin, *The Constitution as Compact and as Conscience: Individual Rights Abroad and at Our Gates*, 27 Wm. & Mary L. Rev. 11, 27–34 (1985) (calling the ruling part of a legacy of the Chinese Exclusion Cases and a "pernicious anomaly"); David A. Martin, *Due Process and Membership in the National Community: Political Asylum and Beyond*, 44 U. Pitt. L. Rev. 165, 216–19 (1983) (arguing noncitizens entering the country should be entitled to some procedure); Hiroshi Motomura, *The Curious Evolution of Immigration Law: Procedural Surrogates for Substantive Constitutional Rights*, 92 Colum. L. Rev. 1625, 1632–50 (1992) (describing generally "[t]he Court's readiness to recognize procedural due process as a formal exception to the plenary power doctrine stood in tension with its unwillingness to give the procedural due process requirement any real content"); Gerald L. Neuman, *Federal Courts Issues in Immigration Law*, 78 Tex. L. Rev. 1661, 1661–79 (2000) (describing tension between how the Suspension Clause offers habeas rights to new entrants to the country, but due process does not regulate administrative procedure); Peter H. Schuck, *The Transformation of Immigration Law*, 84 Colum. L. Rev. 1, 19–20 (1984) ("exclusion's extraconstitutional status has encouraged and legitimated some of the most deplorable governmental conduct toward both aliens and American citizens ever recorded in the annals of the Supreme Court").

INTRODUCTORY NOTE ON SHAUGHNESSY V. MEZEI

The Supreme Court relied on *Knauff* in its subsequent decision, *Shaughnessy v. United States ex rel. Mezei,* 345 U.S. 206 (1953). Ignatz Mezei, a noncitizen indefinitely detained at Ellis Island, New York, had filed four habeas petitions, each of which were summarily dismissed. His fifth habeas petition was granted, but the Supreme Court reversed. *Mezei* held that the noncitizen had no remedy for indefinite detention pursuant to the same emergency statutes and regulations at issue in *Knauff,* and it devoted extensive discussion to the connections among the habeas remedy, due process rights, and the immigration power.

Shaughnessy v. United States ex rel. Mezei
United States Supreme Court
345 U.S. 206 (1953)

■ Mr. JUSTICE CLARK delivered the opinion of the Court.

This case concerns an alien immigrant permanently excluded from the United States on security grounds but stranded in his temporary haven on Ellis Island because other countries will not take him back. The issue is whether the Attorney General's continued exclusion of respondent without a hearing amounts to an unlawful detention, so that courts may admit him temporarily to the United States on bond until arrangements are made for his departure abroad. After a hearing on respondent's petition for a writ of habeas corpus, the District Court so held and authorized his temporary admission on $5,000 bond. The Court of Appeals affirmed that action, but directed reconsideration of the terms of the parole. Accordingly, the District Court entered a modified order reducing bond to $3,000 and permitting respondent to travel and reside in Buffalo, New York. Bond was posted and respondent released. Because of resultant serious problems in the enforcement of the immigration laws, we granted certiorari.

Respondent's present dilemma springs from these circumstances: Though, as the District Court observed, "[t]here is a certain vagueness about [his] history", respondent seemingly was born in Gibraltar of Hungarian or Rumanian parents and lived in the United States from 1923 to 1948. In May of that year he sailed for Europe, apparently to visit his dying mother in Rumania. Denied entry there, he remained in Hungary for some 19 months, due to "difficulty in securing an exit permit." Finally, armed with a quota immigration visa issued by the American Consul in Budapest, he proceeded to France and boarded the *Ile de France* in Le Havre bound for New York. Upon arrival on February 9, 1950, he was temporarily excluded from the United States by an immigration inspector acting pursuant to the Passport Act as amended and regulations thereunder. Pending disposition of his case he was received at Ellis Island. After reviewing the evidence, the Attorney General on May 10, 1950, ordered the temporary exclusion to be made permanent without a hearing before a board of special inquiry, on the "basis of information of a confidential nature, the disclosure of which would be prejudicial to the public interest." That determination rested on a finding that respondent's entry would be prejudicial to the public interest for security reasons. But thus far all attempts to effect respondent's departure have failed: Twice he shipped out to return whence he came; France and Great Britain refused him permission to land. The State Department has unsuccessfully negotiated with Hungary for his readmission. Respondent personally applied for entry to about a dozen Latin American countries but all turned him down. So in June 1951 respondent advised the Immigration and Naturalization Service that he would exert no further efforts to depart. In short, respondent sat on Ellis Island because this country shut him out and others were unwilling to take him in.

Asserting unlawful confinement on Ellis Island, he sought relief through a series of habeas corpus proceedings. After four unsuccessful efforts on respondent's part, the United States District Court for the Southern District of New York on November 9, 1951, sustained the writ. The District Judge, vexed by the problem of "an alien who has no place to go", did not question the validity of the exclusion order but deemed further 'detention' after 21 months excessive and justifiable only by affirmative proof of respondent's danger to the public safety. When the Government declined to divulge such evidence, even *in camera*, the District Court directed respondent's conditional parole on bond. By a divided vote, the Court of Appeals affirmed. Postulating that the power to hold could never be broader than the power to remove or shut out and that to "continue an alien's confinement beyond that moment when deportation becomes patently impossible is to deprive him of his liberty", the court found respondent's "confinement" no longer justifiable as a means of removal elsewhere, thus not authorized by statute, and in violation of due process. Judge Learned Hand, dissenting, took a different view: The Attorney General's order was one of "exclusion" and not "deportation"; respondent's transfer from ship to shore on Ellis Island conferred no additional rights; in fact, no alien so situated "can force us to admit him at all."

Courts have long recognized the power to expel or exclude aliens as a fundamental sovereign attribute exercised by the Government's political departments largely immune from judicial control. In the exercise of these powers, Congress expressly authorized the President to impose additional restrictions on aliens entering or leaving the United States during periods of international tension and strife. That authorization, originally enacted in the Passport Act of 1918, continues in effect during the present emergency. Under it, the Attorney General, acting for the President, may shut out aliens whose "entry would be prejudicial to the interest of the United States". And he may exclude without a hearing when the exclusion is based on confidential information the disclosure of which may be prejudicial to the public interest. The Attorney General in this case proceeded in accord with these provisions; he made the necessary determinations and barred the alien from entering the United States.

It is true that aliens who have once passed through our gates, even illegally, may be expelled only after proceedings conforming to traditional standards of fairness encompassed in due process of law. But an alien on the threshold of initial entry stands on a different footing: "Whatever the procedure authorized by Congress is, it is due process as far as an alien denied entry is concerned." And because the action of the executive officer under such authority is final and conclusive, the Attorney General cannot be compelled to disclose the evidence underlying his determinations in an exclusion case; "it is not within the province of any court, unless expressly authorized by law, to review the determination of the political branch of the Government". In a case such as this, courts cannot retry the determination of the Attorney General.

Neither respondent's harborage on Ellis Island nor his prior residence here transforms this into something other than an exclusion proceeding. Concededly, his movements are restrained by authority of the United States, and he may by habeas corpus test the validity of his exclusion. But that is true whether he enjoys temporary refuge on land or remains continuously aboard ship. In sum, harborage at Ellis Island is not an entry into the United States. For purposes of the immigration laws, moreover, the legal incidents of an alien's entry remain unaltered whether he has been here once before or not. He is an entering alien just the same, and may be excluded if unqualified for admission under existing immigration laws. * * *

To be sure, a lawful resident alien may not captiously be deprived of his constitutional rights to procedural due process[,] * * * [but] respondent, apparently without authorization or reentry papers, simply left the United States and remained behind the Iron Curtain for 19 months. * * * That being so, the Attorney General may lawfully exclude respondent without a hearing as authorized by the emergency regulations promulgated pursuant to the Passport Act. Nor need he disclose the evidence upon which that determination rests. United States ex rel. Knauff v. Shaughnessy, 338 U.S. 537 (1950). * * *

Reversed.

■ Mr. JUSTICE BLACK, with whom Mr. JUSTICE DOUGLAS concurs, dissenting.

Mezei came to this country in 1923 and lived as a resident alien in Buffalo, New York, for twenty-five years. He made a trip to Europe in 1948 and was stopped at our shore on his return in 1950. Without charge of or conviction for any crime, he was for two years held a prisoner on Ellis Island by order of the Attorney General. Mezei sought habeas corpus in the District Court. He wanted to go to his wife and home in Buffalo. The Attorney General defended the imprisonment by alleging that it would be dangerous to the Nation's security to let Mezei go home even temporarily on bail. Asked for proof of this, the Attorney General answered the judge that all his information was "of a confidential nature" so much so that telling any of it or even telling the names of any of his secret informers would jeopardize the safety of the Nation. Finding that Mezei's life as a resident alien in Buffalo had been "unexceptional" and that no facts had been proven to justify his continued imprisonment, the District Court granted bail. The Court of Appeals approved. Now this Court orders Mezei to leave his home and go back to his island prison to stay indefinitely, maybe for life.

Mr. JUSTICE JACKSON forcefully points out the danger in the Court's holding that Mezei's liberty is completely at the mercy of the unreviewable discretion of the Attorney General. I join Mr. JUSTICE JACKSON in the belief that Mezei's continued imprisonment without a hearing violates due process of law.

No society is free where government makes one person's liberty depend upon the arbitrary will of another. Dictatorships have done this since time immemorial. They do now. Russian laws of 1934 authorized the People's Commissariat to imprison, banish and exile Russian citizens as well as "foreign subjects who are socially dangerous." Hitler's secret police were given like powers. German courts were forbidden to make any inquiry whatever as to the information on which the police acted. Our Bill of Rights was written to prevent such oppressive practices. Under it this Nation has fostered and protected individual freedom. The Founders abhorred arbitrary one-man imprisonments. Their belief was—our constitutional principles are—that no person of any faith, rich or poor, high or low, native or foreigner, white or colored, can have his life, liberty or property taken "without due process of law." This means to me that neither the federal police nor federal prosecutors nor any other governmental official, whatever his title, can put or keep people in prison without accountability to courts of justice. It means that individual liberty is too highly prized in this country to allow executive officials to imprison and hold people on the basis of information kept secret from courts. It means that Mezei should not be deprived of his liberty indefinitely except as the result of a fair open court hearing in which evidence is appraised by the court, not by the prosecutor.

■ Mr. JUSTICE JACKSON, whom Mr. JUSTICE FRANKFURTER joins, dissenting.

Fortunately it still is startling, in this country, to find a person held indefinitely in executive custody without accusation of crime or judicial trial. Executive imprisonment has been considered oppressive and lawless since John, at Runnymede, pledged that no free man should be imprisoned, dispossessed, outlawed, or exiled save by the judgment of his peers or by the law of the land. The judges of England developed the writ of habeas corpus largely to preserve these immunities from executive restraint. Under the best tradition of Anglo-American law, courts will not deny hearing to an unconvicted prisoner just because he is an alien whose keep, in legal theory, is just outside our gates. Lord Mansfield, in the celebrated case holding that slavery was unknown to the common law of England, ran his writ of habeas corpus in favor of an alien, an African Negro slave, and against the master of a ship at anchor in the Thames. * * *

What is our case? In contemplation of law, I agree, it is that of an alien who asks admission to the country. Concretely, however, it is that of a lawful and law-abiding inhabitant of our country for a quarter of a century, long ago admitted for permanent residence, who seeks to return home. After a foreign visit to his aged and ailing mother that was prolonged by disturbed conditions of Eastern Europe, he obtained a visa for admission issued by our consul and returned to New York. There the Attorney General refused to honor his documents and turned him back as a menace to this Nation's security. This man, who seems to have led a life of unrelieved insignificance, must have been astonished to find himself suddenly putting the Government of the United States in such fear that it was afraid to tell him why it was afraid of him. He was shipped and reshipped to France, which twice refused him landing. Great Britain declined, and no other European country has been found willing to open its doors to him. Twelve countries of the American Hemisphere refused his applications. Since we proclaimed him a Samson who might pull down the pillars of our temple, we should not be surprised if peoples less prosperous, less strongly established and less stable feared to take him off our timorous hands. With something of a record as an unwanted man, neither his efforts nor those of the United States Government any longer promise to find him an abiding place. For nearly two years he was held in custody of the immigration authorities of the United States at Ellis Island, and if the Government has its way he seems likely to be detained indefinitely, perhaps for life, for a cause known only to the Attorney General.

Is respondent deprived of liberty? The Government answers that he was "transferred to Ellis Island on August 1, 1950 for safekeeping," and "is not being detained in the usual sense, but is in custody solely to prevent him from gaining entry into the United States in violation of law. He is free to depart from the United States to any country of his choice." Government counsel ingeniously argued that Ellis Island is his "refuge" whence he is free to take leave in any direction except west. That might mean freedom, if only he were an amphibian! Realistically, this man is incarcerated by a combination of forces which keeps him as effectually as a prison, the dominant and proximate of these forces being the United States immigration authority. It overworks legal fiction to say that one is free in law when by the commonest of common sense he is bound. Despite the impeccable legal logic of the Government's argument on this point, it leads to an artificial and unreal conclusion. We must regard this alien as deprived of liberty, and the question is whether the deprivation is a denial of due process of law.

The Government on this point argues that "no alien has any constitutional right to entry into the United States"; that "the alien has only such rights as Congress sees fit to grant in exclusion proceedings"; that "the so-called detention is still merely a continuation of the exclusion which is specifically authorized by Congress"; that since "the restraint is not incidental to an order [of exclusion] but is itself the effectuation of the exclusion order, there is no limit to its continuance" other than statutory, which means no limit at all. The Government all but adopts the words of one of the officials responsible for the administration of this Act who testified before a congressional committee as to an alien applicant, that "He has no rights." * *

Procedural fairness, if not all that originally was meant by due process of law, is at least what it most uncompromisingly requires. Procedural due process is more elemental and less flexible than substantive due process. It yields less to the times, varies less with conditions, and defers much less to legislative judgment. * * *

If it be conceded that in some way this alien could be confined, does it matter what the procedure is? Only the untaught layman or the charlatan lawyer can answer that procedures matter not. Procedural fairness and regularity are of the indispensable essence of liberty. Severe substantive laws can be endured if they are fairly and impartially applied. * * * Let it not be overlooked that due process of law is not for the sole benefit of an accused. It is the best insurance for the Government itself against those blunders which leave lasting stains on a system of justice but which are bound to occur on *ex parte* consideration. * * *

Our law may, and rightly does, place more restrictions on the alien than on the citizen. But basic fairness in hearing procedures does not vary with the status of the accused. * * *

The most scrupulous observance of due process, including the right to know a charge, to be confronted with the accuser, to cross-examine informers and to produce evidence in one's behalf, is especially necessary where the occasion of detention is fear of future misconduct, rather than crimes committed. * * * Quite unconsciously, I am sure, the Government's theory of custody for "safekeeping" without disclosure to the victim of charges, evidence, informers or reasons, even in an administrative proceeding, has unmistakable overtones of the "protective custody" of the Nazis more than of any detaining procedure known to the common law. Such a practice, once established with the best of intentions, will drift into oppression of the disadvantaged in this country as surely as it has elsewhere. That these apprehensive surmises are not "such stuff as dreams are made on" appears from testimony of a top immigration official concerning an applicant that "He has no rights."

Because the respondent has no right of entry, does it follow that he has no rights at all? Does the power to exclude mean that exclusion may be continued or effectuated by any means which happen to seem appropriate to the authorities? It would effectuate his exclusion to eject him bodily into the sea or to set him adrift in a rowboat. Would not such measures be condemned judicially as a deprivation of life without due process of law? * * *

Exclusion of an alien without judicial hearing, of course, does not deny due process when it can be accomplished merely by turning him back on land or returning him by sea. But when indefinite confinement becomes the means of enforcing exclusion, it seems to me that due process requires that the alien be informed of its grounds and have a fair chance to overcome them. This is the more due him when he is entrapped into leaving the other shore by reliance on a visa which the Attorney General refuses to honor.

It is evident that confinement of respondent no longer can be justified as a step in the process of turning him back to the country whence he came. Confinement is no longer ancillary to exclusion; it can now be justified only as the alternative to normal exclusion. It is an end in itself. * * *

Congress has ample power to determine whom we will admit to our shores and by what means it will effectuate its exclusion policy. The only limitation is that it may not do so by authorizing United States officers to take without due process of law the life, the liberty or the property of an alien who has come within our jurisdiction; and that means he must meet a fair hearing with fair notice of the charges.

It is inconceivable to me that this measure of simple justice and fair dealing would menace the security of this country. No one can make me believe that we are that far gone.

NOTES AND QUESTIONS ON MEZEI

1)   Habeas Access without Due Process Rights. *Knauff* had determined that due process rights did not necessarily apply in exclusion decisions made before entry to the country. The *Mezei* Court cemented this territorial principle. Thus, the Court rejected Justice Jackson's view in his *Mezei* dissent that noncitizens should receive "the right to know a charge, to be confronted with the accuser, to cross-examine informers and to produce evidence in one's behalf." Or was Justice Jackson really concerned with "indefinite confinement" and not with turning away noncitizens at the border without due process? The Court found that whatever process Congress authorizes is acceptable for deciding whether to exclude noncitizens from the country. Those controversial rulings, however, did not bar noncitizens facing exclusion from seeking habeas corpus remedies. They could not obtain relief based on due process challenges to exclusion hearings, to be sure. Nevertheless, the Court entertained both Mezei and Knauff's habeas petitions.

2)   Habeas Corpus Review. If not on theories of due process deprivations, then on what bases can noncitizens like Mezei and Knauff obtain habeas relief? In both decisions, the Court assumed that habeas corpus review, not of the procedures used to reach the decision to deport them, but of the authorization for the immigration decision to detain them, would be permitted. That is, they can challenge the legal and factual bases for determining that they actually belong to a removable category of noncitizens.

3)   Exclusion versus Deportation. As the Court emphasized, the citizenship status of the person in custody plays an important role—as does the location of the custody, in relation to the border. In contrast to the situation of a noncitizen who has not entered U.S. territory, a noncitizen who has already entered may only be removed following proceedings that comply with due process protections.[h] Due process rights attach to noncitizens who have entered, but summary proceedings—with less due process protection—can be used to deny entry to people who have not. In contrast, the Supreme Court has held that previously admitted lawful resident noncitizens who are returning to the United States also receive full due process protections, even before they enter the territory of the United States. They must also receive a hearing in which they can present their case "effectively," because their initial admission to the country and un-surrendered residence (despite temporary travel) gives them a different "constitutional status." Landon v. Plasencia, 459 U.S. 21, 32–34, 37 (1982). Do you think so much should rest on these types of distinctions regarding the status of the noncitizen?

4)   Indefinite Detention. Detainees at the border, who have not entered the United States, can be kept in the kind of limbo that so upset the dissenters in *Mezei* and *Knauff*—and, as we will see, the same concerns with lengthy detentions at the border remain salient today. Removing a noncitizen is often difficult, at some times for diplomatic reasons and because other countries will not accept them. While the removal proceedings remain pending, or while trying to negotiate the removal, a noncitizen can sometimes remain in detention for lengthy periods of time. Should the length of the potential detention affect the habeas inquiry?

---

[h] Yamataya v. Fisher, 189 U.S. 86, 101 (1903).

5)   What Happened to Knauff and Mezei? Although neither obtained any habeas relief, habeas corpus played a key role in *Knauff* and *Mezei*. For both noncitizens, the decisions precipitated favorable press reports, public outcry concerning their cases, Congressional hearings, private relief bills introduced in Congress, new administrative hearings, and finally, their release into the United States. (Justice Jackson alludes to these events as to Knauff in his *Mezei* opinion.) Knauff eventually won a reversal from the Board of Immigration Appeals, which concluded that she did not in fact reveal classified information to officials in Czechoslovakia, and ordered that she be made a legal permanent resident, which the Attorney General did in 1951. She never became a citizen, however. Mezei was ordered freed on parole by the Attorney General, after losing immigration hearings, and was allowed to live in Buffalo, New York, rather than being forced to remain indefinitely on Ellis Island. However, Mezei was never legally admitted into the country.[i]

3. IMMIGRATION CUSTODY AND THE SUSPENSION CLAUSE

NOTE ON HEIKKILA V. BARBER

In *Heikkila v. Barber*, 345 U.S. 229, 235 (1953), a mid-century case that remains as central to understanding the law as it is enigmatic, the Supreme Court confronted a statute that stripped Article III jurisdiction to decide certain immigration issues. It ultimately considered whether judicial review was "required by the Constitution." The Court characterized the 1891 and 1917 Immigration Acts as having limited judicial review "to the fullest extent permitted under the Constitution." The 1917 statute provided that, "In every case where any person is ordered deported from the United States under the provisions of this Act, or of any law or treaty, the decision of the Attorney General shall be final." 8 U.S.C.A. § 155(a). What did "final" mean? The Government argued that "final" meant that there could be no judicial review of any kind. The history of finality in immigration proceedings was particularly prominent in *Heikkila*, which observed that interpretation of statutes designating immigration decisions as "final" "clearly had the effect of precluding judicial intervention in deportation cases except insofar as it was required by the Constitution." Nevertheless, the Supreme Court emphasized that federal courts had continued to review legality of removal in habeas proceedings. *Heikkila* reasoned that because judicial review persisted even when statutes designated initial determinations as "final," the term required only that the determinations be treated as final for administrative purposes.

In *Heikkila*, the Supreme Court concluded that habeas corpus review remained available: "Congress may well have thought that habeas corpus, despite its apparent inconvenience to the alien, should be the exclusive remedy in these cases in order to minimize opportunities for repetitive litigation and consequent delays as well as to avoid possible venue difficulties connected with any other type of action." What makes the decision ambiguous is that the Court did not explain what type of review was affirmatively "required by the Constitution." Nor did the Court directly address whether there might have been a con-

---

[i] See Charles D. Weisselberg, *The Exclusion and Detention of Aliens, Lessons from the Lives of Ellen Knauff and Ignatz Mezei*, 143 U. Pa. L. Rev. 933, 954–85, 963–64 & n.163, 983–84 (1995); *Alien, Long Held, Freed*, N.Y. Times, Aug. 12, 1954, at 10.

stitutional problem with a contrary interpretation. Was it the Suspension Clause that required that habeas corpus review remain available? Was the Court relying on a principle that it would not assume that Congress meant to limit access to habeas corpus, based on other constitutional sources? Subsequent rulings would begin to address those questions directly.

———————

NOTES ON PETITIONS FOR REVIEW FROM 1961–1996

1) The APA and Substantial Evidence Review. Subsequent statutes recognized that habeas could continue to function as a vehicle for judicial review, but they created a division between what could be litigated in a habeas petition and what had to be litigated using a different judicial review device, which they termed a "petition for review." The Supreme Court decided cases in the late 1960s and early 1970s that relaxed the habeas custody requirement of 28 U.S.C. § 2241. Before that time, even if a noncitizen was facing removal, there could be no habeas petition until the noncitizen was in physical custody. There was pressure to find ways to challenge an order of removal earlier in the process. The Administrative Procedure Act (APA), enacted in 1946, required immigrants facing deportation or exclusion orders to seek "substantial evidence" review of immigration agency decisions—an approach the Court ratified. See Wong Yang Sung v. McGrath, 339 U. S. 33 (1950).

Congress then intervened to create an immigration custody-specific approach; the Immigration and Nationality Act of 1952 (INA) provided for notice and hearings before immigration judges, authorized regulations that led to the creation of the Board of Immigration Appeals, and adopted a separate-but-analogous "substantial evidence" standard for reviewing immigration judge findings.

2) Hobbs Act Review. In 1955, the Supreme Court approved APA review of immigration decisions in *Shaughnessy v. Pedreiro,* 349 U. S. 48 (1955). Next, Congress again made review of immigration rulings a separate process, enacting in 1961 a statute requiring that a noncitizen use a "petition for review" filed in a court of appeals, to seek judicial review of a removal order. INA § 106(a), 8 U.S.C. §1105. The statute relied on the established "petition for review" procedure under the Hobbs Act, 28 U.S.C. §§ 2341–2351, placing review of certain administrative decisions in the federal courts of appeals. The 1961 statute required that this procedure be used as the "sole and exclusive" procedure for "judicial review of all final orders of deportation." 8 U.S.C. § 1105a(a). The 1961 statute also provided for deferential review of agency factual determinations—the findings would be conclusive "if supported by reasonable, substantial, and probative evidence on the record considered as a whole." However, the statute also stated that a person "held in custody pursuant to an order of deportation may obtain judicial review thereof by habeas corpus proceedings." 8 U.S.C. § 1105.

3) The Rise of Petitions for Review. In 1963 in *Foti v. INS,* the Supreme Court held that a challenge to the underlying deportation order had to be brought in a petition for review. 375 U.S. 217, 221 (1963). Since 1940, the Attorney General enjoyed and exercised broad discretionary power to suspend a deportation by the then-Immigration and Naturalization Service (INS). Review of an order denying discretionary relief also had to be sought using a "petition for review" in a court of appeals. The Supreme Court held that, because "intent to give Courts of Appeals exclusive jurisdiction to review denials of discretionary relief in deportation proceedings is contained in the legislative history," such common challenges to denial of discretionary relief could only be brought in a petition for review.

As a result of these developments, petitions for review became the main way that noncitizens challenged removal orders. In the context of deportation (now called removal on deportability grounds), only challenges to detention (and not to the underlying deportation decision) could be brought using the general habeas statute, 28 U.S.C. § 2241—although noncitizens could potentially bring other challenges regarding denials of due process or equal protection, or denials of discretionary relief unrelated to deportability. As a result, "'petitions for review' under INA § 106(a) provided the primary avenue of habeas relief in immigration cases." Magana-Pizano v. I.N.S., 200 F.3d 603, 609 (9th Cir. 1999).

4)   Where Habeas was Still Used. There was still a divide between judicial review of excludability and deportability. Agency decisions to exclude at entry were not reviewable using the "petition for review" in a court of appeals. Section 106(b) provided that judicial review of a final order of exclusion could be obtained "by habeas corpus proceedings and not otherwise." Thus, those facing exclusion, like Knauff and Mezei, who had little in the way of process at their underlying hearing, could not take advantage of the somewhat more generous petition for review standard of review, and had to instead pursue habeas remedies.

NOTES ON AEDPA AND IIRIRA

1)   The 1996 Legislation. The primary statutory avenue of habeas relief, INA § 106(a) (8 USC § 1105a), would be repealed in 1996 and replaced by a new section, INA § 242 (8 USC §1252). Section 1252 channeled all judicial review of removal decisions (with limited exceptions) into petitions for review filed in Courts of Appeals. That restriction raised the possibility that a noncitizen might not be able to obtain habeas relief under 28 U.S.C. § 2241, the general statutory source of habeas power for federal courts. Two pieces of 1996 legislation, the Antiterrorism and Effective Death Penalty Act of 1996 (AEDPA) and the Illegal Immigration Reform and Immigrant Responsibility Act of 1996 (IIRIRA), sought to restrict judicial review of immigration decisions.

2)   New Criminal Removability Categories. The legislation tightened the connection between immigration and criminal law, a phenomenon described as the development of "crimmigration."[j] Early immigration laws permitted deportation for serious criminal offenses, such as murder, drug trafficking, and crimes of "moral turpitude." Over time the number of deportable offenses was increased to include many other "aggravated" felonies. See Anti-Drug Abuse Act of 1988, Pub. L. No. 100–690, § 7342–44, 102 Stat. 4181, 4469–71. In 1996, AEDPA and IIRIRA further broadened those categories to include additional drug offenses, property crimes, and violent crimes. Perhaps far more signifi-

---

[j] See Juliet Stumpf, *The Crimmigration Crisis: Immigrants, Crime, and Sovereign Power*, 56 Am. U. L. Rev. 367, 376 (2006) (exploring more generally how immigration law and criminal law have grown together).

cantly, the legislation amended the Code so as to preclude discretionary relief to noncitizens convicted of certain offenses. IIRIRA § 321, 110 Stat. 3009, 3009–627. The result has made removal from the country an important new collateral consequence about which criminal defense lawyers must advise their clients. In *Padilla v. Kentucky,* 130 S.Ct. 1473 (2010), the Supreme Court formally held that the Sixth Amendment effective-assistance-of-counsel right included the right to be informed about the collateral immigration consequences of a criminal conviction.

3) Rise in Removal of Criminal Convicts. The leading categories of offenses committed by noncitizens who are removed (although not all were the reason for the removal) include criminal traffic offenses, drug offenses, immigration-related offenses (such as illegal entry and reentry, false claims of citizenship, and alien smuggling), burglary, and robbery. The Secure Communities program begun in 2008 created information-sharing agreements with ICE and local law enforcement in order to increase detection of noncitizens violating immigration rules.[k] Whether due to expanding categories of crimes requiring removal, or the exercise of discretion to prioritize removal of those with criminal records, removals following criminal convictions have increased from less than 10,000 per year in the 1980s to almost 170,000 per year by 2010. Over 40% of the 387,000 removals conducted in 2010 followed criminal convictions; ICE detained 363,000 people in 2010, down slightly from 2009.[l]

4) The New Nomenclature: Removal. In 1996, Congress also changed the terminology by doing away with the terms "exclusion" and "deportation" and substituted two new terms, "inadmissibility" and "deportability." See 8 U.S.C. § 1101(a)(13) (definition of "admission"), § 1182(a) (inadmissibility grounds), § 1227(a) (deportability grounds). For arriving noncitizens, the change is largely semantic. These noncitizens are now subject to inadmissibility grounds rather than the old exclusion grounds. For noncitizens physically present within the country, however, the new nomenclature can make a difference. Those noncitizens who were admitted are subject to deportability grounds, but those noncitizens who were not (such are those who snuck in over the border or entered without inspection) are subject to inadmissibility grounds, which are sometimes less generous. Both groups—those who were admitted and those who were not—are now subject to a uniform "removal" proceeding if they are physically present, except in unusual circumstances where "expedited removal" might apply. See 8 U.S.C. §§ 1228–1229a.

5) Immigration Custody. Immigrants sometimes bring habeas corpus claims when they are placed into detention. Over 350,000 individuals are held in immigration detention facilities every year. This number represents a sharp increase in a short amount of time; in 1994, the annual detention figure was

[k] See Annual Report, *Immigration Enforcement Actions:* 2010 3–4 (2011) ("2011 Annual Report"). Some traffic offenses, for example, might be aggravated felonies if they were for say, driving while intoxicated. Other minor traffic offenses, like driving without a license, might have lead to the arrest and the determination that the person was in the country illegally—but the minor offense would not itself be deportable. ICE has apparently changed its policy to avoid deportations of traffic violators, however. See Julia Preston, *Fewer Illegal Immigrations Stopped for Traffic Violations Will Face Deportation*, N.Y. Times, April 27, 2012.

[l] Mexican nationals accounted for 61 percent of detainees (but they account for a far lower percentage of detention-bed days because their stays are comparatively short), with the other leading countries of nationality including El Salvador, Guatemala, Honduras, and China. See 2011 Annual Report, supra note k, at 3. In addition, over 500,000 people were apprehended at the border, 97% of which were at the Southwest border.

only about 81,000.[m] This remarkable spike is due largely to an increased Congressional concern with flight by persons facing removal. But in response to criticism of harsh conditions at these detention facilities, the Department of Homeland Security is in the process of implementing reforms.[n]

In all cases, an administrative agency decides whether to initiate removal proceedings. Before 2003, that agency was the INS. Since 2003, the decisions have usually been made by U.S. Immigration and Customs Enforcement (ICE), which resides within the Department of Homeland Security.[o] ICE authorities may issue a Notice to Appear (NTA), ordering an appearance before an immigration judge to determine whether removal is required, and ICE may also arrest a noncitizen. 8 C.F.R. §§ 1003.13–14. The noncitizen may challenge the removal decision at a hearing before an immigration judge, and may seek a discretionary waiver to prevent removal. A noncitizen may be detained during those proceedings because of potential dangerousness and flight risk. Much as is the case for bail standards in criminal cases, the immigration-detention standards require a case-by-case determination.

7) Custody under § 2241. Whether in detention facilities or not, though, noncitizens facing removal are "in custody" for the purposes of the general federal habeas statute, 28 U.S.C. § 2241. When they are subject to a removal order, they are deemed to be "in custody" even if they are not physically detained pursuant to an order of removal. Noncitizens must ultimately be placed in government custody before they can be physically expelled from the country.

8) Immigration Judges. In most cases, an immigration judge holds a hearing to decide whether the noncitizen may be removed. The immigration judges are not Article III judges; rather they are special judges housed in the Executive Office for Immigration Review (EOIR), which is part of the Department of Justice. There are more than 200 immigration judges sitting in more than 50 immigration courts nationwide. The immigration judges preside over hearings involving removal, asylum, and other types of discretionary relief. 8 C.F.R. § 1240.1(a). The noncitizen has the right under the governing regulations to an interpreter and to have counsel present, but no right to have the government provide counsel, as a defendant would in a criminal setting. 8 C.F.R. § 1003.22. The government attorney is referred to as the DHS attorney. The immigration judges render oral and written decisions at the conclusion of the hearings. The hearings are also recorded electronically. 8 C.F.R. § 1240.9.

9) Burdens of Proof and Discretionary Relief. In cases involving deportability grounds, the Government has the burden to establish deportability "by clear and convincing evidence." 8 U.S.C. § 1229a(c)(3)(A). The distinction between removability (an eligibility status) and relief (the ultimate disposition) is also important. Determining whether a person may be removed from the country is often cut and dried. A noncitizen may be removable because of an over-

---

[m] See Anil Kalhan, *Rethinking Immigration Detention*, 110 Colum. L. Rev. Sidebar 42, 45 (2010) (arguing that this growth has been in part "fueled by enforcement policies that subject ever-larger categories of individuals to removal charges and custody").

[n] See Dora Schriro, U.S. Dep't of Homeland Sec., Immigration Detention Overview and Recommendations 2, 10–11 (Oct. 6, 2009); Amnesty International, *Jailed without Justice: Immigration Detention in the USA*, (2009), at http://www.amnestyusa.org/pdfs/Jailed WithoutJustice.pdf; Nina Bernstein, *U.S. to Overhaul Detention Policy for Immigrants*, N.Y. Times, Aug. 6, 2009, at A1.

[o] See The Office of the Chief Immigration Judge, *Immigration Court Practice Manual* at Ch.1 (2008), at http://www.justice.gov/eoir/vll/OCIJPracManual/ocij_page1.htm.

stayed visa, a criminal conviction, or something else. Removability, in fact, is frequently conceded by the noncitizen. Many removable people, however, can be given discretionary relief for humanitarian and administrative reasons, permitting them to remain in the United States despite their removability—a disposition called "cancellation of removal." When a removable noncitizen seeks discretionary relief before an immigration judge, the burden at the hearing is on the noncitizen. 8 U.S.C. § 1229a(c)(4). The Attorney General and the Department of Homeland Security can also grant discretionary relief.

10) Appeals. This Chapter focuses on judicial review, the central subject of the *St. Cyr* case that follows these Notes. Following the final order in administrative proceeding, a noncitizen has thirty days to file a notice of appeal to the Board of Immigration Appeals (BIA), also an administrative court. 8 C.F.R. § 1003.1. If the noncitizen loses in the BIA, then the noncitizen may appeal to a federal court, typically by petitioning a United States Court of Appeals for discretionary review—but sometimes by filing a writ of habeas corpus. The BIA provides a certified copy of the record, including a record of the proceedings before the immigration judge, to the federal court. Under 8 U.S.C. § 1252(d)(1), noncitizens must exhaust administrative remedies before seeking judicial review, although in some circumstances courts excuse exhaustion.[p]

INTRODUCTION TO INS V. ST. CYR

The 1996 legislation permitted noncitizens facing removal to file petitions for review the courts of appeals, but the statute appeared to preclude review of certain discretionary decisions by the Attorney General and to eliminate the ability to exercise that discretion—including discretionary relief to broad classes of noncitizens convicted of felonies. Moreover, the Attorney General interpreted the 1996 legislation to strip jurisdiction to grant discretionary relief to several categories of noncitizens in the first place. In *INS v. St. Cyr*, the Supreme Court had to decide both the scope of discretionary relief and whether there was a habeas forum to challenge the administrative interpretation of the statute.

INS v. St. Cyr
United States Supreme Court
33 U.S. 289 (2001)

■ JUSTICE STEVENS delivered the opinion of the Court.

Both [AEDPA] and [IIRIRA] contain comprehensive amendments to the Immigration and Nationality Act (INA) * * *. This case raises two important questions about the impact of those amendments. The first question is a procedural one, concerning the effect of those amendments on the availability of habeas corpus jurisdiction under 28 U.S.C. § 2241. The se-

---

[p] See, e.g., United States v. Cerna, (2d Cir. 2010) (finding exhaustion not required because alien received ineffective assistance of counsel during administrative proceedings); Schmitt v. Maurer, 451 F.3d 1092 (10th Cir. 2006) (finding exhaustion excused where no remaining administrative remedies existed); Noriega-Lopez v. Ashcroft, 335 F.3d 874 (9th Cir. 2003) (finding motions to reopen or reconsider not "as of right" and therefore not subject to exhaustion requirement); Grullon v. Mukasey, 509 F.3d 107 (2d Cir. 2007) (finding "manifest injustice" would result).

cond question is a substantive one, concerning the impact of the amendments on conduct that occurred before their enactment and on the availability of discretionary relief from deportation.

Respondent, Enrico St. Cyr, is a citizen of Haiti who was admitted to the United States as a lawful permanent resident in 1986. Ten years later, on March 8, 1996, he pleaded guilty in a state court to a charge of selling a controlled substance in violation of Connecticut law. That conviction made him deportable. Under pre-AEDPA law applicable at the time of his conviction, St. Cyr would have been eligible for a waiver of deportation at the discretion of the Attorney General. However, removal proceedings against him were not commenced until April 10, 1997, after both AEDPA and IIRIRA became effective, and, as the Attorney General interprets those statutes, he no longer has discretion to grant such a waiver.

In his habeas corpus petition, respondent has alleged that the restrictions on discretionary relief from deportation contained in the 1996 statutes do not apply to removal proceedings brought against an alien who pleaded guilty to a deportable crime before their enactment. The District Court accepted jurisdiction of his application and agreed with his submission. In accord with the decisions of four other Circuits, the Court of Appeals for the Second Circuit affirmed. The importance of both questions warranted our grant of certiorari.

I

The character of the pre-AEDPA and pre-IIRIRA law that gave the Attorney General discretion to waive deportation in certain cases is relevant to our appraisal of both the substantive and the procedural questions raised by the petition of the Immigration and Naturalization Service (INS).
* * *

Subject to certain exceptions, § 3 of the Immigration Act of 1917 excluded from admission to the United States several classes of aliens, including, for example, those who had committed crimes "involving moral turpitude." The seventh exception provided "[t]hat aliens returning after a temporary absence to an unrelinquished United States domicile of seven consecutive years may be admitted in the discretion of the Secretary of Labor, and under such conditions as he may prescribe." Although that provision applied literally only to exclusion proceedings, and although the deportation provisions of the statute did not contain a similar provision, the INS relied on § 3 to grant relief in deportation proceedings involving aliens who had departed and returned to this country after the ground for deportation arose.

Section 212 of the Immigration and Nationality Act of 1952, which replaced and roughly paralleled § 3 of the 1917 Act, excluded from the United States several classes of aliens, including those convicted of offenses involving moral turpitude or the illicit traffic in narcotics. As with the prior law, this section was subject to a proviso granting the Attorney General broad discretion to admit excludable aliens. That proviso, codified at 8 U.S.C. § 1182(c), stated:

> "Aliens lawfully admitted for permanent residence who temporarily proceeded abroad voluntarily and not under an order of deportation, and who are returning to a lawful unrelinquished domicile of seven consecutive years, may be admitted in the discretion of the Attorney General ..."

Like § 3 of the 1917 Act, § 212(c) was literally applicable only to exclusion proceedings, but it too has been interpreted by the Board of Immigration Appeals (BIA) to authorize any permanent resident alien with "a lawful unrelinquished domicile of seven consecutive years" to apply for a discretionary waiver from deportation. If relief is granted, the deportation proceeding is terminated and the alien remains a permanent resident.

The extension of § 212(c) relief to the deportation context has had great practical importance, because deportable offenses have historically been defined broadly. For example, under the INA, aliens are deportable upon conviction for two crimes of "moral turpitude" (or for one such crime if it occurred within five years of entry into the country and resulted in a jail term of at least one year). In 1988, Congress further specified that an alien is deportable upon conviction for any "aggravated felony," which was defined to include numerous offenses without regard to how long ago they were committed.[4] Thus, the class of aliens whose continued residence in this country has depended on their eligibility for § 212(c) relief is extremely large, and not surprisingly, a substantial percentage of their applications for § 212(c) relief have been granted. Consequently, in the period between 1989 and 1995 alone, § 212(c) relief was granted to over 10,000 aliens.

Three statutes enacted in recent years have reduced the size of the class of aliens eligible for such discretionary relief. In 1990, Congress amended § 212(c) to preclude from discretionary relief anyone convicted of an aggravated felony who had served a term of imprisonment of at least five years. In 1996, in § 440(d) of AEDPA, Congress identified a broad set of offenses for which convictions would preclude such relief. And finally, that same year, Congress passed IIRIRA. That statute, inter alia, repealed § 212(c), and replaced it with a new section that gives the Attorney General the authority to cancel removal for a narrow class of inadmissible or deportable aliens * * *. So narrowed, that class does not include anyone previously "convicted of any aggravated felony." § 1229b(a)(3).

In the Attorney General's opinion, these amendments have entirely withdrawn his § 212(c) authority to waive deportation for aliens previously convicted of aggravated felonies. Moreover, as a result of other amendments adopted in AEDPA and IIRIRA, the Attorney General also maintains that there is no judicial forum available to decide whether these statutes did, in fact, deprive him of the power to grant such relief. As we shall explain below, we disagree on both points. In our view, a federal court does have jurisdiction to decide the merits of the legal question, and the District Court and the Court of Appeals decided that question correctly in this case.

---

[4] See 8 U.S.C. § 1101(a)(43) (1994 ed. and Supp. V). While the term has always been defined expansively, it was broadened substantially by IIRIRA. For example, as amended by that statute, the term includes all convictions for theft or burglary for which a term of imprisonment of at least one year is imposed (as opposed to five years pre-IIRIRA), compare § 1101(a)(43)(G) (1994 ed., Supp. V) with § 1101(a)(43)(G) (1994 ed.), and all convictions involving fraud or deceit in which the loss to the victim exceeds $10,000 (as opposed to $200,000 pre-IIRIRA), compare § 1101(a)(43)(M)(i) (1994 ed., Supp. V) with § 1101(a)(43)(M)(i) (1994 ed.). In addition, the term includes any "crime of violence" resulting in a prison sentence of at least one year (as opposed to five years pre-IIRIRA), compare § 1101(a)(43)(F) (1994 ed., Supp. V) with § 1101(a)(43)(F) (1994 ed.), and that phrase is itself broadly defined. See 18 U.S.C. § 16 ("[A]n offense that has as an element the use, attempted use, or threatened use of physical force against the person or property of another," or "any other offense that is a felony and that, by its nature, involves a substantial risk that physical force against the person or property of another may be used in the course of committing the offense")* * *.

II

The first question we must consider is whether the District Court retains jurisdiction under the general habeas corpus statute, 28 U.S.C. § 2241, to entertain St. Cyr's challenge. His application for a writ raises a pure question of law. He does not dispute any of the facts that establish his deportability or the conclusion that he is deportable. Nor does he contend that he would have any right to have an unfavorable exercise of the Attorney General's discretion reviewed in a judicial forum. Rather, he contests the Attorney General's conclusion that, as a matter of statutory interpretation, he is not eligible for discretionary relief.

The District Court held, and the Court of Appeals agreed, that it had jurisdiction to answer that question in a habeas corpus proceeding. The INS argues, however, that four sections of the 1996 statutes—specifically, § 401(e) of AEDPA and three sections of IIRIRA (8 U.S.C. §§ 1252(a)(1), 1252(a)(2)(C), and 1252(b)(9)—stripped the courts of jurisdiction to decide the question of law presented by respondent's habeas corpus application.

For the INS to prevail it must overcome both the strong presumption in favor of judicial review of administrative action and the longstanding rule requiring a clear statement of congressional intent to repeal habeas jurisdiction. See *Ex parte Yerger*, 8 Wall. 85, 102 (1869) ("We are not at liberty to except from [habeas corpus jurisdiction] any cases not plainly excepted by law"); *Felker v. Turpin*, 518 U.S. 651, 660–661 (1996) (noting that "[n]o provision of Title I mentions our authority to entertain original habeas petitions," and the statute "makes no mention of our authority to hear habeas petitions filed as original matters in this Court"). Implications from statutory text or legislative history are not sufficient to repeal habeas jurisdiction; instead, Congress must articulate specific and unambiguous statutory directives to effect a repeal. *Yerger*, 8 Wall. at 105 ("Repeals by implication are not favored. They are seldom admitted except on the ground of repugnancy; and never, we think, when the former act can stand together with the new act.").

In this case, the plain statement rule draws additional reinforcement from other canons of statutory construction. First, as a general matter, when a particular interpretation of a statute invokes the outer limits of Congress' power, we expect a clear indication that Congress intended that result. Second, if an otherwise acceptable construction of a statute would raise serious constitutional problems, and where an alternative interpretation of the statute is "fairly possible," we are obligated to construe the statute to avoid such problems.

A construction of the amendments at issue that would entirely preclude review of a pure question of law by any court would give rise to substantial constitutional questions. Article I, § 9, cl. 2, of the Constitution provides: "The Privilege of the Writ of Habeas Corpus shall not be suspended, unless when in Cases of Rebellion or Invasion the public Safety may require it." Because of that Clause, some "judicial intervention in deportation cases" is unquestionably "required by the Constitution." *Heikkila v. Barber*, 345 U.S. 229, 235 (1953).

Unlike the provisions of AEDPA that we construed in *Felker v. Turpin*, 518 U.S. 651 (1996), this case involves an alien subject to a federal removal order rather than a person confined pursuant to a state-court conviction. Accordingly, regardless of whether the protection of the Suspension Clause encompasses all cases covered by the 1867 Amendment extending the protection of the writ to state prisoners [ ] or by subsequent legal developments[ ], at the absolute minimum, the Suspension Clause protects the writ "as it existed in 1789."[13]

At its historical core, the writ of habeas corpus has served as a means of reviewing the legality of Executive detention, and it is in that context that its protections have been strongest. In England prior to 1789, in the Colonies, and in this Nation during the formative years of our Government, the writ of habeas corpus was available to nonenemy aliens as well as to citizens. It enabled them to challenge Executive and private detention in civil cases as well as criminal. Moreover, the issuance of the writ was not limited to challenges to the jurisdiction of the custodian, but encompassed detentions based on errors of law, including the erroneous application or interpretation of statutes. It was used to command the discharge of seamen who had a statutory exemption from impressment into the British Navy, to emancipate slaves, and to obtain the freedom of apprentices and asylum inmates. Most important, for our purposes, those early cases contain no suggestion that habeas relief in cases involving Executive detention was only available for constitutional error.

Notwithstanding the historical use of habeas corpus to remedy unlawful Executive action, the INS argues that this case falls outside the traditional scope of the writ at common law. * * * In this case, the INS points out, there is no dispute that the INS had authority in law to hold St. Cyr, as he is eligible for removal. St. Cyr counters that there is historical evidence of the writ issuing to redress the improper exercise of official discretion. * * *

* * * [W]hile the INS' historical arguments are not insubstantial, the ambiguities in the scope of the exercise of the writ at common law identified by St. Cyr, and the suggestions in this Court's prior decisions as to the extent to which habeas review could be limited consistent with the Constitution, convince us that that the Suspension Clause question that would be presented by the INS' reading of the immigration statutes * * * are difficult and significant.[24]

In sum, even assuming that the Suspension Clause protects only the writ as it existed in 1789, there is substantial evidence to support the proposition that pure questions of law like the one raised by the respondent in this case could have been answered in 1789 by a common-law judge with power to issue the writ of habeas corpus. It necessarily follows that a serious Suspension Clause issue would be presented if we were to accept the INS' submission that the 1996 statutes have withdrawn that power from

---

[13] The fact that this Court would be required to answer the difficult question of what the Suspension Clause protects is in and of itself a reason to avoid answering the constitutional questions that would be raised by concluding that review was barred entirely. * * *

[24] The dissent reads into Chief Justice Marshall's opinion in *Ex parte Bollman*, 4 Cranch 75 (1807), support for a proposition that the Chief Justice did not endorse, either explicitly or implicitly. * * * He did note that "the first congress of the United States" acted under "the immediate influence" of the injunction provided by the Suspension Clause when it gave "life and activity" to "this great constitutional privilege" in the Judiciary Act of 1789, and that the writ could not be suspended until after the statute was enacted. 4 Cranch, at 95. That statement, however, surely does not imply that Marshall believed the Framers had drafted a Clause that would proscribe a temporary abrogation of the writ, while permitting its permanent suspension. Indeed, Marshall's comment expresses the far more sensible view that the Clause was intended to preclude any possibility that "the privilege itself would be lost" by either the inaction or the action of Congress. *See, e.g., ibid.* (noting that the Founders "must have felt, with peculiar force, the obligation" imposed by the Suspension Clause).

federal judges and provided no adequate substitute for its exercise. The necessity of resolving such a serious and difficult constitutional issue—and the desirability of avoiding that necessity—simply reinforce the reasons for requiring a clear and unambiguous statement of congressional intent.

Moreover, to conclude that the writ is no longer available in this context would represent a departure from historical practice in immigration law. The writ of habeas corpus has always been available to review the legality of Executive detention. Federal courts have been authorized to issue writs of habeas corpus since the enactment of the Judiciary Act of 1789, and § 2241 of the Judicial Code provides that federal judges may grant the writ of habeas corpus on the application of a prisoner held "in custody in violation of the Constitution or laws or treaties of the United States." Before and after the enactment in 1875 of the first statute regulating immigration, that jurisdiction was regularly invoked on behalf of noncitizens, particularly in the immigration context. * * *

Until the enactment of the 1952 Immigration and Nationality Act, the sole means by which an alien could test the legality of his or her deportation order was by bringing a habeas corpus action in district court. * * * In case after case, courts answered questions of law in habeas corpus proceedings brought by aliens challenging Executive interpretations of the immigration laws.

Habeas courts also regularly answered questions of law that arose in the context of discretionary relief. * * *

Thus, under the pre-1996 statutory scheme—and consistent with its common-law antecedents—it is clear that St. Cyr could have brought his challenge to the BIA's legal determination in a habeas corpus petition under 28 U.S.C. § 2241. The INS argues, however, that AEDPA and IIRIRA contain four provisions that express a clear and unambiguous statement of Congress's intent to bar petitions brought under § 2241, despite the fact that none of them mention that section. The first of those provisions is AEDPA's § 401(e).

While the title of § 401(e)—"ELIMINATION OF CUSTODY REVIEW BY HABEAS CORPUS"—would seem to support the INS' submission, the actual text of that provision does not. As we have previously noted, a title alone is not controlling. The actual text of § 401(e), unlike its title, merely repeals a subsection of the 1961 statute [§ 106(a)(10)] amending the judicial review provisions of the 1952 Immigration and Nationality Act. Neither the title nor the text makes any mention of 28 U.S.C. § 2241. * * *

In any case, whether § 106(a)(10) served as an independent grant of habeas jurisdiction or simply as an acknowledgment of continued jurisdiction pursuant to § 2241, its repeal cannot be sufficient to eliminate what it did not originally grant—namely, habeas jurisdiction pursuant to 28 U.S.C. § 2241. See *Yerger*, 8 Wall. at 105–106 (concluding that the repeal of "an additional grant of jurisdiction" does not "operate as a repeal of jurisdiction theretofore allowed"); *Ex parte McCardle*, 7 Wall. 506, 515 (1869) (concluding that the repeal of portions of the 1867 statute conferring appellate jurisdiction on the Supreme Court in habeas proceedings did "not affect the jurisdiction which was previously exercised").

The INS also relies on three provisions of IIRIRA, now codified at 8 U.S.C. §§ 1252(a)(1), 1252(a)(2)(C), and 1252(b)(9). As amended by § 306 of IIRIRA, 8 U.S.C. § 1252(a)(1) now provides that, with certain exceptions, including those set out in subsection (b) of the same statutory provision, "[j]udicial review of a final order of removal . . . is governed only by" the Hobbs Act's procedures for review of agency orders in the courts of appeals. Similarly, § 1252(b)(9), which addresses the "[c]onsolidation of questions for judicial review," provides that "[j]udicial review of all questions of law and fact, including interpretation and application of constitutional and statutory provisions, arising from any action taken or proceeding brought to remove an alien from the United States under this subchapter shall be available only in judicial review of a final order under this section." Finally, § 1252(a)(2)(C), which concerns "[m]atters not subject to judicial review," states: "Notwithstanding any other provision of law, no court shall have jurisdiction to review any final order of removal against an alien who is removable by reason of having committed" certain enumerated criminal offenses.

The term "judicial review" or "jurisdiction to review" is the focus of each of these three provisions. In the immigration context, "judicial review" and "habeas corpus" have historically distinct meanings. See *Heikkila v. Barber*, 345 U.S. 229 (1953). In *Heikkila*, the Court concluded that the finality provisions at issue "preclud[ed] judicial review" to the maximum extent possible under the Constitution, and thus concluded that the APA was inapplicable. Nevertheless, the Court reaffirmed the right to habeas corpus. * * *

If it were clear that the question of law could be answered in another judicial forum, it might be permissible to accept the INS' reading of § 1252. But the absence of such a forum, coupled with the lack of a clear, unambiguous, and express statement of congressional intent to preclude judicial consideration on habeas of such an important question of law, strongly counsels against adopting a construction that would raise serious constitutional questions. Accordingly, we conclude that habeas jurisdiction under § 2241 was not repealed by AEDPA and IIRIRA.

III * * *

IIRIRA's elimination of any possibility of § 212(c) relief for people who entered into plea agreements with the expectation that they would be eligible for such relief clearly "'attaches a new disability, in respect to transactions or considerations already past.'" Plea agreements involve a *quid pro quo* between a criminal defendant and the government. In exchange for some perceived benefit, defendants waive several of their constitutional rights (including the right to a trial) and grant the government numerous "tangible benefits, such as promptly imposed punishment without the expenditure of prosecutorial resources." There can be little doubt that, as a general matter, alien defendants considering whether to enter into a plea agreement are acutely aware of the immigration consequences of their convictions. Given the frequency with which § 212(c) relief was granted in the years leading up to AEDPA and IIRIRA, preserving the possibility of such relief would have been one of the principal benefits sought by defendants deciding whether to accept a plea offer or instead to proceed to trial. * * *

We find nothing in IIRIRA unmistakably indicating that Congress considered the question whether to apply its repeal of § 212(c) retroactively to such aliens. We therefore hold that § 212(c) relief remains available for aliens, like respondent, whose convictions were obtained through plea agreements and who, notwithstanding those convictions, would have been eligible for § 212(c) relief at the time of their plea under the law then in effect.

The judgment is affirmed.

[The dissenting opinion of JUSTICE O'CONNOR is omitted].

■ JUSTICE SCALIA, with whom THE CHIEF JUSTICE and JUSTICE THOMAS join, and with whom JUSTICE O'CONNOR joins as to Parts I and III, dissenting.

The Court today finds ambiguity in the utterly clear language of a statute that forbids the district court (and all other courts) to entertain the claims of aliens such as respondent St. Cyr, who have been found deportable by reason of their criminal acts. It fabricates a superclear statement, "magic words" requirement for the congressional expression of such an intent, unjustified in law and unparalleled in any other area of our jurisprudence. And as the fruit of its labors, it brings forth a version of the statute that affords *criminal* aliens *more* opportunities for delay-inducing judicial review than are afforded to noncriminal aliens, or even than were afforded to criminal aliens prior to this legislation concededly designed to *expedite* their removal. Because it is clear that the law deprives us of jurisdiction to entertain this suit, I respectfully dissent.

I

In categorical terms that admit of no exception, [IIRIRA] unambiguously repeals the application of 28 U.S.C. § 2241 (the general habeas corpus provision), and of all other provisions for judicial review, to deportation challenges brought by certain kinds of criminal aliens. This would have been readily apparent to the reader, had the Court at the outset of its opinion set forth the relevant provisions of IIRIRA and of its statutory predecessor, [AEDPA]. I will begin by supplying that deficiency, and explaining IIRIRA's jurisdictional scheme. It begins with what we have called a channeling or " 'zipper' clause," —namely 8 U.S.C. § 1252(b)(9). This provision, entitled "Consolidation of questions for judicial review," provides as follows:

"Judicial review of *all* questions of law and fact, including interpretation and application of constitutional and statutory provisions, arising from *any action taken or proceeding brought to remove an alien* from the United States under this subchapter shall be available only in judicial review of a final order under this section." (Emphases added.)

In other words, *if* any review is available of any "questio[n] of law . . . arising from any action taken or proceeding brought to remove an alien from the United States under this subchapter," it is available "only in judicial review of a final order under this section [§ 1252]." What kind of review does that section provide? That is set forth in § 1252(a)(1), which states:

Judicial review of a final order of removal (other than an order of removal without a hearing pursuant to [the expedited-removal provisions for undocumented aliens arriving at the border found in] section 1225(b)(1) of this title) is governed only by chapter 158 of title 28 [the Hobbs Act], except as provided in subsection (b) of this section [which modifies some of the Hobbs Act provisions] and except that the court may not order the taking of additional evidence under section 2347(c) of [Title 28].

In other words, *if* judicial review is available, it consists only of the modified Hobbs Act review specified in § 1252(a)(1).

In some cases (including, as it happens, the one before us), there can be no review at all, because IIRIRA categorically and unequivocally rules out judicial review of challenges to deportation brought by certain kinds of criminal aliens. Section 1252(a)(2)(C) provides:

> "Notwithstanding *any* other provision of law, *no court* shall have jurisdiction to review *any* final order of removal against an alien who is removable by reason of having committed [one or more enumerated] criminal offense[s] [including drug-trafficking offenses of the sort of which respondent had been convicted]." (Emphases added.)

Finally, the pre-IIRIRA antecedent to the foregoing provisions—AEDPA § 401(e) —and the statutory background against which that was enacted, confirm that § 2241 habeas review, in the district court or elsewhere, has been unequivocally repealed. In 1961, Congress amended the Immigration and Nationality Act of 1952 (INA) * * * by directing that the procedure for Hobbs Act review in the courts of appeals "shall apply to, and shall be the *sole and exclusive procedure for*, the judicial review of all final orders of deportation" under the INA. 8 U.S.C. § 1105a(a) (repealed Sept. 30, 1996) (emphasis added). Like 8 U.S.C. § 1252(a)(2)(C), this provision squarely prohibited § 2241 district-court habeas review. At the same time that it enacted this provision, however, the 1961 Congress enacted a specific exception: "any alien held in custody pursuant to an order of deportation may obtain judicial review thereof by habeas corpus proceedings," 8 U.S.C. § 1105a(a)(10). (This would of course have been surplusage had § 2241 habeas review not been covered by the "sole and exclusive procedure" provision.) Section 401(e) of AEDPA repealed this narrow exception, and there is no doubt what the repeal was thought to accomplish: the provision was entitled "ELIMINATION OF CUSTODY REVIEW BY HABEAS CORPUS." It gave universal preclusive effect to the "sole and exclusive procedure" language of § 1105a(a). And it is this regime that IIRIRA has carried forward.

The Court's efforts to derive ambiguity from this utmost clarity are unconvincing. First, the Court argues that §§ 1252(a)(2)(C) and 1252(b)(9) are not as clear as one might think—that, even though they are sufficient to repeal the jurisdiction of the courts of appeals, they do not cover habeas jurisdiction in the district court, since, "[i]n the immigration context, 'judicial review' and 'habeas corpus' have historically distinct meanings[.]" Of course § 1252(a)(2)(C) does not even use the term "judicial review" (it says "jurisdiction to review")—but let us make believe it does. The Court's contention that in this statute it does not include habeas corpus is decisively refuted by the language of § 1252(e)(2), enacted along with §§ 1252(a)(2)(C) and 1252(b)(9): "*Judicial review* of any determination made under section 1225(b)(1) of this title [governing review of expedited removal orders against undocumented aliens arriving at the border] is available in habeas corpus proceedings . . ." (Emphases added.) It is hard to imagine how Congress could have made it any clearer that, when it used the term "judicial review" in IIRIRA, it included judicial review through habeas corpus. * * *

Unquestionably, unambiguously, and unmistakably, IIRIRA expressly supersedes § 2241's general provision for habeas jurisdiction. The Court asserts that *Felker v. Turpin*, 518 U.S. 651 (1996), and *Ex parte Yerger*, 8 Wall. 85(1869), reflect a "longstanding rule requiring a clear statement of congressional intent to repeal habeas jurisdiction[.]" They do no such thing. Those cases simply applied the general principle-not unique to habeas-that "[r]epeals by implication are not favored." *Felker* * * * In the present case, unlike in *Felker* and *Yerger*, none of the statutory provisions relied upon—§ 1252(a)(2)(C), § 1252(b)(9), or 8 U.S.C. § 1105a(a)—requires us to imply from one statutory provision the repeal of another. All by their terms prohibit the judicial review at issue in this case. * * *

It has happened before—too frequently, alas—that courts have distorted plain statutory text in order to produce a "more sensible" result. * * * By authorizing § 2241 habeas review in the district court but foreclosing review in the court of appeals, * * * the Court's interpretation routes all legal challenges to removal orders brought by criminal aliens to the district court, to be adjudicated under that court's § 2241 habeas authority, which specifies no time limits. After review by that court, criminal aliens will presumably have an appeal as of right to the court of appeals, and can then petition this Court for a writ of certiorari. In contrast, noncriminal aliens seeking to challenge their removal orders—for example, those charged with having been inadmissible at the time of entry, with having failed to maintain their nonimmigrant status, with having procured a visa through a marriage that was not bona fide, or with having become, within five years after the date of entry, a public charge, see 8 U.S.C. §§ 1227(a)(1)(A), (a)(1)(C), (a)(1)(G), (a)(5)—will still presumably be required to proceed directly to the court of appeals by way of petition for review, under the restrictive modified Hobbs Act review provisions set forth in § 1252(a)(1), including the 30-day filing deadline, see § 1252(b)(1). * * * The Court has therefore succeeded in perverting a statutory scheme designed to *expedite* the removal of criminal aliens into one that now affords them more opportunities for (and layers of) judicial review (and hence more opportunities for delay) than are afforded *non*-criminal aliens—and more than were afforded criminal aliens prior to the enactment of IIRIRA. This outcome speaks for itself; no Congress ever imagined it.

To excuse the violence it does to the statutory text, the Court invokes the doctrine of constitutional doubt, which it asserts is raised by the Suspension Clause, U.S. Const., Art. I, § 9, cl. 2. * * * The doctrine of constitutional doubt is meant to effectuate, not to subvert, congressional intent, by giving *ambiguous* provisions a meaning that will avoid constitutional peril, and that will conform with Congress's presumed intent not to enact measures of dubious validity. * * * It is a device for interpreting what the statute says—not for *ignoring* what the statute says in order to avoid the trouble of determining whether what it says is unconstitutional. For the reasons I have set forth above, it is crystal clear that the statute before us here bars criminal aliens from obtaining judicial review, including § 2241 district-court review, of their removal orders. It is therefore also crystal clear that the doctrine of constitutional doubt has no application.

In the remainder of this opinion I address the question the Court *should* have addressed: Whether these provisions of IIRIRA are unconstitutional.

II

A

The Suspension Clause of the Constitution, Art. I, § 9, cl. 2, provides as follows:

> "The Privilege of the Writ of Habeas Corpus shall not be suspended, unless when in Cases of Rebellion or Invasion the public Safety may require it."

A straightforward reading of this text discloses that it does not guarantee any content to (or even the existence of) the writ of habeas corpus, but merely provides that the writ shall not (except in case of rebellion or invasion) be suspended. * * *

To "suspend" the writ was not to fail to enact it, much less to refuse to accord it particular content. Noah Webster, in his American Dictionary of the English Language, defined it—with patriotic allusion to the constitutional text—as "[t]o cause to cease for a time from operation or effect; as, to suspend the habeas corpus act." This was a distinct abuse of majority power, and one that had manifested itself often in the Framers' experience: temporarily but entirely eliminating the "Privilege of the Writ" for a certain geographic area or areas, or for a certain class or classes of individuals. Suspension Acts had been adopted (and many more proposed) both in this country and in England during the late 18th century, * * * Typical of the genre was the prescription by the Statute of 1794, 34 Geo. 3, c. 54, § 2, that "'an Act for preventing wrongous imprisonment, and against undue delays in trials', insofar as the same may be construed to relate to the cases of Treason and suspicion of Treason, be suspended [for one year] . . .'"

In the present case, of course, Congress has not temporarily withheld operation of the writ, but has permanently altered its content. That is, to be sure, an act subject to majoritarian abuse, as is Congress's framing (or its determination not to frame) a habeas statute in the first place. But that is not the majoritarian abuse against which the Suspension Clause was directed. It is no more irrational to guard against the common and well known "suspension" abuse, without guaranteeing any particular habeas right that enjoys immunity from suspension, than it is, in the Equal Protection Clause, to guard against unequal application of the laws, without guaranteeing any particular law which enjoys *that* protection. And it is no more acceptable for this Court to write a habeas law, in order that the Suspension Clause might have some effect, than it would be for this Court to write other laws, in order that the Equal Protection Clause might have some effect. * * *

There is, however, another Supreme Court dictum that is unquestionably in point—an unusually authoritative one at that, since it was written by Chief Justice Marshall in 1807. It supports precisely the interpretation of the Suspension Clause I have set forth above. In *Ex parte Bollman*, 4 Cranch 75, one of the cases arising out of the Burr conspiracy, the issue presented was whether the Supreme Court had the power to issue a writ of habeas corpus for the release of two prisoners held for trial under warrant of the Circuit Court of the District of Columbia. Counsel for the detainees asserted not only statutory authority for issuance of the writ, but inherent power. The Court would have nothing to do with that, whether under Article III or any other provision. While acknowledging an inherent power of the courts "over their own officers, or to protect themselves, and their members, from being disturbed in the exercise of their functions," Marshall says that "the power of taking cognizance of any question between individuals, or between the government and individuals,"

"must be given by written law.

"The inquiry, therefore, on this motion will be, whether by any statute compatible with the constitution of the United States, the power to award a writ of *habeas corpus*, in such a case as that of Erick Bollman and Samuel Swartwout, has been given to this court." * * *.[5]

---

[5] The Court claims that I "rea[d] into Chief Justice Marshall's opinion in *Ex parte Bollman* ... support for a proposition that the Chief Justice did not endorse, either explicitly or

There is no more reason for us to believe, than there was for the Marshall Court to believe, that the Suspension Clause means anything other than what it says.

B

* * * If one reads the Suspension Clause as a guarantee of habeas relief, the obvious question presented is: *What* habeas relief? There are only two alternatives, the first of which is too absurd to be seriously entertained. It could be contended that Congress "suspends" the writ whenever it eliminates *any* prior ground for the writ that it adopted. Thus, if Congress should ever (in the view of this Court) have authorized immediate habeas corpus—without the need to exhaust administrative remedies—for a person arrested as an illegal alien, Congress would *never* be able (in the light of sad experience) to revise that disposition. The Suspension Clause, in other words, would be a one-way ratchet that enshrines in the Constitution every grant of habeas jurisdiction. This is, as I say, too absurd to be contemplated, and I shall contemplate it no further.

The other alternative is that the Suspension Clause guarantees the common-law right of habeas corpus, as it was understood when the Constitution was ratified. There is no doubt whatever that this did not include the right to obtain discretionary release. * * *

III * * *

The Court has created a version of IIRIRA that is not only unrecognizable to its framers (or to anyone who can read) but gives the statutory scheme precisely the *opposite* of its intended effect, affording criminal aliens *more* opportunities for delay-inducing judicial review than others have, or even than criminal aliens had prior to the enactment of this legislation. Because § 2241's exclusion of judicial review is unmistakably clear, and unquestionably constitutional, both this Court and the courts below were without power to entertain respondent's claims. I would set aside the judgment of the court below and remand with instructions to have the District Court dismiss for want of jurisdiction. I respectfully dissent from the judgment of the Court.

NOTES AND QUESTIONS ON ST. CYR

1)   **The Limits of Plenary Power.** What does the *St. Cyr* decision suggest about the limits of the immigration power? Recall that the power over individuals for immigration purposes is considered a class of "custody" that is subject to habeas review. In other types of habeas cases, the power to detain is the functional target of the challenge. In immigration cases, however, the detention

----

implicitly." Its support for this claim is a highly selective quotation from the opinion, There is nothing "implici[t]" whatsoever about Chief Justice Marshall's categorical statement that "the power to award the writ [of habeas corpus] by any of the courts of the United States, must be given by written law." If, as the Court concedes, "the writ could not be suspended" * * * within the meaning of the Suspension Clause until Congress affirmatively provided for habeas by statute, then surely Congress may subsequently alter what it had initially provided for, lest the Clause become a one-way ratchet[.] The Court's position that a permanent repeal of habeas jurisdiction is unthinkable (and hence a violation of the Suspension Clause) is simply incompatible with its (and Marshall's) belief that a failure to confer habeas jurisdiction is *not* unthinkable.

may be incidental to the threat of physical removal from the United States—and the removal is the official act that the habeas petitioner is trying to preclude. First, why might one say that *St. Cyr* ultimately failed to test the limits of the plenary power doctrine? Second, in what sense does *St. Cyr* reject the most expansive interpretations of that doctrine?

2)   Executive Detention. Why does the Court call review of executive detention part of the core purpose of habeas corpus? Is this consistent with the historical material presented in Chapter 1 and the beginning of Chapter 2? When the Court invokes the "core" purpose of habeas, what is the Court contrasting? In other words, what is "noncore?"

3)   Judicial Review of Removal. AEDPA and IRRIRA appeared to consolidate judicial review, requiring noncitizens to file petitions for review in the federal Courts of Appeals—including petitions challenging any denial of discretionary relief. 8 U.S.C. § 1252. The Court held that habeas corpus review remained available to noncitizens challenging denial of discretionary relief or removal based on criminal convictions. Does the decision undermine Congressional intent to streamline all removal challenges by channeling them to the Courts of Appeals? Does it also create a perverse result highlighted by Justice Scalia: that noncitizens facing removal for criminal convictions may seek review of removal and denial of discretionary relief using habeas corpus, while noncitizens facing removal on other grounds must use a "petition for review" in a court of appeals?

4)   Avoidance. The Court stated that it interpreted the statutes to avoid "a serious Suspension Clause issue." Did the Court do so by construing the statutes in a manner that in effect changed their meaning and misread congressional intent? Justice Scalia claimed the majority had done just that. If the judicial interpretation altered Congressional meaning or intent, then should the Court have simply reached the Suspension Clause issue?

5)   *Ex Parte Bollman.* What do you make of the contrast in uses of *Bollman* by the majority and the dissent? Each side would like to lay claim to the authority of Chief Justice Marshall. Is the Court's use of the Framer's intent any more convincing than Chief Justice Marshall's in *Bollman*?

6)   The Empty Privilege? What of Justice Scalia's argument that the Suspension Clause does not ensure that the writ has any particular content, but merely that it shall not be suspended? He argues at length that "[t]o 'suspend' the writ was not to fail to enact it, much less to refuse to accord it particular content." Does Congress in fact have an unlimited ability to withdraw habeas jurisdiction from federal courts, so long as those measures stripping habeas jurisdiction are not temporary suspensions? Professor Gerald Neuman called the dissenters' view of the Suspension Clause "astonishing." See Gerald Neuman, *The Habeas Corpus Suspension Clause After INS v. St. Cyr,* 33 Colum. Hum. Rights L. Rev. 555, 557 (2002).

7)   The Scope of the Privilege. Why does the Court assume that the habeas privilege must at least cover what it had reached in 1789? Why does it not consider the argument that the protections of the writ have evolved? Is it possible that some of the writ's parameters should be fixed at their 1789 scope (e.g. its territorial reach) but that, consistent with the writ's design, other parameters (like procedures that make the writ effective) should evolve? Should the

Suspension Clause be interpreted to guarantee some amount of access to an evolving writ?

8) Questions of Law. Why does the Court focus on the ability of a federal judge to review questions of law? Are constitutional questions of law more important and less amenable to Congressional restrictions than other questions of federal law? Does the Suspension Clause assure access to a federal judge to review questions of law?

Did the Court also reach the question whether purely statutory (and not constitutional) questions of law must be reviewed?[q] How about questions regarding exercise of agency discretion? In an omitted portion of his dissent, Justice Scalia claims that, historically, habeas corpus was not used to challenge discretionary relief. As the majority pointed out, however, habeas corpus was traditionally used to examine the issue of eligibility for discretionary review. Historical evidence also suggests that, in the immigration context, habeas corpus had been used to examine facts supporting the decision to detain as well. See James Oldham and Michael J. Wishnie, *The Historical Scope of Habeas Corpus and INS v. St. Cyr*, 16 Geo. Immigr. L.J. 485, 496 (2002).

Why was there no argument that habeas review in this context also reached questions of fact? Did the Court treat fact review as less constitutionally significant, or did the Court fail to address that question because St. Cyr was himself seeking only to bring a legal challenge? What if the noncitizen facing removal contends that the immigration judge relied on erroneous information? Does the Suspension Clause require that a federal judge be permitted to review such questions?

9) District Courts. As Justice Scalia pointed out, the result of this opinion is that those raising challenges relating to removal based on criminal convictions or challenges relating to discretionary relief can get habeas review in federal district courts, and are not limited to review in the Courts of Appeals. Why did the Court hold that federal district courts must remain open to review questions as to the legality of detentions?

10) Coda on *St. Cyr* and Removal Proceedings. In *Calcano-Martinez v. INS*, 533 U.S. 348 (2001), decided the same day, the Supreme Court upheld the constitutionality of the provision that generally channeled judicial review of removal decisions to courts of appeals. After *St. Cyr*, however, habeas review remained available—at least as to questions of law—for criminal aliens and those challenging denials of discretionary relief. The REAL-ID Act of 2005, however, explored in Section 5, would again alter judicial review of removal decisions, in response to the *St. Cyr* decision.

4. WHAT FACT REVIEW DOES THE CONSTITUTION REQUIRE?

The Court's ruling in *St. Cyr* focused on the right to challenge questions of law and constitutional questions, not factual questions. After *St. Cyr,* may Congress sharply restrict fact review, and must Congress pre-

---

[q] Cf. Richard H. Fallon, Jr. and Daniel J. Meltzer, *Habeas Corpus Jurisdiction, Substantive Rights, And The War On Terror*, 120 Harv. L. Rev. 2029, 2099 (2007) (noting that, in *St. Cyr*, the Court "came close to holding" that the petitioner was "constitutionally entitled to review not merely of constitutional but also of statutory questions underlying his claim of unlawful detention")

serve judicial review of legal questions? Before turning to statutes enacted in response to *St. Cyr,* we discuss the development of the "some evidence" and "substantial evidence" rules that have long played a role in the fact-review function performed by Article III courts during immigration habeas proceedings. Over time, the courts began insisting that at least some evidence support immigration custody. Early rulings grew out of challenges to the Chinese Exclusion Acts. As Professor Gerald Neuman describes: "Congress authorized executive officials stationed at seaports and land borders to deny ineligible aliens admission to the United States after proceedings of a summary character." When noncitizens used habeas proceedings to lodge due process objections to this practice, "the Supreme Court insisted that supervision of immigration was an executive, not a judicial function." Gerald L. Neuman, *The Constitutional Requirement of "Some Evidence",* 25 San Diego L. Rev. 631, 637 (1988).

The early assumption that executive fact-finding was unreviewable eventually yielded to "some evidence" review under the Due Process Clause, and, ultimately, to broader review under federal statutes. One early challenge that accelerated the change to a due process rule was brought by a noncitizen detained by the collector of the port of San Francisco. She argued that she should benefit from due process because she had been removed from the steamship and placed onshore in a "mission house" pending review of her habeas petition.

Nishimura Ekiu v. U.S.

United States Supreme Court
142 U.S. 651 (1892)

■ Mr. JUSTICE GRAY * * * delivered the opinion of the court.

* * * It is an accepted maxim of international law that every sovereign nation has the power, as inherent in sovereignty, and essential to self-preservation, to forbid the entrance of foreigners within its dominions, or to admit them only in such cases and upon such conditions as it may see fit to prescribe. In the United States this power is vested in the national government, to which the constitution has committed the entire control of international relations, in peace as well as in war. * * *

The supervision of the admission of aliens into the United States may be intrusted by congress either to the department of state, having the general management of foreign relations, or to the department of the treasury, charged with the enforcement of the laws regulating foreign commerce; and congress has often passed acts forbidding the immigration of particular classes of foreigners, and has committed the execution of these acts to the secretary of the treasury, to collectors of customs, and to inspectors acting under their authority.

An alien immigrant, prevented from landing by any such officer claiming authority to do so under an act of congress, and thereby restrained of his liberty, is doubtless entitled to a writ of *habeas corpus* to ascertain whether the restraint is lawful. And congress may, if it sees fit * * * authorize the courts to investigate and ascertain the facts on which the right to land depends. But, on the other hand, the final determination of those facts may be in trusted by congress to executive officers; and in such a case, as in all others, in which a statute gives a discretionary power to an officer, to be exercised by him upon his own opinion of certain facts, he is made the sole and exclusive judge of the existence of those facts, and no other tribunal, unless expressly authorized by law to do so, is at liberty to re-examine or controvert the sufficiency of the evidence on which he acted It is not within the province of the judiciary to order that foreigners who have never been naturalized, nor acquired any domicile or residence within the United States, nor even been admitted into the country pursuant to law, shall be permitted to enter, in opposition to the constitutional and lawful measures of the legislative and executive branches of the national government. As to such persons, the decisions of executive or administrative officers, acting within powers expressly conferred by congress, are due process of law.

The immigration act of August 3, 1882 * * * imposed a duty of 50 cents for each alien passenger coming by vessel into any port of the United States, to be paid to the collector of customs, and by him into the treasury, to constitute an immigrant fund; by section 2, the secretary of the treasury was charged with the duty of execution the provisions of the act, and with the supervision of the business of immigration to the United States, and, for these purposes, was empowered to make contracts with any state commission, board, or officers, and it was made their duty to go on board vessels and examine the condition of immigrants, "and if on such examination there shall be found among such passengers any convict, lunatic, idiot, or any person unable to take care of himself or herself without becoming a public charge, they shall report the same in writing to the collector of such port, and such persons shall not be permitted to land;" and by section 3, the secretary of the treasury was authorized to establish rules and regulations, and to issue instructions, to carry out this and other immigration laws of the United States.

The doings of Thornley, the state commissioner of immigration, in examining and detaining the petitioner, and in reporting to the collector, appear to have been under that act, and would be justified by the second section thereof, unless that section should be taken to have been impliedly repealed by the last paragraph of section 8 of the act of March 3, 1891, by which all duties imposed and powers confered by that section upon state commissions, boards, or officers, acting under contract with the secretary of the treasury, "shall be performed and exercised, as occasion may arise, by the inspection officers of the United States."

But it is unnecessary to express a definite opinion on the authority of Thornley to inspect and detain the petitioner.

Putting her in the mission-house as a more suitable place than the steam-ship, pending the decision of the question of her right to land, and keeping her there, by agreement between her attorney and the attorney for the United States, until final judgment upon the writ of *habeas corpus*, left her in the same position, so far as regarded her right to land in the United States, as if she never had been removed from the steam-ship.

Before the hearing upon the writ of *habeas corpus*, Hatch was appointed by the secretary of the treasury inspector of immigration at the port of San Francisco, and, after making the inspection and examination required by the act of 1891, refused to allow the petitioner to land, and made a report to the collector of customs, stating facts which tended to show, and which the inspector decided did show, that she was a "person likely to become a public charge," and so within one of the classes of aliens "excluded from admission into the United States" by the first section of that act. And Hatch intervened in the proceedings on the writ of *habeas corpus*, setting up his decision in bar of the writ.

A writ of *habeas corpus* is not like an action to recover damages for an unlawful arrest or commitment, but its object is to ascertain whether the prisoner can lawfully be detained in custody; and, if sufficient ground for his detention by the government is shown, he is not to be discharged for defects in the original arrest or commitment.

The case must therefore turn on the validity and effect of the action of Hatch as inspector of immigration.

Section 7 of the act of 1891 establishes the office of superintendent of immigration, and enacts that he "shall be an officer in the treasury department, under the control and supervision of the secretary of the treasury." By section 8, "the proper inspection officers" are required to go on board any vessel bringing alien immigrants, and to inspect and examine them, and may for this purpose remove and detain them on shore, without such removal being considered a landing; and "shall have power to administer oaths, and to take and consider testimony touching the right of any such aliens to enter the United States, all of which shall be entered of record." "All decisions made by the inspection officers or their assistants touching the right of any alien to land, when adverse to such right, shall be final unless appeal be taken to the superintendent of immigration, whose action shall be subject to review by the secretary of the treasury;" and the secretary of the treasury may prescribe rules for inspection along the borders of Canada, British Columbia, and Mexico, "provided that not exceeding one inspector shall be appointed for each customs district." * * *

It was also argued that Hatch's proceedings did not conform to section 8 of the act of 1891, because it did not appear that he took testimony on oath, and because there was no record of any testimony or of his decision. But the statute does not require inspectors to take any testimony at all, and allows them to decide on their own inspection and examination the question of the right of any alien immigrant to land. The provision relied on merely empowers inspectors to administer oaths, and to take and consider testimony, and requires only testimony so taken to be entered of record.

The decision of the inspector of immigration being in conformity with the act of 1891, there can be no doubt that it was final and conclusive against the petitioner's right to land in the Unites States. * * *

The result is that the act of 1891 is constitutional and valid; the inspector of immigration was duly appointed; his decision against the petitioner's right to land in the United States was within the authority conferred upon him by that act; no appeal having been taken to the superintendent of immigration, that decision was final and conclusive; the petitioner is not unlawfully restrained of her liberty; and the order of the circuit court is affirmed.

NOTES AND QUESTIONS ON EKIU

1) A Habeas Corpus Remedy for Broad Detention Authority. *Ekiu* emphasized that a noncitizen may seek habeas review: a noncitizen "is doubtless entitled to a writ of *habeas corpus* to ascertain whether the restraint is lawful." Consider the following question, which has been posed to you in different ways throughout this Chapter: what value does habeas relief provide if a noncitizen has little basis to challenge a detention because Congress authorizes broad detention and removal powers? What features of immigration proceedings might a noncitizen challenge using habeas corpus?

2)   Defining Lawfulness to Exclude Due Process. The Court held here, long before its rulings in *Knauff* and *Mezei*, that due process rights of a person not yet admitted into the country are extremely limited. What was the nature of the hearing that the officer provided for Ekiu? What did the court mean when it said that "the decisions of executive or administrative officers, acting within powers expressly conferred by congress, are due process of law"? Would it be possible for such officers to act arbitrarily, even pursuant to powers conferred by Congress?

Professor Gerald Neuman has described how, over time "[t]he immigration officials made distressing use of the discretion they had been granted, . . . executive officials regarded the testimony of Chinese witnesses as inherently suspect . . . [and] openly announced a strategy of detecting deceit by isolating arriving Chinese in holding centers and then trapping them in minor testimonial inconsistencies." In response, "[p]rotests against the degrading conduct of the immigration officials were common in this period; one American scholar condemned their 'corruption, oppression, prejudice and intolerance,'" and in 1905 "a boycott of American goods was organized" in China in response to "mistreatment of merchants and students" entering the U.S. See Neuman, *Constitutional Review of "Some Evidence"*, 25 San Diego L. Rev. at 638–639.

3)   Originating Fact Review Paradigm. Does the Supreme Court mean to suggest that a judge conducting habeas review must defer unconditionally to fact finding by the executive? The Court says that the officer "is made the sole and exclusive judge of the existence of those facts, and no other tribunal, unless expressly authorized by law to do so, is at liberty to re-examine or controvert the sufficiency of the evidence on which he acted." The Court adds that another tribunal will not review the "sufficiency of the evidence." What are the separation-of-powers implications of restricting the authority of Article III judges to review executive factfinding, and what are the implications of setting up the rule the other way?

4)   The Rise of Some Evidence Review. Over the next few decades, however, the Court would impose a due process requirement that there be "some evidence" in support of the detention. Thus, the Court noted, "if the Department makes a finding of an essential fact which is unsupported by evidence, the court may intervene by the writ of habeas corpus." United States ex rel. Bilokumsky v. Tod, 263 U.S. 149, 153 (1924). In other contexts the Court has held that due process requires, at minimum, that there be some evidence to support administrative action.[r] That standard did not require the reviewing court to evaluate the evidence that the agency relied upon, but simply required that there be some evidence in the record supportive of the outcome. Perhaps only a completely baseless or arbitrary decision would lack "some evidence" supporting it. Notwithstanding that the standard was extremely deferential, some-evidence review meant that a court could offer relief to a citizen that an inspector, without any support, determined to be an excludable alien.

5)   A Sufficiency of the Evidence Approach. As noted, the 1952 INA permitted administrative review of immigration removal and detention deci-

---

[r] See Gerald Neuman, *The Habeas Corpus Suspension Clause After INS v. St. Cyr*, 33 Colum. Hum. Rights L. Rev. 555, 631-35 (2002).

sions, using a sufficiency of the evidence standard somewhat less deferential to immigration decisions than a "some evidence" standard. The INA some-evidence standard was modeled on the APA provision under which review of an administrative record involved only a determination of whether there was "substantial evidence" to support the outcome. See 5 U.S.C. § 706(2)(E). The substantial evidence standard is also deferential, but far less deferential than the "some evidence" standard.

5. THE REAL-ID ACT

NOTES ON JUDICIAL REVIEW PROVISIONS

1)   Enactment of the REAL-ID Act. The provisions of AEDPA (enacted on April 24, 1996) and IIRIRA (enacted on September 30, 1996) profoundly altered immigration law. As Chapters 3 through 6 explained, AEDPA also had a dramatic effect on federal habeas review of state convictions. The Court's decision in *St. Cyr* was followed by new legislation reshaping immigration habeas and judicial review, crafted in part in response to the *St. Cyr* decision. In 2005, Congress enacted the REAL-ID Act, Pub. L. No. 109–13, Div. B §106, 116 Stat. 231, 310–11.

2)   Consolidation of Petitions for Review. Congress made even more clear that federal Courts of Appeals are the sole forum for judicial review of all removal orders. Recall how Justice Scalia raised the concern that noncitizens with criminal convictions would receive habeas review while others facing removal would not. The REAL-ID Act restored review of all immigration removal decisions using petitions for review as under the 1996 legislation. Accordingly, the Act also sought to assure that there would be only "one bite at the apple" for any challenge to a removal decision.[s] The provisions explicitly eliminate all § 2241 habeas corpus habeas jurisdiction over such matters. The Act provides, under the heading "Exclusive Means of Review":

> Notwithstanding any other provision of law (statutory or nonstatutory), including section 2241 of title 28, or any other habeas corpus provision, and sections 1361 and 1651 of such title, a petition for review filed with an appropriate court of appeals in accordance with this section shall be the sole and exclusive means for judicial review of an order of removal entered or issued under any provision of this chapter, except as provided in subsection (e).

8 U.S.C. § 1252(a)(5). The Act then added, however, that: "Nothing in . . . any . . . provision of this Act (other than this section) which limits or eliminates judicial review, shall be construed as precluding review of constitutional claims or questions of law raised upon a petition for review filed with an appropriate court of appeals in accordance with this section." 8 U.S.C. § 1252(a)(2)(D).

Although REAL-ID used some of what Justice Scalia called "magic words" on the issue of jurisdiction, Congress avoided a full Constitutional confrontation with the Court by vesting the federal circuits with authority to a fairly-broad set of legal and factual questions. REAL-ID explicitly permitted Courts of Appeals, on virtually all petitions for review, to rule on "constitutional claims or questions of law" under the new 242(a)(2)(D) of the INA. In short, the revised

---

[s] Bonhometre v. Gonzales, 414 F.3d 442, 446 (3d Cir. 2005).

statute expressly provided that claims challenging orders of removal do still enjoy a federal forum, and that the forum was exclusive to federal appeals courts. The provision does not apply to orders unrelated to removal, such as challenges to detention in immigration facilities.[t]

To summarize: 8 U.S.C. § 1252(a) has a provision entitled "Exclusive Means of Review;" it vests exclusive jurisdiction over removal orders in the federal Courts of Appeals; it expressly bars other methods of review; and it makes express reference to 28 U.S.C. § 2241, the general grant of habeas corpus power to article III judges. Moreover, § 1252(a) preserves the authority of the appellate courts to review the category of issues that *St. Cyr* identified as necessary to avoid a constitutional problem. As the Third Circuit put it, "In the REAL ID Act, Congress provided precisely what had been lacking in the statutory provisions at issue in *St. Cyr*—a clear statement within the legislation itself explicitly depriving the judiciary of habeas jurisdiction."[u]

3) Judicial Review and Criminal Noncitizens. What was the result of Congress shifting challenges by criminal noncitizens to the petitions-for-review process? The REAL-ID Act contains one additional important provision which interacts with 8 U.S.C. § 1252(a)(2)(D). That provision, 8 U.S.C. § 1252(a)(2)(C) states: "except as provided in subparagraph (D), no court shall have jurisdiction to review any final order of removal against an alien who is removable by reason of having committed a criminal offense covered in [the enumerated sections]." Those enumerated sections include a wide range of criminal offenses that lead to deportation: crimes of "moral turpitude," violations of laws "relating to a controlled substance," persons who have been a "drug abuser or addict," persons who have committed an "aggravated felony" (of which there is an expanding list), certain firearms offenses, failure to register as a sex offender, and other miscellaneous offenses. Will the question whether a noncitizen was convicted of an enumerated crime always be a question of law? Determining whether a crime falls within a specific category is a difficult interpretive task, as the criminal categories often fail to track the criminal law of any given state. That ambiguity, in turn, makes legal advice very difficult to give to noncitizen clients.[v]

4) Judicial Review of Questions of Law for Criminal Noncitizens. As a result of the bar on judicial review for most criminal noncitizens, they may not file petitions of review, but they may bring a petition for review to raise

---

[t] See Ayanbadejo v. Chertoff, 517 F.3d 273, 277–78 (5th Cir. 2008). One question is whether deficient representation by attorneys outside the context of removal proceedings (such as subsequent failure to file a timely petition of review) can escape the REAL-ID Act's jurisdictional provisions and permit habeas jurisdiction. Some courts have held that in such circumstances habeas jurisdiction is proper. See, e.g., Afanwi v. Mukasey, 526 F.3d 788, 795–96 (4th Cir. 2008); Amarjeet Singh v. Gonzales, 499 F.3d 969 (9th Cir. 2007). Similarly, courts have permitted habeas review to challenge the existence of a removal order (and not its merits). See, e.g., Madu v. U.S. Att'y Gen., 470 F.3d 1362, 1367 (11th Cir. 2006); Kumarasamy v. Att'y Gen., 453 F.3d 169, 172 (3d Cir. 2006).

[u] Khouzam v. Att'y General of the U.S., 549 U.S. 235, 245 (3d Cir. 2008).

[v] The complex provisions relating to which criminal offenses require removal do have some narrow exceptions, for example, where the maximum punishment was less than one year and the alien served less than six months, or where the drug offense involved 30 grams or less of marijuana for personal use. See 8 U.S.C. §1182(a)(ii), 1227(B)(i); see also David M. McConnell, *Judicial Review Under the Immigration and Nationality Act: Habeas Corpus And The Coming Of Real ID (1996–2005)*, 51 N.Y.L. Sch. L. Rev. 75, 86–90 (2006–2007) (providing an overview of changes in the criminal deportation grounds); *Lopes v. Gonzales*, 549 U.S. 47 (2006).

"questions of law" and "constitutional claims." Does that sound to you like an adequate and effective substantive for habeas corpus, based on *St. Cyr* and the cases discussed in Chapter 2? Consider that question as you read on about the additional provisions in the Act.

5) Judicial Review Stripping for Discretionary Decisions. The REAL-ID Act also eliminates judicial review for almost all discretionary decisions, but as with criminal convicts, preserves a petition of review to challenge "questions of law" and "constitutional claims."[w] In the bulk of challenges that noncitizens bring in immigration cases, the best hope for relief and the most contested issues may involve requests that the removal be waived or that different status be afforded to prevent removal.[x] Since the REAL-ID Act provisions preserve Court of Appeals review of questions of law and constitutional questions, legal issues raised in challenges to discretionary decisions may still be raised in a petition for review.[y] In doing so, was Congress trying to avoid constitutional problems under *St. Cyr*?

6) Suspension Clause Implications. Do you think that the REAL-ID Act satisfies the Suspension Clause rules set forth in *INS v. St. Cyr*? What was Congress' intent—is the idea that the petition for review procedure is an adequate and effective substitute for habeas corpus? So far, Courts of Appeals have found the Act constitutional.[z] If and when the Supreme Court finally confronts the question, what do you think the Justices will do? Will they find it far more difficult to narrowly construe REAL-ID Act provisions than the provisions at issue in *St. Cyr*?

The back-and-forth between the Court and Congress over what statutory language will strip habeas jurisdiction, is described as a "dialogue" between those two institutions. Your views about whether that is a healthy dialogue may change in the Chapters that follow, as we discuss more polarizing examples, particularly with respect to national security detentions at GTMO.

NOTES ON QUESTIONS OF LAW

1) Preserving Petition-for-Review Jurisdiction Over Legal and Constitutional Questions. REAL-ID sought to satisfy cautionary implications from *St. Cyr* by preserving petition for judicial review of both "questions of law" and "constitutional claims." Why does the statute specify that both "questions of law" and "constitutional claims" may be raised—are constitutional claims "questions of law"—or is the implication that "constitutional claims" may involve mixed questions of law and fact? Federal courts are beginning to address many questions concerning the REAL-ID procedures for reviewing "questions of

---

[w] The statute also creates an exception for discretionary decisions in asylum cases discussed below.

[x] 8 U.S.C. § 1252(a)(2)(B)(i) eliminates judicial review of "any judgment regarding the granting of relief" under the waiver provisions relating to cancellation of removal, voluntary departure, and adjustment of status. The next subsection, (a)(2)(B)(ii), bars judicial review of any other discretionary "decision or action."

[y] See, e.g., Pareja v. Attorney General, 615 F.3d 180, 187–88 (3d Cir. 2010); Montero–Martinez v. Ashcroft, 277 F.3d 1137, 1141-44 (9th Cir. 2002).

[z] See, e.g., Mohamed v Gonzales, 477 F3d 522, 526 (8th Cir 2007) ("Congress has created a remedy as broad in scope as a habeas petition."); Puri v Gonzales, 464 F3d 1038, 1041 (9th Cir 2006) ("The agency is the fact-finding body and this court's review of the administrative proceeding is an adequate substitute for district court habeas corpus jurisdiction.").

law" and "constitutional questions."[aa] Chapter 9 examines similar questions concerning whether post-conviction habeas petitions may challenge state court rulings as "contrary to law" or whether they raised "mixed" questions regarding the application of the law to the facts in a given case.

2)   What About Mixed Questions? If the statute preserves review over mixed questions, then petitions for review may cover a far broader range of situations. For example, although the statute specifies that petitions may be filed concerning questions of law, and while perhaps it means to limit review of questions of fact in cases by criminal noncitizens, it does not specifically limit (or address) litigation of mixed issues of law and fact. For an argument that such review should be preserved, see Aaron G. Leiderman, *Note, Preserving the Constitution's Most Important Human Right: Judicial Review of Mixed Questions Under the REAL ID Act*, 106 Colum. L. Rev. 1367 (2006).

The Courts of Appeals divide over the scope of their review on "questions of law" raised by petitions of review, and whether their appellate power extends to mixed questions of law and fact. The Ninth Circuit has adopted perhaps the broadest view, stating: "the phrase 'questions of law' as it is used in . . . the REAL-ID Act includes review of the application of statutes and regulations to undisputed historical facts." See Ramadan v. Gonzales, 479 F.3d 646, 654 (9th Cir.2007) (per curium). The Seventh Circuit sharply disagreed:

> The panel in Ramadan held that § 242(a)(2)(D) authorizes judicial review of all "mixed questions of law and fact," including all applications of law to fact. Only pure findings of fact are outside the scope of subsection (D), the panel concluded. Because no administrative case can be decided without applying some law to some facts, that understanding of § 242(a)(2)(D) vitiates all clauses in the statute, including § 208(a)(3), that limit judicial review of particular classes of decisions.

Viracacha v. Mukasey, 518 F.3d 511, 515–16 (7th Cir. 2008). The Seventh Circuit added, "[T]he ninth circuit stands alone: at least eight circuits read § 242(a)(2)(D) as limited to pure questions of law." A careful review of decisional law in each jurisdiction, however, reveals that the circuits approach the pertinent question with great variation—by, for example, straining to characterize an issue as a "pure" question of law, when it is probably closer to a mixed question.[bb] The Second Circuit discussed the complexities of such distinctions in Chen v. Gonzales, 471 F.3d 315 (2d Cir. 2006), by beginning with the legislative history:

> The Conference Report makes clear that Congress, in enacting the REAL ID Act, sought to avoid the constitutional concerns outlined by the Supreme Court in *St. Cyr*, which stated that as a result of the Suspension Clause, "*some* judicial intervention in deportation cases is unquestionably required by the Constitution". . .

That passage suggests that REAL-ID Act was intended to preserve traditional habeas review of some sort. The Second Circuit explained: "While the term

---

[aa] See, e.g., Lolong v. Gonzales, 484 F.3d 1173, 1176 (9th Cir. 2007) (en banc).

[bb] See Thomas Alexander Aleinikoff, David A. Martin, Hiroshi Motomura & Maryellen Fullerton, *Immigration and Citizenship: Process and Policy* 1296–97 (7th ed. 2012) ("Those courts that are inclined to preserve as much review as possible tend to find ways to subdivide the questions presented and locate a separately identifiable question of law, or possibly a due process issue. Other courts are more resistant to such arguments by the petitioner.").

'questions of law' undeniably can encompass claims of 'erroneous *application* or interpretation of statutes,' every discretionary determination . . . can in some sense be said to reflect an 'application' of a statute to the facts presented." The Second Circuit took a functional approach to the determination of whether a challenge implicated a question of law:

> The court would need to determine, regardless of the rhetoric employed in the petition, whether it merely quarrels over the correctness of the factual findings or justification for the discretionary choices, in which case the court would lack jurisdiction, or whether it instead raises a "constitutional claim" or "question of law," in which case the court could exercise jurisdiction to review those particular issues.

Do you agree that a court can easily distinguish the situations involving a genuine question of law with those "using the rhetoric of a 'constitutional claim' or 'question of law' to disguise what is essentially a quarrel about fact-finding or the exercise of discretion"? Does the Suspension Clause counsel that judges err on the side of permitting judicial review, or should judges tend to exercise restraint and defer to administrative fact-finding?

NOTES ON QUESTIONS OF FACT

1)   Silence on Questions of Fact. What review remains for questions of fact? For non-criminal noncitizens petitioning for review in the Court of Appeals, the REAL-ID Act retained the IIRIRA language, which itself incorporated pre-existing "substantial evidence" review, providing that "administrative findings of fact are conclusive unless any reasonable adjudicator would be compelled to conclude to the contrary." 8 U.S.C. § 1252(b)(4)(B).[cc]

2)   Residual Habeas Standards? How about criminal alien petitions or petitions regarding discretionary decisions—can they challenge questions of fact? Some lower courts hold they cannot. Most, however, have held the REAL-ID Act treats challenges to denials of discretionary relief litigated in prior habeas petitions as subject to the strictures that formerly applied to those petitions.[dd] What all of this means is that minimal "some evidence" review remains for such challenges, requiring only that the agency have had "some evidence" to support its decision.

3)   Is the Noncitizen a Removable Criminal? One type of question that comes up with particular frequency for criminal noncitizens is a question of

---

[cc] The provision is understood to codify the prior "substantial evidence" review standard, although the statute does not use the same language. See e.g., Xiao Ji Chen v. U.S. Dept. of Justice, 471 F.3d 315, 334 (2d Cir. 2006) ("Under this strict standard of review, we defer to the factual findings of the BIA and the IJ if they are supported by substantial evidence") (citing additional cases). The APA provides "[t]he reviewing court shall . . . hold unlawful and set aside agency action, findings, and conclusions found to be . . . unsupported by substantial evidence in a case . . . reviewed on the record of an agency hearing provided by statute . . . ." 5 U.S.C. § 706(2)(E). The Supreme Court interpreted the predecessor statute to 8 U.S.C. § 1252(b)(4)(B) in *INS v. Elias-Zacarias*, 502 U.S. 478 (1992).

[dd] See, e.g., Kamara v. Attorney Gen. of the United States, 420 F.3d 202, 210–11 (3d Cir. 2005) ("A review for 'constitutional claims or questions of law,' . . . mirrors our previously enunciated standard of review over an alien's habeas petition." (citation omitted)). But see Jean-Pierre v. U.S. Atty. Gen., 500 F.3d 1315, 1321 (7th Cir. 2007) ("In other words, the REAL ID Act prevents us from reviewing factual determinations made by the IJ or BIA in cases involving aliens who have committed a listed criminal offense.").

law: whether the noncitizen was convicted of an "aggravated felony" that qualifies the noncitizen for removal. In a complex twist, *more* fact review is sometimes permitted in that setting, modifying the "categorical approach" that asks whether a crime qualifies a noncitizen for removal.[ee] Instead, courts may look at a more "circumstance-specific" approach, that is, the facts surrounding a crime of conviction that is not defined as "aggravated."

4)   *Nijhawan v. Holder.* In *Nijhawan v. Holder,* the Supreme Court held that a noncitizen could be removed when convicted with co-conspirators of a bank fraud scheme. None of the relevant state criminal statutes required the crime to involve more than $10,000, which was federally required to make the crime "aggravated" and a deportable offense. 8 U.S.C. § 1101(a)(43)(M)(i). As a result, there had been no jury findings on the total amount of money involved in the fraud. The Court, however, found the removal proper, noting that the noncitizen had stipulated that the fraud involved more than $100 million in losses to the banks.[ff]

5)   Looking into the Specific Circumstances to Cancel Removal. Sometimes facts outside the mere existence of a conviction may be pertinent for determining whether a noncitizen committed an "aggravated" criminal offense; noncitizens convicted of aggravated criminal offenses are not eligible for cancellation of removal under 8 U.S.C. § 1229b(a)(3). The BIA has ruled that it is a mixed question of law and fact whether a petty conviction for marijuana possession involving a "small amount" of marijuana, makes it a non-removable offense. The BIA added that the noncitizen may present evidence outside the record of conviction to demonstrate that under the circumstances, the amount was "small" and not purchased for distribution. Matter of Wilmer Rodrigo Castro Rodriguez, 25 I&N Dec. 698 (BIA 2012). Should the REAL-ID Act permit a federal court of appeals to review a BIA determination regarding that mixed question of law and fact? What standard of review should apply?[gg]

[ee] See Matter of Silva-Trevino, 24 I. & N. Dec. 687 (A.G. 2008) ("To determine whether a conviction is for a crime involving moral turpitude, immigration judges and the Board of Immigration Appeals should: (1) look to the statute of conviction under the categorical inquiry and determine whether there is a 'realistic probability' that the State or Federal criminal statute pursuant to which the alien was convicted would be applied to reach conduct that does not involve moral turpitude; (2) if the categorical inquiry does not resolve the question, engage in a modified categorical inquiry and examine the record of conviction, including documents such as the indictment, the judgment of conviction, jury instructions, a signed guilty plea, and the plea transcript; and (3) if the record of conviction is inconclusive, consider any additional evidence deemed necessary or appropriate to resolve accurately the moral turpitude question.").

[ff] Circuits have different in their approaches when and whether to defer to Attorney General determinations regarding whether a criminal conviction satisfies the statutory definitions. See, e.g., Jean-Louis v. Att'y Gen., 582 F.3d 462, 480 (3d Cir. 2009) (endorsing categorical approach); Ali v. Mukasey, 521 F.3d 737 (7th Cir. 2008) (holding that examination of underlying conduct is necessary). See generally Jeremiah J. Farrelly, *Denying Formalism's Apologist's: Reforming Immigration Law's CIMT Analysis,* 82 U. Colo. L. Rev. 877 (2011) (crititicizing CMIT policy).

[gg] The Third Circuit, for example, has applied a "modified categorical approach," treating the question whether the conviction involved a "small amount" as a question of law, and examining only limited facts outside the record of the state conviction: the criminal information, but not representations made in the sentencing document. See Catwell v. Attorney General of U.S., 623 F.3d 199, 207 & n. 15 (3d Cir. 2010).

NOTES ON THE CURRENT USES OF IMMIGRATION HABEAS

1) Non-removal Challenges. The REAL-ID Act places most removal-related challenges back in the Courts of Appeals, but it probably leaves undisturbed the habeas jurisdiction of district courts to review detention decisions. The statute does not explicitly exempt detention-related habeas challenges, but provisions that expressly limit judicial review refer only to removal orders. The REAL-ID Act's legislative history confirms Congressional intent not to limit judicial review for non-detention related challenges.[hh]

2) Status and Expedited Removal. Article III courts also retain habeas authority to review certain status determinations during expedited removal proceedings. Expedited removal is a highly summary removal proceeding that is conducted primarily at or near the border, for persons who have entered the United States, but without inspection, and who were thus not admitted. 8 U.S.C. § 1252(e)(2) provides that habeas review of expedited removal is specifically available for these subjects:

> (A) whether the petitioner is an alien,
>
> (B) whether the petitioner was ordered removed under such section, and
>
> (C) whether the petitioner can prove by a preponderance of the evidence that the petitioner is an alien lawfully admitted for permanent residence, has been admitted as a refugee under section 1157 of this title, or has been granted asylum under section 1158 of this title, such status not having been terminated, and is entitled to such further inquiry as prescribed by the Attorney General pursuant to section 1225(b)(1)(C) of this title.

Why were those three subjects singled out? They each have to do with the person's status—very important but confined questions.

3) Status. The question whether the person is a citizen has always been centrally important. After all, a citizen cannot be removed and immigration authorities have no power over a citizen. That question—whether a person belongs to a category over which officials can lawfully exercise power—goes to a historically-central form of the habeas question, whether a detention is authorized. The INA preserves *de novo* factual review over claims of U.S. citizenship. See 8 U.S.C. § 1252(b)(5)(B). In removal cases, the government always bears the burden of establishing alienage. Citizens retain their U.S. citizenship unless they voluntarily relinquish it. See Afroyim v. Rusk, 387 U.S. 253, 262 (1967). It is possible for U.S. citizens to be deported—not because they are expatriated or denaturalized—but by mistake. One can think of such cases as wrongful deportations—perhaps analogues of wrongful convictions—and they have some similar causes. They may occur because individuals signed settlement agreements misstating their nationality, perhaps to avoid a criminal conviction; they were litigating pro se; they did not realize that they could claim citizenship based, say on birth or derivative citizenship; or they were minors or

---

[hh] H.R. Rep. No. 109–72, 109th Cong., at 175–176 (2005) (Cong. Rep.) (stating that the Act would "not preclude habeas review over challenges to detention that are independent of challenges to removal orders"). See also 8 U.S.C. § 1252(a)(9) (permitting habeas review of final orders "arising from" removal orders); Gerald Neuman, *On the Adequacy of Direct Review After the Real-ID Act of 2005*, 51 N.Y.L.S. Rev. 133, 138, 141 (2006–2007).

mentally ill.[ii] Where does the analogy to "actual innocence" work, and where does it break down?

4)   Asylum. In asylum cases, an INA provision limits review of discretionary decisions, noting that "the Attorney General's discretionary judgment whether to grant relief under section 1158(a) of this title shall be conclusive unless manifestly contrary to the law and an abuse of discretion." 8 U.S.C. § 1252(b)(4)(D) (2000). Although that language is different than the general language in (b)(4)(B), it has been interpreted to continue to provide "substantial evidence" review of administrative factfinding. Why do you think that is?

———————

NOTES ON INSTITUTIONAL CONTEXT OF REMOVAL DECISIONS

1)   The Overburdened BIA. For one view of the constitutionality of the REAL-ID Act, see Hiroshi Motomura, *Immigration Law and Federal Court Jurisdiction Through The Lens Of Habeas Corpus*, 91 Cornell L. Rev. 459 (2006). Professor Motomura explains that an assessment of the Act's constitutionality requires administrative context. First, he notes that the BIA has been part of the DOJ since 1940, and part of the Executive Office for Immigration Review (EOIR) since 1983. In 2002, the new Department of Homeland Security (DHS) assumed the tasks formerly handled by the INS—but the EOIR kept immigration appeals functions within the DOJ. Meanwhile, in "the 1980s and 1990s, the BIA caseload grew steadily" where "the BIA heard 3630 cases in 1983, 8204 cases in 1987, 12,774 cases in 1992, 30,000 cases in 1997, and over 34,000 cases in 2002." The BIA expanded in 1999 from five members who sat en banc, to 23 members who were permitted to hear cases in three-member panels. Yet, Professor Motomura explains, "When even these changes could not keep up with the rising caseload," the BIA adopted, in November 1999, new regulations permitting "a single BIA member to issue an affirmance, without opinion, of the appealed decision if that member found 'that the result reached in the decision under review was correct [and] that any errors in the decision under review were harmless or nonmaterial.'"[jj] Another set of 2002 regulations made it the norm for a single BIA member to decide an appeal.[kk] Those regulations created time limits to expedite BIA decisions and narrowed the standard of review on appeal to a more deferential "clearly erroneous" standard for findings of fact by immigration judges.[ll] At the same time, the regulations reduced the size of the BIA to only eleven members. The result was that "the number of cases that noncitizens filed in court to review BIA decisions grew dramatically."[mm]

2)   BIA Under Attack. All of this restructuring resulted in mounting criticism of BIA decisions—and a marked increase in reversals of BIA decisions in

———————

[ii] See Jacqueline Stevens, *U.S. Government Unlawfully Detaining and Deporting U.S. Citizens As Aliens*, 18 Va. J. Soc. Pol'y & L. 606 (2011) (describing causes of removal of citizens).

[jj] *Id.*; see also 8 C.F.R. §§ 1.1-3.11 (1999).

[kk] See Board of Immigration Appeals: Procedural Reforms to Improve Case Management, 67 Fed. Reg. 54,878 (Aug. 26, 2002) (codified as amended at 8 C.F.R. §1003 (2010)).

[ll] 8 C.F.R. § 1003.1(d)(3)(i); see, e.g., 25 I. & N. Dec. 209 (BIA 2010).

[mm] Motomura, 91 Corn. L. Rev. at 475; see also Organization, Jurisdiction, and Powers of the Board of Immigration Appeals, 8 C.F.R. § 1003.1(e)(4)(i) (2005); John R.B. Palmer, Stephen W. Yale-Loehr & Elizabeth Cronin, *Why are so Many People Challenging Board of Immigration Appeals Decisions in Federal Court? An Empirical Analysis of the Recent Surge in Petitions for Review*, 20 Geo. Immigr. L.J. 1, 29–32 (2005).

the federal circuits. See, e.g. Benslimane v. Gonzales, 430 F.3d 828, 829–30, 833 (7th Cir. 2005) (calling BIA's reasoning "completely arbitrary"); Wang v. Attorney Gen., 423 F.3d 260, 267–68 (3d Cir. 2005) (citing other circuit court opinions and criticizing "tone, the tenor, the disparagement, and the sarcasm" of the immigration judge as "more appropriate to a court television show than a federal court proceeding.").[nn] The changes also created mounting burdens on court of appeals caseloads; petitions for review came to account for about a third of appellant filings in the Second and Ninth Circuits.[oo] Some of the 2002 changes have been reversed or modified. Should changes in the way the BIA reviews decisions require a different standard for review petitions for review of BIA decisions in appellate courts? Does more-restrictive BIA review also support more aggressive federal habeas review of legal questions? Of factual determinations?

3)   Adequate BIA Proceedings? Traditionally, if the administrative factual record is not adequate, then the appellate court may refer the case back to the agency to develop an adequate record. Some appeals courts have avoided the requirement that they "shall decide the petition only on the administrative record on which the order of removal is based," 8 U.S.C. § 1252(b)(4)(A), and that they refrain from "order[ing] the taking additional evidence," INA § 242(a)(1), by transferring the cases to the BIA for further factfinding as permitted by the Hobbs Act—at least where there are reasonable grounds for failing to have presented materials evidence to the agency. See 28 U.S.C. § 2347 (2000). Do such transfers contravene the intent of the statute? Or is it properly consistent with the typical practice associated with an inadequate record—to send it back for further development? Recall from Chapter 2 how in the post-conviction context, the Supreme Court did much the same thing in the *Troy Davis* case.[pp]

   Such questions underscore a problem with federal appeals courts having exclusive jurisdiction—they are not trial courts and are not equipped to conduct factual inquiries. Following IIRIRA AEDPA, and the REAL-ID Act—which have the collective effect of channeling all review of removal orders to the federal appeals courts—can the circuits realistically conduct all judicial review of immigration-related removal decisions? Is there any constitutional problem with channeling such review in intermediate courts rather than in lower courts? *St. Cyr* highlighted the importance of habeas review of legal questions, but the comparative advantage of lower federal courts may be the ability to examine the factual record. Is the post-REAL-ID Act process an "adequate substitute" for habeas corpus?

[nn] See also Jaya Ramji-Nogales, Andrew I. Schoenholtz & Philip G. Schrag, *Refugee Roulette: Disparities in Asylum Adjudication*, 60 Stan. L. Rev. 295, 325–49 (2007); Rachel L. Swarns, *Study Finds Disparities in Judges' Asylum Rulings*, N.Y. Times, July 31, 2006, at A15.

[oo] See Lawrence Baum, *Judicial Specialization and the Adjudication of Immigration Cases*, 59 Duke L.J. 1501, 1519 (2010).

[pp] The REAL-ID Act imposes a 30-day time limit on seeking a petition for review in the Courts of Appeals. 8 U.S.C. § 1252(b)(1). What if newly discovered evidence surfaces later? One court has suggested that in an appropriate case, that time limit might be relaxed. See Wang v. Department of Homeland Security, 484 F.3d 615, 618 (2d Cir. 2007).

NOTE ON STAYS OF REMOVAL

IRRIRA affected another important type of judicial relief. Before that legislation, stays of removal automatically operated pending the filing of a petition of review. When IIRIRA eliminated stays, however, it also added something new, providing that the physical removal of the alien from the country would no longer bar judicial review (even if practically far more difficult) and that "no court shall enjoin the removal of any alien . . . unless the alien shows by clear and convincing evidence that the entry or execution of such order is prohibited as a matter of law." 8 U.S.C. § 1252(f)(2). The Supreme Court in Nken v. Holder, 556 U.S. 418 (2009) held that the provision did not eliminate the authority of a federal court to stay removal, and that, by the provision's terms it applied only to "injunctions." The Court noted that allowing the removal to proceed without considering factors such as the likelihood of success and whether irreparable injury might result, as was traditionally done when evaluating whether to order a stay, "may deprive the movant of his right to petition for review of the removal order." The Court, however, also cautioned against setting the threshold for granting stays too low. Would it have raised constitutional problems to interpret that section to eliminate the ability to obtain any kind of stay or injunction of removal while pursuing judicial review?

NOTE ON EXTRADITION

The United States has extradition treaties with many other countries providing for exchange of prisoners facing criminal charges abroad and for the reciprocal extradition of prisoners abroad who are facing charges in the United States. The Supreme Court has said that the scope of habeas review of a judge's decision to extradite is limited to determining "whether the magistrate had jurisdiction, whether the offense charged is within the treaty and by a somewhat liberal construction, whether there was any evidence warranting the finding that there was reasonable ground to believe the accused guilty." Fernandez v. Phillips, 268 U.S. 311, 312 (1925). Is that 1925 opinion still good law in light of the Suspension Clause holding of *St. Cyr*? Or are decisions to extradite, because they are related to interpretation of treaty obligations, types of foreign policy questions deserving special deference? The federal judge acts as a magistrate conducting a type of probable cause hearing, but a foreign sovereign ultimately takes up the criminal prosecution. Should it be relevant that, once a prisoner is extradited, the prisoner will presumably receive the benefits of the full criminal process available in the receiving country?

Under Article Three of the Convention Against Torture (CAT), countries may not "expel, return, or extradite" a person if there are substantial grounds to believe that the person would be danger of being subject to torture. 136 Cong. Rec. S17486–92 (daily ed., Oct. 27, 1990). Congress has statutorily implemented the treaty as part of the Foreign Affairs Reform and Restructuring Act of 1998 (FARRA). 8 U.S.C. § 1231. That statute states that it is "the policy of the United States not to . . . extradite . . . any person to a country in which there are substantial grounds for believing the person would be in danger of being subjected to torture." The statute requires that "the appropriate agencies . . . prescribe regulations to implement the obligations of the United States under Article 3 of the United Nations Convention Against Torture." Those regulations have been adopted by the Department of State. 22 C.F.R. § 95.2–3.

Extradition and removal may both be terminated based on a claim under the Torture Convention.[qq] The REAL-ID Act also affects these claims under now-familiar language stating that a "petition for review" in the Court of Appeals "shall be the sole and exclusive means for judicial review" of a CAT torture claim, 8 U.S.C.A. § 1252(a)(4), except as permitted under subsection (e), which allows very limited judicial review. Does this arrangement raise Suspension Clause issues, or issues of Convention compliance?

The Ninth Circuit recently addressed those issues in *Trinidad y Garcia v. Thomas,* 683 F.3d 952 (9th Cir. 2012) (en banc). The petitioner alleged that his extradition to the Philippines would violate his CAT rights. A *per curiam* opinion concluded that, where the Secretary of State did not comply with the required regulations implementing CAT and FARRA, a habeas petition could properly be filed in the district court. The judges ruled that "[t]he REAL ID Act can be construed as being confined to addressing final orders of removal, without affecting federal habeas jurisdiction." This petition did not challenge the order of removal, but rather the legality of the extradition proceedings. The scope of judicial review, however, would be highly deferential, examining "the substance of the Secretary's extradition decision" only to assess "compliance with her obligations under domestic law." Do you think that the Ninth Circuit's decision reflects the limited role that habeas plays to reexamine executive decisions? Or is there a Suspension Clause problem with the court declining to examine the merits of the petitioner's CAT claim?

6. LENGTH OF DETENTION PENDING REMOVAL

NOTES ON LENGTH-OF-DETENTION CHALLENGES

1)   Immigration Detention of Noncitizens Seeking Admission. Detention may occur before an order of removal ("pre-order detention"). For noncitizens seeking admission to the U.S., who have not been ordered removed, the government's authority to detain them depends on a number of circumstances. For example, government must detain asylum seekers to determine their eligibility. See 8 U.S.C. §1225(b)(1)(B)(iii)(IV). The government may detain arriving noncitizens to evaluate whether they are inadmissible for medical or mental health reasons. See 8 U.S.C. §1225(a). Arriving noncitizens may also be detained and removed for committing certain crimes. See 8 U.S.C. §1226(c)(1). Noncitizens suspected of involvement in terrorism must be detained based on provisions in the USA PATRIOT Act, discussed in the last Section.

2)   Detention and Removal. Following an order of removal, noncitizens may be detained ("post-order detention") during the pendency of a hearing and appellate review thereof. Over half of noncitizens facing removal for deportability reasons are held in detention facilities. A noted earlier, they may be detained if the Government determines that they are a flight risk, dangerousness, if the reason for the removal is a criminal conviction, and for other reasons. (Many noncitizens fail to appear at their hearings, although the numbers are

---

[qq] See Wang v. Ashcroft, 320 F.3d 130, 141 (2d Cir. 2003); Abra Edwards, Note, *Cornejo-Barreto Revisited: The Availability of a Writ of Habeas Corpus to Provide Relief from Extradition under the Torture Convention,* 43 Va. J. Int'l L. 889 (2003).

dropping, perhaps because detention is so much more common.[rr]) Most noncitizens subject to removal orders must be removed within 90 days and are detained only during that time. 8 U.S.C. §1231(a)(1).

3)   Longer Detention. While the statute provides for post-order detention of a noncitizen for a 90-day statutorily defined "removal period," and while most noncitizens are removed within a few days of this removal order, sometimes there are delays. The removal may be delayed for reasons including: that the destination country's refusal to accept deportees, that the deportee might face torture in the destination country, and that the deportee does not cooperate with efforts to remove. If the noncitizen poses no threat to public safety and cooperates, DHS may provide for supervised release, including on bond, while efforts to remove are pending. 8 U.S.C. §1231(a)(3).

4)   *Zadvydas v. Davis.* In *Zadvydas v. Davis,* 533 U.S. 678 (2001), noncitizens had filed habeas petitions challenging their indefinite detention, which persisted for far longer than the statutorily-specified 90 days. The lengthy detention occurred because the other countries refused to accept the removed noncitizens. The Supreme Court was confronted with the question of whether the statute authorized indefinite detention and, if it did, whether the statute was constitutional. The Court noted, "A statute permitting indefinite detention of an alien would raise a serious constitutional problem." The Court cited to *Mezei* and emphasized that, although "[i]t is well established that certain constitutional protections available to persons inside the United States are unavailable to aliens outside of our geographic borders[,]" there was an important distinction between the Mezei and Zadvydas. Unlike Mezei, who was detained at Ellis Island and was deemed to have not entered the country, Zadvydas was physically present in U.S. territory: "once an alien enters the country, the legal circumstance changes, for the Due Process Clause applies to all 'persons' within the United States, including aliens, whether their presence here is lawful, unlawful, temporary, or permanent."

Rather than strike down the statute under the due process right which it had just held applicable, the Court construed the statute to impose an implied six-month time limit on detention. The Court noted, "Despite this constitutional problem, if Congress has made its [statutory] intent . . . clear, we must give effect to that intent. We cannot find here, however, any clear indication of congressional intent to grant the Attorney General the power to hold indefinitely in confinement an alien ordered removed." The Court imposed a six-month deadline, not to accomplish the removal, but to decide whether removal is anticipated in the "reasonable foreseeable future." Why do you suppose that the Court held that the time period was six months and not the 90 days provided in the statute? The current agency regulations now reflect the Court's holding, but did the Court in effect rewrite the statutes and regulations for immigration detention?[ss]

The Court also emphasized that, as in the civil commitment context, an indefinite detention must be reviewed carefully and on an ongoing basis. The Court emphasized that "[t]he provision authorizing detention does not apply

---

[rr]Exec. Office for Immigration Review, U.S. Dep't of Justice, FY 2008 Statistical Year Book, H2 fig.10, 12 (2009), at http://www.justice.gov/eoir/statspub/fy08syb.pdf.

[ss] See Office of Inspector General, Department of Homeland Security, *ICE's Compliance with Detention Limits for Aliens with a Final Order of Removal from the United States* 10 (2007).

narrowly to "a small segment of particularly dangerous individuals," such as, "say, suspected terrorists," but it instead applies "broadly to aliens ordered removed for many and various reasons, including tourist visa violations." The statute would raise a "serious constitutional problem" if it were to permit "detention that is potentially permanent" for individuals not detained before entry into the U.S. (as in *Mezei*)—at least absent any showing that they pose a danger and absent enhanced procedural protections. Thus, the Court required a burden-shifting scheme whereby if a noncitizen provides "good reason" to believe that there is no significant likelihood of removal in the reasonably foreseeable future, then "the Government must respond with evidence sufficient to rebut that showing."

Justice Scalia dissented, making a point similar to the one he made in *St. Cyr*: under the Court's interpretation, a category of noncitizens facing one consequence (removal for deportability) now enjoy a habeas privilege that remains unavailable to a similarly-situated category of noncitizens facing another (removal for inadmissibility). He stated: "We are offered no justification why an alien under a valid and final order of removal-which has *totally extinguished* whatever right to presence in this country he possessed-has any greater due process right to be released into the country than an alien at the border seeking entry."

Do these decisions suggest that the plenary power doctrine is dead, and that the federal immigration power is meaningfully limited? Does the decision mark "a milestone of moderate promise toward candid adoption of a sensible framework yielding graduated constitutional protections for different categories of aliens"? David A. Martin, *The Graduated Application of Constitutional Protections for Aliens: The Real Meaning of Zadvydas v. Davis*, 2001 Sup. Ct. Rev. 47, 134. Or, in contrast, will "the imperative of migration control, in time, necessitate that *Zadvydas* be limited, distinguished, left standing as a monument but not a signpost?" See T. Alexander Aleinikoff, *Detaining Plenary Power: The Meaning And Impact Of Zadvydas v. Davis*, 16 Geo. Immigr. L.J. 365 (2002). Subsequent precedent seems to suggest that Professor Martin's view may be closer to the correct one; *Zadvydas* has had remarkable staying power.

5) *Clark v. Martinez.* Justice Scalia later authored a majority opinion in *Clark v. Martinez*, affirming and extending *Zadvydas* in ways that addressed the concerns he expressed in his *Zadvydas* dissent. 543 U.S. 371, 386–87 (2005). Once *Zadvydas* interpreted the statute to imply a six-month limitation for removal (with some exceptions), Justice Scalia simply applied it in that way to all noncitizens covered by the statute, thereby avoiding the differential treatment about which he expressed concern in his *Zadvydas* dissent. Therefore, the statute would not authorize indefinite detention of aliens detained pending removal for inadmissibility. As a result, even detainees in the position of Mezei, who had not yet entered the country, may obtain habeas review of their detention. Justice Scalia concluded in *Martinez*:

> The Government fears that the security of our borders will be compromised if it must release into the country inadmissible aliens who cannot be removed. If that is so, Congress can attend to it. But for this Court to sanction indefinite detention in the face of *Zadvydas* would establish within our jurisprudence, beyond the power of Congress to remedy, the dangerous principle that judges can give the same statutory text different meanings in different cases.

6) *Demore v. Kim.* In contrast, in *Demore v. Kim,* 538 U.S. 510 (2003), the Supreme Court held that provisions authorizing "mandatory" detention of certain criminal aliens, before any final order of removal, was constitutional. The Court noted:

> Section 236(c) mandates detention during removal proceedings for a limited class of deportable aliens—including those convicted of an aggravated felony. Congress adopted this provision against a backdrop of wholesale failure by the INS to deal with increasing rates of criminal activity by aliens. Criminal aliens were the fastest growing segment of the federal prison population, already constituting roughly 25% of all federal prisoners, and they formed a rapidly rising share of state prison populations as well. Congress' investigations showed, however, that the INS could not even identify most deportable aliens, much less locate them and remove them from the country. One study showed that, at the then- current rate of deportation, it would take 23 years to remove every criminal alien already subject to deportation. Making matters worse, criminal aliens who were deported swiftly reentered the country illegally in great numbers.

The Court distinguished *Zadvydas*, which dealt with noncitizens who had been ordered removed, but who were being detained indefinitely pending removal, with the mandatory detention during removal proceedings:

> In the present case, the statutory provision at issue governs detention of deportable criminal aliens pending their removal proceedings. Such detention necessarily serves the purpose of preventing deportable criminal aliens from fleeing prior to or during their removal proceedings, thus increasing the chance that, if ordered removed, the aliens will be successfully removed. Respondent disagrees, arguing that there is no evidence that mandatory detention is necessary because the Government has never shown that individualized bond hearings would be ineffective. But . . . in adopting § 236(c), Congress had before it evidence suggesting that permitting discretionary release of aliens pending their removal hearings would lead to large numbers of deportable criminal aliens skipping their hearings and remaining at large in the United States unlawfully.

The Court also noted that "the detention here is of a much shorter duration" and that "in the majority of cases it lasts for less than the 90 days we considered presumptively valid in *Zadvydas*." Justice Souter joined by Justices Stevens and Ginsburg dissented:

> Due process calls for an individual determination before someone is locked away. In none of the cases cited did we ever suggest that the government could avoid the Due Process Clause by doing what § 236(c) does, by selecting a class of people for confinement on a categorical basis and denying members of that class any chance to dispute the necessity of putting them away.

7)   Lower Court Rulings on Mandatory Detention. Perhaps most surprising of all is that following *Demore*, even the mandatory detention provision has been narrowly interpreted by lower courts. Professors Aleinikoff et. al. describe how, "Somewhat surprisingly, the lower courts have found significant constraints on lengthy detention under the mandatory detention provision in

§ 236(c), despite the Supreme Court's apparent endorsement of that provision in *Demore*."[tt]

8)   Substantive Due Process or the Suspension Clause? Can this careful scrutiny of indefinite or lengthy immigration detention be explained by a substantive due process concern with lengthy or indefinite detentions? The Court emphasized the Due Process Clause in each of these rulings. Or is part of the explanation that the Suspension Clause permits habeas corpus scrutiny of detentions, even of detentions that are themselves subjected to minimal due process protection? Or do both due process and habeas corpus explain these rulings?

7. ENEMY ALIENS

Nowhere have the imperatives of "migration control" been felt more strongly than in response to real or perceived national security threats. Immigration laws have long been used to directly target individuals suspected of posing such a threat. Recall how the Alien Friends Act of 1798 permitted the President to approve the summary arrest and then deportation of aliens determined to be "dangerous to the peace and Safety of the United States," leading to controversy and the Act's expiration. Other immigration provisions targeted not enemies or citizens of nations with which we were at war, but other types of dangerous persons. An immigration measure passed in 1903 targeted anarchists and barred entry of those who sought the overthrow of the U.S. or other governments. See Immigration Act of 1903, ch. 1012, § 2, 32 Stat. 1213, 1214 (1903). Over the next few decades, other political radicals, including union organizers, were deported under such provisions. The Palmer Raids in 1919–1920 resulted in deportations of suspected communists by the "alien radical" division of the Justice Department, lead by J. Edgar Hoover.[uu] The question then arose—to what extent would habeas corpus remedies be available to challenge detention decisions?

Ludecke v. Watkins involved a World War II detention, but under the authority of the first federal statute targeting enemy aliens, the Alien Enemies Act of 1798. Act of July 6, 1798, 1 Stat. 577, R.S. s 4067, as amended, 40 Stat. 531, 50 U.S.C. s 21, 50 U.S.C.A. s 21. The Alien Enemies Act permitted removal of citizens of nations with which the U.S. was at war. A German immigrant to the U.S. had been arrested in 1941 and deemed an enemy alien under the 1798 Act by an Alien Enemy Hearing Board, and designated for deportation by the Attorney General. He had left Germany after being placed in a concentration camp in 1934, after earlier having been a high-level supporter of the Nazi party. He came to the U.S. and wrote a book titled "I Knew Hitler: The Story of a Nazi Who Escaped the Blood Purge." Ludecke filed a petition seeking habeas corpus review, arguing that he had not been provided adequate process to challenge the desig-

---

[tt] See Thomas Alexander Aleinikoff, David A. Martin, Hiroshi Motomura & Maryellen Fullerton, *Immigration and Citizenship: Process and Policy* 1257 (7th ed. 2012); see, e.g.; DIOP v. ICE/Homeland Security ("we conclude that the [mandatory detention] statute authorizes only detention for a reasonable period of time"); Casas-Castrillon v. DHS, 535 F.3d 942 (9th Cir. 2008) ("We conclude that a prolonged detention must be accompanied by appropriate procedural safeguards, including a hearing to establish whether releasing the alien would pose a danger to the community or a flight risk.").

[uu] See William Preston, Jr., *Aliens and Dissenters: Federal Suppression of Radicals, 1903–1933* 208–37 (1963); David Cole, *Enemy Aliens*, 54 Stan. L. Rev. 953 (2002).

nation and removal, and that he should have access to judicial review. When you read *Ludecke*, recall the Court's decisions just a few years later in *Knauff* and *Mezei*—here the issue is not that the noncitizen has not yet been admitted to the country, but rather that the case involves a national security detention. Should habeas review be narrower than in typical proceedings challenging immigration detention—or should it simply be confined to the question whether a person was in fact an enemy alien—or should it be broader?

Ludecke v. Watkins

United States Supreme Court
335 U.S. 160 (1948)

■ Mr. JUSTICE FRANKFURTER delivered the opinion of the Court.

The Fifth Congress committed to the President these powers:

> "Whenever there is a declared war between the United States and any foreign nation or government, or any invasion or predatory incursion is perpetrated, attempted, or threatened against the territory of the United States by any foreign nation or government, and the President makes public proclamation of the event, all natives, citizens, denizens, or subjects of the hostile nation or government, being of the age of fourteen years and upward, who shall be within the United States and not actually naturalized, shall be liable to be apprehended, restrained, secured, and removed as alien enemies. The President is authorized, in any such event, by his proclamation thereof, or other public act, to direct the conduct to be observed, on the part of the United States, toward the aliens who become so liable; the manner and degree of the restraint to which they shall be subject and in what cases, and upon what security their residence shall be permitted, and to provide for the removal of those who, not being permitted to reside within the United States, refuse or neglect to depart therefrom; and to establish any other regulations which are found necessary in the premises and for the public safety."

This Alien Enemy Act has remained the law of the land * * *. Throughout these one hundred and fifty years executive interpretation and decisions of lower courts have found in the Act an authority for the President which is now questioned, and the further claim is made that if what the President did comes within the Act, the Congress could not give him such power. Obviously these are issues which properly brought the case here.

> Petitioner, a German alien enemy, was arrested on December 8, 1941, and, after proceedings before an Alien Enemy Hearing Board on January 16, 1942, was interned by order of the Attorney General, dated February 9, 1942.[4] Under authority of the Act of 1798, the President, on July 14, 1945, directed the removal from the United States of all alien enemies "who shall be deemed by the Attorney General to be dangerous to the public peace and safety of the United States." Accordingly, the Attorney General, on January

---

[4] No question has been raised as to the validity of these administrative actions taken pursuant to Presidential Proclamation 2526, dated December 8, 1941, 6 Fed.Reg. 6323, issued under the authority of the Alien Enemy Act.

18, 1946, ordered petitioner's removal.[5] Denial of a writ of habeas corpus for release from detention under this order was affirmed by the court below.

As Congress explicitly recognized in the recent Administrative Procedure Act, some statutes "preclude judicial review." Barring questions of interpretation and constitutionality, the Alien Enemy Act of 1798 is such a statute. Its terms, purpose, and construction leave no doubt. The language employed by the Fifth Congress could hardly be made clearer * * * by the incomplete and not always dependable accounts we have of debates in the early years of Congress. That such was the scope of the Act is established by controlling contemporaneous construction. "The act concerning alien enemies, which confers on the president very great discretionary powers respecting their persons," Marshall, C.J., in *Brown v. United States*, 8 Cranch 110, 126, "appears to me to be as unlimited as the legislature could make it." Washington, J., in *Lockington v. Smith*, 15 Fed.Cas. 758, 761, at page 760, No. 8,448. The very nature of the President's power to order the removal of all enemy aliens rejects the notion that courts may pass judgment upon the exercise of his discretion. * * *

The power with which Congress vested the President had to be executed by him through others. He provided for the removal of such enemy aliens as were "deemed by the Attorney General" to be dangerous. But such a finding, at the President's behest, was likewise not to be subjected to the scrutiny of courts. For one thing, removal was contingent not upon a finding that in fact an alien was "dangerous." The President was careful to call for the removal of aliens "deemed by the Attorney General to be dangerous." But the short answer is that the Attorney General was the President's voice and conscience. A war power of the President not subject to judicial review is not transmuted into a judicially reviewable action because the President chooses to have that power exercised within narrower limits than Congress authorized.

And so we reach the claim that while the President had summary power under the Act, it did not survive cessation of actual hostilities. This claim in effect nullifies the power to deport alien enemies, for such deportations are hardly practicable during the pendency of what is colloquially known as the shooting war. Nor does law lag behind common sense. War does not cease with a cease-fire order, and power to be exercised by the President such as that conferred by the Act of 1798 is a process which begins when war is declared but is not exhausted when the shooting stops.* * * Whether and when it would be open to this Court to find that a war though merely formally kept alive had in fact ended, is a question too fraught with gravity even to be adequately formulated when not compelled. * * * The political branch of the Government has not brought the war with Germany to an end. On the contrary, it has proclaimed that "a state of war still exists." The Court would be assuming the functions of the political agencies of the Government to yield to the suggestion that the unconditional surrender of Germany and the disintegration of the Nazi Reich have left Germany without a government capable of negotiating a treaty of peace. It is not for us to question a belief by the President that enemy aliens who

---

[5] The order recited that the petitioner was deemed dangerous on the basis of the evidence adduced at hearings before the Alien Enemy Hearing Board on January 16, 1942, and the Repatriation Hearing Board on December 17, 1945. The district court which examined these proceedings found that petitioner had notice and a fair hearing and that the evidence was substantial.

were justifiably deemed fit subjects for internment during active hostilities do not lose their potency for mischief during the period of confusion and conflict which is characteristic of a state of war even when the guns are silent but the Peace has not come. These are matters of political judgment for which judges have neither technical competence nor official responsibility.

This brings us to the final question. Is the statute valid as we have construed it? The same considerations of reason, authority, and history, that led us to reject reading the statutory language "declared war" to mean "actual hostilities," support the validity of the statute. The war power is the war power. If the war * * * has not in fact ended, * * * it validly supports the power given to the President by the Act of 1798 in relation to alien enemies. Nor does it require protracted argument to find no defect in the Act because resort to the courts may be had only to challenge the construction and validity of the statute and to question the existence of the "declared war," as has been done in this case.[17] The Act is almost as old as the Constitution, and it would savor of doctrinaire audacity now to find the statute offensive to some emanation of the Bill of Rights. The fact that hearings are utilized by the Executive to secure an informed basis for the exercise of summary power does not argue the right of courts to retry such hearings, nor bespeak denial of due process to withhold such power from the courts.

Such great war powers may be abused, no doubt, but that is a bad reason for having judges supervise their exercise, whatever the legal formulas within which such supervision would nominally be confined. * * * Accordingly, we hold that full responsibility for the just exercise of this great power may validly be left where the Congress has constitutionally placed it—on the President of the United States. The Founders in their wisdom made him not only the Commander-in-Chief but also the guiding organ in the conduct of our foreign affairs. He who was entrusted with such vast powers in relation to the outside world was also entrusted by Congress, almost throughout the whole life of the nation, with the disposition of alien enemies during a state of war. Such a page of history is worth more than a volume of rhetoric.

Judgment affirmed and stay order entered February 2, 1948, vacated.

[The dissenting opinion of JUSTICE BLACK, which was joined by JUSTICES DOUGLAS, MURPHY and RUTLEDGE, is omitted]

■ Mr. JUSTICE DOUGLAS, with whom Mr. JUSTICE MURPHY and Mr. JUSTICE RUTLEDGE, concur, dissenting.

I do not agree that the sole question open on habeas corpus is whether the petitioner is in fact an alien enemy. That delimitation of the historic writ is a wholly arbitrary one. I see no reason for a more narrow range of judicial inquiry here than in habeas corpus arising out of any other deportation proceeding.

It is undisputed that in peacetime an alien is protected by the due process clause of the Fifth Amendment. Federal courts will then determine through habeas corpus whether or not a deportation order is based upon procedures affording due process of law. In deportation proceedings due process requires reasonable notice, a fair hearing, and an order supported by some evidence.

---

[17] The additional question as to whether the person restrained is in fact an alien enemy fourteen years of age or older may also be reviewed by the courts. * * * This question is not raised in this case.

The rule of those cases is not restricted to instances where Congress itself has provided for a hearing. The Japanese Immigrant Case (Kaoru Yamataya v. Fisher), 189 U.S. 86, decided in 1903, so held. The Court in that case held that due process required that deportation be had only after notice and hearing even though there, as here, the statute prescribed no such procedure but entrusted the matter wholly to an executive officer. Consistently with that principle we held in Bridges v. Wixon, that a violation of the rules governing the hearing could be reached on habeas corpus, even though the rules were prescribed not by Congress but by the administrative agency in charge of the deportation proceeding. * * *

The same principles are applicable here. The President has classified alien enemies by regulations of general applicability and has authorized deportation only of those deemed dangerous because they have adhered to an enemy government, or the principles thereof. Petitioner was in fact given a hearing in 1945 before the Repatriation Hearing Board in addition to one in 1942 before the Alien Enemy Hearing Board. The order for his deportation recites that "upon consideration of the evidence presented" before those Boards, the Attorney General, in the words of the Proclamation, deems petitioner "to be dangerous to the public peace and safety of the United States because he has adhered to a government with which the United States is at war or to the principle thereof." Those findings and conclusions and the procedure by which they were reached must conform with the requirements of due process. And habeas corpus is the time-honored procedure to put them to the test.

The inquiry in this type of case need be no greater an intrusion in the affairs of the Executive branch of government than inquiries by habeas corpus in times of peace into a determination that the alien is considered to be an "undesirable resident of the United States." Both involve only a determination that procedural due process is satisfied, that there be a fair hearing, and that the order be based upon some evidence.

The needs of the hour may well require summary apprehension and detention of alien enemies. A nation at war need not be detained by time-consuming procedures while the enemy bores from within. But with an alien enemy behind bars, that danger has passed. If he is to be deported only after a hearing, our constitutional requirements are that the hearing be a fair one. It is foreign to our thought to defend a mock hearing on the ground that in any event it was a mere gratuity. Hearings that are arbitrary and unfair are no hearings at all under our system of government. Against them habeas corpus provides in this case the only protection.

The notion that the discretion of any officer of government can override due process is foreign to our system. Due process does not perish when war comes. It is well established that the war power does not remove constitutional limitations safeguarding essential liberties.

NOTES AND QUESTIONS ON LUDECKE

1)   Enemy Aliens. This is the first time that we have seen the term "enemy alien" used by the Supreme Court. The Court defines an "enemy alien" as a noncitizen who is a citizen of a country with which the U.S. is formally at War (or in limited circumstances based on an invasion.) The Alien Enemy statute provided broadly defined power to deport such "enemy aliens" to the Executive.

Unlike the companion Alien Friends Statute, which was controversial and allowed to expire, this statute remained. Should the power to detain for national security reasons be broader than the immigration power?

2) **Judicial Review and Habeas Review.** That power to detain and deport does not answer (1) whether habeas review remains, (2) whether some other form of judicial review remains, and (3) the scope of any such review. There is very well-pedigreed decisional law requiring a clear statement of any intent to displace habeas review—and the Alien Enemy Act did not address the subject.

3) **Habeas Corpus on Statutory Questions.** In *Ludecke*, the Court found that the War Power "validly supports the power given to the President by the Act of 1798 in relation to alien enemies." 335 U.S. 160 (1948). However, the question as to whether the detention was authorized was separate from the question as to whether habeas corpus could be used to review the detention. Importantly, the court noted that judicial review would be available to examine "the construction and validity of the statute" as well as whether "the person restrained is in fact an enemy alien." This means that habeas corpus may be used to review whether the detention is authorized. The Court's ruling would later assume an important rule in the military detention context, because it again made clear that, even if the detainee cannot or does not assert that his detention is unconstitutional, the court must still examine whether the detention is authorized.

4) **Due Process.** The Court rejected any due process claim, remarking "it would savor of doctrinaire audacity now to find the statute offensive to some emanation of the Bill of Rights." Of course, a factual challenge to the determination that Ludecke fell within the terms of the statute would likely fail; he was a German national and there was the requisite state of war. Ludecke may have instead been claiming that he did not fall within the requisite dangerousness when selected for removal by the Executive. The due process claim, however, might challenge the statutory and administrative process used to make that finding (ultimately the Attorney General's decision)—and the Court refused to consider such a claim. After reading this case, and *Mezei and Knauff,* do you agree with Professor Henry Hart's view that if habeas corpus is available, the Constitution should apply in full? Or has the Supreme Court correctly limited the reach of certain due process rights to noncitizens?

———

NOTES ON THE USA PATRIOT ACT

1) **National Security Immigration Detention.** Following the September 11, 2001 attacks, Congress responded by enacting the USA PATRIOT Act, which contained a provision authorizing prolonged detention. Recall that, after *Zadvydas*, the Government must typically offer reasons for detaining an individual beyond an initial six-month period. Under the USA PATRIOT Act, for a small class of individuals deemed to pose a national security or terrorism threat, an additional six month detention is mandatory, but any additional custody must be certified and reviewed every six months by the Attorney General or a Deputy Attorney General. The Act also makes indefinitely renewable the detention of an alien (1) whose removal is not reasonably foreseeable and (2) who presents a national security threat or has been involved in terrorist activities.[vv] Does this comply with *Zadvdas*, which appeared to require "clear" Congressional intent to detain, by specifically authorizing a category of detentions? The power under the Act apparently has not yet been used.[ww]

2) Material Support. Recall the "mandatory detention" provisions, providing that some types of noncitizens must be detained and cannot be released (that is, released on bail into the U.S.)—if they are subject to removal based on support of terrorism grounds or having committed crimes of "moral turpitude." The USA PATRIOT Act expanded the definition of what constitutes "material support" for terrorist activity. Those provisions contain detailed definitions of what "terrorist activity" means, including to "afford[] material support, including transportation, communications, funds... or training," "for the commission of a terrorist activity" to an individual or to a designated "terrorist organization." 8 U.S.C.A. § 1182(a)(3)(B)(iv). Any noncitizen who "has engaged in a terrorist activity" or whom the Government "has reasonable ground to believe, is engaged in or is likely to engage after entry in any terrorist activity," is inadmissible to the U.S. *Id.* at § 1182(a)(3)(B). The same is true of members or representatives of a terrorist organization. *Id.* at § 1182(a)(3)(B)(iv).

After *St. Cyr.*, a noncitizen sought, in a habeas petition, to challenge his removal for having engaged in terrorist activity in 1978; he argued that the IIRIRA and subsequent legislation that made those who engage in terrorist activity removable should not be made retroactive to him. The petitioner did not challenge his removability for having engaged in terrorist activities. The Second Circuit denied the petition, reasoning that such a person "cannot plausibly claim that they would have acted any differently if they had known" about the subsequent elimination of discretionary relief. *Kelava v. Gonzales*, 434 F.3d 1120, 1124–25 (9th Cir. 2006).

There is also a detailed process by which the Secretary of State may designate an organization as a terrorist organization. 8 U.S.C.A. § 1189.[xx] We will see additional definitions of what it means to support terrorist activity in the next Chapter on military detention. Separate provisions criminalize "material support" for terrorist activities. 18 U.S.C.A. § 2339A–B.

3) Alien Terrorist Removal Court. As part of the IIRIRA, Congress also enacted legislation creating an Alien Terrorist Removal Court (ATRC), which receives cases submitted by the Attorney General, and consisting in five federal district judges serving five-year terms, and appointed by the Chief Justice of the United States. *See* INA §§ 501–507. The ATRC has yet to be used. If used, it would hear removal proceedings to deport noncitizens "on the grounds that the alien is an alien terrorist." 8 U.S.C.A. § 1534(a). Those hearings provide for notice of the nature of the charges, an open public hearing, a right to be represented by counsel, and to introduce evidence and cross-examine witnesses, but not a right to access classified information. *Id.* at § 1534(b)-(c). The ATRC would provide the noncitizen an unclassified digest of the withheld information, unless doing so would cause "serious and irreparable harm"; otherwise, such

---

[vv] Uniting and Strengthening America by Providing Appropriate Tools Required to Intercept and Obstruct Terrorism Act of 2001 (USA PATRIOT ACT), § 412(a), 115 Stat. 350 (enacted Oct. 26, 2001) (codified at 8 U.S.C. § 1226a(a)(6) (2000 ed., Supp. II)).

[ww] See Aleinikoff et al., supra note tt, at 1183.

[xx] Those procedures have themselves been litigated in a series of due process challenges. See, e.g., People's Mojahedin Organization of Iran v. U.S. Dept. of State, 613 F.3d 220 (D.C. Cir. 2010).

classified information is reviewed by the court in camera and ex parte (in which case special counsel with security clearance may be provided). The Government has the burden to prove by the preponderance of the evidence "that the alien is subject to removal because the alien is an alien terrorist." *Id.* at § 1534(g).

Perhaps the procedures have never been used because the Government has never needed the special forum. After all, the Government can already withhold classified information when seeking to remove an alien based on inadmissibility. The Government would only need to use the ATRC if that classified information was absolutely necessary to prove its case for removal of an already-admitted noncitizen; perhaps since the Government already has broad powers to remove, the ATRC has not been invoked.[yy] They certainly provide more procedures than those used in the *Ludecke, Knauff* or *Mezei* cases. If they were used, would the procedures be constitutional?

————

REVIEW EXERCISE

When federal judges review immigration decisions, they no longer primarily use habeas corpus. After *INS v. St. Cyr* and the REAL-ID Act, the petition-for-review procedure allows appeals courts to consider questions of law and constitutional questions, as well as deferential fact-review for certain types of challenges to removal. What Suspension Clause problems have been identified in this Chapter? Could any of those problems be addressed through interpretation of the immigration statutes? If you were to propose legislation designed to create an efficient but also constitutionally adequate system for judicial review of immigration decisions, what role would you provide for habeas corpus review in the federal district courts?

————

————

[yy] See John D. Niles, *Assessing the Constitutionality of the Alien Terrorist Removal Court,* 57 Duke L. J. 1833 (2008); Aleinikoff et al., *supra* note tt, at 1184.

CHAPTER 8

CIVIL DETENTION

INTRODUCTION TO CIVIL DETENTION

Habeas corpus can be used to challenge custody that is civil and not based on a criminal conviction or military authority. In addition to immigration custody, a form of civil custody discussed in the previous Chapter, historically, many prisoners have been civilly committed to asylums and mental hospitals. Today, judges hold other categories of prisoners in custody under civil commitment authority: those in "pretrial" detention pending a criminal trial, sexually-violent predators incapacitated as public dangers, and others subject to some form of preventative detention.

Both federal and state governments have civil detention authority, the latter pursuant to broad police powers. In *Gibbons v. Ogden*, 22 U.S. 1 (1824), the Supreme Court listed several examples of such state power: "quarantine laws, and other regulations of police, respecting the public health in the several States." What must the government show to exercise custody over the prisoner? The answer may depend on the legal source of the government's authority, the factual support for the detention, and the length of the detention. Recall from the last Chapter that the Supreme Court, in *Zadvydas v. United States*, 533 U.S. 678, 699–700 (2001), expressed special concerns when the government detains noncitizens indefinitely. For immigration detention pending removal, the Court emphasized the question whether removal is "reasonably foreseeable" or not. What kind of detention is "reasonable" in other circumstances? What if the detention is justified by military necessity, a public health emergency, or a dangerous mental illness?

Recall that the habeas privilege can only be exercised by a person who is "in custody." Many prisoners challenge an order subjecting them to physical confinement in a jail, prison, or other detention facility. The "custody" requirement, however, does not always require that a prisoner be physically located in such a facility. "Custody" also exists within the meaning of Title 28 if a person is on probation, on parole, or subject to any form of civil or criminal detention. For example, a person is in custody if the person is in a mental institution or is jailed for contempt. When a noncitizen is subject to a removal order in an immigration proceeding, as discussed in Chapter 7, the "custody" requirement is satisfied.

This Chapter is organized around the types of special justifications for civil detention. First, civil detention can be auxiliary to some type of military necessity. Second, detention may be auxiliary to the criminal process. Third, persons may be detained after a criminal sentence has lapsed, allowing ongoing detention of sex offenders and other "dangerous" people. Fourth, the government may exercise civil custody pursuant to some special public-health justification, such as in cases of dangerous mental illness and substance abuse. This Chapter explores how habeas corpus has developed as a way for people to challenge such detentions.

1. Civil Detention Auxiliary to Military Necessity

Note on Mitsuye Endo and American Detention of Japanese Americans During World War II

The United States Government interned about 120,000 people during World War II, most of them of Japanese descent. Sixty percent of the detainees were American citizens. The internment program started with two Executive Orders: (1) Order No. 9066, to clear pacific states of persons who might be sympathetic to enemy invaders;[a] and (2) Order No. 9102, to remove these people to "Japanese Relocation Centers" under the supervision of the War Relocation Authority (WRA). Removed persons were forced to relocate from their homes in Arizona, California, Oregon, and Washington. Such "evacuees" could bring only a few belongings, and were often directed to take only the clothes they were wearing. Because interior states did not want to shoulder the burden of unchecked immigration, the WRA had to quickly build places for the evacuees to live. The WRA placed detainees in one of ten military relocation centers, which were constructed in remote, inland areas throughout the country.

Barbed-wire fences and armed guards surrounded most WRA relocation centers. The physical conditions of confinement were not abysmal; some groups, such as college students and seasonal farm workers, were permitted to leave. Nevertheless, tensions in the centers grew as a result of psychological and physical hardship, the absence of medical care, and growing hostility towards the United States. As the War progressed and the likelihood of another Japanese attack receded, the military justification for detaining those of Japanese descent diminished. To address these changing circumstances, the United States established a loyalty review program, designed to separate loyal from disloyal evacuees and, for the former, to hasten their release from relocation centers.[b]

Mitsuye Endo, a stenographer who had been working for the California Department of Motor Vehicles, was evacuated from her home in Sacramento, California, in July of 1942. She was originally taken to the Tule Lake War Relocation Center in Newell, California. Endo sought to avail herself of U.S. Government's loyalty review program. After proving her loyalty, the government was supposed to release Ms. Endo into an interior community, away from the Pacific Coast. Because so many interior communities were hostile to evacuees, however, the government scrapped the program. The new system required detainees to show that they had an employer or sponsor who would ensure a smooth process of community integration. If detainees were unable to find a suitable employer or sponsor, then the War Relocation Authority was to detain them indefinitely.

Endo completed the paperwork necessary to prove her loyalty, but did not meet the other requirements for release. At that point, she petitioned for habeas relief. While her appeal was pending, the Relocation Authority transferred her to a center in Topaz, Utah. The Government "wanted Endo to drop her

[a] Executive Order No. 9066 was upheld in the anti-canonical decision, *Korematsu v. United States*, 323 U.S. 214 (1944).

[b] See generally *Report of the Comm'n on Wartime Relocation & Internment of Civilians, Personal Justice Denied* 2–7 (1982); *The Mass Internment of Japanese American and the Quest for Legal Redress* (Charles J. McClain ed., 1994); Maisie Conrat & Richard Conrat, *Executive Order 9066: The Internment of 110,000 Japanese Americans* (1992).

suit," and offered her a permit to leave the internment camp if she would leave the West Coast, but she "bravely refused" and as a result "remained in detention for a total of three years." Noah Feldman, *Scorpions: The Battles and Triumphs of FDR's Great Supreme Court Justices* 235 (2010) (*Scorpions*). Her petition reached the U.S. Supreme Court, which issued a landmark decision that not only hastened the end of these detentions, but also announced durable restrictions on the scope of civil detention authority.

Ex parte Mitsuye Endo

United States Supreme Court
323 U.S. 283 (1944)

■ MR. JUSTICE DOUGLAS delivered the opinion of the Court.

* * * Mitsuye Endo * * * is an American citizen of Japanese ancestry. She was evacuated from Sacramento, California, in 1942, pursuant to certain military orders * * * and was removed to the Tule Lake War Relocation Center located at Newell, Modoc County, California. In July, 1942, she filed a petition for a writ of habeas corpus in the District Court of the United States for the Northern District of California, asking that she be discharged and restored to liberty. That petition was denied * * * and an appeal was perfected to the Circuit Court of Appeals in August, 1943. Shortly thereafter [Endo] was transferred from the Tule Lake Relocation Center to the Central Utah Relocation Center located at Topaz, Utah, where she is presently detained. * * *

[The United States formally declared War on Japan on December 8, 1941, a day after the Japanese aerial assault on the Naval Base at Pearl Harbor.] * * * On February 19, 1942, the President promulgated Executive Order No. 9066[.] It recited that "the successful prosecution of the war requires every possible protection against espionage and against sabotage to national-defense material, national-defense premises, and national-defense utilities as defined in Section 4, Act of April 20, 1918, as amended by the Act of November 30, 1940, and the Act of August 21, 1941." * * * And it authorized and directed "the Secretary of War, and the Military Commanders whom he may from time to time designate, whenever he or any designated Commander deems such action necessary or desirable, to prescribe military areas in such places and of such extent as he or the appropriate Military Commander may determine, from which any or all persons may be excluded, and with respect to which, the right of any person to enter, remain in, or leave shall be subject to whatever restrictions the Secretary of War or the appropriate Military Commander may impose in his discretion. The Secretary of War is hereby authorized to provide for residents of any such area who are excluded therefrom, such transportation, food, shelter, and other accommodations as may be necessary, in the judgment of the Secretary of War or the said Military Commander, and until other arrangements are made, to accomplish the purpose of this order."

Lt. General J. L. De Witt, Military Commander of the Western Defense Command, was designated to carry out the duties prescribed by that Executive Order. On March 2, 1942, he promulgated Public Proclamation No. 1 * * * which recited that the entire Pacific Coast of the United States * * * "is particularly subject to attack [and] attempted invasion * * *, and, in connection therewith, is subject to espionage and acts of sabotage, thereby requiring the adoption of military measures necessary to establish safeguards against such enemy operations." It designated certain Military Areas and Zones in the Western Defense Command and announced that certain persons might subsequently be excluded from these areas. On March 16, 1942, General De Witt promulgated Public Proclamation No. 2 which contained similar recitals and designated further Military Areas and Zones. * * *

On March 18, 1942, the President promulgated Executive Order No. 9102 which established in the Office for Emergency Management of the Executive Office of the President the War Relocation Authority. It recited that it was made "in order to provide for the removal from designated areas of persons whose removal is necessary in the interests of national security." It provided for a Director and authorized and directed him to: "formulate and effectuate a program for the removal, from the areas designated from time to time by the Secretary of War or appropriate military commander under the authority of Executive Order No. 9066 of February 19, 1942, of the persons or classes of persons designated under such Executive Order, and for their relocation, maintenance, and supervision." * * *

Congress shortly enacted legislation which * * * ratified and confirmed Executive Order No. 9066. It * * * provided: "That whoever shall enter, remain in, leave, or commit any act in any military area or military zone prescribed, under the authority of an Executive order of the President, by the Secretary of War, or by any military commander designated by the Secretary of War, contrary to the restrictions applicable to any such area or zone or contrary to the order of the Secretary of War or any such military commander, shall, if it appears that he knew or should have known of the existence and extent of the restrictions or order and that his act was in violation thereof, be guilty of a misdemeanor and upon conviction shall be liable to a fine of not to exceed $5,000 or to imprisonment for not more than one year, or both, for each offense."

Beginning on March 24, 1942, a series of 108 Civilian Exclusion Orders were issued by General De Witt pursuant to Public Proclamation Nos. 1 and 2. Appellant's exclusion was effected by Civilian Exclusion Order No. 52, dated May 7, 1942. It ordered that "all persons of Japanese ancestry, both alien and non-alien" be excluded from Sacramento, California, beginning at noon on May 16, 1942. Appellant was evacuated to the Sacramento Assembly Center on May 15, 1942, and was transferred from there to the Tule Lake Relocation Center on June 19, 1942.

On May 19, 1942, General De Witt promulgated Civilian Restrictive Order No. 1 * * * and on June 27, 1942, Public Proclamation No. 8. * * * These prohibited evacuees from leaving Assembly Centers or Relocation Centers except pursuant to an authorization from General De Witt's headquarters. * * *

By letter of August 11, 1942, General De Witt authorized the War Relocation Authority to issue permits for persons to leave these areas. By virtue of that delegation and the authority conferred by Executive Order No. 9102, the War Relocation Authority was given control over the ingress and egress of evacuees from the Relocation Centers where Mitsuye Endo was confined.

The program of the War Relocation Authority is said to have three main features: (1) the maintenance of Relocation Centers as interim places of residence for evacuees; (2) the segregation of loyal from disloyal evacuees; (3) the continued detention of the disloyal and so far as possible the relocation of the loyal in selected communities. In connection with the latter phase of its work the War Relocation Authority established a procedure for obtaining leave from Relocation Centers. That procedure, so far as indefinite leave is concerned, presently provides as follows:

Application for leave clearance is required. An investigation of the applicant is made for the purpose of ascertaining "the probable effect upon the war program and upon the public peace and security of issuing indefinite leave" to the applicant. The grant of leave clearance does not authorize departure from the Relocation Center. Application for indefinite leave must also be made. Indefinite leave may be granted under 14 specified conditions. For example, it may be granted (1) where the applicant proposes to accept an employment offer or an offer of support that has been investigated and approved by the Authority; or (2) where the applicant does not intend to work but has "adequate financial resources to take care of himself" and a Relocation Officer has investigated and approved "public sentiment at his proposed destination", or (3) where the applicant has made arrangements to live at a hotel or in a private home approved by a Relocation Officer while arranging for employment; or (4) where the applicant proposes to accept employment by a federal or local governmental agency; or (5) where the applicant is going to live with designated classes of relatives. * * *

Mitsuye Endo made application for leave clearance on February 19, 1943, after the petition was filed in the District Court. Court. Leave clearance was granted her on August 16, 1943. But she made no application for indefinite leave. * * *

Her petition for a writ of *habeas corpus* alleges that she is a loyal and law-abiding citizen of the United States, that no charge has been made against her, that she is being unlawfully detained, and that she is confined in the Relocation Center under armed guard and held there against her will.

It is conceded by the Department of Justice and by the War Relocation Authority that [Endo] is a loyal and law-abiding citizen. [The DOJ does not claim] that she is detained on any charge or that she is even suspected of disloyalty. Moreover, they do not contend that she may be held any longer in the Relocation Center. They concede that it is beyond the power of the War Relocation Authority to detain citizens against whom no charges of disloyalty or subversiveness have been made for a period longer than that necessary to separate the loyal from the disloyal and to provide the necessary guidance for relocation. But they maintain that detention for an additional period after leave clearance has been granted is an essential step in the evacuation program. Reliance for that conclusion is placed on the following circumstances.

When compulsory evacuation from the West Coast was decided upon, plans for taking care of the evacuees after their detention in the Assembly Centers, to which they were initially removed, remained to be determined. On April 7, 1942, the Director of the Authority held a conference in Salt Lake City with various state and federal officials including the Governors of the inter-mountain states. "Strong opposition was expressed to any type of unsupervised relocation and some of the Governors refused to be responsible for maintenance of law and order unless evacuees brought into their States were kept under constant military surveillance." * * * As stated by General De Witt in his report to the Chief of Staff: "Essentially, military necessity required only that the Japanese population be removed from the coastal area and dispersed in the interior, where the danger of action in concert during any attempted enemy raids along the coast, or in advance thereof as preparation for a full scale attack, would be eliminated. That the evacuation program necessarily and ultimately developed into one of complete Federal supervision, was due primarily to the fact that the interior states would not accept an uncontrolled Japanese migration." * * * The Authority thereupon abandoned plans for assisting groups of evacuees in private colonization and temporarily put to one side plans for aiding the evacuees in obtaining private employment. As an alternative the Authority "concentrated on establishment of Government-operated centers with sufficient capacity and facilities to accommodate the entire evacuee population." Accordingly, it undertook to care for the basic needs of these people in the Relocation Centers, to promote as rapidly as possible the permanent resettlement of as many as possible in normal communities, and to provide indefinitely for those left at the Relocation Centers. An effort was made to segregate the loyal evacuees from the others. The leave program which we have discussed was put into operation and the resettlement program commenced.[19]

It is argued that such a planned and orderly relocation was essential to the success of the evacuation program; that but for such supervision there might have been a dangerously disorderly migration of unwanted people to unprepared communities; that unsupervised evacuation might have resulted in hardship and disorder; that the success of the evacuation program was thought to require the knowledge that the federal government was maintaining control over the evacuated population except as the release of individuals could be effected consistently with their own peace and well-being and that of the nation; that although community hostility towards the evacuees has diminished, it has not disappeared and the continuing control of the Authority over the relocation process is essential to the success of the evacuation program. It is argued that supervised relocation, as the chosen method of terminating the evacuation, is the final step in the entire process and is a consequence of the first step taken. It is conceded that [Endo's] detention pending compliance with the leave regulations is not directly connected with the prevention of espionage and sabotage at the present time. But it is argued that Executive Order No. 9102 confers power to make regulations necessary and proper for controlling situations created by the exercise of the powers expressly conferred for protection against espionage and sabotage. The leave regulations are said to fall within that category.

First. We are of the view that Mitsuye Endo should be given her liberty. In reaching that conclusion we do not come to the underlying constitutional issues which have been argued. For we conclude that, whatever power the War Relocation Authority may have to detain other classes of citizens, it has no authority to subject citizens who are concededly loyal to its leave procedure.

---

[19] There were 108,503 evacuees transferred to Relocation Centers. Final Report, supra, note 2, p. 279. As of July 29, 1944, there were 28,911 on indefinite leave and 61,002 in the Relocation Centers other than Tule Lake. It was sought to assemble at Tule Lake those whose disloyalty was deemed to be established and those who persisted in a refusal to say they would be willing to serve in the armed forces of the United States on combat duty wherever ordered and to swear unqualified allegiance to the United States and forswear any form of allegiance to the Japanese Emperor or any other foreign government, power or organization. This group, together with minor children, totaled 18,684 on July 29, 1944. And see Hearings, Subcommittee on the National War Agencies Appropriation Bill for 1945, p. 611.

It should be noted at the outset that we do not have here a question such as was presented in *Ex parte Milligan* * * * or in *Ex parte Quirin,* * * * where the jurisdiction of military tribunals to try persons according to the law of war was challenged in habeas corpus proceedings. Mitsuye Endo is detained by a civilian agency, the War Relocation Authority, not by the military. Moreover, the evacuation program was not left exclusively to the military; the Authority was given a large measure of responsibility for its execution and Congress made its enforcement subject to civil penalties by the Act of March 21, 1942. Accordingly, no questions of military law are involved.

Such power of detention as the Authority has stems from Executive Order No. 9066. That order is the source of the authority delegated by General De Witt in his letter of August 11, 1942. And Executive Order No. 9102 which created the War Relocation Authority purported to do no more than to implement the program authorized by Executive Order No. 9066.

We approach the construction of Executive Order No. 9066 as we would approach the construction of legislation in this field. That Executive Order must indeed be considered along with the Act of March 21, 1942, which ratified and confirmed it * * * as the Order and the statute together laid such basis as there is for participation by civil agencies of the federal government in the evacuation program. Broad powers frequently granted to the President or other executive officers by Congress so that they may deal with the exigencies of war time problems have been sustained. And the Constitution when it committed to the Executive and to Congress the exercise of the war power necessarily gave them wide scope for the exercise of judgment and discretion so that war might be waged effectively and successfully. At the same time, however, the Constitution is as specific in its enumeration of many of the civil rights of the individual as it is in its enumeration of the powers of his government. Thus it has prescribed procedural safeguards surrounding the arrest, detention and conviction of individuals. Some of these are contained in the Sixth Amendment, compliance with which is essential if convictions are to be sustained. And the Fifth Amendment provides that no person shall be deprived of liberty (as well as life or property) without due process of law. Moreover, as a further safeguard against invasion of the basic civil rights of the individual[, the Suspension Clause appears in Article I, § 9.]

We mention these constitutional provisions not to stir the constitutional issues which have been argued at the bar but to indicate the approach which we think should be made to an Act of Congress or an order of the Chief Executive that touches the sensitive area of rights specifically guaranteed by the Constitution. This Court has quite consistently given a narrower scope for the operation of the presumption of constitutionality when legislation appeared on its face to violate a specific prohibition of the Constitution. We have likewise favored that interpretation of legislation which gives it the greater chance of surviving the test of constitutionality. Those analogies are suggestive here. We must assume that the Chief Executive and members of Congress, as well as the courts, are sensitive to and respectful of the liberties of the citizen. In interpreting a war-time measure we must assume that their purpose was to allow for the greatest possible accommodation between those liberties and the exigencies of war. We must assume, when asked to find implied powers in a grant of legislative or executive authority, that the law makers intended to place no greater restraint on the citizen than was clearly and unmistakably indicated by the language they used.

The Act of March 21, 1942, was a war measure. The House Report * * * stated, "The necessity for this legislation arose from the fact that the safe conduct of the war requires the fullest possible protection against either espionage or sabotage to national defense material, national defense premises, and national defense utilities." That was the precise purpose of Executive Order No. 9066, for, as we have seen, it gave as the reason for the exclusion of persons from prescribed military areas the protection of such property "against espionage and against sabotage." And Executive Order No. 9102 which established the War Relocation Authority did so, as we have noted, "in order to provide for the removal from designated areas of persons whose removal is necessary in the interests of national security." The purpose and objective of the Act and of these orders are plain. Their single aim was the protection of the war effort against espionage and sabotage. It is in light of that one objective that the powers conferred by the orders must be construed.

Neither the Act nor the orders use the language of detention. The Act says that no one shall "enter, remain in leave, or commit any act" in the prescribed military areas contrary to the applicable restrictions. Executive Order No. 9066 subjects the right of any person "to enter, remain in, or leave" those prescribed areas to such restrictions as the military may impose. And apart from those restrictions the Secretary of War is only given authority to afford the evacuees "transportation, food, shelter, and other accommodations." Executive Order No. 9102 authorizes and directs the War Relocation Authority "to formulate and effectuate a program for the removal" of the persons covered by Executive Order No. 9066 from the prescribed military areas and "for their relocation, maintenance, and supervision." And power is given the Authority to make regulations "necessary or desirable to promote effective execution of such program." * * * [T]he legislative history of the Act of March 21, 1942, is silent on detention. And that silence may have special significance in view of the fact that detention in Relocation Centers was no part of the original program of evacuation but developed later to meet what seemed to the officials in charge to be mounting hostility to the evacuees on the part of the communities where they sought to go.

We do not mean to imply that detention in connection with no phase of the evacuation program would be lawful. The fact that the Act and the orders are silent on detention does not of course mean that any power to detain is lacking. Some such power might indeed be necessary to the successful operation of the evacuation program. At least we may so assume. Moreover, we may assume for the purposes of this case that initial detention in Relocation Centers was authorized. But we stress the silence of the legislative history and of the Act and the Executive Orders on the power to detain to emphasize that any such authority which exists must be implied. If there is to be the greatest possible accommodation of the liberties of the citizen with this war measure, any such implied power must be narrowly confined to the precise purpose of the evacuation program.

A citizen who is concededly loyal presents no problem of espionage or sabotage. Loyalty is a matter of the heart and mind not of race, creed, or color. He who is loyal is by definition not a spy or a saboteur. When the power to detain is derived from the power to protect the war effort against espionage and sabotage, detention which has no relationship to that objective is unauthorized.

Nor may the power to detain an admittedly loyal citizen or to grant him a conditional release be implied as a useful or convenient step in the evacuation program, whatever authority might be implied in case of those whose loyalty was not conceded or established. If we assume (as we do) that the original evacuation was justified, its lawful character was derived from the fact that it was an espionage and sabotage measure, not that there was community hostility to this group of American citizens. The evacuation program rested explicitly on the former ground not on the latter as the underlying legislation shows. The authority to detain a citizen or to grant him a conditional release as protection against espionage or sabotage is exhausted at least when his loyalty is conceded. If we held that the authority to detain continued thereafter, we would transform an espionage or sabotage measure into something else. That was not done by Executive Order No. 9066 or by the Act of March 21, 1942, which ratified it. What they did not do we cannot do. Detention which furthered the campaign against espionage and sabotage would be one thing. But detention which has no relationship to that campaign is of a distinct character. Community hostility even to loyal evacuees may have been (and perhaps still is) a serious problem. But if authority for their custody and supervision is to be sought on that ground, the Act of March 21, 1942, Executive Order No. 9066, and Executive Order No. 9102, offer no support. And none other is advanced. To read them that broadly would be to assume that the Congress and the President intended that this discriminatory action should be taken against these people wholly on account of their ancestry even though the government conceded their loyalty to this country. We cannot make such an assumption. * * *

Mitsuye Endo is entitled to an unconditional release by the War Relocation Authority.

Second. The question remains whether the District Court has jurisdiction to grant the writ of *habeas corpus* because of the fact that while the case was pending in the Circuit Court of Appeals [Endo] was moved from the Tule Lake Relocation Center in the Northern District of California where she was originally detained to the Central Utah Relocation Center in a different district and circuit.

That question is not colored by any purpose to effectuate a removal in evasion of the *habeas corpus* proceedings. It appears that [Endo's] removal to Utah was part of a general segregation program involving many of these people and was in no way related to this pending case. Moreover, there is no suggestion that there is no one within the jurisdiction of the District Court who is responsible for the detention of [Endo] and who would be an appropriate respondent. We are indeed advised by the Acting Secretary of the Interior that if the writ issues and is directed to the Secretary of the Interior or any official of the War Relocation Authority (including an assistant director whose office is at San Francisco, which is in the jurisdiction of the District Court), the corpus of [Endo] will be produced and the court's order complied with in all respects. Thus it would seem that the case is not moot. * * *

There are expressions in some of the cases which indicate that the place of confinement must be within the court's territorial jurisdiction in order to enable it to issue the writ. * * * But we are of the view that the court may act if there is a respondent within reach of its process who has custody of the petitioner. As [a prominent state judge has stated:] "The important fact to be observed in regard to the mode of procedure upon this writ is, that it is directed to, and served upon, not the person confined, but his jailer. It does not reach the former except through the latter. The officer or person who serves it does not unbar the prison doors, and set the prisoner free, but the court relieves him by compelling the oppressor to release his constraint. The whole force of the writ is spent upon the respondent." * * *

The judgment is reversed and the cause is remanded to the District Court for proceedings in conformity with this opinion.

Reversed.

NOTES AND QUESTIONS ON ENDO

1) Authorization. The Supreme Court extensively describes the legislative and executive process that resulted in rules authorizing the "evacuation" and subsequent detention of Japanese-Americans. Note that the authorizing Executive Order never mentioned that only persons of Japanese descent would be detained. Why did the Executive avoid that subject? Did that allow the Court to itself avoid difficult questions based on the racial and ethnic composition of the detainees? The language of authorization was important to the results in *Endo* and in *St. Cyr*; and it will be important in the post-9/11 decisions presented in the next Chapter. Why did Congress, in the emergency legislation fail to more clearly specify the authorized detentions? Could Congress have explicitly stated it meant to suspend the writ of habeas corpus? Would the circumstances have justified doing so (i.e., was there a rebellion or invasion)?

2) Clear Statement Rules. Why does *Endo* require that "language of detention" be used to avoid a constitutional issue? This approach prefigures the Supreme Court's analysis in *St. Cyr*. Was there anything unclear about the purpose of the authorizing legislation and regulations? Was there any doubt that Congress or the President envisioned mass detentions? Was the Court placing responsibility for the detentions on the obscure War Relocation Authority? If so, why?

3) Civil commitment. Of what significance was the fact that Endo's commitment was under civil authority? Compare *Endo* to *Ex Parte Milligan*, 71 U.S. 2 (1866), which will be presented in Chapter Nine. Milligan was detained in Indiana and tried before a military commission constituted there. In *Milligan*, the Supreme Court ruled that the military-commission trial was unauthorized and unconstitutional, emphasizing that civilian courts remained open and that charges should have been brought there. Endo and Milligan were both citizens detained in jurisdictions with functioning court systems. In what sense was Endo's commitment under military auspices? As Justice Souter eventually described the facts of *Endo* in a post-9/11 case, "Although a civilian agency authorized by Executive order ran the detention camps, the relocation and detention of American citizens was ordered by the military under authority of the President as Commander in Chief." *Hamdi v. Rumsfeld*, 542 U.S. 507, 547 (2004) (Souter, J., concurring). In *Endo*, the Court narrowly construed the relevant authority. It found the initial detention to have been undertaken during an emergency and for national security reasons, but not the ongoing detention after the decision to grant leave to a loyal citizen had been made.

4) Future Dangerousness. In *Endo*, of what significance was the fact that the detainee was "concededly loyal" and therefore "present[ed] no problem of espionage or sabotage"? How searchingly would a habeas judge scrutinize a case where the Executive claimed the person was not loyal and did pose a threat, but where the detainee disagreed? In contrast, when evaluating the national security detention of prisoners alleged to have been part of Al Qaeda, the D.C. Circuit concluded that whether the prisoner may rejoin the enemy or constitute a future danger is not relevant; all that was relevant was whether they had been part of Al Qaeda. *Awad v. Obama*, 608 F.3d 1 (D.C. Cir. 2010).[c]

5) Individual rights. Which individual rights might Endo's continuing detention implicate? The Supreme Court does not name them, but it calls the issue a "sensitive area." Why didn't the Court name the relevant rights? Contrast that sentiment with the precision of in *Milligan*. In *Milligan*, the Court detailed each constitutional right potentially compromised when Milligan was deprived of a criminal trial and was convicted by a military commission.

6) Jurisdiction Over the Respondent. *Endo's* language concerning habeas jurisdiction and military authority was ultimately very important in the post-9/11 cases, to which this Book turns shortly. *Endo* concluded that, although the prisoner had been moved from the place of initial detention—where she sought the writ—she could still obtain relief because there remained an officer who had been properly served and who had authority to order her release. The focus on *in personam* authority over the jailer is consistent with the common-law history of the writ, emphasized in Chapter 1. That focus is also consistent with the stated goals of the federal post-conviction statute, which Congress enacted to work around the fact that habeas writs generally involved territorial jurisdiction over the jailor, not over the prisoner. See *United States v. Hayman*, 342 U.S. 205 (1952) (excerpted in Chapter 2).

7) The End of Internment. *Endo* was issued on the same day as a much more (in)famous decision in which the Court found constitutional the use of race, ethnicity, and national origin in the initial exclusion and relocation actions. See Korematsu v. United States, 323 U.S. 214, 219–20 (1944).[d] Justice Hugo Black wrote, "Korematsu was not excluded from the Military Area because of hostility to him or his race. He was excluded because we are at war with the Japanese Empire, because the properly constituted military authorities feared an invasion of our West Coast and felt constrained to take proper security measures." Justice Frank Murphy dissented, stating, "Racial discrimination in any form and in any degree has no justifiable part whatever in our democratic way of life."

Note how the *Endo* opinion obliquely refers to *Korematsu*, stating that "[l]oyalty is a matter of the heart and mind not of race, creed, or color," but discusses how Congress must not have intended "this discriminatory action" to be ongoing. In his concurring opinion (omitted here), Justice Murphy put it more sharply: "As stated more fully in my dissenting opinion in [Korematsu], racial

[c] For an argument connecting civil and criminal detention with indefinite detention for national security reasons, see Michael Louis Corrado, *Sex Offenders, Unlawful Combatants, and Preventive Detention*, 84 N.C. L. Rev. 77, 85–100 (2005).

[d] See Dennis J. Hutchinson, *"The Achilles Heel" of the Constitution: Justice Jackson and the Japanese Exclusion Cases*, in 2002 Sup. Ct. Rev. 455, 485 n.99; David Cole, *Enemy Aliens*, 54 Stan. L. Rev. 953, 993 (2002) ("Eight of the nine sitting Justices on today's Supreme Court have stated that [Korematsu] was wrongly decided").

discrimination of this nature bears no reasonable relation to military necessity and is utterly foreign to the ideals and traditions of the American people."

Endo, however, had the effect of hastening the end of the internment program. The Government apparently "got wind of the decision," and the day before it was to be announced, the War Department announced that loyal citizens would be released—which "in practical terms" meant that "the overwhelming majority" of those in the camps would be discharged. See Feldman, *Scorpions*, at 246. President Gerald Ford apologized, calling the internments "wrong"; Congress appointed a Commission to investigate the internments in the 1980's, and reparations were eventually paid by the U.S. Government to the internees.[e] In 1984, the district court granted Fred Korematsu a writ of coram nobis, an extraordinarily rare form of relief in which the convicting court vacates its own judgment. In 1998, Korematsu was awarded the Presidential Medal of Freedom. Korematsu later filed one of the most noteworthy briefs opposing governmental detention in the GTMO cases.

2. CIVIL DETENTION AUXILIARY TO CRIMINAL PROCESS

NOTE ON PRE-TRIAL DETENTION OF DEFENDANT BASED ON FLIGHT RISK AND COMMUNITY SAFETY

Persons may be subject to pre-trial detention while the prosecution prepares for various phases of the criminal proceeding. Pre-trial detention is formally civil, but operates as an adjunct to criminal process. The prisoner has not yet been convicted, but a court may order a defendant that is either sufficiently dangerous or a sufficient "flight risk" to be detained.

1) **The English Bail Statutes.** The most famous habeas statute in Anglo-American legal history—the Habeas Corpus Act of 1679—was more of a bail-reform measure than anything else. Parliament passed the 1679 Act to combat the Crown's widespread practice of holding prisoners who it intended to charge criminally without bail. It provided: "A Magistrate shall discharge prisoners from their Imprisonment taking their Recognizance, with one or more Surety or Sureties, in any Sum according to the Magistrate's discretion, unless it shall appear that the Party is committed for such Matter or offences for which by law the Prisoner is not bailable." The 1679 Act established habeas as a remedy for, among other things, pre-trail detention without bail—although, contrary to the suggestions of many history books, it was not particularly effective in this respect. The spirit of the 1679 Act was frequently defeated by setting excessive bail, a practice that Parliament had to forbid ten years later in the English Bill of Rights. The pertinent part of the English Bill observed that "excessive bail hath been required of persons committed in criminal cases, to elude the benefit of the laws made for the liberty of the subjects[,]" and it therefore provided that "[e]xcessive bail ought not to be required." That provision is the English ancestor of language in the Eighth Amendment to the U.S. Constitution.

2) **American Bail Statutes.** Under the Federal Bail Reform Act of 1966, Congress established as the primary bail-setting criterion the flight risk of the potential bailee. In 1984, Congress amended the statute to add as a criterion

---

[e] Proclamation No. 4417, An American Promise, 41 Fed. Reg. 7741 (Feb. 19, 1976); Civil Liberties Act of 1988, Pub. L. No. 100–383, 102 Stat. 903 (1988) (recognizing "fundamental injustice" of internment and providing restitution).

the safety risk that a potential bailee would present to the community.[f] Thus, as with the rule concerning noncitizens awaiting immigration hearings, discussed in Chapter Three, the two concerns when deciding whether to grant bail are flight risk and public safety. The Supreme Court approved the preventative detention procedures of the Bail Reform Act of 1984, holding that "the Government's regulatory interest in community safety can, in appropriate circumstances, outweigh an individual's liberty interest." *United States v. Salerno*, 481 U.S. 739, 748 (1987). The Court observed that the Act provided for procedures to evaluate dangerousness that comported with the Due Process Clause—that were "specifically designed to further the accuracy of that determination." The Act provided for counsel, that a potential bailee was entitled to cross-examine witnesses at a hearing, and that the Government prove by "clear and convincing evidence" that detention is warranted.

3)   Immediate Appellate Review of Bail Decisions and Habeas Corpus. Pre-trial detention is extremely common both in federal and state courts, but habeas review is not as frequent as the incidence of the custody might suggest. *Salerno* also emphasized that judicial review under the Act included "immediate appellate review of the detention decision [under 18 U.S.C. § 3145]." Because appellate review of the bail determination must happen immediately, courts have held that federal habeas consideration should occur once that remedy is exhausted. See, e.g., *Fassler v. United States*, 858 F.2d 1016, 1017 (5th Cir. 1988) (dismissing habeas petition that "bypassed the expedited appeal procedure noted by the Supreme Court as an essential safeguard provided by the Bail Reform Act."). Because a pre-trial detention decision is subject to immediate review that the prisoner must exhaust before initiating habeas proceedings, defendants rarely mount successful habeas challenges to pre-trial detention.[g] Either a federal court will conclude that the state pre-trial process was sufficient or the issue of pre-trial detention will have been mooted entirely by a judgment of conviction.[h]

4)   A Katrina Exception? One uneasy exception to the general pattern that habeas does not frequently relieve pre-trial detention involves the aftermath of Hurricane Katrina. Thousands of persons who had been in the Orleans Parish Prison in New Orleans, mostly in post-arrest or pre-trial detention, were evacuated from the flooded prison, relocated, and then languished in detention. There were slow executive and judicial responses to these mass detentions, and people were detained for minor traffic violations for many months—even half a year or more—in distant locations making them difficult for relatives to reach. See Brandon L. Garrett & Tania Tetlow, *Criminal Justice Collapse: The Constitution After Hurricane Katrina,* 56 Duke L. J. 127 (2006). Habeas petitions

---

[f] The Court has approved pre-trial detention of the mentally ill. See Jackson v. Indiana, 406 U.S. 715 (1972). The Court has also approved state pre-trial detention of juveniles, noting "the widespread use and judicial acceptance of preventive detention for juveniles." Schall v. Martin, 467 U.S. 253 (1984).

[g] See, e.g., U.S. v. Pipito, 861 F.2d 1006, 1009 (7th Cir. 1987) (affirming district court's refusal to entertain habeas petition when petitioner should have followed § 3145 review procedures instead).

[h] See, e.g., Yohey v. Collins, 985 F.2d 222, 228–29 (5th Cir. 1993) (finding petitioner's claims for habeas relief related to pretrial issues moot by subsequent conviction); Thorne v. Warden, Brooklyn House of Detention of Men, 479 F.2d 297, 299 (2d Cir. 1973) (holding habeas challenge to the legality of petitioner's pretrial detention moot by subsequent conviction); Medina v. People of the State of California, 429 F.2d 1392, 1393 (9th Cir. 1970) (deeming a habeas challenge to unconstitutional bail revocation mooted by subsequent conviction).

514 Civil Detention Chapter 8

were filed in courts around the state, because thousands of people were being detained in temporary facilities—including an outdoor football field. Many were indigent persons who could not afford bail, had not received a preliminary hearing, or had not met with a lawyer. With the courts remaining closed, their post-arrest or pre-trial detention was longer than what a criminal conviction would have enailed. As the months passed, the Louisiana Supreme Court refused to accept habeas filings by these detainees, stating that it was closed and would not reopen, with three justices dissenting. Eventually, New Orleans courts reopened and began to order the release of prisoners. Federal courts granted relief to some prisoners as well.[i]

————

NOTE ON MATERIAL WITNESS DETENTION

1)   The Federal Statute. Ordinarily, a court compels a witness to testify using a subpoena. Sometimes, however, a subpoena will not be sufficient to ensure the presence of its recipient in court. 18 U.S.C. § 3144, sometimes called the "material witness statute," is designed to secure the testifying presence of he witness:

> If . . . the testimony of a person is material in a criminal proceeding, and if it is shown that it may become impracticable to secure the presence of the person by subpoena, a judicial officer may order the arrest of the person and treat the person in accordance with the provisions of [detention and bail applicable to criminal defendants]. No material witness may be detained because of inability to comply with any condition of release if the testimony of such witness can adequately be secured by deposition, and if further detention is not necessary to prevent a failure of justice. Release of a material witness may be delayed for a reasonable period of time until the deposition of the witness can be taken pursuant to the Federal Rules of Criminal Procedure.

States have similar statutes.[j] Material witness detention does not involve a criminal defendant, but rather *non-defendants* who may have information important to the criminal prosecution of *someone else*. The idea that a witness may be arrested and detained pending testimony may strike many as extreme, but the Supreme Court has affirmed that "[t]he duty to disclose knowledge of crime . . . is so vital that one known to be innocent may be detained in the ab-

————

[i] Ansari v. State, 913 So.2d 834 (La. 2005); see also Brandon L. Garrett & Tania Tetlow, 56 Duke L.J. 127, 149–150 (2006) (discussing stopgap solutions to legal problems in aftermath of Katrina).

[j] For example, the material witness laws in New Hampshire and Wyoming are almost identical to § 3144. See N.H. Rev. Stat. Ann. § 597:6-d; Wyo. R. Crim. P. 46.3. Arizona's material witness statute is also similar to § 3144, but it specifies that the impracticability of securing persons to testify must be based on one's immigration status: "If . . . the testimony of a person is material in a criminal proceeding . . . and if it is shown that it may become impracticable to secure the presence of the person by subpoena because of the immigration status of the person, the court may order the temporary detention of the person." Ariz. Rev. Stat. Ann. § 13–4085. Other states, such as Iowa, provide for the arrest of material witnesses: "When a law enforcement officer has probable cause to believe that a person is a necessary and material witness to a felony and that such person might be unavailable for service of a subpoena, the officer may arrest such persons as a material witness with or without an arrest warrant." Iowa Code Ann. § 804.11.

sence of bail, as a material witness." Stein v. New York, 346 U.S. 156, 184 (1953).[k]

2) Material Witness Detention After September 11. After the 9/11 attacks, the Attorney General announced that the material witness detention statute would be used in fighting terrorism. For example, Jose Padilla was initially detained as a material witness, though he was later deemed an "enemy combatant" and placed in military custody. See Rumsfeld v. Padilla, 542 U.S. 426 (2004). The Government may use the material witness statute to arrest and detain grand jury witnesses. See United States v. Awadallah, 349 F.3d 42, 49–51 (2d Cir. 2003) (interpreting "criminal proceeding" in § 3144 to include grand jury proceedings). Commentators have objected to the use of the material witness statute to accomplish, in effect, preventative detention of terror suspects. See Laurie L. Levenson, *Detention, Material Witnesses & the War on Terrorism*, 35 Loy. L.A. L. Rev. 1217, 1225 (2002). The same material witness statute has also been used in immigration prosecutions.[l]

3) *Ashcroft v. al-Kidd*. In *Ashcroft v. al-Kidd*, 131 S. Ct. 2074 (2011), the Court decided a constitutional challenge to the use of the material witness statute in the national security context. Justice Scalia's opinion for the Court summarizes Abdullah al-Kidd's allegations:

> [I]n the aftermath of the September 11th terrorist attacks, then-Attorney General John Ashcroft authorized federal prosecutors and law enforcement officials to use the material-witness statute to detain individuals with suspected ties to terrorist organizations. It is alleged that federal officials had no intention of calling most of these individuals as witnesses, and that they were detained, at Ashcroft's direction, because federal officials suspected them of supporting terrorism but lacked sufficient evidence to charge them with a crime.

> It is alleged that this pretextual detention policy led to the material-witness arrest of al-Kidd, a native-born United States citizen. FBI agents apprehended him in March 2003 as he checked in for a flight to Saudi Arabia. Two days earlier, federal officials had informed a Magistrate Judge that, if al-Kidd boarded his flight, they believed information "crucial" to the prosecution of Sami Omar al-Hussayen would be lost. Al–Kidd remained in federal custody for 16 days and on supervised release until al-Hussayen's trial concluded 14 months later. Prosecutors never called him as a witness.

Al-Kidd maintained a "*Bivens* action" against the federal government, seeking compensatory damages and alleging that the policy violated the Fourth

---

[k] For examples of state cases involving habeas challenges to material witness detention, see, e.g. In re D.W., 20 Cal. Rptr. 3d 274 (Cal. Ct. App. 2004) (granting habeas petition of material witness who was denied counsel and never afforded an opportunity to challenge the allegations requiring her detention as provided by state law); Rodriguez v. Sandstrom, 382 So. 2d 778 (Fla. Dist. Ct. App. 1980) (granting habeas petition of material witness who was detained to assure appearance when no charges were pending against any person in the investigation); State, ex. rel. Dorsey, v. Haines, 579 N.E.2d 541 (Ohio Ct. App. 1991) (granting habeas petition when warrant to detain material witness was not supported by probable cause).

[l] See, e.g., In re Class Action Application of Habeas Corpus on Behalf of All Material Witnesses in the Western District of Texas, 612 F.Supp. 940, 944 (W.D. Tex. 1985) (discussing how most material witnesses in the Western District of Texas are held in connection with cases involving illegal transportation of noncitizens).

Amendment prohibition on pretextual arrest without probable cause.[m] The Government argued that former-Attorney General Ashcroft was entitled to qualified immunity from damages liability. The majority found the Attorney General immune, noting that a warrant authorized al-Kidd's arrest, and that an "affidavit accompanying the warrant application (as al-Kidd concedes) gave individualized reasons to believe that he was a material witness and that he would soon disappear."

Justice Kennedy, in an opinion joined by three other Justices (and where Justice Kagan did not take part in the case), underscored that the decision did not address when material witness detention was consistent with the statute and the Constitution, and he expressed concern with broad use of the statute:

> The scope of the statute's lawful authorization is uncertain. For example, a law-abiding citizen might observe a crime during the days or weeks before a scheduled flight abroad. It is unclear whether those facts alone might allow police to obtain a material witness warrant on the ground that it "may become impracticable" to secure the person's presence by subpoena... The question becomes more difficult if one further assumes the traveler would be willing to testify if asked; and more difficult still if one supposes that authorities delay obtaining or executing the warrant until the traveler has arrived at the airport.

Justice Sotomayor, joined by two other Justices, also concurred, but stated: "Whether the Fourth Amendment permits the pretextual use of a material witness warrant for preventive detention of an individual whom the Government has no intention of using at trial is, in my view, a closer question than the majority's opinion suggests." Discussing the facts in still greater detail, Justice Ginsburg also concurred but with reservations:

> In addressing al-Kidd's Fourth Amendment claim against Ashcroft, the Court assumes at the outset the existence of a *validly obtained* material witness warrant... That characterization is puzzling... Is a warrant "validly obtained" when the affidavit on which it is based fails to inform the issuing Magistrate Judge that "the Government has no intention of using [al-Kidd as a witness] at [another's] trial," ... and does not disclose that al-Kidd had cooperated with FBI agents each of the several times they had asked to interview him ... ?
>
> Casting further doubt on the assumption that the warrant was validly obtained, the Magistrate Judge was not told that al-Kidd's parents, wife, and children were all citizens and residents of the United States. In addition, the affidavit misrepresented that al-Kidd was about to take a one-way flight to Saudi Arabia, with a first-class ticket costing approximately $5,000; in fact, al-Kidd had a round-trip, coach-class ticket that cost $1,700. Given these omissions and misrepresentations, there is strong cause to question the Court's opening assumption—a valid material-witness warrant—and equally strong reason to conclude that a merits determination was neither necessary nor proper.

---

[m] A "*Bivens* action" is a suit against federal officials for violating the Fourth Amendment; because of the centrality of the Fourth Amendment, the *Bivens* remedy is implied by the Constitution and requires no enabling statute. See Bivens v. Six Unknown Named Agents, 403 U.S. 388 (1971). *Al-Kidd* is one of many *Bivens* actions brought against executive officials for post-9/11 detentions; the last Section of Chapter 11 discusses *Bivens* actions in the national security context.

Putting to one side whether the particular Fourth Amendment claim had merit, what sorts of circumstances would permit a federal court to entertain a habeas claim challenging a material witness detention?

———

NOTE ON CIVIL COMMITMENT FOLLOWING SUCCESSFUL INSANITY DEFENSES

The previous Note discussed civil commitment for those defendants convicted of a crime. What about persons tried for crimes and found not guilty by reason of insanity (NGBRI); can the State then switch gears and detain the person civilly? In an answer many students find surprising, the State may do so. In *Jones v. United States*, 463 U.S. 534 (1983), the Court held:

> When a criminal defendant establishes by a preponderance of the evidence that he is not guilty of a crime by reason of insanity, the Constitution permits the Government, on the basis of the insanity judgment, to confine him to a mental institution until such time as he has regained his sanity or is no longer a danger to himself or society.

The *Jones* Court also held that a defendant found NGBRI can be committed for a longer period than he would have been incarcerated had he been convicted. For the State to continue to confine a person found NGBRI, however, it must show that the individual is *presently* mentally ill *and* dangerous. See Foucha v. Louisiana, 504 U.S. 71, 77 (1992).[n]

3. POST-CONVICTION CIVIL DETENTION

NOTE ON POST-CONVICTION DETENTION OF SEXUALLY VIOLENT PREDATORS

Civil detention can occur after a criminal conviction. For examplethe Supreme Court has ruled that a state can indefinitely detain a sex offender even after that person has served a criminal sentence—or without any criminal trial—if it can show that an individual has a harm-threatening mental illness that outweighs the "constitutionally protected interest in avoiding physical restraint." Kansas v. Hendricks, 521 U.S. 346, 356 (1997). Several statutes permit sex violent offenders (SVPs) to be civilly committed after serving their criminal sentences, usually based on a finding that they are mentally ill and pose a danger to others. Several thousand people have been involuntarily committed under SVP statutes, and few have ever been released.[o] Some states have

---

[n] Federal law mandates that a person found NGBRI be committed to a mental facility. 18 U.S.C. § 4243. A hearing must be conducted no later than forty days after the verdict to determine whether the insanity acquittee is entitled to release. 18 U.S.C. § 4243(c). Persons found NGBRI of an offense involving bodily injury or serious damage to a person's property must prove by clear and convincing evidence that their release would not create similar danger due to a present mental disease. *Id.* at § 4243(d). Release of a person found NGBRI for any other offense requires proof by a preponderance of the evidence. *Id.*

[o] See Monica Davey & Abbey Goodnough, *Doubts Rise as States Hold Sex Offenders After Prison*, N.Y. TIMES, Mar. 4, 2007 (finding that only 250 confined under SVP laws had ever been released); Adam Deming, *Sex Offender Civil Commitment Programs: Current Practices, Characteristics, and Resident Demographics*, 36 J. Psychiatry & L. 439, 441 (2009) (describing over 3,500 confined under SVP laws).

enacted statutes permitting indefinite civil commitment of other types of "dangerous" offenders.

The Court examined the constitutional status of such detention through consideration of a Kansas Statute, the Sexually Violent Predator's Act (KSVPA). The KSVPA provided for the civil commitment of individuals who, because of a "mental abnormality" or "personality disorder," are more likely to engage in "predatory acts of sexual violence." These individuals did not have mental diseases or defects that rose to the level necessary for involuntary commitment under general involuntary-commitment procedures. Moreover, the treatment modalities under the general involuntary commitment statute were poor fits for the psychiatric features of those offenders whom the KSVPA targeted. Specifically, the KSVPA put in place commitment procedures for (1) presently-confined inmates convicted of a sexually violent offense, but scheduled for release; (2) a person charged with a sexually violent offense found not competent to stand trial; (3) a person charged with a violent sexual offense found not guilty by reason of insanity; and (4) a person charged with a violent sexual offense found not guilty by reason of a mental disease or defect.

In *Kansas v. Hendricks*, 521 U.S. 346, 360 (1997), which involved a criminally-convicted inmate scheduled for release, the Supreme Court held that, "under the appropriate circumstances and when accompanied by proper procedures, incapacitation may be a legitimate end of the civil law." The Court also explained, "A finding of dangerousness, standing alone, is ordinarily not a sufficient ground upon which to justify indefinite involuntary commitment." Thus, the Court added that "[w]e have sustained civil commitment statutes when they have coupled proof of dangerousness with the proof of some additional factor, such as a 'mental illness' or 'mental abnormality.'"

The Supreme Court later clarified, in another challenge to the Kansas statute, that the dangerousness requirement does not mean a "*total* or *complete* lack of control." Kansas v. Crane, 534 U.S. 407, 411 (2002). The Court highlighted the importance of insisting on a high level of dangerousness, noting that such a "distinction is necessary lest civil commitment become a mechanism for retribution or general deterrence-functions properly those of criminal law, not civil commitment." In dissent, Justice Scalia argued that the Court's reasoning rendered the underlying standard of proof vague, such that a judge would have "not a clue" how to instruct a jury. He asked, "How is one to frame for a jury the degree of 'inability to control' which, in the particular case, the nature of the psychiatric diagnosis, and the severity of the mental abnormality require?" That "lack of control" standard has been the subject of substantial scientific and scholarly criticism.[p]

State courts later had to consider whether there was a federal right to have appointed counsel provide adequate representation at the civil commitment hearings. The Kansas Court of Appeals held that state habeas corpus proceedings could be used to challenge the effectiveness of counsel at a civil

---

[p] See, e.g., Stephen J. Morse, *Protecting Liberty and Autonomy: Desert/Disease Jurisprudence*, 48 San Diego L. Rev. 1077, 1112–14 (2011) ("The American Bar Association and the American Psychiatric Association both supported the movement to abolish control tests for legal insanity on the ground that it was impossible to evaluate lack of control objectively."). Are there better ways to predict future dangerousness? See Jennifer L. Skeem & John Monahan, *Current Directions in Violence Risk Assessment*, 20 Current Directions Psychol. Sci. 38, 39–41 (2011); Christopher Slobogin, *Dangerousness and Expertise Redux*, 56 Emory L. J. 275 (2006).

commitment hearing. See In re Ontiberos, 45 Kan. App. 2d 235, 239 (Kan. Ct. App. 2011). The Virginia Supreme Court held the same. See Jenkins v. Director of Virginia Center for Behavioral Rehabilitation, 624 S.E.2d 453, 460–61 (Va. 2006). In contrast, the Minnesota Court of Appeals held that there is no constitutional right to effective assistance of counsel at civil commitment hearings, and thus habeas petitioners cannot be afforded relief on such grounds. See Beaulieu v. Minnesota, 798 N.W.2d 542, 549–50 (Minn. Ct. App. 2011).

In *United States v. Comstock*, 130 S. Ct. 1949, 1961 (2010), the Court upheld civil commitment of federal prisoners certified as "sexually dangerous persons." That civil commitment provision had been enacted as part of the Adam Walsh Child Protection and Safety Act, 18 U.S.C. § 4248 (2006). The Adam Walsh Act requires proof, by "clear and convincing evidence," that the person "has engaged or attempted to engage in sexual violence or child molestation." The prisoners challenged the Act in motions to dismiss the Government's request for commitment. The Court ruled that "Congress reasonably extended its longstanding civil-commitment system to cover mentally ill and sexually dangerous persons who are already in federal custody, even if doing so detains them beyond the termination of their criminal sentence." The Court added that "the Federal Government is the custodian of its prisoners [and, as such] . . . has the constitutional power to act in order to protect nearby (and other) communities from the danger federal prisoners may pose." While the Court decided that Congress had the power to enact measures "necessary and proper" to its authority to hold federal prisoners, the Court did not address possible due process or other constitutional challenges to the statute.[q] The next case involves a federal habeas challenge to state civil commitment of SVPs.

Seling v. Young

United States Supreme Court
531 U.S. 250 (2001)

■ JUSTICE O'CONNOR delivered the opinion of the Court.

Washington State's Community Protection Act of 1990 authorizes the civil commitment of "sexually violent predators," persons who suffer from a mental abnormality or personality disorder that makes them likely to engage in predatory acts of sexual violence. [Young] is confined as a sexually violent predator at the Special Commitment Center (Center), for which [Seling] is the superintendent. After [Young's] challenges to his commitment in state court proved largely unsuccessful, he instituted a habeas action under 28 U.S.C. § 2254, seeking release from confinement. The Washington Supreme Court had already held that the Act is civil, * * * and this Court held a similar commitment scheme for sexually violent predators in Kansas to be civil on its face, *Kansas v. Hendricks*, 521 U.S. 346 (1997). The

---

[q] After *Comstock*, the Fourth Circuit considered a habeas petition filed by an otherwise release-eligible federal prisoner for whom the Government also sought commitment as a sexually-dangerous person under the Adam Walsh Act. The district court had stayed the habeas proceeding pending *Comstock* and, after the Supreme Court decided *Comstock*, the district court granted the petition. The district court concluded that the Act, as applied, amounted to criminal punishment without due process. See Timms v. Johns, 700 F. Supp. 2d 764 (E.D.N.C. 2010). The Fourth Circuit reversed, ruling that the prisoner could not challenge the Act before having been successfully committed. "[T]he district court's discretion to entertain *habeas* petitions and exercise the power of the writ is not boundless," and the petitioner had "failed to exhaust the alternative remedies available for review of his detention in the pending Commitment Action." Timms v. Johns, 627 F.3d 525, 532 (4th Cir. 2010).

Court of Appeals for the Ninth Circuit nevertheless concluded that [Young] could challenge the statute as being punitive "as applied" to him in violation of the Double Jeopardy and Ex Post Facto Clauses, and remanded the case to the District Court for an evidentiary hearing. * * *

[Young] was convicted of six rapes over three decades. Young was scheduled to be released from prison for his most recent conviction in October 1990. One day prior to his scheduled release, the State filed a petition to commit Young as a sexually violent predator.

At the commitment hearing, Young's mental health experts testified that there is no mental disorder that makes a person likely to reoffend and that there is no way to predict accurately who will reoffend. The State called an expert who testified, based upon a review of Young's records, that Young suffered from a severe personality disorder not otherwise specified with primarily paranoid and antisocial features, and a severe paraphilia, which would be classified as either paraphilia sexual sadism or paraphilia not otherwise specified (rape). * * * In the state expert's opinion, severe paraphilia constituted a mental abnormality under the Act. The State's expert concluded that Young's condition, in combination with the personality disorder, the span of time during which Young committed his crimes, his recidivism, his persistent denial, and his lack of empathy or remorse, made it more likely than not that he would commit further sexually violent acts. The victims of Young's rapes also testified. The jury unanimously concluded that Young was a sexually violent predator.

Young and another individual appealed their commitments in state court, arguing that the Act violated the Double Jeopardy, Ex Post Facto, Due Process, and Equal Protection Clauses of the Federal Constitution. In major respects, the Washington Supreme Court held that the Act is constitutional. * * * To the extent the court concluded that the Act violated due process and equal protection principles, those rulings are reflected in subsequent amendments to the Act.

The Washington court reasoned that the claimants' double jeopardy and ex post facto claims hinged on whether the Act is civil or criminal in nature. Following this Court's precedents, the court examined the language of the Act, the legislative history, and the purpose and effect of the statutory scheme. The court found that the legislature clearly intended to create a civil scheme both in the statutory language and legislative history. The court then turned to examine whether the actual impact of the Act is civil or criminal. The Act, the court concluded, is concerned with treating committed persons for a current mental abnormality, and protecting society from the sexually violent acts associated with that abnormality, rather than being concerned with criminal culpability. The court distinguished the goals of incapacitation and treatment from the goal of punishment. The court found that the Washington Act is designed to further legitimate goals of civil confinement and that the claimants had failed to provide proof to the contrary. * * *

In 1994, after unsuccessful challenges to his confinement in state court, Young filed a habeas action under 28 U.S.C. § 2254 against the superintendent of the Center. Young contended that the Act was unconstitutional and that his confinement was illegal. He sought immediate release. The District Court granted the writ, concluding that the Act violated substantive due process, that the Act was criminal rather than civil, and that it violated the double jeopardy and ex post facto guarantees of the Constitution. The superintendent appealed. While the appeal was pending, this

Court decided *Kansas v. Hendricks*, 521 U.S. 346 (1997), which held that Kansas' Sexually Violent Predator Act, on its face, met substantive due process requirements, was nonpunitive, and thus did not violate the Double Jeopardy and Ex Post Facto Clauses. The Ninth Circuit Court of Appeals remanded Young's case to the District Court for reconsideration in light of *Hendricks.* * * *

On remand, the District Court denied Young's petition. Young appealed and the Ninth Circuit reversed and remanded in part and affirmed in part. * * * The Ninth Circuit affirmed the District Court's ruling that Young's confinement did not violate the substantive due process requirement that the State prove mental illness and dangerousness to justify confinement. * * *

The Ninth Circuit reversed the District Court's determination that because the Washington Act is civil, Young's double jeopardy and ex post facto claims must fail. The "linchpin" of Young's claims, the court reasoned, was whether the Act was punitive "as applied" to Young. The court did not read this Court's decision in *Hendricks* to preclude the possibility that the Act could be punitive as applied. The court reasoned that actual conditions of confinement could divest a facially valid statute of its civil label upon a showing by the clearest proof that the statutory scheme is punitive in effect. * * *

As the Washington Supreme Court held and the Ninth Circuit acknowledged, we proceed on the understanding that the Washington Act is civil in nature. The Washington Act is strikingly similar to a commitment scheme we reviewed four Terms ago in *Kansas v. Hendricks*, 521 U.S. 346 (1997). In fact, Kansas patterned its Act after Washington's. * * * In *Hendricks*, we explained that the question whether an Act is civil or punitive in nature is initially one of statutory construction. * * * A court must ascertain whether the legislature intended the statute to establish civil proceedings. A court will reject the legislature's manifest intent only where a party challenging the Act provides the clearest proof that the statutory scheme is so punitive in either purpose or effect as to negate the State's intention. * * *

We also examined the conditions of confinement provided by the Act. * * * The Court was aware that sexually violent predators in Kansas were to be held in a segregated unit within the prison system. We explained that the Act called for confinement in a secure facility because the persons confined were dangerous to the community. We noted, however, that conditions within the unit were essentially the same as conditions for other involuntarily committed persons in mental hospitals. Moreover, confinement under the Act was not necessarily indefinite in duration. Finally, we observed that in addition to protecting the public, the Act also provided treatment for sexually violent predators. We acknowledged that not all mental conditions were treatable. For those individuals with untreatable conditions, however, we explained that there was no federal constitutional bar to their civil confinement, because the State had an interest in protecting the public from dangerous individuals with treatable as well as untreatable conditions. * * *

We hold that respondent cannot obtain release through an "as-applied" challenge to the Washington Act on double jeopardy and ex post facto grounds * * * [because] an "as-applied" analysis would prove unworkable. Such an analysis would never conclusively resolve whether a particular scheme is punitive and would thereby prevent a final determination of the scheme's validity under the Double Jeopardy and Ex Post Facto Clauses. * * * Unlike a fine, confinement is not a fixed event. As petitioner notes, it extends over time under conditions that are subject to change. The particular features of confinement may affect how a confinement scheme is evaluated to determine whether it is civil rather than punitive, but it remains no less true that the query must be answered definitively. The civil nature of a confinement scheme cannot be altered based merely on vagaries in the implementation of the authorizing statute. * * *

Our decision today does not mean that respondent and others committed as sexually violent predators have no remedy for the alleged conditions and treatment regime at the Center. The text of the Washington Act states that those confined under its authority have the right to adequate care and individualized treatment. * * * As petitioner acknowledges, if the Center fails to fulfill its statutory duty, those confined may have a state law cause of action. It is for the Washington courts to determine whether the Center is operating in accordance with state law and provide a remedy. * * *

State courts, in addition to federal courts, remain competent to adjudicate and remedy challenges to civil confinement schemes arising under the Federal Constitution. * * *

Finally, we note that a § 1983 action against the Center is pending in the Western District of Washington. * * * The Center operates under an injunction that requires it to adopt and implement a plan for training and hiring competent sex offender therapists; to improve relations between residents and treatment providers; to implement a treatment program for residents containing elements required by prevailing professional standards; to develop individual treatment programs; and to provide a psychologist or psychiatrist expert in the diagnosis and treatment of sex offenders to supervise the staff. A Special Master has assisted in bringing the Center into compliance with the injunction. In its most recent published opinion on the matter, the District Court noted some progress at the Center in meeting the requirements of the injunction. * * *

We have not squarely addressed the relevance of conditions of confinement to a first instance determination, and that question need not be resolved here. An Act, found to be civil, cannot be deemed punitive "as applied" to a single individual in violation of the Double Jeopardy and Ex Post Facto Clauses and provide cause for release.

The judgment of the United States Court of Appeals for the Ninth Circuit is therefore reversed, and the case is remanded for further proceedings consistent with this opinion.

It is so ordered.

[A concurring opinion by JUSTICE SCALIA, joined by JUSTICE SOUTER is omitted, as is a concurring opinion by JUSTICE THOMAS and a dissent by JUSTICE STEVENS].

———————

NOTES AND QUESTIONS ON YOUNG

1)   Confinement is Not Fixed. Is civil commitment a moving target? The confinement is an ongoing status, and one that is revisited over time (with reevaluation of the detainee's condition). At the end of its opinion, the Supreme Court indicated that a "first instance" challenge to a civil commitment statute could still be appropriate. Here, an appeal had already been filed in state court, and the Washington Supreme Court agreed that this commitment statute created a constitutionally-permissible civil, non-punitive detention.

2) Section 1983. One reason few prisoners make habeas challenges to civil commitment is that challenges to the constitutionality of the statutory scheme permitting a commitment may be brought in federal court, not using habeas petitions, but instead as civil rights actions under 42 U.S.C. § 1983. They seek a declaration that the statute is unconstitutional or an injunction to improve the conditions of confinement. The Supreme Court mentioned that such litigation had been used to enjoin Washington state. We discuss such civil rights litigation by prisoners in Chapter 11—challenges to conditions of confinement must typically be brought using § 1983 and not habeas corpus. Can ongoing injunctions be better adapted to "conditions that are subject to change"?

3) Habeas Procedure and Civil Commitment. Other features of habeas process may make habeas challenges to civil commitment difficult. In *Martin v. Bartow*, 628 F.3d 871 (7th Cir. 2010), the Seventh Circuit addressed when a civilly committed person may bring a federal habeas petition. AEDPA imposes a one-year statute of limitations on habeas filings. In 1996, Stanley Martin was committed as a sexually violent predator in Wisconsin, after having pleaded guilty to two charges of a nonsexual nature, and his status was reviewed annually. He brought a federal habeas petition in 2005, and the state argued that it was untimely because the one-year limitations period began immediately after his 1996 commitment. The Seventh Circuit emphasized the annual review of his status and that his continuing commitment was based on the prior findings and convictions. As a result, "unlike a conviction and sentence for a discrete criminal offense, a person's current status as a sexually violent person is a determination that is constantly and forever disputable as a matter of constitutional law." Therefore, the appeals court reasoned, Martin's 2005 habeas petition was a timely challenge to his ongoing detention. Is this outcome consistent with a principle that prisoners should be able use habeas review as a final avenue to appeal a conviction?

Civil detainees can continually bring challenges in periodic status reviews, state appeals, and state habeas proceedings; as a result, fewer may seek relief using federal habeas corpus. When they do so, they must exhaust the claim by bringing at least one round of challenges to their civil commitment in state courts. They must also follow the procedures set out in the federal habeas statutes, discussed in Chapters to come. Federal courts have dismissed habeas petitions filed by civilly-committed detainees if they have not exhausted those civil remedies.[r]

NOTE ON INCAPACITATION

Do these rules for civil detention enable what is equivalent to unauthorized criminal punishment without the typical protections that criminal procedure supplies? Consider the degree to which society accepts incapacitation and

---

[r] See, e.g., Archuleta v. Hedrick, 365 F.3d 644 (8th Cir. 2004) (noting "habeas corpus is an extraordinary remedy typically available only when the petitioner has no other remedy" and dismissing petition by federal prisoner where federal civil commitment statute provided a procedure for remedy sought).

prevention of future crime as a legitimate goal of criminal punishment. Paul H. Robinson has argued that "the justice system's focus has shifted from punishing past crimes to preventing future violations through the incarceration and control of dangerous offenders." *Punishing Dangerousness: Cloaking Preventive Detention as Criminal Justice*, 114 Harv. L. Rev. 1429, 1429–31 (2001). Not everyone agrees that incapacitation is a valid objective of civil detention or criminal sanction. See, e.g., Stephen J. Morse, *Blame and Danger: An Essay on Preventive Detention*, 76 B.U. L. Rev. 113, 116–22 (1996) ("[R]eadily available preventive detention may cause society to ignore other, potentially fairer and more effective interventions to prevent violence."). For the argument that a person's inability to be deterred through criminal punishment should be the criteria for preventative detention, see Christopher Slobogin, *A Jurisprudence of Dangerousness*, 98 Nw. U. L. Rev. 1 (2003) ("[T]he core trait that normatively distinguishes the dangerous person who may be preventively detained from the dangerous person who may not be is imperviousness to criminal punishment, or what I shall call undeterrability."); see also Alec Walen, *A Punitive Precondition for Preventive Detention: Lost Status as a Foundation for a Lost Immunity*, 48 San Diego L. Rev. 1229, 1236–37 n.27, 1256, 1259–60 (2011). If you believe that incapacitation is a legitimate goal of criminal punishment, does that help or hurt the case for using civil commitment?

4. PREVENTATIVE AND PUBLIC HEALTH DETENTION

NOTE ON PREVENTATIVE AND PUBLIC HEALTH CIVIL DETENTION

Civil detention that is not premised on a prior conviction, but is based on a substantial state interest, consists of either preventative detention—based on a finding of dangerousness either to oneself or others—or detention in certain other emergency situations designed to protect members of the public. For example, aside from the sex-offender context, other civil detention statutes implement public-health quarantines, enable severe-weather detentions for the homeless, or accompany mandatory drug and alcohol treatment. See Adam Klein & Benjamin Wittes, *Preventative Detention in American Theory and Practice*, 2 Harv. Nat'l Sec. J. 85 (2011).

NOTE ON CIVIL COMMITMENT FOR MENTAL ILLNESS

Many people were once housed in mental hospitals—close to 600,000 patients were housed in public mental hospitals by the mid-twentieth century—but public scrutiny led to de-institutionalization of those hospitals. See Valerie L. Collins, *Camouflaged Legitimacy: Civil Commitment, Property Rights, and Legal Isolation*, 52 How. L. J. 407 (2009). Bernard Harcourt called mental hospitalization part of an "incarceration revolution" that pre-dated the more recent explosion in prison populations. See Bernard E. Harcourt, *From the Asylum to the Prison: Rethinking the Incarceration Revolution*, 84 Tex. L. Rev. 1751 (2006).

In 1975, the Supreme Court held that "a State cannot constitutionally confine without more a nondangerous individual who is capable of surviving safely in freedom by himself or with the help of willing and responsible family members or friends." O'Connor v. Donaldson, 422 U.S. 563, 575 (1975). In *Addington v. Texas*, 441 U.S. 418 (1979), the Court considered what process a person must receive before being civilly committed to a state mental hospital. The Court set itself to the task of locating such custody on a continuum:

> At one end of the spectrum is the typical civil case involving a monetary dispute between private parties. Since society has a minimal concern with the outcome of such private suits, plaintiff's burden of proof is a mere preponderance of the evidence. The litigants thus share the risk of error in roughly equal fashion.

> In a criminal case, on the other hand, the interests of the defendant are of such magnitude that historically and without any explicit constitutional requirement they have been protected by standards of proof designed to exclude as nearly as possible the likelihood of an erroneous judgment. In the administration of criminal justice, our society imposes almost the entire risk of error upon itself. This is accomplished by requiring under the Due Process Clause that the state prove the guilt of an accused beyond a reasonable doubt.

For civil commitment proceedings, the Supreme Court cited to an "intermediate standard," which requires clear and convincing evidence. Recall from the last Chapter how an intermediate standard is also used in some areas of immigration law, including at removal hearings before immigration judges. The Court explained the rule in terms of acceptable error costs:

> The state has a legitimate interest under its *parens patriae* powers in providing care to its citizens who are unable because of emotional disorders to care for themselves; the state also has authority under its police power to protect the community from the dangerous tendencies of some who are mentally ill. Under the Texas Mental Health Code, however, the State has no interest in confining individuals involuntarily if they are not mentally ill or if they do not pose some danger to themselves or others. Since the preponderance standard creates the risk of increasing the number of individuals erroneously committed, it is at least unclear to what extent, if any, the state's interests are furthered by using a preponderance standard in such commitment proceedings.

However, the Court noted that "[t]he heavy standard applied in criminal cases manifests our concern that the risk of error to the individual must be minimized even at the risk that some who are guilty might go free. The full force of that idea does not apply to a civil commitment." The Court emphasized that "even though an erroneous confinement should be avoided in the first instance, the layers of professional review and observation of the patient's condition, and the concern of family and friends generally will provide continuous opportunities for an erroneous commitment to be corrected." Further, the Court justified the less-than-maximal requirement by reference to the inherent limitations of clinical diagnosis:

> Whether the individual is mentally ill and dangerous to either himself or others and is in need of confined therapy turns on the *meaning* of the facts which must be interpreted by expert psychiatrists and psychologists. Given the lack of certainty and the fallibility of psychiatric diagnosis, there is a serious question as to whether a state could ever prove beyond a reasonable doubt that an individual is both mentally ill and likely to be dangerous.

The Court addressed the process required for the custody determination, but not the process required for any subsequent habeas review. However, where the state's burden of proof in the underlying commitment proceeding is lower, a prisoner may find it more difficult to challenge the adequacy of the factual basis for the commitment in a subsequent habeas case.

Should we share the Supreme Court's concern about the imprecise nature of the psychiatric determinations upon which these civil commitments are based? In *Kansas v. Crane*, 434 U.S. 407 (2002), the Court did remark that "the science of psychiatry, which informs but does not control ultimate legal determinations, is an ever-advancing science, whose distinctions do not seek precisely to mirror those of the law."

NOTE ON CIVIL COMMITMENT FOR SUBSTANCE ABUSE

Many states also have statutes permitting involuntary detention of alcohol or drug addicts that pose a danger to themselves, in order to provide mandatory treatment. Although it has never ruled on a challenge to such a statute, the Supreme Court has suggested that "a State might establish a program of compulsory treatment for those addicted to narcotics [which] might require periods of involuntary confinement." Robinson v. California, 370 U.S. 660, 665 (1962).[s] Habeas corpus traditionally has been used to challenge unsupported or noncomplying civil commitments under such statutes. For an opinion by California Supreme Court Chief Judge Roger Traynor finding arbitrary an effort to require substance abusers to sign waiver forms "purporting to dispense with every right granted by the narcotics addict commitment law," and granting the writ, see *In re Walker*, 71 Cal.2d 54, 58–60 (Cal. 1969). Other challenges, however, may be brought using § 1983; such challenges simply seek money damages for allegedly-unconstitutional or illegal commitment. See, e.g. Moline v. City of Castle Rock, 528 F.Supp.2d 1102 (W.D.Wash. 2005).

NOTE ON CIVIL COMMITMENT FOR PUBLIC HEALTH (QUARANTINE)

The government has long used public health problems and quarantines to justify detentions. In *Jacobson v. Massachusetts*, 197 U.S. 11, 27 (1905), the Court emphasized that, "upon the principle of self-defense, of paramount necessity, a community has the right to protect itself against an epidemic of disease which threatens the safety of its members." The Court nonetheless stated that such efforts "are subject to such reasonable conditions as may be deemed by the governing authority [as] essential to the . . . health . . . of the community." The Court suggested that such a detention might last until "the danger of the spread of the disease among the community at large has disappeared." Today, many states have statutes regulating tuberculosis carriers who pose an infection risk.[t] Federal plans now exist to quarantine individuals in the event of an

---

[s] See David F. Chavkin, *"For Their Own Good": Civil Commitment Of Alcohol And Drug-Dependent Pregnant Women*, 37 S.D. L. Rev. 224, 236 (1992).

[t] See Paula Mindes, *Tuberculosis Quarantine: A Review of Legal Issues in Ohio and Other States*, 10 J.L. & Health 403, 420 (1995–96).

outbreak of a pandemic flu.[u] A federal statute provides quarantine authority for purposes of preventing disease transmission. See 42 U.S.C. § 264.

Some state statutes provide for expedited judicial review of detentions.[v] Habeas litigation in this context is infrequent, given that the government exercises only brief custody in emergencies. The "overwhelming majority of such habeas writs are denied, citing either broad police powers or deference to the determinations of health officers."[w] In a case involving fourteen-day detention of a woman at a U.S. Public Health Hospital—due to possible small pox exposure during a trip to Stockholm—the judge denied relief. The court explained that "light use of isolation" would be troubling, but the custody was supported was testimony from "three medical men," and "the consequences of mistaken indulgence can be irretrievably tragic." See United States ex rel. Siegel v. Shinnick, 219 F.Supp. 789 (D.C.N.Y. 1963).

A 1952 decision by the Florida Supreme Court dismissed a habeas petition brought by a person confined in a state sanitarium for people with tuberculosis:

> [W]hat laws or regulations are necessary to protect public health and secure public comfort is a legislative question, and appropriate measures intended and calculated to accomplish these ends are not subject to judicial review . . . except where the regulations adopted for the protection of the public health are arbitrary, oppressive and unreasonable. The court has nothing to do with the wisdom or expediency of the measures adopted.

Moore v. Draper, 57 So. 2d 648 (Fla. 1952). Should habeas review extend farther if the police power or public health justification appears more attenuated? There are reported cases granting habeas corpus where local police had arrested couples for engaging in non-marital sex, but terming it a public health quarantine. For example, a California Court in 1919 released a man and woman who were placed in a "pretended quarantine"—as the court put it—for allegedly violating a local ordinance prohibiting extra-marital relations. The officers claimed that, in their experience "about 90 per cent. of the women so arrested and charged are found to be afflicted with contagious and infectious venereal disease in some form." Ex parte Dillon, 186 P. 170, 171 (Cal. Dist. Ct. App. 1919). Lest one think such litigation is a thing of the past, the American Civil Liberties Union brought a lawsuit in 2007 challenging the placement of an ill tubercular man in a jail cell and not a "least restrictive" environment where he could get medical treatment; the lawsuit resulted in his transfer to a medical facility.[x]

---

[u] See Rebecca Chen, *Closing The Gaps in the U.S. and International Quarantine Systems: Legal Implications of the 2007 Tuberculosis Scare*, 31 Hous. J. Int'l L. 83, 94 (2008).

[v] See, e.g., Wash. Admin. Code § 246–100–055 (2011) ("Any person or group of persons detained by order of a local health officer pursuant to WAC 246–100–040(3) may apply to the court for an order to show cause why the individual or group should not be released; (a) the court shall rule on the application to show cause within forty-eight hours of its filing; (b) if the court grants the application, the court shall schedule a hearing on the order to show cause as soon as practicable; and that (c) the issuance of an order to show cause shall not stay or enjoin an isolation or quarantine order.").

[w] See Christopher Ogolla, *Non-Criminal Habeas Corpus for Quarantine and Isolation Detainees: Serving the Private Right or Violating Public Policy?*, 14 DePaul J. Health Care L. 135, 136 (2011).

[x] See ACLU of Arizona Lawsuit Triggers Transfer of TB Patient to Denver Hospital, *at* http://www.aclu.org/prisoners-rights/aclu-arizona-lawsuit-triggers-transfer-tb-patient-denver-hospital (last visited Feb. 9, 2013).

5. THE BOUNDARIES OF CIVIL DETENTION: CHILD CUSTODY

At common law, habeas corpus was used to determine "the custody of the prisoner according to law." McNally v. Hill, 293 U.S. 131, 136 (1934). Thus, the First Judiciary Act defined its reach as extending to prisoners "in custody." In general, 28 U.S.C. § 2241 extends the federal habeas power only to adjudicate the lawfulness of inmates "in custody."[y] What does it mean for a person to be in custody? A related question involves *when* a prisoner must be in custody for the purposes of a habeas claim. Custody is assessed at the time the habeas petition is filed. Incarceration or actual detention satisfies the requirement, but "custody" has a broader meaning. As the Court has put it, "habeas corpus was made available to challenge less obvious restraints." Preiser v. Rodriguez, 411 U.S. 475, 486 n.7 (1973). The custody requirement is also satisfied if the prisoner was released but remains on probation or parole, or if the prisoner is in civil or criminal detention of any kind, including in a mental institution. See, e.g., Jones v. Cunningham, 371 U.S. 236, 243 (1963) (parole); Wright v. United States, 732 F.2d 1048, 1050 (2d Cir.) (probation); Dow v. Circuit Court of the First Circuit, 995 F.2d 922, 923 (9th Cir.) (1993) (rehabilitation program). In contrast, a person is not "in custody" simply because the person must pay fines, has had a driver's license revoked, is subject to professional discipline, suffers dignitary harm, or loses the right to vote. Is a court hearing a child custody dispute "deciding the lawfulness of custody" within the meaning of the habeas statute?

Lehman v. Lycoming County Children's Services

United States Supreme Court
458 U.S. 502 (1982)

■ JUSTICE POWELL delivered the opinion of the Court.

The question presented is whether the habeas corpus statute, 28 U.S.C. § 2254, confers jurisdiction on the federal courts to consider collateral challenges to state-court judgments involuntarily terminating parental rights.

I

The facts of this case [involve a] Pennsylvania Supreme Court decision terminating the parental rights of petitioner Marjorie Lehman with respect to three sons born in 1963, 1965, and 1969. In 1971, Ms. Lehman discovered that she was pregnant again. Because of housing and other problems related to the care of her sons, Ms. Lehman voluntarily placed them in the legal custody of the Lycoming County Children's Services Agency, and it placed them in foster homes.

Although Ms. Lehman visited her sons monthly, she did not request their return until 1974. At that point, the Lycoming County Children's Services Agency initiated parental termination proceedings. In those proceedings, the Orphan's Court Division of the Lycoming County Court of Common Pleas heard testimony from Agency caseworkers, a psychologist, nutri-

---

[y] The only exception is in 28 U.S.C. § 2241(d)(5), which allows a federal court to issue a writ to allow "prisoners" to testify. Of course, one might legitimately ask when someone might be a "prisoner" but not be "in custody," but suffice it to say that Subsection (d)(5) is nonetheless the only part of § 2241 to which the "in custody" requirement does not formally apply.

tion aides, petitioner, and the three sons. The judge concluded: "[I]t is absolutely clear to the court that, by reason of her very limited social and intellectual development combined with her five-year separation from the children, the mother is incapable of providing minimal care, control and supervision for the three children. Her incapacity cannot and will not be remedied." The court therefore declared that petitioner's parental rights respecting the three sons were terminated.

The Pennsylvania Supreme Court affirmed the termination order based on "parental incapacity, which does not involve parental misconduct." It held that the legislature's power to protect the physical and emotional needs of children authorized termination in the absence of serious harm or risk of serious harm to the children and in the absence of parental misconduct. The court stressed that, "[i]n the instant cases, the basis for termination is several years of demonstrated parental incapacity * * * ." It also held that the statute was not unconstitutionally vague either on its face or as applied.

Petitioner sought this Court's review in a petition for certiorari rather than by appeal. We denied the petition. Petitioner then filed the instant proceeding on January 16, 1979, in the United States District Court for the Middle District of Pennsylvania, seeking a writ of habeas corpus pursuant to 28 U.S.C. 2241 and 2254. Petitioner requested (i) a declaration of the invalidity of the Pennsylvania statute under which her parental rights were terminated; (ii) a declaration that petitioner was the legal parent of the children; and (iii) an order releasing the children to her custody unless within 60 days an appropriate state court judicially determined that the best interest of the children required that temporary custody remain with the State.

The District Court dismissed the petition without a hearing. * * * [T]he court concluded that "the custody maintained by the Respondent over the three Lehman children is not that type of custody to which the federal habeas corpus remedy may be addressed."

Sitting en banc, the Court of Appeals for the Third Circuit affirmed the District Court's order of dismissal * * *.

* * *

The question presented to this Court can be stated more fully as whether federal habeas corpus jurisdiction, under § 2254, may be invoked to challenge the constitutionality of a state statute under which a State has obtained custody of children and has terminated involuntarily the parental rights of their natural parent. * * *

II

A

Petitioner seeks habeas corpus collateral review by a federal court of the Pennsylvania decision. Her application was filed under 28 U.S.C. § 2254(a):

"The Supreme Court, a Justice thereof, a circuit judge, or a district court shall entertain an application for a writ of habeas corpus in behalf of a person in custody pursuant to the judgment of a State court only on the ground that he is in custody in violation of the Constitution or laws or treaties of the United States."

Although the language of § 2254(a), especially in light of § 2241, suggests that habeas corpus is available only to challenge the convictions of prisoners actually in the physical custody of the State, three modern cases have extended it to other situations involving challenges to state-court decisions. * * *

[A]lthough the scope of the writ of habeas corpus has been extended beyond that which the most literal reading of the statute might require, the Court has never considered it a generally available federal remedy for every violation of federal rights. Instead, past decisions have limited the writ's availability to challenges to state-court judgments in situations where—as a result of a state-court criminal conviction—a petitioner has suffered substantial restraints not shared by the public generally. In addition, in each of these cases the Court considered whether the habeas petitioner was "in custody" within the meaning of § 2254.

Ms. Lehman argues that her sons are involuntarily in the custody of the State for purposes of § 2254 because they are in foster homes pursuant to an order issued by a state court. Her sons, of course, are not prisoners. Nor do they suffer any restrictions imposed by a state criminal justice system. These factors alone distinguish this case from all other cases in which this Court has sustained habeas challenges to state-court judgments. Moreover, although the children have been placed in foster homes pursuant to an order of a Pennsylvania court, they are not in the "custody" of the State in the sense in which that term has been used by this Court in determining the availability of the writ of habeas corpus. They are in the "custody" of their foster parents in essentially the same way, and to the same extent, other children are in the custody of their natural or adoptive parents. Their situation in this respect differs little from the situation of other children in the public generally; they suffer no unusual restraints not imposed on other children. They certainly suffer no ["restraint on liberty" or "collateral consequences" that earlier cases have cited as bringing the case within the ambit of the custody requirement]. The "custody" of foster or adoptive parents over a child is not the type of custody that traditionally has been challenged through federal habeas. Ms. Lehman simply seeks to relitigate, through federal habeas, not any liberty interest of her sons, but the interest in her own parental rights.

Although a federal habeas corpus statute has existed ever since 1867, federal habeas has never been available to challenge parental rights or child custody. * * * [F]ederal courts consistently have shown special solicitude for state interests "in the field of family and family-property arrangements." *United States v. Yazell*, 382 U.S. 341, 352 (1966). Under these circumstances, extending the federal writ to challenges to state child-custody decisions—challenges based on alleged constitutional defects collateral to the actual custody decision—would be an unprecedented expansion of the jurisdiction of the lower federal courts.

B

Federalism concerns and the exceptional need for finality in child-custody disputes argue strongly against the grant of Ms. Lehman's petition. The writ of habeas corpus is a major exception to the doctrine of res judicata, as it allows relitigation of a final state-court judgment disposing of precisely the same claims. Because of this tension between the State's interest in finality and the asserted federal interest, federal courts properly have been reluctant to extend the writ beyond its historic purpose. * * *

The State's interest in finality is unusually strong in child-custody disputes. The grant of federal habeas would prolong uncertainty for children such as the Lehman sons, possibly lessening their chances of adoption. It is undisputed that children require secure, stable, long-term, continuous relationships with their parents or foster parents. There is little that can be as detrimental to a child's sound development as uncertainty over whether he is to remain in his current "home," under the care of his parents or foster parents, especially when such uncertainty is prolonged. Extended uncertainty would be inevitable in many cases if federal courts had jurisdiction to relitigate state custody decisions.

III

Petitioner argues that habeas corpus should be available to her because it has been used as a procedure in child-custody cases in various States and in England. She notes that * * * [this] Court indicated that in construing the habeas statute, reference may be made to the common law and to practices in the States and in England. It is true that habeas has been used in child-custody cases in England and in many of the States. * * * As [several] cases illustrate, the term "custody" in 28 U.S.C. § 2255—authorizing federal-court collateral review of federal decisions—could be construed to include the type of custody the Lehman children are subject to, since they are in foster homes pursuant to court orders. But reliance on what may be appropriate within the federal system or within a state system is of little force where—as in this case—a state judgment is attacked collaterally in a federal court. It is one thing to use a proceeding called "habeas corpus" in resolving child-custody disputes within a single system obligated to resolve such disputes. The question in such a case may be which procedure is most appropriate. The system is free to set time limits on the bringing of such actions as well as to impose other requirements to ensure finality and a speedy resolution of disputes in cases involving child custody or termination of parental rights. In this case, however, petitioner would have the federal judicial system entertain a writ that is not time-barred to challenge collaterally a final judgment entered in a state judicial system. * * *

IV

The considerations in a child-custody case are quite different from those present in any prior case in which this Court has sustained federal-court jurisdiction under § 2254. The federal writ of habeas corpus, representing as it does a profound interference with state judicial systems and the finality of state decisions, should be reserved for those instances in which the federal interest in individual liberty is so strong that it outweighs federalism and finality concerns. Congress has indicated no intention that the reach of § 2254 encompass a claim like that of petitioner. We therefore hold that § 2254 does not confer federal-court jurisdiction. The decision below, affirming the denial of a writ of habeas corpus, therefore is affirmed.

It is so ordered.

■ JUSTICE BLACKMUN, with whom JUSTICE BRENNAN and JUSTICE MARSHALL join, dissenting.

Although I can sympathize with what the Court seeks to accomplish in this case today, I cannot reconcile myself to its holding that "§ 2254 does not confer federal-court jurisdiction" * * * to consider collateral challenges to state-court judgments involuntarily terminating parental rights. In my view, the literal statutory requisites for the exercise of § 2254 federal habeas corpus jurisdiction are satisfied here—in particular, the requirement that petitioner's children must be "in custody." Because I believe the Court could have achieved much the same practical result in this area without decreeing a complete withdrawal of federal jurisdiction, I respectfully dissent.

I

Justice Black, speaking for a unanimous Court in *Jones v. Cunningham*, 371 U.S. 236, 243 (1963), observed that * * * [:]

"While limiting its availability to those "in custody," the statute does not attempt to mark the boundaries of "custody" nor in any way other than by use of that word attempt to limit the situations in which the writ can be used. To determine whether habeas corpus could be used to test the legality of a given restraint on liberty, this Court has generally looked to common-law usages and the history of habeas corpus both in England and in this country."

Even a brief historical examination of common-law usages teaches two lessons: first, for centuries, the English and American common-law courts have had the undisputed power to issue writs of habeas corpus ordering the release of children from unlawful custody; and, second, those courts have exercised broad discretion in deciding whether or not to invoke that power in a given case. English common-law courts traditionally were authorized to order the release of minor children from unlawful custody. Relying on the English tradition, American state courts very early asserted their own power to issue common-law habeas writs in child-custody matters.

While acknowledging that "habeas has been used in child-custody cases in England and in many of the States," * * * the Court suggests that a state court derives its authority to issue a writ of habeas corpus in such disputes not from the common law, but from "the fabric of its reserved jurisdiction over child custody matters." * * * While such a conclusion is not illogical, it is surely ahistorical. * * * A state court's traditional power to issue a writ of habeas corpus to free a confined child always has been derived directly from the nature of the writ, not from any reserved jurisdiction over child-custody matters. * * *

The codification of the writ into federal law indicates no congressional intent to contract its common-law scope. * * * Nor, since [the writ was made applicable to state custodians in 1867], has this Court ever held that the congressional purpose originally underlying the statute barred use of the federal writ to free children from unlawful state custody. The Court's more recent precedents have firmly established § 2254's "in custody" requirement as its most flexible element, stressing that the test of "custody" is not present physical restraint, but whether "there are other restraints on a man's liberty, restraints not shared by the public generally, which have been thought sufficient in the English-speaking world to support the issuance of habeas corpus."

Today the Court bows in the direction of this historical precedent only by leaving open the possible availability of federal habeas if a child is actually confined in a state institution, rather than in the custody of a foster parent pursuant to a court order. * * *

First, the Court restrictively reads [the precedential cases] to involve only substantial and unusual restraints suffered by individuals "as a result of a state-court *criminal conviction*." Yet those decisions plainly drew no distinction between criminal and civil detention. To the contrary, they declared in unusually broad and expansive language that the habeas writ must be widely available "as a remedy for severe restraints on individual liberty." * * *

Second, the Court argues that children living with foster parents somehow are not in the State's "custody" because "they suffer no unusual restraints not imposed on other children." Yet because unadopted children whose ties with their natural parents have been severed are wards of the State, the State decides where they will live, reserves the right to move them to new physical settings at will, and consents to their marriage, their enlistment in the Armed Forces, as well as all major decisions regarding medical, psychiatric, and surgical treatment.

This Court has found the statutory concept of "custody" broad enough to confer jurisdiction on federal courts to hear and determine habeas applications from petitioners who have freely traveled across state borders while released on their own recognizance, *Hensley v. Municipal Court*, and who are on unattached, inactive Army Reserve duty, *Strait v. Laird*, 406 U.S. 341 (1972). Under these precedents, I have difficulty finding that minor children, who as state wards are fully subject to state-court custody orders, are not sufficiently and peculiarly restrained to be deemed "in custody" for the purposes of the habeas corpus statute. * * *

Third, the Court asserts that "[f]ederalism concerns and the exceptional need for finality in child-custody disputes argue strongly against the grant of Ms. Lehman's petition." While I am fully sensitive to these concerns, once again I cannot understand how they deprive federal courts of statutory jurisdiction to entertain habeas petitions. Although the Court's decisions involving collateral attack by state prisoners against state criminal convictions have recognized similar federalism and finality concerns, they have never held that those interests erect jurisdictional bars to relief. * * *

II

As a matter of history and precedent, then, "[t]here can be no question of a federal district court's power to entertain an application for a writ of habeas corpus in a case such as this * * * . The issue . . . goes rather to the appropriate exercise of that power." *Francis v. Henderson*, 425 U.S. at 538–539. In my view, the difficult discretionary question in this case is whether, 11 years after petitioner voluntarily relinquished her sons to state custody and 4 years after the involuntary termination of her parental rights was affirmed on direct appeal, she remains a proper "next friend" to apply for the federal habeas writ on behalf of her natural children. * * *

On [this] record, I believe that the District Court could have found, as a discretionary matter, that petitioner had not made a sufficient showing that she acted in the interests of the children to warrant issuing her the writ as their "next friend." Indeed, I believe that the common-law habeas corpus tradition would have supported recognition of broad district court discretion to withhold the writ in all but the most extraordinary cases, where the district court had strong reason to believe both that the conditions of the child's confinement unconstitutionally constrained that child's liberty, and that release of the child to his natural parent very likely would serve the child's best interest.

* * * Because the Court overrides contrary history and precedent to find that habeas jurisdiction does not lie, I dissent.

NOTES AND QUESTIONS ON LEHMAN

1) A Non-Textualist, Ahistorical Interpretation. As the majority opinion notes, 28 U.S.C. § 2254(a) provided that habeas run on "behalf of a person in custody pursuant to the judgment of a State court." The statute did not say that the state judgment in question be a criminal conviction, and Congress presumably knew how to specify that subset of judgments if it wanted to. Moreover, as Justice Blackmun emphasized, habeas was in fact used by English judges to consider child custody, so there is nothing historically implausible involving this particular use of the writ. Professor Paul Halliday has described how King's Bench Justices intervened in a range of family disputes. Not only did they use habeas corpus to resolve child custody disputes—including to "permit women, even minors, to determine custody disputes for themselves"—but also "to release wives from abusive husbands," to investigate "allegations of lunacy that led to confinement," and to intervene in "marriage disputes" in which offending parties were imprisoned. Paul Halliday, *Habeas Corpus: From England to Empire* 122–133 (2010). In *Lehman*, what is unusual about the alignment of opinions on the textualist question? Is a textualist approach usually used to expand or to restrict relief? What about the ordinary interpretive result of recourse to history at the founding?

2) Jurisdictional Limits versus Relief on the Merits. The dissenters would presumably prefer to frame limits on habeas relief in child custody situations as substantive limits on merits relief, rather than as a jurisdictional limitation on federal courts. The majority phrases its concerns over recognizing jurisdiction in several ways, but the various rationales all reflect a fundamental concern that states not be second-guessed in their child-custody determinations. Do you think that recognizing such interests requires a jurisdictional limitation (as the majority argues), or do you think that a rule pertaining to substantive limits on relief would be sufficient (as the dissent argues)? Could federal courts accommodate the substantial interest in the finality of state child-custody determinations by recognizing jurisdiction but withholding relief in most cases? What would such a rule look like?

3) The Elasticity of "Custody." What would be the practical implications of a broad reading of "custody" to include child custody? What other sorts of judgments involve some form of custody order that are not a state conviction? Note, for example, that child custody may be adjusted at any time based on changing circumstances and the "best interests" of the child, under different state law tests. See, e.g. June Carbone & Naomi Cahn, *Judging Families*, 77 UMKC L. Rev. 267, 288 (2008) (explaining that custody determinations are made "at the state level in accordance with legislation that varies from state-to-state, but that also typically adopts a relatively open-ended 'best interest of the child' standard"). Family court judges may have special expertise in reaching judgments as to what is in the best interests of the child. On the other hand, many state courts still permit state habeas to be used to challenge child custody decisions. See, e.g., In re Marriage of Osborne, 21 Kan. App. 2d 374, 380 (1995) ("[t]he appropriate remedy for a third party seeking custody is a suit in equity or a habeas corpus action."). Is the explanation that complex value judgments must be made to decide what is in the best interests of a child? Professors Carbone and Cahn point out that "[f]amily law is on the front lines of a culture war . . . Issues such as abortion, gay marriage, nonmarital parenthood, and teen sexuality are symbols of cultural division." Carbone and Cahn, *Judg-*

ing Families, 77 UMKC L. Rev. at 267. How do the various forms of civil custody discussed differ from the child custody at issue here?

4)   Domestic Relations Exceptionalism or Coverture? Is this case part of a general reluctance among federal judges to handle family law matters? Think of the domestic relations exception to diversity jurisdiction in the federal courts, which is entirely judge-made and not based on any historical or textual understanding of the diversity statute. See, Ankenbrandt v. Richards, 504 U.S. 689 (1992) ("We thus are content to rest our conclusion that a domestic relations exception exists as a matter of statutory construction not on the accuracy of the historical justifications on which it was seemingly based, but rather on Congress' apparent acceptance of this construction of the diversity jurisdiction provisions . . ."). In *Ankenbrandt,* the Court noted there also that "state courts are more eminently suited to work of this type than are federal courts, which lack the close association with state and local government organizations dedicated to handling issues that arise out of conflicts over divorce, alimony, and child custody decrees." The exception was first announced in *Barber v. Barber,* 62 U.S. (21 How.) 582 (1859).

For criticism of the domestic relations exception, see Jill Elaine Hasday, *Federalism and the Family Reconstructed,* 45 UCLA L. Rev. 1297, 1307 (1998); Judith Resnik, *"Naturally" Without Gender: Women, Jurisdiction, and the Federal Courts,* 66 N.Y.U. L. Rev. 1682 (1991). Professor Hasday argues that the exception had its origins in coverture, and that "the history of this exception, and its very reason for coming into being in the nineteenth century, are inextricably connected to a legal view of women that is unconstitutional under modern equal protection doctrine." Is the *Lehman* Court selectively relying on tradition—not common law—but a more troubling nineteenth-century view of localism in family law that treats women as lacking certain legal capacity? To frame the question more broadly, should *Lehman* be read as an idiosyncratic child-custody exception, and part of a general reluctance to reach family law cases? Or should it be read as a more general statement about the required relationship between custody and a criminal judgment—and a case seeking to narrow the types of custody cognizable on federal habeas?

5)   Review Question. Suppose that a prisoner was civilly committed after serving a sentence for a sex offense. He is then released. Under state law, he must register as a sex offender, which deprives him of certain liberties. He files a federal habeas petition and argues that the state sex-offender registration statute does not exempt people who pose "no risk" of danger, and that his registration is required only on the ground that he was previously convicted. Does a lack of state process for determining future dangerousness require greater habeas scrutiny—or since the type of "custody" here is not a physical commitment, and is premised on a prior conviction, does the state have to do less to justify its decision? See Connecticut Dept. of Public Safety v. Doe, 538 U.S. 1, 7–8 (2003).

CHAPTER 9

MILITARY COMMISSIONS

1. INTRODUCTORY NOTES ON THE LAW OF WAR AND MILITARY CUSTODY

A quintessential use of the habeas privilege is to challenge military custody. There are several types of military custody, ranging from detention under the authority of a military commission to "detention to prevent a combatant's return to the battlefield," the latter of which a Supreme Court plurality called "a fundamental incident of waging war." Hamdi v. Rumsfeld, 542 U.S. 507, 519 (2004). As you read the cases that follow, be careful to distinguish between "substantive" questions about the lawfulness of military custody and "remedial" questions about whether a prisoner may use the habeas privilege to challenge it. We have arranged this Chapter in a way that highlights the difference.

The military's power to detain individuals does not flow from Article III. The custodial authority instead arises under the constitutional articles that specify legislative and executive power. By contrast, the availability of the habeas privilege to challenge military custody *does* involve tough Article III questions. Usually, the first step in answering the substantive question whether the United States is exercising lawful military custody involves identifying the source of constitutional and/or statutory power under which the military claims authority to detain a prisoner.

The Notes that follow provide a brief overview of the body of international law—implemented and supplemented by statutes and regulations—that governs military detention. We define key terms that will appear throughout this Chapter: the law of war, prisoners of war (POWs), courts martial, enemy aliens, enemy combatants, and military commissions. The second Section explores the relationship between the habeas privilege and power exercised by military commissions, examining military tribunals during the Civil War, World War II, and following the September 11, 2001 attacks.

NOTES ON THE LAW OF WAR

1)   Law of War. The Latin phrase *jus in bello* means "law in war," and refers to a body of international law governing armed conflicts.[a] There are a number of sources for the international law that applies to armed conflicts, including customary international law and treaties such as the Geneva and Hague Con-

---

[a] This body of law is often called the "law of war," but perhaps a more descriptively-accurate term is "the law of armed conflict." The relevant law reaches belligerency that does not involve a formal declaration of war, and formal declarations of war are now rare. Those approaching *jus in bello* from a human-rights perspective prefer the term "international humanitarian law" (IHL). We use "law of war" chiefly because the Supreme Court opinions appearing in this Chapter do so.

ventions. These sources constitute international law generally, and they represent the substantive law of war.[b]

The law of war has a rich legal history in the United States. One of the first sets of modern rules reflecting law-of-war principles was issued to the Union Army during the Civil War. General Order No. 100 was titled "Instructions for the Government of Armies of the United States in the Field."[c] A modern U.S. Defense Department directive on the law of war expressly references the scope of the law of war and identifies its international origins:

> That part of international law that regulates the conduct of armed hostilities . . . is often called the "law of armed conflict." The law of war encompasses all international law for the conduct of hostilities binding on the United States or its individual citizens, including treaties and international agreements to which the United States is a party, and applicable customary international law.[d]

2)   The Geneva Conventions. Perhaps the most critical treaties regarding detentions and armed conflicts are the four Geneva Conventions, concluded after World War II. The subject matter ranges from treatment of the wounded and sick in the field (the first Convention) and at sea (the second)—to the Conventions of greatest interest here—the third, which relates to Prisoners of War (POWs), and the fourth, which relates to protection of civilians.[e] As the "Common Articles" (the initial provisions that appear in all four Conventions) explain, the Geneva Conventions apply exclusively (with the exception of Common Article 3, described next) to states that are parties to the treaties (High Contracting Parties). The Geneva Conventions define international armed conflicts quite precisely, but the definition and scope of non-international armed conflicts remains contested. All countries have ratified the Geneva Conventions.[f] One theme this Chapter explores is the friction between a body of international law developed to govern nation states, and its application to a "war on terror" waged against more loosely-defined, non-nation-state groups (i.e. the Taliban and Al Qaeda) that do not themselves abide by the law of war.

3)   Common Article 3. Common Article 3 applies to conflicts termed "not of an international character"—the meaning of which has been the source of some controversy. In general, Common Article 3 applies to conflicts between a High Contracting Party and non-state armed groups (often fighting within the bor-

---

[b] For treatises on the subject, see Leslie C. Green, *The Contemporary Law of Armed Conflict* (2d ed. 2000); Adam Roberts & Richard Guelff, *Documents on the Laws of War* (3d ed. 2000).

[c] For extended treatments of this set of rules, also known as Lieber's Code, after its drafter, Professor Francis Lieber, see, e.g., Richard Shelly Hartigan, *Lieber's Code and the Law of War* 20–23 (1983); John Fabian Witt, *Lincoln's Code: The Laws of War in American History* (2012); David Glazier, Ignorance is Not Bliss: *The Law of Belligerent Occupation and the U.S. Invasion of Iraq*, 58 Rutgers L. Rev. 121, 147, 151-58 (2005).

[d] Dep't of Def. Directive 2311.01E, para. 3.1 (May 9, 2006).

[e] Convention for the Amelioration of the Condition of the Wounded and Sick in Armed Forces in the Field art. 3, Aug. 12, 1949, 6 U.S.T. 3114, 75 U.N.T.S. 31 (Geneva Convention I); Convention for the Amelioration of the Condition of the Wounded, Sick, and Shipwrecked Members of Armed Forces at Sea art. 3, Aug. 12, 1949, 6 U.S.T. 3217, 75 U.N.T.S. 85 (Geneva Convention II); Convention Relative to the Treatment of Prisoners of War art. 3, Aug. 12, 1949, 6 U.S.T. 3316, 75 U.N.T.S. 135, (Geneva Convention III); Convention Relative to the Protection of Civilian Persons in Time of War art. 3, Aug. 12, 1949, 6 U.S.T. 3516, 75 U.N.T.S. 287 (Geneva Convention IV).

[f] Int'l Comm. Of the Red Cross, Geneva Conventions of 1949 Achieve Universal Acceptance (Aug. 21, 2006).

ders of a High Contracting Party) or to conflicts between two non-state armed groups. Common Article 3 states in part:

> (1) Persons taking no active part in the hostilities, including members of armed forces who have laid down their arms and those placed hors de combat by sickness, wounds, detention, or any other cause, shall in all circumstances be treated humanely, without any adverse distinction founded on race, colour, religion or faith, sex, birth or wealth, or any other similar criteria.

Common Article 3 adds that such persons should be protected from "outrages upon personal dignity, in particular, humiliating and degrading treatment." Common Article 3(d) also prohibits "[t]he passing of sentences and the carrying out of executions without previous judgment pronounced by a regularly constituted court affording all the judicial guarantees which are recognized as indispensable by civilized peoples." Thus, even in non-international conflicts where non-POWs are detained and prosecuted, they have a right to be tried before "a regularly constituted court." We will soon discuss what that broadly-phrased requirement means.

4)   POWs in International Armed Conflicts. POWs are an important prisoner category. Except for Common Article 3, the Geneva Conventions apply only to international conflicts; POW status therefore attaches only in international conflicts covered by those Conventions. The Geneva Conventions do not provide any protections to citizens of the *detaining* power, under the assumption that the detaining country will offer protections when it detains its own citizens.

Some of the most detailed and best-known provisions of the Geneva Conventions relate to POWs, such as the rule that captured POWs must only provide their "name, rank, and serial number." Geneva Convention III, art. 17. The Third Geneva Convention defines POWs as including several categories of people "who have fallen into the power of the enemy." Geneva Convention III, art. 4.[g] POWs may not be prosecuted for acts that they performed during a war and that were consistent with the Geneva Conventions, such as killing enemy forces. Punishment for such acts is foreclosed by what is termed "combatant immunity." POWs, however, may be prosecuted for violating the law of war—performing belligerent acts not permitted by the Conventions—such as torture or killing civilians. Who or what entity decides whether a person should be detained as a POW? Article 5 states:

> Should any doubt arise as to whether persons, having committed a belligerent act and having fallen into the hands of the enemy, belong to any of the categories enumerated in Article 4, such persons shall enjoy the protection of the present Convention until such time as their status has been determined by a competent tribunal.

What is a "competent tribunal," commonly called an "Article 5 tribunal"? The Convention says no more about what such a tribunal need involve.

---

[g] These categories include, for example, "[m]embers of the armed forces of a Party to the conflict, as well as members of militias or volunteer corps forming part of such armed forces." These categories also include other, less organized forces that belong to a High Contracting Party, so long as such groups: are commanded by a person responsible for subordinates, have a fixed and distinctive sign, carry arms openly, and follow "the laws and customs of war." POW categories may also include non-soldiers who accompany the armed forces, such as contractors and war correspondents.

U.S. Army Regulations implement rules for treatment of persons captured during armed conflicts. The regulations for convening a "competent tribunal" to decide whether to detain an individual as a POW do not require a full-fledged military trial, because such tribunals may be convened in the field during an armed conflict.[h]

In addition, if a POW is charged with war crimes, then the POW "shall not be deprived of the rights of fair and regular trial prescribed by the present Convention." Geneva Convention IV, art. 5. Such a trial may be before a civilian court or before a military court martial (the tribunal that would try a member of a country's own armed forces). Courts martial possess "the essential guarantees of independence and impartiality as generally recognized," and require that the parties tried receive a meaningful defense and are represented by counsel. See Geneva Convention III, art. 84, 105.

Parties must "humanely treat" POWs and protect them from harm. POWs, however, may be kept in camps and interned, subject to rules about their treatment and discipline. The Third Geneva Convention applies to POWs until "their final release and repatriation," and they must be "released and repatriated without delay after the cessation of active hostilities." Geneva Convention III, art. 118.

5) Non-International Conflicts. The role of international law is far less clear in cases involving non-POW combatants and in non-international conflicts such as insurgencies and civil wars. Common Article 3 applies, as noted, to non-international conflicts, but it is very brief and not very specific. A more detailed 1977 protocol (often called "Additional Protocol II") was designed to apply to certain non-international conflicts and to supplement the Geneva Conventions, but it has *not* been ratified by the United States.[i]

6) Unlawful Enemy Combatants. Some states and scholars believe that international law recognizes three categories of individuals in armed conflict: combatants, civilians, and "unlawful enemy combatants." Unlawful enemy combatants are members of an armed group that is fighting a state, where the group does not meet the requirements of the Third Geneva Convention. On the one hand, unlawful enemy combatants are like lawful combatants in the sense that the states they are fighting may target them at any time or may detain them until the end of hostilities. On the other hand, unlike POWs, unlawful enemy combatants are not entitled to combatant immunity for acts they under-

---

[h] See Army Regulation 190–8, at http://www.apd.army.mil/pdffiles/r190_8.pdf (last visited on Jan. 27, 2013). The tribunal "shall be composed of three commissioned officers, one of whom must be of a field grade," convened by a commander. Army Regulation 190–8, at 1-6. The tribunal members and a recorder are sworn, a "written record" of the proceedings is made, and the record is open except for the deliberation. See *id.* The persons whose status is being determined are told of their rights, may attend the open portions, can testify, and can call witnesses "if reasonably available." Afterwards, using a preponderance of the evidence standard, a written report is completed and a determination is made. See *id.* An innocent civilian may be released or sent home immediately, while others may be detained as enemy prisoners of war. A Staff Judge Advocate reviews these determinations for legal sufficiency. See *id.*

[i] See Protocol Additional to the Geneva Conventions of 12 August 1949, and relating to the Protection of Victims of Non-International Armed Conflicts, 8 June 1977 (Additional Protocol II). For example, Additional Protocol II would provide additional treatment protections to individuals not taking part in those conflicts, including detainees. See Additional Protocol II, art. 4, and 5. It also would provide greater procedural protections during criminal prosecutions. See id. at art. 6.

take during the conflict (such as killing enemy soldiers).ʲ The Supreme Court offered the following guidance in *Ex parte Quirin*, 317 U.S. 1, 30 (1942):

> By universal agreement and practice the law of war draws a distinction between the armed forces and the peaceful populations of belligerent nations and also between those who are lawful and unlawful combatants. Lawful combatants are subject to capture and detention as prisoners of war by opposing military forces. Unlawful combatants are likewise subject to capture and detention, but in addition they are subject to trial and punishment by military tribunals for acts which render their belligerency unlawful. The spy who secretly and without uniform passes the military lines of a belligerent in time of war, seeking to gather military information and communicate it to the enemy, or an enemy combatant who without uniform comes secretly through the lines for the purpose of waging war by destruction of life or property, are familiar examples of belligerents who are generally deemed not to be entitled to the status of prisoners of war, but to be offenders against the laws of war subject to trial and punishment by military tribunals.

NOTE ON COURTS MARTIAL

Courts martial have jurisdiction to try and punish, among others, members of the United States Armed Forces. Article I, § 8, cl. 14 gives Congress the power to "make Rules for the Government and Regulation of the land and naval Forces." That grant of legislative authority includes the power to create courts martial. For much of American history—until 1950—Congress maintained bifurcated treatment of the Armed Forces. Because ship captains had historically enjoyed considerable power and discretion, the Navy remained subject only to deferential legislative rules and to nonstatutory "international law of the sea." The Army, on the other hand, was subject to a frequently revised body of positive law. In 1950, Congress passed the Uniform Code of Military Justice (UCMJ) that, as the legislation's title suggests, unified the military law applicable to all Armed Forces members. The UCMJ authorizes the use of courts martial to try military personnel for law-of-war violations, military offenses, and common-law crimes. UCMJ §§ 877–934. The UCMJ also authorizes the use of courts martial to try any "[p]risoners of war in custody of the armed forces." Id. § 802(a)(9). An armed forces member can also, "upon request," have a case transferred to a civilian court for trial. Id. § 818.

NOTE ON MILITARY COMMISSIONS

In *Hamdan v. Rumsfeld*, 548 U.S. 557 (2006), presented in the next Section, the Supreme Court described the origins of military commissions: "The military commission, a tribunal neither mentioned in the Constitution nor created by statute, was born of military necessity." Early military commissions in the United States were informal tribunals created by the military outside the

---

ʲ See Ingrid Detter, *The Law of War* 148 (2d ed. 2000) (distinguishing between lawful combatants, who are immunized from personal liability for their acts of belligerency, and unlawful enemy combatants, who may be tried, convicted, and punished for such acts).

courts martial process (1) to substitute for civilian courts when martial law was in place, (2) to substitute for such courts during military occupation of enemy territory, and, (3) to serve as a "law of war commission" for trying enemies who violated the law of war.[k] The judge presiding over a military commission proceeding is a military officer, and the commission does not derive its authority from Article III. Congress, in enacting the UCMJ, provided "concurrent jurisdiction" to convene such commissions as an alternative to courts martial. 10 U.S.C. § 821. Such commissions could theoretically convene to try U.S. servicemen, but courts martial have always been the exclusive forum for such proceedings. The power to exercise military custody, however, also includes the power to detain and punish members of *enemy* forces.

An "enemy alien," who is a civilian citizen of a country with which the United States is in a state of declared war, is considered distinct from an "enemy combatant," an enemy adversary engaged in belligerency against the United States. As noted, if a person designated as a POW does not violate the law of war, then the POW is to be released when hostilities end. In contrast, enemies that violated the law of war may be tried for war crimes. In a conflict between signatories, the Geneva Conventions provide that any POW must be tried for war crimes before a tribunal that would try a member of the state's own armed forces; whether military commissions may be used for that purpose is less clear. In a non-international conflict, Article 3 of the Geneva Conventions requires only that "a regularly constituted court" adjudicate charges against persons tried. During the years following the 9/11 attacks, the Supreme Court had to decide whether more informally-conducted military commissions violated the Geneva Conventions and the statutes regulating military trials (the UCMJ).

Now you are familiar with enough terminology to classify challenges to military power. A detainee may challenge military custody on the grounds that (1) there is not constitutional, statutory, or international-law authority for indefinitely detaining a prisoner without a military trial; (2) there is not authority for the exercise of power pursuant to a military commission; (3) there is not authority for a military commission to try a particular type of offense; (4) a detainee is in military custody in derogation of certain constitutional, statutory, or international-law rights, the protections of which the detainee should have enjoyed in the determination of the detainee's eligibility for a particular form of military custody (e.g., due process); (5) factual error in a status determination. The cases in the next Section examine the connection between the substantive authority to detain military prisoners and the prisoners' remedial entitlement to the privilege of habeas corpus.

---

[k] See also David Glazier, *Kangaroo Court or Competent Tribunal?: Judging the 21st Century Military Commission*, 89 Va. L. Rev. 2005, 2027–34 (2003) (describing use of commissions for crimes committed by servicemen that were not within the then-statutory jurisdiction of courts martial). The power of the Executive to convene such commissions absent a statute is unclear; the Court has at least suggested that "controlling necessity" might give the President authority to convene them. Ex parte Milligan, 71 U.S. (4 Wall) 139–40 (1866).

2. THE SUSPENSION CLAUSE AND LAW OF WAR COMMISSIONS

INTRODUCTORY NOTE ON EX PARTE MILLIGAN

As the Civil War was beginning, Confederate sympathizers began destroying strategically-important bridges near Baltimore, Maryland. Congress was adjourned, so President Lincoln unilaterally authorized his commanders to suspend the habeas privilege on April 27, 1861, an action without prior or subsequent precedent. See William H. Rehnquist, *All The Laws But One: Civil Liberties in Wartime* 21–25 (1998) (*All the Laws But One*). Whether the President has unilateral suspension power remains in doubt,[1] but Congress rendered the issue moot by authorizing Lincoln's suspension after the fact. Specifically, Congress enacted The Habeas Corpus Suspension Act on March 3, 1863, which provided procedures for suspending the habeas privilege and for judicial review. Chapter 2 discusses this suspension episode in great detail. *Ex parte Milligan*, 71 U.S. 2 (1866), excerpted below, was a decision interpreting the 1863 statute, rendered amidst a brutal legal and political struggle over the meaning of secession and the form that Reconstruction was to take.

Lambdin P. Milligan was a so-called "Copperhead Democrat"—a Democrat from a northern state who opposed the Civil War and who favored immediate restoration of the rebellious states after the war ended. Milligan was a lawyer who believed in the legality of secession, and he mounted an unsuccessful campaign during the 1864 Indiana gubernatorial primary. He was also a member of an order of the "Sons of Liberty," a Civil War secessionist organization with influence throughout Indiana, Illinois, Kentucky, Missouri, and Ohio. See Rehnquist, *All the Laws But One*, at 83. Milligan and several other Sons were accused of a plot to seize a cache of Union Army weapons, to free imprisoned Confederate soldiers, and to take over Indiana and surrounding states. Milligan was detained in Indiana, a northern state in which the habeas privilege was not suspended.

Indiana's incumbent Republican governor Oliver Morton was running for reelection in 1864, and he pushed for Milligan to be tried by military commission. Milligan was charged with: "(1) Conspiracy against the Government of the United States; (2) Affording aid and comfort to rebels against the authority of the United States; (3) Inciting insurrection; (4) Disloyal practices; and (5) Violation of the laws of war." Military commissions convicted all of the alleged conspirators and sentenced them to death by hanging. When Governor Morton became confident that he would be reelected, he recommended that the sentences be commuted. General Robert E. Lee had surrendered at Appomattox, and President Lincoln, sensing the destabilizing effect that the executions could have, agreed with Governor Morton. John Wilkes Booth then assassinated President Lincoln. President Andrew Johnson, who was dealing with the fall-

---

[1] In *Ex parte Merryman*, Chief Justice Roger B. Taney, sitting as a Circuit Justice, stated that Lincoln's unilateral suspension was unconstitutional: "These great and fundamental laws, which congress itself could not suspend, have been disregarded and suspended, like the writ of habeas corpus, by a military order, supported by force of arms." 17 F. Cas. 144, 152 (C.C.D. Md. 1861). President Lincoln did not comply with the order to release Merryman. Although federal authorities eventually charged Merryman, he was released on bail and the charges were subsequently dropped. See Daniel A. Farber, *Lincoln's Constitution* 87–88 (2003).

out, had no intention of commuting the sentences. Just nine days before his execution date, Milligan filed a habeas corpus petition challenging his conviction and capital sentence. The Government argued, among other things, that the habeas privilege had been suspended during the hostilities and, therefore, that Milligan's habeas petition should not be considered.[m] *Milligan* spoke directly to the federal government's authority to organize Reconstruction in light of the numerous threats and conspiracies to undermine it.

Ex parte Milligan

United States Supreme Court
71 U.S. 2 (1866)

■ Mr. JUSTICE DAVIS delivered the opinion of the court.

[Military authorities arrested Milligan at his home on October 5, 1864. He appeared before a military commission on October 21, 1864, where he was charged, convicted, and capitally sentenced. He was to be executed on May 19, 1865. On January 2, 1865, after the military commission's proceedings had concluded, the federal circuit court for the district of Indiana empaneled a grand jury to determine whether Milligan violated any federal law and, if so, to make presentments. The grand jury adjourned twenty-five days later, on January 27, 1865, without indicting or making a presentment against Milligan. No charges against Milligan were pending in a civilian court. He filed a federal habeas petition in the Indiana federal district court on May 10, 1865.]

Milligan insists that said military commission had no jurisdiction to try him [on any charges] because he was a citizen of the United States and the State of Indiana, and had not been, since the commencement of the late Rebellion, a resident of any of the States whose citizens were arrayed against the government, and that the right of trial by jury was guaranteed to him by the Constitution of the United States.

The prayer of the petition was that, under [Habeas Corpus Suspension Act of 1863], he may be brought before the court and either turned over to the proper civil tribunal to be proceeded against according to the law of the land or discharged from custody altogether. * * *

During the late wicked Rebellion, the temper of the times did not allow that calmness in deliberation and discussion so necessary to a correct conclusion of a purely judicial question. Then, considerations of safety were mingled with the exercise of power; and feelings and interests prevailed which are happily terminated. * * * We approach the investigation of this case, fully sensible of the magnitude of the inquiry and the necessity of full and cautious deliberation.

* * * The President was authorized by [the Suspension Act] to suspend the privilege of the writ of *habeas corpus* whenever, in his judgment, the public safety required, and he did [so on September 15, 1863]. The suspension of the writ does not authorize the arrest of anyone, but simply denies to one arrested the privilege of this writ in order to obtain his liberty.

---

[m] For a detailed exploration of these events, see Curtis A. Bradley, *The Story of* Ex parte Milligan*: Military Trials, Enemy Combatants, and Congressional Authorization, in Presidential Power Stories* (Curtis A. Bradley and Christopher H. Schroeder eds., 2009).

It is proper, therefore, to inquire under what circumstances the courts could rightfully refuse to grant this writ, and when the citizen was at liberty to invoke its aid.

The second and third sections of the [Suspension Statute] are explicit on these points. * * * The public safety demanded, if the President thought proper to arrest a suspected person, that he should not be required to give the cause of his detention on return to a writ of habeas corpus. But it was not contemplated that such person should be detained in custody beyond a certain fixed period unless [he was indicted or presented]. The Secretaries of State and War were directed to furnish to the judges of the courts of the United States a list of the names of all parties, not prisoners of war, resident in their respective jurisdictions, who then were or afterwards should be held in custody by the authority of the President, and who were citizens of states in which the administration of the laws in the Federal tribunals was unimpaired. After the list was furnished, if a grand jury of the district convened and adjourned, and did not indict or present one of the persons thus named, he was entitled to his discharge * * *. The refusal or omission to furnish the list could not operate to the injury of anyone who was not indicted or presented by the grand jury, for, if twenty days had elapsed from the time of his arrest and the termination of the session of the grand jury, he was equally entitled to his discharge as if the list were furnished, and any credible person, on petition verified by affidavit, could obtain the judge's order for that purpose.

* * * It was the manifest design of Congress to secure a certain remedy by which anyone deprived of liberty could obtain it if there was a judicial failure to find cause of offence against him. Courts are not, always, in session, and can adjourn on the discharge of the grand jury, and before those who are in confinement could take proper steps to procure their liberation. To provide for this contingency, authority was given to the judges out of court to grant relief to any party who could show that, under the law, he should be no longer restrained of his liberty. * * *

The controlling question in the case is this: upon the facts stated in Milligan's petition and the exhibits filed, had the military commission mentioned in it jurisdiction legally to try and sentence him? Milligan, not a resident of one of the rebellious states or a prisoner of war, but a citizen of Indiana * * * and never in the military or naval service, [is arrested and imprisoned by the United States military] on certain criminal charges preferred against him, tried, convicted, and sentenced to be hanged by a military commission, organized under the direction of the military commander of the military district of Indiana. Had this tribunal the legal power and authority to try and punish this man?

No graver question was ever considered by this court, * * * for it is the birthright of every American citizen when charged with crime to be tried and punished according to law. * * *

Have any of the rights guaranteed by the Constitution been violated in the case of Milligan? and, if so, what are they?

Every trial involves the exercise of judicial power, and from what source did the military commission that tried him derive their authority? Certainly no part of judicial power of the country was conferred on them, because the Constitution expressly vests it "in one supreme court and such inferior courts as the Congress may from time to time ordain and establish," and it is not pretended that the commission was a court ordained and established by Congress. They cannot justify on the mandate of the President, because he is controlled by law, and has his appropriate sphere of duty, which is to execute, not to make, the laws, and there is "no unwritten criminal code to which resort can be had as a source of jurisdiction."

But it is said that the jurisdiction is complete under the "laws and usages of war."

[Those laws and usages] can never be applied to citizens in states which have upheld the authority of the government, and where the courts are open and their process unobstructed. * * * [I]n Indiana, the Federal authority was always unopposed, and its courts always open to hear criminal accusations and redress grievances, and no usage of war could sanction a military trial there for any offence whatever of a citizen in civil life in nowise connected with the military service. Congress could grant no such power[.] * * *

Why was he not delivered to the Circuit Court of Indiana to be proceeded against according to law? No reason of necessity could be urged against it, because Congress had declared penalties against the offences charged, provided for their punishment, and directed that court to hear and determine them. And soon after this military tribunal was ended, the Circuit Court met * * * and adjourned. It needed no bayonets to protect it, and required no military aid to execute its judgments. It was held * * * by judges commissioned during the Rebellion, who were provided with juries, upright, intelligent, and selected by a marshal appointed by the President. The government had no right to conclude that Milligan, if guilty, would not receive in that court merited punishment, for its records disclose that it was constantly engaged in the trial of similar offences, and was never interrupted in its administration of criminal justice. If it was dangerous, in the distracted condition of affairs, to leave Milligan unrestrained of his liberty * * *, the law said arrest him, confine him closely, render him powerless to do further mischief, and then present his case to the grand jury of the district * * * and, if indicted, try him according to the course of the common law. * * *

Another guarantee of freedom was broken when Milligan was denied a trial by jury. * * * [That right] is *now* assailed, but if ideas can be expressed in words and language has any meaning, *this right*—one of the most valuable in a free country—is preserved to everyone accused of crime who is not attached to the army or navy or militia in actual service. * * * The sixth amendment affirms that "in all criminal prosecutions the accused shall enjoy the right to a speedy and public trial by an impartial jury," language broad enough to embrace all persons and cases; but the fifth, recognizing the necessity of an indictment, or presentment, before any one can be held to answer for high crimes, "excepts cases arising in the land or naval forces, or in the militia, when in actual service, in time of war or public danger;" and the framers of the Constitution, doubtless, meant to limit the right of trial by jury, in the sixth amendment, to those persons who were subject to indictment or presentment in the fifth.

The discipline necessary to the efficiency of the army and navy, required other and swifter modes of trial than are furnished by the common law courts; and, in pursuance of the power conferred by the Constitution, Congress has declared the kinds of trial, and the manner in which they shall be conducted, for offences committed while the party is in the military or naval service. Every one connected with these branches of the public service * * * surrenders his right to be tried by the civil courts. All other persons, citizens of states where the courts are open, if charged with crime, are guaranteed the inestimable privilege of trial by jury. This privilege is a vital principle, underlying the whole administration of criminal justice; it is not held by sufferance, and cannot be frittered away on any plea of state or political necessity. * * *

It is claimed that martial law covers * * * the proceedings of this military commission. The proposition is this: that in a time of war the commander of an armed force * * * has the power, within the lines of his military district, to suspend all civil rights and their remedies, and subject [citizens and soldiers to] the rule of his will; and in the exercise of his lawful authority cannot be restrained, except by his superior officer or the President of the United States. * * * Civil liberty and this kind of martial law cannot endure together; the antagonism is irreconcilable; and, in the conflict, one or the other must perish.

This nation, as experience has proved, cannot always remain at peace * * *. Wicked men, ambitious of power, with hatred of liberty and contempt of law, may fill the place once occupied by Washington and Lincoln, and if this right is conceded, and the calamities of war again befall us, the dangers to human liberty are frightful to contemplate. [Our fathers] knew—the history of the world told them—the nation they were founding * * * would be involved in war; * * * and that unlimited power, wherever lodged at such a time, was especially hazardous to freemen. * * * [T]hey secured the inheritance they had fought to maintain by incorporating in a written constitution the safeguards which time had proved were essential to its preservation. Not one of these safeguards can the President or Congress or the Judiciary disturb, except the one concerning the writ of habeas corpus.

It is essential to the safety of every government that, in a great crisis like the one we have just passed through, there should be a power somewhere of suspending the writ of habeas corpus. * * * In the emergency of the times, an immediate public investigation according to law may not be possible, and yet the period to the country may be too imminent to suffer such persons to go at large. * * * The Constitution goes no further. It does not say, after a writ of habeas corpus is denied a citizen, that he shall be tried otherwise than by the course of the common law; if it had intended this result, it was easy, by the use of direct words, to have accomplished it. * * *

* * * [T]his is not a question of the power to proclaim martial law when war exists in a community and the courts and civil authorities are overthrown. Nor is it a question what rule a military commander * * * can impose on states in rebellion to cripple their resources and quell the insurrection. The jurisdiction claimed is much more extensive. The necessities of the service during the late Rebellion required that the loyal states should be placed within the limits of certain military districts and commanders appointed in them, and it is urged that this, in a military sense, constituted them the theater of military operations, and as, in this case, Indiana had been and was again threatened with invasion by the enemy, the occasion was furnished to establish martial law. The conclusion does not follow from the premises. If armies were collected in Indiana, they were to be employed in another locality, where the laws were obstructed and the national authority disputed. On her soil there was no hostile foot * * *. Martial law cannot arise from a *threatened* invasion. The necessity must be actual and present, the invasion real, such as effectually closes the courts and deposes the civil administration.

It is difficult to see how the *safety* for the country required martial law in Indiana. If any of her citizens were plotting treason, the power of arrest could secure them until the government was prepared for their trial, when the courts were open and ready to try them. It was as easy to protect witnesses before a civil as a military tribunal, and as there could be no wish to convict except on sufficient legal evidence, surely an ordained and establish court was better able to judge of this than a military tribunal composed of gentlemen not trained to the profession of the law. * * *

If the military trial of Milligan was contrary to law, then he was entitled, on the facts stated in his petition, to be discharged from custody by the terms of the act of Congress of March 3d, 1863. * * *

■ [CHIEF JUSTICE CHASE, joined by JUSTICES WAYNE, SWAYNE, and MILLER, concurring:]

* * *[The Court's opinion] asserts not only that the military commission held in Indiana was not authorized by Congress, but that it was not in the power of Congress to authorize it, from which it may be thought to follow that Congress has no power to indemnify the officers who composed the commission against liability in civil courts for acting as members of it.

We cannot agree to this.

* * * [We concur] in what is said of the writ of habeas corpus and of its suspension, with two reservations: (1) that, in our judgment, when the writ is suspended, the Executive is authorized to arrest, as well as to detain, and (2) that there are cases in which, the privilege of the writ being suspended, trial and punishment by military commission, in states where civil courts are open, may be authorized by Congress, as well as arrest and detention.

* * * Congress had power, though not exercised, to authorize the military commission which was held in Indiana. * * *

* * * Congress has power to raise and support armies, to provide and maintain a navy, to make rules for the government and regulation of the land and naval forces, and to provide for governing such part of the militia as may be in the service of the United States.

* * * [T]he power to make rules for the government of the army and navy is a power to provide for trial and punishment by military courts without a jury. It has been so understood and exercised from the adoption of the Constitution to the present time.

Nor * * * does the fifth, or any other amendment, abridge that power. "Cases arising in the land and naval forces, or in the militia in actual service in time of war or public danger," are expressly excepted from the fifth amendment, "that no person shall be held to answer for a capital or otherwise infamous crime, unless on a presentment or indictment of a grand jury," and it is admitted that the exception applies to the other amendments as well as to the fifth.

* * * The states, most jealous of encroachments upon the liberties of the citizen, when proposing additional safeguards in the form of amendments, excluded specifically from their effect cases arising in the government of the land and naval forces. * * *

We think, therefore, that the power of Congress in the government of the land and naval forces and of the militia is not at all affected by the fifth or any other amendment. * * * [I]s it impossible to imagine cases in which citizens conspiring or attempting the destruction or great injury of the national forces may be subjected by Congress to military trial and punishment in the just exercise of this undoubted constitutional power? Congress is but the agent of the nation, and does not the security of individuals against the abuse of this, as of every other, power depend on the intelligence and virtue of the people, on their zeal for public and private liberty, upon official responsibility secured by law, and upon the frequency of elections, rather than upon doubtful constructions of legislative powers?

But we do not put our opinion that Congress might authorize such a military commission as was held in Indiana upon the power to provide for the government of the national forces.

Congress has the power not only to raise and support and govern armies, but to declare war. It has therefore the power to provide by law for carrying on war. This power necessarily extends to all legislation essential to the prosecution of war with vigor and success except such as interferes with the command of the forces and the conduct of campaigns. That power and duty belong to the President as commander-in-chief. * * *

The power to make the necessary laws is in Congress, the power to execute in the President. Both powers imply many subordinate and auxiliary powers. Each includes all authorities essential to its due exercise. * * *

* * * [W]hen the nation is involved in war, and some portions of the country are invaded, and all are exposed to invasion, it is within the power of Congress to determine in what states or district such great and imminent public danger exists as justifies the authorization of military tribunals for the trial of crimes and offences against the discipline or security of the army or against the public safety.

* * * [Indiana] was the theatre of military operations, had been actually invaded, and was constantly threatened with invasion. It appears also that a powerful secret association, composed of citizens and others, existed within the state, under military organization, conspiring against the draft and plotting insurrection, the liberation of the prisoners of war at various depots, the seizure of the state and national arsenals, armed cooperation with the enemy, and war against the national government.

* * * [I]n such a time of public danger, Congress had power under the Constitution to provide for the organization of a military commission and [for trial of conspirators thereby]. The fact that the Federal courts were open was regarded by Congress as a sufficient reason for not exercising the power, but that fact could not deprive Congress of the right to exercise it. Those courts might be open and undisturbed in the execution of their functions, and yet wholly incompetent to avert threatened danger or to punish, with adequate promptitude and certainty, the guilty conspirators. * * *

We think that the power of Congress, in such times and in such localities, to authorize trials for crimes against the security and safety of the national forces may be derived from its constitutional authority to raise and support armies and to declare war, if not from its constitutional authority to provide for governing the national forces. * * *

_____

NOTES AND QUESTIONS ON MILLIGAN

1) **Military Commissions.** As described earlier, the term "military commission" can be used colloquially to refer to any tribunal operating under military

authority. Some military commissions operate under shared sovereign authority and are therefore denominated as "international," such as those used in Nuremburg after the end of World War II. Chapter 10 explores the law-of-war commissions at the center of the modern national security detention cases, and *Milligan* has assumed elevated importance in those disputes. A military commission does not derive its authority from Article III; thus, the Court's remark in *Milligan*: "Certainly no part of judicial power of the country was conferred on them, because the Constitution expressly vests it 'in one supreme court and such inferior courts as the Congress may from time to time ordain and establish[.]'" Can you now see (1) why the prospect of a military commission is fraught with constitutional questions, and (2) what sorts of separation-of-powers questions arise?

2)   The Habeas Corpus Suspension Act of 1863 and Lincoln's Suspension. The Court is not terrifically clear in its statutory holding. The majority and dissenting opinions both agree that the Habeas Corpus Suspension Act of 1863 did not permit the military to keep Milligan in custody, but there are several reasons why Milligan's privilege may not have been suspended. See An Act Relating to Habeas Corpus and Regulating Judicial Proceedings in Certain Cases, ch. 81, 12 Stat. 755 (1863). Section 1 of the 1863 Suspension Act authorized the President to suspend the writ, and specifies the effect of the suspension:

> [D]uring the present rebellion, the President of the United States, whenever, in his judgment, the public safety may require it, is authorized to suspend the privilege of the writ of habeas corpus in any case throughout the United States, or any part thereof.

> [During the suspension], no military or other officer shall be compelled, in answer to any writ of habeas corpus, to return the body of any person or persons detained by him by authority of the President; ... further proceedings under the writ of habeas corpus shall be suspended by the judge or court having issued the said writ, so long as said suspension by the President shall remain in force, and said rebellion continue.

Note that Section 1 only authorized the President to suspend the privilege; thus, the President still needed to initiate the actual suspension. After the suspension commenced, a covered prisoner remained unable to assert the privilege "so long as said suspension by the President" is operative *and* so long as "said rebellion continue." (Emphasis added.) President Lincoln then initiated the suspension with Proclamation 104 on September 15, 1863:

> I, Abraham Lincoln, ... do hereby proclaim ... that the privilege of the writ of habeas corpus is suspended throughout the United States in the several cases before mentioned, and that this suspension will continue throughout the duration of the said rebellion or until this proclamation shall, by a subsequent one to be issued by the President of the United States, be modified or revoked ....

Milligan was almost certainly covered by the initial suspension, which was not geographically qualified. General Robert E. Lee surrendered to General Ulysses S. Grant on April 9, 1865. One might argue that the suspension became inoperative at that time, but President Johnson did not formally revoke the suspension until December 1, 1865. If Milligan was arrested in 1864 and filed a habeas petition on May 10, 1865, and if the Supreme Court decided the case in 1866, should Milligan's petition be dismissed because the privilege had been suspended?

3) Statutory Process. The Supreme Court did not seem willing to rest its opinion on the argument that the suspension period had lapsed by the time it decided the case, but instead appeared to believe that Milligan was not afforded process that he was to receive in lieu of some sort of habeas proceeding.[n] In Section 2 of the 1863 Suspension Act, Congress required that the Secretaries of State and War provide a list of individuals, like Milligan, detained as something other than POWs. Section 3 then provided that, if the Secretaries did not furnish the list within twenty days of arrest (or passage of the Act), or if the grand jury had not indicted or presented the individual when its session ended, then the judge was obligated to discharge the prisoner. U.S. officers failing to obey that order could be indicted for a misdemeanor, fined, and serve up to six months in jail.[o] In Milligan's case, the grand jury's session was terminated without it having indicted or presented him, so he was entitled to discharge. Why would the Court have preferred a statutory Section 2 and Section 3 ruling over a Statutory section 1 ruling? In a strict sense, is *Milligan* a Suspension Clause case?

4) Rebellion or Invasion. The Article I, § 9 suspension conditions permit Congress to suspend the privilege only "when in Cases of Rebellion or Invasion the public Safety may require it." In passing the 1863 Suspension Act, Congress invoked its power under the rebellion condition. Does the Clause restrict the geographic scope of permissible suspension? Is there anything about the Clause that prevents Congress from suspending it in a non-rebellious jurisdiction? Does the word "when" provide a temporal restriction, rather than a geographic one?

Recall again Chief Justice Marshall's closing language in *Bollman*: "If at any time the public safety should require [suspension], it is for the legislature to say so. That question depends on political considerations, on which the legislature is to decide." In light of *Milligan*, do you think a federal court should have the authority to review the following issues: (1) whether there has been a suspension; (2) whether there is a rebellion or invasion; or (3) whether the public safety requires the suspension? What are the costs and benefits of judicial review in such cases?

5) Power to Arrest versus Power to Detain. Having determined that Milligan's habeas privilege was not suspended, why did the Court keep going? As the Court stated, "The suspension of the writ does not authorize the arrest of anyone, but simply denies to one arrested the privilege of this writ in order to obtain his liberty." Once it determined that a federal court could require the custodian (the military) to show cause for the detention, the Supreme Court had to actually determine whether the detention could be unlawful under the facts alleged.

6) Could Congress Authorize the Military Trial? In determining the lawfulness of custody, one of the central issues may be whether the officer or tribunal that has convicted or sentenced the prisoner had power to do so. In

---

[n] See Bradley, *Story of* Ex parte Milligan, supra note m, at 93.

[o] There was some confusion about whether Milligan fit under Section 2 or Section 3 because he did not allege any facts about the list. The Court determined that, insofar as he would be entitled to release under either Section, resolving that issue was unnecessary.

Milligan, the question that most clearly divides the Justices is the issue of whether Congress, pursuant to some express or implied emergency power, could have authorized the military commissions to try civilian citizens. The potential sources of power the concurring opinion identifies are all in Article I, § 8: Congress might permissibly authorize commissions as necessary and proper to its enumerated powers to "declare War," to "raise and support Armies," or to "provide and maintain a Navy." The majority believed that the jury-trial right in the Sixth Amendment trumped any auxiliary power, and that military-commission convictions of civilians in non-rebellious states violated that right. Why is the interpretation of the Fifth Amendment important to this question? Why does the majority think that the Fifth Amendment does not except military commissions from the Sixth Amendment rule in this case?

Recall that the Court heard *Milligan* at the beginning of Reconstruction. Even though the Supreme Court had decided the case in October, it did not issue a written opinion until December 1866. The opinion was widely understood to express the Court's disposition toward Reconstruction generally. In response, Congress enacted legislation that stripped the Court of conventional appellate jurisdiction to review habeas corpus decisions in the lower courts. Congress later restored that jurisdiction. We discussed this back-and-forth in detail in Chapters 2 and 3.

7)   Executive Power During Wartime. Does *Milligan* indicate whether the President could unilaterally create military commissions? Congress has always carefully specified the jurisdiction of courts martial, but not for military commissions, which the Executive may informally convene. Article II declares the President to be the "Commander in Chief of the Army and Navy of the United States." Would the Commander-in-Chief power authorize the President to create the same types of military commissions that Congress is authorized to create as necessary and proper to its Article I military powers? Might the answer to that question vary depending on what type of military commission is involved, whether it is trying prisoners for violating the law of war, or whether it is trying civilians?

8)   Emergency Power. Especially in the last decade, *Milligan* has reemerged as a seminal American decision on emergency government power. What are the institutional constraints of each branch of government during crises? If you represented the Government in post-9/11 litigation, and were seeking to defend the use of military commissions to try noncitizen detainees for law of war violations, how would you rely on the *Milligan* decision?

9)   Citizenship and Prisoner of War Status. Remember that the Court expressly limited its decision to cases in which the prisoner was a resident of a non-rebellious state, is not a prisoner of war, and is an American citizen. What if Milligan had been a non-citizen who came to the U.S. to join the Confederate cause? Or what if he had been held as a prisoner of war?

10) Was Milligan Alive? When the Court decided *Milligan,* it did not even know whether he was still alive. In an omitted part of the opinion, the Court wrote:

> [T]he inference is that [Milligan] is alive; for otherwise learned counsel would not appear for him and urge this court to decide his case. It can never be in this country of written constitution and laws, with a judicial department to interpret them, that any chief magistrate would be so far

forgetful of his duty, as to order the execution of a man who denied the jurisdiction that tried and convicted him; after his case was before Federal judges with power to decide it, who, being unable to agree on the grave questions involved, had, according to known law, sent it to the Supreme Court of the United States for decision. But even the suggestion is injurious to the Executive, and we dismiss it from further consideration.

What was the point of explaining at length why Milligan was probably alive, only to dismiss the mere discussion of it as improper? Can judicial officers order executions despite the pendency of federal cases seeking to challenge the death sentence (or even pendency in the Supreme Court)? Could a court punish an officer for executing a prisoner whose case was still under review? In any event, Milligan was in fact alive; after the case was over, he was discharged and returned to Indiana, where he resumed his legal career.

NOTES ON WORLD WAR II MILITARY COMMISSIONS

1) **Duncan v. Kahahamoku and the Role of Civilian Courts.** In *Milligan,* the Supreme Court emphasized that a prisoner could be tried for conspiracy in civilian courts and that the law of war "can never be applied to citizens in states which have upheld the authority of the government, and where the courts are open and their process unobstructed." The habeas privilege was again suspended in Hawaii after the Japanese attack on Pearl Harbor in 1941. As it had in *Milligan,* in *Duncan v. Kahahamoku,* 327 US 304, 323 (1946), the Court held that the suspension of the privilege, intended to complement martial law in Hawaii, "was not intended to authorize the supplanting of courts by military tribunals," and that prisoners could not be prosecuted in military tribunals for civilian crimes. Is the test, then, whether the same charges could have been brought in civilian courts?

2) **Ex Parte Quirin.** *Ex parte Quirin,* a seminal World War II enemy-combatant case, involved the law-of-war commission trial of eight Nazi saboteurs landing on U.S. shores. 317 U.S. 1 (1942).[p] One of them was an American citizen. The saboteurs had actually been living in the United States before returning to the German Reich in 1933. They eventually received explosives training there and were apprehended while attempting to reenter the United States. President Roosevelt convened a secret military commission that convicted all eight men and sentenced them to death. The prisoners filed habeas petitions seeking relief on the ground that the commission both lacked power to sentence them and violated certain protections specified in the Bill of Rights. President Roosevelt eventually commuted two of the sentences, but chose not to proceed with the others without the imprimatur of the Supreme Court.

In *Quirin,* the Supreme Court determined that (1) Congress had the authority to constitute military commissions under Article I, § 8, cl. 10; (2) Con-

---

[p] There are several fascinating historical works involving the behind-the-scenes activity in *Quirin.* See, e.g., 39 Landmark Briefs and Arguments of the Supreme Court of the United States: Constitutional Law 498–504 (1975); Boris I. Bittker, *The World War II German Saboteurs' Case and Writs of Certiorari Before Judgment by the Court of Appeals: A Tale of Nunc Pro Tunc Jurisdiction,* 14 Const. Comment. 431, 440, 441 n.21 (1997); Robert E. Cushman, *Ex parte Quirin et al.—The Nazi Saboteur Case,* 28 Cornell L.Q. 54, 58 (1942); G. Edward White, *Felix Frankfurter's "Soliloquy" in Ex parte Quirin: Nazi Sabotage & Constitutional Conundrums,* 5 Green Bag 2d 423 (2002).

gress had authorized the military commissions through the Articles of War; (3) the President lawfully executed that authorized power; and (4) the prisoners did not have the Fifth and Sixth Amendment rights for which they alleged violations. *Quirin* explained that the World War II military commission, in contrast to the commission in *Milligan*, was appropriate because it tried offenses against the law of war. This jurisdiction remained lawful even when civilian courts were open and operating. *Quirin* began by stating, "We must therefore first inquire whether any of the acts charged is an offense against the law of war cognizable before a military tribunal." *Quirin* considered insignificant the fact that no codified law of war could serve as a guide. "It is no objection that Congress in providing for the trial of such offenses has not itself undertaken to codify that branch of international law or to mark its precise boundaries, or to enumerate or define by statute all the acts which that law condemns." The Court was deferential to Congress' choice to simply adopt "the system of common law applied by military tribunals . . . ." The Court added:

> By universal agreement and practice the law of war draws a distinction between the armed forces and the peaceful populations of belligerent nations and also between those who are lawful and unlawful combatants. Lawful combatants are subject to capture and detention as prisoners of war by opposing military forces. Unlawful combatants are likewise subject to capture and detention, but in addition they are subject to trial and punishment by military tribunals for acts which render their belligerency unlawful.

The citizenship status of the U.S. saboteur did not affect the result:

> Citizenship in the United States of an enemy belligerent does not relieve him from the consequences of a belligerency which is unlawful because in violation of the law of war. Citizens who associate themselves with the military arm of the enemy government, and with its aid, guidance and direction enter this country bent on hostile acts are enemy belligerents within the meaning of the Hague Convention and the law of war.

Why do you think *Quirin* came out differently than *Milligan*? Was it that *Milligan* did not involve war crimes, but crimes that could be tried in civilian courts, which were open and available? Was it that *Milligan* involved U.S. citizens detained in the United States?

3)   Is *Quirin* Inconsistent with *Milligan*? Supreme Court Justices have themselves struggled to reconcile the cases. Justice Scalia would later describe *Quirin's* attempt to distinguish *Milligan* as "not this Court's finest hour." He reasoned that, while the difference between law-of-war commissions and other types of military tribunals was not significant, the citizenship status of the detainee was. See Hamdi v. Rumsfeld, 542 U.S. 507, 570–72 (2004) (Scalia, J., dissenting). "Though treason often occurred in wartime, there was, absent provision for special treatment in a congressional suspension of the writ, no exception to the right to trial by jury for citizens who could be called 'belligerent' or 'prisoners of war.'" Justice Scalia could only envision a justified departure from that rule because the *Quirin* defendants were "admitted enemy invaders[.]" In *Hamdi*, Justice Scalia would argue that—absent circumstances where those facts are contested, during periods of non-suspension, and where the courts remain open—a citizen is entitled either to a civilian trial or to release.[q]

3. MILITARY COMMISSION PROCEDURES

Habeas corpus challenges to a military commission may question whether the commission has authority to hear a prisoner's case, whether it has jurisdiction over a class of detainee, whether it has jurisdiction over particular crimes, whether the proceeding was within the scope of authorizing orders, whether commissions used adequate procedures, and whether there was an adequate factual basis for the commission's determinations. The Court had not addressed many of those questions in the past. Although *Quirin* concluded that the contested military commissions were lawfully constituted, the Supreme Court declined to review the procedures by which President Roosevelt ordered the military trials conducted.

Nor could federal courts review factual issues, as the Court emphasized in *In re Yamashita*: "If the military tribunals have lawful authority to hear, decide and condemn, their action is not subject to judicial review merely because they have made a wrong decision on disputed facts." 327 U.S. 1, 8 (1946). *Yamashita* involved an American military trial, conducted in Manila, of a Japanese Imperial Army General accused of allowing his troops to commit atrocities against civilians and prisoners of war. The Court noted that General Yamashita was represented by six military lawyers and that "[t]hroughout the proceedings . . . defense counsel . . . demonstrated their professional skill and resourcefulness and their proper zeal for the defense with which they were charged." Yamashita was given a death sentence, and, after General Douglas MacArthur and the Philippine Supreme Court both refused to overturn it, he sought writs of certiorari, prohibition, and habeas corpus in the U.S. Supreme Court. The Court denied all three writs, ruling on the merits that the Manila military commissions had authority to hear the cases and that the "petitioner was charged with violation of the law of war." The Court noted that, although the Manila Commissions failed to comply with procedures specified in the Geneva Convention of 1929, those procedures applied only to POWs and not to enemy combatants charged with violating the law of war. The Court emphasized that military commissions retain their "traditional jurisdiction over enemy combatants."

NOTE ON MILITARY DETENTIONS AND STATUTORY JURISDICTION

Geographically speaking, how far does the writ "run"? Does the extraterritorial scope of the writ turn on the sovereign identity of the jailor, the citizenship of the prisoner, or both? At their most abstract, these are not entirely novel questions. Habeas corpus figured prominently in English imperial governance of faraway lands. As Professor Halliday has observed, "No dominion of the

---

[q] For additional scholarship discussing *Quirin* and *Milligan*, see Amanda Tyler, *The Forgotten Core Meaning of the Suspension Clause*, 125 Harv. L. Rev. 901, 1016 (2012) (arguing that historical evidence, consistent with *Milligan* but not consistent with the result in *Quirin*, shows that "as a general rule domestic legal protections enjoyed by persons within protection may not be displaced by the laws of war."); Richard H. Fallon, Jr., Essay, *The Supreme Court, Habeas Corpus, and the War on Terror: An Essay on Law and Political Science*, 110 Colum. L. Rev. 352, 389 (2010) (describing implications of both cases for national security detention).

king was exempt from habeas corpus, even those palatinates or other special places within the British Isles and far beyond them, where process from King's Bench normally did not go." They did so to "ensure proper behavior by all who acted in the King's name." Paul D. Halliday, *Habeas Corpus: From England to Empire* 34 (2010). At English common law, habeas corpus acted upon the jailor *in personam.* As long as the jailor could be brought before the court, a judge could issue the writ and call the jailor to account. In fact, "[a]s a writ originating in the prerogative, habeas corpus was concerned with jailers more than with prisoners." Paul D. Halliday and G. Edward White, *The Suspension Clause: English Text, Imperial Contexts, and American Implications,* 94 Va. L. Rev. 575, 713 (2008). The source of habeas power in American government, however, is not royal prerogative; it is the Constitution (and the habeas statutes passed pursuant thereto). Do the unique features of the American Constitution limit the territorial scope of habeas relief?

The Court did not permit enemy combatants to exercise the habeas privilege at all in *Hirota v. MacArthur,* 338 U.S. 197 (1948). A number of Japanese prisoners sentenced by the Allied Powers' International Military Tribunal for the Far East jointly sought an *original* habeas writ from the Supreme Court. The petitioners included Koki Hirota, a former Japanese Prime Minister. The Court's per curiam opinion states that because the Far East military tribunal was "not a tribunal of the United States," the "courts of the United States" lacked power to scrutinize the custody. In determining the availability of the privilege, the brief opinion not only relied upon notions of territorial jurisdiction, but also the prior and ongoing involvement of other sovereign powers. (In *Hirota,* the Supreme Court may have—and almost certainly should have—relied upon the absence of its appellate jurisdiction to review decisions of the international tribunal.[r]) As a result, the Court did not adjudicate the lawfulness of Hirota's custody in light of the procedures used by the Far East tribunal.

One common thread in these opinions has been the territorial jurisdiction of federal courts to issue writs of habeas corpus. Below, we separate the problem into parts. The Supreme Court's approach to territorial jurisdiction has evolved over time, becoming far more flexible. At common law, the writ would run broadly to the sovereign's agents—and that history most influenced the Court in *Boumediene v. Bush,* 553 U.S. 723 (2008), excerpted in the next Chapter. Although the U.S. practice has at times adopted a more constrained view of territorial jurisdiction, the Court has not been clear as to what source restricts the territorial scope of the writ—the Suspension Clause, Article III, statutes, or common law.

---

[r] The Supreme Court later called it a "slip of an opinion" and noted "those familiar with the history of the period would appreciate the possibility of confusion over who General MacArthur took orders from." *Munaf v. Geren,* 553 U.S. 674, 687 (2008); see also *id.* at 688 n.3 (noting the possible lack of appellate jurisdiction in *Hirota*). For scholarship exploring *Hirota,* see Aziz Z. Huq, *The Hirota Gambit,* 63 N.Y.U. Annual Survey of Am. Law 63 (2007) (criticizing "purported exception" to habeas jurisdiction premised in *Hirota*); Stephen I. Vladeck, *Deconstructing Hirota: Habeas Corpus, Citizenship, and Article III,* 95 Geo. L. J. 1497 (2007) (arguing that *Hirota* does not stand for the proposition that Article III jurisdiction does not reach persons detained abroad).

NOTE ON DETERMINING APPROPRIATE UNITED STATES DISTRICT COURT

Early decisions suggested that the language in § 2241, stating that a federal judge may grant the writ of habeas corpus "within their respective jurisdictions," meant that a judge could only do so where the petitioner was in custody in the relevant district court's territorial jurisdiction. See Ahrens v. Clark, 335 U.S. 188 (1948). The *Ahrens* rule explains why the Manila detainees like Yamashita filed original habeas petitions with the U.S. Supreme Court; they were all detained outside the territorial jurisdiction of any district court.[s] Amendments to § 2241 broadened, for practical reasons, the territorial habeas jurisdiction of certain federal courts. For example, a 1966 amendment revised § 2241(d) to permit federal prisoners to file certain habeas-like § 2255 petitions either in the district of their conviction or their confinement. In *Braden v. 30th Judicial Cir. Ct.*, 410 U.S. 484 (1973), the Court effectively overruled *Ahrens*, holding that a district court could issue the writ if it simply had "jurisdiction over the custodian." That language, as discussed in Chapter 1, is consonant with common-law habeas practice: "jurisdiction" referred to power to hale a jailer before the court to account for the legality of the detention.

INTRODUCTORY NOTE ON DETENTION IN FOREIGN JURISDICTIONS

In *Johnson v. Eisentrager*, the Supreme Court confronted a new custodial configuration: enemy aliens detained by the U.S. military abroad. 339 U.S. 763 (1950). There, the Court decided whether the habeas privilege was available to enemy aliens who had been convicted of violating the law of war. The prisoners were initially detained in China. They were moved, in U.S. custody and during the Allied Powers' postwar occupation, to Germany's Landsberg Prison.

Johnson v. Eisentrager
United States Supreme Court
339 U.S. 763 (1950)

■ Mr. JUSTICE JACKSON delivered the opinion of the Court.

The ultimate question in this case is one of jurisdiction of civil courts of the United States *vis-a-vis* military authorities in dealing with enemy aliens overseas. * * * These prisoners have been convicted of violating laws of war, by engaging in, permitting or ordering continued military activity against the United States[, in China,] after surrender of Germany and before surrender of Japan. * * * They * * * were taken into custody by the United States Army after the Japanese surrender and were tried and convicted by a Military Commission constituted by our Commanding General at Nanking by delegation from the Commanding General, United States Forces, China Theatre, pursuant to authority specifically granted by the Joint Chiefs of Staff of the United States. The Commission sat in China, with express consent of the Chinese Government. The proceeding was con-

---

[s] Two additional early cases in which the Court did not discuss jurisdiction, but appeared to assume jurisdiction was proper, involved American servicemen or ex-servicemen detained overseas. See Burns v. Wilson, 346 U.S. 137 (1953); U.S. ex rel. Toth v. Quarles, 350 U.S. 11 (1955).

ducted wholly under American auspices and involved no international participation. After conviction, the sentences were duly reviewed and, with immaterial modification, approved by military reviewing authority.

[The Prisoners are now held in U.S. military custody at Landsberg Prison in Germany.]

The petition prays an order that the prisoners be produced before the District Court, that it may inquire into their confinement and order them discharged from such offenses and confinement. It is claimed that their trial, conviction and imprisonment violate Articles I and III of the Constitution, and the Fifth Amendment thereto, and other provisions of the Constitution and laws of the United States and provisions of the Geneva Convention governing treatment of prisoners of war.

* * * [In the litigation below, the Court of Appeals ultimately] concluded that any person, including an enemy alien, deprived of his liberty anywhere under any purported authority of the United States is entitled to the writ if he can show that extension to his cases of any constitutional rights or limitations would show his imprisonment illegal; [and] that, although no statutory jurisdiction of such cases is given, courts must be held to possess it as part of the judicial power of the United States * * *. * * *

We are cited to no instance where a court [in any country] has issued it on behalf of an alien enemy who, at no relevant time and in no stage of his captivity, has been within its territorial jurisdiction. Nothing in the text of the Constitution extends such a right, nor does anything in our statutes. * * *

I.

Modern American law has come a long way since the time when outbreak of war made every enemy national an outlaw, subject to both public and private slaughter, cruelty and plunder. But even by the most magnanimous view, our law does not abolish inherent distinctions recognized throughout the civilized world between citizens and aliens, nor between aliens of friendly and of enemy allegiance, nor between resident enemy aliens who have submitted themselves to our laws and nonresident enemy aliens who at all times have remained with, and adhered to, enemy governments.

With the citizen we are now little concerned, except to set his case apart as untouched by this decision and to take measure of the difference between his status and that of all categories of aliens. Citizenship as a head of jurisdiction and a ground of protection was old when Paul invoked it in his appeal to Caesar. * * * If a person's claim to United States citizenship is denied by any official, Congress has directed our courts to entertain his action to declare him to be a citizen "regardless of whether he is within the United States or abroad." * * * Because the Government's obligation of protection is correlative with the duty of loyal support inherent in the citizen's allegiance, Congress has directed the President to exert the full diplomatic and political power of the United States on behalf of any citizen, but of no other, in jeopardy abroad. When any citizen is deprived of his liberty by any foreign government, it is made the duty of the President to demand the reasons and, if the detention appears wrongful, to use means not amounting to acts of war to effectuate his release. It is neither sentimentality nor chauvinism to repeat that "Citizenship is a high privilege."

The alien, to whom the United States has been traditionally hospitable, has been accorded a generous and ascending scale of rights as he increases his identity with our society. Mere lawful presence in the country creates an implied assurance of safe conduct and gives him certain rights; they become more extensive and secure when he makes preliminary declaration of intention to become a citizen, and they expand to those of full citizenship upon naturalization. During his probationary residence, this Court has steadily enlarged his right against Executive deportation except upon full and fair hearing. * * * And, at least since 1886, we have extended to the person and property of resident aliens important constitutional guaranties—such as the due process of law of the Fourteenth Amendment. * * *

It is war that exposes the relative vulnerability of the alien's status. The security and protection enjoyed while the nation of his allegiance remains in amity with the United States are greatly impaired when his nation takes up arms against us. While his lot is far more humane and endurable than the experience of our citizens in some enemy lands, it is still not a happy one. But disabilities this country lays upon the alien who becomes also an enemy are imposed temporarily as an incident of war and not as an incident of alienage. * * *

* * * With confirmation of recent history, we may reiterate this Court's earlier teaching that in war "every individual of the one nation must acknowledge every individual of the other nation as his own enemy—because the enemy of his country." * * *

The United States does not invoke this enemy allegiance only for its own interest, but respects it also when to the enemy's advantage. * * * Thus the alien enemy status carries important immunities as well as disadvantages. The United States does not ask him to violate his allegiance or to commit treason toward his own country for the sake of ours. This also is the doctrine and the practice of other states comprising our Western Civilization.

The essential pattern for seasonable Executive constraint of enemy aliens, not on the basis of individual prepossessions for their native land but on the basis of political and legal relations to the enemy government, * * * was established by the Alien Enemy Act of 1798. * * * [T]his enactment was never repealed. Executive power over enemy aliens, undelayed and unhampered by litigation, has been deemed, throughout our history, essential to war-time security. This is in keeping with the practices of the most enlightened of nations and has resulted in treatment of alien enemies more considerate than that which has prevailed among any of our enemies and some of our allies. * * *

The resident enemy alien is constitutionally subject to summary arrest, internment and deportation whenever a "declared war" exists. Courts will entertain his plea for freedom from Executive custody only to ascertain the existence of a state of war and whether he is an alien enemy and so subject to the Alien Enemy Act. Once these jurisdictional elements have been determined, courts will not inquire into any other issue as to his internment. * * *

II.

The foregoing demonstrates how much further we must go if we are to invest these enemy aliens, resident, captured and imprisoned abroad, with standing to demand access to our courts.

We are here confronted with a decision whose basic premise is that these prisoners are entitled, as a constitutional right, to sue in some court of the United States for a writ of habeas corpus. To support that assumption we must hold that a prisoner of our military authorities is constitutionally entitled to the writ, even though he (a) is an enemy alien; (b) has never been or resided in the United States; (c) was captured outside of our territory and there held in military custody as a prisoner of war; (d) was tried and convicted by a Military Commission sitting outside the United States; (e) for offenses against laws of war committed outside the United States; (f) and is at all times imprisoned outside the United States.

* * * [T]he privilege of litigation has been extended to aliens, whether friendly or enemy, only because permitting their presence in the country implied protection. No such basis can be invoked here, for these prisoners at no relevant time were within any territory over which the United States is sovereign, and the scenes of their offense, their capture, their trial and their punishment were all beyond the territorial jurisdiction of any court of the United States.

Another reason for a limited opening of our courts to resident aliens is that among them are many of friendly personal disposition to whom the status of enemy is only one imputed by law. But these prisoners were actual enemies, active in the hostile service of an enemy power There is no fiction about their enmity. Yet the decision below confers upon them a right to use our courts, free even of the limitation we have imposed upon resident alien enemies, to whom we deny any use of our courts that would hamper our war effort or aid the enemy.

A basic consideration in habeas corpus practice is that the prisoner will be produced before the court. This is the crux of the statutory scheme established by the Congress; indeed, it is inherent in the very term "habeas corpus." And though production of the prisoner may be dispensed with where it appears on the face of the application that no cause for granting the writ exists, we have consistently adhered to and recognized the general rule. To grant the writ to these prisoners might mean that our army must transport them across the seas for hearing. This would require allocation of shipping space, guarding personnel, billeting and rations. It might also require transportation for whatever witnesses the prisoners desired to call as well as transportation for those necessary to defend legality of the sentence. The writ, since it is held to be a matter of right, would be equally available to enemies during active hostilities as in the present twilight between war and peace. Such trials would hamper the war effort and bring aid and comfort to the enemy. They would diminish the prestige of our commanders, not only with enemies but with wavering neutrals. It would be difficult to devise more effective fettering of a field commander than to allow the very enemies he is ordered to reduce to submission to call him to account in his own civil courts and divert his efforts and attention from the military offensive abroad to the legal defensive at home. Nor is it unlikely that the result of such enemy litigiousness would be a conflict between judicial and military opinion highly comforting to enemies of the United States.

Moreover, we could expect no reciprocity for placing the litigation weapon in unrestrained enemy hands. The right of judicial refuge from military action, which it is proposed to bestow on the enemy, can purchase no equivalent for benefit of our citizen soldiers. Except England, whose law appears to be in harmony with the views we have expressed, and other English-speaking peoples in whose practice nothing has been cited to the contrary, the writ of habeas corpus is generally unknown. * * *

Despite this, the doors of our courts have not been summarily closed upon these prisoners. Three courts have considered their application and have provided their counsel opportunity to advance every argument in their support and to show some reason in the petition why they should not be subject to the usual disabilities of non-resident enemy aliens. * * * [W]e arrive at the same conclusion the Court reached in each of those cases, viz.: that no right to the writ of habeas corpus appears.

III.

The Court of Appeals dispensed with all requirement of territorial jurisdiction based on place of residence, captivity, trial, offense, or confinement. It could not predicate relief upon any intraterritorial contact of these prisoners with our laws or institutions. Instead, it gave our Constitution an extraterritorial application to embrace our enemies in arms. * * *

* * * [T]he claim [that the] prisoners are asserting and the court below sustained * * * amounts to a right not to be tried at all for an offense against our armed forces. * * * The decision below would extend coverage of our Constitution to nonresident alien enemies denied to resident alien enemies. The latter are entitled only to judicial hearing to determine what the petition of these prisoners admits: that they are really alien enemies. When that appears, those resident here may be deprived of liberty by Executive action without hearing. While this is preventive rather than punitive detention, no reason is apparent why an alien enemy charged with having committed a crime should have greater immunities from Executive action than one who it is only feared might at some future time commit a hostile act.

If the Fifth Amendment confers its rights on all the world except Americans engaged in defending it, the same must be true of the companion civil-rights Amendments, for none of them is limited by its express terms, territorially or as to persons. Such a construction would mean that during military occupation irreconcilable enemy elements, guerrilla fighters, and "were-wolves" could require the American Judiciary to assure them freedoms of speech, press, and assembly as in the First Amendment, right to bear arms as in the Second, security against "unreasonable" searches and seizures as in the Fourth, as well as rights to jury trial as in the Fifth and Sixth Amendments.

Such extraterritorial application of organic law would have been so significant an innovation in the practice of governments that, if intended or apprehended, it could scarcely have failed to excite contemporary comment. Not one word can be cited. No decision of this Court supports such a view. None of the learned commentators on our Constitution has ever hinted at it. The practice of every modern government is opposed to it.

We hold that the Constitution does not confer a right of personal security or an immunity from military trial and punishment upon an alien enemy engaged in the hostile service of a government at war with the United States. * * *

For reasons stated, the judgment of the Court of Appeals is reversed and the judgment of the District Court dismissing the petition is affirmed.

Reversed.

■ Mr. JUSTICE BLACK, with whom Mr. JUSTICE DOUGLAS and Mr. JUSTICE BURTON concur, dissenting.

* * * In Parts I, II, and III of its opinion, the Court apparently holds that no American court can even consider the jurisdiction of the military tribunal to convict and sentence these prisoners for the alleged crime. * * *

[I]t is based on the facts that (1) they were enemy aliens who were belligerents when captured, and (2) they were captured, tried, and imprisoned outside our realm, never having been in the United States.

The contention that enemy alien belligerents have no standing whatever to contest conviction for war crimes by habeas corpus proceedings has twice been emphatically rejected by a unanimous Court. * * * If the opinion thus means, and it apparently does, that these petitioners are deprived of the privilege of habeas corpus solely because they were convicted and imprisoned overseas, the Court is adopting a broad and dangerous principle. The range of that principle is underlined by the argument of the Government brief that habeas corpus is not even available for American citizens convicted and imprisoned in Germany by American military tribunals. While the Court wisely disclaims any such necessary effect for its holding, rejection of the Government's argument is certainly made difficult by the logic of today's opinion. * * *

It has always been recognized that actual warfare can be conducted successfully only if those in command are left the most ample independence in the theatre of operations. Our Constitution is not so impractical or inflexible that it unduly restricts such necessary independence. It would be fantastic to suggest that alien enemies could hail our military leaders into judicial tribunals to account for their day to day activities on the battlefront. Active fighting forces must be free to fight while hostilities are in progress. But that undisputable axiom has no bearing on this case or the general problem from which it arises. * * *

Conquest by the United States * * * does not mean tyranny. For our people "choose to maintain their greatness by justice rather than violence." Our constitutional principles are such that their mandate of equal justice under law should be applied as well when we occupy lands across the sea as when our flag flew only over thirteen colonies. Our nation proclaims a belief in the dignity of human beings as such, no matter what their nationality or where they happen to live. Habeas corpus, as an instrument to protect against illegal imprisonment, is written into the Constitution. Its use by courts cannot in my judgment be constitutionally abridged by Executive or by Congress. I would hold that our courts can exercise it whenever any United States official illegally imprisons any person in any land we govern. Courts should not for any reason abdicate this, the loftiest power with which the Constitution has endowed them.

NOTES AND QUESTIONS ON EISENTRAGER

1)   **Discrete Inquiries.** As you work through the following notes, be sure to pay attention to which type of question you might be answering. First, does a federal court have habeas jurisdiction to even examine the military custody? (Put another way, is the prisoner entitled to ask for a habeas remedy?) Second, was the military commission lawfully constituted under the Constitution and pertinent statutes? Third, did the military commission have authority over this prisoner? Fourth, what rights does a prisoner have in a proceeding before the military commission?

2)   **Territorial Scope of the Writ.** The prisoners in *Eisentrager* were initially detained and tried before a military commission in China and then brought to a prison in Germany. Which of these locations was dispositive? Would the

case have come out differently if the prisoners were detained abroad, but then tried in the United States? Would the case have come out differently if the prisoners were detained in the United States, but then received military trials in Germany? To answer such questions, recall how the Court identified six different features of the case that disfavored habeas jurisdiction, which included the fact that the prisoner:

> (a) is an enemy alien; (b) has never been or resided in the United States; (c) was captured outside of our territory and there held in military custody as a prisoner of war; (d) was tried and convicted by a military commission sitting outside the United States; (e) for offenses against laws of war committed outside the United States; (f) and is at all times imprisoned outside the United States.

Which of the six factors were most important to the result in *Eisentrager*? What result would *Eisentrager* require if the United States exercised complete control over a prison facility, but it was not a territorial sovereign?

These six factors went on to assume great importance in the Court's post-9/11 cases. Compare the contrasting view of the *Eisentrager* dissent, which believed that these factors were irrelevant because a court may exercise habeas jurisdiction whenever "any United States official illegally imprisons any person in any land we govern." The *Eisentrager* majority, in contrast, reasoned that "[t]he privilege of litigation has been extended to aliens, whether friendly or enemy, only because permitting their presence in the country implied protection." *Eisentrager*'s emphasis on the physical presence of the prisoner—the site of the crime, the custody, or the trial—accounted for the dissent's concern that the decision "permits the executive branch, by deciding where its prisoners will be tried and imprisoned, to deprive all federal courts of their power to protect against a federal executive's illegal incarcerations." How salient is the dissent's concern?

3) Citizenship. Would *Eisentrager*'s reasoning ensure review for American citizens, or would citizenship be an insufficient territorial nexus to trigger federal habeas jurisdiction? In *Reid v. Covert*, 354 U.S. 1, 30 (1957) (plurality opinion), the Court, relying on *Milligan*, held that citizens and civilian dependents of armed forces members could not be tried by courts martial abroad (in Japan and England). The Plurality emphasized that territory did not matter: "When the Government reaches out to punish a citizen who is abroad, the shield which the Bill of Rights and other parts of the Constitution provide to protect his life and liberty should not be stripped away just because he happens to be in another land." This shift in emphasis—away from territoriality—contrasted with the reasoning the "Insular Cases," which had emphasized that constitutional rights followed territorial jurisdiction. See, e.g. In re Ross, 140 U.S. 453, 464 (1891) ("The Constitution can have no operation in another country."). *Eisentrager* also focused on the citizenship of the prisoner, suggesting in several places that noncitizens do not enjoy the same habeas privilege as citizens do. Subsequent chapters will examine whether such a proposition remains viable today. An English common-law judge—focused not on the rights of the prisoner, but rather on the franchise and obligations of the jailor—would not have made much of citizenship. Common-law courts often granted the writ to aliens, particularly so that they might escape impressment in the Royal Navy. See Halliday, *From England to Empire*, at 206–207. As Professor Halliday describes, subjecthood—not citizenship—was the dispositive feature of access to the habeas privilege.

4) A Personal Return. Remember that a habeas writ is an *in personam* order to the custodian. *Eisentrager* raises the specter of military commanders haled into court as habeas respondents. Such circumstances, the Supreme Court explains, would diminish both the prestige of the commanders and the efficacy of their command. The dissenters responded forcefully on this point. With respect to its discussion of military leaders, the Court must have been speaking figuratively because the commanders do not have to be physically present during any habeas proceeding; they are respondents in name only. (In post-conviction review of state sentences, the state's warden is the nominal respondent.) In what ways might a habeas proceeding tax the prestige and efficacy of military leadership, even if the military is represented by legal counsel? Does the analysis change materially, as the dissent suggests, when active conflict ceases?

5) Merits Review. Once a judge has habeas jurisdiction, what other question(s) does the judge have to answer in order to decide whether to release a prisoner? Does the judge simply examine whether the prisoner could be tried for war crimes. Could a judge also examine whether the charges were sufficiently supported?

6) Alien Enemies. The term "enemy alien" is a term of art. As *Eisentrager* explains, the term was originally used in the Alien Enemy Act of 1798, a statute passed alongside the more-famous-but-subsequently-repealed Alien and Sedition Act. The term referred to an alien *who was a citizen of a country with which the United States was at war.* An alien enemy was distinct from a prisoner of war, a member of an enemy state's military who met the formal requirement under the Geneva Conventions for having engaged in lawful acts of belligerency. The term "alien enemy" is problematic when applied in post-9/11 cases, which involve international terrorist groups and not declared wars against nation-states. After September 11, the Bush Administration began to use the term "enemy combatant" to refer to individuals detained for national security reasons. Should a prisoner's entitlement to habeas turn on these status classifications?

7) Habeas as a Due Process Derivative. The prisoners argued that they were constitutionally entitled to habeas process because (1) they were entitled to Fifth Amendment due process protections and (2) the habeas privilege springs from the Fifth Amendment. Should an individual's constitutional rights obligate a judge to consider habeas claims more carefully? Does that theory present habeas more as an issue of judicial power or as an issue of individual rights? Which perspective do you think the Court's opinion takes?

8) *Quirin*. The *Eisentrager* dissent argued that, in *Quirin*, the Court afforded German prisoners the habeas privilege, notwithstanding a Presidential Proclamation to the contrary. *Quirin*, the *Eisentrager* dissent observed, did entertain the habeas petitions before denying relief. *Quirin*, however, could also be distinguished on the grounds specified in the majority opinion: that the German saboteurs were placed under civil arrest; that the Attorney General oversaw their prosecution; that they waived arraignment before a civilian court; that they were acting, arrested, tried, and imprisoned outside a theatre of military operations; and that neither the federal government nor the states were under any form of military control. Do you think that the *Eisentrager* Court correctly distinguished *Quirin*?

**9)   *Yamashita.* ***Eisentrager* also had to find a way to distinguish *In re Yamashita*, 327 U.S. 1 (1946). You encountered *Yamashita* briefly in the material that introduced *Eisentrager*. Tomoyuki Yamashita, nicknamed the "Tiger of Malaya," was a general in the Japanese Imperial Army during World War II. Japan committed a number of war crimes during its occupation of Singapore, including several massacres on his watch. (Yamashita's personal, as opposed to supervisory, responsibility for the atrocities remains a matter of academic disagreement.) An American military commission tried and sentenced Yamashita to death. After the Philippine Supreme Court refused habeas relief and after General Douglas MacArthur refused to modify the sentence, Yamashita sought review in the United States Supreme Court.[t] (The U.S. Supreme Court had appellate jurisdiction over the orders of the Philippine Supreme Court because the Philippines was, at that time, subject to American insular jurisdiction.) *Yamashita* denied all relief, but stated:

> [Congress] has not foreclosed [prisoners'] right to contend that the Constitution or laws of the United States withhold authority to proceed with the trial. It has not withdrawn, and the Executive branch of the government could not, unless there was suspension of the writ, withdraw from the courts the duty and power to make such inquiry into the authority of the commission as may be made by habeas corpus.

The *Eisentrager* majority distinguished *Yamashita* on the grounds that Yamashita committed war crimes and that Yamashita was both detained and tried in a United States jurisdiction. The dissent in *Eisentrager* correctly observed that *Yamashita* did not expressly predicate its decision on any of those "heads of jurisdiction." Do you think those factors should go to the "substantive" question of whether the military custody was lawful or to the "remedial" question of whether a prisoner is entitled to seek habeas review of that custody? Should they go to both?

10) Lothar Eisentrager and Landsberg Prison. Did the underlying charges against these prisoners matter to the Supreme Court? The Court describes how these individuals violated the law of war by continuing hostilities after surrender. In doing so, they lost protections traditionally afforded to POWs, who are entitled to release once hostilities are over. For an excellent description of the German prisoners, their intelligence activities in Shanghai, China before their detention, and the litigation that led to the Supreme Court decision, see Charles Lane, *Shanghaied*, 7 Green Bag 2d 247 (2004). Lane describes how the military commission trial in Shanghai "was no kangaroo court" and "the Germans' American defense lawyers fought vigorously" to challenge the jurisdiction and procedures of the military commission. As the Court noted, although Eisentrager and 19 others were convicted, 6 others were acquitted. Ironically, the Landsberg prison used by the U.S. to detain war criminals was the same prison both where Adolf Hitler had been held after his failed 1923 putsch and where he had written Mein Kampf. Apparently, the Administration had in fact intended to release the convicts because their crimes "were more technical than real," but first wanted to secure a favorable ruling from the Supreme Court. All

---

[t] Yamashita sought petitions for writs of certiorari, prohibition, and habeas corpus.

of the prisoners were released after the Court's decisions, following "further investigation of the case by a U.S. army inquiry commission." *Id.* at 256.

────────

NOTES ON HAMDAN V. RUMSFELD AND POST-9/11 MILITARY COMMISSIONS

1)   *Hamdan v. Rumsfeld* and the Legal Status of Post-9/11 Executive Commissions under the Geneva Conventions. The next Chapter will discuss in some detail the habeas litigation brought by detainees at the Guantánamo Bay Naval Base in Cuba, or GTMO. Most of those cases challenged indefinite detention at GTMO. In *Hamdan v. Rumsfeld*, 548 U.S. 557 (2006), however, a GTMO detainee challenged the lawfulness of a military commission created under the Detainee Treatment Act of 2005 (DTA), 119 Stat. 2739, and to be conducted under procedures created in Military Commission Order No. 1 (August 31, 2005). He filed his habeas petition before any military commission trial took place. In *Hamdan*, the United States argued that the military commission had authority to try the detainee for a conspiracy offense because such authority existed under federal statutes and under the law of war. *Hamdan* was one of the first post-9/11 Supreme Court decisions to reject claims of executive authority made in the wake of the attacks.

2)   The Facts in *Hamdan*. Salim Hamdan had been charged with conspiracy during a period from 1996 to 2001. Specifically, paragraph 12 of the indictment alleged that he "willfully and knowingly joined an enterprise of persons who shared a common criminal purpose and conspired and agreed with [named members of al Qaeda] to commit the following offenses triable by military commission: attacking civilians; attacking civilian objects; murder by an unprivileged belligerent; and terrorism." The Government argued that Congress had created military authority to try Hamdan on the conspiracy charge under both the DTA and the Authorization for the Use of Military Force (AUMF), 115 Stat. 224, the latter of which Congress passed days after the 9/11 attacks. Central to the detentions of prisoners after 9/11—and to the military commissions used to try them—was an argument that they were not POWs under the Geneva Conventions. Instead, the Government argued, they were "enemy combatants" that received far less protection under domestic and international law.

3)   The *Hamdan* Statutory Holding. The Court ruled against the United States, and first concluded that neither the DTA nor the AUMF authorized the military commission to try the conspiracy offense. The Court explained that, in combination with the UCMJ, the DTA and the AUMF "at most acknowledge a general Presidential authority to convene military commissions in circumstances where justified under the 'Constitution and laws,' including the law of war." A plurality then held that the law of war did not authorize the commission to try Hamdan on the conspiracy offense. (Justice Kennedy did not join the portion of the opinion involving the law-of-war authority to convene the commission, which is discussed in Note 5.)

4)   Military Commission Procedures. The Court did not address whether the conflict with al Qaeda was one to which the Third Geneva Convention applied—that is, whether the conflict was between signatories. (Afghanistan was a "High Contracting Party" but al Qaeda was not.) Instead, the Court found that all detainees—even enemy combatants—are covered under Common Article 3 of the Geneva Conventions. That coverage is not dependent on the signatory status of the belligerent enemies. Common Article 3 provides that a "regularly constituted" court be made available even to non-POWs, "affording all the judicial guarantees which are recognized as indispensable by civilized peoples."

The Court then found unlawful the procedures to be used at the GTMO military commissions. (Justice Kennedy joined all but a small part of this opinion.) The Court rested that conclusion on the UCMJ, which not only "conditions the President's use of military commissions on compliance . . . with the American common law of war[,]" but also on compliance with international law and its own regulations for military trials. The Court contrasted the GTMO commission procedures with those required under the UCMJ and under the Geneva Conventions. For example, the GTMO commissions would not permit the accused and counsel to be present at any part of the proceeding that was closed or classified, and they would be denied access to such evidence. In contrast, the right to be present is a "fundamental" part of the UCMJ procedures. Any evidence could be admitted at the commissions, including evidence obtained through coercion. A two-thirds vote of the commission members could result in a guilty verdict. The Court underscored that "[n]othing in the record before us demonstrates that it would be impracticable to apply court-martial rules in this case. There is no suggestion, for example, of any logistical difficulty in securing properly sworn and authenticated evidence or in applying the usual principles of relevance and admissibility." Scholars have debated whether military commissions must adopt the UCMJ procedures for courts martial.[u]

5)   The *Hamdan* Plurality on the Law of War. Writing for a plurality in Section V of the opinion and joined by Justices Souter, Breyer, and Ginsburg (Chief Justice Roberts did not participate in the decision), Justice Stevens emphasized that the conspiracy offense was not a violation of the law of war, and was therefore "not triable by law-of-war military commission." The federal statute regulating military proceedings, the UCMJ, restricted military commissions to offenses that "by statute or by the law of war may be tried by" such military commissions. 10 U.S.C. § 821. In *Quirin,* the Court had noted, "An important incident to the conduct of war is the adoption of measures by the military command not only to repel and defeat the enemy, but to seize and subject to disciplinary measures those enemies who in their attempt to thwart or impede our military effort have violated the law of war." The Court explained that Hamdan's trial was not intended to "dispense swift justice . . . on the battlefield" and that he was not charged with violating the law of war or acting in battle, but with entering a conspiracy years before September 11, 2001: "None of the overt acts alleged to have been committed in furtherance of the agreement is itself a war crime, or even necessarily occurred during time of, or in a theater of, war." The Plurality concluded that non-law of war uses of military commissions are far more restricted, such as to the situation in which civilian courts are not operative.

6)   Justice Thomas's *Hamdan* Dissent. Justice Thomas, joined by Justices Scalia and Alito, dissented. Justice Thomas disputed the conclusion that conspiracy could not be charged in a military commission and that the conduct of law of war commissions was inflexible. Justice Thomas concluded, "The judg-

---

[u] See, e.g., Curtis A. Bradley & Jack L. Goldsmith, *Congressional Authorization and the War on Terrorism*, 118 Harv. L. Rev. 2047, 2130 n. 366 (2005) (expressing skepticism that UCMJ-level procedures might be required in military commission proceedings).

ment of the political branches that Hamdan . . . must be held accountable before military commissions for their involvement with and membership in an unlawful organization dedicated to inflicting massive civilian casualties is supported by virtually every relevant authority, including all of the authorities invoked by the plurality today." Justice Thomas also disputed whether Geneva Conventions Common Article 3 applied, was judicially enforceable, or would result in any relief to the petitioner.

7) Authorization and Justice Breyer's Concurrence. Justice Breyer, concurring along with Justices Souter, Kennedy, and Ginsburg, concluded, "Congress has denied the President the legislative authority to create military commissions of the kind at issue here. Nothing prevents the President from returning to Congress to seek the authority he believes necessary." Commentators have debated the meaning of the AUMF and whether it authorized the President to convene military tribunals. See, e.g. Curtis A. Bradley & Jack L. Goldsmith, *Congressional Authorization and the War on Terrorism*, 118 Harv. L. Rev. 2047, 2127–28 (2005) (arguing that the AUMF was broad enough to authorize the executive to constitute the commissions); Neal K. Katyal & Laurence H. Tribe, *Waging War, Deciding Guilt: Trying the Military Tribunals*, 111 YALE L.J. 1259, 1308 (2002) (arguing that the Bush Administration set up the military commissions at issue in *Hamdan* without Congressional authorization). How broadly would you read the AUMF, and what interpretive tools would you use to discern its meaning? Does your answer depend on what force authorizations have historically done, or is it based in a practical sense that Congress should specifically outline the power necessary to use force?

8) Updated Procedures and "Black Sites." Days after the *Hamdan* decision, the Defense Department issued a memo instructing that Common Article 3 be followed by the military.[v] Faced with the Court's ruling that Article 3 applied to all detentions, the Central Intelligence Agency closed its "black sites."[w]

9) Hamdan Released. Hamdan was released following the Court's decision, after 7 years at GTMO. He was not released immediately, however. Following the 2006 decision, Congress passed a new Military Commissions Act, and Hamdan then received a military commission trial under the revised procedures. See Military Commissions Act of 2006, Pub.L. No. 109–366, 120 Stat. 2600. The jury sentenced him to only 66 months, giving him credit for 61 months already spent at GTMO. Hamdan was thereafter sent home to Yemen in 2008, to serve the five months remaining on his sentence.[x]

10) Conviction Reversed. Hamdan challenged his military commission conviction on appeal. He had been convicted of "material support for terrorism," which was one of the war crimes specified by the Military Commissions Act of 2006. See 10 U.S.C. § 950t(25); see also 10 U.S.C. § 950v(b)(25) (2006) (previous

---

[v] Memorandum from Gordon England, Deputy Sec'y of Defense, on the Application of Common Article 3 of the Geneva Conventions to the Treatment of Detainees in the Department of Defense to Department of Defense Officials (July 7, 2006). A subsequent executive order may have adopted somewhat more relaxed procedures. See Interpretation of the Geneva Conventions Common Article 3 as Applied to a Program of Detention and Interrogation Operated by the Central Intelligence Agency, Exec Order No 13340, 72 Fed Reg 40707 (2007). Subsequent federal legislation regarding military commissions is discussed *infra*.

[w] See Dafna Linzer and Glenn Kessler, *Decision to Move Detainees Resolved Two-Year Debate Among Bush Advisers*, Wash Post, Sept. 8, 2006.

[x] See Josh White and William Branigin, *Hamdan To Be Sent To Yemen: Bin Laden Driver Spent 7 Years at Guantánamo*, Washington Post, November 25, 2008.

codification of same provision). His conviction, however, was based on actions he took years before, from 1996 to 2001, and chiefly based on his role as Osama Bin Laden's personal driver and bodyguard. At the time that Hamdan was alleged to be conspirator, the federal statute authorized military commissions to try only violations of the "law of war." 10 U.S.C. § 821. The D.C. Circuit reversed his conviction, concluding: "consistent with Congress's stated intent and so as to avoid a serious Ex Post Facto Clause issue, we interpret the Military Commissions Act of 2006 not to authorize retroactive prosecution of crimes that were not prohibited as war crimes triable by military commission under U.S. law at the time the conduct occurred." In enacting the statute, Congress had noted that "This chapter does not establish new crimes that did not exist before its enactment, but rather codifies those crimes for trial by military commission." The D.C. Circuit reasoned:

> When Hamdan committed the conduct in question, the international law of war proscribed a variety of war crimes, including forms of terrorism. At that time, however, the international law of war did not proscribe material support for terrorism as a war crime. Indeed, the Executive Branch acknowledges that the international law of war did not—and still does not—identify material support for terrorism as a war crime. Therefore, the relevant statute at the time of Hamdan's conduct—10 U.S.C. § 821—did not proscribe material support for terrorism as a war crime.

Hamdan v. U.S., 696 F.3d 1238 (D.C. Cir. 2012). Judge Kavanaugh, writing separately, noted his view that although Congress had not done so when Hamdan committed the conduct, "Congress has authority under Article I, § 8 to establish material support for terrorism as a war crime that, when committed by an alien, may be tried by military commission."

11) Domestic Statutes and the Law of War. As this Chapter has described, U.S. Armed Forces regulations implement the law of war, the executive is bound by it, and the Supreme Court cites to it. Moreover, statutes expressly incorporate it. The next Chapter will discuss an important provision that incorporates the law of war: "Detention under the law of war without trial until the end of the hostilities authorized by the Authorization for Use of Military Force." See National Defense Authorization Act of 2012, Pub. L. No. 112–81, §§1021–1034, 125. Stat. 1298, 1562–1573. That statutory provision was enacted only after the Supreme Court intervened in a series of landmark habeas corpus decisions, to which the next Chapter turns, regarding the Government's indefinite detention of individuals for national security reasons.

CHAPTER 10

NATIONAL SECURITY DETENTION

INTRODUCTION TO NATIONAL SECURITY DETENTION

The last Chapter explored the law of war and the use of military commissions. This Chapter turns to the role of habeas corpus when the military detains prisoners indefinitely, and where the prisoners are *not* being held pending any official proceeding. We place particular emphasis on post-9/11 indefinite detention.[a] The U.S. military began holding national security detainees at the Guantánamo Bay Naval Base in Cuba (GTMO) during the years immediately following the 9/11 attacks. The Administration housed prisoners at GTMO because it believed prisoners detained outside the territorial United States would not enjoy rights or remedies under the U.S. Constitution. In the first Section, we discuss the Supreme Court's ruling in *Hamdi v. Rumsfeld*, 542 U.S. 507 (2004), and its aftermath. *Hamdi* analyzed the relationship between the habeas privilege, the Due Process Clause, and Congressional authorization to indefinitely detain a citizen as an "enemy combatant."

In the second Section, we discuss the Supreme Court's ruling in *Boumediene v. Bush*, 553 U.S. 723 (2008), the most important of the post-9/11 cases. *Boumediene* held that the noncitizens at GTMO may use habeas process to challenge their indefinite detentions. Although the Court held that the GTMO detainees enjoyed the habeas privilege, the Court did not address the scope of the Executive's authority to detain prisoners there nor the precise procedures that lower federal courts should follow when reviewing their habeas petitions. In the third Section, we discuss post-*Boumediene* developments, emphasizing how the lower courts have struggled to give meaning to the habeas procedures outlined by the Supreme Court.

1. INTRODUCTION TO INDEFINITE DETENTION

As an alternative to killing belligerents in combat, the military detains prisoners of war (POWs) for the duration of the hostilities so that they do not rejoin the battle. (The military must detain enemy soldiers who surrender, rather than use force against them.) The Supreme Court elaborated on the features of such detention in *Ex Parte Quirin*:

---

[a] We do not call post-9/11 operations the "War on Terror" because the use of that phrase is contentious and is no longer used officially. The Defense Department had titled its operations a "Global War on Terror" but, in 2009, changed the title to "Overseas Contingency Operation." See Scott Wilson & Al Kamen, *"Global War on Terror" is Given a New Name*, Wash. Post, March 25, 2009 (quoting Defense Department memo stating: "[t]his administration prefers to avoid using the term 'Long War' or 'Global War on Terror' [GWOT.] Please use 'Overseas Contingency Operation'" and citing "critics abroad and at home, including some within the U.S. military," who objected to the phrase "war on terror"). See also Bruce Ackerman, *Terrorism and the Constitutional Order*, 75 Fordham L. Rev. 475, 477 (2006) ("Terrorism is merely the name of a technique: the intentional attack on innocent civilians. . . . Once we allow ourselves to declare war on a technique, we open up a dangerous path, authorizing the government to lash out at amorphous threats without the need to define them").

An important incident to the conduct of war is the adoption of measures by the military command not only to repel and defeat the enemy, but to seize and subject to disciplinary measures those enemies who in their attempt to thwart or impede our military effort have violated the law of war.

In *Hamdi* (excerpted below), a plurality of the Court described "detention to prevent a combatant's return to the battlefield" as "a fundamental incident of waging war." That statement reflects a generally-agreed-upon consensus for POWs, but less clear are the circumstances under which non-POW combatants may be detained; as Chapter 9 explained, the Geneva Conventions are largely inapplicable to non-international armed conflicts.

Most of the cases discussed in this Chapter involve post-9/11 indefinite military detention. These detentions occurred in locations around the world, although the most prominent cases involved detainees at GTMO. The Government asserted an authority, grounded in the congressional authorization to use military force in response to the attacks, to indefinitely detain and interrogate detainees without charging them, without providing them access to counsel or federal judicial review, and without designating them as POWs. In some cases, the United States asserted an inherent Executive power to detain prisoners—a theory of detention under which the military would need no congressional authorization to exercise certain types of custody. The last Chapter discussed *Hamdan v. Rumsfeld*, 548 U.S. 557 (2006), a decision that rejected an aggressive assertion of Executive authority in a military commission case. Over the course of the seven years following the 9/11 attacks, the Supreme Court dismantled the broadest assertions of executive detention authority and the most restrictive habeas-stripping legislation.

INTRODUCTORY NOTE ON HAMDI V. RUMSFELD

In several key national-security detention cases, the Justices may have been thinking about more than just the formal merits of the habeas petitions before the Supreme Court. For example, on the morning of oral arguments in *Hamdi*, reporters broke the story of abuse at Abu Ghraib prison, an Iraqi facility used by United-States-led coalition forces to house detainees during the war in Iraq. Those stories included deeply-disturbing pictures capturing physical and psychological abuse. The story about and images from Abu Ghraib may have validated a growing public concern about American treatment of its military prisoners. At oral argument in *Hamdi* that day, the U.S. Solicitor General felt the need to emphasize the "judgment of those involved" in making GTMO detention decisions and that "the last thing you want to do is torture somebody."[b]

As you read the cases in this Chapter, ask yourself an atmospheric question—whether different legislative and executive policies might have averted unfavorable judicial intervention. When reading *Hamdi*, also remain mindful that Justice O'Connor announces the *judgment* of the Court, but that her opinion is only for a plurality. Also, pay particular attention to how the *Hamdi* plurality distinguishes between the due process right that is the subject of the ha-

---

[b] See Jonathan Hafetz, *Habeas Corpus After 9/11* 117 (2011).

beas challenge and the "habeas process" to which a prisoner is entitled when litigating the claim.

Hamdi v. Rumsfeld

United States Supreme Court
542 U.S. 507 (2004)

■ JUSTICE O'CONNOR announced the judgment of the Court and delivered an opinion, in which THE CHIEF JUSTICE, JUSTICE KENNEDY, and JUSTICE BREYER join.

At this difficult time in our Nation's history, we are called upon to consider the legality of the Government's detention of a United States citizen on United States soil as an "enemy combatant" and to address the process that is constitutionally owed to one who seeks to challenge his classification as such. * * * We hold that although Congress authorized the detention of combatants in the narrow circumstances alleged here, due process demands that a citizen held in the United States as an enemy combatant be given a meaningful opportunity to contest the factual basis for that detention before a neutral decisionmaker.

I

On September 11, 2001, the al Qaeda terrorist network used hijacked commercial airliners to attack prominent targets in the United States. Approximately 3,000 people were killed in those attacks. One week later, * * * Congress passed a resolution authorizing the President to "use all necessary and appropriate force against those nations, organizations, or persons he determines planned, authorized, committed, or aided the terrorist attacks" or "harbored such organizations or persons, in order to prevent any future acts of international terrorism against the United States by such nations, organizations or persons." Authorization for Use of Military Force (AUMF), 115 Stat. 224. Soon thereafter, the President ordered United States Armed Forces to Afghanistan, with a mission to subdue al Qaeda and quell the Taliban regime that was known to support it.

This case arises out of the detention of a man whom the Government alleges took up arms with the Taliban during this conflict. His name is Yaser Esam Hamdi. Born in Louisiana in 1980, Hamdi moved with his family to Saudi Arabia as a child. By 2001, the parties agree, he resided in Afghanistan. At some point that year, he was seized by members of the Northern Alliance, a coalition of military groups opposed to the Taliban government, and eventually was turned over to the United States military. The Government asserts that it initially detained and interrogated Hamdi in Afghanistan before transferring him to the United States Naval Base in Guantánamo Bay in January 2002. In April 2002, upon learning that Hamdi is an American citizen, authorities transferred him to a naval brig in Norfolk, Virginia, where he remained until a recent transfer to a brig in Charleston, South Carolina. The Government contends that Hamdi is an "enemy combatant," and that this status justifies holding him in the United States indefinitely—without formal charges or proceedings—unless and until it makes the determination that access to counsel or further process is warranted.

In June 2002, Hamdi's father, Esam Fouad Hamdi, filed the present petition for a writ of habeas corpus under 28 U.S.C. § 2241 in the Eastern District of Virginia, naming as petitioners his son and himself as next friend. The elder Hamdi alleges in the petition that he has had no contact with his son since the Government took custody of him in 2001, and that the Government has held his son "without access to legal counsel or notice of any charges pending against him." * * * Hamdi's father has asserted in documents [filed in conjunction with his petition] that his son went to Afghanistan to do "relief work," and that he had been in that country less than two months before September 11, 2001, and could not have received military training. The 20-year-old was traveling on his own for the first time, his father says, and "[b]ecause of his lack of experience, he was trapped in Afghanistan once the military campaign began."

The District Court found that Hamdi's father was a proper next friend, appointed the federal public defender as counsel for the petitioners, and ordered that counsel be given access to Hamdi. The United States Court of Appeals for the Fourth Circuit reversed that order, holding that the District Court had failed to extend appropriate deference to the Government's security and intelligence interests. It directed the District Court to consider "the most cautious procedures first," and to conduct a deferential inquiry into Hamdi's status. It opined that "if Hamdi is indeed an 'enemy combatant' who was captured during hostilities in Afghanistan, the government's present detention of him is a lawful one."

On remand, the Government * * * attached to its response a declaration from one Michael Mobbs (hereinafter Mobbs Declaration), who identified himself as Special Advisor to the Under Secretary of Defense for Policy. Mobbs indicated that in this position, he has been "substantially involved with matters related to the detention of enemy combatants in the current war against the al Qaeda terrorists and those who support and harbor them (including the Taliban)." He expressed his "familiar[ity]" with Department of Defense and United States military policies and procedures applicable to the detention, control, and transfer of al Qaeda and Taliban personnel, and declared that "[b]ased upon my review of relevant records and reports, I am also familiar with the facts and circumstances related to the capture of . . . Hamdi and his detention by U.S. military forces."

Mobbs then set forth what remains the sole evidentiary support that the Government has provided to the courts for Hamdi's detention. The declaration states that Hamdi "traveled to Afghanistan" in July or August 2001, and that he thereafter "affiliated with a Taliban military unit and received weapons training." It asserts that Hamdi "remained with his Taliban unit following the attacks of September 11" and that, during the time when Northern Alliance forces were "engaged in battle with the Taliban," "Hamdi's Taliban unit surrendered" to those forces, after which he "surrender[ed] his Kalishnikov assault rifle" to them. The Mobbs Declaration also states that, because al Qaeda and the Taliban "were and are hostile forces engaged in armed conflict with the armed forces of the United States," "individuals associated with" those groups "were and continue to be enemy combatants." Mobbs states that Hamdi was labeled an enemy combatant "[b]ased upon his interviews and in light of his association with the Taliban." According to the declaration, a series of "U.S. military screening team[s]" determined that Hamdi met "the criteria for enemy combatants," and "[a] subsequent interview of Hamdi has confirmed the fact that he surrendered and gave his firearm to Northern Alliance forces, which supports his classification as an enemy combatant."

[The district court determined that the Mobbs declaration was not sufficient to justify Hamdi's detention. It ordered the government to turn over numerous documents that it deemed necessary to conduct meaningful *in camera* review of the detention: Hamdi's statements, witness notes, lists of his interrogators, statements by Northern Alliance members, a catalogue of the sites at which Hamdi was detained and interrogated, and the identities of United States officials who had determined that Hamdi was an enemy combatant and that he should be moved to a naval brig. The Fourth Circuit reversed, stressing that it was "undisputed that Hamdi was captured in a zone of active combat in a foreign theater of conflict." It further determined that no further factual development, including a hearing, was necessary or proper, and that the Mobbs declaration, "if accurate," sufficiently justified the conclusion that the President's detention of Hamdi was a constitutional exercise of executive war power.]

The Fourth Circuit denied rehearing en banc, and we granted certiorari * * *. We now vacate the judgment below and remand.

II

The threshold question before us is whether the Executive has the authority to detain citizens who qualify as "enemy combatants." There is some debate as to the proper scope of this term * * *. [The Government] has made clear, however, that, for purposes of this case, the "enemy combatant" that it is seeking to detain is an individual who, it alleges, was "part of or supporting forces hostile to the United States or coalition partners" in Afghanistan and who "engaged in an armed conflict against the United States" there. We therefore answer only the narrow question before use: whether the detention of citizens falling within that definition is authorized.

The Government maintains that no explicit congressional authorization is required, because the Executive possesses plenary authority to detain pursuant to Article II of the Constitution. We do not reach the question whether Article II provides such authority, however, because we agree with the Government's alternative position, that Congress has in fact authorized Hamdi's detention, through the AUMF.

Our analysis on that point, set forth below, substantially overlaps with our analysis of Hamdi's principal argument for the illegality of his detention. He posits that his detention is forbidden by 18 U.S.C. § 4001(a). Section 4001(a) states that "[n]o citizen shall be imprisoned or otherwise detained by the United States except pursuant to an Act of Congress." * * * [W]e conclude that the AUMF is explicit congressional authorization for the detention of individuals in the narrow category we describe (assuming, without deciding, that such authorization is required), and that the AUMF satisfied § 4001(a)'s requirement that a detention be "pursuant to an Act of Congress" (assuming, without deciding, that § 4001(a) applies to military detentions).

The AUMF authorizes the President to use "all necessary and appropriate force" against "nations, organizations, or persons" associated with the September 11, 2001, terrorist attacks. There can be no doubt that individuals who fought against the United States in Afghanistan as part of the Taliban, an organization known to have supported the al Qaeda terrorist network responsible for those attacks, are individuals Congress sought to target in passing the AUMF. We conclude that detention of individuals falling into the limited category we are considering, for the duration of the particular conflict in which they were captured, is so fundamental and accepted an incident to war as to be an exercise of the "necessary and appropriate force" Congress has authorized the President to use.

The capture and detention of lawful combatants and the capture, detention, and trial of unlawful combatants, by "universal agreement and practice," are "important incident[s] of war." The purpose of detention is to prevent captured individuals from returning to the field of battle and taking up arms once again. * * *

There is no bar to this Nation's holding one of its own citizens as an enemy combatant. In *Quirin*, one of the detainees, Haupt, alleged that he was a naturalized United States citizen. We held that "[c]itizens who associate themselves with the military arm of the enemy government, and with its aid, guidance and direction enter this country bent on hostile acts, are enemy belligerents within the meaning of . . . the law of war." While Haupt was tried for violations of the law of war, nothing in *Quirin* suggests that his citizenship would have precluded his mere detention for the duration of the relevant hostilities. * * *

* * * [I]t is of no moment that the AUMF does not use specific language of detention. Because detention to prevent a combatant's return to the battlefield is a fundamental incident of waging war, in permitting the use of "necessary and appropriate force," Congress has clearly and unmistakably authorized detention in the narrow circumstances considered here.

Hamdi objects, nevertheless, that Congress has not authorized the *indefinite* detention to which he is now subject. The Government responds that "the detention of enemy combatants during World War II was just as 'indefinite' while that war was being fought." * * * If the Government does not consider this unconventional war won for two generations, and if it maintains during that time that Hamdi might, if released, rejoin forces fighting against the United States, then the position it has taken throughout the litigation of this case suggests that Hamdi's detention could last for the rest of his life.

It is a clearly established principle of the law of war that detention may last no longer than active hostilities. See Article 118 of the Geneva Convention (III) Relative to the Treatment of Prisoners of War ("Prisoners of war shall be released and repatriated without delay after the cessation of active hostilities"). * * *

Hamdi contends that the AUMF does not authorize indefinite or perpetual detention. Certainly, we agree that indefinite detention for the purpose of interrogation is not authorized. Further, we understand Congress' grant of authority for the use of "necessary and appropriate force" to include the authority to detain for the duration of the relevant conflict, and our understanding is based on longstanding law-of-war principles. * * * [While the United States is actively fighting the Taliban in Afghanistan, it] may detain, for the duration of these hostilities, individuals legitimately determined to be Taliban combatants who "engaged in an armed conflict against the United States." If the record establishes that United States troops are still involved in active combat in Afghanistan, those detentions are part of the exercise of "necessary and appropriate force," and therefore are authorized by the AUMF. * * *

III

Even in cases in which the detention of enemy combatants is legally authorized, there remains the question of what process is constitutionally due to a citizen who disputes his enemy-combatant status. * * * [We must carefully examine] both of the writ of habeas corpus, which Hamdi now seeks to employ as a mechanism of judicial review, and of the Due Process Clause, which informs the procedural contours of that mechanism in this instance.

A

* * * All agree that, absent suspension, the writ of habeas corpus remains available to every individual detained within the United States. * * * All agree suspension of the writ has not occurred here. Thus, it is undisputed that Hamdi was properly before an Article III court to challenge his detention under 28 U.S.C. § 2241. Further, all agree that § 2241 and its companion provisions provide at least a skeletal outline of the procedures to be afforded a petitioner in federal habeas review. Most notably, § 2243 provides that "the person detained may, under oath, deny any of the facts set forth in the return or allege any other material facts," and § 2246 allows the taking of evidence in habeas proceedings by deposition, affidavit, or interrogatories.

The simple outline of § 2241 makes clear both that Congress envisioned that habeas petitioners would have some opportunity to present and rebut facts and that courts in cases like this retain some ability to vary the ways in which they do so as mandated by due process. * * *

B

First, the Government urges * * * that because it is "undisputed" that Hamdi's seizure took place in a combat zone, the habeas determination can be made purely as a matter of law, with no further hearing or factfinding necessary. This argument is easily rejected. * * * [T]he circumstances surrounding Hamdi's seizure cannot in any way be characterized as "undisputed," as "those circumstances are neither conceded in fact, nor susceptible to concession in law, because Hamdi has not been permitted to speak for himself or even through counsel as to those circumstances." Further, the "facts" that constitute the alleged concession are insufficient to support Hamdi's detention. Under the definition of enemy combatant that we accept today as falling within the scope of Congress' authorization, Hamdi would need to be "part of or supporting forces hostile to the United States or coalition partners" and "engaged in an armed conflict against the United States" to justify his detention in the United States for the duration of the relevant conflict. The habeas petition states only that "[w]hen seized by the United States Government, Mr. Hamdi resided in Afghanistan." An assertion that one *resided* in a country in which combat operations are taking place is not a concession that one was "*captured* in a zone of active combat" operations in a foreign theater of war, and certainly is not a concession that one was "part of or supporting forces hostile to the United States or coalition partners" and "engaged in an armed conflict against the United States." Accordingly, we reject any argument that Hamdi has made concessions that eliminate any right to further process.

C

The Government's second argument requires closer consideration. This is the argument that further factual exploration is unwarranted and inappropriate in light of the extraordinary constitutional interests at stake. * * * At most, the Government argues, courts should review its determination that a citizen is an enemy combatant under a very deferential "some evidence" standard. Under this review, a court would assume the accuracy of the Government's articulated basis for Hamdi's detention, as set forth in the Mobbs Declaration, and assess only whether that articulated basis was a legitimate one.

In response, Hamdi emphasizes that this Court consistently has recognized that an individual challenging his detention may not be held at the will of the Executive without recourse to some proceeding before a neutral tribunal to determine whether the Executive's asserted justifications for that detention have basis in fact and warrant in law. *See, e.g., Zadvydas v. Davis*, 533 U.S. 678, 690 (2001); *Addington v. Texas*, 441 U.S. 418, 425–427 (1979). * * *

[These positions] emphasize the tension that often exists between the autonomy that the Government asserts is necessary in order to pursue effectively a particular goal and the process that a citizen contends he is due before he is deprived of a constitutional right. The ordinary mechanism that we use for balancing such serious competing interests, and for determining the procedures that are necessary to ensure that a citizen is not "deprived of life, liberty, or property, without due process of law," is the test that we articulated in *Mathews v. Eldridge*, 424 U.S. 319 (1976). * * * *Mathews* dictates that the process due in any given instance is determined by weighing "the private interest that will be affected by the official action" against the Government's asserted interest, "including the function involved" and the burdens the Government would face in providing greater process. The *Mathews* calculus then contemplates a judicious balancing of these concerns, through an analysis of "the risk of an erroneous deprivation" of the private interest if the process were reduced and the "probable value, if any, of additional or substitute procedural safeguards." We take each of these steps in turn.

1

It is beyond question that substantial interests lie on both sides of the scale in this case. Hamdi's "private interest . . . affected by the official action[]" is the most elemental of liberty interests—the interest in being free from physical detention by one's own government. * * *

Nor is the weight on this side of the *Mathews* scale offset by the circumstances of war or the accusation of treasonous behavior, for "[i]t is clear that commitment for any purpose constitutes a significant deprivation of liberty that requires due process protection" * * *. [T]he risk of erroneous deprivation of a citizen's liberty in the absence of sufficient process here is very real. Moreover, as critical as the Government's interest may be in detaining those who actually pose an immediate threat to the national security of the United States during ongoing international conflict, history and common sense teach us that an unchecked system of detention carries the potential to become a means for oppression and abuse of others who do not present that sort of threat. * * * [O]ur starting point for the *Mathews v. Eldridge* analysis is unaltered by the allegations surrounding the particular detainee or the organizations with which he is alleged to have associated. We reaffirm today the fundamental nature of a citizen's right to be free from involuntary confinement by his own government without due process of law, and we weigh the opposing governmental interests against the curtailment of liberty that such confinement entails.

2

On the other side of the scale are the weighty and sensitive governmental interests in ensuring that those who have in fact fought with the enemy during a war do not return to battle against the United States. As discussed above, the law of war and the realities of combat may render such detentions both necessary and appropriate, and our due process analysis need not blink at those realities. Without doubt, our Constitution recognizes that core strategic matters of warmaking belong in the hands of those who are best positioned and most politically accountable for making them. * * *

3

* * * With due recognition of these competing concerns, we believe that neither the process proposed by the Government nor the process apparently envisioned by the District Court below strikes the proper constitutional balance when a United States citizen is detained in the United States as an enemy combatant. * * *

We therefore hold that a citizen-detainee seeking to challenge his classification as an enemy combatant must receive notice of the factual basis for his classification, and a fair opportunity to rebut the Government's factual assertions before a neutral decisionmaker. * * *

At the same time, the exigencies of the circumstances may demand that, aside from these core elements, enemy-combatant proceedings may be tailored to alleviate their uncommon potential to burden the Executive at a time of ongoing military conflict. Hearsay, for example, may need to be accepted as the most reliable available evidence from the Government in such a proceeding. Likewise, the Constitution would not be offended by a presumption in favor of the Government's evidence, so long as that presumption remained a rebuttable one and fair opportunity for rebuttal were provided. Thus, once the Government puts forth credible evidence that the habeas petitioner meets the enemy-combatant criteria, the onus could shift to the petitioner to rebut that evidence with more persuasive evidence that he falls outside the criteria. A burden-shifting scheme of this sort would meet the goal of ensuring that the errant tourist, embedded journalist, or local aid worker has a chance to prove military error while giving due regard to the Executive once it has put forth meaningful support for its conclusion that the detainee is in fact an enemy combatant. * * *

We think it unlikely that this basic process will have the dire impact on the central functions of warmaking that the Government forecasts. The parties agree that initial captures on the battlefield need not receive the process we have discussed here; that process is due only when the determination is made to *continue* to hold those who have been seized. The Government has made clear in its briefing that documentation regarding battlefield detainees already is kept in the ordinary course of military affairs. Any factfinding imposition created by requiring a knowledgeable affiant to summarize these records to an independent tribunal is a minimal one. Likewise, arguments that military officers ought not have to wage war under the threat of litigation lose much of their steam when factual disputes at enemy-combatant hearings are limited to the alleged combatant's acts. This focus meddles little, if at all, in the strategy or conduct of war, inquiring only into the appropriateness of continuing to detain an individual claimed to have taken up arms against the United States. * * *

D

In so holding, we necessarily reject the Government's assertion that separation of powers principles mandate a heavily circumscribed role for the courts in such circumstances. Indeed, the position that the courts must forgo any examination of the individual case and focus exclusively on the legality of the broader detention scheme cannot be mandated by any reasonable view of separation of powers, as this approach serves only to *condense* power into a single branch of government. We have long since made clear that a state of war is not a blank check for the President when it comes to the rights of the Nation's citizens. * * * Likewise, we have made clear that, unless Congress acts to suspend it, the Great Writ of habeas corpus allows the Judicial Branch to play a necessary role in maintaining this delicate balance of governance, serving as an important judicial check on the Executive's discretion in the realm of detentions. * * * Absent suspension of the writ by Congress, a citizen detained as an enemy combatant is entitled to this process.

Because we conclude that due process demands some system for a citizen-detainee to refute his classification, the proposed "some evidence" standard is inadequate. Any process in which the Executive's factual assertions go wholly unchallenged or are simply presumed correct without any opportunity for the alleged combatant to demonstrate otherwise falls constitutionally short. * * * [W]e have utilized the "some evidence" standard in the past as a standard of review, not as a standard of proof. That is, it primarily has been employed by courts in examining an administrative record developed after an adversarial proceeding—one with process at least of the sort that we today hold is constitutionally mandated in the citizen enemy-combatant setting. This standard therefore is ill suited to the situation in which a habeas petitioner has received no prior proceedings before any tribunal and had no prior opportunity to rebut the Executive's factual assertions before a neutral decisionmaker.* * *

* * * Aside from unspecified "screening" processes and military interrogations in which the Government suggests Hamdi could have contested his classification, Hamdi has received no process. An interrogation by one's captor, however effective an intelligence-gathering tool, hardly constitutes a constitutionally adequate factfinding before a neutral decisionmaker. * * * Plainly, the "process" Hamdi has received is not that to which he is entitled under the Due Process Clause.

There remains the possibility that the standards we have articulated could be met by an appropriately authorized and properly constituted military tribunal. * * * In the absence of such process, however, a court that receives a petition for a writ of habeas corpus from an alleged enemy combatant must itself ensure that the minimum requirements of due process are achieved. * * *

The judgment of the United States Court of Appeals for the Fourth Circuit is vacated, and the case is remanded for further proceedings.

It is so ordered.

■ JUSTICE SOUTER, with whom JUSTICE GINSBURG joins, concurring in part, dissenting in part, and concurring in the judgment. * * *

* * * The plurality * * * accept[s] the Government's position that if Hamdi's designation as an enemy combatant is correct, his detention * * * is authorized by [the AUMF]. Here, I disagree and respectfully dissent. The Government has failed to demonstrate that the [AUMF] authorizes the detention complained of here even on the facts the Government claims. If the Government raises nothing further than the record now shows, the Non-Detention Act entitles Hamdi to be released.

* * * Since the [AUMF] was adopted one week after the attacks of September 11, 2001, it naturally speaks with some generality, but its focus is

clear, and that is on the use of military power. It is fairly read to authorize the use of armies and weapons, whether against other armies or individual terrorists. But * * * it never so much as uses the word detention, and there is no reason to think Congress might have perceived any need to augment Executive power to deal with dangerous citizens within the United States, given the well-stocked statutory arsenal of defined criminal offenses covering the gamut of actions that a citizen sympathetic to terrorists might commit. * * *

■ JUSTICE SCALIA, with whom JUSTICE STEVENS joins, dissenting.

[Hamdi], a presumed American citizen, has been imprisoned without charge or hearing in the Norfolk and Charleston Naval Brigs for more than two years, on the allegation that he is an enemy combatant who bore arms against his country for the Taliban. His father claims * * * that he is an inexperienced aid worker caught in the wrong place at the wrong time. * * *

Where the Government accuses a citizen of waging war against it, our constitutional tradition has been to prosecute him in federal court for treason or some other crime. Where the exigencies of war prevent that, the Constitution's Suspension Clause allows Congress to relax the usual protections temporarily. Absent suspension, however, the Executive's assertion of military exigency has not been thought sufficient to permit detention without charge. No one contends that the [AUMF], on which the Government relies to justify its actions here, is an implementation of the Suspension Clause. Accordingly, I would reverse the decision below.

I

The very core of liberty secured by our Anglo-Saxon system of separated powers has been freedom from indefinite imprisonment at the will of the Executive. Blackstone stated this principle clearly:

" * * * To bereave a man of life, or by violence to confiscate his estate, without accusation or trial, would be so gross and notorious an act of despotism, as must at once convey the alarm of tyranny throughout the whole kingdom. But confinement of the person, by secretly hurrying him to gaol, where his sufferings are unknown or forgotten; is a less public, a less striking, and therefore a more dangerous engine of arbitrary government. . .

"To make imprisonment lawful, it must either be, by process from the courts of judicature, or by warrant from some legal officer, having authority to commit to prison; which warrant must be in writing, under the hand and seal of the magistrate, and express the causes of the commitment, in order to be examined into (if necessary) upon a *habeas corpus*. If there be no cause expressed, the gaoler is not bound to detain the prisoner. For the law judges in this respect, . . . that it is unreasonable to send a prisoner, and not to signify withal the crimes alleged against him."

These words were well known to the Founders. Hamilton quoted from this very passage in The Federalist No. 84. The two ideas central to Blackstone's understanding—due process as the right secured, and habeas corpus as the instrument by which due process could be insisted upon by a citizen illegally imprisoned—found expression in the Constitution's Due Process and Suspension Clauses.

The gist of the Due Process Clause, as understood at the founding and since, was to force the Government to follow those common-law procedures traditionally deemed necessary before depriving a person of life, liberty, or property. When a citizen was deprived of liberty because of alleged criminal conduct, those procedures typically required committal by a magistrate followed by indictment and trial. The Due Process Clause "in effect affirms the right of trial according to the process and proceedings of the common law."

To be sure, certain types of permissible *non* criminal detention—that is, those not dependent upon the contention that the citizen had committed a criminal act—did not require the protections of criminal procedure. However, these fell into a limited number of well-recognized exceptions—civil commitment of the mentally ill, for example, and temporary detention in quarantine of the infectious. It is unthinkable that the Executive could render otherwise criminal grounds for detention noncriminal merely by disclaiming an intent to prosecute, or by asserting that it was incapacitating dangerous offenders rather than punishing wrongdoing. * * *

The writ of habeas corpus was preserved in the Constitution—the only common-law writ to be explicitly mentioned. Hamilton lauded "the establishment of the writ of *habeas corpus*" in his Federalist defense as a means to protect against "the practice of arbitrary imprisonments . . . in all ages, [one of] the favourite and most formidable instruments of tyranny." Indeed, availability of the writ under the new Constitution (along with the requirement of trial by jury in criminal cases) was his basis for arguing that additional, explicit procedural protections were unnecessary.

II

The allegations here, of course, are no ordinary accusations of criminal activity. Yaser Esam Hamdi has been imprisoned because the Government believes he participated in the waging of war against the United States. The relevant question, then, is whether there is a different, special procedure for imprisonment of a citizen accused of wrongdoing by *aiding the enemy in wartime.*

A

Justice O'Connor, writing for a plurality of this Court, asserts that captured enemy combatants (other than those suspected of war crimes) have traditionally been detained until the cessation of hostilities and then released. That is probably an accurate description of wartime practice with respect to enemy aliens. The tradition with respect to American citizens, however, has been quite different. Citizens aiding the enemy have been treated as traitors subject to the criminal process.

As early as 1350, England's Statute of Treasons made it a crime to "levy War against our Lord the King in his Realm, or be adherent to the King's Enemies in his Realm, giving to them Aid and Comfort, in the Realm, or elsewhere." * * * Subjects accused of levying war against the King were routinely prosecuted for treason. * * * The Founders inherited the understanding that a citizen's levying war against the Government was to be punished criminally. The Constitution provides: "Treason against the United States, shall consist only in levying War against them, or in adhering to their Enemies, giving them Aid and Comfort"; and establishes a heightened proof requirement (two witnesses) in order to "convic[t]" of that offense. Article III, § 3, cl. 1.

In more recent times, too, citizens have been charged and tried in Article III courts for acts of war against the United States, even when their noncitizen co-conspirators were not. * * *

* * * The only citizen other than Hamdi known to be imprisoned in connection with military hostilities in Afghanistan against the United States was subjected to criminal process and convicted upon a guilty plea.

B

There are times when military exigency renders resort to the traditional criminal process impracticable.   English law accommodated such exigencies by allowing legislative suspension of the writ of habeas corpus for brief periods. * * * Where the Executive has not pursued the usual course of charge, committal, and conviction, it has historically secured the Legislature's explicit approval of a suspension. In England, Parliament on numerous occasions passed temporary suspensions in times of threatened invasion or rebellion. Not long after Massachusetts had adopted a clause in its constitution explicitly providing for habeas corpus, it suspended the writ in order to deal with Shay's Rebellion.

Our Federal Constitution contains a provision explicitly permitting suspension, but limiting the situations in which it may be invoked * * * . Although this provision does not state that suspension must be effected by, or authorized by, a legislative act, it has been so understood, consistent with English practice and the Clause's placement in Article I.

The Suspension Clause was by design a safety valve, the Constitution's only "express provision for exercise of extraordinary authority because of a crisis." * * *

III

Of course the extensive historical evidence of criminal convictions and habeas suspensions does not *necessarily* refute the Government's position in this case. When the writ is suspended, the Government is entirely free from judicial oversight. It does not claim such total liberation here, but argues that it need only produce what it calls "some evidence" to satisfy a habeas court that a detained individual is an enemy combatant. * * *

Further evidence comes from this Court's decision in *Ex parte Milligan*. There, the Court issued the writ to an American citizen who had been tried by military commission for offenses that included conspiring to overthrow the Government, seize munitions, and liberate prisoners of war. The Court rejected in no uncertain terms the Government's assertion that military jurisdiction was proper "under the 'laws and usages of war'":

> "It can serve no useful purpose to inquire what those laws and usages are, whence they originated, where found, and on whom they operate; they can never be applied to citizens in states which have upheld the authority of the government, and where the courts are open and their process unobstructed."

Milligan is not exactly this case, of course, since the petitioner was threatened with death, not merely imprisonment. But the reasoning and conclusion of *Milligan* logically cover the present case. The Government justifies imprisonment of Hamdi on principles of the law of war and admits that, absent the war, it would have no such authority. But if the law of war cannot be applied to citizens where courts are open, then Hamdi's imprisonment without criminal trial is no less unlawful than Milligan's trial by military tribunal.

* * * [C]riminal process was viewed as the primary means—and the only means absent congressional action suspending the writ—not only to punish traitors, but to incapacitate them.

The proposition that the Executive lacks indefinite wartime detention authority over citizens is consistent with the Founders' general mistrust of military power permanently at the Executive's disposal. In the Founders' view, the "blessings of liberty" were threatened by "those military establishments which must gradually poison its very fountain." No fewer than 10 issues of the Federalist were devoted in whole or part to allaying fears of oppression from the proposed Constitution's authorization of standing armies in peacetime. Many safeguards in the Constitution reflect these concerns. Congress's authority "[t]o raise and support Armies" was hedged with the proviso that "no Appropriation of Money to that Use shall be for a longer Term than two Years." Except for the actual command of military forces, all authorization for their maintenance and all explicit authorization for their use is placed in the control of Congress under Article I, rather than the President under Article II. As Hamilton explained, the President's military authority would be "much inferior" to that of the British King * * *. A view of the Constitution that gives the Executive authority to use military force rather than the force of law against citizens on American soil flies in the face of the mistrust that engendered these provisions.

IV

The Government argues that our more recent jurisprudence ratifies its indefinite imprisonment of a citizen within the territorial jurisdiction of federal courts. It places primary reliance upon *Ex parte Quirin*, 317 U.S. 1 (1942), a World War II case upholding the trial by military commission of eight German saboteurs, one of whom, Hans Haupt, was a U.S. citizen. The case was not this Court's finest hour. The Court upheld the commission and denied relief in a brief *per curiam* issued the day after oral argument concluded: a week later the Government carried out the commission's death sentence upon six saboteurs, including Haupt. The Court eventually explained its reasoning in a written opinion issued several months later.

* * * In *Quirin* it was uncontested that the petitioners were members of enemy forces. They were "*admitted* enemy invaders," * * * and it was "undisputed" that they had landed in the United States in service of German forces. The specific holding of the Court was only that, "upon the *conceded* facts," the petitioners were "plainly within [the] boundaries" of military jurisdiction. But where those jurisdictional facts are *not* conceded— where the petitioner insists that he is *not* a belligerent—Quirin left the pre-existing law in place: Absent suspension of the writ, a citizen held where the courts are open is entitled either to criminal trial or to a judicial decree requiring his release.

V

* * * The plurality finds justification for Hamdi's imprisonment in the [AUMF] * * *. This is not remotely a congressional suspension of the writ, and no one claims that it is. Contrary to the plurality's view, I do not think this statute even authorizes detention of a citizen with the clarity necessary to satisfy the interpretive canon that statutes should be construed so as to avoid grave constitutional concerns; with the clarity necessary to comport with cases such as *Ex parte Endo*, 323 U.S. 283, 300 (1944), and *Duncan v. Kahanamoku*, 327 U.S. 304, 314–316, 324 (1946); or with the clarity necessary to overcome the statutory prescription that "[n]o citizen shall be imprisoned or otherwise detained by the United States except pursuant to an Act of Congress." But even if it did, I would not permit it to overcome Hamdi's entitlement to habeas corpus relief. The Suspension Clause of the Constitution, which carefully circumscribes the conditions

under which the writ can be withheld, would be a sham if it could be evaded by congressional prescription of requirements *other than the common-law requirement of committal for criminal prosecution* that render the writ, though available, unavailing. If the Suspension Clause does not guarantee the citizen that he will either be tried or released, unless the conditions for suspending the writ exist and the grave action of suspending the writ has been taken; if it merely guarantees the citizen that he will not be detained unless Congress by ordinary legislation says he can be detained; it guarantees him very little indeed.

* * * As usual, the major effect of [the Plurality's] constitutional improvisation is to increase the power of the Court. Having found a congressional authorization for detention of citizens where none clearly exists; and having discarded the categorical procedural protection of the Suspension Clause; the plurality then proceeds, under the guise of the Due Process Clause, to prescribe what procedural protections *it* thinks appropriate. It "weigh[s] the private interest . . . against the Government's asserted interest," and—just as though writing a new Constitution—comes up with an unheard-of system in which the citizen rather than the Government bears the burden of proof, testimony is by hearsay rather than live witnesses, and the presiding officer may well be a "neutral" military officer rather than judge and jury. It claims authority to engage in this sort of "judicious balancing" from *Mathews v. Eldridge*, a case involving . . . *the withdrawal of disability benefits!* Whatever the merits of this technique when newly recognized property rights are at issue (and even there they are questionable), it has no place where the Constitution and the common law already supply an answer.

Having distorted the Suspension Clause, the plurality finishes up by transmogrifying the Great Writ—disposing of the present habeas petition by remanding for the District Court to "engag[e] in a factfinding process that is both prudent and incremental." "In the absence of [the Executive's prior provision of procedures that satisfy due process], . . . a court that receives a petition for a writ of habeas corpus from an alleged enemy combatant must itself ensure that the minimum requirements of due process are achieved." This judicial remediation of executive default is unheard of. The role of habeas corpus is to determine the legality of executive detention, not to supply the omitted process necessary to make it legal. It is not the habeas court's function to make illegal detention legal by supplying a process that the Government could have provided, but chose not to. If Hamdi is being imprisoned in violation of the Constitution (because without due process of law), then his habeas petition should be granted; the Executive may then hand him over to the criminal authorities, whose detention for the purpose of prosecution will be lawful, or else must release him. * * *

VI

Several limitations give my views in this matter a relatively narrow compass. They apply only to citizens, accused of being enemy combatants, who are detained within the territorial jurisdiction of a federal court. This is not likely to be a numerous group; currently we know of only two, Hamdi and Jose Padilla. Where the citizen is captured outside and held outside the United States, the constitutional requirements may be different. Moreover, even within the United States, the accused citizen-enemy combatant may lawfully be detained once prosecution is in progress or in contemplation. The Government has been notably successful in securing conviction, and hence long-term custody or execution, of those who have waged war against the state.

I frankly do not know whether these tools are sufficient to meet the Government's security needs, including the need to obtain intelligence through interrogation. It is far beyond my competence, or the Court's competence, to determine that. But it is not beyond Congress's. If the situation demands it, the Executive can ask Congress to authorize suspension of the writ—which can be made subject to whatever conditions Congress deems appropriate, including even the procedural novelties invented by the plurality today. To be sure, suspension is limited by the Constitution to cases of rebellion or invasion. But whether the attacks of September 11, 2001, constitute an "invasion," and whether those attacks still justify suspension several years later, are questions for Congress rather than this Court. If civil rights are to be curtailed during wartime, it must be done openly and democratically, as the Constitution requires, rather than by silent erosion through an opinion of this Court. * * *

■ JUSTICE THOMAS, dissenting.

The Executive Branch, acting pursuant to the powers vested in the President by the Constitution and with explicit congressional approval, has determined that Yaser Hamdi is an enemy combatant and should be detained. This detention falls squarely within the Federal Government's war powers, and we lack the expertise and capacity to second-guess that decision. As such, petitioners' habeas challenge should fail, and there is no reason to remand the case. The plurality reaches a contrary conclusion by failing adequately to consider basic principles of the constitutional structure as it relates to national security and foreign affairs and by using the balancing scheme of *Mathews v. Eldridge*. I do not think that the Federal Government's war powers can be balanced away by this Court. Arguably, Congress could provide for additional procedural protections, but until it does, we have no right to insist upon them. But even if I were to agree with the general approach the plurality takes, I could not accept the particulars. The plurality utterly fails to account for the Government's compelling interests and for our own institutional inability to weigh competing concerns correctly. I respectfully dissent. * * *

The plurality * * * qualifies its recognition of the President's authority to detain enemy combatants in the war on terrorism in ways that are at odds with our precedent. * * * I do not believe that we may diminish the Federal Government's war powers by reference to a treaty and certainly not to a treaty that does not apply. Further, we are bound by the political branches' determination that the United States is at war. And, in any case, the power to detain does not end with the cessation of formal hostilities. * * *

Accordingly, the President's action here is "supported by the strongest of presumptions and the widest latitude of judicial interpretation."[2] * * *

III

I agree with the plurality that the Federal Government has power to detain those that the Executive Branch determines to be enemy combatants. But I do not think that the plurality has adequately explained the

[2] It could be argued that the habeas statutes are evidence of congressional intent that enemy combatants are entitled to challenge the factual basis for the Government's determination. But factual development is needed only to the extent necessary to resolve the legal challenge to the detention.

breadth of the President's authority to detain enemy combatants, an authority that includes making virtually conclusive factual findings. In my view, the structural considerations discussed above, as recognized in our precedent, demonstrate that we lack the capacity and responsibility to second-guess this determination.

This makes complete sense once the process that is due Hamdi is made clear. As an initial matter, it is possible that the Due Process Clause requires only "that our Government must proceed according to the 'law of the land'—that is, according to written constitutional and statutory provisions."* * *

* * * In this context, due process requires nothing more than a good-faith executive determination. To be clear: The Court has held that an executive, acting pursuant to statutory and constitutional authority may, consistent with the Due Process Clause, unilaterally decide to detain an individual if the executive deems this necessary for the public safety even if he is mistaken.

I therefore cannot agree with Justice Scalia's conclusion that the Government must choose between using standard criminal processes and suspending the writ. Justice Scalia relies heavily upon *Ex Parte Milligan*, and three cases decided by New York state courts in the wake of the War of 1812 * * *. I admit that *Milligan* supports his position. But because the Executive Branch there, unlike here, did not follow a specific statutory mechanism provided by Congress, the Court did not need to reach the broader question of Congress' power, and its discussion on this point was arguably dicta.

More importantly, the Court referred frequently and pervasively to the criminal nature of the proceedings instituted against Milligan. In fact, this feature serves to distinguish the state cases as well. * * *

Although I do acknowledge that the reasoning of these cases might apply beyond criminal punishment, the punishment-nonpunishment distinction harmonizes all of the precedent. And, subsequent cases have at least implicitly distinguished *Milligan* in just this way. Finally, *Quirin* overruled *Milligan* to the extent that those cases are inconsistent. Because the Government does not detain Hamdi in order to punish him, as the plurality acknowledges, *Milligan* and the New York cases do not control. * * *

Finally, Justice Scalia's position raises an additional concern. Justice Scalia apparently does not disagree that the Federal Government has all power necessary to protect the Nation. If criminal processes do not suffice, however, Justice Scalia would require Congress to suspend the writ. But the fact that the writ may not be suspended "unless when in Cases of Rebellion or Invasion the public Safety may require it[]" * * * poses two related problems. First, this condition might not obtain here or during many other emergencies during which this detention authority might be necessary. Congress would then have to choose between acting unconstitutionally and depriving the President of the tools he needs to protect the Nation. Second, I do not see how suspension would make constitutional otherwise unconstitutional detentions ordered by the President. It simply removes a remedy. Justice Scalia's position might therefore require one or both of the political branches to act unconstitutionally in order to protect the Nation. But the power to protect the Nation must be the power to do so lawfully.

Accordingly, I conclude that the Government's detention of Hamdi as an enemy combatant does not violate the Constitution. By detaining

Hamdi, the President, in the prosecution of a war and authorized by Congress, has acted well within his authority. Hamdi thereby received all the process to which he was due under the circumstances. I therefore believe that this is no occasion to balance the competing interests, as the plurality unconvincingly attempts to do.

IV

Although I do not agree with the plurality that the balancing approach of *Mathews v. Eldridge* * * * is the appropriate analytical tool with which to analyze this case, I cannot help but explain that the plurality misapplies its chosen framework, one that if applied correctly would probably lead to the result I have reached. * * * At issue here is the far more significant interest of the security of the Nation. The Government seeks to further that interest by detaining an enemy soldier not only to prevent him from rejoining the ongoing fight. Rather, as the Government explains, detention can serve to gather critical intelligence regarding the intentions and capabilities of our adversaries, a function that the Government avers has become all the more important in the war on terrorism.

Additional process, the Government explains, will destroy the intelligence gathering function. It also does seem quite likely that, under the process envisioned by the plurality, various military officials will have to take time to litigate this matter. And though the plurality does not say so, a meaningful ability to challenge the Government's factual allegations will probably require the Government to divulge highly classified information to the purported enemy combatant, who might then upon release return to the fight armed with our most closely held secrets. * * *

Ultimately, the plurality's dismissive treatment of the Government's asserted interests arises from its apparent belief that enemy-combatant determinations are not part of "the actual prosecution of a war"or one of the "central functions of warmaking." This seems wrong: Taking and holding enemy combatants is a quintessential aspect of the prosecution of war. Moreover, this highlights serious difficulties in applying the plurality's balancing approach here. First, in the war context, we know neither the strength of the Government's interests nor the costs of imposing additional process.

Second, it is at least difficult to explain why the result should be different for other military operations that the plurality would ostensibly recognize as "central functions of warmaking." * * * Because a decision to bomb a particular target might extinguish *life* interests, the plurality's analysis seems to require notice to potential targets. To take one more example, in November 2002, a Central Intelligence Agency (CIA) Predator drone fired a Hellfire missile at a vehicle in Yemen carrying an al Qaeda leader, a citizen of the United States, and four others. It is not clear whether the CIA knew that an American was in the vehicle. But the plurality's due process would seem to require notice and opportunity to respond here as well. I offer these examples not because I think the plurality would demand additional process in these situations but because it clearly would not. The result here should be the same. * * *

Undeniably, Hamdi has been deprived of a serious interest, one actually protected by the Due Process Clause. Against this, however, is the Government's overriding interest in protecting the Nation. * * *

I acknowledge that under the plurality's approach, it might, at times, be appropriate to give detainees access to counsel and notice of the factual basis for the Government's determination.　　But properly accounting for the Government's interests also requires concluding that access to counsel and to the factual basis would not always be warranted. Though common sense suffices, the Government thoroughly explains that counsel would often destroy the intelligence gathering function. Equally obvious is the Government's interest in not fighting the war in its own courts and protecting classified information. * * *

For these reasons, I would affirm the judgment of the Court of Appeals.

———

NOTES AND QUESTIONS ON HAMDI AND INDEFINITE DETENTION

1)　Counting Votes. The bottom line in *Hamdi* was that the Fourth Circuit's judgment was reversed and Hamdi's detention was not authorized on the record before the Supreme Court. Beyond that holding, consider the Justices' configurations for the following: (1) whether the Constitution permits the indefinite detention of citizen-enemy combatants; (2) whether the AUMF permits the indefinite detention of citizen-enemy combatants; (3) whether the President can detain citizen-enemy combatants without an authorizing statute; (4) whether the Constitution requires the judiciary to make an individualized combatant status determination (and if so, what process is due); (5) whether there is a habeas remedy to challenge the detention of citizen-enemy combatants; and (6) whether the Constitution requires the judiciary to make an individualized combatant status determination as part of the habeas remedy.

2)　The AUMF. Under the AUMF, the President was authorized "to use all necessary and appropriate force against those nations, organizations, or persons he determines planned, authorized, committed, or aided the terrorist attacks that occurred on September 11, 2001, or harbored such organizations or persons, in order to prevent any future acts of international terrorism against the United States by such nations, organizations or persons." Authorization for Use of Military Force Joint Resolution, Pub. L. 107–40, 115 Stat. 224. The Government could have made two different arguments—that the AUMF both authorized indefinite detention and suspended the habeas privilege—but it made only the former.

a)　As a suspension statute. That authorization does not include "language of detention," but rather discusses "necessary and appropriate force." If the AUMF language regarding "necessary and appropriate force" was broad enough to set up military commissions and detain prisoners, could it not operate as a suspension of the privilege? Should the Court have adopted a clear statement rule on this particular question? Even if Congress had suspended the privilege, would the suspension have been effective? If that suspension were improper, would a challenge to it be justiciable?

b)　As authorization for detention. *Hamdi* held that the AUMF authorized some indefinite detention. (The four Justices in Justice O'Connor's bloc, plus Justice Thomas.) Parts of the *Hamdi* plurality opinion dealing with the issue of statutory authorization, which were omitted here, discussed the Emergency Detention Act of 1950, 18 U.S.C. § 4001(a), which states that "[n]o citizen shall be imprisoned or otherwise detained by the United States except pursuant to an Act of Congress." Does that Act provide a clear statement rule of its own? Is it a particularly powerful statute given the language in *Endo* requiring "specific language of detention?" The Act was passed, the *Hamdi* plurality noted, because "Congress was particularly concerned about the possibility that the Act could be used to reprise the Japanese internment camps of World War II." The Government argued that the AUMF authorized the detention of individuals like Hamdi. Do you agree that the AUMF's reference to "necessary and appropriate force" includes the power to indefinitely detain citizen-enemy combatants?

The O'Connor plurality believed that the AUMF permitted such detention because it was a necessary incident of the military action that Congress authorized. The plurality reasoned that, because detention inheres in the sovereign prosecution of a war, the AUMF need not use "specific language of detention" as required in *Endo* and by the Emergency Detention Act of 1950. When the AUMF was passed one week after September 11, 2001, do you think Congress considered the scope of detention that would result? Might Congress have assumed, given past practice, that enemy detainees would either be designated as POWs, that they would face criminal charges, or that they woud be subjected to military process under the law of war?

If the AUMF authorizes detention, then whose detention does it authorize and for what purpose? The statute nowhere contains the term "enemy combatant," which was a term of art used by the Executive after 9/11 to describe, among others, GTMO detainees. Any enemy combatant status designation meant that a detainee was not a POW, and therefore not entitled to certain legal protections. During the oral arguments, Justice Scalia, addressing the question of what the term "enemy combatant" meant, humorously commented, "it means someone who is combating." The plurality noted, "[T]he Government has never provided any court with the full criteria that it uses in classifying individuals" as enemy combatants. Must the detainee have "planned, authorized, committed, or aided" the terrorists behind the 9/11 attacks? Do you agree with Justice O'Connor in that the scope of the authorization should be limited to indefinite detention for the purposes of incapacitation only—not for the purposes of interrogation?

3)   Clear Language of Detention. Only Justices Souter and Ginsburg doubted whether the AUMF authorized such detention on its own terms. They argued that the AUMF's focus was on authorizing war, not detention: "its focus is clear, and that is on the use of military power." They highlighted that, similar to the statute in *Endo*, the AUMF does not include clear language of detention. They argued that such an authorization of war must be understood as limited by traditional usages and the law of war. Finally, they emphasized that "even if history had spared us the cautionary example of the internments in World War II, even if there had been no *Korematsu*, and *Endo* had set out no principle of statutory interpretation, there would be a compelling reason to . . . demand manifest authority to detain before detention is authorized." That reason they cited was an interest in separated powers, whereby executive detention requires Congressional authorization. Justices Souter and Ginsburg concluded that, if prisoners were being detained not as POWs, without access to counsel, or otherwise in violation of the Geneva Conventions, then their detention would be illegal and their release justified. Do you agree that simply because a detention is "illegal" there must be a habeas remedy?

Justices Scalia and Stevens, on the other hand, argued that the issue of whether the AUMF purported to authorize indefinite detention did not matter. Absent an outright suspension of the privilege, they reasoned, the AUMF was incapable of authorizing the indefinite detention of a citizen. Do you agree with their interpretation of *Milligan* as strictly forbidding the indefinite detention of a citizen, absent a suspension? In other words, do you think the Suspension Clause forbids any restriction on habeas relief other than a suspension statute?

4) Scholarship on the AUMF. Professors Curtis Bradley and Jack Goldsmith have prominently argued that the language of the AUMF should play a central role in any analysis of post-9/11 executive detention power, and they give a favorable account of how the AUMF figured prominently in the *Hamdi* analysis. See Curtis Bradley & Jack Goldsmith, *Congressional Authorization and the War on Terrorism*, 118 HARV. L. REV. 2047 (2005). They conclude that the AUMF provides authority comparable to a declaration of war. Despite its sweeping generality, they argue, courts should look to the law of war and international law to interpret the AUMF. Others favor the more limited and "clear statement" approach adopted by Justices Souter and Ginsburg. Eschewing both of the previously-mentioned positions, the D.C. Circuit has suggested that it would be "mistaken" to treat the "war powers granted by" the AUMF as "limited by the international laws of war." *Al-Bihani v. Obama*, 590 F.3d 866, 871 (D.C. Cir. 2010); but see *Al-Bihani v. Obama*, 619 F.3d 1, 1 (2010) (Sentelle, J., concurring in denial of rehearing en banc) (declining rehearing en banc because that statement was dictum). Is the D.C. Circuit's view (dicta or not) consistent with the *Hamdi* plurality?

The meaning of the AUMF is crucial. After all, although the AUMF may clearly authorize force in Afghanistan against those harboring Al Qaeda, does it similarly authorize the detention of those who are said to be members of new Al Qaeda cells formed since the 9/11 attacks? Does it authorize detention of individuals who are members of Al Qaeda groups in other countries, such as Yemen? Does it authorize the detention of individuals who solely provide financial support to Al Qaeda? Does it authorize the detention of individuals who provided transportation or housing to Al Qaeda members but were not part of the "command structure"?

5) The Executive Power Theory. The Government argued both that the AUMF authorized the President to indefinitely detain citizen-enemy combatants and, in the alternative, that the President needed no such authorization because the detention was legal under the Article II War Powers. Because the Supreme Court determined (by a vote of five to four, with Justice Thomas agreed joining the plurality on this proposition) that the AUMF did authorize indefinite citizen-enemy detention, it did not reach the executive power argument. Justice Thomas, however, also signaled his willingness to accept the executive power position, and he would continue to vote for or signal his receptivity to it in other post-9/11 cases.

What was that theory, exactly? Article II, § 2, cl. 1 provides that "[t]he President shall be Commander in Chief of the Army and Navy of the United States." Moreover, there is considerable case law that supports the proposition that the President has all power that is required to prosecute that responsibility—to take care that the President "faithfully execute" the laws.[c] In *Hamdi*,

---

[c] See, e.g., Johnson v. Eisenstrager, 339 U.S. 763, 785 ("And, of course, grant of war power includes all that is necessary and proper for carrying these powers into execution"); Fleming v.

the Government relied heavily on *Quirin* and argued that the President's auxiliary war power includes "the authority to capture and detain enemy combatants in wartime, at least for the duration of a conflict." *Quirin*, however, was a military commission case and discussed the authority of the President as Commander in Chief to create military commissions to try enemy soldiers for law-of-war violations. Does *Quirin* answer whether the Executive has the power to indefinitely detain citizen-enemy combatants? Should the Court have discussed whether the Executive had the power to detain citizens? Should habeas review be available to challenge an exercise of executive authority to detain citizen enemy-combatants?

6)   The Due Process Clause. Note that, in justifying the holding, the *Hamdi* Plurality eschews the Suspension Clause in favor of the Due Process Clause. Justice Scalia instead argued in dissent that the Suspension Clause ensures release and is connected with a view of due process that a citizen may only be prosecuted for treason in civilian courts. For the argument that the Due Process Clause itself guarantees a habeas privilege to prisoners, see Martin H. Redish and Colleen McNamara, *Habeas Corpus, Due Process and the Suspension Clause: A Study in the Foundations of American Constitutionalism*, 96 Va. L. Rev. 1361 (2010).

7)   Prior Process. In order to decide whether *Hamdi* received *due* process, the Court had to examine what process *Hamdi* had already received. What procedures did the Government use to reach the decision that he should be detained as an enemy combatant—in other words, what process did the Government use to make the "status determination"? What would you suppose comprised the Government's "screening" after Hamdi was initially captured and turned over by allied forces in Afghanistan? What further evaluation do you suppose occurred subsequent to that initial screening? Why did the Government later reject his requests for access to counsel?

8)   Due Process Balancing. The plurality applies the due process balancing test from *Mathews v. Eldridge*, 424 U.S. 319 (1976)—a decision concerning what procedures should be applied before taking away social security disability benefits. Was *Eldridge* really the "ordinary" test to be used? *Eldridge* is used to evaluate administrative process—and its balancing test has been much criticized in that context.[d] The *Eldridge* test had rarely been used in a criminal context, and it had never been used to assess habeas procedures. The *Hamdi* plurality did not purport to assign particular weights to the interests at stake. Weighty interests lie on each side of the scale—the detainee's interest in not being detained indefinitely, the government's national security interests—and

---

Page, 50 U.S. 603, 615 (1850) ("As commander-in-chief, he is authorized to direct the movements of the naval and military forces placed by law at his command, and to employ them in the manner he may deem most effectual to harass and conquer and subdue the enemy."). Auxiliary war power derives from several places in Article II. Article II vests all of the "executive power" in the President. Art II, § 1, cl. 1. It also makes the President the Commander in Chief of the Army and Navy, Art. II, § 2, cl. 1, and it empowers him to appoint and commission officers of the United States. Art. II, § 3, cl. 1. Finally, Article requires the President to "take Care that the Laws be faithfully executed." Art. II, § 3.

[d] For critiques on the use of *Eldridge* in administrative law, see Jerry L. Mashaw, *The Supreme Court's Due Process Calculus for Administrative Adjudication in Mathews v. Eldridge: Three Factors in Search of a Theory of Value*, 44 U. Chi. L. Rev. 28, 53–54 (1976); Edward L. Rubin, *Due Process and the Administrative State*, 72 Cal. L. Rev. 1044, 1046 (1984); Richard B. Saphire, *Specifying Due Process Values*, 127 U. Pa. L. Rev. 111, 155 (1978); Lawrence B. Solum, *Procedural Justice*, 78 S. Cal. L. Rev. 181, 252–53 (2004).

there exists a risk of erroneous deprivation. Can such weighty interests on both sides of the scale be balanced? Did the Court purport to balance them? Could the plurality instead have described minimum procedures required by due process, without using a balancing approach at all? What would the merits of a more categorical approach accomplish? In his dissent, Justice Thomas stated that he did "not think that the Federal Government's war powers [could] be balanced away by this Court." He noted that, during wartime, such interests may be obscured. He commented, "Taking and holding enemy combatants is a quintessential aspect of the prosecution of war," but that "in the war context, we know neither the strength of the Government's interests nor the costs of imposing additional process." For scholarly criticism of the use of the *Eldridge* analysis in *Hamdi*, see, for example, Tung Yin, *Procedural Due Process to Determine "Enemy Combatant" Status in the War on Terrorism*, 73 Tenn. L. Rev. 351, 355, 398–99, 400 (2006) (observing "the interests on both sides can be described with apocalyptic intensity" and predicting that the balancing test is "likely to succumb to a result-oriented malleability").

9) What Process is Due? After *Hamdi,* what procedures must the Government use to assess whether detainees are in fact enemy combatants? The plurality does not define who or what constitutes an enemy combatant. (You will soon see that the Government's terminology shifted in response to *Hamdi*, in part to facilitate a change in policy towards those prisoners that fell within the ambit of the decision.) Could the Government reintroduce the same Mobbs declaration and adequately support Hamdi's detention? Would *Hamdi* require the Government to continue to give a detainee like Hamdi access to a lawyer?

What type of hearing must the district court conduct on remand following *Hamdi*? The plurality was clear that the district court must be able to review facts and not just law; Hamdi's goal was to challenge the factual basis for his designation as an enemy combatant. Thus, the plurality stated that the process must not permit "the Executive's factual assertions [to] go wholly unchallenged[,]" and that those assertions may not be "simply presumed correct." Would *Hamdi* have access to discovery in order to counter the Executive's factual assertions? What if the Government states that all records aside from the Mobbs declaration are classified? Could the Government benefit from an evidentiary presumption in its favor? Although the plurality stated that there could be some presumption or burden shifting, it rejected the possibility that such a presumption might attach where the custody was supported merely "some evidence" against the detainee. (Recall the limited use of the "some evidence" test in the immigration context from Chapter 7.) Also, although *Hamdi* received access to counsel and would receive a chance to rebut the Government's assertions before a neutral decision-maker, the exact contours of the required process remained quite vague and were only outlined by way of dicta.

10) A Competent Tribunal? Nor did the plurality address whether the process due had to take the form of a habeas corpus proceeding. More precisely, the plurality opinion did not distinguish between the process that must be part of the combatant status determination and the process that must be available to conduct federal habeas review of custody pursuant to that determination. Could the Government conduct its screening before a military tribunal? The plurality suggested as much in dicta, citing to army regulations implementing Article 5 of the Third Geneva Convention concerning the screening of detainees who assert POW status (Army Regulation 190–8, Enemy Prisoners of War, Retained Personnel, Civilian Internees and Other Detainees § 1–6 (1997)), and implying that it could supply the required process.[e] Had the Government made such a "competent tribunal" available, could the *Hamdi* litigation have been avoided? The plurality also suggested the Suspension Clause ensures some amount of process, as set out in the relevant habeas statutes. What role, then, did the due process analysis play? If the Government provided process that complied with the *Eldridge* test, would habeas corpus still be available? The plurality suggested that it would, at least to allow examination of whether the Government had in fact provided adequate process is the custody determination. Would habeas corpus still be available to examine whether the detention was authorized?

11) Habeas Process. The Supreme Court did not rely on the Suspension Clause, at least not explicitly. The plurality, however, also cited to 42 U.S.C. § 2241 and companion provisions, which "provide at least a skeletal outline of the procedures to be afforded a petitioner in federal habeas review." Those procedures allow, among other things, "the taking of evidence in habeas proceedings by deposition, affidavit, or interrogatories." Could the Court have instead used the habeas statutes more explicitly as the source to develop the procedures to be used to evaluate Hamdi's detention? Or is Justice Scalia correct in that habeas corpus simply requires that Hamdi be released? As he put it, habeas corpus examines legality of detention and does not "supply the omitted process necessary to make it legal." For the argument that the Court could have relied more on habeas process, see Jonathan Hafetz, *Habeas Corpus, Judicial Review, and Limits On Secrecy In Detentions At Guantánamo*, 5 Cardozo Pub. L. Pol'y & Ethics J. 127, 157–78 (2006). For the argument that the Court should have more straightforwardly relied on the Suspension Clause, see Brandon L. Garrett, *Habeas Corpus and Due Process*, 98 Cornell L. Rev. 47 (2012). Professor Amanda Tyler agrees that the Due Process Clause governs but that it should have provided Hamdi with more than just a hearing. See Amanda Tyler, *Is Suspension a Political Question?*, 59 Stan. L. Rev. 333, 384 n. 20 (2006). Professor Trevor Morrison has explored implications of Justice Scalia's views, which he helpfully terms "suspension-as-authorization." Trevor W. Morrison, *Hamdi's Habeas Puzzle: Suspension as Authorization?*, 91 Cornell L. Rev. 411, 424 (2006).

12) Enough About Process Already. For the criticism that the Court should instead focus more carefully on the substantive individual rights, see Jenny S. Martinez, *Process and Substance in the "War on Terror,"* 108 Colum. L. Rev. 1013, 1016 (2008). Professor Martinez noted that "[t]he most important legal questions in the 'war on terror' involve profound infringements of individual rights—torture and other forms of cruel treatment, imprisonment, deportation, scrutiny of private phone calls and personal records." But the judicial rulings instead focused on questions of jurisdiction, habeas corpus procedures and the like. Does that tell you something about habeas corpus as a vehicle for vindicating individual rights? Is there a reason why habeas corpus might be only a limited remedy for certain types of constitutional violations?

---

[e] Amici emphasized longstanding U.S. compliance with Article 5 of the Geneva Conventions and the provision of a "competent tribunal" to detainees during wartime, arguing "[p]aradoxically, the United States invokes the laws of war as the source of its authority to detain Petitioner, yet refuses to abide by the clear mandates of the Geneva Conventions that lie at the heart of these laws of war." Brief of Amicus Curiae Experts on the Law of War in Support of Petitioners, Hamdi v. Rumsfeld, No. 03–6696, at 11 (2004). However, the plurality did not address whether the U.S. was in violation of any treaty obligations and only made the brief reference to the army regulations implementing Article 5.

13) Length of National Security Detention. What significance did the *Hamdi* plurality attach to the fact that Hamdi's detention was not only indefinite, but—based on the Government's position—that it could potentially "last for the rest of his life"? President George W. Bush had told Congress: "Our war on terror begins with al Qaeda, but it does not end there. It will not end until every terrorist group of global reach has been found, stopped and defeated."[f] On the one hand, the plurality noted that active combat in Afghanistan was still ongoing. On the other hand, the *Hamdi* cited *Zadvydas v. Davis*, 533 U.S. 678, 690 (2001) regarding indefinite immigration detention, discussed in Chapter 7, and *Addington v. Texas*, 441 U.S. 418, 425–427 (1979) regarding civil detention, discussed in Chapter 8. How do you think the length of detention should figure into the determination of whether a prisoner enjoys a statutory or constiutional habeas privilege?

14) Military Strikes. In dissent, Justice Thomas also asked "why the result should be different for other military operations." He went on:

> To take one more example, in November 2002, a Central Intelligence Agency (CIA) Predator drone fired a Hellfire missile at a vehicle in Yemen carrying an al Qaeda leader, a citizen of the United States, and four others. . . . It is not clear whether the CIA knew that an American was in the vehicle. But the plurality's due process would seem to require notice and opportunity to respond here as well.

He added, "I offer these examples not because I think the plurality would demand additional process in these situations but because it clearly would not. The result here should be the same." Such remote drone missile attacks have only escalated since the Court's *Hamdi* decision. Is treating an individual as a military target really no different than an indefinite detention, as Justice Thomas suggested? In contrast to the result in *Hamdi,* federal courts have rejected due process challenges to decisions to target individuals using such remote missiles. The most prominent was a challenge to the targeting of a U.S. citizen, Anwar Al-Awlaki. (His father was the petitioner.) The federal court dismissed the challenge, finding that, among other things, the political-question doctrine barred consideration of a challenge to authorization for missile targeting.[g] Al-Awlaki was later killed in a drone attack in Yemen.[h]

15) Hamdi's Release. After the decision, and having earlier maintained that Hamdi posed such danger that he should not be allowed to meet with counsel, the Government released him on the condition that he return to Saudi Arabia, renounce his U.S. citizenship, and agree to restrictions on his travel. The settlement agreement is available online.[i]

---

[f] Address to a Joint Session of Congress and the American People (Sept. 20, 2001).

[g] Al-Aulaqi v. Obama, NO. CIV. A. 10–1469 JDB, 727 F.Supp.2d 1 (D.D.C., December 07, 2010).

[h] See Mark Mazzetti, Eric Schmitt and Robert F. Worth, *Two-Year Manhunt Led to Killing of Awlaki in Yemen,* N.Y. Times, Sept. 30, 2011.

[i] Settlement Agreement, Yaser Esam Hamdi v. Donald Rumsfeld (Sept. 17, 2004), at http://news.findlaw.com/hdocs/docs/hamdi/91704stlagrmnt.html.

NOTES ON THE POST-9/11 IMPORTANCE OF TERRITORIAL JURISDICTION

1) Territorial Jurisdiction Revisited. The military had initially taken Hamdi to GTMO, but then moved him to the United States because it realized that he was an American citizen. Why do you think that the Government decided to move him from GTMO to the mainland U.S. after learning that he was a citizen?

2) *Rumsfeld v. Padilla* and the Proper Respondent. The Supreme Court confronted a problem involving the designation of a proper respondent in *Rumsfeld v. Padilla*, 542 U.S. 426 (2004). Jose Padilla was the only other American citizen detained as an enemy combatant in the mainland United States but, unlike Hamdi, he was not seized abroad. Should the fact that he was seized in the United States make a difference as to habeas review of his case? The government brought him to New York pursuant to a warrant in a grand jury investigation of the 9/11 attacks in the Southern District of New York. Meanwhile, the President concluded that it was "consistent with U.S. law and the laws of war for the Secretary of Defense to detain Mr. Padilla as an enemy combatant." Padilla filed his habeas petition in New York, but once he was designated as an enemy combatant, the military transferred him to a Navy brig in Charleston, S.C. The Supreme Court concluded that the Navy brig commander in South Carolina was the proper respondent and that the habeas petition should have been filed there. The Court emphasized, "The federal habeas statute straightforwardly provides that the proper respondent to a habeas petition is 'the person who has custody over [the petitioner].'"

Recall earlier rulings concerning territorial jurisdiction. The Supreme Court's ruling in *Braden v. 30th Judicial Circuit Court of Ky.*, 410 U.S. 484, 495 (1973) stated—contrary to its earlier ruling in *Ahrens v. Clark*, 335 U.S. 188 (1948)—that the prisoner's presence within the territorial jurisdiction of the district court is not "an invariable prerequisite" to the exercise of federal habeas jurisdiction because "the writ of habeas corpus does not act upon the prisoner who seeks relief, but upon the person who holds him in what is alleged to be unlawful custody." *Padilla*, however, emphasized that *Braden* involved an individual detained overseas, outside the jurisdiction of any district court. The Court held that Donald Rumsfeld, the Secretary of Defense, was not the proper respondent named in a habeas petition when the "immediate physical custodian" could be served in another district court. *Padilla* also distinguished *Endo*, explaining that, "when the Government moves a habeas petitioner after she properly files a petition naming her immediate custodian, the District Court retains jurisdiction and may direct the writ to any respondent within its jurisdiction who has legal authority to effectuate the prisoner's release." Padilla was ultimately transferred to Florida, where he was convicted of conspiracy in a federal court. Should a prisoner have to name the custodian most immediately responsible for the custody, or should a prisoner be able to name someone up the chain of command? Which way would history, *Endo*, and practical considerations cut?

3) *Rasul v. Bush*. Very few of the post-9/11 detainees were American citizens, as Justice Scalia noted in his *Hamdi* dissent. Most of the GTMO detainees were noncitizens. Why detain them on a remote naval base held by the U.S. under a long-term lease agreement with Cuba, rather than bring them to the territorial United States? A key rationale for detaining individuals at GTMO was that the location would place the detainees outside the habeas jurisdiction of any court. The Supreme Court dealt a sharp blow to that rationale in *Rasul v. Bush*, 542 U.S. 466 (2004), decided the same day as *Hamdi*. Citizens of Australia and Kuwait, all captured in Afghanistan after 9/11, were being indefinitely detained as enemy combatants at GTMO. Lower courts had applied the *Eisentrager* factors and concluded that they lacked jurisdiction to entertain habeas petitions filed by noncitizens detained abroad.

In *Rasul*, the Supreme Court reversed those lower-court decisions, holding that GTMO detainees could invoke federal jurisdiction under the generally-applicable habeas corpus statute, 28 U.S.C. § 2241. The opinion, by Justice Stevens, emphasized *Braden* and the idea that physical presence in a territory is no longer an "invariable prerequisite" to habeas jurisdiction. The Court also emphasized that the relevant lease agreements gave the U.S. "complete jurisdiction and control" over GTMO, thereby making it, in effect, a piece of U.S. territory for the purposes of habeas inquiries. The Court added, "The courts of the United States have traditionally been open to nonresident aliens." The Court concluded—prematurely—that "[n]o party questions the District Court's jurisdiction over petitioners' custodians. . . Section 2241, by its terms, requires nothing more."

Justice Kennedy concurred, for a slightly different reason, distinguishing the factors highlighted by the Court in *Eisentrager* and emphasizing how "Guantánamo Bay is in every practical respect a United States territory, and it is one far removed from any hostilities." He also noted that, unlike the military commissions conducted in *Eisentrager*, "Indefinite detention without trial or other proceeding presents altogether different considerations. It allows friends and foes alike to remain in detention. It suggests a weaker case of military necessity and much greater alignment with the traditional function of habeas corpus."

Justice Scalia dissented, and was joined by Chief Justice Rehnquist and Justice Thomas. Justice Scalia argued that—as in *Eisentrager*—when a noncitizen is detained abroad, practical reasons counsel *against* extending the privilege to the detainees. He argued:

> The consequence of this holding, as applied to aliens outside the country, is breathtaking. It permits an alien captured in a foreign theater of active combat to bring a § 2241 petition against the Secretary of Defense. Over the course of the last century, the United States has held millions of alien prisoners abroad. . . . The Court's unheralded expansion of federal-court jurisdiction is not even mitigated by a comforting assurance that the legion of ensuing claims will be easily resolved on the merits.

Rasul made it difficult to evade the reach of judicial process by detaining enemy combatants at GTMO—unless Congress rewrote the statute. The Court, however, did not specify which rights habeas petitioners might assert, if any, now that their habeas petitions were to be entertained. How would the "legion of ensuing claims" be resolved?

2. THE *BOUMEDIENE* DECISION

*INTRODUCTORY NOTES ON POST-*HAMDI *STATUTORY DEVELOPMENTS*

1) **Regulations Following *Rasul* and *Hamdi*.** *Rasul* and *Hamdi* prompted several years of sustained habeas litigation, new executive procedures, and new legislation designed to restrict habeas relief. The Secretary of Defense issued a Memo that established combatant status review tribunals (CSRTs) to determine whether a detainee was an unlawful "enemy combatant." A CSRT consisted of three military officers who were tasked with this responsibility.[j] The Memo establishing the CSRTs defined an "enemy combatant" as "an individual who was part of or supporting Taliban or al Qaeda forces, or associated forces that are engaged in hostilities against the United States or its coalition partners." This definition somewhat tracked the language in the AUMF. Note that the citizenship of the detainee was not part of the Memo's definition.

Detainees brought federal habeas challenges to that CSRT process. One district judge took the view that noncitizens detained outside the U.S. lacked rights under the Due Process Clause, and dismissed the petitions.[k] A second judge disagreed and concluded they had due process rights.[l] Meanwhile, Congress intervened to restrict such habeas challenges.

2) **The DTA.** The Detainee Treatment Act of 2005 (DTA), Pub. L. No. 109–148, 119 Stat. 2680, 2739–42 (2005), followed the Court's decisions in *Rasul* and *Hamdi*. The DTA added Subsection (e) to 28 U.S.C. § 2241, the general grant of habeas authority. Subsection (e) stated that "no court, justice, or judge shall have jurisdiction to hear or consider" any action or "an application for a writ of habeas corpus filed by or on behalf of an alien detained by the Department of Defense at [GTMO]," except that the Court of Appeals for the District of Columbia could hear questions concerning compliance with DTA procedures for conducting military commissions and reviewing the status of detainees and the constitutionality of those procedures:

> (i) whether the status determination of the [CSRT] with regard to such alien was consistent with the standards and procedures specified by the Secretary of Defense . . . and (ii) to the extent the Constitution and laws of the United States are applicable, whether the use of such standards and procedures to make the determination is consistent with the Constitution and laws of the United States.

Id. at § 1005(e)(2)(C). The DTA also explicitly authorized military commission trials of enemy aliens. Finally, the DTA contained a provision stating that "[t]his section shall take effect on the date of the enactment of this Act." *Id.* at § 1005(h)(1).

3) ***Hamdan v. Rumsfeld* and Retroactive Application of the DTA.** Did the DTA provisions divesting federal judges of power to hear petitions from GTMO detainees apply to cases pending when the DTA was enacted? The Court decided that question in *Hamdan v. Rumsfeld*, 548 U.S. 557 (2006), the

---

[j] Memorandum from Deputy Secretary of Defense Paul Wolfowitz re: Order Establishing Combatant Status Review Tribunal (July 7, 2004).

[k] Khalid v. Bush, 355 F.Supp.2d 311, 314 (D.D.C. 2005).

[l] In re Guantánamo Detainee Cases, 355 F.Supp.2d 443, 464 (D.D.C. 2005).

military commission case that you read in Chapter 9. Salim Hamdan, a GTMO detainee, challenged the lawfulness of a military commission created under the 2005 DTA and to be conducted under procedures created in Military Commission Order No. 1 (August 31, 2005). As described in Chapter 9, Hamdan did not follow the DTA procedures and instead filed a habeas petition before his military commission trial commenced. The Court, in an opinion authored by Justice Stevens, interpreted the DTA to apply only prospectively, allowing habeas review in federal district courts for all detainees whose petitions were pending when Congress enacted the DTA. Citing to "[o]rdinary principles of statutory construction" and a presumption against retroactivity, *Hamdan* held that the DTA did not apply to pending cases.

Justice Scalia, joined by Justices Thomas and Alito, dissented, arguing that "[a]n ancient and unbroken line of authority attests that statutes ousting jurisdiction unambiguously apply to cases pending at their effective date." He concluded, "The Court's interpretation transforms a provision abolishing jurisdiction over all Guantánamo-related habeas petitions into a provision that retains jurisdiction over cases sufficiently numerous to keep the courts busy for years to come." To be sure, with the procedures held *not* to apply retroactively and the DTA having been enacted in 2005, several years after September 11, 2001, the DTA could not apply to the population present at GTMO as of 2005. Because no new detainees were being brought to GTMO and the detainee population had by then reached its peak, this interpretation effectively guaranteed the habeas privilege for the entire GTMO population. As discussed in the prior Chapter, the Court also ruled that Hamdan could not be tried by a military commission.

4) The Military Commissions Act of 2006. Following *Hamdan*, Congress enacted the Military Commissions Act of 2006 (MCA), which made clear that the restrictions on habeas jurisdiction applied to all GTMO cases, including those pending at the time the DTA was enacted. This clarity forced the Supreme Court to directly address whether these limits on federal habeas jurisdiction violated the Suspension Clause. Recall how, in *St. Cyr,* the Court emphasized that the relevant immigration reforms neither mentioned habeas corpus nor affected the text of the general habeas corpus statute, 28 U.S.C. § 2241. To avoid similar ambiguity, the MCA amended 28 U.S.C. § 2241 to include a new subsection (e):

> (e)(1) No court, justice, or judge shall have jurisdiction to hear or consider an application for a writ of habeas corpus filed by or on behalf of an alien detained by the United States who has been determined by the United States to have been properly detained as an enemy combatant or is awaiting such determination.

> (2) Except as provided in paragraphs (2) and (3) of section 1005(e) of the Detainee Treatment Act of 2005 (10 U.S.C. 801 note), no court, justice, or judge shall have jurisdiction to hear or consider any other action against the United States or its agents relating to any aspect of the detention, transfer, treatment, trial, or conditions of confinement of an alien who is or was detained by the United States and has been determined by the United States to have been properly detained as an enemy combatant or is awaiting such determination.

The new statute incorporated provisions of the DTA and was passed on September 27, 2006 as an amendment to the 2006 Defense Appropriations Act. In place of habeas process, the MCA provided for very limited judicial review, exclusively by the federal Court of Appeals for the District of Columbia. It also confined that review to questions regarding the constitutionality of the military commissions, combatant status review procedures, and compliance with those procedures. Responding to *Hamdan*, the MCA § 7(b) included the following language about its effective date:

> The amendment made by [MCA § 7(a)] shall take effect on the date of the enactment of this Act, and shall apply to all cases, without exception, pending on or after the date of the enactment of this Act which relate to any aspect of the detention, transfer, treatment, trial, or conditions of detention of an alien detained by the United States since September 11, 2001.

The MCA forced the question of whether Congress could impose dramatic restrictions on judicial review of noncitizen detention.

INTRODUCTORY NOTE ON BOUMEDIENE V. BUSH

Lakhdar Boumediene was detained at GTMO along with five Algerian men, each accused of having links to al-Qaeda and planning to bomb a U.S. Embassy.[m] The consolidated cases were dismissed by the D.C. Circuit, which reasoned that: the prisoners were held outside the U.S.; they had no constitutional rights under either the Suspension Clause or the Due Process Clause; and Congress had stripped federal courts of jurisdiction.[n]

The Supreme Court initially denied certiorari. Boumediene v. Bush, 549 U.S. 1328 (2007). An order denying certiorari would ordinarily end the matter; the Court very rarely reverses course after denying certiorari, and had not done so in decades. Three months later, however, Lt. Col. Stephen Abraham, a reserve intelligence officer and attorney who served on a CSRT panel, filed a supplemental declaration. In that declaration, he stated that the CSRT process failed to satisfy even minimal procedural standards. Lt. Col. Abraham explained that he was part of a CSRT panel that had unanimously concluded that a detainee was not an enemy combatant, but that they were told to reconsider. He stated that, when the CSRT panelists refused to change their ruling, the panelists were replaced.[o] That declaration was widely credited with causing the unusual events that unfolded on the Supreme Court docket after the Abraham declaration was filed.[p] The Supreme Court eventually granted the certiorari petition.

In *Boumediene v. Bush*, 553 U.S. 723 (2008), excerpted below, the Court reversed the D.C. Circuit and held, for the first time, that Congress violated the Suspension Clause. As you read the lengthy majority opinion, consider why, in Part III, the Court first discusses the history of habeas corpus. Ask yourself what view of the Suspension Clause the Court adopts. Next consider why the

---

[m] Andy Worthington, *Profiles: Odah and Boumediene*, BBC News, Dec. 4, 2007.

[n] Boumediene v. Bush, 476 F.3d 981 (D.C. Cir. 2007).

[o] See Reply to Opposition to Petition for Rehearing app., Al Odah v. United States, 551 U.S. 1161 (2007) (No. 06–1196).

[p] See William Glaberson, *In Shift, Justices Agree to Review Detainees' Case*, N.Y. Times, June 30, 2007.

Court adopts, in Part IV, a multifactor test for habeas jurisdiction, whether that test is properly drawn from the *Eisentrager* case, and whether it was applied properly. Justice Scalia's dissent primarily responds to that portion of the opinion and should be read in conjunction with Part IV. Finally, consider what specific reasons the Court relied upon, in Part V, to conclude that Congress had unconstitutionally impaired the privilege by failing to provide an adequate substitute for habeas review, and ask what roles the doctrines of adequate and effective substitutes for habeas and due process played in the analysis. Chief Justice Roberts' dissent primarily responds to that portion of the opinion and should be read in conjunction with Part V.

Boumediene v. Bush

United States Supreme Court
553 U.S. 723 (2008)

■ JUSTICE KENNEDY delivered the opinion of the Court.

Petitioners are aliens designated as enemy combatants and detained at the United States Naval Station at Guantánamo Bay, Cuba. * * *

Petitioners present a question not resolved by our earlier cases relating to the detention of aliens at Guantánamo: whether they have the constitutional privilege of habeas corpus, a privilege not to be withdrawn except in conformance with the Suspension Clause * * *. We hold these petitioners do have the habeas corpus privilege. Congress has enacted a statute, the Detainee Treatment Act of 2005 (DTA) that provides certain procedures for review of the detainees' status. We hold that those procedures are not an adequate and effective substitute for habeas corpus. Therefore § 7 of the Military Commissions Act of 2006 (MCA), 28 U.S.C.A. § 2241(e), operates as an unconstitutional suspension of the writ. We do not address whether the President has authority to detain these petitioners nor do we hold that the writ must issue. These and other questions regarding the legality of the detention are to be resolved in the first instance by the District Court. * * *

I

* * * Some of these individuals were apprehended on the battlefield in Afghanistan, others in places as far away from there as Bosnia and Gambia. All are foreign nationals, but none is a citizen of a nation now at war with the United States. Each denies he is a member of the al Qaeda terrorist network that carried out the September 11 attacks or of the Taliban regime that provided sanctuary for al Qaeda. Each petitioner appeared before a separate CSRT; was determined to be an enemy combatant; and has sought a writ of habeas corpus in the United States District Court for the District of Columbia.

[Following remand after the Court's decision in *Rasul*], Congress passed the DTA. * * * [T]he DTA amended 28 U.S.C. § 2241 to provide that "no court, justice, or judge shall have jurisdiction to hear or consider . . . an application for a writ of habeas corpus filed by or on behalf of an alien detained by the Department of Defense at Guantánamo Bay, Cuba." [The DTA] further provides that the Court of Appeals for the District of Columbia Circuit shall have "exclusive" jurisdiction to review decisions of the CSRTs.

In *Hamdan v. Rumsfeld*, the Court held this provision did not apply to cases (like petitioners') pending when the DTA was enacted. Congress responded by passing the MCA, which again amended § 2241. * * *

The Court of Appeals concluded that MCA § 7 must be read to strip from it, and all federal courts, jurisdiction to consider petitioners' habeas corpus applications; that petitioners are not entitled to the privilege of the writ or the protections of the Suspension Clause; and, as a result, that it was unnecessary to consider whether Congress provided an adequate and effective substitute for habeas corpus in the DTA.

We granted certiorari.

II

* * * In *Hamdan* the Court found it unnecessary to address the petitioner's Suspension Clause arguments but noted the relevance of the clear statement rule in deciding whether Congress intended to reach pending habeas corpus cases. * * * This interpretive rule facilitates a dialogue between Congress and the Court.

* * * [W]e cannot ignore that the MCA was a direct response to *Hamdan*'s holding that the DTA's jurisdiction-stripping provision had no application to pending cases. * * * [T]he MCA deprives the federal courts of jurisdiction to entertain the habeas corpus actions now before us.

III

* * * [W]e must determine whether petitioners are barred from seeking the writ or invoking the protections of the Suspension Clause either because of their status, *i.e.*, petitioners' designation by the Executive Branch as enemy combatants, or their physical location, *i.e.*, their presence at Guantánamo Bay. * * *

We begin with a brief account of the history and origins of the writ. Our account proceeds from two propositions. First, protection for the privilege of habeas corpus was one of the few safeguards of liberty specified in a Constitution that, at the outset, had no Bill of Rights. In the system conceived by the Framers the writ had a centrality that must inform proper interpretation of the Suspension Clause. Second, to the extent there were settled precedents or legal commentaries in 1789 regarding the extraterritorial scope of the writ or its application to enemy aliens, those authorities can be instructive for the present cases.

A

The Framers viewed freedom from unlawful restraint as a fundamental precept of liberty, and they understood the writ of habeas corpus as a vital instrument to secure that freedom. Experience taught, however, that the common-law writ all too often had been insufficient to guard against the abuse of monarchial power. That history counseled the necessity for specific language in the Constitution to secure the writ and ensure its place in our legal system.

Magna Carta decreed that no man would be imprisoned contrary to the law of the land. Important as the principle was, the Barons at Runnymede prescribed no specific legal process to enforce it. * * * [G]radually the writ of habeas corpus became the means by which the promise of Magna Carta was fulfilled.

The development was painstaking, even by the centuries-long measures of English constitutional history. * * * Even so, from an early date it was understood that the King, too, was subject to the law. * * * Still, the writ proved to be an imperfect check. Even when the importance of the writ was well understood in England, habeas relief often was denied by the courts or suspended by Parliament. Denial or suspension occurred in times of political unrest, to the anguish of the imprisoned and the outrage of those in sympathy with them.

A notable example from this period was *Darnel's Case,* 3 How. St. Tr. 1 (K.B. 1627). * * * [I]n a display of the Stuart penchant for authoritarian excess, Charles I demanded that Darnel and at least four others lend him money. Upon their refusal, they were imprisoned. The prisoners sought a writ of habeas corpus; and the King filed a return in the form of a warrant signed by the Attorney General. The court held this was a sufficient answer and justified the subjects' continued imprisonment.

There was an immediate outcry of protest. The House of Commons promptly passed the Petition of Right, which condemned executive "impris-on[ment] without any cause" shown, and declared that "no freeman in any such manner as is before mencioned [shall] be imprisoned or deteined." Yet a full legislative response was long delayed. The King soon began to abuse his authority again, and Parliament was dissolved. * * * Civil strife and the Interregnum soon followed, and not until 1679 did Parliament try once more to secure the writ, this time through the Habeas Corpus Act of 1679. The Act, which later would be described by Blackstone as the "stable bulwark of our liberties," established procedures for issuing the writ; and it was the model upon which the habeas statutes of the 13 American Colonies were based.

This history was known to the Framers. It no doubt confirmed their view that pendular swings to and away from individual liberty were endemic to undivided, uncontrolled power. * * * That the Framers considered the writ a vital instrument for the protection of individual liberty is evident from the care taken to specify the limited grounds for its suspension: "The Privilege of the Writ of Habeas Corpus shall not be suspended, unless when in Cases of Rebellion or Invasion the public Safety may require it." The word "privilege" was used, perhaps, to avoid mentioning some rights to the exclusion of others. (Indeed, the only mention of the term "right" in the Constitution, as ratified, is in its clause giving Congress the power to protect the rights of authors and inventors. See Art. I, § 8, cl. 8.). * * * The Clause protects the rights of the detained by a means consistent with the essential design of the Constitution. It ensures that, except during periods of formal suspension, the Judiciary will have a time-tested device, the writ, to maintain the "delicate balance of governance" that is itself the surest safeguard of liberty. The Clause protects the rights of the detained by affirming the duty and authority of the Judiciary to call the jailer to account. The separation-of-powers doctrine, and the history that influenced its design, therefore must inform the reach and purpose of the Suspension Clause.

B

The broad historical narrative of the writ and its function is central to our analysis, but we seek guidance as well from founding-era authorities addressing the specific question before us: whether foreign nationals, apprehended and detained in distant countries during a time of serious threats to our Nation's security, may assert the privilege of the writ and seek its protection. The Court has been careful not to foreclose the possibility that the protections of the Suspension Clause have expanded along with post-1789 developments that define the present scope of the writ. But the analysis may begin with precedents as of 1789, for the Court has said that "at the absolute minimum" the Clause protects the writ as it existed when the Constitution was drafted and ratified.

* * * The Government argues the common-law writ ran only to those territories over which the Crown was sovereign. Petitioners argue that jurisdiction followed the King's officers. Diligent search by all parties reveals no certain conclusions. In none of the cases cited do we find that a common-law court would or would not have granted, or refused to hear for lack of jurisdiction, a petition for a writ of habeas corpus brought by a prisoner deemed an enemy combatant, under a standard like the one the Department of Defense has used in these cases, and when held in a territory, like Guantánamo, over which the Government has total military and civil control.

We know that at common law a petitioner's status as an alien was not a categorical bar to habeas corpus relief. *See, e.g., Sommersett's Case,* 20 How. St. Tr. 1, 80–82 (1772) (ordering an African slave freed upon finding the custodian's return insufficient) * * *. We know as well that common-law courts entertained habeas petitions brought by enemy aliens detained in England-"entertained" at least in the sense that the courts held hearings to determine the threshold question of entitlement to the writ.* * *

We find the evidence as to the geographic scope of the writ at common law informative, but, again, not dispositive. Petitioners argue the site of their detention is analogous to two territories outside of England to which the writ did run: the so-called "exempt jurisdictions," like the Channel Islands; and (in former times) India. There are critical differences between these places and Guantánamo, however.

* * *[C]ommon-law courts granted habeas corpus relief to prisoners detained in the exempt jurisdictions. But these areas, while not in theory part of the realm of England, were nonetheless under the Crown's control. And there is some indication that these jurisdictions were considered sovereign territory. Because the United States does not maintain formal sovereignty over Guantánamo Bay, see Part IV, *infra,* the naval station there and the exempt jurisdictions discussed in the English authorities are not similarly situated.

Petitioners and their *amici* further rely on cases in which British courts in India granted writs of habeas corpus to noncitizens detained in territory over which the Moghul Emperor retained formal sovereignty and control. The analogy to the present cases breaks down, however, because of the geographic location of the courts in the Indian example. The Supreme Court of Judicature (the British Court) sat in Calcutta; but no federal court sits at Guantánamo. The Supreme Court of Judicature was, moreover, a special court set up by Parliament to monitor certain conduct during the British Raj. * * *

The Government argues, in turn, that Guantánamo is more closely analogous to Scotland and Hanover, territories that were not part of England but nonetheless controlled by the English monarch (in his separate capacities as King of Scotland and Elector of Hanover). Lord Mansfield can be cited for the proposition that, at the time of the founding, English courts lacked the "power" to issue the writ to Scotland and Hanover, territories Lord Mansfield referred to as "foreign." But what matters for our purposes is why common-law courts lacked this power. Given the English Crown's delicate and complicated relationships with Scotland and Hanover in the 1700's, we cannot disregard the possibility that the common-law courts' refusal to issue the writ to these places was motivated not by formal legal constructs but by what we would think of as prudential concerns. * * *

The prudential barriers that may have prevented the English courts from issuing the writ to Scotland and Hanover are not relevant here. We have no reason to believe an order from a federal court would be disobeyed at Guantánamo. No Cuban court has jurisdiction to hear these petitioners' claims, and no law other than the laws of the United States applies at the naval station. * * * Each side in the present matter argues that the very lack of a precedent on point supports its position. The Government points out there is no evidence that a court sitting in England granted habeas relief to an enemy alien detained abroad; petitioners respond there is no evidence that a court refused to do so for lack of jurisdiction.

Both arguments are premised, however, upon the assumption that the historical record is complete and that the common law, if properly understood, yields a definite answer to the questions before us. There are reasons to doubt both assumptions. Recent scholarship points to the inherent shortcomings in the historical record. [*See* Paul D. Halliday & G. Edward White, *The Suspension Clause: English Text, Imperial Contexts, and American Implications*, 94 VA. L. REV. 575, 588–93 (2008).] And given the unique status of Guantánamo Bay and the particular dangers of terrorism in the modern age, the common-law courts simply may not have confronted cases with close parallels to this one. We decline, therefore, to infer too much, one way or the other, from the lack of historical evidence on point.

IV

Drawing from its position that at common law the writ ran only to territories over which the Crown was sovereign, the Government says the Suspension Clause affords petitioners no rights because the United States does not claim sovereignty over the place of detention.

Guantánamo Bay is not formally part of the United States. And under the terms of the lease between the United States and Cuba, Cuba retains "ultimate sovereignty" over the territory while the United States exercises "complete jurisdiction and control." Under the terms of the 1934 Treaty, however, Cuba effectively has no rights as a sovereign until the parties agree to modification of the 1903 Lease Agreement or the United States abandons the base.

The United States contends, nevertheless, that Guantánamo is not within its sovereign control. This was the Government's position well before the events of September 11, 2001. And in other contexts the Court has held that questions of sovereignty are for the political branches to decide. * * * We therefore do not question the Government's position that Cuba, not the United States, maintains sovereignty, in the legal and technical sense of the term, over Guantánamo Bay. But this does not end the analysis.

* * * For the reasons indicated above, the history of common-law habeas corpus provides scant support for this proposition; and, for the reasons indicated below, that position would be inconsistent with our precedents and contrary to fundamental separation-of-powers principles.

A

* * * The Framers foresaw that the United States would expand and acquire new territories. * * * In particular, there was no need to test the

limits of the Suspension Clause because, as early as 1789, Congress extended the writ to the Territories.

Fundamental questions regarding the Constitution's geographic scope first arose at the dawn of the 20th century when the Nation acquired noncontiguous Territories: Puerto Rico, Guam, and the Philippines—ceded to the United States by Spain at the conclusion of the Spanish-American War—and Hawaii—annexed by the United States in 1898. At this point Congress chose to discontinue its previous practice of extending constitutional rights to the territories by statute.

In a series of opinions later known as the Insular Cases, the Court addressed whether the Constitution, by its own force, applies in any territory that is not a State. The Court held that the Constitution has independent force in these territories, a force not contingent upon acts of legislative grace. Yet it took note of the difficulties inherent in that position. * * *

These considerations resulted in the doctrine of territorial incorporation, under which the Constitution applies in full in incorporated Territories surely destined for statehood but only in part in unincorporated Territories. * * * But, as early as * * * 1922, the Court took for granted that even in unincorporated Territories the Government of the United States was bound to provide to noncitizen inhabitants "guaranties of certain fundamental personal rights declared in the Constitution." * * *

Practical considerations weighed heavily as well in *Johnson v. Eisentrager,* 339 U.S. 763 (1950), where the Court addressed whether habeas corpus jurisdiction extended to enemy aliens who had been convicted of violating the laws of war. The prisoners were detained at Landsberg Prison in Germany during the Allied Powers' postwar occupation. The Court stressed the difficulties of ordering the Government to produce the prisoners in a habeas corpus proceeding. It "would require allocation of shipping space, guarding personnel, billeting and rations" and would damage the prestige of military commanders at a sensitive time. In considering these factors the Court sought to balance the constraints of military occupation with constitutional necessities. * * *

True, the Court in *Eisentrager* denied access to the writ, and it noted the prisoners "at no relevant time were within any territory over which the United States is sovereign, and [that] the scenes of their offense, their capture, their trial and their punishment were all beyond the territorial jurisdiction of any court of the United States." The Government seizes upon this language as proof positive that the *Eisentrager* Court adopted a formalistic, sovereignty-based test for determining the reach of the Suspension Clause. We reject this reading for three reasons.

First, we do not accept the idea that the above-quoted passage from *Eisentrager* is the only authoritative language in the opinion and that all the rest is dicta. The Court's further determinations, based on practical considerations, were integral to Part II of its opinion and came before the decision announced its holding.

Second, because the United States lacked both *de jure* sovereignty and plenary control over Landsberg Prison, it is far from clear that the *Eisentrager* Court used the term sovereignty only in the narrow technical sense and not to connote the degree of control the military asserted over the facility. The Justices who decided *Eisentrager* would have understood sovereignty as a multifaceted concept. * * *

Third, if the Government's reading of *Eisentrager* were correct, the opinion would have marked not only a change in, but a complete repudiation of, the Insular Cases' * * * functional approach to questions of extraterritoriality. * * * Nothing in *Eisentrager* says that *de jure* sovereignty is or has ever been the only relevant consideration in determining the geographic reach of the Constitution or of habeas corpus. * * * A constricted reading of *Eisentrager* overlooks * * * the idea that questions of extraterritoriality turn on objective factors and practical concerns, not formalism.

C

* * * In addition to the practical concerns discussed above, the *Eisentrager* Court found relevant that each petitioner:

> "(a) is an enemy alien; (b) has never been or resided in the United States; (c) was captured outside of our territory and there held in military custody as a prisoner of war; (d) was tried and convicted by a Military Commission sitting outside the United States; (e) for offenses against laws of war committed outside the United States; (f) and is at all times imprisoned outside the United States."

Based on this language from *Eisentrager*, and the reasoning in our other extraterritoriality opinions, we conclude that at least three factors are relevant in determining the reach of the Suspension Clause: (1) the citizenship and status of the detainee and the adequacy of the process through which that status determination was made; (2) the nature of the sites where apprehension and then detention took place; and (3) the practical obstacles inherent in resolving the prisoner's entitlement to the writ.

Applying this framework, we note at the onset that the status of these detainees is a matter of dispute. Petitioners, like those in *Eisentrager*, are not American citizens. But the petitioners in *Eisentrager* did not contest, it seems, the Court's assertion that they were "enemy alien[s]." In the instant cases, by contrast, the detainees deny they are enemy combatants. They have been afforded some process in CSRT proceedings to determine their status; but, unlike in *Eisentrager*, there has been no trial by military commission for violations of the laws of war. The difference is not trivial. The records from the *Eisentrager* trials suggest that, well before the petitioners brought their case to this Court, there had been a rigorous adversarial process to test the legality of their detention. The *Eisentrager* petitioners were charged by a bill of particulars that made detailed factual allegations against them. To rebut the accusations, they were entitled to representation by counsel, allowed to introduce evidence on their own behalf, and permitted to cross-examine the prosecution's witnesses.

In comparison the procedural protections afforded to the detainees in the CSRT hearings are far more limited, and, we conclude, fall well short of the procedures and adversarial mechanisms that would eliminate the need for habeas corpus review. Although the detainee is assigned a "Personal Representative" to assist him during CSRT proceedings, the Secretary of the Navy's memorandum makes clear that person is not the detainee's lawyer or even his "advocate." The Government's evidence is accorded a presumption of validity. The detainee is allowed to present "reasonably available" evidence, but his ability to rebut the Government's evidence against him is limited by the circumstances of his confinement and his lack of counsel at this stage. And although the detainee can seek review of his status determination in the Court of Appeals, that review process cannot cure all defects in the earlier proceedings.

As to the second factor relevant to this analysis, the detainees here are similarly situated to the *Eisentrager* petitioners in that the sites of their apprehension and detention are technically outside the sovereign territory of the United States. * * * But there are critical differences between Landsberg Prison, circa 1950, and the United States Naval Station at Guantánamo Bay in 2008. Unlike its present control over the naval station, the United States' control over the prison in Germany was neither absolute nor indefinite. Like all parts of occupied Germany, the prison was under the jurisdiction of the combined Allied Forces. The United States was therefore answerable to its Allies for all activities occurring there. The Allies had not planned a long-term occupation of Germany, nor did they intend to displace all German institutions even during the period of occupation. The Court's holding in *Eisentrager* was thus consistent with the Insular Cases, where it had held there was no need to extend full constitutional protections to territories the United States did not intend to govern indefinitely. Guantánamo Bay, on the other hand, is no transient possession. In every practical sense Guantánamo is not abroad; it is within the constant jurisdiction of the United States. * * *

As to the third factor, we recognize, as the Court did in *Eisentrager*, that there are costs to holding the Suspension Clause applicable in a case of military detention abroad. Habeas corpus proceedings may require expenditure of funds by the Government and may divert the attention of military personnel from other pressing tasks. While we are sensitive to these concerns, we do not find them dispositive. Compliance with any judicial process requires some incremental expenditure of resources. Yet civilian courts and the Armed Forces have functioned alongside each other at various points in our history. The Government presents no credible arguments that the military mission at Guantánamo would be compromised if habeas corpus courts had jurisdiction to hear the detainees' claims. And in light of the plenary control the United States asserts over the base, none are apparent to us.

The situation in *Eisentrager* was far different, given the historical context and nature of the military's mission in post-War Germany. When hostilities in the European Theater came to an end, the United States became responsible for an occupation zone encompassing over 57,000 square miles with a population of 18 million. * * * In addition to supervising massive reconstruction and aid efforts the American forces stationed in Germany faced potential security threats from a defeated enemy. In retrospect the post-War occupation may seem uneventful. But at the time *Eisentrager* was decided, the Court was right to be concerned about judicial interference with the military's efforts to contain "enemy elements, guerilla fighters, and 'werewolves.'"

Similar threats are not apparent here; nor does the Government argue that they are. * * *

It is true that before today the Court has never held that noncitizens detained by our Government in territory over which another country maintains *de jure* sovereignty have any rights under our Constitution. But the cases before us lack any precise historical parallel. They involve individuals detained by executive order for the duration of a conflict that, if measured from September 11, 2001, to the present, is already among the longest wars in American history. The detainees, moreover, are held in a territory that, while technically not part of the United States, is under the complete and total control of our Government. Under these circumstances the lack of a precedent on point is no barrier to our holding.

We hold that Art. I, § 9, cl. 2, of the Constitution has full effect at Guantánamo Bay. If the privilege of habeas corpus is to be denied to the detainees now before us, Congress must act in accordance with the requirements of the Suspension Clause. * * * The MCA does not purport to be a formal suspension of the writ; and the Government, in its submissions to us, has not argued that it is. Petitioners, therefore, are entitled to the privilege of habeas corpus to challenge the legality of their detention.

V

In light of this holding the question becomes whether the statute stripping jurisdiction to issue the writ avoids the Suspension Clause mandate because Congress has provided adequate substitute procedures for habeas corpus. The Government submits there has been compliance with the Suspension Clause because the DTA review process in the Court of Appeals * * * provides an adequate substitute. [The DTA] granted that court jurisdiction to consider

"(i) whether the status determination of the [CSRT] . . . was consistent with the standards and procedures specified by the Secretary of Defense . . . and (ii) to the extent the Constitution and laws of the United States are applicable, whether the use of such standards and procedures to make the determination is consistent with the Constitution and laws of the United States."

* * *

A

Our case law does not contain extensive discussion of standards defining suspension of the writ or of circumstances under which suspension has occurred. This simply confirms the care Congress has taken throughout our Nation's history to preserve the writ and its function. * * *

There are exceptions, of course. Title I of the Antiterrorism and Effective Death Penalty Act of 1996 (AEDPA), § 106, 110 Stat. 1220, contains certain gatekeeping provisions that restrict a prisoner's ability to bring new and repetitive claims in "second or successive" habeas corpus actions. We upheld these provisions against a Suspension Clause challenge in *Felker v. Turpin*, 518 U.S. 651, 662–664 (1996). The provisions at issue in *Felker*, however, did not constitute a substantial departure from common-law habeas procedures. The provisions, for the most part, codified the longstanding abuse-of-the-writ doctrine. AEDPA applies, moreover, to federal, postconviction review after criminal proceedings in state court have taken place. As of this point, cases discussing the implementation of that statute give little helpful instruction (save perhaps by contrast) for the instant cases, where no trial has been held.

The two leading cases addressing habeas substitutes, *Swain v. Pressley*, 430 U.S. 372 (1977), and *United States v. Hayman*, 342 U.S. 205 (1952), likewise provide little guidance here. The statutes at issue were attempts to streamline habeas corpus relief, not to cut it back.

The statute discussed in *Hayman* was 28 U.S.C. § 2255. It replaced traditional habeas corpus for federal prisoners (at least in the first instance) with a process that allowed the prisoner to file a motion with the sentencing court on the ground that his sentence was, *inter alia*, "'imposed in violation of the Constitution or laws of the United States.'" The purpose and effect of the statute was not to restrict access to the writ but to make postconviction proceedings more efficient. It directed claims not to the court that had territorial jurisdiction over the place of the petitioner's confinement but to the sentencing court, a court already familiar with the facts of the case. * * *

The statute in *Swain* applied to prisoners in custody under sentence of the Superior Court of the District of Columbia. Before enactment of the District of Columbia Court Reform and Criminal Procedure Act of 1970 (D.C. Court Reform Act), those prisoners could file habeas petitions in the United States District Court for the District of Columbia. The Act, which was patterned on § 2255, substituted a new collateral process in the Superior Court for the pre-existing habeas corpus procedure in the District Court. But, again, the purpose and effect of the statute was to expedite consideration of the prisoner's claims, not to delay or frustrate it. * * *

Unlike in *Hayman* and *Swain*, here we confront statutes, the DTA and the MCA, that were intended to circumscribe habeas review. * * * To the extent any doubt remains about Congress' intent, the legislative history confirms what the plain text strongly suggests: In passing the DTA Congress did not intend to create a process that differs from traditional habeas corpus process in name only. It intended to create a more limited procedure. * * *

It is against this background that we must interpret the DTA and assess its adequacy as a substitute for habeas corpus. The present cases thus test the limits of the Suspension Clause in ways that *Hayman* and *Swain* did not.

B

We do not endeavor to offer a comprehensive summary of the requisites for an adequate substitute for habeas corpus. We do consider it uncontroversial, however, that the privilege of habeas corpus entitles the prisoner to a meaningful opportunity to demonstrate that he is being held pursuant to "the erroneous application or interpretation" of relevant law. And the habeas court must have the power to order the conditional release of an individual unlawfully detained-though release need not be the exclusive remedy and is not the appropriate one in every case in which the writ is granted. These are the easily identified attributes of any constitutionally adequate habeas corpus proceeding. But, depending on the circumstances, more may be required.

Indeed, common-law habeas corpus was, above all, an adaptable remedy. Its precise application and scope changed depending upon the circumstances. It appears the common-law habeas court's role was most extensive in cases of pretrial and noncriminal detention, where there had been little or no previous judicial review of the cause for detention. * * *

The idea that the necessary scope of habeas review in part depends upon the rigor of any earlier proceedings accords with our test for procedural adequacy in the due process context. See Mathews v. Eldridge, 424 U.S. 319, 335 (1976) (noting that the Due Process Clause requires an assessment of, *inter alia*, "the risk of an erroneous deprivation of [a liberty interest;] and the probable value, if any, of additional or substitute procedural safeguards").* * *

Where a person is detained by executive order, rather than, say, after being tried and convicted in a court, the need for collateral review is most pressing. A criminal conviction in the usual course occurs after a judicial hearing before a tribunal disinterested in the outcome and committed to procedures designed to ensure its own independence. These dynamics are not inherent in executive detention orders or executive review procedures. In this context the need for habeas corpus is more urgent. The intended duration of the detention and the reasons for it bear upon the precise scope of the inquiry. Habeas corpus proceedings need not resemble a criminal trial, even when the detention is by executive order. But the writ must be effective. The habeas court must have sufficient authority to conduct a meaningful review of both the cause for detention and the Executive's power to detain.

To determine the necessary scope of habeas corpus review, therefore, we must assess the CSRT process, the mechanism through which petitioners' designation as enemy combatants became final. Whether one characterizes the CSRT process as direct review of the Executive's battlefield determination that the detainee is an enemy combatant—as the parties have and as we do—or as the first step in the collateral review of a battlefield determination makes no difference in a proper analysis of whether the procedures Congress put in place are an adequate substitute for habeas corpus. What matters is the sum total of procedural protections afforded to the detainee at all stages, direct and collateral.

Petitioners identify what they see as myriad deficiencies in the CSRTs. The most relevant for our purposes are the constraints upon the detainee's ability to rebut the factual basis for the Government's assertion that he is an enemy combatant. As already noted, at the CSRT stage the detainee has limited means to find or present evidence to challenge the Government's case against him. He does not have the assistance of counsel and may not be aware of the most critical allegations that the Government relied upon to order his detention. The detainee can confront witnesses that testify during the CSRT proceedings. But given that there are in effect no limits on the admission of hearsay evidence—the only requirement is that the tribunal deem the evidence "relevant and helpful"—the detainee's opportunity to question witnesses is likely to be more theoretical than real.

The Government defends the CSRT process, arguing that it was designed to conform to the procedures suggested by the plurality in *Hamdi*. * * * [The *Hamdi*] plurality concentrated on whether the Executive had the authority to detain and, if so, what rights the detainee had under the Due Process Clause. True, there are places in the Hamdi plurality opinion where it is difficult to tell where its extrapolation of § 2241 ends and its analysis of the petitioner's Due Process rights begins. But the Court had no occasion to define the necessary scope of habeas review, for Suspension Clause purposes, in the context of enemy combatant detentions. The closest the plurality came to doing so was in discussing whether, in light of separation-of-powers concerns, § 2241 should be construed to forbid the District Court from inquiring beyond the affidavit *Hamdi's* custodian provided in answer to the detainee's habeas petition. The plurality answered this question with an emphatic "no."

Even if we were to assume that the CSRTs satisfy due process standards, it would not end our inquiry. * * * Although we make no judgment as to whether the CSRTs, as currently constituted, satisfy due process standards, we agree with petitioners that, even when all the parties involved in this process act with diligence and in good faith, there is considerable risk of error in the tribunal's findings of fact. * * * And given that the consequence of error may be detention of persons for the duration of hostilities that may last a generation or more, this is a risk too significant to ignore.

For the writ of habeas corpus, or its substitute, to function as an effective and proper remedy in this context, the court that conducts the habeas proceeding must have the means to correct errors that occurred during the CSRT proceedings. This includes some authority to assess the sufficiency of the Government's evidence against the detainee. It also must have the authority to admit and consider relevant exculpatory evidence that was not introduced during the earlier proceeding. Federal habeas petitioners long have had the means to supplement the record on review, even in the postconviction habeas setting. Here that opportunity is constitutionally required.

Consistent with the historic function and province of the writ, habeas corpus review may be more circumscribed if the underlying detention proceedings are more thorough than they were here. * * * The extent of the showing required of the Government in these cases is a matter to be determined. We need not explore it further at this stage. We do hold that when the judicial power to issue habeas corpus properly is invoked the judicial officer must have adequate authority to make a determination in light of the relevant law and facts and to formulate and issue appropriate orders for relief, including, if necessary, an order directing the prisoner's release. * * *

VI

* * *

B

In the DTA Congress sought to consolidate review of petitioners' claims in the Court of Appeals. Channeling future cases to one district court would no doubt reduce administrative burdens on the Government. This is a legitimate objective that might be advanced even without an amendment to § 2241. If, in a future case, a detainee files a habeas petition in another judicial district in which a proper respondent can be served, the Government can move for change of venue to the court that will hear these petitioners' cases, the United States District Court for the District of Columbia. * * *

Another of Congress' reasons for vesting exclusive jurisdiction in the Court of Appeals, perhaps, was to avoid the widespread dissemination of classified information. * * * We make no attempt to anticipate all of the evidentiary and access-to-counsel issues that will arise during the course of the detainees' habeas corpus proceedings. We recognize, however, that the Government has a legitimate interest in protecting sources and methods of intelligence gathering; and we expect that the District Court will use its discretion to accommodate this interest to the greatest extent possible. * * *

These and the other remaining questions are within the expertise and competence of the District Court to address in the first instance. * * *

Our opinion does not undermine the Executive's powers as Commander in Chief. On the contrary, the exercise of those powers is vindicated, not eroded, when confirmed by the Judicial Branch. Within the Constitution's separation-of-powers structure, few exercises of judicial power are as legitimate or as necessary as the responsibility to hear challenges to the authority of the Executive to imprison a person. Some of these petitioners have been in custody for six years with no definitive judicial determination as to the legality of their detention. Their access to the writ is a necessity to determine the lawfulness of their status, even if, in the end, they do not obtain the relief they seek. * * *

It bears repeating that our opinion does not address the content of the law that governs petitioners' detention. That is a matter yet to be determined. We hold that petitioners may invoke the fundamental procedural protections of habeas corpus. The laws and Constitution are designed to survive, and remain in force, in extraordinary times. Liberty and security can be reconciled; and in our system they are reconciled within the framework of the law. The Framers decided that habeas corpus, a right of first importance, must be a part of that framework, a part of that law.

The determination by the Court of Appeals that the Suspension Clause and its protections are inapplicable to petitioners was in error. The judgment of the Court of Appeals is reversed. The cases are remanded to the Court of Appeals with instructions that it remand the cases to the District Court for proceedings consistent with this opinion.

It is so ordered.

[JUSTICE SOUTER, joined by JUSTICES GINSBURG and BREYER, concurred to emphasize that the Court's earlier opinion in *Rasul* suggested this eventual course and that the Court was being adequately deferential to the other branches.]

■ CHIEF JUSTICE ROBERTS, with whom JUSTICE SCALIA, JUSTICE THOMAS, and JUSTICE ALITO join, dissenting.

Today the Court strikes down as inadequate the most generous set of procedural protections ever afforded aliens detained by this country as enemy combatants. The political branches crafted these procedures amidst an ongoing military conflict, after much careful investigation and thorough debate. The Court rejects them today out of hand, without bothering to say what due process rights the detainees possess, without explaining how the statute fails to vindicate those rights, and before a single petitioner has exhausted the procedures under the law. And to what effect? The majority merely replaces a review system designed by the people's representatives with a set of shapeless procedures to be defined by federal courts at some future date. One cannot help but think, after surveying the modest practical results of the majority's ambitious opinion, that this decision is not really about the detainees at all, but about control of federal policy regarding enemy combatants.

* * * Habeas is most fundamentally a procedural right, a mechanism for contesting the legality of executive detention. The critical threshold question in these cases, prior to any inquiry about the writ's scope, is whether the system the political branches designed protects whatever rights the detainees may possess. If so, there is no need for any additional process, whether called "habeas" or something else.

* * * How the detainees' claims will be decided now that the DTA is gone is anybody's guess. But the habeas process the Court mandates will most likely end up looking a lot like the DTA system it replaces, as the district court judges shaping it will have to reconcile review of the prisoners' detention with the undoubted need to protect the American people from the terrorist threat—precisely the challenge Congress undertook in drafting the DTA. All that today's opinion has done is shift responsibility for those sensitive foreign policy and national security decisions from the elected branches to the Federal Judiciary. * * *

It is grossly premature to pronounce on the detainees' right to habeas without first assessing whether the remedies the DTA system provides vindicate whatever rights petitioners may claim. The plurality in *Hamdi v. Rumsfeld*, 542 U.S. 507, 533 (2004), explained that the Constitution guaranteed an American *citizen* challenging his detention as an enemy combatant the right to "notice of the factual basis for his classification, and a fair opportunity to rebut the Government's factual assertions before a neutral decisionmaker." The plurality specifically stated that constitutionally adequate collateral process could be provided "by an appropriately authorized and properly constituted military tribunal," given the "uncommon potential to burden the Executive at a time of ongoing military conflict." This point is directly pertinent here, for surely the Due Process Clause does not afford *non*-citizens in such circumstances greater protection than citizens are due.

If the CSRT procedures meet the minimal due process requirements outlined in *Hamdi*, and if an Article III court is available to ensure that these procedures are followed in future cases, * * * there is no need to reach the Suspension Clause question. Detainees will have received all the process the Constitution could possibly require, whether that process is called "habeas" or something else. The question of the writ's reach need not be addressed.

Because the central purpose of habeas corpus is to test the legality of executive detention, the writ requires most fundamentally an Article III court able to hear the prisoner's claims and, when necessary, order release. See *Brown v. Allen*, 344 U.S. 443, 533 (1953) (Jackson, J., concurring in result). Beyond that, the process a given prisoner is entitled to receive depends on the circumstances and the rights of the prisoner. See *Mathews v. Eldridge*, 424 U.S. 319, 335 (1976). After much hemming and hawing, the majority appears to concede that the DTA provides an Article III court competent to order release. The only issue in dispute is the process the Guantánamo prisoners are entitled to use to test the legality of their detention. *Hamdi* concluded that American citizens detained as enemy combatants are entitled to only limited process, and that much of that process could be supplied by a military tribunal, with review to follow in an Article III court. That is precisely the system we have here. It is adequate to vindicate whatever due process rights petitioners may have.

* * * The Court reaches the opposite conclusion partly because it misreads the statute. The majority appears not to understand how the review system it invalidates actually works—specifically, how CSRT review and review by the D.C. Circuit fit together. After briefly acknowledging in its recitation of the facts that the Government designed the CSRTs "to comply with the due process requirements identified by the plurality in *Hamdi*," the Court proceeds to dismiss the tribunal proceedings as no more than a suspect method used by the Executive for determining the status of the detainees in the first instance. This leads the Court to treat the review the DTA provides in the D.C. Circuit as the only opportunity detainees have to challenge their status determination.

First of all, the majority is quite wrong to dismiss the Executive's determination of detainee status as no more than a "battlefield" judgment, as if it were somehow provisional and made in great haste. In fact, detainees are designated "enemy combatants" only after "multiple levels of review by military officers and officials of the Department of Defense."

The majority is equally wrong to characterize the CSRTs as part of that initial determination process. They are instead a means for detainees to challenge the Government's determination. The Executive designed the CSRTs to mirror Army Regulation 190–8, * * * the very procedural model the plurality in *Hamdi* said provided the type of process an enemy combatant could expect from a habeas court. The CSRTs operate much as habeas courts would if hearing the detainee's collateral challenge for the first time: They gather evidence, call witnesses, take testimony, and render a decision on the legality of the Government's detention. If the CSRT finds a particular detainee has been improperly held, it can order release. * * *

The use of a military tribunal such as the CSRTs to review the aliens' detention should be familiar to this Court in light of the *Hamdi* plurality, which said that the due process rights enjoyed by *American citizens* detained as enemy combatants could be vindicated "by an appropriately authorized and properly constituted military tribunal." The DTA represents Congress's considered attempt to provide the accused alien combatants detained at Guantánamo a constitutionally adequate opportunity to contest their detentions before just such a tribunal.

But Congress went further in the DTA. CSRT review is just the first tier of collateral review in the DTA system. The statute provides additional review in an Article III court. Given the rationale of today's decision, it is well worth recalling exactly what the DTA provides in this respect. The statute directs the D.C. Circuit to consider whether a particular alien's status determination "was consistent with the standards and procedures specified by the Secretary of Defense" *and* "whether the use of such standards and procedures to make the determination is consistent with the Constitution and laws of the United States." That is, a court determines whether the CSRT procedures are constitutional, and a *court* determines whether those procedures were followed in a particular case.

By virtue of its refusal to allow the D.C. Circuit to assess petitioners' statutory remedies, and by virtue of its own refusal to consider, at the outset, the fit between those remedies and due process, the majority now finds itself in the position of evaluating whether the DTA system is an adequate substitute for habeas review without knowing what rights either habeas or the DTA is supposed to protect. The majority attempts to elide this problem by holding that petitioners have a right to habeas corpus and then comparing the DTA against the "historic office" of the writ. But habeas is, as the majority acknowledges, a flexible remedy rather than a substantive right. Its "precise application . . . change[s] depending upon the circumstances." The shape of habeas review ultimately depends on the nature of the rights a petitioner may assert. * * *

The scope of federal habeas review is traditionally more limited in some contexts than in others, depending on the status of the detainee and the rights he may assert. See *I.N.S. v. St. Cyr*, 533 U.S. 289, 306 (2001)] ("In [immigration cases], other than the question whether there was some evidence to support the [deportation] order, the courts generally did not review factual determinations made by the Executive" (footnote omitted)) * * *

Declaring that petitioners have a right to habeas in no way excuses the Court from explaining why the DTA does not protect whatever due process or statutory rights petitioners may have. Because if the DTA provides a means for vindicating petitioners' rights, it is necessarily an adequate substitute for habeas corpus. See *Swain v. Pressley*, 430 U.S. 372, 381 (1977); *United States v. Hayman*, 342 U.S. 205, 223 (1952).

For my part, I will assume that any due process rights petitioners may possess are no greater than those of American citizens detained as enemy combatants. * * *

The majority rests its decision on abstract and hypothetical concerns. Step back and consider what, in the real world, Congress and the Executive have actually granted aliens captured by our Armed Forces overseas and found to be enemy combatants:

• The right to hear the bases of the charges against them, including a summary of any classified evidence.

• The ability to challenge the bases of their detention before military tribunals modeled after Geneva Convention procedures. Some 38 detainees have been released as a result of this process.

• The right, before the CSRT, to testify, introduce evidence, call witnesses, question those the Government calls, and secure release, if and when appropriate.

• The right to the aid of a personal representative in arranging and presenting their cases before a CSRT.

• Before the D.C. Circuit, the right to employ counsel, challenge the factual record, contest the lower tribunal's legal determinations, ensure compliance with the Constitution and laws, and secure release, if any errors below establish their entitlement to such relief.

In sum, the DTA satisfies the majority's own criteria for assessing adequacy. This statutory scheme provides the combatants held at Guantánamo greater procedural protections than have ever been afforded alleged enemy detainees—whether citizens or aliens—in our national history.

* * *

So who has won? Not the detainees. The Court's analysis leaves them with only the prospect of further litigation to determine the content of their new habeas right, followed by further litigation to resolve their particular cases, followed by further litigation before the D.C. Circuit—where they could have started had they invoked the DTA procedure. Not Congress, whose attempt to "determine—through democratic means—how best" to balance the security of the American people with the detainees' liberty interests has been unceremoniously brushed aside. Not the Great Writ, whose majesty is hardly enhanced by its extension to a jurisdictionally quirky outpost, with no tangible benefit to anyone. Not the rule of law, unless by that is meant the rule of lawyers, who will now arguably have a greater role than military and intelligence officials in shaping policy for alien enemy combatants. And certainly not the American people, who today lose a bit more control over the conduct of this Nation's foreign policy to unelected, politically unaccountable judges.

I respectfully dissent.

■ JUSTICE SCALIA, with whom THE CHIEF JUSTICE, JUSTICE THOMAS, and JUSTICE ALITO join, dissenting.

Today, for the first time in our Nation's history, the Court confers a constitutional right to habeas corpus on alien enemies detained abroad by our military forces in the course of an ongoing war. * * * The writ of habeas corpus does not, and never has, run in favor of aliens abroad; the Suspension Clause thus has no application, and the Court's intervention in this military matter is entirely *ultra vires*.

I shall devote most of what will be a lengthy opinion to the legal errors contained in the opinion of the Court. Contrary to my usual practice, however, I think it appropriate to begin with a description of the disastrous consequences of what the Court has done today.

I

America is at war with radical Islamists. * * *

The game of bait-and-switch that today's opinion plays upon the Nation's Commander in Chief will make the war harder on us. It will almost certainly cause more Americans to be killed. * * * The President relied on our settled precedent in *Johnson v. Eisentrager,* 339 U.S. 763 (1950), when he established the prison at Guantánamo Bay for enemy aliens. Citing that case, the President's Office of Legal Counsel advised him "that the great weight of legal authority indicates that a federal district court could not properly exercise habeas jurisdiction over an alien detained at [Guantánamo Bay]." Memorandum from Patrick F. Philbin and John C. Yoo, Deputy Assistant Attorneys General, Office of Legal Counsel, to William J. Haynes II, General Counsel, Dept. of Defense (Dec. 28, 2001). Had the law been otherwise, the military surely would not have transported prisoners there, but would have kept them in Afghanistan, transferred them to another of our foreign military bases, or turned them over to allies for detention. Those other facilities might well have been worse for the detainees themselves. * * *

But it does not matter. The Court today decrees that no good reason to accept the judgment of the other two branches is "apparent." * * * Henceforth, as today's opinion makes unnervingly clear, how to handle enemy prisoners in this war will ultimately lie with the branch that knows least about the national security concerns that the subject entails.

II

A

* * * The writ as preserved in the Constitution could not possibly extend farther than the common law provided when that Clause was written. See Part III, *infra.* The Court admits that it cannot determine whether the writ historically extended to aliens held abroad, and it concedes (necessarily) that Guantánamo Bay lies outside the sovereign territory of the United States. Together, these two concessions establish that it is (in the Court's view) perfectly ambiguous whether the common-law writ would have provided a remedy for these petitioners. If that is so, the Court has no basis to strike down the Military Commissions Act, and must leave undisturbed the considered judgment of the coequal branches.

How, then, does the Court weave a clear constitutional prohibition out of pure interpretive equipoise? The Court resorts to "fundamental separation-of-powers principles" to interpret the Suspension Clause. * * *

That approach distorts the nature of the separation of powers and its role in the constitutional structure. The "fundamental separation-of-powers principles" that the Constitution embodies are to be derived not from some judicially imagined matrix, but from the sum total of the individual separation-of-powers provisions that the Constitution sets forth. Only by considering them one-by-one does the full shape of the *Constitution's* separation-of-powers principles emerge. It is nonsensical to interpret those provisions themselves in light of some general "separation-of-powers principles" dreamed up by the Court. * * *

B

The Court purports to derive from our precedents a "functional" test for the extraterritorial reach of the writ, which shows that the Military Commissions Act unconstitutionally restricts the scope of habeas. That is remarkable because the most pertinent of those precedents, *Johnson v. Eisentrager,* conclusively establishes the opposite. There we were confronted with the claims of 21 Germans held at Landsberg Prison, an American military facility located in the American Zone of occupation in postwar Germany. They had been captured in China, and an American military commission sitting there had convicted them of war crimes—collaborating with the Japanese after Germany's surrender. Like the petitioners here, the Germans claimed that their detentions violated the Constitution and international law, and sought a writ of habeas corpus. Writing for the Court, Justice Jackson held that American courts lacked habeas jurisdiction * * *.

The Court would have us believe that *Eisentrager* rested on "[p]ractical considerations," such as the "difficulties of ordering the Government to produce the prisoners in a habeas corpus proceeding." Formal sovereignty, says the Court, is merely one consideration "that bears upon which constitutional guarantees apply" in a given location. This is a sheer rewriting of the case. *Eisentrager* mentioned practical concerns, to be sure—but not for the purpose of determining *under what circumstances* American courts could issue writs of habeas corpus for aliens abroad. It cited them to support its *holding* that the Constitution does not empower courts to issue writs of habeas corpus to aliens abroad *in any circumstances.* * * *

The category of prisoner comparable to these detainees are not the *Eisentrager* criminal defendants, but the more than 400,000 prisoners of war detained in the United States alone during World War II. Not a single one was accorded the right to have his detention validated by a habeas corpus action in federal court—and that despite the fact that they were present on U.S. soil. * * *

* * * The rule that aliens abroad are not constitutionally entitled to habeas corpus has not proved unworkable in practice; if anything, it is the Court's "functional" test that does not (and never will) provide clear guidance for the future. *Eisentrager* forms a coherent whole with the accepted proposition that aliens abroad have no substantive rights under our Constitution. Since it was announced, no relevant factual premises have changed. It has engendered considerable reliance on the part of our military. And, as the Court acknowledges, text and history do not clearly compel a contrary ruling. It is a sad day for the rule of law when such an important constitutional precedent is discarded without an apologia, much less an apology. * * *

III

Putting aside the conclusive precedent of *Eisentrager,* it is clear that the original understanding of the Suspension Clause was that habeas corpus was not available to aliens abroad * * *. It is entirely clear that, at English common law, the writ of habeas corpus did not extend beyond the sovereign territory of the Crown. To be sure, the writ had an "extraordinary territorial ambit," because it was a so-called "prerogative writ," which, unlike other writs, could extend beyond the realm of England to other places where the Crown was sovereign. * * *

But prerogative writs could not issue to foreign countries, even for British subjects; they were confined to the King's dominions—those areas over which the Crown was sovereign. Thus, the writ has never extended to Scotland, which, although united to England when James I succeeded to the English throne in 1603, was considered a foreign dominion under a different Crown—that of the King of Scotland. * * * Despite three opening briefs, three reply briefs, and support from a legion of *amici*, petitioners have failed to identify a single case in the history of Anglo-American law that supports their claim to jurisdiction. * * *

Today the Court warps our Constitution in a way that goes beyond the narrow issue of the reach of the Suspension Clause, invoking judicially brainstormed separation-of-powers principles to establish a manipulable "functional" test for the extraterritorial reach of habeas corpus (and, no doubt, for the extraterritorial reach of other constitutional protections as well). It blatantly misdescribes important precedents, most conspicuously Justice Jackson's opinion for the Court in *Johnson v. Eisentrager*. It breaks a chain of precedent as old as the common law that prohibits judicial inquiry into detentions of aliens abroad absent statutory authorization. And, most tragically, it sets our military commanders the impossible task of proving to a civilian court, under whatever standards this Court devises in the future, that evidence supports the confinement of each and every enemy prisoner.

The Nation will live to regret what the Court has done today. I dissent.

NOTES AND QUESTIONS ON BOUMEDIENE

1) Overview of the Decision. Professor Ronald Dworkin called *Boumediene* "one of the most important decisions by the Court in recent years"—although the full effect of the outcome remains to be seen.[q] The *Boumediene* opinion can be divided into three parts. First, in Part III of the opinion, the Supreme Court held that the Constitution protected a habeas privilege that Congress could not eliminate. Because the constitutionally-protected privilege was at least as broad as the privilege was in 1789, the Court settled on a particular history of the common-law writ. (The Court also used the Habeas Corpus Act of 1679 as a benchmark for the privilege's meaning at the American founding.) Second, in Part IV of the opinion, the Court held that the noncitizen detainees were entitled to the habeas privilege notwithstanding that (1) they were detained at GTMO, a location over which the U.S. exercises only *de facto* sovereignty, and (2) they were noncitizens that the executive had designated as unlawful enemy combatants. Third, in Part V of the opinion, the Court expounded on the minimal protections that the Suspension Clause affords to military detainees, saying more about the meaning of the "privilege" of the writ than the Court had in any prior decision. Although the Court held that the privilege entitled prisoners to certain remedial process, it left open the "substantive" questions surrounding whether the detentions were lawful.

2) Revising the Historical Record. The Supreme Court frequently clears its throat in important habeas decisions with historical accounts of the writ. (Think back to *Fay v. Noia*, the post-conviction case discussed in Chapter 4.) What purposes do such accounts of the writ serve? One of the things that

---

[q] Ronald Dworkin, *Why It Was a Great Victory*, N.Y. Rev. Books, Aug. 14, 2008, at 18.

makes *Boumediene* remarkable is that the opinion replaces hagiography with historiography—emphasizing the inadequacies in the historical record. The Court cited repeatedly to a study by Professors Paul Halliday and G. Edward White—an exhaustive inventory of how King's Bench used the common law writ in the three centuries preceding the American Revolution.[r] What did the Court mean when it observed that there were "inherent shortcomings in the historical record," and that the few written decisions upon which prior opinions had relied were not good representations of common-law habeas practice? Does this passage—expressing misgivings about the historical record—embody a disciplinary humility on the part of the Justices, or is it an attempt to evade established precedent about the historical record (if there is such a thing)? After all, a historian would say that a historical record is never "complete" and certainly never conclusive. Can history be used to answer current legal questions? What does *Boumediene* suggest about the way that the Court should use history?

The Supreme Court ultimately concluded that, although the English common-law writ extended to all sorts of unusual territories, no English analogy was on point. It reasoned that GTMO detention was novel, and that there existed no controlling precedent on the precise set of custodial conditions there. Even if some form of analogous custody were addressed by a common-law decision, should such precedent matter to the Court today? As Professor Daniel J. Meltzer commented:

> [T]here is something more than a bit strange in trying to determine from the scanty available records whether the modern American naval base at Guantánamo Bay is more like eighteenth-century Scotland, Berwick-upon-Tweed, Ireland, or areas in the Indian subcontinent in which the East India Company operated but which remained under the formal sovereignty of the Moghul Emperor.[s]

3)   The Suspension Clause. The Court held that detainees at Guantánamo are "entitled to the privilege of habeas corpus to challenge the legality of their detention." The holdings that Congress could not impair the privilege by stripping federal jurisdiction over detainee claims, and that the Suspension Clause was the source of the privilege, were momentous. *Boumediene* was the first time that the Court had clearly described how the Clause provides an affirmative guarantee of access to meaningful judicial review of detention.[t] Recall Justice Scalia's position in *St. Cyr*: that Congress, so long as it does not temporarily withdraw the writ, may permanently strip habeas jurisdiction. Is that view still tenable after *Boumediene*?

4)   *Boumediene* and the Madisonian Compromise. Recall that the Madisonian Compromise was that the Constitution would not require the existence of lower federal courts. Could the Supreme Court have heard *Boumediene* if it were filed as an original matter there, rather than as an appeal from the D.C. Circuit? For the view that "the Court challenged, sub

---

[r] *Boumediene*, 553 U.S. at 741 (citing Paul D. Halliday and G. Edward White, *The Suspension Clause: English Text, Imperial Contexts, and American Implications*, 94 Va. L. Rev. 575 (2008)).

[s] Daniel J. Meltzer, *Habeas Corpus, Suspension, and Guantánamo: The Boumediene Decision*, 2008 Sup. Ct. Rev. 1.

[t] See *id.* at 1 (the Court "for the first time, clearly held" that the Suspension Clause "affirmatively guarantees access to the courts to seek the writ of habeas corpus (or an adequate substitute) in order to test the legality of executive detention.").

silentio, the continued soundness of the Madisonian Compromise—the blackletter view that the Constitution does not require the existence of any federal court other than the Supreme Court," see Lumen N. Mulligan, *Did the Madisonian Compromise Survive Detention at Guantánamo?*, 85 N.Y.U. L. Rev. 535, 539 (2010). What is the theory that could ever support such a finding? Does Professor Mulligan overstate the tension between *Boumediene* and the Madisonian compromise?

5) The Role of Territorial Jurisdiction in Determining Applicability of the Privilege. The Supreme Court explored whether precedent, particularly *Eisentrager*, rendered as dispositive the location of custody. The United States emphasized that it does not have *de jure* sovereignty over GTMO. The D.C. Circuit had denied relief, finding no jurisdiction over the claims and holding that "the Constitution does not confer rights on aliens without property or presence within the United States." The Supreme Court accepted the Government's premise—that the United States was not a *de jure* sovereign at GTMO—but rejected the conclusion that the habeas inquiry ended there. Rather than treating the location of custody as dispositive, the Court adopted a "functional approach" to the question of extraterritorial jurisdiction. The Court's approach—which reflected Justice Kennedy's *Rasul* concurrence[u]—emphasized that the absence of jurisdiction in *Eisentrager* was a result of practical constraints not present in *Boumediene*. The Court distilled a three-part test to be used to determine the reach of the Suspension Clause:

> (1) the citizenship and status of the detainee and the adequacy of the process through which that status determination was made; (2) the nature of the sites where apprehension and then detention took place; and (3) the practical obstacles inherent in resolving the prisoner's entitlement to the writ.

The test should be split into six factors, since the first and second "parts" each have multiple sub-parts: (1) citizenship, (2) status, (3) adequacy of the process through which the status determination was made, (4) site of apprehension, (5) site of detention, and (6) practical obstacles. Should *de jure* sovereignty over territory be dispositive, or did the Court properly adopt a multi-factor test?

Some of these factors relate to the question of territorial jurisdiction. Some of these factors, however—which are formally Suspension Clause assurances—are expressed in due process terminology. Why is the adequacy of process relevant *both* to jurisdiction to hear a habeas petition and also to a subsequent adjudication of the claim on the merits? Compare this multi-factor test to personal jurisdiction tests you have encountered in civil procedure. Is the use of a multi-factor test for habeas jurisdiction problematic? Other jurisdiction tests are similarly multi-factored. For example, a court conducting the due process personal jurisdiction analysis considers "minimum contacts" with the forum, procedural fairness ("traditional notions of fair play and substantial justice"), as well as other state and judicial interests (such as "the interstate judicial system's interest in obtaining the most efficient resolution of controversies)."[v] *Boumediene* adopts something like a Suspension Clause variation on a personal

---

[u] On the potentially broader implications of the Court's approach for extraterritorial application of constitutional rights, see Gerald L. Neuman, *The Extraterritorial Constitution After Boumediene v. Bush*, 82 S. Cal. L. Rev. 259 (2009).

[v] World-Wide Volkswagen Corp. v. Woodson, 444 U.S. 286, 292, 297 (1980) (internal quotations omitted).

jurisdiction test—which was perhaps no surprise given the due process approach espoused by the plurality in *Hamdi.*

Sometimes the factors are difficult to consider in isolation. For instance, sometimes the questions involve the military or other executive procedures used to determine enemy combatant status and citizenship. As the Court noted, the status of the detainee is itself a factor that might remain in dispute because the ability to investigate the question may have been limited.[w] Do you agree with the Court's interpretation of *Eisentrager*? Or do you agree with Justice Scalia that *Eisentrager* did not make practical considerations relevant to whether habeas jurisdiction exists?

6)   Due Process? Unlike *Hamdi*, which was formally about the due process rights of an American citizen, *Boumediene* does not reason through the due process rights of prisoners designated as enemy combatants. Chief Justice Roberts expressed frustration at the Court's insistence on reaching the remedial questions before the substantive ones, accusing the majority of being "grossly premature to pronounce on the detainees' right to habeas without first assessing whether the remedies the DTA system provides vindicate whatever rights petitioners may claim." Why didn't the Court address whether the CSRTs and DTA review met the requirements of the Due Process clause? Is *Boumediene* about whether the procedures afford due process, or whether they are adequate and effective to test the lawfulness of detention? If the question is whether the district court had habeas jurisdiction, could the sequencing of its habeas decision be justified on the ground that it must be decided before "merits" consideration?

Which framing of the question is more solicitous of detainee rights? In any event, the procedures the Court teased from the Suspension Clause look very much like the due process principles announced in *Hamdi.* The Court discussed the features of a "meaningful opportunity" to contest the CSRT custody determination, such as the ability to review exculpatory evidence and develop facts. For the argument that the Court correctly located the procedural requirements for scrutinizing custody in the Suspension Clause (and not in the Due Process Clause), see Brandon L. Garrett, *Habeas Corpus and Due Process*, 98 Cornell L. Rev. 47 (2012).

7)   Adequate Substitute for Habeas Corpus. While the Supreme Court found the CSRT procedures to be lacking, Chief Justice Roberts countered that the whole of the DTA procedure, which included D.C. Circuit review of the CSRT determination, was an "adequate substitute" for habeas corpus. All of the Justices appeared to agree that, in theory, there could be an "adequate substitute" for habeas review—even in executive-detention contexts. The majority emphasized, however, that, in any context where the custody determination reflects no judicial process, habeas process plays a particularly crucial role. What about the DTA, specifically, made it inadequate as a substitute for the CSRT process used by the military?

8)   Distinguishing Habeas Substitutes. In addressing whether the statutory procedures were an adequate and effective substitute for habeas process, the majority inventoried post-conviction statutes that the Supreme Court had previously found constitutional. What accounts for different constitutional ha-

---

[w] See David Franklin, *Enemy Combatants and the Jurisdictional Fact Doctrine,* 29 Cardozo L. Rev. 1001, 1028 (2008).

beas requirements in post-conviction and executive detention contexts? The Court also briefly cited to AEDPA provisions, noting that it had sustained successive-petition provisions against a Suspension Clause challenge in *Felker v. Turpin*, 518 U.S. 651, 662–664 (1996). The Court, however, noted that the AEDPA provisions "did not constitute a substantial departure from common-law habeas procedures" and that, unlike in the post-conviction context, the GTMO detainees were subject to a custody determination lacking any judicial process. Rather than make such distinctions, should the Court have simply said there is no substitute for habeas scrutiny of executive detention that has not been subjected to judicial review?

9) Questions of Fact and Law. Compare *Boumediene's* holding that the habeas substitute has to include the power to review facts with the holding in *St. Cyr,* presented in Chapter 7, in which the Court emphasized that the Suspension Clause ensured access to federal judicial review of constitutional claims and legal questions. What explains the difference between the outcomes in the two cases? Are they inconsistent, or was the Court focused on different facets of collateral review in different cases. Do you think *St. Cyr's* emphasis on authority to review legal questions reflected trust in the ability of the BIA to develop the factual record in immigration cases? Did the Court have less confidence in the factfinding procedures in place under the DTA and MCA? In thinking through the answers to these questions and how they played out different in *Boumediene* and *St. Cyr*, note that whether a person can be classified as an "enemy combatant" is a mixed question of law and fact.

10) Boumediene's Release. On May 15, 2009, like Hamdi and Hamdan, Boumediene was released. Judge Richard J. Leon ordered the discharge, granting his habeas petition and finding that his detention was not factually supported. The Government, however, had a difficult time finding countries to accept Boumediene, as well as some of the other GTMO detainees freed in *Boumediene's* wake. Eventually, France agreed to accept Boumediene.[x] Boumediene himself later wrote: "Some American politicians say that people at Guantánamo are terrorists, but I have never been a terrorist. Had I been brought before a court when I was seized, my children's lives would not have been torn apart, and my family would not have been thrown into poverty." He concluded: "I'm told that my Supreme Court case is now read in law schools. Perhaps one day that will give me satisfaction, but so long as Guantánamo stays open and innocent men remain there, my thoughts will be with those left behind in that place of suffering and injustice."[y]

11) Open Question: What is the Scope of Detention Authority? Some of the most important information in these Notes is not about what *Boumediene* did, but about what it didn't do. *Boumediene* held that the Suspension Clause requires a habeas privilege to be available to challenge custody, or that some substitute exist to perform that same function. The Supreme Court clearly held that federal district courts must be the locus of such review, and not just the D.C. Circuit Court of Appeals as under the DTA and MCA. The Court may have done so to direct federal judges to focus on both legal and factual questions. However, one question that *Boumediene* left unanswered involves the substantive scope of detention authority, stating: "It bears repeating that our opinion

---

[x] See Edward Cody, *Ex-Detainee Describes Struggle for Exoneration*, Washington Post, May 26, 2009; Boumediene v. Bush, 579 F. Supp. 2d 191, 193 (D.D.C. 2008).

[y] Lakhdar Boumediene, *My Guantánamo Nightmare*, N.Y. Times, Jan. 7, 2012.

does not address the content of the law that governs petitioners' detention. That is a matter yet to be determined." For that reason, Curtis Bradley commented that the Court "did not impose any specific restrictions on the executive's detention, treatment, or trial of the detainees." Professor Bradley added: "In other words, *Boumediene* was more about preserving a role for the courts than about prohibiting the executive from exercising statutorily conferred authority." Curtis A. Bradley, *Clear Statement Rules And Executive War Powers*, 33 Harv. J.L. & Pub. Pol'y 139 (2010). Do you agree with that statement?

12) Open Question: What Procedures Must be Followed? Tacking the way of the *Hamdi* plurality, *Boumediene* also declined to describe precisely what procedures lower courts must follow. The Court stated that a detainee must have a meaningful opportunity to be heard before and to present potentially exculpatory evidence to a federal district court. Why was an opportunity to be heard before a federal district court crucial? Again consider the constitutional source of that requirement. Was the process required by the Suspension Clause, or by the Due Process Clause? Was it required so as to make the process an adequate and effective alternative to habeas corpus? If so, then do the procedural requirements reflect a concept of adequacy and effectiveness under *Swain* and *Hayman*? Consider the requirements of those post-conviction cases. In response to *Boumediene*, could Congress constitutionally pass new legislation creating an enhanced detainee review procedure that was administrative in nature?

13) Open Question: What is the Standard of Proof? *Boumediene* also failed to specify the underlying standard of proof necessary to show lawful detention: "The extent of the showing required of the Government in these cases is a matter to be determined." In response to *Boumediene,* could Congress constitutionally pass new legislation permitting limited factual and legal review of detention decisions in federal court—but imposing a presumption that the government's evidence is valid, and maintaining the same "preponderance of the evidence" standard used in the CSRTs? Could Congress impose a "some evidence" standard?

14) Implications for Immigration Habeas? Professor Gerald Neuman suggests that the Court's "innovation"—insofar as it chose a particular combination of Suspension Clause and Due Process analysis—"invites future debate" and has profound implications, including for habeas review of immigration custody. See Gerald L. Neuman, *The Habeas Corpus Suspension Clause after* Boumediene v. Bush, 110 Colum. L. Rev. 537, 578 (2010). For example, as discussed in Chapter 7, under provisions of the immigration code added in 1996, an "expedited removal" may take place without the otherwise-commonplace hearing procedures. 8 U.S.C. §§ 1225(b)(1), 1252(a)(1), 1252(e) (2006). Those expedited removal procedures typically apply at the border (and airports), but they may also be extended to noncitizens detained within the country— noncitizens who are deemed inadmissible because they entered the country without inspection. As Professor Neuman describes, "The opportunity to be heard in expedited removal proceedings is extremely limited. The individual is confronted by an immigration officer and held largely incommunicado." Neuman, *Suspension Clause after* Boumediene, 110 Colum. L. Rev. at 572. The provisions seek to limit judicial review. They allow a habeas court to consider "whether the petitioner is an alien, whether the petitioner was ordered removed under § 235(b)(1), and whether the petitioner is entitled to diversion into a fuller hearing as a lawful permanent resident, admitted refugee, or asylee." 8

U.S.C. § 1252(e)(2), (e)(3), & (e)(5). The provisions do not allow challenges to other factual determinations, nor to the constitutionality of the statute itself.

Such treatment may not violate the Due Process Clause where the noncitizen is denied entry at the border (recall *Knauff v. Shaughnessy*, 338 U.S. 537 (1950), and *Shaughnessy v. United States ex rel. Mezei*, 345 U.S. 206 (1953) from Chapter 7), but what about a situation in which the noncitizen is detained *within* the country? Immigration officials are authorized to use expedited removal for individuals found within 100 miles of the U.S.-Mexico border. If *Boumediene* requires that any noncitizen receive minimal process as required by the Suspension Clause, then has the Court departed from the territorial focus of *Knauff* and *Mezei*? If so, then how would the *Boumediene* analysis proceed? What would the result be? What alternative process might a court require? Professor Neuman adds, "After *Boumediene*, it is unclear whether the Suspension Clause would require that aliens facing expedited removal from the interior receive no factual review, 'some evidence' review, or fuller factual review than in ordinary deportation proceedings." Neuman, *The Habeas Corpus Suspension Clause after* Boumediene v. Bush, 110 Colum. L. Rev. at 577.

15) Implications for Post-Conviction Review of Actual Innocence Claims. Does *Boumediene* suggest that habeas corpus serves a special purpose to review factual support for convictions? As you learned in Chapter 3, *Herrera v. Collins*, 506 U.S. 390 (1993), failed to recognize (except for the sake of argument) that innocence alone could be a constitutional basis for habeas relief. The Court noted that such a claim would be "disruptive of our federal system" and that "federal habeas corpus courts sit to ensure that individuals are not imprisoned in violation of the Constitution—not to correct errors of fact." Could the *Boumediene* Court's methodology "supply a new doctrinal foundation for a constitutional right to challenge a death sentence based on subsequently obtained evidence of actual innocence"? Neuman, *Suspension Clause after* Boumediene, 110 Colum. L. Rev. at 563–64; *see also* Brandon L. Garrett, *Habeas Corpus and Due Process*, 98 Corn. L. Rev. at 121 (exploring the relationship between fact review of combatant status in military detention cases with innocence review in post-conviction cases). For example, if no prior court has adequately examined new evidence of innocence, then does the Suspension Clause mandate federal habeas corpus review that includes a factual inquiry? Does this suggest a reason for federal judges to create exceptions to the strict rules surrounding evidentiary hearings in federal post-conviction proceedings, or to grant discovery more liberally? Given the *Boumediene* Court's emphasis on how GTMO detainees had not received prior judicial review, how should courts apply *Boumediene* to post-conviction proceedings, where prisoners have received a criminal trial?

NOTE ON THE GUANTÁNAMO POPULATION

The first detainees arrived at GTMO in January 2002. From a high of almost 700 detainees, the population steadily declined. It is now less than 200 detainees. About 600 detainees have been transferred abroad. Professor Aziz Z. Huq has compiled data concerning the population of detainees at Guantánamo over time.

Aziz Z. Huq, Trends in Guantánamo Detainee Population, 2002–2009

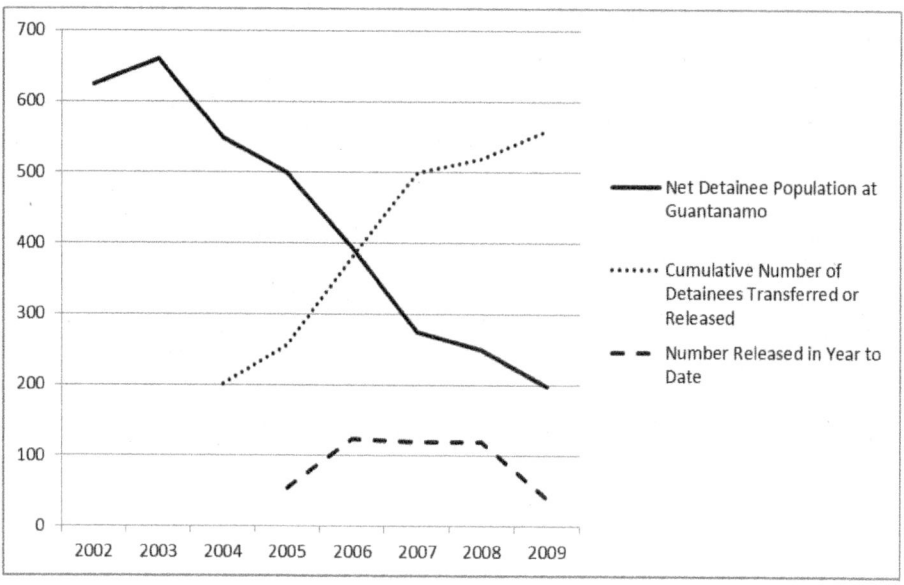

As you can see, in Professor Huq's chart, the GTMO population was at its height in 2003. Aziz Z. Huq, *What Good is Habeas?*, 26 Const. Commentary 385 (2010).[z] Since about 2004, the United States has transferred no new detainees to GTMO—nor does it intend to do so in the future.[aa]

What was *Boumediene* good for? Beginning in 2004, there have been steady releases and transfers from GTMO. As you can see, however, most releases occurred prior to *Boumediene*. Of the 560 detainees released at the time of Professor Huq's writing, only 21 of them—or 3.75%—were discharged pursuant to habeas orders. Moreover, Professor Huq points out, although federal courts have granted writs of habeas corpus filed post-*Boumediene,* the release orders have been honored only after the Government gave its consent. Indeed, most release orders state that the Government must first make "all necessary and appropriate diplomatic steps to facilitate" a release. Are there ways in which *Boumediene* might have affected custody that are not captured in the chart?

3. Post-*Boumediene* Developments

A. Substantive Standards for Detention

Introductory Notes on GTMO Detention After Boumediene

1)   The Military Commissions Act of 2009. *Boumediene* involved a challenge to the authority to undertake indefinite detention and not to the military

---

[z] This chart is reproduced with permission and with modifications only to its formatting, from Aziz Z. Huq, *What Good is Habeas?*, 26 Const. Commentary 385 (2010).

[aa] See Carol Rosenberg, *Pentagon: 'No Vacancy' at Guantánamo Camps,* Miami Herald, Oct. 18, 2011.

commission procedures struck down in *Hamdan*. The Military Commissions Act of 2009 (2009 MCA) replaced the process created following the *Hamdan* decision. See Title XVIII of the National Defense Authorization Act for Fiscal Year 2010, Pub.L. 111–84, 123 Stat. 2190 (Oct. 29, 2009). The 2009 MCA added procedural safeguards and aligned the commissions process with international law norms. The 2009 MCA used the term "unprivileged enemy belligerents" and not the term "enemy combatants" to describe the category of prisoners over whom the commissions have jurisdiction—signaling a change in approach towards applicability of international law and mirroring the language of the Geneva Convictions. 10 U.S.C. § 948c. The statute also prohibits the use of any statements that were the product of torture, and defined torture as cruel, inhuman or degrading treatment consistent with the United Nations Torture Convention. 10 U.S.C. § 948r(a). Now prisoners may be represented by military lawyers of their own choosing, with additional qualifications required in capital cases. 10 U.S.C. § 949a(b)(2)(C) (2009). The 2009 MCA also references the federal Classified Information Protection Act to provide the standards for treatment of classified information. See 10 U.S.C. § 949a(b)(3)(D).

2) DTA Review Unavailable. Although *Boumediene* did not reach the issue whether detainees could choose to pursue DTA review—except to say that detainees need not exhaust DTA review in the D.C. Circuit—the appeals court eventually decided that issue. It concluded that, in light of the persistent availability of habeas corpus review, DTA review was no longer available. See *Bismullah v. Gates*, 551 F.3d 1068 (D.C. Cir. 2009).

3) The D.C. Circuit Goes Back to Work. Recall the significant issues left open by *Boumediene*. Those issues include the substantive scope of detention authority, the procedural rights that attach in the exercise of that authority, and the standards of proof to be used when adjudicating it. Chief Justice Roberts, in his *Boumediene* dissent, expressed the fear that the result of the Court's decision would be "shapeless procedures." Others described the decisional law that followed, largely on these questions, as a new common law of detention. See Nathaniel H. Nesbitt, Note, *Meeting Boumediene's Challenge*, 95 Minn. L. Rev. 244 (2010); Benjamin Wittes et al., Brooking Inst., *The Emerging Law of Detention: The Guantánamo Habeas Cases as Lawmaking* (2010). The D.C. Circuit noted that *Boumediene* did not provide "a detailed procedural regime[,]" but rather issued "a spare but momentous guarantee that a 'judicial officer must have adequate authority to make a determination in light of the relevant law and facts,'" resulting in process that evolves "in the shadow of *Boumediene*." *Al-Bihani v. Obama*, 590 F.3d 866, 880, 887 (D.C. Cir. 2010) (quoting *Boumediene*, 128 S.Ct. at 2271).

4) Responses to *Boumediene* in the D.C. Circuit. *Boumediene* might be seen as a rebuke to the D.C. Circuit's handling of the GTMO habeas petitions, and the decision was not welcomed warmly by some judges on the D.C. appeals court. Judge A. Raymond Randolph authored the D.C. Circuit's overturned opinion in *Boumediene*. He has become a leading critic of post-9/11 Supreme Court decisions, which generally protect a role for federal judges in the national-security detention context. Judge Randolph joined Judge Laurence Silberman in an opinion that described *Boumediene* as a "charade" producing a "mess." *Esmail v. Obama*, 639 F.3d 1075, 1078 (D.C. Cir. 2011) (Silberman, J., concurring). A decision discussed further below, *Al-Bihani v. Obama*, 590 F.3d 866 (D.C. Cir. 2010), was authored by another outspoken critic of *Boumediene*, Judge Janice Brown. In *Al-Bihani*, the D.C. Circuit rejected the proposition that the law of war controlled the Government's power to detain GTMO prisoners indefinitely, and it instead located an enhanced detention power in the emanations from several domestic statutes relating to military trials of enemy combatants. *Al-Bihani* also strongly indicated that the Government's burden of proof in military detention cases was no more than a preponderance standard, and that hearsay evidence may be broadly admissible. In *Al-Adahi v. Obama*, 613 F.3d 1102 (D.C. Cir. 2010), the D.C. Circuit began to suggest aggressively that the constitution did not even require a preponderance standard and that "some evidence" might be sufficient to justify detention.

While *Boumediene* made clear that the Suspension Clause guarantees the habeas privilege to GTMO detainees, the D.C. Circuit reaffirmed its earlier position that the Due Process Clause does not extend extraterritorially to GTMO detainees. See Rasul v. Myers, 563 F.3d 527, 529 (D.C. Cir. 2009). In a series of decisions, the D.C. Circuit eventually elaborated on what process *Boumediene* required. It relied on *Hamdi* and other sources—including Due Process jurisprudence, post-conviction law, and even constitutional criminal procedure. The following Notes discuss those D.C. Circuit rulings, and explore whether the D.C. Circuit is appropriately implementing *Boumediene*. Professor Stephen Vladeck summarizes the resistance:

> [A] number of scholars, civil liberties groups, and detainee lawyers (not to mention the editorial pages of various major newspapers) have accused the D.C. Circuit in general—and some of its judges in particular—of actively subverting *Boumediene* by adopting holdings and reaching results that have both the intent and the effect of vitiating the Supreme Court's 2008 decision.

Stephen I. Vladeck, *The D.C. Circuit After Boumediene*, 41 Seton Hall L. Rev. 1451, 1453 (2011). To be sure, *Boumediene* delegated many very difficult tasks to the lower courts. Professor Vladeck added, "[I]t seems unfair to claim that, in these contexts, the D.C. Circuit is subverting Supreme Court rules that simply do not exist."

5)   The D.C. Circuit Develops Procedures and Evidentiary Standards. After *Boumediene,* the federal district court in the District of Columbia developed a case management order (CMO) designed to handle the various GTMO habeas petitions. See In re Guantánamo Bay Detainee Litig., Misc. No. 08–0442 (TFH), 2008 WL 4858241 (D.D.C. Nov. 6, 2008), *amended on reconsideration in part by* In re Guantánamo Bay Detainee Litigation, Misc. No. 08–0442 (TFH), 2008 WL 5245890 (D.D.C. Dec 16, 2008). The CMO has been adopted by most of the federal judges in the court, though some judges have adopted it with slight modifications.

6)   Burden Shifting. The CMO "placed upon the Government the burden of establishing, by a preponderance of the evidence, the lawfulness of the petitioner's detention." In response, "The Government was required to submit a return stating the factual and legal bases for detaining that prisoner, who was then required to file a traverse stating the relevant facts in support of his petition and a rebuttal of the Government's legal justification for his detention."

7)   The Discovery Standard. The CMO permitted discovery only "by leave of the Court for good cause shown," and required that requests for discovery (1) "be narrowly tailored"; (2) "specify the discovery sought"; (3) show why the request is "likely to produce evidence that demonstrates that the petitioner's detention is unlawful"; and (4) explain why the request is not "unfairly disruptive nor unduly burdening the Government." Finally, the CMO required the Government to produce "all reasonably available evidence in its possession that tends materially to undermine the information presented to support the government's justification for detaining the petitioner." There are questions, however, about which agencies the CMO applies to, or how to handle relevant information in the possession of the DOJ, the Defense Department, the CIA, and perhaps foreign governments working with those agencies.

In a series of rulings, the D.C. Circuit grappled with the questions that *Boumediene* left outstanding. Generally, the D.C. Circuit affirmed the procedures adopted by the D.C. district courts. The appeals court noted:

> Habeas review for Guantánamo detainees need not match the procedures developed by Congress and the courts specifically for habeas challenges to criminal convictions. Boumediene's holding explicitly stated that habeas procedures for detainees "need not resemble a criminal trial[.]"It instead invited "innovation" of habeas procedure by lower courts, granting leeway for "[c]ertain accommodations [to] be made to reduce the burden habeas corpus proceedings will place on the military."[bb]

NOTES ON THE SCOPE OF DETENTION AUTHORITY

1) Source of Detention Authority. First, in a series of opinions, the D.C. Circuit dealt with the substantive question of who the executive and military may detain. The Bush Administration had asserted that the President had "plenary" authority as Commander-in-Chief to detain individuals labeled as "enemy combatants." In 2009, the Obama Administration, without disavowing an executive power theory, asserted that its authority to detain was based on the AUMF. Consequently, while the Government had asserted that it could detain "those individuals who were part of, or supporting, forces engaged in hostilities against the United States or its coalition partners and allies," it now asserted authority to detain "persons who were part of, or *substantially* supported, Taliban or al-Qaeda forces or associated forces that are engaged in hostilities against the United States or its coalition partners, including any person who has committed a belligerent act, or has directly supported hostilities, in aid of such enemy forces."[cc] Was this any more specific than earlier assertions that "enemy combatants" could be detained?

2) A Functional Test. In *Bensayah v. Obama*, 610 F.3d 718 (D.C. Cir. 2010), the D.C. Circuit concluded that the AUMF authorizes detention of individuals who were functionally "part of" al Qaeda. The Government had by this time "abandoned the term 'enemy combatant' in reference to the scope of its detention authority." In *Bensayah*, the Government again cited to the AUMF standard, claiming "authority to detain individuals who 'were part of, or substantially supported, Taliban or al-Qaida forces or associated forces that are engaged in hostilities against the United States or its coalition partners, including any person who has committed a belligerent act, or has directly sup-

---

[bb] Al-Bihani v. Obama, 590 F.3d 866, 876 (D.C. Cir. 2010) *cert. denied*, 131 S. Ct. 1814 (U.S. 2011).

[cc] Gherebi v. Obama, 609 F. Supp. 2d 43, 53 (D.D.C. 2009) (emphasis in original).

ported hostilities, in aid of such enemy armed forces.'" Similarly, the D.C. Circuit had said that "Once [a petitioner is shown to be] 'part of al Qaeda . . . the requirements of the AUMF [are] satisfied." *Awad v. Obama*, 608 F.3d 1, 11–12 (D.C. Cir. 2010).

What does it mean to be "part of" al Qaeda? The D.C. Circuit has said that the meaning must be determined on a case-by-case basis:

> Although it is clear al Qaeda has, or at least at one time had, a particular organizational structure, . . . the details of its structure are generally unknown, . . . but it is thought to be somewhat amorphous. . . As a result, it is impossible to provide an exhaustive list of criteria for determining whether an individual is "part of" al Qaeda.

Thus, the court explained that judges must use "a functional rather than a formal approach." The court noted: "That an individual operates within al Qaeda's formal command structure is surely sufficient but is not necessary," but "the purely independent conduct of a freelancer is not enough." What guidance does that explanation provide to district courts? Is this "functional" approach too malleable? Does that flexibility help the Government or detainees?

A substantial and growing literature has examined the issue of scope of detention authority. See Ryan Goodman & Derek Jinks, *International Law, U.S. War Powers, and the Global War on Terrorism*, 118 Harv. L. Rev. 2653, 2655–58 (2005). On how the law of war could inform this analysis, see Matthew C. Waxman, *Detention as Targeting: Standards Of Certainty And Detention Of Suspected Terrorists*, 108 Colum. L. Rev. 1365, 1415 (2008).

NOTE ON THE NATIONAL DEFENSE AUTHORIZATION ACT OF 2012

In the National Defense Authorization Act of 2012 (NDAA), Congress ratified an AUMF-based standard. The statute provides for "Detention under the law of war without trial until the end of the hostilities authorized by the Authorization for Use of Military Force." See National Defense Authorization Act of 2012, S. 1867, Sec. 1031–32. Under the heading of "construction," the statute adds that "[n]othing in this section is intended to limit or expand the authority of the President or the scope of the Authorization for Use of Military Force." The statute defined "covered persons" as follows:

> (1) A person who planned, authorized, committed, or aided the terrorist attacks that occurred on September 11, 2001, or harbored those responsible for those attacks.

> (2) A person who was a part of or substantially supported al-Qaeda, the Taliban, or associated forces that are engaged in hostilities against the United States or its coalition partners, including any person who has committed a belligerent act or has directly supported such hostilities in aid of such enemy forces.

Is that detention standard more precise than the standard already used by judges? Or does that language ratify the interpretations of the D.C. Circuit? The statute also repeats that no federal funds may be used to transfer detainees from GTMO without completing a certification process to ensure that the receiving country is not a state sponsor of terrorism and that releasing the individual will not pose a security threat to the United States. The statute does not address procedures for reviewing the merits of detainee claims. Should Congress have addressed procedure and not just the detention standard?

For the following scenarios, assess whether the prisoner is a "part of Al-Qaeda":

(a) Can a person who admittedly spent time in an Al-Qaeda training camp and received training—but who was subsequently accused by Al-Qaeda of being a spy and tortured for months—be entitled to a determination that he renounced his allegiance and is no longer a part of Al-Qaeda at the time he was taken into custody? See Al Ginco v. Obama, 626 F.Supp.2d 123, 128 (D.D.C. 2009)

(b) Is a person who swore the "bayat," or oath of allegiance, to Al-Qaeda in 1990 and fought with them in 1990 and 1991 against communists in Afghanistan, with no further established contacts, still a "part of" Al-Qaeda at the time of his capture in 2002?

(c) What if, subsequent to 1991, this person did no fighting, but did provide some services to Al-Qaeda, such as recruiting, hosting leaders at his house, and transferring money? See Salahi v. Obama, 710 F.Supp.2d 1 (D.D.C. 2010), *vacated and remanded by* Salahi v. Obama, 625 F.3d 745 (D.C. Cir. 2010).

(d) Would a court consider as "part of al Qaeda" a "freelancer" who seeks to emulate Al-Qaeda, and conducts on his own a (botched) suicide bombing against U.S. troops in Afghanistan?

(e) What of a person who admits to having been a top commander in Al-Qaeda in 2002, but says that prior to his detention he had renounced his affiliation with them, joined the civilian government in Afghanistan, and offered to cooperate with the U.S. military?

(f) Is a U.S. citizen who wires money to a cousin in Afghanistan, and knows that his cousin is active in Al-Qaeda, a "part of" Al-Qaeda?

(g) Is a resident alien who lives in New York and believes he is forming a plot to work with Al-Qaeda to bomb a train station in New York, but in fact has been speaking to an undercover F.B.I. agent, a "part of" Al-Qaeda?

(h) Is staying in an Al-Qaeda "guesthouse" in Afghanistan enough, standing on its own, to make a person "part of" Al-Qaeda? See *Al-Bihani*, 590 F.3d at 873 n. 2 (suggesting in dicta that evidence that a detainee "visited Al Qaeda guesthouses . . . would seem to overwhelmingly, if not definitively, justify the government's detention").

―――――――

NOTES ON THE STANDARD OF PROOF AND EVIDENTIARY RULES

1)   A Preponderance Standard. In *Bensayah*, the D.C. Circuit approved the CMO standard of proof, requiring that the Government prove by a "preponderance of the evidence" that an individual was "part of" al Qaeda. This standard would be used to review the custody of the noncitizen GTMO detainees. In

Al-Bihani, the D.C. Circuit also ruled that such a standard would satisfy the mandates of *Hamdi* concerning review of detention of *citizens*:

> In addition to the *Hamdi* plurality's approving treatment of military tribunal procedure, it also described as constitutionally adequate—even for the detention of U.S. citizens—a "burden-shifting scheme" in which the government need only present "credible evidence that the habeas petitioner meets the enemy-combatant criteria" before "the onus could shift to the petitioner to rebut that evidence with more persuasive evidence that he falls outside the criteria."

The D.C. Circuit concluded that such a process "mirrors a preponderance standard." Does a preponderance standard comply with the Suspension Clause, after *Boumediene*? Remember that *Boumediene* rejected the CSRT process, which used a "preponderance" standard.

Should courts use the same standard in detainee cases as they do in ordinary civil tort suits? Recall from Chapter 7 how civil commitment of prisoners in the U.S. requires "clear and convincing" evidence that they pose a danger, and a full adversarial hearing to make that determination. Should more proof be required before indefinitely detaining prisoners? Should a "beyond a reasonable doubt standard" be used as in a criminal case? What are the justifications for setting the standard of proof at a level lower than what is required in a criminal proceeding? Is the lower standard a function of national security interests, of the different custodial authority, or both? Or is there no precise analogy to the situation of these national security detainees?

2)   Hearsay. Al-Bihani had also challenged Government reliance on hearsay (recall the Mobbs Declaration in *Hamdi*). He argued that "government reports of his interrogation answers—which made up the majority, if not all, of the evidence on which the district court relied—and other informational documents were hearsay improperly admitted absent an examination of reliability and necessity." He also argued that "government reports of his interrogation answers were 'double hearsay' because his answers were first translated by an interpreter and then written down by an interrogator." The D.C. Circuit, however, noted that the Confrontation Clause of the Sixth Amendment applies only in criminal prosecutions. The D.C. Circuit further noted that, "[i]n *Hamdi*, the Supreme Court said hearsay 'may need to be accepted as the most reliable available evidence' as long as the petitioner is given the opportunity to rebut that evidence."

3)   Pushing Towards the Constitutional Floor? The D.C. Circuit added that, although a preponderance standard was constitutional, an even more deferential standard would also satisfy constitutional requirements. The *Al-Bihani* court emphasized that it did not reach the question of the "minimum required by the Constitution[,]"and suggested that even "some evidence, reasonable suspicion, or probable cause standard of proof could constitutionally suffice." In *Al-Adahi v. Obama*, 613 F.3d 1101, 1104–1105 (D.C. Cir. 2010), a subsequent D.C. Circuit decision emphasized that it would "assume arguendo" that the Government must meet a preponderance of the evidence standard. The panel, however, invited the Government to advocate a more deferential standard, which the Government declined to do. Specifically, the D.C. Circuit urged the Government to pursue a "some evidence" standard, citing to decisions in immigration removal cases antedating the 1952 Immigration and Nationality

Act.[dd] Justice Roberts had cited to the same standard in his *Boumediene* dissent, noting that the scope of factual review "is traditionally more limited in some contexts than others, depending on the status of the detainee and the rights he may assert," a passage that the D.C. Circuit echoed.[ee] Recall from Chapter 7, however, that the "some evidence" standard for reviewing administrative action is formally the constitutional floor in immigration caselaw, but remains largely absent from most immigration statutes. Somewhat more searching "substantial evidence" review exists in other contexts, and there is de novo review of status questions like claims of citizenship.

Would a "some evidence" standard violate the Suspension Clause, the Due Process Clause, or both, or neither? The *Hamdi* plurality rejected a proposed "some evidence" standard, stating that it does not provide a meaningful opportunity to challenge the determination.[ff] Similarly, *Boumediene* emphasized that habeas corpus must minimally include "some authority to assess the sufficiency of the Government's evidence against the detainee.

4) Bibliography. For commentary on the standard of review problem, see Marc D. Falkoff, *Back to Basics: Habeas Corpus Procedures and Long-Term Executive Detention*, 86 Den. U. L. Rev. 961, 1018 (2009); Matthew C. Waxman, *Guantánamo, Habeas, and Standards of Proof: Viewing the Law Through Multiple Lenses*, 42 Case W. Res. J. Int'l L. 245, 246–56 (2009). Does the precise language of the standard used to evaluate detentions matter? Is it properly labeled a standard of review—used to review a military determination—or a standard of proof used to resolve a habeas petitioner's claim? For a description of the high degree of court-to-court variation in standard of review inquiries and discovery, see Nathaniel H. Nesbitt, *Meeting Boumediene's Challenge: The Emergence of an Effective Habeas Jurisprudence and Obsolescence of New Detention Legislation*, 95 Minn. L. Rev. 244, 268–73 (2010).

NOTES ON DISCOVERY AND RELIABILITY

1) The Discovery Process. In *Al-Bihani*, the D.C. Circuit also held that:

> [T]he standard for disclosure ordered by the district court, coupled with the opportunity to make specific discovery requests, is consistent with the Supreme Court's directive in *Boumediene* that a detainee be provided with the opportunity to challenge 'the sufficiency of the Government's evidence' and to 'supplement the record on review' with additional 'exculpatory evidence.'

The D.C. Circuit added that the Government would not be permitted to "withhold exculpatory evidence because personnel from other agencies will pass only inculpatory evidence on." Al-Bihani had also requested an evidentiary hearing.

[dd] Cf. *St. Cyr*, 522 U.S. at 306 ("Until the enactment of the 1952 Immigration and Nationality Act, the sole means by which an alien could test the legality of his or her deportation order was by bringing a habeas corpus action in district court . . . In such cases, other than the question whether there was some evidence to support the order, the courts generally did not review factual determinations made by the Executive."). See generally Gerald L. Neuman, *The Constitutional Requirement of "Some Evidence,"* 25 San Diego L. Rev. 631-35 (1988).

[ee] See *Boumediene*, 553 U.S. at 814 (Roberts, C.J., dissenting).

[ff] *Hamdi*, 542 U.S. at 537 ("Because we conclude that due process demands some system for a citizen-detainee to refute his classification, the proposed 'some evidence' standard is inadequate."). Perhaps the plurality should instead have grounded the inadequacy of the "some evidence" standard in the Suspension Clause and not in the Due Process Clause.

The D.C. Circuit found denial of a hearing appropriate, noting that in post-conviction cases—under 28 U.S.C. § 2254(e)(2)—district courts have discretion to conduct such hearings only under limited circumstances. The court reasoned that there was a "full habeas hearing" and that "the district court did hear the facts of Al-Bihani's case and provided ample opportunity in conference and in a hearing for the parties to air concerns over evidence."

2)   Hearsay. The Federal Rules of Evidence apply in habeas proceedings. The *Hamdi* plurality, however, noted that hearsay evidence may need to be accepted as the most reliable evidence in detainee challenges. In response, the D.C. Circuit has said that hearsay is "always admissible" in detainee challenges, but with a caveat—the court must still weigh the reliability of the evidence. See *Al-Bihani*, 590 F.3d at 879.

3)   Admissibility and Torture. Government use of harsh interrogation techniques in the wake of the 9/11 attacks created difficult problems when relying on the resulting statements to support indefinite detentions. For example, in granting the writ in *Al Rabiah v. United States*, the district court cited a Fifth Amendment voluntariness test and concluded that there was credible evidence that the detainee had been severely tortured. See 658 F.Supp. 2d 11, 32 (D.D.C. 2009). The district court, however, did not formally apply a Fifth Amendment test to decide if the confession statements should have been admissible into evidence, because there was no trial—just a habeas proceeding. Instead, evidence of torture was relevant to the inquiry into whether the confession statements were reliable enough to support the decision to detain. But cf. Al Alwi v. Obama, 653 F.3d 11, 19 (D.C. Cir. 2011) (noting that the clear error review includes questioning reliability of evidence and finding that the district court properly evaluated reliability prior to admitting evidence).

Another district court noted, however, that in criminal cases "confessions or testimony procured by torture are excluded under the Due Process Clause because such admissions would run contrary to 'fundamental principles of liberty and justice which lie at the base of all our civil and political institutions.'" Mohammed v. Obama, 704 F.Supp.2d 1, 24 (D.D.C. 2009). The court recounted a harrowing ordeal:

> Binyamin Mohammed's trauma lasted for two long years. During that time, he was physically and psychologically tortured. His genitals were mutilated. He was deprived of sleep and food. He was summarily transported from one foreign prison to another. Captors held him in stress positions for days at a time. He was forced to listen to piercingly loud music and the screams of other prisoners while locked in a pitch-black cell. All the while, he was forced to inculpate himself and others in various plots to imperil Americans.

The court concluded that, despite the detail of his statements, "lengthy prior torture" rendered them unreliable because "coercive tactics" can lead to "confabulation" and creation of "false memories." As a result, the court granted the writ and ordered his release.[gg] Do you think that evidence resulting from torture should only be screened for its reliability, or should the courts address whether the Constitution or treaties protect such detainees from torture?

[gg] In contrast, for a decision finding that effects of prior torture had dissipated by the same later statements were made to interrogators, see Anam v. Obama, 696 F.Supp.2d 1, 7, 10 (D.D.C. 2010).

B. THE RETURN OF EXTRATERRITORIALITY

INTRODUCTORY NOTES ON NEW EXTRATERRITORIAL QUESTIONS

1) *Munaf v. Geren.* The Supreme Court issued its opinion in *Munaf v. Geren*, 553 U.S. 674 (2008), the same day as it issued *Boumediene*. The two opinions form bookends of sorts, with *Boumediene* addressing the habeas privilege and *Munaf* addressing the substantive scope of detention. In *Munaf*, the habeas petitioners were two U.S. citizens travelling in Iraq, and were captured by coalition forces for allegedly committing "hostile and warlike acts." They were given hearings before U.S. military officers, they were determined to pose a threat to Iraqi security, and then they were imprisoned. The Court described the nature of their custody:

> The Multinational Force–Iraq (MNF–I) is an international coalition force operating in Iraq composed of 26 different nations, including the United States. The force operates under the unified command of United States military officers, at the request of the Iraqi Government, and in accordance with United Nations (U. N.) Security Council Resolutions. Pursuant to the U. N. mandate, MNF–I forces detain individuals alleged to have committed hostile or warlike acts in Iraq, pending investigation and prosecution in Iraqi courts under Iraqi law.

The Court held that, although they were detained by a multinational force, the generally-applicable habeas statute, 28 U.S.C. § 2241, runs to all persons "in custody under or by color of the authority of the United States" and that the U.S. had custody of both persons. *Munaf* noted, though, that these petitioners were also U.S. citizens. The Court distinguished *Hirota v. MacArthur*, which involved a war-crime conviction of a noncitizen before a multinational-force entity. Chief Justice Roberts, who wrote for the Court, observed wryly:

> Although those familiar with the history of the period would appreciate the possibility of confusion over who General MacArthur took orders from, the Court concluded that the sentencing tribunal was "not a tribunal of the United States." The Court then held that, "[u]nder the foregoing circumstances," United States courts had "no power or authority to review, to affirm, set aside or annul the judgments and sentences" imposed by that tribunal. . .

> The Government argues that the multinational character of the MNF–I, like the multinational character of the tribunal at issue in Hirota, means that it too is not a United States entity subject to habeas. In making this claim, the Government acknowledges that the MNF–I is subject to American authority, but contends that the same was true of the tribunal at issue in *Hirota*. In *Hirota*, the Government notes, the petitioners were held by the United States Eighth Army, which took orders from General MacArthur . . . , and were subject to an "unbroken" chain of U. S. command, ending with the President of the United States . . .

> The Court in *Hirota*, however, may have found it significant, in considering the nature of the tribunal established by General MacArthur, that the Solicitor General expressly contended that General MacArthur, as pertinent, was not subject to United States authority.

In short, in unanimously affirming the habeas jurisdiction of federal courts, *Munaf* distinguished between the power exercised by the MNF-I and that exercised by the Far East Military Tribunal in Manila. How does the "wry" characterization of General MacArthur reflect that distinction?

Although the Court recognized the habeas power of federal courts, it denied relief on the merits. The petitioners had asked that the district court prohibit the U.S. from transferring them to Iraqi authorities for criminal prosecution. The Court ruled that such a remedy was not available, stating that the ordinary habeas remedy is release and not prohibition of transfer. The Court also noted that Iraq had the sovereign right to prosecute the prisoners for offenses committed on Iraqi soil: "To allow United States courts to intervene in an ongoing foreign criminal proceeding and pass judgment on its legitimacy seems at least as great an intrusion as the plainly barred collateral review of foreign convictions."

2)   The Torture Claim. Finally, the Court responded to the petitioners' argument that they would be tortured if handed to Iraqi authorities: "Petitioners here allege only the possibility of mistreatment in a prison facility; this is not a more extreme case in which the Executive has determined that a detainee is likely to be tortured but decides to transfer him anyway." The Government had taken the position that, although it was concerned about torture in some parts of the Iraqi system, the Justice Ministry that would have custody over the two petitioners "generally met internationally accepted standards for basic prisoner needs." In *Munaf*, the prisoners had argued very briefly that a statute—the Foreign Affairs Reform and Restructuring Act of 1998 (FARRA), Pub. L. No. 105–277, div. G, § 2242, 112 Stat. 2681, 2681–822 (codified at 8 U.S.C. § 1231)—allowed them to raise and prevail on their torture claims. Specifically, FARRA imposes certain preconditions on transfers to countries where the prisoner alleges torture would occur upon transfer. In *Munaf*, however, the Court expressly reserved the FARRA question, reasoning that the issue had been inadequately briefed in the lower-court and certiorari-stage proceedings.

3)   Subsequent CAT Litigation. Recall from Chapter 7 that the Convention Against Torture (CAT) limits the signatories' ability to extradite prisoners, and that specific Immigration and Nationality Act (INA) provisions regulate CAT challenges to removal. Also recall the FARRA issue reserved in *Munaf*. One of the petitioners in the *Munaf* litigation, who was detained in Iraq, argued on remand and in an amended habeas petition that the Suspension Clause, Due Process Clause, and various statutes entitled him to "a right to judicial review of conditions in the receiving country before he may be transferred." Omar v. McHugh, 646 F.3d 13, 18 (D.C. Cir. 2011). The D.C. Circuit affirmed the order rejecting the petition, explaining that "[t]hose facing extradition traditionally have not been able to maintain habeas claims to block transfer based on conditions in the receiving country." *Omar* also underscored that the REAL-ID Act says that "only immigration transferees have a right to judicial review of conditions in the receiving country, during a court's review of a final order of removal." *Omar* reasoned that persons facing transfer from military custody lack access to such judicial review because they are not facing removal and cannot petition for review available under the REAL-ID Act. In the extradition context, courts perform only a very-deferential, "some-evidence" review of the extradition decision. If *Omar* correctly interpreted the REAL-ID Act, then does the Act unconstitutionally suspend the habeas privilege by barring judicial review? After *Boumediene*, does the Suspension Clause require more meaningful review than "some evidence" review under the Due Process Clause? Should the D.C. Circuit have avoided that consequence by interpreting the Real-ID Act as regulating challenges to removal (which is all it does by its terms) and not restricting habeas corpus review of other non-removal decisions? The D.C. Circuit briefly called the suggestion that habeas corpus alone guarantees a right to meaningful judicial review of extradition "absurd" and "frivolous."

The Ninth Circuit *en banc* decision in *Trinidad y Garcia v. Thomas*, 683 F.3d 952 (9th Cir. 2012), which Chapter 7 discusses in reference to the REAL ID Act, also extended *Munaf* to the context of domestic extradition. *Trinidad y Garcia* held that, because the petitioner argued that extradition would violate the CAT, a federal court must determine whether the Secretary of State complied with statutory process in determining whether the petitioner would face torture upon completion of the transfer. *Trinidad y Garcia* held that, after having determined whether the Secretary had met the certification requirements, the judge should conduct no further review, since any "substantive due process claim is foreclosed by [*Munaf*]."

4) Scholarly Views on Habeas Jurisdiction and Foreign Prison Facilities. For the view that habeas jurisdiction runs to GTMO but not to Iraq or Afghanistan, see Richard H. Fallon, Jr. and Daniel J. Meltzer, *Habeas Corpus Jurisdiction, Substantive Rights, and the War on Terror*, 120 Harv. L. Rev. 2029 (2007). For the view that habeas jurisdiction, in a deferential form, should run to noncitizens detained abroad, see David A. Martin, *Offshore Detainees and the Role of Courts After Rasul v. Bush: The Underappreciated Virtues of Deferential Review*, 25 B.C. Third World L.J. 125 (2005).

INTRODUCTORY NOTE ON AL-MAQALEH V. GATES *AND BAGRAM*

No new prisoners have been brought to GTMO for years. For some time, Bagram Theater Internment Facility (BTIF) at the Bagram Airbase in Afghanistan appeared to take GTMO's place, housing detainees captured in Afghanistan and in other countries around the world. As Professor Aziz Z. Huq described, the Bagram detainee population grew while the GTMO population fell: "At a minimum, the trend line for Bagram raises the possibility that increased judicial scrutiny of Guantánamo results not in less detention, but rather detention in a different location." Aziz Z. Huq, *What Good is Habeas?*, 26 Const. Comment. at 407. Given the many hundreds of prisoners indefinitely detained at Bagram, one of the first logical questions after *Boumediene* involved whether the writ ran to that facility in Afghanistan. Justice Scalia complained in his *Boumediene* dissent that the Court's functional test "does not (and never will) provide clear guidance for the future." The D.C. Circuit then had to examine how to apply that test to the Bagram base.

Al-Maqaleh v. Gates

United States Court of Appeals for the District of Columbia
605 F.3d 84 (2010)

■ SENTELLE, Chief Judge:

Three detainees at Bagram Air Force Base in Afghanistan petitioned the district court for habeas corpus relief from their confinement by the

United States military. Appellants (collectively "the United States" or "the government") moved to dismiss for lack of jurisdiction based on § 7(a) of the Military Commissions Act of 2006 (MCA). The district court [a]greed with the United States that § 7(a) of the MCA purported to deprive the court of jurisdiction, but held that this section could not constitutionally be applied to deprive the court of jurisdiction under the Supreme Court's test articulated in *Boumediene v. Bush,* 553 U.S. 723 (2008). The court therefore denied the motion to dismiss but certified the three habeas cases for interlocutory appeal * * * . * * * [A]pplying the Supreme Court decision in *Boumediene,* we determine that the district court did not have jurisdiction to consider the petitions for habeas corpus. We therefore reverse the order of the district court and order that the petitions be dismissed.

I. Background

A. *The Petitioners*

All three petitioners are being held as unlawful enemy combatants at the Bagram Theater Internment Facility on the Bagram Airfield Military Base in Afghanistan. Petitioner Fadi Al-Maqaleh is a Yemeni citizen who alleges he was taken into custody in 2003. While Al-Maqaleh's petition asserts "on information and belief" that he was captured beyond Afghan borders, a sworn declaration from Colonel James W. Gray, Commander of Detention Operations, states that Al-Maqaleh was captured in Zabul, Afghanistan. Redha Al-Najar is a Tunisian citizen who alleges he was captured in Pakistan in 2002. Amin Al-Bakri is a Yemeni citizen who alleges he was captured in Thailand in 2002. Both Al-Najar and Al-Bakri allege they were first held in some other unknown location before being moved to Bagram.

B. *The Place of Confinement*

The Bagram Airfield Military Base is the largest military facility in Afghanistan occupied by United States and coalition forces. The United States entered into an "Accommodation Consignment Agreement for Lands and Facilities at Bagram Airfield" with the Islamic Republic of Afghanistan in 2006, which "consigns all facilities and land located at Bagram Airfield ... owned by [Afghanistan,] or Parwan Province, or private individuals, or others, for use by the United States and coalition forces for military purposes." * * * The Agreement refers to Afghanistan as the "host nation" and the United States "as the lessee." The leasehold created by the agreement is to continue "until the United States or its successors determine that the premises are no longer required for its use."

Afghanistan remains a theater of active military combat. The United States and coalition forces conduct "an ongoing military campaign against al Qaeda, the Taliban regime, and their affiliates and supporters in Afghanistan." These operations are conducted in part from Bagram Airfield. Bagram has been subject to repeated attacks from the Taliban and al Qaeda, including a March 2009 suicide bombing striking the gates of the facility, and Taliban rocket attacks in June of 2009 resulting in death and injury to United States service members and other personnel.

While the United States provides overall security to Bagram, numerous other nations have compounds on the base. Some of the other nations control access to their respective compounds. The troops of the other nations are present at Bagram both as part of the American-led military coalition in Afghanistan and as members of the International Security Assistance Force (ISAF) of the North Atlantic Treaty Organization. * * * According to the United States, as of February 1, 2010, approximately 38,000 non-

United States troops were serving in Afghanistan as part of the ISAF, representing 42 other countries. * * *

C. *The Litigation*

Appellees in this action, three detainees at Bagram, filed habeas petitions against the President of the United States and the Secretary of Defense in the district court. The government moved to dismiss for lack of jurisdiction, relying principally upon § 7(a) of the [MCA]. * * * The district court, recognizing that the issue of whether the court had jurisdiction presented a controlling question of law as to which there were substantial grounds for difference of opinion, certified the question for interlocutory appeal * * * .

II. Analysis

A. *The Legal Framework*

* * * Applying the "common threat" to the question of the jurisdiction of United States courts to consider habeas petitions from detainees in Guantánamo, the [*Boumediene*] Court concluded that "at least three factors are relevant in determining the reach of the Suspension Clause." Those three factors, which we must apply today in answering the same question as to detainees at Bagram, are: (1) the citizenship and status of the detainee and the adequacy of the process through which that status determination was made; (2) the nature of the sites where apprehension and then detention took place; and (3) the practical obstacles inherent in resolving the prisoner's entitlement to the writ. Applying these factors to the detainees at Guantánamo, the Court held that the petitioners had the protection of the Suspension Clause.

B. *Application to the Bagram Petitioners*

Our duty, as explained above, is to determine the reach of the right to habeas corpus and therefore of the Suspension Clause to the factual context underlying the petitions we consider in the present appeal. In doing so, we are controlled by the Supreme Court's interpretation of the Constitution in *Eisentrager* as construed and explained in the Court's more recent opinion in *Boumediene*. * * * [W]e reexamine the issue and ultimately [reverse the district court].

* * * The United States would like us to hold that the *Boumediene* analysis has no application beyond territories that are, like Guantánamo, outside the *de jure* sovereignty of the United States but are subject to its *de facto* sovereignty. As the government puts it in its reply brief, "[t]he real question before this Court, therefore, is whether Bagram may be considered effectively part of the United States in light of the nature and history of the U.S. presence there." We disagree.

Relying upon three independent reasons, the Court in *Boumediene* expressly repudiated the argument of the United States in that case to the effect "that the *Eisentrager* Court adopted a formalistic, sovereignty-based test for determining the reach of the Suspension Clause." Briefly put, the High Court rejected that argument first on the basis that the *Eisentrager* Court's further analysis beyond recitations concerning sovereignty would not have been undertaken by the Court if the sovereignty question were determinative. The *Boumediene* Court explicitly did "not accept the idea that . . . the [sovereignty discussion] from *Eisentrager* is the only authoritative language in the opinion and that all the rest is dicta. The Court's further determinations, based on practical considerations, were integral to

Part II of its opinion and came before the decision announced its holding." Second, the Court rejected the Government's reading of *Eisentrager* because the meaning of the word "sovereignty" in the *Eisentrager* opinion was not limited to the "narrow technical sense" of the word and could be read "to connote the degree of control the military asserted over the facility." The third reason is the one we noted above, that is, that the Court concluded that such a reading of *Eisentrager* as proposed by the United States "would have marked not only a change in, but a complete repudiation of, the Insular Cases' * * * functional approach to questions of extraterritoriality."

True, the second factor articulated in *Boumediene* for rejecting the government's reading of *Eisentrager* might apply differently in this case because of differences in the levels of control over the military facilities. But we must keep in mind that the second factor is only one of the three reasons offered by the *Boumediene* Court for the rejection of "a formalistic, sovereignty-based test for determining the reach of the Suspension Clause." Whatever the force of the second reason offered by the Court in *Boumediene,* the first and third reasons make it plain that the Court's understanding of *Eisentrager,* and therefore of the reach of the Suspension Clause, was based not on a formalistic attachment to sovereignty, but on a consideration of practical factors as well. * * * We therefore reject the proposition that *Boumediene* adopted a bright-line test with the effect of substituting *de facto* for *de jure* in the otherwise rejected interpretation of *Eisentrager.*

For similar reasons, we reject the most extreme position offered by the petitioners. At various points, the petitioners seem to be arguing that the fact of United States control of Bagram under the lease of the military base is sufficient to trigger the extraterritorial application of the Suspension Clause, or at least satisfy the second factor of the three set forth in *Boumediene.* Again, we reject this extreme understanding. Such an interpretation would seem to create the potential for the extraterritorial extension of the Suspension Clause to noncitizens held in any United States military facility in the world, and perhaps to an undeterminable number of other United States-leased facilities as well. * * * Having rejected the bright-line arguments of both parties, we must proceed to their more nuanced arguments, and reach a conclusion based on the application of the Supreme Court's enumerated factors to the case before us.

The first of the enumerated factors is "the citizenship and status of the detainee and the adequacy of the process through which that status determination was made." Citizenship is, of course, an important factor in determining the constitutional rights of persons before the court. It is well established that there are "constitutional decisions of [the Supreme] Court expressly according differing protection to aliens than to citizens." However, clearly the alien citizenship of the petitioners in this case does not weigh against their claim to protection of the right of habeas corpus under the Suspension Clause. So far as citizenship is concerned, they differ in no material respect from the petitioners at Guantánamo who prevailed in *Boumediene.* As to status, the petitioners before us are held as enemy aliens. But so were the *Boumediene* petitioners. While the *Eisentrager* petitioners were in a weaker position by having the status of war criminals, that is immaterial to the question before us. This question is governed by *Boumediene* and the status of the petitioners before us again is the same as the Guantánamo detainees, so this factor supports their argument for the extension of the availability of the writ.

So far as the adequacy of the process through which that status determination was made, the petitioners are in a stronger position for the availability of the writ than were either the *Eisentrager* or *Boumediene* petitioners. As the Supreme Court noted, the *Boumediene* petitioners were in a very different posture than those in *Eisentrager* in that "there ha[d] been no trial by military commission for violations of the laws of war." Unlike the *Boumediene* petitioners or those before us, "[t]he *Eisentrager* petitioners were charged by a bill of particulars that made detailed factual allegations against them." The *Eisentrager* detainees were "entitled to representation by counsel, allowed to introduce evidence on their own behalf, and permitted to cross-examine the prosecution's witnesses" in an adversarial proceeding. The status of the *Boumediene* petitioners was determined by Combatant Status Review Tribunals (CSRTs) affording far less protection. Under the CSRT proceeding, the detainee, rather than being represented by an attorney, was advised by a "Personal Representative" who was "not the detainee's lawyer or even his 'advocate.'" * * *

The status of the Bagram detainees is determined not by a Combatant Status Review Tribunal but by an "Unlawful Enemy Combatant Review Board" (UECRB). As the district court correctly noted, proceedings before the UECRB afford even less protection to the rights of detainees in the determination of status than was the case with the CSRT. Therefore, as the district court noted, "while the important adequacy of process factor strongly supported the extension of the Suspension Clause and habeas rights in *Boumediene,* it even more strongly favors petitioners here." * * * However, we do not stop with the first factor.

The second factor, "the nature of the sites where apprehension and then detention took place," weighs heavily in favor of the United States. Like all petitioners in both *Eisentrager* and *Boumediene,* the petitioners here were apprehended abroad. While this in itself would appear to weigh against the extension of the writ, it obviously would not be sufficient, otherwise *Boumediene* would not have been decided as it was. However, the nature of the place where the detention takes place weighs more strongly in favor of the position argued by the United States and against the extension of habeas jurisdiction than was the case in either *Boumediene* or *Eisentrager.* In the first place, while *de facto* sovereignty is not determinative, for the reasons discussed above, the very fact that it was the subject of much discussion in *Boumediene* makes it obvious that it is not without relevance. As the Supreme Court set forth, Guantánamo Bay is "a territory that, while technically not part of the United States, is under the complete and total control of our Government." While it is true that the United States holds a leasehold interest in Bagram, and held a leasehold interest in Guantánamo, the surrounding circumstances are hardly the same. The United States has maintained its total control of Guantánamo Bay for over a century, even in the face of a hostile government maintaining *de jure* sovereignty over the property. In Bagram, while the United States has options as to duration of the lease agreement, there is no indication of any intent to occupy the base with permanence, nor is there hostility on the part of the "host" country. Therefore, the notion that *de facto* sovereignty extends to Bagram is no more real than would have been the same claim with respect to Landsberg in the *Eisentrager* case. While it is certainly realistic to assert that the United States has *de facto* sovereignty over Guantánamo, the same simply is not true with respect to Bagram. Though the site of detention analysis weighs in favor of the United States and against the petitioners, it is not determinative.

But we hold that the third factor, that is "the practical obstacles inherent in resolving the prisoner's entitlement to the writ," particularly when considered along with the second factor, weighs overwhelmingly in favor of the position of the United States. It is undisputed that Bagram, indeed the entire nation of Afghanistan, remains a theater of war. Not only does this suggest that the detention at Bagram is more like the detention at Landsberg than Guantánamo, the position of the United States is even stronger in this case than it was in *Eisentrager*. As the Supreme Court recognized in *Boumediene,* even though the active hostilities in the European theater had "c[o]me to an end," at the time of the *Eisentrager* decision, many of the problems of a theater of war remained * * *.

In ruling for the extension of the writ to Guantánamo, the Supreme Court expressly noted that "[s]imilar threats are not apparent here." In the case before us, similar, if not greater, threats are indeed apparent. The United States asserts, and petitioners cannot credibly dispute, that all of the attributes of a facility exposed to the vagaries of war are present in Bagram. The Supreme Court expressly stated in *Boumediene* that at Guantánamo, "[w]hile obligated to abide by the terms of the lease, the United States is, for all practical purposes, answerable to no other sovereign for its acts on the base. Were that not the case, *or if the detention facility were located in an active theater of war,* arguments that issuing the writ would be 'impractical or anomalous' would have more weight." * * *

We are supported in this conclusion by the rationale of *Eisentrager,* which was not only not overruled, but reinforced by the language and reasoning just referenced from *Boumediene.* * * * While it is true, as the Supreme Court noted in *Boumediene,* that the United States forces in Germany in 1950 faced the possibility of unrest and guerilla warfare, operations in the European theater had ended with the surrender of Germany and Italy years earlier. Bagram remains in a theater of war. * * *

We do not ignore the arguments of the detainees that the United States chose the place of detention and might be able "to evade judicial review of Executive detention decisions by transferring detainees into active conflict zones, thereby granting the Executive the power to switch the Constitution on or off at will." However, that is not what happened here. * * * We need make no determination on the importance of this possibility, given that it remains only a possibility; its resolution can await a case in which the claim is a reality rather than a speculation. In so stating, we note that [*Boumediene*] did not dictate that the three enumerated factors are exhaustive. It only told us that "*at least* three factors" are relevant. Perhaps such manipulation by the Executive might constitute an additional factor in some case in which it is in fact present. However, the notion that the United States deliberately confined the detainees in the theater of war rather than at, for example, Guantánamo, is not only unsupported by the evidence, it is not supported by reason. To have made such a deliberate decision to "turn off the Constitution" would have required the military commanders or other Executive officials making the situs determination to anticipate the complex litigation history set forth above and predict the *Boumediene* decision long before it came down.

Also supportive of our decision that the third factor weighs heavily in favor of the United States, as the district court recognized, is the fact that the detention is within the sovereign territory of another nation, which itself creates practical difficulties. Indeed, it was on this factor that the district court relied in dismissing the fourth petition, which was filed by an

Afghan citizen detainee. While that factor certainly weighed more heavily with respect to an Afghan citizen, it is not without force with respect to detainees who are alien to both the United States and Afghanistan. The United States holds the detainees pursuant to a cooperative arrangement with Afghanistan on territory as to which Afghanistan is sovereign. While we cannot say that extending our constitutional protections to the detainees would be in any way disruptive of that relationship, neither can we say with certainty what the reaction of the Afghan government would be.

In sum, taken together, the second and especially the third factors compel us to hold that the petitions should have been dismissed.

CONCLUSION

For the reasons set forth above, we hold that the jurisdiction of the courts to afford the right to habeas relief and the protection of the Suspension Clause does not extend to aliens held in Executive detention in the Bagram detention facility in the Afghan theater of war. We therefore reverse the order of the district court denying the motion for dismissal of the United States and order that the petitions be dismissed for lack of jurisdiction.

So ordered.

———

NOTES AND COMMENTS ON AL-MAQALEH

1) *Eisentrager* **Again.** Which of the three (or six) *Eisentrager* factors seemed to be decisive for the D.C. Circuit judges in *Maqaleh*? How did the D.C. Circuit judges reach their result? The status of the detainees, the place of initial detention, and the adequacy of the process all weighed strongly in favor of jurisdiction. The prisoners' status as noncitizens was no different than that of the prisoners in *Boumediene*. The place of current detention, the more temporary nature of the lease, and the fact that Bagram was situated in an active military theater seemed to outweigh the other factors. The Court in *Boumediene* did not say what weight to give each factor. Do you think that the D.C. Circuit correctly evaluated the factors?

2) **Status.** Did the D.C. Circuit accurately describe the "status" factor? The court noted that the prisoners were not citizens, but that noncitizenship did not prevent them from seeking habeas review. The court also emphasized that the prisoners were "held as enemy aliens." This language was incorrect—at least based on the common understanding of the term "enemy alien"—because the prisoners were not citizens of nations with which the U.S. was at war. The prisoners were being held as "enemy combatants," though they contested that status designation. The court noted that they had been designated for detention based on a screening process less searching than the CSRT process rejected by *Boumediene*. In assessing whether the prisoners could exercise the habeas privilege, should the court have placed more weight on the adequacy of the screening process used at BTIF?

3) **The Future of the BTIF.** What result do you predict, should the issue of whether habeas runs to the BTIF reach the U.S. Supreme Court?

    a) How would the Court rule, applying its test from *Boumediene,* if citizens of countries not at war with the U.S.—say of Yemen, Egypt, and Thailand—are taken into custody in their home countries, brought to Bagram, and then file habeas petitions?

b) Would the result change if the petitioners were Afghan citizens initially captured in Afghanistan, and then detained at Bagram?

c) Would the result change if the petitioners acknowledge that they were "part of" the Taliban, including after the 9/11 attacks?

d) How would the analysis change if more careful screening procedures were used to make the combatant status determinations of the petitioners lodging the habeas challenge? After *Boumediene*, the Government established new enhanced review procedures at BTIF, including review boards that conduct an assessment within 60 days of a detention and every six months thereafter. Much like the CSRT process that the Court reviewed in *Boumediene*, however, the BTIF tribunal consists of military officers and the detainee is assigned a "personal representative" instead of an advocate.[hh]

e) How would the analysis change if, following a hypothetical Human Rights Watch report disclosing widespread torture in Afghan prisons, the detainee was captured in Afghanistan by CIA operatives and then challenged an order transferring him to the custody of Afghan authorities? Now suppose the detainee was captured by U.S. troops in Afghanistan, but was a citizen of another country, say Saudi Arabia, and challenges a decision to transfer him back into the custody of the Saudi government?

4) Executive Power. Should *Maqaleh* ultimately be understood as deferential to executive power? For the view that it should, see Stephen I. Vladeck, *The Unreviewable Executive: Kiyemba, Maqaleh, and the Obama Administration*, 26 Const. Comment. 603, 623 (2010) ("Arguments against the power of the federal courts to entertain habeas petitions from individuals in federal custody, or to be able to fashion appropriate relief in cases in which the petitioners prevail on the merits, are inherently arguments in favor of the Executive."). Does the decision allow the executive to "switch the Constitution on or off at will" by moving detainees to BTIF to avoid judicial intervention? Kal Raustiala, Al Maqaleh v. Gates, *605 F.3d 84. U.S. Court of Appeals for the D.C. Circuit, May 21, 2010*, 104 Am. J. Int'l L. 647, 652 (2010). The Government stopped moving persons detained outside Afghanistan to the BTIF, perhaps to avoid creating new questions regarding the reach of habeas corpus.[ii]

5) Transferring BTIF Detainees. In 2012, after negotiations with the Afghani President, the U.S. agreed to transfer authority over Bagram to the Afghans. Detainees, however, apparently cannot be released except after consultation with U.S. military. The U.S. administrative scheme for reviewing detentions may be replaced by Afghan custody over the detainees and an Afghan administrative scheme. The fate of the Bagram detention site after NATO operations are scheduled to end in 2014 is "still undetermined."[jj] U.S. involvement in Afghanistan may end before the U.S. Supreme Court revisits the D.C. Circuit's opinion in *Maqaleh*.

[hh] See Michael J. Buxton, *No Habeas for You! Al Maqaleh v. Gates, The Bagram Detainees, and the Global Insurgency*, 60 Am. U. L. Rev. 519 (2010).

[ii] See Eric Schmitt, *Closing Jail in Bagram is a Puzzle for Obama*, N.Y. Times, Jan. 29, 2009.

[jj] Ray Norland, *As Bagram Detainees are Transferred, U.S. Keeps its Grip*, N.Y. Times, May 30, 2012.

C. THE REMEDY OF RELEASE

INTRODUCTORY NOTE ON KIYEMBA V. OBAMA

At common law, recall how the remedy of release was central to the judge's habeas power. The judge could grant the writ and order the body of the prisoner produced; after hearing from the jailer, the judge might order the prisoner released from the courtroom. In *Boumediene,* the Supreme Court emphasized the centrality of the remedy of release. The Court underscored that "the central purpose of habeas corpus is to test the legality of executive detention," and that "the writ requires most fundamentally an Article III court able to hear the prisoner's claims and, when necessary, order release." Recall the events preceding the order granting certiorari in *Boumediene*—where there was evidence that, when a CSRT panel actually recommended a release, its decisions were overturned.

GTMO detainees, however, were not personally flown to courtrooms in Washington D.C. to have their cases heard by federal judges, nor was it clear that federal judges could simply order detainees released from GTMO. After all, the detainees could not be released into Cuba. Moreover, even as GTMO detainees increasingly obtained relief after *Boumediene,* the United States faced serious practical difficulties finding countries willing to receive them. The problem was not an entirely novel one; recall the Supreme Court's decisions concerning indefinite detention pending removal in the immigration context (Chapter 7). Those immigration removal cases, however, involved persons detained in the territorial United States, and they often involved far less politically-fraught custody. In the *"Kiyemba"* litigation, the first circuit decision of which is excerpted below, the D.C. Circuit confronted the question of what the discharge remedy means in the national security detention context.

Kiyemba v. Obama (Kiyemba I)

United States Court of Appeals for the District of Columbia
555 F.3d 1022 (2009)

■ RANDOLPH, Senior Circuit Judge:

Seventeen Chinese citizens currently held at Guantánamo Bay Naval Base, Cuba, brought petitions for writs of habeas corpus. Each petitioner is an ethnic Uighur, a Turkic Muslim minority whose members reside in the Xinjiang province of far-west China. The question is whether, as the district court ruled, petitioners are entitled to an order requiring the government to bring them to the United States and release them here.

Sometime before September 11, 2001, petitioners left China and traveled to the Tora Bora mountains in Afghanistan, where they settled in a camp with other Uighurs. Petitioners fled to Pakistan when U.S. aerial strikes destroyed the Tora Bora camp. Eventually they were turned over to the U.S. military, transferred to Guantánamo Bay and detained as "enemy combatants."

Evidence produced at hearings before Combatant Status Review Tribunals in Guantánamo indicated that at least some petitioners intended to fight the Chinese government, and that they had received firearms training at the camp for this purpose. The Tribunals determined that the petitioners could be detained as enemy combatants because the camp was run by the

Eastern Turkistan Islamic Movement, a Uighur independence group the military believes to be associated with al Qaida or the Taliban, and which the State Department designated as a terrorist organization three years after the petitioners' capture.

In the *Parhat* case, the court ruled that the government had not presented sufficient evidence that the Eastern Turkistan Islamic Movement was associated with al Qaida or the Taliban, or had engaged in hostilities against the United States or its coalition partners. Parhat therefore could not be held as an enemy combatant. The government saw no material differences in its evidence against the other Uighurs, and therefore decided that none of the petitioners should be detained as enemy combatants.

Releasing petitioners to their country of origin poses a problem. Petitioners fear that if they are returned to China they will face arrest, torture or execution. United States policy is not to transfer individuals to countries where they will be subject to mistreatment. Petitioners have not sought to comply with the immigration laws governing an alien's entry into the United States. Diplomatic efforts to locate an appropriate third country in which to resettle them are continuing. In the meantime, petitioners are held under the least restrictive conditions possible in the Guantánamo military base.

As relief in their habeas cases, petitioners moved for an order compelling their release into the United States. Although the district court assumed that the government initially detained petitioners in compliance with the law, the court thought the government no longer had any legal authority to hold them. As to the appropriate relief, the court acknowledged that historically the authority to admit aliens into this country rested exclusively with the political branches. Nevertheless, the court held that the "exceptional" circumstances of this case and the need to safeguard "an individual's liberty from unbridled executive fiat," justified granting petitioners' motion.

Our analysis begins with * * * the ancient principle that a nation-state has the inherent right to exclude or admit foreigners and to prescribe applicable terms and conditions for their exclusion or admission. * * *

For more than a century, the Supreme Court has recognized the power to exclude aliens as "inherent in sovereignty, necessary for maintaining normal international relations and defending the country against foreign encroachments and danger—-a power to be exercised exclusively by the political branches of government" and not "granted away or restrained on behalf of any one." The Chinese Exclusion Case, 130 U.S. 581, 609 (1889). * * *

* * * Policies pertaining to the entry of aliens and their right to remain here are peculiarly concerned with the political conduct of government." * * * As a result, it "is not within the province of any court, unless expressly authorized by law, to review the determination of the political branch of the Government to exclude a given alien." With respect to these seventeen petitioners, the Executive Branch has determined not to allow them to enter the United States. The critical question is: what law "expressly authorized" the district court to set aside the decision of the Executive Branch and to order these aliens brought to the United States and released in Washington, D.C.?

The district court cited no statute or treaty authorizing its order, and we are aware of none. As to the Constitution, the district court spoke only generally. The court said there were "constitutional limits," that there was some "constitutional imperative," that it needed to protect "the fundamental right of liberty." These statements suggest that the court may have had the Fifth Amendment's due process clause in mind. But the due process clause cannot support the court's order of release. Decisions of the Supreme Court and of this court—decisions the district court did not acknowledge— hold that the due process clause does not apply to aliens without property or presence in the sovereign territory of the United States.

The district court also sought to support its order by invoking the idea embodied in the maxim *ubi jus, ibi remedium*—where there is a right, there is a remedy. We do not believe the maxim reflects federal statutory or constitutional law. Not every violation of a right yields a remedy, even when the right is constitutional. Application of the doctrine of sovereign immunity to defeat a remedy is one common example. Another example, closer to this case, is application of the political question doctrine. More than that, the right-remedy dichotomy is not so clear-cut. * * * Whatever the force of this maxim, it cannot overcome established law that an "alien who seeks admission to this country may not do so under any claim of right. Admission of aliens to the United States is a privilege granted by the sovereign United States Government. * * *

Much of what we have just written served as the foundation for the Supreme Court's opinion in *Shaughnessy v. United States ex rel. Mezei,* 345 U.S. 206 (1953), a case analogous to this one in several ways. The government held an alien at the border (Ellis Island, New York). He had been denied entry into the United States under the immigration laws. But no other country was willing to receive him. The Court ruled that the alien, who petitioned for a writ of habeas corpus, had not been deprived of any constitutional rights. In so ruling the Court necessarily rejected the proposition that because no other country would take Mezei, the prospect of indefinite detention entitled him to a court order requiring the Attorney General to release him into the United States. As the Supreme Court saw it, the Judiciary could not question the Attorney General's judgment. * * *

And so we ask again: what law authorized the district court to order the government to bring petitioners to the United States and release them here? It cannot be that because the court had habeas jurisdiction, *see Boumediene v. Bush,* 553 U.S. 723 (2008), it could fashion the sort of remedy petitioners desired. * * * Petitioners and the amici supporting them invoke the tradition of the Great Writ as a protection of liberty. As part of that tradition, they say, a court with habeas jurisdiction has always had the power to order the prisoner's release if he was being held unlawfully. But as in *Munaf v. Geren,* petitioners are not seeking "simple release." Far from it. They asked for, and received, a court order compelling the Executive to release them into the United States outside the framework of the immigration laws. Whatever may be the content of common law habeas corpus, we are certain that no habeas court since the time of Edward I ever ordered such an extraordinary remedy.

An undercurrent of petitioners' arguments is that they deserve to be released into this country after all they have endured at hands of the United States. But such sentiments, however high-minded, do not represent a legal basis for upsetting settled law and overriding the prerogatives of the political branches. We do not know whether all petitioners or any of them would qualify for entry or admission under the immigration laws. We do know that there is insufficient evidence to classify them as enemy combatants—enemies, that is, of the United States. But that hardly qualifies petitioners for admission. Nor does their detention at Guantánamo for many years entitle them to enter the United States. Whatever the scope of habeas corpus, the writ has never been compensatory in nature. The government has represented that it is continuing diplomatic attempts to find an appropriate country willing to admit petitioners, and we have no reason to doubt that it is doing so. Nor do we have the power to require anything more.

————

NOTES AND QUESTIONS ON KIYEMBA I

1)   The Remedy of Release. One question that *Kiyemba I* and other D.C. Circuit GTMO rulings raised is whether the lower courts were being faithful to the Supreme Court's directives in *Hamdi* and *Boumediene*. In *Boumediene*, the Supreme Court held that "the habeas court must have the power to order the conditional release of an individual unlawfully detained." The Supreme Court however, also explained that "release need not be the exclusive remedy and is not the appropriate one in every case in which the writ is granted." Against that backdrop, was the *Kiyemba* court right to suggest that the type of release requested was "extraordinary"? As discussed, a common law habeas proceeding required that a prisoner be brought before the judge—and a release order allowed the prisoner simply to walk out the courtroom door. Could a federal judge similarly order that prisoners be brought from GTMO to a federal courtroom in Washington D.C.?

2)   Immigration and Habeas. Note *Kiyemba I*'s emphasis on the unique prerogative of the federal government under American immigration law. (Also recall the discussion of plenary power doctrine in Chapter 7.) *Kiyemba I* invites interesting detention questions that lie at the intersection of immigration and military law. The habeas power to release would not include, *Kiyemba I* reasoned, the power to order a release *into the United States*. Such a remedy would interfere with plenary power over immigration. Is a GTMO detainee like an immigrant awaiting admission to the United States in the landmark immigration decisions *Kiyemba I* invokes? Should the outcome or remedy reflect the fact that these prisoners were brought to GTMO against their will?

Judge Rogers concurred in the judgment, but argued that the majority "ignores the very purpose of the Great Writ and its province as a check on arbitrary Executive power. The power to grant the writ means the power to order release." Judge Rogers argued that the district court should have inquired further into whether immigration statutes could permit transfer to the United States. See also Caprice L. Roberts, *Rights, Remedies, and Habeas Corpus— The Uighurs, Legally Free while Actually Imprisoned*, 24 Geo. Imm. L.J. 1 (2009) (providing a detailed overview of the *Kiyemba* litigation and arguing that lower courts mistakenly relied on immigration precedent).

3)   A Political Question? Consider the brief reference to the political-question doctrine—what role should that concept play in judicial review of national security and detentions? If the chief rationale was compliance with immigration laws, then in what way are immigration decisions "political questions"? The "political-question" doctrine typically applies to matters that are the sole responsibility of another branch, such as foreign affairs. See, e.g., Oetjen v. Central Leather Co., 246 U.S. 297 (1918) (holding that the identity of a territorial sovereign is a political question). Or was the political-questions argument that the actions of the executive should be essentially "unreviewable"? See Stephen L. Vladeck, *The Unreviewable Executive: Kiyemba, Maqaleh, and the Obama Administration,* 26 Const. Comm. 603 (2010).

4) Deterrence. After *Kiyemba I,* what incentive will the United States have to justify a national security detention if it knows that, even if a judge recognizes that custody is unlawful, such a finding need not trigger a remedy? What other costs might the United States sustain if detentions are ultimately determined to be unlawful? See Jon Connolly and Marc D. Falkoff, *Habeas, Information Asymmetries, and the War on Terror,* 41 Seton Hall L. Rev. 1361 (2011) (describing how habeas review has an "information-forcing" function that improves the quality of Government justification of custody).

5) Release and Relocation. All of the seventeen Uighur detainees were subsequently given offers of resettlement. After *Kiyemba I,* four were resettled in the Bermudas, two in Switzerland, and six in Palau. The U.S. Supreme Court vacated its order granting certiorari in *Kiyemba* in light of these "new developments." Kiyemba v. Obama, 130 S. Ct. 1235, 1235 (2010) (per curiam). The five remaining Uighurs had offers of resettlement from various countries, but did not accept them, asserting concerns about torture in the receiving country.

On remand, the D.C. Circuit denied release requests of the five remaining Uighurs, emphasizing that Congress had since spoken: "In seven separate enactments—five of which remain in force today—Congress has prohibited the expenditure of any funds to bring any Guantánamo detainee to the United States." Kiyemba v. Obama, 605 F.3d 1046, 1047–48 (D.C. Cir. 2010) (per curiam) (*Kiyemba II*). Was it Congress, by passing legislation barring expenditures on such transfers, that made it impossible to release these detainees into the U.S.?

The Supreme Court denied the certiorari petition to review that decision. Kiyemba v. Obama, 131 S. Ct. 1631 (2011). Justice Breyer issued a statement in conjunction with the order denying certiorari, joined by Justices Kennedy, Ginsburg, and Sotomayor (Justice Kagan did not participate). That statement read, in part:

> In my view, these offers, the lack of any meaningful challenge as to their appropriateness, and the Government's uncontested commitment to continue to work to resettle petitioners transform petitioners' claim. Under present circumstances, I see no Government-imposed obstacle to petitioners' timely release and appropriate resettlement. Accordingly, I join in the Court's denial of certiorari. Should circumstances materially change, however, petitioners may of course raise their original issue (or related issues) again in the lower courts and in this Court.

Two more Uighurs were subsequently resettled in El Salvador. As of winter 2012, three of the original seventeen Uighur detainees remained at GTMO.[kk]

6) Release from Custody and Collateral Consequences of Executive Detention. What happens after the United States releases a GTMO detainee? Most have already been released, and the government has said that it (eventu-

---

[kk] See Jane Sutton, *Two Uighur Detainees Sent to El Salvador,* N.Y. TIMES, April 20, 2012, at A9.

ally) plans to close the base. Can a former GTMO detainee still pursue habeas remedies? A habeas petition under § 2241 can only be brought by a person in "custody." A person who still faces "collateral consequences" of confinement, such as a criminal record, parole supervision, and the like, however, may continue to pursue habeas in order to challenge the conviction. See, e.g. Spencer v. Kemna, 523 U.S. 1, 8 (1998) (noting how the Court "[i]n recent decades . . . [has] been willing to presume that a wrongful criminal conviction has continuing collateral consequences"). What collateral consequences flow from having been detained at Guantánamo?

In another case, two detainees argued that, after their transfer from GTMO, they faced travel restrictions, including: placement on the federal No Fly list, being barred from entry to the U.S. under 8 U.S.C. § 1182(9)(A), and being labeled as enemy combatants. See Gul v. Obama, 652 F.3d 12, 20–21 (D.C. Cir. 2011). On the basis of the enemy-combatant label, the former detainees argued that the United States might target and kill them, and that they were subject to stigma and reputational harm. The D.C. Circuit found that none of those collateral consequences allowed the former GTMO detainees to pursue post-transfer litigation. The appeals court found the claim of possible targeting "speculative" and that travel restrictions would remain in place even if the former GTMO detainees succeeded in a habeas challenge. The appeals court concluded that "the label 'enemy combatant' brings with it neither a 'concrete effect' nor a 'civil disability' susceptible to judicial correction." Do you think that the D.C. Circuit was correct? Does *Gul* give the United States greater incentives to release and transfer detainees? Does it go too far to reduce the ability of detainees to obtain a remedy for an unlawful detention?

7)   **Recidivism and Terrorism.** If national security detention is, like its civil counterpart, based on a prediction that individuals are too dangerous to be released—even if they have been charged with no crime—how well can we predict that danger? Is having been a "part of" Al Qaeda a good proxy for future dangerousness? From *Hamdi* through the present, the United States and its courts have expressed the concern that detainees "might, if released, rejoin forces fighting against the United States." A March 7, 2011 Executive Order states that "continued law of war detention is warranted for a detainee subject to [p]eriodic review . . . if it is necessary to protect against a significant threat to the security of the United States." How good is the Government at predicting which detainees pose a future threat and which can be safely released? How does one predict the risk that a person will engage in terrorist acts? Very little is known about either question. See John Monahan, *The Individual Risk Assessment of Terrorism,* 18 Psychol. Pub Polc'y & Law 167 (2012). The United States has also claimed that many who have been released from GTMO have rejoined the enemy—but those claims are "highly contested." Do judges, legislators, and executive officials need better information to form a sound detention policy?

NOTES ON THE FUTURE OF NATIONAL SECURITY DETENTION

1)   **More Federal Legislation?** Judge Brown concurred in the opinion in *Al-Bihani* to note that "[t]he Supreme Court in *Boumediene* and *Hamdi* charged this court and others with the unprecedented task of developing rules to review

the propriety of military actions during a time of war, relying on common law tools." She further explained:

> The common law process depends on incrementalism and eventual correction, and it is most effective where there are a significant number of cases brought before a large set of courts, which in turn enjoy the luxury of time to work the doctrine supple. None of those factors exist in the Guantánamo context. The number of Guantánamo detainees is limited and the circumstances of their confinement are unique. . . [I]n the midst of an ongoing war, time to entertain a process of literal trial and error is not a luxury we have.

Judge Brown added that, "[h]aving been repeatedly rebuffed, . . . Congress may understandably be reluctant to return to this arena to craft appropriate habeas standards as it has done for other habeas contexts in the past." However, "looking backward may not be enough in this new war. The saying that generals always fight the last war is familiar, but familiarity does not dull the maxim's sober warning." Judge Brown concluded: "Both the rule of law and the nation's safety will benefit from an honest assessment of the new challenges we face, one that will produce an appropriately calibrated response." The legislative intervention Judge Brown contemplated never materialized. As noted, although the NDAA addressed the authorization for detention, it did not address procedures for judicial review.

2) Habeas, What is it Good For? As Professor Deborah Pearlstein has put it:

> Since the United States began detaining people . . . as part of global counterterrorism operations, U.S. detention programs have spawned more than 200 different lawsuits producing 6 Supreme Court decisions, 4 major pieces of legislation, at least 7 executive orders across 2 presidential administrations, more than 100 books, 231 law review articles (counting only those with the word "Guantánamo" in the title), dozens of reports by nongovernmental organizations, and countless news and analysis articles from media outlets in and out of the mainstream.[ll]

After *Boumediene,* and in light of the NDAA of 2012 and D.C. Circuit rulings, does the Government have clearer guidance on how to proceed should it decide to detain non-citizens abroad as part of its effort to combat international terrorism?

3) Substitution Effects. Has habeas corpus unduly restricted U.S. military options? Will the Government, as Justice Scalia suggested, increasingly hand individuals off to allies, or as Justice Thomas suggested, instead target and kill enemies? In a future conflict, do you think GTMO will be used again, or will other detention facilities be created abroad? Would doing so allow the military to escape the protections afforded by habeas corpus? Does the Suspension Clause permit national security and liberty to coexist? Do you agree or disagree with Justice Kennedy's statement in *Boumediene* that "Security subsists, too, in fidelity to freedom's first principles"?

[ll] Deborah N. Pearlstein, *Detention Debates,* 110 Mich. L. Rev. 1045, 1045 (2012).

CHAPTER 11

POST-CONVICTION PROCEDURE

INTRODUCTION

This Chapter explores the procedural rules that govern habeas filings. Habeas proceedings are nominally civil, but they follow a special set of rules promulgated under the Rules Enabling Act, 28 U.S.C. § 2072 (REA). Those rules are very different from the Federal Rules of Civil Procedure (FRCP). These habeas rules apply during post-conviction challenges; they do not govern habeas review of executive detention. The first Section of Chapter 11 explores these rules, which frequently displace the more generally-applicable FRCP. As the earlier post-conviction chapters described, for example, habeas petitioners do not have the broad discovery privileges that civil litigants ordinarily enjoy under the FRCP. Nor do federal habeas cases follow the same process in federal court; questions of jurisdiction and burdens of pleading are handled quite differently in post-conviction litigation.

The second Section develops how the Supreme Court regulates the boundary between habeas corpus actions and other forms of civil rights litigation, particularly the various types of prisoner claims brought under 18 U.S.C. § 1983. The Court polices that boundary so that prisoners do not use other types of civil rights litigation to avoid the more-stringent requirements of habeas law. If a prisoner could file a § 1983 action and avoid the procedural rules restricting habeas relief—such as exhaustion, the statute of limitations, abuse of the writ, and the like—then those habeas rules would serve little practical function. Balanced against the concern that prisoners might use civil rights actions to circumvent restrictive habeas procedures is the reality that many constitutional grievances may be better suited to other forms of civil rights litigation than to habeas corpus. Non-habeas vehicles are particularly appropriate when the constitutional claims do not relate to the legality of the custody. Recent cases challenging execution protocols or seeking access to post-conviction DNA testing, however, raise more complicated questions about how to define the boundary between habeas corpus and other forms of civil rights litigation.

1. CONFLICTING FEDERAL RULES OF PROCEDURE

Habeas corpus is a *sui generis* cause of action. A post-conviction proceeding is formally considered a *civil* case, but the underlying claim usually asserts a constitutional right of *criminal* procedure. In part because habeas proceedings are neither fish nor fowl, federal post-conviction review is now subject to a unique set of procedural rules, promulgated under the REA. The REA authorizes the creation of uniform procedural rules in the federal courts. State-inmate proceedings are subject to the "Rules Governing Section 2254 Cases" (Section 2254 Rules) and federal-inmate proceedings are subject of the "Rules Governing Section 2255 Cases" (Section 2255 Rules). Both sets of rules were drafted in 1976 and took effect in 1977. For legislative history concerning the adoption of those rules, see H.R. Rep. No. 94–

1471, 94th Cong., 2nd Sess. 1, 5 (1976). The Section 2254 Rules and the Section 2255 Rules are both included in the Appendix at the end of this Book.

FRCP 81(a)(4) provides that the FRCP "apply to proceedings for habeas corpus . . . to the extent that the practice in those proceedings: (A) is not specified in a federal statute, the Rules Governing Section 2254 Cases, or the Rules Governing Section 2255 Cases; and (B) has previously conformed to the practice in civil actions." The Section 2254 Rules have a reciprocal provision, stating that the FRCP, "to the extent that they are not inconsistent with any statutory provisions or these rules, may be applied to a [habeas] proceeding[.]" See Section 2254 Rule 12. Section 2255 Rule 12 is almost identical, except that, in the post-conviction proceeding, it permits a federal court to apply Federal Rules of Civil *and Criminal* procedure that are not inconsistent with the Section 2255 Rules. Many (but not all) of the questions in this Section involve situations in which the decision whether to apply an interpretation of a Federal Rule of Procedure is outcome determinative.

A. Pleading

You have already encountered many procedural doctrines in post-conviction cases: nonretroactivity, the statute of limitations, procedural default, etc. You should resist any temptation to use familiar labels such as "jurisdictional rule" and "affirmative defense" to classify them. The Supreme Court continues to grapple with the mischief that such labeling causes. Writing for the majority in a recent habeas case, Justice Sonia Sotomayor observed that the Supreme Court "has endeavored in recent years to 'bring some discipline' to the use of the term 'jurisdictional.' Recognizing our 'less than meticulous' use of the term in the past, we have pressed a stricter distinction between truly jurisdictional rules, which govern a court's 'adjudicatory authority,' and nonjurisdictional 'claim-processing rules,' which do not." Gonzalez v. Thaler, 132 S.Ct. 641, 648 (2012) (internal citations omitted). How habeas litigants plead, forfeit, or waive each procedural doctrine requires lawyers to consult rapidly-changing decisional law.

The 28 U.S.C. § 2244(b) rules regarding successive petitions are the most conventionally "jurisdictional" of all the habeas restrictions. Although successive-petition doctrines were once affirmative defenses that a government party could waive or forfeit, AEDPA reconstituted those doctrines as mandatory limits on the habeas jurisdiction of federal courts. The rest of the habeas procedural limits that Chapter 4 presents, however, are not issues that lawyers would traditionally describe as jurisdictional.[a]

Procedural default, exhaustion, nonretroactivity, and the statute of limitations are each subject to pleading requirements that do not square perfectly with traditional concepts of jurisdictional rules or affirmative defenses. As you read the following cases, keep the following concepts in mind: whether a court may impose a procedural bar *sua sponte*, whether *sua sponte* authority turns on whether the court is a trial or an appeals court, whether a procedural bar can be forfeited or whether it must be ex-

---

[a] Exhaustion is also subject to specific statutory pleading requirement. Section 2254(b)(3) provides that: "A State shall not be deemed to have waived the exhaustion requirement or be estopped from reliance upon the requirement unless the State, through counsel, expressly waives the requirement."

pressly waived, and whether the term "affirmative defense" remains a meaningful way of describing a particular rule.

Granberry v. Greer

United States Supreme Court
481 U.S. 129 (1987)

■ JUSTICE STEVENS delivered the opinion of the Court.

[Granberry], a state prisoner, applied to the District Court for the Southern District of Illinois for a writ of habeas corpus pursuant to 28 U.S.C. § 2254. [Illinois argued] that the petition failed to state a claim upon which relief could be granted. The District Court * * * dismissed the petition on the merits. When [Granberry] appealed to the Court of Appeals for the Seventh Circuit, [Illinois] for the first time interposed the defense that [Granberry] had not exhausted his state remedies. In response, [Granberry] contended that the State had waived that defense by failing to raise it in the District Court. The Court of Appeals rejected the waiver argument[.] * * *

How an appellate court ought to handle a nonexhausted habeas petition when the State has not raised this objection in the district court is a question that might be answered in three different ways. We might treat the State's silence on the matter as a procedural default precluding the State from raising the issue on appeal. At the other extreme, we might treat nonexhaustion as an inflexible bar to consideration of the merits of the petition by the federal court, and therefore require that a petition be dismissed when it appears that there has been a failure to exhaust. Or, third[,] we might adopt an intermediate approach and direct the courts of appeals to exercise discretion in each case to decide whether the administration of justice would be better served by insisting on exhaustion or by reaching the merits of the petition forthwith.

We have already decided that the failure to exhaust state remedies does not deprive an appellate court of jurisdiction to consider the merits of a habeas corpus application. * * *

We have also expressed our reluctance to adopt rules that allow a party to withhold raising a defense until after the "main event"—in this case, the proceeding in the District Court—is over. Although the record indicates that the State's failure to raise the nonexhaustion defense in this case was the result of inadvertence, rather than a matter of tactics, it seems unwise to adopt a rule that would permit, and might even encourage, the State to seek a favorable ruling on the merits in the district court while holding the exhaustion defense in reserve for use on appeal if necessary. * * *

We are not persuaded by either of the extreme positions. The appellate court is not required to dismiss for nonexhaustion notwithstanding the State's failure to raise it, and the court is not obligated to regard the State's omission as an absolute waiver of the claim. * * *

[In its answer, a State] has a duty to advise the district court whether the prisoner has, in fact, exhausted all available state remedies. As this case demonstrates, however, there are exceptional cases in which the State fails * * * to raise an arguably meritorious nonexhaustion defense. The State's omission in such a case makes it appropriate for the court of appeals to take a fresh look at the issue. The court should determine whether the interests of comity and federalism will be better served by addressing the merits forthwith or by requiring a series of additional state and district court proceedings before reviewing the merits of the petitioner's claim.

If, for example, the case presents an issue on which an unresolved question of fact or of state law might have an important bearing, both comity and judicial efficiency may make it appropriate for the court to insist on complete exhaustion to make sure that it may ultimately review the issue on a fully informed basis. On the other hand, if it is perfectly clear that the applicant does not raise even a colorable federal claim, the interests of the petitioner, the warden, the state attorney general, the state courts, and the federal courts will all be well served even if the State fails to raise the exhaustion defense, the district court denies the habeas petition, and the court of appeals affirms the judgment of the district court forthwith.

Conversely, if a full trial has been held in the district court and it is evident that a miscarriage of justice has occurred, it may also be appropriate for the court of appeals to hold that the nonexhaustion defense has been waived in order to avoid unnecessary delay in granting relief that is plainly warranted. * * *

In this case, the Court of Appeals simply held that the nonexhaustion defense could not be waived, and made no attempt to determine whether the interests of justice would be better served by addressing the merits of the habeas petition or by requiring additional state proceedings before doing so. Accordingly, we vacate the judgment of the Court of Appeals and remand the case for further proceedings consistent with this opinion.

It is so ordered.

———

NOTES AND QUESTIONS ON GRANBERRY

1) **The Middle Ground.** The Supreme Court said it could consider three options in determining how to treat forfeiture of the State's exhaustion defense, and it chose the middle ground. At one extreme, the Court could treat exhaustion as a condition of federal subject-matter jurisdiction. A party may raise subject-matter jurisdiction at any stage in a case, or a court may consider it *sua sponte*. If exhaustion were a pure jurisdictional defense, a federal appellate court would have to dismiss the petition for non-exhaustion without respect to the preference of the State party. (Prior to *Granberry*, a majority of circuit courts took the jurisdictional approach.) Should the Supreme Court have treated exhaustion as a question of subject matter jurisdiction? Is a failure to exhaust like the absence of diversity or federal question jurisdiction, which require that a federal court dismiss a civil suit? Recall the history of the exhaustion rule from Chapter 4. What about the exhaustion rule makes it such a poor candidate for treatment as a jurisdictional condition?

At the other extreme, the Supreme Court discussed treating the exhaustion rule as an ordinary affirmative defense. Section 2254 Rule 5 requires that a habeas respondent's answer "must state whether any claim in the petition is barred by a failure to exhaust state remedies[ ]." In civil practice, parties are ordinarily foreclosed from raising on appeal any issue, defense, or claim not made at trial. See Weinberger v. Salfi, 422 U.S. 749, 764 (1975). Except for the most serious constitutional errors, parties are usually foreclosed from raising such errors for the first time on appeal in a criminal case. See Fed. Rule Crim. Proc. 52(b); United States v. Olano, 507 U.S. 725, 732 (1993). What about the exhaustion rule justifies the middle-ground exception to forfeiture that *Granberry* creates?

2)   Different Rules for Trial Courts? *Granberry* was formally a rule about the authority of a federal appellate court to impose an exhaustion bar *sua sponte*. If an appellate court can impose an exhaustion rule *sua sponte*, then is there any reason to deny that authority to district courts? After *Granberry*, several circuits held that district courts had authority to issue *sua sponte* dismissals for non-exhaustion. See, e.g., Hampton v. Miller, 927 F.2d 429, 431 (8th Cir. 1991) (underscoring the authority of district courts to abrogate forfeiture); Plunkett v. Johnson, 828 F.2d 954, 956 (2d Cir. 1987) (same).

3)   The State Interest. How does *Granberry* promote or undermine state interests? On the one hand, it promotes state comity by giving state courts the opportunity to resolve any claim before federal adjudication. On the other hand, how does a rule that potentially overrules a state pleading decision promote the interest of the state in question? The *Granberry* rule might be one of the few situations where the interests in "comity" and "federalism" point in different ways. The interest in comity is an interest in respecting the privilege of a *state court* to decide an issue first. An interest in federalism, however, could be stated more broadly as an interest that the state sovereign has in its capacity as a *federal litigant*. Do you think, from a policy perspective, the interest in federalism or the interest in comity should predominate in this type of case?

4)   Miscarriage of Justice. Writing for the Court, Justice Stevens stated: "[I]f a full trial has been held in the district court and it is evident that a miscarriage of justice has occurred, it may also be appropriate for the court of appeals to hold that the nonexhaustion defense has been waived in order to avoid unnecessary delay in granting relief that is plainly warranted." Under *Granberry*, then, a federal court could ignore nonexhaustion if the state waived it and if the court believed that the claim was "plainly" meritorious. There might be efficiency gains from permitting a federal court to honor a forfeiture. Why treat a "plainly" meritorious claim in a case where there would be a miscarriage of justice differently? If the court knows that the claim will eventually be granted, would state exhaustion be a waste of time—because the federal court will ultimately adjudicate the claim on the merits and grant relief? How does such a rule implicate comity? If the purpose of the exhaustion defense is to give state courts the first opportunity to correct constitutional error, then does the plainly-meritorious-claim exception undermine that purpose?

5)   Meritless Claims. As *Granberry* noted, one of the reasons why a federal court might impose a forfeited exhaustion defense is to avoid frivolous litigation involving a meritless claim. See also Barrett v. Acevedo, 169 F.3d 1155, 1162 (8th Cir. 1999) ("[J]udicial economy sometimes dictates reaching the merits if the merits are easily resolvable against a petitioner while the procedural bar issues are complicated.") In fact, the State will sometimes want to waive exhaustion on meritless claims to expedite executions. See Alan W. Clarke, *Procedural Labyrinths And The Injustice Of Death: A Critique Of Death Penalty Habeas Corpus (Part One)*, 29 U. Rich. L. Rev. 1327, 1836 (1985). AEDPA retained this principle when it reformulated the forfeiture rules in 1996 (see Note 8, *infra*). The efficiency advantages of such a rule appear obvious, but how does it accommodate interests in comity and finality?

6)   State Sandbagging. In *Granberry*, the Court remarked: "We have also expressed our reluctance to adopt rules that allow a party to withhold raising a defense until after the 'main event'—in this case, the proceeding in the District Court—is over." What incentive might the State have in withholding the exhaustion defense? Cf. Harris v. Scully, 779 F.2d 875, 878 (2d Cir. 1985) (expressing misgivings about the State's failure to raise exhaustion before lawyers and courts spent considerable time litigating and adjudicating other issues). Does *Granberry* aggravate this problem, or could the *Granberry* rule contain the problem by incorporating state gamesmanship as one of the criteria by which a court decides to impose the bar *sua sponte*? Should a prisoner be left sitting in jail when a State withholds the exhaustion defense in hopes of getting a favorable decision on the merits?

7)   Equity. Exhaustion conforms to a pattern of state habeas defenses in the following respect: the defense was created by federal judges and was later codified by Congress. Is there anything in the equitable origins of exhaustion that renders the *Granberry* exception appropriate? To put the question a different way, does the fact that the exhaustion defense was an equitable doctrine mean that federal courts should have a corresponding equitable power to cure or abrogate a state forfeiture? If the answer is yes, then should the forfeiture rule work differently for statutory defenses with no common law antecedent, such as a statute of limitations?

8)   The New Statutory Waiver Rule. AEDPA basically codified *Granberry*, with some minor differences. 28 U.S.C. § 2254(b)(3) now provides: "A State shall not be deemed to have waived the exhaustion requirement or be estopped from reliance upon the requirement unless the State, through counsel, expressly waives the requirement." A few observations: first, with respect to the authority to impose the exhaustion defense *sua sponte*, the statute appears to make no distinction between the authority of federal district and appellate courts. Second, the State cannot inadvertently forfeit or be estopped from relying on the exhaustion rule; AEDPA *requires* federal courts to impose the exhaustion rule, unless a State party expressly waives it.[b] Third, § 2254(b)(2) foreclosed the option, mentioned in *Granberry*, for a court to refuse to consider exhaustion where a claim is plainly meritorious: "An application for a writ of habeas corpus may be denied on the merits, notwithstanding the failure of the applicant to exhaust the remedies available in the courts of the State."

The major post-AEDPA question, then, is how a State "expressly" waives the exhaustion rule. What happens if a State bases its waiver on a flawed legal conclusion? Should a court deem the defense waived, in the sense that it was done so knowingly and intelligently?[c] How do the statutory changes affect the twin interests in comity and finality? To the extent that exhaustion and proce-

---

[b] At least one circuit has held that a federal court may abrogate an express waiver if the interest in comity requires it to do so. See Earhart v. Johnson, 132 F.3d 1062, 1065 (5th Cir. 1998).

[c] Cf. Sharrieff v. Cathel, 574 F.3d 225, 228, 229–30 (3d Cir. 2009) ("The fact that the State based its concession on a flawed legal conclusion is of no consequence; its concession clearly, explicitly, and unambiguously relinquished and abandoned its right to assert the nonexhaustion defense."). Should § 2254(b)(3) be construed to impose a "magic words" requirement, or can the state "expressly waive" the defense simply by manifesting intent to waive? Cf. D'Ambrosio v. Bagley, 527 F.3d 489, 496–97 (6th Cir. 2008) (remarking that "waiver is traditionally defined as an intentional relinquishment or abandonment of a known right" and holding that "[t]he warden expressly waived the exhaustion requirement because her counsel's conduct during the district court proceedings manifested a clear and unambiguous intent to waive the requirement") (internal quotation marks omitted).

dural default are different sides of the same coin, how should a *Granberry*-like principle apply in contexts where a claim may be procedurally defaulted?

NOTE ON TREST V. CAIN *AND* FORFEITURE OF PROCEDURAL DEFAULT

In *Trest v. Cain*, 522 U.S. 87 (1997), the Supreme Court addressed the forfeiture rules for procedural default. In *Trest*, the federal court of appeals affirmed an order denying the writ, reasoning that Trest had procedurally defaulted his claims. Neither Trest nor Louisiana raised the issue of procedural default before the lower courts. The appeals court apparently believed that, once it realized procedural default was an issue, it *had to* impose the bar without respect to the advocacy of the parties. In a unanimous opinion by Justice Breyer, the Supreme Court reversed: "A court of appeals is not 'required' to raise the issue of procedural default *sua sponte*. It is not as if the presence of a procedural default deprived the federal court of jurisdiction, for this Court has made clear that in the habeas context, a procedural default, that is, a critical failure to comply with state procedural law, is not a jurisdictional matter."

In dicta, *Trest* also remarked that "procedural default is normally a defense that the State is obligated to raise and preserve if it is not to lose the right to assert the defense thereafter." (Internal alterations, citations, and quotation marks omitted.) Citing to some confusion in the lower courts, *Trest* declined to answer a related question—whether a court is *permitted* to impose a forfeited procedural default defense *sua sponte*.[d] Do you think comity, finality, and federalism require that procedural default be treated the same way as exhaustion? What are the costs and benefits of allowing an appeals court to impose a nonjurisdictional defense *sua sponte*? Should the authority to impose the defense *sua sponte* be different in the federal district court? Should it matter whether the waiver was intentional or inadvertent? Does the waiver rule reflect the status of procedural default as a judge-made rule? How does the answer to *that* question bear on waiver analysis of a statute of limitations defense?

NOTES ON DAY V. MCDONOUGH *AND* FORFEITURE OF LIMITATIONS

Recall that, in contrast to the other habeas procedural doctrines, the AEDPA statute of limitations has no judge-made antecedent. 28 U.S.C. § 2244(d)(1) provides that: "A 1-year period of limitation *shall apply* to an application for a writ of habeas corpus by a person in custody pursuant to the judgment of a State court." (Emphasis added.) In light of the language of the statute, as well as the decision in *Granberry*, how would you expect the Supreme Court to treat the statute of limitations: as an unwaivable rule of subject matter jurisdiction, as an affirmative defense subject to the ordinary treatment of such defenses under the FRCP, or as something in between? Indeed, the Su-

---

[d] Compare Esslinger v. Davis, 44 F.3d 1515, 1525–1528 (11th Cir. 1995) (remarking that allowing courts to abrogate State waiver of a procedural default defense promotes no important federal interest), with Hardiman v. Reynolds, 971 F.2d 500, 502–505 (10th Cir. 1992) (reasoning that comity and judicial efficiency may justify a court raising state procedural default *sua sponte*.)

preme Court has located timeliness rules along this spectrum. Compare John R. Sand & Gravel Co. v. United States, 552 U.S. 130 (2008) (treating the limitations period for suits against the United States in the Court of Federal Claims as a jurisdictional rule because it served "a broader system-related goal") and Allen v. Siebert 552 U.S. 3, 7 (2007) (noting that "statutes of limitations are often affirmative defenses" and citing FRCP 8(c), which lists statutes of limitations among affirmative defenses). In *Day v. McDonough*, the Supreme Court considered the scope of a district court's authority to impose an otherwise-forfeited AEDPA limitations defense.

In *Day*, Florida had conceded in its answer that Day's federal habeas petition was timely, apparently because Florida had miscomputed the statutory tolling period. Under Eleventh circuit precedent for proper accounting of the tolling period, however, the federal petition was filed late. In ordinary civil litigation—under FRCP 8(c), 12(b), and 15(a)—an affirmative defense is waived if a party omits it from the answer. In *Day*, however, the district court imposed the limitations bar *sua sponte*. Writing for the Court, which affirmed, Justice Ginsburg framed the issue as follows: "The question presented is whether a federal court lacks authority, on its own initiative, to dismiss a habeas petition as untimely, once the State has answered the petition without contesting its timeliness." Justice Ginsburg held that a federal court had the authority to impose the defense *sua sponte*—at least in the situation before the Court, in which forfeiture was the result of a computational error.

Justice Ginsburg began by recognizing that, because the statute of limitations was nonjurisdictional, federal courts were not *obligated* to raise the issue *sua sponte*. She likened the limitations defense to "other threshold barriers—exhaustion of state remedies, procedural default, nonretroactivity—courts have typed nonjurisdictional, . . . recognizing that those defenses implicate values beyond the concerns of the parties." (Internal alterations omitted). Does the statute of limitations "implicate values beyond the concerns of the parties," and, if so, should the Supreme Court treat forfeiture of the limitations defense in the same way it treated forfeiture of the other "threshold barriers?" Justice Ginsburg supported "intermediate" treatment for the limitations defense because Section 2254 Rule 5 provides that a State habeas answer "must state whether any claim in the petition is barred by a failure to exhaust state remedies, a procedural bar, non-retroactivity, or a statute of limitations." She considered the analogy sufficient to justify similar treatment under the federal rules, citing *Granberry* (exhaustion), *Caspari* (nonretroactivity), and *Trest* (procedural default). *Day* formally held "that district courts are permitted, but not obliged, to consider, *sua sponte*, the timeliness of a state prisoner's habeas petition. We so hold, noting that it would make scant sense to distinguish in this regard AEDPA's time bar from other threshold constraints on federal habeas petitioners."

Justice Scalia dissented, writing for an unusual lineup that included Justices Breyer and Thomas. He emphasized that FRCP 81 and Section 2254 Rule 11 required federal courts to apply the FRCP unless there existed some inconsistency between the FRCP and the habeas rules or statute. He argued that, when a State omits a limitations defense from its Answer, forfeiture under Section 2254 Rule 5(b) was consistent with the FRCP. Justice Scalia then directly attacked the notion that forfeiture of the limitations defense should be treated the same way as forfeiture of other habeas defenses with common law antecedents:

Unlike AEDPA's statute of limitations, these defenses were all created by the habeas courts themselves, in the exercise of their traditional equitable discretion, because they were seen as necessary to protect the interests of comity and finality that federal collateral review of state criminal proceedings necessarily implicates. Unlike these other defenses, no time limitation—not even equitable laches—was imposed to vindicate comity and finality. AEDPA's 1-year limitations period is entirely a recent creature of statute. If comity and finality did not compel any time limitation at all, it follows a fortiori that they do not compel making a legislatively created, forfeitable time limitation nonforfeitable.... The Court's reliance on preexisting equitable doctrines like procedural default and nonretroactivity is, therefore, utterly misplaced. Nothing in our tradition of refusing to dismiss habeas petitions as untimely justifies the Court's decision to beef up the presumptively forfeitable "limitations period" of §2244(d) by making it the subject of *sua sponte* dismissal.

Do you think that it follows necessarily that, because the limitations period was statutorily (rather than judicially) created, the interests of comity and finality should not dictate the terms of forfeiture? Did AEDPA reflect the same purposes that prompted judges to create the habeas rules to which the majority analogized? If so, why should they not dictate an analogous forfeiture rule?

In support of the intermediate rule, Justice Ginsburg also reasoned that, rather than impose the limitations defense *sua sponte*, the district court could have alerted Florida to its miscalculation and permitted Florida to amend its Answer under FRCP 15(a). For that reason, Justice Ginsburg stated, prohibiting a federal court from reaching the same result faster would make little sense. (Justice Ginsburg's position seems predicated on the idea that computational error was the only reason that Florida forfeited the limitations defense.) Justice Scalia, however, believed that, "[i]f there truly were no 'dispositive difference' between following and disregarding the rules that Congress has enacted, the natural conclusion would be that there is no compelling reason to disregard the Civil Rules." He further observed that "there already exists a well-developed body of law to govern the district courts' exercise of discretion under Rule 15(a)." Do you agree that the two methods of considering the limitations defense are functionally equivalent, and what is the implication of your answer?

B. POST-JUDGMENT MOTIONS AND SUCCESSIVE PETITIONS

Pleading requirements are not the only context in which the FRCP potentially conflict with habeas statutes and doctrine. Another major conflict occurs *after* a federal district court has issued a final judgment in a habeas case. FRCP 60(b) provides that:

On motion and just terms, the court may relieve a party or its legal representative from a final judgment, order, or proceeding for the following reasons: (1) mistake, inadvertence, surprise, or excusable neglect; (2) newly discovered evidence that, with reasonable diligence, could not have been discovered in time to move for a new trial under Rule 59(b); (3) fraud (whether previously called intrinsic or extrinsic), misrepresentation, or misconduct by an opposing party; (4) the judgment is void; (5) the judgment has been satisfied, released, or discharged; it is based on an earlier judgment that has been reversed or vacated; or applying it prospectively is no longer equitable; or (6) any other reason that justifies relief.

Rule 60(c)(1) also furnishes a rough timing requirement: "A motion under Rule 60(b) must be made within a reasonable time—and for reasons (1), (2), and (3) no more than a year after the entry of the judgment or order or the date of the proceeding."

FRCP 60(b) specifically requires that post-judgment relief be available in certain circumstances, and one of the most frequently asserted grounds for Rule 60(b) relief is a Supreme Court decision announced shortly after a judgment becomes final. Not all Supreme Court decisions are "new" substantive rules of criminal procedure, however. Some simply clarify the application of the habeas statutes, and such situations present difficulties for federal courts that must reconcile FRCP 60(b) with the successive habeas petition rules contained in 28 U.S.C. § 2244(b). In *Gonzalez v. Crosby*, 545 U.S. 524 (2005), excerpted below, the Court decided a case in this posture, setting forth principles for resolving conflicts between the habeas statutes and other sources of federal law.

Gonzalez v. Crosby

United States Supreme Court
545 U.S. 524 (2005)

■ JUSTICE SCALIA delivered the opinion of the Court.

After the federal courts denied petitioner habeas corpus relief from his state conviction, he filed a motion for relief from that judgment, pursuant to Federal Rule of Civil Procedure 60(b). The question presented is whether, in a habeas case, such motions are subject to the additional restrictions that apply to "second or successive" habeas corpus petitions under the provisions of * * * 28 U. S. C. § 2244(b).

I

Petitioner Aurelio Gonzalez pleaded guilty in Florida Circuit Court to one count of robbery with a firearm. He filed no appeal and began serving his 99-year sentence in 1982. Some 12 years later, petitioner began to seek relief from his conviction. He filed two motions for state postconviction relief, which the Florida courts denied. Thereafter, in June 1997, petitioner filed a federal habeas petition in the United States District Court for the Southern District of Florida, alleging that his guilty plea had not been entered knowingly and voluntarily.

Upon the State's motion, the District Court dismissed petitioner's habeas petition as barred by AEDPA's statute of limitations, 28 U. S. C. § 2244(d). Under Eleventh Circuit precedent, petitioner's filing deadline, absent tolling, was April 23, 1997, one year after AEDPA's statute of limitations took effect. * * * [T]he District Court concluded that the limitations period was not tolled during the 163-day period while petitioner's second motion for state postconviction relief was pending. Section 2244(d)(2) tolls the statute of limitations during the pendency of "properly filed" applications only, and the District Court thought petitioner's motion was not "properly filed" because it was both untimely and successive. * * *

On November 7, 2000, we held in *Artuz v. Bennett* that an application for state postconviction relief can be "properly filed" even if the state courts dismiss it as procedurally barred. Almost nine months later, petitioner filed in the District Court a pro se "Motion to Amend or Alter Judgment," contending that the District Court's time-bar ruling was incorrect under *Artuz's* construction of § 2244(d), and invoking Federal Rule of Civil Procedure 60(b)(6), which permits a court to relieve a party from the effect of a final judgment. The District Court denied the motion, and petitioner appealed.

[The Eleventh Circuit held that] * * * any postjudgment motion under Rule 60(b) save one alleging fraud on the court under Rule 60(b)(3)—was in substance a second or successive habeas corpus petition. * * *

We granted certiorari.

II

Rule 60(b) allows a party to seek relief from a final judgment, and request reopening of his case, under a limited set of circumstances including fraud, mistake, and newly discovered evidence. Rule 60(b)(6), the particular provision under which petitioner brought his motion, permits reopening when the movant shows "any * * * reason justifying relief from the operation of the judgment" other than the more specific circumstances set out in Rules 60(b)(1)–(5). The mere recitation of these provisions shows why we give little weight to respondent's appeal to the virtues of finality. That policy consideration, standing alone, is unpersuasive in the interpretation of a provision whose whole purpose is to make an exception to finality. The issue here is whether the text of Rule 60(b) itself, or of some other provision of law, limits its application in a manner relevant to the case before us.

AEDPA did not expressly circumscribe the operation of Rule 60(b). (By contrast, AEDPA directly amended other provisions of the Federal Rules.) * * * Rule 60(b), like the rest of the Rules of Civil Procedure, applies in [Section 2254(d)] only "to the extent that [it is] not inconsistent with" applicable federal statutory provisions and rules. 28 U. S. C. § 2254 Rule 11; see Fed. Rule Civ. Proc. 81(a)(2). The relevant provisions of the [28 U.S.C. § 2244(b)] impose three requirements on second or successive habeas petitions: First, any claim that has already been adjudicated in a previous petition must be dismissed. Second, any claim that has not already been adjudicated must be dismissed unless it relies on either a new and retroactive rule of constitutional law or new facts showing a high probability of actual innocence. Third, before the district court may accept a successive petition for filing, the court of appeals must determine that it presents a claim not previously raised that is sufficient to meet § 2244(b)(2)'s new-rule or actual-innocence provisions. We proceed to consider whether these provisions limit the application of Rule 60(b) to the present case.

A

"As a textual matter, § 2244(b) applies only where the court acts pursuant to a prisoner's 'application' for a writ of habeas corpus." We therefore must decide whether a Rule 60(b) motion filed by a habeas petitioner is a "habeas corpus application" as the statute uses that term.

Under § 2244(b), the first step of analysis is to determine whether a "claim presented in a second or successive habeas corpus application" was also "presented in a prior application." If so, the claim must be dismissed; if not, the analysis proceeds to whether the claim satisfies one of two narrow exceptions. In either event, it is clear that for purposes of §2244(b) an "application" for habeas relief is a filing that contains one or more "claims." That definition is consistent with the use of the term "application" in the other habeas statutes in chapter 153 of title 28. These statutes, and our own decisions, make clear that a "claim" as used in §2244(b) is an asserted federal basis for relief from a state court's judgment of conviction.

In some instances, a Rule 60(b) motion will contain one or more "claims." For example, it might straightforwardly assert that owing to "excusable neglect," Fed. Rule Civ. Proc. 60(b)(1), the movant's habeas petition had omitted a claim of constitutional error, and seek leave to present that claim. Similarly, a motion might seek leave to present "newly discovered evidence," Fed. Rule Civ. Proc. 60(b)(2), in support of a claim previously denied. Or a motion might contend that a subsequent change in substantive law is a "reason justifying relief," Fed. Rule Civ. Proc. 60(b)(6), from the previous denial of a claim. Virtually every Court of Appeals to consider the question has held that such a pleading, although labeled a Rule 60(b) motion, is in substance a successive habeas petition and should be treated accordingly.

We think those holdings are correct. A habeas petitioner's filing that seeks vindication of such a claim is, if not in substance a "habeas corpus application," at least similar enough that failing to subject it to the same requirements would be "inconsistent with" the statute. Using Rule 60(b) to present new claims for relief from a state court's judgment of conviction— even claims couched in the language of a true Rule 60(b) motion— circumvents AEDPA's requirement that a new claim be dismissed unless it relies on either a new rule of constitutional law or newly discovered facts. The same is true of a Rule 60(b)(2) motion presenting new evidence in support of a claim already litigated: even assuming that reliance on a new factual predicate causes that motion to escape § 2244(b)(1)'s prohibition of claims "presented in a prior application," § 2244(b)(2)(B) requires a more convincing factual showing than does Rule 60(b). Likewise, a Rule 60(b) motion based on a purported change in the substantive law governing the claim could be used to circumvent § 2244(b)(2)(A)'s dictate that the only new law on which a successive petition may rely is "a new rule of constitutional law, made retroactive to cases on collateral review by the Supreme Court, that was previously unavailable." In addition to the substantive conflict with AEDPA standards, in each of these three examples use of Rule 60(b) would impermissibly circumvent the requirement that a successive habeas petition be precertified by the court of appeals as falling within an exception to the successive-petition bar.

In most cases, determining whether a Rule 60(b) motion advances one or more "claims" will be relatively simple. A motion that seeks to add a new ground for relief * * * will of course qualify. A motion can also be said to bring a "claim" if it attacks the federal court's previous resolution of a claim on the merits,[4] since alleging that the court erred in denying habeas relief on the merits is effectively indistinguishable from alleging that the movant is, under the substantive provisions of the statutes, entitled to habeas relief. That is not the case, however, when a Rule 60(b) motion attacks, not the substance of the federal court's resolution of a claim on the merits, but some defect in the integrity of the federal habeas proceedings.

---

[4] The term "on the merits" has multiple usages. We refer here to a determination that there exist or do not exist grounds entitling a petitioner to habeas corpus relief under 28 U.S.C. § 2254(a) and (d). When a movant asserts one of those grounds (or asserts that a previous ruling regarding one of those grounds was in error) he is making a habeas corpus claim. He is not doing so when he merely asserts that a previous ruling which precluded a merits determination was in error—for example, a denial for such reasons as failure to exhaust, procedural default, or statute-of-limitations bar.

B

When no "claim" is presented, there is no basis for contending that the Rule 60(b) motion should be treated like a habeas corpus application. If neither the motion itself nor the federal judgment from which it seeks relief substantively addresses federal grounds for setting aside the movant's state conviction, allowing the motion to proceed as denominated creates no inconsistency with the habeas statute or rules. Petitioner's motion in the present case, which alleges that the federal courts misapplied the federal statute of limitations set out in §2244(d), fits this description. * * *

Rule 60(b) has an unquestionably valid role to play in habeas cases. The Rule is often used to relieve parties from the effect of a default judgment mistakenly entered against them, a function as legitimate in habeas cases as in run-of-the-mine civil cases. The Rule also preserves parties' opportunity to obtain vacatur of a judgment that is void for lack of subject-matter jurisdiction—a consideration just as valid in habeas cases as in any other, since absence of jurisdiction altogether deprives a federal court of the power to adjudicate the rights of the parties. In some instances, we may note, it is the State, not the habeas petitioner, that seeks to use Rule 60(b), to reopen a habeas judgment granting the writ.

Moreover, several characteristics of a Rule 60(b) motion limit the friction between the Rule and the successive-petition prohibitions of AEDPA, ensuring that our harmonization of the two will not expose federal courts to an avalanche of frivolous postjudgment motions. First, Rule 60(b) contains its own limitations, such as the requirement that the motion "be made within a reasonable time" and the more specific 1-year deadline for asserting three of the most open-ended grounds of relief (excusable neglect, newly discovered evidence, and fraud). Second, our cases have required a movant seeking relief under Rule 60(b)(6) to show "extraordinary circumstances" justifying the reopening of a final judgment. Such circumstances will rarely occur in the habeas context. Third, Rule 60(b) proceedings are subject to only limited and deferential appellate review. * * *

Because petitioner's Rule 60(b) motion challenges only the District Court's previous ruling on the AEDPA statute of limitations, it is not the equivalent of a successive habeas petition. The Eleventh Circuit therefore erred in holding that petitioner did not qualify even to seek Rule 60(b) relief.

III

Although the Eleventh Circuit's reasoning is inconsistent with our holding today, we nonetheless affirm its denial of petitioner's Rule 60(b) motion.

[The Court held that the post-judgment change in law was insufficient to support a Rule 60(b) grant.]

* * *

We hold that a Rule 60(b)(6) motion in a § 2254 case is not to be treated as a successive habeas petition if it does not assert, or reassert, claims of error in the movant's state conviction. A motion that, like petitioner's, challenges only the District Court's failure to reach the merits does not warrant such treatment, and can therefore be ruled upon by the District Court without precertification by the Court of Appeals pursuant to §2244(b)(3). In this case, however, petitioner's Rule 60(b)(6) motion fails to set forth an "extraordinary circumstance" justifying relief. For that reason, we affirm the judgment of the Court of Appeals.

It is so ordered.

[The concurring opinion of Justice Breyer and the dissenting opinion of Justice Stevens are omitted.]

***

NOTES AND QUESTIONS ON GONZALEZ V. CROSBY

1) A Choice of Law Analysis. The question in *Gonzalez v. Crosby* involves a choice of law between FRCP 60(b)(6) and 28 U.S.C. § 2244(b). Whether the two potential sources of law conflict turns on an interpretation of § 2244(b)—namely, whether it applies to any form of relief requested after a federal district court has entered judgment in a habeas case. That application of § 2244(b) seems too broad; the interpretation would seem to encompass even things plainly permitted under the statute, such as appeals. At the other end of the spectrum, a prisoner should not be able to take what would otherwise be a claim that is jurisdictionally disqualified because it is successive or abusive, repackage it as part of an FRCP 60(b) request, and force the court into a more forgiving inquiry. In *Gonzalez v. Crosby*, the Court was forced to identify a line, on one side of which fell nominal FRCP 60(b) issues that were really just successive or abusive claims in disguise, and on the other side of which were issues that were properly presented in a postjudgment motion. On what side of the line does the issue in *Gonzalez* fall, according to the Court?

2) "On the Merits" and Postjudgment Motions. Perhaps the most important language in *Gonzalez* is in footnote 4, in which the Court held that FRCP 60(b) may be used when the issue urged in the postjudgment motion is not a challenge to the "merits" of the habeas disposition. As footnote 4 recognizes, "on the merits" means different things in different contexts. Justice Scalia defines "on the merits" in this context to mean a challenge to "a determination that there exist or do not exist grounds entitling a petitioner to habeas corpus relief under 28 U.S.C. § 2254(a) and (d)." Why does Justice Scalia pick this particular set of habeas challenges? Should *Gonzalez v. Crosby* apply to all postjudgment challenges, or just to those under FRCP 60(b)? FRCP 59(e) permits a party to file a motion to alter or amend the judgment within 28 days after the trial court enters judgment. Should the content of a FRCP 59(e) motion be restricted in the same way that the content of an FRCP 60(b) motion is, or does the time limit change the analysis somewhat? The Supreme Court has not decided this issue, although several circuits have held that *Gonzalez v. Crosby* does not apply to motions under FRCP 59(e). See, e.g., Howard v. United States, 533 F.3d 472, 275 (6th Cir. 2008) ("Because [an FRCP 59(e)] motion only 'operates to suspend the finality of the [district court's] judgment,' . . . it is not a collateral action. . . [Extending] *Gonzalez* to [FRCP 59(e)] motions would attribute to Congress the unlikely intent to preclude broadly the reconsideration of just-entered judgments.").

3) "On the Merits" and Procedural Defenses. Prior to *Gonzalez v. Crosby,* many federal courts observed something close to a *per se* rule that any FRCP 60(b) motion containing a habeas issue was to be treated as a successive petition. In *Gonzalez* itself, an *en banc* panel of the 11th Circuit held that only FRCP 60(b)(3) motions—those alleging fraud on the court—were to be treated as containing issues outside of the successive petition framework. The Supreme Court unanimously rejected that rule. Also in footnote 4, *Gonzalez v. Crosby* explains that an FRCP 60(b) motion is not "on the merits" if it "merely asserts that a previous ruling which precluded a merits determination was in error— for example, a denial for such reasons as failure to exhaust, procedural default, or statute-of-limitations bar." Why are such challenges in the FRCP 60(b) posture not treated as successive petitions? Should any procedural challenge avoid the "on the merits" rule in *Gonzalez*? Should an allegation that the federal court committed procedural error in its factfinding be considered a challenge "on the merits," or should it be treated under the FRCP 60(b) rubric? What about an allegation that the procedural error in factfinding was committed by the state court?

4) **Applying FRCP 60(b) to Nonmerits Challenges.** Assuming that a federal court determines that a challenge under FRCP 60(b) is not "on the merits" and that it should therefore be analyzed under the FRCP, what questions does a federal court ask? *Gonzalez v. Crosby* makes clear that a prisoner must show extraordinary circumstances, and, in an unexcerpted portion of the opinion, the Court nests a diligence rule inside the extraordinary circumstances requirement: "The change in the law worked by *Artuz* [*v. Bennett*, 531 U.S. 4 (2000),] is all the less extraordinary in petitioner's case, because of his lack of diligence in pursuing review of the statute-of-limitations issue." In what ways are the substantive restrictions under the FRCP 60(b) rubric weaker than the restrictions imposed under the § 2244(b) framework? (One major difference is that an FRCP 60(b) motion need not be authorized by a court of appeals before the federal district court can decide the merits of the issues presented in the request for relief.)

5) **Extraordinary Circumstances.** Under FRCP 60(b), what is an extraordinary circumstance that qualifies the issue presented in the motion for consideration? *Gonzalez v. Crosby* clearly holds that a subsequent change in law can constitute an extraordinary circumstance that would permit the district court to reopen the judgment. The Court, however, was careful to note—in an unexcerpted part of the opinion—that "not every interpretation of the federal statutes setting forth the requirements for habeas provides cause for reopening cases long since final." Aside from a supervening change in statutory habeas law, what else might constitute "extraordinary circumstances" under FRCP 60(b)?

6) **Review Exercise.** Suppose that a state prisoner came into court with a mixed petition containing exhausted *Brady* and IAC claims. In January of 2012 the federal trial court held that the IAC claim was procedurally defaulted, and that the default was unexcused because the prisoner failed to show cause. The Supreme Court then decided *Martinez v. Ryan* on March 20, 2012. In *Martinez*, the Court held that the ineffective assistance of state post-conviction counsel could constitute "cause" for excusing an otherwise-defaulted IAC claim. Sixty-five days after the judgment, the prisoner obtains an order holding the appeal in abeyance while the prisoner returns to the district court to file a motion under FRCP 60(b)(6). In the FRCP 60(b) motion, filed seventy days after the judgment, the prisoner claims that the default of the IAC claim would have been excused under *Martinez*. If you were the federal district court judge, how would you rule on the motion, and why would you rule that way?

C. CERTIFICATES OF APPEALABILITY

One context in which the federal habeas statute plainly trumps the ordinary FRCP is with respect to the "notice of appeal." A notice of appeal is a short document that an appellant files with the federal district court, and filing triggers the jurisdiction of the appropriate federal appeals court. FRCP 3(a)(1) governs ordinary as-of-right appeals: "An appeal permitted by law as of right from a district court to a court of appeals may be taken only by filing a notice of appeal with the district clerk within the [specified] time . . . ." In cases under §§ 2254 and 2255, however, a prisoner seeking to appeal an adverse judgment cannot do so simply by filing a notice. The prisoner must obtain a "certificate of appealability" (COA). A COA is basically a certification that the controversy is sufficiently meritorious to warrant appellate consideration.

Understanding the role of the COA requires a brief digression on the Rules and statutory provisions governing the form of appeals in §§ 2254 & 2255 cases. Before AEDPA, a habeas petitioner (but not a prisoner seeking relief under § 2255) had to obtain a "certificate of probable cause" (CPC), which similarly certified that a controversy merited appellate review. AEDPA replaced the CPC with the COA, applied the COA requirement to both state and federal inmates, and specified the standard for issuing the COA. For the most part, AEDPA codified the CPC standard that the Supreme Court announced in *Barefoot v. Estelle*, 463 U.S. 880 (1983). Under 28 U.S.C. § 2253(c)(2), a COA should issue only when a prisoner "has made a substantial showing of the denial of a constitutional right." Under § 2253(c)(3), any order granting the COA must specify the issue deserving of appellate consideration.

The pertinent Rules of Procedure complement the COA requirement. Rule 11—for both § 2254 and § 2255 cases—requires parties to file and judges to decide COA applications. Federal Rule of Appellate Procedure 22(b) complements the Rules for Section 2254 and Section 2255 cases, and it also makes clear that no entity affiliated with the state or the federal government need seek a COA to appeal the lower court decision. Under § 2253(c), a "circuit justice or judge" may issue a COA.

INTRODUCTORY NOTE ON SLACK v. MCDANIEL

28 U.S.C. § 2254(c)(3) states that a COA should issue upon a "substantial showing of the denial of a constitutional right," but the merit of the constitutional claim is not necessarily the dispute in every federal habeas case. In many cases, a district court will have denied or dismissed a claim based on a procedural doctrine—something that has little to do with the merits. In such situations, should the same COA standard apply, and should the federal courts determine only whether the underlying constitutional claim has merit? Or, alternatively, should federal courts also look at the correctness of the lower-court procedural ruling? For example, if a prisoner lodges an IAC claim in a federal habeas petition and if a federal district judge rules that the claim is untimely under § 2244(d), then what analysis does a federal judge conduct in order to determine whether a COA should issue? Should a judge simply ask whether the IAC claim makes a substantial showing of a constitutional violation, or should the judge also inquire as to the relative merit of the procedural issue? Consider that question as you read *Slack v. McDaniel*, 529 U.S. 473 (2000).

Slack v. McDaniel

United States Supreme Court
529 U.S. 473 (2000)

■ JUSTICE KENNEDY delivered the opinion of the Court.

We are called upon to resolve a series of issues regarding the law of habeas corpus, including questions of the proper application of [AEDPA]. We hold as follows:

* * * Second, when the district court denies a habeas petition on procedural grounds without reaching the prisoner's underlying constitutional claim, a COA should issue (and an appeal of the district court's order may be taken) if the prisoner shows, at least, that jurists of reason would find it debatable whether the petition states a valid claim of the denial of a constitutional right, and that jurists of reason would find it debatable whether the district court was correct in its procedural ruling.

Third, a habeas petition which is filed after an initial petition was dismissed without adjudication on the merits for failure to exhaust state remedies is not a "second or successive" petition as that term is understood in the habeas corpus context. Federal courts do, however, retain broad powers to prevent duplicative or unnecessary litigation.

I

Petitioner Antonio Slack was convicted of second-degree murder in Nevada state court in 1990. His direct appeal was unsuccessful. On November 27, 1991, Slack filed a petition for writ of habeas corpus in federal court under 28 U.S.C. § 2254. Early in the federal proceeding, Slack decided to litigate claims he had not yet presented to the Nevada courts. [The court therefore dismissed the petition as mixed]. Accordingly, Slack filed a motion seeking to hold his federal petition in abeyance while he returned to state court to exhaust the new claims. Without objection by the State, the District Court ordered the habeas petition dismissed "without prejudice." The order, dated February 19, 1992, further stated, "Petitioner is granted leave to file an application to renew upon exhaustion of all State remedies."

After an unsuccessful round of state postconviction proceedings, Slack filed a new federal habeas petition on May 30, 1995. * * * On December 24, 1997, counsel filed an amended petition presenting 14 claims for relief. The State moved to dismiss the petition. As its first ground, the State argued that Slack's petition must be dismissed because it was [still] a mixed petition * * *. As its second ground, the State * * * contended that, under the established rule in the Ninth Circuit, claims Slack had not raised in his 1991 federal habeas petition must be dismissed as an abuse of the writ.

The District Court granted the State's motion. First, the court [held] that Slack's 1995 petition was "[a] second or successive petition," even though his 1991 petition had been dismissed without prejudice for a failure to exhaust state remedies. The court then invoked the abuse of the writ doctrine to dismiss with prejudice the claims Slack had not raised in the 1991 petition. This left Slack with four claims, each having been raised in the 1991 petition; but one of these, the court concluded, had not yet been presented to the state courts. The court therefore dismissed Slack's remaining claims because they were in a mixed petition. Here, Slack seeks to challenge the dismissal of claims as abusive; he does not contend that all claims presented in the amended petition were exhausted.

The District Court's dismissal order was filed March 30, 1998. On April 29, 1998, Slack filed in the District Court a pleading captioned "Notice of Appeal." Consistent with Circuit practice, the court treated the notice as an application for a certificate of probable cause (CPC) under the pre-AEDPA version of 28 U.S.C. § 2253; and it denied a CPC, concluding the appeal would raise no substantial issue. The Court of Appeals likewise denied a CPC. As a result, Slack was not permitted to take an appeal of the order dismissing his petition. We granted certiorari. Slack contends that he is entitled to an appeal of the dismissal of his petition, arguing that the District Court was wrong to hold that his 1995 petition was "second or successive." We agree that Slack's 1995 petition was not second or successive, but first we must resolve two preliminary questions.

II

[The Court first determined that AEDPA applied to the rules of appellate jurisdiction, and that Slack had to obtain a COA to appeal the trial court decision.]

III

As AEDPA applied, the Court of Appeals should have treated the notice of appeal as an application for a COA. To evaluate whether the Court of Appeals should have granted a COA, we must determine what the habeas applicant must show to satisfy the requirements of §2253(c).

Citing §2253(c)'s requirement that a COA may issue only upon the "substantial showing of the denial of a constitutional right," the State contends that no appeal can be taken if the District Court relies on procedural grounds to dismiss the petition. According to the State, only constitutional rulings may be appealed. Under this view, a state prisoner who can demonstrate he was convicted in violation of the Constitution and who can demonstrate that the district court was wrong to dismiss the petition on procedural grounds would be denied relief. We reject this interpretation. The writ of habeas corpus plays a vital role in protecting constitutional rights. In setting forth the preconditions for issuance of a COA under §2253(c), Congress expressed no intention to allow trial court procedural error to bar vindication of substantial constitutional rights on appeal.

Our conclusion follows from AEDPA's present provisions, which incorporate earlier habeas corpus principles. Under AEDPA, a COA may not issue unless "the applicant has made a substantial showing of the denial of a constitutional right." Except for substituting the word "constitutional" for the word "federal," § 2253 is a codification of the CPC standard announced in *Barefoot v. Estelle*. Congress had before it the meaning *Barefoot* had given to the words it selected; and we give the language found in § 2253(c) the meaning ascribed it in *Barefoot*, with due note for the substitution of the word "constitutional." To obtain a COA under § 2253(c), a habeas prisoner must make a substantial showing of the denial of a constitutional right, a demonstration that, under *Barefoot*, includes showing that reasonable jurists could debate whether (or, for that matter, agree that) the petition should have been resolved in a different manner or that the issues presented were ["adequate to deserve encouragement to proceed further."]

Where a district court has rejected the constitutional claims on the merits, the showing required to satisfy §2253(c) is straightforward: The petitioner must demonstrate that reasonable jurists would find the district court's assessment of the constitutional claims debatable or wrong. The issue becomes somewhat more complicated where, as here, the district court dismisses the petition based on procedural grounds. We hold as follows: When the district court denies a habeas petition on procedural grounds without reaching the prisoner's underlying constitutional claim, a COA should issue when the prisoner shows, at least, that jurists of reason would find it debatable whether the petition states a valid claim of the denial of a constitutional right and that jurists of reason would find it debatable whether the district court was correct in its procedural ruling. This construction gives meaning to Congress' requirement that a prisoner demonstrate substantial underlying constitutional claims and is in conformity with the meaning of the "substantial showing" standard provided in *Barefoot* and adopted by Congress in AEDPA. Where a plain procedural bar is present and the district court is correct to invoke it to dispose of the case, a reasonable jurist could not conclude either that the district court erred in dismissing the petition or that the petitioner should be allowed to proceed further. In such a circumstance, no appeal would be warranted.

Determining whether a COA should issue where the petition was dismissed on procedural grounds has two components, one directed at the underlying constitutional claims and one directed at the district court's procedural holding. Section 2253 mandates that both showings be made before the court of appeals may entertain the appeal. Each component of the § 2253(c) showing is part of a threshold inquiry, and a court may find that it can dispose of the application in a fair and prompt manner if it proceeds first to resolve the issue whose answer is more apparent from the record and arguments. The recognition that the "Court will not pass upon a constitutional question although properly presented by the record, if there is also present some other ground upon which the case may be disposed of" allows and encourages the court to first resolve procedural issues. * * *

In this case, Slack did not attempt to make a substantial showing of the denial of a constitutional right, instead arguing only that the District Court's procedural rulings were wrong. We will not attempt to determine whether Slack could make the required showing of constitutional error, for the issue was neither briefed nor presented below because of the view that the CPC, rather than COA, standards applied. It will be necessary to consider the matter upon any remand for further proceedings. We will, however, address the second component of the § 2253(c) inquiry, whether jurists of reason could conclude that the District Court's dismissal on procedural grounds was debatable or incorrect. * * *

The District Court dismissed claims Slack failed to raise in his 1991 petition based on its conclusion that Slack's 1995 petition was a second or successive habeas petition. This conclusion was wrong. A habeas petition filed in the district court after an initial habeas petition was unadjudicated on its merits and dismissed for failure to exhaust state remedies is not a second or successive petition.

Slack commenced this habeas proceeding in the District Court in 1995, before AEDPA's effective date. Because the question whether Slack's petition was second or successive implicates his right to relief in the trial court, pre-AEDPA law governs, though we do not suggest the definition of second or successive would be different under AEDPA. * * *

The phrase "second or successive petition" is a term of art given substance in our prior habeas corpus cases. * * * *Rose v. Lundy* held that a federal district court must dismiss habeas corpus petitions containing both exhausted and unexhausted claims. The opinion, however, contemplated that the prisoner could return to federal court after the requisite exhaustion. It was only if a prisoner declined to return to state court and decided to proceed with his exhausted claims in federal court that the possibility arose that a subsequent petition would be considered second or successive and subject to dismissal as an abuse of the writ. * * *

The State contends that the prisoner, upon his return to federal court, should be restricted to the claims made in his initial petition. [This result] would limit a prisoner to claims made in a pleading that is often uncounseled, hand-written, and pending in federal court only until the state identifies one unexhausted claim. The proposed rule would bar the prisoner from raising nonfrivolous claims developed in the subsequent state exhaustion proceedings contemplated by the Rose dismissal, even though a federal court had yet to review a single constitutional claim. This result would be contrary to our admonition that the complete exhaustion rule is not to "trap the unwary pro se prisoner." It is instead more appropriate to treat the initial mixed petition as though it had not been filed, subject to whatever conditions the court attaches to the dismissal. *Rose v. Lundy* dictated that, whatever particular claims the petition contained, none could be considered by the federal court.

Slack's 1991 petition was dismissed under the procedure established in Rose v. Lundy. No claim made in Slack's 1991 petition was adjudicated during the three months it was pending in federal court. As such, the 1995 petition should not have been dismissed on the grounds that it was second or successive. * * *

IV

Slack has demonstrated that reasonable jurists could conclude that the District Court's abuse of the writ holding was wrong, for we have determined that a habeas petition filed after an initial petition was dismissed under *Rose v. Lundy* without an adjudication on the merits is not a "second or successive" petition. Whether Slack is otherwise entitled to the issuance of a COA is a question to be resolved first upon remand. The decision of the Court of Appeals is reversed, and the case is remanded for further proceedings consistent with this opinion.

It is so ordered.

[The opinion of JUSTICE STEVENS, partially concurring and concurring in the judgment, is omitted.]

[The opinion of JUSTICE SCALIA, partially concurring and partially dissenting, is omitted.]

NOTES AND QUESTIONS ON SLACK AND ON § 2253

1) The "Straightforward" Case. *Slack* states: "Where a district court has rejected the constitutional claims on the merits, the showing required to satisfy § 2253(c) is straightforward: The petitioner must demonstrate that reasonable jurists would find the district court's assessment of the constitutional claims debatable or wrong." As it turns out, the COA requirement is not straightforward, even in the merits context. Does a federal court have to determine whether reasonable jurists could disagree over the abstract merit of the claim or whether it would survive a § 2554(d) analysis?

The Supreme Court confronted a dispute over the COA standard in *Miller-El v. Cockrell*, 537 U.S. 322 (2003) (*Miller-El I*). As you might recall from the discussion of *Miller-El II*, from Chapter 8, Thomas Jo Miller-El had made a *Batson* challenge to his Texas capital sentence—alleging racially-motivated jury strikes under *Batson v. Kentucky*, 476 U.S. 79 (1986). Specifically, because the COA standard requires (at least) an assessment of the claim itself, the question remained how and to what degree the COA determination should account for the lower court's treatment of the claim under § 2254(d). *Miller-El I* put it this way:

> [Section] 2253(c) permits the issuance of a COA only where a petitioner has made a "substantial showing of the denial of a constitutional right." . . . Under the controlling standard, a petitioner must [show "that reasonable jurists could debate whether (or, for that matter, agree that) the petition should have been resolved in a different manner or that the issues presented were adequate to deserve encouragement to proceed further."]

> The COA determination under §2253(c) requires an overview of the claims in the habeas petition and a general assessment of their merits. We look to the District Court's application of AEDPA to petitioner's constitutional claims and ask whether that resolution was debatable amongst jurists of reason. This threshold inquiry does not require full consideration of the factual or legal bases adduced in support of the claims. In fact, the statute forbids it. When a court of appeals side steps this process by first deciding the merits of an appeal, and then justifying its denial of a COA based on its adjudication of the actual merits, it is in essence deciding an appeal without jurisdiction.

> . . . [A] court of appeals should not decline the application for a COA merely because it believes the applicant will not demonstrate an entitlement to relief. . . It is consistent with § 2253 that a COA will issue in some instances where there is no certainty of ultimate relief. . .

> Our holding should not be misconstrued as directing that a COA always must issue. Statutes such as AEDPA have placed more, rather than fewer, restrictions on the power of federal courts to grant writs of habeas corpus to state prisoners. The concept of a threshold, or gateway, test was not the innovation of AEDPA. Congress established a threshold prerequisite to appealability in 1908, in large part because it was "concerned with the increasing number of frivolous habeas corpus petitions challenging capital sentences which delayed execution pending completion of the appellate process[.]" . . .

> A prisoner seeking a COA must prove "something more than the absence of frivolity," or the existence of mere "good faith" on his or her part. We do not require petitioner to prove, before the issuance of a COA, that some jurists would grant the petition for habeas corpus. Indeed, a claim can be debatable even though every jurist of reason might agree, after the COA has been granted and the case has received full consideration, that petitioner will not prevail.

Miller-El's reference to the federal district court determination is confusing. Most recitations of the COA standard have simply required an assessment of the claim's merit—a "substantial showing of a violation of a constitutional right." In his concurring opinion, Justice Scalia underscored the unnecessary confusion that the *Miller-El I* standard might create:

> Less clear from the Court's opinion . . . is why a "circuit justice or judge," in deciding whether to issue a COA, must "look to the District Court's application of AEDPA to [a habeas petitioner's] constitutional claims and ask whether that resolution was debatable amongst jurists of reason." How the district court applied AEDPA has nothing to do with whether a COA applicant has made "a substantial showing of the denial of a constitutional right," as required by 28 U.S.C. § 2253(c)(2), so the AEDPA standard should seemingly have no role in the COA inquiry. . .

> The Court today imposes another additional requirement: a circuit justice or judge must deny a COA, even when the habeas petitioner has made a substantial showing that his constitutional rights were violated, if all reasonable jurists would conclude that a substantive provision of the federal habeas statute bars relief. To give an example, suppose a state prisoner presents a constitutional claim that reasonable jurists might find debatable, but is unable to find any "clearly established" Supreme Court precedent in support of that claim (which was previously rejected on the merits in state-court proceedings). Under the Court's view, a COA must be denied, even if the habeas petitioner satisfies the "substantial showing of the denial of a constitutional right" requirement of §2253(c)(2), because all reasonable jurists would agree that habeas relief is impossible to obtain under §2254(d).

What do you think the appropriate role of the district Court opinion should be? The concerns of Justice Scalia notwithstanding, the standard practice is to show that the underlying constitutional claim is debatable, rather than that the application of § 2254(d) to that claim is debatable. See, e.g., Smith v. Dretke, 422 F.3d 269, 273 (5th Cir. 2005) ("At the COA stage, we do not apply the deferential AEDPA standard of review to examine the merits of the habeas application."). Is the practice of evaluating the claim in a vacuum consistent with the idea that AEDPA simply codified *Barefoot*?

2) Who Issues COAs? 28 U.S.C. § 2253(c)(1) provides that a "circuit justice or judge" can issue a COA. A strict textual reading of the statute produces some interesting insights. First, the word "circuit" does not obviously modify "judge." So there are two plausible readings of the statute. In the first, § 2253(c)(1) gives COA authority to a "circuit justice" and to a "judge;" in the second, the provision gives the authority to a "circuit justice" and to a "[circuit] judge." A "circuit justice" is the Supreme Court Justice who "rides circuit in a federal appellate jurisdiction."[e] An interpretation that distributed the word "circuit" such that it modifies "judge" would mean that district court judges could not issue COAs. An interpretation that did not distribute the word "circuit" such that it modifies "judge" would mean that any federal judicial officer could issue a COA, and that is indeed the observed rule.

Less clear from the statutory text, however, is whether a *court* could issue a COA. At least as a textual matter, the phrase "circuit justice or judge" does not appear to vest authority in a circuit court to certify an appeal. Federal Rule of Appellate Procedure (FRAP) 22(b), however, states:

---

[e] Prisoners do make COA applications to Supreme Court Justices sitting in their individual capacities, although, to our knowledge, no such application has been granted.

> In a habeas corpus proceeding in which the detention complained of arises out of process issued by a State court, an appeal by the applicant for the writ may not proceed unless a district or a circuit judge issues a certificate of appealability pursuant to section 2253(c) of title 28, United States Code ... If the district judge has denied the certificate, the applicant for the writ may then request issuance of the certificate by a circuit judge. If such a request is addressed to the court of appeals, it shall be deemed addressed to the judges thereof and shall be considered by a circuit judge or judges as the court deems appropriate. If no express request for a certificate is filed, the notice of appeal shall be deemed to constitute a request addressed to the judges of the court of appeals.

Moreover, FRAP 27(c) also states:

> In addition to the authority expressly conferred by these rules or by law, a single judge of a court of appeals may entertain and may grant or deny any request for relief which under these rules may properly be sought by motion, except that a single judge may not dismiss or otherwise determine an appeal or other proceeding, and except that a court of appeals may provide by order or rule that any motion or class of motions must be acted upon by the court. The action of a single judge may be reviewed by the court.

Does the combination of FRAP 22 and 27 convince you that a *circuit court panel* should be able to dispose of a COA application? With respect to the power of individual judges to issue COAs, do the FRAP trump the statute, or do they plausibly shed light on how it should be interpreted? Does your answer change if you know that the FRAP 22 Advisory Committee's notes state that "28 U.S.C. § 2253 does not authorize the court of appeals as a court to grant a certificate of probable cause[?]" In *Hohn v. United States*, 524 U.S. 236 (1998), the Supreme Court nonetheless decided that circuit panels could decide COA applications: "It is more consistent with the Federal Rules and the uniform practice of the courts of appeals to construe § 2253(c)(1) as conferring the jurisdiction to issue certificates of appealability upon the court of appeals rather than by a judge acting under his or her own seal." (*Hohn* also held that the Supreme Court could conduct certiorari review of COA dispositions in the federal circuit courts.)

3)   Is 28 U.S.C. § 2253(c) a "Jurisdictional" Rule? Section 2253(c) states that a COA must "indicate which specific issue or issues satisfy the [COA standard]." What happens if a court grants a COA, but does not indicate the issue on which a prisoner made a "substantial showing of the denial of a constitutional right"? Does a "non-indicating" order granting a COA deprive a court of appellate jurisdiction to review the case? *Gonzalez v. Thaler*, 132 S.Ct. 641 (2012), held that a non-indicating COA still triggers appellate jurisdiction. In *Gonzalez*, the Fifth Circuit granted a COA under *Slack*—on a procedural issue—without indicating on which of the underlying constitutional claims Gonzalez had made a substantial showing. The Supreme Court held that the only jurisdictional prerequisite for appellate review is the presence of a COA under § 2253(c)(1), and that any defects—real or alleged—under § 2253(c)(2) or (c)(3) did not void appellate jurisdiction. Consider not only whether you agree with the textualist assessment of § 2253(c), but also whether you think the outcome in *Gonzalez* promotes or undermines the putative purposes of AEDPA.

4)   Treatment of Nonconstitutional Claims. Before AEDPA, a claimant seeking a certificate of probable cause needed to make a substantial showing of the denial of a *federal* right. 28 U.S.C. § 2253(c)(2), however, now provides that a COA should not issue unless a claimant makes a "substantial showing of the denial of a *constitutional* right." (Emphasis added.) Although the vast majority of state claimants allege constitutional violations in their federal habeas petitions, some do allege violations of statutes or treaties. The federal circuits are divided on the question of whether COAs may issue for adverse rulings on such challenges.[f] In *Medellín v. Dretke*, 544 U.S. 660 (2005), the Supreme Court dismissed a prisoner's certiorari petition as improvidently granted. Among others, one reason it gave for dismissing the petition was: "Medellín requires a [COA] in order to pursue the merits of his claim on appeal. A [COA] may be granted only where there is 'a substantial showing of the denial of a constitutional right.' To obtain the necessary certificate of appealability to proceed in the Court of Appeals, Medellín must demonstrate that his allegation of a treaty violation could satisfy this standard." (Internal citations omitted.) In her opinion dissenting from the dismissal, Justice O'Connor observed that the Court had not resolved whether "prisoners may only appeal district courts' adverse decisions involving constitutional rights" or whether AEDPA's use of the word "constitutional" was a "shorthand for all of the federal claims traditionally heard in habeas." For this question, should federal courts honor a strict reading of the text, or should they treat AEDPA as having codified *Barefoot*?

5) Special Solicitude in Capital Cases. Although the proposition that "death is different" remains controversial, courts generally recognize that, in capital cases, any doubts about whether a COA should issue are to be resolved in favor of the claimant.[g] Why is death different, and should the principle be limited to certain types of questions in the COA (questions that go to guilt, or questions that go to sentencing)? Do you think the special treatment given to capital cases is a feature of the statutory text or legislative intent, or is it a result of the special equitable authority that judges have in federal habeas cases? If the latter, then do you think such an exercise of equitable authority is appropriate?

2. THE BOUNDARIES WITH SECTION 1983

A habeas writ is one of many types of relief that prisoners may seek in connection with their detention. Prisoners may seek monetary compensation by complaining about prison conditions, treatment, or disciplinary decisions; they may challenge denial of parole; and they may challenge their arrest and conviction as wrongful. For example, in 2010, prisoners filed 20,319 habeas petitions in federal courts, but that they filed even more

---

[f] Compare, e.g., Murphy v. Netherland, 116 F.3d 97, 99–100 (4th Cir. 1997) ("Murphy's argument that his rights under the Vienna Convention were violated does not satisfy section 2253(c)(2)'s requirement because even if the Vienna Convention on Consular Relations could be said to create individual rights (as opposed to setting out the rights and obligations of signatory nations), it certainly does not create constitutional rights.") with Gomez v. Dretke, 422 F.3d 264, 266–68 (5th Cir. 2005) (rejecting state argument that § 2253(c)(2) strips power to hear appeals from prisoners on treaty-based claims that they lost in the district courts).

[g] See, e.g., Graves v. Cockrell, 351 F.3d 143, 150 (5th Cir. 2003) (2003) ("Any doubt regarding whether to grant a COA is resolved in favor of the petitioner, and the severity of the penalty may be considered in making this determination."); Valerio v. Crawford, 306 F.3d 742, 767 (9th Cir. 2004) (*en banc*) ("Because this is a capital case, we resolve in Valerio's favor any doubt about whether he has met the standard for a COA.")

non-habeas civil suits, including 17,348 civil rights suits and 7,540 suits challenging prison conditions.[h]

The civil claims of these prisoners may overlap with claims they bring in their habeas petitions. The central civil rights statute, 42 U.S.C. § 1983, originally passed as part the Civil Rights Act of 1871, provides:

> Every person who, under color of any statute, ordinance, regulation, custom, or usage, of any State or Territory or the District of Columbia, subjects, or causes to be subjected, any citizen of the United States or other person within the jurisdiction thereof to the deprivation of any rights, privileges, or immunities secured by the Constitution and laws, shall be liable to the party injured in an action at law, suit in equity, or other proper proceeding for redress.

Section 1983 and habeas cases have much in common. Both actions seek remedies for violations of federal law. The habeas statute, however, does not permit an action at law for money damages or for redress. The habeas statute instead permits a prisoner to seek discharge from unlawful custody. By the late 1960's, the Supreme Court began to interpret both the civil rights and habeas statutes more expansively. At the same time, the Warren Court recognized more constitutional rules of criminal procedure, creating more opportunities for prisoners to bring habeas and civil rights actions. Immediately following these developments, prisoners brought class actions in federal court. Among other things, they complained of improper sentencing and lack of access to legal materials, and they challenged the death penalty as cruel and unusual punishment. Prisoners sometimes labeled these challenges as § 1983 actions, sometimes they labeled the challenges as habeas claims, and they sometimes switched the label back and forth in the middle of the litigation.[i]

INTRODUCTORY NOTE ON PRE-HECK CASES

Eventually, the Supreme Court began to police the boundaries between habeas and other types of civil rights cases. The Court was particularly concerned that prisoners might improperly exploit developments in § 1983 in order to escape the procedural restrictions on habeas relief. As the cases and discussion in this Section demonstrate, prisoners can use habeas actions to challenge conditions of confinement. In some circumstances, habeas corpus is the exclusive remedy—for example, where the prisoner seeks to challenge the conviction or seeks release from prison. In other circumstances, however, a prisoner may use a Section 1983 suit.

A line of cases culminating in *Heck v. Humphrey*, 512 U.S. 477 (1994), eventually established a general principle: challenges that necessarily invalidate a conviction or sentence must be brought in a habeas corpus action, while more indirect challenges—to things like prison conditions—must be brought in a § 1983 lawsuit. The Supreme Court's central goal was to ensure that prison-

---

[h] See U.S. Courts, *Judicial Business of the U.S. Courts* Table C-2 (2010), at http://www.uscourts.gov/uscourts/Statistics/JudicialBusiness/2010/appendices/C02Sep10.pdf (last visited Mar. 15, 2013).

[i] See Randy Hertz and James S. Liebman, *Federal Habeas Corpus Practice and Procedure* § 11.4[b] & n.9 (6th ed. 2011) (*FHCPP*). See also Brandon L. Garrett, *Aggregation in Criminal Law*, 95 Cal. L. Rev. 383, 404–410 (2007) (describing the demise of the habeas class action as a result of the AEDPA and other procedural bars).

ers challenging their convictions complied with the procedural rules and caselaw governing habeas corpus, and that they did not use § 1983 to circumvent that law. Over time, however, the Supreme Court faced more cases that raised difficult questions of categorization.

The first in the line of cases, *Preiser v. Rodriguez*, 411 U.S. 425 (1973), involved several New York prisoners who lost good-time credits because of adverse results in disciplinary proceedings. They brought § 1983 actions in federal court, alleging that their good-time credits were unconstitutionally reduced. They also argued that, if their credits were restored, then they would be entitled to immediate release. Noting that "the essence of habeas corpus is an attack by a person in custody upon the legality of that custody," the Court held that the claims fell within the "traditional scope of habeas corpus" and that habeas corpus was the exclusive remedy. Indeed, "[e]ven if the restoration of the respondents' credits would not have resulted in their immediate release, but only in shortening the length of their actual confinement in prison, habeas corpus would have been their appropriate remedy." What supported this result?

The Supreme Court emphasized that the federal habeas statute requires the exhaustion of state remedies prior to filing a habeas petition. As a result, "[i]t would wholly frustrate explicit congressional intent to hold that the respondents in the present case could evade this requirement by the simple expedient of putting a different label on their pleadings." The Court noted that reasons of comity supported the result—and that state judges may be in a better position to address such claims in the first instance. The Court emphasized that "[i]n New York, for example, state judges sit on a regular basis at all but one of the State's correctional facilities, and thus inmates may present their grievances to a court at the place of their confinement, where the relevant records are available and where potential witnesses are located."

Preiser did not seek to comprehensively address all of the circumstances when a federal court might permit a prisoner to file a Section 1983 claim. The Court merely ruled that, "when a state prisoner is challenging the very fact or duration of his physical imprisonment, and the relief he seeks is a determination that he is entitled to immediate release or a speedier release from that imprisonment, his sole federal remedy is a writ of habeas corpus." The Court, however, ultimately rejected a piecemeal approach to defining the border between § 1983 and habeas claims.

Heck v. Humphrey

United States Supreme Court
512 U.S. 477 (1994)

■ JUSTICE SCALIA delivered the opinion of the Court.

This case presents the question whether a state prisoner may challenge the constitutionality of his conviction in a suit for damages under 42 U.S.C. § 1983.

I

Petitioner Roy Heck was convicted in Indiana state court of voluntary manslaughter for the killing of Rickie Heck, his wife, and is serving a 15-year sentence in an Indiana prison. While the appeal from his conviction was pending, petitioner, proceeding pro se, filed this suit in Federal District Court under 42 U.S.C. § 1983 * * *. The complaint alleged that respondents, acting under color of state law, had engaged in an "unlawful, unreasonable, and arbitrary investigation" leading to [Heck's] arrest; "knowingly destroyed" evidence "which was exculpatory in nature and could have proved [Heck's] innocence"; and caused "an illegal and unlawful voice identification procedure" to be used at [Heck's] trial. The complaint sought, among other things, compensatory and punitive monetary damages. It did not ask for injunctive relief, and petitioner has not sought release from custody in this action.

The District Court dismissed the action without prejudice, because the issues it raised "directly implicate the legality of [Heck's] confinement," While petitioner's appeal to the Seventh Circuit was pending, the Indiana Supreme Court upheld his conviction and sentence on direct appeal; his first petition for a writ of habeas corpus in Federal District Court was dismissed because it contained unexhausted claims; and his second federal habeas petition was denied, and the denial affirmed by the Seventh Circuit.

When the Seventh Circuit reached [Heck's] appeal from dismissal of his § 1983 complaint, it affirmed the judgment and approved the reasoning of the District Court: "If, regardless of the relief sought, the plaintiff [in a federal civil rights action] is challenging the legality of his conviction,[2] so that if he won his case the state would be obliged to release him even if he hadn't sought that relief, the suit is classified as an application for habeas corpus and the plaintiff must exhaust his state remedies, on pain of dismissal if he fails to do so." Heck filed a petition for certiorari, which we granted.

II

This case lies at the intersection of the two most fertile sources of federal-court prisoner litigation—the Civil Rights Act of 1871, Rev.Stat. § 1979, as amended, 42 U.S.C. § 1983, and the federal habeas corpus statute, 28 U.S.C. § 2254. Both of these provide access to a federal forum for claims of unconstitutional treatment at the hands of state officials, but they differ in their scope and operation. In general, exhaustion of state remedies "is not a prerequisite to an action under § 1983," even an action by a state prisoner. The federal habeas corpus statute, by contrast, requires that state prisoners first seek redress in a state forum. * * *

The common-law cause of action for malicious prosecution provides the closest analogy to claims of the type considered here because, unlike the related cause of action for false arrest or imprisonment, it permits damages for confinement imposed pursuant to legal process. "If there is a false arrest claim, damages for that claim cover the time of detention up until issuance of process or arraignment, but not more." But a successful malicious prosecution plaintiff may recover, in addition to general damages, "compensation for any arrest or imprisonment, including damages for discomfort or injury to his health, or loss of time and deprivation of the society." * * *

One element that must be alleged and proved in a malicious prosecution action is termination of the prior criminal proceeding in favor of the

---

[2] Neither in his petition for certiorari nor in his principal brief on the merits did petitioner contest the description of his monetary claims (by both the District Court and the Court of Appeals) as challenging the legality of his conviction. Thus, the question we understood to be before us was whether money damages premised on an unlawful conviction could be pursued under § 1983. . . . We also decline to pursue, without implying the nonexistence of, another issue, suggested by the Court of Appeals' statement that, if petitioner's "conviction were proper, this suit would in all likelihood be barred by res judicata." The res judicata effect of state-court decisions in § 1983 actions is a matter of state law.

accused. This requirement "avoids parallel litigation over the issues of probable cause and guilt * * * and it precludes the possibility of the claimant succeeding in the tort action after having been convicted in the underlying criminal prosecution, in contravention of a strong judicial policy against the creation of two conflicting resolutions arising out of the same or identical transaction." Furthermore, "to permit a convicted criminal defendant to proceed with a malicious prosecution claim would permit a collateral attack on the conviction through the vehicle of a civil suit." This Court has long expressed similar concerns for finality and consistency and has generally declined to expand opportunities for collateral attack * * *. We think the hoary principle that civil tort actions are not appropriate vehicles for challenging the validity of outstanding criminal judgments applies to § 1983 damages actions that necessarily require the plaintiff to prove the unlawfulness of his conviction or confinement, just as it has always applied to actions for malicious prosecution.

We hold that, in order to recover damages for allegedly unconstitutional conviction or imprisonment, or for other harm caused by actions whose unlawfulness would render a conviction or sentence invalid,[6] a § 1983 plaintiff must prove that the conviction or sentence has been reversed on direct appeal, expunged by executive order, declared invalid by a state tribunal authorized to make such determination, or called into question by a federal court's issuance of a writ of habeas corpus, 28 U.S.C. § 2254. A claim for damages bearing that relationship to a conviction or sentence that has not been so invalidated is not cognizable under § 1983. Thus, when a state prisoner seeks damages in a § 1983 suit, the district court must consider whether a judgment in favor of the plaintiff would necessarily imply the invalidity of his conviction or sentence; if it would, the complaint must be dismissed unless the plaintiff can demonstrate that the conviction or sentence has already been invalidated. But if the district court determines that the plaintiff's action, even if successful, will not demonstrate the invalidity of any outstanding criminal judgment against the plaintiff, the action should be allowed to proceed,[7] in the absence of some other bar to the suit.[8] * * *

---

[6] An example of this latter category—a § 1983 action that does not seek damages directly attributable to conviction or confinement but whose successful prosecution would necessarily imply that the plaintiff's criminal conviction was wrongful—would be the following: A state defendant is convicted of and sentenced for the crime of resisting arrest, defined as intentionally preventing a peace officer from effecting a lawful arrest. (This is a common definition of that offense.) He then brings a § 1983 action against the arresting officer, seeking damages for violation of his Fourth Amendment right to be free from unreasonable seizures. In order to prevail in this § 1983 action, he would have to negate an element of the offense of which he has been convicted. Regardless of the state law concerning res judicata, the § 1983 action will not lie.

[7] For example, a suit for damages attributable to an allegedly unreasonable search may lie even if the challenged search produced evidence that was introduced in a state criminal trial resulting in the § 1983 plaintiff's still—outstanding conviction. Because of doctrines like independent source and inevitable discovery, and especially harmless error, such a § 1983 action, even if successful, would not necessarily imply that the plaintiff's conviction was unlawful. In order to recover compensatory damages, however, the § 1983 plaintiff must prove not only that the search was unlawful, but that it caused him actual, compensable injury, which, we hold today, does not encompass the "injury" of being convicted and imprisoned (until his conviction has been overturned).

[8] For example, if a state criminal defendant brings a federal civil-rights lawsuit during the pendency of his criminal trial, appeal, or state habeas action, abstention may be an appropriate response to the parallel state-court proceedings. * * * Moreover, we do not decide whether abstention might be appropriate in cases where a state prisoner brings a § 1983 dam-

Applying these principles to the present action, in which both courts below found that the damages claims challenged the legality of the conviction, we find that the dismissal of the action was correct. The judgment of the Court of Appeals for the Seventh Circuit is

Affirmed.

_____

NOTES AND QUESTIONS ON HECK

1) Violation and Remedies. What is the constitutional violation for which Roy Heck sought redress? What remedies did Heck seek? Could he seek them in a habeas corpus petition?

2) Favorably Terminated Convictions. The Supreme Court required that, in order for a prisoner to pursue a § 1983 challenge, the prisoner's conviction or sentence must have been terminated. That is, the conviction or sentence must have been reversed on appeal, vacated on collateral review, set aside by executive order, or "declared invalid by a state tribunal authorized to make such determination." In *Heck*, the Court adopted this "favorable termination" requirement from the common law action for malicious prosecution. The *Heck* favorable termination requirement is exacting. That a sentence has been served is not enough; the conviction or sentence must have been reversed or legally invalidated. How often will one of those outcomes occur, in light of the fact that appeals, collateral relief, and pardons are increasingly rare?

3) "Necessarily Imply the Invalidity." Heck's conviction had not been invalidated in some other proceeding. The bar against pursuing a § 1983 case seeking damages or an injunction—the "*Heck* bar"—does not apply if the § 1983 challenge does not itself "necessarily imply the invalidity" of the conviction or sentence. Why didn't Heck's § 1983 challenge "necessarily" implicate the invalidity of his conviction?

The Supreme Court suggests, in footnotes 6 and 7, that a claim seeking damages for an unreasonable search or seizure in violation of the Fourth Amendment would imply the invalidity of the conviction—if the conviction was for resisting arrest. If, however, the challenge sought damages for the unconstitutional search and seizure, but the conviction was for homicide and was based on other evidence, then the *Heck* bar would not preclude a civil suit.

Would the *Heck* bar preclude a lawsuit alleging that police suppressed exculpatory evidence at trial? Would it bar a lawsuit seeking damages against police who secured a coerced confession that was central to the prosecution's case-in-chief? Would it bar a lawsuit seeking damages for excessive force when police made an arrest for possession of an illegal firearm?

4) The Intersection of Section 1983 and Habeas. The Supreme Court noted that the case raised an issue "at the intersection of the "two most fertile sources of federal-court prisoner litigation," 28 U.S.C. § 1983 and 42 U.S.C. § 2254. Justice Souter, in his concurring opinion, described how § 1983 and § 2254 were on a "collision course," given the breadth of both remedies. The Court resolved the conflict by ruling out relief under § 1983. Although the

_____

ages suit raising an issue that also could be grounds for relief in a state-court challenge to his conviction or sentence.

Court emphasized that § 1983 generally does not require exhaustion of state remedies, is that what the Court's rule requires when a civil rights action might call into question a criminal conviction? The Court said: "We do not engraft an exhaustion requirement upon § 1983, but rather deny the existence of a cause of action." All of the Justices agreed that a civil rights action becomes cognizable only after obtaining a vacatur of the sentence of conviction, including through habeas remedies. What would happen if the result had been different and the "collision" had occurred? For one, prisoners like Heck could file actions seeking damages for their wrongful convictions. In doing so, they might not just be seeking damages. Prisoners might file those civil suits alleging that their constitutional rights were violated during their prosecution, outside of the appeals and habeas process, and use § 1983 as a way to avoid the restrictions that limit habeas filings.

5) Malicious Prosecution. The common-law tort of malicious prosecution permits a person to sue officials for intentionally or maliciously pursuing a criminal case without probable cause, where the case was dismissed. What role does the claim of malicious prosecution play in the Supreme Court's reasoning? In other words, why are limits on common law malicious-prosecution claims used to reason through the appropriate limits on federal civil rights remedies? The Court describes as a "hoary principle" the idea that tort actions are not "appropriate vehicles for challenging the validity of outstanding criminal judgments." Should the elements of common-law tort claims be used to interpret a civil rights statute? Justice Souter, joined by three others, concurred in the result only, arguing that: "I do not think that the existence of the tort of malicious prosecution alone provides the answer." Justice Souter would have required the same result, that a state prisoner must pursue federal habeas remedies before filing a § 1983 petition, but objected to "style, not substance." He would have grounded the result in a statutory interpretation reading "the 'general' Section 1983 statute in light of the 'specific federal habeas corpus statute,'" and its policy "embodied in its exhaustion requirement, § 2254(b), that state courts be given the first opportunity to review constitutional claims bearing upon a state prisoner's release from custody." In omitted passages, the majority and Justice Souter disagreed about whether, in that common law context, a plaintiff must show that that the prosecution has ceased, or whether the plaintiff actually had to show favorable termination in the form of a reversed conviction. Justice Souter did not view the favorable-termination requirement in malicious prosecution cases as a strict or formal rule requiring a reversed conviction or sentence. One practical consequence is that Justice Souter would have allowed a prisoner who was no longer in custody (and who could not pursue habeas) to pursue a § 1983 suit, even if the prisoner's conviction had not been reversed.

6) Preclusion. In *Allen v. McCurry*, 449 US 90 (1980), McCurry argued at trial that heroin seized by police should be suppressed because it was obtained unlawfully. He argued that, because *Stone v. Powell* (excerpted in Chapter 3) rendered his Fourth Amendment claim non-cognizable on federal habeas review, his § 1983 damages claim was the only means to litigate the issue. The officers argued that, because the trial court had considered and rejected the Fourth Amendment claim at the suppression hearing, a federal court was collaterally estopped from revisiting the question. (Collateral estoppels is basically the same concept as issue preclusion. *Res judicator*, or claim preclusion, would not apply because the individual officers were not parties to the criminal trial, in which the State is the prosecuting party.) *McCurry* held that collateral estoppels could apply, and remanded for the lower courts to consider whether collateral estoppels in fact barred the suit.[j]

If the criminal conviction had been overturned, then there would no longer be a final judgment deserving of preclusive effect in a subsequent civil case. If a criminal conviction is treated as a final and valid judgment, unless overturned, would its preclusive effect generate the same result as under the rule adopted by the Court in *Heck*? (*Heck* expressly declined to address this question in footnote 2.) As another alternative, could federal judges simply stay civil rights actions until all habeas proceedings were completed? Indeed, the Supreme Court stated that, for cases not barred by *Heck*, "if a state criminal defendant brings a federal civil-rights lawsuit during the pendency of his criminal trial, appeal, or state habeas action, abstention may be an appropriate response to the parallel state-court proceedings." Cf. Younger v. Harris, 401 U.S. 37 (1971) (holding that federal courts should abstain from hearing tort claims involving issues that may be resolved in a pending state criminal proceeding).

7) Effect on Statutes of Limitation. The Court also held that "[u]nder our analysis the statute of limitations poses no difficulty while the state challenges are being pursued, since the § 1983 claim has not yet arisen." In other words, because the claim does not become cognizable until the conviction or sentence is invalidated, the limitations period does not commence. Perhaps, then, if Heck later had his conviction overturned, he could then bring civil claims—including claims under § 1983—at that time.

NOTES ON PAROLE CHALLENGES

1) Good-time Credits and Parole Challenges. A series of post-*Preiser* and post-*Heck* rulings concerned challenges to procedures for deciding whether to award "good-time credits" towards early release or parole. In *Edwards v. Ballios*, 520 U.S. 641 (1997), the Supreme Court held that a suit seeking to restore good time credits must be brought in a habeas corpus action. Similarly, in *Spencer v. Kaman*, 523 U.S. 1 (1998), the Court held that a challenge to a parole revocation must be brought in a habeas action. In *Spencer*, three Justices agreed that the result might be different—that the challenge to the parole revocation might not have to be in a habeas format—if the convict was no longer in custody and could not pursue habeas remedies. The Court has not yet answered whether the "favorable termination" requirement in *Heck* would bar a civil suit by someone who could not pursue habeas either.

Whether habeas or § 1983 is the right vehicle for a civil rights claim might also depend on the remedy the prisoner seeks. In *Wilkinson v. Dotson*, 544 U.S. 76 (2005), a prisoner brought Ex Post Facto and due process challenges to new parole guidelines, arguing that the guidelines should not be applied retroactively to his case. Because he sought a new parole hearing "under constitutionally proper procedures"—i.e., an injunction—the Court held that the claim needed to be pressed in a § 1983 action. He did not seek "an injunction ordering his immediate or speedier release into the community," but rather one seeking to alter disciplinary proceeding practices; "a favorable judgment" would not "nec-

---

[j] The suit then proceeded to a one-day trial. The verdict was directed for the officers, and one of the officers prevailed in a counterclaim and obtained a $105,000 judgment against McCurry. See McCurry v. Allen, 688 F.2d 581, 584 (8th Cir. 1982).

essarily imply the invalidity" of his conviction or sentence. Is the remedial variable in the habeas-versus-§ 1983 decision consistent with the essential features of the writ?

2)   The Prison Litigation Reform Act of 1996. At the same time that Congress passed AEDPA, which imposed new procedural restrictions on federal habeas litigation, it also ratified the Prison Litigation Reform Act of 1996 (PLRA), which was designed to restrict § 1983 prisoner litigation. While § 1983 does not require a prisoner to exhaust administrative remedies before seeking relief under the statute, the PLRA created a requirement that inmates "exhaust prison grievance remedies before initiating a lawsuit." The PLRA also requires that courts screen complaints to assess whether the complaints are "frivolous, malicious, or fail[] to state a claim." 28 U.S.C. § 1915A(a)–(b).[k] Courts have held that, for some conditions-of-confinement claims, § 1983, and not habeas corpus, is the only appropriate vehicle. See Randy Hertz and James S. Liebman, *Federal Habeas Corpus Practice and Procedure* § 9.1 & n.33 (6th ed. 2011) (*FHCPP*). For example, prisoners cannot seek money damages—like the prisoner sought in *Heck*—in a habeas action. Should conditions-of-confinement claims be cognizable on habeas review? Is there some sense in which that type of suit is a challenge to "custody?"

NOTES ON DNA EXONERATE CIVIL SUITS

1)   Exonerations and Civil Suits. One result of the *Heck* rule is that a suit seeking relief for a wrongful conviction is not ripe until the conviction has been vacated or otherwise invalidated. Section 1983 does not have its own statute of limitations; instead, the relevant state law limitations period for an analogous tort case applies, and the typical state limitations period is just a few years. Recall that the *Heck* ripeness rule means that the statute of limitations is not triggered until a court invalidates the conviction. As a result, a former prisoner may seek relief for a wrongful conviction years—or even decades—after the conviction itself. That aspect of the Court's ruling in *Heck* became important in cases in which DNA technology allowed some prisoners to obtain new evidence of innocence, and then obtain their release and the vacatur of their convictions. Following their DNA exonerations, these former inmates have brought § 1983 claims that have resulted in landmark, multi-million dollar verdicts. After all, in those cases, the innocence of the former inmate may be hard to contest; a jury instead tends to focus its attention on what it was like for an innocent person to be in prison for many years, and what missteps led to the wrongful conviction in the first place. See generally Brandon L. Garrett, *Innocence, Harmless Error, and Federal Wrongful Conviction Law*, 2005 Wis. L. Rev. 35.

2)   Criminal Procedure Rights in Civil Rights Suits. The civil rights lawsuits raise interesting theoretical and doctrinal problems, because many exonerated plaintiffs assert criminal-procedure and fair-trial rights—but they do so in a § 1983 civil suit. As a result, wrongful-conviction suits implicate the same intersection that occupied the *Heck* Court. Wrongful-conviction suits also raise analogous questions about whether the elements of the civil rights statute

---

[k] See Kermit Roosevelt III, *Exhaustion under the Prison Litigation Reform Act: The Consequences of Procedural Error*, 52 Emory L.J. 1771 (2003); Margo Schlanger, *Inmate Litigation*, 116 Harv. L. Rev. 1557 (2003).

should displace post-conviction doctrines. For example, *Brady* claims do not require that the prosecution act in "bad faith." *Brady* claims require an objective assessment of whether the exculpatory evidence that was suppressed was "material" or would have reasonably prejudiced the trial outcome. In a civil rights lawsuit, perhaps courts should instead use a causation analysis, rather than a materiality and prejudice analysis.

3) Restrictions on § 1983 Suits. Although the Supreme Court, in decisions like *Heck*, has attempted to limit the use of civil rights actions to circumvent post-conviction restrictions, the civil rights statutes have their own fairly onerous restrictions. Section 1983 has been interpreted to include a series of immunity doctrines that provide defenses for individual officers from damages liability. As in *Heck,* the Court developed those immunity defenses by drawing from common-law doctrine at the time that § 1983 was drafted. For example, prosecutors receive absolute immunity for their conduct as officers of the court; the Court has reasoned that the drafters of § 1983 would not have intended to displace common law prosecutorial immunity. In *Ambler v. Pittman*, the Court commented that "this immunity does leave the genuinely wronged defendant without civil redress against a prosecutor whose malicious or dishonest action deprives him of liberty. But the alternative of qualifying a prosecutor's immunity would disserve the broader public interest." 424 U.S. 409, 427 (1973). In contrast, law enforcement officers receive qualified immunity, which protects them from damages for conduct that was reasonable in light of clearly established constitutional law. (Note the resemblance of the qualified-immunity standard to the nonretroactivity rule and to 28 U.S.C. § 2254(d).[1]) Municipalities may only be held liable for facially-unconstitutional policies or for "deliberate indifference" to constitutional violations. See City of Canton v. Harris, 489 U.S. 378, 398 (1989). For example, the Supreme Court held, in *Connick v. Thompson*, 131 S.Ct. 1350 (2011), that the New Orleans District Attorney's Office could not be civilly liable for a serious *Brady* violation. Even though the office withheld exculpatory forensic evidence in a death penalty case, the Court held that civil liability was inappropriate because it was not "obvious" that additional training on *Brady* obligations was necessary, and because there was not strong enough evidence that there was a pattern of prior violations.

4) Outcomes in Exoneree Civil Rights Suits. As a result of those immunity doctrines and limitations on civil rights liability, success in federal wrongful-conviction lawsuits is not a given. Many DNA exonerees have been unable to obtain compensation using § 1983. See Brandon L. Garrett, *Convicting the Innocent: Where Criminal Prosecutions Go Wrong* 235 (2011). Several of the wrongful-conviction lawsuits that were brought using traditional civil rights vehicles, however, have generated systemic reforms of police practices, frequently through settlement. For example, the City of Cleveland, Ohio paid $1.6 million to settle a lawsuit filed by Anthony Michael Green, a man convicted of rape and exonerated by DNA testing after 16 years in prison. False testimony by a crime lab analyst had contributed to his wrongful conviction. As part of the

---

[1] Cf. Harlow v. Fitzgerald, 457 U.S. 800, 818 (1982) (describing absolute immunity for certain executive officials and the objective reasonableness standard for qualified immunity); Imbler v. Pachtman, 424 U.S. 409, 427–431 (1973) (describing contours of absolute immunity for prosecutions).

settlement, though, the City also agreed to conduct a year-long audit of old crime lab cases, supervised by a special master.[m]

5) No-fault Compensation Statutes. Partly in reaction to the difficulty of obtaining federal civil rights remedies, twenty-five states, the District of Columbia, and the federal government have enacted statutory compensation schemes to provide no-fault compensation to the wrongly convicted. The statutes typically require a showing that a conviction was invalidated for reasons having to do with innocence; some require an executive pardon on innocence grounds. Those statutes may result in faster relief to exonerees, although such statutes do not result in the kind of discovery and inquiry into the cause of a wrongful conviction that might occur during § 1983 litigation. Most exonerees received less than $50,000 per year of wrongful incarceration under these statutes—far less than they might receive at a civil jury trial. Some statutes are more generous; Texas now provides $80,000 for each year behind bars, lifetime annuity payments, and social services such as job training, financial advising, tuition credits, and medical treatment.[n]

INTRODUCTORY NOTE ON ACCESS TO POST-CONVICTION DNA TESTING

The Supreme Court has also had to confront whether a § 1983 lawsuit could be used not to obtain compensation, but to access post-conviction DNA testing in an effort to prove innocence. In the two cases that follow, the Court addressed whether there is a constitutional right to DNA testing, and whether a DNA test would "necessarily imply" the invalidity of a conviction under *Heck*.

District Attorney's Office for Third Judicial Dist. v. Osborne

United States Supreme Court
557 U.S. 52 (2009)

■ CHIEF JUSTICE ROBERTS delivered the opinion of the Court.

DNA testing has an unparalleled ability both to exonerate the wrongly convicted and to identify the guilty. It has the potential to significantly improve both the criminal justice system and police investigative practices. The Federal Government and the States have recognized this, and have developed special approaches to ensure that this evidentiary tool can be effectively incorporated into established criminal procedure-usually but not always through legislation.

Against this prompt and considered response, the respondent, William Osborne, proposes a different approach: the recognition of a freestanding and far-reaching constitutional right of access to this new type of evidence. The nature of what he seeks is confirmed by his decision to file this lawsuit

---

[m] See Andrew Tilghman and S.K. Bardwell, *City Looks to Ohio for Fix of Crime Lab Woes*, Houston Chron., Aug. 19, 2004.

[n] See Brandon L. Garrett, *Convicting the Innocent: Where Criminal Prosecutions Go Wrong* 236–237 (2011); Adele Bernhard, *Justice Still Fails: A Review of Recent Efforts to Compensate Individuals Who Have Been Unjustly Convicted and Later Exonerated*, 52 Drake L. Rev. 703 (2004).

in federal court under 42 U.S.C. § 1983, not within the state criminal justice system. This approach would take the development of rules and procedures in this area out of the hands of legislatures and state courts shaping policy in a focused manner and turn it over to federal courts applying the broad parameters of the Due Process Clause. There is no reason to constitutionalize the issue in this way. Because the decision below would do just that, we reverse.

I

A

This lawsuit arose out of a violent crime committed 16 years ago, which has resulted in a long string of litigation in the state and federal courts. On the evening of March 22, 1993, two men driving through Anchorage, Alaska, solicited sex from a female prostitute, K.G. She agreed to perform fellatio on both men for $100 and got in their car. The three spent some time looking for a place to stop and ended up in a deserted area near Earthquake Park. When K.G. demanded payment in advance, the two men pulled out a gun and forced her to perform fellatio on the driver while the passenger penetrated her vaginally, using a blue condom she had brought. The passenger then ordered K.G. out of the car and told her to lie face-down in the snow. Fearing for her life, she refused, and the two men choked her and beat her with the gun. When K.G. tried to flee, the passenger beat her with a wooden axe handle and shot her in the head while she lay on the ground. They kicked some snow on top of her and left her for dead. * * *

K.G. did not die; the bullet had only grazed her head. Once the two men left, she found her way back to the road, and flagged down a passing car to take her home. Ultimately, she received medical care and spoke to the police. At the scene of the crime, the police recovered a spent shell casing, the axe handle, some of K.G.'s clothing stained with blood, and the blue condom. * * *

Six days later, two military police officers at Fort Richardson pulled over Dexter Jackson for flashing his headlights at another vehicle. In his car they discovered a gun (which matched the shell casing), as well as several items K.G. had been carrying the night of the attack. The car also matched the description K.G. had given to the police. Jackson admitted that he had been the driver during the rape and assault, and told the police that William Osborne had been his passenger. * * * Other evidence also implicated Osborne. K.G. picked out his photograph (with some uncertainty) and at trial she identified Osborne as her attacker. Other witnesses testified that shortly before the crime, Osborne had called Jackson from an arcade, and then driven off with him. An axe handle similar to the one at the scene of the crime was found in Osborne's room on the military base where he lived.

The State also performed DQ Alpha testing on sperm found in the blue condom. DQ Alpha testing is a relatively inexact form of DNA testing that can clear some wrongly accused individuals, but generally cannot narrow the perpetrator down to less than 5% of the population. * * * The semen found on the condom had a genotype that matched a blood sample taken from Osborne, but not ones from Jackson, K. G., or a third suspect named James Hunter. Osborne is black, and approximately 16% of black individuals have such a genotype. In other words, the testing ruled out Jackson and Hunter as possible sources of the semen, and also ruled out over 80% of other black individuals. The State also examined some pubic hairs found at the scene of the crime, which were not susceptible to DQ Alpha testing, but which state witnesses attested to be similar to Osborne's.

B

Osborne and Jackson were convicted by an Alaska jury of kidnaping, assault, and sexual assault. * * * [Osborne's] conviction and sentence were affirmed on appeal.

Osborne then sought postconviction relief in Alaska state court. He claimed that he had asked his attorney, Sidney Billingslea, to seek more discriminating restriction-fragment-length-polymorphism (RFLP) DNA testing during trial, and argued that she was constitutionally ineffective for not doing so. Billingslea testified that after investigation, she had concluded that further testing would do more harm than good. * * * Because she believed Osborne was guilty, ["]insisting on a more advanced * * * DNA test would have served to prove that Osborne committed the alleged crimes.["] The Alaska Court of Appeals concluded that Billingslea's decision had been strategic and rejected Osborne's claim.

In this proceeding, Osborne also sought the DNA testing that Billingslea had failed to perform, relying on an Alaska postconviction statute, Alaska Stat. § 12.72 (2008), and the State and Federal Constitutions. In two decisions, the Alaska Court of Appeals concluded that Osborne had no right to the RFLP test. According to the court, § 12.72 "apparently" did not apply to DNA testing that had been available at trial. The court found no basis in our precedents for recognizing a federal constitutional right to DNA evidence. After a remand for further findings, the Alaska Court of Appeals concluded that Osborne could not claim a state constitutional right either, because the other evidence of his guilt was too strong and RFLP testing was not likely to be conclusive. Two of the three judges wrote separately to say that "[i]f Osborne could show that he were in fact innocent, it would be unconscionable to punish him," and that doing so might violate the Alaska Constitution.

The court relied heavily on the fact that Osborne had confessed to some of his crimes in a 2004 application for parole-in which it is a crime to lie. In this statement, Osborne acknowledged forcing K.G. to have sex at gunpoint, as well as beating her and covering her with snow. He repeated this confession before the parole board. Despite this acceptance of responsibility, the board did not grant him discretionary parole. * * *

Meanwhile, Osborne had also been active in federal court, suing state officials under 42 U.S.C. § 1983. He claimed that the Due Process Clause and other constitutional provisions gave him a constitutional right to access the DNA evidence for what is known as short-tandem-repeat (STR) testing (at his own expense). This form of testing is more discriminating than the DQ Alpha or RFLP methods available at the time of Osborne's trial. [After the District Court concluded *Heck* barred the suit and then the Court of Appeals reversed, the District Court then concluded there was a due process right to disclose exculpatory evidence, recognized in Brady v. Maryland and Osborne had a "potentially viable" claim of "actual innocence."]

We granted certiorari to decide whether Osborne's claims could be pursued using § 1983, and whether he has a right under the Due Process Clause to obtain postconviction access to the State's evidence for DNA testing. We now reverse on the latter ground.

II

Modern DNA testing can provide powerful new evidence unlike anything known before. Since its first use in criminal investigations in the mid-1980s, there have been several major advances in DNA technology, culminating in STR technology. * * * The dilemma is how to harness DNA's power to prove innocence without unnecessarily overthrowing the established system of criminal justice.

That task belongs primarily to the legislature. [The States are currently engaged in serious, thoughtful examinations] of how to ensure the fair and effective use of this testing within the existing criminal justice framework. Forty-six States have already enacted statutes dealing specifically with access to DNA evidence. * * * The State of Alaska itself is considering joining them. The Federal Government has also passed the Innocence Protection Act of 2004, which allows federal prisoners to move for court-ordered DNA testing under certain specified conditions. That Act also grants money to States that enact comparable statutes, and as a consequence has served as a model for some state legislation. At oral argument, Osborne agreed that the federal statute is a model for how States ought to handle the issue. * * *

These laws recognize the value of DNA evidence but also the need for certain conditions on access to the State's evidence. A requirement of demonstrating materiality is common, but it is not the only one. * * * States also impose a range of diligence requirements. Several require the requested testing to "have been technologically impossible at trial." Others deny testing to those who declined testing at trial for tactical reasons.

Alaska is one of a handful of States yet to enact legislation specifically addressing the issue of evidence requested for DNA testing. But that does not mean that such evidence is unavailable for those seeking to prove their innocence. * * *

Under the State's general postconviction relief statute, a prisoner may challenge his conviction when "there exists evidence of material facts, not previously presented and heard by the court, that requires vacation of the conviction or sentence in the interest of justice." Such a claim is exempt from otherwise applicable time limits if "newly discovered evidence," pursued with due diligence, "establishes by clear and convincing evidence that the applicant is innocent." * * *

III

The parties dispute whether Osborne has invoked the proper federal statute in bringing his claim. He sued under the federal civil rights statute, 42 U.S.C. § 1983, which gives a cause of action to those who challenge a State's "deprivation of any rights . . . secured by the Constitution." The State insists that Osborne's claim must be brought under 28 U.S.C. § 2254, which allows a prisoner to seek "a writ of habeas corpus . . . on the ground that he is in custody in violation of the Constitution."

While Osborne's claim falls within the literal terms of § 1983, we have also recognized that § 1983 must be read in harmony with the habeas statute. * * * Osborne responds that his claim does not sound in habeas at all. Although invalidating his conviction is of course his ultimate goal, giving him the evidence he seeks "would not necessarily imply the invalidity of [his] confinement." If he prevails, he would receive only *access* to the DNA, and even if DNA testing exonerates him, his conviction is not automatically invalidated. He must bring an entirely separate suit or a petition for clemency to invalidate his conviction. If he were proved innocent, the State might also release him on its own initiative, avoiding any need to pursue habeas at all.

While we granted certiorari on this question, our resolution of Osborne's claims does not require us to resolve this difficult issue. Accordingly, we will assume without deciding that the Court of Appeals was correct that *Heck* does not bar Osborne's § 1983 claim. Even under this assumption, it was wrong to find a due process violation.

IV

A

"No State shall ... deprive any person of life, liberty, or property, without due process of law." U.S. Const., Amdt. 14, § 1. This Clause imposes procedural limitations on a State's power to take away protected entitlements. * * * Osborne argues that access to the State's evidence is a "process" needed to vindicate his right to prove himself innocent and get out of jail. Process is not an end in itself, so a necessary premise of this argument is that he has an entitlement (what our precedents call a "liberty interest") to prove his innocence even after a fair trial has proved otherwise. We must first examine this asserted liberty interest to determine what process (if any) is due.

In identifying his potential liberty interest, Osborne first attempts to rely on the Governor's constitutional authority to "grant pardons, commutations, and reprieves." Alaska Const., Art. III, § 21. That claim can be readily disposed of. We have held that noncapital defendants do not have a liberty interest in traditional state executive clemency, to which no particular claimant is *entitled* as a matter of state law. * * *

Osborne does, however, have a liberty interest in demonstrating his innocence with new evidence under state law. As explained, Alaska law provides that those who use "newly discovered evidence" to "establis[h] by clear and convincing evidence that [they are] innocent" may obtain "vacation of [their] conviction or sentence in the interest of justice." This "state-created right can, in some circumstances, beget yet other rights to procedures essential to the realization of the parent right." * * *

A criminal defendant proved guilty after a fair trial does not have the same liberty interests as a free man. At trial, the defendant is presumed innocent and may demand that the government prove its case beyond reasonable doubt. But "[o]nce a defendant has been afforded a fair trial and convicted of the offense for which he was charged, the presumption of innocence disappears." *Herrera v. Collins*, 506 U.S. 390, 399 (1993).* * *

The State accordingly has more flexibility in deciding what procedures are needed in the context of postconviction relief. "[W]hen a State chooses to offer help to those seeking relief from convictions," due process does not "dictat[e] the exact form such assistance must assume." *Pennsylvania v. Finley*, 481 U.S. 551, 559 (1987). Osborne's right to due process is not parallel to a trial right, but rather must be analyzed in light of the fact that he has already been found guilty at a fair trial, and has only a limited interest in postconviction relief. *Brady* is the wrong framework.

Instead, the question is whether consideration of Osborne's claim within the framework of the State's procedures for postconviction relief "offends some principle of justice so rooted in the traditions and conscience of our people as to be ranked as fundamental," or "transgresses any recognized principle of fundamental fairness in operation." *Medina v. California*, 505 U.S. 437, 446, 448 (1992) (internal quotation marks omitted); see *Herrera, supra*, at 407–408 (applying *Medina* to postconviction relief for actual innocence); *Finley, supra*, at 556 (postconviction relief procedures are constitutional if they "compor[t] with fundamental fairness"). Federal courts may upset a State's postconviction relief procedures only if they are fundamentally inadequate to vindicate the substantive rights provided.

We see nothing inadequate about the procedures Alaska has provided to vindicate its state right to postconviction relief in general, and nothing inadequate about how those procedures apply to those who seek access to DNA evidence. Alaska provides a substantive right to be released on a sufficiently compelling showing of new evidence that establishes innocence. It exempts such claims from otherwise applicable time limits.

* * * These procedures are not without limits. The evidence must indeed be newly available to qualify under Alaska's statute, must have been diligently pursued, and must also be sufficiently material. These procedures are similar to those provided for DNA evidence by federal law and the law of other States, and they are not inconsistent with the "traditions and conscience of our people" or with "any recognized principle of fundamental fairness."

And there is more. While the Alaska courts have not had occasion to conclusively decide the question, the Alaska Court of Appeals has suggested that the State Constitution provides an additional right of access to DNA. * * *

To the degree there is some uncertainty in the details of Alaska's newly developing procedures for obtaining postconviction access to DNA, we can hardly fault the State for that. Osborne has brought this § 1983 action without ever using these procedures in filing a state or federal habeas claim relying on actual innocence. In other words, he has not tried to use the process provided to him by the State or attempted to vindicate the liberty interest that is now the centerpiece of his claim. When Osborne did request DNA testing in state court, he sought RFLP testing that had been available at trial, not the STR testing he now seeks, and the state court relied on that fact in denying him testing under Alaska law. * * *

As a fallback, Osborne also obliquely relies on an asserted federal constitutional right to be released upon proof of "actual innocence." Whether such a federal right exists is an open question. We have struggled with it over the years, in some cases assuming, arguendo, that it exists while also noting the difficult questions such a right would pose and the high standard any claimant would have to meet. * * * In this case too we can assume without deciding that such a claim exists, because even if so there is no due process problem. Osborne does not dispute that a federal actual innocence claim (as opposed to a DNA access claim) would be brought in habeas. If such a habeas claim is viable, federal procedural rules permit discovery "for good cause." 28 U.S.C. § 2254 Rule 6. * * *

B

The Court of Appeals below relied only on procedural due process, but Osborne seeks to defend the judgment on the basis of substantive due process as well. He asks that we recognize a freestanding right to DNA evidence untethered from the liberty interests he hopes to vindicate with it. We reject the invitation and conclude, in the circumstances of this case, that there is no such substantive due process right. * * * There is no long history of such a right, and "[t]he mere novelty of such a claim is reason enough to process' sustains it."

And there are further reasons to doubt. The elected governments of the States are actively confronting the challenges DNA technology poses to our criminal justice systems and our traditional notions of finality, as well as the opportunities it affords. To suddenly constitutionalize this area would short-circuit what looks to be a prompt and considered legislative response. The first DNA testing statutes were passed in 1994 and 1997. * * * In the past decade, 44 States and the Federal Government have followed suit, reflecting the increased availability of DNA testing. * * *

Establishing a freestanding right to access DNA evidence for testing would force us to act as policymakers, and our substantive-due-process rulemaking authority would not only have to cover the right of access but a myriad of other issues. We would soon have to decide if there is a constitutional obligation to preserve forensic evidence that might later be tested. If so, for how long? Would it be different for different types of evidence? Would the State also have some obligation to gather such evidence in the first place? How much, and when? No doubt there would be a miscellany of other minor directives. * * *

DNA evidence will undoubtedly lead to changes in the criminal justice system. It has done so already. The question is whether further change will primarily be made by legislative revision and judicial interpretation of the existing system, or whether the Federal Judiciary must leap ahead-revising (or even discarding) the system by creating a new constitutional right and taking over responsibility for refining it. * * *

The judgment of the Court of Appeals is reversed, and the case is remanded for further proceedings consistent with this opinion.

It is so ordered.

■ JUSTICE ALITO, with whom JUSTICE KENNEDY joins, and with whom JUSTICE THOMAS joins as to Part II, concurring.

* * *We have never previously held that a state prisoner may seek discovery by means of a § 1983 action, and we should not take that step here. I would hold that respondent's claim (like all other Brady claims) should be brought in habeas. * * *

■ JUSTICE STEVENS, with whom JUSTICE GINSBURG and JUSTICE BREYER join, and with whom JUSTICE SOUTER joins as to Part I, dissenting.

The State of Alaska possesses physical evidence that, if tested, will conclusively establish whether respondent William Osborne committed rape and attempted murder. If he did, justice has been served by his conviction and sentence. If not, Osborne has needlessly spent decades behind bars while the true culprit has not been brought to justice. The DNA test Osborne seeks is a simple one, its cost modest, and its results uniquely precise. Yet for reasons the State has been unable or unwilling to articulate, it refuses to allow Osborne to test the evidence at his own expense and to thereby ascertain the truth once and for all.

On two equally problematic grounds, the Court today blesses the State's arbitrary denial of the evidence Osborne seeks. First, while acknowledging that Osborne may have a due process right to access the evidence under Alaska's postconviction procedures, the Court concludes that Osborne has not yet availed himself of all possible avenues for relief in state court. As both a legal and factual matter, that conclusion is highly suspect.

More troubling still, based on a fundamental mischaracterization of the right to liberty that Osborne seeks to vindicate, the Court refuses to acknowledge "in the circumstances of this case" any right to access the evidence that is grounded in the Due Process Clause itself. Because I am convinced that Osborne has a constitutional right of access to the evidence he wishes to test and that, on the facts of this case, he has made a sufficient showing of entitlement to that evidence, I would affirm the decision of the Court of Appeals. * * *

NOTES AND QUESTIONS ON OSBORNE AND ON POST-CONVICTION DNA TESTING

1)   **The Scope of the Due Process Right.** *Osborne* relied on prior decisions, such as Pennsylvania v. Finley, 481 U.S. 551 (1987), which had held that there is no constitutional right to effective assistance of counsel during state post-conviction proceedings. *Osborne* did, however, validate a procedural due process right to non-arbitrary treatment during post-conviction proceedings. Also consider the Supreme Court's observation that the state need not provide a mechanism for post-conviction review in the first place. How meaningful is the procedural due process right to non-arbitrary proceedings?

2)   **Implications of *Osborne*.** If the state court denies relief by incorrectly interpreting a DNA statute to bar testing, does that decision violate due process? If the state statute bars access to DNA in all cases except homicide cases, and a rape convict seeks a DNA test, can that convict obtain relief by relying on *Osborne*? What if the state statute bars DNA tests for any person who had confessed to the crime, or any person who had pleaded guilty? Does the Court suggest that more robust procedures, like those specified in the federal Innocence Project Act (detailed in Chapter 6), provide a model?

3)   **Habeas Discovery.** What do you make of the Court's suggestion that Osborne could file a habeas petition, claim innocence, and seek DNA testing in discovery? Does this suggestion mean that, on habeas review, federal courts may grant discovery even if the underlying constitutional claim—a freestanding innocence claim under *Herrera*—has not yet been recognized by the Supreme Court? Does the suggestion mean that the Court might extend a hypothetical *Herrera* claim to non-death penalty cases (like Osborne's)? For additional discussion of these possible implications, see Brandon L. Garrett, *DNA and Due Process*, 78 Ford. L. Rev. 2919 (2010).

Osborne was also decided before *Cullen v. Pinholster*, 131 S.Ct. 1388 (2011), in which the Supreme Court held that a question under § 2254(d)(1)—the rule that the writ may issue for state merits decisions that are contrary to or an unreasonable application of clearly established federal law—must be resolved in light only of evidence presented to a state court. After *Pinholster*, federal courts are much less likely to allocate resources towards new federal factfinding. What impact does such a development have on the idea, expressed in *Osborne*, that prisoners might make collateral use of discovery in federal habeas proceedings?

4)   Comity. Modern habeas law reflects, in large part, a principle that federal courts should not unduly interfere with state criminal judgments. Even if a state has a post-conviction DNA statute, what damage to state interests occurs if there is also a federal constitutional entitlement to post-conviction DNA testing? In light of the number of states that have post-conviction DNA access statutes, how severely would a federal constitutional rule interfere with state interests? As is the case in many situations where the Court contemplates a due process issue, *Osborne* considered the potential disruption a decision might cause in other states. Is Alaska an outlier, such that recognizing a right to access DNA would not affect many other states? Or is the Court right to stay out of a complicated policy area involving new technology?

5)   Human Error. What do you make of the Court's frank admission that the criminal justice system sometimes makes mistakes, and that DNA testing can expose these errors? Is the majority being sincere—why not encourage the use of DNA testing to catch the mistakes that our system sometimes makes? Is there a way to reconcile the "frank admission" with the outcome in the case? Is the separation of powers rationale persuasive?

6)   What Next? The Court noted that Osborne had previously confessed in parole hearings. What options does Osborne have to continue to pursue DNA testing? What impact might his post-conviction confession have on how his claims might be received? Alaska, following this decision, enacted a detailed and fairly-broad DNA access statute. See Alaska Stat. Ann. § 12.73.010. How do you evaluate, then, of the State's strenuous objections to DNA testing in this particular case? What would happen if Osborne did get the DNA test, and it excluded him?

7)   *Skinner v. Switzer.* In *Skinner v. Switzer*, 131 S. Ct. 1388 (2011), the Supreme Court addressed the *Heck* issue left unanswered in *Osborne*: whether an inmate can use a § 1983 suit to access post-conviction DNA testing? In 1995, a Texas court convicted and capitally sentenced Henry Skinner for murdering his girlfriend and her two sons, with whom he lived. Before trial, the State tested some crime-scene evidence. Some of it inculpated Skinner, and some did not. The State left untested several pieces of evidence, including knives found at the scene, an axe handle, vaginal swabs, fingernail clippings, and hair samples. The Court held that a § 1983 suit could be used to seek DNA testing, invoking the procedural due process right recognized in *Osborne*. The Court emphasized that the Circuits that already allow such claims had experienced no "litigation flood, or even rainfall." That proposition is consistent with the fact that pretrial DNA testing is now routine. The Court also emphasized that Skinner would need to show that he was denied due process when denied relief under the Texas DNA access statute. Justice Thomas dissented, arguing that § 1983 should not "[intrude] into the boundaries of habeas corpus." Recall how, in *Osborne*, the Court suggested that DNA testing might also be obtained by requesting discovery after filing a federal habeas petition. As a result, post-conviction DNA testing can be requested in both habeas and § 1983 litigation.

Hill v. McDonough

United States Supreme Court
547 U.S. 573 (2006)

■ JUSTICE KENNEDY delivered the opinion of the Court.

Petitioner Clarence E. Hill challenges the constitutionality of a three-drug sequence the State of Florida likely would use to execute him by lethal injection. Seeking to enjoin the procedure, he filed this action in the United States District Court for the Northern District of Florida, pursuant to * * * 42 U.S.C. § 1983. The District Court and the Court of Appeals for the Eleventh Circuit construed the action as a petition for a writ of habeas corpus and ordered it dismissed for noncompliance with the requirements for a second and successive petition. The question before us is whether Hill's claim must be brought by an action for a writ of habeas corpus under the statute authorizing that writ, 28 U.S.C. § 2254, or whether it may proceed as an action for relief under 42 U.S.C. § 1983.

This is not the first time we have found it necessary to discuss which of the two statutes governs an action brought by a prisoner alleging a constitutional violation. See, e.g., *Nelson v. Campbell*, 541 U.S. 637 (2004); *Heck v. Humphrey*, 512 U.S. 477 (1994); *Preiser v. Rodriguez*, 411 U.S. 475 (1973). Hill's suit, we now determine, is comparable in its essentials to the action the Court allowed to proceed under § 1983 in *Nelson*. In accord with that precedent we now reverse.

I

In the year 1983, Hill was convicted of first-degree murder and sentenced to death. When his conviction and sentence became final some five years later, the method of execution then prescribed by Florida law was electrocution. On January 14, 2000-four days after the conclusion of Hill's first, unsuccessful round of federal habeas corpus litigation-Florida amended the controlling statute to provide: "A death sentence shall be executed by lethal injection, unless the person sentenced to death affirmatively elects to be executed by electrocution." The now-controlling statute, which has not been changed in any relevant respect, does not specify a particular lethal injection procedure. Implementation is the responsibility of the Florida Department of Corrections. * * * The department has not issued rules establishing a specific lethal injection protocol, and its implementing policies and procedures appear exempt from Florida's Administrative Procedure Act.

After the statute was amended to provide for lethal injection, the Florida Supreme Court heard a death row inmate's claim that the execution procedure violated the Eighth Amendment's prohibition of cruel and unusual punishments. In [that case], the complainant, who had acquired detailed information about the procedure from the State, contended the planned three-drug sequence of injections would cause great pain if the drugs were not administered properly. The Florida Supreme Court rejected this argument as too speculative.

On November 29, 2005, the Governor of Florida signed Hill's death warrant, which ordered him to be executed on January 24, 2006. Hill requested information about the lethal injection protocol, but the department provided none. * * *. Hill then challenged, for the first time, the State's lethal injection procedure. On December 15, 2005, he filed a successive postconviction petition in state court, relying upon the Eighth Amendment. The trial court denied Hill's request for an evidentiary hearing and dismissed his claim as procedurally barred. The Florida Supreme Court affirmed on January 17, 2006. * * *

Three days later—and four days before his scheduled execution—Hill brought this action in District Court pursuant to 42 U.S.C. § 1983. Assuming the State would use the procedure discussed at length in the Sims decision, * * * Hill alleged that the first drug injected, sodium pentothal, would not be a sufficient anesthetic to render painless the administration of the second and third drugs, pancuronium bromide and potassium chloride. There was an ensuing risk, Hill alleged, that he could remain conscious and suffer severe pain as the pancuronium paralyzed his lungs and body and the potassium chloride caused muscle cramping and a fatal heart attack. The complaint sought an injunction "barring defendants from executing Plaintiff in the manner they currently intend."

The District Court found that under controlling Eleventh Circuit precedent the § 1983 claim was the functional equivalent of a petition for writ of habeas corpus. * * * Because Hill had sought federal habeas corpus relief in an earlier action, the District Court deemed his petition successive and thus barred for failure to obtain leave to file from the Court of Appeals as required by 28 U.S.C. § 2244(b). On the day of the scheduled execution the Court of Appeals affirmed. * * * After issuing a temporary stay of execution, this Court granted Hill's petition for certiorari and continued the stay pending our resolution of the case.

II

"Federal law opens two main avenues to relief on complaints related to imprisonment: a petition for habeas corpus, 28 U.S.C. § 2254, and a complaint under the Civil Rights Act of 1871, Rev. Stat. § 1979, as amended, 42 U.S.C. § 1983. Challenges to the validity of any confinement or to particulars affecting its duration are the province of habeas corpus." An inmate's challenge to the circumstances of his confinement, however, may be brought under § 1983.

In *Nelson* we addressed whether a challenge to a lethal injection procedure must proceed as a habeas corpus action. The complainant had severely compromised peripheral veins, and Alabama planned to apply an invasive procedure on his arm or leg to enable the injection. He sought to enjoin the procedure, alleging it would violate the Eighth Amendment. The Court observed that the question whether a general challenge to a method of execution must proceed under habeas was a difficult one. The claim was not easily described as a challenge to the fact or duration of a sentence; yet in a State where the legislature has established lethal injection as the method of execution, "a constitutional challenge seeking to permanently enjoin the use of lethal injection may amount to a challenge to the fact of the sentence itself."

Nelson did not decide this question. The lawsuit at issue, as the Court understood the case, did not require an injunction that would challenge the sentence itself. The invasive procedure in Nelson was not mandated by law, and the inmate appeared willing to concede the existence of an acceptable alternative procedure. Absent a finding that the challenged procedure was necessary to the lethal injection, the Court concluded, injunctive relief would not prevent the State from implementing the sentence. * * *

In the case before us we conclude that Hill's § 1983 action is controlled by the holding in *Nelson*. Here, as in *Nelson*, Hill's action if successful would not necessarily prevent the State from executing him by lethal injection. The complaint does not challenge the lethal injection sentence as a general matter but seeks instead only to enjoin respondents "from executing [Hill] in the manner they currently intend." * * * Hill concedes that "other methods of lethal injection the Department could choose to use would be constitutional,"* * *. Florida law, moreover, does not require the department of corrections to use the challenged procedure.* * *

Respondents and the States as amici frame their argument differently. * * * They rely on cases barring § 1983 damages actions that, if successful, would imply the invalidation of an existing sentence or confinement. Those cases, they contend, demonstrate that the test of whether an action would undermine a sentence must "be applied functionally." By the same logic, it is said, a suit should be brought in habeas if it would frustrate the execution as a practical matter. * * * As discussed above, and at this stage of the litigation, the injunction Hill seeks would not necessarily foreclose the State from implementing the lethal injection sentence under present law, and thus it could not be said that the suit seeks to establish "unlawfulness [that] would render a conviction or sentence invalid." Any incidental delay caused by allowing Hill to file suit does not cast on his sentence the kind of negative legal implication that would require him to proceed in a habeas action.

III

Filing an action that can proceed under § 1983 does not entitle the complainant to an order staying an execution as a matter of course. * * * We state again, as we did in *Nelson*, that a stay of execution is an equitable remedy. It is not available as a matter of right, and equity must be sensitive to the State's strong interest in enforcing its criminal judgments without undue interference from the federal courts. * * * Thus, like other stay applicants, inmates seeking time to challenge the manner in which the State plans to execute them must satisfy all of the requirements for a stay, including a showing of a significant possibility of success on the merits. * * *

The equities and the merits of Hill's underlying action are also not before us. We reverse the judgment of the Court of Appeals and remand the case for further proceedings consistent with this opinion.

It is so ordered.

NOTES AND QUESTIONS ON HILL AND ON METHOD-OF-EXECUTION CHALLENGES

1) **Civil Procedure.** What remedy did Hill seek? On its face, would that remedy prevent the State from executing him? And why did Hill want to bring the Eighth Amendment challenge to lethal injection protocols in a § 1983 case, and not in a habeas petition? Did the Supreme Court correctly apply the rule of the *Preiser* line of cases?

2) **Death Penalty Litigation.** An overriding concern in the Supreme Court's capital habeas decisions, and of Congress when enacting AEDPA, was limiting delays in capital litigation. The Court expressed concern that last-ditch § 1983 suits could be used to further delay executions. How effective will § 1983 litigation be in light of the Court's comments highlighting how federal judges do not necessarily need to grant stays of execution? For an exploration of how

federal courts have imported procedural bars from habeas to limit § 1983 method-of-execution challenges, see Liam Montgomery, *The Unrealized Promise of Section 1983 Method-of-Execution Challenges*, 94 Va. L. Rev. 1987 (2008).

3)   The Eighth Amendment. For many years, the standard three-drug lethal injection cocktail has largely consisted of the following chemical sequence: sodium thiopental (an anesthetic agent), pancuronium bromide (a paralytic agent); and potassium chloride (which induces cardiac arrest). The three drugs are not mixed, and states administer them sequentially. Because most doctors believe that the Hippocratic Oath forbids them from participating in the injection protocol, lethal injections are usually conducted by warden personnel that are not physicians. Moreover, states conduct many lethal injections in modified spaces that once housed electric chairs. Medical professionals recently began to argue that the anesthetic agent was not working, but that the paralytic agent prevented the outward manifestation of physical pain. *Baze v. Rees*, 553 U.S. 35 (2008), was the culmination of litigation involving many of these objections.

In *Baze*, the Supreme Court rejected an Eighth Amendment challenge to lethal injection protocols. It held that, for an inmate to prevail, there must be a "substantial risk of serious harm" or an "objectively intolerable risk of harm." It reasoned: "[s]imply because an execution method may result in pain, either by accident or as an inescapable consequence of death, does not establish the sort of 'objectively intolerable risk of harm' that qualifies as cruel and unusual." Does this holding mean that—as was arguably the case in *Osborne* and *Skinner*—there is a § 1983 vehicle in theory, but the constitutional right is so limited that there will be little practical remedy in fact?

After *Baze*, the manufacturer of sodium thiopental—responding to public pressure—decided it would no longer allow the chemical to be used in the lethal injection sequence. Many states had already started to shift to a different anesthetic agent, pentobarbital. The decision by the sodium thiopental manufacturer accelerated that change. Some states have moved away from a sequenced cocktail entirely, and now simply administer a lethal dose of the pentobarbital. See, e.g., Beaty v. Brewer, 649 F.3d 1071 (9th Cir. 2011) (denying rehearing en banc) (affirming district court's denial of death row inmate's request for an injunction staying execution, objecting to the replacement of sodium thiopental with pentobarbital). But cf. id. at 1076 (Reinhardt, J., dissenting) ("When the State has created a constitutional issue by changing the method of execution only eighteen hours before that ultimate and irreversible act is to take place, we must permit the person to be executed adequate time to prepare his challenge.").

NOTES ON BIVENS AND NATIONAL SECURITY DETENTION

1)   *Bivens* Remedies. Section 1983 allows plaintiffs to sue state officials for constitutional violations; there is no comparable statute for suits involving constitutional violations committed by federal officers. In *Bivens v. Six Unknown Named Agents of the F.B.I.*, 403 U.S. 388 (1971), however, the Supreme Court held that federal officials may be sued for violation of Fourth Amendment rights, under an implied-cause-of-action theory. That is, the Court found that such lawsuits may be brought in federal court—implying a cause of action from the Constitution—in the absence of any statute explicitly creating a right to sue. While lower courts initially assumed that *Bivens* provided a cause of action for any constitutional violation by a federal official, the Supreme Court has sharply limited the availability of *Bivens* remedies. The Court has repeatedly rejected efforts to extend *Bivens* to claims beyond a select few constitutional torts: Fourth Amendment claims, Fifth Amendment due process claims, and Eighth Amendment violations. The Court has held that no *Bivens* remedy is available when there (1) is an alternative existing remedy protecting the interest that the plaintiff seeks to vindicate, or (2) there are "special factors counseling hesitation" to recognize a *Bivens* remedy such as non-interference with military affairs or federal personnel policy. See Alexander A. Reinert, *Measuring the Success of* Bivens *Litigation and its Consequences for the Individual Liability Model*, 62 Stan. L. Rev. 809, 823–24 (2010) (describing the development of the Court's *Bivens* doctrine).

2)   Post-9/11 *Bivens* Litigation. Post-9/11 national-security detentions and interrogations resulted in a series of *Bivens* suits against federal officials. The plaintiffs in the suits face a series of procedural obstacles that has some parallels to the obstacles that national-security detainees face in habeas litigation. See George D. Brown, *Counter-Counter-Terrorism Via Lawsuit—The Bivens Impasse*, 82 S. Cal. L. Rev 841 (2009). Evidentiary concerns, judicial abstention, and pleading requirements all play an important role in national security-related *Bivens* litigation.

3)   State Secrets Privilege. The presence of classified national-security information is an important issue, as it is in habeas challenges to national-security detentions. The Government has asserted the "state secrets" privilege and argued that suits must be dismissed if litigation would risk disclosure of such secrets. In *El-Masri v. United States*, the Fourth Circuit dismissed a *Bivens* challenge to an "extraordinary rendition" on that ground. 479 F.3d 296, 302 (4th Cir. 2007).

4)   *Bivens* "Special Factors." A series of federal court rulings interpreted the scope of *Bivens* in national-security detention cases, have applied the Supreme Court's "special factors" test for deciding whether to permit a *Bivens* remedy. For example, in *Arar v. Ashcroft*, 585 F.3d 559 (2d Cir. 2009) (en banc), the Second Circuit dismissed a case in which a noncitizen brought a Fifth Amendment challenge to an extraordinary rendition to Syria. The Second Circuit did not decide whether the plaintiff was subjected to torture, instead finding that "special factors" militated against extending *Bivens* to such situations. The Second Circuit emphasized that it was reluctant to intrude in national-security matters; it also noted the presence of classified information and the availability of immigration remedies. The dissent would have reached the merits of the *Bivens* claim, describing the facts as follows:

> During his first twelve days in Syrian detention, Arar was interrogated for eighteen hours per day and was physically and psychologically tortured. He was beaten on his palms, hips, and lower back with a two-inch-thick electric cable. His captors also used their fists to beat him on his stomach, his face, and the back of his neck. He was subjected to excruciating pain and pleaded with his captors to stop, but they would not. He was placed in a room where he could hear the screams of other detainees being tortured and was told that he, too, would be placed in a spine-breaking "chair," hung upside down in a "tire" for beatings, and subjected to electric shocks. To lessen his exposure to the torture, Arar falsely confessed, among other

things, to having trained with terrorists in Afghanistan, even though he had never been to Afghanistan and had never been involved in terrorist activity.

5) Qualified Immunity. Just as in § 1983 litigation, *Bivens* defendants enjoy the defense of absolute or qualified immunity. Officials protected by qualified immunity may argue that they acted reasonably in light of clearly established law. See Padilla v. Yoo, 678 F.3d 748 (9th Cir. 2012) (dismissing suit by Jose Padilla challenging the author of DOJ Office of Legal Counsel legal opinions, which had approved enhanced interrogation techniques, and ruling that it was not clearly established then that "cruel, inhuman, or degrading treatment" violated substantive due process, nor was it clearly established whether such treatment was torture). In *Ali v. Rumsfeld,* 649 F.3d 762, 773 (D.C. Cir. 2011), the D.C. Circuit found that the officials benefited from the defense of qualified immunity, and emphasized that the "danger of obstructing U.S. national security policy" was a factor that counseled against permitting a *Bivens* remedy. The D.C. Circuit analogized the concern to that expressed by the Supreme Court in *Johnson v. Eisentrager,* 339 U.S. 763, 779 (1950), in that the appeals court believed that civil trials would "hamper the war effort and bring aid and comfort to the enemy." Of course, in *Eisentrager*, the Supreme Court was ruling on whether to permit habeas proceedings to challenge military detentions. Do civil suits by noncitizens seeking damages for alleged torture by military personnel raise the same issues?

6) Heightened Pleading. In what is also a landmark civil procedure case, the Supreme Court emphasized the need for heightened pleading when bringing *Bivens* suits against high-level officials regarding national-security-detention policymaking. See Ashcroft v. Iqbal, 556 U.S. 662 (2009). Nevertheless, some argue that rulings in these *Bivens* cases do not reflect general civil litigation doctrine, but that they instead receive different treatment due to national security concerns. See Stephen I. Vladeck, *The New National Security Canon,* 61 Am. U. L. Rev. 1295 (2012).

CHAPTER 12

THE FUTURE OF HABEAS CORPUS

INTRODUCTION

This Book concludes with a focus on broader questions of institutional design and custodial process. In Section 1, we examine proposals for improving existing federal habeas statutes and for experimenting in the states, including alternatives to post-conviction review. In Section 2, we explore common themes across all forms of sovereign custody—executive, civil, and criminal. In each area, you have already thought about how the Constitution generally, and the Suspension Clause specifically, guarantees the habeas privilege. In each area, the habeas process will reflect the process producing the underlying custody determination, and will be particularly sensitive to whether the underlying custodial process observed certain due process rights.[a] Not only is a habeas proceeding a forum in which prisoners may redress constitutional grievances, but it is also a vehicle for developing and refining constitutional rights that implicate federalism, the separation of powers, and the relationship between individuals and the state.

1. INSTITUTIONAL DESIGN

How would you improve or reform our system of habeas corpus review, particularly our process for post-conviction litigation? Which statutes or doctrines would you target? Or should our post-conviction system be scrapped? How should we replace it? Judges, lawyers, and scholars have made many creative proposals over the years, and jurisdictions have adopted some of them. Those approaches include efforts to streamline or narrow post-conviction review, to create alternatives to the typical post-conviction process, and to better remedy certain types of errors.

————

NOTES ON FEDERAL LEGISLATIVE REFORM

1) **Improving Existing Federal Statutes.** In the past twenty years, various legislative proposals have either changed or sought to change the availability of certain categories of habeas review. AEDPA, IIRIRA, the REAL-ID Act, the DTA, and the MCA all recalibrated review—sometimes dramatically—for different types of government detention. There have been a series of proposals to revisit each of those pieces of legislation. Although some proposals are designed to relax the existing restrictions on judicial review, most are introduced to bolster them.

---

[a] For some of the Authors thoughts on the relationship between habeas and due process, see Brandon L. Garrett, *Habeas Corpus and Due Process*, 98 Corn. L. Rev. 97 (2012); Lee B. Kovarsky, Lee Kovarsky, *Custodial and Collateral Process: A Response to Professor Garrett*, 98 Cornell L. Rev. Online 1 (2013).

2)   Channeling. For example, would you alter the balance struck by the RE-AL-ID Act, which, as discussed in Chapter 7, centralized review of challenges to removal? Congress did channel appellate review of GTMO litigation through the D.C. Circuit, and—although the Supreme Court struck down MCA § 7—the GTMO litigation remains consolidated in the District Court for the District of Columbia. Why did the Supreme Court reject a D.C. Circuit-centered approach in *Boumediene*—and does that rejection suggest that the REAL-ID Act may be constitutionally suspect? In what ways has Congress enhanced the role of federal appeals courts in post-conviction litigation? To put the question in a slightly different way, is there any analogy to be made between the centralization of national-security-detention review and the gatekeeping functions of appeals courts in post-conviction proceedings? Would you consider similar gatekeeping roles for the D.C. Circuit if a federal district court retained some subsequent authority to consider the merits of the national-security-detention cases?

3)   Procedural Rules. Imagine yourself as having the power to design legislation. How would you draft or alter the procedural rules that govern federal post-conviction filings? Would you adopt, for the first time, a statutory provision governing procedural defaults? How would you decide what the optimal standards should be? Congress often enacts major habeas legislation hastily; if you could study the issues as carefully as you could, what data would you want? What values would inform your drafting of procedural rules? Would the emphasis be, as in Professor Paul Bator's view, preserving the finality of state court judgments? See Paul M. Bator, *Finality in Criminal Law and Federal Habeas Corpus for State Prisoners*, 76 Harv. L.R. 441, 466 (1963). Would the emphasis of these new procedural rules be to preserve comity, in which federal judges honor the reasoning and decisions of state judges? Would the emphasis be to prevent strategic behavior by inmates—e.g., lack of diligence, sandbagging, delay tactics, and piecemeal litigation? Would the emphasis be to encourage lawyers to focus their representation of criminal defendants at trial or appellate proceedings?

Would you alter AEDPA's statute of limitations? If so, how? Would the emphasis be on speeding the disposition of habeas petitions? Recall how Congress sought to reduce delays by enacting AEDPA, but the time between judgment and federal habeas disposition has only increased. Have changes to the habeas statutes necessarily accomplished their intended goals? If legislative changes do sometimes have counter-intuitive effects, why?

Or should the emphasis be preserving some flexibility to examine certain types of claims? Some scholars have advocated relaxing procedural barriers that restrict federal habeas litigation. See, e.g., Gary Peller, *In Defense of Federal Habeas Corpus Relitigation*, 16 Harv. C.R.-C.L. L. Rev. 579, 690–91 (1982). If procedural restrictions should be relaxed, then what is the best way to do so? Should the procedural rules have exceptions depending on the type of claim? Should there be more rules like that of *Martinez v. Ryan*—allowing an ineffective-lawyer excuse for forfeiting a "substantial" IAC claim at the first state opportunity to file it? Should the procedural rules have other equitable exceptions based on poor representation, like the equitable tolling rule the Court recognized in *Holland v. Florida*, 130 S.Ct. 2549 (U.S. 2010)? Should there be more exceptions involving state-created obstacles or evidence of a miscarriage of justice? Recall how Judge Henry Friendly argued that innocence should be central to federal habeas inquiry; in fact, he argued that, absent evidence of innocence, a federal judge should not consider a habeas petition. See Henry J. Friendly, *Is*

Innocence Irrelevant? Collateral Attack on Criminal Judgments, 38 U. Chi. L. Rev. 142, 142 (1970). Would you change the way that facts are developed in federal habeas proceedings? Would you alter AEDPA's evidentiary hearing restrictions? Do all the exceptions and caveats create an administrative interest in having fewer, clearer rules?

4) Merits Review. The most controversial AEDPA provision was the limitation on relief in 28 U.S.C. § 2254(d). Section 2254(d) has raised a series of difficult interpretive issues. Would you change § 2254(d) if you redrafted it and, if so, how? Would you specify what counts as state court adjudication "on the merits"? Would you adjust what it means for state courts to have "reasonably" decided legal questions, mixed legal questions, and pure fact questions? Would you review only to the reasoning *actually* used by state judges? See Steven Semeraro, *A Reasoning-Process Review Model for Federal Habeas Corpus*, 94 J. Crim. L. & Criminology 897, 927–28 (2004). Is there anything about the statutory interpretation of § 2254(d) that you might change?

5) Complexity. Recall Justice Blackmun's dissent in *Coleman v. Thomson*: "I believe that the Court is creating a Byzantine morass of arbitrary, unnecessary, and unjustifiable impediments to the vindication of federal rights." 501 U.S. 722, 759 (1991) (Blackmun, J., dissenting). Why have the rules become so complicated? Does the fault lie with the Supreme Court? Or with Congress' interventions, particularly AEDPA? Is there any way for the Court to cut through the Gordian knot and make the federal habeas procedures simpler? Would expanding *Stone v. Powell*, 428 U.S. 465 (1976)—which held that Fourth Amendment violations were not cognizable on federal collateral review—to other types of constitutional claims simplify habeas litigation? See Brian M. Hoffstadt, *How Congress Might Redesign a Leaner, Cleaner Writ of Habeas Corpus*, 49 Duke L.J. 947 (2000). Could Congress simplify the procedures and rules for granting merits relief? Why have the rules become so complicated over time, and what interests does that complexity serve? Are the rules simply traps for unwary *pro se* habeas petitioners? Do they make the work of federal judges needlessly difficult? Or do they try to arrive at the right balance, to sift through the meritless petitions to locate those that truly deserve special attention and relief? And, after considering the federal rules, think about the answers you might give for the same questions addressed to improving *state* post-conviction law.

6) Grand Bargains. There is a tradition of habeas reform proposals that focus on linking procedural restrictions on "downstream" post-conviction review to "upstream" reforms—one could call it a quid pro quo or a "grand bargain" approach. Measures that would restrict access to habeas remedies would be connected to reforms providing greater resources earlier on in the criminal or collateral process. The report by what was known as the "Powell Committee"— formed in June 1988 and chaired by then-retired Supreme Court Justice Louis Powell—emphasized the need to address endemic delays and piecemeal litigation. Ad Hoc Comm. on Federal Habeas Corpus in Capital Cases, *Report on Habeas Corpus in Capital Cases*, 45 Crim. L. Rep. (BNA) 3239, 3239–40 (Sept. 27, 1989). It also underscored the "need for qualified counsel to represent inmates in collateral review." The Powell Committee Report called for special provisions limiting federal habeas filings for death row inmates, including by imposing a six month time period for filing a federal habeas petition. These expedited procedures, however, could only be used if they were provided "competent counsel" during state collateral review," with "standards for competency" to evaluate whether counsel was in fact competent.

7)   AEDPA Capital Opt-in Procedures. Seven years later, Congress adopted a variant of the quid pro quo proposed by the Powell Committee. AEDPA included a set of capital opt-in procedures, through which states that provide adequate and effective indigent capital defense benefit from expedited habeas review. See 28 U.S.C. §§ 2261–2266. One of these provisions reads:

> This chapter is applicable if a State established by statute, rule of its court of last resort, or by another agency authorized by State law, a mechanism for the appointment, compensation, and payment of reasonable litigation expenses of competent counsel in State post-conviction proceedings brought by indigent prisoners whose capital convictions and sentences have been upheld on direct appeal to the court of last resort in the State or have otherwise become final for State law purposes. The rule of court or statute must provide standards for competency for the appointment of such counsel.

28 U.S.C. § 2261(b). Federal courts have held that states must not only adopt or certify opt-in preconditions, but that they must in fact comply with those requirements.[b]

Should a state in fact provide death row inmates such competent post-conviction counsel, several provisions would further limit federal habeas review of petitions filed by death row inmates. Rather than the one-year AEDPA statute of limitations, a 180-day statute of limitations would apply, just as the Powell Committee recommended. 28 U.S.C. § 2263(a). Intending, at least, to further expedite matters, the statute provided that the federal judge "shall render a final determination and enter a final judgment on any application . . . in a capital case not later than 180 days after the date on which the application is filed." 28 U.S.C. § 2266(b)(1)(A).

No state has successfully opted into those procedures. Although some states claimed to have complied with the requirements, federal courts disagreed.[c] Why do you think states have not opted in? Was the reward for opting in too small? Or did opting in require a state to enact an unnecessarily-expensive system for providing competent and reasonably well-compensated state counsel? Why do you think AEDPA's quid pro quo approach failed? See Betsy See Dee Sanders Parker, *The Antiterrorism and Effective Death Penalty Act ("AEDPA"): Understanding the Failures of State Opt-In Mechanisms*, 92 Iowa L. Rev. 1969 (2007).

---

[b] Cf. Spears v. Stewart, 283 F.3d 992, 997, 1002–04 (9th Cir. 2002) (finding that Arizona statute did not completely satisfy opt-in standards because of lengthy delays in appointment of counsel); Tucker v. Catoe, 221 F.3d 600, 604–05 (4th Cir. 2000) ("[A] state must not only enact a 'mechanism' and standards for post-conviction review counsel, but those mechanisms and standards must in fact be complied with before the state may invoke the time limitations of 28 U.S.C. § 2263.")

[c] See, e.g., Ashmus v. Woodford, 202 F.3d 1160, 1167 (9th Cir. 2000) ("The State of California has offered no evidence that . . . it had established by rule of its court of last resort or by statute a mechanism for the appointment, compensation and payment of reasonable expenses for collateral counsel.") (internal quotation marks omitted); Hall v. Luebbers, 341 F.3d 706, 712 (8th Cir. 2003) (rejecting Missouri's claim to comply with the opt-in provisions); Perillo v. Johnson, 205 F.3d 775, 793 (5th Cir. 2000) (rejecting Texas' claim to comply with the opt-in provisions).

Congress responded to state inaction by passing a revision to the opt-in procedures. The provision would permit the United States Attorney General (AG) to determine whether a State established "a mechanism for the appointment, compensation, and payment of reasonable litigation expenses of competent counsel" in state habeas proceedings by indigent death row prisoners. The provision also limits the authority of federal courts to review whether a state successfully opted in, by placing exclusive and *de novo* review of such determinations in the D.C. Circuit. See USA Patriot Improvement and Reauthorization Act of 2005, Pub. L. No. 109–177, 120 Stat. 192, 250 (codified at 28 U.S.C. § 2261(b) (2006)). The new provisions appeared to remove two previously-imposed conditions for opt-in status: reasonable compensation of appointed counsel and actual adequacy of counsel. Although the AG drafted procedures for assessing the competency of state counsel, 28 U.S.C. § 2265(b), with final regulations published in 2008, Certification Process for State Capital Counsel Systems, 73 Fed. Reg. 75, 327 (Dec. 11, 2008), the regulations were challenged in federal court, and they did not take effect.[d] AEDPA's opt-in provisions remain dormant.

8) Scholarly Proposals. Scholars continue to bemoan the configuration and efficacy of federal habeas corpus review. For example, Professor Larry Yackle calls the area an "intellectual disaster area." Larry W. Yackle, *The Figure in the Carpet*, 78 Tex. L. Rev. 1731, 1765 (2000). Professor Yackle suggests that "we need to take a deep breath, recognize the mess we have made of things, and start over." Larry W. Yackle, *State Convicts and Federal Courts: Reopening the Habeas Corpus Debate*, 91 Cornell L. Rev. 541, 542, 553 (2006). He proposes that federal district courts be given the authority to review state convictions directly—after review in state court concludes—thereby avoiding any *Teague*-like bar. He proposes that, because such a regime would allow unencumbered, mandatory federal review of a conviction before it becomes final, any subsequent federal habeas review would be quite limited. Ask yourself a couple of questions about Professor Yackle's proposal. First, why would it avoid the *Teague* bar? Second, would the proposal really mollify those concerned about federal interference in state criminal process?

Professor Jordan Steiker has offered a different proposal, limited to death penalty cases, but it also involves a larger direct-review role for federal appellate courts courts. See Jordan Steiker, *Restructuring Post-Conviction Review of Federal Constitutional Claims Raised by State Prisoners: Confronting the New Face of Excessive Proceduralism*, 1998 U. Chi. Legal F. 315, 320–21 (the proposal would "[a]llow all state death-row inmates to litigate record federal constitutional claims in the federal courts of appeal immediately after relief is denied by the highest state court on direct review."). Consider another issue, which you might fairly consider in conjunction with Professor Yackle's proposal: in what ways is review by federal appeals courts different from certiorari proceedings in the Supreme Court, the latter of which is also direct review?

---

[d] Habeas Corpus Res. Ctr. v. U.S. Dep't of Justice, No. C 08–2649 CW, 2009 WL 185423, at *4 (N.D. Cal. Jan. 20, 2009). For a detailed discussion of the development of these regulations and efforts to challenge them, see Casey C. Kannenberg, *Wading Through The Morass Of Modern Federal Habeas Review Of State Capital Prisoners' Claims*, 28 Quinnipiac L. Rev. 107 (2009). The Obama administration subsequently sought to withdraw the final regulations. See Certification Process for State Capital Counsel Systems: Removal of Final Rule, 75 Fed. Reg. 29,217 (May 25, 2010). The Attorney General has never determined that any state has successfully complied by providing sufficiently competent counsel for death row prisoners during state post-conviction proceedings.

Professor James Liebman has proposed that a more expansive approach be adopted to provide better representation and resources on the front end of criminal process. Professor Liebman's approach focuses on trial representation in capital cases, and not on state post-conviction litigation; he provides a "plan for (1) narrowing the range of cases that are charged capitally, (2) carefully testing capital charges at trial, and (3) narrowing post-trial review of the fewer and more reliable capital sentences that result." James Liebman, *The Overproduction of Death*, 100 Colum. L. Rev. 2030, 2156 (2000); see also James S. Liebman, *Opting for Real Death Penalty Reform*, 63 Ohio St. L.J. 315 (2002) (supporting a similar proposal). Allocating greater trial resources to a more limited set of capital trials would, Professor Liebman argues, justify back-end restrictions on the relitigation of capital sentencing questions.[e]

Professors Joseph Hoffman and Nancy King offered a related-but-broader proposal in an article and then a book, but without any formal tradeoff. They argued: "Not only is habeas futile, it is expensive for both federal and state taxpayers. One out of every fourteen civil cases filed in federal district court is a habeas challenge by a state prisoner. Most of these cases are not summarily dismissed." Joseph L. Hoffmann and Nancy J. King, *Rethinking the Federal Role in State Criminal Justice*, 84 N.Y.U. L. Rev. 89 (2009); see also Nancy J. King and Joseph L. Hoffmann, *Habeas for the Twenty-First Century: Uses, Abuses, and the Future of the Great Writ* (2011) (discussing proposal in greater detail). In their book, they observe that, "[f]or the vast majority of the more than two million people now incarcerated in America, the Great Writ is a pipe dream." Professors Hoffman and King proposed to eliminate post-conviction habeas review for all noncapital prisoners, provided the federal government increased funding for indigent defense and preserved review for claims of actual innocence.

In response, Professors John H. Blume, Sheri Lynn Johnson and Keir M. Weyble wrote that, although "the existing system of habeas review for non-capital cases is not without problems and could stand to be improved in a variety of ways," it still serves important purposes. John H. Blume, Sheri Lynn Johnson and Keir M. Weyble. *In Defense of Noncapital Habeas: A Reply to Hoffman and King*, 96 Cornell L. Rev. 435, 439 (2011). They disagreed with Hoffman and King's interpretation of empirical data suggesting low reversal rates in non-capital habeas filings. Professor Blume et al. argued: "If the prospect of subsequent federal habeas review were removed, there is every reason to believe that relief rates in state courts would go down, not because the number of deserving cases would be lessened, but because a key incentive for state courts to acknowledge and remedy constitutional error would be absent." They also ask "why states should be trusted to institute reforms without an incentive," particularly when states did not do so in response to AEDPA's opt-in procedures. What lessons should we take from the failure of AEDPA's opt-in procedures? Professor Blume et al. observed that "federal habeas has something genuinely important to offer the non-capital state prisoner who manages to avoid or overcome the procedural traps: a new review of the issues by a life-tenured, Article III judge."

---

[e] For another detailed quid pro quo reform proposal focusing on death penalty litigation, see Andrew Hammel, *Diabolical Federalism: A Functional Critique and Proposed Reconstruction of Death Penalty Federal Habeas*, 39 Am. Crim. L. Rev. 1, 42 (2002).

One of the authors of this Book argued that, although Hoffman and King "correctly observe that state criminal and post-conviction representation is abysmal," how to change federal habeas corpus to address that concern is a very different question. See Lee Kovarsky, *Habeas Verité,* 47 Tulsa L. Rev. 13, 18 (2011). If it were true that so few habeas litigants prevail because meritorious claims are dismissed, then "society would want fewer habeas restrictions, not more." Further, Professor Kovarsky agues that, at least historically speaking, "habeas has primarily been a vehicle for judges to rule on what kinds of imprisonment were unlawful." Do you think, as Professors King and Hoffman argue, that the states are unlikely to give short shrift to certain constitutional protections?

Regardless of whether you think proposals that Congress eliminate all or most post-conviction review of state convictions are sound policy, do you think that the Supreme Court would find such an elimination of post-conviction review constitutional under the Suspension Clause? Others suggest the opposite approach: solving the problem of costly and protracted capital litigation by abolishing the death penalty. The American Law Institute adopted that view in 2010, noting the decline in the use of the death penalty and citing to "unsuccessful efforts to constitutionally regulate the death penalty." See Carol S. Steiker and Jordan M. Steiker, *Part II: Report to the ALI Concerning Capital Punishment,* 89 Tex. L. Rev. 367, 420 (2010) (recommending abolition, and describing not only burdens on the post-conviction process, but how in some states "the burdens imposed by capital cases on appellate courts compromise the ability of those courts to manage their competing commitments on the civil and non-capital side.").

9)　Structural Reform Litigation. Others have proposed new mechanisms to allow federal habeas judges to address structural deficiencies, beyond the ability to simply grant relief in individual cases. See, e.g., Eve Brensike Primus, *A Structural Vision of Habeas Corpus,* 98 Cal. L. Rev. 1 (2010) (proposing that habeas review be reconfigured to facilitate structural reform in states with widespread constitutional problems in criminal adjudication). Recall Chapter 11's discussion of civil procedure and habeas procedure. Section 1983 permits "systemic" litigation because the Federal Rules of Civil Procedure allow class actions; in contrast, the federal habeas ruls make bringing such cases difficult. Professor Primus argues that "one important function of the Great Writ is to prevent states from ignoring defendants' federal rights systematically." Professor Primus proposes that a prisoner be permitted "to come forward with some evidence that the error in his case was part of a pattern of errors and not simply an individual mistake." Federal judges would be empowered to conduct an evidentiary hearing and to craft injunctive remedies in order to address systemic patterns of constitutional violations. Should federal judges focus more on systemic violations than on ad hoc or idiosyncratic errors? Cf. Ann Woolhandler, *Demodeling Habeas,* 45 Stan. L. Rev. 575 (1993) (describing Supreme Court efforts "to deny remedies when violations occur through ad hoc official illegality, while constitutional violations occurring under statutes or through continuing policies are more readily subject to full review").

In fact, at one time, inmates actually used collective actions to raise systemic challenges; habeas class actions, however, have disappeared over the past two decades. See Note, *Multiparty Federal Habeas Corpus,* 81 Harv. L. Rev. 1482, 1491 (1968). These habeas class actions became impossible once procedural bars such as exhaustion and abuse of the writ started to corrode the common interests of potential classes. See Brandon L. Garrett, *Aggregation in Criminal Law*, 95 Calif. L. Rev. 383 (2007). Can you see why habeas class actions are now problematic? As Professor Garrett explains, however, the trend away from habeas class actions has not entirely stopped courts from experimenting with structural remedies in remarkable ways. For example, some trial courts have conducted system-wide inquiries into IAC claims, by consolidating cases before trial.[f] Higher state courts have also conducted state-wide inquiries into misconduct at forensic crime laboratories, and then granted state post-conviction relief to affected prisoners. See, e.g., In re an Investigation of The W. Va. State Police Crime Lab., Serology Div., 438 S.E.2d 501, 502–03 (W. Va. 1993) (reporting results of an audit of crime lab work that state supreme court ordered following a wrongful conviction, and ordering reexamination of additional closed cases and the certification of the crime lab by an accrediting agency). Although most examples come from state courts, federal courts also experiment with collectivized post-conviction inquiry—particularly when judges can consolidate cases. Judge Jack Weinstein, of the United States District Court for the Eastern District of New York, for example, appointed a Special Master to review the entire backlog of hundreds of federal habeas petitions in the District. See In re Habeas Corpus Cases, 298 F. Supp. 2d 303, 317 (E.D.N.Y. 2003). Do you think that post-conviction process should have a broader systemic focus than that implicated by individual cases? Do you think that judges should specialize and encourage other judges to send cases to a Special Master? Or do these administrative and public law models undermine the traditional model of an individual judge examining the custody of an individual prisoner?

NOTES ON HABEAS AND THE ROLE OF COUNSEL

1) The Sixth Amendment. Under modern retroactivity jurisprudence, one of the two exceptions to the rule against retroactivity is for "watershed" rules of criminal procedure. See Teague v. Lane, 489 U.S. 288, 311 (1989). The Warren Court decided *Gideon v. Wainwright,* 372 U.S. 335 (1963), recognizing an indigent felony defendant's Sixth Amendment right to counsel. *Gideon* is the only criminal procedure decision the Court has been able to specify as a "watershed" ruling. See Whorton v. Bockting, 549 U.S. 406, 417, 421 (2007). A consistent theme across post-conviction law is that judges must reckon with the quality of lawyering provided to criminal defendants. Context-specific questions about the performance of a prisoner's lawyer are not yet a central theme in national-security-detention law. Although the *Hamdi* plurality did not reach whether the prisoner was entitled to a lawyer, it did pause to note that, during the early phases of his legal challenge, he had been denied counsel. In *Boumediene*, the Court distinguished prior military commission trials—with adversary hearings and in which detainees were represented by counsel—from the Combatant Status Review Tribunal (CSRT) process in which detainees received "personal representatives" but not lawyers. There is some focus on a right-to-counsel in im-

---

[f] See, e.g., State v. Peart, 621 So. 2d 780 (La. 1993) (finding that procedures for the provision of "indigent defense services in Section E of Orleans Criminal District Court is in many respects so lacking that defendants who must depend on it are not likely to be receiving the reasonably effective assistance of counsel the constitution guarantees"). Courts have conducted state-wide proportionality review of death penalty charging. See, e.g., In re Proportionality Review Project II, 757 A.2d 168 (N.J. 2000); In re Proportionality Review Project, 735 A.2d 528, 532–33 (N.J. 1999).

migration proceedings. While in immigration proceedings at the BIA, noncitizens do not have a right to appointed counsel; in *Padilla v. Kentucky,* 559 U.S. 356 (2010), however, the Court held that noncitizens have a right to be effectively advised, during plea bargaining in criminal cases, as to collateral immigration consequences of a conviction.

2) The Impact of Right to Counsel on Post-Conviction Litigation. In the state post-conviction setting, the quality of lawyering (or the lack thereof) is a pervasive problem. The Supreme Court has held, however, that there is no right to effective assistance of counsel during post-conviction proceedings. As a result, post-conviction litigants are mostly *pro se*, but must comply with highly-technical legal rules. Moreover, a state post-conviction setting, where the prisoner is ordinarily unrepresented, is the very forum in which the prisoner is usually capable of and permitted to challenge the ineffective assistance of their trial lawyer. That circumstance created the bind that the Court tried to address in *Martinez v. Ryan,* 132 S.Ct. 1309 (U.S. 2012). *Martinez* emphasized the importance of being able to assert such claims at the initial level of state review, and excusing forfeiture of "substantial" IAC claims if the forfeiture was itself the result of deficient state post-conviction representation.

Despite the modest exception created to remedy inadvertent state habeas waiver of IAC claims, IAC claims are by no means easy to win. IAC inquiry entails deferential collateral review of counsel's performance, and also requires that the claimant make a difficult prejudice showing. At the same time, however, IAC claims are the most commonly-raised post-conviction challenge. One reason may be their breadth. IAC claims can involve a wide range of theories about what went wrong at the criminal trial—so long as those failures can be attributed to defense counsel. In fact, the Supreme Court recently expanded the scope of Sixth Amendment effective-assistance requirements to all "critical" phases of the criminal process, including plea bargaining. See Lafler v. Cooper, 132 S. Ct. 1376 (U.S. 2012); Missouri v. Frye, 132 S. Ct. 1399 (U.S. 2012).

3) Reconsidering the Role Post-Conviction Counsel. Do the Supreme Court and Congress need to rethink the role of post-conviction counsel, particularly with respect to IAC claims? Is bolstering post-conviction representation a way to ensure higher-quality representation at all phases of the criminal process? If the quality of the representation throughout the criminal process improves, does that diminish the need for post-conviction litigation? Are there other ways to ensure that criminal defendants receive sound representation, aside from providing hard-to-come-by money to pay for lawyers? Could enhanced discovery from the prosecution, or more judicial supervision and screening of evidence, also help to ensure fairer and more accurate outcomes? Could interventions into the plea bargaining process improve outcomes to lessen the need for post-conviction scrutiny of lawyering?

––––––

NOTES ON NATIONAL SECURITY COURTS

1) National Security Courts. In the national-security-detention context, scholars have proposed the creation of specialized courts, using federal judges, to apply specific procedures for reviewing national-security detention.[g] Imagine

––––––

[g] See, e.g., Glenn Sulmasy, *The National Security Court System: A Natural Evolution of Justice in an Age of Terror* 175–93 (2009); Benjamin Wittes, *Law and the Long War: The Fu-*

that such a court would have highly streamlined procedures, perhaps like the CSRT process. What if the court provided detainees with advisers but no lawyers, and little in the way of any discovery? Recall that *Boumediene* emphasized the "deference" that is appropriate where there exists sufficient prior judicial process; the national security detention courts would provide judicial process, administered by Article III judges. *Boumediene* also emphasized other constitutionally-required features of national security detention litigation—for example, access to exculpatory evidence was "constitutionally required." *Boumediene* also added that military courts, for example, might provide the requisite process only if they had a sufficiently "adversarial structure," including a provision for appointed counsel.

2)   Pros and Cons. What are the arguments in favor of creating a national-security court? Would such a court focus on substantive questions and policy more than federal judges have in the federal judges' rulings on habeas petitions? See Jenny S. Martinez, *Process and Substance in the "War on Terror,"* 108 Colum. L. Rev. 1013 (2008) (criticizing reluctance to reach substantive questions in national security detention litigation). What are the arguments in favor of continuing to adjudicate national-security-detention cases using habeas corpus? How should a court rule on the constitutionality of such a national-security court?

3)   Other Specialized National-Security Courts. Recall from Chapter 7 that, in 1996, Congress enacted legislation providing for a specialized Alien Terrorist Removal Court (ATRC), which would offer specialized procedures—more sensitive to concerns regarding classified information—in removal proceedings. Those ATRC procedures, however, remain dormant. Are there other types of national-security-related procedures for which you can imagine a need to create an alternative to regularly-constituted courts with habeas corpus review? Or as a result of habeas litigation, has the D.C. Circuit, together with the U.S. District Court for the District of Columbia, in effect become our national security court?

NOTES ON STATE HABEAS REFORM

1)   State Post-conviction Statutes. Federal post-conviction procedure is determined in part by the state proceedings that come before federal review. Exhaustion rules turn on the availability of state remedies; procedural default law requires an inquiry into the circumstances surrounding state forfeiture; and the statute of limitations tolls during the pendency of "properly filed" state post-conviction applications. In other words, how state proceedings unfold affects how well federal judges can do their jobs, as well as the deference that those prior state proceedings receive. In particular, *Martinez* created incentives for state courts reviewing habeas petitions to ensure that state post-conviction lawyers develop "substantial" IAC claims. *Cullen v. Pinholster*, 131 S.Ct. 1388 (2011), created incentives for inmates to exhaust not only their claims, but also the factual evidence in state proceedings. How do you feel about the proposition

---

ture of Justice in the Age of Terrorism 176–78 (2008); Jack Goldsmith & Neal Katyal, *The Terrorist' Court*, N.Y. Times, July 11, 2007. But see Stephen I. Vladeck, *The Case Against National Security Courts*, 45 Willamette L. Rev. 505 (2009).

that the teeth of federal procedural obstacles are sharper when state process is sufficient? How often is state process sufficient?

2) Blurring the Lines between Appellate and Post-Conviction Review. Some states have also created expedited post-conviction review of capital sentences. Because no state has successfully opted in to the AEDPA fast-track provisions, there is no comparable expedited federal post-conviction process. Some states have created other ways to raise factual challenges and claims of innocence in consolidated appeals—seeking to expedite consideration of factual issues even before the conviction becomes final upon the conclusion of direct review. See Keith A. Findley, *Innocence Protection in the Appellate Process*, 93 Marq. L. Rev. 591, 604 (2009). Of course, state post-conviction review is fairly cursory, infrequently involves evidentiary hearings, and usually results in summary dispositions. At what stage of criminal process should our society invest most in evidentiary review and factual investigation—during trials, appeals, state post-conviction proceedings, or federal habeas proceedings?

3) Laboratories of Experimentation. States are also laboratories of habeas experimentation, which might provide lessons for federal habeas design. State post-conviction statutes are of fairly recent vintage, and some parts of them are smaller-scale experiments. In Chapter 3, we discussed how, in response to the advent of modern DNA testing, states created new "writs of innocence" and other statutory vehicles for state judges to consider newly-discovered evidence of innocence and to order DNA testing. State limitations statutes have become more forgiving in cases involving newly-discovered evidence of innocence, particularly in comparison to their federal habeas corpus counterpart, 28 U.S.C. § 2244(d).

NOTES ON INNOCENCE COMMISSIONS

1) The Concept of Innocence Commissions. One response to failures of the criminal justice system has been to convene blue-ribbon commissions to study problems and suggest reforms. Professor Barry Scheck and Peter Neufeld, the founders of the Innocence Project, have argued that, "[i]n the United States, there are strict and immediate investigative measures taken when an airplane falls from the sky, a plane's fuel tank explodes on the runway, or a train derails," but that, "[t]he American criminal justice system, in sharp contrast, has no institutional mechanism to evaluate its equivalent of a catastrophic plane crash, the conviction of an innocent person." However, "reforms recommended by study commissions, which are mainstream, sensible, and bipartisan, seem to be ignored." Barry C. Scheck & Peter J. Neufeld, *Toward the Formation of "Innocence Commissions" in America*, 86 Judicature 98, 104 n.24 (2002). Rather than simply convene blue-ribbon commissions, they called for the creation of "Innocence Commissions" that would serve as standing bodies to conduct formal inquiries and recommend reforms. Just as states have standing sentencing commissions to draft sentencing guidelines, or crime commissions to examine issues of importance to law enforcement, an Innocence Commission would serve to investigate ways to improve the accuracy of the criminal justice system. In response to wrongful convictions, several states have created such entities.

2)   The CCRC Model. One model came from the United Kingdom. In 1997, the UK created a Criminal Cases Revision Commission to serve as an independent executive agency with full subpoena power to review convictions. It cannot reverse convictions, but refers cases to appellate courts, recommending that convictions be vacated—and many hundreds of convictions in the U.K. have been reversed as a result. See Criminal Cases Review Commission, at www.ccrc.gov.uk/about.htm/ (last visited Mar. 14, 2013); see also Jerome M. Maiatico, *All Eyes on Us: A Comparative Critique of the North Carolina Innocence Inquiry Commission,* 56 Duke L.J. 1345 (2007) (comparing North Carolina and U.K. commissions).

3)   The Inquiry Model. In Canada, a person can request that the Minister of Justice convene a Criminal Conviction Review Group (made up of attorneys from the Canadian Department of Justice) to examine cases and make recommendations to the minister. See Canada Criminal Code, R.S.C., ch. C-46, § 696.1-696.6 (1985) (providing procedures for the Minister to conduct special reviews of criminal cases and correct wrongful convictions.) The Minister can order a new trial or hearing, or refer a case to a court. The Minister can also order a formal inquiry examining what caused a wrongful conviction. Several inquiry reports have recommended and led to the implementation of sweeping reforms. See, e.g., Hon. Fred Kaufman, *Report of the Kaufman Commission on Proceedings Involving Guy Paul Morin* (1998) (making 119 recommendations for reforms, including regarding the admissibility and regulation of forensic science and the reliability of informant testimony).

4)   North Carolina Commissions. In North Carolina, a series of high-profile DNA exonerations lead to the creation, in 2002, of a North Carolina Actual Innocence Commission, tasked with both recommending changes to improve criminal procedure and creating a mechanism to investigate claims of innocence. See Christine C. Mumma, *"The North Carolina Actual Innocence Commission: Unknown Perspectives Joined by a Common Cause,"* 52 Drake L. Rev. 647 (2004). The Commission quickly assessed practices in the state regarding eyewitness identifications, leading to the enactment of an Eyewitness Identification Reform Act. See N.C. Gen. Stat. § 15A- 284.50–53 (2002). At the urging of commission members, North Carolina then enacted a law that required the recording of interrogations in homicide cases, enhanced the preservation of evidence and access to DNA testing, and expanded post-exoneration support for the wrongfully convicted. See N.C. Gen. Stat. § 15A- 211 (2009).

Based on the Commission's work, North Carolina created a second Commission in 2006: the North Carolina Innocence Inquiry Commission. See N.C. Gen. Stat. § 15A-1460–75 (2006). A panel of eight members serving three-year terms and including a judge, prosecutor, criminal defense lawyer, sheriff, victim's advocate, and members of the public, conducts innocence-based inquiries into criminal convictions. The Commission director administers rules for screening cases and coordinates the investigations. If five of the eight panel members agree that a defendant deserves judicial review, the Chief Justice of the North Carolina Supreme Court appoints a three-judge panel, which may vacate the conviction if they unanimously agree there is "clear and convincing evidence" of factual innocence. The Inquiry Commission has recommended judicial review in several cases and has screened hundreds. In 2010, the Inquiry Commission recommended that Gregory Taylor be exonerated, and after the three-judge panel agreed, he became the first person exonerated due to the work of an innocence commission in the United States.[h]

5) Other Innocence Commissions. Outside North Carolina, no states have established administrative bodies designed to review innocence cases. More than ten other states have created or begun to create innocence commissions, but they all lack formal power either to make recommendations or to review cases. Some commissions have nonetheless issued influential policy recommendations and reports. For example, the Illinois Commission on Capital Punishment issued a detailed report with recommendations, some of which were incorporated in legislation, including a requirement that homicide interrogations be videotaped. See 725 Ill. Comp. Stat. Ann. 5/103–2.1 (2006). A California commission recommended comprehensive reform that the legislature passed, but the Governor vetoed them.[i]

6) A Proposed Federal Criminal Justice Commission. Meanwhile, the U.S. Senate did not vote on a proposal to create a National Criminal Justice Commission, which would have more broadly examined reforms to the criminal justice system.[j]

7) Innocence-Based Reform. With some subtle changes, courts could accommodate innocence claims within the existing structure of habeas law, and without adding new entities to review convictions. As noted throughout this Book, some scholars have argued that innocence claims be given priority in federal post-conviction review, and that federal post-conviction review even be restricted to litigation of innocence claims. See, e.g., Henry J. Friendly, *Is Innocence Irrelevant? Collateral Attack on Criminal Judgments*, 38 U. Chi. L. Rev. 142 (1970) (arguing that colorable claims of factual innocence should be the central focus of federal habeas corpus review); John C. Jeffries, Jr. & William J. Stuntz, *Ineffective Assistance and Procedural Default in Federal Habeas Corpus*, 57 U. Chi. L. Rev. 679, 680, 691–92 (1990) (arguing that the question when reviewing otherwise defaulted ineffective assistance of counsel claims should be "whether consideration of a defaulted claim would present a realistic possibility of correcting an unjust conviction or sentence of death"). Although federal habeas statutes permit prisoners with innocence claims to proceed, they do so only by removing procedural bars to litigation of other constitutional challenges, and not by providing relief based on innocence alone. (Innocence is necessary but not sufficient to habeas relief.) In contrast, state and federal DNA-access and writ-of-innocence-type statutes, discussed in Chapters 3 and 6, do allow inmates to obtain and courts to consider new evidence of innocence. What role should innocence play in federal habeas corpus? If the Supreme Court were to

---

[h] See Robbie Brown, *Judges Free Inmate on Recommendation of Special Panel*, New York Times, February 17, 2010.

[i] See Stanley Z. Fisher, *Convictions of Innocent Persons in Massachusetts: An Overview*, 12 B.U. Pub. Int. L.J. 1 (2002); John T. Rago, *A Fine Line between Chaos & Creation: Lessons on Innocence Reform from the Pennsylvania Eight*, 12 Widener L. Rev. 359 (2006); Radley Balko, "Schwarzenegger Vetoes Justice," FOXNews.com, November 5, 2007; *Innocence Commissions in the U.S.*, at www.innocenceproject.org/Content/415.php (last visited Mar. 14, 2013); Cal. Comm'n on the Fair Admin. of Justice, Final Report (2008), at www.ccfaj.org/documents/CCFAJFinalReport.pdf (last visited Mar. 14, 2013); New York State Justice Task Force, http://www.nyjusticetaskforce.com/ (last visited Mar. 14, 2013); Commission on Capital Punishment, State of Illinois, *Report of the Governor's Commission on Capital Punishment* (2002), at www.idoc.state.il.us/ccp/ccp/reports/commissionreport/index.htm (last visited Mar. 14, 2013).

[j] See S. 714, National Criminal Justice Commission Act of 2010.

recognize a freestanding innocence claim, in what situations would that holding make a difference?

2. REVISITING THE CONSTITUTIONAL STRUCTURE OF HABEAS CORPUS

CONCLUDING NOTES ON THE SUSPENSION CLAUSE

1)   **After *Boumediene*.** Recall how Justice Scalia expressed perhaps the most restrictive view of the Suspension Clause in his dissent in *INS v. St. Cyr*, arguing that the Suspension Clause "does not guarantee any content to (or even the existence of) the writ of habeas corpus." 533 U.S. 280, 337 (2001) (Scalia, J., dissenting). Does that view comport with the interpretations of the Suspension Clause that we have seen across different areas of habeas jurisprudence—immigration custody, civil detention law, national-security detention, and post-conviction review? The Supreme Court basically avoided the subject prior to *Boumediene*, stating, for example, that the Suspension Clause might "at the absolute minimum" protect the writ "as it existed in 1789." *St. Cyr*, 533 U.S. at 315.

What made *Boumediene* so striking was that, for the first time, the Supreme Court held that the Constitution extended, to certain persons, "the fundamental procedural protections of habeas corpus." *Boumediene v. Bush*, 553 U.S. 723, 798 (2008). Prior to *Boumediene*, the Court had consistently avoided addressing whether the Constitution affirmatively guarantees some access to habeas corpus. But what does that holding mean, and does it apply to any other forms of custody that we have studied? When the Court says that "[h]abeas is at its core a remedy for unlawful executive detention," *Munaf v. Geren*, 553 U.S. 674, 693 (2008), does that mean that the Suspension Clause does less work outside the executive detention context? *Boumediene* was certainly careful to say that post-conviction review is different, because federal judges defer to a prior criminal proceeding in an Article III court.

2)   **Impact on Immigration Habeas.** Recall questions about whether the existing mechanisms for reviewing immigration custody may, after *St. Cyr*, be constrained by the Suspension Clause. At a minimum, *St. Cyr* suggests that there must be some judicial review in the federal appeals courts—even if that review is not denominated as a habeas corpus proceeding. The Second Circuit has adopted a more flexible view of the mixed questions it could review in removal proceedings, citing to the Suspension Clause:

> The Conference Report makes clear that Congress, in enacting the REAL ID Act, sought to avoid the constitutional concerns outlined by the Supreme Court in St. Cyr, which stated that as a result of the Suspension Clause, "some judicial intervention in deportation cases is unquestionably required by the Constitution . . . ."

Chen v. U.S., 471 F.3d 315, 326 (2d Cir. 2006) (quoting *St. Cyr*, 533 U.S. at 300). Broad review of status claims—when the prisoner argues that they are a citizen, for example—receive *de novo* review under the immigration statutes, and Congress preserved habeas review over status-related questions for expedited removal proceedings. See 8 U.S.C. § 1252(b)(5)(B); 8 U.S.C. § 1252(e)(2). In contrast, for criminal aliens that have previously been convicted, the REAL-

ID Act sharply limits review to questions of law and constitutional questions. Does this limitation reflect some view of the Suspension Clause?

3)　The Suspension Clause and Post-Conviction Habeas. What role does the Suspension Clause play in post-conviction proceedings, in which there has been a prior criminal trial (or a guilty plea)? Is there any analogy involving the concept of "innocence" in the immigration-habeas context (arguing that I am a citizen and cannot be deported), the national security detention context (I am not an enemy combatant), and the post-conviction context (I did not commit the crime)—or do the substantive and procedural differences demand different treatment of the factual questions raised in each area?

Professor Gerald Neuman has suggested that, after *Boumediene,* the Supreme Court's failure to recognize a freestanding innocence claim may stand on weaker constitutional ground. See Gerald L. Neuman, *The Habeas Corpus Suspension Clause after* Boumediene v. Bush, 110 Colum. L. Rev. 537, 563–64 (2010). Do you think Professor Neuman is right? Will the Court ever revisit *Herrera v. Collins,* 506 U.S. 390 (1993), the case that most extensively discussed the possibility of a freestanding innocence claim? Recall that the Court has had multiple chances to do so and continues to assume for the sake of argument only that some freestanding innocence claim might exist under the Constitution.

4)　History. How should the history of the Suspension Clause influence the analysis? The Supreme Court describes habeas corpus as "a writ antecedent to statute, and throwing its root deep into the genius of the common law." Williams v. Kaiser, 323 U.S. 471, 484 n.2 (1945). In an influential piece of scholarship, Professors Paul D. Halliday and G. Edward White describe how the Suspension Clause incorporated the English common law writ. See *The Suspension Clause: English Text, Imperial Contexts, and American Implications,* 94 Va. L. Rev. 575 (2008). Professor Halliday's work has been particularly influential in generating scholarly reconsideration of the nature and practice of the common-law habeas writ. See Stephen I. Vladeck, *The New Habeas Revisionism,* 124 Harv. L. Rev. 941, 966–78 (2011).

The Supreme Court often relies on common-law history of the writ—but even if the common-law writ predated statutes, modern statutes are here to stay. Post-conviction statutes like AEDPA, immigration statutes like the REAL-ID act, or national security statutes like the MCA all raise quite novel issues. In each area we have studied, there is a separation-of-powers issue involving the degree to which Congress may limit the habeas authority of federal judges. Do you think that judges should retain a common-law habeas power if the Framers had such a power in mind? Now consider the premise: having read the materials in this Book, do you believe that the historical record yields precise answers regarding what the Framers meant when they drafted the Suspension Clause?

Is the constitutionally-or-statutorily-required function of the writ frozen in time? Or does the constitutionally-required scope of the habeas writ evolve? Could judges invoke that historical evolution to assert authority to review custody, and to resist statutory incursions? Are judges foreclosed from assertion of such authority if the "evolving" paradigm is rejected? Could judges act more like common law judges did, by using more flexible procedures? Cf. Eric M. Freedman, *Habeas Corpus in Three Dimensions: Dimension I: Habeas as a Common Law Writ,* 46 Harv C.R.-C.L. L. Rev. 591, 595, 617 (2011) (describing the emergence of American habeas practice from a system of common law writs and suggesting that modern judges give more consideration to "the history of habeas corpus as a common law writ."). Consider the argument that we now live in an era of statutes, in which Congress supervises and defines the work of federal judges. In what ways does that proposition bear theories of enhanced executive power, under which both Congress and the judiciary defer to the executive in national-security matters, including military and national-security detention?

5)   A POW Detention Hypothetical. Imagine a future conflict during which the military detains tens of thousands of POWs. Each POW receives procedure commensurate with that status, including, if the status is unclear, military hearings under Article 5 of the Geneva Conventions. Such hearings may be quite rudimentary, however, involving a "competent tribunal," but with no specific procedures required by the Geneva Conventions. Suppose that thousands of the POWs demand access to habeas review and then file habeas petitions. They claim that they were not combatants fighting for an enemy state, but that they were private mercenaries or noncombatants and should be released. What should a federal judge do? Should the judge rule that the competent-tribunal screening by the military, following army regulations, is sufficient? Should federal habeas review be available? Should the answer depend on where the POWs are detained? Should it depend on other practical factors?

6)   Post-Conviction Hypotheticals. Imagine that, as in the prior hypothetical, thousands of North Carolina inmates seek post-conviction review. All were convicted in part because of forensic evidence that had been tested at the North Carolina Crime Lab. They all file habeas petitions arguing that the crime lab—now closed due to a major scandal—botched the fingerprint, blood-work, DNA, or other forensics in their cases. They argue that the scandal has, for the first time, brought to light these systemic laboratory errors. They argue that the § 2244(d) limitations periods applicable to the laboratory-related claims are just starting, for at least two reasons: because the new information provides the factual predicate for their claims and because evidence of misconduct had been concealed from their lawyers. For some prisoners, this petition would be successive (and, for many of those, it would contain new claims); for others, this petition would be their first. As an administrative matter, how should the district court handle these habeas cases? Should the court appoint a single judge to handle them, and should the judge appoint a Special Master? Should there be consolidated evidentiary hearings? Or should the cases be taken one at a time?

Now consider a second post-conviction scenario. What if a state prisoner files a federal petition and argues that, after *Pinholster*, the state court employed inadequate fact-finding procedures and did not conduct an evidentiary hearing. Suppose that, because of *Pinholster*, the federal court does not let the prisoner develop the facts surrounding the claim. Could the prisoner argue that the Constitution prevents such an interpretation of AEDPA, which would be the final step precluding any fact-development of a constitutional claim? Could the prisoner rely on *Boumediene* in making the argument that some factual review is required by the Constitution? See Samuel R. Wiseman, *Habeas After Pinholster*, 53 B.C. L. Rev. 953, 994–95 (2012). How do you interpret the *Boumediene* language that "the necessary scope of habeas review in part depends upon the rigor of any earlier proceedings"? How does the fact that this is a *state* prisoner claim affect your answer? Could you be an "originalist" and still argue that *Boumediene* protects some form of habeas review for state prisoners?

CONCLUDING NOTES ON DUE PROCESS

1) Ubiquity of Due Process Claims. Habeas petitioners usually bring either "straightforward" due process claims, or other constitutional claims that are incorporated against the states via the Due Process Clause. Dating back to *Brown v. Allen*, 344 U.S. 443 (1953), these evolving due process and criminal procedure norms regulate and place stress on state criminal (and now collateral) adjudication.

2) Due Process Analysis. Recall a passage from *Boumediene,* where the Supreme Court suggested that the Due Process Clause influenced its analysis:

> The idea that the necessary scope of habeas review in part depends upon the rigor of any earlier proceedings accords with our test for procedural adequacy in the due process context. See Mathews v. Eldridge, 424 U.S. 319, 335 (1976) (noting that the Due Process Clause requires an assessment of, inter alia, "the risk of an erroneous deprivation of [a liberty interest] and the probable value, if any, of additional or substitute procedural safeguards").

That due process drives the constitutionally required scope of habeas review is a prominent theme in this Book. Due process questions focus on different issues than does habeas review, however. The Court emphasized how procedural due process rules generally seek to prevent "mistaken or unjustified deprivation of life, liberty, or property." Carey v. Piphus, 435 U.S. 247, 259 (1978).

3) Influence of the Inapplicability of Due Process. Does due process influence habeas corpus in a negative way—if the prisoner lacks due process rights, then will the prisoner lack habeas corpus rights as well? In its immigration rulings, the Court has focused on the distinction between admissibility—noncitizens deemed not yet admitted and therefore without due process rights—and noncitizens admitted but facing deportation, for whom more procedural protections attach. On the other hand, in *Boumediene*, the Court did not treat due process as a limit or a constraint on habeas corpus. Further, longstanding immigration rulings affirmed that habeas plays a limited role in requiring review of detention, despite the fact that detainees might lack due process rights. Do innocence-based exceptions to habeas procedural restrictions reflect a view of the role that habeas plays—or do they instead reflect a due process concern with accuracy in adjudication?

4) Should Due Process Affect Habeas Process? Scholars have argued that due process analysis should affect the quality and quantity of federal postconviction review. Professor Samuel Wiseman has argued that the Due Process Clause could guarantee a "fundamentally fair proceeding in the state postconviction process." Samuel R. Wiseman, *Habeas After Pinholster,* 53 B.C. L. Rev. 953, 999 (2012). Professor Justin Marceau has argued that the Due Process Clause compels federal habeas review of constitutional claims that did not receive "full and fair" state adjudication. See Justin F. Marceau, *Don't Forget Due Process: The Path Not (Yet) Taken in § 2254 Habeas Corpus Adjudications,* 62 Hastings L.J. 1, 4–5, 62–63 (2010). Other scholars distinguish the purposes of due process from habeas process. For the argument that due process focuses on the adequacy of the procedures used to place a person in custody, but habeas corpus focuses on judicial review of the authorization of each individual detention, see Brandon L. Garrett, *Habeas Corpus and Due Process,* 98 Cornell L. Rev. 47 (2012). Nevertheless, that view does not consider habeas and due process as unrelated. Habeas process may be far more important and robust when the scope of the prior process used to establish the custody of a prisoner was lacking.

———

CONCLUDING NOTES ON ARTICLE III

Do federal judges have a special constitutional responsibility, under Article III, to ensure that prisoners are detained only consistent with the U.S. Constitution and federal law? Recall from Chapter 5 Judge John T. Noonan's argument that Article III precluded Congress from using AEPDA provisions to unduly constrain the power of a federal judge to rule on whether the constitutional rights of a prisoner had been violated. What roles does Article III play in obligating, say, federal judges to conduct a certain level of review of habeas petitions? One of the authors of this Book has argued that "Article III combines with the Suspension Clause to guarantee habeas process and to specify the exclusive conditions by which Congress may restrict it." See Lee Kovarsky, *A Constitutional Theory of Habeas Power,* 97 Va. L. Rev. __ (forthcoming 2013). What cases have you read that support Professor Kovarsky's view that the combination of the Suspension Clause and Article III requires that federal judges be able to effectively review federal authority to detain a prisoner?

Outside the executive detention context, can an Article III theory explain the approach that the Supreme Court has taken towards interpreting statutes such as AEDPA? What cases that you have read suggest otherwise—that Article III does not create any such obligation of federal judges to independently review habeas petitions? For an argument that Article III combines with the Supremacy Clause to ensure some level of meaningful federal habeas review for state prisoners, see James S. Liebman and William F. Ryan, *"Some Effectual Power": The Quantity and Quality of Decisionmaking Required of Article III Courts,* 98 Colum. L. Rev. 696, 887 (1998).

———

CONCLUDING NOTE

We have brought together the different threads of habeas corpus law by asking whether they share something more than a focus on whether custody is legal. Who gets to ask the question, who gets to answer it, for which sovereigns, and—most importantly—what does the concept of "lawful custody" even mean? On the constitutional front, the Suspension Clause, Article III, and substantive constitutional rights work together to define the scope of the habeas privilege. On the statutory front, the scope and manner of applying the habeas remedy depends on a number of different provisions, the precise mix of which frequently turns on the custodial form at issue. Perhaps most importantly, modern habeas law represents the accumulated legacy of judging. The writ's form and function is the stuff of common-law judicial officers protecting their turf against insurgent courts; of Supreme Court Justices preserving federal judicial power to decide questions that other coordinate federal branches try to foreclose; of sovereign judiciaries working through the unique features of American federalism; and of judges trying to reconcile state power, security, and individual liberty. The Framers of the U.S. Constitution envisioned that habeas corpus would reprise its common law role in every day life and in national emergencies. Federal habeas rulings affect the most important matters of public policy, including crime control, defense lawyering, the death penalty, wrongful convictions, immigration, national security, military justice, and federalism. We hope that you now have a stronger grasp on why the position of habeas corpus in our modern legal environment remains as complex, contested, and as Great as ever.

STATUTORY APPENDIX

APPENDIX A

SELECTED PROVISIONS OF THE U.S. CONSTITUTION

ARTICLE I

SECTION 9, CL. 2. The Privilege of the Writ of Habeas Corpus shall not be suspended, unless when in Cases of Rebellion or Invasion the public Safety may require it.

ARTICLE III

SECTION 1. The judicial Power of the United States, shall be vested in one supreme Court, and in such inferior Courts as the Congress may from time to time ordain and establish. The Judges, both of the supreme and inferior Courts, shall hold their Offices during good Behaviour, and shall, at stated Times, receive for their Services, a Compensation, which shall not be diminished during their Continuance in Office.

SECTION 2. The judicial Power shall extend to all Cases, in Law and Equity, arising under this Constitution, the Laws of the United States, and Treaties made, or which shall be made, under their Authority;—to all Cases affecting Ambassadors, other public Ministers and Consuls;—to all Cases of admiralty and maritime Jurisdiction;—to Controversies to which the United States shall be a Party;—to Controversies between two or more States;—between a State and Citizens of another State;—between Citizens of different States;—between Citizens of the same State claiming Lands under Grants of different States, and between a State, or the Citizens thereof, and foreign States, Citizens or Subjects.

In all Cases affecting Ambassadors, other public Ministers and Consuls, and those in which a State shall be Party, the supreme Court shall have original Jurisdiction. In all the other Cases before mentioned, the supreme Court shall have appellate Jurisdiction, both as to Law and Fact, with such Exceptions, and under such Regulations as the Congress shall make.

AMENDMENT V

No person shall be held to answer for a capital, or otherwise infamous crime, unless on a presentment or indictment of a grand jury, except in cases arising in the land or naval forces, or in the militia, when in actual service in time of war or public danger; nor shall any person be subject for the same offense to be twice put in jeopardy of life or limb; nor shall be compelled in any criminal case to be a witness against himself, nor be deprived of life, liberty, or property, without due process of law; nor shall private property be taken for public use, without just compensation.

AMENDMENT VI

In all criminal prosecutions, the accused shall enjoy the right to a speedy and public trial, by an impartial jury of the state and district wherein the crime shall have been committed, which district shall have been previously ascertained by law, and to be informed of the nature and cause of the accusation; to be confronted with the witnesses against him; to have compulsory process for obtaining witnesses in his favor, and to have the assistance of counsel for his defense.

AMENDMENT XIV

SECTION 1. All persons born or naturalized in the United States, and subject to the jurisdiction thereof, are citizens of the United States and of the state wherein they reside. No state shall make or enforce any law which shall abridge the privileges or immunities of citizens of the United States; nor shall any state deprive any person of life, liberty, or property, without due process of law; nor deny to any person within its jurisdiction the equal protection of the laws.

APPENDIX B

SELECTED FEDERAL STATUTES

TITLE 8 U.S.C.:

§ 1252. Judicial review of orders of removal.

(a) Applicable provisions

    (1) General orders of removal

Judicial review of a final order of removal (other than an order of removal without a hearing pursuant to section 1225(b)(1) of this title) is governed only by chapter 158 of Title 28, except as provided in subsection (b) of this section and except that the court may not order the taking of additional evidence under section 2347(c) of such title.

    (2) Matters not subject to judicial review

        (A) Review relating to section 1225(b)(1) of this title

Notwithstanding any other provision of law (statutory or nonstatutory), including section 2241 of Title 28, or any other habeas corpus provision, and sections 1361 and 1651 of such title, no court shall have jurisdiction to review—

            (i) except as provided in subsection (e) of this section, any individual determination or to entertain any other cause or claim arising from or relating to the implementation or operation of an order of removal pursuant to section 1225(b)(1) of this title,

            (ii) except as provided in subsection (e) of this section, a decision by the Attorney General to invoke the provisions of such section,

            (iii) the application of such section to individual aliens, including the determination made under section 1225(b)(1)(B) of this title, or

            (iv) except as provided in subsection (e) of this section, procedures and policies adopted by the Attorney General to implement the provisions of section 1225(b)(1) of this title.

        (B) Denials of discretionary relief

Notwithstanding any other provision of law (statutory or nonstatutory), including section 2241 of Title 28, or any other habeas corpus provision, and sections 1361 and 1651 of such title, and except as provided in subparagraph (D), and regardless of whether the judgment, decision, or action is made in removal proceedings, no court shall have jurisdiction to review—

            (i) any judgment regarding the granting of relief under section 1182(h), 1182(i), 1229b, 1229c, or 1255 of this title, or

            (ii) any other decision or action of the Attorney General or the Secretary of Homeland Security the authority for which is specified under this subchapter to be in the discretion of the Attorney General or the Secretary of Homeland Security, other than the granting of relief under section 1158(a) of this title.

(C) Orders against criminal aliens

Notwithstanding any other provision of law (statutory or nonstatutory), including section 2241 of Title 28, or any other habeas corpus provision, and sections 1361 and 1651 of such title, and except as provided in subparagraph (D), no court shall have jurisdiction to review any final order of removal against an alien who is removable by reason of having committed a criminal offense covered in section 1182(a)(2) or 1227(a)(2)(A)(iii), (B), (C), or (D) of this title, or any offense covered by section 1227(a)(2)(A)(ii) of this title for which both predicate offenses are, without regard to their date of commission, otherwise covered by section 1227(a)(2)(A)(i) of this title.

(D) Judicial review of certain legal claims

Nothing in subparagraph (B) or (C), or in any other provision of this chapter (other than this section) which limits or eliminates judicial review, shall be construed as precluding review of constitutional claims or questions of law raised upon a petition for review filed with an appropriate court of appeals in accordance with this section.

(3) Treatment of certain decisions

No alien shall have a right to appeal from a decision of an immigration judge which is based solely on a certification described in section 1229a(c)(1)(B) of this title.

(4) Claims under the United Nations Convention

Notwithstanding any other provision of law (statutory or nonstatutory), including section 2241 of Title 28, or any other habeas corpus provision, and sections 1361 and 1651 of such title, a petition for review filed with an appropriate court of appeals in accordance with this section shall be the sole and exclusive means for judicial review of any cause or claim under the United Nations Convention Against Torture and Other Forms of Cruel, Inhuman, or Degrading Treatment or Punishment, except as provided in subsection (e) of this section.

(5) Exclusive means of review

Notwithstanding any other provision of law (statutory or nonstatutory), including section 2241 of Title 28, or any other habeas corpus provision, and sections 1361 and 1651 of such title, a petition for review filed with an appropriate court of appeals in accordance with this section shall be the sole and exclusive means for judicial review of an order of removal entered or issued under any provision of this chapter, except as provided in subsection (e) of this section. For purposes of this chapter, in every provision that limits or eliminates judicial review or jurisdiction to review, the terms "judicial review" and "jurisdiction to review" include habeas corpus review pursuant to section 2241 of Title 28, or any other habeas corpus provision, sections 1361 and 1651 of such title, and review pursuant to any other provision of law (statutory or nonstatutory).

(b) Requirements for review of orders of removal

With respect to review of an order of removal under subsection (a)(1) of this section, the following requirements apply:

(1) Deadline

The petition for review must be filed not later than 30 days after the date of the final order of removal.

(2) Venue and forms

The petition for review shall be filed with the court of appeals for the judicial circuit in which the immigration judge completed the proceedings. The record and briefs do not have to be printed. The court of appeals shall review the proceeding on a typewritten record and on typewritten briefs.

(3) Service

(A) In general

The respondent is the Attorney General. The petition shall be served on the Attorney General and on the officer or employee of the Service in charge of the Service district in which the final order of removal under section 1229a of this title was entered.

(B) Stay of order

Service of the petition on the officer or employee does not stay the removal of an alien pending the court's decision on the petition, unless the court orders otherwise.

(C) Alien's brief

The alien shall serve and file a brief in connection with a petition for judicial review not later than 40 days after the date on which the administrative record is available, and may serve and file a reply brief not later than 14 days after service of the brief of the Attorney General, and the court may not extend these deadlines except upon motion for good cause shown. If an alien fails to file a brief within the time provided in this paragraph, the court shall dismiss the appeal unless a manifest injustice would result.

(4) Scope and standard for review

Except as provided in paragraph (5)(B)—

(A) the court of appeals shall decide the petition only on the administrative record on which the order of removal is based,

(B) the administrative findings of fact are conclusive unless any reasonable adjudicator would be compelled to conclude to the contrary,

(C) a decision that an alien is not eligible for admission to the United States is conclusive unless manifestly contrary to law, and

(D) the Attorney General's discretionary judgment whether to grant relief under section 1158(a) of this title shall be conclusive unless manifestly contrary to the law and an abuse of discretion.

No court shall reverse a determination made by a trier of fact with respect to the availability of corroborating evidence, as described in section 1158(b)(1)(B), 1229a(c)(4)(B), or 1231(b)(3)(C) of this title, unless the court finds, pursuant to with subsection (b)(4)(B) of this section, that a reasonable trier of fact is compelled to conclude that such corroborating evidence is unavailable.

(5) Treatment of nationality claims

(A) Court determination if no issue of fact

If the petitioner claims to be a national of the United States and the court of appeals finds from the pleadings and affidavits that no genuine issue of material fact about the petitioner's nationality is presented, the court shall decide the nationality claim.

(B) Transfer if issue of fact

If the petitioner claims to be a national of the United States and the court of appeals finds that a genuine issue of material fact about the petitioner's nationality is presented, the court shall transfer the proceeding to the district court of the United States for the judicial district in which the petitioner resides for a new hearing on the nationality claim and a decision on that claim as if an action had been brought in the district court under section 2201 of Title 28.

(C) Limitation on determination

The petitioner may have such nationality claim decided only as provided in this paragraph.

(6) Consolidation with review of motions to reopen or reconsider

When a petitioner seeks review of an order under this section, any review sought of a motion to reopen or reconsider the order shall be consolidated with the review of the order.

(7) Challenge to validity of orders in certain criminal proceedings

(A) In general

If the validity of an order of removal has not been judicially decided, a defendant in a criminal proceeding charged with violating section 1253(a) of this title may challenge the validity of the order in the criminal proceeding only by filing a separate motion before trial. The district court, without a jury, shall decide the motion before trial.

(B) Claims of United States nationality

If the defendant claims in the motion to be a national of the United States and the district court finds that—

(i) no genuine issue of material fact about the defendant's nationality is presented, the court shall decide the motion only on the administrative record on which the removal order is based and the administrative findings of fact are conclusive if supported by reasonable, substantial, and probative evidence on the record considered as a whole; or

(ii) a genuine issue of material fact about the defendant's nationality is presented, the court shall hold a new hearing on the nationality claim and decide that claim as if an action had been brought under section 2201 of Title 28.

The defendant may have such nationality claim decided only as provided in this subparagraph.

(C) Consequence of invalidation

If the district court rules that the removal order is invalid, the court shall dismiss the indictment for violation of section 1253(a) of this title. The United States Government may appeal the dismissal to the court of appeals for the appropriate circuit within 30 days after the date of the dismissal.

(D) Limitation on filing petitions for review

The defendant in a criminal proceeding under section 1253(a) of this title may not file a petition for review under subsection (a) of this section during the criminal proceeding.

(8) Construction

This subsection—

(A) does not prevent the Attorney General, after a final order of removal has been issued, from detaining the alien under section 1231(a) of this title;

(B) does not relieve the alien from complying with section 1231(a)(4) of this title and section 1253(g) [FN1] of this title; and

(C) does not require the Attorney General to defer removal of the alien.

(9) Consolidation of questions for judicial review

Judicial review of all questions of law and fact, including interpretation and application of constitutional and statutory provisions, arising from any action taken or proceeding brought to remove an alien from the United States under this subchapter shall be available only in judicial review of a final order under this section. Except as otherwise provided in this section, no court shall have jurisdiction, by habeas corpus under section 2241 of Title 28 or any other habeas corpus provision, by section 1361 or 1651 of such title, or by any other provision of law (statutory or nonstatutory), to review such an order or such questions of law or fact.

(c) Requirements for petition

A petition for review or for habeas corpus of an order of removal—

(1) shall attach a copy of such order, and

(2) shall state whether a court has upheld the validity of the order, and, if so, shall state the name of the court, the date of the court's ruling, and the kind of proceeding.

(d) Review of final orders

A court may review a final order of removal only if—

(1) the alien has exhausted all administrative remedies available to the alien as of right, and

(2) another court has not decided the validity of the order, unless the reviewing court finds that the petition presents grounds that could not have been presented in the prior judicial proceeding or that the remedy provided by the prior proceeding was inadequate or ineffective to test the validity of the order.

(e) Judicial review of orders under section 1225(b)(1)

(1) Limitations on relief

Without regard to the nature of the action or claim and without regard to the identity of the party or parties bringing the action, no court may—

(A) enter declaratory, injunctive, or other equitable relief in any action pertaining to an order to exclude an alien in accordance with section 1225(b)(1) of this title except as specifically authorized in a subsequent paragraph of this subsection, or

(B) certify a class under Rule 23 of the Federal Rules of Civil Procedure in any action for which judicial review is authorized under a subsequent paragraph of this subsection.

(2) Habeas corpus proceedings

Judicial review of any determination made under section 1225(b)(1) of this title is available in habeas corpus proceedings, but shall be limited to determinations of—

(A) whether the petitioner is an alien,

(B) whether the petitioner was ordered removed under such section, and

(C) whether the petitioner can prove by a preponderance of the evidence that the petitioner is an alien lawfully admitted for permanent residence, has been admitted as a refugee under section 1157 of this title, or has been granted asylum under section 1158 of this title, such status not having been terminated, and is entitled to such further inquiry as prescribed by the Attorney General pursuant to section 1225(b)(1)(C) of this title.

(3) Challenges on validity of the system

(A) In general

Judicial review of determinations under section 1225(b) of this title and its implementation is available in an action instituted in the United States District Court for the District of Columbia, but shall be limited to determinations of—

(i) whether such section, or any regulation issued to implement such section, is constitutional; or

(ii) whether such a regulation, or a written policy directive, written policy guideline, or written procedure issued by or under the authority of the Attorney General to implement such section, is not consistent with applicable provisions of this subchapter or is otherwise in violation of law.

(B) Deadlines for bringing actions

Any action instituted under this paragraph must be filed no later than 60 days after the date the challenged section, regulation, directive, guideline, or procedure described in clause (i) or (ii) of subparagraph (A) is first implemented.

(C) Notice of appeal

A notice of appeal of an order issued by the District Court under this paragraph may be filed not later than 30 days after the date of issuance of such order.

(D) Expeditious consideration of cases

It shall be the duty of the District Court, the Court of Appeals, and the Supreme Court of the United States to advance on the docket and to expedite to the greatest possible extent the disposition of any case considered under this paragraph.

(4) Decision

In any case where the court determines that the petitioner—

(A) is an alien who was not ordered removed under section 1225(b)(1) of this title, or

(B) has demonstrated by a preponderance of the evidence that the alien is an alien lawfully admitted for permanent residence, has been admitted as a refugee under section 1157 of this title, or has been granted asylum under section 1158 of this title, the court may order no remedy or relief other than to require that the petitioner be provided a hearing in accordance with section 1229a of this title. Any alien who is provided a hearing under section 1229a of this title pursuant to this paragraph may thereafter obtain judicial review of any resulting final order of removal pursuant to subsection (a)(1) of this section.

(5) Scope of inquiry

In determining whether an alien has been ordered removed under section 1225(b)(1) of this title, the court's inquiry shall be limited to whether such an order in fact was issued and whether it relates to the petitioner. There shall be no review of whether the alien is actually inadmissible or entitled to any relief from removal.

(f) Limit on injunctive relief

(1) In general

Regardless of the nature of the action or claim or of the identity of the party or parties bringing the action, no court (other than the Supreme Court) shall have jurisdiction or authority to enjoin or restrain the operation of the provisions of part IV of this subchapter, as amended by the Illegal Immigration Reform and Immigrant Responsibility Act of 1996, other than with respect to the application of such provisions to an individual alien against whom proceedings under such part have been initiated.

(2) Particular cases

Notwithstanding any other provision of law, no court shall enjoin the removal of any alien pursuant to a final order under this section unless the alien shows by clear and convincing evidence that the entry or execution of such order is prohibited as a matter of law.

(g) Exclusive jurisdiction

Except as provided in this section and notwithstanding any other provision of law (statutory or nonstatutory), including section 2241 of Title 28, or any other habeas corpus provision, and sections 1361 and 1651 of such title, no court shall have jurisdiction to hear any cause or claim by or on behalf of any alien arising from the decision or action by the Attorney General to commence proceedings, adjudicate cases, or execute removal orders against any alien under this chapter.

Title 10 U.S.C.:

§ 1002. Uniform Standards for the Interrogation of Persons Under the Detention of the Department of Defense.

(a) In general.—No person in the custody or under the effective control of the Department of Defense or under detention in a Department of

Defense facility shall be subject to any treatment or technique of interrogation not authorized by and listed in the United States Army Field Manual on Intelligence Interrogation.

(b) Applicability.—Subsection (a) [of this note] shall not apply with respect to any person in the custody or under the effective control of the Department of Defense pursuant to a criminal law or immigration law of the United States.

(c) Construction.—Nothing in this section [this note] shall be construed to affect the rights under the United States Constitution of any person in the custody or under the physical jurisdiction of the United States."

§ 1005. Procedures for Status Review of Detainees Outside the United States.

(a) Submittal of procedures for status review of detainees at Guantanamo Bay, Cuba, and in Afghanistan and Iraq.—

(1) In general.—Not later than 180 days after the date of the enactment of this Act [Dec. 30, 2005], the Secretary of Defense shall submit to the Committee on Armed Services and the Committee on the Judiciary of the Senate and the Committee on Armed Services and the Committee on the Judiciary of the House of Representatives a report setting forth—

(A) the procedures of the Combatant Status Review Tribunals and the Administrative Review Boards established by direction of the Secretary of Defense that are in operation at Guantanamo Bay, Cuba, for determining the status of the detainees held at Guantanamo Bay or to provide an annual review to determine the need to continue to detain an alien who is a detainee; and

(B) the procedures in operation in Afghanistan and Iraq for a determination of the status of aliens detained in the custody or under the physical control of the Department of Defense in those countries.

(2) Designated Civilian Official.—The procedures submitted to Congress pursuant to paragraph (1)(A) shall ensure that the official of the Department of Defense who is designated by the President or Secretary of Defense to be the final review authority within the Department of Defense with respect to decisions of any such tribunal or board (referred to as the 'Designated Civilian Official') shall be a civilian officer of the Department of Defense holding an office to which appointments are required by law to be made by the President, by and with the advice and consent of the Senate.

(3) Consideration of new evidence.—The procedures submitted under paragraph (1)(A) shall provide for periodic review of any new evidence that may become available relating to the enemy combatant status of a detainee.

(b) Consideration of statements derived with coercion.—

(1) Assessment.—The procedures submitted to Congress pursuant to subsection (a)(1)(A) shall ensure that a Combatant Status Review Tribunal or Administrative Review Board, or any similar or successor administrative tribunal or board, in making a determi-

nation of status or disposition of any detainee under such procedures, shall, to the extent practicable, assess—

(A) whether any statement derived from or relating to such detainee was obtained as a result of coercion; and

(B) the probative value (if any) of any such statement.

(2) Applicability.—Paragraph (1) applies with respect to any proceeding beginning on or after the date of the enactment of this Act [Dec. 30, 2005].

(c) Report on modification of procedures.—The Secretary of Defense shall submit to the committees specified in subsection (a)(1) a report on any modification of the procedures submitted under subsection (a). Any such report shall be submitted not later than 60 days before the date on which such modification goes into effect. * * *

(e) Judicial review of detention of enemy combatants.—

(1) In general.—[Omitted; amended 28 U.S.C.A. § 2241]

(2) Review of decisions of Combatant Status Review Tribunals of propriety of detention.—

(A) In general.—Subject to subparagraphs (B), (C), and (D), the United States Court of Appeals for the District of Columbia Circuit shall have exclusive jurisdiction to determine the validity of any final decision of a Combatant Status Review Tribunal that an alien is properly detained as an enemy combatant.

(B) Limitation on claims.—The jurisdiction of the United States Court of Appeals for the District of Columbia Circuit under this paragraph shall be limited to claims brought by or on behalf of an alien—

(i) who is, at the time a request for review by such court is filed, detained by the United States; and

(ii) for whom a Combatant Status Review Tribunal has been conducted, pursuant to applicable procedures specified by the Secretary of Defense.

(C) Scope of review.—The jurisdiction of the United States Court of Appeals for the District of Columbia Circuit on any claims with respect to an alien under this paragraph shall be limited to the consideration of—

(i) whether the status determination of the Combatant Status Review Tribunal with regard to such alien was consistent with the standards and procedures specified by the Secretary of Defense for Combatant Status Review Tribunals (including the requirement that the conclusion of the Tribunal be supported by a preponderance of the evidence and allowing a rebuttable presumption in favor of the Government's evidence); and

(ii) to the extent the Constitution and laws of the United States are applicable, whether the use of such standards and procedures to make the determination is consistent with the Constitution and laws of the United States.

(D) Termination on release from custody.—The jurisdiction of the United States Court of Appeals for the District of Columbia Circuit with respect to the claims of an alien under this paragraph shall cease upon the release of such alien from the custody of the Department of Defense.

[(3) Repealed. Pub.L. 111–84, Div. A, Title XVIII, § 1803(b)(1), formerly § 1803(b), Oct. 28, 2009, 123 Stat. 2612, as renumbered § 1803(b)(1) by Pub.L. 111–383, Div. A, Title X, § 1075(d)(21), Jan. 7, 2011, 124 Stat. 4374]

(4) Respondent.—The Secretary of Defense shall be the named respondent in any appeal to the United States Court of Appeals for the District of Columbia Circuit under this subsection.

(f) Construction.—Nothing in this section [this note] shall be construed to confer any constitutional right on an alien detained as an enemy combatant outside the United States.

(g) United States defined.—For purposes of this section, the term 'United States', when used in a geographic sense, is as defined in section 101(a)(38) of the Immigration and Nationality Act [8 U.S.C.A. § 1101(a)(38)] and, in particular, does not include the United States Naval Station, Guantanamo Bay, Cuba.

(h) Effective date.—

(1) In general.—This section [this note] shall take effect on the date of the enactment of this Act [Dec. 30, 2005].

(2) Review of combatant status tribunal and military commission decisions.—Paragraphs (2) and (3) of subsection (e) [of this note] shall apply with respect to any claim whose review is governed by one of such paragraphs and that is pending on or after the date of the enactment of this Act [Dec. 30, 2005].

TITLE 28 U.S.C.:

§ 2241. Power to grant writ.

(a) Writs of habeas corpus may be granted by the Supreme Court, any justice thereof, the district courts and any circuit judge within their respective jurisdictions. The order of a circuit judge shall be entered in the records of the district court of the district wherein the restraint complained of is had.

(b) The Supreme Court, any justice thereof, and any circuit judge may decline to entertain an application for a writ of habeas corpus and may transfer the application for hearing and determination to the district court having jurisdiction to entertain it.

(c) The writ of habeas corpus shall not extend to a prisoner unless—

(1) He is in custody under or by color of the authority of the United States or is committed for trial before some court thereof; or

(2) He is in custody for an act done or omitted in pursuance of an Act of Congress, or an order, process, judgment or decree of a court or judge of the United States; or

(3) He is in custody in violation of the Constitution or laws or treaties of the United States; or

(4) He, being a citizen of a foreign state and domiciled therein is in custody for an act done or omitted under any alleged right, title, authority, privilege, protection, or exemption claimed under the commission, order or sanction of any foreign state, or under color thereof, the validity and effect of which depend upon the law of nations; or

(5) It is necessary to bring him into court to testify or for trial.

(d) Where an application for a writ of habeas corpus is made by a person in custody under the judgment and sentence of a State court of a State which contains two or more Federal judicial districts, the application may be filed in the district court for the district wherein such person is in custody or in the district court for the district within which the State court was held which convicted and sentenced him and each of such district courts shall have concurrent jurisdiction to entertain the application. The district court for the district wherein such an application is filed in the exercise of its discretion and in furtherance of justice may transfer the application to the other district court for hearing and determination.

(e)

(1) No court, justice, or judge shall have jurisdiction to hear or consider an application for a writ of habeas corpus filed by or on behalf of an alien detained by the United States who has been determined by the United States to have been properly detained as an enemy combatant or is awaiting such determination.

(2) Except as provided in paragraphs (2) and (3) of section 1005(e) of the Detainee Treatment Act of 2005 (10 U.S.C. 801 note), no court, justice, or judge shall have jurisdiction to hear or consider any other action against the United States or its agents relating to any aspect of the detention, transfer, treatment, trial, or conditions of confinement of an alien who is or was detained by the United States and has been determined by the United States to have been properly detained as an enemy combatant or is awaiting such determination.

§ 2242. Application

Application for a writ of habeas corpus shall be in writing signed and verified by the person for whose relief it is intended or by someone acting in his behalf.

It shall allege the facts concerning the applicant's commitment or detention, the name of the person who has custody over him and by virtue of what claim or authority, if known.

It may be amended or supplemented as provided in the rules of procedure applicable to civil actions.

If addressed to the Supreme Court, a justice thereof or a circuit judge it shall state the reasons for not making application to the district court of the district in which the applicant is held.

§ 2243. Issuance of writ; return; hearing; decision.

A court, justice or judge entertaining an application for a writ of habeas corpus shall forthwith award the writ or issue an order directing the respondent to show cause why the writ should not be granted, unless it appears from the application that the applicant or person detained is not entitled thereto.

The writ, or order to show cause shall be directed to the person having custody of the person detained. It shall be returned within three days unless for good cause additional time, not exceeding twenty days, is allowed.

The person to whom the writ or order is directed shall make a return certifying the true cause of the detention.

When the writ or order is returned a day shall be set for hearing, not more than five days after the return unless for good cause additional time is allowed.

Unless the application for the writ and the return present only issues of law the person to whom the writ is directed shall be required to produce at the hearing the body of the person detained.

The applicant or the person detained may, under oath, deny any of the facts set forth in the return or allege any other material facts.

The return and all suggestions made against it may be amended, by leave of court, before or after being filed.

The court shall summarily hear and determine the facts, and dispose of the matter as law and justice require.

§ 2244. Finality of determination.

(a) No circuit or district judge shall be required to entertain an application for a writ of habeas corpus to inquire into the detention of a person pursuant to a judgment of a court of the United States if it appears that the legality of such detention has been determined by a judge or court of the United States on a prior application for a writ of habeas corpus, except as provided in section 2255.

(b)

(1) A claim presented in a second or successive habeas corpus application under section 2254 that was presented in a prior application shall be dismissed.

(2) A claim presented in a second or successive habeas corpus application under section 2254 that was not presented in a prior application shall be dismissed unless—

(A) the applicant shows that the claim relies on a new rule of constitutional law, made retroactive to cases on collateral review by the Supreme Court, that was previously unavailable; or

(B)

(i) the factual predicate for the claim could not have been discovered previously through the exercise of due diligence; and

(ii) the facts underlying the claim, if proven and viewed in light of the evidence as a whole, would be sufficient to establish by clear and convincing evidence that, but for constitutional error, no reasonable factfinder would have found the applicant guilty of the underlying offense.

(3)

    (A) Before a second or successive application permitted by this section is filed in the district court, the applicant shall move in the appropriate court of appeals for an order authorizing the district court to consider the application.

    (B) A motion in the court of appeals for an order authorizing the district court to consider a second or successive application shall be determined by a three-judge panel of the court of appeals.

    (C) The court of appeals may authorize the filing of a second or successive application only if it determines that the application makes a prima facie showing that the application satisfies the requirements of this subsection.

    (D) The court of appeals shall grant or deny the authorization to file a second or successive application not later than 30 days after the filing of the motion.

    (E) The grant or denial of an authorization by a court of appeals to file a second or successive application shall not be appealable and shall not be the subject of a petition for rehearing or for a writ of certiorari.

(4) A district court shall dismiss any claim presented in a second or successive application that the court of appeals has authorized to be filed unless the applicant shows that the claim satisfies the requirements of this section.

(c) In a habeas corpus proceeding brought in behalf of a person in custody pursuant to the judgment of a State court, a prior judgment of the Supreme Court of the United States on an appeal or review by a writ of certiorari at the instance of the prisoner of the decision of such State court, shall be conclusive as to all issues of fact or law with respect to an asserted denial of a Federal right which constitutes ground for discharge in a habeas corpus proceeding, actually adjudicated by the Supreme Court therein, unless the applicant for the writ of habeas corpus shall plead and the court shall find the existence of a material and controlling fact which did not appear in the record of the proceeding in the Supreme Court and the court shall further find that the applicant for the writ of habeas corpus could not have caused such fact to appear in such record by the exercise of reasonable diligence.

(d)

(1) A 1-year period of limitation shall apply to an application for a writ of habeas corpus by a person in custody pursuant to the judgment of a State court. The limitation period shall run from the latest of—

    (A) the date on which the judgment became final by the conclusion of direct review or the expiration of the time for seeking such review;

    (B) the date on which the impediment to filing an application created by State action in violation of the Constitution or laws of the United States is removed, if the applicant was prevented from filing by such State action;

(C) the date on which the constitutional right asserted was initially recognized by the Supreme Court, if the right has been newly recognized by the Supreme Court and made retroactively applicable to cases on collateral review; or

(D) the date on which the factual predicate of the claim or claims presented could have been discovered through the exercise of due diligence.

(2) The time during which a properly filed application for State post-conviction or other collateral review with respect to the pertinent judgment or claim is pending shall not be counted toward any period of limitation under this subsection.

§ 2245. Certificate of trial judge admissible in evidence.

On the hearing of an application for a writ of habeas corpus to inquire into the legality of the detention of a person pursuant to a judgment the certificate of the judge who presided at the trial resulting in the judgment, setting forth the facts occurring at the trial, shall be admissible in evidence. Copies of the certificate shall be filed with the court in which the application is pending and in the court in which the trial took place.

§ 2246. Evidence; depositions; affidavits.

On application for a writ of habeas corpus, evidence may be taken orally or by deposition, or, in the discretion of the judge, by affidavit. If affidavits are admitted any party shall have the right to propound written interrogatories to the affiants, or to file answering affidavits.

§ 2247. Documentary evidence.

On application for a writ of habeas corpus documentary evidence, transcripts of proceedings upon arraignment, plea and sentence and a transcript of the oral testimony introduced on any previous similar application by or in behalf of the same petitioner, shall be admissible in evidence.

§ 2248. Return or answer; conclusiveness.

The allegations of a return to the writ of habeas corpus or of an answer to an order to show cause in a habeas corpus proceeding, if not traversed, shall be accepted as true except to the extent that the judge finds from the evidence that they are not true.

§ 2249. Certified copies of indictment, plea and judgment; duty of respondent.

On application for a writ of habeas corpus to inquire into the detention of any person pursuant to a judgment of a court of the United States, the respondent shall promptly file with the court certified copies of the indictment, plea of petitioner and the judgment, or such of them as may be material to the questions raised, if the petitioner fails to attach them to his petition, and same shall be attached to the return to the writ, or to the answer to the order to show cause.

§ 2250. Indigent petitioner entitled to documents without cost.

If on any application for a writ of habeas corpus an order has been made permitting the petitioner to prosecute the application in forma pauperis, the clerk of any court of the United States shall furnish to the petitioner without cost certified copies of such documents or parts of the record on file in his office as may be required by order of the judge before whom the application is pending.

§ 2251. Stay of State court proceedings

(a) In general.—

(1) Pending matters.—A justice or judge of the United States before whom a habeas corpus proceeding is pending, may, before final judgment or after final judgment of discharge, or pending appeal, stay any proceeding against the person detained in any State court or by or under the authority of any State for any matter involved in the habeas corpus proceeding.

(2) Matter not pending.—For purposes of this section, a habeas corpus proceeding is not pending until the application is filed.

(3) Application for appointment of counsel.—If a State prisoner sentenced to death applies for appointment of counsel pursuant to section 3599(a)(2) of title 18 in a court that would have jurisdiction to entertain a habeas corpus application regarding that sentence, that court may stay execution of the sentence of death, but such stay shall terminate not later than 90 days after counsel is appointed or the application for appointment of counsel is withdrawn or denied.

(b) No further proceedings.—After the granting of such a stay, any such proceeding in any State court or by or under the authority of any State shall be void. If no stay is granted, any such proceeding shall be as valid as if no habeas corpus proceedings or appeal were pending.

§ 2252. Notice.

Prior to the hearing of a habeas corpus proceeding in behalf of a person in custody of State officers or by virtue of State laws notice shall be served on the attorney general or other appropriate officer of such State as the justice or judge at the time of issuing the writ shall direct.

§ 2253. Appeal.

(a) In a habeas corpus proceeding or a proceeding under section 2255 before a district judge, the final order shall be subject to review, on appeal, by the court of appeals for the circuit in which the proceeding is held.

(b) There shall be no right of appeal from a final order in a proceeding to test the validity of a warrant to remove to another district or place for commitment or trial a person charged with a criminal offense against the United States, or to test the validity of such person's detention pending removal proceedings.

(c)

(1) Unless a circuit justice or judge issues a certificate of appealability, an appeal may not be taken to the court of appeals from—

(A) the final order in a habeas corpus proceeding in which the detention complained of arises out of process issued by a State court; or

(B) the final order in a proceeding under section 2255.

(2) A certificate of appealability may issue under paragraph (1) only if the applicant has made a substantial showing of the denial of a constitutional right.

(3) The certificate of appealability under paragraph (1) shall indicate which specific issue or issues satisfy the showing required by paragraph (2).

§ 2254. State custody; remedies in Federal courts.

(a) The Supreme Court, a Justice thereof, a circuit judge, or a district court shall entertain an application for a writ of habeas corpus in behalf of a person in custody pursuant to the judgment of a State court only on the ground that he is in custody in violation of the Constitution or laws or treaties of the United States.

(b)

(1) An application for a writ of habeas corpus on behalf of a person in custody pursuant to the judgment of a State court shall not be granted unless it appears that—

(A) the applicant has exhausted the remedies available in the courts of the State; or

(B)(i) there is an absence of available State corrective process; or

(ii) circumstances exist that render such process ineffective to protect the rights of the applicant.

(2) An application for a writ of habeas corpus may be denied on the merits, notwithstanding the failure of the applicant to exhaust the remedies available in the courts of the State.

(3) A State shall not be deemed to have waived the exhaustion requirement or be estopped from reliance upon the requirement unless the State, through counsel, expressly waives the requirement.

(c) An applicant shall not be deemed to have exhausted the remedies available in the courts of the State, within the meaning of this section, if he has the right under the law of the State to raise, by any available procedure, the question presented.

(d) An application for a writ of habeas corpus on behalf of a person in custody pursuant to the judgment of a State court shall not be granted with respect to any claim that was adjudicated on the merits in State court proceedings unless the adjudication of the claim—

(1) resulted in a decision that was contrary to, or involved an unreasonable application of, clearly established Federal law, as determined by the Supreme Court of the United States; or

(2) resulted in a decision that was based on an unreasonable determination of the facts in light of the evidence presented in the State court proceeding.

(e)

(1) In a proceeding instituted by an application for a writ of habeas corpus by a person in custody pursuant to the judgment of a State court, a determination of a factual issue made by a State court shall be presumed to be correct. The applicant shall have the burden of rebutting the presumption of correctness by clear and convincing evidence.

(2) If the applicant has failed to develop the factual basis of a claim in State court proceedings, the court shall not hold an evidentiary hearing on the claim unless the applicant shows that—

(A) the claim relies on—

(i) a new rule of constitutional law, made retroactive to cases on collateral review by the Supreme Court, that was previously unavailable; or

(ii) a factual predicate that could not have been previously discovered through the exercise of due diligence; and

(B) the facts underlying the claim would be sufficient to establish by clear and convincing evidence that but for constitutional error, no reasonable factfinder would have found the applicant guilty of the underlying offense.

(f) If the applicant challenges the sufficiency of the evidence adduced in such State court proceeding to support the State court's determination of a factual issue made therein, the applicant, if able, shall produce that part of the record pertinent to a determination of the sufficiency of the evidence to support such determination. If the applicant, because of indigency or other reason is unable to produce such part of the record, then the State shall produce such part of the record and the Federal court shall direct the State to do so by order directed to an appropriate State official. If the State cannot provide such pertinent part of the record, then the court shall determine under the existing facts and circumstances what weight shall be given to the State court's factual determination.

(g) A copy of the official records of the State court, duly certified by the clerk of such court to be a true and correct copy of a finding, judicial opinion, or other reliable written indicia showing such a factual determination by the State court shall be admissible in the Federal court proceeding.

(h) Except as provided in section 408 of the Controlled Substances Act, in all proceedings brought under this section, and any subsequent proceedings on review, the court may appoint counsel for an applicant who is or becomes financially unable to afford counsel, except as provided by a rule promulgated by the Supreme Court pursuant to statutory authority. Appointment of counsel under this section shall be governed by section 3006A of title 18.

(i) The ineffectiveness or incompetence of counsel during Federal or State collateral post-conviction proceedings shall not be a ground for relief in a proceeding arising under section 2254.

§ 2255. Federal custody; remedies on motion attacking sentence.

(a) A prisoner in custody under sentence of a court established by Act of Congress claiming the right to be released upon the ground that the sentence was imposed in violation of the Constitution or laws of the United States, or that the court was without jurisdiction to impose such sentence, or that the sentence was in excess of the maximum authorized by law, or is otherwise subject to collateral attack, may move the court which imposed the sentence to vacate, set aside or correct the sentence.

(b) Unless the motion and the files and records of the case conclusively show that the prisoner is entitled to no relief, the court shall cause notice thereof to be served upon the United States attorney, grant a prompt hearing thereon, determine the issues and make findings of fact and conclusions of law with respect thereto. If the court finds that the judgment was rendered without jurisdiction, or that the sentence imposed was not authorized by law or otherwise open to collateral attack, or that there has been such a denial or infringement of the constitutional rights of the prisoner as to render the judgment vulnerable to collateral attack, the court shall vacate and set the judgment aside and shall discharge the prisoner or resentence him or grant a new trial or correct the sentence as may appear appropriate.

(c) A court may entertain and determine such motion without requiring the production of the prisoner at the hearing.

(d) An appeal may be taken to the court of appeals from the order entered on the motion as from a final judgment on application for a writ of habeas corpus.

(e) An application for a writ of habeas corpus in behalf of a prisoner who is authorized to apply for relief by motion pursuant to this section, shall not be entertained if it appears that the applicant has failed to apply for relief, by motion, to the court which sentenced him, or that such court has denied him relief, unless it also appears that the remedy by motion is inadequate or ineffective to test the legality of his detention.

(f) A 1-year period of limitation shall apply to a motion under this section. The limitation period shall run from the latest of—

(1) the date on which the judgment of conviction becomes final;

(2) the date on which the impediment to making a motion created by governmental action in violation of the Constitution or laws of the United States is removed, if the movant was prevented from making a motion by such governmental action;

(3) the date on which the right asserted was initially recognized by the Supreme Court, if that right has been newly recognized by the Supreme Court and made retroactively applicable to cases on collateral review; or

(4) the date on which the facts supporting the claim or claims presented could have been discovered through the exercise of due diligence.

(g) Except as provided in section 408 of the Controlled Substances Act, in all proceedings brought under this section, and any subsequent proceedings on review, the court may appoint counsel, except as provided by a rule promulgated by the Supreme Court pursuant to statutory authority. Appointment of counsel under this section shall be governed by section 3006A of title 18.

(h) A second or successive motion must be certified as provided in section 2244 by a panel of the appropriate court of appeals to contain—

(1) newly discovered evidence that, if proven and viewed in light of the evidence as a whole, would be sufficient to establish by clear and convincing evidence that no reasonable factfinder would have found the movant guilty of the offense; or

(2) a new rule of constitutional law, made retroactive to cases on collateral review by the Supreme Court, that was previously unavailable.

APPENDIX C

TREATIES OF THE UNITED STATES

GENEVA CONVENTION (IV) RELATIVE TO THE PROTECTION OF CIVILIAN PERSONS IN TIME OF WAR (GENEVA CONVENTION IV)

UNITED STATES OF AMERICA
Multilateral
Protection of War Victims
Prisoners of War
Convention, with annexes, dated at Geneva August 12, 1949.

Ratification advised by the Senate of the United States of America,
subject to a statement, July 6, 1955;
Ratified by the President of the United States of America,
subject to said statement, July 14, 1955;
Ratification of the United States of America deposited with the
Swiss Federal Council August 2, 1955;
Proclaimed by the President of the United States of America
August 30, 1955;
Date of entry into force with respect to the United States
ofAmerica: February 2, 1956.
February 2, 1956.

GENERAL PROVISIONS

ARTICLE 1

The High Contracting Parties undertake to respect and to ensure respect for the present Convention in all circumstances.

ARTICLE 2

In addition to the provisions which shall be implemented in peace time, the present Convention shall apply to all cases of declared war or of any other armed conflict which may arise between two or more of the High Contracting Parties, even if the state of war is not recognized by one of them.

The Convention shall also apply to all cases of partial or total occupation of the territory of a High Contracting Party, even if the said occupation meets with no armed resistance.

Although one of the Powers in conflict may not be a party to the present Convention, the Powers who are parties thereto shall remain bound by it in their mutual relations. They shall furthermore be bound by the Convention in relation to the said Power, if the latter accepts and applies the provisions thereof.

ARTICLE 3

In the case of armed conflict not of an international character occurring in the territory of one of the High Contracting Parties, each Party to the conflict shall be bound to apply, as a minimum, the following provisions:

(1) Persons taking no active part in the hostilities, including members of armed forces who have laid down their arms and those placed *hors de combat* by sickness, wounds, detention, or any other cause, shall in all circumstances be treated humanely, without any adverse distinction founded on race, colour, religion or faith, sex, birth or wealth, or any other similar criteria.

To this end the following acts are and shall remain prohibited at any time and in any place whatsoever with respect to the above-mentioned persons:

(a) violence to life and person, in particular murder of all kinds, mutilation, cruel treatment and torture;

(b) taking of hostages;

(c) outrages upon personal dignity, in particular, humiliating and degrading treatment;

(d) the passing of sentences and the carrying out of executions without previous judgment pronounced by a regularly constituted court affording all the judicial guarantees which are recognized as indispensable by civilized peoples.

ARTICLE 4

A. Prisoners of war, in the sense of the present Convention, are persons belonging to one of the following categories, who have fallen into the power of the enemy:

(1) Members of the armed forces of a Party to the conflict, as well as members of militias or volunteer corps forming part of such armed forces.

(2) Members of other militias and members of other volunteer corps, including those of organized resistance movements, belonging to a Party to the conflict and operating in or outside their own territory, even if this territory is occupied, provided that such militias or volunteer corps, including such organized resistance movements, fulfil the following conditions:

(a) that of being commanded by a person responsible for his subordinates;

(b) that of having a fixed distinctive sign recognizable at a distance;

(c) that of carrying arms openly;

(d) that of conducting their operations in accordance with the laws and customs of war.

(3) Members of regular armed forces who profess allegiance to a government or an authority not recognized by the Detaining Power.

(4) Persons who accompany the armed forces without actually being members thereof, such as civilian members of military aircraft crews,

war correspondents, supply contractors, members of labour units or of services responsible for the welfare of the armed forces, provided that they have received authorization from the armed forces which they accompany, who shall provide them for that purpose with an identity card similar to the annexed model.

(5) Members of crews, including masters, pilots and apprentices, of the merchant marine and the crews of civil aircraft of the Parties to the conflict, who do not benefit by more favourable treatment under any other provisions of international law.

(6) Inhabitants of a non-occupied territory, who on the approach of the enemy spontaneously take up arms to resist the invading forces, without having had time to form themselves into regular armed units, provided they carry arms openly and respect the laws and customs of war.

B. The following shall likewise be treated as prisoners of war under the present Convention:

(1) Persons belonging, or having belonged, to the armed forces of the occupied country, if the occupying Power considers it necessary by reason of such allegiance to intern them, even though it has originally liberated them while hostilities were going on outside the territory it occupies, in particular where such persons have made an unsuccessful attempt to rejoin the armed forces to which they belong and which are engaged in combat, or where they fail to comply with a summons made to them with a view to internment.

(2) The persons belonging to one of the categories enumerated in the present Article, who have been received by neutral or non-belligerent Powers on their territory and whom these Powers are required to intern under international law, without prejudice to any more favourable treatment which these Powers may choose to give and with the exception of Articles 8, 10, 15, 30, fifth paragraph, 58–67, 92, 126 and, where diplomatic relations exist between the Parties to the conflict and the neutral or non-belligerent Power concerned, those Articles concerning the Protecting Power. Where such diplomatic relations exist, the Parties to a conflict on whom these persons depend shall be allowed to perform towards them the functions of a Protecting Power as provided in the present Convention, without prejudice to the functions which these Parties normally exercise in conformity with diplomatic and consular usage and treaties.

C. This Article shall in no way affect the status of medical personnel and chaplains as provided for in Article 33 of the present Convention.

GENERAL PROTECTION OF PRISONERS OF WAR

ARTICLE 12

Prisoners of war are in the hands of the enemy Power, but not of the individuals or military units who have captured them. Irrespective of the individual responsibilities that may exist, the Detaining Power is responsible for the treatment given them.

ARTICLE 13

Prisoners of war must at all times be humanely treated. Any unlawful act or omission by the Detaining Power causing death or seriously endangering the health of a prisoner of war in its custody is prohibited, and will be regarded as a serious breach of the present Convention. In particular, no prisoner of war may be subjected to physical mutilation or to medical or scientific experiments of any kind which are not justified by the medical, dental or hospital treatment of the prisoner concerned and carried out in his interest.

Likewise, prisoners of war must at all times be protected, particularly against acts of violence or intimidation and against insults and public curiosity.

Measures of reprisal against prisoners of war are prohibited.

ARTICLE 84

A prisoner of war shall be tried only by a military court, unless the existing laws of the Detaining Power expressly permit the civil courts to try a member of the armed forces of the Detaining Power in respect of the particular offence alleged to have been committed by the prisoner of war.

In no circumstances whatever shall a prisoner of war be tried by a court of any kind which does not offer the essential guarantees of independence and impartiality as generally recognized, and, in particular, the procedure of which does not afford the accused the rights and means of defence provided for in Article 105.

ARTICLE 118

Prisoners of war shall be released and repatriated without delay after the cessation of active hostilities.

APPENDIX D

EXECUTIVE ORDERS OF THE UNITED STATES

EXECUTIVE ORDER NO. 13425

Ex. Ord. No. 13425, "Trial of Alien Unlawful Enemy Combatants by Military Commission", Feb. 14, 2007, 72 F.R. 7737, is set out as a note under 10 U.S.C.A. § 948b.

Section 3 of that Order provided as follows:

Sec. 3. Supersedure. This order supersedes any provision of the President's Military Order of November 13, 2001 (66 Fed. Reg. 57,833), that relates to trial by military commission, specifically including:

   (a) section 4 of the Military Order; and

   (b) any requirement in section 2 of the Military Order, as it relates to trial by military commission, for a determination of:

      (i) reason to believe specified matters; or

      (ii) the interest of the United States.

EXECUTIVE ORDER NO. 13492

REVIEW AND DISPOSITION OF INDIVIDUALS DETAINED AT THE GUANTÁNAMO BAY NAVAL BASE AND CLOSURE OF DETENTION FACILITIES

By the authority vested in me as President by the Constitution and the laws of the United States of America, in order to effect the appropriate disposition of individuals currently detained by the Department of Defense at the Guantánamo Bay Naval Base (Guantánamo) and promptly to close detention facilities at Guantánamo, consistent with the national security and foreign policy interests of the United States and the interests of justice, I hereby order as follows:

§ 1. **Definitions.** As used in this order:

   (a) "Common Article 3" means Article 3 of each of the Geneva Conventions.

   (b) "Geneva Conventions" means:

      (i) the Convention for the Amelioration of the Condition of the Wounded and Sick in Armed Forces in the Field, August 12, 1949 (6 UST 3114);

      (ii) the Convention for the Amelioration of the Condition of Wounded, Sick and Shipwrecked Members of Armed Forces at Sea, August 12, 1949 (6 UST 3217);

      (iii) the Convention Relative to the Treatment of Prisoners of War, August 12, 1949 (6 UST 3316); and

(iv) the Convention Relative to the Protection of Civilian Persons in Time of War, August 12, 1949 (6 UST 3516).

(c) "Individuals currently detained at Guantánamo" and "individuals covered by this order" mean individuals currently detained by the Department of Defense in facilities at the Guantánamo Bay Naval Base whom the Department of Defense has ever determined to be, or treated as, enemy combatants.

§ 2. Findings.

(a) Over the past 7 years, approximately 800 individuals whom the Department of Defense has ever determined to be, or treated as, enemy combatants have been detained at Guantánamo. The Federal Government has moved more than 500 such detainees from Guantánamo, either by returning them to their home country or by releasing or transferring them to a third country. The Department of Defense has determined that a number of the individuals currently detained at Guantánamo are eligible for such transfer or release.

(b) Some individuals currently detained at Guantánamo have been there for more than 6 years, and most have been detained for at least 4 years. In view of the significant concerns raised by these detentions, both within the United States and internationally, prompt and appropriate disposition of the individuals currently detained at Guantánamo and closure of the facilities in which they are detained would further the national security and foreign policy interests of the United States and the interests of justice. Merely closing the facilities without promptly determining the appropriate disposition of the individuals detained would not adequately serve those interests. To the extent practicable, the prompt and appropriate disposition of the individuals detained at Guantánamo should precede the closure of the detention facilities at Guantánamo.

(c) The individuals currently detained at Guantánamo have the constitutional privilege of the writ of habeas corpus. Most of those individuals have filed petitions for a writ of habeas corpus in Federal court challenging the lawfulness of their detention.

(d) It is in the interests of the United States that the executive branch undertake a prompt and thorough review of the factual and legal bases for the continued detention of all individuals currently held at Guantánamo, and of whether their continued detention is in the national security and foreign policy interests of the United States and in the interests of justice. The unusual circumstances associated with detentions at Guantánamo require a comprehensive interagency review.

(e) New diplomatic efforts may result in an appropriate disposition of a substantial number of individuals currently detained at Guantánamo.

(f) Some individuals currently detained at Guantánamo may have committed offenses for which they should be prosecuted. It is in the interests of the United States to review whether and how any such individuals can and should be prosecuted.

(g) It is in the interests of the United States that the executive branch conduct a prompt and thorough review of the circumstances of the individuals currently detained at Guantánamo who have been charged with offenses before military commissions pursuant to the Military Commissions Act of 2006, Public Law 109–366, as well as of the military commission process more generally.

§ 3. Closure of Detention Facilities at Guantánamo. The detention facilities at Guantánamo for individuals covered by this order shall be closed as soon as practicable, and no later than 1 year from the date of this order. If any individuals covered by this order remain in detention at Guantánamo at the time of closure of those detention facilities, they shall be returned to their home country, released, transferred to a third country, or transferred to another United States detention facility in a manner consistent with law and the national security and foreign policy interests of the United States.

§ 4. Immediate Review of All Guantánamo Detentions.

    (a) Scope and Timing of Review. A review of the status of each individual currently detained at Guantánamo (Review) shall commence immediately.

    (b) Review Participants. The Review shall be conducted with the full cooperation and participation of the following officials:

        (1) the Attorney General, who shall coordinate the Review;

        (2) the Secretary of Defense;

        (3) the Secretary of State;

        (4) the Secretary of Homeland Security;

        (5) the Director of National Intelligence;

        (6) the Chairman of the Joint Chiefs of Staff; and

        (7) other officers or full-time or permanent part-time employees of the United States, including employees with intelligence, counterterrorism, military, and legal expertise, as determined by the Attorney General, with the concurrence of the head of the department or agency concerned.

APPENDIX E

RULES OF HABEAS PROCEDURE

ORDERS OF THE SUPREME COURT OF THE UNITED STATES ADOPTING AND AMENDING RULES GOVERNING SECTION 2254 AND 2255 PROCEEDINGS IN THE UNITED STATES DISTRICT COURTS

ORDER OF APRIL 26, 1976

1. That the rules and forms governing proceedings in the United States District Courts under Section 2254 and Section 2255 of Title 28, United States Code, as approved by the Judicial Conference of the United States be, and they hereby are, prescribed pursuant to Section 2072 of Title 28, United States Code and Sections 3771 and 3772 of Title 18, United States Code.

2. That the aforementioned rules and forms shall take effect August 1, 1976, and shall be applicable to all proceedings then pending except to the extent that in the opinion of the court their application in a particular proceeding would not be feasible or would work injustice.

3. That THE CHIEF JUSTICE be, and he hereby is, authorized to transmit the aforementioned rules and forms governing Section 2254 and Section 2255 proceedings to the Congress in accordance with the provisions of Section 2072 of Title 28 and Sections 3771 and 3772 of Title 18, United States Code.

Rules Governing § 2254 Cases

Rule 1. Scope

(a) **Cases Involving a Petition under 28 U.S.C. § 2254.** These rules govern a petition for a writ of habeas corpus filed in a United States district court under 28 U.S.C. § 2254 by:

(1) a person in custody under a state-court judgment who seeks a determination that the custody violates the Constitution, laws, or treaties of the United States; and

(2) a person in custody under a state-court or federal-court judgment who seeks a determination that future custody under a state-court judgment would violate the Constitution, laws, or treaties of the United States.

(b) **Other Cases.** The district court may apply any or all of these rules to a habeas corpus petition not covered by Rule 1(a).

Rule 2. The Petition

(a) **Current Custody; Naming the Respondent.** If the petitioner is currently in custody under a state-court judgment, the petition must name as respondent the state officer who has custody.

(b) **Future Custody; Naming the Respondents and Specifying the Judgment.** If the petitioner is not yet in custody—but may be subject to future custody—under the state-court judgment being contested, the petition must name as respondents both the officer who has current custody and the attorney general of the state where the judgment was entered. The petition must ask for relief from the state-court judgment being contested.

(c) **Form.** The petition must:

(1) specify all the grounds for relief available to the petitioner;

(2) state the facts supporting each ground;

(3) state the relief requested;

(4) be printed, typewritten, or legibly handwritten; and

(5) be signed under penalty of perjury by the petitioner or by a person authorized to sign it for the petitioner under 28 U.S.C. § 2242.

(d) **Standard Form.** The petition must substantially follow either the form appended to these rules or a form prescribed by a local district-court rule. The clerk must make forms available to petitioners without charge.

(e) **Separate Petitions for Judgments of Separate Courts.** A petitioner who seeks relief from judgments of more than one state court must file a separate petition covering the judgment or judgments of each court.

Rule 3. Filing the Petition; Inmate Filing

(a) **Where to File; Copies; Filing Fee.** An original and two copies of the petition must be filed with the clerk and must be accompanied by:

(1) the applicable filing fee, or

(2) a motion for leave to proceed in forma pauperis, the affidavit required by 28 U.S.C. § 1915, and a certificate from the warden or other appropriate officer of the place of confinement showing the amount of money or securities that the petitioner has in any account in the institution.

(b) **Filing.** The clerk must file the petition and enter it on the docket.

(c) **Time to File.** The time for filing a petition is governed by 28 U.S.C. § 2244(d).

(d) **Inmate Filing.** A paper filed by an inmate confined in an institution is timely if deposited in the institution's internal mailing system on or before the last day for filing. If an institution has a system designed for legal mail, the inmate must use that system to receive the benefit of this rule. Timely filing may be shown by a declaration in compliance with 28 U.S.C. § 1746 or by a notarized statement, either of which must set forth the date of deposit and state that first-class postage has been prepaid.

Rule 4. Preliminary Review; Serving the Petition and Order

The clerk must promptly forward the petition to a judge under the court's assignment procedure, and the judge must promptly examine it. If it plainly appears from the petition and any attached exhibits that the petitioner is not entitled to relief in the district court, the judge must dismiss the petition and direct the clerk to notify the petitioner. If the petition is not dismissed, the judge must order the respondent to file an answer, motion, or other response within a fixed time, or to take other action the judge may order. In every case, the clerk must serve a copy of the petition and any order on the respondent and on the attorney general or other appropriate officer of the state involved.

Rule 5. The Answer and the Reply

(a) When Required. The respondent is not required to answer the petition unless a judge so orders.

(b) Contents: Addressing the Allegations; Stating a Bar. The answer must address the allegations in the petition. In addition, it must state whether any claim in the petition is barred by a failure to exhaust state remedies, a procedural bar, non-retroactivity, or a statute of limitations.

(c) Contents: Transcripts. The answer must also indicate what transcripts (of pretrial, trial, sentencing, or post-conviction proceedings) are available, when they can be furnished, and what proceedings have been recorded but not transcribed. The respondent must attach to the answer parts of the transcript that the respondent considers relevant. The judge may order that the respondent furnish other parts of existing transcripts or that parts of untranscribed recordings be transcribed and furnished. If a transcript cannot be obtained, the respondent may submit a narrative summary of the evidence.

(d) Contents: Briefs on Appeal and Opinions. The respondent must also file with the answer a copy of:

(1) any brief that the petitioner submitted in an appellate court contesting the conviction or sentence, or contesting an adverse judgment or order in a post-conviction proceeding;

(2) any brief that the prosecution submitted in an appellate court relating to the conviction or sentence; and

(3) the opinions and dispositive orders of the appellate court relating to the conviction or the sentence.

(e) Reply. The petitioner may submit a reply to the respondent's answer or other pleading within a time fixed by the judge.

Rule 6. Discovery

(a) Leave of Court Required. A judge may, for good cause, authorize a party to conduct discovery under the Federal Rules of Civil Procedure and may limit the extent of discovery. If necessary for effective discovery, the judge must appoint an attorney for a petitioner who qualifies to have counsel appointed under 18 U.S.C. § 3006A.

(b) Requesting Discovery. A party requesting discovery must provide reasons for the request. The request must also include any proposed interrogatories and requests for admission, and must specify any requested documents.

(c) Deposition Expenses. If the respondent is granted leave to take a deposition, the judge may require the respondent to pay the travel expenses, subsistence expenses, and fees of the petitioner's attorney to attend the deposition.

Rule 7. Expanding the Record

(a) In General. If the petition is not dismissed, the judge may direct the parties to expand the record by submitting additional materials relating to the petition. The judge may require that these materials be authenticated.

(b) Types of Materials. The materials that may be required include letters predating the filing of the petition, documents, exhibits, and answers under oath to written interrogatories propounded by the judge. Affidavits may also be submitted and considered as part of the record.

(c) Review by the Opposing Party. The judge must give the party against whom the additional materials are offered an opportunity to admit or deny their correctness.

Rule 8. Evidentiary Hearing

(a) Determining Whether to Hold a Hearing. If the petition is not dismissed, the judge must review the answer, any transcripts and records of state-court proceedings, and any materials submitted under Rule 7 to determine whether an evidentiary hearing is warranted.

(b) Reference to a Magistrate Judge. A judge may, under 28 U.S.C. § 636(b), refer the petition to a magistrate judge to conduct hearings and to file proposed findings of fact and recommendations for disposition. When they are filed, the clerk must promptly serve copies of the proposed findings and recommendations on all parties. Within 14 days after being served, a party may file objections as provided by local court rule. The judge must determine de novo any proposed finding or recommendation to which objection is made. The judge may accept, reject, or modify any proposed finding or recommendation.

(c) Appointing Counsel; Time of Hearing. If an evidentiary hearing is warranted, the judge must appoint an attorney to represent a petitioner who qualifies to have counsel appointed under 18 U.S.C. § 3006A. The judge must conduct the hearing as soon as practicable after giving the attorneys adequate time to investigate and prepare. These rules do not limit the appointment of counsel under § 3006A at any stage of the proceeding.

Rule 9. Second or Successive Petitions

Before presenting a second or successive petition, the petitioner must obtain an order from the appropriate court of appeals authorizing the district court to consider the petition as required by 28 U.S.C. § 2244(b)(3) and (4).

Rule 10. Powers of a Magistrate Judge

A magistrate judge may perform the duties of a district judge under these rules, as authorized under 28 U.S.C. § 636.

Rule 11. Certificate of Appealability; Time to Appeal

(a) Certificate of Appealability. The district court must issue or deny a certificate of appealability when it enters a final order adverse to the applicant. Before entering the final order, the court may direct the parties to submit arguments on whether a certificate should issue. If the court issues a certificate, the court must state the specific issue or issues that satisfy the showing required by 28 U.S.C. § 2253(c)(2). If the court denies a certificate, the parties may not appeal the denial but may seek a certificate from the court of appeals under Federal Rule of Appellate Procedure 22. A motion to reconsider a denial does not extend the time to appeal.

(b) Time to Appeal. Federal Rule of Appellate Procedure 4(a) governs the time to appeal an order entered under these rules. A timely notice of appeal must be filed even if the district court issues a certificate of appealability.

Rule 12. Applicability of the Federal Rules of Civil Procedure

The Federal Rules of Civil Procedure, to the extent that they are not inconsistent with any statutory provisions or these rules, may be applied to a proceeding under these rules.

*ORDERS OF THE SUPREME COURT OF THE UNITED STATES
ADOPTING AND AMENDING RULES GOVERNING SECTION 2255
PROCEEDINGS*
ORDER OF APRIL 26, 1976

1. That the rules and forms governing proceedings in the United States District Courts under Section 2254 and Section 2255 of Title 28, United States Code, as approved by the Judicial Conference of the United States be, and they hereby are, prescribed pursuant to Section 2072 of Title 28, United States Code and Sections 3771 and 3772 of Title 18, United States Code.

2. That the aforementioned rules and forms shall take effect August 1, 1976, and shall be applicable to all proceedings then pending except to the extent that in the opinion of the court their application in a particular proceeding would not be feasible or would work injustice.

3. That THE CHIEF JUSTICE be, and he hereby is, authorized to transmit the aforementioned rules and forms governing Section 2254 and Section 2255 proceedings to the Congress in accordance with the provisions of Section 2072 of Title 28 and Sections 3771 and 3772 of Title 18, United States Code.

Rules Governing § 2255 Cases

Rule 1. Scope

These rules govern a motion filed in a United States district court under 28 U.S.C. § 2255 by:

(a) a person in custody under a judgment of that court who seeks a determination that:

(1) the judgment violates the Constitution or laws of the United States;

(2) the court lacked jurisdiction to enter the judgment;

(3) the sentence exceeded the maximum allowed by law; or

(4) the judgment or sentence is otherwise subject to collateral review; and

(b) a person in custody under a judgment of a state court or another federal court, and subject to future custody under a judgment of the district court, who seeks a determination that:

(1) future custody under a judgment of the district court would violate the Constitution or laws of the United States;

(2) the district court lacked jurisdiction to enter the judgment;

(3) the district court's sentence exceeded the maximum allowed by law; or

(4) the district court's judgment or sentence is otherwise subject to collateral review.

Rule 2. The Motion

(a) Applying for Relief. The application must be in the form of a motion to vacate, set aside, or correct the sentence.

(b) Form. The motion must:

(1) specify all the grounds for relief available to the moving party;

(2) state the facts supporting each ground;

(3) state the relief requested;

(4) be printed, typewritten, or legibly handwritten; and

(5) be signed under penalty of perjury by the movant or by a person authorized to sign it for the movant.

(c) Standard Form. The motion must substantially follow either the form appended to these rules or a form prescribed by a local district-court rule. The clerk must make forms available to moving parties without charge.

(d) Separate Motions for Separate Judgments. A moving party who seeks relief from more than one judgment must file a separate motion covering each judgment.

Rule 4. Preliminary Review

(a) Referral to a Judge. The clerk must promptly forward the motion to the judge who conducted the trial and imposed sentence or, if the judge who imposed sentence was not the trial judge, to the judge who conducted the proceedings being challenged. If the appropriate judge is not available, the clerk must forward the motion to a judge under the court's assignment procedure.

(b) Initial Consideration by the Judge. The judge who receives the motion must promptly examine it. If it plainly appears from the motion, any attached exhibits, and the record of prior proceedings that the moving party is not entitled to relief, the judge must dismiss the motion and direct the clerk to notify the moving party. If the motion is not dismissed, the judge must order the United States attorney to file an answer, motion, or other response within a fixed time, or to take other action the judge may order.

Rule 8. Evidentiary Hearing

(a) Determining Whether to Hold a Hearing. If the motion is not dismissed, the judge must review the answer, any transcripts and records of prior proceedings, and any materials submitted under Rule 7 to determine whether an evidentiary hearing is warranted.

(b) Reference to a Magistrate Judge. A judge may, under 28 U.S.C. § 636(b), refer the motion to a magistrate judge to conduct hearings and to file proposed findings of fact and recommendations for disposition. When they are filed, the clerk must promptly serve copies of the proposed findings and recommendations on all parties. Within 14 days after being served, a party may file objections as provided by local court rule. The judge must determine de novo any proposed finding or recommendation to which objection is made. The judge may accept, reject, or modify any proposed finding or recommendation.

(c) Appointing Counsel; Time of Hearing. If an evidentiary hearing is warranted, the judge must appoint an attorney to represent a moving party who qualifies to have counsel appointed under 18 U.S.C. § 3006A. The judge must conduct the hearing as soon as practicable after giving the attorneys adequate time to investigate and prepare. These rules do not limit the appointment of counsel under § 3006A at any stage of the proceeding.

(d) Producing a Statement. Federal Rule of Criminal Procedure 26.2(a)-(d) and (f) applies at a hearing under this rule. If a party does not comply with a Rule 26.2(a) order to produce a witness's statement, the court must not consider that witness's testimony.

INDEX

References are to Pages

ABUSE OF THE WRIT

Deliberate Bypass, 247, 248, 380

    Generally, 73, 95–96, 187, 245, 247, 248–65, 380, 653, 707

ACCURACY, 160, 163, 407, 711

ADMINISTRATIVE PROCEDURE ACT (APA), 457, 479, 483 fn.cc

ADMISSIBILITY (NONCITIZENS), 459, 491, 717

AGGRAVATED FELONIES, 50, 458–59, 463, 484, 492

ALIEN ENEMIES ACT, 445, 493

ALIEN FRIENDS ACT, 445, 493

ALIEN TERRORIST REMOVAL COURT (ATRC), 444, 499–500, 710

ANTITERRORISM AND EFFECTIVE DEATH PENALTY ACT (AEDPA)

Filing Data, 420

Illegal Immigration Reform and Immigrant Responsibility Act of 1996 (IIRIRA), 458–79

Legislative History, 318–21

Limits on relief, 75–76, 95–96, 169, 173, 179, 189–91, 214, 243–45, 261–81, 296–97, 299–304, 314, 321–78, 654–76

    Generally, 41, 50, 72–73, 75–76, 95–96, 134, 137, 151, 165, 169, 173, 179, 189–91, 214, 227, 243–45, 261–81, 296–97, 299–304, 314–15, 318–21, 321–79, 384–95, 414–16, 523, 622–23, 654–76, 684, 697, 702–07, 711, 715–16, 718

Section 2255, effects on, 421–25, 429, 432–39

APPEALS

Certificates of probable cause, 668, 670, 675, 680

Certificates of appealability

    Generally, 32, 33, 40, 88–89, 91–97, 170–74, 177–78, 180, 226–28, 266–68, 312, 314–15, 317, 419–20, 426, 429–30, 446, 461, 473, 486–87, 523, 656, 659, 666, 668–77, 682–83, 705, 711

APPELLATE JURISDICTION (HABEAS CORPUS AS A FORM OF), 12, 20–33, 38–41, 45, 48, 79–81, 86, 88–97, 99–106, 113, 178, 200, 265, 552, 556, 668–76

ARTICLE III, 12, 18, 20, 22, 28–33, 39, 44, 46, 48, 49, 52–53, 71, 75, 82, 85–88, 92, 96, 97, 113 fn.e, 130, 178, 299, 456, 460, 475, 478, 480, 485, 537, 542, 550, 556, 614, 615, 645, 706, 710, 714, 718

ASYLUM, 460, 465, 481 fn.w, 485–86, 489, 501, 728–29

***ATKINS* CLAIMS,** 140, 281, 343, 383, 393,

AUTHORIZATION FOR THE USE OF MILITARY FORCE (AUMF), 566, 568, 573–76, 580–81, 589–91, 598, 629

AUTHORIZATION, MOTIONS FOR, 96, 265–66, 280, 423

BAGRAM AIRFIELD MILITARY BASE (BTIF), 637, 643–44

BAIL

    Generally, 19, 22, 27, 61–62, 85, 175, 460, 512–13

Bail Reform Act of 1966, 512–13

Bail Reform Act of 1984, 512–13

BOARD OF IMMIGRATION APPEALS (BIA), 457, 461, 484, 486–87, 623, 709

***BRADY* CLAIMS,** 138–40, 164, 172, 216, 217 fn.o, 218, 228, 230, 249, 271–72, 356–57, 387–93, 399, 667, 685, 688, 689–92

CERTIFICATES OF APPEALABILITY, 235, 356, 367, 376, 668–76

CHILD CUSTODY, 528, 534–35

CHINESE EXCLUSION ACTS, 443, 445–46, 449, 475

CITIZENSHIP, 444, 485, 552, 554, 558, 563–64, 576, 595, 598, 607, 621–22, 633, 639–40, 643

CIVIL COMMITMENT, 490, 501, 510, 517–19, 522–26, 632

CLEAR STATEMENT RULES, 51, 91, 96, 215, 464, 466–69, 472, 480, 498, 510, 589, 591, 602, 624

COGNIZABILITY, 12, 37, 38, 99–101, 105, 134, 141–50, 151, 154, 158, 160, 162, 167, 177, 209, 212, 242, 254, 262, 302, 304 fn.f, 409, 418–20, 535, 554, 680, 682–84, 703

COMBATANT STATUS REVIEW TRIBUNAL (CSRT), 598, 600, 601, 607, 609, 611–16, 622, 641, 643–45, 708, 710

COMITY, 100, 114, 130, 169, 177–79, 181, 187–92, 248, 264, 271–74, 276–77, 316, 339, 380–81, 408–09, 421, 426, 657–59, 661, 678, 694, 702

COMPETENT TRIBUNAL, 37, 85, 104, 107–08, 113, 539–40, 593–94, 716

CONFESSIONS, COERCED, 4–5, 10–11, 122–23, 128, 192, 199, 399

CONSTITUTIONAL CONVENTION, 19, 20, 44–48

CONTEMPORANEOUS OBJECTION, 203–10, 213, 428

CONVENTION AGAINST TORTURE (CAT), 488–89, 636

CORAM NOBIS, WRIT OF, 439–40

CORRECTIVE PROCESS, 110, 113, 116–19, 129, 142, 147–48, 159, 180

COURT OF APPEALS, D.C. CIRCUIT, 631–37

COURTS MARTIAL, 541–42, 552, 563, 567

CUSTODY REQUIREMENT, 34, 40–41, 134–35, 417–18, 459–60, 500, 528–35, 596, 635, 650, 678, 683

DATA
2007 Habeas Study, 136–38, 151, 173, 190, 191 fn's i & j, 243, 245 fn.t, 266, 296, 301 fn.b, 379

DEPARTMENT OF HOMELAND SECURITY (DHS), 460, 486, 490

DEPORTABILITY, 446, 459

DEPORTATION. 446–47, 455, 457–59

DETAINEE TREATMENT ACT OF 2005 (DTA), 566, 598–99, 600–10, 613–15, 622–23, 627

DICTA, 32, 34, 61, 83, 201 fn.m, 205, 246, 331, 334, 337, 344–45, 426, 587, 593, 606, 639, 659

DISCHARGE, 512, 551

DISCOVERY, 383, 593, 625, 628–29, 633–34, 680, 693–94, 751

DISCRETIONARY RELIEF (IMMIGRATION REMOVAL), 457–66, 473

DNA
Generally, 150–51, 161, 199, 228, 237, 241–42, 411–12, 684–86, 687–94
Post-conviction testing, 150–51, 161–65, 244, 441–42, 687–94,

DOMESTIC RELATIONS EXCEPTION, 535

DOYLE ERROR, 401–08

DUE PROCESS
Due Process Clause, 132, 151, 158–61, 192, 314, 402, 443, 449, 475, 490, 492–93, 496, 513, 520, 525, 571, 577, 580–82, 585, 587–88, 592, 594, 598, 600, 610–11, 614, 622, 624–25, 628, 633–34, 636–37, 647, 687–90, 693, 717–18
Generally, 100, 113, 164, 343, 455, 478, 493, 498, 564, 592, 622, 693, 717

ENEMY ALIENS, 444, 465, 493, 497, 537, 557, 598, 643

ENEMY COMBATANTS
Generally, 540–41
Unlawful, 540–41, 553, 556, 564, 566, 573–88, 589, 593, 596–98, 599, 601, 607, 611, 613–16, 627, 629, 643, 650
Unprivileged enemy belligerents, 627

EVIDENTIARY HEARINGS
Diligence, 347, 353–54, 355, 385–95, 425
"Failed to develop", 347, 369, 375, 385–95
Generally, 129, 159, 163, 257, 301, 347–57, 377 fn.cc, 379–95, 425–26, 634, 695, 703, 707, 711, 716

EXCLUDABILITY, 446–47

EXCLUSION, 446–48, 451–55, 458–59

EXCLUSIONARY RULE, 147–149, 299, 304–05

EXHAUSTION
Generally, 129, 130, 169, 173–91, 213–14, 217, 245, 274, 276, 278, 280, 319–20, 380–81, 426, 461, 653–59, 660, 678, 682, 684 fn.k, 707, 710
Mechanics, 180–81
Mixed Petitions, 181–91

EXONERATION, 150–51, 164, 240, 684, 712

EXPEDITED REMOVAL, 459, 485, 624–25

EXTRADITION, 488–89, 636–37

EXTRATERRITORIALITY, 488–89, 636–37

FEDERAL RULES (UNDER RULES ENABLING ACT)

Federal Rules of Civil Procedure, 383, 396, 653–54, 659–62, 666–68, 707, 728, 751, 753

Federal Rules of Criminal Procedure, 383, 429, 514

Rules in Section 2254 Proceedings, 653–61

Rules in Section 2255 Proceedings, 653

FINALITY, 12, 38–39, 100, 151, 155, 159–60, 162, 164, 169, 181, 187, 205, 226, 245, 247, 248, 259, 266, 272–74, 280, 319, 408–09, 421, 424, 428, 429, 439–40, 456, 534, 657–59, 661, 666, 702

FORCE ACT OF 1833, 72, 77

FORD CLAIMS, 140–41, 264, 343–44

FRANK, LEO, 106, 111–12

FUGITIVE SLAVE ACT, 72 fn.w, 76–77, 82

FULL AND FAIR REVIEW, 73, 147–48, 149–50, 319–20, 377, 379, 381, 717

GENEVA CONVENTIONS

Common Article 3, 538–39, 567

Third Convention, 536–40, 558, 564, 566–68, 576, 593–94, 616, 716

GUANTANAMO BAY NAVAL BASE (GTMO), 53, 71–72, 566–68, 596–96, 572, 598–99, 619–21, 625–26

HABEAS CORPUS ACT OF 1679, 14, 16–17, 19, 31, 39, 45 fn.b, 47 fn.i, 512, 603, 619

HABEAS CORPUS ACT OF 1867, 2, 8, 9, 12, 41, 65, 67, 72–74, 89–91, 92–95, 99–101, 108, 114, 124, 126, 130, 133, 141–42, 174, 194, 204, 314, 336, 464–66, 530, 532

HABEAS CORPUS SUSPENSION ACT OF 1863, 543, 550

HARMLESS ERROR

Generally, 162, 301, 395–416

Chapman, 217 fn.o, 396–401

Kotteakos, 400–01, 408–10, 414

Plea Bargains, 399–400

HEARSAY, 315, 579, 628, 632, 634

HISTORIOGRAPHY, 200, 620

HISTORY, COMMON LAW, 1–2, 12–15, 16 fn.m, 17, 19, 21, 28, 30, 33, 38–39, 41–42, 43, 47 fn's i & j, 49–53, 62, 86 fn.cc, 104, 133, 246, 266, 304, 395, 439–40, 511, 556, 563, 619–20, 715–16

HOBBS ACT, 457, 467–70, 487

IMMIGRATION

Deportation, 446–47, 455, 457–59

Exclusion, 446–48, 451–55, 458–59

Illegal Immigration Reform and Immigrant Responsibility Act of 1996 (IIRIRA), 50–51, 458–59, 459–79, 480, 700

Inadmissibility, 459

Judges, 460–61, 486–87

Removal, 484–88

Waiver of Removal, 50, 460, 462, 481

INEFFECTIVE ASSISTANCE OF COUNSEL ("IAC") CLAIMS, 67, 147–40, 149, 171–72, 213, 217–20, 226–30, 243, 247, 260, 315, 334–34, 336, 340, 344, 346, 354, 356–57, 377, 379, 393, 399, 415, 420, 426, 430, 667–68, 702, 708–10

INCAPACITATION, 518, 523–24

INDEFINITE DETENTION, 481–93, 571–72, 576, 589–95, 597, 626

INNOCENCE

Freestanding Innocence, 151–62, 163–65, 217

Gateways, 160–61, 230–31, 231–44, 260, 263, 296, 394

Innocence Commissions, 711, 713

Innocence Protection Act of 2004, 441–42

Sentencing Innocence, 165–67, 423

State Innocence Statutes, 163–65

INTERNMENT, OF JAPANESE AMERICANS, 502, 510, 590

JURISDICTION, TERRITORIAL, 41, 53, 64, 67, 76, 82, 455, 473, 511, 556–57, 562–63, 596, 621, 625, 628, 635, 645

KING'S BENCH, 1, 17, 32, 35, 105, 440, 534, 556, 620

LACHES, 404, 661

LAW OF WAR, 537–41, 553–55, 566–69

LINCOLN, PRESIDENT ABRAHAM, 54–55, 60–61, 543, 550

MADISONIAN COMPROMISE, 20, 45, 52, 86–87, 131, 178, 620–21

MALICIOUS PROSECUTIONS, 681–82, 685

MANDATORY DETENTION, 492–93

MASSIAH CLAIMS, 257–58

MATERIAL SUPPORT, 499, 568–69

MATERIAL WITNESS DETENTION, 514–16

McVEIGH, TIMOTHY, 261, 320

MILITARY COMMISSIONS
Generally, 541–69
Military Commissions Act of 2006, 71, 599–602, 609–10, 624, 638
Military Commissions Act of 2009, 627

MIRANDA CLAIMS, 150

MISCARRIAGE OF JUSTICE, 167, 180, 211, 214, 216–18, 229–31, 242, 260, 262–63, 295 fn.hh, 296, 339, 381, 393–94, 419 fn.e, 420, 430–31, 441, 657, 702

MIXED QUESTIONS OF LAW AND FACT, 130, 133, 315, 322, 332, 335, 481–82, 484, 623, 703, 714

NATIONAL DEFENSE AUTHORIZATION ACT OF 2012 (2012), 569, 630–31, 651

NATIONAL SECURITY COURTS, 709–10

NEW EVIDENCE, 151, 160, 163–64, 180, 230–31, 243–44, 247, 260, 263, 269, 302 fn.c, 354–57, 375, 379, 385, 394, 412, 422, 426, 625, 684, 713, 730

NONRETROACTIVITY, *see Retroactivity*

OPT–IN PROCEDURES, 267, 704–06

ORIGINAL HABEAS WRITS, 21–35, 44, 87–97, 97, 278

PARKER COMMITTEE, 318–19

PAROLE, CHALLENGES TO, 676, 683

PENRY CASES, 345

PERSONAL LIBERTY LAWS, 76

PETITIONS FOR REVIEW, 457–58, 461, 473, 479–82, 487

PLEA BARGAINING, 340–41, 399–400, 709

PLEADING, 169, 214, 267, 410, 653–61

PLENARY POWER DOCTRINE, 444–46, 472–73, 491, 648

POLICE POWERS, 501, 527

POWELL COMMITTEE, 319–20, 703–04

PRECLUSION, 166, 682

PREVENTATIVE DETENTION, 513, 515, 524

PRISON LITIGATION REFORM ACT OF 1996 (PLRA), 684

PRISONERS OF WAR (POWS), 539–43, 566–67, 571–72, 590, 593

PRIVILEGE, 2, 13–14, 17–21, 32–35, 39, 42, 43–54, 60–64, 75, 83, 86, 383, 447–48, 473, 491, 501, 537, 543–44, 550–51, 553, 556–57, 563–64, 566, 571, 589, 591–92, 599, 601, 619–21, 623, 627–28, 653, 657, 677, 699

PROCEDURAL DEFAULT
Adequacy, 191, 200–01, 214
Cause, 216–17
Deliberate Bypass, 201–02
Generally, 129, 151, 161, 169, 173, 180, 186, 191–244, 245, 247, 248, 258, 259–60, 263, 268, 280, 296, 302, 313, 356–57, 380–82, 392–94, 426–32, 654, 669, 660–61, 667, 702, 710, 713
Independence, 191, 201, 214
Mechanics, 213–18
Miscarriage of justice, 217, 218–29, 229–44
Prejudice, 217, 228

PUBLIC HEALTH DETENTION, 501, 524, 526–27

QUALIFIED IMMUNITY, 299, 334, 411, 516, 685, 700

QUARANTINE, 501, 524, 526–27

QUESTIONS OF FACT, 354–78, 474, 482–84, 623

QUESTIONS OF LAW, 303–57, 444, 474, 479–83, 715

REAL–ID ACT, 474, 479–87, 489, 500, 636–37, 701–02

RECONSTRUCTION, 2, 53, 77 fn.aa, 88–89, 91, 95, 99, 543–44, 552, 608

RELEASE, 509, 540, 568, 576, 580–82, 585, 588, 593, 610, 612, 614, 615, 623, 626, 636, 645–49

REMOVAL, 484–88

RETROACTIVITY
Generally, 262, 268–69, 303–06, 313–18, 338, 421 fn.i, 439, 599, 708
Linkletter Standard 304, 307–08
Teague Bar
Generally, 300, 306–18, 335, 421–22, 705, 708

New and retroactive rule exception, 314

Watershed criminal procedure rule exception, 314–15

RETURN, 14–16, 41, 55, 61, 67, 77, 564, 628

RIGHT TO COUNSEL, 149, 213, 216, 218–20, 257 fn.v, 260, 708–09

RULES ENABLING ACT (REA), 653

SANDBAGGING, 212, 657, 702

SAVINGS CLAUSE (SECTION 2255), 65, 67, 420–21, 432–39

SECTION 1983, 523, 676–698, 707

SECTION 2254(d) (UNDER TITLE 28)
Generally, 41,134, 170 fn.a, 227 266, 299–303, 379, 384, 414–15, 421, 673–74, 703

Subsection 1
Generally, 318–58, 693

clearly established federal law, 334, 344–46

"contrary to" clause, 333–34, 339–41

"on the merits" requirement, 301–03

"unreasonable application" clause, 334, 342–44

Subsection 2, 358–78, 385

SENTENCING CLAIMS, 140–41, 165–67, 230, 263, 334, 345–46, 409, 418–19, 431, 439, 676, 706

SENTENCING GUIDELINES, 167, 419, 431, 711

SEXUALLY VIOLENT PREDATORS, 517–23

SIXTH AMENDMENT
Generally, 67, 137, 149, 257, 295, 303, 315, 340, 358, 398, 459, 552, 554, 632, 708–09

See also Ineffective Assistance of Counsel ("IAC") Claims

SLAVERY, 54, 76, 86 fn.dd, 445

SOME EVIDENCE REVIEW, 475, 478–79, 483, 577, 580, 583, 593, 615, 625, 628, 632–33, 636

STAR CHAMBER, 14, 16 fn.m

STATE POST–CONVICTION REVIEW, 2, 32, 35, 40, 75, 105, 119, 170–73, 227, 274, 276, 278, 354, 356, 421, 564, 693, 707, 711

STATE RECORD, 300, 347, 354, 375, 378–79, 382

STATUTE OF LIMITATIONS
For Federal Prisoners, 424–25

For State Prisoners, 266–97

Tolling (equitable)
Generally, 281–97

Diligence, 295

Extraordinary circumstances, 294–95

Tolling (statutory)
Generally, 267, 269 fn.ee, 270, 271–81, 425, 660

"other collateral review", 271–76

"pending", 276–78

"pertinent judgment or claim", 280–81

"properly filed", 278–80

STAY AND ABEYANCE, 190–91, 272, 280, 357–58

***STRICKLAND* CLAIMS,** *see Ineffective Assistance of Counsel ("IAC") Claims*

STRUCTURAL ERROR, 396, 398–400, 409

STRUCTURAL REFORM LITIGATION, 707

SUBSTANCE ABUSE, 345, 501, 526

SUBSTANTIAL AND INJURIOUS EFFECT, 217 fn.o, 400, 408, 410, 414–15

SUBSTANTIVE DUE PROCESS, 159, 493, 637, 700

SUCCESSIVE PETITIONS
Generally, 73, 95–96, 134, 162, 169, 230, 243, 244–97, 393, 422–23, 429, 432, 437–39, 654, 661–68

See also Abuse of the Writ

SUMMARY DENIALS, 301–02

SUPREMACY, 11, 33, 48, 76, 86, 299, 336, 445, 718

SUSPENSION
Executive Suspension, 54–61

Generally, 18–21

Suspension Clause, 44–52, 53–63,67, 71, 73–76, 336, 432, 437, 456–7, 473–74, 481, 551, 592, 594, 620–25, 633, 636, 714–15

UNIFORM CODE OF MILITARY JUSTICE (UCMJ), 541–42, 566–67

***WIGGINS* CLAIMS,** 140, 377